INTRODUCTION TO PHILOSOPHY OF RELIGION

READINGS

James Kellenberger

PEARSON

Prentice
Hall

Upper Saddle River, NJ 07458

To Anne

Library of Congress Cataloging-in-Publication Data

Introduction to philosophy of religion: readings / edited by J. Kellenberger.
p. cm.
Includes bibliographical references and index.
ISBN-13: 978-0-13-151764-6 (alk. paper)
ISBN-10: 0-13-151764-3 (alk. paper)
1. Religion-Philosophy.   2. Christianity and other religions.   3. Bible-Introductions.
4. Religions.
I. Kellenberger, James.
BL51.1659 2006
210–dc22

2006021403

Senior Acquisitions Editor: Mical Moser
Editor-in-Chief: Sarah Touborg
Editorial Assistant: Carla Worner
Asst. Marketing Manager: Andrea Messineo
Senior Managing Editor: Joanne Riker
Production Liaison: Fran Russello
Manufacturing Buyer: Christina Amato
Art Director, Cover: Jayne Conte
Manager, Cover Visual Research & Permissions: Karen Sanatar
Composition/Full-Service Project Management: GGS Book Services/
Karpagam Jagadeesan
Printer/Binder: RR Donnelley & Sons Company

Credits and acknowledgments borrowed from other sources and reproduced, with
permission, in this textbook appear on appropriate page within text.

Pearson Education LTD. London
Pearson Education Singapore, Pte. Ltd
Pearson Education, Canada, Ltd
Pearson Education–Japan
Pearson Education Australia PTY, Limited

Pearson Education North Asia Ltd
Pearson Educación de Mexico, S.A. de C.V.
Pearson Education Malaysia, Pte. Ltd
Pearson Education, Upper Saddle River,
New Jersey

10 9 8 7 6 5 4 3 2 1

ISBN : 0-13-151764-3

Contents

Preface

Many of the readings in this collection cover a number of traditional issues in philosophy of religion; however some of the chapters of this collection and their readings are devoted to issues that are not usually covered in introductions to philosophy of religion. And the first chapter is not an "issue" chapter at all. It is a background chapter on the religions of the world with readings from the scriptures and other religious writings of Hinduism, Buddhism, Judaism, Christianity, and Islam. One of the issues covered by this book is the issue of religious plurality or diversity—How should we understand the relationship between the various religions of the world? The readings in the first chapter help provide a useful background for a discussion of the plurality issue. Moreover these readings help students understand aspects of other issues. For instance, they bring into relief the difference between theistic and non-theistic religions and so are pertinent to understanding the scope or applicability of the arguments for the existence of God as well as the traditional religious problem of evil.

Among the chapters of this collection that contain traditional readings on traditional issues is the second chapter, in which there are familiar readings presenting the Ontological, Cosmological, Teleological, and Moral Arguments. These readings relate to a discussion of the logical status of the familiar arguments for the existence of God. The third chapter is one of the chapters that contain readings relating to an issue not usually covered in introductions to philosophy of religion. It contains readings that bear on the issue of the *relevance* for faith of the arguments for God's existence, an issue that readings in collections like this one rarely address but which for many may be more pressing than the issue of the logical strength of the arguments for God's existence. In another case Chapter 4 on the reasonableness of religious belief contains a reading by William James, in which he argues for the right to believe religiously, a reading by Alvin Plantinga, in which he advances his theory of proper basic beliefs, and a reading by William Alston on reliabilism. The fifth chapter contrasts with the fourth in presenting less traditional readings that relate to the possibility of a religious discovery of God in accord with a discovery model implicit in a strain of religious sensibility.

Sometimes when a chapter covers a traditional issue some of the readings in the chapter are more traditional and some are less traditional. In Chap. 6 on the religious problem of evil the readings include Fyoder Dostyoevsky's "Rebellion" from *The Brothers Karamazov* (in which Ivan relates evils done to children), a selection from David Hume's *Dialogues Concerning Natural Religion*, John Hick's presentation of an Irenaean theodicy, and H. J. McCloskey's "God and Evil," all of which are fairly traditional readings on this issue; also included is another selection from *The Brothers Karamazov*, not traditionally included (in which we see the reaction of Alyosha, Ivan's brother, to evil), as well as a less traditional reading by this collection's editor on how an understanding of evil is significantly affected by the perspective of a faith like the faith of Job. Again, in Chapter 7 on miracles there is the traditional "Of Miracles" from David Hume's *Enquiry*, and selections from Richard Swinburne's *The Concept of Miracle*, as well as less traditional discussions of non-intervention concepts of *miracle* that are identifiable in religious sensibilities. Though the readings focus mainly on philosophical discussions of the issues, some of the readings consult various religious sensibilities to help frame a number of the issues discussed.

Also to be noted as a distinctive feature of this collection is a section in Chapter 9 with readings on the gender-of-God issue, which augments a section of the same chapter that has more traditional readings on the issue of the factual meaning of religious language. In Chapter 10 this collection provides readings on religious realism and the meaning of God, where the issue is whether all that is essential to religion, or theistic religion, is retained in the absence of belief in a transcendent "metaphysical" God. And the text ends with two chapters of readings on the contemporary issue of religious plurality.

A range of philosophical and religious perspectives is reflected in the readings in the issue chapters. These include the theological perspectives of St. Thomas Aquinas, John Calvin, and Karl Rahner, the analytic perspectives of Alvin Plantinga and William Alston, the modern perspectives of Blaise Pascal, William James and W. K. Clifford, the contemporary perspectives of John Hick and Don Cupitt, the continental perspectives of Soren Kierkegaard and Friedrich Nietzsche, and the feminist/theological perspectives of Sally McFague and Rosemary Reuther.

Each chapter has an introduction. The first chapter has an introduction that relates an appreciation of the different religions of the world to an understanding of at least some issues in philosophy of religion, and each succeeding chapter has an introduction that describes the issue of the chapter and relates the readings of the chapter to that issue.

This collection can be used with *Introduction to Philosophy of Religion*, written by the editor of this collection. Chapters in that text are coordinated with the chapters of this collection. However, the two books can be used independently.

My preparation of this collection was aided by reassigned time granted to me by the Department of Philosophy and the College of Humanities at California State University, Northridge, for which I am grateful. Among the people at Prentice Hall who helped bring this book to completion I am particularly indebted to Frances Russello and Peggy Davis in Production and to Mical Moser and Carla Worner for their editorial support. Carla Worner's support over the years in which this book was being prepared was invaluable, and to her special thanks are due. I wish to thank the reviewers of this book Edward Wierenga, University of Rochester; Lauress L. Wilkins, Regis College; Laur Duhan Kaplan, University of North Carolina at Charlotte. Finally, I am very grateful to Karpagam Jagadeesan for her careful copyediting of this collection.

James Kellenberger

About the Author

James Kellenberger is the author of several books in philosophy of religion and philosophy of ethics. He is Professor of Philosophy at California State University, Northridge, and has taught courses in philosophy of religion for many years.

Introduction

Readings in Philosophy of Religion

All of the readings in this collection bear on issues in philosophy of religion; however they do not all do so in the same way. Most of the readings in the various chapters are philosophical. They contain philosophical reflection on issues relating to religion or to particular religious traditions. The readings in the first chapter, though, are purely religious. They are drawn from the scriptural and written traditions of five major religions. Most of us in the contemporary world are acquainted with religion in one way or another, but few of us have an acquaintance with the range of world religions. For this reason, and because we will better appreciate the issues philosophy of religion reflects on if we have an acquaintace with the phenomena of religion and their range, our first chapter consists of readings from the religious traditions themselves.

The philosophical readings, on the other hand, address issues in philosophy of religion. These issues are the subjects of Chapters 2 through 12. Many of the philosophical readings in this collection are taken from what is called "analytic philosophy." Others come from philosophical writers who stand closer to some theological tradition than do most analytic philosophers. Others come from writers who are religious thinkers, in the sense that they have reflected on religion, but who may or may not label themselves as philosophers. Philosophy endeavors to be objective and to pursue issues with intellectual honesty, but of course as rigorous as philosophical writers may be the specific background and commitments of philosphers can influence their reflections, if only in the questions they think important and the assuptions they make. For these reasons there has been an effort to include philosophical writers, in a broad construction of "philosophy," who come from a variety of backgrounds. This collection includes contributions from Christian writers with various perspectives (John Hick and Don Cupitt) and writers from other religious traditions (Martin Buber, Shavesh Thakur, Abu Hamid al Ghazali, and Black Elk). It includes writers sympathetic to religion (William James, John Hick and Alvin Plantinga) and writers who are not (W. K. Clifford, Bertrand Russell, and Sigmund Freud). It includes Western writers (ranging from David Hume to Blaise Pascal) and Eastern writers (Shavesh Thakur). It includes medieval writers (St. Anselm, St. Thomas Aquinas, and Julian of Norwich), modern writers (Immanuel Kant and William James), and contemporary writers (William Alston and D. Z. Phillips). It includes feminist writers (Sally McFague and Rosemary Reuther). And it includes analytic writers (Alvin Plantinga and William Alston) and Continental writers (Søren Kierkegaard, Miguel de Unamuno, and Friederich Nietzsche).

The issues in philosophy of religion addressed by the writers in this collection are religious and philosophical in that they arise where religion and philosophy meet. They arise at those points where we may raise a philosophical question about some religious belief or practice or concept. We should appreciate, however, that the issues in philosophy of religion may well arise *within* religion, so that the philosophical questioner and the religiously committed individual are one and the same person. So it is that in the thirteenth century St. Thomas Aquinas, who as a Christian saint is of course a religious believer, asks the question "Whether God exists?" and answers it by advancing philosophical reasoning to show that God exists. Other times philosophical questions about religion may come from critics who stand outside religion, but even in these cases those within religion may address the questions raised. The basic questions asked in philosophy of religion at the deepest level constitute human issues. They arise from our human condition, as do all the original questions of philosophy. They arise from our human condition as it expresses itself in religious belief and practice.

This collection provides readings that address ten issues in philosophy of religion. Chapter 2 contains readings that present and critically examine several traditional arguments, or proposed proofs, for the existence of God. There are, however, *two* important questions to be asked about the proposed proofs. One question is about whether they do in fact prove the existence of God. This is the concern of Chapter 2. The other question is about the *relevance* of these arguments for religious belief, a question that we can ask even if we become convinced that one or more of the arguments for God's existence work. This question is the concern of Chapter 3.

Finding a proof for the existence of God is not the only way to make religion, or religious belief in God, reasonable. In Chapter 4 readings by authors with different perspectives will discuss various other ways that religious belief might be shown to be reasonable. In Chapter 5 readings will address the possibility that religion is reasonable because it has a basis in a kind of experience that is open to human beings.

The readings in Chapter 6 will discuss the Religious Problem of Evil. The Problem of Evil is a problem that arises within religions where there is a belief in God and God is believed to be all-good and all-powerful, as in traditional Christianity and Judaism. The Religious Problem of Evil may be stated this way: If God is all-good and all-powerful, how can there be such a God when that God allows such evils in the world to exist?

The subject of Chapter 7 is the issue of miracles. Roughly a miracle, in the religious traditions of Judaism, Christianity, and Islam, is an act of God, something that God does in our world. This means that *if* there are miracles in this religious sense, then there must be a God who performs them. The questions here are: Is any report of a miracle true? And, more fundamentally, Are miracles even possible?

Chapter 8 will take up the question of the relationship between religion and morality. We speak of "Christian ethics," "Jewish ethics," and "Buddhist ethics." How are they related, and is non-religious morality connected to religion? Is religion in some way the foundation of morality? Or is morality independent of religion?

The readings in Chapter 9 will take up questions that have to do with "religious language," in particular language about God. Questions that arise here are: Can we say anything about God in a "factual" sense? And if we can, can we say anything about God in a literal sense? Or, at best, can we only metaphorically speak of God? Is it metaphorical to say God is merciful? Related is the gender issue. If God is a loving Father, is God a male or masculine? Can God just as well be conceived of or imaged as a loving Mother?

The issue of religious realism is addressed by the readings of Chapter 10. The issue of religious realism asks this question: Does the religious meaning of God require that God be a transcendent being that exists independently of religious and spiritual practice? Realism answers this question by saying that yes, God must be understood as having a "real" existence over and above the practice and belief of those who are religious. Those who think that realism is misconceived say that it is time for a new meaning of God (or sometimes they say a return to the original meaning) that does not require any reference to a transcendent being.

The readings in Chapters 11 and 12 will treat the issue of religious plurality. This is the issue that arises from the fact that there are many different religions in the world. This issue asks: How should we understand there being many, diverse religions in the world? The question, put another way, is: How are the different religions of the world related to one another? This issue is given two chapters because there are several important but distinguishable resolutions proposed for it.

These issues in philosophy of religion, we should appreciate, relate to us whether we are religious or not. Consider the issue of religious plurality, the issue of Chapters 11 and 12. If I am religious—a Muslim, say—I will ask how my religion, Islam, relates to other religions, like Judaism and Christianity. If I am not religious, I still may wonder how the different religions relate to one another. Whether we are religious or not, we all live in the same world, and in that world various religions exist side by side. If we are going to understand one another, we should understand the religious commitment of others, even if it is not our own commitment. This reason becomes more pressing as cultures and religions more and more intermingle and geographical isolation becomes a thing of the past.

The chapters of this anthology parallel the chapters in the Prentice-Hall *Introduction to Philosophy of Religion* written by the editor, and the two volumes may be used together. However, the readings speak for themselves, and this anthology may also be used independently.

Chapter 1

Religions of the World

The purpose of this first chapter of selections from religious texts is to provide readers with an initial acquaintance with important texts of several world religions and thereby an acquaintance with those world religions themselves. It may be that many will have a personal acquaintance with one religion or another and some may have a personal acquaintance with more than one religion, but probably many, like most of us in the broader American culture, will not have a personal acquaintance with all five of the world religions represented in this chapter. The initial acquaintance with these world religions provided by this chapter's readings has relevance for many of the philosophical issues that relate to religion. In an obvious way it bears on the philosophical issue of *religious plurality*, the issue of how to understand the relationship between the different religions of the world. However, it also has relevance for an understanding of other issues in philosophy of religion. For instance, it will help provide us with an understanding of how the heritage of issues relating to the existence of God and to belief in God, such as, the issue of *proving the existence of God*, can only be raised in regard to some religious traditions.

The chapter contains readings from five of the major religious traditions of the world. In most cases the reading is from the scripture of the religion. The scripture of a religion is a text that the religion recognizes as having special authority. But in some cases an important religious text may not be scriptural. For instance, in those different forms of Indian religion known as Hinduism the *Bhagavad-Gita* has special religious significance, but it is not scriptural. It is accepted as "remembered," not as "revealed."

Hinduism

Hinduism is the main religion of the Indian sub-continent, although there are Hindu communities in many parts of the world, including the United States, Europe, and Africa. Hinduism has no required set of beliefs or "creed" and it has no primary religious authority or leader analogous to the Roman Catholic Pope. In the complex of religious practice and belief that is Hinduism, there are three different *margas*, or paths to salvation or liberation (or moksha): the path of devotion, the path of action, and the path of knowledge. They can be combined or one can be emphasized.

The path of devotion (*bhakti*), with its various forms of worship, has had a wider appeal than the more austere ways of knowledge and action. It is the way of *bhakti* or devotion that Krishna recommends in the *Bhagavad Gita*. Many different gods may be worshipped, such as Ganesha the elephant god, Kama the god of love, or the mother goddess in various forms, including the fierce Kali or the gracious and kind Parvati. Hindus may worship the three gods of the Trimurti, Brahma the creator, Shiva the destroyer and Vishnu the preserver. Both Shiva and Vishnu have many devotees in India. Brahma the creator has no cult of devotees, although he has several temples and is important in Hindu art. Also important religiously, and from a devotional standpoint, are the avatars of Vishnu, especially Krishna, who, since the *Bhagavad Gita* is regarded as a deity in his own right. The birthday of Lord Krishna is celebrated throughout India. Another of Vishnu's avatars, Rama, the hero of the *Ramayana*, is also considered a god in his own right. There are nine main avatars of Vishnu, Krishna being the eighth and Rama the seventh, but in addition there are innumerable other avatars of Vishnu claimed by the followers of Vishnu. The devotional form of Hinduism allows the worship of the one God through the worship of any of several gods, and often this is done quite consciously. This practice is called henotheism and is distinguished from unqualified polytheism.

Contrasting with devotional Hinduism is the Vedanta, or "end of the Vedas," teaching of Shankara. Shankara in the eighth or early ninth century of the Common Era provided a systematic treatment of the Upanishadic teaching that the highest reality is an impersonal Absolute. Shankara's teaching, called *advaita*, is monistic or nondualistic. In this teaching all is one, so that there ultimately is no distinction between this and that, between knower and known, between *Brahman*, the impersonal Absolute, and *atman*, the soul of the individual. Release or moksha, for this strain of Hinduism, is attained not through worship and devotion, but through overcoming the illusion of diversity, which is done through the practice of piety, virtue, and meditation. Finally the layers of illusion, built up by the *karma* of this life or earlier lives, are shed and true Being, Consciousness, and Bliss (*sat-chit-ananda*) is attained.

Some Hindus are in the tradition of Hinduism by virtue of their meditative approach to the impersonal reality of Brahman. Many Hindus are in the tradition of Hinduism by virtue of their following the path of devotion. Their worship may be of Vishnu or it may be of Shiva or Kali. Or their worship may be of the one God through their worship of Vishnu or another god of the Hindu pantheon.

from The Bhagavad-Gita

The *Bhagavad-Gita* is a part of the *Mahabharata*, an epic poem that is the longest poem ever written. The *Bhagavad-Gita* can be read alone, however, and often is by Hindus and others. In the *Gita* a warrior, Arjuna, is having a conversation with his charioteer before a great battle. The charioteer is none other than the god Krishna, an *avatar*, or incarnation, of Vishnu. The Lord Krishna gives advice to Arjuna regarding his duty (dharma) and teaches the path of devotion or faith. The following selection, which is a little less than a quarter of the *Gita*, contains material from near the beginning and all of two chapters, including the last.

From the *Bhagavad-Gita*. Mount Vernon, New York: Peter Pauper Press, 1952. Reprinted by permission of Peter Pauper Press © 1952.

The Grief of Arjuna

1

ARJUNA SAID:

28 As I look upon all these kinfolk meeting for battle, O Krishna,

29 My limbs grow weak, and my mouth goes dry. Trembling comes upon my body, my hair stands on end;

30 My bow falls from my hand, and my skin burns. I cannot stand in my place; my mind whirls.

31 Unlucky are all the omens that I behold, O Long-Haired One. I see no blessing from the slaying of my own kinfolk in strife;

32 I desire not victory, O Krishna, nor kingship, nor delights. What good to me is kingship, O Lord of the Herds, or pleasures, or life?

33 Those for whose sake I desired kingship, pleasures, and delights stand here in battle-array, offering up their lives and wealth.

34 Teachers, fathers, sons; and grandsires, uncles, fathers-in-law; grandsons, brothers-in-law, kinsmen too.

35 These though they smite me I would not smite, O Madhu-Slayer, even for the sake of empire over the Three Worlds. Much less for the sake of things of this earth.

36 What pleasure can there be to us, O Troubler of the Folk, from slaughter of Dhritarashtra's folk? Guilt indeed must lodge with us for doing these to death with our armed hand.

37 Therefore it is not right that we should slay Dhritarashtra's folk, our kinsmen; for if we do to death our own kin, how can we walk in joy, Madhu Lord?

38 Although these my enemies, whose wits are overthrown by greed, see not the guilt of destroying a family, see not the sin of treason to friends,

39 Yet how, O Troubler of the Folk, shall we with clear sight not see the sin of destroying a family? Clearly we must ourselves hold back from this guilt.

40 With the destruction of a family comes the destruction of the ancient laws of that family; when laws are destroyed, lawlessness falls upon the family.

41 When lawlessness has come upon it, O Krishna, the women fall to sin; and from the women's sinning, O thou of Vrishni's race, castes become confounded.

42 The confounding of caste brings to hell both the family's slayers and the family itself; for their ancestors fall, being deprived of the offerings of the sacred rice cakes and water.

43 By this guilt of the destroyers of a family, which makes castes to be confounded, the everlasting laws of race and laws of family are overthrown.

44 Hell is the dwelling ordained for men whose laws of family are overthrown, O Troubler of the Folk; thus have we heard.

45 Alas, it is a heavy sin we have resolved on, to slay our kin from lust after the sweets of kingship!

46 Far better for me if Dhritarashtra's men, with their armed hand, should slay me in the strife—unresisting and weaponless.

SANJAYA SAID:

47 So spoke Arjuna, and sank down on the seat of his chariot in the field of war; and he let fall his bow and arrows, for his heart was heavy with sorrow.

The Way of the Rule

2

SANJAYA SAID:

Thus was he stricken by pity and despair, with clouded eyes full of tears; and the Slayer of Madhu spoke to him these words:

1

THE LORD SPOKE:

O Arjuna, whence, in your hour of crisis, comes upon you this depression unworthy of your noble race, dishonorable, and contrary to the attainment of heaven?

2

Yield not to unmanliness, O Pritha's son; it is not for you. Cast off this base faintness of heart and rise up, O terror of the foe!

3

ARJUNA ASKED:

O Madhu's Slayer, O smiter of foes, how can I contend in the strife with my arrows against Bhishma and Drona, who are worthy of my reverence?

4

It were better to live by beggary in this world than to kill such noble masters; were I to slay my masters, all I should enjoy here of wealth and desires would be stained by blood.

5

We know not which is better for us, that we should overcome them or they should overcome us; before us stand arrayed Dhritarashtra's folk, whom if we slay we shall have no wish to live.

6

My soul stricken with unmanliness, my mind all unsure of the Law, I implore Thee, O Krishna, tell me clearly what will be the better way. I am Thy disciple; teach me, who am come to Thee for refuge.

7

I can see no way to cast out the sorrow that withers my limbs, no, not though I win wide lordship without rival on earth and even to lordship over the gods.

8

SANJAYA SAID:

So spoke the Wearer of the Hair-Knot, frightener of foes, to the High-Haired One: "I will not make war!" he said to the Lord Krishna, and made an end of speaking.

9

And as he sat despairing between the two hosts (O thou of Bharata's race) the High-Haired One, seeming to smile, spoke these words to him:

10

THE LORD SPOKE:

You have grieved over those for whom grief is unmeet, though you speak words of understanding. But the truly learned grieve not for the dead or the living.

11

Never have I not been, never have you not been, and never have these princes of men not been; and never shall the time come when all of us shall not still be.

12

As the tenant Soul goes through childhood and manhood and old age in this body, so does it pass to other bodies; therefore the wise man is not confused.

13

It is the touchings of the senses, O Kunti's son, that beget cold and heat, pleasure and pain; it is they that come and go, that do not abide; endure them bravely, O you of Bharata's race.

14

Truly, the man whom these do not disturb, indifferent alike to pain and to pleasure, and wise, is fit for immortality, O chief of men.

15

There cannot be being for what is unreal; what is real can never become non-being. The bounds of these twain have been beheld by those who have seen the truth.

16

Know that That which pervades this universe is imperishable; there is no one who can ever destroy the Indestructible.

17

These bodies are perishable; but the dwellers in these bodies are eternal, indestructible, incomprehensible. Therefore fight, O you of Bharata's race.

18

He who thinks this Self to be a slayer, and he who thinks this Self to be slain, are both without discernment; the Soul slays not, neither is it slain.

19

It never is born, and never dies, nor may it, being in being, descend into non-being; this unborn, everlasting, abiding Ancient is not slain when the body is slain.

20

Knowing this Soul to be imperishable, everlasting, unborn, changeless, how can you think, O Arjuna, to slay it or to make it slain?

21

As a man lays aside outworn garments and takes others that are new, so the Body-Dweller puts away outworn bodies and goes to others that are new.

22

Weapons cannot pierce It, fires cannot burn It, waters cannot wet It, winds cannot dry It.

23

Not to be pierced is This, not to be burned, nor to be wetted, nor likewise to be dried; everlasting is This, dwelling in all things, firm, motionless, everlasting.

24

Unmanifested is This, unthinkable This, unalterable This; therefore, knowing It to be so, you do not do well to grieve.

25

Even though you believe It must pass everlastingly through births and everlastingly through deaths, nevertheless, O strong of arm, you should not grieve thus.

26

For, to that which is born, the coming of death is certain, and to that which is dead, the coming of new birth is certain. Therefore grieve not over the inevitable.

27

All born beings are in their beginnings unshown, in their midway states are shown, and for their endings, O you of Bharata's race, are unshown again; what lament should there be for this?

28

Some look upon this Soul as a marvel; as a marvel another tells of it; and as a marvel another hears of it; but though all hear of this Soul none knows It.

29

For all time this Body-Dweller may not be wounded, O you of Bharata's stock, in the body of any being. Therefore you should not sorrow for any being.

30

Looking likewise on your own law, you should not be dismayed; for to a noble warrior there is nothing higher than a righteous war.

31

Happy the noble warriors, O son of Pritha, who find such a war coming unsought to them, as an open door to Paradise.

32

But if you will not wage this lawful battle, then will you fail your own law and your honor, and incur sin.

33

The people will name you with dishonor; and to a man of fame dishonor is worse than death.

34

These lords of great chariots will think you have held back from the battle through fear; and you will come to be lightly thought of by those who formerly were eager to pay you honor.

35

Those who seek your hurt will utter many words of ill speech, crying out against you for your faintness; now what could be more painful than this?

36

If you fall in battle, you win Paradise; if you conquer, you have the joys of the earth; therefore rise up resolute for the fray, O son of Kunti.

37

Holding yourself with the same indifference to pleasure and to pain, gain and loss, conquest and defeat, make yourself ready for the fight; in this way you can incur no stain of sin.

38

Thus have I declared to you the wisdom of Self-Realization. Now hear of the wisdom of Yoga, by knowing which you will cast off the bonds of Karma, of cause and effect in action. 39

Here there is no failure of enterprise, here there is no backsliding. Even a very little practice of this Law saves you from the dread of continued rebirth. 40

The Nature of Brahma

8

ARJUNA SAID:

What is Brahma? What is the Self? What is Action? What is the realm of Things? What is the realm of Gods? 1

Who dwells in our body as the deity of sacrifice, and how does he dwell there, O Destroyer of Madhu? And how mayest Thou be known even at the hour of our death? 2

THE LORD SPOKE:

Brahma is the Imperishable, the Supreme; the Nature of each is called the One over Self; the creative force that makes born beings arise into existence bears the name of Karma. 3

The One over earthly things is mutable Nature; the One over Gods is the cosmic spirit; the One over sacrifice is Myself, here in this body, O best of men. 4

He who at his last hour, when he casts off the body, goes hence remembering Me, goes assuredly into My being. 5

Whatsoever state of being a man remembers at his end in leaving the body, to that same state he goes, O son of Kunti, being absorbed in the thought thereof. 6

Therefore at all times remember Me, and act; if your mind and understanding are devoted to Me, you will assuredly come to Me. 7

O son of Pritha, he who meditates on the Supreme Being, and with practiced mind remains unwavering, he goes to the heavenly Supreme on whom his thought dwells. 8

He who thinks of the Omniscient, the Ancient, the Ruler, the minutest of the minute, the sustainer of all; whose form is inconceivable, self-effulgent like the sun, and beyond the darkness of ignorance, 9

At his time of going hence; with steadfast wisdom, guided by devotion and force of the Rule, setting the life-force properly midway between the brows, he comes to the heavenly Supreme. 10

I will tell you briefly of that state which Veda-knowers call the Imperishable; ascetics void of passion enter this state; and in desire of it men observe chastity and self-control. 11

Closing all doors, shutting the mind within the heart, bringing the life-force into the head, entering the concentration of the Rule, 12

Uttering *Om*, the one-syllabled symbol of the inexpressible Brahma, and remembering Me—he who does this as he departs, leaves the body and enters the supreme way. 13

To the man of the Rule everlastingly under the Rule, who always and everlastingly with undivided mind remembers Me, I am easy to win, O son of Pritha. 14

The great-souled ones, having reached Me, never again re-enter rebirth, the inconstant home of sorrows, for they have reached perfection. 15

All realms, even up to the Braham-realm, O Arjuna, are subject to rebirth; but for those who have come to Me, O son of Kunti, there is no birth again. 16

They who know the Day of Brahma to endure for a thousand ages and the Night of Brahma to endure for a thousand ages are true knowers of night and day. 17

At the dawning of this Day all existence springs from the unshown state; and at the falling of this Night it dissolves into the unshown again. 18

This same multitude of beings, rising to birth after birth, dissolves away without will of its own at the coming of the Night, O son of Pritha, and rises once again at coming of the Day. 19

But there is another Existence beyond this, an Unshown beyond this Unshown, an ancient eternal Existence, which is in all born beings, but perishes not with them. 20

This Unshown Being is called "the Imperishable." This, they say, is the Way Supreme, from which, once won, men return not to rebirth; and this is My supreme abode. 21

This is the Supreme Self, wherein all beings abide, wherewith this whole universe is filled; and is to be won, O son of Pritha, by undivided devotion. 22

Now I will declare the times when the men of the Rule go hence never to return; also the times when, departing, they will come back to rebirth. 23

Fire, light, day, the waxing half of the moon, the six months of the sun's northern course—in these times the knowers of Brahma go hence, and come to Brahma. 24

Smoke, night, the waning half of the moon, the six months of the sun's southern course—in these times the man of the Rule receives the light of the moon, and returns. 25

Light and dark; these are the two everlasting ways of the world; by the one a man never comes back again, by the other he returns. 26

Knowing these two paths, no man of the Rule, O son of Pritha, is ever bewildered; therefore be at all times guided by the Rule, Arjuna. 27

The man of the Rule, knowing well the fruits of righteousness promised for Veda-study, offerings, mortifications, and almsgiving, passes beyond them and beyond this present universe, and reaches the primeval Supreme Abode. 28

The Path of Liberation

18

ARJUNA SAID:

I am eager, O Mighty-Armed One, to know the true nature of renunciation and relinquishment. O High-Haired One, Kesin's slayer. 1

THE LORD SPOKE:

Putting aside all the works of desire which are done for return, is called renunciation; surrender of the fruit of all works is called relinquishment. 2

Some sages say that all action should be renounced as a fault; others say that works of sacrifice, almsgiving, and mortification should not be renounced. 3

Now hear from Me the true word concerning such renunciation, O best of Bharatas; for renunciation, O tiger among men, has been explained as threefold. 4

Acts of sacrifice, almsgiving, and mortification should not be renounced, but should indeed be performed; sacrifice, almsgiving, and mortification are purifying to the wise. 5

But even these works must be done with relinquishment of attachment and all thought of reward; this, O Son of Pritha, is my final and best word. 6

To renounce a duty is not right; to renounce it through delusion is a working of the Darkness Mood. 7

To renounce a duty out of fear of its difficulty or painfulness is a renunciation of the Fiery Mood; there is no reward for such renunciation. 8

But to perform a duty merely because it is a duty, without emotional attachment and without thought of reward, is to act from the Goodness Mood. 9

The relinquisher, enveloped in Goodness, enlightened, and with doubts destroyed, does not hate unpleasant works, and does not become attached to pleasant ones. 10

For the body-bearer is not able to surrender works altogether; but he that surrenders the reward of works is called the relinquisher. 11

After death there are three kinds of reward for the doer of works: pleasing, unpleasing, and mixed. But for the relinquisher there is no need for reward. 12

Now learn from Me, O Mighty-Armed, the five causes of all actions, as declared in the Vedanta. 13

The body, the self, the senses, the functions, and the fifth of these, Providence: 14

These five are the causes of every action, good or bad, that man sets himself to do, whether with body, or with speech, or with mind. 15

This being so, he who in imperfect understanding sees his Self alone as the doer, is blinded by his foolishness. 16

He who knows that his Self is not the doer, whose understanding is not defiled, does no slaughter even though he slay these people, nor is he fettered by his act. 17

The Knowledge, the Knowable, and the Knower are the threefold incitement to action; the Instrument, the Action, and the Agent are the threefold realization of action. 18

Knowledge, Action, and Agent, according to the science of the moods, are of three kinds: hear too about this. 19

The knowledge whereby a man beholds one unchangeable Being in all beings, the Undivided in the divided, is of the Goodness Mood. 20

The knowledge whereby a man perceives diverse and various existences in diverse and varying beings is knowledge of the Fiery Mood. 21

But that which believes a simple life is the whole, which in its smallness sees not the cause, or the eternal reality, this is knowledge of the Darkness Mood. 22

The action that is duty, free of attachment, and done without passion or hatred by one seeking no reward, is said to be of the Goodness Mood. 23

But work done by one seeking to gratify his desires, or with thought of "I"; or with great effort, is said to be of the Fiery Mood. 24

The work that is undertaken from bewilderment, without heed to future consequence, destruction, harm, or one's own powers, is said to be of Darkness. 25

A worker is of Goodness who is free from attachment, speaks not of himself, his constancy and vigor, and is unmoved by success or failure. 26

27 A worker is of Fieryness who is passionate, wishful for rewards, greedy; a doer of harm, impure; who is moved by joy and grief.

28 A worker is of Darkness who is unsteady, vulgar, obstinate, deceitful, malicious; who is lazy, despondent and delaying.

29 Now hear, O Wealth-Winner, the three-fold division of understanding and constancy according to the Moods, set forth fully and clearly:

30 O son of Pritha, that understanding is of the Goodness Mood which knows when to act and when to refrain, what is right and what is wrong, what to fear and what not to fear, what is slavery and what is deliverance.

31 O son of Pritha, that understanding is of the Fiery Mood, which fails to know right from wrong, proper from improper.

32 O son of Pritha, that understanding is of the Darkness Mood which, enveloped in gloom, confuses right with wrong, and twists all things into their contraries.

33 O son of Pritha, that constancy is of the Goodness Mood which, by concentration, controls the actions of mind, breath, and senses.

34 O Arjuna, that constancy is of the Fiery Mood which holds to duty, pleasure and wealth in obstinate desire for rewards.

35 That constancy is of the Darkness Mood whereby fools never put aside sleep, fear, sorrow, despair, and vanity.

36 Now, O Bharata-prince, hear from Me the three kinds of happiness. First, that happiness wherein a man may rejoice by long practice, and which brings him to the end of sorrow:

37 This, which at first is like poison and in its ripening is like ambrosia, is the pleasure of Goodness, born of the clearness of one's own understanding of the Self.

38 And that which is at first like ambrosia and in its ripening like poison, which comes from union of the senses with the objects of their desire, is the pleasure of Fieryness.

39 That pleasure which begins and ends in self-delusion, which comes from sleep, indolence, and self-deception, is the pleasure of Darkness.

40 There is not, either on earth or in heaven among the gods, anything that is free from these three Nature-born Moods.

41 The works of Brahmans, lords, men of affairs and serfs, O frightener of the foe, are different from each other by virtue of the different Moods by which they spring from Nature.

42 Restraint of mind and senses, austerity, purity, patience, uprightness, knowledge, discernment, and faith in God, are the natural duties of the Brahman, born in him.

43 Bravery, heroic temper, steadiness, skill; not fleeing in battle, generosity and princeliness are the natural duties of the lord.

44 Tilling the ground, herding cattle, and trading are the natural duties of practical men of affairs, and the natural duty of the serf is service.

45 Only as each man devotes himself to his own proper duty does he attain to consummation. Hear how by devotion to his proper duty he wins consummation.

46 A man wins consummation by worshipping, with his proper work and duty, Him who pervades the universe and is the source of all.

47 There is more happiness in following one's own duty without skill, than in doing another's duty well. To do the work assigned by Nature incurs no sin.

No one should forsake the work to which he is born, even though it is faulty; for all undertakings are clouded by faults as fire is by smoke. 48

He whose understanding is without attachment, who has wholly conquered self, and who is freed of desires, wins, by this relinquishment, the supreme consummation. 49

Learn from Me briefly, O son of Kunti, how he who has won such consummation wins to Brahma, the highest goal of knowledge. 50

Possessed of purified understanding, restraining self by firmness, relinquishing sweet sound and all other objects of the senses; casting aside passion and hatred, 51

Living alone away from men, eating little, restraining speech, body, and mind, given over to the Rule of meditation, turned everlastingly to passionlessness, 52

Free from egotism, from force, pride, desire, wrath, and possession, without thought of a "mine," and at peace, one becomes fit for Brahmahood. 53

Becoming Brahma, he is clear of spirit, he grieves not and desires not; indifferent towards all earthly beings, he wins to supreme devotion to Me. 54

By devotion he recognizes Who and What I am; thus knowing Me in verity, he speedily enters into Me. 55

Even though he is a doer of many works, by taking refuge in Me he attains by My grace to the eternal changeless home. 56

Cast off, in your mind, all thoughts of actions; look at Me as Supreme; with steadfastness of understanding fix your thoughts firmly on Me. 57

With your thoughts on Me, you shall pass beyond all obstacles; but if from self-interest you do not listen to Me, you shall be lost. 58

In self-interest you say: "I will not do battle!" But your resolve is vain: Nature will compel you. 59

Fettered to the actions born of your own nature, you must do battle despite the delusions of your self-conceit. 60

The Lord dwells in the heart of all born beings, O Arjuna, and with magic makes them spin about as though set upon a wheel. 61

Seek refuge with your whole soul, O Bharata's son, in Him; by His grace you shall win supreme peace, the everlasting realm. 62

Thus have I set forth to you the deepest of deep knowledge; ponder upon it in its fullness, and do as you will. 63

Hear again My supreme word, deepest of all; because you are exceedingly beloved of Me, therefore I speak for your best good. 64

Fix your mind on Me, be devoted to Me, sacrifice to Me, prostrate yourself to Me: so shall you come to Me. I promise you this truly, for you are dear to Me. 65

Surrendering all duties, come for refuge to Me alone. Grieve not, for I will deliver you from all sins. 66

This is never to be spoken of by you to anyone not austere in living, not devout, not dutiful, or not respectful to Me. 67

But he who in supreme devotion toward Me shall recite this supreme secret among My worshippers, he shall assuredly come to Me. 68

None among men can do me more acceptable service; none shall be dearer to Me on earth than he. 69

And he who shall read and study this sacred dialogue between us—he shall worship Me bringing knowledge as his sacrificial offering. This is My thought. 70

And he who listens to it with faith and without scoffings—even he, liberated from evil, shall attain to the happy worlds of the workers of holiness. 71

Have you heard this, O son of Pritha, with mind wholly intent? now has the bewilderment of your ignorance vanished, O Wealth-Winner? 72

ARJUNA SPOKE:

My bewilderment has vanished; I have regained understanding by Thy grace, O Never-Falling. I stand free from doubt. I will do Thy word. 73

SANJAYA SPOKE:

Thus did I hear this wondrous, hair-stirring dialogue of Krishna and the great-hearted son of Pritha. 74

By the grace of Vyasa I heard this supreme secret from Krishna, the Lord of the Rule, himself reciting his Rule. 75

O king, each time I remember this wondrous and holy dialogue of the Long-Haired One and Arjuna, I rejoice again. 76

And each time I remember the exceedingly wondrous form of the Lord, great astonishment comes upon me, O king, and I rejoice again. 77

Wherever Krishna is, the Lord of the Rule; wherever the archer is, Pritha's son, there, I know, are fortune, victory, welfare and good life. 78

Buddhism

Buddhism was founded in India by Siddartha Gautama in the sixth century B.C.E In traditional Buddhist belief, Gautama Buddha, or the Buddha, renounced his life as a prince and followed a religious quest for seven years. When he was thirty-five he sat beneath a tree and after forty-nine days of meditation attained enlightenment. The Buddha lived many years and during that time gave sermons and taught the dharma (teaching, truth) to his followers. In the centuries that followed Buddhism spread to Southeast Asia, China, and Japan, as well as to Eastern countries, and developed into different schools, with different teachings. The three major schools of Buddhism are Theravada (the way of the elders), Mahayana (the great vehicle), and Vajrayana, the main form of Buddhism in the Himalayan region. Especially for Mahayana Buddhism, the bodhisattva ideal is important.

Siddhartha, the historical Buddha, is a man, not a god. While for Buddhism there are gods, Buddhist gods are, like other beings, caught up in the cycle of rebirth (as opposed to the God of the Western monotheistic traditions, for which God traditionally is the supreme being and creator of the world). Nirvana is the ultimate goal of virtually all Buddhism, a "blowing out" of desire or craving: an enlightenment, a realization and overcoming of ignorance that releases one from the karmic cycle of rebirth. Even Mahayana bodhisattvas, who out of compassion do not enter Nirvana, are on the path to Nirvana. Buddhism is a *way* or *path*, a way or path to Nirvana. It is not a faith in a deity or a seeking of a faith-relationship to a deity. All humans and all sentient beings are potential Buddhas, and for Buddhism all are on the journey to the final realization of their Buddhahood.

from The Dhammapada

The *Dhammapada* is a collection of verses derived from talks given by the Buddha. "Dhamma" is a variant of "dharma" (teaching, truth) that is used in Buddhism and "pada" refers to the state of transcendental existence. The *Dhammapada* was written down in different languages (Prakrit, Pali, and Sanskrit) about 500 years after the death of the Buddha by followers in different schools of Buddhism. In each version the *Dhammapada* contains moral and spiritual precepts taught by the Buddha, and in each version verses are grouped into blocks or chapters according to theme. There are verses from several chapters in the following selection.

Several important Buddhist teachings are presented in our selection. These include *Nirvana* (Chap. 5, verse 75), conquering oneself (Chap. 8, verse 105), the Four Noble Truths (Chap. 14, verses 190-191) (In a fuller statement the Four Noble Truths are (1) existence is sorrow, (2) the cause of sorrow is craving, (3) this craving and its sorrow can be overcome, (4) this can be done by following eight stages or the Noble Eightfold Path, which calls for right-mindedness, right speech, right action and more.), overcoming craving (Chap. 24, verse 353), reincarnation and gaining release from rebirth (through attaining Nirvana) (Chap. 26, verse 423).

A Buddha (Chap. 14) is an enlightened one. A *brāhmin* (Chap. 26) is one who is spiritually advanced through personal attainment. In Hinduism a *brahmin* is a member of the highest, priestly caste. For Buddhism, in contrast with traditional Hinduism, spiritual status is not a matter of family or inheritance, and the true *brahmin* has come to that position through personal effort.*

The Dhammapada

1
Contrary Ways

'He insulted me, he hurt me, he defeated me, he robbed me.' Those who think such thoughts will not be free from hate. 3

'He insulted me, he hurt me, he defeated me, he robbed me.' Those who think not such thoughts will be free from hate. 4

For hate is not conquered by hate: hate is conquered by love. This is a law eternal. 5

5
The Fool

'These are my sons. This is my wealth.' In this way the fool troubles himself. He is not even the owner of himself: how much less of his sons and of his wealth! 62

If a fool can see his own folly, he in this at least is wise; but the fool who thinks he is wise, he indeed is the real fool. 63

If during the whole of his life a fool lives with a wise man, he never knows the path of wisdom as the spoon never knows the taste of the soup. 64

* From *The Dhammapada* (The path of perfection) translated with an introduction by Juan Mascaró (Penguin Classics , 1973). Copyright © Juan Mascaró, 1973.

A wrong action may not bring its reaction at once, even as fresh milk turns not sour at once: like a smouldering fire concealed under ashes it consumes the wrongdoer, 71 the fool.

And if ever to his own harm the fool increases in cleverness, this only destroys his own mind and his fate is worse than 72 before.

For he will wish for reputation, for precedence among the monks, for authority in the monasteries and for veneration 73 amongst the people.

'Let householders and hermits, both, think it was I who did that work; and let them ever ask me what they should do or not do.' These are the thoughts of the fool, 74 puffed up with desire and pride.

But one is the path of earthly wealth, and another is the path of NIRVANA. Let the follower of Buddha think of this and, without striving for reputation, let him 75 ever strive after freedom.

6
The Wise Man

He who for himself or others craves not for sons or power or wealth, who puts not his own success before the success of righteousness, he is virtuous, and right- 84 eous, and wise.

Few cross the river of time and are able to reach NIRVANA. Most of them run up 85 and down only on this side of the river.

But those who when they know the law follow the path of the law, they shall reach the other shore and go beyond the realm 86 of death.

87 Leaving behind the path of darkness and following the
path of light, let the wise man leave his home life and go into a life of freedom. In

solitude that few enjoy, let him find his joy supreme: free from possessions, free from desires, and free from whatever may darken his mind. 88

8
Better than a Thousand

Better than a thousand useless words is one single word that gives peace. 100

Better than a thousand useless verses is one single verse that gives peace. 101

Better than a hundred useless poems is one single poem that gives peace. 102

If a man should conquer in battle a thou- 103 sand and a
thousand more, and another man should 104 conquer him
self, his would be the greater victory, because the greatest of victories is the victory over oneself; and neither the gods in heaven above nor the demons down below can turn into defeat the victory of such a man. 105

Better than a hundred years lived in vice, without contemplation, is one single day of life lived in virtue and in deep contemplation. 110

Better than a hundred years lived in ignorance, without contemplation, is one single day of life lived in wisdom and in deep contemplation. 111

13
Arise! Watch

Live not a low life; remember and forget not; follow not wrong ideas; sink not into the world. 167

Arise! Watch. Walk on the right path. He who follows the right path has joy in this world and in the world beyond. 168

Follow the right path: follow not the wrong path. He who follows the right path has joy 169 in this world and in the world beyond.

When a man considers this world as a bubble of froth, and as the illusion of an appearance, then the king of death has no 170 power over him.

Come and look at this world. It is like a royal painted chariot wherein fools sink. 171 The wise are not imprisoned in the chariot.

He who in early days was unwise but later found wisdom, he sheds a light over the world like that of the moon when free 172 from clouds.

14

The Buddha

By what earthly path could you entice the Buddha who, enjoying all, can wander through the pathless ways of the Infinite?— the Buddha who is awake, whose victory cannot be turned into defeat, and whom no 179 one can conquer?

By what earthly path could you entice the Buddha who, enjoying all, can wander through the pathless ways of the Infinite?— the Buddha who is awake, whom the net 180 of poisonous desire cannot allure?

Even the gods long to be like the Buddhas who are awake and watch, who find peace in contemplation and who, calm and steady, 181 find joy in renunciation.

He who goes for refuge to Buddha, to Truth and to those whom he taught, he goes indeed to a great refuge. Then he 190 sees the four great truths:

Sorrow, the cause of sorrow, the end of sorrow, and the path of eight stages which 191 leads to the end of sorrow.

That is the safe refuge, that is the refuge supreme. If a man goes to that refuge, he 192 is free from sorrow.

16

Transient Pleasures

He who does what should not be done and fails to do what should be done, who forgets the true aim of life and sinks into transient pleasures—he will one day envy the man who lives in high contemplation. 209

Let a man be free from pleasure and let a man be free from pain; for not to have pleasure is sorrow and to have pain is also sorrow. 210

Be therefore not bound to pleasure for the loss of pleasure is pain. There are no fetters for the man who is beyond pleasure and pain. 211

From pleasure arises sorrow and from pleasure arises fear. If a man is free from pleasure, he is free from fear and sorrow. 212

From passion arises sorrow and from passion arises fear. If a man is free from passion, he is free from fear and sorrow. 213

24

Cravings

Leave the past behind; leave the future behind; leave the present behind. Thou art then ready to go to the other shore. Never more shalt thou return to a life that ends in death. 348

The man who is disturbed by wrong thoughts, whose selfish passions are strong and who only seeks sensuous pleasures, increases his craving desires and makes stronger the chains he forges for himself. 349

But he who enjoys peaceful thoughts, who considers the sorrows of pleasure, and who ever remembers the light of his life—he will see the end of his cravings, he will break the chains of death. 350

He has reached the end of his journey, he
trembles not, his cravings are gone, he is
free from sin, he has burnt the thorns of
351   life: this is his last mortal body.

He is free from lust, he is free from
greed, he knows the meaning of words,
and the meaning of their combinations,
he is a great man, a great man who sees
352   the Light: this is his last mortal body.

I have conquered all; I know all, and my life
is pure; I have left all, and I am free from
craving. I myself found the way. Whom
353   shall I call Teacher? Whom shall I teach?

The gift of Truth conquers all gifts. The
taste of Truth conquers all sweetness.
The Joy of Truth conquers all pleasures.
354   The loss of desires conquers all sorrows.

26
The Brahmin

He for whom things future or past or
present are nothing, who has nothing and
desires nothing—him I call a Brahmin.   421

He who is powerful, noble, who lives a
life of inner heroism, the all-seer, the all-
conqueror, the ever-pure, who has
reached the end of the journey, who like
Buddha is awake—him I call a Brahmin.   422

He who knows the river of his past lives
and is free from life that ends in death, who
knows the joys of heaven and the sorrows
of hell, for he is a seer whose vision is pure,
who in perfection is one with the Supreme
Perfection—him I call a Brahmin.   423

from The Diamond Sutra

The Diamond Sutra (sometimes called *The Diamond-Cutter*) expounds Buddhist
teachings in the Mahayana tradition. The Sanskrit word *sutra* means thread or
suture, and a sutra is a book of rules or precepts. *The Diamond Sutra* is a part of
the Mahayana prajna or wisdom literature, and a Chinese translation of *The
Diamond Sutra* is the oldest printed book known.[1]

Buddhist, and specifically Mahayana, themes that are present in *The
Diamond Sutra* include the following:

The Mahayana understanding of the *Bodhisattva*, according to which a
bodhisattva is one who at the threshold of the release of Nirvana holds back out
of compassion for others and their suffering. In *The Diamond Sutra* the Buddha
teaches that the Bodhisattva practices charity with no attachment to appearances
(Sec. 3) and has no desire for rewards (Sec. 28).

The doctrine of *sunyata* or emptiness, according to which conceptual distinctions are illusory, appearances are a delusion, and peace requires detachment
from appearances and distinctions (Secs. 9, 32).

Following the theme of emptiness are the related themes that the Buddha's
Teaching or Dharma is beyond declaration (Secs. 15, 21), the theme of the illusion of the ego or soul (or "I-ness") (Sec. 25), and the theme of there being no
"marks" of a Buddha (Secs. 20, 26).

Other themes are Nirvana (Sec. 3), and the theme that the Buddha's teaching is like a raft (Sec. 6). It is a vehicle to get humans to the further shore (that of
enlightenment and release) and there to be set down. Mahayana means great
vehicle, one that will carry many.

---

[1] *The Concise Encyclopedia of Living Faiths*, edited by R.C. Zaehner (London: Hutchinson, 1959) p. 322.

The Lord, or World-Honored One, who expounds the teachings of the sutra, is the Buddha, Gautama Buddha. A *bhikshu* (Sec. 1) is a monk or friar in an order founded by Gautama Buddha and a *bhikshuni* is a nun in that order. Subhuti is a disciple or pupil of the Buddha. *Tathagata* is another designation for the Buddha. A venerable one (Sec. 2) is an Arhat, a monk who has attained enlightenment or Nirvana.*

The Diamond Sutra

1

The Convocation of the Assembly

THUS HAVE I HEARD: Upon a time Buddha sojourned in Anāthapindika's park by Shravasti with a great company of *bhikshus*, even twelve hundred and fifty.

One day, at the time for breaking fast, the World-Honored One enrobed and, carrying his bowl, made his way into the great city of Shravasti to beg for his food. In the midst of the city he begged from door to door according to rule. This done, he returned to his retreat and took his meal. When he had finished he put away his robe and begging bowl, washed his feet, arranged his seat, and sat down.

2

Subhūti Makes a Request

Now in the midst of the assembly was the venerable Subhūti. Forthwith he arose, uncovered his right shoulder, knelt upon his right knee, and respectfully raising his hands with palms joined, addressed Buddha thus: World-Honored One, it is most precious how mindful the Tathāgata is of all the bodhisattvas, protecting and instructing them so well! World-Honored One, if good men and good women seek the consummation of incomparable enlightenment, by what criteria should they abide and how should they control their thoughts?

Buddha said: Very good, Subhūti! Just as you say, the Tathāgatha is ever mindful of all the bodhisattvas, protecting and instructing them well. Now listen and take my words to heart: I will declare to you by what criteria good men and good women seeking the consummation of incomparable enlightenment should abide, and how they should control their thoughts.

Said Subhūti: Pray, do, World-Honored One. With joyful anticipation we long to hear.

3

The Real Teaching of the Great Way

Buddha said: Subhūti, all the bodhisattva heroes should discipline their thoughts as follows: All living creatures of whatever class, born from eggs, from wombs, from moisture, or by transformation, whether with form or without form, whether in a state of thinking or exempt from thought necessity, or wholly beyond all thought realms—all these are caused by me to attain unbounded liberation nirvāna. Yet when vast, uncountable, immeasurable numbers of beings have thus been liberated, verily no being has been liberated. Why is this, Subhūti? It is because no bodhisattva who is a real bodhisattva cherishes the idea of an ego entity, a personality, a being, or a separated individuality.

* From *The Diamond Sutra.*

4

Even the Most Beneficent Practices Are Relative

Furthermore, Subhūti, in the practice of charity a bodhisattva should be detached. That is to say, he should practice charity without regard to appearances—without regard to sound, odor, touch, flavor, or any quality. Subhūti, thus should the bodhisattva practice charity without attachment. Wherefore? In such a case his merit is incalculable.

Subhūti, what do you think? Can you measure all the space extending eastward?

No, World-Honored One, I cannot.

Then can you, Subhūti, measure all the space extending southward, westward, northward, or in any other direction, including nadir and zenith?

No, World-Honored One, I cannot.

Well, Subhūti, equally incalculable is the merit of the bodhisattva who practices charity without any attachment to appearances. Subhūti, bodhisattvas should persevere one-pointedly in this instruction.

5

Understanding the Ultimate Principle of Reality

Subhūti, what do you think? Is the Tathāgata to be recognized by some material characteristic?

No, World-Honored One; the Tathāgata cannot be recognized by any material characteristic. Wherefore? Because the Tathāgata has said that material characteristics are not, in fact, material characteristics.

Buddha said: Subhūti, wheresoever are material characteristics there is delusion; but whoso perceives that all characteristics are in fact no-characteristics, perceives the Tathāgata.

6

Rare Is True Faith

Subhūti said to Buddha: World-Honored One, will there always be men who will truly believe after coming to hear these teachings?

Buddha answered: Subhūti, do not utter such words! At the end of the last five-hundred-year period following the passing of the Tathāgata, there will be self-controlled men, rooted in merit, coming to hear these teachings, who will be inspired with belief. But you should realize that such men have not strengthened their root of merit under just one buddha, or two buddhas, or three, or four, or five buddhas, but under countless buddhas; and their merit is of every kind. Such men, coming to hear these teachings, will have an immediate uprising of pure faith, Subhūti; and the Tathāgata will recognize them. Yes, he will clearly perceive all these of pure heart, and the magnitude of their moral excellences. Wherefore? It is because such men will not fall back to cherishing the idea of an ego entity, a personality, a being, or a separated individuality. They will neither fall back to cherishing the idea of things as having intrinsic qualities, nor even of things as devoid of intrinsic qualities.

Wherefore? Because if such men allowed their minds to grasp and hold on to anything they would be cherishing the idea of an ego entity, a personality, a being, or a separated individuality; and if they grasped and held on to the notion of things as having intrinsic qualities they would be cherishing the idea of an ego entity, a personality, a being, or a separated individuality. Likewise, if they grasped and held on to the notion of things as devoid of intrinsic qualities they would be cherishing the idea of an ego entity, a personality, a being, or a separated individuality. So you should not be attached to things as being possessed of, or devoid of, intrinsic qualities.

This is the reason why the Tathāgata always teaches this saying: My teaching of the good law is to be likened unto a raft. The buddha-teaching must be relinquished; how much more so misteaching!

7

Great Ones, Perfect Beyond Learning, Utter No Words of Teaching

Subhūti, what do you think? Has the Tathāgata attained the consummation of incomparable enlightenment? Has the Tathāgata a teaching to enunciate?

Subhūti answered: As I understand Buddha's meaning there is no formulation of truth called consummation of incomparable enlightenment. Moreover, the Tathāgata has no formulated teaching to enunciate. Wherefore? Because the Tathāgata has said that truth is uncontainable and inexpressible. It neither is nor is not.

Thus it is that this unformulated principle is the foundation of the different systems of all the sages.

8

The Fruits of Meritorious Action

Subhūti, what do you think? If anyone filled three thousand galaxies of worlds with the seven treasures and gave all away in gifts of alms, would he gain great merit?

Subhūti said: Great indeed, World-Honored One! Wherefore? Because merit partakes of the character of no-merit, the Tathāgata characterized the merit as great.

Then Buddha said: On the other hand, if anyone received and retained even only four lines of this discourse and

taught and explained them to others, his merit would be the greater. Wherefore? Because, Subhūti, from this discourse issue forth all the buddhas and the consummation of incomparable enlightenment teachings of all the buddhas.

Subhūti, what is called "the religion given by Buddha" is not, in fact, buddha-religion.

9

Real Designation Is Undesignate

Subhūti, what do you think? Does a disciple who has entered the stream of the holy life say within himself, "I obtain the fruit of a stream entrant?"

Subhūti said: No, World-Honored One. Wherefore? Because "stream entrant" is merely a name. There is no stream entering. The disciple who pays no regard to form, sound, odor, taste, touch, or any quality is called a stream entrant.

Subhūti, what do you think? Does an adept who is subject to only one more rebirth say within himself, "I obtain the fruit of a once-to-be-reborn?"

Subhūti said: No, World-Honored One. Wherefore? Because "once-to-be-reborn" is merely a name. There is no passing away nor coming into existence. [The adept who realizes] this is called "once-to-be-reborn."

Subhūti, what do you think? Does a venerable one who will never more be reborn as a mortal say within himself, "I obtain the fruit of a nonreturner?"

Subhūti said: No, World-Honored One. Wherefore? Because "nonreturner" is merely a name. There is no nonreturning; hence the designation "nonreturner."

Subhūti, what do you think? Does a holy one say within himself, "I have obtained perfective enlightenment?"

Subhūti said: No, World-Honored One. Wherefore? Because there is no such condition as that called "perfective enlightenment." World-Honored One, if a holy one of perfective enlightenment said to himself, "Such am I," he would necessarily partake of the idea of an ego entity, a personality, a being, or a separated individuality. World-Honored One, when the Buddha declares that I excel among holy men in the yoga of perfect quiescence, in dwelling in seclusion, and in freedom from passions, I do not say within myself, "I am a holy one of perfective enlightenment, free from passions." World-Honored One, if I said within myself, "Such am I," you would not declare, "Subhūti finds happiness abiding in peace, in seclusion in the midst of the forest." This is because Subhūti abides nowhere: therefore he is called "Subhūti, Joyful Abider in Peace, Dweller in Seclusion in the Forest."

10

Setting Forth Pure Lands

Buddha said: Subhūti, what do you think? In the remote past when the Tathāgata was with Dīpamkara Buddha, did he have any degree of attainment in the good law?

No, World-Honored One. When the Tathāgata was with Dī-pamkara Buddha he had no degree of attainment in the good law.

Subhūti, what do you think? Does a bodhisattva set forth any majestic buddha-lands?

No, World-Honored One. Wherefore? Because "setting forth majestic buddha-lands" is not a majestic setting forth; this is merely a name.

[Then Buddha continued:] Therefore, Subhūti, all bodhisattvas, lesser and great, should develop a pure, lucid mind, not depending upon sound, flavor, touch, odor, or any quality. A bodhisattva should develop a mind that alights upon nothing whatsoever; and so should he establish it.

Subhūti, this may be likened to a human frame as large as the mighty Mount

Sumeru. What do you think? Would such a body be great?

Subhūti replied: Great indeed, World-Honored One. This is because Buddha has explained that no body is called a great body.

11

The Superiority of Unformulated Truth

Subhūti, if there were as many Ganges rivers as the sand grains of the Ganges, would the sand grains of them all be many?

Subhūti said: Many indeed, World-Honored One! Even the Ganges rivers would be innumerable; how much more so would be their sand grains!

Subhūti, I will declare a truth to you. If a good man or good woman filled three thousand galaxies of worlds with the seven treasures for each sand grain in all those Ganges rivers, and gave all away in gifts of alms, would he gain great merit?

Subhūti answered: Great indeed, World-Honored One!

Then Buddha declared: Nevertheless, Subhūti, if a good man or good woman studies this discourse only so far as to receive and retain four lines, and teaches and explains them to others, the consequent merit would be far greater.

12

Veneration of the True Doctrine

Furthermore, Subhūti, you should know that wheresoever this discourse is proclaimed, by even so little as four lines, that place should be venerated by the whole realms of gods, men, and titans, as though it were a Buddha shrine. How much more is this so in the case of one who is able to receive and retain the whole and read and recite it throughout! Subhūti, you should know that such a one attains the highest and most wonderful truth. Wheresoever this sacred discourse may be found there should you comport yourself as though in the presence of Buddha and disciples worthy of honor.

13

How This Teaching Should Be Received and Retained

At that time Subhūti addressed Buddha, saying: World-Honored One, by what name should this discourse be known, and how should we receive and retain it?

Buddha answered: Subhūti, this discourse should be known as the Diamond of the Perfection of Transcendental Wisdom—thus should you receive and retain it. Subhūti, what is the reason herein? According to the buddha-teaching, the perfection of transcendental wisdom is not really such. "Perfection of transcendental wisdom" is just the name given to it. Subhūti, what do you think? Has the Tathāgata a teaching to enunciate?

Subhūti replied to Buddha: World-Honored One, the Tathāgata has nothing to teach.

Subhūti, what do you think? Would there be many molecules in [the composition of] three thousand galaxies of worlds?

Subhūti said: Many, indeed, World-Honored One!

Subhūti, the Tathāgata declares that all these molecules are not really such; they are called "molecules." [Furthermore,] the Tathāgata declares that a world is not really a world; it is [merely] called a world.

Subhūti, what do you think? May the Tathāgata be perceived by the thirty-two physical peculiarities [of an outstanding sage]?

No, World-Honored One, the Tathāgata may not be perceived by these thirty-two marks. Wherefore? Because the Tathāgata has explained that the thirty-two marks are not really such; they are [merely] called the thirty-two marks.

Subhūti, if on the one hand a good man or a good woman sacrifices as many lives as the sand grains of the Ganges, and on the other hand anyone receives and retains even only four lines of this discourse, and teaches and explains them to others, the merit of the latter will be the greater.

15

The Incomparable Value of This Teaching

Subhūti, if on the one hand, a good man or a good woman performs in the morning as many charitable acts of self-denial as the sand grains of the Ganges, and performs as many again in the noonday and as many again in the evening, and continues so doing throughout numberless ages, and, on the other hand, anyone listens to this discourse with heart of faith and without contention, the latter would be the more blessed. But how can any comparison be made with one who writes it down, receives it, retains it, and explains it to others!

Subhūti, we can summarize the matter by saying that the full value of this discourse can be neither conceived nor estimated, nor can any limit be set to it. The Tathāgata has declared this teaching for the benefit of initiates of the great way; he has declared it for the benefit of initiates of the supreme way. Whosoever can receive and retain this teaching, study it, recite it, and spread it abroad will be clearly perceived and recognized by the Tathāgata and will achieve a perfection of merit beyond measurement or calculation—a perfection of merit unlimited and inconceivable. In every case such a one will exemplify the Tathāgata-consummation of the incomparable enlightenment. Wherefore? Because, Subhūti, those who find consolation in limited doctrines involving the conception of an ego entity, a personality, a being, or a separated individuality, are unable to accept, receive, study, recite, and openly explain this discourse.

Subhūti, in every place where this discourse is to be found the whole realms of gods, men, and titans should offer worship; for you must know that such a place is sanctified like a shrine and should properly be venerated by all with ceremonial obeisance and circumambulation and with offerings of flowers and incense.

16
Purgation through Suffering the Retribution for Past Sins

Furthermore, Subhūti, if it be that good men and good women who receive and retain this discourse are downtrodden, their evil destiny is the inevitable retributive result of sins committed in their past mortal lives. By virtue of their present misfortunes the reacting effects of their past will be thereby worked out, and they will be in a position to attain the consummation of incomparable enlightenment.

Subhūti, I remember the infinitely remote past before Dīpamkara Buddha. There were eighty-four thousand myriads of multimillions of buddhas, and to all these I made offerings; yes, all these I served without the least trace of fault. Nevertheless, if anyone is able to receive, retain, study, and recite this discourse at the end of the last [five-hundred-year] period he will gain such a merit that mine in the service of all the buddhas could not be reckoned as one-hundredth part of it, not even one-thousandth part of it, not even one thousand-myriad-multimillionth part of it—indeed, no such comparison is possible.

Subhūti, if I fully detailed the merit gained by good men and good women coming to receive, retain, study, and recite this discourse in the last period,

my hearers would be filled with doubt and might become disordered in mind, suspicious and unbelieving. You should know, Subhūti, that the significance of this discourse is beyond conception; likewise the fruit of its rewards is beyond conception.

19
Absolute Reality Is the Only Foundation

Subhūti, what do you think? If anyone filled three thousand galaxies of worlds with the seven treasures and gave all away in gifts of alms, would he gain great merit?

Yes, indeed, World-Honored One, he would gain great merit!

Subhūti, if such merit was real, the Tathāgata would not have declared it to be great, but because it is without a foundation the Tathāgata characterized it as "great."

20
The Unreality of Phenomenal Distinctions

Subhūti, what do you think? Can the Buddha be perceived by his perfectly formed body?

No, World-Honored One, the Tathāgata cannot be perceived by his perfectly formed body, because the Tathāgata teaches that a perfectly formed body is not really such; it is merely called a perfectly formed body.

Subhūti, what do you think? Can the Tathāgata be perceived by means of any phenomenal characteristic?

No, World-Honored One, the Tathāgata may not be perceived by any phenomenal characteristic, because the Tathāgata teaches that phenomenal characteristics are not really such; they are merely called phenomenal characteristics.

21

Words Cannot Express Truth; That Which Words Express Is Not Truth

Subhūti, do not say that the Tathāgata conceives the idea "I must set forth a teaching." For if anyone says that the Tathāgata sets forth a teaching he really slanders Buddha and is unable to explain what I teach. As to any truth-declaring system, truth is undeclarable; so "an enunciation of truth" is just the name given to it.

Thereupon, Subhūti spoke these words to Buddha: World-Honored One, in the ages of the future will there be men coming to hear a declaration of this teaching who will be inspired with belief?

And Buddha answered: Subhūti, those to whom you refer are neither living beings nor not-living beings. Wherefore? Because, Subhūti, these "living beings" are not really such; they are just called by that name.

22

It Cannot Be Said That Anything Is Attainable

Then Subhūti asked Buddha: World-Honored One, in the attainment of the consummation of incomparable enlightenment did Buddha make no acquisition whatsoever?

Buddha replied: Just so, Subhūti. Through the consummation of incomparable enlightenment I acquired not even the least thing; wherefore it is called "consummation of incomparable enlightenment."

23

The Practice of Good Works Purifies the Mind

Furthermore, Subhūti, *This* is altogether everywhere, without differentiation or degree; wherefore it is called "consummation of incomparable enlightenment." It is straightly attained by freedom from separate personal selfhood and by cultivating all kinds of goodness.

Subhūti, though we speak of "goodness," the Tathāgata declares that there is no goodness; such is merely a name.

24

The Incomparable Merit of This Teaching

Subhūti, if there be one who gives away in gifts of alms a mass of the seven treasures equal in extent to as many mighty Mount Sumerus as there would be in three thousand galaxies of worlds, and if there be another who selects even only four lines from this discourse upon the perfection of transcendental wisdom, receiving and retaining them, and clearly expounding them to others, the merit of the latter will be so far greater than that of the former that no conceivable comparison can be made between them.

25

The Illusion of Ego

Subhūti, what do you think? Let no one say the Tathāgata cherishes the idea "I must liberate all living beings." Allow no such thought, Subhūti. Wherefore? Because in reality there are no living beings to be liberated by the Tathāgata. If there were living beings for the Tathāgata to liberate, he would partake in the idea of selfhood, personality, ego entity, and separate individuality.

Subhūti, though the common people accept egoity as real, the Tathāgata declares that ego is not different from nonego. Subhūti, those whom the Tathāgata referred to as "common people" are not really common people; such is merely a name.

26

The Body of Truth Has No Marks

Subhūti, what do you think? May the Tathāgata be perceived by the thirty-two marks [of a great man]?

Subhūti answered: Yes, certainly the Tathāgata may be perceived thereby.

Then Buddha said: Subhūti, if the Tathāgata may be perceived by such marks, any great imperial ruler is the same as the Tathāgata.

Subhūti then said to Buddha: World-Honored One, as I understand the meaning of Buddha's words the Tathāgata may not be perceived by the thirty-two marks.

Whereupon the World-Honored One uttered this verse:

Who sees me by form,
Who seeks me in sound,
Perverted are his footsteps upon the way;
For he cannot perceive the Tathāgata.

27

It Is Erroneous to Affirm That All Things Are Ever Extinguished

Subhūti, if you should conceive the idea that the Tathāgata attained the consummation of incomparable enlightenment by reason of his perfect form, do not countenance such thoughts. The Tathāgata's attainment was not by reason of his perfect form. [On the other hand] Subhūti, if you should conceive the idea that anyone in whom dawns the consummation of incomparable enlightenment declares that all manifest standards are ended and extinguished, do not countenance such thoughts. Wherefore? Because the man in whom the consummation of incomparable enlightenment dawns does not affirm concerning any formula that it is finally extinguished.

28

Attachment to Rewards of Merit

Subhūti, if one bodhisattva bestows in charity sufficient of the seven treasures to fill as many worlds as there be sand grains in the river Ganges, and another, realizing that all things are egoless, attains perfection through patient forbearance, the merit of the latter will far exceed that of the former. Why is this, Subhūti? It is because all bodhisattvas are insentient as to the rewards of merit.

Then Subhūti said to Buddha: What is this saying, World-Honored One, that bodhisattvas are insentient as to rewards of merit?

[And Buddha answered:] Subhūti, bodhisattvas who achieve merit should not be fettered with desire for rewards. Thus it is said that the rewards of merit are not received.

29

Perfect Tranquillity

Subhūti, if anyone should say that the Tathāgata comes or goes or sits or reclines, he fails to understand my teaching. Why? Because *Tathāgata* has neither whence nor whither, therefore is he called "Tathāgata."

30

The Integral Principle

Subhūti, if a good man or a good woman ground an infinite number of galaxies of worlds to dust, would the resulting minute particles be many?

Subhūti replied: Many indeed, World-Honored One! Wherefore? Because if such were really minute particles Buddha would not have spoken of them as minute particles. For as to this, Buddha has declared that they are not really such. "Minute particles" is just the name given to them. Also, World-Honored One, when the Tathāgata speaks of galaxies of worlds these are not worlds; for if reality could be predicated of a world it would be a self-existent cosmos, and the Tathāgata teaches that there is really no such thing. "Cosmos" is merely a figure of speech.

[Then Buddha said:] Subhūti, words cannot explain the real nature of a cosmos. Only common people fettered with desire make use of this arbitrary method.

31
Conventional Truth Should Be Cut Off

Subhūti, if anyone should say that Buddha declares any conception of egoity, do you consider he would understand my teaching aright?

No, World-Honored One, such a man would not have any sound understanding of the Tathāgata's teaching, because the World-Honored One declares that notions of selfhood, personality, entity, and separate individuality, as really existing, are erroneous—these terms are merely figures of speech.

[Thereupon Buddha said:] Subhūti, those who aspire to the consummation of incomparable enlightenment should recognize and understand all varieties of things in the same way and cut off the arising of [views that are mere] aspects. Subhūti, as regards aspects, the Tathāgata

declares that in reality they are not such. They are [merely] called "aspects."

32
The Delusion of Appearances

Subhūti, someone might fill innumerable worlds with the seven treasures and give all away in gifts of alms, but if any good man or any good woman awakens the thought of enlightenment and takes even only four lines from this discourse, reciting, using, receiving, retaining, and spreading them abroad and explaining them for the benefit of others, it will be far more meritorious.

Now in what manner may he explain them to others? By detachment from appearances—abiding in real truth. So I tell you:

Thus shall ye think of all this fleeting world:
A star at dawn, a bubble in a stream;
A flash of lightning in a summer cloud,
A flickering lamp, a phantom, and a dream.

When Buddha finished this discourse the venerable Subhūti, together with the *bhikshus*, *bhikshunis*, lay brothers and sisters, and the whole realms of gods, men, and titans, were filled with joy by his teaching, and taking it sincerely to heart they went their ways.

Judaism

Judaism is the religion of the Jewish people. Traditionally Judaism traces its origin to Abraham and the covenant that Abraham made with God, according to which the Jewish people would be God's chosen people. Important in the Jewish tradition are the commands of God, given to Moses, and the subsequent instructions communicated by prophets like Isaiah.

Judaism is the oldest of the three Abrahamic religions whose heritages traditionally reach back to Abraham (the other major monotheistic religions, Christianity and Islam, being the other two). In the Jewish tradition the story of Abraham is told in Genesis, the first book of the *Tanakh*, or Jewish Bible. (The

Tanakh corresponds to the Christian Old Testament.) In the story in Genesis God makes a covenant with Abraham. Abraham and his wife Sarah have a son, Isaac, and through him God renews his covenant for all his descendants. Isaac and his wife Rebekah in turn have a son, Jacob (in the Judaic and Christian traditions God is sometimes referred to as "the God of Abraham, Isaac, and Jacob"). In the traditional story in Genesis Jacob and his two wives Leah and Rachel have twelve sons and a daughter, and God gives Jacob the new name of Israel. Jacob's, or Israel's, sons multiply and the house of Israel becomes the "Children of Israel." Judah and Benjamin are two of Jacob's sons, and in time the tribes of Judah and Benjamin form the powerful Kingdom of Judah. (Hence the name Judaism.) In the tenth century B.C.E. David became the second King of Judah and all Israel and captured Jerusalem, which became the City of David. Known as "the Psalmist," David is traditionally regarded as the author of many of the psalms in the Bible in the Book of Psalms.

However in traditional Jewish belief hundreds of years before the Kingdom of Judah was formed, there was an event that is of great significance for Judaism. That event is Moses' leading the Israelites out of Egyptian bondage to the land promised to them by God. Moses is for orthodox Jews the author of the Penatuch, the first five books of the Jewish Bible (and of the Christian Bible). The Five Books of Moses constitute the *Torah*. Torah means "teaching." While Torah applies specifically to the Five Books of Moses, Torah can be used more widely to mean the entire Tanakh or even the spiritual tradition of Judaism. Torah, as the Five Books of Moses, tells the story of Moses' leading the people of Israel—the Children of Israel—out of Egyptian bondage and to deliverance. As Moses is the founder of Judaism this great event, which occurred about 1280 B.C.E., is looked upon as the founding event of Judaism. The journey of the Israelites through the desert to the promised land lasted many years. In traditional belief, during this time Moses received from God the 613 commandments about how the people of Israel are to walk in God's way. Hence the Torah contains both the story of Moses' leading the Israelites out of Egypt to God's promised land and God's law and instruction for the people of Israel.

Tanakh

The Tanakh is the Jewish Bible or Holy Scriptures. The Tenekh is divided into three parts: Torah (The Five Books of Moses), Nev'im (The Prophets) and Kethuvim (The Writings). In our selection we have passages from books from each of these parts.*

from Torah Genesis

The Torah, consisting of the Five Books of Moses, was canonized, or officially accepted as scripture around 400 C.E. Genesis is the first of the five book of Torah. Our selection from Genesis includes God's creation (Gen. 1 and 2), the covenant with Abraham (Gen. 17), Abraham's trial of faith (Gen. 22), and God's blessing and renaming Jacob (Gen. 35).

Genesis

1

When God began to create[a] heaven and earth— [2]the earth being unformed and void, with darkness over the surface of the deep and a wind from[b] God sweeping over the water— [3]God said, "Let there be light"; and there was light. [4]God saw that the light was good, and God separated the light from the darkness. [5]God called the light Day, and the darkness He called Night. And there was evening and there was morning, a first day.[c]

[6]God said, "Let there be an expanse in the midst of the water, that it may separate water from water." [7]God made the expanse, and it separated the water which was below the expanse from the water which was above the expanse. And it was so. [8]God called the expanse Sky. And there was evening and there was morning, a second day.

[9]God said, "Let the water below the sky be gathered into one area, that the dry land may appear." And it was so. [10]God called the dry land Earth, and the gathering of waters He called Seas. And God saw that this was good. [11]And God said, "Let the earth sprout vegetation: seed-bearing plants, fruit trees of every kind on earth that bear fruit with the seed in it." And it was so. [12]The earth brought forth vegetation: seed-bearing plants of every kind, and trees of every kind bearing fruit with the seed in it. And God saw that this was good. [13]And there was evening and there was morning, a third day.

[14]God said, "Let there be lights in the expanse of the sky to separate day from night; they shall serve as signs for the set times—the days and the years; [15]and they shall serve as lights in the expanse of the sky to shine upon the earth." And it was so. [16]God made the two great lights, the greater light to dominate the day and the lesser light to dominate the night, and the stars. [17]And God set them in the expanse of the sky to shine upon the earth, [18]to dominate the day and the night, and to separate light from darkness. And God saw that this was good. [19]And there was evening and there was morning, a fourth day.

[20]God said, "Let the waters bring forth swarms of living creatures, and birds that fly above the earth across the expanse of the sky." [21]God created the great sea monsters, and all the living creatures of every kind that creep, which the waters brought forth in swarms, and all the winged birds of every kind. And God saw that this was good. [22]God blessed them, saying, "Be fertile and increase, fill the waters in the seas, and let the birds increase on the earth." [23]And there was evening and there was morning, a fifth day.

[24]God said, "Let the earth bring forth every kind of living creature: cattle, creeping things, and wild beasts of every kind." And it was so. [25]God made wild beasts of every kind and cattle of every kind, and all kinds of creeping things of the earth. And God saw that this was good. [26]And God said, "Let us make man in our image, after our likeness. They shall rule the fish of the sea, the birds of the sky, the cattle, the whole earth, and all the creeping things that creep on earth." [27]And God created man in His image, in the image of God He created him; male and female He created them. [28]God blessed them and God said to them, "Be fertile and increase, fill the earth and master it; and rule the fish of the sea, the birds of the sky, and all the living things that creep on earth."

[a] *Others "In the beginning God created."* [b] *Others "the spirit of."* [c] *Others "one day."*

²⁹God said, "See, I give you every seed-bearing plant that is upon all the earth, and every tree that has seed-bearing fruit; they shall be yours for food. ³⁰And to all the animals on land, to all the birds of the sky, and to everything that creeps on earth, in which there is the breath of life, [I give] all the green plants for food." And it was so. ³¹And God saw all that He had made, and found it very good. And there was evening and there was morning, the sixth day.

2

The heaven and the earth were finished, and all their array. ²On the seventh day God finished the work that He had been doing, and He ceased[a] on the seventh day from all the work that He had done. ³And God blessed the seventh day and declared it holy, because on it God ceased from all the work of creation that He had done. ⁴Such is the story of heaven and earth when they were created.

When the LORD God made earth and heaven—when no shrub of the field was yet on earth and no grasses of the field had yet sprouted, because the LORD God had not sent rain upon the earth and there was no man to till the soil, but a flow would well up from the ground and water the whole surface of the earth—the LORD God formed man[b] from the dust of the earth.[c] He blew into his nostrils the breath of life, and man became a living being.

⁸The LORD God planted a garden in Eden, in the east, and placed there the man whom He had formed. ⁹And from the ground the LORD God caused to grow every tree that was pleasing to the sight and good for food, with the tree of life in the middle of the garden, and the tree of knowledge of good and bad.

¹⁰A river issues from Eden to water the garden, and it then divides and becomes four branches. ¹¹The name of the first is Pishon, the one that winds through the whole land of Havilah, where the gold is. (¹²The gold of that land is good; bdellium is there, and lapis lazuli.[d]) ¹³The name of the second river is Gihon, the one that winds through the whole land of Cush. ¹⁴The name of the third river is Tigris, the one that flows east of Asshur. And the fourth river is the Euphrates.

¹⁵The LORD God took the man and placed him in the garden of Eden, to till it and tend it. ¹⁶And the LORD God commanded the man, saying, "Of every tree of the garden you are free to eat; ¹⁷but as for the tree of knowledge of good and bad, you must not eat of it; for as soon as you eat of it, you shall die."

¹⁸The LORD God said, "It is not good for man to be alone; I will make a fitting helper for him." ¹⁹And the LORD God formed out of the earth all the wild beasts and all the birds of the sky, and brought them to the man to see what he would call them; and whatever the man called each living creature, that would be its name. ²⁰And the man gave names to all the cattle and to the birds of the sky and to all the wild beasts; but for Adam no fitting helper was found. ²¹So the LORD God cast a deep sleep upon the man; and, while he slept, He took one of his ribs and closed up the flesh at that spot. ²²And the LORD God fashioned the rib that He had taken from the man into a woman; and He brought her to the man. ²³Then the man said,

"This one at last
Is bone of my bones
And flesh of my flesh.

---

[a] Or "rested."   [b] Heb. 'adam.   [c] Heb. 'adamah.   [d] Others "onyx"; meaning of Heb. shoham uncertain.

This one shall be called Woman,[e]
For from man[f] was she taken.”

[24]Hence a man leaves his father and mother and clings to his wife, so that they become one flesh.

17

When Abram was ninety-nine years old, the LORD appeared to Abram and said to him, “I am El Shaddai.[a] Walk in My ways and be blameless. [2]I will establish My covenant between Me and you, and I will make you exceedingly numerous.”

[3]Abram threw himself on his face; and God spoke to him further, [4]“As for Me, this is My covenant with you: You shall be the father of a multitude of nations. [5]And you shall no longer be called Abram, but your name shall be Abraham,[b] for I make you the father of a multitude of nations. [6]I will make you exceedingly fertile, and make nations of you; and kings shall come forth from you. [7]I will maintain My covenant between Me and you, and your offspring to come, as an everlasting covenant throughout the ages, to be God to you and to your offspring to come. [8]I assign the land you sojourn in to you and your offspring to come, all the land of Canaan, as an everlasting holding. I will be their God.”

[9]God further said to Abraham, “As for you, you and your offspring to come throughout the ages shall keep My covenant. [10]Such shall be the covenant between Me and you and your offspring to follow which you shall keep: every male among you shall be circumcised. [11]You shall circumcise the flesh of your foreskin, and that shall be the sign of the covenant between Me and you. [12]And throughout the generations, every male among you shall be circumcised at the age of eight days. As for the homeborn slave and the one bought from an outsider who is not of your offspring, [13]they must be circumcised, homeborn, and purchased alike. Thus shall My covenant be marked in your flesh as an everlasting pact. [14]And if any male who is uncircumcised fails to circumcise the flesh of his foreskin, that person shall be cut off from his kin; he has broken My covenant.”

[15]And God said to Abraham, “As for your wife Sarai, you shall not call her Sarai, but her name shall be Sarah.[c] [16]I will bless her; indeed, I will give you a son by her. I will bless her so that she shall give rise to nations; rulers of peoples shall issue from her.” [17]Abraham threw himself on his face and laughed, as he said to himself, “Can a child be born to a man a hundred years old, or can Sarah bear a child at ninety?” [18]And Abraham said to God, “O that Ishmael might live by Your favor!” [19]God said, “Nevertheless, Sarah your wife shall bear you a son, and you shall name him Isaac;[d] and I will maintain My covenant with him as an everlasting covenant for his offspring to come. [20]As for Ishmael, I have heeded you.[e] I hereby bless him. I will make him fertile and exceedingly numerous. He shall be the father of twelve chieftains, and I will make of him a great nation. [21]But My covenant I will maintain with Isaac, whom Sarah shall bear to you at this season next year.” [22]And when He was done speaking with him, God was gone from Abraham.

[23]Then Abraham took his son Ishmael, and all his homeborn slaves and all those he had bought, every male in Abraham’s household, and he circumcised

---

[e] *Heb. 'ishshah.*   [f] *Heb. 'ish.*
[a] *Traditionally rendered “God Almighty.”*   [b] *Understood as “father of a multitude.”*   [c] *I.e., “princess.”*
[d] *Heb. Yiṣḥaq, from ṣaḥaq, “laugh.”*   [e] *Heb. shema‘tikha, play on “Ishmael.”*

the flesh of their foreskins on that very day, as God had spoken to him. ²⁴Abraham was ninety-nine years old when he circumcised the flesh of his foreskin, ²⁵and his son Ishmael was thirteen years old when he was circumcised in the flesh of his foreskin. ²⁶Thus Abraham and his son Ishmael were circumcised on that very day; ²⁷and all his household, his homeborn slaves and those that had been bought from outsiders, were circumcised with him.

22

Some time afterward, God put Abraham to the test. He said to him, "Abraham," and he answered, "Here I am." ²And He said, "Take your son, your favored one, Isaac, whom you love, and go to the land of Moriah, and offer him there as a burnt offering on one of the heights that I will point out to you." ³So early next morning, Abraham saddled his ass and took with him two of his servants and his son Isaac. He split the wood for the burnt offering, and he set out for the place of which God had told him. ⁴On the third day Abraham looked up and saw the place from afar. ⁵Then Abraham said to his servants, "You stay here with the ass. The boy and I will go up there; we will worship and we will return to you."

⁶Abraham took the wood for the burnt offering and put it on his son Isaac. He himself took the firestone^a and the knife; and the two walked off together. ⁷Then Isaac said to his father Abraham, "Father!" And he answered, "Yes, my son." And he said, "Here are the firestone and the wood; but where is the sheep for the burnt offering?" ⁸And Abraham said, "God will see to the sheep for His burnt offering, my son." And the two of them walked on together.

⁹They arrived at the place of which God had told him. Abraham built an altar there; he laid out the wood; he bound his son Isaac; he laid him on the altar, on top of the wood. ¹⁰And Abraham picked up the knife to slay his son. ¹¹Then an angel of the LORD called to him from heaven: "Abraham! Abraham!" And he answered, "Here I am." ¹²And he said, "Do not raise your hand against the boy, or do anything to him. For now I know that you fear God, since you have not withheld your son, your favored one, from Me." ¹³When Abraham looked up, his eye fell upon a^b ram, caught in the thicket by its horns. So Abraham went and took the ram and offered it up as a burnt offering in place of his son. ¹⁴And Abraham named that site Adonai-yireh,^c whence the present saying, "On the mount of the LORD there is vision."^d

¹⁵The angel of the LORD called to Abraham a second time from heaven, ¹⁶and said, "By Myself I swear, the LORD declares: Because you have done this and have not withheld your son, your favored one, ¹⁷I will bestow My blessing upon you and make your descendants as numerous as the stars of heaven and the sands on the seashore; and your descendants shall seize the gates of their foes. ¹⁸All the nations of the earth shall bless themselves by your descendants, because you have obeyed My command." ¹⁹Abraham then returned to his servants, and they departed together for Beer-sheba; and Abraham stayed in Beer-sheba.

35

God said to Jacob, "Arise, go up to Bethel and remain there; and build an altar there to the God who appeared to you when you were fleeing from your brother

---

^a Lit. "fire."   ^b Reading 'chad with many Heb. mss. and ancient versions; text 'ahar "after."
^c I.e., "the Lord will see"; cf. v. 8.   ^d Heb. Behar Adonai yera'eh.

Esau." ²So Jacob said to his household and to all who were with him, "Rid yourselves of the alien gods in your midst, purify yourselves, and change your clothes. ³Come, let us go up to Bethel, and I will build an altar there to the God who answered me when I was in distress and who has been with me wherever I have gone." ⁴They gave to Jacob all the alien gods that they had, and the rings that were in their ears, and Jacob buried them under the terebinth that was near Shechem. ⁵As they set out, a terror from God fell on the cities round about, so that they did not pursue the sons of Jacob.

⁶Thus Jacob came to Luz—that is, Bethel—in the land of Canaan, he and all the people who were with him. ⁷There he built an altar and named the site El-bethel,ᵃ for it was there that God had revealed Himself to him when he was fleeing from his brother.

⁸Deborah, Rebekah's nurse, died, and was buried under the oak below Bethel; so it was named Allon-bacuth.ᵇ

⁹God appeared again to Jacob on his arrival from Paddan-aram, and He blessed him. ¹⁰God said to him,

"You whose name is Jacob,
You shall be called Jacob no more,
But Israel shall be your name."

Thus He named him Israel.
¹¹And God said to him,

"I am El Shaddai.ᶜ
Be fertile and increase;
A nation, yea an assembly of nations,
Shall descend from you.
Kings shall issue from your loins.
¹²The land that I assigned to Abraham
    and Isaac
I assign to you;
And to your offspring to come
Will I assign the land."

¹³God parted from him at the spot where He had spoken to him; ¹⁴and Jacob set up a pillar at the site where He had spoken to him, a pillar of stone, and he offered a libation on it and poured oil upon it. ¹⁵Jacob gave the site, where God had spoken to him, the name of Bethel.

from Torah Exodus

Exodus is the second book of Torah. In our selection God gives Moses the Ten Commandments, the core of the law of Moses.

Exodus

20

God spoke all these words,ᵃ saying:

²I the LORD am your God who brought you out of the land of Egypt, the house of bondage: ³You shall have no other gods besides Me.

⁴You shall not make for yourself a sculptured image, or any likeness of what is in the heavens above, or on the earth

---

ᵃ *"The God of Bethel."*   ᵇ *Understood as "the oak of the weeping."*   ᶜ *Cf. 17.1.*
ᵃ *Tradition varies as to the division of the Commandments in vv. 2–14, and as to the numbering of the verses from 13 on.*

below, or in the waters under the earth. ⁵You shall not bow down to them or serve them. For I the LORD your God am an impassioned God, visiting the guilt of the parents upon the children, upon the third and upon the fourth generations of those who reject Me, ⁶but showing kindness to the thousandth generation of those who love Me and keep My commandments.

⁷You shall not ᵇ-swear falsely by-ᵇ the name of the LORD your God; for the LORD will not clear one who swears falsely by His name.

⁸Remember the sabbath day and keep it holy. ⁹Six days you shall labor and do all your work, ¹⁰but the seventh day is a sabbath of the LORD your God: you shall not do any work—you, your son or daughter, your male or female slave, or your cattle, or the stranger who is within your settlements. ¹¹For in six days the LORD made heaven and earth and sea, and all that is in them, and He rested on the seventh day; therefore the LORD blessed the sabbath day and hallowed it.

¹²Honor your father and your mother, that you may long endure on the land that the LORD your God is assigning to you.

¹³You shall not murder.

You shall not commit adultery.

You shall not steal.

You shall not bear false witness against your neighbor.

¹⁴You shall not covet your neighbor's house: you shall not covet your neighbor's wife, or his male or female slave, or his ox or his ass, or anything that is your neighbor's.

¹⁵All the people witnessed the thunder and lightning, the blare of the horn and the mountain smoking; and when the people saw it, they fell back and stood at a distance. ¹⁶"You speak to us," they said to Moses, "and we will obey; but let not God speak to us, lest we die." ¹⁷Moses answered the people, "Be not afraid; for God has come only in order to test you, and in order that the fear of Him may be ever with you, so that you do not go astray." ¹⁸So the people remained at a distance, while Moses approached the thick cloud where God was.

from Torah Leviticus

Leviticus is the third book of Torah. while the core of the law of Moses is the Ten Commandments, there are in torah hundreds of commandmensts given by God to the people of Israel. Traditionally there are 613. In our selection God gives to Moses a number of specific commandments relating to matters ranging from how crops are to be harvested to how those who are aged are to be treated.

Leviticus

19

The LORD spoke to Moses, saying: ²Speak to the whole Israelite community and say to them:

You shall be holy, for I, the LORD your God, am holy.

³You shall each revere his mother and his father, and keep My sabbaths: I the LORD am your God.

⁴Do not turn to idols or make molten gods for yourselves: I the LORD am your God.

ᵇ-ᵇ *Others "take in vain."*

⁵When you sacrifice an offering of well-being to the LORD, sacrifice it so that it may be accepted on your behalf. ⁶It shall be eaten on the day you sacrifice it, or on the day following; but what is left by the third day must be consumed in fire. ⁷If it should be eaten on the third day, it is an offensive thing, it will not be acceptable. ⁸And he who eats of it shall bear his guilt, for he has profaned what is sacred to the LORD; that person shall be cut off from his kin.

⁹When you reap the harvest of your land, you shall not reap all the way to the edges of your field, or gather the gleanings of your harvest. ¹⁰You shall not pick your vineyard bare, or gather the fallen fruit of your vineyard; you shall leave them for the poor and the stranger: I the LORD am your God.

¹¹You shall not steal; you shall not deal deceitfully or falsely with one another. ¹²You shall not swear falsely by My name, profaning the name of your God: I am the LORD.

¹³You shall not defraud your fellow. You shall not commit robbery. The wages of a laborer shall not remain with you until morning.

¹⁴You shall not insult the deaf, or place a stumbling block before the blind. You shall fear your God: I am the LORD.

¹⁵You shall not render an unfair decision: do not favor the poor or show deference to the rich; judge your kinsman fairly. ¹⁶Do not ᵃ-deal basely with-ᵃ your countrymen. Do not ᵇ-profit by-ᵇ the blood of your fellow: I am the LORD.

¹⁷You shall not hate your kinsfolk in your heart. Reprove your kinsman butᶜ incur no guilt because of him. ¹⁸You shall not take vengeance or bear a grudge against your countrymen. Love your fellow as yourself: I am the LORD.

¹⁹You shall observe My laws.

You shall not let your cattle mate with a different kind; you shall not sow your field with two kinds of seed; you shall not put on cloth from a mixture of two kinds of material.

²⁰If a man has carnal relations with a woman who is a slave and has been designated for another man, but has not been redeemed or given her freedom, there shall be an indemnity; they shall not, however, be put to death, since she has not been freed. ²¹But he must bring to the entrance of the Tent of Meeting, as his guilt offering to the LORD, a ram of guilt offering. ²²With the ram of guilt offering the priest shall make expiation for him before the LORD for the sin that he committed; and the sin that he committed will be forgiven him.

²³When you enter the land and plant any tree for food, you shall regard its fruit as forbidden.ᵈ Three years it shall be forbiddenᵈ for you, not to be eaten. ²⁴In the fourth year all its fruit shall be set aside for jubilation before the LORD; ²⁵and only in the fifth year may you use its fruit—that its yield to you may be increased: I the LORD am your God.

²⁶You shall not eat anything with its blood. You shall not practice divination or soothsaying. ²⁷You shall not round off the side-growth on your head, or destroy the side-growth of your beard. ²⁸You shall not make gashes in your flesh for the dead, or incise any marks on yourselves: I am the LORD.

²⁹Do not degrade your daughter and make her a harlot, lest the land fall into harlotry and the land be filled with depravity. ³⁰You shall keep My sabbaths and venerate My sanctuary: I am the LORD.

³¹Do not turn to ghosts and do not inquire of familiar spirits, to be defiled by them: I the LORD am your God.

ᵃ⁻ᵃ *Others "go about as a talebearer among"; meaning of Heb. uncertain.*
ᵇ⁻ᵇ *Lit. "stand upon"; precise meaning of Heb. phrase uncertain.*   ᶜ *Exact force of we uncertain.*
ᵈ *Heb. root ʻrl, commonly "to be uncircumcised."*

³²You shall rise before the aged and show deference to the old; you shall fear your God: I am the LORD.

³³When a stranger resides with you in your land, you shall not wrong him. ³⁴The stranger who resides with you shall be to you as one of your citizens; you shall love him as yourself, for you were strangers in the land of Egypt: I the LORD am your God.

³⁵You shall not falsify measures of length, weight, or capacity. ³⁶You shall have an honest balance, honest weights, an honest *ephah*, and an honest *hin*.

I the LORD am your God who freed you from the land of Egypt. ³⁷You shall faithfully observe all My laws and all My rules: I am the LORD.

from Torah Deuteronomy

Deuteronomy is the fifth book of Torah. Deuteronomy 6.4-9 is known as the Shema. It is said in morning and evening prayers.

Deuteronomy

6

And this is the Instruction—the laws and the rules—that the LORD your God has commanded [me] to impart to you, to be observed in the land that you are about to cross into and occupy, ²so that you, your children, and your children's children may revere the LORD your God and follow, as long as you live, all His laws and commandments that I enjoin upon you, to the end that you may long endure. ³Obey, O Israel, willingly and faithfully, that it may go well with you and that you may increase greatly [in] ᵃ⁻ᵃ land flowing with milk and honey,⁻ᵃ as the LORD, the God of your fathers, spoke to you.

⁴Hear, O Israel! The LORD is our God, the LORD alone.ᵇ ⁵You shall love the LORD your God with all your heart and with all your soul and with all your might. ⁶Take to heart these instructions with which I charge you this day. ⁷Impress them upon your children. Recite them when you stay at home and when you are away, when you lie down and when you get up. ⁸Bind them as a sign on your hand and let them serve as a symbolᶜ on your forehead;ᵈ ⁹inscribe them on the door-posts of your house and on your gates.

from Nevi'im Isaiah

In our selection the prophet Isaiah speaks to the people of Israel—those of the "House of Jacob"—and urges them to seek the instruction of the Lord, and not to follow the ways of the Philistines, whose "land is full of idols."

ᵃ⁻ᵃ *According to Ibn Ezra, this phrase connects with the end of v. 1.*
ᵇ *Cf. Rashbam and Ibn Ezra; see Zech. 14.9. Others "The LORD our God, the LORD is one."*
ᶜ *Others "frontlet"; cf. Exod. 13.16.* ᵈ *Lit. "between your eyes"; cf. Exod. 13.9.*

Isaiah

2

The word that Isaiah son of Amoz prophesied concerning Judah and Jerusalem.

2 In the days to come,
The Mount of the LORD's House
Shall stand firm above the mountains
And tower above the hills;
And all the nations
Shall gaze on it with joy.
3 And the many peoples shall go and say:
"Come,
Let us go up to the Mount of the LORD,
To the House of the God of Jacob;
That He may instruct us in His ways,
And that we may walk in His paths."
For instruction shall come forth[a] from
    Zion,
The word of the LORD from Jerusalem.
4 Thus He will judge among the nations
And arbitrate for the many peoples,
And they shall beat their swords into
    plowshares[b]
And their spears into pruning hooks:
Nation shall not take up
Sword against nation;
They shall never again know[c] war.

5 O House of Jacob!
Come, let us walk
By the light of the LORD.
6 For you have forsaken [the ways of] your
    people,
O House of Jacob!
[d-]For they are full [of practices] from the
    East,
And of soothsaying like the Philistines;

They abound in customs[e] of the aliens.[-d]
Their land is full of silver and gold,   7
There is no limit to their treasures;
Their land is full of horses,
There is no limit to their chariots.
And their land is full of idols;   8
They bow down to the work of their
    hands,
To what their own fingers have wrought.
But man shall be humbled,   9
And mortal brought low—
[f-]Oh, do not forgive them![-f]

Go deep into the rock,   10
Bury yourselves in the ground,
Before the terror of the LORD
And His dread majesty!
Man's haughty look shall be brought low,   11
And the pride of mortals shall be
    humbled.
None but the LORD shall be
Exalted in that day.

For the LORD of Hosts has ready a day   12
Against all that is proud and arrogant,
Against all that is lofty—so that it is
    brought low:
Against all the cedars of Lebanon,   13
Tall and stately,
And all the oaks of Bashan;
Against all the high mountains   14
And all the lofty hills;
Against every soaring tower   15
And every mighty wall;
Against all the [g-]ships of Tarshish[-g]   16
And all the gallant barks.
Then man's haughtiness shall be   17
    humbled

---

[a] *I.e., oracles will be obtainable.*   [b] *More exactly, the iron points with which wooden plows were tipped.*
[c] *Cf. Judg. 3.2.*
[d-d] *Emendation yields "For they are full of divination/and have abundance of soothsaying,/Like Philistines/And like alien folk."*   [e] *Cf. Targum; lit. "children."*
[f-f] *Meaning of Heb. uncertain. Emendation yields "And their idols with them"; cf. vv. 17–21.*
[g-g] *Probably a type of large ship.*

And the pride of man brought low.
None but the LORD shall be
Exalted in that day.

18 As for idols, they shall vanish completely.
19 And men shall enter caverns in the rock
And hollows in the ground—
Before the terror of the LORD
And His dread majesty,
When He comes forth to overawe the earth.

20 On that day, men shall fling away,
To the ^h-flying foxes^-h and the bats,
The idols of silver
And the idols of gold
Which they made for worshiping.
And they shall enter the clefts in the 21
    rocks
And the crevices in the cliffs,
Before the terror of the LORD
And His dread majesty,
When He comes forth to overawe
    the earth.

Oh, cease to glorify man, 22
Who has only a breath in his nostrils!
For by what does he merit esteem?

from Nevi'im Micah

In our selection Micah reproaches the people of the Lord and tells them that what
the Lord requires is not burnt offerings, but that they "walk modestly" with God.

Micah

6

Hear what the LORD is saying:
Come, present [My] case before the
    mountains,
And let the hills hear you pleading.

2 Hear, you mountains, the case of the
    LORD—
^a-You firm-^a foundations of the earth!
For the LORD has a case against His
    people,
He has a suit against Israel.

3 "My people!
What wrong have I done you?
What hardship have I caused you?
Testify against Me.

4 In fact,
I brought you up from the land of Egypt,
I redeemed you from the house of
    bondage,
And I sent before you
Moses, Aaron, and Miriam.
"My people, 5
Remember what Balak king of Moab
Plotted against you,
And how Balaam son of Beor
Responded to him.
[Recall your passage]
From Shittim to Gilgal^b—
And you will recognize
The gracious acts of the LORD."

With what shall I approach the LORD, 6
Do homage to God on high?
Shall I approach Him with burnt
    offerings,
With calves a year old?
Would the LORD be pleased with 7
    thousands of rams,
With myriads of streams of oil?

---

^h-h *Exact meaning of Heb. uncertain.*
^a-a *Emendation yields "Give ear, you."* ^b *I.e., the crossing of the Jordan; see Josh. 3.1, 14—4.19.*

Shall I give my first-born for my
   transgression,
The fruit of my body for my sins?

8   "He has told you, O man, what is good,
And what the LORD requires of you:
Only to do justice
And to love goodness,
And c-to walk modestly with your God;-c

9   d-Then will your name achieve wisdom."-d

Hark! The LORD
Summons the city:
e-Hear, O scepter;

10   For who can direct her
but you?-e
Will I overlook,f in the wicked man's house,
The granaries of wickedness
And the accursed short *ephah?*g

11   Shall heh be acquitted despite wicked
   balances
And a bag of fraudulent weights?—

12   iWhose rich men are full of lawlessness,
And whose inhabitants speak treachery,
With tongues of deceit in their mouths.

13   I, in turn, have beaten you sore,
Have stunned [you] for your sins:

14   You have been eating without getting
   your fill,
e-And there is a gnawing at your vitals;
You have been conceiving without
   bearing young,-e
And what you bore I would deliver to
   the sword.

15   You have been sowing, but have nothing
   to reap;
You have trod olives, but have no oil for
   rubbing,
And grapesj but have no wine to drink.

16   Yet k-you have kept-k the laws of Omri,

And all the practices of the House of Ahab,
And have followed what they devised.
Therefore I will make you an object of
   horror
And l-her inhabitants-l an object of hissing;m
And you shall bear the mockery of peoplesn

7

Woe is me!a
I am become like leavings of a fig harvest,
Like gleanings when the vintage is over,
There is not a cluster to eat,
Not a ripe fig I could desire.
The pious are vanished from the land,   2
None upright are left among men;
All lie in wait to commit crimes,
One traps the other in his net.
b-They are eager to do evil: 3
The magistrate makes demands,
And the judge [judges] for a fee;
The rich man makes his crooked plea,
And they grant it.-b
The best of them is like a prickly shrub;   4
The [most] upright, worse than a barrier
   of thorns.
b-On the day you waited for,-b your
   doom has come—
Now their confusion shall come to pass.
Trust no friend,   5
Rely on no intimate;
Be guarded in speech
With her who lies in your bosom.
For son spurns father,   6
Daughter rises up against mother,
Daughter-in-law against mother-in-law—
A man's own household
Are his enemies.
Yet I will look to the LORD,   7
I will wait for the God who saves me,
My God will hear me.

c-c *Or "It is prudent to serve your God."*   d-d *Emendation yields "And it is worthwhile to revere His name."*
e-e *Meaning of Heb. uncertain.*   f *Taking ish as from nashah "to forget"; cf. Deut. 32.18.*
g *Cf. Amos 8.4—5.*   h *Heb. "I"; change of vocalization yields "Will I acquit him."*
i *This verse would read well after "city" in v. 9.*   j *Lit. "new wine."*   k-k *Heb. "is kept."*
l-l *I.e., those of the city of v. 9, apparently Samaria.*   m *See note at Jer. 18.16.*   n *Heb. "My people."*
a *The speaker is feminine (cf. 'elohayikh, v. 10), probably Samaria personified; cf. note l-l at 6.16.*
b-b *Meaning of Heb. uncertain.*

8 Do not rejoice over me,
O my enemy!^c
Though I have fallen, I rise again;
Though I sit in darkness, the LORD is
    my light.

9 I must bear the anger of the LORD,
Since I have sinned against Him,
Until He champions my cause
And upholds my claim.
He will let me out into the light;
I will enjoy vindication by Him.

10 When my enemy^c sees it,
She shall be covered with shame,
She who taunts me with "Where is He,
The LORD your God?"
My eyes shall behold her [downfall];
Lo, she shall be for trampling
Like mud in the streets.

11 A day for mending your walls^d—
That is a far-off day.

12 This is rather a day when to you
[Tramplers] will come streaming
From Assyria and the towns of Egypt—
From [every land from] Egypt to the
    Euphrates,
From sea to sea and from mountain to
    mountain—

13 And your^c land shall become a desolation—
Because of those who dwell in it—
As the fruit of their misdeeds.

14 Oh, shepherd Your people with Your staff,
Your very own flock.

May they who dwell isolated
^f-In a woodland surrounded by farmland^-f
Graze^g Bashan and Gilead
As in olden days.

15 ^h-I will show him^-h wondrous deeds
As in the days when You sallied forth
    from the land of Egypt.

16 Let nations behold and be ashamed
Despite all their might;
Let them put hand to mouth;
Let their ears be deafened!

17 Let them lick dust like snakes,
Like crawling things on the ground!
^b-Let them come trembling out of their
    strongholds^-b
To the LORD our God;
Let them fear and dread You!

18 Who is a God like You,
Forgiving iniquity
And remitting transgression;
Who has not maintained His
    wrath forever
Against the remnant of His own people,
Because He loves graciousness!

19 He will take us back in love;
He will cover up our iniquities,
You will hurl all our^i sins
Into the depths of the sea.
You will keep faith with Jacob,
Loyalty to Abraham,

20 As You promised on oath to our fathers
In days gone by.

from Kethuvim Psalms

The Book of Psalms consists of psalms, or songs or poems, many of which are hymns. While the psalms have more than one author, David, as the "Psalmist," is traditionally regarded as the author of the psalms. David is King David. He lived about 1000 B.C.E. and figures in several biblical narratives. He is the David in the story of David and Goliath (1 Samuel 17) as well as King David.

^c *Heb. feminine, apparently referring to Damascus.*
^d *To keep out tramplers (end of preceding verse); cf. Isa. 5.5; Ps. 80.13–14.*   ^e *Heb. "the."*
^f-f *I.e., the land west of the Jordan, which is represented as far less fertile than adjacent regions.*
^g *Emendation yields "possess."*   ^h-h *Emendation yields "Show us."*   ^i *Heb. "their."*

The Psalms is one of the places in the Bible that one may go to fill in the Biblical concept of God. It is in the Book of Psalms that we are told that God's "steadfast love endures for ever" (Ps. 106). In our selection, in Ps. 90, we find the idea that God exists "from eternity to eternity" or "from everlasting to everlasting." We also find in the Psalms an expression of a wide spectrum of religious feelings or emotions, ranging from despair/distress to praise, hope, thankfulness, awe, and penitence. Above all, though, the Psalms express the Psalmist's sense of God's presence, as in Pss. 3, 19, 84 and 121 in our selection.

Psalms

BOOK ONE

1

Happy is the man who has not followed
    the counsel of the wicked,
    or taken the path of sinners,
    or joined the company of the insolent;
2 rather, the teaching of the LORD is his delight,
    and he studies[a] that teaching day and night.
3 He is like a tree planted beside streams of water,
    which yields its fruit in season,
    whose foliage never fades,
    and whatever [b-]it produces thrives.[-b]

4 Not so the wicked;
    rather, they are like chaff that wind blows away.
5 Therefore the wicked will not survive judgment,
    nor will sinners, in the assembly of the righteous.
6 For the LORD cherishes the way of the righteous,
    but the way of the wicked is doomed.

2

Why do nations assemble,
    and peoples plot[a] vain things;

kings of the earth take their stand,   2
and regents intrigue together
    against the LORD and against His anointed?
"Let us break the cords of their yoke,   3
    shake off their ropes from us!"
He who is enthroned in heaven laughs;   4
    the Lord mocks at them.
Then He speaks to them in anger,   5
    terrifying them in His rage,
    "But I have installed My king   6
    on Zion, My holy mountain!"
Let me tell of the decree: 7
    the LORD said to me,
    b-"You are My son,
    I have fathered you this day.-b
Ask it of Me,   8
    and I will make the nations your domain;
    your estate, the limits of the earth.
You can smash them with an iron mace,   9
    shatter them like potter's ware."

So now, O kings, be prudent;   10
    accept discipline, you rulers of the earth!
Serve the LORD in awe;   11
    c-tremble with fright,-c
    d-pay homage in good faith,-d   12
    lest He be angered, and your way be doomed

---

[a] *Or "recites"; lit. "utters."*   [b-b] *Or "he does prospers."*
[a] *Lit. "utter."*   [b-b] *Compare 2 Sam. 7.14, and Ps. 89.27 ff.*
[c-c] *Meaning of Heb. uncertain; others "rejoice with trembling."*   [d-d] *Meaning of Heb. uncertain.*

in the mere flash of His anger.
Happy are all who take refuge in Him.

3

A psalm of David when he fled from his son Absalom.

2 O LORD, my foes are so many!
Many are those who attack me;
3   many say of me,
    "There is no deliverance for him through God."
        Selah[a].
4 But You, O LORD, are a shield about me,
    my glory, He who holds my head high.
5 I cry aloud to the LORD,
    and He answers me from His holy mountain.
        Selah.
6 I lie down and sleep and wake again,
    for the LORD sustains me.
7 I have no fear of the myriad forces
    arrayed against me on every side.
8 Rise, O LORD!
Deliver me, O my God!
For You slap all my enemies in the face;[b]
    You break the teeth of the wicked.
9 Deliverance is the LORD's;
    Your blessing be upon Your people!
        Selah.

14

[a]For the leader. Of David.

The benighted man thinks,
  [b-]"God does not care."[-b]
Man's deeds are corrupt and loathsome;
    no one does good.
2 The LORD looks down from heaven on mankind
    to find a man of understanding,
    a man mindful of God.
3 All have turned bad,
altogether foul;
    there is none who does good,
    not even one.
4 Are they so witless, all those evildoers,
    who devour my people as they devour food,
    and do not invoke the LORD?
5 There they will be seized with fright,
    for God is present in the circle of the righteous.
6 You may set at naught the counsel of the lowly,
    but the LORD is his refuge.

7 O that the deliverance of Israel might come from Zion!
When the LORD restores the fortunes of His people,
    Jacob will exult, Israel will rejoice.

19

For the leader. A psalm of David.

2 The heavens declare the glory of God,
    the sky proclaims His handiwork.
3 Day to day makes utterance,
    night to night speaks out.
4 There is no utterance,
    there are no words,
    [a-]whose sound goes unheard.[-a]
5 Their voice[b] carries throughout the earth,
    their words to the end of the world.
6 He placed in them[c] a tent for the sun,
    who is like a groom coming forth from the chamber,
    like a hero, eager to run his course.
7 His rising-place is at one end of heaven,
    and his circuit reaches the other;
    nothing escapes his heat.

8 The teaching of the LORD is perfect,
    renewing life;
    the decrees of the LORD are enduring,
    making the simple wise;

---

[a] *A liturgical direction of uncertain meaning.*   [a] *Cf. Ps. 53.*   [b-b] *Lit. "There is no God"; cf. Ps. 10.4.*
[a-a] *With Septuagint, Symmachus, and Vulgate; or "their sound is not heard."*
[b] *Cf. Septuagint, Symmachus, and Vulgate; Arabic qawwah, "to shout."*   [c] *Viz., the heavens.*

9   The precepts of the LORD are just,
        rejoicing the heart;
        the instruction of the LORD is lucid,
        making the eyes light up.
10   The fear of the LORD is pure,
        abiding forever;
        the judgments of the LORD are true,
        righteous altogether,
11   more desirable than gold,
        than much fine gold;
        sweeter than honey,
        than drippings of the comb.
12   Your servant pays them heed;
        in obeying them there is much reward.
13   Who can be aware of errors?
        Clear me of unperceived guilt,
14   and from ᵈ-willful sins-ᵈ keep Your
            servant;
        let them not dominate me;
        then shall I be blameless
        and dear of grave offense.
15   May the words of my mouth
        and the prayer of my heartᵉ
        be acceptable to You,
        O LORD, my rock and my redeemer.

65

For the leader. A psalm of David. A song.

2   Praise befits You in Zion, O God;
        vows are paid to You;
3   all mankindᵃ comes to You,
        You who hear prayer.
4   When all manner of sins overwhelm me,
        it is You who forgive our iniquities.
5   Happy is the man You choose and bring
            near
        to dwell in Your courts;
        may we be sated with the blessings of
            Your house,
        Your holy temple.

6   Answer us with victory through awesome
            deeds,
        O God, our deliverer,

in whom all the ends of the earth
and the distant seas
put their trust;
who by His power fixed the mountains   7
    firmly,
who is girded with might,
who stills the raging seas,   8
the raging waves,
and tumultuous peoples.
Those who live at the ends of the earth   9
    are awed by Your signs;
You make the lands of sunrise and sun-
    set shout for joy.
You take care of the earth and irrigate it;   10
    You enrich it greatly,
    with the channel of God full of water;
    You provide grain for men;
    for so do You prepare it.
Saturating its furrows,   11
    leveling its ridges,
    You soften it with showers,
    You bless its growth.
You crown the year with Your bounty;   12
    fatness is distilled in Your paths;
    the pasturelands distill it;   13
    the hills are girded with joy.
The meadows are clothed with flocks,   14
    the valleys mantled with grain;
    they raise a shout, they break into
        song.

66

For the leader. A song. A psalm.

Raise a shout for God, all the earth;   2
    sing the glory of His name,
    make glorious His praise.
Say to God,   3
    "How awesome are Your deeds,
    Your enemies cower before Your great
        strength;
    all the earth bows to You,   4
    and sings hymns to You;
    all sing hymns to Your name."
                                    Selah.

ᵈ⁻ᵈ *Or "arrogant men"; cf. Ps. 119.51.*   ᵉ *For* leb *as a source of speech, see note to Eccl. 5.1.*   ᵃ *Lit. "flesh."*

5 Come and see the works of God,
   who is held in awe by men for His acts.
6 He turned the sea into dry land;
   they crossed the river on foot;
   we therefore rejoice in Him.
7 He rules forever in His might;
   His eyes scan the nations;
   let the rebellious not assert themselves.
                                    Selah.

8 O peoples, bless our God,
   celebrate His praises;
9 who has granted us life,
   and has not let our feet slip.

10 You have tried us, O God,
    refining us, as one refines silver.
11 You have caught us in a net,
    ᵃ⁻caught us in trammels.⁻ᵃ
12 You have let men ride over us;
    we have endured fire and water,
    and You have brought us through to
       prosperity.

13 I enter Your house with burnt offerings,
    I pay my vows to You,
14 [vows] that my lips pronounced,
    that my mouth uttered in my distress.
15 I offer up fatlings to You,
    with the odor of burning rams;
    I sacrifice bulls and he-goats.
                                    Selah.
16 Come and hear, all God-fearing men,
    as I tell what He did for me.
17 I called aloud to Him,
    glorification on my tongue.
18 Had I an evil thought in my mind,
    the Lᴏʀᴅ would not have listened.
19 But God did listen;
    He paid heed to my prayer.
20 Blessed is God who has not turned away
    my prayer,
    or His faithful care from me.

84

For the leader; on the *gittith*. Of the
Korahites. A psalm.

How lovely is Your dwelling-place,   2
   O Lᴏʀᴅ of hosts.
I long, I yearn for the courts of the Lᴏʀᴅ; 3
   my body and soul shout for joy to the
      living God.
Even the sparrow has found a home,   4
   and the swallow a nest for herself
   in which to set her young,
   near Your altar, O Lᴏʀᴅ of hosts,
   my king and my God.
Happy are those who dwell in Your house;   5
   they forever praise You.
                                    Selah.

Happy is the man who finds refuge in You,   6
   whose mind is on the [pilgrim] highways.
They pass through the Valley of Baca,   7
   ᵃ⁻regarding it as a place of springs,
   as if the early rain had covered it with
      blessing.⁻ᵃ
They go from ᵇ⁻rampart to rampart,⁻ᵇ   8
   appearing before God in Zion.
O Lᴏʀᴅ, God of hosts,   9
   hear my prayer;
   give ear, O God of Jacob.
                                    Selah.
O God, behold our shield,   10
   look upon the face of Your anointed.

Better one day in Your courts than a   11
      thousand [anywhere else];
   I would rather stand at the threshold
      of God's house
   than dwell in the tents of the wicked.
For the Lᴏʀᴅ God is sunᶜ and shield;   12
   the Lᴏʀᴅ bestows grace and glory;
   He does not withhold His bounty from
      those who live
   without blame.
O Lᴏʀᴅ of hosts,   13
   happy is the man who trusts in You.

ᵃ⁻ᵃ *Lit. "put a trammel on our loins."*
ᵃ⁻ᵃ *Meaning of Heb. uncertain.*   ᵇ⁻ᵇ *Others "strength to strength."*   ᶜ *Or "bulwark," with Targum; cf. Isa. 54.12.*

90

A prayer of Moses, the man of God.

O Lord, You have been our refuge in
    every generation.

2 Before the mountains came into being,
    before You brought forth the earth
    and the world,
    from eternity to eternity You are God.

3 You return man to dust;[a]
    You decreed, "Return you mortals!"

4 [b-]For in Your sight a thousand years
    are like yesterday that has past,
    like a watch of the night.

5 You engulf men in sleep;[-b]
    at daybreak they are like grass that
    renews itself;

6   at daybreak it flourishes anew;

    by dusk it withers and dries up.

7 So we are consumed by Your anger,
    terror-struck by Your fury.

8 You have set our iniquities before You,
    our hidden sins in the light of Your face.

9 All our days pass away in Your wrath;
    we spend our years like a sigh.

10 The span of our life is seventy years,
    or, given the strength, eighty years;
    but the [b-]best of them[-b] are trouble
    and sorrow.
    They pass by speedily, and we [c-]are in
    darkness.[-c]

11 Who can know Your furious anger?
    Your wrath matches the fear of You.

12 Teach us to count our days rightly,
    that we may obtain a wise heart.

Turn, O LORD!   13
How long?
Show mercy to Your servants.
Satisfy us at daybreak with Your steadfast   14
    love
    that we may sing for joy all our days.
Give us joy for as long as You have   15
    afflicted us,
    for the years we have suffered misfortune.
Let Your deeds be seen by Your servants,   16
    Your glory by their children.
May the favor of the LORD, our God, be   17
    upon us;
    let the work of our hands prosper,
    O prosper the work of our hands!

121

A song for ascents.

I turn my eyes to the mountains;
    from where will my help come?
My help comes from the LORD,   2
    maker of heaven and earth.
He will not let your foot give way;   3
    your guardian will not slumber;
See, the guardian of Israel   4
    neither slumbers nor sleeps!
The LORD is your guardian;   5
    the LORD is your protection
    at your right hand.
By day the sun will not strike you,   6
    nor the moon by night.
The LORD will guard you from all harm;   7
    He will guard your life.
The LORD will guard your going and   8
    coming
    now and forever.

from Kethuvim Job

The Book of Job tells the story of Job, who was "blameless and upright" but who
suffered the loss of his possessions and family and is afflicted with the suffering
of disease. It is an exploration of the human situation in which, through no fault
of their own, men and women are visited with great evil and suffering.

[b-b] *Meaning of Heb. uncertain.*   [c-c] *Or "fly away."*

Our selection begins with the prologue (Chaps. 1 and 2). It sets the stage for the dialogue between Job and his friends, who remonstrate with him. In our selection, in Chap. 3, Job curses the day of his birth, and in Chap. 19 he claims that God has wronged him and yet proclaims that he knows his "Vindicator lives." In Chap. 38 the Lord replies to Job out of the tempest, and in Chap. 42 Job relents and the Lord shows favor to him.

Job

1

There was a man in the land of Uz named Job. That man was blameless and upright; he feared God and shunned evil. [2]Seven sons and three daughters were born to him; [3]his possessions were seven thousand sheep, three thousand camels, five hundred yoke of oxen and five hundred she-asses, and a very large household. That man was wealthier than anyone in the East.

[4]It was the custom of his sons to hold feasts, each on his set day in his own home. They would invite their three sisters to eat and drink with them. [5]When a round of feast days was over, Job would send word to them to sanctify themselves, and, rising early in the morning, he would make burnt offerings, one for each of them; for Job thought, "Perhaps my children have sinned and blasphemed God in their thoughts." This is what Job always used to do.

[6]One day the divine beings presented themselves before the LORD, [a-]and the Adversary[-a] came along with them. [7]The LORD said to the Adversary, "Where have you been?" The Adversary answered the LORD, "I have been roaming all over the earth." [8]The LORD said to the Adversary, "Have you noticed My servant Job? There is no one like him on earth, a blameless and upright man who fears God and shuns evil!" [9]The Adversary answered the LORD, "Does Job not have

good reason to fear God? [10]Why, it is You who have fenced him round, him and his household and all that he has. You have blessed his efforts so that his possessions spread out in the land. [11]But lay Your hand upon all that he has and he will surely blaspheme You to Your face." [12]The LORD replied to the Adversary, "See, all that he has is in your power; only do not lay a hand on him." The Adversary departed from the presence of the LORD.

[13]One day, as his sons and daughters were eating and drinking wine in the house of their eldest brother, [14]a messenger came to Job and said, "The oxen were plowing and the she-asses were grazing alongside them [15]when Sabeans attacked them and carried them off, and put the boys to the sword; I alone have escaped to tell you." [16]This one was still speaking when another came and said, "God's fire fell from heaven, took hold of the sheep and the boys, and burned them up; I alone have escaped to tell you." [17]This one was still speaking when another came and said, "A Chaldean formation of three columns made a raid on the camels and carried them off and put the boys to the sword; I alone have escaped to tell you." [18]This one was still speaking when another came and said, "Your sons and daughters were eating and drinking wine in the house of their eldest brother[19] when suddenly a mighty wind came from the wilderness. It struck the four corners of the house so that

---

a-a *Heb.* ha-satan.

it collapsed upon the young people and they died; I alone have escaped to tell you." ²⁰Then Job arose, tore his robe, cut off his hair, and threw himself on the ground and worshiped. ²¹He said, "Naked came I out of my mother's womb, and naked shall I return there; the LORD has given, and the LORD has taken away; blessed be the name of the LORD."

²²For all that, Job did not sin nor did he cast reproach on God.

2

One day the divine beings presented themselves before the LORD. The Adversary came along with them to present himself before the LORD. ²The LORD said to the Adversary, "Where have you been?" The Adversary answered the LORD, "I have been roaming all over the earth." ³The LORD said to the Adversary, "Have you noticed My servant Job? There is no one like him on earth, a blameless and upright man who fears God and shuns evil. He still keeps his integrity; so you have incited Me against him to destroy him for no good reason." ⁴The Adversary answered the LORD, ᵃ-"Skin for skin⁻ᵃ—all that a man has he will give up for his life. ⁵But lay a hand on his bones and his flesh, and he will surely blaspheme You to Your face." ⁶So the LORD said to the Adversary, "See, he is in your power; only spare his life." ⁷The Adversary departed from the presence of the LORD and inflicted a severe inflammation on Job from the sole of his foot to the crown of his head. ⁸He took a potsherd to scratch himself as he sat in ashes. ⁹His wife said to him, "You still keep your integrity! Blaspheme God and die!" ¹⁰But he said to her, "You talk as any shameless woman

might talk! Should we accept only good from God and not accept evil?" For all that, Job said nothing sinful.

¹¹When Job's three friends heard about all these calamities that had befallen him, each came from his home—Eliphaz the Temanite, Bildad the Shuhite, and Zophar the Naamathite. They met together to go and console and comfort him. ¹²When they saw him from a distance, they could not recognize him, and they broke into loud weeping; each one tore his robe and threw dust into the air onto his head. ¹³They sat with him on the ground seven days and seven nights. None spoke a word to him for they saw how very great was his suffering.

3

ᵃAfterward, Job began to speak and cursed the day of his birth. ²Job spoke up and said:

³Perish the day on which I was born,
And the night it was announced,
"A male has been conceived!"
⁴May that day be darkness;
May God above have no concern for it;
May light not shine on it;
⁵May darkness and deep gloom reclaim it;
May a pall lie over it;
May ᵇ⁻what blackens⁻ᵇ the day terrify it.
⁶May obscurity carry off that night;
May it not be counted among the days of the year;
May it not appear in any of its months;
⁷May that night be desolate;
May no sound of joy be heard in it;
⁸May those who cast spells upon the dayᶜ damn it,
Those prepared to disable Leviathan;

ᵃ⁻ᵃ *Apparently a proverb whose meaning is uncertain.*
ᵃ *There are many difficulties in the poetry of Job, making the interpretation of words, verses, and even chapters uncertain. The rubric "Meaning of Heb. uncertain" in this book indicates only some of the extreme instances.*
ᵇ⁻ᵇ *Meaning of Heb. uncertain.*
ᶜ *Or "sea," taking Heb.* yorn *as equivalent of* yam; *compare the combination of sea with Leviathan in Ps. 74.13, 14 and with Dragon in Job 7.12; cf. also Isa. 27.1.*

⁹May its twilight stars remain dark;
May it hope for light and have none;
May it not see the glimmerings of the
dawn—
¹⁰Because it did not block my mother's
womb,
And hide trouble from my eyes.

¹¹Why did I not die at birth,
Expire as I came forth from the womb?
¹²Why were there knees to receive me,
Or breasts for me to suck?
¹³For now would I be lying in repose,
asleep and at rest,
¹⁴With the world's kings and counselors
who rebuild ruins for themselves,
¹⁵Or with nobles who possess gold and
who fill their houses with silver.
¹⁶Or why was I not like a buried stillbirth,
Like babies who never saw the light?
¹⁷There the wicked cease from troubling;
There rest those whose strength is spent.
¹⁸Prisoners are wholly at ease;
They do not hear the taskmaster's voice.
¹⁹Small and great alike are there,
And the slave is free of his master.

19

Job said in reply:

²How long will you grieve my spirit,
And crush me with words?
³ᵃ⁻Time and again⁻ᵃ you humiliate me,
And are not ashamed to abuse me.
⁴If indeed I have erred,
My error remains with me.
⁵Though you are overbearing toward me,
Reproaching me with my disgrace,
⁶Yet know that God has wronged me;
He has thrown up siege works around me.
⁷I cry, "Violence!" but am not answered;
I shout, but can get no justice.
⁸He has barred my way; I cannot pass;
He has laid darkness upon my path.
⁹He has stripped me of my glory,

Removed the crown from my head.
¹⁰He tears down every part of me; I perish;
He uproots my hope like a tree.
¹¹He kindles His anger against me;
He regards me as one of His foes.
¹²His troops advance together;
They build their road toward me
And encamp around my tent.
¹³He alienated my kin from me;
My acquaintances disown me.
¹⁴My relatives are gone;
My friends have forgotten me.
¹⁵My dependents and maidservants
regard me as a stranger;
I am an outsider to them.
¹⁶I summon my servant but he does not
respond;
I must myself entreat him.
¹⁷My odor is repulsive to my wife;
I am loathsome to my children.
¹⁸Even youngsters disdain me;
When I rise, they speak against me.
¹⁹All my bosom friends detest me;
Those I love have turned against me.
²⁰My bones stick to my skin and flesh;
I escape with the skin of my teeth.

²¹Pity me, pity me! You are my friends;
For the hand of God has struck me!
²²Why do you pursue me like God,
ᵇ⁻Maligning me insatiably?⁻ᵇ
²³O that my words were written down;
Would they were inscribed in a record,
²⁴Incised on a rock forever
With iron stylus and lead!
²⁵But I know that my Vindicator lives;
In the end He will testify on earth—
²⁶This, after my skin will have been
peeled off.
But I would behold God while still in my
flesh,
²⁷I myself, not another, would behold Him;
Would see with my own eyes:
My heartᶜ pines within me.
²⁸You say, "How do we persecute him?

ᵃ⁻ᵃ *Lit. "Ten times."*   ᵇ⁻ᵇ *Lit. "You are not satisfied with my flesh."*   ᶜ *Lit. "kidneys."*

The root of the matter is in him."[d]
[29]Be in fear of the sword,
For [your] fury is iniquity worthy of the
   sword;
Know there is a judgment!

23

Job said in reply:

[2]Today again my complaint is bitter;
[a-]My strength is spent[-a] on account of
   my groaning.
[3]Would that I knew how to reach Him,
How to get to His dwelling-place.
[4]I would set out my case before Him
And fill my mouth with arguments.
[5]I would learn what answers He had for me
And know how He would reply to me.
[6]Would He contend with me
   overbearingly?
Surely He would not accuse me!
[7]There the upright would be cleared
   by Him,
And I would escape forever from my judge.

[8]But if I go East—He is not there;
West—I still do not perceive Him;
[9]North—since He is concealed, I do not
   behold Him;
South—He is hidden, and I cannot see
   Him.
[10]But He knows the way I take;
Would He assay me, I should emerge
   pure as gold.
[11]I have followed in His tracks,
Kept His way without swerving,
[12]I have not deviated from what His lips
   commanded;
I have treasured His words more than
   my daily bread.
[13]He is one; who can dissuade Him?
Whatever He desires, He does.
[14]For He will bring my term to an end,
But He has many more such at His
   disposal.

[15]Therefore I am terrified at His
   presence;
When I consider, I dread Him.
[16]God has made me fainthearted;
Shaddai has terrified me.
[17]Yet I am not cut off by the darkness;
He has concealed the thick gloom
   from me.

38

Then the LORD replied to Job out of the
tempest and said:

[2]Who is this who darkens counsel,
Speaking without knowledge?
[3]Gird your loins like a man;
I will ask and you will inform Me.

[4]Where were you when I laid the earth's
   foundations?
Speak if you have understanding.
[5]Do you know who fixed its dimensions
Or who measured it with a line?
[6]Onto what were its bases sunk?

Who set its cornerstone
[7]When the morning stars sang together
And all the divine beings shouted for joy?

[8]Who closed the sea behind doors
When it gushed forth out of the womb,
[9]When I clothed it in clouds,
Swaddled it in dense clouds,
[10]When I made breakers My limit for it,
And set up its bar and doors,
[11]And said, "You may come so far and no
   farther;
Here your surging waves will stop"?

[12]Have you ever commanded the day to
   break,
Assigned the dawn its place,
[13]So that it seizes the corners of the earth
And shakes the wicked out of it?
[14]It changes like clay under the seal

---

[d] *With many mss. and versions; printed editions, "me."*   [a-a] *Lit. "My hand is heavy."*

Till [its hues] are fixed like those of a
    garment.
15Their light is withheld from the wicked,
And the upraised arm is broken.

42

Job said in reply to the LORD:

2I know that You can do everything,
That nothing you propose is impossible
    for You.
3Who is this who obscures counsel
    without knowledge?
Indeed, I spoke without understanding
Of things beyond me, which I did not
    know.
4Hear now, and I will speak;
I will ask, and You will inform me.
5I had heard You with my ears,
But now I see You with my eyes;
6Therefore, I recant and relent,
Being but dust and ashes.

7After the LORD had spoken these
words to Job, the LORD said to Eliphaz the
Temanite, "I am incensed at you and your
two friends, for you have not spoken the
truth about Me as did My servant Job. 8Now
take seven bulls and seven rams and go to
My servant Job and sacrifice a burnt offering
for yourselves. And let Job, My servant,
pray for you; for to him I will show favor
and not treat you vilely, since you have not
spoken the truth about Me as did My servant Job." 9Eliphaz the Temanite and Bildad
the Shuhite and Zophar the Naamathite
went and did as the LORD had told them,
and the LORD showed favor to Job. 10The
LORD restored Job's fortunes when
he prayed on behalf of his friends, and the
LORD gave Job twice what he had before.
11All his brothers and sisters and all
his former friends came to him and had a
meal with him in his house. They con-
soled and comforted him for all the misfortune that the LORD had brought upon
him. Each gave him one *kesitah*a and each
one gold ring. 12Thus the LORD blessed
the latter years of Job's life more than the
former. He had fourteen thousand sheep,
six thousand camels, one thousand yoke
of oxen, and one thousand she-asses. 13He
also had seven sons and three daughters.
14The first he named Jemimah, the second Keziah, and the third Keren-
happuch. 15Nowhere in the land were
women as beautiful as Job's daughters to
be found. Their father gave them estates
together with their brothers. 16Afterward,
Job lived one hundred and forty years to
see four generations of sons and grandsons. 17So Job died old and contented.

from The Zohar

Within Judaism different forms or traditions have developed over the centuries.
One of these is the *Kabbalah* (literally, tradition; that is, the esoteric tradition of
mysticism). Religious mysticism is a form of religious expression and sensibility
that is found in most religious traditions; it typically stresses feeling and experience. Jewish mysticism is traditionally claimed to be as old as the prophets. A
main text of the kabbalistic movement is the *Zohar* (the Book of Splendor), published in 1285. It was, it seems, written by the Spanish kabbalist Moses de Leon,
although in the kabbalistic tradition it was attributed to Rabbi Simeon bar Yohai,
a famous third century rabbi. In this tradition the *Ein Soph* is the ultimate reality
of God beyond all specification and differentiation, that from which all creation
emanates. The *Zohar* in the sixteenth century came to have wide acceptance
within the Jewish community and exerted influence on Christian thought.

This reading consists of two short sections from the *Zohar*. The first of these two sections is "The Creation of *Elohim*." Elohim is one of the names by which God was known by the early writers of the Bible. In it Moses de Leon speaks of "the Concealed One who is not known," that is, the *Ein Sof* (the Infinite or ultimate reality of God beyond all differentiation).*

The Creation of Elohim

In the Beginning

When the King conceived ordaining
He engraved engravings in the luster
    on high.
A blinding spark flashed
within the Concealed of the Concealed
from the mystery of the Infinite,
a cluster of vapor in formlessness,
set in a ring,
not white, not black, not red, not green,
no color at all.
When a band spanned, it yielded radiant
    colors.
Deep within the spark gushed a flow
imbuing colors below,
concealed within the concealed of the
    mystery of the Infinite.
The flow broke through and did not
    break through its aura.
It was not known at all
until, under the impact of breaking
    through,
one high and hidden point shone.
Beyond that point, nothing is known.
So it is called Beginning,
the first command of all.

"The enlightened will shine like the
    zohar of the sky, and those who
    make the masses righteous

will shine like the stars forever and
ever"
        (Daniel 12:3).

Zohar, Concealed of the Concealed,
    struck its aura.
The aura touched and did not touch this
    point.
Then this Beginning emanated
and made itself a palace for its glory and
    its praise.
There it sowed the seed of holiness
to give birth
for the benefit of the universe.
The secret is:
"Her stock is a holy seed"
        (Isaiah 6:13).

Zohar, sowing a seed for its glory
like the seed of fine purple silk.
The silkworm wraps itself within and
    makes itself a palace.
This palace is its praise and a benefit
    to all.

With the Beginning
the Concealed One who is not known
    created the palace.
This palace is called *Elohim*.
The secret is:
"With Beginning, _____ created
    Elohim"
        (Genesis 1:1).

* Excerpts from ZOHAR: *The Book of Enlightenment*, from the classics of western spirituality, translation and introduction by Daniel Chanan Matt, copyright © 1983 by Daniel Chanan Matt, Paulist Press, Inc., New York/Mahwah, N.J. used with permission of Paulist Press. *www.paulistpress.com*

The Hidden Light

God said, "Let there be light!"
And there was light.
(Genesis 1:3)

This is the light that the Blessed Holy
    One created at first.
It is the light of the eye.
It is the light that the Blessed Holy One
    showed the first Adam;
with it he saw from one end of the world
    to the other.
It is the light that the Blessed Holy One
    showed David;
he sang its praise:
"How great is Your good that You have
    concealed for those who fear You!"
                (Psalms 31:20).
It is the light that the Blessed Holy One
    showed Moses;
with it he saw from Gilead to Dan.
But when the Blessed Holy One saw
that three wicked generations would arise:
    the generation of Enosh, the
        generation of the Flood,
    and the generation of the Tower of
        Babel,
He hid the light away so they would not
    make use of it.
The Blessed Holy One gave it to Moses
and he used it for the three unused
    months of his gestation,
as it is said:
"She concealed him for three months"
                (Exodus 2:2).
When three months had passed, he was
    brought before Pharaoh
and the Blessed Holy One took it away
    from him
until he stood on Mt. Sinai to receive the
    Torah.
Then He gave him back that light;
he wielded it his whole life long
and the children of Israel could not come
    near him

until he put a veil over his face,
as it is said:
"They were afraid to come near him"
                (Exodus 34:30).
He wrapped himself in it as in a *tallit*,
as it is written:
"He wraps Himself in light as in a
    garment"
                (Psalms 104:2).

"'Let there be light!' And there was
    light."
Every subject of the phrase "And there
    was"
exists in this world and in the world that
    is coming.

Rabbi Isaac said,
"The light created by the Blessed Holy
    One in the act of Creation
flared from one end of the world to the
    other
and was hidden away.
Why was it hidden away?
So the wicked of the world would not
    enjoy it
and the worlds would not enjoy it
    because of them.
It is stored away for the righteous,
for the Righteous One!
As it is written:
'Light is sown for the righteous one,
joy for the upright in heart'
                (Psalms 97:11).
Then the worlds will be fragrant, and all
    will be one.
But until the day when the world that is
    coming arrives,
it is stored and hidden away. . . ."

Rabbi Judah said
"If it were completely hidden
the world would not exist for even a
    moment!

Rather, it is hidden and sown like a seed
that gives birth to seeds and fruit.
Thereby the world is sustained.
Every single day, a ray of that light
    shines into the world
and keeps everything alive,
for with that ray the Blessed Holy One
    feeds the world.
And everywhere that Torah is studied
    at night
one thread-thin ray appears from that
    hidden light

and flows down upon those absorbed
    in her,
as it is written:
'By day *YHVH* will enjoin His love;
in the night His song is with me'
                (Psalms 42:9),
as we have already established. . . .

Since the first day, it has never been fully
    revealed,
but it plays a vital role in the world,
renewing every day the act of
    Creation!"

Christianity

Christianity is historically the second of the Western monothesitic religions. It's founder is Jesus of Nazareth, believed by Christians to be the Son of God. Christians accept the Tanakh or Jewish Bible as the Old Testament, but the Christian Bible also includes the New Testament, which contains the Christian message and teachings. Christianity, like Judaism, is Abrahamic in that it traces its heritage back to Abraham, and, like Judaism, it is covenantal. However, it teaches a new covenant and accepts Jesus as the Savior of all who believe in him.

Jesus of Nazareth is for traditional Christians Jesus Christ (Christ is the Greek word for Messiah). Jesus was a Jew who began his ministry among the Children of Israel in Palestine, as the land of his birth has been called since Roman times. However, his message in the Christian tradition is not for Jews alone but for all men and women. For traditional Christians Jesus is the Messiah and Savior for all the world. The central belief of Christians is not so much in a doctrine as a belief in Jesus Christ as the Savior and the Son of God.

Although the Common Era is otherwise known as the Christian Era, Jesus was born a few years before the beginning of the Common Era. In traditional Christian belief, Jesus was conceived in his mother Mary by the Holy Spirit while she was a virgin. He was born in Bethlehem and grew up in Nazareth, about sixty miles north of Jerusalem, and so is known as Jesus of Nazareth. Almost all that is known about the life of Jesus has its source in the four Gospels, the first four books of the New Testament. These are the Gospel according to Matthew, according to Mark, according to Luke, and according to John. While the Gospels do not agree in every particular, taken together they present the story of Jesus' life.

The New Testament

The four Gospels were written in the first century of the Common Era. The word "gospel" derives from an Anglo-Saxon word, *god-spell*, which means good news or good tidings. Each Gospel tells the story of Jesus' life and death and recounts his teachings. Also in the New Testament are the epistles or letters, many of which were written by Paul. In our selection we have passages from three of the Gospels and from three epistles.*

from The Gospel According to Matthew

In this selection from The Gospel According to Matthew there is a geneology of Jesus showing his line of descent from Abraham and through David (Chap. 1), an account of Jesus' baptism by John (Chap. 3), and an account of Jesus' temptation by the devil (Chap. 4). Chap. 5 contains the Beatitudes or Jesus' pronouncement of the blessedness of the lowly, the humble, the merciful, the pure in heart, the persecuted, and those who seek after righteousness and peace. Jesus often taught using parables, and in Chap. 13 he says why he speaks in parables.

The Gospel According to Matthew

1

The book of the genealogy of Jesus Christ, the son of David, the son of Abraham.

[2]Abraham was the father of Isaac, and Isaac the father of Jacob, and Jacob the father of Judah and his brothers, [3]and Judah the father of Perez and Zerah by Tamar, and Perez the father of Hezron, and Hezron the father of Ram,[a] [4]and Ram[a] the father of Ammin'adab, and Ammin'adab the father of Nahshon, and Nahshon the father of Salmon, [5]and Salmon the father of Bo'az by Rahab, and Bo'az the father of Obed by Ruth, and Obed the father of Jesse, [6]and Jesse the father of David the king.

And David was the father of Solomon by the wife of Uri'ah, [7]and Solomon the father of Rehobo'am, and Rehobo'am the father of Abi'jah, and Abi'jah the father of Asa,[b] [8]and Asa[b] the father of Jehosh'aphat, and Jehosh'aphat the father of Joram, and Joram the father of Uzzi'ah, [9]and Uzzi'ah the father of Jotham, and Jotham the father of Ahaz, and Ahaz the father of Hezeki'ah, [10]and Hezeki'ah the father of Manas'seh, and Manas'seh the father of Amos,[c] and Amos[c] the father of Josi'ah, [11]and Josi'ah the father of Jechoni'ah and his brothers, at the time of the deportation to Babylon.

[12]And after the deportation to Babylon: Jechoni'ah was the father of Sheal'ti-el,[d] and She-al'ti-el[d] the father of Zerub'babel, [13]and Zerub'babel the father of Abi'ud, and Abi'ud the father of Eli'akim, and Eli'akim the father of Azor, [14]and Azor the father of Zadok, and Zadok the father of Achim, and Achim the father of Eli'ud, [15]and Eli'ud the father of Elea'zar, and Elea'zar the father of Matthan, and Matthan the father of Jacob, [16]and Jacob the father of Joseph the husband of Mary, of whom Jesus was born, who is called Christ.

[a] Greek *Aram*   [b] Greek *Asaph*   [c] Other authorities read *Amon*   [d] Greek *Salathiel*

17So all the generations from Abraham to David were fourteen generations, and from David to the deportation to Babylon fourteen generations, and from the deportation to Babylon to the Christ fourteen generations.

3

In those days came John the Baptist, preaching in the wilderness of Judea, 2"Repent, for the kingdom of heaven is at hand." 3For this is he who was spoken of by the prophet Isaiah when he said,

"The voice of one crying in the
  wilderness:
Prepare the way of the Lord,
make his paths straight."

4Now John wore a garment of camel's hair, and a leather girdle around his waist; and his food was locusts and wild honey. 5Then went out to him Jerusalem and all Judea and all the region about the Jordan, 6and they were baptized by him in the river Jordan, confessing their sins. 7But when he saw many of the Pharisees and Sad'ducees coming for baptism, he said to them, "You brood of vipers! Who warned you to flee from the wrath to come? 8Bear fruit that befits repentance, 9and do not presume to say to yourselves, 'We have Abraham as our father'; for I tell you, God is able from these stones to raise up children to Abraham. 10Even now the axe is laid to the root of the trees; every tree therefore that does not bear good fruit is cut down and thrown into the fire.

11"I baptize you with water for repentance, but he who is coming after me is mightier than I, whose sandals I am not worthy to carry; he will baptize you with the Holy Spirit and with fire. 12His winnowing fork is in his hand, and he will clear his threshing floor and gather his wheat into the granary, but the chaff he will burn with unquenchable fire."

13Then Jesus came from Galilee to the Jordan to John, to be baptized by him. 14John would have prevented him, saying, "I need to be baptized by you, and do you come to me?" 15But Jesus answered him, "Let it be so now; for thus it is fitting for us to fulfil all righteousness." Then he consented. 16And when Jesus was baptized, he went up immediately from the water, and behold, the heavens were openedg and he saw the Spirit of God descending like a dove, and alighting on him; 17and lo, a voice from heaven, saying, "This is my beloved Son,h with whom I am well pleased."

4

Then Jesus was led up by the Spirit into the wilderness to be tempted by the devil. 2And he fasted forty days and forty nights, and afterward he was hungry. 3And the tempter came and said to him, "If you are the Son of God, command these stones to become loaves of bread." 4But he answered, "It is written,

'Man shall not live by bread alone,
but by every word that proceeds
from the mouth of God.'"

5Then the devil took him to the holy city, and set him on the pinnacle of the

---

g Other ancient authorities add *to him*   h Or *my Son, my* (or *the*) *Beloved*
3. 4: 2 Kings 1. 8; Zech. 13. 4; Lev. 11. 22.   3. 7: Mt. 12. 34; 23. 33; 1 Thess. 1. 10.   3. 9: Jn. 8. 33;
Rom. 4. 16.   3. 10: Mt. 7. 19.   3. 12: Mt. 13. 30.   3. 13–17: Mk. 1. 9–11; Lk. 3. 21–22; Jn. 1. 31–34.
3. 17: Mt. 12. 18; 17. 5; Mk. 9. 7; Lk. 9. 35; Ps. 2. 7; Is. 42. 1.   4. 1–11: Mk. 1. 12–13; Lk. 4. 1–13;
Heb. 2. 18; 4. 15.   4. 2: Ex. 34. 28; 1 Kings 19. 8.   4. 4: Deut. 8. 3.   4. 5: Mt. 27. 53; Neh. 11. 1;
Dan. 9. 24; Rev. 21. 10.   4. 6: Ps. 91. 11–12.

temple, [6]and said to him, "If you are the Son of God, throw yourself down; for it is written,

'He will give his angels charge of you,'

and

'On their hands they will bear you up, lest you strike your foot against a stone.'"

[7]Jesus said to him, "Again it is written, 'You shall not tempt the Lord your God.'" [8]Again, the devil took him to a very high mountain, and showed him all the kingdoms of the world and the glory of them; [9]and he said to him, "All these I will give you, if you will fall down and worship me." [10]Then Jesus said to him, "Begone, Satan! for it is written,

'You shall worship the Lord your God and him only shall you serve.'"

[11]Then the devil left him, and behold, angels came and ministered to him.

[12]Now when he heard that John had been arrested, he withdrew into Galilee; [13]and leaving Nazareth he went and dwelt in Caper'na-um by the sea, in the territory of Zeb'ulun and Naph'tali, [14]that what was spoken by the prophet Isaiah might be fulfilled:

[15]"The land of Zeb'ulun and the land of Naph'tali,
toward the sea, across the Jordan,
Galilee of the Gentiles—
[16]the people who sat in darkness
have seen a great light,

and for those who sat in the region
and shadow of death
light has dawned."

[17]From that time Jesus began to preach, saying, "Repent, for the kingdom of heaven is at hand."

[18]As he walked by the Sea of Galilee, he saw two brothers, Simon who is called Peter and Andrew his brother, casting a net into the sea; for they were fishermen [19]And he said to them, "Follow me, and I will make you fishers of men." [20]Immediately they left their nets and followed him. [21]And going on from there he saw two other brothers, James the son of Zeb'edee and John his brother, in the boat with Zeb'edee their father, mending their nets, and he called them.[22] Immediately they left the boat and their father, and followed him.

[23]And he went about all Galilee, teaching in their synagogues and preaching the gospel of the kingdom and healing every disease and every infirmity among the people. [24]So his fame spread throughout all Syria, and they brought him all the sick, those afflicted with various diseases and pains, demoniacs, epileptics, and paralytics, and he healed them. And great crowds followed him from Galilee and the Decap'olis and Jerusalem and Judea and from beyond the Jordan.

5

Seeing the crowds, he went up on the mountain, and when he sat down his disciples came to him. [2]And he opened his mouth and taught them, saying:

"[3]Blessed are the poor in spirit, for theirs is the kingdom of heaven.

4. 7: Deut. 6. 16.   4. 10: Deut. 6. 13; Mk. 8. 33.   4. 11: Mt. 26. 53; Lk. 22. 43.   4. 12: Mk. 1. 14; Lk.   4. 14; Mt. 14. 3; Jn. 1. 43.   4. 13: Jn. 2. 12; Mk. 1. 21; Lk. 4. 23.   4. 15: Is. 9. 1–2.   4. 17: Mk. 1. 15; Mt. 3. 2; 10. 7.   4. 18–22: Mk. 1. 16–20; Lk. 5. 1–11; Jn. 1. 35–42.   4. 23–25: Mk. 1. 39; Lk. 4. 15, 44; Mt. 9. 35; Mk. 3. 7–8; Lk. 6. 17.   5. 1–12: Lk. 6. 17, 20–23; Mk. 3. 13; Jn. 6. 3.   5. 3: Mk. 10. 14; Lk. 22. 29.

[4]"Blessed are those who mourn, for they shall be comforted.

[5]"Blessed are the meek, for they shall inherit the earth.

[6]"Blessed are those who hunger and thirst for righteousness, for they shall be satisfied.

[7]"Blessed are the merciful, for they shall obtain mercy.

[8]"Blessed are the pure in heart, for they shall see God.

[9]"Blessed are the peacemakers, for they shall be called sons of God.

[10]"Blessed are those who are persecuted for righteousness' sake, for theirs is the kingdom of heaven.

[11]"Blessed are you when men revile you and persecute you and utter all kinds of evil against you falsely on my account. [12]Rejoice and be glad, for your reward is great in heaven, for so men persecuted the prophets who were before you.

[13]"You are the salt of the earth; but if salt has lost its taste, how shall its saltness be restored? It is no longer good for anything except to be thrown out and trodden under foot by men.

[14]"You are the light of the world.

A city set on a hill cannot be hid. Nor do men light a lamp and put it under a bushel, but on a stand, and it gives light to all in the house. [16]Let your light so shine before men, that they may see your good works and give glory to your Father who is in heaven. . .".

13

That same day Jesus went out of the house and sat beside the sea. [2]And great crowds gathered about him, so that he got into a boat and sat there; and the whole crowd stood on the beach. [3]And he told them many things in parables, saying: "A sower went out to sow. [4]And as he sowed, some seeds fell along the path, and the birds came and devoured them. [5]Other seeds fell on rocky ground, where they had not much soil, and immediately they sprang up, since they had no depth of soil, [6]but when the sun rose they were scorched; and since they had no root they withered away. [7]Other seeds fell upon thorns, and the thorns grew up and choked them. [8]Other seeds fell on good soil and brought forth grain, some a hundredfold, some sixty, some thirty. [9]He who has ears,[b] let him hear."

[10]Then the disciples came and said to him, "Why do you speak to them in parables?" And he answered them, "To you it has been given to know the secrets of the kingdom of heaven, but to them it has not been given. [12]For to him who has will more be given, and he will have abundance; but from him who has not, even what he has will be taken away. [13]This is why I speak to them in parables, because seeing they do not see, and hearing they do not hear, nor do they understand. . .".

from The Gospel According to Luke

In this selection from The Gospel According to Luke there is in Chap. 10 the parable of the Good Samaritan. In Chap. 11 Jesus teaches his disciples the Lord's Prayer, and in Chap. 15 Jesus tells the parable of the Prodigal Son. Selections from Chaps. 22–24 present the narrative of Jesus' crucifixion and resurrection as it is found in The Gospel According to Luke.

5. 4: Is. 61. 2; Jn. 16. 20; Rev. 7. 17. 5. 5: Ps. 37. 11.   5. 6: Is. 55. 1–2; Jn. 4. 14; 6. 48–51.
5. 8: Ps. 24. 4; Heb. 12. 14; 1 Jn. 3. 2; Rev. 22. 4. 5. 10: 1 Pet. 3. 14; 4. 14.
5. 12: 2 Chron. 36. 16; Mt. 23. 37; Acts 7. 52; 1 Thess. 2. 15; Jas. 5. 10.
5. 13: Mk. 9. 49–50; Lk. 14. 34–35.   5. 14: Eph. 5. 8; Phil. 2. 15; Jn. 8. 12.

The Gospel According to Luke

Luke 10

²⁵And behold, a lawyer stood up to put him to the test, saying, "Teacher, what shall I do to inherit eternal life?" ²⁶He said to him, "What is written in the law? How do you read?" ²⁷And he answered, "You shall love the Lord your God with all your heart, and with all your soul, and with all your strength, and with all your mind; and your neighbor as yourself." ²⁸And he said to him, "You have answered right; do this, and you will live."

²⁹But he, desiring to justify himself, said to Jesus, "And who is my neighbor?" ³⁰Jesus replied, "A man was going down from Jerusalem to Jericho, and he fell among robbers, who stripped him and beat him, and departed, leaving him half dead. ³¹Now by chance a priest was going down that road; and when he saw him he passed by on the other side. ³²So likewise a Levite, when he came to the place and saw him, passed by on the other side. ³³But a Samaritan, as he journeyed, came to where he was; and when he saw him, he had compassion, ³⁴and went to him and bound up his wounds, pouring on oil and wine; then he set him on his own beast and brought him to an inn, and took care of him. ³⁵And the next day he took out two denarii and gave them to the innkeeper, saying, 'Take care of him; and whatever more you spend, I will repay you when I come back.' ³⁶Which of these three, do you think, proved neighbor to the man who fell among the robbers?" ³⁷He said, "The one who showed mercy on him." And Jesus said to him, "Go and do likewise."

³⁸Now as they went on their way, he entered a village; and a woman named Martha received him into her house. ³⁹And she had a sister called Mary, who sat at the Lord's feet and listened to his teaching. ⁴⁰But Martha was distracted with much serving; and she went to him and said, "Lord, do you not care that my sister has left me to serve alone? Tell her then to help me." ⁴¹But the Lord answered her, "Martha, Martha, you are anxious and troubled about many things; ⁴²one thing is needful.ʲ Mary has chosen the good portion, which shall not be taken away from her."

11

He was praying in a certain place, and when he ceased, one of his disciples said to him, "Lord, teach us to pray, as John taught his disciples." ²And he said to them, "When you pray, say:

"Father, hallowed be thy name. Thy kingdom come. ³Give us each day our daily bread;ᵏ ⁴and forgive us our sins, for we ourselves forgive every one who is indebted to us; and lead us not into temptation."

⁵And he said to them, "Which of you who has a friend will go to him at midnight and say to him, 'Friend, lend me three loaves; ⁶for a friend of mine has arrived on a journey, and I have nothing to set before him'; ⁷and he will answer from within, 'Do not bother me; the door is now shut, and my children are with me in bed; I cannot get up and give you anything'?

ⁱ The denarius was worth about twenty cents ʲ Other ancient authorities read *few things are needful, or only one* ᵏ Or *our bread for the morrow*
10. 23–24: Mt. 13. 16–17; Jn. 8. 56; Heb. 11. 13; 1 Pet. 1. 10–12. 10. 25–28: Mt. 22. 34–39; Mk. 12. 28–31. 10. 25: Mk. 10. 17; Mt. 19. 16; Lk. 18. 18. 10. 27: Deut. 6. 5; Lev. 19. 18; Rom. 13. 9; Gal. 5. 14; Jas. 2. 8. 10. 28: Lk. 20. 39; Lev. 18. 5. 10. 33: Lk. 9. 51–56; 17. 11–19; Jn. 4. 4–42. 10. 38–42: Jn. 12. 1–3; 11. 1–45. 10. 41: Lk. 7. 13. 11. 1: Mk. 1. 35; Lk. 3. 21; 5. 16; 6. 12; 9. 18. 28; 5. 33; 7. 18. 11. 2–4: Mt. 6. 9–13. 11. 4: Mk. 11. 25; Mt. 18. 35. 11. 5–8: Lk. 1–6. 1–8.

[8]I tell you, though he will not get up and give him anything because he is his friend, yet because of his importunity he will rise and give him whatever he needs. [9]And I tell you, Ask, and it will be given you; seek, and you will find: knock, and it will be opened to you. [10]For every one who asks receives, and he who seeks finds, and to him who knocks it will be opened. [11]What father among you, if his son asks for a fish, will instead of a fish give him a serpent; [12]or if he asks for an egg, will give him a scorpion? [13]If you then, who are evil, know how to give good gifts to your children, how much more will the heavenly Father give the Holy Spirit to those who ask him!"

15

Now the tax collectors and sinners were all drawing near to hear him. [2]And the Pharisees and the scribes murmured, saying, "This man receives sinners and eats with them."

[3]So he told them this parable: [4]"What man of you, having a hundred sheep, if he has lost one of them, does not leave the ninety-nine in the wilderness, and go after the one which is lost, until he finds it? [5]And when he has found it, he lays it on his shoulders, rejoicing. [6]And when he comes home, he calls together his friends and his neighbors, saying to them, 'Rejoice with me, for I have found my sheep which was lost.' [7]Just so, I tell you, there will be more joy in heaven over one sinner who repents than over ninety-nine righteous persons who need no repentance.

[8]"Or what woman, having ten silver coins,[t] if she loses one coin, does not light a lamp and sweep the house and seek diligently until she finds it? [9]And when she has found it, she calls together her friends and neighbors, saying, 'Rejoice with me, for I have found the coin which I had lost.' [10]Just so, I tell you, there is joy before the angels of God over one sinner who repents."

[11]And he said, "There was a man who had two sons; [12]and the younger of them said to his father, 'Father, give me the share of property that falls to me.' And he divided his living between them. [13]Not many days later, the younger son gathered all he had and took his journey into a far country, and there he squandered his property in loose living. [14]And when he had spent everything, a great famine arose in that country, and he began to be in want. [15]So he went and joined himself to one of the citizens of that country, who sent him into his fields to feed swine. [16]And he would gladly have fed on[u] the pods that the swine ate; and no one gave him anything. [17]But when he came to himself he said, 'How many of my father's hired servants have bread enough and to spare, but I perish here with hunger! [18]I will arise and go to my father, and I will say to him, "Father, I have sinned against heaven and before you; [19]I am no longer worthy to be called your son; treat me as one of your hired servants."' [20]And he arose and came to his father. But while he was yet at a distance, his father saw him and had compassion, and ran and embraced him and kissed him. [21]And the son said to him, 'Father, I have sinned against heaven and before you; I am no longer worthy to be called your son.' [22]But the father said to his servants, 'Bring quickly the best robe, and put it on him; and put a ring on his hand, and shoes on his feet; [23]and bring the fatted calf and kill it, and let us eat and make merry; [24]for this my son was dead, and is alive again; he was lost, and is found.' And they began to make merry.

[t] The drachma, rendered here by *silver coin*, was about sixteen cents   [u] Other ancient authorities read *filled his belly with*

14. 27: Mt. 16. 24; Mk. 8. 34; Lk. 9. 23.   14. 33: Lk. 18. 29–30; Phil. 3. 7. 14. 34–35: Mt. 5. 13; Mk. 9. 49–50; Mt. 11. 15.   15. 1–2: Lk. 5. 29–30; 19. 7.   15. 4–7: Mt. 18. 10–14.   15. 7: Jas. 5. 20; Lk. 19. 10; 15. 10.   15. 11: Mt. 21. 28.   15. 12: Deut. 21. 15–17.

^{25}"Now his elder son was in the field; and as he came and drew near to the house, he heard music and dancing. ^{26}And he called one of the servants and asked what this meant. ^{27}And he said to him, 'Your brother has come, and your father has killed the fatted calf, because he has received him safe and sound.' ^{28}But he was angry and refused to go in. His father came out and entreated him, ^{29}but he answered his father, 'Lo, these many years I have served you, and I never disobeyed your command; yet you never gave me a kid, that I might make merry with my friends. ^{30}But when this son of yours came, who has devoured your living with harlots, you killed for him the fatted calf!' ^{31}And he said to him, 'Son, you are always with me, and all that is mine is yours. ^{32}It was fitting to make merry and be glad, for this your brother was dead, and is alive; he was lost, and is found.'"

22

^{39}And he came out, and went, as was his custom, to the Mount of Olives; and the disciples followed him. ^{40}And when he came to the place he said to them, "Pray that you may not enter into temptation." ^{41}And he withdrew from them about a stone's throw, and knelt down and prayed, ^{42}"Father, if thou art willing, remove this cup from me; nevertheless not my will, but thine, be done." ^{43}And there appeared to him an angel from heaven, strengthening him. ^{44}And being in an agony he prayed more earnestly; and his sweat became like great drops of blood falling down upon the ground.[1] ^{45}And when he rose from prayer, he came to the disciples and found them sleeping for sorrow, ^{46}and he said to them, "Why do you sleep? Rise and pray that you may not enter into temptation."

^{47}While he was still speaking, there came a crowd, and the man called Judas, one of the twelve, was leading them. He drew near to Jesus to kiss him; ^{48}but Jesus said to him, "Judas, would you betray the Son of man with a kiss?" ^{49}And when those who were about him saw what would follow, they said, "Lord, shall we strike with the sword?" ^{50}And one of them struck the slave of the high priest and cut off his right ear. ^{51}But Jesus said, "No more of this!" And he touched his ear and healed him. ^{52}Then Jesus said to the chief priests and captains of the temple and elders, who had come out against him, "Have you come out as against a robber, with swords and clubs? ^{53}When I was with you day after day in the temple, you did not lay hands on me. But this is your hour, and the power of darkness."

^{54}Then they seized him and led him away, bringing him into the high priest's house. Peter followed at a distance; ^{55}and when they had kindled a fire in the middle of the courtyard and sat down together, Peter sat among them. ^{56}Then a maid, seeing him as he sat in the light and gazing at him, said, "This man also was with him." ^{57}But he denied it, saying, "Woman, I do not know him." ^{58}And a little later some one else saw him and said, "You also are one of them." But Peter said, "Man, I am not." ^{59}And after an interval of about an hour still another insisted, saying, "Certainly this man also was with him; for he is a Galilean." ^{60}But Peter said, "Man, I do not know what you are saying." And immediately, while he was still speaking, the cock crowed. ^{61}And the Lord turned and looked at Peter. And Peter remembered the word of the Lord, how he had said to him, "Before the cock crows today, you will deny me three times." ^{62}And he went out and wept bitterly.

^{63}Now the men who were holding Jesus mocked him and beat him; ^{64}they also blindfolded him and asked him, "Prophesy! Who is it that struck you?" ^{65}And they spoke many other words against him, reviling him.

[1] Other ancient authorities omit verses 43 and 44

66When day came, the assembly of the elders of the people gathered together, both chief priests and scribes; and they led him away to their council, and they said, 67"If you are the Christ, tell us." But he said to them, "If I tell you, you will not believe; 68and if I ask you, you will not answer. 69But from now on the Son of man shall be seated at the right hand of the power of God." 70And they all said, "Are you the Son of God, then?" And he said to them, "You say that I am." 71And they said, "What further testimony do we need? We have heard it ourselves from his own lips."

23

Then the whole company of them arose, and brought him before Pilate. 2And they began to accuse him, saying, "We found this man perverting our nation, and forbidding us to give tribute to Caesar, and saying that he himself is Christ a king." 3And Pilate asked him, "Are you the King of the Jews?" And he answered him, "You have said so." 4And Pilate said to the chief priests and the multitudes, "I find no crime in this man." 5But they were urgent, saying, "He stirs up the people, teaching throughout all Judea, from Galilee even to this place."

6When Pilate heard this, he asked whether the man was a Galilean. 7And when he learned that he belonged to Herod's jurisdiction, he sent him over to Herod, who was himself in Jerusalem at that time. 8When Herod saw Jesus, he was very glad, for he had long desired to see him, because he had heard about him, and he was hoping to see some sign done by him. 9So he questioned him at some length; but he made no answer. 10The chief priests and the scribes stood by, vehemently accusing him. 11And Herod with his soldiers treated him with contempt and mocked him; then, arraying him in gorgeous apparel, he sent him back to Pilate. 12And Herod and Pilate became friends with each other that very day, for before this they had been at enmity with each other.

13Pilate then called together the chief priests and the rulers and the people, 14and said to them, "You brought me this man as one who was perverting the people; and after examining him before you, behold, I did not find this man guilty of any of your charges against him; 15neither did Herod, for he sent him back to us. Behold, nothing deserving death has been done by him; 16I will therefore chastise him and release him."[m]

18But they all cried out together, "Away with this man, and release to us Barab'bas"—19a man who had been thrown into prison for an insurrection started in the city, and for murder. 20Pilate addressed them once more, desiring to release Jesus; 21but they shouted out, "Crucify, crucify him!" 22A third time he said to them, "Why, what evil has he done? I have found in him no crime deserving death; I will therefore chastise him and release him." 23But they were urgent, demanding with loud cries that he should be crucified. And their voices prevailed. 24So Pilate gave sentence that their demand should be granted. 25He released the man who had been thrown into prison for insurrection and murder, whom they asked for; but Jesus he delivered up to their will.

44It was now about the sixth hour, and there was darkness over the whole land[q] until the ninth hour, 45while the sun's light failed;[r] and the curtain of the temple was torn in two. 46Then Jesus, crying with a loud voice, said, "Father, into thy hands I commit my spirit!" And having said this he breathed his last. 47Now when the centurion saw what had taken place, he praised

[m] Here, or after verse 19, other ancient authorities add verse 17, *Now he was obliged to release one man to them at the festival* [q] Or *earth*

[r] Or *the sun was eclipsed*. Other ancient authorities read *the sun was darkened*

God, and said, "Certainly this man was innocent!" [48]And all the multitudes who assembled to see the sight, when they saw what had taken place, returned home beating their breasts. [49]And all his acquaintances and the women who had followed him from Galilee stood at a distance and saw these things.

[50]Now there was a man named Joseph from the Jewish town of Arimathe'a. He was a member of the council, a good and righteous man, [51]who had not consented to their purpose and deed, and he was looking for the kingdom of God. [52]This man went to Pilate and asked for the body of Jesus. [53]Then he took it down and wrapped it in a linen shroud, and laid him in a rock-hewn tomb, where no one had ever yet been laid. [54]It was the day of Preparation, and the sabbath was beginning.[s] [55]The women who had come with him from Galilee followed, and saw the tomb, and how his body was laid; [56]then they returned, and prepared spices and ointments.

On the sabbath they rested according to the commandment.

24

But on the first day of the week, at early dawn, they went to the tomb, taking the spices which they had prepared. [2]And they found the stone rolled away from the tomb, [3]but when they went in they did not find the body.[t] [4]While they were perplexed about this, behold, two men stood by them in dazzling apparel; [5]and as they were frightened and bowed their faces to the ground, the men said to them, "Why do you seek the living among the dead?[u] [6]Remember how he told you, while he was still in Galilee, [7]that the Son of man must be delivered into the hands of sinful men, and be crucified, and on the third day rise." [8]And they remembered his words, [9]and returning from the tomb they told all this to the eleven and to all the rest.

from The Gospel According to John

In this selection from The Gospel According to John we read in Chap. 1 that in the beginning (of all things) was the Word, and we are told that the Word was God, and in verse 14 we are told that the Word became flseh. The Greek for "word" is *logos*, which in Greek religion and philosophy in the first century of the Common Era had a range of meanings. In The Gospel According to John *logos* means God's activity and purpose. When the Gospel says that the *logos* or Word became flesh the reference is to Jesus Christ as the incarnation of God, in whom God's activity enters the world. Chap. 2 tells of Jesus' turning water into wine at a marriage celebration at Cana.

The Gospel According to John

1

In the beginning was the Word, and the Word was with God, and the Word was God. [2]He was in the beginning with God; [3]all things were made through him, and without him was not anything made that was made. [4]In him was life,[a] and the life was the light of men. [5]The light

[s] Greek *was dawning*   [t] Other ancient authorities add *of the Lord Jesus*
[u] Other ancient authorities add *He is not here, but has risen*
[a] Or *was not anything made. That which has been made was life in him*

shines in the darkness, and the darkness has not overcome it.

⁶There was a man sent from God, whose name was John. ⁷He came for testimony, to bear witness to the light, that all might believe through him. ⁸He was not the light, but came to bear witness to the light.

⁹The true light that enlightens every man was coming into the world. ¹⁰He was in the world, and the world was made through him, yet the world knew him not. ¹¹He came to his own home, and his own people received him not. ¹²But to all who received him, who believed in his name, he gave power to become children of God; ¹³who were born, not of blood nor of the will of the flesh nor of the will of man, but of God.

¹⁴And the Word became flesh and dwelt among us, full of grace and truth; we have beheld his glory, glory as of the only Son from the Father. ¹⁵(John bore witness to him, and cried, "This was he of whom I said, 'He who comes after me ranks before me, for he was before me.'") ¹⁶And from his fulness have we all received, grace upon grace. ¹⁷For the law was given through Moses; grace and truth came through Jesus Christ. ¹⁸No one has ever seen God; the only Son,ᵇ who is in the bosom of the Father, he has made him known.

2

On the third day there was a marriage at Cana in Galilee, and the mother of Jesus was there; ²Jesus also was invited to the marriage, with his disciples. ³When the wine failed, the mother of Jesus said to him, "They have no wine." ⁴And Jesus said to her, "O woman, what have you to do with me? My hour has not yet come." ⁵His mother said to the servants, "Do whatever he tells you." ⁶Now six stone jars were standing there, for the Jewish rites of purification, each holding twenty or thirty gallons. ⁷Jesus said to them, "Fill the jars with water." And they filled them up to the brim. ⁸He said to them, "Now draw some out, and take it to the steward of the feast." So they took it. ⁹When the steward of the feast tasted the water now become wine, and did not know where it came from (though the servants who had drawn the water knew), the steward of the feast called the bridegroom ¹⁰and said to him, "Every man serves the good wine first; and when men have drunk freely, then the poor wine; but you have kept the good wine until now." ¹¹This, the first of his signs, Jesus did at Cana in Galilee, and manifested his glory; and his disciples believed in him.

¹²After this he went down to Caper'naum, with his mother and his brothers and his disciples; and there they stayed for a few days.

¹³The Passover of the Jews was at hand, and Jesus went up to Jerusalem. ¹⁴In the temple he found those who were selling oxen and sheep and pigeons, and the money-changers at their business. ¹⁵And making a whip of cords, he drove them all, with the sheep and oxen, out of the temple; and he poured out the coins of the money-changers and overturned their tables. ¹⁶And he told those who sold the pigeons, "Take these things away; you shall not make my Father's house a house of trade." ¹⁷His disciples remembered that it was written, "Zeal for thy house will consume me." ¹⁸The Jews then said to him, "What sign have you to show us for doing this?" ¹⁹Jesus answered them, "Destroy this temple, and in three days I will raise it up." ²⁰The Jews then said, "It has taken forty-six years to build this temple, and will you raise it up in three

ᵇ Other ancient authorities read *God*

days?" [21]But he spoke of the temple of his body. [22]When therefore he was raised from the dead, his disciples remembered that he had said this; and they believed the scripture and the word which Jesus had spoken.

from The Letter of Paul to the Romans

In the first century of the Common Era many of the early Christians were from the Jewish community, but there was also an effort by some in the early church to take the Christian message beyond Palestine to Gentiles (that is, to non-Jews). Chief among these early missionaries to Gentile populations was Paul. In this selection from Paul's letter to the Romans Paul says that he is eager to preach the gospel to Greeks, to Romans, and to all Gentiles. He also proclaims that God's deity is to be seen "in the things that have been made."

The Letter of Paul to the Romans

1

Paul, a servant[a] of Jesus Christ, called to be an apostle, set apart for the gospel of God [2]which he promised beforehand through his prophets in the holy scriptures, [3]the gospel concerning his Son, who was descended from David according to the flesh [4]and designated Son of God in power according to the Spirit of holiness by his resurrection from the dead, Jesus Christ our Lord, [5]through whom we have received grace and apostleship to bring about the obedience of faith for the sake of his name among all the nations, [6]including yourselves who are called to belong to Jesus Christ;

[7]To all God's beloved in Rome, who are called to be saints:

Grace to you and peace from God our Father and the Lord Jesus Christ.

[8]First, I thank my God through Jesus Christ for all of you, because your faith is proclaimed in all the world. [9]For God is my witness, whom I serve with my spirit in the gospel of his Son, that without ceasing I mention you always in my prayers, [10]asking that somehow by God's will I may now at last succeed in coming to you. [11]For I long to see you, that I may impart to you some spiritual gift to strengthen you, [12]that is, that we may be mutually encouraged by each other's faith, both yours and mine. [13]I want you to know, brethren, that I have often intended to come to you (but thus far have been prevented), in order that I may reap some harvest among you as well as among the rest of the Gentiles. [14]I am under obligation both to Greeks and to barbarians, both to the wise and to the foolish: [15]so I am eager to preach the gospel to you also who are in Rome.

[16]For I am not ashamed of the gospel: it is the power of God for salvation to every one who has faith, to the Jew first and also to the Greek. [17]For in it the righteousness of God is revealed through faith for faith; as it is written, "He who through faith is righteous shall live."[b]

[18]For the wrath of God is revealed from heaven against all ungodliness and

---

[a] Or *slave*   [b] Or *The righteous shall live by faith*

wickedness of men who by their wickedness suppress the truth. [19]For what can be known about God is plain to them, because God has shown it to them. [20]Ever since the creation of the world his invisible nature, namely, his eternal power and deity, has been clearly perceived in the things that have been made. So they are without excuse; [21]for although they knew God they did not honor him as God or give thanks to him, but they became futile in their thinking and their senseless minds were darkened. [22]Claiming to be wise, they became fools, [23]and exchanged the glory of the immortal God for images resembling mortal man or birds or animals or reptiles.

from The First Letter of Paul to the Corinthians

In his first letter to the Corinthians (in Greece) Paul says that if he has faith, but does not have love, he is nothing. Paul names the three Christian virtues of faith, hope, and love. Love, he proclaims, is the greatest of these.

The First Letter of Paul to the Corinthians

13

If I speak in the tongues of men and of angels, but have not love, I am a noisy gong or a clanging cymbal. [2]And if I have prophetic powers, and understand all mysteries and all knowledge, and if I have all faith, so as to remove mountains, but have not love, I am nothing. [3]If I give away all I have, and if I deliver my body to be burned, but have not love, I gain nothing.

[4]Love is patient and kind; love is not jealous or boastful; [5]it is not arrogant or rude. Love does not insist on its own way; it is not irritable or resentful; [6]it does not rejoice at wrong, but rejoices in the right. [7]Love bears all things, believes all things, hopes all things, endures all things.

[8]Love never ends; as for prophecies, they will pass away; as for tongues, they will cease; as for knowledge, it will pass away. [9]For our knowledge is imperfect and our prophecy is imperfect; [10]but when the perfect comes, the imperfect will pass away. [11]When I was a child, I spoke like a child, I thought like a child, I reasoned like a child; when I became a man, I gave up childish ways. [12]For now we see in a mirror dimly, but then face to face. Now I know in part; then I shall understand fully, even as I have been fully understood. [13]So faith, hope, love abide, these three; but the greatest of these is love.

from The First Letter of John

In this selection from John's first letter we are told in Chap. 2 that in those who keep the word of God the love of God is perfected and that he who loves his brother abides in the light. In Chap. 4 we are told that those who abide in love abide in God.

The First Letter of John

1

That which was from the beginning, which we have heard, which we have seen with our eyes, which we have looked upon and touched with our hands, concerning the word of life—[2]the life was made manifest, and we saw it, and testify to it, and proclaim to you the eternal life which was with the Father and was made manifest to us—[3]that which we have seen and heard we proclaim also to you, so that you may have fellowship with us; and our fellowship is with the Father and with his Son Jesus Christ. [4]And we are writing this that our[a] joy may be complete.

[5]This is the message we have heard from him and proclaim to you, that God is light and in him is no darkness at all. [6]If we say we have fellowship with him while we walk in darkness, we lie and do not live according to the truth; [7]but if we walk in the light, as he is in the light, we have fellowship with one another, and the blood of Jesus his Son cleanses us from all sin. [8]If we say we have no sin, we deceive ourselves, and the truth is not in us. [9]If we confess our sins, he is faithful and just, and will forgive our sins and cleanse us from all unrighteousness. [10]If we say we have not sinned, we make him a liar, and his word is not in us.

2

My little children, I am writing this to you so that you may not sin; but if any one does sin, we have an advocate with the Father, Jesus Christ the righteous; [2]and he is the expiation for our sins, and not for ours only but also for the sins of the whole world. [3]And by this we may be sure that we know him, if we keep his commandments. [4]He who says "I know him" but disobeys his commandments is a liar, and the truth is not in him; [5]but whoever keeps his word, in him truly love for God is perfected. By this we may be sure that we are in him: [6]he who says he abides in him ought to walk in the same way in which he walked.

[7]Beloved, I am writing you no new commandment, but an old commandment which you had from the beginning; the old commandment is the word which you have heard. [8]Yet I am writing you a new commandment, which is true in him and in you, because[b] the darkness is passing away and the true light is already shining. [9]He who says he is in the light and hates his brother is in the darkness still. [10]He who loves his brother abides in the light, and in it[c] there is no cause for stumbling. [11]But he who hates his brother is in the darkness and walks in the darkness, and does not know where he is going, because the darkness has blinded his eyes.

[12]I am writing to you, little children, because your sins are forgiven for his sake. [13]I am writing to you, fathers, because you know him who is from the beginning. I am writing to you, young men, because you have overcome the evil one. [14]I write to you, children, because you know the Father. I write to you, fathers, because you know him who is from the beginning. I write to you, young men, because you are strong, and the word of God abides in you, and you have overcome the evil one.

---

[a] Other ancient authorities read *your*   [b] Or *that*   [c] Or *him*

4

Beloved, do not believe every spirit, but test the spirits to see whether they are of God; for many false prophets have gone out into the world. [2]By this you know the Spirit of God: every spirit which confesses that Jesus Christ has come in the flesh is of God, [3]and every spirit which does not confess Jesus is not of God. This is the spirit of antichrist, of which you heard that it was coming, and now it is in the world already. [4]Little children, you are of God, and have overcome them; for he who is in you is greater than he who is in the world. [5]They are of the world, therefore what they say is of the world, and the world listens to them. [6]We are of God. Whoever knows God listens to us, and he who is not of God does not listen to us. By this we know the spirit of truth and the spirit of error.

[7]Beloved, let us love one another; for love is of God, and he who loves is born of God and knows God. [8]He who does not love does not know God; for God is love. [9]In this the love of God was made manifest among us, that God sent his only Son into the world, so that we might live through him. [10]In this is love, not that we loved God but that he loved us and sent his Son to be the expiation for our sins. [11]Beloved, if God so loved us, we also ought to love one another. [12]No man has ever seen God; if we love one another, God abides in us and his love is perfected in us.

[13]By this we know that we abide in him and he in us, because he has given us of his own Spirit. [14]And we have seen and testify that the Father has sent his Son as the Savior of the world. [15]Whoever confesses that Jesus is the Son of God, God abides in him, and he in God. [16]So we know and believe the love God has for us. God is love, and he who abides in love abides in God, and God abides in him. [17]In this is love perfected with us, that we may have confidence for the day of judgment, because as he is so are we in this world. [18]There is no fear in love, but perfect love casts out fear. For fear has to do with punishment, and he who fears is not perfected in love. [19]We love, because he first loved us. [20]If any one says, "I love God," and hates his brother, he is a liar; for he who does not love his brother whom he has seen, cannot[h] love God whom he has not seen. [21]And this commandment we have from him, that he who loves God should love his brother also.

Islam

Islam, historically the third Western monotheistic religion, dates from the seventh century of the Common Era, when Muhammad, the founder of Islam lived. Muhammad is accepted as the prophet or messenger of Allah (Allah is the Arabic word for God). In Islamic belief, there have been a number of prophets who have received God's message. Abraham, Moses, and Jesus are accepted as prophets. Muhammad, however, is accepted by Muslims as the seal of the prophets, the final prophet to whom God's final word has been revealed.

Muhammad, the Prophet of Allah, was born in 570. As a young man he was a shepherd and camel driver. Later he went to work for a rich widow named Khadijah. He did well in her employ, managing caravans. They were attracted to each other and in time were married and had several children. While

[h] Other ancient authorities read *how can he*

Muhammad later would have several wives, he took no other wife while Khadijah was alive. During the time of his marriage to Khadijah, Muhammad's faith in the one God deepened and for several years he would leave Mecca and take solitary month-long retreats in a cave on nearby Mount Hira.

In 610 there occurred what in the Islamic tradition is called the Night of Power and Glory. The angel Gabriel appeared to Muhammad and summoned him to be the messenger of Allah. This occurrence distressed Muhammad, but outside the cave he heard the same Voice telling him, "O Muhammad, you are Allah's messenger." Muhammad returned home and told Khadijah of his experience, and the two of them consulted her elderly cousin who knew the Jewish and Christian scriptures. Khadijah's cousin reassured Muhammad and, according to tradition, told him that his experience must be the beginning of prophecy and there would come to him the Great Law, as it had come to Moses. In the time that followed Muhammad received other messages from the Voice, and he came to accept himself as Prophet and Apostle, as the Voice proclaimed.

In this way the *Qur'an* (or Koran), the sacred book of Islam, was revealed to Muhammad. The messages that constitute the Qur'an came to Muhammad over most of his life in Mecca and Medina. At first passages were memorized by the Prophet's hearers, and those who could write wrote them down on what was available. In 651-52, twenty years after Muhammad's death, a written Qur'an was put into canonical form, with 114 suras (sections or chapters). In its entirety the Qur'an is about the length of the Christian New Testament. Strictly it exists only in Arabic. The Qur'an cannot be translated into other languages, and in this it is unlike the Christian Bible and the Jewish Bible (although there is some controversy about translating the Hebrew Bible). Still the Qur'an has been put into English and other languages because many Muslims do not speak or read Arabic.

The Qur'an

The Qur'an (or Koran) is the Holy Book or scripture of Islam. In the Islamic tradition it was revealed to Muhammad by the angel Gabriel who called Muhammad to be the messenger of God. It is the primary source of the sharia or the religious law of Islam. In our selection there are passages from several suras, or chapters, of the Qur'an and several short suras in their entirety, including the Opening or Exordium.*

Sura I The Opening

This sura, the first sura of the Qur'an, is the most often recited sura in the Qur'an. Every sura, except one, Sura IX Repentance, begins with "In the name of Allah, the Compassionate, the Merciful." Since "Allah" is Arabic for "God" our translation reads "In the name of God. . . ."

---

* From *The Koran*, translated from the Arabic by J. M. Rodwell, 1909.

Sura I—The Opening

In the Name of God, the Compassionate, the Merciful

PRAISE be to God, Lord of the worlds!
The compassionate, the merciful!
King on the day of reckoning!
Thee *only* do we worship, and to Thee
    do we cry for help.

Guide Thou us on the straight path,
The path of those to whom Thou hast
    been gracious;—with whom thou
    art not angry, and who go not
    astray.

from Sura II The Cow

In this sura and others "we" is Allah, God (verse 81). This sura is typical of the suras of the Qur'an in that God, "We," is speaking to Muhammad as "thou" (verse 90) and instructing him with "SAY [and there follows a revealed message to be communicated to the people]," as in verse 88.

    In verse 81, the first verse in our reading, God says that he gave Moses the Book (as the Torah) and inspired Jesus with the Holy Spirit. Islam recognizes Jews and Christians as "people of the Book." However, the message of the Prophet, the revelation of the Qur'an, is God's final revelation.

Sura II—The Cow

Moreover, to Moses gave we "the Book," and we raised up apostles after him; and to Jesus, son of Mary, gave we clear proofs *of his mission*, and strengthened him by the Holy Spirit. So oft then as an apostle cometh to you with that which your souls desire not, swell ye with pride, and treat some as impostors, and slay others?

    And they say, "Uncircumcised are our hearts." Nay! God hath cursed them in their infidelity: few are they who believe!

    And when a Book had come to them from God, confirming that which they had received already—although they had before prayed for victory over those who believed not—yet when that Koran come to them, of which they had knowledge, they did not recognise it. The curse of God on the infidels!

    For a vile price have they sold themselves, by not believing what God hath sent down, envious of God's sending down his grace on such of his servants as he pleaseth: and they have brought on themselves wrath upon wrath. And for the unbelievers is a disgraceful chastisement.

    And when it is said to them, "Believe in what God hath sent down," they say, "In that which hath been sent down to us we believe:" but what hath since been sent down they disbelieve, although it be the truth confirmatory of their own Scriptures. SAY: Why then have ye of old slain God's prophets, if ye are indeed believers?

Moreover, Moses came unto you with proofs of his mission. Then in his absence ye took the calf *for your God*, and did wickedly.

And when we accepted your covenant, and uplifted the mountain over you, *we said*, "Take firm hold on what we have given you, and hearken." They said, "We have hearkened and have rebelled:" then were they made to drink down the calf into their hearts for their ingratitude.

SAY: A bad thing hath your faith commanded you, if ye be indeed believers.

SAY: If the future dwelling place with God be specially for you, but not for the rest of mankind, then wish for death, if ye are sincere:

But never can they wish for it, because of that which their own hands have sent on before them! And God knoweth the offenders.

90 And thou wilt surely find them of all men most covetous of life, beyond even the polytheists. To be kept alive a thousand years might one of them desire: but that he may be preserved alive, shall no one reprieve himself from the punishment! And God seeth what they do.

SAY: Whoso is the enemy of Gabriel—For he it is who by God's leave hath caused *the Koran* to descend on thy heart, the confirmation of previous revelations, and guidance, and good tidings to the faithful—

Whoso is an enemy to God or his angels, or to Gabriel, or to Michael, *shall have God as his enemy:* for verily God is an enemy to the Infidels.

Moreover, clear signs have we sent down to thee, and none will disbelieve them but the perverse.

Oft as they have formed an engagement *with thee*, will some of them set it aside? But most of them believe not.

And when there came to them an apostle from God, affirming the previous revelations made to them, some of those to whom the Scriptures were given, threw the Book of God behind their backs as if they knew it not:

And they followed what the Satans read in the reign of Solomon: not that Solomon was unbelieving, but the Satans were unbelieving. Sorcery did they teach to men, and what had been revealed to the two angels, Harut and Marut, at Babel. Yet no man did these two teach until they had said, "We are only a temptation. Be not then an unbeliever." From these two did men learn how to cause division between man and wife: but unless by leave of God, no man did they harm thereby. They learned, indeed, what would harm and not profit them; and yet they knew that he who bought that art should have no part in the life to come! And vile the price for which they have sold themselves,—if they had but known it!

But had they believed and feared God, better surely would have been the reward from God,—if they had but known it!

O ye who believe! say not to our apostle, "Raina" (Look at us); but say, "Ondhorna" (Regard us). And attend to this; for, the Infidels shall suffer a grievous chastisement.

The unbelievers among the people of the Book, and among the idolaters, desire not that any good should be sent down to you from your Lord: but God will shew His special mercy to whom He will, for He is of great bounty.

Whatever verses we cancel, or cause 100 thee to forget, we bring a better or its like. Knowest thou not that God hath power over all things?

Knowest thou not that the dominion of the Heavens and of the Earth is God's? and that ye have neither patron nor helper, save God?

Would ye ask of your apostle what of old was asked of Moses? But he who exchangeth faith for unbelief, hath already erred from the even way.

Many of the people of the Book desire to bring you back to unbelief after ye have believed, out of selfish envy, even after the truth hath been clearly shewn them. But forgive them, and shun them till God shall come in with His working. Truly God hath power over all things.

And observe prayer and pay the legal impost: and whatever good thing ye have sent on before for your soul's sake, ye shall find it with God. Verily God seeth what ye do.

110   And they say, "None but Jews or Christians shall enter Paradise:" This is their wish. SAY: Give your proofs if ye speak the truth.

But they who set their face with resignation Godward, and do what is right,— their reward is with their Lord; no fear shall come on them, neither shall they be grieved.

Moreover, the Jews say, "The Christians lean on nought:"

"On nought lean the Jews," say the Christians: Yet both are readers of the Book. So with like words say they who have no knowledge. But on the resurrection day, God shall judge between them as to that in which they differ.

And who committeth a greater wrong than he who hindereth God's name from being remembered in his temples, and who hasteth to ruin them? Such men cannot enter them but with fear. Their's is shame in this world, and a severe torment in the next.

The East and the West is God's: therefore, whichever way ye turn, there is the face of God: Truly God is immense and knoweth all.

And they say, "God hath a son:" No! Praise be to Him! But—His, whatever is in the Heavens and the Earth! All obeyeth Him,

Sole maker of the Heavens and of the Earth! And when He decreeth a thing, He only saith to it, "Be," and it is.

And they who have no knowledge say, "Unless God speak to us, or thou shew us a sign . . . !" So, with like words, said those who were before them: their hearts are alike: Clear signs have we already shewn for those who have firm faith:

Verily, with the Truth have we sent thee, a bearer of good tidings and a warner: and of the people of Hell thou shalt not be questioned.

But until thou follow their religion, neither Jews nor Christians will be satisfied with thee. SAY: Verily, guidance of God,— that is the guidance! And if, after "the Knowledge" which hath reached thee, thou follow their desires, thou shalt find neither helper nor protector against God.

They to whom we have given the Book, and who read it as it ought to be read,—these believe therein: but whoso believeth not therein, shall meet with perdition.

O children of Israel! remember my favour wherewith I have favoured you, and that high above all mankind have I raised you:

And dread the day when not in aught shall soul satisfy for soul, nor shall any ransom be taken from it, nor shall any intercession avail, and they shall not be helped.

When his Lord made trial of Abraham by commands which he fulfilled, He said, "I am about to make thee an Imâm to mankind:" he said, "Of my offspring also:" "My covenant," said God, "embraceth not the evil doers."

And remember when we appointed the Holy House[1] as man's resort and safe retreat, and said, "Take ye the station of

[1] The Ka'ba

Abraham for a place of prayer:" And we commanded Abraham and Ismael, "Purify my house for those who shall go in procession round it, and those who shall abide there for devotion, and those who shall bow down and prostrate themselves."

120   And when Abraham said, "Lord! make this secure land, and supply its people with fruits, such of them as believe in God and in the last day:" He said, "And whoso believeth not, for a little while will I bestow good things on him; then will I drive him to the torment of the Fire!" An ill passage!

And when Abraham, with Ismael, raised the foundations of the House, *they said*, "O our Lord! accept *it* from us; for thou art the Hearer, the Knower.

O our Lord! make us also Muslims, and our posterity a Muslim people; and teach us our holy rites, and be turned towards us, for thou art He who turneth, the Merciful.

O our Lord! raise up among them an apostle who may rehearse thy signs unto them, and teach them 'the Book,' and Wisdom, and purify them: for thou art the Mighty, the Wise."

And who but he that hath debased his soul to folly will mislike the faith of Abraham, when we have chosen him in this world, and in the world to come he shall be of the Just?

When his Lord said to him, "Resign thyself to me," he said, "I resign myself to the Lord of the Worlds."

And this to his children did Abraham bequeath, and Jacob also, *saying*, "O my children! truly God hath chosen a religion for you; so die not unless ye be also Muslims."

Were ye present when Jacob was at the point of death? when he said to his sons, "Whom will ye worship when I am gone?" They said, "We will worship thy God and the God of thy fathers Abraham and Ismael and Isaac, one God, and to Him are we surrendered (Muslims)."

That people have now passed away; they have the reward of their deeds, and ye shall have the meed of yours: but of their doings ye shall not be questioned.

They say, moreover, "Become Jews or Christians that ye may have the *true* guidance." SAY: Nay! the religion of Abraham, the sound in faith, and not one of those who join gods with God!

Say ye: "We believe in God, and that   130 which hath been sent down to us, and that which hath been sent down to Abraham and Ismael and Isaac and Jacob and the tribes: and that which hath been given to Moses and to Jesus, and that which was given to the prophets from their Lord. No difference do we make between any of them: and to God are we resigned (Muslims)."

If therefore they believe even as ye believe, then have they true guidance; but if they turn back, then do they cut themselves off *from you:* and God will suffice *to protect* thee against them, for He is the Hearer, the Knower.

Islam is the Baptism of God, and who is better to baptise than God? And Him do we serve.

SAY: Will ye dispute with us about God? when He is our Lord and your Lord! We have our works and ye have your works; and we are sincerely His.

Will ye say, "Verily Abraham, and Ismael, and Isaac, and Jacob, and the tribes, were Jews or Christians?" SAY: Who knoweth best, ye, or God? And who is more in fault than he who concealeth the witness which he hath from God? But God is not regardless of what ye do.

That people have now passed away: they have the reward of their deeds, and for you is the meed of yours; but of their doings ye shall not be questioned.

from Sura XIX Mary

In this sura Mary, in accord with Christian belief, is recognized as giving birth to Jesus while a virgin, and Jesus is recognized as a "servant of God," ordained as a prophet, to whom God has given "the Book."

Sura XIX.—Mary

In the Name of God, the Compassionate, the Merciful

KAF. HA. YA. AIN. SAD. A recital of thy Lord's mercy to his servant Zachariah;

When he called upon his Lord with secret calling,

And said: "O Lord, verily my bones are weakened, and the hoar hairs glisten on my head,

And never, Lord, have I prayed to thee with ill success.

But now I have fears for my kindred after me; and my wife is barren:

Give me, then, a successor as thy special gift, who shall be my heir and an heir of the family of Jacob: and make him, Lord, well pleasing to thee."

—"O Zachariah! verily we announce to thee a son,—his name John:

That name We have given to none before him."

He said: "O my Lord! how when my wife is barren shall I have a son, and when I have now reached old age, failing in my powers?"

10 He said: "So shall it be. Thy Lord hath said, Easy is this to me, for I created thee aforetime when thou wast nothing."

He said: "Vouchsafe me, O my Lord! a sign." He said: "Thy sign shall be that for three nights, though sound in health, thou speakest not to man."

And he came forth from the sanctuary to his people, and made signs to them to sing praises morn and even.

We said: "O John! receive the Book with purpose of heart:"—and We bestowed on him wisdom while yet a child;

And mercifulness from Ourself, and purity; and pious was he, and duteous to his parents; and not proud, rebellious.

And peace was on him on the day he was born, and the day of his death, and *shall be* on the day when he shall be raised to life!

And make mention in the Book, of Mary, when she went apart from her family, eastward,

And took a veil *to shroud herself* from them: and we sent our spirit to her, and he took before her the form of a perfect man.

She said: "I fly for refuge from thee to the God of Mercy! If thou fearest Him, *begone from me*."

He said: "I am only a messenger of thy Lord, that I may bestow on thee a holy son."

She said: "How shall I have a son, 20 when man hath never touched me? and I am not unchaste."

He said: "So shall it be. Thy Lord hath said: 'Easy is this with me;' and we will make him a sign to mankind, and a mercy from us. For it is a thing decreed."

And she conceived him, and retired with him to a far-off place.

And the throes came upon her by the trunk of a palm. She said: "Oh, would that I had died ere this, and been a thing forgotten, forgotten quite!"

And one cried to her from below her: "Grieve not thou, thy Lord hath provided a streamlet at thy feet:—

And shake the trunk of the palm-tree toward thee: it will drop fresh ripe dates upon thee.

Eat then and drink, and be of cheerful eye: and shouldst thou see a man,

Say,—Verily, I have vowed abstinence to the God of mercy.—To no one will I speak this day."

Then came she with the babe to her people, bearing him. They said, "O Mary! now hast thou done a strange thing!

O sister of Aaron! Thy father was not a man of wickedness, nor unchaste thy mother."

30 And she made a sign *to them, pointing* towards the babe. They said, "How shall we speak with him who is in the cradle, an infant?"

It said, "Verily, I am the servant of God; He hath given me the Book, and He hath made me a prophet;

And He hath made me blessed wherever I may be, and hath enjoined me prayer and almsgiving so long as I shall live;

And to be duteous to her that bare me: and he hath not made me proud, depraved.

And the peace of God was on me the day I was born, and will be the day I shall die, and the day I shall be raised to life."

This is Jesus, the son of Mary; this is a statement of the truth concerning which they doubt.

It beseemeth not God to beget a son. Glory be to Him! when he decreeth a thing, He only saith to it, Be, and it Is.

And verily, God is my Lord and your Lord; adore Him then. This is the right way.

But the Sects have fallen to variance among themselves *about Jesus:* but woe, because of the assembly of a great day, to those who believe not!

Make them hear, make them behold the day when they shall come before us! But the offenders this day are in a manifest error.

Warn them of the day of sighing 40 when the decree shall be accomplished, while they are *sunk* in heedlessness and while they believe not.

Verily, we will inherit the earth and all who are upon it. To us shall they be brought back.

Sura XXXII Adoration

In this sura Allah tells the Prophet that it is He, God, who has created the heavens and the earth, and God proclaims a day of judgment on which believers and disbelievers will be separated. The "He" in verse 2 is Muhammad. The Djinn (verse 13) are supernatural spirits that may be either good or evil.

Sura XXXII.—Adoration

In the Name of God, the Compassionate, the Merciful.

ELIF. LAM. MIM. This Book is without a doubt a Revelation sent down from the Lord of the Worlds.

Will they say, He hath forged it? Nay, it is the truth from thy Lord that

thou mayest warn a people to whom no warner hath come before thee, that haply they may be guided.

God it is who hath created the Heavens and the Earth and all that is between them in six days; then ascended his throne. Save Him ye have no patron, and none to plead for you. Will ye not then reflect?

From the Heaven to the Earth He governeth all things: hereafter shall they come up to him on a day whose length shall be a thousand of such years as ye reckon.

This is He who knoweth the unseen and the seen; the Mighty, the Merciful,

Who hath made everything which he hath created most good; and began the creation of man with clay;

Then ordained his progeny from germs of life, from sorry water:

Then shaped him, and breathed of His Spirit into him, and gave you hearing and seeing and hearts: what little thanks do ye return!

And they say, "What! when we shall have lain hidden in the earth, shall we become a new creation?"

Yea, they deny that they shall meet their Lord.

SAY: The angel of death who is charged with you shall cause you to die: then shall ye be returned to your Lord.

Couldst thou but see when the guilty shall droop their heads before their Lord, *and cry,* "O our Lord! we have seen and we have heard: return us then *to life:* we will do that which is right. Verily we believe firmly!"

(Had we pleased we had certainly given to every soul its guidance. But true shall be the word which hath gone forth from me—I will surely fill hell with Djinn and men together.)

"Taste then the recompense of your having forgotten the meeting with this your day. We, too, have forgotten you: taste then an eternal punishment for that which ye have wrought."

They only believe in our signs, who, when mention is made of them, fall down in ADORATION, and celebrate the praise of their Lord, and are not puffed up with disdain:

Who, as they raise them from their couches, call on their Lord with fear and desire, and give alms of that with which we have supplied them.

No soul knoweth what joy of the eyes is reserved *for the good* in recompense of their works.

Shall he then who is a believer be as he who sinneth grossly? they shall not be held alike.

As to those who believe and do that which is right, they shall have gardens of eternal abode as the meed of their works:

But as for those who grossly sin, their abode shall be the fire: so oft as they shall desire to escape out of it, back shall they be turned into it. And it shall be said to them, Taste ye the torment of the fire, which ye treated as a lie.

And we will surely cause them to taste a punishment yet nearer at hand, besides the greater punishment, that haply they may turn to us *in penitence.*

Who acteth worse than he who is warned by the signs of his Lord, then turneth away from them? We will surely take vengeance on the guilty ones.

We heretofore gave the Book *of the law* to Moses: have thou no doubt as to our meeting with him: and we appointed it for the guidance of the children of Israel.

And we appointed Imams from among them who should guide after our command when they had themselves endured with constancy, and had firmly believed in our signs.

Now thy Lord! He will decide between them on the day of resurrection as to the subject of their disputes.

Is it not notorious to them how many generations, through whose abodes they walk, we have destroyed before them? Truly herein are signs: will they not then hear?

See they not how we drive the rain to some parched land and thereby bring forth corn of which their cattle and themselves do eat? Will they not then behold?

They say, "When will this decision take place? Tell us, if ye are men of truth?"

SAY: On the day of that decision, the faith of infidels shall not avail them, and they shall have no further respite.

Stand aloof from them then, and wait thou, for they too wait. 30

Sura LV The Merciful

Every sura except one begins with "In the name of God, the Compassionate, the Merciful." Mercy is one of the Attributes of Allah, and this sura describes and celebrates the merciful blessings of God. The "etc." that recurs in this sura stands for a refrain of "then of the bounties of your Lord would ye twain [humans and djinn] deny?" which occurs in verse 11.

Sura LV.—The Merciful

In the Name of God, the Compassionate, the Merciful

THE God of MERCY hath taught the Koran,
Hath created man,
Hath taught him articulate speech.
The Sun and the Moon have each their times,
And the plants and the trees bend in adoration.
And the Heaven, He hath reared it on high, and hath
appointed the balance;
That in the balance ye should not transgress.
Weigh therefore with fairness, and scant not the balance.
And the Earth, He hath prepared it for the living tribes:
10 Therein are fruits, and the palms with sheathed clusters,
And the grain with its husk, and the fragrant plants.
Which then of the bounties of your Lord will ye twain deny?
He created man of clay like that of the potter.

And He created the djinn of pure fire:
Which then of the bounties, etc.
He is the Lord of the East,
He is the Lord of the West:
Which, etc.
He hath let loose the two seas which meet each other:
Yet between them is a barrier which they 20
overpass not:
Which, etc.
From each he bringeth up pearls both great and small:
Which, etc.
And His are the ships towering up at sea like mountains:
Which, etc.
All on the earth shall pass away,
But the face of thy Lord shall abide resplendent with majesty and glory:
Which, etc.
To Him maketh suit all that is in the Heaven and the Earth.
Every day doth some new work employ Him:
Which, etc. 30
We will find leisure *to judge* you, O ye men and djinn:

Which, etc.

O company of djinn and men, if ye can overpass the bounds of the Heavens and the Earth, then overpass them. But by *our* leave only shall ye overpass them:

Which, etc.

A bright flash of fire shall be hurled at you both, and molten brass, and ye shall not defend yourselves from it:

Which, etc.

When the Heaven shall be cleft asunder, and become rose red, like stained leather:

Which, etc.

On that day shall neither man nor djinn be asked of his sin:

40 Which, etc.

By their tokens shall the sinners be known, and they shall be seized by their forelocks and their feet:

Which, etc.

"This is Hell which sinners treated as a lie."

To and fro shall they pass between it and the boiling water:

Which, etc.

But for those who dread the majesty of their Lord shall be two gardens:

Which, etc.

With o'erbranching trees in each:

Which, etc.

50 In each two fountains flowing:

Which, etc.

In each two kinds of every fruit:

Which, etc.

On couches with linings of brocade shall they recline, and the fruit of the two gardens shall be within easy reach:

Which, etc.

Therein shall be the damsels with retiring glances, whom nor man nor djinn hath touched before them:

Which, etc.

Like jacynths and pearls:

Which, etc.

Shall the reward of good be aught but good?   60

Which, etc.

And beside these shall be two other gardens:

Which, etc.

Of a dark green:

Which, etc.

With gushing fountains in each:

Which, etc.

In each fruits and the palm and the pomegranate:

Which, etc.

In each, the fair, the beauteous ones: 70

Which, etc.

With large dark eyeballs, kept close in their pavilions:

Which, etc.

Whom man hath never touched, nor any djinn:

Which, etc.

Their spouses on soft green cushions and on beautiful carpets shall recline:

Which, etc.

Blessed be the name of thy Lord, full of majesty and glory.

Sura XCIII The Brightness

In this sura God gives assurance to Muhammad that "thy Lord hath not forsaken thee," and there is an expression of the Islamic recognition of charity for those in need.

Sura XCIII.—The Brightness

*In the Name of God, the Compassionate,
the Merciful*

By the noon-day BRIGHTNESS,
And by the night when it darkeneth!
Thy Lord hath not forsaken thee, neither
hath he been displeased.
And surely the Future shall be better for
thee than the Past,
And in the end shall thy Lord be boun-
teous to thee and thou be satisfied.

Did he not find thee an orphan and gave
thee a home?
And found thee erring and guided thee,
And found thee needy and enriched thee.
As to the orphan therefore wrong him
not;
And as to him that asketh of thee, chide   10
him not away;
And as for the favours of thy Lord tell
them abroad.

Sura CVII Religion

Giving to those in need and daily prayer are religiously required by Islam. In
this sura it is made plain that it is heedful prayer that is required, and that charity
or doing good is required, not the mere appearance of charity that impresses
others.

Sura CVII.—Religion

*In the Name of God, the Compassionate,
the Merciful*

What thinkest thou of him who treateth
our RELIGION as a lie?
He it is who thrusteth away the orphan,

And stirreth not *others* up to feed
the poor.
Woe to those who pray,
But in their prayer are careless;
Who make a shew of devotion,
But refuse help to the needy.

Sura CXII The Unity

This sura is regarded by Muslims as a short expression of their faith. It clearly
articulates the oneness of God, the dependence of all upon God, and the uniqueness of God.

Sura CXII.—The Unity

*In the Name of God, the Compassionate,
the Merciful*

Say: He is God alone:
God the eternal!

He begetteth not, and He is not
begotten;
And there is none like unto Him.

Chapter **2**

Proving God's Existence

In the West for nearly a millennium arguments for the existence of God have been formulated in an effort to prove that there is a God. Often, although not always, these arguments have been advanced by Christian thinkers. A notable exception is Moses Maimonides, the great Jewish thinker, who in the twelfth century provided more than one argument for the existence of God. Efforts to prove that God exists are not a thing of the past. There are contemporary philosophers who put forward and espouse one or another argument for God's existence. Arguments for the existence of God are usually put into one of four main categories: Ontological, Cosmological, Teleological, and Moral.

The Ontological Argument was first formulated by St. Anselm in the second half of the eleventh century. Anselm's effort was not to prove God's existence so that he might believe there is a God. Anselm already was a believer; in fact he was a Benedictine monk when he formulated his Ontological Argument. Anselm tried to prove that God exists and is as we believe God to be (has the divine perfections) in order that "understanding" might be given to his faith. Anselm's argument is "ontological" because it is based on ontology, the "being" of God, or what God is by the very concept of God. The argument that Anselm devised is *a priori* in that it relies only on knowledge we have "before observation." That is, it does not rely upon any observations about the world. If Anselm is right, the nature, or the idea of God, necessitates that God exists in reality. While Anselm's argument has drawn much criticism over the centuries, it has also had its supporters. In the seventeenth century René Descartes offered his version of it, and it has its proponents today.

The Cosmological Argument no less than the Ontological seeks to demonstrate the existence of God. It's most renown champion is St. Thomas Aquinas, who provided "five ways" of proving God's existence in the thirteenth century, all or most of which are versions of the Cosmological Argument. It is "cosmological" because it depends on facts about the "cosmos," the world or universe. The facts the argument in one version or another cites are very general: there is motion or there is cause and effect, for instance. Still the facts it relies upon are facts that must be observed, and so it does not use a priori reasoning.

The Teleological Argument is sometimes called the argument from design. It is "teleological" because it cites purpose or design in the natural world. It came into prominence in the eighteenth century. Unlike the Ontological Argument and like the Cosmological it relies upon observations, but unlike the Cosmological it in some formulations brings forward detailed observations, for it looks for design in the world as a whole and in even its minute parts. It may not be accidental that the Teleological Argument rose with the early flourishing of the empirical sciences. Unlike the first two arguments the Teleological Argument is an argument by analogy and seeks to establish the existence of God (and God's divine attributes or perfections) only with probability.

It is sometimes remarked that the Cosmological and Teleological Arguments are closer to religious, or to theistic religious, sensibilities and have more intuitive appeal to the religious than the Ontological Argument. It may well be true that if a general sampling of religious believers in God tried to prove the existence of God most would come up with a version of the Cosmological or the Teleological Argument. The Cosmological Argument, after all, relates closely to the religious belief that God created the universe. Similarly, the Teleological Argument relates closely to the religious belief that God, as the creator of all that is, is the creator of the intricate design we find throughout nature. It should be observed, however, that the Ontological Argument is also close to religious sensibility, for it relates closely to the fundamental religious belief that God is the supreme being. In this way it too is closely connected to religious belief and sensibility, even though the a priori and conceptual reasoning it employs is less likely to be anticipated by either the religious or the nonreligious.

A fourth argument is the Moral Argument. It does not depend on a priori reasoning based on the idea of God or on general or detailed observations about the natural world, but on the nature and coherence of human morality. It is a "practical" argument in that it argues that the coherence of morality requires that the existence of God be postulated.

This chapter contains readings setting forth each of these four arguments for the existence of God, as well as critical evaluations of the first three arguments.

The Ontological Argument

The Ontological Argument seeks to prove the existence of God, reasoning from the idea or "being" of God and using a priori reasoning. Originally formulated by St. Anselm in the eleventh century, it has both detractors and supporters in the present day.

ST. ANSELM

from The Proslogion

Anselm presents the reasoning of the Ontological Argument in Chapter 2 of his *Proslogion*, which is only a page in length. His reasoning may be presented in three steps. The first step is the premise:

1. God is by definition that-than-which-nothing-greater-can-be-thought.

Anselm is not saying that this is the only concept of God, but he is saying that his reasoning will apply when what we mean by "God" is the supreme being, understood as that-than-which-nothing-greater-can-be-thought. Anselm is confident that this is what "we" believe God to be, that is, what those in Anselm's Christian tradition, and in the broader Western theistic tradition, and perhaps not in it alone, believe God to be; and in Anselm's day, as in ours, it is not unnatural to think of God as the supreme being.

The second step in Anselm's reasoning is this crucial premise, which Anselm takes to be self-evident:

2. That which exists in reality as well as in the understanding is greater than that which exists in the understanding alone.

The third step in Anselm's argument is Anselm's use of *reductio ad absurdum* reasoning. Anselm tentatively assumes that God, the supreme being, or that-than-which-a-greater-cannot-be-thought, exists "only in the understanding" and not in reality—which is the opposite of what he wants to prove. He then deduces an absurdity (a contradiction, the most serious kind of absurdity) from this assumption along with what Anselm takes to be an indisputable truth, namely that it is greater to exist in reality as well as in the understanding than it is to exist in the understanding alone (step 2 in his argument). And then, from this deduced absurdity, he concludes that his tentative assumption must be false and it must therefore be true that God exists not only in our understanding as a concept, but also in reality. In this way Anselm's Ontological Argument concludes that, since God is the supreme being (a being than-which-a-greater-cannot-be-thought), God must exist; otherwise there would be a yet greater being we could conceive of, namely one that *did* exist in reality.

In our reading we have Chapters 2, 3, 4, 5, and 15 of the *Proslogion*. Chapter 2 of Anselm's *Proslogion* contains the Ontological Argument in Anselm's succinct statement. Chapter 3 elaborates the argument, or, for some (Norman Malcolm in particular), contains a second version of the Ontological Argument. Chapter 4 addresses a question that Anselm finds he must address about the possibility of saying or thinking that God does not exist. If Anselm's first concern is to prove God's existence, his second concern is to prove that God is as we believe God to be. Chapter 5 addresses Anselm's second concern. Chapter 15 sheds light on the extent Anselm thought we could conceive of God.

The "fool" in Chapter 2 who does not understand that God exists is the fool of the Psalms. Psalm 14 begins with "The fool says in his heart, 'There is no God.'"

From *The Prayers and Meditations of Saint Anslem* translated with an introduction by Sister Benedicta Ward, with a forward by R. W. Southern (Penguin Classics, 1973). Copyright © Benedicta Ward, 1973. Foreword Copyright © R. W. Southern, 1973.

CHAPTER 2

That God really exists

Now, Lord, since it is you who gives understanding to faith, grant me to understand as well as you think fit, that you exist as we believe, and that you are what we believe you to be. We believe that you are that thing than which nothing greater can be thought. Or is there nothing of that kind in existence, since 'the fool has said in his heart, there is no God'? But when the fool hears me use this phrase, 'something than which nothing greater can be thought', he understands what he hears; and what he understands is in his understanding, even if he does not understand that it exists. For it is one thing to have something in the understanding, but quite another to understand that it actually exists. It is like a painter who, when he thinks out beforehand what he is going to create, has it in his understanding, but he does not yet understand it as actually existing because he has not yet painted it. But when he has painted it, he both has it in his understanding and actually has it, because he has created it. So the fool has to agree that the concept of something than which nothing greater can be thought exists in his understanding, since he understood what he heard and whatever is understood is in the understanding. And certainly that than which nothing greater can be thought cannot exist only in the understanding. For if it exists only in the understanding, it is possible to think of it existing also in reality, and that is greater. If that than which nothing greater can be thought exists in the understanding alone, then this thing than which nothing greater can be thought is something than which a greater can be thought. And this is clearly impossible. Therefore there can be no doubt at all that something than which a greater cannot be thought exists both in the understanding and in reality.

CHAPTER 3

That Which it is Not Possible to Think of as Not Existing

This is so truly, that it is not possible to think of it not existing. For it is possible to think of something existing which it is not possible to think of as not existing, and that is greater than something that can be thought not to exist. If that than which nothing greater can be thought, can be thought of as not existing, then that than which nothing greater can be thought is not the same as that than which nothing greater can be thought. And that simply will not do. Something than which nothing greater can be thought so truly exists that it is not possible to think of it as not existing.

This being is yourself, our Lord and God. Lord my God, you so truly are, that it is not possible to think of you as not existing. And rightly so. For if someone's mind could think of something better than you, the creature would rise higher than its creator and would judge its creator; which is clearly absurd. For whatever exists except you alone can be thought of as not existing. Therefore you alone of all most truly are, and you exist most fully of all things. For nothing else is as true as that, and therefore it has *less* existence. So why does the fool say in his heart, 'there is no God', when it is perfectly clear to the reasoning mind that you exist most fully of all? Why, except that he is indeed stupid and a fool?

CHAPTER 4

That What the Fool said in his Heart is Something that it is Not Possible to Think

Now how has he 'said in his heart' what it is not possible to think; for how could he avoid thinking that which he 'said in his heart', for to say in one's heart is to think. But if he really did, or rather because he really did, both think, because he said in his heart, and not say in his heart, because he was not able to think, then there is not only one way of saying in one's heart and thinking. For in a way one thinks a thing when one thinks the word that signifies the thing; but one thinks it in another way when the thing itself is understood. So in one way it is possible to entertain the concept that God does not exist, but not in the other way. For no one who truly understands that which God is, can think that God does not exist, though he may say those words in his heart, either without any, or with a special, meaning. For God is that than which nothing greater can be thought. Whoever truly understands this, understands that he is of such a kind of existence that he cannot be thought not to exist. So whoever understands this to be the nature of God, cannot think of him as not existing.

Thank you, good Lord, thank you, for it was by your gift that I first believed, and now by your illumination I understand; if I did not want to believe that you existed, still I should not be able not to understand it.

CHAPTER 5

God is Whatever it is Better To Be than Not To Be; He Exists in Himself Alone; and He Creates Everything Else Out Of Nothing

What are you, then, Lord God, you than whom nothing greater can be thought? What are you but that which exists alone over all things, and has made everything else out of nothing? For whatever is not that, is something less than can be thought; but this cannot be thought about you. Then what good can be lacking to the highest good, through whom all other good exists? So you are just, true, blessed, and whatever it is better to be than not to be. For it is better to be just than unjust, blessed than not blessed.

CHAPTER 15

That He is Greater Than it is Possible to Think

Lord, you are then not only that than which nothing greater can be thought; you are something greater than it is possible to think about. For since it is possible to think that this could exist, if you are not that thing, then a greater than you can be thought; and that will not do.

GAUNILO

A Reply on Behalf of the Fool

It did not take long for Anselm's Ontological Argument to draw criticism. The first critic of the Ontological Argument was Anselm's contemporary, Gaunilo, who was a Benedictine monk, like Anselm. Gaunilo of course believed in God, but he did not think that Anselm's Ontological Argument proved God's existence. And so Gaunilo wrote a reply, which, referring to the Fool of the Psalms, he entitled *A Reply on Behalf of the Fool*. In his reply Gaunilo constructs an argument parallel to Anselm's, except it is about a "Lost Island." Gaunilo imagines someone telling him about this island and telling him that it has all kinds of "riches and delights in abundance" and is "more excellent than all other lands." Now, says Gaunilo, he has no trouble understanding this description of the Lost Island. But what if the person telling him about the island goes on to reason that this island must exist in reality, since it is the most excellent island, and it is more excellent to exist in reality as well as in the mind than in the mind alone? Well, says Gaunilo, he is not sure who the greater fool would be, he himself if he accepted this reasoning or the person making this Lost Island argument if he thought it really proved the existence of the Lost Island.*

A Reply to the Foregoing by a Certain Writer on Behalf of the Fool

[1.] To one doubting whether there is, or denying that there is, something of such a nature than which nothing greater can be thought, it is said here [in the *Proslogion*] that its existence is proved, first because the very one who denies or doubts it already has it in his mind, since when he hears it spoken of he understands what is said; and further, because what he understands is necessarily such that it exists not only in the mind but also in reality. And this is proved by the fact that it is greater

*From *St. Anselm's Proslogion*, edited and translated by M.J. Charlesworth, Oxford University Press, 1965. Reprinted by permission of Oxford University Press.

to exist both in the mind and in reality than in the mind alone. For if this same being exists in the mind alone, anything that existed also in reality would be greater than this being, and thus that which is greater than everything would be less than some thing and would not be greater than everything, which is obviously contradictory. Therefore, it is necessarily the case that that which is greater than everything, being already proved to exist in the mind, should exist not only in the mind but also in reality, since otherwise it would not be greater than everything.

[2.] But he [the Fool] can perhaps reply that this thing is said already to exist in the mind only in the sense that I understand what is said. For could I not say that all kinds of unreal things, not existing in themselves in any way at all, are equally in the mind since if anyone speaks about them I understand whatever he says? Unless perhaps it is manifest that this being is such that it can be entertained in the mind in a different way from unreal or doubtfully real things, so that I am not said to think of or have in thought what is heard, but to understand and have it in mind, in that I cannot really think of this being in any other way save by understanding it, that is to say, by grasping by certain knowledge that the thing itself actually exists. But if this is the case, first, there will be no difference between having an object in mind (taken as preceding in time), and understanding that the object actually exists (taken as following in time), as in the case of the picture which exists first in the mind of the painter and then in the completed work. And thus it would be scarcely conceivable that, when this object had been spoken of and heard, it could not be thought not to exist in the same way in which God can [be thought] not to exist. For if He

cannot, why put forward this whole argument against anyone denying or doubting that there is something of this kind? Finally, that it is such a thing that, as soon as it is thought of, it cannot but be certainly perceived by the mind as indubitably existing, must be proved to me by some indisputable argument and not by that proposed, namely, that it must already be in my mind when I understand what I hear. For this is in my view like [arguing that] any things doubtfully real or even unreal are capable of existing if these things are mentioned by someone whose spoken words I might understand, and, even more, that [they exist] if, though deceived about them as often happens, I should believe them [to exist]— which argument I still do not believe!

[3.] Hence, the example of the painter having the picture he is about to make already in his mind cannot support this argument. For this picture, before it is actually made, is contained in the very art of the painter and such a thing in the art of any artist is nothing but a certain part of his very understanding, since as St. Augustine says [*In Iohannem*, tract. 1, n. 16], 'when the artisan is about actually to make a box he has it beforehand in his art. The box which is actually made is not a living thing, but the box which is in his art is a living thing since the soul of the artist, in which these things exist before their actual realization, is a living thing'. Now how are these things living in the living soul of the artist unless they are identical with the knowledge or understanding of the soul itself? But, apart from those things which are known to belong to the very nature of the mind itself, in the case of any truth perceived by the mind by being either heard or understood, then it cannot be doubted that this truth is one thing and that the understanding which grasps it is another.

Therefore even if it were true that there was something than which nothing greater could be thought, this thing, heard and understood, would not, however, be the same as the not-yet-made picture is in the mind of the painter.

[4.] To this we may add something that has already been mentioned, namely, that upon hearing it spoken of I can so little think of or entertain in my mind this being (that which is greater than all those others that are able to be thought of, and which it is said can be none other than God Himself) in terms of an object known to me either by species or genus, as I can think of God Himself, whom indeed for this very reason I can even think does not exist. For neither do I know the reality itself, nor can I form an idea from some other things like it since, as you say yourself, it is such that nothing could be like it. For if I heard something said about a man who was completely unknown to me so that I did not even know whether he existed, I could nevertheless think about him in his very reality as a man by means of that specific or generic notion by which I know what a man is or men are. However, it could happen that, because of a falsehood on the part of the speaker, the man I thought of did not actually exist, although I thought of him nevertheless as a truly existing object—not this particular man but any man in general. It is not, then, in the way that I have this unreal thing in thought or in mind that I can have that object in my mind when I hear 'God' or 'something greater than everything' spoken of. For while I was able to think of the former in terms of a truly existing thing which was known to me, I know nothing at all of the latter save for the verbal formula, and on the basis of this alone one can scarcely or never think of any truth. For when one thinks in this way, one thinks not so much of the word itself, which is indeed a real thing (that is to say, the sound of the letters or syllables), as of the meaning of the word which is heard. However, it [that which is greater than everything] is not thought of in the way of one who knows what is meant by that expression—thought of, that is, in terms of the thing [signified] or as true in thought alone. It is rather in the way of one who does not really know this object but thinks of it in terms of an affection of his mind produced by hearing the spoken words, and who tries to imagine what the words he has heard might mean. However, it would be astonishing if he could ever [attain to] the truth of the thing. Therefore, when I hear and understand someone saying that there is something greater than everything that can be thought of, it is agreed that it is in this latter sense that it is in my mind and not in any other sense. So much for the claim that that supreme nature exists already in my mind.

[5.] That, however, [this nature] necessarily exists in reality is demonstrated to me from the fact that, unless it existed, whatever exists in reality would be greater than it and consequently it would not be that which is greater than everything that undoubtedly had already been proved to exist in the mind. To this I reply as follows: if something that cannot even be thought in the true and real sense must be said to exist in the mind, then I do not deny that this also exists in my mind in the same way. But since from this one cannot in any way conclude that it exists also in reality, I certainly do not yet concede that it actually exists, until this is proved to me by an indubitable argument. For he who claims that it actually exists because otherwise it would not be that which is greater than everything does not consider carefully enough whom he is addressing. For I certainly do not yet admit this greater [than everything] to be any truly existing thing; indeed I doubt or even deny it. And I do not concede that it exists in a different way from that—if one ought to speak of 'existence' here—when the mind tries to imagine a completely unknown thing on the basis of the spoken words alone. How then can it be proved to me on that basis that that which is greater than everything truly exists in reality (because it is evident that it is greater than all others) if I keep on denying and also doubting that this is evident and do not admit that this greater [than everything] is either in my mind or thought, not even in the sense in which many doubtfully real and unreal things are? It must first of all be proved to me then that this same greater than everything truly exists in reality somewhere, and then only will the fact that it is greater than everything make it clear that it also subsists in itself.

[6.] For example: they say that there is in the ocean somewhere an island which, because of the difficulty (or rather the impossibility) of finding that which does not exist, some have called the '*Lost Island*'. And the story goes that it is blessed with all manner of priceless riches and delights in abundance, much more even than the Happy Isles, and, having no owner or inhabitant, it is superior everywhere in abundance of riches to all those other lands that men inhabit. Now, if anyone tell me that it is like this, I shall easily understand what is said, since nothing is difficult about it. But if he should then go on to say, as though it were a logical consequence of this: You cannot any more doubt that this island that is more excellent than all other lands truly exists somewhere in reality than you

can doubt that it is in your mind; and since it is more excellent to exist not only in the mind alone but also in reality, therefore it must needs be that it exists. For if it did not exist, any other land existing in reality would be more excellent than it, and so this island, already conceived by you to be more excellent than others, will not be more excellent. If, I say, someone wishes thus to persuade me that this island really exists beyond all doubt, I should either think that he was joking, or I should find it hard to decide which of us I ought to judge the bigger fool—I, if I agreed with him, or he, if he thought that he had proved the existence of this island with any certainty, unless he had first convinced me that its very excellence exists in my mind precisely as a thing existing truly and indubitably and not just as something unreal or doubtfully real.

[7.] Thus first of all might the Fool reply to objections. And if then someone should assert that this greater [than everything] is such that it cannot be thought not to exist (again without any other proof than that otherwise it would not be greater than everything), then he could make this same reply and say: When have I said that there truly existed some being that is 'greater than everything', such that from this it could be proved to me that this same being really existed to such a degree that it could not be thought not to exist? That is why it must first be conclusively proved by argument that there is some higher nature, namely that which is greater and better than all the things that are, so that from this we can also infer everything else which necessarily cannot be wanting to what is greater and better than everything. When, however, it is said that this supreme being cannot be *thought* not to exist, it would perhaps be better to say that it cannot be *understood* not to exist nor even to be able not to exist. For, strictly speaking, unreal things cannot be *understood*, though certainly they can be *thought* of in the same way as the Fool *thought* that God does not exist. I know with complete certainty that I exist, but I also know at the same time nevertheless that I can not-exist. And I *understand* without any doubt that that which exists to the highest degree, namely God, both exists and cannot not exist. I do not know, however, whether I can *think* of myself as not existing while I know with absolute certainty that I do exist; but if I can, why cannot [I do the same] with regard to

anything else I know with the same certainty? If however I cannot, this will not be the distinguishing characteristic of God [namely, to be such that He cannot be thought not to exist].

[8.] The other parts of this tract are argued so truly, so brilliantly and so splendidly, and are also of so much worth and instinct with so fragrant a perfume of devout and holy feeling, that in no way should they be rejected because of those things at the beginning (rightly intuited, but less surely argued out). Rather the latter should be demonstrated more firmly and so everything received with very great respect and praise.

ST. THOMAS AQUINAS

Whether the Existence of God is Self-Evident? (Summa Theologica I, q.2, a.1)

St. Thomas Aquinas, who wrote in the thirteenth century, is the author of the *Summa Theologica*, a massive work in which he addressed many of the theological and religious questions of Christianity. It is in this work that Aquinas criticizes the reasoning of the Ontological Argument. Aquinas was like Anselm in believing in God. Furthermore he was like Anselm in believing that the existence of God can be proven. However, Aquinas implicitly objected to the reasoning of the Ontological Argument on the grounds that the existence of God is not self-evident to us human beings. In the format that Aquinas uses in the *Summa Theologica* he breaks down large "questions" into "articles." Here the "question" is "The Existence of God" and the first "article" is "Whether the existence of God is self-evident?" Within the article Aquinas considers and replies to "objections," but his own view is contained in the central portion of the article that begins with the phrase "*I answer that*."

Question II

The Existence of God

First Article

WHETHER THE EXISTENCE OF
GOD IS SELF-EVIDENT?

We proceed thus to the First Article:—
Objection 1. It seems that the existence of God is self-evident. For those things are said to be self-evident to us the knowledge of which exists naturally in us, as we can see in regard to first principles. But as Damascene says, *the knowledge of God is naturally implanted in all.*[10] Therefore the existence of God is self-evident.

Obj. 2. Further, those things are said to be self-evident which are known as soon as the terms are known, which the Philosopher says is true of the first principles of demonstration.[11] Thus, when the nature of a whole and of a part is known, it is at once recognized that every whole is greater than its part. But as soon as the signification of the name *God* is understood, it is at once seen that God exists. For by this name is signified that thing than which nothing greater can be conceived. But that which exists actually and mentally is greater than that which exists only mentally. Therefore, since as soon as the name *God* is understood it exists mentally, it also follows that it exists actually. Therefore the proposition *God exists* is self-evident.

Obj. 3. Further, the existence of truth is self-evident. For whoever denies the existence of truth grants that truth does not exist: and, if truth does not exist, then the proposition *Truth does not exist* is true: and if there is anything true, there must be

truth. But God is truth itself: *I am the way, the truth, and the life* (*Jo.* xiv. 6). Therefore *God exists* is self-evident.

On the contrary, No one can mentally admit the opposite of what is self-evident, as the Philosopher states concerning the first principles of demonstration.[12] But the opposite of the proposition *God is* can be mentally admitted: *The fool said in his heart, There is no God* (*Ps.* lii. 1). Therefore, that God exists is not self-evident.

I answer that, A thing can be self-evident in either of two ways: on the one hand, self-evident in itself, though not to us; on the other, self-evident in itself, and to us. A proposition is self-evident because the predicate is included in the essence of the subject: *e.g., Man is an animal,* for animal is contained in the essence of man. If, therefore, the essence of the predicate and subject be known to all, the proposition will be self-evident to all; as is clear with regard to the first principles of demonstration, the terms of which are certain common notions that no one is ignorant of, such as being and non-being, whole and part, and the like. If, however, there are some to whom the essence of the predicate and subject is unknown, the proposition will be self-evident in itself, but not to those who do not know the meaning of the predicate and subject of the proposition. Therefore, it happens, as Boethius says, that there are some notions of the mind which are common and self-evident only to the learned, as that incorporeal substances are not in space.[13] Therefore I say that this proposition, *God exists,* of itself is self-evident, for the predicate is

[10] *De Fide Orth.*, 1, 1; 3 CPG 94, 789; 793.   [11] *Post. Anal.*, 1, 3 (726 18).
[12] *Metaph.*, III, 3 (1005b 11); *Post. Anal.*, I, 10 (76b 23).   [13] *De Hebdom.* (PL 64, 1311).

the same as the subject, because God is His own existence as will be hereafter shown.[14] Now because we do not know the essence of God, the proposition is not self-evident to us, but needs to be demonstrated by things that are more known to us, though less known in their nature—namely, by His effects.

Reply Obj. 1. To know that God exists in a general and confused way is implanted in us by nature, inasmuch as God is man's beatitude. For man naturally desires happiness, and what is naturally desired by man is naturally known by him. This, however, is not to know absolutely that God exists; just as to know that someone is approaching is not the same as to know that Peter is approaching, even though it is Peter who is approaching; for there are many who imagine that man's perfect good, which is happiness, consists in riches, and others in pleasures, and others in something else.

Reply Obj. 2. Perhaps not everyone who hears this name *God* understands it to signify something than which nothing greater can be thought, seeing that some have believed God to be a body.[15] Yet, granted that everyone understands that by this name *God* is signified something than which nothing greater can be thought, nevertheless, it does not therefore follow that he understands that what the name signifies exists actually, but only that it exists mentally. Nor can it be argued that it actually exists, unless it be admitted that there actually exists something than which nothing greater can be thought; and this precisely is not admitted by those who hold that God does not exist.

Reply Obj. 3. The existence of truth in general is self-evident, but the existence of a Primal Truth is not self-evident to us.

IMMANUEL KANT

The Impossibility of an Ontological Proof of the Existence of God

One of the most serious criticisms of the Ontological Argument is credited to Immanuel Kant. Kant was an eighteenth-century German philosopher who wrote on many philosophical subjects, including the limitations of reason and the nature of morality. His criticism of the Ontological Argument, offered about 700 after Anselm's writing of the *Proslogion*, is inspired by René Descartes' seventeenth-century version of the Ontological Argument. (Kant refers to the "Cartesian argument.") Kant's criticism is that the argument assumes that "existence" is like "omnipotence" in being a predicate that can add to the concept of God (and name one of God's perfections or attributes), and this is a wrong assumption about "existence."*

---

[14] Q. 3, a. 4.   [15] Cf. C. G., 1, 20.—Also Aristotle, Phys., 1, 4 (187a 12); St. Augustine, *De Civit. Dei*, VIII, 2; 5 (PL 41, 226; 239); De Haeres, 46, 50, 86 (PL 42, 35; 39; 46); *De Genesi ad Litt.*, X, 25, (PL 34, 427; Maimonides, *Guide*, 1, 53 (p. 72).

* From *Critique of Pure Reason*, translated by J. M. D. Meiklejohn.

SECTION IV

Of the Impossibility of an Ontological Proof of the Existence of God

IT is evident from what has been said that the conception of an absolutely necessary being is a mere idea, the objective reality of which is far from being established by the mere fact that it is a need of reason. On the contrary, this idea serves merely to indicate a certain unattainable perfection, and rather limits the operations than, by the presentation of new objects, extends the sphere of the understanding. But a strange anomaly meets us at the very threshold; for the inference from a given existence in general to an absolutely necessary existence seems to be correct and unavoidable, while the conditions of the *understanding* refuse to aid us in forming any conception of such a being.

Philosophers have always talked of an *absolutely necessary* being, and have nevertheless declined to take the trouble of conceiving whether—and how—a being of this nature is even cogitable, not to mention that its existence is actually demonstrable. A verbal definition of the conception is certainly easy enough: it is something the non-existence of which is impossible. But does this definition throw any light upon the conditions which render it impossible to cogitate the non-existence of a thing—conditions which we wish to ascertain, that we may discover whether we think anything in the conception of such a being or not? For the mere fact that I throw away, by means of the word *unconditioned*, all the conditions which the understanding habitually requires in order to regard anything as necessary, is very far from making clear whether by means of the conception of the unconditionally necessary I think of something, or really of nothing at all.

Nay, more, this chance-conception, now become so current, many have en-deavoured to explain by examples which seemed to render any inquiries regarding its intelligibility quite needless. Every geometrical proposition—a triangle has three angles—it was said, is absolutely necessary; and thus people talked of an object which lay out of the sphere of our understanding as if it were perfectly plain what the conception of such a being meant.

All the examples adduced have been drawn, without exception, from *judgements*, and not from *things*. But the unconditioned necessity of a judgement does not form the absolute necessity of a thing. On the contrary, the absolute necessity of a judgement is only a conditioned necessity of a thing, or of the predicate in a judgement. The proposition above-mentioned does not enounce that three angles necessarily exist, but, upon condition that a triangle exists, three angles must necessarily exist—in it. And thus this logical necessity has been the source of the greatest delusions. Having formed an *a priori* conception of a thing, the content of which was made to embrace existence, we believed ourselves safe in concluding that, because existence belongs necessarily to the object of the conception (that is, under the condition of my positing this thing as given), the existence of the thing is also posited necessarily, and that it is therefore absolutely necessary—merely because its existence has been cogitated in the conception.

If, in an identical judgement, I annihilate the predicate in thought, and retain the subject, a contradiction is the result; and hence I say, the former belongs necessarily to the latter. But if I suppress both subject and predicate in thought, no contradiction arises; for there *is nothing* at all, and therefore no means of forming a contradiction. To suppose the existence of a triangle and not that of its three angles, is self-contradictory; but to suppose the non-existence of both triangle and angles is perfectly admissible. And so is it with the conception of an absolutely necessary being. Annihilate its existence in thought, and you annihilate the thing itself with all its predicates; how then can there be any room for contradiction? Externally, there is nothing to give rise to a contradiction, for a thing cannot be necessary externally; nor internally, for, by the annihilation or suppression of the thing itself, its internal properties are also annihilated. God is omnipotent—that is a necessary judgement. His omnipotence cannot be denied, if the existence of a Deity is posited—the existence, that is, of an infinite being, the two conceptions being identical. But when you say, *God does not exist*, neither omnipotence nor any other predicate is affirmed; they must all disappear with the subject, and in this judgement there cannot exist the least self-contradiction.

You have thus seen that when the predicate of a judgement is annihilated in thought along with the subject, no internal contradiction can arise, be the predicate what it may. There is no possibility of evading the conclusion—you find yourselves compelled to declare: There are certain subjects which cannot be annihilated in thought. But this is nothing more than saying: There exist subjects which are absolutely necessary—the very hypothesis which you are called upon to establish. For I find myself unable to form the

slightest conception of a thing which when annihilated in thought with all its predicates, leaves behind a contradiction; and contradiction is the only criterion of impossibility in the sphere of pure *a priori* conceptions.

Against these general considerations, the justice of which no one can dispute, one argument is adduced, which is regarded as furnishing a satisfactory demonstration from the fact. It is affirmed that there is one and only one conception, in which the non-being or annihilation of the object is self-contradictory, and this is the conception of an *ens realissimum*. It possesses, you say, all reality, and you feel yourselves justified in admitting the possibility of such a being. (This I am willing to grant for the present, although the existence of a conception which is not self-contradictory is far from being sufficient to prove the possibility of an object.)[1] Now the notion of all reality embraces in it that of existence; the notion of existence lies, therefore, in the conception of this possible thing. If this thing is annihilated in thought, the internal possibility of the thing is also annihilated, which is self-contradictory.

I answer: It is absurd to introduce—under whatever term disguised—into the conception of a thing, which is to be cogitated solely in reference to its possibility, the conception of its existence. If this is admitted, you will have apparently gained the day, but in reality have enounced nothing but a mere tautology. I ask, is the proposition, *this or that thing* (which I am admitting to be possible) *exists*, an analytical or a synthetical proposition? If the

---

[1] A conception is always possible, if it is not self-contradictory. This is the logical criterion of possibility, distinguishing the object of such a conception from the *nihil negativum*. But it may be, notwithstanding, an empty conception, unless the objective reality of this synthesis, but which it is generated, is demonstrated; and a proof of this kind must be based upon principles of possible experience, and not upon the principle of analysis or contradiction. This remark may be serviceable as a warning against concluding, from the possibility of a conception—which is logical—the possibility of a thing—which is real.

former, there is no addition made to the subject of your thought by the affirmation of its existence; but then the conception in your minds is identical with the thing itself, or you have supposed the existence of a thing to be possible, and then inferred its existence from its internal possibility—which is but a miserable tautology. The word *reality* in the conception of the thing, and the word *existence* in the conception of the predicate, will not help you out of the difficulty. For, supposing you were to term all positing of a thing *reality*, you have thereby posited the thing with all its predicates in the conception of the subject and assumed its actual existence, and this you merely repeat in the predicate. But if you confess, as every reasonable person must, that every existential proposition is synthetical, how can it be maintained that the predicate of existence cannot be denied without contradiction?—a property which is the characteristic of analytical propositions, alone.

I should have a reasonable hope of putting an end for ever to this sophistical mode of argumentation, by a strict definition of the conception of existence, did not my own experience teach me that the illusion arising from our confounding a logical with a real predicate (a predicate which aids in the determination of a thing) resists almost all the endeavours of explanation and illustration. A *logical predicate* may be what you please, even the subject may be predicated of itself; for logic pays no regard to the content of a judgement. But the determination of a conception is a predicate, which adds to and enlarges the conception. It must not, therefore, be contained in the conception.

Being is evidently not a real predicate, that is, a conception of something which is added to the conception of some other thing. It is merely the positing of a thing, or of certain determinations in it. Logically, it is merely the copula of a judgement. The proposition, *God is omnipotent*, contains two conceptions, which have a certain object or content; the word *is*, is no additional predicate—it merely indicates the relation of the predicate to the subject. Now, if I take the subject (God) with all its predicates (omnipotence being one), and say: *God is*, or, *There is a God*, I add no new predicate to the conception of God, I merely posit or affirm the existence of the subject with all its predicates—I posit the *object* in relation to my *conception*. The content of both is the same; and there is no addition made to the conception, which expresses merely the possibility of the object, by my cogitating the object—in the expression, it *is*—as absolutely given or existing. Thus the real contains no more than the possible. A hundred real dollars contain no more than a hundred possible dollars. For, as the latter indicate the conception, and the former the object, on the supposition that the content of the former was greater than that of the latter, my conception would not be an expression of the whole object, and would consequently be an inadequate conception of it. But in reckoning my wealth there may be said to be more in a hundred real dollars than in a hundred possible dollars—that is, in the mere conception of them. For the real object—the dollars—is not analytically contained in my conception, but forms a synthetical addition to my conception, (which is merely a determination of my mental state), although this objective reality—this existence—apart from my conceptions, does not in the least degree increase the aforesaid hundred dollars.

By whatever and by whatever number of predicates—even to the complete determination of it—I may cogitate a thing, I do not in the least augment the object of my conception by the addition of the statement: *This thing exists*. Otherwise, not exactly the same, but something more than what was cogitated in my conception, would exist, and I could not affirm that the exact object of my conception had real existence. If I cogitate a thing as containing all modes of reality except one, the mode of reality which is absent is not added to the conception of the thing by the affirmation that the thing exists; on the contrary, the thing exists—if it exist at all—with the same defect as that cogitated in its conception; otherwise not that which was cogitated, but something different, exists. Now, if I cogitate a being as the highest reality, without defect or imperfection, the question still remains—whether this being exists or not? For, although no element is wanting in the possible real content of my conception, there is a defect in its relation to my mental state, that is, I am ignorant whether the cognition of the object indicated by the conception is possible *a posteriori*. And here the cause of the present difficulty becomes apparent. If the question regarded an object of sense merely, it would be impossible for me to confound the conception with the existence of a thing. For the conception merely enables me to cogitate an object as according with the general conditions of experience; while the existence of the object permits me to cogitate ··· At the same time, this connection with the world of experience does not in the least augment the conception, although a possible perception has been added to the experience of the mind. But if we cogitate existence by the pure category alone, it is not to be wondered at, that we should find ourselves unable to present any criterion sufficient to distinguish it from mere possibility.

Whatever be the content of our conception of an object, it is necessary to go beyond it, if we wish to predicate existence of the object. In the case of sensuous objects, this is attained by their connection according to empirical laws with some one of my perceptions; but there is no means of cognizing the existence of objects of pure thought, because it must be cognized completely *a priori*. But all our knowledge of existence (be it immediately by perception, or by inferences connecting some object with a perception) belongs entirely to the sphere of experience—which is in perfect unity with itself; and although an existence out of this sphere cannot be absolutely declared to be impossible, it is a hypothesis the truth of which we have no means of ascertaining.

The notion of a Supreme Being is in many respects a highly useful idea; but for the very reason that it is an idea, it is incapable of enlarging our cognition with regard to the existence of things. It is not even sufficient to instruct us as to the possibility of a being which we do not know to exist. The analytical criterion of possibility, which consists in the absence of contradiction in propositions, cannot be denied it. But the connection of real properties in a thing is a synthesis of the possibility of which an *a priori* judgement cannot be formed, because these realities are not presented to us specifically; and even if this were to happen, a judgement would still be impossible, because the criterion of the possibility of synthetical cognitions must be sought for in the world of experience, to which the object of an idea cannot belong. And thus the celebrated Leibnitz has utterly failed in his attempt to establish upon *a priori* grounds the possibility of this sublime ideal being.

The celebrated ontological or Cartesian argument for the existence of a Supreme Being is therefore insufficient; and we may as well hope to increase our stock of knowledge by the aid of mere ideas, as the merchant to augment his wealth by the addition of noughts to his cash-account.

The Cosmological Argument

The Cosmological Argument seeks to demonstrate the existence of God by reasoning from the observable "effects" of God in the world. It's most well-known proponent, St. Thomas Aquinas provides us with several versions of this argument in his *Summa Theologica*.

ST. THOMAS AQUINAS

Whether God Exists? (Summa Theologica I, q.2, a.3)

Although Aquinas criticized the reasoning of the Ontological Argument and any effort to prove the existence of God from our understanding of God's nature or essence, Aquinas did believe that God's existence could be demonstrated, not a priori, but by "His effects," which, for Aquinas, we can observe in the world about us, or the cosmos. In the *Summa Theologica*, after criticizing the reasoning of the Ontological Argument, Aquinas almost immediately goes on to provide five related "ways" of proving God's existence, each or most being a form of the Cosmological Argument. They all are based on what Aquinas thought were indisputable facts about the observable world. One proceeds from the observation that some things are in motion; one cites the fact that things are caused; another cites the fact that it is possible for things in nature not to exist; another cites the different degrees of certain properties or perfections in things (Aquinas names goodness, truth, nobility, "and the like"); and one is based on how natural objects act for some end (as Aquinas thought stones did when they were dropped and fall to earth). Some commentators suggest that the fourth "way," which cites gradations in such "perfections" as goodness and nobility, is "not clearly cosmological," and some commentators say that the fifth "way" is a version of the design argument, or "points forward" to it, as one has observed.[1] The basic logical difference between Anselm's argument and the five arguments of Aquinas is that Anselm's a priori reasoning did not rely on observations about the world, but instead relied upon conceptual points that he thought were self-evident (before or independently of any observations), while Aquinas does cite and rely upon some basic observations about the world, such as that some things are in motion. If we look at his arguments we can see that some of his basic facts are more questionable than others. For instance, in today's scientific era many would deny that inanimate bodies like stones act for some end. But, on the other hand, some of the basic facts he relies upon in his arguments do seem to be beyond dispute, such as, that some things are in motion and that some things cause other things.

---

[1] Donald F. Burrill suggests that the fourth way is "not clearly cosmological" in his Introduction to *The Cosmological Argument*, edited by Donald F. Burrill (Garden City, N.Y.: Anchor Books, 1967) p. 2, footnote 2; John Hick observes that the fifth way "points forward" to the design argument in *The Existence of God* (New York: Macmillan, 1964) p. 82.

The main idea underlying Aquinas' approach is that the world we live in and observe can be explained only by the existence of God. This underlying main idea is most clear in the first three "ways," the argument from motion, the argument from the order of causes, and the argument from possibility and necessity.

In the page or so that forms the *I answer that* portion of his "article" Aquinas provides his "five ways" of proving the existence of God.*

Third Article

WHETHER GOD EXISTS?

We proceed thus to the Third Article:—
Objection 1. It seems that God does not exist; because if one of two contraries be infinite, the other would be altogether destroyed. But the name *God* means that He is infinite goodness. If, therefore, God existed, there would be no evil discoverable; but there is evil in the world. Therefore God does not exist.

Obj. 2. Further, it is superfluous to suppose that what can be accounted for by a few principles has been produced by many. But it seems that everything we see in the world can be accounted for by other principles, supposing God did not exist. For all natural things can be reduced to one principle, which is nature; and all voluntary things can be reduced to one principle, which is human reason, or will. Therefore there is no need to suppose God's existence.

On the contrary, It is said in the person of God: *I am Who am* (*Exod.* iii, 14).

I answer that, The existence of God can be proved in five ways.

The first and more manifest way is the argument from motion. It is certain, and evident to our senses, that in the world some things are in motion. Now whatever is moved is moved by another, for nothing can be moved except it is in potentiality to that towards which it is moved; whereas a thing moves inasmuch as it is in act. For motion is nothing else than the reduction of something from potentiality to actuality. But nothing can be reduced from potentiality to actuality, except by something in a state of actuality. Thus that which is actually hot, as fire, makes wood, which is potentially hot, to be actually hot, and thereby moves and changes it. Now it is not possible that the same thing should be at once in actuality and potentiality in the same respect, but only in different respects. For what is actually hot cannot simultaneously be potentially hot; but it is simultaneously potentially cold. It is therefore impossible that in the same respect and in the same way a thing should be both mover and moved, *i.e.*, that it should move itself. Therefore, whatever is moved must be moved by another. If that by which it is moved be itself moved, then this also must needs be moved by another, and that by another again. But this cannot go on to infinity, because then there would be no first mover, and, consequently, no other mover, seeing that subsequent movers move only inasmuch as they are moved by the first mover; as the staff moves only because it is moved by the hand. Therefore it is necessary to arrive at a first mover, moved by no other; and this everyone understands to be God.

The second way is from the nature of efficient cause. In the world of sensible things we find there is an order of efficient causes. There is no case known (neither is it, indeed, possible) in which a thing is found to be the efficient cause of itself; for so it would be prior to itself, which is impossible. Now in efficient causes it is not possible to go on to infinity, because in all efficient causes following in order, the first is the cause of the intermediate cause, and the intermediate is the cause of the ultimate cause, whether the intermediate cause be several, or one only. Now to take away the cause is to take away the effect. Therefore, if there be no first cause among efficient causes, there will be no ultimate, nor any intermediate, cause. But if in efficient causes it is possible to go on to infinity, there will be no first efficient cause, neither will there be an ultimate effect, nor any intermediate efficient causes; all of which is plainly false. Therefore it is necessary to admit a first efficient cause, to which everyone gives the name of God.

The third way is taken from possibility and necessity, and runs thus. We find in nature things that are possible to be and not to be, since they are found to be generated, and to be corrupted, and consequently, it is possible for them to be and not to be. But it is impossible for these always to exist, for that which can not-be at some time is not. Therefore, if everything can not-be, then at one time there was nothing in existence. Now if this were true, even now there would be nothing in existence, because that which does not exist begins to exist only through something already existing. Therefore, if at one time nothing was in existence, it would have been impossible for anything to have begun to exist; and thus even now nothing would be in existence—which is absurd. Therefore, not all beings are merely possible, but there must exist something the existence of which is

necessary. But every necessary thing either has its necessity caused by another, or not. Now it is impossible to go on to infinity in necessary things which have their necessity caused by another, as has been already proved in regard to efficient causes. Therefore we cannot but admit the existence of some being having of itself its own necessity, and not receiving it from another, but rather causing in others their necessity. This all men speak of as God.

The fourth way is taken from the gradation to be found in things. Among beings there are some more and some less good, true, noble, and the like. But *more* and *less* are predicated of different things according as they resemble in their different ways something which is the maximum, as a thing is said to be hotter according as it more nearly resembles that which is hottest; so that there is something which is truest, something best, something noblest, and, consequently, something which is most being, for those things that are greatest in truth are greatest in being, as it is written in *Metaph*. ii.[18] Now the maximum in any genus is the cause of all in that genus, as fire, which is the maximum of heat, is the cause of all hot things, as is said in the same book.[19] Therefore there must also be something which is to all beings the cause of their being, goodness, and every other perfection; and this we call God.

The fifth way is taken from the governance of the world. We see that things which lack knowledge, such as natural bodies, act for an end, and this is evident from their acting always, or nearly always, in the same way, so as to obtain the best result. Hence it is plain that they achieve their end, not fortuitously, but designedly.

[18] *Metaph*. Ia, 1 (993b 30).   [19] *Ibid*. (993b 25).

Now whatever lacks knowledge cannot move towards an end, unless it be directed by some being endowed with knowledge and intelligence; as the arrow is directed by the archer. Therefore some intelligent being exists by whom all natural things are directed to their end; and this being we call God.

Reply Obj. 1. As Augustine says: *Since God is the highest good, He would not allow any evil to exist in His works, unless His omnipotence and goodness were such as to bring good even out of evil.*[20] This is part of the infinite goodness of God, that He should allow evil to exist, and out of it produce good.

Reply Obj. 2. Since nature works for a determinate end under the direction of a higher agent, whatever is done by nature must be traced back to God as to its first cause. So likewise whatever is done voluntarily must be traced back to some higher cause other than human reason and will, since these can change and fail; for all things that are changeable and capable of defect must be traced back to an immovable and self-necessary first principle, as has been shown.

F.C. COPLESTON AND BERTRAND RUSSELL

The Existence of God—A Debate

In 1948 F.C. Copleston and Bertrand Russell had a radio debate on the existence of God, a portion of which—the part that forms our reading—relates to the question of whether there must be a cause of the universe, and so to the reasoning of the Cosmological Argument. F.C. Copleston is Father Copleston a Jesuit priest, and also a historian and defender of Aquinas' reasoning. Bertrand Russell, one of the most influential philosophers of the twentieth century, wavered between atheism and agnosticism; in this debate he proclaims himself to be an agnostic.

Copleston in the exchange expresses a religious sensibility that is in sympathy with Aquinas' intuition, and Russell expresses a very different sensibility. Copleston expresses the intuition that of course we can raise "the question of the existence of the this sorry scheme of things—of the whole universe." For Russell really all we can or should say is "that the universe is just there, and that's all," and, he says, "the notion of the world [or universe] having an explanation is a mistake." Copleston backs up his viewpoint by referring to his and Aquinas' distinction between a temporal phenomenal series and a nontemporal series, especially as it applies to Aquinas' third way. Whether or not the phenomenal series is infinite, Copleston argues, still we can ask of it as a whole—of the whole universe of contingent things—Why should it exist? Russell on his side argues that a fallacy or mistake is involved, and he provides an analogy. While every person has a mother, it is a mistake to think that therefore the human race has a mother, and similarly it is a mistake to reason that since everything in the universe has a cause therefore

[20] *Enchir.*, XI (PL 40, 236).

the universe has a cause. If Copleston were reasoning this way, then, as he sees, he would be committing a fallacy. But he is not, he says. His reasoning is not that just as every contingent object in the phenomenal series has a phenomenal cause so the whole series must have a phenomenal cause. It is that the phenomenal series *as a whole* must have a "transcendent" or necessary cause. Still, says Russell, it is misguided to think that the universe as a whole needs or has a cause.*

The Existence of God

A DEBATE BETWEEN BERTRAND RUSSELL
AND FATHER F. C. COPLESTON, S.J.

This debate was originally broadcast in 1948 on the Third Programme of the B.B.C. It was published in *Humanitas* for the autumn of 1948 and is here reprinted with the kind permission of Father Copleston.

COPLESTON: As we are going to discuss the existence of God, it might perhaps be as well to come to some provisional agreement as to what we understand by the term 'God.' I presume that we mean a supreme personal being—distinct from the world and creator of the world. Would you agree—provisionally at least—to accept this statement as the meaning of the term 'God'?

RUSSELL: Yes, I accept this definition.

COPLESTON: Well, my position is the affirmative position that such a being actually exists, and that His existence can be proved philosophically. Perhaps you would tell me if your position is that of agnosticism or of atheism. I mean, would you say that the non-existence of God can be proved?

RUSSELL: No, I should not say that: my position is agnostic.

COPLESTON: Would you agree with me that the problem of God is a problem of great importance? For example, would you agree that if God does not exist, human beings and human history can

have no other purpose than the purpose they choose to give themselves, which—in practice—is likely to mean the purpose which those impose who have the power to impose it?

RUSSELL: Roughly speaking, yes, though I should have to place some limitation on your last clause.

COPLESTON: Would you agree that if there is no God—no absolute Being—there can be no absolute values? I mean, would you agree that if there is no absolute good that the relativity of values results?

RUSSELL: No, I think these questions are logically distinct. Take, for instance, G. E. Moore's *Principia Ethica*, where he maintains that there is a distinction of good and evil, that both of these are definite concepts. But he does not bring in the idea of God to support that contention.

COPLESTON: Well, suppose we leave the question of good till later, till we come to the moral argument, and I give first a metaphysical argument. I'd like to put the main weight on the metaphysical argument based on Leibniz's argument from 'Contingency' and then later we might discuss the moral argument. Suppose I give a brief statement on the metaphysical argument and that then we go on to discuss it?

RUSSELL: That seems to me to be a very good plan.

* From Bertrand Russell, *Why I Am Not A Christian: And Other Essays on Religion and Related Subjects*, pp. 225–236. London: George Allen & Unwin, 1957. Reprinted by permission.

The Argument from Contingency

COPLESTON: Well, for clarity's sake, I'll divide the argument into distinct stages. First of all, I should say, we know that there are at least some beings in the world which do not contain in themselves the reason for their existence. For example, I depend on my parents, and now on the air, and on food, and so on. Now, secondly, the world is simply the real or imagined totality or aggregate of individual objects, none of which contain in themselves alone the reason for their existence. There isn't any world distinct from the objects which form it, any more than the human race is something apart from the members. Therefore, I should say, since objects or events exist, and since no object of experience contains within itself the reason of its existence, this reason, the totality of objects, must have a reason external to itself. That reason must be an existent being. Well, this being is either itself the reason for its own existence, or it is not. If it is, well and good. If it is not, then we must proceed farther. But if we proceed to infinity in that sense, then there's no explanation of existence at all. So, I should say, in order to explain existence, we must come to a being which contains within itself the reason for its own existence, that is to say, which cannot not-exist.

RUSSELL: This raises a great many points and it is not altogether easy to know where to begin, but I think that, perhaps, in answering your argument, the best point at which to begin is the question of necessary being. The word 'necessary' I should maintain, can only be applied significantly to propositions. And, in fact, only to such as are analytic—that is to say—such as it is self-contradictory to deny. I could only admit a necessary being if there were a being whose existence it is self-contradictory to deny. I should like to know whether you would accept Leibniz's division of propositions into truths of reason and truths of fact. The former—the truths of reason—being necessary.

COPLESTON: Well, I certainly should not subscribe to what seems to be Leibniz's idea of truths of reason and truths of fact, since it would appear that, for him, there are in the long run only analytic propositions. It would seem that for Leibniz truths of fact are ultimately reducible to truths of reason. That is to say, to analytic propositions, at least for an omniscient mind. Well, I couldn't agree with that. For one thing, it would fail to meet the requirements of the experience of freedom. I don't want to uphold the whole philosophy of Leibniz. I have made use of his argument from contingent to necessary being, basing the argument on the principle of sufficient reason, simply because it seems to me a brief and clear formulation of what is, in my opinion, the fundamental metaphysical argument for God's existence.

RUSSELL: But, to my mind, 'a necessary proposition' has got to be analytic. I don't see what else it can mean. And analytic propositions are always complex and logically somewhat late. 'Irrational animals are animals' is an analytic proposition; but a proposition such as 'This is an animal' can never be analytic. In fact, all the propositions that can be analytic are somewhat late in the build-up of propositions.

COPLESTON: Take the proposition 'If there is a contingent being then there is a necessary being.' I consider that that proposition hypothetically expressed is a necessary proposition. If you are going to call every necessary proposition an analytic proposition, then—in order to avoid a dispute in terminology—I would agree to call it analytic, though I don't consider it a tautological proposition. But the proposition is a necessary proposition only on the supposition that there is a contingent being. That there is a contingent being actually existing has to be discovered by experience, and the proposition that there is a contingent being is certainly not an analytic proposition, though once you know, I should maintain, that there is a contingent being, it follows of necessity that there is a necessary being.

RUSSELL: The difficulty of this argument is that I don't admit the idea of a necessary being and I don't admit that there is any particular meaning in calling other beings 'contingent.' These phrases don't for me have a significance except within a logic that I reject.

COPLESTON: Do you mean that you reject these terms because they won't fit in with what is called 'modern logic'?

RUSSELL: Well, I can't find anything that they could mean. The word 'necessary,' it seems to me, is a useless word, except as applied to analytic propositions, not to things.

COPLESTON: In the first place, what do you mean by 'modern logic'? As far as I know, there are somewhat differing systems. In the second place, not all modern logicians surely would admit the meaninglessness of metaphysics. We both know, at any rate, one very eminent modern thinker whose knowledge of modern logic was profound, but who certainly did not think that metaphysics are meaningless or, in particular, hat the problem of God is meaningless. Again, even if all modern logicians held that metaphysical terms are meaningless, it would not follow that they were right. The proposition that metaphysical terms are meaningless seems to me to be a proposition based on an assumed philosophy. The dogmatic position behind it seems to be this: What will not go into my machine is non-existent, or it is meaningless; it is the expression of emotion. I am simply trying to point out that anybody who says that a particular system of modern logic is the sole criterion of meaning is saying something that is over

dogmatic; he is dogmatically insisting that a part of philosophy is the whole of philosophy. After all, a 'contingent' being is a being which has not in itself the complete reason for its existence, that's what I mean by a contingent being. You know, as well as I do, that the existence of neither of us can be explained without reference to something or somebody outside us, our parents, for example. A 'necessary' being, on the other hand, means a being that must and cannot not-exist. You may say that there is no such being, but you will find it hard to convince me that you do not understand the terms I am using. If you do not understand them, then how can you be entitled to say that such a being does not exist, if that is what you do say?

RUSSELL: Well, there are points here that I don't propose to go into at length. I don't maintain the meaningless of metaphysics in general at all. I maintain the meaningless of certain particular terms—not on any general ground, but simply because I've not been able to see an interpretation of those particular terms. It's not a general dogma—it's a particular thing. But those points I will leave out for the moment. And I will say that what you have been saying brings us back, it seems to me, to the ontological argument that there is a being whose essence involves existence, so that his existence is analytic. That seems to me to be impossible, and it raises, of course, the question what one means by existence, and as to this, I think a subject named can never be significantly said to exist but only a subject described. And that existence, in fact, quite definitely is not a predicate.

COPLESTON: Well, you say, I believe, that is bad grammar, or rather bad syntax to say for example 'T. S. Eliot exists'; one ought to say, for example, 'He, the author of *Murder in the Cathedral*, exists.' Are you going to say that the proposition, 'The cause of the world exists,' is without meaning? You may say that the world has no cause; but I fail to see how you can say that the proposition that 'the cause of the world exists' is meaningless. Put it in the form of a question: 'Has the world a cause?' or 'Does a cause of the world exist?' Most people surely would understand the question, even if they don't agree about the answer.

RUSSELL: Well, certainly the question 'Does the cause of the world exist?' is a question that has meaning. But if you say 'Yes, God is the cause of the world' you're using God as a proper name; then 'God exists' will not be a statement that has meaning; that is the position that I'm maintaining. Because, therefore, it will follow that it cannot be an analytic proposition ever to say that this or that exists. For example, suppose you take as your subject 'the existent round-square,' it would look like an analytic proposition that 'the existent round-square exists,' but it doesn't exist.

COPLESTON: No, it doesn't, then surely you can't say it doesn't exist unless you have a conception of what existence is. As to the phrase 'existent round-square,' I should say that it has no meaning at all.

RUSSELL: I quite agree. Then I should say the same thing in another context in reference to a 'necessary being.'

COPLESTON: Well, we seem to have arrived at an impasse. To say that a necessary being is a being that must exist and cannot not-exist has for me a definite meaning. For you it has no meaning.

RUSSELL: Well, we can press the point a little, I think. A being that must exist and cannot not-exist, would surely, according to you, be a being whose essence involves existence.

COPLESTON: Yes, a being the essence of which is to exist. But I should not be willing to argue the existence of God simply from the idea of His essence because I don't think we have any clear intuition of God's essence as yet. I think we have to argue from the world of experience to God.

RUSSELL: Yes, I quite see the distinction. But, at the same time, for a being with sufficient knowledge it would be true to say 'Here is this being whose essence involves existence!'

COPLESTON: Yes, certainly if anybody saw God, he would see that God must exist.

RUSSELL: So that I mean there is a being whose essence involves existence although we don't know that essence. We only know there is such a being.

COPLESTON: Yes, I should add we don't know the essence *a priori*. It is only *a posteriori* through our experience of the world that we come to a knowledge of the existence of that being. And then one argues, the essence and existence must be identical. Because if God's essence and God's existence was not identical, then some sufficient reason for this existence would have to be found beyond God.

RUSSELL: So it all turns on this question of sufficient reason, and I must say you haven't defined 'sufficient reason' in a way that I can understand—what do you mean by sufficient reason? You don't mean cause?

COPLESTON: Not necessarily. Cause is a kind of sufficient reason. Only contingent being can have a cause. God is His own sufficient reason; and He is not cause of Himself. By sufficient reason in the full sense I mean an explanation adequate for the existence of some particular being.

RUSSELL: But when is an explanation adequate? Suppose I am about to make a flame with a match. You may say that the adequate explanation of that is that I rub it on the box.

COPLESTON: Well, for practical purposes—but theoretically, that is only a partial explanation. An adequate explanation must ultimately be a total explanation, to which nothing further can be added.

RUSSELL: Then I can only say that you're looking for something which can't be got, and which one ought not to expect to get.

COPLESTON: To say that one has not found it is one thing; to say that one should not look for it seems to me rather dogmatic.

RUSSELL: Well, I don't know. I mean, the explanation of one thing is another thing which makes the other thing dependent on yet another, and you have to grasp this sorry scheme of things entire to do what you want, and that we can't do.

COPLESTON: But are you going to say that we can't, or we shouldn't even raise the question of the existence of the whole of this sorry scheme of things—of the whole universe?

RUSSELL: Yes. I don't think there's any meaning in it at all. I think the word 'universe' is a handy word in some connections, but I don't think it stands for anything that has a meaning.

COPLESTON: If the word is meaningless, it can't be so very handy. In any case, I don't say that the universe is something different from the objects which compose it (I indicated that in my brief summary of the proof), what I'm doing is to look for the reason, in this case the cause of the objects—the real or imagined totality of which constitute what we call the universe. You say, I think that the universe—or my existence if you prefer, or any other existence—is unintelligible?

RUSSELL: First may I take up the point that if a word is meaningless it can't be handy. That sounds well but isn't in fact correct. Take, say, such a word as 'the' or 'than.' You can't point to any object that those words mean, but they are very useful words; I should say the same of 'universe.' But leaving that point, you ask whether I consider that the universe is unintelligible. I shouldn't say unintelligible—I think it is without explanation. Intelligible, to my

mind, is a different thing. Intelligible has to do with the thing itself intrinsically and not with its relations.

COPLESTON: Well, my point is that what we call the world is intrinsically unintelligible, apart from the existence of God. You see, I don't believe that the infinity of the series of events—I mean a horizontal series, so to speak—if such an infinity could be proved, would be in the slightest degree relevant to the situation. If you add up chocolates you get chocolates after all and not a sheep. If you add up chocolates to infinity, you presumably get an infinite number of chocolates. So if you add up contingent beings to infinity, you still get contingent beings, not a necessary being. An infinite series of contingent beings will be, to my way of thinking, as unable to cause itself as one contingent being. However, you say, I think, that it is illegitimate to raise the question of what will explain the existence of any particular object?

RUSSELL: It's quite all right if you mean by explaining it, simply finding a cause for it.

COPLESTON: Well, why stop at one particular object? Why shouldn't one raise the question of the cause of the existence of all particular objects?

RUSSELL: Because I see no reason to think there is any. The whole concept of cause is one we derive from our observation of particular things; I see no reason whatsoever to suppose that the total has any cause whatsoever.

COPLESTON: Well, to say that there isn't any cause is not the same thing as saying that we shouldn't look for a cause. The statement that there isn't any cause should come, if it comes at all, at the end of the enquiry, not the beginning. In any case, if the total has no cause, then to my way of thinking it must be its own cause, which seems to me impossible. Moreover, the statement that the world is simply there if in answer to a question, presupposes that the question has meaning.

RUSSELL: No, it doesn't need to be its own cause, what I'm saying is that the concept of cause is not applicable to the total.

COPLESTON: Then you would agree with Sartre that the universe is what he calls 'gratuitous'?

RUSSELL: Well, the word 'gratuitous' suggests that it might be something else; I should say that the universe is just there, and that's all.

COPLESTON: Well, I can't see how you can rule out the legitimacy of asking the question how the total, or anything at all comes to be there. Why something rather than nothing, that is the question? The fact that we gain our knowledge of causality empirically, from particular causes, does not rule out the possibility of asking what the cause of the series is. If the word 'cause' were meaningless or if it could be shown that Kant's view of the matter were correct, the question would be illegitimate I agree; but you don't seem to hold that the word 'cause' is meaningless, and I do not suppose you are a Kantian.

RUSSELL: I can illustrate what seems to me your fallacy. Every man who exists has a mother, and it seems to me your argument is that therefore the human race must have a mother, but obviously the human race hasn't a mother—that's a different logical sphere.

COPLESTON: Well, I can't really see any parity. If I were saying 'every object has a phenomenal cause, therefore, the whole series has a phenomenal cause,' there would be a parity; but I'm not saying that; I'm saying, every object has a phenomenal cause if you insist on the infinity of the series—but the series of phenomenal causes, is an insufficient explanation of the series. Therefore, the series has not a phenomenal cause but a transcendent cause.

RUSSELL: That's always assuming that not only every particular thing in the world, but the world as a whole must have a cause. For that assumption I see no ground whatever. If you'll give me a ground I'll listen to it.

COPLESTON: Well, the series of events is either caused or it's not caused. If it is caused, there must obviously be a cause outside the series. If it's not caused then it's sufficient to itself, and if it's sufficient to itself it is what I call necessary. But it can't be necessary since each member is contingent, and we've agreed that the total is no reality apart from its members, therefore, it can't be necessary. Therefore, it can't be (caused)—uncaused—therefore it must have a cause. And I should like to observe in passing that the statement 'the world is simply there and is inexplicable' can't be got out of logical analysis.

RUSSELL: I don't want to seem arrogant, but it does seem to me that I can conceive things that you say the human mind can't conceive. As for things not having a cause, the physicists assure us that individual quantum transition in atoms have no cause.

COPLESTON: Well, I wonder now whether that isn't simply a temporary inference.

RUSSELL: It may be, but it does show that physicists' minds can conceive it.

COPLESTON: Yes, I agree, some scientists—physicists—are willing to allow for indetermination within a restricted field. But very many scientists are not so willing. I think that Professor Dingle, of London University, maintains that the Heisenberg uncertainty principle tells us something about the success (or the lack of it) of the present atomic theory in correlating observations, but not about nature in itself, and many physicists would accept this view. In any case, I don't see how physicists can fail to accept the theory in practice, even if they don't do so in theory. I cannot see how science could be conducted on any other assumption than that of order and intelligibility in nature. The physicist presupposes, at least tacitly, that there is some sense in investigating nature and looking for the causes of events, just as the detective presupposes that there is some sense in looking for the cause of a murder. The metaphysician assumes that there is sense in looking for the reason or cause of phenomena, and, not being a Kantian, I consider that the metaphysician is as justified in his assumption as the physicist. When Sartre, for example, says that the world is gratuitous, I think that he has not sufficiently considered what is implied by 'gratuitous.'

RUSSELL: I think—there seems to me a certain unwarrantable extension here; a physicist looks for causes; that does not necessarily imply that there are causes everywhere. A man may look for gold without assuming that there is gold everywhere; if he finds gold, well and good, if he doesn't he's had bad luck. The same is true when the physicists look for causes. As for Sartre, I don't profess to know what he means, and I shouldn't like to be thought to interpret him, but for my part, I do think the notion of the world having an explanation is a mistake. I don't see why one should expect it to have, and I think what you say about what the scientist assumes is an over-statement.

COPLESTON: Well, it seems to me that the scientist does make some such assumption. When he experiments to find out some particular truth, behind that experiment lies the assumption that the universe is not simply discontinuous. There is the possibility of finding out a truth by experiment. The experiment may be a bad one, it may lead to no result, or not to the result that he wants, but that at any rate there is the possibility, through experiment, of finding out the truth that he assumes. And that seems to me to assume an ordered and intelligible universe.

RUSSELL: I think you're generalising more than is necessary. Undoubtedly the scientist assumes that this sort of thing is likely to be found and will often be found. He does not assume that it will be found, and that's a very important matter in modern physics.

COPLESTON: Well, I think he does assume or is bound to assume it tacitly in practice. It may be that, to quote Professor Haldane, 'when I light the gas under the kettle, some of the water molecules will fly off as vapour, and there is no way of finding out which will do so,' but it doesn't follow necessarily that the idea of chance must be introduced except in relation to our knowledge.

RUSSELL: No it doesn't—at least if I may believe what he says. He's finding out quite a lot of things—the scientist is finding out quite a lot of things that are happening in the world, which are, at first, beginnings of causal chains—first causes which haven't in themselves got causes. He does not assume that everything has a cause.

COPLESTON: Surely that's a first cause within a certain selected field. It's a relatively first cause.

RUSSELL: I don't think he'd say so. If there's a world in which most events, but not all, have causes, he will then be able to depict the probabilities and uncertainties by assuming that this particular event you're interested in probably has a cause. And since in any case you won't get more than probability that's good enough.

COPLESTON: It may be that the scientist doesn't hope to obtain more than probability, but in raising the question he assumes that the question of explanation has a meaning. But your general point then, Lord Russell, is that it's illegitimate even to ask the question of the cause of the world?

RUSSELL: Yes, that's my position.

COPLESTON: If it's a question that for you has no meaning, it's of course very difficult to discuss it, isn't it?

RUSSELL: Yes, it is very difficult. What do you say—shall we pass on to some other issue?

The Teleological Argument

The Teleological Argument, or "design argument" is an argument by analogy. In basic form it argues that the world is like a human contrivance, such as a watch, in one respect (they both show purpose or design) and so probably they are alike in another respect (they both were created by an intelligence), the intelligence that created the world being God. Historically, the chief proponent of the Teleological Argument is William Paley, who published his *Natural Theology* in 1802. In it Paley sought to show that the design exhibited by the world showed that there is an intelligent Creator and also that the Creator has the traditional attributes of God, such as omnipotence (is all-powerful) and omniscience (is all-knowing). In fact Paley thought that the detailed design of such "works of nature" as the eye, was sufficient to show that there is a divine creator.

The chief critic of the Teleological Argument is generally thought to be David Hume. Hume, who was the earlier writer, was not addressing Paley, but the reasoning embodied in the Teleological Argument, which was well known before Paley's celebrated formulation of the argument. Hume's criticisms are in his *Dialogues Concerning Natural Religion*, published more than twenty years before Paley's *Natural Theology*. Paley did not consider Hume's criticisms—perhaps because he, along with many other contemporaries, accepted it that Hume had been refuted. Today Hume's forceful and detailed criticisms of the reasoning of the Teleological Argument are duly recognized.

WILLIAM PALEY

from Natural Theology

Just after the close of the eighteenth century, in 1802, William Paley published his *Natural Theology*, in which there is an influential form of the Teleological Argument. Paley, who was a theologian and the Archdeacon of Carlisle (in the Church of England), called his work "natural theology" because (like Anselm and Aquinas) he set out to use only "natural" reason, or the reason that human beings naturally have, and because (like Aquinas) he appealed to what we can observe in nature. His argument and other versions of the Teleological Argument are like the forms of the Cosmological Argument in that they consult and reason from observations about the world. A main difference is that those who advance versions of the Teleological Argument cite a pervasive presence of *design* that they find throughout nature. The Teleological Argument is often called the argument from design or the design argument.

While the Teleological Argument or design argument for God's existence could be put in a deductive form (and Aquinas' fifth way, which is deductive, is sometimes said to be a form of the design argument, or to "point forward" to the design argument), the Teleological Argument as presented by Paley is an argument by analogy. Paley's reasoning is that since these human creations and natural objects are similar in one respect (they exhibit design), they are similar in another respect (they both are created by an intelligence).

In our reading we have Chapters 1, 6, 24, and selections from Chap. 3. Chapters 1 and 3 contain Paley's reasoning that the world as much as human contrivances has an intelligent creator. In Chapter 6 Paley argues that the eye is sufficient to show there is a divine creator, and in Chap. 24 Paley addresses the attributes of God.*

CHAPTER 1

State of the Argument

In crossing a heath, suppose I pitched my foot against a *stone* and were asked how the stone came to be there, I might possibly answer that for anything I knew to the contrary it had lain there forever; nor would it, perhaps, be very easy to show the absurdity of this answer. But suppose I had found a *watch* upon the ground, and it should be inquired how the watch happened to be in that place, I should hardly think of the answer which I had before given, that for anything I knew the watch might have always been there. Yet why should not this answer serve for the watch as well as for the stone; why is it not as admissible in the second case as in the first? For this reason, and for no other, namely, that when we come to inspect the watch, we perceive—what we could not discover in the stone—that its several parts are framed and put together for a purpose, e.g., that they are so formed and adjusted as to produce motion, and that motion so regulated as to point out the hour of the day; that if the different parts had been differently shaped from what they are,

or placed after any other manner or in any other order than that in which they are placed, either no motion at all would have been carried on in the machine, or none which would have answered the use that is now served by it. To reckon up a few of the plainest of these parts and of their offices, all tending to one result: we see a cylindrical box containing a coiled elastic spring, which, by its endeavor to relax itself, turns round the box. We next observe a flexible chain—artificially wrought for the sake of flexure—communicating the action of the spring from the box to the fusee. We then find a series of wheels, the teeth of which catch in and apply to each other, conducting the motion from the fusee to the balance and from the balance to the pointer, and at the same time, by the size and shape of those wheels, so regulating that motion as to terminate in causing an index, by an equable and measured progression, to pass over a given space in a given time. We take notice that the wheels are made of brass, in order to keep them from rust; the springs of

* From William Paley, *Natural Theology*, first published 1802.

steel, no other metal being so elastic; that over the face of the watch there is placed a glass, a material employed in no other part of the work, but in the room of which, if there had been any other than a transparent substance, the hour could not be seen without opening the case. This mechanism being observed—it requires indeed an examination of the instrument, and perhaps some previous knowledge of the subject, to perceive and understand it; but being once, as we have said, observed and understood—the inference we think is inevitable, that the watch must have had a maker—that there must have existed, at some time and at some place or other, an artificer or artificers who formed it for the purpose which we find it actually to answer, who completely comprehended its construction and designed its use.

I. Nor would it, I apprehend, weaken the conclusion, that we had never seen a watch made—that we had never known an artist capable of making one—that we were altogether incapable of executing such a piece of workmanship ourselves, or of understanding in what manner it was performed; all this being no more than what is true of some exquisite remains of ancient art, of some lost arts, and, to the generality of mankind, of the more curious productions of modern manufacture. Does one man in a million know how oval frames are turned? Ignorance of this kind exalts our opinion of the unseen and unknown artist's skill, if he be unseen and unknown, but raises no doubt in our minds of the existence and agency of such an artist, at some former time and in some place or other. Nor can I perceive that it varies at all the inference, whether the question arise concerning a human agent or concerning an agent of a different species, or an agent possessing in some respects a different nature.

II. Neither, secondly, would it invalidate our conclusion, that the watch sometimes went wrong or that it seldom went exactly right. The purpose of the machinery, the design, and the designer might be evident, and in the case supposed, would be evident, in whatever way we accounted for the irregularity of the movement, or whether we could account for it or not. It is not necessary that a machine be perfect in order to show with what design it was made: still less necessary, where the only question is whether it were made with any design at all.

III. Nor, thirdly, would it bring any uncertainty into the argument, if there were a few parts of the watch, concerning which we could not discover or had not yet discovered in what manner they conduced to the general effect; or even some parts, concerning which we could not ascertain whether they conduced to that effect in any manner whatever. For, as to the first branch of the case, if by the loss, or disorder, or decay of the parts in question, the movement of the watch were found in fact to be stopped, or disturbed, or retarded, no doubt would remain in our minds as to the utility or intention of these parts, although we should be unable to investigate the manner according to which, or the connection by which, the ultimate effect depended upon their action or assistance; and the more complex the machine, the more likely is this obscurity to arise. Then, as to the second thing supposed, namely, that there were parts which might be spared without prejudice to the movement of the watch, and that we had proved this by experiment, these superfluous parts, even if we were completely assured that they were such, would not vacate the reasoning which we had instituted concerning other parts. The indication of contrivance remained, with respect to them, nearly as it was before.

IV. Nor, fourthly, would any man in his senses think the existence of the watch with its various machinery accounted for, by being told that it was one out of possible combinations of material forms; that whatever he had found in the place where he found the watch, must have contained some internal configuration or other; and that this configuration might be the structure now exhibited, namely, of the works of a watch, as well as a different structure.

V. Nor, fifthly, would it yield his inquiry more satisfaction, to be answered that there existed in things a principle of order, which had disposed the parts of the watch into their present form and situation. He never knew a watch made by the principle of order; nor can he even form to himself an idea of what is meant by a principle of order distinct from the intelligence of the watchmaker.

VI. Sixthly, he would be surprised to hear that the mechanism of the watch was no proof of contrivance, only a motive to induce the mind to think so:

VII. And not less surprised to be informed that the watch in his hand was nothing more than the result of the laws of *metallic* nature. It is a perversion of language to assign any law as the efficient, operative cause of any thing. A law presupposes an agent, for it is only the mode according to which an agent proceeds: it implies a power, for it is the order according to which that power acts. Without this agent, without this power, which are both distinct from itself, the *law* does nothing, is nothing. The expression, "the law of metallic nature," may sound strange and harsh to a philosophic ear; but it seems quite as justifiable as some others which are more familiar to him, such as "the law of vegetable nature," "the law of animal nature," or, indeed, as "the law of nature" in general, when assigned as the cause of phenomena, in exclusion of agency and power, or when it is substituted into the place of these.

VIII. Neither, lastly, would our observer be driven out of his conclusion or from his confidence in its truth by being told that he knew nothing at all about the matter. He knows enough for his argument; he knows the utility of the end; he knows the subserviency and adaptation of the means to the end. These points being known, his ignorance of other points, his doubts concerning other points affect not the certainty of his reasoning. The consciousness of knowing little need not beget a distrust of that which he does know.

CHAPTER 3

Application of the Argument

. . . every indication of contrivance, every manifestation of design which existed in the watch, exists in the works of nature, with the difference on the side of nature of being greater and more, and that in a degree which exceeds all computation. I mean that the contrivances of nature surpass the contrivances of art in the complexity, subtlety, and curiosity of the mechanism; and still more, if possible, do they go beyond them in number and variety; yet, in a multitude of cases, are not less evidently mechanical, not less evidently contrivances, not less evidently accommodated to their end or suited to their office than are the most perfect productions of human ingenuity.

I know no better method of introducing so large a subject than that of comparing a single thing with a single thing: an eye, for example, with a telescope. As far as the examination of the instrument goes, there is precisely the same proof that the eye was made for vision as there is that the telescope was made for assisting it. They are made upon the same principles, both being adjusted to the laws by which the transmission and refraction of rays of light are regulated. I speak not of the origin of the laws themselves; but such laws being fixed, the construction in both cases is adapted to them. For instance, these laws require, in order to produce the same effect, that rays of light in passing from water into the eye should be refracted by a more convex surface than when it passes out of air into the eye. Accordingly, we find that the eye of a fish, in that part of it called the crystalline lens, is much rounder than the eye of terrestrial animals. What plainer manifestation of design can there be than this difference? What could a mathematical instrument maker have done more to show his knowledge of his principle, his application of that knowledge, his suiting of his means to his end— I will not say to display the compass or excellence of his skill and art, for in these all comparison is indecorous, but to testify counsel, choice, consideration, purpose?

To some it may appear a difference sufficient to destroy all similitude between the eye and the telescope, that the one is a perceiving organ, the other an unperceiving instrument. The fact is that they are both instruments. And as to the mechanism, at least as to the mechanism being employed, and even as to the kind of it, this circumstance varies not the analogy at all. For observe what the constitution of the eye is. It is necessary, in order to produce distinct vision, that an image or picture of the object be formed at the bottom of the eye. Whence this necessity arises, or how the picture is connected with the sensation or contributes to it, it may be difficult, nay, we will confess, if you please, impossible for us to search out. But the present question is not concerned in the inquiry. It may be true that in this and in other instances we trace mechanical contrivance a certain way, and that then we come to something which is not mechanical, or which is inscrutable. But this affects not the certainty of our investigation, as far as we have gone. The difference between an animal and an automatic statue consists in this, that in the animal we trace the mechanism to a certain point, and then we are stopped, either the mechanism being too subtle for our discernment, or something else beside the known laws of mechanism taking place; whereas, in the automaton, for the comparatively few motions of which it is capable, we trace the mechanism throughout. But, up to the limit, the reasoning is as clear and certain in the one case as in the other. In the example before us it is a matter of certainty, because it is a matter which experience and observation demonstrate, that the formation of an image at the bottom of the eye is necessary to perfect vision. The formation then of such an image being necessary—no matter how— to the sense of sight and to the exercise of that sense, the apparatus by which it is formed is constructed and put together not only with infinitely more art, but upon the selfsame principles of art as in the telescope or the camera obscura. The perception arising from the image may be laid out of the question; for the production of the image, these are instruments of the same kind. The end is the same, the means are the same. The purpose in both is alike, the contrivance for accomplishing that purpose is in both alike. The lenses of the telescopes and humors of the eye bear a complete resemblance to one another, in their figure, their position, and in their power over the rays of light, namely, in bringing each pencil to a point at the right distance from the lens; namely, in the eye, at the exact place where the membrane is spread to receive it. How is it possible, under circumstances of such dose affinity, and under the operation of equal evidence, to exclude contrivance from the one, yet to acknowledge the proof of contrivance having been employed, as the plainest and clearest of all propositions, in the other?

The resemblance between the two cases is still more accurate, and obtains in more points than we have yet represented, or than we are, on the first view of the subject, aware of. In dioptric telescopes there is an imperfection of this nature. Pencils of light in passing through glass lenses are separated into different colors, thereby tinging the object, especially the edges of it, as if it were viewed through a prism. To correct this inconvenience had been long a desideratum in the art. At last it came into the mind of a sagacious optician to inquire how this matter was managed in the eye, in which there was exactly the same difficulty to contend with as in the telescope. His observation taught him that in the eye the evil was cured by combining lenses composed of different substances, that is, of substances which possessed different refracting powers. Our artist borrowed thence his hint and produced a correction of the defect by imitating, in glasses made from different materials, the effects of the different humors through which the rays of light pass before they reach the bottom of the eye. Could this be in the eye without purpose, which suggested to the optician the only effectual means of attaining that purpose?

But further, there are other points not so much perhaps of strict resemblance between the two as of superiority of the eye over the telescope, yet of a superiority which, being founded in the laws that regulate both, may furnish topics of fair and just comparison. Two things were wanted to the eye, which were not wanted, at least in the same degree, to the telescope; and these were the adaptation of the organ, first, to different degrees of light, and secondly, to the vast diversity of distance at which objects are viewed by the naked eye, namely, from a few inches to as many miles. These difficulties present not themselves to the maker of the telescope. He wants all the light he can get; and he never directs his instrument to objects near at hand. In the eye, both these cases were to be provided for; and for the purpose of providing for them, a subtle and appropriate mechanism is introduced.

Observe a newborn child first lifting up its eyelids. What does the opening of the curtain discover? The anterior part of two pellucid globes, which, when they come to be examined, are found to be constructed upon strict optical principles—the selfsame principles upon which we ourselves construct optical instruments. We find them perfect for the purpose of forming an image by refraction, composed of parts executing different offices, one part having fulfilled its office upon the pencil of light, delivering it over to the action of another part, that to a third, and so onward: the progressive action depending for its success upon the nicest and minutest adjustment of the parts concerned, yet these parts so in fact adjusted as to produce, not by a simple action or effect but by a combination of actions and effects, the result which is ultimately wanted. And forasmuch as this organ would have to operate under different circumstances with strong degrees of light and with weak degrees upon near objects and upon remote ones, and these differences demanded, according to the laws by which the transmission of light is regulated, a corresponding diversity of structure—that the aperture, for example, through which the light passes should be larger or less, the lenses rounder or flatter, or that their distance from the tablet upon which the picture is delineated should be shortened or lengthened—this, I say, being the case, and the difficulty to which the eye was to be adapted, we find its several parts capable of being occasionally changed, and a most artificial apparatus provided to produce that change. This is far beyond the common regulator of a watch, which requires the touch of a foreign hand to set it; but it is not altogether unlike Harrison's contrivance for making a watch regulate itself, by inserting within it a machinery which, by the artful use of the different expansion of metals, preserves the equability of the motion under all the various temperatures of heat and cold in which the instrument may happen to be placed. The ingenuity of this last contrivance has been justly praised. Shall, therefore, a structure which differs from it chiefly by surpassing it be accounted no contrivance at all; or, if it be a contrivance, that it is without a contriver?

One question may possibly have dwelt in the reader's mind during the perusal of these observations, namely, why should not the Deity have given to the animal the faculty of vision *at once*? Why this circuitous perception; the ministry of so many means; an element provided for the purpose; reflected from opaque substances, refracted through transparent ones, and both according to precise laws; then a complex organ, an intricate and artificial apparatus, in order, by the operation of this element and in conformity with the restrictions of these laws, to produce an image upon a membrane communicating with the brain? Wherefore all this? Why make the difficulty in order to surmount it? If to perceive objects by some other mode than that of touch, or objects which lay out of the reach of that sense, were the thing proposed, could not a simple volition of the Creator have communicated the capacity? Why resort to

contrivance where power is omnipotent? Contrivance, by its very definition and nature, is the refuge of imperfection. To have recourse to expedients implies difficulty, impediment restraint, defect of power. This question belongs to the other senses as well as to sight; to the general functions of animal life, as nutrition, secretion, respiration; to the economy of vegetables—and indeed to almost all the operations of nature. The question, therefore, is of very wide extent; and among other answers which may be given to it, beside reasons of which probably we are ignorant, one answer is this: it is only by the display of contrivance that the existence, the agency, the wisdom of the Deity *could* be testified to his rational creatures. This is the scale by which we ascend to all the knowledge of our Creator which we possess, so far as it depends upon the phenomena or the works of nature. Take away this, and you take away from us every subject of observation and ground of reasoning; I mean, as our rational faculties are formed at present. Whatever is done, God could have done without the intervention of instruments or means; but it is in the construction of instruments, in the choice and adaptation of means, that a creative intelligence is seen. It is this which constitutes the order and beauty of the universe. God, therefore, has been pleased to prescribe limits to his own power and to work his ends within those limits. The general laws of matter have perhaps prescribed the nature of these limits; its inertia; its reaction; the laws which govern the communication of motion, the refraction and reflection of light, and the constitution of fluids nonelastic and elastic, the transmission of sound through the latter; the laws of magnetism, of electricity, and probably others yet undiscovered. These are general laws; and when a particular purpose is to be effected, it is not by making a new law, nor by the suspension of the old ones, nor by making them wind and bend, and yield to the occasion—for nature with great steadiness adheres to and supports them—but it is, as we have seen in the eye, by the interposition of an apparatus corresponding with these laws, and suited to the exigency which results from them, that the purpose is at length attained. As we have said, therefore, God prescribes limits to his power that he may let in the exercise and thereby exhibit demonstrations of his wisdom. For then—that is, such laws and limitations being laid down—it is as though one Being should have fixed certain rules, and, if we may so speak, provided certain materials, and afterwards have committed to another Being, out of these materials and in subordination to these rules, the task of drawing forth a creation: a supposition which evidently leaves room and induces indeed a necessity for contrivance. Nay, there may be many such agents, and many ranks of these. We do not advance this as a doctrine either of philosophy or of religion; but we say that the subject may safely be represented under this view, because the Deity, acting himself by general laws, will have the same consequences upon our reasoning as if he had prescribed these laws to another. It has been said that the problem of creation was "attraction and matter being given, to make a world out of them"; and, as above explained, this statement perhaps does not convey a false idea.

CHAPTER 6

The Argument Cumulative

Were there no example in the world of contrivance except that of the *eye*, it would be alone sufficient to support the conclusion which we draw from it, as to the necessity of an intelligent Creator. It could never be got rid of, because it could not be accounted for by any other supposition which did not contradict all the principles we possess of knowledge— the principles according to which things do, as often as they can be brought to the test of experience, turn out to be true or false. Its coats and humors, constructed as the lenses of a telescope are constructed, for the refraction of rays of light to a point, which forms the proper action of the organ; the provision in its muscular tendons for turning its pupil to the object, similar to that which is given to the telescope by screws, and upon which power of direction in the eye the exercise of its office as an optical instrument depends; the further provision for its defense, for its constant lubricity and moisture, which we see in its socket and its lids, in its glands for the secretion of the matter of tears, its outlet or communication with the nose for carrying off the liquid after the eye is washed with it; these provisions compose altogether an apparatus, a system of parts, a preparation of means, so manifest in their design, so exquisite in their contrivance, so successful in their issue, so precious, and so infinitely beneficial in their use, as, in my opinion, to bear down all doubt that can be raised upon the subject.

And what I wish, under the title of the present chapter, to observe is that, if other parts of nature were inaccessible to our inquiries, or even if other parts of nature presented nothing to our examination but disorder and confusion, the validity of this example would remain the same. If there were but one watch in the world, it would not be less certain that it had a maker. If we had never in our lives seen any but one single kind of hydraulic machine, yet if of that one kind we understood the mechanism and use, we should be as perfectly assured that it proceeded from the hand and thought and skill of a workman, as if we visited a museum of the arts and saw collected there twenty different kinds of machines for drawing water, or a thousand different kinds for other purposes. Of this point each machine is a proof independently of all the rest. So it is with the evidences of a divine agency. The proof is not a conclusion which lies at the end of a chain of reasoning, of which chain each instance of contrivance is only a link, and of which, if one link fail, the whole fails; but it is an argument separately supplied by every separate example. An error in stating an example affects only that example. The argument is cumulative in the fullest sense of that term. The eye proves it without the ear; the ear without the eye. The proof in each example is complete; for when the design of the part and the conduciveness of its structure to that design is shown, the mind may set itself at rest; no future consideration can detract anything from the force of the example.

CHAPTER 24

Of the Natural Attributes of the Deity

It is an immense conclusion that there is a God—a perceiving, intelligent, designing Being, at the head of creation, and from whose will it proceeded. The *attributes* of such a Being, suppose his reality to be proved, must be adequate to the magnitude, extent, and multiplicity of his operations, which are not only vast beyond comparison with those performed by any other power, but so far as respects our conceptions of them, infinite, because they are unlimited on all sides.

Yet the contemplation of a nature so exalted, however surely we arrive at the proof of its existence, overwhelms our faculties. The mind feels its powers sink under the subject. One consequence of which is that from painful abstraction the thoughts seek relief in sensible images, whence may be deduced the ancient and almost universal propensity to idolatrous substitutions. They are the resources of a laboring imagination. False religions usually fall in with the natural propensity; true religions, or such as have derived themselves from the true, resist it.

It is one of the advantages of the revelations which we acknowledge, that while they reject idolatry with its many pernicious accompaniments, they introduce the Deity to human apprehension under an idea more personal, more determinate, more within its compass, than the theology of nature can do. And this they do by representing him exclusively under the relation in which he stands to ourselves; and for the most part, under some precise character, resulting from that relation or from the history of his providences; which method suits the span of our intellects much better than the universality which enters into the idea of God, as deduced from the views of nature. When, therefore, these representations are well founded in point of authority—for all depends upon that—they afford a condescension to the state of our faculties, of which they who have most reflected on the subject will be the first to acknowledge the want and the value.

Nevertheless, if we be careful to imitate the documents of our religion by confining our explanations to what concerns ourselves, and do not affect more precision in our ideas than the subject allows of, the several terms which are employed to denote the attributes of the Deity may be made, even in natural religion, to bear a sense consistent with truth and reason and not surpassing our comprehension.

These terms are omnipotence, omniscience, omnipresence, eternity, self-existence, necessary existence, spirituality.

"Omnipotence," "omniscience," "infinite" power, "infinite" knowledge are *superlatives* expressing our conception of these attributes in the strongest and most elevated terms which language supplies. We ascribe power to the Deity under the name of "omnipotence," the strict and correct conclusion being that a power which could create such a world as this is must be, beyond all comparison, greater than any which we experience in ourselves, than any which we observe in other visible agents, greater also than any which we can want, for our individual protection and preservation, in the Being upon whom we depend. It is a power likewise to which we are not authorized, by our observation or knowledge, to assign any limits of space or duration.

Very much of the same sort of remark is applicable to the term "omniscience"—infinite knowledge, or infinite wisdom. In strictness of language, there is a difference between knowledge and wisdom, wisdom always supposing action and action directed by it. With respect to the first, namely, *knowledge*, the Creator must know intimately the constitution and properties of the things which he created, which seems also to imply a foreknowledge of their action upon one another and of their changes; at least, so far as the same result from trains of physical and necessary causes. His omniscience also, as far as respects things present, is deducible from his nature, as an intelligent being, joined with the extent, or rather the universality of his operations. Where he acts, he is; and where he is, he perceives. The *wisdom* of the Deity, as testified in the works of creation, surpasses all idea we have of wisdom drawn from the highest intellectual operations of the highest class of intelligent beings with whom we are acquainted; and, which is of the chief importance to us, whatever be its compass or extent which it is evidently impossible that we should be able to determine, it must be adequate to the conduct of that order of things under which we live. And this is enough. It is of very inferior consequence by what terms we express our notion, or rather our admiration of this attribute. The terms which the piety and the usage of language have rendered habitual to us may be as proper as any other. We can trace this attribute much beyond what is necessary for any conclusion to which we have occasion to apply it. The degree of knowledge and power requisite for the formation of created nature cannot, with respect to us, be distinguished from infinite.

The divine "omnipresence" stands, in natural theology, upon this foundation: in every part and place of the universe with which we are acquainted we perceive the exertion of a power which we believe, mediately or immediately, to proceed from the Deity. For instance, in what part or point of space that has ever been explored do we not discover attraction? In what regions do we not find light? In what accessible portion of our globe do we not meet with gravity, magnetism, electricity, together with the properties also and powers of organized substances, of vegetable, or of animated nature? Nay, further, we may ask, what kingdom is there of nature, what corner of space, in which there is anything that can be examined by us, where we do not fall upon contrivance and design? The only reflection perhaps which arises in our minds from this view of the world around us is that the laws of nature everywhere prevail, that they are uniform and universal. But what do you mean by the laws of nature or by any law? Effects are produced by power not by laws. A law cannot execute itself. A law refers us to an agent. Now, an agency so general as that we cannot discover its absence, or assign the place in which some effect of its continued energy is not found, may, in popular language at least, and perhaps without much deviation from philosophical strictness, be called universal; and with not quite the same but with no inconsiderable propriety the person or being in whom that power resides or from whom it is derived may be taken to be omnipresent. He who upholds all things by his power may be said to be everywhere present.

This is called a virtual presence. There is also what metaphysicians denominate an essential ubiquity, and which idea the language of Scripture seems to favor; but the former, I think, goes as far as natural theology carries us.

"Eternity" is a negative idea clothed with a positive name. It supposes, in that to which it is applied, a present existence, and is the negation of a beginning or an end of that existence. As applied to the Deity, it has not been controverted by those who acknowledge a Deity at all. Most assuredly, there never was a time in which nothing existed, because that condition must have continued. The universal *blank* must have remained; nothing could rise up out of it, nothing could ever have existed since, nothing could exist now. In strictness, however, we have no concern with duration prior to that of the visible world. Upon this article, therefore, of theology it is sufficient to know that the contriver necessarily existed before the contrivance.

"Self-existence" is another negative idea, namely, the negation of a preceding cause, as of a progenitor, a maker, an author, a creator.

"Necessary existence" means demonstrable existence.

"Spirituality" expresses an idea made up of a negative part and of a positive part. The negative part consists in the exclusion of some of the known properties of matter, especially of solidity, of the *vis inertiae*, and of gravitation. The positive part comprises perception, thought, will, power, *action*; by which last term is meant the origination of motion, the quality, perhaps, in which resides the essential superiority of spirit over matter, "which cannot move, unless it be moved; and cannot but move, when impelled by another." I apprehend that there can be no difficulty in applying to the Deity both parts of this idea.

DAVID HUME

from Dialogues Concerning Natural Religion

We have in our selection Part II and Part V of Hume's *Dialogues*. In the *Dialogues* Cleanthes champions "natural religion," or reasoning to the existence of God from nature by means of the Teleological Argument. Philo, speaking for Hume himself, criticizes Cleanthes' reasoning. In Part II Cleanthes gives us a formulation of the argument, and Hume begins his criticism. In Part V the concern is reasoning to the attributes of God. Lucretius' exclamation in Latin near the beginning of Part V is a question. Shortened and paraphrased it is: "Who is mighty enough to rule the universe?" The immediately following Latin quotation from Tully, or Marcus Tullius Cicero (usually called Cicero), contains a similar question. Shortened and paraphrased it is: "What means of production could the architect of the universe have used?"*

PART II

I must own, *Cleanthes*, said *Demea*, that nothing can more surprise me, than the light, in which you have, all along, put this argument. By the whole tenor of your discourse, one would imagine that you were maintaining the being of a God, against the cavils of atheists and infidels; and were necessitated to become a champion for that fundamental principle of all religion. But this, I hope, is not, by any means, a question among us. No man; no man, at least, of common sense, I am persuaded, ever entertained a serious doubt with regard to a truth so certain and self-evident. The question is not concerning the BEING but the NATURE of GOD. This I affirm, from the infirmities of human understanding, to be altogether incomprehensible and unknown to us. The essence of that supreme mind, his attributes, the manner of his existence, the very nature of his duration; these and every particular, which regards so divine a being, are mysterious to men. Finite, weak, and blind creatures, we ought to humble ourselves in his august presence, and, conscious of our frailties, adore in silence his infinite perfections which eye hath not seen, ear hath not heard, neither hath it entered into the heart of man to conceive them. They are covered in a deep cloud from human curiosity: It is profaneness to attempt penetrating through these sacred obscurities: And next to the impiety of denying his existence, is the temerity of prying into his nature and essence, decrees and attributes.

But lest you should think, that my *piety* has here got the better of my *philosophy*, I shall support my opinion, if it needs any support, by a very great authority. I might cite all the divines almost, from the foundation of Christianity, who have ever treated of this or any other theological subject: But I shall confine myself, at present, to one equally celebrated for piety and philosophy. It is *Father Malebranche*, who, I remember,

---

* From David Hume, *Dialogues Concerning Natural Religion*, 1779.

thus expresses himself.* 'One ought not so much (says he) to call God a spirit, in order to express positively what he is, as in order to signify that he is not matter. He is a being infinitely perfect: of this we cannot doubt. But in the same manner as we ought not to imagine, even supposing him corporeal, that he is clothed with a human body, as the *Anthropomorphites* asserted, under colour that that figure was the most perfect of any; so neither ought we to imagine, that the spirit of God has human ideas or bears *any* resemblance to our spirit; under colour that we know nothing more perfect than a human mind. We ought rather to believe, that as he comprehends the perfections of matter without being material . . . he comprehends also the perfections of created spirits, without being spirit, in the manner we conceive spirit: That his true name is *He that is*, or, in other words, Being without restriction, All Being, the Being infinite and universal.'

After so great an authority, *Demea*, replied *Philo*, as that which you have produced, and a thousand more, which you might produce, it would appear ridiculous in me to add my sentiment, or express my approbation of your doctrine. But surely, where reasonable men treat these subjects, the question can never be concerning the *being* but only the *nature* of the deity. The former truth, as you well observe, is unquestionable and self-evident. Nothing exists without a cause; and the original cause of this universe (whatever it be) we call GOD; and piously ascribe to him every species of perfection. Whoever scruples this fundamental truth deserves every punishment, which can be inflicted among philosophers, *to wit*, the greatest ridicule, contempt and disapprobation. But as all perfection is entirely relative, we ought never to imagine, that we

comprehend the attributes of this divine being, or to suppose, that his perfections have any analogy or likeness to the perfections of a human creature. Wisdom, thought, design, knowledge; these we justly ascribe to him; because these words are honourable among men, and we have no other language or other conceptions, by which we can express our adoration of him. But let us beware, lest we think, that our ideas anywise correspond to his perfections, or that his attributes have any resemblance to these qualities among men. He is infinitely superior to our limited view and comprehension; and is more the object of worship in the temple than of disputation in the schools.

In reality, *Cleanthes*, continued he, there is no need of having recourse to that affected scepticism, so displeasing to you, in order to come at this determination. Our ideas reach no farther than our experience: We have no experience of divine attributes and operations: I need not conclude my syllogism: You can draw the inference yourself. And it is a pleasure to me (and I hope to you too) that just reasoning and sound piety here concur in the same conclusion, and both of them establish the adorably mysterious and incomprehensible nature of the supreme being.

Not to lose any time in circumlocutions, said *Cleanthes*, addressing himself to *Demea*, much less in replying to the pious declamations of *Philo*; I shall briefly explain how I conceive this matter. Look round the world: Contemplate the whole and every part of it: You will find it to be nothing but one great machine, subdivided into an infinite number of lesser machines, which again admit of subdivisions, to a degree beyond what human senses and faculties can trace and explain. All these various machines, and even their

* Recherche de la Verite. Liv.3. Chap. 9.

most minute parts, are adjusted to each other with an accuracy, which ravishes into admiration all men, who have ever contemplated them. The curious adapting of means to ends, throughout all nature, resembles exactly, though it much exceeds, the productions of human contrivance; of human design, thought, wisdom, and intelligence. Since therefore the effects resemble each other, we are led to infer, by all the rules of analogy, that the causes also resemble; and that the author of nature is somewhat similar to the mind of man; though possessed of much larger faculties, proportioned to the grandeur of the work, which he has executed. By this argument *a posteriori*, and by this argument alone, do we prove at once the existence of a deity, and his similarity to human mind and intelligence.

I shall be so free, *Cleanthes*, said *Demea*, as to tell you, that from the beginning I could not approve of your conclusion concerning the similarity of the deity to men; still less can I approve of the mediums, by which you endeavour to establish it. What! No demonstration of the being of God! No abstract arguments! No proofs *a priori*! Are these which have hitherto been so much insisted on by philosophers all fallacy, all sophism? Can we reach no farther in this subject than experience and probability? I will not say, that this is betraying the cause of a deity: But surely, by this affected candour, you give advantages to atheists, which they never could obtain, by the mere dint of argument and reasoning.

What I chiefly scruple in this subject, said *Philo*, is not so much, that all religious arguments are by *Cleanthes* reduced to experience, as that they appear not to be even the most certain and irrefragable of that inferior kind. That a stone will fall, that fire will burn, that the earth has solidity, we have observed a thousand and a thousand times; and when any new instance of this nature is presented, we draw without hesitation the accustomed inference. The exactly similarity of the cases gives us a perfect assurance of a similar event; and a stronger evidence is never desired nor sought after. But wherever you depart, in the least, from the similarity of the cases, you diminish proportionably the evidence; and may at last bring it to a very weak *analogy*, which is confessedly liable to error and uncertainty. After having experienced the circulation of the blood in human creatures, we make no doubt, that it takes place in *Titius* and *Maevius*: But from its circulation in frogs and fishes, it is only a presumption, though a strong one, from analogy, that it takes place in men and other animals. The analogical reasoning is much weaker, when we infer the circulation of the sap in vegetables from our experience, that the blood circulates in animals; and those, who hastily followed that imperfect analogy, are found, by more accurate experiments, to have been mistaken.

If we see a house, *Cleanthes*, we conclude, with the greatest certainty, that it had an architect or builder, because this is precisely that species of effect, which we have experienced to proceed from that species of cause. But surely you will not affirm, that the universe bears such a resemblance to a house, that we can with the same certainty infer a similar cause, or that the analogy is here entire and perfect. The dissimilitude is so striking, that the utmost you can here pretend to is a guess, a conjecture, a presumption concerning a similar cause; and how that pretension will be received in the world, I leave you to consider.

It would surely be very ill received, replied *Cleanthes*; and I should be deservedly blamed and detested, did I allow, that the proofs of a deity amounted to no more than a guess or conjecture.

But is the whole adjustment of means to ends in a house and in the universe so slight a resemblance? The economy of final causes? The order, proportion, and arrangement of every part? Steps of a stair are plainly contrived, that human legs may use them in mounting; and this inference is certain and infallible. Human legs are also contrived for walking and mounting; and this inference, I allow, is not altogether so certain, because of the dissimilarity which you remark; but does it, therefore, deserve the name only of presumption or conjecture?

Good God! cried *Demea*, interrupting him, where are we? Zealous defenders of religion allow, that the proofs of a deity fall short of perfect evidence! And you, *Philo*, on whose assistance I depended, in proving the adorable mysteriousness of the divine nature, do you assent to all these extravagant opinions of *Cleanthes*? For what other name can I give them? Or why spare my censure, when such principles are advanced, supported by such an authority, before so young a man as *Pamphilus*?

You seem not to apprehend, replied *Philo*, that I argue with *Cleanthes* in his own way; and by showing him the dangerous consequences of his tenets, hope at last to reduce him to our opinion. But what sticks most with you, I observe, is the representation which *Cleanthes* has made of the argument *a posteriori*; and finding that that argument is likely to escape your hold and vanish into air, you think it so disguised that you can scarcely believe it to be set in its true light. Now, however much I may dissent, in other respects, from the dangerous principle of *Cleanthes*, I must allow, that he has fairly represented that argument; and I shall endeavour so to state the matter to you that you will entertain no farther scruples with regard to it.

Were a man to abstract from everything which he knows or has seen, he would be altogether incapable, merely from his own ideas, to determine what kind of scene the universe must be, or to give the preference to one state or situation of things above another. For as nothing which he clearly conceives could be esteemed impossible or implying a contradiction, every chimera of his fancy would be upon an equal footing; nor could he assign any just reason, why he adheres to one idea or system, and rejects the others, which are equally possible.

Again; after he opens his eyes, and contemplates the world as it really is, it would be impossible for him, at first, to assign the cause of any one event, much less, of the whole of things or of the universe. He might set his fancy a-rambling; and she might bring him in an infinite variety of reports and representations. These would all be possible; but being all equally possible, he would never, of himself, give a satisfactory account for his preferring one of them to the rest. Experience alone can point out to him the true cause of any phenomenon.

Now, according to this method of reasoning, *Demea*, it follows (and is, indeed, tacitly allowed by *Cleanthes* himself) that order, arrangement, or the adjustment of final causes is not, of itself, any proof of design; but only so far as it has been experienced to proceed from that principle. For aught we can know *a priori*, matter may contain the source or spring of order originally, within itself, as well as mind does; and there is no more difficulty in conceiving, that the several elements, from an internal unknown cause, may fall into the most exquisite arrangement, than to conceive that their ideas, in the great, universal mind, from a like internal, unknown cause, fall into that arrangement. The equal possibility of both these suppositions is allowed. But by experience we find (according to Cleanthes), that there is a difference between them. Throw several pieces of steel together, without shape or form; they will never arrange themselves so as to compose a watch: Stone, and mortar, and wood, without an architect, never erect a house. But the ideas in a human mind, we see, by an unknown, inexplicable economy, arrange themselves so as to form the plan of a watch or house. Experience, therefore, proves, that there is an orginal principle of order in mind, not in matter. From similar effects we infer similar causes. The adjustment of means to ends is alike in the universe, as in a machine of human contrivance. The causes, therefore, must be resembling.

I was from the beginning scandalized, I must own, with this resemblance, which is asserted, between the deity and human creatures; and must conceive it to imply such a degradation of the supreme being as no sound theist could endure. With your assistance, therefore, *Demea*, I shall endeavour to defend what you justly call the adorable mysteriousness of the divine nature, and shall refute this reasoning of *Cleanthes*; provided he allows, that I have made a fair representation of it.

When *Cleanthes* has assented, *Philo*, after a short pause, proceeded in the following manner.

That all inferences, *Cleanthes*, concerning fact are founded on experience, and that all experimental reasonings are founded on the supposition, that similar causes prove similar effects, and similar effects similar causes; I shall not, at present, much dispute with you. But observe, I entreat you, with what extreme caution all just reasoners proceed in the transferring of experiments to similar cases. Unless the cases be exactly similar, they repose no perfect confidence in applying their past observation to any particular phenomenon. Every alteration of circumstances occasions a doubt concerning the event; and it requires new

experiments to prove certainly, that the new circumstances are of no moment or importance. A change in bulk, situation, arrangement, age, disposition of the air, or surrounding bodies; any of these particulars may be attended with the most unexpected consequences: And unless the objects be quite familiar to us, it is the highest temerity to expect with assurance, after any of these changes, an event similar to that which before fell under our observation. The slow and deliberate steps of philosophers here, if anywhere, are distinguished from the precipitate march of the vulgar, who, hurried on by the smallest similitude, are incapable of all discernment or consideration.

But can you think, *Cleanthes*, that your usual phlegm and philosophy have been preserved in so wide a step as you have taken, when you compared to the universe houses, ships, furniture, machines; and from their similarity in some circumstances inferred a similarity in their causes? Thought, design, intelligence, such as we discover in men and other animals, is no more than one of the springs and principles of the universe, as well as heat or cold, attraction or repulsion, and a hundred others, which fall under daily observation. It is an active cause, by which some particular parts of nature, we find, produce alterations on other parts. But can a conclusion, with any propriety, be transferred from parts to the whole? Does not the great disproportion bar all comparison and inference? From observing the growth of a hair, can we learn anything concerning the generation of a man? Would the manner of a leaf's blowing, even though perfectly known, afford us any instruction concerning the vegetation of a tree?

But allowing that we were to take the *operations* of one part of nature upon another for the foundation of our judgement concerning the *origin* of the whole (which never can be admitted) yet why select so minute, so weak, so bounded a principle as the reason and design of animals is found to be upon this planet? What peculiar privilege has this little agitation of the brain which we call thought, that we must thus make it the model of the whole universe? Our partiality in our own favour does indeed present it on all occasions: But sound philosophy ought carefully to guard against so natural an illusion.

So far from admitting, continued *Philo*, that the operations of a part can afford us any just conclusion concerning the origin of the whole, I will not allow any one part to form a rule for another part, if the latter be very remote from the former. Is there any reasonable ground to conclude, that the inhabitants of other planets possess thought, intelligence, reason, or anything similar to these faculties in men? When nature has so extremely diversified her manner of operation in this small globe; can we imagine, that she incessantly copies herself throughout so immense a universe? And if thought, as we may well suppose, be confined merely to this narrow corner, and has even there so limited a sphere of action; with what propriety can we assign it for the original cause of all things? The narrow views of a peasant, who makes his domestic economy the rule for the government of kingdoms, is in comparison a pardonable sophism.

But were we ever so much assured, that a thought and reason, resembling the human, were to be found throughout the whole universe, and were its activity elsewhere vastly greater and more commanding than it appears in this globe: Yet I cannot see why the operations of a world, constituted, arranged, adjusted, can with any propriety be extended to a world, which is in its embryo-state, and is advancing towards that constitution and arrangement. By observation, we know somewhat of the economy, action, and nourishment of a finished animal; but we must transfer with great caution that observation to the growth of a foetus in the womb, and still more, to the formation of an animalcule in the loins of its male-parent. Nature, we find, even from our limited experience, possesses an infinite number of springs and principles, which incessantly discover themselves on every change of her position and situation. And what new and unknown principles would actuate her in so new and unknown a situation, as that of the formation of a universe, we cannot, without the utmost temerity, pretend to determine.

A very small part of this great system, during a very short time, is very imperfectly discovered to us: And do we thence pronounce decisively concerning the origin of the whole?

Admirable conclusion! Stone, wood, brick, iron, brass, have not, at this time, in this minute globe of earth, an order or arrangement without human art and contrivance: Therefore the universe could not originally attain its order and arrangement, without something similar to human art. But is a part of nature a rule for another part very wide of the former? Is it a rule for the whole? Is a very small part a rule for the universe? Is nature in one situation, a certain rule for nature in another situation, vastly different from the former?

And can you blame me, *Cleanthes*, if I here imitate the prudent reserve of *Simonides*, who, according to the noted story, being asked by *Hiero*, *What God was?*, desired a day to think of it, and then two days more; and after that manner continually prolonged the term, without ever bringing in his definition or description? Could you even blame me, if I had answered at first, *that I did not know*, and was sensible that this subject lay vastly beyond the reach of my faculties? You might cry out sceptic and railer, as much as you pleased: But having found, in so many other subjects, much more familiar, the imperfections and even contradictions of human reason, I never should expect any success from its feeble conjectures, in a subject, so sublime, and so remote from the sphere of our observation. When two *species* of objects have always been observed to be conjoined together, I can *infer*, by custom, the existence of one wherever I *see* the existence of the other: And this I call an argument from experience. But how this argument can have place, where the objects, as in the present case, are single, individual, without parallel, or specific resemblance, may be difficult to explain. And will any man tell me with a serious countenance, that an orderly universe must arise from some thought and art, like the human; because we have experience of it? To ascertain this reasoning, it were requisite, that we had experience of the origin of worlds; and it is not sufficient surely, that we have seen ships and cities arise from human art and contrivance . . .

Philo was proceeding in this vehement manner, somewhat between jest and earnest, as it appeared to me; when he observed some signs of impatience in *Cleanthes*, and then immediately stopped short. What I had to suggest, said *Cleanthes*, is only that you would not abuse terms, or make use of popular expressions to subvert philosophical reasonings. You know, that the vulgar often distinguish reason from experience, even where the question relates only to matter of fact and existence; though it is found, where that *reason* is properly analysed, that it is nothing but a species of experience. To prove by experience the origin of the universe from mind is not more contrary to common speech than to prove the motion of the earth from the same principle. And a caviller might raise all the same objections to the *Copernican* system, which you have urged against my reasonings. Have you other earths, might he say, which you have seen to move? Have . . .

Yes! cried *Philo*, interrupting him, we have other earths. Is not the moon another earth, which we see to turn round its centre? Is not Venus another earth, where we observe the same phenomenon? Are not the revolutions of the sun also a confirmation, from analogy, of the same theory? All the planets, are they not earths, which revolve about the sun? Are not the satellites moons, which move round Jupiter and Saturn, and along with these primary planets, round the sun? These analogies and resemblances, with others which I have not mentioned, are the sole proofs of the *Copernican* system: And to you it belongs to consider, whether you have any analogies of the same kind to support your theory.

In reality, *Cleanthes*, continued he, the modern system of astronomy is now so much received by all inquirers, and has become so essential a part even of our earliest education, that we are not commonly very scrupulous in examining the reasons, upon which it is founded. It is now become a matter of mere curiosity to study the first writers on that subject, who had the full force of prejudice to counter, and were obliged to turn their arguments on every side, in order to render them popular and convincing. But if we peruse *Galileo's* famous Dialogues concerning the system of the world, we shall find, that that great genius, one of the sublimest that ever existed, first bent all his endeavours to prove, that there was no foundation for the distinction commonly made between elementary and celestial substances. The Schools, proceeding from the illusions of sense, had carried this distinction very far; and had established the latter substances to be ingenerable, incorruptible, unalterable, impassible; and had assigned all the opposite qualities to the former. But *Galileo*, beginning with the moon, proved its similarity in every particular to the earth; its convex figure, its natural darkness when not illuminated, its density, its distinction into solid and liquid, the variations of its phases, the mutual illuminations of the earth and moon, their mutual eclipses, the inequalities of the lunar surface, etc. After many instances of this kind, with regard to all the planets, men plainly saw, that these bodies became proper objects of experience; and that the similarity of their nature enabled us to extend the same arguments and phenomena from one to the other.

In this cautious proceeding of the astronomers, you may read your own condemnation, *Cleanthes*; or rather may see, that the subject in which you are engaged exceeds all human reason and inquiry. Can you pretend to show any such similarity between the fabric of a house, and the generation of a universe? Have you ever seen nature in any such situation as resembles the first arrangement of the elements? Have worlds ever been formed under your eye? And have you had leisure to observe the whole progress of the phenomenon, from the first appearance of order to its final consumation? If you have, then cite your experience, and deliver your theory.

PART V

But to show you still more inconveniences, continued *Philo*, in your anthropomorphism; please to take a new survey of your principles. *Like effects prove like causes*. This is the experimental argument; and this, you say too, is the sole theological argument. Now it is certain, that the liker the effects are, which are seen, and the liker the causes, which are inferred, the stronger is the argument. Every departure on either side diminishes the probability, and renders the experiment less conclusive. You cannot doubt of the principle: Neither ought you reject its consequences.

All the new discoveries in astronomy, which prove the immense grandeur and magnificence of the works of nature, are so many additional arguments for a deity, according to the true system of theism: But according to your hypothesis of experimental theism they become so many objections, by removing the effect still farther from all resemblance to the effects of human art and contrivance. For if *Lucretius*,* even following the old system of the world, could exclaim:

Quis regere immensi summam; quis habere profundi
Indu manu validas potis est moderanter habenas?
Quis pariter coelos omnes convertere? et omnes
Ignibus aetheriis terras suffire feraces?
Omnibus inque locis esse omni tempore praesto?

If *Tully*† esteemed this reasoning so natural as to put it into the mouth of his *Epicurean. Quibus enim oculis animi intueri potuit vester* **Plato** *fabricam illam tanti operis, qua construi a deo atque aedificare mundum facit? quae molitio? quae ferramenta? qui vectes? quae machinae? qui ministri tant: muneris fuerunt? quemadmodum autem obedire et parere voluntati architecti*

---

* Lib. II. 1094   † De. nat. Deor. Lib. 1.

aer, ignis, aqua, terra potuerunt? If this argument, I say, had any force in former ages; how much greater must it have at present; when the bounds of nature are so infinitely enlarged, and such a magnificent scene is opened to us? It is still more unreasonable to form our idea of so unlimited a cause from our experience of the narrow productions of human design and invention.

The discoveries by microscopes, as they open a new universe in miniature, are still objections, according to you; arguments, according to me. The farther we push our researches of this kind, we are still led to infer the universal cause of all to be vastly different from mankind, or from any object of human experience and observation.

And what say you to the discoveries in anatomy, chemistry, botany? . . . These surely are no objections, replied *Cleanthes*: They only discover new instances of art and contrivance. It is still the image of mind reflected on us from innumerable objects. Add, a mind *like the human*, said *Philo*. I know of no other, replied *Cleanthes*. And the liker, the better, insisted *Philo*. To be sure, said *Cleanthes*.

Now, *Cleanthes*, said *Philo*, with an air of alacrity and triumph, mark the consequences. *First*. By this method of reasoning, you renounce all claim to infinity in any of the attributes of the deity. For as the cause ought only to be proportioned to the effect, and the effect, so far as it falls under our cognizance, is not infinite; What pretensions have we, upon your suppositions, to ascribe that attribute to the divine being? You will still insist, that, by removing him so much from all similarity to human creatures, we give into the most arbitrary hypothesis, and at the same time, weaken all proofs of his existence.

Secondly. You have no reason, on your theory, for ascribing perfection to the deity, even in his finite capacity; or for supposing him free from every error, mistake, or incoherence, in his undertakings. There are many inexplicable difficulties in the works of nature, which, if we allow a perfect author to be proved *a priori*, are easily solved, and become only seeming difficulties from the narrow capacity of man, who cannot trace infinite relations. But according to your method of reasoning, these difficulties become all real; and perhaps will be insisted on, as new instances of likeness to human art and contrivance. At least, you must acknowledge, that it is impossible for us to tell, from our limited views, whether this system contains any great faults, or deserves any considerable praise, if compared to other possible, and even real systems. Could a peasant, if the *Aeneid* were read to him, pronounce that poem to be absolutely faultless, or even assign it to its proper rank among the productions of human wit; he, who had never seen any other production?

But were this world ever so perfect a production, it must still remain uncertain, whether all the excellences of the work can justly be ascribed to the workman. If we survey a ship, what an exalted idea must we form of the ingenuity of the carpenter, who framed so complicated useful and beautiful a machine? And what surprise must we entertain, when we find him a stupid mechanic, who imitated others, and copied an art, which, through a long succession of ages, after multiplied trials, mistakes, corrections, deliberations, and controversies, had been gradually improving? Many worlds might have been botched and bungled, throughout an eternity, ere this system was struck out: Much labour lost: Many fruitless trials made: And a slow, but continued improvement carried on during infinite ages in the art of world-making. In such subjects, who can determine, where the truth; nay, who can conjecture where the probability, lies; amidst a great number of hypotheses, which may be proposed, and a still greater number, which may be imagined?

And what shadow of an argument, continued *Philo*, can you produce from your hypothesis, to prove the unity of the deity? A great number of men join in building a house or ship, in rearing a city, in framing a commonwealth: Why may not several deities combine in contriving and framing a world? This is only so much greater similarity to human affairs. By sharing the work among several, we may so much farther limit the attributes of each, and get rid of that extensive power and knowledge, which must be supposed in one deity, and which, according to you, can only serve to weaken the proof of his existence. And if such foolish, such vicious creatures as man can yet often unite in framing and executing one plan, how much more those deities or demons, whom we may suppose several degrees more perfect?

To multiply causes without necessity is indeed contrary to true philosophy: But this principle applies not to the present case. Were one deity antecedently proved by your theory, who were possessed of every attribute, requisite to the production of the universe; it would be needless, I own (though not absurd) to suppose any other deity existent. But while it is still a question, whether all these attributes are united in one subject, or dispersed among several independent beings: By what phenomena in nature can we pretend to decide the controversy? Where we see a body raised in a scale, we are sure that there is in the opposite scale, however concealed from sight, some counterpoising weight equal to it: But it is still allowed to doubt, whether that weight be an aggregate of several distinct bodies, or one uniform united mass. And if the

weight requisite very much exceeds anything which we have ever seen conjoined in any single body; the former supposition becomes still more probable and natural. An intelligent being of such vast power and capacity, as is necessary to produce the universe, or to speak in the language of ancient philosophy, so prodigious an animal, exceeds all analogy and even comprehension.

But farther, *Cleanthes*; men are mortal, and renew their species by generation; and this is common to all living creatures. The two great sexes of male and female, says *Milton*, animate the world. Why must this circumstance, so universal, so essential, be excluded from those numerous and limited deities? Behold, then, the theogeny of ancient times brought back upon us.

And why not become a perfect anthropomorphite? Why not assert the deity or deities to be corporeal, and to have eyes, a nose, mouth, ears, etc. *Epicurus* maintained, that no man had ever seen reason but in a human figure; therefore, the gods must have a human figure. And this argument, which is deservedly so much ridiculed by *Cicero*, becomes, according to you, solid and philosophical.

In a word, *Cleanthes*, a man, who follows your hypothesis, is able, perhaps, to assert, or conjecture, that the universe, some time, arose from some thing like design: But beyond that position he cannot ascertain one single circumstance, and is left afterwards to fix every point of his theology, by the utmost licence of fancy and hypothesis. This world, for aught he knows, is very faulty and imperfect, compared to a superior standard; and was only the first rude essay of some infant deity, who afterwards abandoned it, ashamed of his lame performance: It is the work only of some dependent, inferior deity; and is the object of derision to his superiors: It is the production of old age and dotage in some superannuated deity; and ever since his death, has run on at adventures, from the first impulse and active force, which it received from him . . . You justly give signs of horror, *Demea*, at these strange suppositions: But these, and a thousand more of the same kind, are *Cleanthes'* suppositions, not mine. From the moment the attributes of the deity are supposed finite, all these have a place. And I cannot, for my part, think, that so wild and unsettled a system of theology is, in any respect, preferable to none at all.

These suppositions I absolutely disown; cried *Cleanthes*: They strike me, however, with no horror; especially, when proposed in that rambling way, in which they drop from you. On the contrary, they give me pleasure, when I see, that, by the utmost indulgence of your imagination, you never get rid of the hypothesis of design in the universe; but are obliged, at every turn, to have recourse to it. To this concession I adhere steadily; and this I regard as a sufficient foundation for religion.

The Moral Argument

The Moral Argument for the existence of God is different from the other three in that it is a "practical" argument. It does not endeavor to prove with certainty or probability that God exists. It rather argues that we need to *assume* that God exists—or, in Kant's language, *postulate* God's existence—in order for our moral practice to make sense and have coherence.

IMMANUEL KANT

The Existence of God as A Postulate of Pure Practical Reason

While Kant rejected the reasoning of the Ontological Argument (and of other arguments for the existence of God), he did think that our morality requires us to postulate God's existence. The reason it does so depends on points that Kant believes are essential for the coherent practice of morality, namely, that we have an obligation to strive for the *summum bonum* or "highest good," and that that good includes our being "worthy of happiness" (which we will be only by virtue of being moral), and that happiness will be proportionate to our morality. But it requires God's guarantee for the *summum bonum* to be possible of attainment (and immortality is required as well). So, Kant reasons, since our being moral requires the hope for the attainment of what we are obligated to strive for, and that attainment requires God's existence, morality itself, to be coherent, requires us to postulate God's existence.

From Immanuel Kant, *Critique of Practical Reason*, translated by T. K. Abbott.

V. *The Existence of God as a Postulate of Pure Practical Reason*

In the foregoing analysis the moral law led to a practical problem which is prescribed by pure reason alone, without the aid of any sensible motives, namely, that of the necessary completeness of the first and principal element of the *summum bonum*, viz., Morality; and as this can be perfectly solved only in eternity, to the postulate of *immortality*. The same law must also lead us to affirm the possibility of the second element of the *summum bonum*, viz., Happiness proportioned to that morality, and this on grounds as disinterested as before, and solely from impartial reason; that is, it must lead to the supposition of the existence of a cause adequate to this effect; in other words, it must postulate the *existence of God*, as the necessary condition of the possibility of the *summum bonum* (an object of the will which is necessarily connected with the moral legislation of pure reason). We proceed to exhibit this connection in a convincing manner.

Happiness is the condition of a rational being in the world with whom *everything goes according to his wish and will*; it rests, therefore, on the harmony of physical nature with his whole end, and likewise with the essential determining principle of his will. Now the moral law as a law of freedom commands by determining principles, which ought to be quite independent on nature and on its harmony with our faculty of desire (as springs). But the acting rational being in the world is not the cause of the world and of nature itself. There is not the least ground, therefore, in the moral law for a necessary connection between morality and proportionate happiness in a being that belongs to the world as part of it, and therefore dependent on it, and which for that reason cannot by his will be a cause of this nature, nor by his own power make it thoroughly harmonize, as far as his happiness is concerned, with his practical principles. Nevertheless, in the practical problem of pure reason, i.e., the necessary pursuit of the *summum bonum*, such a connection is postulated as necessary: we ought to endeavor to promote the *summum bonum*, which, therefore, must be possible. Accordingly, the existence of a cause of all nature, distinct from nature itself, and containing the principle of this connection, namely, of the exact harmony of happiness with morality, is also *postulated*. Now, this supreme cause must contain the principle of the harmony of nature, not merely with a law of the will of rational beings, but with the conception of this *law*, in so far as they make it the *supreme determining principle of the will*, and consequently not merely with the form of morals, but with their morality as their motive, that is, with their moral character. Therefore, the *summum bonum* is possible in the world only on the supposition of a Supreme Being[1] having a causality corresponding to moral character. Now a being that is capable of acting on the conception of laws is an *intelligence* (a rational being), and the causality of such a being according to this conception of laws is his *will*; therefore the supreme cause of nature, which must be presupposed as a condition

---

[1] [The original has "a Supreme Nature." *Natur*, however, almost invariably means "physical nature"; therefore Hartenstein supplies the words "cause of" before "nature." More probably *Natur* is a slip for *Ursache*, "cause."]

of the *summum bonum* is a being which is the cause of nature by *intelligence* and *will*, consequently its author, that is God. It follows that the postulate of the possibility of the *highest derived good* (the best world) is likewise the postulate of the reality of a *highest original good*, that is to say, of the existence of God. Now it was seen to be a duty for us to promote the *summum bonum*; consequently it is not merely allowable, but is a necessity connected with duty as a requisite, that we should presuppose the possibility of this *summum bonum*; and as this is possible only on condition of the existence of God, it inseparably connects the supposition of this with duty; that is, it is morally necessary to assume the existence of God.

It must be remarked here that this moral necessity is subjective, that is, it is a want, and not *objective*, that is, itself a duty, for there cannot be a duty to suppose the existence of anything (since this concerns only the theoretical employment of reason). Moreover, it is not meant by this that it is necessary to suppose the existence of God *as a basis of all obligation in general* (for this rests, as has been sufficiently proved, simply on the autonomy of reason itself). What belongs to duty here is only the endeavor to realize and promote the *summum bonum* in the world, the possibility of which can therefore be postulated; and as our reason finds it not conceivable except on the supposition of a supreme intelligence, the admission of this existence is therefore connected with the consciousness of our duty, although the admission itself belongs to the domain of speculative reason. Considered in respect of this alone, as a principle of explanation, it may be called a *hypothesis*, but in reference to the intelligibility of an object given us by the moral law (the *summum bonum*), and consequently of a requirement for practical purposes, it may be called *faith*, that is to say a pure *rational faith*, since

pure reason (both in its theoretical and its practical use) is the sole source from which it springs.

From this *deduction* it is now intelligible why the *Greek* schools could never attain the solution of their problem of the practical possibility of the *summum bonum*, because they made the rule of the use which the will of man makes of his freedom the sole and sufficient ground of this possibility, thinking that they had no need for that purpose of the existence of God. No doubt they were so far right that they established the principle of morals of itself independently on this postulate, from the relation of reason only to the will, and consequently made it the *supreme* practical condition of the *summum bonum*; but it was not therefore the *whole* condition of its possibility. The *Epicureans* had indeed assumed as the supreme principle of morality a wholly false one, namely, that of happiness, and had substituted for a law a maxim of arbitrary choice according to every man's inclination; they proceeded, however, *consistently* enough in this, that they degraded their *summum bonum* likewise just in proportion to the meanness of their fundamental principle, and looked for no greater happiness than can be attained by human prudence (including temperance and moderation of the inclinations), and this, as we know, would be scanty enough and would be very different according to circumstances; not to mention the exceptions that their maxims must perpetually admit and which make them incapable of being laws. The *Stoics*, on the contrary, had chosen their supreme practical principle quite rightly, making virtue the condition of the *summum bonum*; but when they represented the degree of virtue required by its pure law as fully attainable in this life, they not only strained the moral powers of the *man* whom they called *the wise* beyond all the limits of his nature, and assumed a thing that contradicts all our knowledge of men, but also and principally they would not allow the second *element* of the *summum bonum*, namely, happiness, to be properly a special object of human desire, but made their *wise man*, like a divinity in his consciousness of the excellence of his person, wholly independent on nature (as regards his own contentment); they exposed him indeed to the evils of life, but made him not subject to them (at the same time representing him also as free from moral evil). They thus, in fact, left out the second element of the *summum bonum*, namely, personal happiness, placing it solely in action and satisfaction with one's own personal worth, thus including it in the consciousness of being morally minded, in which they might have been sufficiently refuted by the voice of their own nature.

The doctrine of Christianity,[1] even if we do not yet consider it as a religious doctrine, gives, touching this point, a conception of the *summum bonum* (the Kingdom of God), which alone satisfies the strictest demand of practical reason. The moral law is holy (unyielding) and demands holiness of morals, although all the moral perfection to which man can attain is still only virtue, that is, a rightful disposition arising from *respect* for the law, implying consciousness of a constant propensity to transgression, or at least a want of purity, that is, a mixture of many spurious (not moral) motives of obedience to the law, consequently a self-esteem combined with humility. In respect, then, of the holiness which the Christian law requires, this leaves the creature nothing but a progress *in infinitum*, but for that very reason it justifies him in hoping for an endless duration of his existence. The *worth* of a character *perfectly* accordant with the moral law is

---

[1] It is commonly held that the Christian precept of morality has no advantage in respect of purity over the moral conceptions of the Stoics; the distinction between them is, however, very obvious. The Stoic system made the consciousness of strength of mind the pivot on which all moral dispositions should turn; and although its disciples spoke of duties and even defined them very well, yet they placed the spring and proper determining principle of the will in an elevation of the mind above the lower springs of the senses, which owe their power only to weakness of mind. With them, therefore, virtue was a sort of heroism in the *wise man* who, raising himself above the animal nature of man, is sufficient for himself, and while he prescribes duties to others is himself raised above them, and is not subject to any temptation to transgress the moral law. All this, however, they could not have done if they had conceived the law in all its purity and strictness, as the precept of the Gospel does. When I give the name *idea* to a perfection to which nothing adequate can be given in experience, it does not follow that the moral ideas are something transcendent, that is, something of which we could not even determine the concept adequately, or of which it is uncertain whether there is any object corresponding to it at all, as is the case with the ideas of speculative reason; on the contrary, being types of practical perfection, they serve as the indispensable rule of conduct and likewise as the *standard of comparison*. Now if I consider *Christian morals* on their philosophical side, then compared with the ideas of the Greek schools, they would appear as follows: the ideas of the *Cynics*, the *Epicureans*, the *Stoics*, and the *Christians* are: *simplicity of nature, prudence, wisdom,* and *holiness.* In respect of the way of attaining them, the Greek schools were distinguished from one another thus, that the Cynics only required *common sense*, the others the path of *science*, but both found the mere *use of natural powers* sufficient for the purpose. Christian morality, because its precept is framed (as a moral precept must be) so pure and unyielding, takes from man all confidence that he can be fully adequate to it, at least in this life, but again sets it up by enabling us to hope that if we act as well as it is in our *power* to do, then what is not in our power will come in to our aid from another source, whether we know how this may be or not. Aristotle and Plato differed only as to the origin of our moral conception.

infinite, since the only restriction on all possible happiness in the judgment of a wise and all-powerful distributor of it is the absence of conformity of rational beings to their duty. But the moral law of itself does not *promise* any happiness, for according to our conceptions of an order of nature in general, this is not necessarily connected with obedience to the law. Now Christian morality supplies this defect (of the second indispensable element of the *summum bonum*) by representing the world, in which rational beings devote themselves with all their soul to the moral law, as a *kingdom of God*, in which nature and morality are brought into a harmony foreign to each of itself, but a holy Author who makes the derived *summum bonum* possible. *Holiness* of life is prescribed to them as a rule even in this life, while the welfare proportioned to it, namely, *bliss*, is represented as attainable only in an eternity; because the *former* must always be the pattern of their conduct in every state, and progress towards it is already possible and necessary in this life; while the *latter*, under the name of happiness, cannot be attained at all in this world (so far as our own power is concerned), and therefore is made simply an object of hope. Nevertheless, the Christian principle of *morality* itself is not theological (so as to be heteronomy), but is autonomy of pure practical reason, since it does not make the knowledge of God and His will the foundation of these laws, but only of the attainment of the *summum bonum*, on condition of following these laws, and it does not even place the proper *spring* of this obedience in the desired results, but solely in the conception of duty, as that of which the faithful observance alone constitutes the worthiness to obtain those happy consequences.

In this manner the moral laws lead through the conception of the *summum bonum* as the object and final end of pure practical reason to *religion*, that is, to the *recognition of all duties as divine commands, not as sanctions*,[1] *that is to say, arbitrary ordinances of a foreign will and contingent in themselves*, but as essential *laws* of every free will in itself, which, nevertheless, must be regarded as commands of the Supreme Being, because it is only from a morally perfect (holy and good) and at the same time all-powerful will, and consequently only through harmony with this will, that we can hope to attain the *summum bonum* which the moral law makes it our duty to take as the object of our endeavors. Here again, then, all remains disinterested and founded merely on duty; neither fear nor hope being made the fundamental springs, which if taken as principles would destroy the whole moral worth of actions. The moral law commands me to make the highest possible good in a world the ultimate object of all my conduct. But I cannot hope to effect this otherwise than by the harmony of my will with that of a holy and good Author of the world; and although the conception of the *summum bonum* as a whole, in which the greatest happiness is conceived as combined in the most exact proportion with the highest degree of moral perfection (possible in creatures), includes *my own happiness*, yet it is not that this is the determining principle of the will which is enjoined to promote the *summum bonum*, but the moral law, which, on the contrary, limits by strict conditions my unbounded desire of happiness.

Hence also morality is not properly the doctrine how we should *make* ourselves happy, but how we should become *worthy* of happiness. It is only when religion is added that there also comes in the

---

[1] [The word "sanction" is here used in the technical German sense, which is familiar to students of history in connection with the "Pragmatic Sanction."]

hope of participating some day in happiness in proportion as we have endeavored to be not unworthy of it.

A man is *worthy* to possess a thing or a state when his possession of it is in harmony with the *summum bonum*. We can now easily see that all worthiness depends on moral conduct, since in the conception of the *summum bonum* this constitutes the condition of the rest (which belongs to one's state), namely, the participation of happiness. Now it follows from this that *morality* should never be treated as a *doctrine of happiness*, that is, an instruction how to become happy; for it has to do simply with the rational condition (*conditio sine qua non*) of happiness, not with the means of attaining it. But when morality has been completely expounded (which merely imposes duties instead of providing rules for selfish desires), then first, after the moral desire to promote the *summum bonum* (to bring the kingdom of God to us) has been awakened, a desire founded on a law, and which could not previously arise in any selfish mind, and when for the behoof of this desire the step to religion has been taken, then this ethical doctrine may be also called a doctrine of happiness because the *hope* of happiness first begins with religion only.

We can also see from this that, when we ask what is *God's ultimate end* in creating the world, we must not name the *happiness* of the rational beings in it, but the *summum bonum*, which adds a further condition to that wish of such beings, namely, the condition of being worthy of happiness, that is, the *morality* of these same rational beings, a condition which alone contains the rule by which only they can hope to share in the former at the hands of a *wise* Author.[1] For as *wisdom* theoretically considered signifies the *knowledge of the summum bonum*, and practically *the accordance of the will with the summum bonum*, we cannot attribute to a supreme independent wisdom an end based merely on *goodness*. For we cannot conceive the action of this goodness (in respect of the happiness of rational beings) as suitable to the highest original good, except under the restrictive conditions of harmony with the holiness of His will. Therefore those who placed the end of creation in the glory of God (provided that this is not conceived anthropomorphically as a desire to be praised) have perhaps hit upon the best expression. For nothing glorifies God more than that which is the most estimable thing in the world, respect for His command, the observance of the holy duty that His law imposes on us, when there is added thereto His glorious plan of crowning such a beautiful order of things with corresponding happiness. If the latter (to speak humanly) makes Him worthy of love, by the *former* He is an object of adoration. Even men can never acquire respect by benevolence alone, though they may gain love, so that the greatest beneficence only

---

[1] In order to make these characteristics of these conceptions clear, I add the remark that whilst we ascribe to God various attributes, the quality of which we also find applicable to creatures, only that in Him they are raised to the highest degree, e.g., power, knowledge, presence, goodness, &c., under the designations of omnipotence, omniscience, omnipresence, &c., there are three that are ascribed to God exclusively, and yet without the addition of greatness, and which are all moral. He is the *only holy*, the *only blessed*, the *only wise*, because these conceptions already imply the absence of limitation. In the order of these attributes He is also the *holy lawgiver* (and creator), the *good governor* (and preserver), and the *just judge*, three attributes which include everything by which God is the object of religion, and in conformity with which the metaphysical perfections are added of themselves in the reason.

procures them honor when it is regulated by worthiness.

That in the order of ends, man (and with him every rational being) is *an end in himself*, that is, that he can never be used merely as a means by any (not even by God) without being at the same time an end also himself, that therefore *humanity* in our person must be *holy* to ourselves, this follows now of itself because he is the *subject*[1] *of the moral law*, in other words, of that which is holy in itself, and on account of which and in agreement with which alone can anything be termed holy. For this moral law is founded on the autonomy of his will, as a free will which by its universal laws must necessarily be able to agree with that to which it is to submit itself.

---

[1] [That the ambiguity of the word *subject* may not mislead the reader, it may be remarked that it is here used in the psychological sense *subjectum legis*, not *subjectus legi*.]

Chapter **3**

Religious Faith and Proving God's Existence

There are two major questions to ask about the arguments or offered proofs for the existence of God. The first question to be asked about each argument is whether it is *logically strong*. Does the argument logically prove, or show to be probable, the existence of God? The readings of the last chapter relate to this question.

The other question to be asked about the arguments for the existence of God is: What is their *relevance* for religious faith? If we focus on the question "*Can* the existence of God be proven?" we may overlook the question of relevance, as many have. But it is just as important as the question of logical strength, if not more important. Say that we have somehow proven that God exists. Now the question comes up: What does this mean religiously? What relevance does this proof have for a religious life? Is such a proof a great support for religion (or those religions that believe in God, the theistic religions)? Or is such a proof actually detrimental to religious faith and commitment? Is such a proof needed by religion? Would such a proof bolster religious faith and make it stronger, or would it do just the reverse?

Over time four distinct answers to the relevance question have emerged. Each is significantly different from the others. Taken together they present us with a gamut of reactions.

1. A proof for the existence of God is relevant to religious faith in that there must be such a proof in order for faith in God to be proper.
2. A proof for the existence of God is in a way relevant to religious faith in that, while proper faith does not require a proof of God's existence, such a proof is helpful to the religious and does not hurt depth in religion.
3. Proofs for the existence of God are irrelevant to religious faith and can be distracting to the religious.
4. A proof for the existence of God is relevant to religious faith in a negative way in that such a proof would destroy faith.

Each of these four answers has seemed right to serious thinkers who have addressed this question, and many but not all of these thinkers have been committed religious individuals. All four answers have been fervently held because each answer has some kind of support.

The readings in this chapter are arranged under the four headings provided by the four answers to the relevance question. In the context of the discussion of this chapter a "proof" can be a conclusive argument or only very strong evidence for God's existence.

1.   A Proof for the Existence of God is Relevant to Religious Faith in that there must be Such a Proof in Order for Faith in God to be Proper.

W. K. CLIFFORD

from The Ethics of Belief

W. K. Clifford was a nineteenth-century philosopher and mathematician. In his essay "The Ethics of Belief" he maintained that "It is wrong always, everywhere, and for anyone to believe anything on insufficient evidence." If Clifford is right, then it is morally or epistemically wrong to believe there is a God on insufficient evidence. Proper belief, for Clifford, may not require a logical demonstration, but proper belief does require a "proof" in the sense of sufficient evidence. In our reading from "The Ethics of Belief" Clifford defends his claim and also considers when it is proper to believe on the "warrant" of authority.*

The Ethics of Belief[1]

I.—THE DUTY OF INQUIRY

A SHIPOWNER was about to send to sea an emigrant-ship. He knew that she was old, and not over-well built at the first; that she had seen many seas and climes, and often had needed repairs. Doubts had been suggested to him that possibly she was not seaworthy. These doubts preyed upon his mind and made him unhappy; he thought that perhaps he ought to have her thoroughly overhauled and refitted, even though this should put him to great expense. Before the ship sailed, however, he succeeded in overcoming these melancholy reflections. He said to himself that she had gone safely through so many voyages and weathered so many storms that it was idle to suppose she would not come safely home from this trip also. He would put his trust in Providence, which could hardly fail to protect all these unhappy families that were leaving their fatherland to seek for better times elsewhere. He would dismiss from his mind all ungenerous suspicions about the honesty of builders and contractors. In such ways he acquired a sincere and comfortable conviction that his vessel was thoroughly safe and seaworthy; he watched her departure with a light heart, and benevolent wishes for

* From W. K. Clifford, *Lectures and Essays*, 1886.
[1] *Contemporary Review*, January 1877.

the success of the exiles in their strange new home that was to be; and he got his insurance-money when she went down in mid-ocean and told no tales.

What shall we say of him? Surely this, that he was verily guilty of the death of those men. It is admitted that he did sincerely believe in the soundness of his ship; but the sincerity of his conviction can in no wise help him, because *he had no right to believe on such evidence as was before him*. He had acquired his belief not by honestly earning it in patient investigation, but by stifling his doubts. And although in the end he may have felt so sure about it that he could not think otherwise, yet inasmuch as he had knowingly and willingly worked himself into that frame of mind, he must be held responsible for it.

Let us alter the case a little, and suppose that the ship was not unsound after all; that she made her voyage safely, and many others after it. Will that diminish the guilt of her owner? Not one jot. When an action is once done, it is right or wrong for ever; no accidental failure of its good or evil fruits can possibly alter that. The man would not have been innocent, he would only have been not found out. The question of right or wrong has to do with the origin of his belief, not the matter of it; not what it was, but how he got it; not whether it turned out to be true or false, but whether he had a right to believe on such evidence as was before him.

There was once an island in which some of the inhabitants professed a religion teaching neither the doctrine of original sin nor that of eternal punishment. A suspicion got abroad that the professors of this religion had made use of unfair means to get their doctrines taught to children. They were accused of wresting the laws of their country in such a way as to remove children from the care of their natural and legal guardians; and even of stealing them away and keeping them concealed from their friends and relations. A certain number of men formed themselves into a society for the purpose of agitating the public about this matter. They published grave accusations against individual citizens of the highest position and character, and did all in their power to injure these citizens in the exercise of their professions. So great was the noise they made, that a Commission was appointed to investigate the facts; but after the Commission had carefully inquired into all the evidence that could be got, it appeared that the accused were innocent. Not only had they been accused on insufficient evidence, but the evidence of their innocence was such as the agitators might easily have obtained, if they had attempted a fair inquiry. After these disclosures the inhabitants of that country looked upon the members of the agitating society, not only as persons whose judgment was to be distrusted, but also as no longer to be counted honourable men. For although they had sincerely and conscientiously believed in the charges they had made, *yet they had no right to believe on such evidence as was before them*. Their sincere convictions, instead of being honestly earned by patient inquiring, were stolen by listening to the voice of prejudice and passion.

Let us vary this case also, and suppose, other things remaining as before, that a still more accurate investigation proved the accused to have been really guilty. Would this make any difference in the guilt of the accusers? Clearly not; the question is not whether their belief was true or false, but whether they entertained it on wrong grounds. They would no doubt say, "Now you see that we were right after all; next time perhaps you will believe us." And they might be believed, but they would not thereby become honourable men. They would not be innocent, they would only be not found out. Every one of them, if he chose to examine himself *in foro conscientice*, would know that he had acquired and nourished a belief, when he had no right to believe on such evidence as was before him; and therein he would know that he had done a wrong thing.

It may be said, however, that in both of these supposed cases it is not the belief which is judged to be wrong, but the action following upon it. The shipowner might say, "I am perfectly certain that my ship is sound, but still I feel it my duty to have her examined, before trusting the lives of so many people to her." And it might be said to the agitator, "However convinced you were of the justice of your cause and the truth of your convictions, you ought not to have made a public attack upon any man's character until you had examined the evidence on both sides with the utmost patience and care."

In the first place, let us admit that, so far as it goes, this view of the case is right and necessary; right, because even when a man's belief is so fixed that he cannot think otherwise, he still has a choice in regard to the action suggested by it, and so cannot escape the duty of investigating on the ground of the strength of his convictions; and necessary, because those who are not yet capable of controlling their feelings and thoughts must have a plain rule dealing with overt acts.

But this being premised as necessary, it becomes clear that it is not sufficient, and that our previous judgment is required to supplement it. For it is not possible so to sever the belief from the action it suggests as to condemn the one without condemning the other. No man holding a strong belief on one side of a question, or even wishing to hold a belief on one side, can investigate it with such fairness and completeness as if he were really in doubt and unbiassed; so that the existence of a belief not founded on fair inquiry unfits a man for the performance of this necessary duty.

Nor is that truly a belief at all which has not some influence upon the actions of him who holds it. He who truly believes that which prompts him to an action has looked upon the action to lust after it, he has committed it already in his heart. If a belief is not realised immediately in open deeds, it is stored up for the guidance of the future. It goes to make a part of that aggregate of beliefs which is the link between sensation and action at every moment of all our lives, and which is so organised and compacted together that no part of it can be isolated from the rest, but every new addition modifies the structure of the whole. No real belief, however trifling and fragmentary it may seem, is ever truly insignificant; it prepares us to receive more of its like, confirms those which resembled it before, and weakens others; and so gradually it lays a stealthy train in our inmost thoughts, which may some day explode into overt action, and leave its stamp upon our character for ever.

And no one man's belief is in any case a private matter which concerns himself alone. Our lives are guided by that general conception of the course of things which has been created by society for social purposes. Our words, our phrases, our forms and processes and modes of thought, are common property, fashioned and perfected from age to age; an heirloom which every succeeding generation inherits as a precious deposit and a sacred trust to be handed on to the next one, not unchanged but enlarged and purified, with some clear marks of its proper handiwork. Into this, for good or ill, is woven every belief of every man who has speech of his fellows. An awful privilege, and an awful responsibility, that we should help to create the world in which posterity will live.

In the two supposed cases which have been considered, it has been judged wrong to believe on insufficient evidence, or to nourish belief by suppressing doubts and avoiding investigation. The reason of this judgment is not far to seek: it is that in both these cases the belief held by one man was of great importance to other men. But forasmuch as no belief held by one man, however seemingly trivial the belief, and however obscure the believer, is ever actually insignificant or without its effect on the fate of mankind, we have no choice but to extend our judgment to all cases of belief whatever. Belief, that sacred faculty which prompts the decisions of our will, and knits into harmonious working all the compacted energies of our being, is ours not for ourselves, but for humanity. It is rightly used on truths which have been established by long experience and waiting toil, and which have stood in the fierce light of free and fearless questioning. Then it helps to bind men together, and to strengthen and direct their common action. It is desecrated when given to unproved and unquestioned statements, for the solace and private pleasure of the believer; to add a tinsel splendour to the plain straight road of our life and display a bright mirage beyond it; or even to drown the common sorrows of our kind by a self-deception which allows them not only to cast down, but also to degrade us. Whoso would deserve well of his fellows in this matter will guard the purity of his belief with a very fanaticism of jealous care, lest at any time it should rest on an unworthy object, and catch a stain which can never be wiped away.

It is not only the leader of men, statesman, philosopher, or poet, that owes this bounden duty to mankind. Every rustic who delivers in the village alehouse his slow, infrequent sentences, may help to kill or keep alive the fatal superstitions which clog his race. Every hard-worked wife of an artisan may transmit to her children beliefs which shall knit society together, or rend it in pieces. No simplicity of mind, no obscurity of station, can escape the universal duty of questioning all that we believe.

It is true that this duty is a hard one, and the doubt which comes out of it is often a very bitter thing. It leaves us bare and powerless where we thought that we were safe and strong. To know all about anything is to know how to deal with it under all circumstances. We feel much happier and more secure when we think we know precisely what to do, no matter what happens, than when we have lost our way and do not know where to turn. And if we have supposed ourselves to know all about anything, and to be capable of doing what is fit in regard to it, we naturally do not like to find that we are really ignorant and powerless, that we have to begin again at the beginning, and try to learn what the thing is and how it is to be dealt with—if indeed anything can be learnt about it. It is the sense of power attached to a sense of knowledge that makes men desirous of believing, and afraid of doubting.

This sense of power is the highest and best of pleasures when the belief on which it is founded is a true belief, and has been fairly earned by investigation. For then we may justly feel that it is common property, and holds good for others as well as for ourselves. Then we may be glad, not that *I* have learned secrets by which I am safer and stronger, but that *we men* have got mastery over more of the world; and we shall be strong, not for ourselves, but in the name of Man and in his strength. But if the belief has been accepted on insufficient evidence, the pleasure is a stolen one. Not only does it deceive ourselves by giving us a sense of power which we do not really possess, but it is sinful, because it is stolen in defiance of our duty to mankind. That duty is to guard ourselves from such beliefs as from a pestilence, which may shortly master our own body and then spread to the rest of the town. What would be thought of one who, for the sake of a sweet fruit, should deliberately run the risk of bringing a plague upon his family and his neighbours?

And, as in other such cases, it is not the risk only which has to be considered; for a bad action is always bad at the time when it is done, no matter what happens afterwards. Every time we let ourselves believe for unworthy reasons, we weaken our powers of self-control, of doubting, of judicially and fairly weighing evidence. We all suffer severely enough from the maintenance and support of false beliefs and the fatally wrong actions which they lead to, and the evil born when one such belief is entertained is great and wide. But a greater and wider evil arises when the credulous character is maintained and supported, when a habit of believing for unworthy reasons is fostered and made permanent. If I steal money from any person, there may be no harm done by the mere transfer of possession; he may not feel the loss, or it may prevent him from using the money badly. But I cannot help doing this great wrong towards Man, that I make myself dishonest. What hurts society is not that it should lose its property, but that it should become a den of thieves; for then it must cease to be society. This is why we ought not to do evil that good may come; for at any rate this great evil has come, that we have done evil and are made wicked thereby. In like manner, if I let myself believe anything on insufficient evidence, there may

be no great harm done by the mere belief; it may be true after all, or I may never have occasion to exhibit it in outward acts. But I cannot help doing this great wrong towards Man, that I make myself credulous. The danger to society is not merely that it should believe wrong things, though that is great enough; but that it should become credulous, and lose the habit of testing things and inquiring into them; for then it must sink back into savagery.

The harm which is done by credulity in a man is not confined to the fostering of a credulous character in others, and consequent support of false beliefs. Habitual want of care about what I believe leads to habitual want of care in others about the truth of what is told to me. Men speak the truth to one another when each reveres the truth in his own mind and in the other's mind; but how shall my friend revere the truth in my mind when I myself am careless about it, when I believe things because I want to believe them, and because they are comforting and pleasant? Will he not learn to cry, "Peace," to me, when there is no peace? By such a course I shall surround myself with a thick atmosphere of falsehood and fraud, and in that I must live. It may matter little to me, in my cloud-castle of sweet illusions and darling lies; but it matters much to Man that I have made my neighbours ready to deceive. The credulous man is father to the liar and the cheat; he lives in the bosom of this his family, and it is no marvel if he should become even as they are. So closely are our duties knit together, that whoso shall keep the whole law, and yet offend in one point, he is guilty of all.

To sum up: it is wrong always, everywhere, and for any one, to believe anything upon insufficient evidence.

If a man, holding a belief which he was taught in childhood or persuaded of afterwards, keeps down and pushes away any doubts which arise about it in his mind, purposely avoids the reading of books and the company of men that call in question or discuss it, and regards as impious those questions which cannot easily be asked without disturbing it—the life of that man is one long sin against mankind.

If this judgment seems harsh when applied to those simple souls who have never known better, who have been brought up from the cradle with a horror of doubt, and taught that their eternal welfare depends on *what* they believe, then it leads to the very serious question, *Who hath made Israel to sin?*

It may be permitted me to fortify this judgment with the sentence of Milton[1]—

"A man may be a heretic in the truth; and if he believe things only because his pastor says so, or the assembly so determine, without knowing other reason, though his belief be true, yet the very truth he holds becomes his heresy."

And with this famous aphorism of Coleridge[2]—

"He who begins by loving Christianity better than Truth, will proceed by loving his own sect or Church better than Christianity, and end in loving himself better than all."

Inquiry into the evidence of a doctrine is not to be made once for all, and then taken as finally settled. It is never lawful to stifle a doubt; for either it can be honestly answered by means of the inquiry already made, or else it proves that the inquiry was not complete.

"But," says one, "I am a busy man; I have no time for the long course of study which would be necessary to make me in any degree a competent judge of certain questions, or even able to understand the nature of the arguments." Then he should have no time to believe.

* * * * * * * * * * * * * * * * * * *

And if we admit for the sake of argument (for it seems that we cannot do more) that the progress made by Moslem nations in certain cases was really due to the system formed and sent forth into the world by Mohammed, we are not at liberty to conclude from this that he was inspired to declare the truth about things which we cannot verify. We are only at liberty to infer the excellence of his moral precepts, or of the means which he devised for so working upon men as so get them obeyed, or of the social and political machinery which he set up. And it would require a great amount of careful examination into the history of those nations to determine which of these things had the greater share in the result. So that here again it is the Prophet's knowledge of human nature, and his sympathy with it, that are verified; not his divine inspiration or his knowledge of theology.

If there were only one Prophet, indeed, it might well seem a difficult and even an ungracious task to decide upon what points we would trust him, and on what we would doubt his authority; seeing what help and furtherance all men have gained in all ages from those who saw more clearly, who felt more strongly, and who sought the truth with more single heart than their weaker brethren. But there is not only one Prophet; and while the consent of many upon that which, as men, they had real means of knowing and did know, has endured to the end, and been honourably built into the great

[1] *Areopagitica.* [2] *Aids to Reflection.*

fabric of human knowledge, the diverse witness of some about that which they did not and could not know remains as a warning to us that to exaggerate the prophetic authority is to misuse it, and to dishonour those who have sought only to help and further us after their power. It is hardly in human nature that a man should quite accurately gauge the limits of his own insight; but it is the duty of those who profit by his work to consider carefully where he may have been carried beyond it. If we must needs embalm his possible errors along with his solid achievements, and use his authority as an excuse for believing what he cannot have known, we make of his goodness an occasion to sin.

To consider only one other such witness: the followers of the Buddha have at least as much right to appeal to individual and social experience in support of the authority of the Eastern saviour. The special mark of his religion, it is said, that in which it has never been surpassed, is the comfort and consolation which it gives to the sick and sorrowful, the tender sympathy with which it soothes and assuages all the natural griefs of men. And surely no triumph of social morality can be greater or nobler than that which has kept nearly half the human race from persecuting in the name of religion. If we are to trust the accounts of his early followers, he believed himself to have come upon earth with a divine and cosmic mission to set rolling the wheel of the law. Being a prince, he divested himself of his kingdom, and of his free will became acquainted with misery, that he might learn how to meet and subdue it. Could such a man speak falsely about solemn things? And as for his knowledge, was he not a man miraculous with powers more than man's? He was born of woman

without the help of man; he rose into the air and was transfigured before his kinsmen; at last he went up bodily into heaven from the top of Adam's Peak. Is not his word to be believed in when he testifies of heavenly things?

If there were only he, and no other, with such claims! But there is Mohammed with his testimony; we cannot choose but listen to them both. The Prophet tells us that there is one God, and that we shall live for ever in joy or misery, according as we believe in the Prophet or not. The Buddha says that there is no God, and that we shall be annihilated by and by if we are good enough. Both cannot be infallibly inspired; one or other must have been the victim of a delusion, and thought he knew that which he really did not know. Who shall dare to say which? and how can we justify ourselves in believing that the other was not also deluded?

We are led, then, to these judgments following. The goodness and greatness of a man do not justify us in accepting a belief upon the warrant of his authority, unless there are reasonable grounds for supposing that he knew the truth of what he was saying. And there can be no grounds for supposing that a man knows that which we, without ceasing to be men, could not be supposed to verify.

If a chemist tells me, who am no chemist, that a certain substance can be made by putting together other substances in certain proportions and subjecting them to a known process, I am quite justified in believing this upon his authority, unless I know anything against his character or his judgment. For his professional training is one which tends to encourage veracity and the honest pursuit of truth, and to produce a dislike of hasty conclusions and slovenly investigation. And I have reasonable ground for supposing that he knows the truth of what he is saying, for although I am no chemist, I can be made to understand so much of the methods and processes of the science as makes it conceivable to me that, without ceasing to be man, I might verify the statement. I may never actually verify it, or even see any experiment which goes towards verifying it; but still I have quite reason enough to justify me in believing that the verification is within the reach of human appliances and powers, and in particular that it has been actually performed by my informant. His result, the belief to which he has been led by his inquiries, is valid not only for himself but for others; it is watched and tested by those who are working in the same ground, and who know that no greater service can be rendered to science than the purification of accepted results from the errors which may have crept into them. It is in this way that the result becomes common property, a right object of belief, which is a social affair and matter of public business. Thus it is to be observed that his authority is valid because there are those who question it

and verify it; that it is precisely this process of examining and purifying that keeps alive among investigators the love of that which shall stand all possible tests, the sense of public responsibility as of those whose work, if well done, shall remain as the enduring heritage of mankind.

But if my chemist tells me that an atom of oxygen has existed unaltered in weight and rate of vibration throughout all time I have no right to believe this on his authority, for it is a thing which he cannot know without ceasing to be man. He may quite honestly believe that this statement is a fair inference from his experiments, but in that case his judgment is at fault. A very simple consideration of the character of experiments would show him that they never can lead to results of such a kind; that being themselves only approximate and limited, they cannot give us knowledge which is exact and universal. No eminence of character and genius can give a man authority enough to justify us in believing him when he makes statements implying exact or universal knowledge.

T. H. HUXLEY

from Agnosticism

T. H. Huxley was a nineteenth century scientist. He recognized Charles Darwin's contribution to biology and publicly defended Darwin's evolutionary theory. In our selection from his "Agnosticism" he explains how "agnostic" means something distinguishable from "infidel" or "unbeliever." He also considers the evidential weight of biblical "testimony," and he tells us how he came to coin the term "agnostic."

From T.H. Huxley, *Lectures and Essays*, 1910.

Agnosticism

(1889)

Within the last few months, the public has received much and varied information on the subject of agnostics, their tenets, and even their future. Agnosticism exercised the orators of the Church Congress at Manchester. It has been furnished with a set of "articles" fewer, but not less rigid, and certainly not less consistent than the thirty-nine; its nature has been analyzed, and its future severely predicted by the most eloquent of that prophetical school whose Samuel is Auguste Comte. It may still be a question, however, whether the public is as much the wiser as might be expected, considering all the trouble that has been taken to enlighten it. Not only are the three accounts of the agnostic position sadly out of harmony with one another, but I propose to show cause for my belief that all three must be seriously questioned by any one who employs the term "agnostic" in the sense in which it was originally used. The learned Principal of King's College, who brought the topic of Agnosticism before the Church Congress, took a short and easy way of settling the business:—

> But if this be so, for a man to urge, as an escape from this article of belief, that he has no means of a scientific knowledge of the unseen world, or of the future, is irrelevant. His difference from Christians lies not in the fact that he has no knowledge of these things, but that he does not believe the authority on which they are stated. He may prefer to call himself an Agnostic; but his real name is an older one—he is an infidel; that is to say, an unbeliever. The word infidel, perhaps, carries an unpleasant significance. Perhaps it is right that it should. It is, and it ought to be, an unpleasant thing for a man to have to say plainly that he does not believe in Jesus Christ.[1]

So much of Dr. Wace's address either explicitly or implicitly concerns me, that I take upon myself to deal with it; but, in so doing, it must be understood that I speak for myself alone. I am not aware that there is any sect of Agnostics; and if there be, I am not its acknowledged prophet or pope. I desire to leave to the Comtists the entire monopoly of the manufacture of imitation ecclesiasticism.

Let us calmly and dispassionately consider Dr. Wace's appreciation of agnosticism. The agnostic, according to his view, is a person who says he has no means of attaining a scientific knowledge of the unseen world or of the future; by which somewhat loose phraseology Dr. Wace presumably means the theological unseen world and future. I cannot think this description happy, either in form or substance, but for the present it may pass. Dr. Wace continues, that it is not "his difference from Christians." Are there

---

[1] In this place there are references to the late Archbishop of York which are of no importance to my main argument, and which I have expunged because I desire to obliterate the traces of a temporary misunderstanding with a man of rare ability, candor, and wit, for whom I entertained a great liking and no less respect. I rejoice to think now of the (then) Bishop's cordial hail the first time we met after our little skirmish, "Well, is it to be peace or war?" I replied, "A little of both." But there was only peace when we parted, and ever after.

then any Christians who say that they know nothing about the unseen world and the future? I was ignorant of the fact, but I am ready to accept it on the authority of a professional theologian, and I proceed to Dr. Wace's next proposition.

The real state of the case, then, is that the agnostic "does not believe the authority" on which "these things" are stated, which authority is Jesus Christ. He is simply an old-fashioned "infidel" who is afraid to own to his right name. As "Presbyter is priest writ large," so is "agnostic" the mere Greek equivalent for the Latin "infidel." There is an attractive simplicity about this solution of the problem; and it has that advantage of being somewhat offensive to the persons attacked, which is so dear to the less refined sort of controversialist. The agnostic says, "I cannot find good evidence that so and so is true." "Ah," says his adversary, seizing his opportunity, "then you declare that Jesus Christ was untruthful, for he said so and so"; a very telling method of rousing prejudice. But suppose that the value of the evidence as to what Jesus may have said and done, and as to the exact nature and scope of his authority, is just that which the agnostic finds it most difficult to determine. If I venture to doubt that the Duke of Wellington gave the command "Up, Guards, and at 'em!" at Waterloo, I do not think that even Dr. Wace would accuse me of disbelieving the Duke. Yet it would be just as reasonable to

do this as to accuse any one of denying what Jesus said, before the preliminary question as to what he did say is settled.

Now, the question as to what Jesus really said and did is strictly a scientific problem, which is capable of solution by no other methods than those practiced by the historian and the literary critic. It is a problem of immense difficulty, which has occupied some of the best heads in Europe for the last century; and it is only of late years that their investigations have begun to converge towards one conclusion.[2]

That kind of faith which Dr. Wace describes and lauds is of no use here. Indeed, he himself takes pains to destroy its evidential value.

"What made the Mahommedan world? Trust and faith in the declarations and assurances of Mahommed. And what made the Christian world? Trust and faith in the declarations and assurances of Jesus Christ and His Apostles." The triumphant tone of this imaginary catechism leads me to suspect that its author has hardly appreciated its full import. Presumably, Dr. Wace regards Mahommed as an unbeliever, or, to use the term which he prefers, infidel; and considers that his assurances have given rise to a vast delusion which has led, and is leading, millions of men straight to everlasting punishment. And this being so, the "Trust and faith" which have "made the Mahommedan world," in

[2] Dr. Wace tells us, "It may be asked how far we can rely on the accounts we possess of our Lord's teaching on these subjects." And he seems to think the question appropriately answered by the assertion that it "ought to be regarded as settled by M. Renan's practical surrender of the adverse case." I thought I knew M. Renan's works pretty well, but I have contrived to miss this "practical" (I wish Dr. Wace had defined the scope of that useful adjective) surrender. However, as Dr. Wace can find no difficulty in pointing out the passage of M. Renan's writings, by which he feels justified in making his statement, I shall wait for further enlightenment, contenting myself, for the present, with remarking that if M. Renan were to retract and do penance in Notre-Dame tomorrow for any contributions to Biblical criticism that may be specially his property, the main results of that criticism, as they are set forth in the works of Strauss, Baur, Reuss, and Volkmar, for example, would not be sensibly affected.

just the same sense as they have "made the Christian world," must be trust and faith in falsehoods. No man who has studied history, or even attended to the occurrences of everyday life, can doubt the enormous practical value of trust and faith; but as little will he be inclined to deny that this practical value has not the least relation to the reality of the objects of that trust and faith. In examples of patient constancy of faith and of unswerving trust, the *Acta Martyrum* do not excel the annals of Babism.

The discussion upon which we have now entered goes so thoroughly to the root of the whole matter; the question of the day is so completely, as the author of "Robert Elsmere" says, the value of testimony, that I shall offer no apology for following it out somewhat in detail; and, by way of giving substance to the argument, I shall base what I have to say upon a case, the consideration of which lies strictly within the province of natural science, and of that particular part of it known as the physiology and pathology of the nervous system.

I find, in the second Gospel (chap. v.), a statement, to all appearance intended to have the same evidential value as any other contained in that history. It is the well-known story of the devils who were cast out of a man, and ordered, or permitted to enter into a herd of swine, to the great loss and damage of the innocent Gerasene, or Gadarene, pig owners. There can be no doubt that the narrator intends to convey to his readers his own conviction that this casting out and entering in were effected by the agency of Jesus of Nazareth; that, by speech and action, Jesus enforced this conviction; nor does any inkling of the legal and moral difficulties of the case manifest itself.

On the other hand, everything that I know of physiological and pathological science leads me to entertain a very strong conviction that the phenomena ascribed to possession are as purely natural as those which constitute smallpox; everything that I know of anthropology leads me think that the belief in demons and demoniacal possession is a mere survival of a once universal superstition, and that its persistence, at the present time, is pretty much in the inverse ratio of the general instruction, intelligence, and sound judgment of the population among whom it prevails. Everything that I know of law and justice convinces me that the wanton destruction of other people's property is a misdemeanor of evil example. Again, the study of history, and especially of that of the fifteenth, sixteenth, and seventeenth centuries, leaves no shadow of doubt on my mind that the belief in the reality of possession and of witchcraft, justly based, alike by Catholics and Protestants, upon this and innumerable other passages in both the Old and New Testaments, gave rise, through the special influence of Christian ecclesiastics, to the most horrible persecutions and judicial murders of thousands upon thousands of innocent men, women, and children. And when I reflect that the record of a plain and simple declaration upon such an occasion as this, that the belief in witchcraft and possession is wicked nonsense, would have rendered the long agony of medieval humanity impossible, I am prompted to reject, as dishonoring, the supposition that such declaration was withheld out of condescension to popular error.

"Come forth, thou unclean spirit, out of the man" (Mark v. 8),[3] are the words attributed to Jesus. If I declare, as I

---

[3] Here, as always, the revised version is cited.

have no hesitation in doing, that I utterly disbelieve in the existence of "unclean spirits," and, consequently, in the possibility of their "coming forth" out of a man, I suppose that Dr. Wace will tell me I am disregarding the testimony "of our Lord." For, if these words were really used, the most resourceful of reconcilers can hardly venture to affirm that they are compatible with a disbelief "in these things." As the learned and fair-minded, as well as orthodox, Dr. Alexander remarks, in an editorial note to the article "Demoniacs," in the "Biblical Cyclopædia" (vol. i, p. 664, note):—

> . . . On the lowest grounds on which our Lord and His Apostles can be placed they must, at least, be regarded as *honest* men. Now, though honest speech does not require that words should be used always and only in their etymological sense, it does require that they should not be used so as to affirm what the speaker knows to be false. Whilst, therefore, our Lord and His Apostles might use the word δαιμονίζεσναι, or the phrase, δαιμόνιον, ἔχεσιν as a popular description of certain diseases, without giving in to the belief which lay at the source of such a mode of expression, they could not speak of demons entering into a man, or being cast out of him, without pledging themselves to the belief of an actual possession of the man by the demons. (Campbell, *Prel. Diss.* vi. 1, 10.) If, consequently, they did not hold this belief, they spoke not as honest men.

The story which we are considering does not rest on the authority of the second Gospel alone. The third confirms the second, especially in the matter of commanding the unclean spirit to come

out of the man (Luke viii. 29); and, although the first Gospel either gives a different version of the same story, or tells another of like kind, the essential point remains: "If thou cast us out, send us away into the herd of swine. And He said unto them: Go!" (Matt. viii. 31, 32).

If the concurrent testimony of the three synoptics, then, is really sufficient to do away with all rational doubt as to a matter of fact of the utmost practical and speculative importance—belief or disbelief in which may affect, and has affected, men's lives and their conduct towards other men, in the most serious way—then I am bound to believe that Jesus implicitly affirmed himself to possess a "knowledge of the unseen world," which afforded full confirmation of the belief in demons and possession current among his contemporaries. If the story is true, the medieval theory of the invisible world may be, and probably is, quite correct; and the witch-finders, from Sprenger to Hopkins and Mather, are much-maligned men.

On the other hand, humanity, noting the frightful consequences of this belief; common sense, observing the futility of the evidence on which it is based, in all cases that have been properly investigated; science, more and more seeing its way to inclose all the phenomena of so-called "possession" within the domain of pathology, so far as they are not to be relegated to that of the police—all these powerful influences concur in warning us, at our peril, against accepting the belief without the most careful scrutiny of the authority on which it rests.

I can discern no escape from this dilemma: either Jesus said what he is reported to have said, or he did not. In the former case, it is inevitable that his authority on matters connected with the "unseen world" should be roughly shaken; in the latter, the blow falls upon the authority of the synoptic Gospels. If their report on a matter of such stupendous and far-reaching practical import as this is untrustworthy, how can we be sure of its trustworthiness in other cases?

* * * * * * * * * * * * * * * * * * *

From what precedes, I think it becomes sufficiently clear that Dr. Wace's account of the origin of the name of "Agnostic" is quite wrong. Indeed, I am bound to add that very slight effort to discover the truth would have convinced him that, as a matter of fact, the term arose otherwise. I am loath to go over an old story once more; but more than one object which I have in view will be served by telling it a little more fully than it has yet been told.

Looking back nearly fifty years, I see myself as a boy, whose education has been interrupted, and who, intellectually, was left, for some years, altogether to his own devices. At that time, I was a voracious and omnivorous reader; a dreamer and speculator of the first water, well endowed with that splendid courage in attacking any and every subject, which is the blessed compensation of youth and inexperience. Among the books and essays, on all sorts of topics from metaphysics to heraldry, which I read at this time, two left indelible impressions on my mind. One was Guizot's "History of Civilization," the other was Sir William Hamilton's essay "On the Philosophy of the Unconditioned," which I came upon, by chance, in an odd volume of the "Edinburgh Review." The latter was certainly strange reading for a boy, and I could not possibly have understood a great deal of it;[8] nevertheless, I devoured it with avidity, and it stamped upon my mind the strong conviction that, on even the most solemn and important of questions, men are apt to take cunning phrases for answers; and that the limitation of our faculties, in a great number of cases, renders real answers to such questions, not merely actually impossible, but theoretically inconceivable.

Philosophy and history having laid hold of me in this eccentric fashion, have never loosened their grip. I have no pretension to be an expert in either subject; but the turn for philosophical and historical reading, which rendered Hamilton and Guizot attractive to me, has not only filled many lawful leisure hours, and still more sleepless ones, with the repose of changed mental occupation, but has not unfrequently disputed my proper work-time with my liege lady, Natural Science. In this way I have found it possible to cover a good deal of ground in the territory of philosophy; and all the more easily that I have never cared much about A's or B's opinions, but have rather sought to know what answer he had to give to the questions I had to put to him—that of the limitation of possible knowledge being the chief. The ordinary examiner, with his "State the views of So-and-so," would have floored me at any time. If he had said what do *you* think about any given problem, I might have got on fairly well.

The reader who has had the patience to follow the enforced, but unwilling, egotism of this veritable history (especially if his studies have led him in the same direction), will now see why my mind steadily gravitated towards the conclusions of Hume and Kant, so well stated by the latter in a sentence, which I have quoted elsewhere.

---

[8] Yet I must somehow have laid hold of the pith of the matter, for, many years afterwards, when Dean Mansel's Bampton Lectures were published, it seemed to me I already knew all that this eminently agnostic thinker had to tell me.

"The greatest and perhaps the sole use of all philosophy of pure reason is, after all, merely negative, since it serves not as an organon for the enlargement [of knowledge], but as a discipline for its delimitation; and, instead of discovering truth, has only the modest merit of preventing error."[9]

* * * * * * * * * * * * * * * * * * *

This was my situation when I had the good fortune to find a place among the members of that remarkable confraternity of antagonists, long since deceased, but of green and pious memory, the Metaphysical Society. Every variety of philosophical and theological opinion was represented there, and expressed itself with entire openness; most of my colleagues were -*ists* of one sort or another; and, however kind and friendly they might be, I, the man without a rag of a label to cover himself with, could not fail to have some of the uneasy feelings which must have beset the historical fox when, after leaving the trap in which his

tail remained, he presented himself to his normally elongated companions. So I took thought, and invented what I conceived to be the appropriate title of "agnostic." It came into my head as suggestively antithetic to the "gnostic" of Church history, who professed to know so much about the very things of which I was ignorant; and I took the earliest opportunity of parading it at our Society, to show that I, too, had a tail, like the other foxes. To my great satisfaction, the term took; and when the *Spectator* had stood godfather to it, any suspicion in the minds of respectable people, that a knowledge of its parentage might have awakened was, of course, completely lulled.

That is the history of the origin of the terms "agnostic" and "agnosticism"; and it will be observed that it does not quite agree with the confident assertion of the reverend Principal of King's College, that "the adoption of the term agnostic is only an attempt to shift the issue, and that it involves a mere evasion" in relation to the Church and Christianity.

ALFRED, LORD TENNYSON

from In Memoriam

Alfred, Lord Tennyson was a Victorian poet who was very popular in Britain during the nineteenth century. He is "Lord Tennyson" because Queen Victoria made him a baron in 1884 when he was 75. Our reading consists of two verses from his long poem "In Memoriam," which he wrote in memory of his good friend Arthur Hallam. These two verses capture the idea of the "devout skeptic," one who wishes to believe in God, but will not dishonestly believe in the face of "honest doubt."*

[9] *Kritik der reinen Vernunft*. Edit. Hartenstein, p. 256.
* From *An Oxford Anthology of English Poetry*, by Howard Foster Lowry with the assistance of Howard C. Horsford. New York: Oxford University Press, 1956

from In Memoriam

LV

The wish, that of the living whole
    No life may fail beyond the grave,
    Derives it not from what we have
The likest God within the soul?

Are God and Nature then at strife,
    That Nature lends such evil dreams?
    So careful of the type she seems,
So careless of the single life;

That I, considering everywhere
    Her secret meaning in her deeds,
    And finding that of fifty seeds
She often brings but one to bear,

I falter where I firmly trod,
    And falling with my weight of cares
    Upon the great world's altar-stairs
That slope thro' darkness up to God,

I stretch lame hands of faith, and grope,
    And gather dust and chaff, and call
    To what I feel is Lord of all,
And faintly trust the larger hope.

XCVI

You say, but with no touch of scorn,
    Sweet-hearted, you, whose light-blue
      eyes

Are tender over drowning flies,
You tell me, doubt is Devil-born.

I know not: one indeed I knew
    In many a subtle question versed,
    Who touch'd a jarring lyre at first,
But ever strove to make it true:

Perplext in faith, but pure in deeds,
    At last he beat his music out.
    There lives more faith in honest
      doubt,
Believe me, than in half the creeds.

He fought his doubts and gather'd
      strength,
    He would not make his judgment
      blind,
    He faced the spectres of the mind
And laid them: thus he came at length

To find a stronger faith his own;
    And Power was with him in the night,
    Which makes the darkness and the
      light,
And dwells not in the light alone,

But in the darkness and the cloud,
    As over Sinaï's peaks of old,
    While Israel made their gods of gold,
Altho' the trumpet blew so loud.

H.H. PRICE

from Faith and Belief

The twentieth-century philosopher H. H. Price was concerned with the question of how one could be a philosopher and believe in God. If one believes in God and is a philosopher, then surely, Price says, "he ought to have good reasons for this belief of his." In our reading Price explores how such a philosopher, or anyone, might proceed by "entertaining" the "theistic hypothesis."

The *Te Deum*, from which Price quotes, is a hymn praising God. The Latin lines Price quotes translate as "We praise you O God, we acknowledge you as Lord . . . heaven and earth are full of the majesty of your glory."*

Faith and Belief

It may happen to a person that he realizes, with surprise perhaps, that he cannot help believing in God. This realization may come upon him suddenly, or it may dawn on him gradually over a period of time. He may or may not be able to recall some particular experience from which this belief-state appears to have resulted. If he can recall such an experience, he will probably prefer not to talk about it except to intimate friends, or not even to them. But at any rate his present condition is that he cannot help believing in God. He would not wish to give up this belief, even if he thought it psychologically possible for him to do so. It is the most precious possession that he has, and far from wishing to give it up, he would wish anyone else to be in a similar condition.

All the same, if the person we are speaking of happens to be a philosopher, it may well seem to him that he is in a very painful dilemma. Surely he ought to have good reasons for this belief of his. But it is very difficult to think of any, and not very difficult to think of pretty strong-looking reasons against it, from the ancient ones which constitute the Problem of Evil to the modern contention that the basic propositions of theism are unfalsifiable and therefore void of content.

* * * * * * * * * * * * * * * * * * * *

The painful dilemma of the philosopher is here represented as a conflict between duty and inclination. But it could also be represented as a conflict between two duties. For if someone does believe in God, he may well think he has a duty to God to continue believing in him, come what may, or at least to try to. And this duty, which he has (or sincerely thinks he has) as a religious person, may conflict with his duty as a philosopher to give up a belief which he can find no reason for holding, or at least to try his best to give it up.

But have we stated the problem correctly? Is there perhaps something inappropriate, out of place, in the suggestion that one should look for 'evidence' in favour of 'the theistic hypothesis'? If believing in God were just a case of believing *that*, of course the demand for evidence would be appropriate. But is it a case of believing *that*? Are we accepting a hypothesis when we believe in God, and has religion much to do with hypotheses at all?

The trouble is that the verb 'to believe' has two distinct functions. It

---

* From *Faith and the Philosophers*, edited by John Hick. New York: St. Martin's Press, 1964. Reproduced with permission of Palgrave Macmillan.

corresponds both to the noun 'faith' and to the noun 'belief'. A man who has faith in God is called a believer, and a man who has none is called an unbeliever. But in the other sense of the word 'belief', the propositional sense as we might call it, there are no unbelievers. There is no human being who believes no propositions at all. But there are very many human beings who have no faith in God.

The philosopher said he found himself believing in God. But the attitude in which he found himself to be was one of faith, rather than believing 'that'. The difference between these two attitudes may be brought out in another way. A person might believe that God exists and that he loves every one of us. He might believe these propositions with complete conviction. Yet such a person might still be completely irreligious. He might have no faith in God at all. He might not love him at all, nor even try to, nor trust him at all, nor pray to him, nor adore him. His metaphysical outlook, one might say, is theistic. But from the religious, as opposed to the theoretical, point of view, such a person might as well be an atheist. Perhaps there is even a sense in which he *is* an atheist, despite the strength of his theistic convictions. Or shall we say that he is an 'anti-God' theist? This presumably is the position of the devils mentioned in St. James's Epistle: 'Thou believest that there is one God. Thou doest well. The devils also believe, and tremble.'[1]

A more common situation (at least it used to be) is that of the person called in Catholic countries a *pococurante*—'one who cares little'. 'Oh, yes, of course there is a God and of course he loves every one of us, and no doubt he asks each one of us to love him. But what of it?' That is his attitude. *He* might as well be an agnostic, although metaphysically he is a convinced theist. At least, he has this in common with the agnostic, that both of them are in an attitude of indifference, though in the agnostic it is a state of cognitive indifference (suspense of judgement) whereas in the *pococurante* it is an indifference of the heart or of the will.

It is not of course that the man who has faith disbelieves these theistic propositions, or doubts them. It is rather that he does *more* than believe them. He has, or he claims to have, some sort or degree of personal relationship with the Being about whom these propositions are asserted. Faith, I would suggest, is not a propositional attitude at all. It is more like an attitude of loving adherence to a person, or at least to a Being with whom one may have personal relations. It is as if (in the old feudal manner) one had given one's allegiance to someone and accepted him—voluntarily and gladly—as one's lord. It is like an act of homage, but a continuing one, repeated whenever your thoughts turn towards him. And when your thoughts do turn towards him, it is not as if you were thinking of someone absent and far away; as Blondel, in the mediaeval story, might have thought with devoted loyalty of his lord King Richard, far away in a prison somewhere in Austria. No, the lord to whom you have given your allegiance is not far away from any one of us. We can address him whenever we will, and when we do, it is not like talking to empty air on the off-chance that someone may hear. It is like speaking to someone in whose presence you are.

If this is what the attitude of faith is like, or what it feels like to be in it, does believing 'that' have much to do with it?

[1] Chapter 2, verse 19.

Is it a propositional attitude at all? If you find yourself addressing someone and giving your allegiance to him, it is a little late in the day to ask the question 'Does he exist?' and look for evidence to support the hypothesis that he does. Such a question does not even occur to your mind. So if we use the word 'belief', we have to describe the man who has faith ('a believer') as one who believes *in* God, and distinguish between believing 'in' and believing 'that'. The term 'belief in' emphasizes the trust which is an essential part of the faith attitude. It does not sufficiently emphasize the love which is also an essential part of it. Still, it might be argued that one cannot trust someone unless one loves him at least a little. At any rate, it seems clear that 'faith without love' is a contradiction. Whereas 'believing *that* . . . without love' is no contradiction at all, even though the propositions believed are propositions about God.

* * * * * * * * * * * * * * * * * * * *

Faith, then, is something very unlike belief 'that' and certainly not reducible to it nor definable in terms of it. Yet we should be going too far if we said that faith has no connection whatever with believing 'that'. Beliefs 'that' are usually the precursors of faith, or at any rate propositional attitudes are, as we shall see presently. Moreover, beliefs 'that' are among the results of it. Those who have faith in God believe that he will be gracious to them in future as he has been in the past, that he loves not only themselves but everyone else too, that therefore they should try to love others because he does, and that he will help them to do this if they ask him, and humbly acknowledge the lack of love which is their present condition. But if a person has faith in God, does he believe *that* God loves him, even though as a result of his faith he does believe that God loves others? Surely

when a person is actually in the faith attitude, he would never say he believed that God loves him. It is rather that he *feels* God's love for him or feels the loving welcome he receives, like the Prodigal Son in the parable. It does not seem to be a matter of believing at all.

Again, even though we have actually been in the faith attitude sometimes, our faith may still be a very weak and vacillating one. (Hence it is proper to pray to God to make it firmer.) We may easily lapse out of the faith attitude even when we have occasionally been in it. In those periods of lapse—and they may be long—we have to fall back, as it were, on believing 'that', and even God's very existence may become a matter of believing 'that'. When we were actually in the faith attitude the question 'Does he exist?' did not even arise. We may remember that it did not, and how it seemed to us then that we were somehow in his presence. Or perhaps we do not remember this, because there is something in us which makes us wish to forget it. What Freud called 'active forgetting' plays a part in the lives of religious persons too, though Freud did not have them in mind when he first introduced this concept. Since it is theistic religion that we are considering, it is love which comes first, here as elsewhere. There is something in us (perhaps in everyone) which makes us wish to love God. But perhaps there is also something in us which makes us wish *not* to love him, nor to have anything to do with him, and even to wish that he did not exist. It is worth while to bear this possibility in mind when theism is described as 'wishful thinking'. There may be some wishful thinking in atheism too, and in agnosticism. Denial or doubt, or even suspense of judgement, *can* be 'wishful', as much as affirmation.

But even though we do have some memory of what it felt like to be in the faith attitude, and do recall (vaguely at least) how it seemed to us then that we were somehow in God's presence and feeling the loving welcome which we received—even so, we may begin to wonder whether this experience really was what it seemed to be at the time when we had it. Then the best we can manage is to believe *that* he exists and *that* he loves us, and *that* he will give us his aid to return to the faith attitude, if we sincerely wish for his aid and ask him to give it.

In this case our evidence for our beliefs 'that' is our own rather hazy memory of what it was like to be actually in the faith attitude. It may be almost like the evidence of testimony, though not quite. It may be almost, though not quite, as if another person were telling us about an experience which *he* had had. To put it another way: a faith attitude which is weak and vacillating, so that we are in it sometimes and at other times lapse out of it, can be regarded as a symptom of a divided personality, or at least of some degree of dissociation. There are some grounds for regarding it so, if conflicting wishes have something to do with this vacillation, as I have suggested they have. They are what one might call 'deep' wishes to. Both the wish to love God and the wish to have nothing to do with him are wishes which are close, as it were, to the centre of our personalities.

* * * * * * * * * * * * * * * * * * * *

The practices recommended are of at least two kinds. First, there are what may be called meditative practices. Here we voluntarily and privately fix our thoughts on the basic theistic propositions themselves. At this stage it is quite proper to describe these propositions as the contents of 'the theistic hypothesis'; for it *is* to us a hypothesis when we set out upon the activity of seeking. At this stage it is not necessary that we should believe it,

still less that we should believe it with full conviction. If we do believe it, the only evidence we have for it at this stage is the evidence of testimony, the testimony of religious persons. But all that is required of us is the suspension of disbelief; or if any more is required, it amounts only to 'suspecting that'—the traditional name for the lowest possible degree of belief, the minimum departure from the purely neutral attitude of suspense of judgement. This does not come to more than would be expressed by saying 'possibly the theistic hypothesis is not altogether false' or 'possibly there is after all something in it'.

The important thing at this stage is not the degree of belief (if any) that we have. What matters is that we should be *interested* in these theistic propositions and willing to take them seriously. What we have to do is to entertain them attentively and repeatedly, to ruminate upon them or let our thoughts dwell upon them, and to consider what it would be like if they were true. We can do this not only at set times, but at odd moments too, when we are walking in the street or sitting in the train. We may assist ourselves by reading some of the parables by which these propositions are illustrated in the Scriptures. To illustrate the proposition 'God loves every one of us' we can ruminate upon the parable of the Prodigal Son, for example. If any words have power, surely the words of the Gospel parables do. Not indeed if they just go in at one ear and out at the other (as they may, through sheer familiarity); but if they are ruminated upon, and pictured as far as possible in mental imagery, they have power to change a man's whole life. What our thoughts dwell on matters more than what we believe in the believing 'that' sense. As has been suggested already, a person might believe all the basic propositions of theism with complete and unshakeable conviction without either seeking for God or finding him.

The process I have been trying to describe may remind the reader of Newman's distinction between 'real' and 'notional' assent. We are not discussing assent at present, but only entertaining. Nevertheless, Newman's distinction applies to entertaining also, as he himself makes clear. (His name for entertaining is 'the apprehension of a proposition'.) The meditative practices I have described are intended to produce a change in our manner of entertaining the basic propositions of theism. Previously we had entertained them in a merely notional manner. But gradually, as a result of these meditative practices, we come to entertain them in a 'real' manner; or if one likes to put it so, we come to 'realize' what their import is, not indeed completely (no human being could), but to a much greater degree than we did before.

But these meditative practices, however important they are, are not the only ones which are recommended to those who wish to 'seek for God'. There are also others, equally inward, which are of a more directly devotional kind; and they raise more difficulties both for the person who is trying to practise them and for the philosopher who is trying to understand what is going on. For here we are recommended to take up emotional and conative attitudes and not merely cognitive ones. There are such forms of speech as prayers, hymns of praise and pious ejaculations.[1]

These are very typical expressions of the religious life, much more so than sentences in the indicative mood. We are now recommended not merely to listen to them, or read them, thoughtfully and attentively, but also to use them ourselves. We are to try to pray to God, inwardly, in our own hearts. Try to thank him, inwardly, for the blessings you have received. Consider such words of praise and adoration as the first few lines of the *Te Deum. Te Deum laudamus, Te Dominum confitemur . . . pleni sunt caeli et terra maiestate gloriae tuae.* Try to say them yourself, not just as splendid poetry, but as if you really meant what you say.

How can we possibly carry out such instructions? Surely we could only say such things if we had faith in God already, and a pretty firm faith too? But at present we are no more than 'seekers' and are not even sure that any such Being exists at all. It might not be too difficult to utter such words outwardly, just joining in with the congregation in church in public prayers, thanksgivings and praises; though even so, our 'seeker', if he is a reflective person, might wonder what on earth it is that he is doing. But saying such things inwardly, in inner speech, in the privacy of our own hearts, is a much more difficult matter, if our attitude is only one of taking a hypothesis seriously and suspecting that there might possibly be some truth in it.

Nevertheless, it can, I think, be done. So far as overt action is concerned, it is quite possible to act on a hypothesis, to do voluntarily things we should have done if we believed or knew it to be true, and to continue pertinaciously doing them for quite a long period. Sometimes we have to act in this way in order to find out whether a hypothesis *is* true. It is surely a mistake to suppose, as some do, that resolute and pertinacious action is only possible when we are already in a state of complete conviction. Human nature is not quite so weak as all that.

Now this applies to inward doing too. The inward use of these devotional

[1] For example the one attributed to St. Francis: *Deus meus et omnia!*

expressions is a kind of inward 'acting as if'. When a man is seeking for God he can act (inwardly) as he thinks a person would who had found him. To put it another way, he can try, voluntarily, to 'assume the role' of such a person, to put himself into such a person's shoes and speak (inwardly) as such a person would speak. He is doing something like what an actor does—the kind of actor who not only says the lines which are assigned to Hamlet in the play, but tries to feel as Hamlet may be supposed to have felt, or to 'identify' himself with the part that he is playing. It would seem that we all have this capacity for voluntarily 'assuming a role', and it could be argued, I think, that it is a more important capacity than we suppose. It enables one to experiment, as it were, with the possibility of being quite a different sort of person. The reading of imaginative literature has a rather similar function, and these devotional practices we are discussing could be regarded as imaginative exercises. One is trying to imagine what it would be like to be someone for whom the Lord's Prayer or the lines I quoted from the *Te Deum* are 'natural' things to say, the spontaneous and unforced expression of one's own emotional and conative attitudes. Such exercises are probably difficult for must of us. That is not a reason for refusing to try them. But we are not likely to have much success in them unless we have undertaken the meditative practices first, and so made ourselves able to entertain the basic theistic propositions in a 'real' and not merely 'notional' manner. In the devotional practices we have to act (inwardly) 'as if' there was a God who loves us all, and we can hardly do so unless we have ruminated for a considerable time on this proposition, and also perhaps on parables designed to illustrate it and 'bring home to us' what its import is.

So far, while we are only seeking, it is proper to speak of the theistic hypothesis and to ask what evidence we have for it. If I am right, the only evidence we have for it at this stage is the evidence of testimony. Whatever weight we give to this testimony and whatever personal respect we have for one or two of those who offer it, such evidence is nothing like conclusive. Perhaps we may think that if the theistic hypothesis were true, the evidence for it *ought* to have been conclusive. There is a story about a celebrated philosopher who was the guest of honour at a dinner of a society of agnostics. One of them asked him, 'What would you say if God himself suddenly appeared among us in this room?' The philosopher replied: 'God,' I should say, 'why did you make the evidence for your existence so inadequate?' This is indeed a problem which may trouble us. Perhaps the solution of it has something to do with the 'uncompellable' character of love. If the evidence had been conclusive and obvious to all, we should have been compelled to believe that God exists and perhaps also that he loves every one of us. But this would only be the settling of a theoretical question, no doubt a very important question, in the sense that the answers to many other theoretical questions depend on the answer given to this one. And what good would there be in settling this theoretical question, if one had no love at all for the Being whose existence was thus conclusively established? Perhaps God's will or plan was that we should love him; and love cannot be compelled, even if assent can. Love has to be given freely, if given at all. But if God must be sought for at the expense of considerable effort and trouble, and can only be found by those who wish to find him, they will love him when and if they do find him. We might even say that when of their own free will they undertook the search, and persisted in it in spite of disappointments, they were already being moved by a kind of incipient love for him. This perhaps is the interpretation of Pascal's paradox 'Thou couldst not seek me unless thou hadst already found me'.

The process of seeking may be long. There may be ups and downs in it. There may be times when it feels hopeless, when you do not seem to be making any progress at all and are tempted to give it up. There may be other times when you seem to be getting nearer, or even to have arrived just for a moment, and then you slip back again. It might also be said that the process of seeking never ends. To use a human analogy: suppose you have heard of some very wonderful person and want to meet him. You now have what you wished for; but once you have it, you wish for more. You do not have to seek for *him* any longer, but you still seek for something—to be as well acquainted with him as he will allow you to be.

So much for 'seeking'. But what of 'finding'? The 'finding', I suggest, is just the establishment of the personal relationship of faith *in* God. This, as has been said already, is not a propositional attitude at all. In the 'seeking' stage we were concerned with propositions all the time. We did not necessarily have to believe them, but our minds were continually occupied with them. In the meditational practices we tried to 'realize' the import of these propositions; in the devotional practices we tried to act (inwardly) as if they were true. These propositions purported to describe someone. We were by no means sure that there was any entity to which these descriptions applied. But now we begin to have experiences of being somehow in personal touch with One whom these descriptions fit. It is no longer a matter of speaking (inwardly) *as if* we were addressing him in a loving and reverent manner, or of voluntarily 'assuming the role' of one who does. Instead, we find ourselves actually addressing him (inwardly, in the privacy of our own minds and hearts) and now we use these devotional expressions spontaneously, without effort, just because it is the natural and appropriate thing to do. They are just the natural overflowing, as it were, of the attitude of personal devotion in which we now find ourselves to be—to our own surprise, perhaps. We use these expressions because that is how we feel towards Someone in whose presence we seem to be, Someone who seems to be giving us a loving welcome now that we are there.

Have we found him? Perhaps it might be more appropriate to say that he has found us. But even so, there is still some cognitive factor on our side. If he has found us, still, in some way or other, we are conscious that he has. The word 'encounter', which theologians sometimes use, has a similar implication. There is no encounter between A and B unless each of them is in some manner or degree *aware* of the other when they meet. If I encounter the Chief Constable in the lane, or he encounters me, it is not enough that he sees me or hears me say 'Good morning'. It is also necessary that I should see or hear *him*. Or if I am half-blind and three-quarters deaf (as this analogy would perhaps require) I must have some sort of visual or auditory perception of him, however dim and confused, or feel the touch of his hand if nothing else. And if the Chief Constable was looking for me and contrived the encounter himself, then certainly he has found me. But still in a sense I have found him too, even though he himself arranged that I should.

2.   A Proof for the Existence of God is in a Way Relevant to Religious Faith in that, while Proper Faith Does Not Require a Proof of God's Existence, such a Proof is Helpful to the Religious and Does Not Hurt Depth in Religion.

ST. THOMAS AQUINAS

from Summa Theologica, Parts I and II

For Aquinas, it is possible to prove that God exists, using the Cosmological Argument. He also believed that it is possible to prove other propositions about God, such as, that God is perfect and that God is one. Such provable propositions Aquinas called "preambles" to faith and he distinguished them from "articles of faith," which are above reason and must be accepted on faith. Aquinas did not think that everyone could master the proofs of the preambles. But some would be able to, and they would then attain *scientia* or "scientific knowledge" of the preambles (by "scientific knowledge" Aquinas meant a kind of systematic knowledge gained by reasoning). Aquinas understood that most would not be intellectual enough to master the proofs and gain scientific knowledge. It would remain open to them, however, to accept the preambles by faith. So the preambles could be accepted by faith or they could be known to be true with scientific knowledge by a given individual. But if one attained scientific knowledge of a preamble, then one no longer accepted it on faith: scientific knowledge ruled out faith. This was all right for Aquinas in that scientific knowledge did not weaken religious commitment. In this way, for Aquinas, at least one form of acceptance of the preambles of faith, either scientific knowledge or faith, was available to everyone, and neither form of acceptance was religiously hurtful. Aquinas went on to add that faith also provided the many believers who were unable to master the proofs with *a kind* of knowledge "free of doubt and uncertainty." He used the Latin word *cognitio* to name this kind of knowledge (from which in English we get "cognition").

In our reading we have several articles by Aquinas from Parts I and II of the *Summa Theologica*. In *ST* I, q.2, a.2 "Whether it can be Demonstrated that God Exists?" Aquinas claims that the existence of God can be demonstrated through his "effects," and in his reply to the first objection Aquinas distinguishes between "articles of faith" and "preambles to the articles." (In *ST* I, q.2, a.3, which we have in Chapter 2, Aquinas, using his "five ways," goes on to try to prove from God's "effects" that God exists.) In *ST* I, q.4, a.1 "Whether God is Perfect?" he endeavors to prove that God is perfect. In *ST* I, q.11, a.3 "Whether God is One?" he endeavors to prove that God is one and not many. In *ST* II-II, q.1, a.5 "Whether those things that are of Faith can be an Object of Science?" Aquinas clarifies the relationship between accepting a proposition on faith and knowing it by "science." In *ST* II-II, q.2, a.4 "Whether it is Necessary to Believe Those Things which can be Proven by Natural Reason?" Aquinas makes it clear that when human beings accept divine truths "delivered to them by way of faith" they are given a kind of knowledge "free of doubt and uncertainty."*

ST I, q. 2, a. 2

Second Article

WHETHER IT CAN BE DEMONSTRATED THAT GOD EXISTS?

We proceed thus to the Second Article:—
Objection 1. It seems that the existence of God cannot be demonstrated. For it is an article of faith that God exists. But what is of faith cannot be demonstrated, because a demonstration produces scientific knowledge, whereas faith is of the unseen, as is clear from the Apostle (*Heb.* xi. 1). Therefore it cannot be demonstrated that God exists.

Obj. 2. Further, essence is the middle term of demonstration. But we cannot know in what God's essence consists, but solely in what it does not consist, as Damascene says.[16] Therefore we cannot demonstrate that God exists.

Obj. 3. Further, if the existence of God were demonstrated, this could only be from His effects. But His effects are not proportioned to Him, since He is infinite and His effects are finite, and between the finite and infinite there is no proportion. Therefore; since a cause cannot be demonstrated by an effect not proportioned to it, it seems that the existence of God cannot be demonstrated.

On the contrary, The Apostle says: *The invisible things of Him are clearly seen, being understood by the things that are made* (*Rom.* i. 20). But this would not be unless the existence of God could be demonstrated through the things that are made; for the first thing we must know of anything is, whether it exists.

I answer that, Demonstration can be made in two ways: One is through the cause, and is called *propter quid*, and this is to argue from what is prior absolutely. The other is through the effect, and is called a demonstration *quia*; this is to argue from what is prior relatively only to us. When an effect is better known to us than its cause, from the effect we proceed to the knowledge of the cause. And from every effect the existence of its proper cause can be demonstrated, so long as its effects are better known to us; because, since every effect depends upon its cause, if the effect exists, the cause must preexist. Hence the existence of God, in so far as it is not self-evident to us, can be demonstrated from those of His effects which are known to us.

Reply Obj. 1. The existence of God and other like truths about God, which can be known by natural reason, are not articles of faith, but are preambles to the articles; for faith presupposes natural

[16] *De Fide Orth.*, I, 4 (PG 94, 800).

knowledge, even as grace presupposes nature and perfection the perfectible. Nevertheless, there is nothing to prevent a man, who cannot grasp a proof, from accepting, as a matter of faith, something which in itself is capable of being scientifically known and demonstrated.

Reply Obj. 2. When the existence of a cause is demonstrated from an effect, this effect takes the place of the definition of the cause in proving the cause's existence. This is especially the case in regard to God, because, in order to prove the existence of anything, it is necessary to accept as a middle term the meaning of the name, and not its essence, for the question of its

essence follows on the question of its existence. Now the names given to God are derived from His effects, as will be later shown.[17] Consequently, in demonstrating the existence of God from His effects, we may take for the middle term the meaning of the name *God*.

Reply Obj. 3. From effects not proportioned to the cause no perfect knowledge of that cause can be obtained. Yet from every effect the existence of the cause can be clearly demonstrated, and so we can demonstrate the existence of God from His effects; though from them we cannot know God perfectly as He is in His essence.

ST I, q. 4, a. 1

First Article

WHETHER GOD IS PERFECT?

We proceed thus to the First Article:—
Objection 1. It seems that to be perfect does not belong to God. For we say that a thing is perfect if it is completely made. But it does not befit God to be made. Therefore, neither does it befit Him to be perfect.

Obj. 2. Further, God is the first beginning of things. But the beginnings of things seem to be imperfect, for a seed is the beginning of animals and plants. Therefore God is imperfect.

Obj. 3. Further, as has been shown above, God's essence is being itself.[2] But being itself seems most imperfect, since it is most universal and receptive of all modification. Therefore God is imperfect.

On the contrary, It is written: *Be you perfect as also your heavenly Father is perfect* (*Matt.* v. 48).

I answer that, As the Philosopher relates,[3] some ancient philosophers, namely, the Pythagoreans and Speusippus, did not predicate *best* and *most perfect* of the first principle. The reason was that the ancient philosophers considered only a material principle; and a material principle is most imperfect. For since matter as such is merely potential, the first material principle must be absolutely potential, and thus most imperfect. Now God is the first principle, not material, but in the order of efficient cause, which must be most perfect. For just as matter, as such, is merely potential, so an agent, as such, is in a state of actuality. Hence, the first active principle must needs be most actual, and therefore most perfect; for a thing is said to be perfect in proportion to its actuality,

[17] Q. 13, a. I.   [2] Q. 3, a. 4.   [3] *Metaph.*, XI, 7 (1072b 30).

because we call that perfect which lacks nothing of the mode of its perfection.

Reply Obj. 1. As Gregory says: *Though our lips can only stammer, we yet chant the high things of God.*[4] For that which has not been made is improperly called perfect. Nevertheless, because things which come to be are then called perfect when from potentiality they are brought into actuality, this term *perfect* signifies by extension whatever is not wanting in actual being, whether this be by way of having been produced or not.

Reply Obj. 2. The material principle which with us is found to be imperfect, cannot be absolutely first, but is preceded by something perfect. For the seed, though it be the principle of the animal generated through it, has previous to it the animal or plant from which it came. Because, previous to that which is potential, must be that which is actual, since a potential being can be reduced to act only by some being already actual.

Reply Obj. 3. Being itself is the most perfect of all things, for it is compared to all things as that which is act; for nothing has actuality except so far as it is. Hence being is the actuality of all things, even of forms themselves. Therefore it is not compared to other things as the receiver is to the received, but rather as the received to the receiver. When therefore I speak of the being of man, or of a horse, or of anything else, being is considered as a formal principle, and as something received, and not as that to which being belongs.

ST I, q.11, a. 3

Third Article

WHETHER GOD IS ONE?

We proceed thus to the Third Article:—
Objection 1. It seems that God is not one. For it is written, *For there be many gods and many lords* (*1 Cor.* viii. 5).

Obj. 2. Further, *one*, as the principle of number, cannot be predicated of God, since quantity is not predicated of God; likewise, neither can *one* which is convertible with *being* be predicated of God, because it imports privation, and every privation is an imperfection, which cannot apply to God. Therefore God is not one.

On the contrary, It is written, *Hear, O Israel, the Lord our God is one Lord* (*Deut.* vi. 4).

I answer that, It can be shown from three sources that God is one. First from His simplicity. For it is manifest that the reason why any singular thing is *this particular thing* is because it cannot be communicated to many, since that whereby Socrates is a man can be communicated to many, whereas what makes him this particular man is communicable only to one. Therefore, if Socrates were a man by what makes him to be this particular man, as there cannot be many Socrateses, so there could not in that way be many men. Now this belongs to God alone; for God Himself is His own nature, as was shown above.[7] Therefore, in the very same way God is God and this God. It is impossible therefore that there should be many gods.

[4] *Moral.*, V, 36 (PL 75, 715).
[7] Q. 3, a. 3.

Secondly, this is proved from the infinity of His perfection. For it was shown above that God comprehends in Himself the whole perfection of being.[8] If, then, many gods existed, they would necessarily differ from each other. Something, therefore, would belong to one which did not belong to another. And if this were a privation, one of them would not be absolutely perfect; but if a perfection, one of them would be without it. So it is impossible for many gods to exist. Hence also the ancient philosophers, constrained as it were by truth, when they asserted an infinite principle, asserted likewise that there was only one such principle.

Thirdly, this is shown from the unity of the world. For all things that exist are seen to be ordered to each other since some serve others. But things that are diverse do not come together in the same order unless they are ordered thereto by some one being. For many are reduced into one order by one better than by many: because one is the *per se* cause of one, and many are only the accidental cause of one, inasmuch as they are in some way one. Since, therefore, what is first is most perfect, and is so *per se* and not accidentally, it must be that the first which reduces all into one order should be only one. And this is God.

Reply Obj. 1. Gods are called many by the error of some who worshipped many deities, thinking as they did that the planets and other stars were gods, and also the particular parts of the world. Hence the Apostle adds: *Our God is one*, etc. (*1 Cor.* viii. 6).

Reply Obj. 2. *One* which is the principle of number is not predicated of God, but only of material things. For *one* which is the principle of number belongs to the *genus* of mathematicals, which are material in being, and abstracted from matter only in idea. But *one* which is convertible with being is something metaphysical and does not, in being, depend on matter. And although in God there is no privation, still, according to the mode of our apprehension, He is known to us by way only of privation and remotion. Thus there is no reason why certain privative terms should not be predicated of God, for instance, that He is *incorporeal*, and *infinite*; and in the same way it is said of God that He is *one*.

ST II–II, q. 1, a. 5

Fifth Article

WHETHER THOSE THINGS THAT ARE OF FAITH CAN BE AN OBJECT OF SCIENCE?

We proceed thus to the Fifth Article:—
Objection 1. It would seem that those things that are of faith can be an object of science. For where science is lacking there is ignorance, since ignorance is the opposite of science. Now we are not in ignorance of those things we have to believe, since ignorance of such things belongs to unbelief, according to *1 Tim.* i. 13: *I did it ignorantly in unbelief.* Therefore things that are of faith can be an object of science.

[8] Q. 4, a. 2.

Obj. 2. Further, Science is acquired by arguments. Now sacred writers employ arguments to inculcate things that are of faith. Therefore such things can be an object of science.

Obj. 3. Further, Things which are demonstrated are an object of science, since a *demonstration is a syllogism that produces science.* Now certain matters of faith have been demonstrated by the philosophers, such as the existence and unity of God, and so forth. Therefore things that are of faith can be an object of science.

Obj. 4. Further, Opinion is further from science than faith is, since faith is said to stand between opinion and science. Now opinion and science can, in a way, be about the same object, as is stated in *Posterior Analytics* i.[18] Therefore faith and science can be about the same object also.

On the contrary, Gregory says that *when a thing is manifest, it is the object, not of faith, but of perception.*[19] Therefore things that are of faith are not the object of perception, whereas what is an object of science is the object of perception. Therefore there can be no faith about things which are an object of science.

I answer that, All science is derived from self-evident and therefore *seen* principles; and so all objects of science must needs be, in a fashion, seen.

Now, as was stated above, it is impossible that one and the same thing should be believed and seen by the same person. Hence it is equally impossible for one and the same thing to be an object of science and of belief for the same person. It may happen, however, that a thing which is an object of vision or science for one, is believed by another; for we hope to see some day what we now believe about the Trinity, according to *1 Cor.* xiii. 12: *We see now through a glass in a dark manner; but then face to face.* And this vision the angels possess already, so that what we believe, they see. In like manner, it may also happen that what is an object of vision or scientific knowledge for one man, even in the state of a wayfarer, is, for another man, an object of faith, because he does not know it by demonstration.

Nevertheless, that which is proposed to be believed equally by all is equally unknown by all as an object of science. Such are the things which are of faith absolutely. Consequently, faith and science are not about the same things.

Reply Obj. 1. Unbelievers are in ignorance of things that are of faith, for neither do they see or know them in themselves, nor do they know them to be credible. The faithful, on the other hand, know them, not as by demonstration, but by the light of faith which makes them see that they ought to believe them, as was stated above.

Reply Obj. 2. The arguments employed by holy men to prove things that are of faith are not demonstrations; they are either persuasive arguments showing that what is proposed to our faith is not impossible, or else they are proofs drawn from the principles of faith, *i.e.,* from the authority of Holy Scripture, as Dionysius declares.[20] Whatever is based on these principles is as well proved in the eyes of the faithful as a conclusion drawn from self-evident principles is in the eyes of all. Hence, again, theology is a science, as we stated at the outset of this work.[21]

Reply Obj. 3. Things which can be proved by demonstration are reckoned among what is of faith, not because they are believed absolutely by all, but because they are a necessary presupposition to matters of faith; so that those who do not

---

[18] Aristotle, *Post. Anal*, I, 33 (89a 25).   [19] *In Evang.*, II, hom. 26 (PL 76, 1202).
[20] *De Div. Nom.*, II, 2 (PG 3, 640).   [21] *S. T.*, I, q. 1, a. 2.

know them by demonstration must possess them at least by faith.

Reply Obj. 4. As the Philosopher says, *science and opinion about the same object can certainly be in different men,*[22] as we have stated above about science and faith; yet it is possible for one and the same man to have science and faith about the same thing relatively, *i.e.,* in relation to the object, but not in the same respect. For it is possible for the same person, about one and the same object, to know one thing and to have an opinion about another; and, in like manner, one may know by demonstration the unity of God, and believe that there are three Persons in God. On the other hand, in one and the same man, about the same object, and in the same respect, science is incompatible with either opinion or faith, but for different reasons. For science is incompatible with opinion about the same object absolutely, for the reason that science demands that its object should be deemed impossible to be otherwise, whereas it is essential to opinion that its object should be deemed possible to be otherwise. But that which is the object of faith, because of the certainty of faith, is also deemed impossible to be otherwise; and the reason why science and faith cannot be about the same object, and in the same respect, is because the object of science is something seen, whereas the object of faith is the unseen, as was stated above.

ST II-II, q. 2, a. 4

Fourth Article

WHETHER IT IS NECESSARY TO BELIEVE THOSE THINGS WHICH CAN BE PROVED BY NATURAL REASON?

We proceed thus to the Fourth Article:—
Objection 1. It would seem unnecessary to believe those things which can be proved by natural reason. For nothing is superfluous in God's works, much less even than in the works of nature. Now it is superfluous to employ other means, where one already suffices. Therefore it would be superfluous to receive by faith things that can be known by natural reason.

Obj. 2. Further, Those things must be believed which are the object of faith. Now science and faith are not about the same object, as was stated above.[18] Since, therefore, all things that can be known by natural reason are an object of science, it seems that there is no need to believe what can be proved by natural reason.

Obj. 3. Further, All things knowable by science would seem to have one nature; so that if some of them are proposed to man as objects of faith, in like manner the others should also be believed. But this is not true. Therefore it is not necessary to believe those things which can be proved by natural reason.

On the contrary, It is necessary to believe that God is one and incorporeal; which things philosophers prove by natural reason.

---

[22] *Post. Anal.,* I, 33 (89b 2).
[18] Q. 1, a. 5.

I answer that, It is necessary for man to receive by faith not only things which are above reason, but also those which can be known by reason; and this for three motives. First, in order that man may arrive more quickly at the knowledge of divine truth. For the science to whose province it belongs to prove the existence of God and many other such truths is the last of all to offer itself to human inquiry, since it presupposes many other sciences; so that it would be far along in life that man would arrive at the knowledge of God. The second reason is, in order that the knowledge of God may be more widespread. For many are unable to make progress in the study of science, either through dullness of ability, or through having a number of occupations and temporal needs, or even through laziness in learning; and all these persons would be altogether deprived of the knowledge of God, unless divine things were brought to their knowledge by way of faith. The third reason is for the sake of certitude. For human reason is very deficient in things concerning God. A sign of this is that philosophers, in their inquiry into human affairs by natural investigation, have fallen into many errors, and have disagreed among themselves. And consequently, in order that men might have knowledge of God, free of doubt and uncertainty, it was necessary for divine truths to be delivered to them by way of faith, being told to them, as it were, by God Himself Who cannot lie.

Reply Obj. 1. The inquiry of natural reason does not suffice mankind for the knowledge of divine truths, even of those that can be proved by reason; and so it is not superfluous if these be believed.

Reply Obj. 2. Science and faith cannot be in the same subject and about the same object; but what is an object of science for one can be an object of faith for another, as was stated above.[19]

Reply Obj. 3. Although all things that can be known by science have the notion of science in common, they do not all alike lead man to beatitude; and hence they are not all equally proposed to our belief.

3. Proofs for the Existence of God are Irrelevant to Religious Faith and Can be Distracting to the Religious.

NORMAN MALCOLM

from Is It A Religious Belief that "God Exists"?

In Norman Malcolm's essay "Anselm's Ontological Arguments" he argues that one version of the Ontological Argument is logically sound and does prove that God must exist. At the end of that essay, however, he raises the question of the relation of the Ontological Argument to religious belief. He goes on to allow

[19] *Ibid.*

that on might accept the argument as logically sound and yet not have a "living faith." In our reading in this chapter Malcolm uses the same distinction between kinds of *belief* cited by H. H. Price: belief *that* God exists and belief *in* God. Malcolm addresses the question whether the belief that God exists is a religious belief at all. His answer may be surprising.*

Is It A Religious Belief that 'God Exists'?

I admire the strategic plan of Alston's paper, and also the skill and thoroughness of his execution. I think his main results are entirely sound. I agree with his conclusion that even if it is a fact that 'reason-irrelevant' factors are sufficient to produce a belief in God's existence, this could have little or no tendency to show that the belief is false, or probably false, or unworthy of serious acceptance.

I agree also with Alston's comments on the Freudian view that religious belief is a form of neurosis, especially with his observation that we are likely to use the word 'neurosis' ambiguously, sometimes defining a belief as neurotic in terms of its supposed causation, sometimes in terms of its supposed injurious effect on a person's adjustment to reality.

It might be worth remarking that one could not expect a religious man to be well-adjusted to the world, if it is a teaching of his religion that he must cast off worldly considerations. A man who desired to be perfect was enjoined by Jesus to sell his possessions and give to the poor (Matthew 19:21). If any one of us were to believe in his heart that this is necessary and had the courage to act on it, he would thereby begin to live an abnormal life. This would have no tendency to prove that he had a neuropathic temperament, but rather that he was a doer of the word and not a hearer only.

At the same time it could be the case that certain forms of neuropathic disposition do contribute to an acute religious sensitivity. William James has put the point better than I can:

As regards the psychopathic origin of so many religious phenomena, that would not be in the least surprising or disconcerting, even were such phenomena certified from on high to be the most precious of human experiences. No one organism can possibly yield to its owner the whole body of truth. Few of us are not in some way infirm, or even diseased; and our very infirmities help us unexpectedly. In the psychopathic temperament we have the emotionality which is the *sine qua non* of moral perception; we have the intensity and tendency to emphasis which are the essence of practical moral vigour; and we have the love of metaphysics and mysticism which carry one's interests

* From *Faith and the Philosophers*, edited by John Hick. New York: St. Martin's Press, 1964. Reproduced with permission of Palgrave Macmillan.

beyond the surface of the sensible world. What, then, is more natural than that this temperament should introduce one to regions of religious truth, to corners of the universe, which your robust Philistine type of nervous system, forever offering its biceps to be felt, thumping its breast, and thanking Heaven that it hasn't a single morbid fibre in its composition, would be sure to hide forever from its self-satisfied possessors. (*The Varieties of Religious Experience*, Lecture I.)

The points of my disagreement with Alston occur only on the periphery of his paper. Although he thinks there is no logical impossibility in the supposition that belief in God could be produced by some 'reason-irrelevant' natural causation, yet he also thinks there would be something unsuitable about it. He would be 'mildly surprised' to learn that God did allow the belief in himself to be produced in this manner. I do not think I have any inclination to feel that this sequence of cause and effect would be somehow inappropriate. If such a causal explanation were true, then that is the way (or one way) God does it! Suppose we learned that the dividing of the Red Sea, which permitted the Israelites to escape from the Egyptians, was probably caused by a strong wind. Would there be anything inappropriate in the thought that this is how God accomplished his purpose? I cannot see that there would. Suppose there was a certain stimulation of the brain that produced a belief in God, and another that made one believe in one's country, or in science, or in psychoanalysis. Would this form of causation be more unsuitable in the first case than in the others?

A possible source of confusion may be the assumption that if belief in God was produced by reason-irrelevant natural causes, then the belief would have no rational content: one would not be able to expound or discuss one's belief in an intelligible way. I should agree that this would be a pretty poor sort of belief in God, hardly worthy of the name. But why would it have to be like that? Why could not some form of purely natural causation, even physiological, cause a man to have a belief in God that was full of intelligible content, so that he could relate this belief to Scripture, to the theological structure of his particular faith, and to the problems of human life?

Another objection which may be felt is that if a reason-irrelevant natural cause produced a belief in the existence of God, then the man who held this belief would not have any reasons or grounds for it. At least it would be true that reasoning did not help to produce his belief, this being so by hypothesis. One may think that the belief in God's existence, if one has it, *ought* to be, in part at least, derived from *grounds* of some sort. Does Alston think this? I suspect that he is pulled in opposite directions. On the one hand, he explicitly declares that there is nothing logically wrong with the idea that God might arrange that the belief in his existence was produced by reason-irrelevant natural causes. On the other hand, Alston confesses that he would be (mildly) *surprised* at such an arrangement. It is evident that his inclination to assume that God would not operate in that way is *a priori*; it is not based on some knowledge of how he normally does things. Thus it seems to me that Alston is inclined to deny, but also has some inclination to accept, the *a priori* proposition that if things were the way they ought (ideally) to be, the belief in God's existence would be derived, in part at least, from *grounds* for believing in his existence.

Behind the inclination to accept this proposition there stands the assumption that it must be *possible* for a person to have grounds for believing in the existence of God. Alston makes this assumption whole-heartedly. He says, for example, that if we could not have any '*a posteriori* grounds for deciding' whether God exists, this would be 'a severe blow to theistic belief'. He says that he feels confident that 'the order, or lack thereof, in the world, the existence of evil, and the facts of human morality, are the right sort of thing to consider . . . if we are looking for positive or negative evidence' of God's existence. Toward the end of his paper he draws the conclusion that 'in religion as elsewhere there is no substitute for the detailed examination of evidence which has a direct bearing on the truth or falsity of a given belief'.

Although I am in nearly perfect agreement with every detail of Alston's attack on the idea that a natural causal explanation of religious belief would or could undermine its truth or respectability, there is in the background of his work an assumption that seems to me to be unrealistic. The assumption is that there is a particular belief, namely, the belief that God exists, and with this belief as with any other we must make a distinction between causes of the belief and grounds or evidence for its truth.

What is unrealistic about this assumption? First of all, I must confess that the supposed *belief that God exists* strikes me as a problematic concept, whereas *belief in God* is not problematic. Some people believe in God and some do not. Some believe in God more (or less) strongly at one time than another.

Belief in God is partly, but only partly, analogous to belief in one's friend or one's doctor. Belief in another human being primarily connotes trust or faith in him. You believe in your friend: that is, you trust him to keep his word or to defend your interests. You believe in your doctor: that is, you trust his skill or his humane interest in his patients. You might trust someone *as* a typist but not *as* a translator. When you believe in a person what it is that you trust him to do (or to say or to think) would depend, of course, on the particular circumstances of the case.

Belief in a person primarily connotes trust or faith: but this is not so of belief in God. A man could properly be said to believe in God whose chief attitude toward God was *fear*. ('A sword is sent upon you, and who may turn it back?') But if you were enormously afraid of another human being you could not be said to believe in him. At least you would not believe in him *in so far* as you were afraid of him: whereas the fear of God is one form of belief in him.

I am suggesting that *belief-in* has a wider meaning when God is the object of it than when a human being is. Belief in God encompasses not only trust but also awe, dread, dismay, resentment and perhaps even hatred. Belief in God will involve some affective state or attitude, having God as its object, and those attitudes could vary from reverential love to rebellious rejection.

Now one is inclined to say that if a person believes in God surely he believes that God exists. It is far from clear what this is supposed to mean. Of course, if 'believing that God exists' is understood to mean the same as 'believing in God' (and this is not an entirely unnatural use of language) then there is no problem. But the inclination we are discussing is to hold that you could believe *that* God exists without believing *in* God. As I understand it, we are supposed to think that one could believe that God exists but at the same time have no affective attitude toward God. The belief that he exists would come first and the affective attitude might or might not come later. The belief that he exists would not logically imply any affective attitude toward him, but an affective attitude toward him would logically imply the belief that he exists.

If we are assuming a Jewish or Christian conception of God I do not see how one can make the above separation. If one conceived of God as the almighty creator of the world and judge of mankind how could one believe that he exists, but not be touched *at all* by awe or dismay or fear? I am discussing logic, not psychology. Would a belief that he exists, if it were completely non-affective, really be a belief that he exists? Would it be anything at all? What is the 'form of life' into which it would enter? What difference would it make whether anyone did or did not have this belief? So many philosophers who discuss these matters assume that the first and great question is to decide whether God exists: there will be time enough later to determine how one should regard him. I think, on the contrary, that a 'belief that God exists', if it was logically independent of any and all ways of regarding him, would be of no interest, not even to God.

JOHN CALVIN

from Concerning Faith, Together with an Explanation of The Creed, which They Call Apostolic

John Calvin, one of the leaders of the Protestant Reformation, was a Reformer and theologian. In our reading we have a section of Chap. Two of Calvin's *Institutes of the Christian Religion*, 1536 edition. Our reading consists of the section of the chapter in which Calvin distinguishes between "two kinds of faith."

Calvin says that there is one kind of faith when we believe that God exists or things about the life of Christ. This kind of faith is of "no importance," says Calvin. For, Calvin observes, referring to a passage in the New Testament, this kind of faith is held in common with "the devils," who, being acutely aware of God's existence, believe that God exists and that there is one God. (The passage referred to by Calvin is James 2.19, the same

From *Calvin: Institutes of the Christian Religion* (Library of Christian Classics) edited by John T. McNeill. Used by permission of Westminster John Knox Press.

passage referred to by H. H. Price.) The other kind of faith occurs when we "believe, not only that God and Christ exist, but also in God and Christ." It requires *in addition to the belief that God exists*, the hope and trust of belief *in*, or faith *in*, God.

CHAPTER 2

Concerning Faith, Together with an Explanation of The Creed, which They Call Apostolic

It can be understood sufficiently well from the discussion in the previous chapter what the Lord, by means of the law, has commanded us to do. Furthermore, if we should have fallen in part from the observance of the law, he decrees wrath and the terrible judgment of eternal death. Again, to fulfill the law, as the law requires, is not only difficult, but absolutely above our strength and beyond all our capacities. Wherefore, if we look only at ourselves, and think about what things may be worthy of us, there is nothing left of genuine hope, but, having been rejected by God, death and most certain confusion remain. And it has been explained already that there is but one way of escaping such a calamity, and one way which may restore us to a better condition, namely, the mercy of God which we most certainly experience, if we accept it with firm faith and rest securely in it. It remains for us to state the nature of this faith. This we may easily learn from the creed (which they call apostolic) which consists in a brief digest, and so to speak, as a certain epitome of the faith in which the Catholic Church concurs.

But before we proceed further, we must remember that there are two kinds of faith. The one kind is this: if anyone believes that God exists, or regards as true history that which he is told of Christ. This is as when we pronounce as true past events which are being reported, or present events which we witness. Now this kind of faith is of no importance, and as such is unworthy to be called faith. If any man should boast of such a faith, let him understand that he has it in common with the devils (James 2:19), its only outcome being that the devils are terrified, shaken, and confounded all the more. The other kind of faith is when we believe, not only that God and Christ exist, but also believe in God and in Christ, truly acknowledging God as our God and Christ as our Saviour. This, indeed, is not only to consider true all that which is written or said about God and Christ, but to put all our hope and trust in one God and Christ, and to be made steadfast by this knowledge that we do not doubt at all about the good pleasure of God toward us; that we may be firmly persuaded that whatever is necessary for us, not only in spirit, but also in body, will be given to us by him; that we may certainly expect that he will fulfill whatever the Scriptures promise concerning him; that we should not doubt at all that Christ is for us Jesus, that is, Saviour; that as we obtain the remission of sins and sanctification through him, so also salvation is given to us; that at last we may be led into the kingdom of God which will be revealed at the last day. And so this, indeed, is the capital part and, so to speak, almost the sum of those things which the Lord promises and offers to us in his Holy Word. This is the goal which he sets up in Scripture. This is the target which he places before us.

MARTIN BUBER

from Eclipse of God

Martin Buber, whose best known work may be *I and Thou*, was an important Jewish thinker who reflected on the nature of faith and religious belief. He wrote *Eclipse of God* near the middle of the twentieth century. In the preface to *Eclipse of God* Buber recounts an encounter he had with one who said he felt no need of God. Buber says that he felt challenged by this man and his attitude, and he proceeded to try to shake his sense of security by challenging his *Weltanschauung* or world view. He does so with an argument to the effect that we need God to account for perception. We need God to hold together the three "worlds" consisting of the world of our subjective experience, the world of objects "out there," and their meeting in the phenomenon of human perception. Buber's argument may not be all that forceful logically. But it does convince the man who felt no need of God. He says to Buber, "You are right." Buber, though, is not elated. He is dismayed. Why is he? Because, as he says, he had opened to this man the way to belief in "the God of the Philsophers," not the God of Religion, to whom one may say "Thou" and with whom one may enter into a trusting faith relationship.*

On three successive evenings I spoke at the adult folk-school of a German industrial city on the subject "Religion as Reality." What I meant by that was the simple thesis that "faith" is not a feeling in the soul of man but an entrance into reality, an entrance into the *whole* reality without reduction and curtailment. This thesis is simple but it contradicts the usual way of thinking. And so three evenings were necessary to make it clear, and not merely three lectures but also three discussions which followed the lectures. At these discussions I was struck by something which bothered me. A large part of the audience was evidently made up of workers but none of them spoke up. Those who spoke and raised questions, doubts, and reflections were for the most part students (for the city had a famous old university). But all kinds of other circles were also represented; the workers alone remained silent. Only at the conclusion of the third evening was this silence, which had by now become painful for me, explained. A young worker came up to me and said: "Do you know, we can't speak in there, but if you would meet with us to-morrow, we could talk together the whole time." Of course I agreed.

* From Martin Buber, *Eclipse of God*. New York: Harper & Row, 1952. Reprinted by permission.

The next day was a Sunday. After dinner I came to the agreed place and now we talked together well into the evening. Among the workers was one, a man no longer young, whom I was drawn to look at again and again because he listened as one who really wished to hear. Real listening has become rare in our time. It is found most often among workers, who are not indeed concerned about the person speaking, as is so often the case with the *bourgeois* public, but about what he has to say. This man had a curious face. In an old Flemish altar picture representing the adoration of the shepherds one of them, who stretches out his arms toward the manger, has such a face. The man in front of me did not look as if he might have any desire to do the same; moreover, his face was not open like that in the picture. What was notable about him was that he heard and pondered, in a manner as slow as it was impressive. Finally, he opened his lips as well. "I have had the experience," he explained slowly and impressively, repeating a saying which the astronomer Laplace is supposed to have used in conversation with Napoleon, "that I do not need this hypothesis 'God' in order to be quite at home in the world." He pronounced the word "hypothesis" as if he had attended the lectures of the distinguished natural scientist who had taught in that industrial and university city and had died shortly before. Although he did not reject the designation "God" for his idea of nature, that naturalist spoke in a similar manner whether he pursued zoology or *Weltanschauung*.

The brief speech of the man struck me; I felt myself more deeply challenged than by the others. Up till then we had certainly debated very seriously, but in a somewhat relaxed way; now everything had suddenly become severe and hard. How should I reply to the man? I pondered awhile in the now severe atmosphere. It came to me that I must shatter the security of his *Weltanschauung*, through which he thought of a "world" in which one "felt at home." What sort of a world was it? What we were accustomed to call world was the "world of the senses," the world in which there exists vermilion and grass green, C major and B minor, the taste of apple and of wormwood. Was this world anything other than the meeting of our own senses with those unapproachable events about whose essential definition physics always troubles itself in vain? The red that we saw was neither there in the "things," nor here in the "soul." It at times flamed up and glowed just so long as a red-perceiving eye and a red-engendering "oscillation" found themselves over against each other. Where then was the world and its security? The unknown "objects" there, the apparently so well-known and yet not graspable "subjects" here, and the actual and still so evanescent meeting of both, the "phenomena"—was that not already three worlds which could no longer be comprehended from one alone? How could we in our thinking place together these worlds so divorced from one another? What was the being that gave this "world," which had become so questionable, its foundation?

When I was through a stern silence ruled in the now twilit room. Then the man with the shepherd's face raised his heavy lids, which had been lowered the whole time, and said slowly and impressively, "You are right."

I sat in front of him dismayed. What had I done? I had led the man to the threshold beyond which there sat enthroned the majestic image which the great physicist, the great man of faith, Pascal, called the God of the Philosophers. Had I wished for that? Had I not rather wished to lead him to the other, Him whom Pascal called the

God of Abraham, Isaac, and Jacob, Him to whom one can say Thou.

It grew dusk, it was late. On the next day I had to depart I could not remain, as I now ought to do; I could not enter into the factory where the man worked, become his comrade, live with him, win his trust through real life-relationship, help him to walk with me the way of the creature who *accepts* the creation. I could only return his gaze.

SØREN KIERKEGAARD

from "Subjective Truth, Inwardness; Truth is Subjectivity"

Søren Kierkegaard was a Danish religious thinker who lived in the first half of the nineteenth century. He wrote many books trying to bring out the true character of religious faith, which he understood as being passionate and life-claiming. Some books he wrote under his own name, but for several he used a pseudonym. Especially in his pseudonymous books he was concerned to challenge the members of "christendom" to recognize the full demands of faith. Because of his emphasis on individual freedom, the passion and anguish of faith, the inwardness of the religious individual, and the life-involving demands of faith Kierkegaard is often regarded as the "father of existentialism." In this reading Kierkegaard says that the important kind of truth in religion is "subjectivity," as opposed to the "objective" truth of WHAT is believed, and in this reading he gives us the "parable of the idol-woshipper," as we may call it. Our reading is taken from his *Concluding Unscientific Postscript*, perhaps his best known work.*

from Subjective Truth, Inwardness; Truth is Subjectivity

When the question about truth is asked objectively, truth is reflected upon objectively as an object to which the knower relates himself. What is reflected upon is not the relation but that what he relates himself to is the truth, the true. If only that to which he relates himself is the truth, the true, then the subject is in the truth. When the question

* From KIERKEGAARD, SØREN; CONCLUDING UNSCIENTIFIC POSTSCRIPT TO PHILOSOPHICAL FRAGMENTS (2 vols.). © 1992 Princeton University Press. Reprinted by permission of Princeton University Press.

about truth is asked subjectively, the individual's relation is reflected upon subjectively. If only the how of this relation is in truth, the individual is in truth, even if he in this way were to relate himself to untruth.*

Let us take the knowledge of God as an example. Objectively, what is reflected upon is that this is the true God; subjectively, that the individual relates himself to a something *in such a way* that his relation is in truth a God-relation. Now, on which side is the truth? Alas, must we not at this point resort to mediation and say: It is on neither side; it is in the mediation? Superbly stated, if only someone could say how an existing person goes about being in mediation, because to be in mediation is to be finished; to exist is to become. An existing person cannot be in two places at the same time, cannot be subject-object. When he is closest to being in two places at the same time, he is in passion; but passion is only momentary, and passion is the highest pitch of subjectivity.

The existing person who chooses the objective way now enters upon all approximating deliberation intended to bring forth God objectively, which is not achieved in all eternity, because God is a subject and hence only for subjectivity in inwardness. The existing person who chooses the subjective way instantly comprehends the whole dialectical difficulty because he must use some time, perhaps a long time, to find God objectively. He comprehends this dialectical difficulty in all its pain, because he must resort to God at that very moment, because every moment in which he does not have God is wasted.** At that very moment he has God, not by virtue of any objective deliberation but by virtue of the infinite passion of inwardness. The objective person is not bothered by dialectical difficulties such as what it means to put a whole research period into finding God, since it is indeed possible that the researcher would die tomorrow, and if he goes on living, he cannot very well regard God as something to be taken along at his convenience, since God is something one takes along *à tout prix* [at any price], which, in passion's understanding, is the true relationship of inwardness with God.

It is at this point, dialectically so very difficult, that the road swings off for the person who knows what it means to think dialectically and, existing, to think dialectically, which is quite different from sitting as a fantastical being at a desk and writing about something one has never done oneself, quite different from writing *de omnibus dubitandum* and then as an existing person being just as credulous as the most sensate human being. It is here that the road swings off, and the change is this: whereas objective knowledge goes along leisurely on the

---

* The reader will note that what is being discussed here is essential truth, or the truth that is related essentially to existence, and that it is specifically in order to clarify it as inwardness or as subjectivity that the contrast is pointed out.

** In this way God is indeed a postulate, but not in the loose sense in which it is ordinarily taken. Instead, it becomes clear that this is the only way an existing person enters into a relationship with God: when the dialectical contradiction brings passion to despair and assists him in grasping God with "the category of despair" (faith), so that the postulate, far from being the arbitrary, is in fact *necessary* defense [N ø d værge], self-defense; in this way God is not a postulate, but the existing person's postulating of God is—a necessity [*Nødvendighed*].

long road of approximation, itself not actuated by passion, to subjective knowledge every delay is a deadly peril and the decision so infinitely important that it is immediately urgent, as if the opportunity had already passed by unused.

Now, if the problem is to calculate where there is more truth (and, as stated, simultaneously to be on both sides equally is not granted to an existing person but is only a beatifying delusion for a deluded *I-I*), whether on the side of the person who only objectively seeks the true God and the approximating truth of the God-idea or on the side of the person who is infinitely concerned that he in truth relate himself to God with the infinite passion of need— then there can be no doubt about the answer for anyone who is not totally botched by scholarship and science. If someone who lives in the midst of Christianity enters, with knowledge of the true idea of God, the house of God, the house of the true God, and prays, but prays in untruth, and if someone lives in an idolatrous land but prays with all the passion of infinity, although his eyes are resting upon the image of an idol—where, then, is there more truth? The one prays in truth to God although he is worshiping an idol; the other prays in untruth to the true God and is therefore in truth worshiping an idol.

* * * * * * * * * * * * * * * * * *

Objectively the emphasis is on what is said; subjectively the emphasis is on how *it is said*. This distinction applies even esthetically and is specifically expressed when we say that in the mouth of this or that person something that is truth can become untruth. Particular attention should be paid to this distinction in our day, for if one were to express in a single sentence the difference between ancient

times and our time, one would no doubt have to say: In ancient times there were only a few individuals who knew the truth; now everyone knows it, but inwardness has an inverse relation to it. Viewed esthetically, the contradiction that emerges when truth becomes untruth in this and that person's mouth is best interpreted comically. Ethically-religiously, the emphasis is again on: *how*. But this is not to be understood as manner, modulation of voice, oral delivery, etc., but it is to be understood as the relation of the existing person, in his very existence, to what is said. Objectively, the question is only about categories of thought; subjectively, about inwardness. At its maximum, this "how" is the passion of the infinite, and the passion of the infinite is the very truth. But the passion of the infinite is precisely subjectivity, and thus subjectivity is truth. From the objective point of view, there is no infinite decision, and thus it is objectively correct that the distinction between good and evil is canceled, along with the principle of contradiction, and thereby also the infinite distinction between truth and falsehood. Only in subjectivity is there decision, whereas wanting to become objective is untruth. The passion of the infinite, not its content, is the deciding factor, for its content is precisely itself. In this way the subjective "how" and subjectivity are the truth.

But precisely because the subject is existing, the "how" that is subjectively emphasized is dialectical also with regard to time. In the moment of the decision of passion, where the road swings off from objective knowledge, it looks as if the infinite decision were thereby finished. But at the same moment, the existing person is in the temporal realm, and the subjective "how" is transformed into a striving that is motivated and repeatedly refreshed by the decisive passion of the infinite, but it is nevertheless a striving.

4. A Proof for The Existence of God is Relevant to Religious Faith in A Negative Way in that Such a Proof Would Destroy Faith.

MIGUEL DE UNAMUNO

from The Agony of Christianity

Miguel de Unamuno was a Spanish thinker and philosopher whose life spanned the nineteenth and twentieth centuries. He gave a great deal of importance to faith, but he was convinced that true faith is marked by the agony of doubt and uncertainty. Much of his characterization of faith draws upon his Spanish and Catholic culture, although Unamuno was also influenced by the existentialist thought of Søren Kierkegaard. Our reading is from his *The Agony of Christianity*.*

III. What is Christianity?

Christianity must be defined agonically and polemically in terms of struggle. Perhaps it would be better to determine first what Christianity is not.

In Spanish, the oracular suffix *ismo* of *cristianismo*, "Christianism," carries with it the suggestion that Christianity is a doctrine like Platonism, Aristotelianism, Cartesianism, Kantianism, or Hegelianism. But this is not the fact of the matter. On the other hand we also have the splendid word *cristiandad*, which, signifying as it does the quality of being a Christian—as the word humanity signifies being a human being—has come to mean the community of Christians: Christendom. But this is manifestly an absurdity, for community kills Christianity, which involves only isolated souls. No one, of course, speaks of Platonianity, Aristotelianity, Cartesianity, Kantianity, or Hegelianity. And Hegelianity, the quality of being Hegelian, could

not be the same as Hegelity, the quality of being Hegel. Nevertheless, we do not distinguish between Christianity and *Christity*. For the quality of being Christian is the quality of being Christ. The Christian makes himself a Christ. St. Paul sensed this fact, for he felt Christ being born, agonize, and die in him.

St. Paul was the first great mystic, the first Christian properly so called. Though St. Peter was the first to whom the Master appeared, St. Paul beheld Christ within himself; Christ appeared to him, even though he believed that Christ had died and been buried (1 Cor. 15:3–8). And when he was caught up to the third heaven, without knowing whether in his body or out of it, for concerning such matters only God knows (many centuries later Teresa of Jesus will repeat the same thought) he heard "unspeakable words" ("dichos

* From KERRIGAN, ANTHONY; SELECTED WORKS OF MIGUEL De UNAMUNO, VOL. 3 © Princeton University Press, 1995 renewed PUP. Reprinted by permission of Princeton Univeristy Press.

indecibles," in Spanish, "unspeakable speakings," ἄρρρητα ῥήματα), an antithesis very much in the style of agonic mysticism (which is the mystical agony), which proceeds by antithesis, paradoxes, and even by tragic play upon words. For mystic agony plays upon words, plays upon the Word. It plays at creating the Word, as perhaps God played at creating the World, not so as to play with it later but to play in creation, inasmuch as the creation was a game. Once created, He delivered it over to the disputes of men and the agonies of the religions in search of God. And as for St. Paul, when he was caught up to the third heaven, to paradise, he heard *unspeakable words* not given to man to speak (2 Cor. 12:4).

Whoever feels incapable of understanding and sensing this experience, of knowing it in a biblical sense, of engendering and creating it in himself, let him renounce the comprehension not only of Christianity, but of anti-Christianity as well, of history itself, of life itself, of reality, of personality. Let him take up what is commonly called politics—aye, party politics at that—or let him turn to scholarship, devote himself to sociology, or to archeology.

Whoever or whatever one knows with mystic knowledge, through the interpenetration of essences, whether it be Christ, or any living, eternal man, or any and all human or divine power, it always comes to the same: that the knower becomes, in knowing, the known; the lover, in loving, the beloved.

When Lev Shestov, for example, discusses the thoughts of Pascal, he appears disinclined to grasp the fact that to be a Pascalian is not merely to accept his thoughts: it is also to be Pascal, to become Pascal. For my part, it has chanced that on several occasions,

whenever I have encountered in some book a man rather than a philosopher or a savant or a thinker, when I encountered a soul rather than a doctrine, I have exclaimed: "But I have been this man myself!" And thus I have lived again with Pascal in his own century and place, and I have lived again with Kierkegaard in Copenhagen, and so with others. And are these phenomena perhaps not the supreme proof of the immortality of the soul? May not these people live in me as I live in them? I shall know, after death, if I thus live on in others. Though even today may not some number of people outside me feel they live in me, even if I do not feel myself in them? What consolation! Leon Shestov opines that "Pascal carries with him no solace, no consolation," and further, that "he annihilates every kind of consolation." Many would agree, but how erroneously! There is no greater consolation than that which springs from dis-consolation, just as there is no more creative hope than that found in the hopelessly despairing, the desperate.

Men seek peace, they say. But do they—really? They are also said to seek liberty. Not so. They look for peace in time of war—and for war in time of peace. They seek liberty under tyranny— and tyranny when they are free.

And as far as liberty and tyranny are concerned, we should not say *homo homini lupus*, man acts like a wolf among men, but rather *homo homini agnus*, man acts like a lamb among men. The tyrant did not make the slave; the slave created the tyrant. A man offered to shoulder his brother, carry him on his back, and it was not the brother who forced him to do so. Man is essentially idle, and in his idleness he is horrified by responsibility.

Returning once again to the subject of mystic knowledge, let us recall the words of Spinoza: *Non ridere, non lugere, neque detestari, sed intelligere*: we should neither laugh, nor lament, nor detest—only understand. But—*intelligere*: understand? No; rather know in the biblical sense; love—*sed amare*. Spinoza spoke of "intellectual love"; but Spinoza was, like Kant, a bachelor and may have died a virgin. Spinoza and Kant and Pascal were bachelors; they were never, apparently, fathers; and neither were they monks in the Christian sense of the word.

Christianity, or better, Christendom, from the time of its birth in St. Paul, has not been a doctrine, though it has expressed itself dialectically. It has been a way of life, of struggle, an agony. The doctrine has been the Gospel; the Glad Tidings. Christianity has been a preparation for death and resurrection, for eternal life. If Christ be not risen from the dead, then we are of all men most miserable, cried St. Paul.

* * * * * * * * * * * * * * * * * * * *

And hence we have doubt, *dubium*, and struggle, *duellum*, and agony. The Epistles of St. Paul offer us the highest example of agonic style: not dialectic, but agonic, for there is no dialogue in it, but only strife and contention.

SØREN KIERKEGAARD

from "Subjective Truth, Inwardness; Truth is Subjectivity"

In the previous selection from Kierkegaard's writing, in the last section, we drew upon Kierkegaard's thinking as it relates to the religious perspective that proofs for the existence of God are irrelevant to faith, and even detrimental. Now, in this section, we need to turn to another and different aspect of his thinking. In the work in which we find the parable of the idol-worshipper Kierkegaard goes on to develop a "definition" of faith, and that definition is informed by and sustains the different form of religious sensibility that underlies the fourth answer: a proof of God's existence is so antithethical to religious faith that it would destroy it.

Paraphrased, Kierkegaard's definition of faith is that faith is the inward passion that arises from the constant struggle to hold fast in belief an "objective uncertainty," something that is uncertain. Without risk, Kierkegaard says, there is no faith. And risk requires uncertainty. Moreover, for Kierkegaard, the greater the risk the greater the faith. The object of religious belief or faith is the greatest uncertainty there can be. Kierkegaard called it "the absurd." It is the "contradiction" that the eternal (which exists outside time and is timeless) became temporal (and so existed in time). For Kierkegaard the absurd that faith must hold fast is that the eternal truth entered into time and took on human form. Kierkegaard has in mind the Christian idea of the incarnation in which the eternal God became a temporal man, Jesus of Nazareth; and here again we see his distinctly Christian thinking. However, although he does not say so, this idea of the absurd applies to Judaism and Islam as well, for in both these religions the eternal God enters into time to interact with men and women. For Kierkegaard, because the absurd is the greatest possible uncertainty, the faith that embraces it in belief—*religious* faith—is the greatest possible faith. This reading, like the previous selection from Kierkegaard's writing, is taken from a chapter of his *Concluding Unscientific Postscript* entitled "Subjective Truth, Inwardness; Truth is Subjectivity."*

from Subjective Truth, Inwardness; Truth is Subjectivity

When subjectivity is truth, the definition of truth must also contain in itself an expression of the antithesis to objectivity, a memento of that fork in the road, and this expression will at the same time indicate the resilience of the inwardness. Here is such a definition of truth: *An objective uncertainty, held fast through appropriation with the most passionate inwardness, is the truth*, the highest truth there is for an *existing* person. At the point where the road swings off (and where that is cannot be stated objectively, since it is precisely subjectivity), objective knowledge is suspended. Objectively he then has only uncertainty, but this is precisely what intensifies the infinite passion of inwardness, and truth is precisely the daring venture of choosing the objective uncertainty with the passion of the infinite. I observe nature in order to find God, and I do indeed see omnipotence and wisdom, but I also see much that

troubles and disturbs. The *summa summarum* [sum total] of this is an objective uncertainty, but the inwardness is so very great, precisely because it grasps this objective uncertainty with all the passion of the infinite. In a mathematical proposition, for example, the objectivity is given, but therefore its truth is also an indifferent truth.

But the definition of truth stated above is a paraphrasing of faith. Without risk, no faith. Faith is the contradiction between the infinite passion of inwardness and the objective uncertainty. If I am able to apprehend God objectively, I do not have faith; but because I cannot do this, I must have faith. If I want to keep myself in faith, I must continually see to it that I hold fast the objective uncertainty, see to it that in the objective uncertainty I am "out on 70,000 fathoms of water" and still have faith.*

* From KIERKEGAARD, SØREN; CONCLUDING UNSCIENTIFIC POSTSCRIPT TO PHILOSOPHICAL FRAGMENTS (2 vols.). © 1992 Princeton University Press. Reprinted by permission of Princeton University Press.

When the eternal truth relates itself to an existing person, it becomes the paradox. Through the objective uncertainty and ignorance, the paradox thrusts away in the inwardness of the existing person. But since the paradox is not in itself the paradox, it does not thrust away intensely enough, for without risk, no faith; the more risk, the more faith; the more objective reliability, the less inwardness (since inwardness is subjectivity); the less objective reliability, the deeper is the possible inwardness. When the paradox itself is the paradox, it thrusts away by virtue of the absurd, and the corresponding passion of inwardness is faith.

But subjectivity, inwardness, is truth; if not, we have forgotten the Socratic merit. But when the retreat out of existence into eternity by way of recollection has been made impossible, then, with the truth facing one as the paradox, in the anxiety of sin and its pain, with the tremendous risk of objectivity, there is no stronger expression for inwardness than—to have faith. But without risk, no faith, not even the Socratic faith, to say nothing of the kind we are discussing here.

When Socrates believed that God is, he held fast the objective uncertainty with the entire passion of inwardness, and faith is precisely in this contradiction, in this risk. Now it is otherwise. Instead of the objective uncertainty, there is here the certainty that, viewed objectively, it is the absurd, and this absurdity, held fast in the passion of inwardness, is faith. Compared with the earnestness of the absurd, the Socratic ignorance is like a witty jest, and compared with the strenuousness of faith, the Socratic existential inwardness resembles Greek nonchalance.

What, then, is the absurd? The absurd is that the eternal truth has come into existence in time, that God has come into existence, has been born, has grown up, etc., has come into existence exactly as an individual human being, indistinguishable from any other human being, inasmuch as all immediate recognizability is pre-Socratic paganism and from the Jewish point of view is idolatry. Every qualification of that which actually goes beyond the Socratic must essentially have a mark of standing in relation to the god's having come into existence, because faith, *sensu strictissimo* [in the strictest sense], as explicated in *Fragments*, refers to coming into existence. When Socrates believed that God is [*er til*], he no doubt perceived that where the road swings off there is a road of objective approximation, for example, the observation of nature, world history, etc. His merit was precisely to shun this road, where the quantifying siren song spellbinds and tricks the existing person. In relation to the absurd, the objective approximation resembles the comedy *Misforstaaelse paa Misforstaaelse* [Misunderstanding upon Misunderstanding], which ordinarily is played by assistant professors and speculative thinkers.

It is by way of the objective repulsion that the absurd is the dynamometer of faith in inwardness. So, then, there is a man who wants to have faith; well, let the comedy begin. He wants to have faith, but he wants to assure himself with the aid of objective deliberation and approximation. What happens? With the aid of approximation, the absurd becomes something else; it becomes probable, it becomes more probable, it may become to a high degree and exceedingly probable. Now he is all set to believe it, and he dares to say of himself that he does not believe as shoemakers and tailors and simple folk do, but only after long deliberation. Now he is all set to believe it, but, lo and behold, now it has indeed become impossible to believe it. The almost probable, the probable, the to-a-high-degree and exceedingly probable—that he can almost know, or as good as know, to a higher degree and exceedingly almost *know*—but *believe* it, that cannot be done, for the absurd is precisely the object of faith and only that can be believed.

Chapter **4**

Is Religious Belief Reasonable?

Many who are religious may never have asked themselves if their religious belief is reasonable, just as they may never have asked if God's existence can be proven. However, in the contemporary world where there is a great respect for science, being unreasonable can be a serious charge. Most of us, religious or not, would like to think that in most if not all things we are reasonable. This holds for the religious in accepting their religious belief, and it holds for those who reject religion because they believe it is unreasonable to accept religious belief in this day and age.

Among those who endeavor to be reasonable, religious individuals, if they are to avoid compartmentalization, will want to believe that their religious belief is reasonable or rational. On the other hand, those who reject religion because it is unreasonable or not rational or not grounded in reality, had better be confident that it truly is not reasonable. In this way, in some form, the question of whether religion is reasonable or rational addresses both the religious and those who reject religion.

In fact the question of the reasonableness of religious belief has a long history within religious reflection. The question of how faith and reason are related, and the question of how revelation and philosophy are related, go back to the early centuries of the Common Era. Thinkers in all three of the great monotheistic traditions of the West—Judaism, Christianity and Islam—reflected on the relationship between faith and reason, or, as it has been expressed, the relationship between Jerusalem and Athens (Jerusalem being the "home" of Christianity and of Judaism, and a sacred city for Islam, and Athens being the "home" of Western philosophy).

While there is a strain of religious sensibility that regards faith as deeply opposed to reason—represented by Unamuno and, at times, by Kierkegaard—the effort to show how reason and faith are compatible goes back to the beginning of the common Era. In the first century of the Common Era the Jewish thinker Philo of Alexandria tried to bring together the teachings of Moses in the Tenakh or Old Testament and the thought of the Greek philosopher Plato. Several centuries later the Christian thinker Augustine of Hippo, or St. Augustine, whose life bridged the fourth and fifth centuries, reflected on the relationship between faith and reason. In the Islamic tradition Avicenna (Ibn Sinā in Arabic), who lived 980–1030 C.E., and Averroes (Ibn Rushd in Arabic), who lived 1126–98 C.E., reflected on the Greek philosophical heritage. The Jewish thinker Moses Maimonides, who was born in the early part of the twelfth century, and the Christian thinkers St. Anselm of Canterbury in the eleventh century and St. Thomas Aquinas in the thirteenth century all offered arguments for the existence of God.

Usually those who have tried to prove the existence of God have wanted to show, not only that God exists, but that reason does not go counter to what faith accepts. The efforts to prove the existence of God embodied in the three traditional arguments, the Ontological, Cosmological, and Teleological Arguments, rely upon "natural reason" to "prove" the existence of God. They try either to show with a conclusive demonstration that God exists or to establish that there is strong evidence that God exists. However, well before Paley's attempt in the early nineteenth century to prove the existence of God with the Teleological Argument, some had begun to question the ability of natural reason to prove that there is a God. And so other ways were sought to show that religious faith was reasonable.

In this chapter we have four readings from four philosophers who address the question of the reasonableness of religious belief in different ways. None of these ways consists of an effort to prove that God exists. Each is an attempt to show that there is a way that belief that there is a God can be reasonable independently of proving that God exists. We shall begin with Pascal, a seventeenth-century author, and then move to William James, a nineteenth-century philosopher. The chapter concludes with two contemporary philosophers, Alvin Plantinga and William Alston, who address the issue of the reasonableness of religion in new and distinctive ways.

BLAISE PASCAL
The Wager

Blaise Pascal lived in France in the seventeenth century. He was a scientist and a mathematician, and he was also a committed religious believer. Over a number of years he wrote notes or reflections, most or all of which are on religious matters, directly or indirectly. He did not publish them during his lifetime, but after his death they were collected and published as the *Pensées* (or, in English, *Thoughts*). Many of his "thoughts" are only one sentence long, some a page long, and a few are longer. Pascal reflects on many religious themes in the *Pensées*, but the "thought" for which he is most often remembered is one several pages long that begins with *Infini-rien* (Infinity-nothing) and is usually given the title "The Wager." It is this "thought" that constitutes our reading. In it Pascal argues for a way that religious belief in God might be reasonable that does not rely upon proving that God exists. Pascal in fact assumes in "The Wager" that reason *cannot* prove either that God exists or that God does not exist.

"The Wager" in part takes the form of a dialogue, and Pascal imagines himself speaking directly to those who are faced with the question of whether to believe in God. Is there or is there not a God? Natural reason, Pascal allows, cannot decide this question. Nevertheless, we have to risk believing one way of the other. We "must bet. There is no option," Pascal maintains. We must either believe there is a God or not believe there is a God. So everyone faces the question

"Should I believe or not?" Which is the best bet, the better wager, to believe or not to believe? And everyone must decide, "must bet."

In "The Wager" Pascal introduces a sense of "reason" different from the sense of "reason" used by those who those who, like Aquinas, put forward "proofs" of God's existence. Reason in the sense of truth-proving natural reason cannot decide the question of God's existence, Pascal says. But reason in the sense of prudential reason, or benefit-calculating reason, can decide what is most reasonable to believe, what is most in a person's interest to believe; and that, concludes Pascal, is to believe that God exists.*

Infinity—Nothing: The Wager

Infinity—nothing. Our soul is cast into the body, where it finds number, time, and dimensions. On these it reasons, calling them natural and necessary, and it can believe in nothing else.

A unit joined to infinity adds nothing to it, any more than one foot added to infinite length. The finite is annihilated in the presence of infinity, and becomes a pure zero. So is our intellect before God, so is our justice before divine justice. But there is not so much disproportion between our justice and God's as there is between unity and infinity.

God's justice must be vast, like His compassion. Now justice towards the reprobate is less vast, and must be less amazing than mercy towards the elect.

We know that there is an infinite, and do not know its nature. As we know it to be untrue that numbers are finite, it is therefore true that there is a numerical infinity. But we do not know its nature; it cannot be even and it cannot be odd, for the addition of a unit cannot change it. Nevertheless it is a number, and all numbers are either even or odd (this is certainly true of every finite number). So, we may well know that there is a God without knowing what He is.

Is there no substantial truth, seeing that there are so many truths that are not the truth itself?

We know then the existence and nature of the finite, because we too are finite and have extension. We know the existence of the infinite, and do not know its nature, because it has extension like us, but unlike us no limits. But we know neither the existence nor the nature of God, because He has neither extension nor limits.

But by faith we know that He exists; in glory we shall know His nature. Now I have already shown that we can very well know a thing exists without knowing its nature.

Let us now speak according to the light of nature.

If there is a God, He is infinitely incomprehensible, since, being undivided and without limits, He bears no relation to us. We are, therefore, incapable of knowing either what He is, or whether He exists. This being so, who will be so rash as to decide the question? Not we who bear no relation to Him.

Who, then, will blame Christians for being unable to give a reason for their belief, since they profess a religion which they cannot explain by reason? In proclaiming it to the world, they declare

* From *Pensées* by Blaise Pascal, translated with a revised introduction by A. J. Krailsheimer (Penguin Classics 1966, Revised edition 1995). Copyright © A. J. Krailsheimer, 1966, 1995.

that it is a foolishness, *stultitiam*,—and then you complain that they do not prove it. If they proved it, they would be denying their own statement; their lack of proof shows that they are not lacking in sense.

'Yes, but although this excuses those who present religion in that way, and we cannot, therefore, blame them for doing so without advancing reasons, it does not excuse those who accept it.'

Let us then examine this point, and say: 'Either God is, or He is not.' But which side shall we take? Reason can decide nothing here; there is an infinite chaos between us. A game is on, at the other side of this infinite distance, and the coin will fall heads or tails. Which will you gamble on? According to reason you cannot gamble on either; according to reason you cannot defend either choice.

But do not blame those who have decided for making a wrong choice; you know nothing about the matter.

'No, I shall not blame them for the choice they have made, but for making any choice at all. For the man who calls heads and the man who calls tails have made the same mistake. They are both wrong: the proper thing is not to bet at all.'

Yes, but you must bet. There is no option; you have embarked on the business. Which will you choose, then? Let us see. Since you must choose, let us see which will profit you less. You have two things to lose: truth and good, and two things to stake: your reason and your will, your knowledge and your happiness. And your nature has two things to avoid: error and misery. Since you must necessarily choose, it is no more unreasonable to make one choice than the other. That is one point cleared up. But your happiness? Let us weigh the gain and loss in calling heads, that God exists. Let us estimate the two chances; if you win, you win everything; if you lose, you lose nothing. Do not hesitate, then; gamble on His existence.

'This is splendid. Yes, I must make the bet; but perhaps I shall stake too much.'

Let us see. There being an equal chance of gain or loss, supposing you had two lives to gain for one, you might still gamble. But if you stood to gain three you would have to (being compelled to take part in the game). And since you have, to play you would be foolish not to stake your one life for three in a game where the chances of gain and loss are equal. But here there is an eternity of life and happiness to be won. And this being so, even if there were an infinity of chances and only one in your favour, you would be right to stake one life against two; and it would be absurd, since you are compelled to play, to refuse to stake one life against three in a game in which one of an infinity of chances is in your favour, if what you stood to gain was an infinity of infinite happiness. But there *is* an infinity of infinite happiness to be gained, there is one chance of winning against a finite number of chances that you will lose, and what you are staking is finite. And so, since you are compelled to play, you would be mad to cling to your life instead of risking it for an infinite gain, which is as liable to turn up as a loss—of nothing.

For it is no use saying that our gain is uncertain, and that the infinite distance between the certainty of what we stake and the uncertainty of what we gain puts the finite good which we certainly risk on a level with the infinite, which is uncertain. This is not the case. Every gambler risks a certain sum to gain an uncertain one; and yet when he, stakes a finite certainty to gain a finite uncertainty, he is not acting unreasonably. There is not an infinite difference between the certainty of the stake and the uncertainty of the gain; not at all. There is, indeed, an infinity between the certainty of gain and the certainty of loss. But the uncertainty of winning is proportionate to the certain amount of the stake, and the odds in favour of gain or loss.[1] If therefore there are as many chances on one side as on the other, the odds are equal; and the fixed sum at stake is equal to the uncertain gain; there is no infinity of difference between them. And so our argument is infinitely strong when only the finite is at stake in a game in which the chances of gain and loss are equal, and infinity is to be won. This is demonstrable; and if men are susceptible to any truth, here is one.

'I confess and admit it. But yet, is there no way of seeing the face of the cards?'. . .

Yes, Holy Scripture and other writings, etc.

'Yes. But my hands are tied and my mouth is gagged. I am forced to play, and I am not free. Something holds me back, for I am so made that I cannot believe. What would you have me do?'

What you say is true. But at least be aware that your inability to believe arises from your passions. For your reason urges you to it, and yet you find it impossible. Endeavour, therefore, to gain conviction, not by an increase of divine proofs, but by the diminution of your passions. You wish to come to faith, but do not know the way. You wish to cure yourself of unbelief, and you ask for remedies. Learn from those who have been hampered like you, and who now stake all their possessions. These are the people who know the road that you wish to follow; they are cured of the disease of which you wish to be cured. Follow the way by which they began: by behaving as if they believed, by taking holy water, by having masses said, etc. This will bring you to belief in the natural way, and will soothe your mind.

'But that is just what I am afraid of.'

And why? What have you to lose?

But to show you that this will lead you there, it is this that will lessen your passions, which are your great obstacles. (*End of this discourse.*) Now what harm will come to you if you follow this course? You will be faithful, honest, humble, grateful, generous, a sincere friend, and a truthful man. Certainly you will be without those poisonous pleasures, ambition and luxury. But will you not have others? I tell you that you will gain in this life, and that at every step you take on this road you will see such certainty of gain and such nothingness in your stake that you will finally realize you have gambled on something certain and infinite, and have risked nothing for it.

'Oh your words transport me, ravish me, etc.'

If this argument pleases you, and seems convincing, let me say that it is the utterance of a man who has knelt before and after, praying that infinite and undivided Being to whom he submits all he has that He may bring all your being likewise into submission, for your own good and His glory, and that thus strength may be brought into touch with weakness.

WILLIAM JAMES

from The Will to Believe

William James in our reading from "The Will to Believe" criticizes Pascal's wager thinking, but he also tries to extend and correct it. Pascal was right, James thought, that there are instances where it is permissible to believe

[1] e.g. in buying a lottery ticket, we are buying a proportion of the total chances of winning, which is decided by the number of tickets sold.

when there is no proof, no deciding evidence, but Pascal left something out. He left out the role of our "passional nature"—our personal fears, hopes, desires—and these, James argues, in certain cases, can provide a justification for our choosing to believe in God if evidence cannot decide the matter. James argues for this in the essay in our reading, which he entitled "The Will to Believe," but he might better have entitled his essay "The Right to Believe," for in fact, as he says in the introductory page to his essay (not in our selection), he is going to offer "a defense of our right to adopt a believing attitude in religious matters." He argues for our *epistemic right* (that is, our belief-related right) to hold a religious belief—at least under certain circumstances.

James starts his essay by distinguishing several kinds of belief-options. We face a belief option when we have a decision or a choice between beliefs, even if it is only a choice between believing something and not believing it. But not all belief-options are the same. James draws to our attention three kinds. One kind of belief-option is that between *live* beliefs or possible beliefs. A belief-option of this sort James calls a *living option* (vs. a *dead option*). Belief-options can also be *forced* (vs. *avoidable*) and *momentous* (vs. *trivial*).

When a belief-option is *living, forced*, and *momentous* James calls it a *genuine option*. James argues for an important thesis about genuine options. He offers it as a general thesis, but, as he is aware, it has great significance for religious belief and for our right to believe religiously. His thesis is: "Our passional nature not only lawfully may, but must decide an option between propositions [that is, between proposed beliefs] whenever it is a genuine option that cannot by its nature be decided on intellectual grounds."

If James is right, then there are times when it is epistemically permissible to believe without sufficient "intellectual grounds." This would mean that W. K. Clifford was wrong when he claimed that it is always wrong to believe on insufficient evidence. In his essay James acknowledges Clifford and his thesis, and he in effect argues that it should be modified.*

The Will to Believe[1]

I

Let us give the name of *hypothesis* to anything that may be proposed to our belief; and just as the electricians speak of live and dead wires, let us speak of any hypothesis as either *live* or *dead*. A live hypothesis is one which appeals as a real possibility to him to whom it is proposed.

If I ask you to believe in the Mahdi, the notion makes no electric connection with your nature—it refuses to scintillate with any credibility at all. As an hypothesis it is completely dead. To an Arab, however (even if he be not one of the Mahdi's followers), the hypothesis is among the mind's possibilities: it is alive. This shows

---

* From William James, "The Will to Belive".
[1] An Address to the Philosophical Clubs of Yale and Brown Universities. Published in the *New World*, June, 1896.

that deadness and liveness in an hypothesis are not intrinsic properties, but relations to the individual thinker. They are measured by his willingness to act. The maximum of liveness in an hypothesis means willingness to act irrevocably. Practically, that means belief; but there is some believing tendency wherever there is willingness to act at all.

Next, let us call the decision between two hypotheses an *option*. Options may be of several kinds. They may be—first, *living* or *dead*; secondly, *forced* or *avoidable*; thirdly, *momentous* or *trivial*; and for our purposes we may call an option a *genuine* option when it is of the forced, living, and momentous kind.

1. A living option is one in which both hypotheses are live ones. If I say to you: "Be a theosophist or be a Mohammedan," it is probably a dead option, because for you neither hypothesis is likely to be alive. But if I say: "Be an agnostic or be a Christian," it is otherwise: trained as you are, each hypothesis makes some appeal, however small, to your belief.

2. Next, if I say to you: "Choose between going out with your umbrella or without it," I do not offer you a genuine option, for it is not forced. You can easily avoid it by not going out at all. Similarly, if I say, "Either love me or hate me," "Either call my theory true or call it false," your option is avoidable. You may remain indifferent to me, neither loving nor hating, and you may decline to offer any judgment as to my theory. But if I say, "Either accept this truth or go without it," I put on you a forced option, for there is no standing place outside of the alternative. Every dilemma based on a complete logical disjunction, with no possibility of not choosing, is an option of this forced kind.

3. Finally, if I were Dr. Nansen and proposed to you to join my North Pole expedition, your option would be momentous; for this would probably be your only similar opportunity, and your choice now would either exclude you from the North Pole sort of immortality altogether or put at least the chance of it into your hands. He who refuses to embrace a unique opportunity loses the prize as surely as if he tried and failed. *Per contra*, the option is trivial when the opportunity is not unique, when the stake is insignificant, or when the decision is reversible if it later prove unwise. Such trivial options abound in the scientific life. A chemist finds an hypothesis live enough to spend a year in its verification: he believes in it to that extent. But if his experiments prove inconclusive either way, he is quit for his loss of time, no vital harm being done.

It will facilitate our discussion if we keep all these distinctions well in mind.

II

The next matter to consider is the actual psychology of human opinion. When we look at certain facts, it seems as if our passional and volitional nature lay at the root of all our convictions. When we look at others, it seems as if they could do nothing when the intellect had once said its say. Let us take the latter facts up first.

Does it not seem preposterous on the very face of it to talk of our opinions being modifiable at will? Can our will either help or hinder our intellect in its perceptions of truth? Can we, by just willing it, believe that Abraham Lincoln's existence is a myth, and that the portraits of him in *McClure's Magazine* are all of some one else? Can we, by any effort of our will, or by any strength of wish that it were true, believe ourselves well and about when we are roaring with rheumatism in bed, or feel certain that the sum of the two one-dollar bills in our pocket must be a hundred dollars? We can *say* any of these things, but we are absolutely impotent to believe them; and of just such things is the whole fabric of the truths that we do believe in made up—matters of fact, immediate or remote, as Hume said, and relations between ideas, which are either there or not there for us if we see them so, and which if not there cannot be put there by any action of our own.

In Pascal's *Thoughts* there is a celebrated passage known in literature as Pascal's wager. In it he tries to force us into Christianity by reasoning as if our concern with truth resembled our concern with the stakes in a game of chance. Translated freely his words are these: You must either believe or not believe that God is—which will you do? Your human reason cannot say. A game is going on between you and the nature of things which at the day of judgment will bring out either heads or tails. Weigh what your gains and your losses would be if you should stake all you have on heads, or God's existence: if you win in such case, you gain eternal beatitude; if you lose, you lose nothing at all. If there were an infinity of chances, and only one for God in this wager, still you ought to stake your all on God; for though you surely risk a finite loss by this procedure, any finite loss is reasonable, even a certain one is reasonable, if there is but the possibility of infinite gain. Go, then, and take holy water, and have masses said; belief will come and stupefy your scruples—*Cela vous fera croire et vous abêtira*. Why should you not? At bottom, what have you to lose?

You probably feel that when religious faith expresses itself thus, in the language of the gaming-table, it is put to its last trumps. Surely Pascal's own personal belief in masses and holy water had far other springs; and this celebrated page of his is but an argument for others, a last desperate snatch at a weapon against the hardness of the unbelieving heart. We feel that a faith in masses and holy water adopted wilfully after such a mechanical calculation would lack the inner soul of faith's reality; and if we were ourselves in the place of the Deity, we should probably take particular pleasure in cutting off believers of this pattern from their infinite reward. It is evident that unless there be some pre-existing tendency to believe in masses and holy water, the option offered to the will by Pascal is not a living option. Certainly no Turk ever took to masses and holy water on its account; and even to us Protestants these means of salvation seem such foregone impossibilities that Pascal's logic, invoked for them specifically, leaves us unmoved. As well might the Mahdi write to us, saying, "I am the Expected One whom God has created in his effulgence. You shall be infinitely happy if you confess me; otherwise you shall be cut off from the light of the sun. Weigh, then, your infinite gain if I am genuine against your finite sacrifice if I am not!" His logic would be that of Pascal; but he would vainly use it on us, for the hypothesis he offers us is dead. No tendency to act on it exists in us to any degree.

The talk of believing by our volition seems, then, from one point of view, simply silly. From another point of view it is worse than silly, it is vile. When one turns to the magnificent edifice of the physical sciences, and sees how it was reared; what thousands of disinterested moral lives of men lie buried in its mere foundations; what patience and postponement, what choking down of preference, what submission to the icy laws of outer fact are wrought into its very stones and mortar; how absolutely impersonal it stands in its vast augustness—then how besotted and contemptible seems every little sentimentalist who comes blowing his voluntary smoke-wreaths, and pretending to decide things from out of his private dream! Can we wonder if those bred in the rugged and manly school of science should feel like spewing such subjectivism out of their mouths? The whole system of loyalties which grow up in the schools of science go dead against its toleration; so that it is only natural that those who have caught the scientific fever should pass over to the opposite extreme, and write sometimes as if the incorruptibly truthful intellect ought positively to prefer bitterness and unacceptableness to the heart in its cup.

It fortifies my soul to know
That though I perish, Truth is so—

sings Clough, while Huxley exclaims: "My only consolation lies in the reflection that, however bad our posterity may become, so far as they hold by the plain rule of not pretending to believe what they have no reason to believe, because it may be to their advantage so to pretend [the word 'pretend' is surely here redundant], they will not have reached the lowest depth of immorality." And that delicious *enfant terrible* Clifford writes: "Belief is desecrated when given to unproved and unquestioned statements for the solace and private pleasure of the believer. . . . Whoso would deserve well of his fellows in this matter will guard the purity of his belief with a very fanaticism of jealous care, lest at any time it should rest on an unworthy object, and catch a stain which can never be wiped away. . . . If [a] belief has been accepted on insufficient evidence [even though the belief be true, as Clifford on the same page explains] the pleasure is a stolen one. . . . It is sinful because it is stolen in defiance of our duty to mankind. That duty is to guard ourselves from such beliefs as from a pestilence which may shortly master our own body and then spread to the rest of the town. . . . It is wrong always, everywhere, and for every one, to believe anything upon insufficient evidence."

III

All this strikes one as healthy, even when expressed, as by Clifford, with somewhat too much of robustious pathos in the voice. Free will and simple wishing do seem, in the matter of our credences, to be only fifth wheels to the coach. Yet if any one should thereupon assume that intellectual insight is what remains after wish and will and sentimental preference have taken wing, or that pure reason is what then settles our opinions, he would fly quite as directly in the teeth of the facts.

It is only our already dead hypotheses that our willing nature is unable to bring to life again. But what has made them dead for us is for the most part a previous action of our willing nature of an antagonistic kind. When I say "willing nature," I do not mean only such deliberate volitions as may have set up habits of belief that we cannot now escape from—I mean all such factors of belief as fear and hope, prejudice and passion, imitation and partisanship, the circumpressure of our caste and set. As a matter of fact we find ourselves believing, we hardly know how or why. Mr. Balfour gives the name of "authority" to all those influences, born of the intellectual climate, that make hypotheses possible or impossible for us, alive or dead. Here in this room, we all of us believe in molecules and the conservation of energy, in democracy and necessary progress, in Protestant Christianity and the duty of fighting for "the doctrine of the immortal Monroe," all for no reasons worthy of the name. We see into these matters with no more inner clearness, and probably with much less, than any disbeliever in them might possess. His unconventionality would probably have some grounds to show for its conclusions; but for us, not insight, but the *prestige* of the opinions, is what makes the spark shoot from them and light up our sleeping magazines of faith. Our reason is quite satisfied, in nine hundred and ninety-nine cases out of every thousand of us, if it can find a few arguments that will do to recite in case our credulity is criticized by some one else. Our faith is faith in some one else's faith, and in the greatest matters this is most the case. Our belief in truth itself, for instance, that there is a truth, and that our minds and it are made for each other—what is it but a passionate affirmation of desire, in which our social system backs us up? We want to have a truth; we want to believe that our experiments and studies and discussions must put us in a continually better and better position towards it; and on this line we agree to fight out our thinking lives. But if a Pyrrhonistic sceptic asks us *how we know* all this, can our logic find a reply? No! certainly it cannot. It is just one volition against another—we willing to go in for life upon a trust or assumption which he, for his part, does not care to make.[2]

As a rule we disbelieve all facts and theories for which we have no use. Clifford's cosmic emotions find no use for Christian feelings. Huxley belabors the bishops because there is no use for sacerdotalism in his scheme of life. Newman, on the contrary, goes over to Romanism, and finds all sorts of reasons good for staying there, because a priestly system is for him an organic need and delight. Why do so few "scientists" even look at the evidence for telepathy, so called? Because they think, as a leading

biologist, now dead, once said to me, that even if such a thing were true, scientists ought to band together to keep it suppressed and concealed. It would undo the uniformity of Nature and all sorts of other things without which scientists cannot carry on their pursuits. But if this very man had been shown something which as a scientist he might *do* with telepathy, he might not only have examined the evidence, but even have found it good enough. This very law which the logicians would impose upon us—if I may give the name of logicians to those who would rule out our willing nature here—is based on nothing but their own natural wish to exclude all elements for which they, in their professional quality of logicians, can find no use.

Evidently, then, our non-intellectual nature does influence our convictions. There are passional tendencies and volitions which run before and others which come after belief, and it is only the latter that are too late for the fair; and they are not too late when the previous passional work has been already in their own direction. Pascal's argument, instead of being powerless, then seems a regular clincher, and is the last stroke needed to make our faith in masses and holy water complete. The state of things is evidently far from simple; and pure insight and logic, whatever they might do ideally, are not the only things that really do produce our creeds.

IV

Our next duty, having recognized this mixed-up state of affairs, is to ask whether it be simply reprehensible and pathological, or whether, on the con-

[2] Compare the admirable page 310 in S. H. Hodgson's *Time and Space*, London, 1865.

trary, we must treat it as a normal element in making up our minds. The thesis I defend is, briefly stated, this: *Our passional nature not only lawfully may, but must, decide an option between propositions, whenever it is a genuine option that cannot by its nature be decided an intellectual grounds; for to say, under such circumstances, "Do not decide, but leave the question open," is itself a passional decision— just like deciding yes or no—and is attended with the same risk of losing the truth.* The thesis thus abstractly expressed will, I trust, soon become quite clear. But I must first indulge in a bit more of preliminary work.

* * * * * * * * * * * * * * * * * * *

VII

One more point, small but important, and our preliminaries are done. There are two ways of looking at our duty in the matter of opinion—ways entirely different, and yet ways about whose difference the theory of knowledge seems hitherto to have shown very little concern. *We must know the truth*; and *we must avoid error*—these are our first and great commandments as would-be knowers; but they are not two ways of stating an identical commandment, they are two separable laws. Although it may indeed happen that when we believe the truth *A*, we escape as an incidental consequence from believing the falsehood *B*, it hardly ever happens that by merely disbelieving *B* we necessarily believe *A*. We may in escaping *B* fall into believing other falsehoods, *C* or *D*, just as bad as *B*; or we may escape *B* by not believing anything at all, not even *A*.

Believe truth! Shun error!—these, we see, are two materially different laws; and by choosing between them we may end by coloring differently our whole intellectual life. We may regard the chase for truth as paramount, and the avoidance of error as secondary; or we may, on the other hand, treat the avoidance of error as more imperative, and let truth take its chance. Clifford, in the instructive passage which I have quoted, exhorts us to the latter course. Believe nothing, he tells us, keep your mind in suspense forever, rather than by closing it on insufficient evidence incur the awful risk of believing lies. You, on the other hand, may think that the risk of being in error is a very small matter when compared with the blessings of real knowledge, and be ready to be duped many times in your investigation rather than postpone indefinitely the chance of guessing true. I myself find it impossible to go with Clifford. We must remember that these feelings of our duty about either truth or error are in any case only expressions of our passional life. Biologically considered, our minds are as ready to grind out falsehood as veracity, and he who says, "Better go without belief forever than believe a lie!" merely shows his own preponderant private horror of becoming a dupe. He may be critical of many of his desires and fears, but this fear he slavishly obeys. He cannot imagine any one questioning its binding force. For my own part, I have also a horror of being duped; but I can believe that worse things than being duped may happen to a man in this world: so Clifford's exhortation has to my ears a thoroughly fantastic sound. It is like a general informing his soldiers that it is better to keep out of battle forever than to risk a single wound. Not so are victories either over enemies or over nature gained. Our errors are surely not such awfully solemn things. In a world where we are so certain to incur them in spite of all our caution, a certain lightness of heart seems healthier than this excessive nervousness on their behalf. At any rate, it seems the fittest thing for the empiricist philosopher.

VIII

And now, after all this introduction, let us go straight at our question. I have said, and now repeat it, that not only as a matter of fact do we find our passional nature influencing us in our opinions, but that there are some options between opinions in which this influence must be regarded both as an inevitable and as a lawful determinant of our choice.

I fear here that some of you my hearers will begin to scent danger, and lend an inhospitable ear. Two first steps of passion you have indeed had to admit as necessary—we must think so as to avoid dupery, and we must think so as to gain truth; but the surest path to those ideal consummations, you will probably consider, is from now onwards to take no further passional step.

Well, of course, I agree as far as the facts will allow. Wherever the option between losing truth and gaining it is not momentous, we can throw the chance of *gaining truth* away, and at any rate save ourselves from any chance of *believing falsehood*, by not making up our minds at all till objective evidence has come. In scientific questions, this is almost always the case; and even in human affairs in general, the need of acting is seldom so urgent that a false belief to act on is better than no belief at all. Law courts, indeed, have to decide on the best evidence attainable for the moment, because a judge's duty is to make law as well as to ascertain it, and (as a learned judge once said to me) few cases are worth spending much time over: the great thing is to have them decided on *any* acceptable principle, and got out of the way. But in our dealings with objective nature we obviously are recorders, not makers, of the truth; and decisions for the mere sake of deciding promptly and getting on to the next business would be wholly out of place. Throughout the breadth of physical nature facts are what they are quite independently of us, and seldom is there any such hurry about them that the risks of being duped by believing a premature theory need be faced. The questions here are always trivial options, the hypotheses are hardly living (at any rate not living for us spectators), the choice between believing truth or falsehood is seldom forced. The attitude of sceptical balance is therefore the absolutely wise one if we would escape mistakes. What difference, indeed, does it make to most of us whether we have or have not a theory of the Röntgen rays, whether we believe or not in mind-stuff, or have a conviction about the causality of conscious states? It makes no difference. Such options are not forced on us. On every account it is better not to make them, but still keep weighing reasons *pro et contra* with an indifferent hand.

I speak, of course, here of the purely judging mind. For purposes of discovery such indifference is to be less highly recommended, and science would be far less advanced than she is if the passionate desires of individuals to get their own faiths confirmed had been kept out of the game. See for example the sagacity which Spencer and Weismann now display. On the other hand, if you want an absolute duffer in an investigation, you must, after all, take the man who has no interest whatever in its results: he is the warranted incapable, the positive fool. The most useful investigator, because the most sensitive observer, is always he whose eager interest in one side of the question is balanced by an equally keen nervousness lest he become deceived.[3] Science has

---

[3] Compare Wilfrid Ward's Essay, "The Wish to Believe," in his *Witnesses to the Unseen*, Macmillan & Co., 1893.

organized this nervousness into a regular *technique*, her so-called method of verification; and she has fallen so deeply in love with the method that one may even say she has ceased to care for truth by itself at all. It is only truth as technically verified that interests her. The truth of truths might come in merely affirmative form, and she would decline to touch it. Such truth as that, she might repeat with Clifford, would be stolen in defiance of her duty to mankind. Human passions, however, are stronger than technical rules. "*Le cœur a ses raisons*," as Pascal says, "*que la raison ne connaît pas*"; and however indifferent to all but the bare rules of the game the umpire, the abstract intellect, may be, the concrete players who furnish him the materials to judge of are usually, each one of them, in love with some pet "live hypothesis" of his own. Let us agree, however, that wherever there is no forced option, the dispassionately judicial intellect with no pet hypothesis, saving us, as it does, from dupery at any rate, ought to be our ideal.

The question next arises: Are there not somewhere forced options in our speculative questions, and can we (as men who may be interested at least as much in positively gaining truth as in merely escaping dupery) always wait with impunity till the coercive evidence shall have arrived? It seems *a priori* improbable that the truth should be so nicely adjusted to our needs and powers as that. In the great boarding-house of nature, the cakes and the butter and the syrup seldom come out so even and leave the plates so clean. Indeed, we should view them with scientific suspicion if they did.

IX

Moral questions immediately present themselves as questions whose solution cannot wait for sensible proof. A moral question is a question not of what sensibly exists, but of what is good, or would be good if it did exist. Science can tell us what exists; but to compare the *worths*, both of what exists and of what does not exist, we must consult not science, but what Pascal calls our heart. Science herself consults her heart when she lays it down that the infinite ascertainment of fact and correction of false belief are the supreme goods for man. Challenge the statements, and science can only repeat it oracularly, or else prove it by showing that such ascertainment and correction bring man all sorts of other goods which man's heart in turn declares. The question of having moral beliefs at all or not having them is decided by our will. Are our moral preferences true or false, or are they only odd biological phenomena, making things good or bad for *us*, but in themselves indifferent? How can your pure intellect decide? If your heart does not *want* a world of moral reality, your head will assuredly never make you believe in one. Mephistophelian scepticism, indeed, will satisfy the head's play-instincts much better than any rigorous idealism can. Some men (even at the student age) are so naturally cool-hearted that the moralistic hypothesis never has for them any pungent life, and in their supercilious presence the hot young moralist always feels strangely ill at ease. The appearance of knowingness is on their side, of *naïveté* and gullibility on his. Yet, in the inarticulate heart of him, he clings to it that he is not a dupe, and that there is a realm in which (as Emerson says) all their wit and intellectual superiority is no better than the cunning of a fox. Moral scepticism can no more be refuted or proved by logic than intellectual scepticism can. When we stick to it that there *is* truth (be it of either kind), we do so with our whole nature, and resolve to stand or fall by the results. The sceptic with his whole nature adopts the doubting attitude; but which of us is the wiser, Omniscience only knows.

Turn now from these wide questions of good to a certain class of questions of fact, questions concerning personal relations, states of mind between one man and another. *Do you like me or not?*—for example. Whether you do or not depends, in countless instances, on whether I meet you half-way, am willing to assume that you must like me, and show you trust and expectation. The previous faith on my part in your liking's existence is in such cases what makes your liking come. But if I stand aloof, and refuse to budge an inch until I have objective evidence, until you shall have done something apt, as the absolutists say, *ad extorquendum assensum meum*, ten to one your liking never comes. How many women's hearts are vanquished by the mere sanguine insistence of some man that they *must* love him! he will not consent to the hypothesis that they cannot. The desire for a certain kind of truth here brings about that special truth's existence; and so it is in innumerable cases of other sorts. Who gains promotions, boons, appointments, but the man in whose life they are seen to play the part of live hypotheses, who discounts them, sacrifices other things for their sake before they have come, and takes risks for them in advance? His faith acts on the powers above him as a claim, and creates its own verification.

A social organism of any sort whatever, large or small, is what it is because each member proceeds to his own duty with a trust that the other members will simultaneously do theirs. Wherever a desired result is achieved by the co-operation of many independent persons, its existence as a fact is a pure consequence of the precursive faith in one another of those immediately concerned. A government, an army, a commercial system, a ship, a college, an athletic team, all exist on this condition, without which not only is nothing achieved, but nothing is even attempted. A whole train of passengers (individually brave enough) will be looted by a few highwaymen, simply because the latter can count on one another, while each passenger fears that if he makes a movement of resistance, he will be shot before any one else backs him up. If we believed that the whole car-full would rise at once with us, we should each severally rise, and train-robbing would never even be attempted. There are, then, cases where a fact cannot come at all unless a preliminary faith exists in its coming. *And where faith in a fact can help create the fact*, that would be an insane logic which should say that faith running ahead of scientific evidence is the "lowest kind of immorality" into which a thinking being can fall. Yet such is the logic by which our scientific absolutists pretend to regulate our lives!

X

In truths dependent on our personal action, then, faith based on desire is certainly a lawful and possibly an indispensable thing.

But now, it will be said, these are all childish human cases, and have nothing to do with great cosmical matters, like the question of religious faith. Let us then pass on to that. Religions differ so much in their accidents that in discussing the religious question we must make it very generic and broad. What then do we now mean by the religious hypothesis? Science says things are; morality says some things are better than other things; and religion says essentially two things.

First, she says that the best things are the more eternal things, the overlapping things, the things in the universe that throw the last stone, so to speak, and say the final word. "Perfection is eternal"—this phrase of Charles Secrétan seems a good way of putting this first affirmation of religion, an affirmation which obviously cannot yet be verified scientifically at all.

The second affirmation of religion is that we are better off even now if we believe her first affirmation to be true.

Now, let us consider what the logical elements of this situation are *in case the religious hypothesis in both its branches be really true.* (Of course, we must admit that possibility at the outset. If we are to discuss the question at all, it must involve a living option. If for any of you religion be a hypothesis that cannot, by any living possibility, be true, then you need go no farther. I speak to the "saving remnant" alone.) So proceeding, we see, first, that religion offers itself as a *momentous* option. We are supposed to gain, even now, by our belief, and to lose by our non-belief, a certain vital good. Secondly, religion is a *forced* option, so far as that good goes. We cannot escape the issue by remaining sceptical and waiting for more light, because, although we do avoid error in that way *if religion be untrue*, we lose the good, *if it be true*, just as certainly as if we positively chose to disbelieve. It is as if a man should hesitate indefinitely to ask a certain woman to marry him because he was not perfectly sure that she would prove an angel after he brought her home. Would he not cut himself off from that particular angel-possibility as decisively as if he went and married some one else? Scepticism, then, is not avoidance of option; it is option of a certain particular kind of risk. *Better risk loss of truth than chance of error*—that is your faith-vetoer's exact position. He is actively playing his stake as much as the believer is; he is backing the field against the religious hypothesis, just as the believer is backing the religious hypothesis against the field. To preach scepticism to us as a duty until "sufficient evidence" for religion be found, is tantamount therefore to telling us, when in presence of the religious hypothesis, that to yield to our fear of its being error is wiser and better than to yield to our hope that it may be true. It is not intellect against all passions, then; it is only intellect with one passion laying down its law. And by what, forsooth, is the supreme wisdom of this passion warranted? Dupery for dupery, what proof is there that dupery through hope is so much worse than dupery through fear? I, for one, can see no proof; and I simply refuse obedience to the scientist's command to imitate his kind of option, in a case where my own stake is important enough to give me the right to choose my own form of risk. If religion be true and the evidence for it be still insufficient, I do not wish, by putting your extinguisher upon my nature (which feels to me as if it had after all some business in this matter), to forfeit my sole chance in life of getting upon the winning side— that chance depending, of course, on my willingness to run the risk of acting as if my passional need of taking the world religiously might be prophetic and right.

All this is on the supposition that it really may be prophetic and right, and that, even to us who are discussing the matter, religion is a live hypothesis which may be true. Now, to most of us religion comes in a still further way that makes a veto on our active faith even more illogical. The more perfect and more eternal aspect of the universe is represented in our religions as having personal form. The universe is no longer a mere *It* to us, but a *Thou*, if we are religious; and any relation that may be possible from person to person might be possible here. For instance, although in one sense we are passive portions of the universe, in another we show a curious autonomy, as if we were small active centres on our own account. We feel, too, as if the appeal of religion to us were made to our own active good-will, as if evidence might be forever withheld from us unless we met the hypothesis half-way. To take a trivial illustration: just as a man who in a company of gentlemen made no advances, asked a warrant for every concession, and believed no one's word without proof, would cut himself off by such churlishness from all the social rewards that a more trusting spirit would earn—so here, one who should shut himself up in snarling logicality and try to make the gods extort his recognition willy-nilly, or not get it at all, might cut himself off forever from his only opportunity of making the gods' acquaintance. This feeling, forced on us we know not whence, that by obstinately believing that there are gods (although not to do so would be so easy both for our logic and our life) we are doing the universe the deepest service we can, seems part of the living essence of the religious hypothesis. If the hypothesis *were* true in all its parts, including this one, then pure intellectualism, with its veto on our making willing advances, would be an absurdity; and some participation of our sympathetic nature would be logically required. I, therefore, for one, cannot see my way to accepting the agnostic rules for truth-seeking, or wilfully agree to keep my willing nature out of the game. I cannot do so for this plain reason, that *a rule of thinking which would absolutely prevent me from acknowledging certain kinds of truth if those kinds of truth were really there, would be an irrational rule*. That for me is the long and short of the formal logic of the situation, no matter what the kinds of truth might materially be.

I confess I do not see how this logic can be escaped. But sad experience makes me fear that some of you may still shrink from radically saying with me, *in abstracto*, that we have the right to believe at our own risk any hypothesis that is live enough to tempt our will. I suspect, however, that if this is so, it is because you have got away from the abstract logical point of view altogether, and are thinking (perhaps without realizing it) of some particular religious hypothesis which for you is dead. The freedom to "believe what we will" you apply to the case of some patent superstition; and the faith you think of is the faith defined by the schoolboy when he said, "Faith is when you believe something that you know ain't true." I can only repeat that this is misapprehension. *In concreto*, the freedom to believe can only cover living options which the intellect of the individual cannot by itself resolve; and living options never seem absurdities to him who has them to consider. When I look at the religious question as it really puts itself to concrete men, and when I think of all the possibilities which both practically and theoretically it involves, then this command that we shall put a stopper on our heart, instincts, and courage, and *wait*—acting of course meanwhile more or less as if religion were *not* true[4]—till doomsday, or till such time as our intellect and senses working together may have raked in evidence enough—this command, I say, seems to me the queerest idol ever manufactured in

---

[4] Since belief is measured by action, he who forbids us to believe religion to be true, necessarily also forbids us to act as we should if we did believe it to be true. The whole defence of religious faith hinges upon action. If the action required or inspired by the religious hypothesis is in no way different from that dictated by the naturalistic hypothesis, then religious faith is a pure superfluity, better pruned away, and controversy about its legitimacy is a piece of idle trifling, unworthy of serious minds. I myself believe, of course, that the religious hypothesis gives to the world an expression which specifically determines our reactions, and makes them in a large part unlike what they might be on a purely naturalistic scheme of belief.

the philosophic cave. Were we scholastic absolutists, there might be more excuse. If we had an infallible intellect with its objective certitudes, we might feel ourselves disloyal to such a perfect organ of knowledge in not trusting to it exclusively, in not waiting for its releasing word. But if we are empiricists, if we believe that no bell in us tolls to let us know for certain when truth is in our grasp, then it seems a piece of idle fantasticality to preach so solemnly our duty of waiting for the bell. Indeed we *may* wait if we will— I hope you do not think that I am denying that—but if we do so, we do so at our peril as much as if we believed. In either case we *act*, taking our life in our hands. No one of us ought to issue vetoes to the other, nor should we bandy words of abuse. We ought, on the contrary, delicately and profoundly to respect one another's mental freedom: then only shall we bring about the intellectual republic; then only shall we have that spirit of inner tolerance without which all our outer tolerance is soulless, and which is empiricism's glory; then only shall we live and let live, in speculative as well as in practical things.

I began by a reference to Fitz-James Stephen; let me end by a quotation from him. "What do you think of yourself? What do you think of the world?... These are questions with which all must deal as it seems good to them. They are riddles of the Sphinx, and in some way or other we must deal with them.... In all important transactions of life we have to take a leap in the dark.... If we decide to leave the riddles unanswered, that is a choice; if we waver in our answer, that, too, is a choice: but whatever choice we make, we make it at our peril. If a man chooses to turn his back altogether on God and the future, no one can prevent him; no one can show beyond reasonable doubt that he is mistaken. If a man thinks otherwise and acts as he thinks, I do not see that any one can prove that *he* is mistaken. Each must act as he thinks best; and if he is wrong, so much the worse for him. We stand on a mountain pass in the midst of whirling snow and blinding mist, through which we get glimpses now and then of paths which may be deceptive. If we stand still we shall be frozen to death. If we take the wrong road we shall be dashed to pieces. We do not certainly know whether there is any right one. What must we do? 'Be strong and of a good courage.' Act for the best, hope for the best, and take what comes.... If death ends all, we cannot meet death better."[5]

W.K. CLIFFORD

from The Ethics of Belief

W. K. Clifford in "The Ethics of Belief" maintains that "It is wrong always, everywhere, and for anyone to believe anything on insufficient evidence." If Clifford is right, then it is morally or epistemically wrong to believe there is a God on insufficient evidence. Conversely, for William James, if evidence cannot decide the religious belief option, and we *must* decide because the option is genuine and so a forced option for us, then our passional nature may decide because it must decide.

---

[5] *Liberty, Equality, Fraternity*, p. 353, 2d edition. London, 1874.

Both Clifford and James use the language of morality, the language of permissibility, duty, and rights. James says that when we are faced with a genuine option and intellectual evidence is not available, we may either believe or not believe. In such a case we have the right to believe. Clifford maintains that we have *no* right to believe on insufficient evidence. So, in the event sufficient evidence for religious belief is unavailable, Clifford and James are in clear opposition as to whether we have a right to believe religiously. James is aware of this opposition and he speaks directly to Clifford's claim, mentioning Clifford by name. Clifford, who died in 1879, well before James published "The Will to Believe," had no opportunity to reply. Still, it is clear that the two are in definite opposition and, as it were, in dialogue.

For James there are *two* laws of epistemic duty. One is that we must know the truth. The second is that we must avoid error. Clifford favors the second duty, as James sees it. In order to meet the duty to avoid error Clifford will reserve judgment when intellectual evidence is not sufficient, as is the case with the religious belief option. This is his right, James says. When we are faced with a genuine option and intellectual evidence is not available, we may either believe or not believe; we have the right to go either way in accord with the epistemic duty we see as more important, given our passional nature. But then, James insists, just as Clifford has the right not to believe religiously, he, William James, and others, have the right to believe religiously. Clifford is not wrong to withhold his belief: that is his right. He is wrong, however, in denying the right of others to believe at their own risk. For this reason James concludes that Clifford is wrong in his central thesis that no one ever has the right to believe when there is insufficient evidence. Finally, then, if James is right, religious belief in the eternal, or in God, is epistemically proper even if evidence is not available, if we are faced with a genuine option and our passional needs and desires lead us to believe.

Still, Clifford might have a reply. One duty, James says, is that we must "know" the truth. Or, as he also puts it "believe" the truth or "gain" the truth. One might reply on behalf of Clifford that, while there is an epistemic duty regarding the truth, it is the duty to *seek* the truth, and the way we do this is by means of investigation and inquiry; and unless and until we have sufficient evidence we should not believe something to be true. So it remains, Clifford would conclude, that we have no epistemic right to believe on insufficient evidence. The reading from W. K. Clifford's "The Ethics of Belief" is in Chapter 3.

ALVIN PLANTINGA

from Reason and Belief in God

Alvin Plantinga is among those contemporary philosophers of religion who have challenged Clifford's principle and sought ways of understanding religious belief, and what might make it acceptable or rational or justified or, to use a single general term, epistemically proper, that would *not* require religious belief to rest upon sufficient evidence. In doing this they are like William James to an extent, but they go beyond James in seeking ways that religious belief can be proper quite independently of any reference to evidence, whether or not evidence is available.

In our reading Plantinga defends the claim that belief in God is epistemically proper because it is a "properly basic belief." Plantinga suggests that each individual has what he calls a "noetic structure." A person's noetic structure contains all that person's beliefs. Many of these beliefs are held on the basis of other beliefs. They have an evidential support or basis in these other beliefs and so are what Plantinga calls *nonbasic* beliefs. Many of our beliefs are not like this, Plantinga suggests. Many of our beliefs are not held on the basis of other beliefs. These beliefs Plantinga calls *basic beliefs*. Examples of basic beliefs that Plantinga gives are the belief that he is seeing a tree and the belief that he had breakfast this morning.

Typically, he says, the belief that he is seeing a tree and the belief that he had breakfast are basic beliefs for him because usually he does not hold these beliefs on the basis of any other beliefs, and so too for most of us. Plantinga does not think that we can draw up a single list of basic beliefs for everyone and a single list of nonbasic beliefs for everyone. We cannot because what is a basic belief for him and his noetic structure may not be a basic belief for you and your noetic stucture, and because, while a belief like the belief that he sees a tree is *typically* a basic belief for him, in some cases he may hold it on the basis of some such proposition as "though the light is bad, I can still see clearly enough." Plantinga admits that "it is not altogether easy to say" when a belief is basic for a person, but he is confident that some beliefs of a person are basic and some are not.

In the way of thinking about belief and its epistemic propriety that Plantinga develops in our reading there are two ways a belief can be epistemically proper for a person. One way is that it is supported by the other beliefs in that person's noetic structure, so that those other beliefs provide evidential support for it. This is how nonbasic beliefs are made epistemically proper for a person. The other way a belief can be epistemically proper is that it is a "properly basic belief"—not just basic, but *properly* basic.

Plantinga argues that for religious believers, or for Christians, the belief that God exists may well be properly basic. Our reading consists of selections from his article "Reason and Belief in God," in which he advances this argument.*

Reason and Belief in God

Belief in God is the heart and center of the Christian religion—as it is of Judaism and Islam. Of course Christians may disagree, at least in emphasis, as to how to think of God; for example, some may emphasize his hatred of sin; others, his love of his creatures. Furthermore, one may find, even among professedly Christian theologians, supersophisticates who proclaim the liberation of Christianity from belief in God, seeking to replace it by trust in "Being itself" or the "Ground of

* From *Faith and Rationality: Reason and Belief in God*, N. Wolterstorff & A. Plantinga, eds. Copyright 1983 by University of Notre Dame Press. Notre Dame IN 46556.

Being" or some such thing. It remains true, however, that belief in God is the foundation of Christianity.

In this essay I want to discuss a connected constellation of questions: Does the believer-in-God accept the existence of God by *faith*? Is belief in God contrary to reason, unreasonable, irrational? Must one have *evidence* to be rational or reasonable in believing in God? Suppose belief in God is *not* rational; does that matter? And what about proofs of God's existence? Many Reformed or Calvinist thinkers and theologians have taken a jaundiced view of natural theology, thought of as the attempt to give proofs or arguments for the existence of God; are they right? What underlies this hostility to an undertaking that, on the surface, at least, looks perfectly harmless and possibly useful? These are some of the questions I propose to discuss. They fall under the general rubric *faith and reason*, if a general rubric is required. I believe Reformed or Calvinist thinkers have had important things to say on these topics and that their fundamental insights here are correct. What they say, however, has been for the most part unclear, ill-focused, and unduly inexplicit. I shall try to remedy these ills; I shall try to state and clearly develop their insight; and I shall try to connect these insights with more general epistemological considerations.

Like the Missouri River, what I have to say is best seen as the confluence of three streams—streams of clear and limpid thought, I hasten to add, rather than turbid, muddy water. These three streams of thought are first, reflection on the evidentialist objection to theistic belief, according to which belief in God is unreasonable or irrational because there is insufficient evidence for it; second, reflection on the Thomistic conception of faith and reason; and third, reflection on the Reformed rejection to natural theology. In Part I I shall explore the evidentialist objection, trying to see more clearly just what it involves and what it presupposes. Part II will begin with a brief look at Thomas Aquinas' views on faith and knowledge; I shall argue that the evidentialist objection and the Thomistic conception of faith and knowledge can be traced back to a common root in *classical foundationalism*—a pervasive and widely accepted picture or total way of looking at faith, knowledge, belief, rationality, and allied topics. I shall try to characterize this picture in a revealing way and then go on to argue that classical foundationalism is both false and self-referentially incoherent; it should therefore be summarily rejected. In Part III I shall explore the Reformed rejection of natural theology; I will argue that it is best understood as an implicit rejection of classical foundationalism in favor of the view that belief in God is properly basic. What the Reformers meant to hold is that it is entirely right, rational, reasonable, and proper to believe in God without any evidence or argument at all; in this respect belief in God resembles belief in the past, in the existence of other persons, and in the existence of material objects. I shall try to state and clearly articulate this claim and in Part IV to defend it against objections.

＊ ＊ ＊ ＊ ＊ ＊ ＊ ＊ ＊ ＊ ＊ ＊ ＊ ＊ ＊ ＊ ＊ ＊ ＊

PART I

The Evidentialist Objection to Belief in God

My first topic, then, is the evidentialist objection to theistic belief. Many philosophers—W. K. Clifford,[1] Brand

---

[1] W. K. Clifford, "The Ethics of Belief" in *Lectures and Essays* (London: Macmillan, 1879), pp. 345 f.

Blanshard,[2] Bertrand Russell,[3] Michael Scriven,[4] and Anthony Flew,[5] to name a few—have argued that belief in God is irrational or unreasonable or not rationally acceptable or intellectually irresponsible or somehow noetically below par because, as they say, there is *insufficient evidence* for it. Bertrand Russell was once asked what he would say if, after dying, he were brought into the presence of God and asked why he had not been a believer. Russell's reply: "I'd say 'Not enough evidence God! Not enough evidence!'"[6] We may have our doubts as to just how that sort of response would be received; but Russell, like many others, held that theistic belief is unreasonable because there is insufficient evidence for it.

* * * * * * * * * * * * * * * * * * * *

B. Foundationalism

Aquinas and the evidentialist objector concur, then, in holding that belief in God is rationally acceptable only if there is evidence for it—only if, that is, it is probable with respect to some body of propositions that constitutes the evidence. And here we can get a better understanding of Aquinas and the evidentialist objector if we see them as accepting some version of *classical foundationalism*. This is a *picture* or total way of looking at faith, knowledge, justified belief, rationality, and allied topics. This picture has been enormously popular in Western thought; and despite a substantial opposing groundswell, I think it remains the dominant way of thinking about these topics. According to the foundationalist some propositions are properly basic and some are not; those that are not are rationally accepted only on the basis of *evidence*, where the evidence must trace back, ultimately, to what *is* properly basic. The existence of God, furthermore, is not among the propositions that are properly basic; hence a person is rational in accepting theistic belief only if he has evidence for it. The vast majority of those in the western world who have thought about our topic have accepted some form of classical foundationalism. The evidentialist objection to belief in God, furthermore, is obviously rooted in this way of looking at things. So suppose we try to achieve a deeper understanding of it.

Earlier I said the first thing to see about the evidentialist objection is that it is a *normative* contention or claim. The same thing must be said about foundationalism: this thesis is a normative thesis, a thesis about how a system of beliefs *ought* to be structured, a thesis about the properties of a correct, or acceptable, or rightly structured system of beliefs. According to the foundationalist there are norms, or duties, or obligations with respect to belief just as there are with respect to actions. To conform to these duties and obligations is to be rational; to fail to measure up to them is to be irrational. To be rational, then, is to exercise one's epistemic powers *properly*—to exercise them in such a way

[2] Brand Blanshard, *Reason and Belief* (London: Allen & Unwin, 1974), pp. 400 f.
[3] Bertrand Russell, "Why I am not a Christian" in *Why I Am Not a Christian* (New York: Simon & Schuster, 1957), p. 3 ff.
[4] Michael Scriven, *Primary Philosophy* (New York: McGraw-Hill, 1966), p. 87 ff.
[5] Anthony Flew, *The Presumption of Atheism* (London: Pemberton, 1976), pp. 22 ff.
[6] Wesley Salmon, "Religion & Science: A New Look at Hume's Dialogues," *Philosophical Studies* 33 (1978): 176.

as to go contrary to none of the norms for such exercise.

* * * * * * * * * * * * * * * * * * * *

I think we can understand foundationalism more fully if we introduce the idea of a *noetic structure*. A person's noetic structure is the set of propositions he believes, together with certain epistemic relations that hold among him and these propositions. As we have seen, some of my beliefs may be based upon others; it may be that there are a pair of propositions A and B such that I believe B, and believe A *on the basis of B*. An account of a person's noetic structure, then, would specify which of his beliefs are basic and which nonbasic. Of course it is abstractly possible that *none* of his beliefs is basic; perhaps he holds just three beliefs, A, B, and C, and believes each of them on the basis of the other two. We might think this improper or irrational, but that is not to say it could not be done. And it is also possible that *all* of his beliefs are basic; perhaps he believes a lot of propositions but does not believe any of them on the basis of any others. In the typical case, however, a noetic structure will include both basic and nonbasic beliefs. It may be useful to give some examples of beliefs that are often basic for a person. Suppose I seem to see a tree; I have that characteristic sort of experience that goes with perceiving a tree. I may then believe the proposition that I see a tree. It is *possible* that I believe that proposition *on the basis of* the proposition that I seem to see a tree; in the typical case, however, I will not believe the former on the basis of the latter because in the typical case I will not believe the latter at all. I will not be paying any attention to my experience but will be concentrating on the tree. Of course I *can* turn my attention to my experience, notice how things look to me, and acquire the belief that I seem to see something that looks like *that*; and if you

challenge my claim that I see a tree, perhaps I *will* thus turn my attention to my experience. But in the typical case I will not believe that I see a tree on the basis of a proposition about my experience; for I believe A on the basis of B only if I believe B, and in the typical case where I perceive a tree I do not believe (or entertain) any propositions about my experience. Typically I take such a proposition as basic. Similarly, I believe I had breakfast this morning; this too is basic for me. I do not believe this proposition on the basis of some proposition about my experience—for example, that I seem to remember having had breakfast. In the typical case I will not have even considered *that* question—the question whether I *seem* to remember having had breakfast; instead I simply believe that I had breakfast; I take it as basic.

Second, an account of a noetic structure will include what we might call an index of *degree* of belief. I hold some of my beliefs much more firmly than others. I believe both that $2 + 1 = 3$ and that London, England, is north of Saskatoon, Saskatchewan; but I believe the former more resolutely than the latter. Some beliefs I hold with maximum firmness; others I do in fact accept, but in a much more tentative way.

* * * * * * * * * * * * * * * * * * * *

Third, a somewhat vaguer notion: an account of S's noetic structure would include something like an index of *depth of ingression*. Some of my beliefs are, we might say, on the periphery of my noetic structure. I accept them, and may even accept them firmly, but I could give them up without much change elsewhere in my noetic structure. I believe there are some large boulders on the top of the Grand Teton. If I come to give up this belief (say by climbing it and not finding any), that change need not have extensive reverberations throughout the rest of my noetic structure; it could be accommodated with minimal alteration elsewhere. So its depth of ingression into my noetic structure is not great. On the other hand, if I were come to believe that there simply is no such thing as the Grand Teton, or no mountains at all, or no such thing as the state of Wyoming, that would have much greater reverberations. And suppose I were to come to think there had not been much of a past (that the world was created just five minutes ago, complete with all its apparent memories and traces of the past) or that there were not any other persons: these changes would have even greater reverberations; these beliefs of mine have great depth of ingression into my noetic structure.

* * * * * * * * * * * * * * * * * * *

Now foundationalism is best construed, I think, as a thesis about *rational* noetic structures. A noetic structure is rational if it could be the noetic structure of a person who was completely rational. To be completely rational, as I am here using the term, is not to believe only what is true, or to believe all the logical consequences of what one believes, or to believe all necessary truths with equal firmness, or to be uninfluenced by emotion in forming belief; it is, instead, to do the right thing with respect to one's believings. It is to violate no epistemic duties. From this point of view, a rational person is one whose believings meet the appropriate standards; to criticize a person as irrational is to criticize her for failing to fulfill these duties or responsibilities, for failing to conform to the relevant norms or standards. To draw the ethical analogy, the irrational is the impermissible; the rational is the permissible.

* * * * * * * * * * * * * * * * * * *

A rational noetic structure, then, is one that could be the noetic structure of a wholly rational person; and foundationalism, as I say, is a thesis about such noetic structures. We may think of the foundationalist as beginning with the observation that some of our beliefs are based upon others. According to the foundationalist a rational noetic structure will *have a foundation*—a set of beliefs not accepted on the basis of others; in a rational noetic structure some beliefs will be basic. Nonbasic beliefs, of course, will be accepted on the basis of other beliefs, which may be accepted on the basis of still other beliefs, and so on until the foundations are reached. In a rational noetic structure, therefore, every nonbasic belief is ultimately accepted on the basis of basic beliefs.

* * * * * * * * * * * * * * * * * * *

According to the foundationalist, therefore, every rational noetic structure has a foundation, and all nonbasic beliefs are ultimately accepted on the basis of beliefs in the foundations. But a belief cannot properly be accepted on the basis of just *any* other belief; in a rational noetic structure, *A* will be accepted on the basis of *B* only if *B supports A* or is a member of a set of beliefs that together support *A*. It is not clear just what this relation—call it the "supports" relation—is; and different foundationalists propose different candidates. Presumably, however, it lies in the neighborhood of *evidence*; if *A* supports *B*, then *A* is evidence for *B*, or makes *B* evident; or perhaps *B* is likely or probable with respect to *B*. This relation admits of degrees. My belief that Feike can swim is supported by my knowledge that nine out of ten Frisians can swim and Feike is a Frisian; it is supported more strongly by my knowledge that the evening paper contains a picture of Feike triumphantly finishing first in the fifteen-hundred meter freestyle in the 1980 summer Olympics. And the foundationalist holds, sensibly enough, that in a rational noetic structure the strength of a nonbasic belief will depend upon the degree of support from foundational beliefs.

* * * * * * * * * * * * * * * * * * *

By way of summary, then, let us say that according to foundationalism: (1) in a rational noetic structure the believed-on-the-basis-of relation is asymmetric and irreflexive, (2) a rational noetic structure has a foundation, and (3) in a rational noetic structure nonbasic belief is proportional in strength to support from the foundations.

* * * * * * * * * * * * * * * * * * *

PART IV

Is Belief in God Properly Basic?

According to the Reformed thinkers discussed in the last section the answer is "Yes indeed." I enthusiastically concur in this contention, and in this section I shall try to clarify and develop this view and defend it against some objections. I shall argue first that one who holds that belief in God is properly basic is not thereby committed to the view that just about *anything* is; I shall argue secondly that even if belief in God is accepted as basic, it is not *groundless*; I shall argue thirdly that one who accepts belief in God as basic may nonetheless be open to arguments *against* that belief; and finally I shall argue that the view I am defending is not plausibly thought of as a species of *fideism*.

A. The Great Pumpkin Objection

It is tempting to raise the following sort of question. If belief in God is properly basic, why cannot *just any* belief be properly basic? Could we not say the same for any bizarre aberration we can think of? What about voodoo or astrology? What about the belief that the Great Pumpkin returns every Halloween? Could I properly take *that* as basic? Suppose I believe that if I flap my arms with sufficient vigor, I can take off and fly about the room; could I defend myself against the charge of irrationality by claiming this belief is basic? If we say that belief in God is properly basic, will we not be committed to holding that just anything, or nearly anything, can properly be taken as basic, thus throwing wide the gates to irrationalism and superstition?

Certainly not. According to the Reformed epistemologist certain beliefs are properly basic in certain circumstances; those same beliefs may *not* be properly basic in other circumstances. Consider the belief that I see a tree: this belief is properly basic in circumstances that are hard to describe in detail, but include my being appeared to in a certain characteristic way; that same belief is not properly basic in circumstances including, say, my knowledge that I am sitting in the living room listening to music with my eyes closed. What the Reformed epistemologist holds is that there are widely realized circumstances in which belief in God is properly basic; but why should that be thought to commit him to the idea that just about *any* belief is properly basic in any circumstances, or even to the vastly weaker claim that for any belief there are circumstances in which it is properly basic? Is it just that he rejects the criteria for proper basicality purveyed by classical foundationalism? But why should *that* be thought to commit him to such tolerance of irrationality? Consider an analogy. In the palmy days of positivism the positivists went about confidently wielding their verifiability criterion and declaring meaningless much that was clearly meaningful. Now suppose someone rejected a formulation of that criterion—the one to be found in the second edition of A. J. Ayer's *Language, Truth and Logic*, for example. Would that mean she was committed to holding that

(1) T' was brillig; and the slithy toves did gyre and gymble in the wabe,

contrary to appearances, makes good sense? Of course not. But then the same goes for the Reformed epistemologist: the fact that he rejects the criterion of proper basicality purveyed by classical foundationalism does not mean that he is committed to supposing just anything is properly basic.

But what then is the problem? Is it that the Reformed epistemologist not only rejects those criteria for proper basicality but seems in no hurry to produce what he takes to be a better substitute? If he has no such criterion, how can he fairly reject belief in the Great Pumpkin as properly basic?

This objection betrays an important misconception. How *do* we rightly arrive at or develop criteria for meaningfulness, or justified belief, or proper basicality? Where do they come from? Must one have such a criterion before one can sensibly make any judgments—positive or negative—about proper basicality? Surely not. Suppose I do not know of a satisfactory substitute for the criteria proposed by classical foundationalism; I am nevertheless entirely within my epistemic rights in holding that certain propositions in certain conditions are not properly basic.

Some propositions seem self-evident when in fact they are not; that is the lesson of some of the Russell paradoxes. Nevertheless it would be irrational to take as basic the denial of a proposition that seems self-evident to you. Similarly, suppose it seems to you that you see a tree; you would then be irrational in taking as basic the proposition that you do not see a tree or that there are no trees. In the same way, even if I do not know of some illuminating criterion of meaning, I can quite properly declare (1) (above) meaningless.

And this raises an important question—one Roderick Chisholm has taught us to ask.[39] What is the status of criteria for knowledge, or proper basicality, or justified belief? Typically these are universal statements. The modern foundationalist's criterion for proper basicality, for example, is doubly universal:

(2) For any proposition *A* and person *S*, *A* is properly basic for *S* if and only if *A* is incorrigible for *S* or self-evident to *S*.

But how could one know a thing like that? What are its credentials? Clearly enough, (2) is not self-evident or just obviously true. But if it is not, how does one arrive at it? What sorts of arguments would be appropriate? Of course a foundationalist might find (2) so appealing he simply takes it to be true, neither offering argument for it nor accepting it on the basis of other things he believes. If he does so, however, his noetic structure will be self-referentially incoherent. (2) itself is neither self-evident nor incorrigible; hence if he accepts (2) as basic, the modern foundationalist violates in accepting it the condition of proper basicality he himself lays down. On the other hand, perhaps the foundationalist will try to produce some argument for it from premises that are self-evident or incorrigible: it is exceeding hard to see,

---

[39] Roderick Chisholm, *The Problem of the Criterion* (Milwaukee: Marquette University Press, 1973), pp. 14 ff.

however, what such an argument might be like. And until he has produced such arguments, what shall the rest of us do—we who do not find (2) at all obvious or compelling? How could he use (2) to show us that belief in God, for example, is not properly basic? Why should we believe (2) or pay it any attention?

The fact is, I think, that neither (2) nor any other revealing necessary and sufficient condition for proper basicality follows from clearly self-evident premises by clearly acceptable arguments. And hence the proper way to arrive at such a criterion is, broadly speaking, *inductive*. We must assemble examples of beliefs and conditions such that the former are obviously properly basic in the latter, and examples of beliefs and conditions such that the former are obviously *not* properly basic in the latter. We must then frame hypotheses as to the necessary and sufficient conditions of proper basicality and test these hypotheses by reference to those examples. Under the right conditions, for example, it is clearly rational to believe that you see a human person before you: a being who has thoughts and feelings, who knows and believes things, who makes decisions and acts. It is clear, furthermore, that you are under no obligation to reason to this belief from others you hold; under those conditions that belief is properly basic for you. But then (2) must be mistaken; the belief in question, under those circumstances, is properly basic, though neither self-evident nor incorrigible for you. Similarly, you may seem to remember that you had breakfast this morning, and perhaps you know of no reason to suppose your memory is playing you tricks. If so, you are entirely justified in taking that belief as basic. Of course it is not properly basic on the criteria offered by classical foundationalists, but that

fact counts not against you but against those criteria.

* * * * * * * * * * * * * * * * * * * *

Accordingly, criteria for proper basicality must be reached from below rather than above; they should not be presented *ex cathedra* but argued to and tested by a relevant set of examples. But there is no reason to assume, in advance, that everyone will agree on the examples. The Christian will of course suppose that belief in God is entirely proper and rational; if he does not accept this belief on the basis of other propositions, he will conclude that it is basic for him and quite properly so. Followers of Bertrand Russell and Madelyn Murray O'Hare may disagree; but how is that relevant? Must my criteria, or those of the Christian community, conform to their examples? Surely not. The Christian community is responsible to *its* set of examples, not to theirs.

* * * * * * * * * * * * * * * * * * * *

So, the Reformed epistemologist can properly hold that belief in the Great Pumpkin is not properly basic, even though he holds that belief in God is properly basic and even if he has no full-fledged criterion of proper basicality. Of course he is committed to supposing that there is a relevant *difference* between belief in God and belief in the Great Pumpkin if he holds that the former but not the latter is properly basic. But this should prove no great embarrassment; there are plenty of candidates. These candidates are to be found in the neighborhood of the conditions that justify and ground belief in God—conditions I shall discuss in the next section. Thus, for example, the Reformed epistemologist may concur with Calvin in holding that God has implanted in us a natural tendency to see his hand in the world around us; the same cannot be said for the Great Pumpkin, there being no Great Pumpkin and no natural tendency to accept beliefs about the Great Pumpkin.[40]

B. The *Ground* of Belief in God

My claim is that belief in God is properly basic; is does not follow, however, that it is *groundless*. Let me explain. Suppose we consider perceptual beliefs, memory beliefs, and beliefs ascribing mental states to other persons, such beliefs as:

(3) I see a tree,

(4) I had breakfast this morning,

and

(5) That person is in pain.

Although beliefs of this sort are typically taken as basic, it would be a mistake to describe them as *groundless*. Upon having experience of a certain sort, I believe that I am perceiving a tree. In the typical case I do not hold this belief on the basis of other beliefs; it is nonetheless not groundless. My having that characteristic sort of experience—to use Professor Chisholm's language, my being appeared treely to—plays a crucial role in the formation of that belief. It also plays a crucial role in its *justification*. Let us say that a belief is *justified* for a person at a time if (a) he is violating no epistemic duties and is within his epistemic rights in accepting it then and (b) his noetic structure is not defective by virtue of his then accepting it.[41] Then my being appeared to in this characteristic way (together with other circumstances) is what confers on me the right to hold the belief in question; this is what justifies me in accepting it. We could say, if we wish, that this experience is what justifies me in holding it; this is the *ground* of my justification, and, by extension, the ground of the belief itself.

If I see someone displaying typical pain behavior, I take it that he or she is in pain. Again, I do not take the displayed behavior as *evidence* for that belief; I do not infer that belief from others I hold; I do not accept it on the basis of other beliefs. Still, my perceiving the pain behavior plays a unique role in the formation and justification of that belief; as in the previous case it forms the ground of my justification for the belief in question. The same holds for memory beliefs. I seem to remember having breakfast this morning; that is, I have an inclination to believe the proposition that I had breakfast, along with a certain past-tinged experience that is familiar to all but hard to describe. Perhaps we should say that I am appeared to pastly; but perhaps that insufficiently distinguishes the experience in question from that accompanying beliefs about the past not grounded in my own memory. The phenomenology of memory is a rich and unexplored realm; here I have no time to explore it. In this case as in the others, however, there is a justifying circumstance present, a condition that forms the ground of my justification for accepting the memory belief in question.

In each of these cases a belief is taken as basic, and in each case *properly* taken as basic. In each case there is some circumstance or condition that confers justification; there is a circumstance that serves as the *ground* of justification. So in each case

---

[40] For further comment on the Great Pumpkin objection see Alvin Plantinga, "On Reformed Epistemology," *Reformed Journal*, April 1982.

[41] I do not mean to suggest, of course, that if a person believes a true proposition and is justified (in this sense) in believing it, then it follows that he *knows* it; that is a different (and stronger) sense of the term.

there will be some true proposition of the sort

(6) In condition C, S is justified in taking p as basic.

Of course C will vary with p. For a perceptual judgment such as

(7) I see a rose-colored wall before me

C will include my being appeared to in a certain fashion. No doubt C will include more. If I am appeared to in the familiar fashion but know that I am wearing rose-colored glasses, or that I am suffering from a disease that causes me to be thus appeared to, no matter what the color of the nearby objects, then I am not justified in taking (7) as basic. Similarly for memory. Suppose I know that my memory is unreliable; it often plays me tricks. In particular, when I seem to remember having breakfast, then, more often than not, I have not had breakfast. Under these conditions I am not justified in taking it as basic that I had breakfast, even though I seem to remember that I did.

So being appropriately appeared to, in the perceptual case, is not sufficient for justification; some further condition—a condition hard to state in detail—is clearly necessary. The central point here, however, is that a belief is properly basic only in certain conditions; these conditions are, we might say, the ground of its justification and, by extension, the ground of the belief itself. In this sense basic beliefs are not, or are not necessarily, *groundless* beliefs.

Now similar things may be said about belief in God. When the Reformers claim that this belief is properly basic, they do not mean to say, of course, that there are no justifying circumstances for it, or that it is in that sense groundless or gratuitous. Quite the contrary. Calvin holds that God "reveals and daily discloses himself in the whole workmanship of the universe," and the divine art "reveals itself in the innumerable and yet distinct and well ordered variety of the heavenly host." God has so created us that we have a tendency or disposition to see his hand in the world about us. More precisely, there is in us a disposition to believe propositions of the sort *this flower was created by God* or *this vast and intricate universe was created by God* when we contemplate the flower or behold the starry heavens or think about the vast reaches of the universe.

Calvin recognizes, at least implicitly, that other sorts of conditions may trigger this disposition. Upon reading the Bible, one may be impressed with a deep sense that God is speaking to him. Upon having done what I know is cheap, or wrong, or wicked, I may feel guilty in God's sight and form the belief *God disapproves of what I have done*. Upon confession and repentance I may feel forgiven, forming the belief *God forgives me for what I have done*. A person in grave danger may turn to God, asking for his protection and help; and of course he or she then has the belief that God is indeed able to hear and help if he sees fit. When life is sweet and satisfying, a spontaneous sense of gratitude may well up within the soul; someone in this condition may thank and praise the Lord for his goodness, and will of course have the accompanying belief that indeed the Lord is to be thanked and praised.

There are therefore many conditions and circumstances that call forth belief in God: guilt, gratitude, danger, a sense of God's presence, a sense that he speaks, perception of various parts of the universe. A complete job would explore the phenomenology of all these conditions and of more besides. This is a large and important topic, but here I can only point to the existence of these conditions.

Of course none of the beliefs I mentioned a moment ago is the simple belief that God exists. What we have instead are such beliefs as:

(8) God is speaking to me,
(9) God has created all this,
(10) God disapproves of what I have done,
(11) God forgives me,

and

(12) God is to be thanked and praised.

These propositions are properly basic in the right circumstances. But it is quite consistent with this to suppose that the proposition *there is such a person as God* is neither properly basic nor taken as basic by those who believe in God. Perhaps what they take as basic are such propositions as (8)–(12), believing in the existence of God on the basis of propositions such as those. From this point of view it is not wholly accurate to say that it is belief in God that is properly basic; more exactly, what are properly basic are such propositions as (8)–(12), each of which self-evidently entails that God exists. It is not the relatively high-level and general proposition *God exists* that is properly basic, but instead propositions detailing some of his attributes or actions.

Suppose we return to the analogy between belief in God and belief in the existence of perceptual objects, other persons, and the past. Here too it is relatively specific and concrete propositions rather than their more general and abstract colleagues that are properly basic. Perhaps such items as:

(13) There are trees,
(14) There are other persons,

and

(15) The world has existed for more than five minutes

are not in fact properly basic; it is instead such propositions as:

(16) I see a tree,
(17) That person is pleased,

and

(18) I had breakfast more than an hour ago

that deserve that accolade. Of course propositions of the latter sort immediately and self-evidently entail propositions of the former sort, and perhaps there is thus no harm in speaking of the former as properly basic, even though so to speak is to speak a bit loosely.

The same must be said about belief in God. We may say, speaking loosely, that belief in God is properly basic; strictly speaking, however, it is probably not that proposition but such propositions as (8)–(12) that enjoy that status. But the main point, here, is this: belief in God, or (8)–(12), are properly basic; to say so, however, is not to deny that there are justifying conditions for these beliefs, or conditions that confer justification on one who accepts them as basic. They are therefore not groundless or gratuitous.

WILLIAM ALSTON

from Perceiving God

William Alston is another contemporary philosopher who has given us a new way of understanding religious belief and its epistemic propriety that does not appeal to sufficient evidence. Alston appeals to religious experience, or a special form of religious experience that he calls "putative direct awareness of God" or putative "direct perception of God" in his effort to show that religious belief is rational and that persons can be justified in holding religious beliefs about God. (Alston uses the word "putative"—that is, "reputed" or, roughly, "alleged"—to leave it open in his discussion whether what he is calling "perceptions of God" are genuine perceptions or not. Many of his readers will not accept it that there is a God of whom there can be genuine perceptions, although many will accept it, and he wants to address both groups of readers.) Unlike Plantinga, Alston has no objection to the idea that there are grounds for religious belief in God in the sense of "grounds" in which grounds support the truth of the belief that God exists. However he does not argue that since there is (putative) religious experience of God, or perceptions of God, we should on this basis alone conclude that belief in God is justified or rational. His reasoning importantly involves a reference to what he calls *doxastic practices*.

What Alston means by a "doxastic practice" is a belief-forming practice (*doxa* is Greek for opinion or belief, and is a root for words like "orthodox"). A doxastic practice is a means or mechanism that we employ, perhaps without conscious attention, to form our beliefs. He recognizes several doxastic practices. One, for Alston, is the doxastic practice we use to form our beliefs about the physical world around us. Another is the doxastic practice used to form beliefs by memory. Furthermore, for Alston, there is a "mystical perceptual doxastic practice" (or "mystical practice" or "MP" for short). MP is the practice of "M-belief formation on the basis of mystical perception (plus, in some cases, background beliefs)," where an "M-belief" is a belief that God is manifested to one in some way, as when one believes that God is giving one support in one's life.

Alston's "central thesis" is that a person can be justified in holding M-beliefs—beliefs that God has been manifested in some way to one—by virtue of perceiving God being a certain way or doing something (like giving one support). The belief that God exists is not itself an M-belief, but the truth of any M-belief entails the truth of "God exists," so that if a person's M-belief is justified so too will be that person's belief in God's existence. For Alston there is not just one religious mystical perceptual doxastic practice, or MP. Instead there are different mystical doxastic practices in the different religions, so that the Hindu practice is different from the Christian practice. Within Christianity there is the "Christian Mystical Perceptual Doxastic Practice," as Alston calls it (or "Christian mystical practice" or "CMP" for short).

What Alston argues is that a religious belief that God has done something in one's life—that God was present in one's suffering or that God has looked upon one and let His mercy flood over one or that the Holy Spirit has strengthened one in her life—is rational because the doxastic practice by which religious persons—specifically, Christians—form these beliefs on the basis of experiences of God, CMP, is rationally believed to be a reliable doxastic practice. Alston argues that, generally, beliefs formed by a reliable doxastic practice, or one rationally believed to be reliable, are justified or epistemically proper. Since

CMP is a doxastic practice that is rationally taken to be reliable, the beliefs it produces are justified or epistemically proper. For the obvious reason Alston's view is called *reliabilism*.

Our Reading consists of part of the Introduction to Alston's *Perceiving God* and selections from Chap. 5 "The Christian Mystical Perceptual Doxastic Practice (CMP)," in which he argues that the "mystical experience belief forming practice" satisfies the conditions for rational acceptance.*

Perceiving God

Introduction

The central thesis of this book is that experiential awareness of God, or as I shall be saying, the *perception* of God, makes an important contribution to the grounds of religious belief. More specifically, a person can become justified in holding certain kinds of beliefs about God by virtue of perceiving God as being or doing so-and-so. The kinds of beliefs that can be so justified I shall call "M-beliefs" ('M' for *manifestation*). M-beliefs are beliefs to the effect that God is doing something currently vis-à-vis the subject—comforting, strengthening, guiding, communicating a message, sustaining the subject in being—or to the effect that God has some (allegedly) perceivable property—goodness, power, lovingness. The intuitive idea is that by virtue of my being aware of God as sustaining me in being I can justifiably believe that God *is* sustaining me in being. This initial formulation will undergo much refinement in the course of the book.

One qualification should be anticipated right away. The above formulation of my central thesis seems to be referring to God and thus to presuppose that God exists. Moreover, in using the "success" terms, 'the awareness of God' and 'the perception of God', it seems to presuppose that people are sometimes genuinely aware of God and do genuinely perceive God. Since the book is designed for a general audience that includes those who do not antecedently accept those presuppositions, this is undesirable. We can avoid these presuppositions by the familiar device of specifying the experiences in question as those that are *taken by the subject* to be an awareness of God (or would be so taken if the question arose). One can agree that there are experiences that satisfy this description even if one does not believe that God exists or that people ever genuinely perceive Him.

This is basically a work in epistemology, the epistemology of religious perceptual beliefs. I will go into descriptive questions concerning the experience of God, but only so far as is required for the epistemological project. I will set the treatment of our central problem in the context of a general epistemology, though, naturally, we will not be able to give a full presentation of the latter. The reader is warned, however, that fairly

---

heavy doses of abstract epistemological discussion can be expected, especially in Chapters 3 and 4. For those whose interests lie elsewhere, Chapter 3, after section ii, could safely be skimmed or omitted.

At the outset I should make it explicit that though I will be concerned with the epistemic value of the perception of God, I by no means suppose that to be its only, or even its most important, value. From a religious point of view, or more specifically from a Christian point of view, the chief value of the experience of God is that it enables us to enter into personal relationships with God; most importantly, it makes it possible for us to enjoy the relation of loving communion with God for which we were created. But my topic in this book will be the function of the experience of God in providing information about God and our relations to Him.

I have been speaking in terms of epistemic *justification*, rather than in terms of *knowledge*, and the focus will be on the former rather than on the latter. This is partly because I can't *know* that God is loving unless it is *true* that God is loving, and the latter in turn implies that God exists, something I will not be arguing for in this book, except by way of arguing that some beliefs about God are justified. It is also partly because of difficult and controverted questions as to just what is required for knowledge. I will make a few remarks on the knowledge of God in section vii of Chapter 7, but no proper treatment will be attempted.[1]

How wide a net am I casting with my notion of (putative) perception of God? This depends on the concept of God by reference to which we determine whether a given person takes a given experience to be a perception of God. We might be using the term to cover any supposed object of religious worship or anything taken as metaphysically ultimate. However, I will be concentrating more narrowly on the concept of God as it has developed in the major theistic religions—Judaism, Christianity, and Islam. This means that our examples of (putative) perception of God will be taken from those traditions and will be cases in which the subject takes him/herself to be aware of a being that exhibits the features deemed crucial in those traditions for the status of divinity. Moreover, since, as I will be arguing, we cannot look on M-belief formation as a single unified doxastic (belief-forming) practice, we will be forced to think in terms of the form such a practice takes within one or another religious tradition. For this purpose I choose the Christian tradition, the one I know best and, to some extent, from the inside. Although the main lines of the epistemological discussion are intended to have general application, it will be more effective to discuss a particular practice as an exemplar, rather than to say everything in maximally general terms. Other traditions will come into the picture not only as other cases of the general phenomenon, but also as giving rise to incompatible bodies of belief and thus posing problems for the epistemic claims made for Christian perceptual beliefs about God. This side of the matter will be addressed in Chapter 7.

I want to make explicit at the outset that my project here is to be distinguished from anything properly called an "argument from religious experience"

[1] For an approach to the topic in terms of reliability theory see Alston 1991b.

for the existence of God.[2] The thesis defended here is not that the existence of God provides the best explanation for facts about religious experience or that it is possible to *argue* in any way from the latter to the former. It is rather that people sometimes do perceive God and thereby acquire justified beliefs about God. In the same way, if one is a direct realist about sense perception, as I am, one will be inclined to hold not that internal facts about sense experience provide one with premises for an effective argument to the existence of external physical objects, but rather that in enjoying sense experience one thereby perceives external physical objects and comes to have various justified beliefs about them, without the necessity of exhibiting those beliefs (or their propositional contents) as the conclusion of any sort of argument.

Am I suggesting that the belief in the *existence* of God is susceptible of a perceptual justification? Well, yes and no. Typically those who take themselves to perceive God are already firmly convinced of the reality of God, and so they don't suppose that to be (part of) what they learn from the experience. In the same way I was already firmly convinced of the existence of the furniture in my house before I cast my eyes on it

this morning. What one typically takes oneself to learn from a particular perception is that, e.g., God is communicating a message to me now or that the furniture is in the same arrangement today as yesterday. Nevertheless, there are exceptions. I sometimes see some item of furniture for the first time, and thereby perceptually learn of its existence as well as of some of its properties. And more than one person has passed from unbelief to belief through (putatively) experientially encountering God. Moreover, there is the point nicely made by Alvin Plantinga (1983, p. 81) that even if 'God exists' is not the propositional content of typical theistic perceptual beliefs,[3] those propositional contents self-evidently entail it. 'God is good' or 'God gave me courage to meet that situation' self-evidently entail 'God exists', just as 'That tree is bare' or 'That tree is tall' self-evidently entail 'That tree exists'. Hence if the former beliefs can be perceptually justified, they can serve in turn, by one short and unproblematic step, to justify the belief in God's existence.

I have been speaking of the perception of God as serving to justify beliefs with a restricted range of propositional contents—M-beliefs. That implies that if the complete belief system of a religion

[2] Most discussions of the place of "religious experience" in the epistemology of religious belief are carried on in terms of such an argument. See, e.g., Mackie 1982, chap. 10, and O'Hear 1984, chap. 2. Swinburne 1979, chap. 13, casts his discussion in terms of such an argument, even though what he defends is more like what I am defending in this book. (See Chapter 5, section ii, for a comparison of my enterprise with Swinburne's.) Even those who unambiguously think of the matter as I do sometimes fall into thinking of the problem as one of whether "religious experience" furnishes sufficient "evidence" for the existence of God. See, e.g., Gutting 1982, pp. 147–49. The discussion of this whole area would be greatly improved by one's keeping in mind the distinction between holding that certain experiences constitute veridical perceptions of God, and holding that certain experiences can be used as premises in an argument (explanatory or otherwise) to the existence of God.
[3] 'Perceptual belief' is my term, not Plantinga's. He speaks of "properly basic beliefs". See Chapter 5, section ii, on the relation of my views to Plantinga's.

is to be justified, there will have to be other grounds as well. The only alternative would be that the whole system can be built up on the basis of M-beliefs by acceptable modes of derivation; and that seems unlikely, especially for a historical religion like Christianity, to which claims about God's action in history are essential. Thus even if the claims of this book for the perceptual justification of M-beliefs are made out, there is the further problem of how this fits into the total basis for a religious belief system. That issue will be broached in the final chapter, though a full treatment lies outside the bounds of this book.

In the present intellectual climate it would be well to make it explicit that this discussion is conducted from a full-bloodedly realist perspective, according to which in religion as elsewhere we mean what we assert to be true of realities that are what they are regardless of what we or other human beings believe of them, and regardless of the "conceptual scheme" we apply to them (except, of course, when what we are talking about is our thought, belief, or concepts). I take this to be a fundamental feature of human thought and talk. Thus, in epistemically evaluating the practice of forming M-beliefs I am interested in whether that practice yields beliefs that are (often) true in this robustly realist sense—not, or not just, in whether it yields beliefs that conform to the rules of the relevant language-game, or beliefs that carry out some useful social function. I must confess that I cannot provide an external proof that this practice, or any other doxastic

practice, achieves that result, as I shall make fully explicit in Chapters 3 and 4. Such support as I muster for that conclusion will be of a different sort. Nevertheless, what I am interested in determining, so far as in me lies, is whether the practice succeeds in accurately depicting a reality that is what it is however we think of it.

Even if our age were firmly realist in its predilections, my central thesis would still be in stark contradiction to assumptions that are well nigh universally shared in intellectual circles.[4] It is often taken for granted by the wise of this world, believers and unbelievers alike, that "religious experience" is a purely subjective phenomenon. Although it may have various psychosocial functions to play, any claims to its cognitive value can be safely dismissed without a hearing. It is the purpose of this book to challenge that assumption and to marshal the resources that are needed to support its rejection.

Although it is no part of my aim here to explain why people hold religious beliefs, I will mention one possible bearing of the book on a question of that sort. Contemporary American nonbelieving academics, in philosophy and elsewhere, often find it curious that some of their intelligent and highly respected colleagues are believers even though they do not claim to possess any conclusive arguments for their religious beliefs. I believe that what is revealed in this book concerning the role of the experience of God in providing grounds, both psychological and epistemic, for religious belief can help to explain this phenomenon.[5]

---

[4] Though not in the population at large.
[5] I throw this out as a suggestion. I have no relevant statistical surveys in my pocket.

CHAPTER 5

The Christian Mystical Perceptual Doxastic Practice (CMP)

iii Reasons for Denying that CMP Is a Full-fledged, Experiential Doxastic Practice

A. Partial Distribution of Mystical Perception

First, there is the point touched on in Chapter 4 (section v) to the effect that CMP, and indeed MP generally—unlike SP [sense perceptual doxastic practice] and memory, introspective, and reasoning practices—is not universally engaged in by normal adult human beings. That was brought up in Chapter 4 in connection with the question of whether social establishments should be allowed to confer prima facie rationality only on universal practices. There I argued that there is no reason to suppose that a practice engaged in by some proper part of the population is less likely to be a source of truth than one we all engage in. No doubt, this fact of partial distribution makes for various difficulties in discussing the problems of this book. When we are doing the epistemology of sense perception or memory or inductive reasoning, we can proceed on the assurance that all our readers are fellow participants. No such assumption can be made here. Nevertheless, I see no real reason for supposing that the partiality of participation derogates from the epistemic claims of a doxastic practice. Indeed, I do not find this consideration bulking large in the writings of my opponents, though it may exercise a sub rosa influence on unfavorable evaluations of MP. Thus it is worth pointing out that a priori it seems just as likely that some aspects of reality are accessible only to persons who satisfy certain conditions not satisfied by all human beings, as that some aspects are equally accessible to all. I cannot see any a priori reason for denigrating a practice either for being universal or for being partial. We have to learn from experience which features of the world are equally open to all and which are open only to an elite. Moreover, quite apart from the religious case, we can see many belief-forming practices, universally regarded as rational, that are practiced by only a small minority. Higher mathematics and theoretical physics certainly satisfy this description. But what about *experiential* doxastic practices? Well, in acknowledging SP to be universal we were speaking too roughly. There are large stretches of the territory that are open to all normal human beings, but there are also restricted domains that are available only to a chosen few. Only the connoisseur can perceptually discriminate the taste and smell of wines so finely as to be able to tell by tasting a wine from what Burgundy commune or Bordeaux chateau it originated. Relatively few persons can follow inner voices in complex orchestral performances. But such belief-forming practices are not denied epistemic credentials on the grounds of narrow distribution.[14]

---

[14] At this point the reader might protest. "In those sensory discrimination cases there are universally available ways to authenticate the alleged discriminatory power. It can be independently determined whether

Moreover, the belief-system ingredient in CMP provides explanation for the partial distribution. This will differ somewhat with the particular theological orientation, but the most basic point is that God has set certain requirements that must be met before He reveals Himself to our experience, at least consistently and with relative fullness. "Blessed are the pure in heart for they shall see God." Again, the details of this vary, but it is generally acknowledged in the tradition that an excessive preoccupation and concern with worldly goods, certain kinds of immorality—particularly self-centeredness and unconcern with one's fellows—and a mind that is closed to the possibility of communion with God, are all antithetical to an awareness of God's presence. This being the case, and given well-known facts about human predilections, it is the reverse of unexpected that not all people should participate in mystical perception.

We can see this criticism from partial distribution to exhibit two vices, each of which we will encounter repeatedly in the ensuing discussion. First, in denigrating CMP for not exhibiting a certain feature of SP, namely, universal distribution, the objector is guilty of what I shall call *epistemic imperialism*, unwarrantedly taking the standards of one doxastic practice as normative for all. The "unwarrantedly" qualification is crucial. Some features of SP are de rigueur for any respectable practice,—for example, embodying certain distinctive input-output functions. But

universal distribution, so I claim, is not one of those. On reflection we can see no reason for supposing that every reliable doxastic practice will be engaged in by all normal, adult human beings. Second, in pointing to uncontroversial examples of reliable doxastic practices with quite restricted distribution—theoretical physics and wine-tasting—I show the objector to be guilty of using an (unwarranted) double standard. CMP is being condemned for features shared by other practices that are approved. This is to apply *arbitrarily* a double standard, as when one takes whites to be innocent until proved guilty but takes blacks to be guilty until proved innocent, or when one requires a higher level of achievement for women than for men in executive positions. Again the qualifiers, "unwarrantedly" and "arbitrarily", are important. There is nothing wrong with applying different standards to two candidates if there is sufficient reason to do so. It is quite in order to require a higher level of education for executives than for manual laborers. But no reason can be given for accepting some doxastic practices that extend only to a certain elite as epistemically in order, and then rejecting CMP *on the very ground* that it is so restricted. Thus the objection from partial distribution is particularly rich in vices. It exhibits two that we shall be encountering repeatedly: (1) *imperialism*, unwarrantedly taking features of one practice to be normative for others, and (2) *double standard*, unwarrantedly making requirements of one practice from which others are exempted.

---

the wine our expert assigned to Chateau Margaux really was made there. But no such public validation is possible for MP." (See. e.g., Daniels 1989, Gale 1991.) That's as it may be. I am by no means claiming that MP is like these sensory-discrimination practices in all epistemically relevant respects. Here I am only making the point that an experiential doxastic practice should not be held suspect just on grounds of partial distribution. The question of the kinds of intersubjective checks available will be addressed later in this chapter.

B. Extent of the Organized Practice

Second, there are doubts as to whether there really is any widely shared *practice* of forming perceptual beliefs about God, as we have depicted doxastic practices. This may be based on a doubt that the formation of such beliefs is widely dispersed in the population. I have already spoken to this in Chapter 1, where I cited sociological studies that indicate that an experiential awareness of God is not at all uncommon (fn. 24). But even if many people form M-beliefs, there is still the question of whether there is a widely shared *practice* of the sort I have labelled 'CMP'. Isn't it more accurate to say that for the most part people who take themselves to perceive God are each "going it alone", doing it on their own, without reliance on the kind of socially established procedures required for a full-blown doxastic practice? No doubt, in Catholic, monastic mystical circles, there is a well-organized practice of cultivating union with God, including putative direct experiential awareness of God, and a standardized set of criteria for distinguishing the real thing from the spurious. But why suppose that other Christians who take themselves to perceive God and who form M-beliefs on that basis are involved in any such practice?

We must be careful not to suppose that the structure of a doxastic practice has to be explicitly formulated in the minds of the participants. Here, as with many other things, the tacit is the normal and the explicit the exception. Just as people internalize and utilize systems of semantic and syntactic rules without ever becoming explicitly aware of them as such, and just as they reason and criticize reasoning in accordance with principles they never explicitly formulate, so it is with doxastic practices. One picks up the mastery of a language from one's social surroundings without any explicit formulation of the structure of the language, and one picks up ways of perceptually recognizing chickens and dogs and houses and apples without anyone ever saying in so many words what the identifying marks are. In the same way one picks up ways of recognizing God and His activities, and criteria for separating veridical perception of God from counterfeits, without any of this ever being explicitly formulated. If rules of speech and of belief formation could not be operative without being verbally articulated, our voices would be stilled and our minds emptied of cognitive content. We are bound together by ties that take hard digging to bring to light. This is not to say that what is internalized in learning CMP is as definite and as uniform across the population as is the structure of a natural language or the marks of sense-perceivable items. But the existence of a socially shared practice is compatible with a certain degree of looseness and individual variation in the constituent rules and criteria.

Considerations like these are sufficient to show that the absence of explicit awareness of the constitutive principles of a doxastic practice on the part of S does not show that S is not a participant. But they do not show that CMP *is* widely engaged in outside monastic circles. An ideally convincing case for this would be difficult to bring off. We would have to show that a significant proportion of mainline Christians who form M-beliefs on the basis of experience mostly do so in accordance with common principles for going from features of the experience to belief contents, and share common grounds for the criticism of such beliefs. The former task is rendered difficult, if not impossible, by our lack of an adequate vocabulary for basic phenomenal qualities of mystical experience. Nevertheless, a survey of reports like those cited in

Chapter 1 strongly suggests that people in the Christian community do tend to make the same or similar attributions to God on the basis of similar experiences. The latter task, determining whether there are common principles of criticism, is somewhat more manageable, though the practical problems of subjecting an adequate sample to the required tests is staggering. But just by doing a survey of the relevant literature we can verify the claim that an over-rider system of the sort I have been describing is often operative. Let's begin with professed mystics in organized monastic communities, who are very much preoccupied with distinguishing genuine from spurious experiences of God and often explicitly discuss criteria. I will restrict myself here to passages from St. Teresa's *Autobiography* (1957). First an expression of concern as to whether certain experiences are genuine.

> His Majesty began to give me the prayer of quiet very frequently, and often the prayer of union too, which lasted for some time. Since there have been cases lately of women who have been grossly deceived and subjected to great illusions through the machinations of the devil, I was very much afraid. For I felt very great delight and sweetness, which it was often beyond my power to avoid. On the other hand I was conscious of a deep inward assurance that this was of God, especially when I was engaged in prayer, and I found that I was the better for these experiences and had developed greater fortitude. But as soon as I became a little distracted, I would be afraid again, and would wonder whether it was not the devil that was suspending my understanding and making me think this a good thing, in order to deprive me of mental prayer, to stop me from my

meditating on the Passion, and to prevent my using my mind. (P. 162)

From time to time St. Teresa identifies some criteria or marks by which the genuine presence of God can be recognized.

> I believe that it is possible to tell whether this state comes from the spirit of God or whether, starting from devotion given us by God, we have attained it by our own endeavours. For if, as I have said before, we try of our own accord to pass on to this quiet of the will, it leads to nothing. Everything is quickly over, and the result is aridity. If it comes from the devil, I think an experienced soul will realize it. For it leaves disquiet behind it, and very little humility, and does not do much to prepare the soul for the effects which are produced when it comes from God. It brings neither light to the understanding nor strength to the will. (P. 108)
>
> I think it possible that a person who has laid some request before God with most loving concern may imagine that he hears a voice telling him whether his prayer will be granted or not. This may well be, though once he has heard some genuine message, he will see clearly what this voice is, for there is a great difference between the two experiences. If his answer has been invented by the understanding, however subtly it may be contrived, he perceives the intellect ordering the words and speaking them. It is just as if a person were composing a speech... and the understanding will then realize that it is not listening but working, and that the words it is inventing are imprecise and fanciful; they have not the clarity of the real locution. In such cases it is in our power to deflect our attention, just as we can stop speaking

and be silent. But in the true locution, this cannot be done. Another sign, which is the surest of all, is that these false locutions leave no results, whereas when the Lord speaks, words lead to deeds; and although the words may be of reproof and not of devotion, they prepare the soul, make it ready, and move it to tenderness. (P. 175)

By now I have had so much experience of the devil's work that he knows I can recognize him and so torments me less in these ways than he used to. His part in an experience can be detected by the restlessness and discomfort with which it begins, by the turmoil that he creates in the soul so long as it lasts, also by the darkness and affliction into which he plunges it, and by its subsequent dryness and indisposition for prayer or anything else that is good . . . In true humility, on the other hand, although the soul knows its wretchedness, and although we are distressed to see what we are, there is no attendant turmoil or spiritual unrest. True humility does not bring darkness or aridity, but on the contrary gives the soul peace, sweetness, and light. (P. 215)

. . . I merely believed the revelation to be true in the sense that it was not contrary to what is written in the Holy Scriptures, or to the laws of the Church, which we are obliged to keep. (P. 239)

If it proceeded from our own mind, not only would it not have the great effects that is has, but it would have none at all . . . instead of being restored and fortified, the soul will become wearier; it will become exhausted and nauseated. But it is impossible to exaggerate the riches that accompany a true vision; it brings health and comfort even to the body. I advanced this argument, amongst others, when they told me—as they often did—that my visions were of the devil and were all imaginary . . . I once said to some of these people whom I used to consult: "If you were to tell me that someone I knew well and to whom I had just been talking is not really himself, and that I was imagining things and you knew what the truth really was, I would believe your statement rather than my own eyes. But if this person had left me some jewels as a pledge of his great love, and if I were still holding them, and if I had possessed no jewels before and now found myself rich where I had been poor, I could not possibly believe that this was delusion, even if I wanted to." I said too that I could show them these jewels, for everyone who knew me saw clearly that my soul had changed . . . I could not believe, therefore, that if the devil were doing this in order to deceive me and drag me down to hell, he would adopt means so contrary to his purpose as to take away my vices and give me virtues and strength instead. For I clearly saw that these visions had made me a different person. (P. 202)

From such passages spiritual directors and mystical theologians have distilled criteria of genuine perceptions of God. Here is a selection from a list given in de Guibert (1953).[15]

---

[15] See also Parente 1945. These two are simply plucked from a large number of books of spiritual direction that say essentially the same thing. For a famous Protestant treatment see Jonathan Edwards, *A Treatise Concerning Religious Affections* (1746), ed. John E. Smith (New Haven, Conn.: Yale University Press, 1959).

True	False
Intellect	
1. Not concerned with useless affairs	Futile, useless, vain preoccupations
2. Discretion	Exaggerations, excesses
Will	
1. Interior peace	Perturbation, disquiet
2. Trust in God	Presumption or despair
3. Patience in pains	Impatience with trials
4. Simplicity, sincerity	Duplicity, dissimulation
5. Charity that is meek, kindly, self-forgetful	False, bitter pharisaical zeal

I know of no canonical systematization of these criteria, but it seems to me highly plausible to take the moral criteria to be the most fundamental. The criteria of conformity to the tradition (Scripture and the Church) are obviously derivative. For how was that tradition built up, except by taking some phenomena rather than others as involving genuine perception of God? As for the way in which the locutions or whatever are presented, it seems plausible to suppose that whatever phenomenal character we fasten on—distinctness, seeming to come from beyond oneself, or whatever—this could possibly be a result of psychological processes within oneself if those processes are sufficiently blocked off from consciousness. But the fruits of the experience in the way of sanctification of the individual are another matter. As Teresa says, if a pledge of jewels has been left, it is difficult not to believe that this is the real thing. We might think of mystics as learning from experience which phenomenal features are regularly correlated with the kinds of results (humility, love, joy, peace, etc.) that would be expected from prolonged contact with God; these features can then be taken as derivative marks of genuineness.

Thus "professional" mystics, more generally, persons under spiritual direction, do recognize and use a fairly definite set of criteria of genuineness. With "amateurs", whose participation in the practice is not explicitly organized, the picture is not so clear. For one thing, the reports here are very sketchy. Even if one or another of these persons is sufficiently reflective to articulate her overrider system, they have not written extensively enough to communicate it to us. Moreover, there is no doubt but that they take a less critical attitude toward their mystical experiences than do monastics. Not being under the supervision of a spiritual adviser and lacking contact with others who have had longer experience in the things of the spirit, they are not so sensitized to the possibilities of delusion and the need for external criteria; hence they tend much more to repose complete confidence in their spontaneous understanding of their experiences.

Nevertheless, it is unlikely that a contemporary educated believer should suppose it to be impossible that what seems to be a direct awareness of God is delusory. Our contemporaries are more likely, if anything, to suppose that the chances are against such experiences being veridical. Hence when such a person finds herself spontaneously believing that she is experiencing God, she is unlikely to be unaware of the possibility that the experience may not be what it seems, even if in the heat of the moment this idea does not occur to her. And it is quite plausible that if she goes so far as to explicitly raise the question of genuineness, the kinds of criteria mentioned above would appeal to her as the right ones to use: conformity with the tradition, concordance with what God could be expected to be, do, or say, and fruits in the way of spiritual development. Hence, though direct evidence is in short supply, I think it quite plausible to suppose that CMP, as I have described it, is widespread at various levels of explicitness within the Christian community. However, I want to emphasize that the extent of distribution is not crucial for my central contentions. Even if CMP were confined to monastics or to other very restricted groups, it would still be worthy of consideration as a possible source of epistemic justification.

To provide a bit of evidence for the claims of the previous paragraph, I will quote some unpublished remarks of Robert M. Adams, made in the course of commenting on a precursor of Chapter 1.

> ... I would like to reflect on a religious experience of my own adolescence. I wanted to feel God's presence in prayer. After a time of looking for it, I noticed a certain feeling that I commonly had when I prayed. It was in some ways rather like a sensation. I wondered whether this could be the experience of the presence of God. I think I sometimes took it to be so. But was it really so? Did I perceive God in that experience? I had my doubts then, and I have them now.
>
> The experience certainly did have a content that went beyond anything I could convey discursively. One who had not had a similar experience could not know exactly what I felt ... I do remember some of my misgivings about it, however. One main misgiving I would express, in the context of my present remarks, by a question about what I felt that went beyond anything I could grasp or express discursively. Was it something about *God*, or only something about *me*? Of

course, in those moments when I believed the experience to be genuine I took myself to be feeling the presence of a God who had all the attributes I believed God to have—but that's discursive content. ...

> A more disturbing doubt about my adolescent feeling of God's presence in prayer has to do with its causes. Was it something I was doing to myself? Was it perhaps a distinctive complex bodily sensation caused by squeezing my eyelids shut very hard and unconsciously controlling my breathing in a certain way? Or was it simply begotten of my imagination by my desire to feel God's presence?

I certainly do not wish to suggest that a brilliant, sophisticated philosopher like Robert Adams, even as an adolescent, is typical of the amateur mystic. Nevertheless, I find in this account a nice presentation of doubts that would naturally occur to a person in the contemporary world who tends to suppose himself to be directly aware of God. And though Adams does not get so far here as to excogitate ways of resolving his question, it would be natural to go from his questionings to criteria not unlike those of Teresa.

C. Not a Genuine Source of New Information

But even if CMP is admitted to be a genuine doxastic practice, there may still be doubts as to whether it is one that is capable of forming new beliefs from experiential input. It may be suspected that what the practice amounts to is just reading one's prior religious beliefs into a cognitively indifferent experiential matrix, rather than forming new beliefs on the basis of experience, plugging into a genuinely new source of information.

Even when we discount all the identifiable conditions in which illusions, dreams, deceptions and mistakes occur . . . one influence is likely to remain which disposes him or her to have or to interpret numinous experience in a particular way. That influence is the cultural and religious environment of the person; the possession of one world view rather than another, or at the very least, familiarity with, or concern with, one system of ideas rather than another. Now there is ample evidence to show that numinous religious experiences are frequently received as, indeed are normally articulated by means of, the religious forms, symbols and figures with which one is familiar, and these may be as incompatibly different as a feeling of union with the god at a Dionysian festival on an Aegean island, or a vision of the Blessed Virgin Mary in a Dublin suburb. To put it baldly: one encounters what one has been brought up to expect to encounter. This, not the independent existence of multiple and incompatible external objects, seems to account for the similarities of what is reported as the object of religious experience within a given community, and for differences between communities with differing world views.[16]

This claim is closely connected with a similar charge I considered in Chapter 1 to the effect that mystical experiences are not genuinely perceptual, even phenomenologically, since the subjects are just reading antecedent beliefs into essentially subjective experiences. The difference between the two claims is this. In Chapter 1 we were considering whether our subjects were correct in taking their experiences to be phenomenologically of a perceptual sort, involving an experiential presentation of something or other to one's awareness as so-and-so. We may take that question to have been settled in the affirmative. That is the way the experience presents itself to its subjects. Now we are asking about the belief formation that stems from that experiential presentation. To what extent is it a source of new information, and to what extent does it just read back to the subject the beliefs the subject brings to the experience?

Even though the questions are different, we can draw on some of the same points in answering this one. First let's separate the charge that one brings an antecedently possessed conceptual scheme to one's experience from the charge that one acquires no new beliefs. The former clearly holds as much for SP as for CMP. When I look around me I typically make use of my familiar and much used concepts of houses, trees, grass, and so on, in recognizing what I see and forming beliefs about them. And so it is with CMP. The Christian typically brings the conceptual framework of Christian theology to her putative experience of God and makes use of it in construing what she is perceiving and how that is presenting itself to her. To be sure, perception *can* lead to conceptual development, in both SP and MP. People and societies do acquire new concepts and modify old concepts over time, and presumably their experience plays some role in this. Indeed, how did the individual

---

[16] J. C. A. Gaskin, *The Quest for Eternity* (New York: Penguin Books, 1984), pp. 101–2. Gaskin is making a number of points simultaneously here, including the problem posed by the plurality of incompatible forms of MP. Here I am concerned with the point that the content of the experience is determined by one's antecedent beliefs.

acquire the concepts that she possessed prior to a particular experience? Past experiences played some role in this unless the concepts were purely innate. Nevertheless, I dare say that the overwhelming majority of perceptual situations, both SP and CMP, involve the application of antecedently possessed concepts. The main point I want to make is that in neither case does this have any tendency to prevent one from genuinely perceiving objective realities or gaining new information about them. If it did we would rarely learn anything in sense perception. Indefinitely many specific bits of information can be formulated by the same conceptual scheme, and the fact that I antecedently possess the concepts that I use to articulate a given perception has no tendency to show that I already had the information I claim to derive from that perception.

But what about the second charge? Does the alleged mystic perceiver learn anything genuinely new in her perception, or is she just reading antecedently held beliefs into it? In considering this question we can usefully distinguish two relations of a particular perceptual belief to the perceiver's prior stock of beliefs. First, the belief may represent a net addition to the stock. This is frequently the case in both SP and MP. As for the latter, remember that M-beliefs often concern God's specific relation to the individual perceiver at the moment, and this kind of information obviously was not in the background belief system. I don't already know or believe, prior to the experience, that God is comforting or upbraiding me at that moment, or that God tells me then what I ought to concentrate on now. Second, the perception may present what one already knows or believes, save for updating. I look at my

house as I approach and it presents itself to my experience as shingled. But I already knew that it was shingled; the only possibility for a net increment is that I learn from the perception that it is still shingled. Likewise, in MP God may appear to me in an experience as supremely loving, but I already firmly believed that. There isn't even any significant updating to be derived here, if one can assume that changes in the divine nature are out of the question. Even so, the experience can add to my total sum of justification for believing that God is loving, even if it doesn't add to the firmness of the belief.[17] And of course, there are obvious noncognitive advantages in experiencing God's love in addition to just believing or knowing "at a distance" that it is there.

But though these considerations draw the teeth of the claim that CMP cannot be a source of new beliefs, it must be acknowledged that CMP does not typically alter the major outlines of a person's faith. Ordinarily the subject already has a more or less firm Christian faith, which is left largely unchanged by mystical experience. What the experience does yield, cognitively, is: (a) information about God's particular relations to the subject; (b) additional grounds for beliefs already held, particularly the belief that God does exist; (c) additional "insight" into facets of the scheme. Examples of the latter range from the more to the less controversial. On the former end are reports by St. Teresa to have gained new understanding of such doctrines as the Trinity and the Incarnation by having "seen" how God is three persons or how the divine and human natures of Christ are united.[18] On the less controversial side is the fact that one has more of a

---

[17] If a belief is already maximally firm, them obviously, any additional support I acquire for it will not make it firmer.
[18] St. Teresa 1957, chap. 39, pp. 304–5.

grasp of what a certain fact is like by having experienced it, rather that just believed it. I may believe on general grounds that my wife loves me, but I have a much fuller sense of what this love is like if I have experienced a variety of manifestations. And so it is here.

I would like to stress that even if one acquired no new beliefs at all from CMP, it could provide additional justification for old beliefs. In the final chapter I will address the question of how mystical perception interacts with other grounds for religious belief in the total spectrum of such grounds. There we will note how perceiving God can shore up the belief system at points at which it would otherwise be a bit shaky.

D. Obvious Differences between Sense Experience and Mystical Experience

In Chapter 1, section viii, I pointed out some of the obvious and important differences between mystical experience and sense experience. Sense experience is continuously, insistently, and unavoidably present during all our waking hours; mystical experience, except for a few choice souls, is a rare phenomenon. Sense experience, especially vision, is vivid and richly detailed, bursting with information, more than we can possibly encode; mystical experience is usually but dim, meager, and obscure. The net effect of these differences is to render MP much less useful as a source of information, even if its epistemic credentials are in order. One might think that these differences could not possibly be adduced by any reasonable person as a reason for refusing to take seriously the idea that MP is a genuine source of knowledge and/or justified belief; but that would be a mistake. Daniels (1989) points out that whereas sense perception reveals indefinitely many trivial and unimportant facts about its objects, along with things of interest to us, mystical perception reveals only what is of such supreme importance as to call forth affective reactions of ecstasy, joy, and peace.

> People with sight notice and can attest to complexes of things whose presence or absence is indifferent to their desires: like the textures and gradations of hues and shades of color on the ceiling of an office they find themselves in or the pattern of cracks in a sidewalk. . . . Gifted musicians, judging contests of their juniors, may hear in great detail aspects of performances that, while not thoroughly abysmal, are quite undistinguished and forgettable. (P. 493)

On the other hand:

> Those who claim to have religious experiences tend not to acquire complexes of trivial, unimportant beliefs from them. This lack is a very significant one. Claims of religious experience tend to be just too important and too narrowly focused and simple. Is it that the religious simply fail to report to the rest of us or to each other the trivial yet complex webs of facts their religious experiences reveal? If the answer is no, then we must begin to entertain suspicions that the explanation for these experiences does not lie in any perceived religious reality, but is rather the effect of some other cause—perhaps excessive emotion and fervor, perhaps the belief that since God causes everything, His hand will be seen in the exceptional experiences life does bring. (Pp. 498–99)

Daniels has identified one possible explanation of the difference cited. But perhaps this explanation will seem less compelling when we reflect that the difference in question is simply one aspect of the difference I have already noted as to the amount of informational content. Since SP, particularly vision, carries such an overload of information it is not at all surprising that much of it will be trivial and uninteresting. Whereas, given the meager content of mystical experience, there is no room, so to speak, for a lot of surplus baggage. If I'm walking to California from New York, I won't take along all the unnecessary frills I would take if I were driving. Of course, it is *conceivable* that a much thinner mode of experience would carry the same proportion of the uninteresting, but it seems much more plausible that details unrelated to our needs would be found in modes of cognition that are overloaded with information. Whether we think of perception as designed by God, or as "selected" by evolution, its basic function is to give us information that we need for the conduct of life. A meager source would have to concentrate on what is important, or it would not be chosen or selected at all. Only the rich source can "afford" to give us lots of extras. Hence I can't see that the restriction of MP to what is of interest counts against its epistemic pretensions.

E. Checks and Tests of Particular Perceptual Beliefs

We have been making much of the fact that overrider systems are essential to doxastic practices, and we have brought out something of the character of the overrider system to be found in CMP. Interestingly enough, a favorite criticism of MP has been its lack of an effective overrider system. A much-discussed statement of this criticism is found in Martin 1959.

There are no tests agreed upon to establish genuine experience of God and distinguish it decisively from the nongenuine. Indeed, many theologians deny the possibility of any such test or set of tests. (P. 67)

It is only when one comes to such a case as knowing God that the society of tests and checkup procedures, which surround other instances of knowing, completely vanishes. What is put in the place of these tests and checking procedures is an immediacy of knowledge that is supposed to carry its own guarantee. (P. 70)

Because "having direct experience of God" does not admit the relevance of a society of tests and checking procedures, it tends to place itself in the company of the other ways of knowing which preserve their self-sufficiency, "uniqueness", and "incommunicability" by making a psychological and not an existential claim. For example, "I seem to see a piece of blue paper", requires no further test or checking procedure in order to be considered true. (P. 72)

. . . the religious statement "I have direct experience of God" is of a different status from the physical object statement "I see a star" and shows a distressing similarity to the low-claim assertion "I seem to see a star." (P. 75)

A terminological note before we proceed. I have taken Martin's reference to "a society of tests and checkup procedures" to be equivalent to my "over-rider system". And yet tests can have a positive as well as a negative outcome; they do not always override. Actually I have been thinking of my "overrider systems" in this way all along, though the term fails to indicate that. From now on, whether I speak of "checks and tests" or "overrider systems", I should be taken as thinking of procedures and criteria for testing beliefs for correctness and putative justifications for efficacy, where these tests may have either a positive or a negative outcome.

As these quoted passages indicate, Martin takes the lack of such checking procedures to cancel out any objective truth claim that goes beyond a report of one's present conscious experience. I won't spend any time on this charge; it is based on a public empirical verifiability criterion of meaningfulness that I see no reason to accept. Apart from reliance on such a criterion the lack of checks and tests cannot prevent one from *claiming*, as an objective truth, that God is, or is doing, so-and-so. The charge I will take seriously is epistemic. The lack of a system of checks and tests prevents M-beliefs from being experientially justified. We find this version in Rowe (1982), where he alleges that the absence of effective checking procedures prevents the application of Swinburne's "principle of credulity" to mystical experience, where the principle of credulity is roughly equivalent to our claim that established experiential doxastic practices confer prima facie justification on their outputs.

> . . . there is an important difference between (1) knowing how to proceed to find positive reasons, if there should be any, for rejecting an experience as probably delusive, and (2) not knowing how to proceed to find such positive reasons if there should be any. When we are in situation (1), as we clearly are in the case of those who habitually drink alcohol to excess and report experiences which they take to be of rats and snakes, the application of the principle of credulity is clearly in order. But when we are in situation (2) as we seem to be in the case of reli-

gious experience, I am doubtful that the application of the principle of credulity is warranted. Since we don't know what circumstances make for delusory religious experiences . . . we can't really go about the process of determining whether there are or are not positive reasons for thinking religious experiences to be probably delusive. (Pp. 90–91)

But, contra Martin and Rowe, there are, as we have seen, such checking procedures.

* * * * * * * * * * * * * * * * * * * *

The specific theses of these authors differ somewhat. I have already noted that O'Hear, for example, is pursuing a line that takes explanatory efficacy to be epistemologically crucial. But they all [various critical authors] take it that the lack in CMP of the kinds of checks from other observers that is characteristic of SP is a serious epistemological defect and that it prevents us from supposing M-beliefs based on mystical perception to be in a strong epistemic position. I shall be discussing this charge in my own terms, taking it to amount to the claim that since CMP lacks this kind of check by other observers it does not have the kind of overrider system that a doxastic practice must possess if it is to confer prima facie justification on its outputs. Experientially based beliefs must be subject to test by the experience of other observers in the SP way if they are to count as prima facie justified by that experience. The price of justification for an objective claim about the world is subjection to an appropriate objective scrutiny by other members of the community. *Objective* epistemic worth requires *intersubjective* validation. Otherwise we are left with only the subject's predilection for a particular interpretation.

This is a powerfully tempting position. Our conviction that sense perception puts us in effective cognitive contact with a surrounding world is intimately tied up with the fact that when we compare our perceptual beliefs with those of relevant others, they exhibit a massive commonality. And if we can have no such interpersonal confirmation how can we distinguish veridical perception from dreams and fancies? Nevertheless, I am going to resist the temptation. The argument rests on an unjustified, and unjustifiable, assumption: that reports of perception of God are properly treated in the same way as reports of perception of the physical environment, so that if the former cannot be validated in the same way as the latter they have no epistemic standing as objective claims. But there is no reason to suppose it *appropriate* to require the same checks and tests for them as for sense-perceptual reports, and every (or at least sufficient) reason to suppose it inappropriate. Here we have what is perhaps our most glaring example of epistemic *imperialism*, unwarrantedly subjecting the outputs of one doxastic practice to the requirements of another.

The first step in this defense is to point out that CMP is a different doxastic practice from SP and to ask why we should suppose that beliefs from the one practice should be subject to the same tests as beliefs from the other in order that the

former be rationally respectable. We do not generally accept such cross-practice extrapolations. Consider an analogous critique of introspective reports—for example, that I now feel excited. Here too the report cannot be assessed on the basis of whether other people experience the same thing under the same conditions. Even if they don't that has no tendency to show that I didn't feel excited. But this will not lead most of us to deny that such beliefs can be justified.[29] We would simply point out that we should not expect beliefs about one's own conscious states to be subject to the same sorts of tests as beliefs about ships and sealing wax. Tests of a public sort can be given to determine the subject's mastery of mentalistic language and her general reliability as a reporter. But as for particular reports, if we can assume general competence, there is no appeal beyond her word. The formation of beliefs about one's own conscious states belongs to a different doxastic practice with a different range of inputs, different input-output functions, a different conceptual scheme, a different subject matter, and different criteria of justification.[30]

This example is designed to suggest the *possibility* that it is just as inappropriate to subject perceptual beliefs about God to the tests of SP as to subject introspective beliefs to such tests, and that the inability to do so will have no more epistemic significance than the inability to use perceptual checks on mathematical

---

[29] It is true that the behaviorist movement in psychology sought to ban introspective reports from the data base of psychology precisely on the ground that they were not intersubjectively testable in the way sense-perceptual reports of the environment are. But this behaviorist ruling concerned what should be required of data for purposes of science; it was not a question of general epistemic status. In any event, if my opponents' case is supported by behaviorist psychology, I take that to be a point in my favor.
[30] I do not follow Martin in supposing that since CMP does not make provision for the same kind of intersubjective corroboration as SP, its outputs are like those of introspection in their subject matter. I introduce introspective practice simply to illustrate the point that one cannot assume that the same sorts of tests are available in all doxastic practices, even in all experiential doxastic practices.

statements, or mathematical checks on perceptual reports. But so far I have only adumbrated a possibility. To get beyond this we must look into CMP itself for some internal reason why confirmation by other observers, as we have it in SP, is not to be expected here.

To do this I must return to the point that the checking system of a practice is typically built up, in good part, on the basis of what we have learned from that practice itself. In particular, in experiential practices like SP and CMP, the general picture of the subject matter that forms an important part of the checking system, is constructed, at least in part, on the basis of what that very practice has taught us. And whatever we know about the conditions that make for accurate or inaccurate perception, we have come to know by relying on the deliverances of perception. How could we know anything about what makes for accurate perception of the physical environment except by using perception to determine what the environment is actually like at a given time and place, what a given subject perceives it to be then and there, and how it is with that subject at that time. If we couldn't rely on sense perception we would never find out anything about these matters. Likewise, in CMP we would have no basis for judgments as to the conditions that make for accurate or inaccurate perception if had no knowledge of the nature and purposes of God to go on; and this knowledge is derived, at least to a considerable extent, from CMP itself. Thus, to a large extent at least, the practice supplies both the tester and the testee; it grades its own examinations. There is a certain circularity involved in supporting the choice of tests. One has to use the practice, including the tests in question, to show that these tests are the right ones to use. Choosing tests in an "inside" job. And this circularity

attaches as fully to universal practices like SP that are taken, in practice, to be unproblematic, as it does to controversial practices like CMP.

Note the difference, as well as the connection, between this point and the earlier point that in checking a perceptual report we make use of what we have learned perceptually. Here we are making a similar point concerning judgments as to what tests are appropriate in a given practice. Putting the two points together, we can say that we perforce make use of what we have learned from a given practice, both in deciding how to go about checking particular outputs of the practice, for accuracy and for epistemic status, and in carrying out such checks in particular cases.

Now let's apply the general point about what is involved in choosing a test for a practice, to the consensual validation test that CMP does not share with SP. And let's begin by asking what SP has taught us about its subject matter that makes it possible and appropriate to hold perceptual beliefs subject to such a test. The basic point is this. We have learned from SP that there are dependable regularities in the behavior of physical objects, including their interaction with the human perceptual apparatus, and we have learned what some of these regularities are. To take some modest examples, we have learned that plants mostly just stay where they are, open to the observation of anyone who is in the right place in the right conditions, whereas animals move around a lot and you can't depend on one staying at the same place over a long period of time. We have gained a lot of empirical knowledge of the dependence of visual perception on lighting, distance of the object from the observer, angle of observation, and other factors. It is because we are cognizant of regularities like this that we are in a position to spell out the conditions under which an observer will perceive a reported object if it really is there. And, to repeat, it is from SP itself that we have learned all this. Hence it is on the basis of what SP has revealed about the nature of its subject matter that we take its deliverances to be subject to assessment in terms of the perceptions of properly qualified others.

A quite different picture of the subject matter of CMP (God and His relations to His creation) has been built up on the basis of CMP and other sources, including revelation[31] and natural theology. God has not revealed to us, nor have we discovered by mystical perception or natural theology, any dependable regularities in divine behavior, particularly regularities in God's interactions with human perceivers. The Christian scheme does include certain basic points about the character and purposes of God, and about patterns in His behavior toward us in the course of history. God can be depended on to work for our salvation from sin, to keep His promises, and to see to it that the church continues to proclaim His message to mankind. Moreover, the scheme does include, as we have seen, some identification of factors that tell for or against openness to the awareness of God. But all this is far from yielding usable recipes for what God will do under certain circumstances. No amount of knowledge of God's essential nature will enable one to predict just when He would punish the Israelites by delivering them to their enemies, or just when He would deliver them from captivity. It is part of the Christian picture that God will forgive those who sincerely repent; but woe to one who supposes that some conditions ascertainable by us will infallibly lead to divine forgiveness. The sufficient condition, "true repentance", is itself such that no effectively ascertainable set of conditions guarantees that it obtains. And most germane to the present concern, such awareness as we have of what is conducive to spiritual receptivity, definitely does not provide any assurance that one who satisfies certain effectively identifiable requirements will experience the presence of God. A constant refrain of the great Christian mystics is that the direct awareness of God is not within our control; we can help to make ourselves receptive, but it is God Himself who determines the time and place, and even whether it will occur in this life.[32]

Moreover, it is not just that we have not discovered any such dependable regularities; the scheme implies that we should not expect to do this. The nature of God and our relations thereto are such that this is simply not in the cards. The rationale for this thesis differs somewhat in various theologies, but both the following themes appear frequently. (1) Divine transcendence. God is infinite; we are finite. How can we hope to attain as adequate a cognitive grasp of the nature and activity of God as we do of finite substances? Our intellect is suited to the knowledge of finite things; there we can discern regularities that enable us to predict and control and to set up tests of the sorts we have been discussing. But why should we expect any such cognitive achievements with respect to an infinite creator? (2) It is presumably true that God could reveal

[31] Revelation might or might not be a form of mystical perception.
[32] Even if there are regularities in divine appearances to our experience, the sufficient conditions of such appearances are not at all within our control, or even effectively recognizable by us. Thus a knowledge of such regularities would not put us in a position to carry out decisive tests by other observers, for we would not be in a position to get other observers in the right position or even to determine when they are.

more than He has about regular patterns in His behavior. But it would be contrary to His sovereignty to do so. He is not subject to natural laws, for He is their author. Any regularities in His behavior are due, at least in large part, to His free choice. Moreover, it is essential to His status as Lord of all that He is not beholden to any creature to respond to conditions in one way rather than another. It would thus be contrary to the fundamental conditions of the divine-human relationship that God should put into our possession a set of recipes that could be used to predict and control His actions. That would be to give us a degree of control highly unbefitting our place in reality.[33]

The upshot of all this is that while what we have learned about the physical world from SP gives us the wherewithal to hold particular perceptual reports subject to a decisive test in terms of what relevant others perceive, what we have learned about God and His relations to His creation, from CMP and other sources, gives us reason to suppose that no such tests are available here. And lest one think that this is just an ad hoc move to escape a difficulty, the features of the Christian scheme that imply this were basic to the scheme long before anyone thought of making unfavorable epistemic comparisons with SP. Thus it is an unthinking parochialism or chauvinism, or epistemic *imperialism* as we have been saying, to suppose the CMP is properly

assessed in terms of the checks and tests appropriate to SP. Judging CMP outputs on the basis of SP tests is no more appropriate than evaluating introspective, memory, or mathematical beliefs by the same tests. The objection to CMP I have been considering is guilty of the same kind of chauvinism as Plato's and Descartes's low assessment of SP as lacking the precision, stability, and certainty of mathematics and Hume's low assessment of inductive reasoning as lacking the conclusiveness of deductive reasoning. These last analogues highlight the way in which I have been stressing the irreducible plurality of doxastic practices in the tradition of Reid and Wittgenstein. Like them, I have been insisting that the criteria of justification are quite different for different doxastic practices, and only confusion results from an attempt to subject the outputs of one practice to the standards of another, without good reason for supposing that those standards carry over.

An even more striking manifestation of SP imperialism is to simply proceed on the assumption that SP is normative without even making the assumption explicit. A particularly glaring example of this is found in Gaskin 1984 (chap. 4). He begins by distinguishing between *experience of an externally existing object* and *experience of an internally existing object*. He *defines* the former as "experience such that any other person rightly and possibly situated, with normally functioning *senses,*

---

[33] Another idea along this line is that if God were to allow us to have as much knowledge of Him as would be required for checks of the SP sort, that would destroy His "epistemic distance" from us, which is itself a necessary condition of our having a free choice as to whether to believe in Him and live according to His commandments. The idea is that if the existence, nature, purposes, and activities of God were to become obvious to us, we would not have a choice as to whether to trust in Him and live the kind of life he enjoins on us. (See Hick 1966, chap. 6, for a well-known exposition of this view.) I have not included this point in the text because I find it unpersuasive. Even if we were as certain of the basic outlines of Christian doctrine as we are of the physical world, I fear that not all of us would automatically lead the new life of the Spirit.

powers of attention, and a suitable conceptual understanding, will have the same or a closely similar experience" (P. 80; my italics). He then has no difficulty in showing that mystical experiences are not "experiences of an externally existing object"! The game has been rigged from the start.

I am quite prepared to recognize that a checking system of the sort we have in SP is an epistemic desideratum. If we were shaping the world to our heart's desire, I dare say we would arrange for all our fallible doxastic practices to include such checks.[34] It certainly puts us in a better position to distinguish between correct and incorrect perceptual beliefs than what we have in CMP. But though this shows that CMP is epistemically inferior to SP in this respect, that is not the same as showing that CMP is unreliable or not rationally engaged in, or that its outputs are not prima facie justified. These conclusions would follow only if the possession of a checking system of the SP sort were not only *a* way of being epistemically acceptable, but the only way. And there is no reason to make the stronger claim. I have already given examples of practices universally regarded as intellectually respectable that involve no such tests. My opponent may still insist that any acceptable *experiential* doxastic practice that issues beliefs about what goes beyond the subject's experience must provide for its outputs being checkable in this way. But what is the basis of this requirement? How can it stand in the face of the fact that the system of belief associated with CMP and

built up, at least in part, on its basis, implies that no such checking system is to be expected even if CMP is as reliable as you please?

The point that the standard tests within a doxastic practice are based on the account of the subject matter that is developed within that practice is crucial to the pluralistic epistemology I am employing here. Once this point is fully appreciated it should break the hold exercised on us by our most deeply rooted and widely shared practices like SP. Because we have been so thoroughly immersed in this practice since long before the age of reflection, since it is second nature to us and no doubt contains many elements of first nature as well, we naturally fall into thinking that any objective experiential claims must be subject to *its* tests and must successfully pass them if they are to be intellectually respectable. But once we realize that the relevance of these tests to sense-perceptual beliefs is not an a priori truth but rather is based on empirical results obtained within SP, we can be open to the possibility that a different structure of the same generic sort is to be found in other experiential doxastic practices, a possibility that is realized in forms of MP. The tests that have been built up within CMP have the same *sort* of justification as the tests of SP, namely being based on the picture of the subject matter that is associated with the practice and that is, in whole or part, built up on the basis of the output of that practice. Thus when CMP does not utilize some test that is crucial in SP, that is no reason

---

[34] Actually, if we had our druthers, we would undoubtedly arrange for our doxastic practices to be much less fallible than SP, so as to stand in no need for an elaborate overrider system. This observation provides another reason for resisting SP imperialism. Since SP itself is not as epistemically ideal as it might conceivably be, why should we take its constitution to be obligatory for other experiential doxastic practices?

to condemn CMP as lacking in justificatory force, any more than the fact that SP does not utilize some test that is crucial in CMP is a reason to downgrade SP epistemically. It is because of the central place SP occupies in our lives that we are drawn to set it up as judge over practices like CMP and not vice versa. But, on rational reflection, we can see that colonial rule is no more appropriate in the one direction than in the other. Once we realize the internal source of the checks and tests of any doxastic practice, we will lose our tendency to entrust imperial control over its fellows to any of these essentially sovereign spheres of cognition.

To put the point most succinctly, the character of CMP is such that even if it is as reliable a cognitive access to God as you like, it still would not make provision for an effective check on particular perceptual beliefs by the perceptions of others. Hence the absence of any such provision cannot be used to cast doubt on its cognitive reliability or on the rationality of engaging in it. Since what it purports to give us information about is not such as to allow for usable formulations of the conditions an observer must satisfy in order to serve as a relevant check on the observations of another, we would still not have any such checks available, however accurate a picture CMP is giving us of that sphere of reality. Hence the lack of such tests is no basis for a criticism of its epistemic pretensions.

iv. Conclusion

Let's take it, then, that CMP is a functioning, socially established, perceptual doxastic practice with distinctive experiential inputs, distinctive input-output functions, a distinctive conceptual scheme, and a rich, internally justified overrider system. As such, it possesses a prima facie title to being rationally engaged in, and its outputs are thereby prima facie justified, *provided we have no sufficient reason to regard it as unreliable or otherwise disqualified for rational acceptance.*

Works Cited in the Text

Daniels, Charles B. 1989. "Experiencing God". *Philosophy and Phenomenological Research*, 49: 487–99.

de Guibert, Joseph, S. J. 1953. *The Theology of the Spiritual Life*. New York: Sheed & Ward.

Martin, C.B. 1959. *Religious Belief*. Ithaca, N.Y.: Cornell University Press.

O'Hear, Anthony. 1984. *Experience, Explanation, and Faith*. London: Routledge & Kegan Paul.

Plantinga, Alvin. 1983. "Reason and Belief in God". In *Faith and Rationality*, ed. A. Plantinga and N. Wolterstorff. Notre Dame, Ind.: University of Notre Dame Press.

Rowe, William L. 1982. "Religious Experience and the Principle of Credulity". *International Journal for Philosophy of Religion*, 13: 85–92.

Teresa, St., of Avila. 1957. *The Life of St. Teresa of Avila by Herself*, trans. J.M. Cohen. London: Penguin Books.

Chapter **5**

Religious Discovery

The last chapter contains readings from the works of four thinkers who are sympathetic to religion and seek to show in their different ways how religious belief might be epistemically proper. Each does so using a theory of epistemic justification that he brings to religion. While such efforts have their place and their value, in this chapter there are readings that start with religious sensibility rather than epistemological theory.

The readings in this chapter relate to a particular kind of religious experience, which from a religious standpoint is considered to be an experience of God's presence in the world, found in our experience of both the grand and the commonplace aspects of our lives. This kind of religious experience has seemed to some to be a way of *discovering* God. While this kind of religious experience may be commonplace in various religious traditions, in the traditions of Judaism and Christianity it is evident in the inspiration of many of the Psalms, as when the Psalmist says "I lift up my eyes to the hills" (Ps. 121) or "How lovely is thy dwelling place" (Ps. 84). When the Psalmist looks upon the hills, he finds new strength and his spirit is lifted up. He looks upon a natural scene—perhaps a range of hills or the sun setting—and his thought is "how lovely!" (Pss. 84, 121, and other psalms from the Tanakh are in Chapter 1 in the section on Judaism.)

Many people, of course, have had something like this experience of looking upon a mountain range or a vista of natural beauty. In a way, then, something like the experience of the Psalmist is fairly common—with this difference: the Psalmist, unlike many, finds God's presence in what he beholds. So, after lifting up his eyes to the hills and finding there new strength, he continues, "From whence does my help come? My help comes from the Lord." And in Ps. 84 the Psalmist is referring to God's tabernacle or temple as "thy dwelling place"—not all of nature, although God's greater dwelling place, in the Psalms, may be all of nature or God's creation, just as God is "enthroned in the heavens" in one psalm. (Ps. 123).

We should appreciate that this kind of religious experience has occurred in other theistic traditions. For instance, it is to be found in Islam in the Sufi tradition. It is also identifiable in Native American religious traditions. In these different religious traditions that which is discovered or whose presence is felt may be differently named and characterized, and different religious practices may surround the underlying religious experience. Moreover, if we were to broaden the definition of this kind of religious experience to an experience of Religious Reality in what is around us we could then relate this kind of experience to non-theistic traditions like Buddhism and nondevotional Hinduism. Within Judaism and Christianity this kind of religious experience is not limited to the Book of Psalms. The tradition of this experience runs as a distinct thread of religious sensibility through much of the Judaic and Christian heritages, but in a clear way its "home," within Judaism and Christianity, is the Psalms.

In this chapter all the readings relate to the kind of religious experience described. However the readings are of two sorts. On the one hand there are selections from different religious traditions that express or refer to this kind of religious experience. These include selections from St. Bonaventura and John Calvin in the Christian tradition, from Martin Buber in the Jewish tradition, from Abu Hamid al-Ghazali in the Islamic tradition, and from Little Wound and Wallace Black Elk, who are Native Americans. On the other hand there are selections from two writers, Friedrich Nietzsche and Sigmund Freud, who are critical of religion and whose criticisms relate to this kind of religious experience, especially as it occurs in the Jewish and Christian traditions.

ST. BONAVENTURA

from The Mind's Road to God

St. Bonaventura, like St. Thomas Aquinas, lived in the thirteenth century. It is said that what Aquinas did for theology in the Middle Ages Bonaventura did for spirituality. A Franciscan, he was greatly influenced by the life of St. Francis. In *The Mind's Road to God* Bonaventura evinces the sensibility of the Psalms when he says that "with respect to the mirror of sensible things God is contemplated not only *through* them, as by His traces, but also *in* them, in so far as He is in them by essence, potency, and presence." He also says, echoing The Letter of Paul to the Romans (which is in Chapter 1 in the section on Christianity), that "the invisible things of God are clearly seen, from the creation of the world." Our reading is taken from this short mystical treatise by Bonaventura.*

CHAPTER 2

Of the Reflection of God in His Traces in the Sensible World

1. But since with respect to the mirror of sensible things it happens that God is contemplated not only *through* them, as by His traces, but also *in* them, in so far as He is in them by essence, potency, and presence; and to consider

* BOAS, GEORGE, BONAVENTURA: THE MINDS ROAD TO GOD, 1st Edition © 1953, pp. 14, 17–26. Reprinted by permission of Pearson Education Inc., Upper Saddle River, NJ.

this is higher than the preceding; therefore a consideration of this sort holds next place as a second step in contemplation, by which we should be led to the contemplation of God in all creatures which enter into our minds through the bodily senses.

* * * * * * * * * * * * * * * * * * * *

7. These all, however, are traces in which we can see the reflection of our God. For since the apprehended species is a likeness produced in the medium and then impressed upon the organ itself, and by means of that impression leads to its principle and source—that is to say, to the object of knowledge—manifestly it follows that the eternal light generates out of itself a likeness or coequal radiance which is consubstantial and coeternal. And He Who is the image and likeness of the invisible God [Col., 1, 15] and "the brightness of His glory and the figure of His substance" [Hebr., 1, 3], He Who is everywhere through His primal generation, as an object generates its likeness in the whole medium, is united by the grace of union to an individual of rational nature—as a species to a corporeal organ—so that by that union He may lead us back to the Father as to the primordial source and object. If then all knowable things can generate their likeness (*species*), obviously they proclaim that in them as in a mirror can be seen the eternal generation of the Word, the Image, and the Son, eternally emanating from God the Father.

8. In this way the species, delighting us as beautiful, pleasant, and wholesome, implies that in that first species is the primal beauty, pleasure, and wholesomeness in which is the highest proportionality and equality to the generator. In this is power, not through imagination, but entering our minds through the truth of apprehension. Here is impression, salubrious and satisfying, and expelling all lack in the apprehending mind. If, then, delight is the conjunction of the harmonious, and the likeness of God alone is the most highly beautiful, pleasant, and wholesome, and if it is united in truth and in inwardness and in plenitude which employs our entire capacity, obviously it can be seen that in God alone is the original and true delight, and that we are led back to seeking it from all other delights.

9. By a more excellent and immediate way are we led by judgment into seeing eternal truths more surely. For if judgment comes about through the reason's abstracting from place, time, and change, and therefore from dimension, succession, and transmutation, by the immutable, illimitable, and endless reason, and if there is nothing immutable, illimitable, and endless except the eternal, then all which is eternal is God or is in God. If, then, all things of which we have more certain judgments are judged by this mode of reasoning, it is clear that this is the reason of all things and the infallible rule and light of truth, in which all things shine forth infallibly, indestructibly, indubitably, irrefragably, unquestiona-bly, unchangeably, boundlessly, endlessly, indivisibly, and intellectually. And therefore those laws by which we make certain judgments concerning all sensible things which come into our consideration—since they [the laws] are infallible and indubitable rules of the apprehending intellect—are indelibly stored up in the memory as if always present, are irrefra-gable and unquestionable rules of the judging intellect. And this is so because, as Augustine says [*Lib. Arb.*, II, ch. 4], no one judges these things except by these rules. It must thus be true that they are incommutable and incorruptible since they are necessary, and boundless since

they are illimitable, endless since eternal. Therefore they must be indivisible since intellectual and incorporeal, not made but uncreated, eternally existing in eternal art, by which, through which, and in accordance with which all things possessing form are formed. Neither, therefore, can we judge with certainty except through that which was not only the form producing all things but also the preserver of all and the distinguisher of all, as the being who preserves the form in all things, the directing rule by which our mind judges all things which enter into it through the senses.

10. This observation is extended by a consideration of the seven different kinds of number by which, as if by seven steps, we ascend to God. Augustine shows this in his book *On the True Religion* and in the sixth book *On Music*, wherein he assigns the differences of the numbers as they mount step by step from sensible things to the Maker of all things, so that God may be seen in all.

For he says that numbers are in bodies and especially in sounds and words, and he calls these *sonorous*. Some are abstracted from these and received into our senses, and these he calls *heard*. Some proceed from the soul into the body, as appears in gestures and bodily movements, and these he calls *uttered*. Some are in the pleasures of the senses which arise from attending to the species which have been received, and these he calls *sensual*. Some are retained in the memory, and these he calls *remembered*. Some are the bases of our judgments about all these, and these he calls *judicial*, which, as has been said above, necessarily transcend our minds because they are infallible and incontrovertible. By these there are imprinted on our minds the *artificial* numbers which Augustine does not include in this classification because they are connected with the judicial numbers from which flow the uttered numbers out of which are created the numerical forms of those things made by art. Hence, from the highest through the middle to the lowest, there is an ordered descent. Thence do we ascend step by step from the sonorous numbers by means of the uttered, the sensual, and the remembered.

Since, therefore, all things are beautiful and in some way delightful, and beauty and delight do not exist apart from proportion, and proportion is primarily in number, it needs must be that all things are rhythmical (*numerosa*). And for this reason number is the outstanding exemplar in the mind of the Maker, and in things it is the outstanding trace leading to wisdom. Since this is most evident to all and closest to God, it leads most directly to God as if by the seven differentiae. It causes Him to be known in all corporeal and sensible things while we apprehend the rhythmical, delight in rhythmical proportions, and through the laws of rhythmical proportions judge irrefragably.

11. From these two initial steps by which we are led to seeing God in His traces, as if we had two wings falling to our feet, we can determine that all creatures of this sensible world lead the mind of the one contemplating and attaining wisdom to the eternal God; for they are shadows, echoes, and pictures, the traces, simulacra, and reflections of that First Principle most powerful, wisest, and best; of that light and plenitude; of that art productive, exemplifying, and ordering, given to us for looking upon God. They are signs divinely bestowed which, I say, are exemplars or rather exemplifications set before our yet untrained minds, limited to sensible things, so that through the sensibles which they see they may be carried forward to the intelligibles

which they do not see, as if by signs to the signified.

12. The creatures of this sensible world signify the invisible things of God [Rom., 1, 20], partly because God is of all creation the origin, exemplar, and end, and because every effect is the sign of its cause, the exemplification of the exemplar, and the way to the end to which it leads; partly from its proper representation; partly from prophetic prefiguration; partly from angelic operation; partly from further ordination. For every creature is by nature a sort of picture and likeness of that eternal wisdom, but especially that which in the book of Scripture is elevated by the spirit of prophecy to the prefiguration of spiritual things. But more does the eternal wisdom appear in those creatures in whose likeness God wished to appear in angelic ministry. And most specially does it appear in those which He wished to institute for the purpose of signifying which are not only signs according to their common name but also Sacraments.

13. From all this it follows that the invisible things of God are clearly seen, from the creation of the world, being understood by the things that are made; so that those who are unwilling to give heed to them and to know God in them all, to bless Him and to love Him, are inexcusable [Rom., 1, 20], while they are unwilling to be carried forth from the shadows into the wonderful light of God [1 Cor., 15, 57]. But thanks be to God through Jesus Christ our Lord, Who has transported us out of darkness into His wonderful light, when through these lights given from without we are disposed to re-enter into the mirror of our mind, in which the divine lights shine [1 Peter, 2, 9].

JOHN CALVIN

from The Knowledge of God Shines Forth in the Fashioning of the Universe and the Continuing Government of it

John Calvin, the sixteenth-century Protestant Reformer, also stands in the tradition of the religious sensibility of the Psalms. In the *The Institutes of the Christian Religion* Calvin, says that God "revealed himself and daily discloses himself in the whole workmanship of the universe." In a reference to Ps. 11, Calvin says, "since the glory of his power and wisdom shine more brightly above, heaven is often called his palace," but, he continues, "wherever you cast your eyes there is no spot in the universe wherein you cannot discern at least some sparks of his glory." Our reading consists of two sections from Bk 1, Chap. Five of Calvin's *Institutes*, 1559, 1560 edition.

From *Calvin: Institutes of the Christian Religion* (Library of Christian Classics) edited by John T. McNeill. Used by permission of Westminster John Knox Press.

CHAPTER 5

The Knowledge of God Shines Forth in the Fashioning of the Universe and the Continuing Government of it

(God manifested in his created works, 1–10)

1. The Clarity of God's Self-Disclosure Strips Us of Every Excuse

The final goal of the blessed life, moreover, rests in the knowledge of God (cf. John 17:3). Lest anyone, then, be excluded from access to happiness, he not only sowed in men's minds that seed of religion of which we have spoken but revealed himself and daily discloses himself in the whole workmanship of the universe. As a consequence, men cannot open their eyes without being compelled to see him. Indeed, his essence is incomprehensible; hence, his divineness far escapes all human perception. But upon his individual works he has engraved unmistakable marks of his glory, so clear and so prominent that even unlettered and stupid folk, cannot plead the excuse of ignorance. Therefore the prophet very aptly exclaims that he is "clad with light as with a garment" (Ps. 104:2 p.). It is as if he said: Thereafter the Lord began to show himself in the visible splendor of his apparel, ever since in the creation of the universe he brought forth those insignia whereby he shows his glory to us, whenever and wherever we cast our gaze. Likewise, the same prophet skillfully compares the heavens, as they are stretched out, to his royal tent and says that he has laid the beams of his chambers on the waters, has made the clouds his chariot, rides on the wings of the wind, and that the winds and lightning bolts are his swift messengers. (Ps. 104:2–4.) And since the glory of his power and wisdom shine more brightly above, heaven is often called his palace (Ps. 11:4). Yet, in the first place, wherever you cast your eyes, there is no spot in the universe wherein you cannot discern at least some sparks of his glory. You cannot in one glance survey this most vast and beautiful system of the universe, in its wide expanse, without being completely overwhelmed by the boundless force of its brightness. The reason why the author of The Letter to the Hebrews elegantly calls the universe the appearance of things invisible (Heb. 11:3) is that this skillful ordering of the universe is for us a sort of mirror in which we can contemplate God, who is otherwise invisible. The reason why the prophet attributes to the heavenly creatures a language known to every nation (Ps. 19:2 ff.) is that therein lies an attestation of divinity so apparent that it ought not to escape the gaze of even the most stupid tribe. The apostle declares this more clearly: "What men need to know concerning God has been disclosed to them, ... for one and all gaze upon his invisible nature, known from the creation of the world, even unto his eternal power and divinity" (Rom. 1:19–20 p.).

2. The Divine Wisdom Displayed for All to See

There are innumerable evidences both in heaven and on earth that declare his wonderful wisdom; not only those more recondite matters for the closer observation of which astronomy, medicine, and all natural science are intended, but also those which thrust themselves upon the sight of even the most untutored and ignorant persons, so that they cannot open their eyes without being compelled to witness them. Indeed, men who have either quaffed or even tasted the liberal arts penetrate with their aid far more deeply into the secrets of the divine wisdom. Yet ignorance of them prevents no one from seeing more than enough of God's workmanship in his creation to lead him to break forth in admiration of the Artificer. To be sure, there is need of art and of more exacting toil in order to investigate the motion of the stars, to determine their assigned stations, to measure their intervals, to note their properties. As God's

providence shows itself more explicitly when one observes these, so the mind must rise to a somewhat higher level to look upon his glory. Even the common folk and the most untutored, who have been taught only by the aid of the eyes, cannot be unaware of the excellence of divine art, for it reveals itself in this innumerable and yet distinct and well-ordered variety of the heavenly host. It is, accordingly, clear that there is no one to whom the Lord does not abundantly show his wisdom. Likewise, in regard to the structure of the human body one must have the greatest keenness in order to weigh, with Galen's skill, its articulation, symmetry, beauty, and use. But yet, as all acknowledge, the human body shows itself to be a composition so ingenious that its Artificer is rightly judged a wonder-worker.

MARTIN BUBER

from I and Thou

Martin Buber, the author of *The Eclipse of God*, was an important Jewish thinker who reflected on religion and morality. The importance of his thought was recognized in Christian circles and generally. Buber in what may be his best know work, *I and Thou*, expressed the religious sensibility of the Psalms in a distinctive way that is grounded in his religious tradition. In *I and Thou*, Buber speaks of an encounter with the Eternal You (or Thou). In the "moment of meeting," Buber says, those meeting the Eternal "receive what [they] did not hitherto have." The selections in this chapter are taken from Part Three of his *I and Thou*.*

THE EXTENDED LINES OF RELATIONS meet in the eternal *Thou*.

Every particular *Thou* is a glimpse through to the eternal *Thou*; by means of every particular *Thou* the primary

word addresses the eternal *Thou*. Through this mediation of the *Thou* of all beings fulfilment, and non-fulfilment, of relations comes to them: the inborn *Thou* is realised in each relation

* Reprinted with the permission of Scribner, an imprint of Simon & Schuster Adult Publishing Group, from I AND THOU by Martin Buber, translated by Ronald Gregor Smith. Copyright © 1958 by Charles Scribner's Sons.

and consummated in none. It is consummated only in the direct relation with the *Thou* that by its nature cannot become *It*.

* * * * * * * * * * * * * * * * * *

MEN HAVE ADDRESSED THEIR ETERNAL *Thou* with many names. In singing of Him who was thus named they always had the *Thou* in mind: the first myths were hymns of praise. Then the names took refuge in the language of *It*; men were more and more strongly moved to think of and to address their eternal *Thou* as an *It*. But all God's names are hallowed, for in them He is not merely spoken about, but also spoken to.

Many men wish to reject the word God as a legitimate usage, because it is so misused. It is indeed the most heavily laden of all the words used by men. For that very reason it is the most imperishable and most indispensable. What does all mistaken talk about God's being and works (though there has been, and can be, no other talk about these) matter in comparison with the one truth that all men who have addressed God had God Himself in mind? For he who speaks the word God and really has *Thou* in mind (whatever the illusion by which he is held), addresses the true *Thou* of his life, which cannot be limited by another *Thou*, and to which he stands in a relation that gathers up and includes all others.

But when he, too, who abhors the name, and believes himself to be godless, gives his whole being to addressing the *Thou* of his life, as a *Thou* that cannot be limited by another, he addresses God.

* * * * * * * * * * * * * * * * * *

EVERY REAL RELATION with a being or life in the world is exclusive. Its *Thou* is freed, steps forth, is single, and confronts you. It fills the heavens. This does not mean that nothing else exists; but all else lives in *its* light As long as the presence of the relation continues, this its cosmic range is inviolable. But as soon as a *Thou* becomes *It*, the cosmic range of the relation appears as an offence to the world, its exclusiveness as an exclusion of the universe.

In the relation with God unconditional exclusiveness and unconditional inclusiveness are one. He who enters on the absolute relation is concerned with nothing isolated any more, neither things nor beings, neither earth nor heaven; but everything is gathered up in the relation. For to step into pure relation is not to disregard everything but to see everything in the *Thou*, not to renounce the world but to establish it on its true basis. To look away from the world, or to stare at it, does not help a man to reach God; but he who sees the world in Him stands in His presence. "Here world, there God" is the language of *It*; "God in the world" is another language of *It*; but to eliminate or leave behind nothing at all, to include the whole world in the *Thou*, to give the world its due and its truth, to include nothing beside God but everything in him—this is full and complete relation.

Men do not find God if they stay in the world. They do not find Him if they leave the world. He who goes out with his whole being to meet his *Thou* and carries to it all being that is in the world, finds Him who cannot be sought.

Of course God is the "wholly Other"; but He is also the wholly Same, the wholly Present. Of course He is the *Mysterium Tremendum* that appears and overthrows; but He is also the mystery of the self-evident, nearer to me than my *I*.

If you explore the life of things and of conditioned being you come to the unfathomable, if you deny the life of things and of conditioned being you stand before nothingness, if you hallow this life you meet the living God.

* * * * * * * * * * * * * * * * * * *

MAN'S SENSE OF *Thou*, which experiences in the relations with every particular *Thou* the disappointment of the change to *It*, strives out but not away from them all to its eternal *Thou*; but not as something is sought: actually there is no such thing as seeking God, for there is nothing in which He could not be found. How foolish and hopeless would be the man who turned aside from the course of his life in order to seek God; even though he won all the wisdom of solitude and all the power of concentrated being he would miss God. Rather is it as when a man goes his way and simply wishes that it might be the way: in the strength of his wish his striving is expressed. Every relational event is a stage that affords him a glimpse into the consummating event. So in each event he does not partake, but also (for he is waiting) does partake, of the one event. Waiting, not seeking, he goes his way; hence he is composed before all things, and makes contact with them which helps them. But when he has *found*, his heart is not turned from them, though everything now meets him in the one event. He blesses every cell that sheltered him, and every cell into which he will yet turn. For this finding is not the end, but only the eternal middle, of the way.

It is a finding without seeking, a discovering of the primal, of origin. His sense of *Thou*, which cannot be satiated till he finds the endless *Thou*, had the *Thou* present to it from the beginning; the presence had only to become wholly real to him in the reality of the hallowed life of the world.

God cannot be inferred in anything—in nature, say, as its author, or in history as its master, or in the subject as the self that is thought in it. Something else is not "given" and God then elicited from it; but God is the Being that is directly, most nearly, and lastingly, over against us, that may properly only be addressed, not expressed.

* * * * * * * * * * * * * * * * * * *

WHAT IS THE ETERNAL, primal phenomenon, present here and now, of that which we term revelation? It is the phenomenon that a man does not pass, from the moment of the supreme meeting, the same being as he entered into it. The moment of meeting is not an "experience" that stirs in the receptive soul and grows to perfect blessedness; rather, in that moment something happens to the man. At times it is like a light breath, at times like a wrestling-bout, but always—it *happens*. The man who emerges from the act of pure relation that so involves his being has now in his being something more that has grown in him, of which he did not know before and whose origin he is not rightly able to indicate. However the source of this new thing is classified in scientific orientation of the world, with its authorised efforts to establish an unbroken causality, we, whose concern is real consideration of the real, cannot have our purpose served with subconsciousness or any other apparatus of the soul. The reality is that we receive what we did not hitherto have, and receive it in such a way that we know it has been given to us. In the language of the Bible, "Those who wait upon the Lord shall renew their strength." In the language of Nietzsche, who in his account remains loyal to reality, "We take and do not ask who it is there that gives."

Man receives, and he receives not a specific "content" but a Presence, a Presence as power. This Presence and this power include three things, undivided, yet in such a way that we may consider them separately. First, there is the whole fulness of real mutual action, of the being raised and bound up in relation: the man can give no account at all of how the binding in relation is brought about, nor does it in any way lighten his life—it makes life heavier, but heavy with meaning. Secondly, there is the inexpressible confirmation of meaning. Meaning is assured. Nothing can any longer be meaningless. The question about the meaning of life is no longer there. But were it there, it would not have to be answered. You do not know how to exhibit and define the meaning of life, you have no formula or picture for it, and yet it has more certitude for you than the perceptions of your senses. What does the revealed and concealed meaning purpose with us, desire from us? It does not wish to be explained (nor are we able to do that) but only to be done by us. Thirdly, this meaning is not that of "another life," but that of this life of ours, not one of a world "yonder" but that of this world of ours, and it desires its confirmation in this life and in relation with this world. This meaning can be received, but not experienced; it cannot be experienced but it can be done, and this is its purpose with us. The assurance I have of it does not wish to be sealed within me, but it wishes to be born by me into the world. But just as the meaning itself does not permit itself to be transmitted and made into knowledge generally current and admissible, so confirmation of it cannot be transmitted as a valid Ought; it is not prescribed, it is not specified on any tablet, to be raised above all men's heads. The meaning that has been received can be proved true by each man only in the singleness of his being and the singleness of his life. As no prescription can lead us to the meeting, so none leads from it. As only acceptance of the Presence is necessary for the approach to the meeting, so in a new sense is it so when we emerge from it. As we reach the meeting with the simple *Thou* on our lips, so with the *Thou* on our lips we leave it and return to the world.

That before which, in which, out of which, and into which we live, even the mystery, has remained what it was. It has become present to us and in its presentness has proclaimed itself to us as salvation; we have "known" it, but we acquire no knowledge from it which might lessen or moderate its mysteriousness. We have come near to God, but not nearer to unveiling being or solving its riddle. We have felt release, but not discovered a "solution." We cannot approach others with what we have received, and say "You must know this, you must do this." We can only go, and confirm its truth. And this, too, is no "ought," but we can, we *must*.

This is the eternal revelation that is present here and now. I know of no revelation and believe in none whose primal phenomenon is not precisely this. I do not believe in a self-naming of God, a self-definition of God before men. The Word of revelation is *I am that I am*. That which reveals is that which reveals. That which is *is*, and nothing more. The eternal source of strength streams, the eternal contact persists, the eternal voice sounds forth, and nothing more.

ABU HAMID AL-GHAZALI

from The Revivification of Religion

Abu Hamid al-Ghazali lived in the twelfth century of the common Era. He established himself as a brilliant philosopher and Islamic theologion, but when he was forty-six he experienced a deep psychological crisis. As a result he turned from his academic teachings toward the Islamic mystical tradition of Sufism to seek true knowledge of God. He wrote several treatises on Sufism, but the one considered his greatest is Ihya 'Ulum al-Din, translated as The Revival of the Religious Sciences or *The Revivification of Religion*. Our reading consists of two selections from that work. The first begins with "All that we behold and perceive with our senses bears undeniable witness to the existence of God and His power and His knowledge and the rest of His attributes . . . ."*

The Revivification of Religion

All that we behold and perceive by our senses bears undeniable witness to the existence of God and His power and His knowledge and the rest of His attributes, whether these things be manifested or hidden, the stone and the clod, the plants and the trees, the living creatures, the heavens and the earth and the stars, the dry land and the ocean, the fire and the air, substance and accident, and indeed we ourselves are the chief witness to Him . . . but just as the bat sees only at night, when the light is veiled by darkness, and cannot therefore see in the daytime, because of the weakness of its sight, which is dazzled by the full light of the sun, so also the human mind is too weak to behold the full glory of the Divine Majesty.

God is One, the Ancient of Days, without prior, Eternal, having no beginning, Everlasting, having no end, continuing for evermore. He is the First and the Last, the Transcendent and the Immanent, Whose wisdom extendeth over all. He cannot be likened to anything else that exists nor is anything like unto Him, nor is He contained by the earth or the heavens, for He is exalted far above the earth and the dust thereof. The fact of His existence is apprehended by men's reason and He will be seen as He is by that gift of spiritual vision, which He will grant unto the righteous, in the Abode of Eternity, when their beatitude shall be made perfect by the vision of His glorious Countenance.

He is the Exalted, Almighty, Puissant, Supreme, Who slumbereth not nor sleepeth: neither mortality nor death have dominion over Him. His is the power and the kingdom and the glory and the majesty and to Him belongs creation and the rule over what He has created: He alone is the Giver of life, He is Omniscient,

---

* From Abu Hamid al-Ghazali, *The Revivification of Religion* in the translation by Margaret Smith.

for His knowledge encompasseth all things, from the deepest depths of the earth to the highest heights of the heavens. Not the smallest atom in the earth or the heavens, but is known unto Him, yea, He is aware of how the ants creep upon the hard rock in the darkness of the night: He perceives the movement of the mote in the ether. He beholds the thoughts which pass through the minds of men, and the range of their fancies and the secrets of their hearts, by His knowledge, which was from aforetime. All that is other than Him— men and jinns, angels and Satan, the heavens and the earth, animate beings, plants, inorganic matter, substance and accident, what is intelligible and what is sensible— all were created by His power out of non-existence. He brought them into being, when as yet they had no being, for from eternity He alone existed and there was no other with Him.

* * * * * * * * * * * * * * * * * * * *

Yet God, for all His unique Majesty and Greatness, differs from earthly kings, in inspiring His creatures to ask and make their plea to Him, for He says: Is there any who calls unto Me? I will answer him Is there any who seeks for forgiveness? I will grant it unto him.

Unlike the rulers of the world, He opens the door and lifts the veil and gives leave to His servants to enter into confidential intercourse with Him through prayer. Nor does He limit Himself to giving them leave, but He shows His loving-kindness by inspiring them with the desire for this, and calling them to Him.

Know that your Companion, Who never forsakes you, whether you are at home or abroad, asleep or awake, in life or in death, is your Lord and Master, your Protector and your Creator, and whenever you remember Him, He is there beside you. For God Most High hath said: "I am the Companion of him who remembers Me." Whenever your heart is stricken with grief for your shortcomings in religion. He is there at hand, continually beside you. For He hath said: "I am with those who are contrite in heart, for My sake," If you but knew Him in truth, you would take Him as your Friend and forsake all others but Him. If you are not able to do that at all times, do not fail to set apart time, both night and day, in which you may commune with your Lord and enjoy His Presence in inward converse with Him, and may know what it means to have continual fellowship with God.

LITTLE WOUND

Wakan

___

L ittle Wound was a Lakota (or Sioux), specifically Oglala, chief and shaman. His statement about the wakan, the mysterious and sacred, and all that is *wakan*, dates from 1896.

Wakan

As the Oglalas speak, this is two words. It is *wa* and it is *kan*. *Wa* means anything which is something. It also means anything with which something can be done. When one says *wakan*, this means anything which is *kan*. *Wakan* is something which is *kan*.

A *wakan* man is one who is wise. It is one who knows the spirits. It is one who has power with the spirits. It is one who communicates with the spirits. It is one who can do strange things. A *wakan* man knows things that the people do not know. He knows the ceremonies and the songs. He can tell the people what their visions mean. He can tell the people what the spirits wish them to do. He can tell what is to be in the future. He can talk with animals and with trees and with stones. He can talk with everything on earth.

The *Wakan Tanka* are those which made everything. They are *Wakanpi*. *Wakanpi* are all things that are above mankind. There are many kinds of the *Wakanpi*. The *Wakan Tanka* are *Wakanpi*. The spirits are *Wakanpi*. The beings that govern things are *Wakanpi*.

The *Wakanpi* have power over everything on earth. They watch mankind all the time. They control everything that mankind does. Mankind should please them in all things. If mankind does not please them, they will do harm to them. They should be pleased by songs and ceremonies. Gifts should be made to them. Mankind should ask them for what they wish. They may be like a father to mankind. But the evil *Wakanpi* are to be feared. They do evil to mankind. There are many of these. The greatest of these is *Iya*. He is *Wakan Tanka*.

Mankind should think about the *Wakanpi* and do what will please them. They should think of them as they think of their fathers and their mothers. But the evil *Wakanpi* they should think of as an enemy.

Animals may be *wakan*. When an animal is *wakan*, then mankind should treat it as if it were one of the *Wakanpi*. Things that do not live may be *wakan*. When anything is food, it is *wakan* because it makes life. When anything is medicine, it is *wakan* for it keeps life in the body. When anything is hard to understand, it is *wakan* because mankind does not know what it is. Anything that is used in the ceremony and songs to the *Wakanpi* is *wakan* because it should not be used for anything else. Little children are *wakan* because they do not speak. Crazy people are *wakan* because the *Wakanpi* are in them. Anything that is very old is *wakan* because no one knows when it was made. Anyone with great power is *wakan* because the *Wakanpi* helps them. Anything that is very dangerous is *wakan* because *Iya*[4] helps it. Anything that is poison or anything that intoxicates is *wakan* because the Sky helps it.

The songs and the ceremonies of the Oglalas are *wakan* because they belong to the *Wakanpi*. A very old man or a very old woman is *wakan* because they know many things. But an old man is not like a *wakan* man. If he has learned the *wakan* things, then he is a *wakan* man. The spirit of every man is *wakan* and the ghost is *wakan*.

Wakan Tanka are many. But they are all the same as one. The evil *Wakan Tanka*

---

[4] *Iya*, the Giant, the God of Evil.

is not one of The *Wakan Tanka*.[5] The *Wakan Tanka* are above all the other *Wakanpi*. The Sun is *Wakan Tanka*, and the Sky and the Earth and the Rock. They are *Wakan Tanka*. *Wakinyan*, this is *Wakan Tanka* but it is different from The *Wakan Tanka*. The Thunderbird and the Wind are *Wakan Tanka* with the Sun and the Sky. The stars are *Wakan Tanka*, but they have nothing to do with the people on the earth. Mankind need pay no attention to the stars.

WALLACE BLACK ELK

from Black Elk: The Sacred Ways of a Lakota

Wallace Black Elk is a Lakota elder and shaman. Born in 1921 on the Rosebud Reservation in South Dakota, he has travelled throughout North America, Europe, and Asia, giving talks and conducting ceremonies. In this selection from his writings he tells of the Chanunpa (or sacred pipe) and its significance in the sacred ways of his people. In Lakota religion Tunkashila is the Grandfather or the male-aspect of the Creator and Grandmother is the female-aspect, knowledge and Earth. Wallace Black Elk speaks of seeing "the wonders and mysteries of Tunkashila." The "breath of spirit" remains because "the wisdom [from Tunkashila] and knowledge [from Grandmother] were placed here." "You can feel it [the spirit], but you can't see it with the naked eye." In this selection Wallace Black Elk provides a distinctive Lakota expression of religious awareness.*

CHAPTER 4

The Chanunpa

The Chanunpa is where I go to school. You see the same thing over and over. I've been going back and forth here for sixty-three years because I've been taught by the Chanunpa. I'm sixty-eight now, so it's been going on for sixty-three years. So I've got just a little jiffy time there, but I sure learned a lot in that

---

[5] Little Wound is apparently referring to the distinction between the superior *Wakan* and the *Wakan* relatives; see document 5. In this instance we have retained the capital *T* in *The* to mark the distinction. The superior *Wakan* are the Sun, Sky, Earth, and Rock (*Sky* is often used as the English translation of *Taku Škanškan*). See Walker to Wissler, January 13, 1915, p. 35 in this volume; Walker, *Sun Dance*, pp. 81, 154–56; Alice C. Fletcher, "Indian Ceremonies," *Report of the Peabody Museum of American Archaeology and Ethnology*, vol. 16 (Salem, Mass.: Salem Press, 1884), pp. 289–95; Dorsey, *Siouan Cults*, pp. 445–47; Frances Densmore, *Teton Sioux Music*, Smithsonian Institution, Bureau of American Ethnology, Bulletin 61 (1918), pp. 205–6.

little jiffy time. It's good. So all of you who have been educated, you should be able to understand the way of the Chanunpa more than what I learned in the little jiffy time spent here.

Right now the Chanunpa, the spirit is kind of wedging its way, finding its way gradually. Sometimes it stops. Then it goes. You never use force. It has to do with the way people move and pray. We pierce in the Sun Dance or go without food or water in order to contact spirit. When that spirit comes, we have all the chance in the world. We could say anything we want there. So I have to prepare myself to be alert as to what I say, what I've been longing to say all my life.

I want to say a lot of things, but I have no one to tell it to. I reported to my senators and congressmen, but they don't have money, and they don't have time for that. They are always counting money first. It seems that they have more important things to talk about than my little worries and sadness and pain and death. But I think we are up against the wall now and have no alternative but to turn to the American Indians. So I think we are at a turning point now. So there's a hope. There's a chance.

The Earth People are rooted in the fire, rock, water, and green. The problem, the saddest part for this society is that if we were to go back to this Earth People philosophy there is no money there. That is really hard for people to understand. It's the saddest part for them, but they have to understand the power of this Chanunpa. One time I was holding this Chanunpa, and the fire came. That power came from the sun. Then the spirit said, "Tunkashila hears you, so he sent me here." Then he talked about a little tiny fire. "This fire that I brought here, I will call it the impenetrable medicine. Now I put this impenetrable

medicine in the bottom of the bowl of that Chanunpa you are holding. It is *wakan* [holy]. I will place it there. So from this bowl through that little tunnel to the mouthpiece of the Chanunpa you will escape with countless people from this nuclear holocaust." So that was his promise. So every time I fill the Chanunpa I look in there and see that light. Then I know the prayer is going to be good.

When we place that medicine, that tobacco in there, it attracts electricity. So you see those lights come in during the ceremony. There are a lot of things you people have to learn. You have to start over again. So I'll put you all back into kindergarten, but this time you're not going to see a dog jump and say "Arf! Arf!" This time you're actually going to hear it talk and learn how to sniff. You're going to learn how to hear, how to taste, and how to feel. You're not just going to rely on your naked eyes. We overload our naked eyes. We overload that little computer chip, so the wires short out. There's an electrical storm going around in our head. So we have a big storm going on in our head. So we have to stay close together and stay behind this Chanunpa. Never sidestep it or go along the side. Don't go in front of it. Let the Chanunpa always lead. That's the instruction that we carry. And that Chanunpa will lead us to safety where there is no end—where there's happiness and joy. There's no pain. There's no death. There won't be anybody coming around to collect rent or taxes or anything. Eventually, the Chanunpa will lead us all back into the hands of Tunkashila. Grandmother, she will cradle us again. She knows that we have been naughty kids, but instead of spanking us, she'll wipe our tears and forgive us. They are the only ones that could forgive. Instead of punishing us, they'll forgive us. So the real amnesty is there. We know that. So don't be afraid. What we left behind, leave it back there. Try to do some good. Let's try to take a step, try to think something good. Try to take a step in a good way. So that is my prayer.

You have to understand this Chanunpa. When we say *Chanunpa*, that's what it means. *Cha* is "a wood." *Nunpa* is "two." The bowl represents the whole world. The stem represents the Tree of Life. Then there is the main Chanunpa. That Chanunpa was first brought to us by the White Buffalo-Calf Maiden. We still carry that original Chanunpa. Orval Looking Horse is the keeper of that Chanunpa. That Chanunpa is like a radio, like a radar. You could communicate from here directly to that main Chanunpa. You could communicate directly with the wisdom. Like I said, Tunkashila is the wisdom itself, and Grandmother is the knowledge.

The buffalo gave his life so we could wear his robe. His blood sifted into the ground and became a stone. So we have a red stone. Also, we have a black stone. That stone represents the universe. It represents the woman. The Tree of Life, the stem part, is the man. So male and female are connected together in that Chanunpa. That spells generation because of the fire, rock, water, and green. So the Chanunpa is very sacred. We didn't carve it; Tunkashila carved it. Then he offered it to his people. So this is the power. So the Chanunpa is sacred of sacreds in the whole universe. It will be known all over the world. That is in our prophecies.

So now we have stone-people-lodges everywhere. We even have one in Tokyo. So in each land, everywhere, you name it. They even have it in Communist countries. I went to East Germany and saw two hundred tipis there. It was really

something. So now the Chanunpa is back there also. So it has traveled all over the world. They say this fireplace, this fire will travel all over the world. That is coming true. You find stone-people-lodges everywhere in the world now. So it will come back again, and the whole universe will be a giant stone-people-lodge. It will be a purification. So it's good to learn our ways.

All the knowledge that is floating around here between the earth and sky was given to me free of charge. It was just given to me. And that knowledge has no end to it. This Chanunpa has no end to it, and that impenetrable medicine is in the bottom of the bowl. So I will escape with countless people from this nuclear destruction. Now I pray to the powers of the Four Winds that my people will lay this fire [nuclear weapons] down before that destruction comes.

I'm glad that there are a lot of young people carrying the Chanunpa now. You have to understand all of this. Always put your people ahead. If you take something to your mouth, always remember the spirit first. When you run into a good thing, like a T-bone steak, take a piece and remember your people first. If you have a piece of meat or a bowl of soup, you look for an elder and you look for an orphan. You feed those two. They are the most poor. They are defenseless. So these two you have to cradle in your arms, and you have to put something in their mouth first. Then Tunkashila will bless you for it, and your day will be long. These are the instructions the Chanunpa carries.

The Chanunpa carries seven rituals. There's a spiritual food-offering ceremony. It's called *wanagi*, or "soul-keeping ceremony." You keep the spirit and you feed it. Then there is the vision quest [*hanbleceya*], Sun Dance, Tossing Ball ceremony, Ghost Dance, Thunder ceremonies, and stone-people-lodge. The path is always the same. There is nothing to change. It's always the same, but today we are only carrying three of those rituals. They are like sacraments to us.

So we have to go step by step. I participate in the rituals every four years. Sometimes the going gets tough. Recently we tried to revive the Tossing Ball ceremony. We talked about those ball-tossing games they play in the schools. So that ball-tossing ceremony is really a global ceremony today. In the ritual we perform it for help and health, but the white man copied it and commercialized it. So now we have all these commercial games like soccer, football, and baseball.

So there is a lot to understand about this Chanunpa. I already told you about making the Chanunpa—how it took me four years to make my first Chanunpa. Then you have to know how to fill the Chanunpa and then how to offer it. We don't put just anything in there. We have a pipe mixture that we make. It is made from four parts red willow bark, one part tobacco, one part *kinic-kinic*, and sprinkled, like peppered, with *tobacco root*. You have to remember how much of each of these to use to make the mixture taste good. You need to know on which moon to gather each one of those plants. If you pick them too early or too late they will taste bitter. You only use certain parts. You don't use the whole plant. Like they call it red willow bark, but what you really use there is that little sheet of green in there between the bark and the wood. You have to scrape that one. Then you have to learn how to dry them and cut them. So there is a lot to learn about how to take care of the Chanunpa.

When you fill the Chanunpa, there is a pipe-filling song that goes with it. During that time everybody should respect that Chanunpa and not talk. They can sing that song if they want to. There is a certain way you put that tobacco [mixture] in there. You have to educate your fingers, your pinch, for that. The old people told me that you have to be really careful when you're accepting the Chanunpa. When you put your mixture into the bowl, you should never put bad words or bad thoughts in that offering. Don't wish bad luck or death or like that. If I hear what's in that Chanunpa, like death or bad luck for someone, I will take that Chanunpa, disconnect it, and return it to that person.

So you have to state your reason. When you offer the Chanunpa you say, "Tunkashila, I offer this Chanunpa." Then you state the reason you are offering it. "I have a dad lying in the hospital with a heart attack. Tunkashila, go there and extend my father's life another day or another moon or another year or another generation." Then you pivot and present the Chanunpa to the medicine man. The medicine man or woman will hold out hands [arms extended and palms upward]. You hold that Chanunpa level in front of you. You hold it with both hands [palms upward]. Then you place it in their hands four times. You don't let it go. You just go there with it and then pull it back. Each time you pull it back, you pray. Then on the fourth time you let it go. He will accept it. When he accepts it, everybody says, "Hi-ho! Hi-ho!" It's like you applaud. You praise, you're thankful, you cheer, you yell, like that. Maybe in Christianity they would say, "Hallelujah. Amen." It's acceptance, because that Chanunpa is going to go before the Creator. That's the reason it's presented this way.

But like I said, if that person puts something in there that doesn't belong in there, then bad thoughts and bad words will be blowing your way. So never take one and put it in the Chanunpa. If you do that, then it is going to happen that way, but that's going to come back to you twice. Eventually, when people do something like that and leave the Chanunpa and go away, then that whole family—just one by one or all in one shot—dies.

So this Chanunpa is really sacred, and we have to be really careful how we handle it. It's not a toy when you have part of the wisdom of the Creator and the power of Grandmother, one drop from each, in your hands. The power is the atom. We call it nuclear bombs or neutron bombs or like that. But that power is in our hands. And that gift, that love, is in our hands.

A lot of Christian people try to interpret God. They say God is love or love is God, like that. People don't really understand. That Chanunpa can destroy with that bad thought or bad word in there. That is why I said that the spirit told me if a bad thought or bad word ever comes to you, to let it go in your ear and out the other ear, but never out of your mouth. If it comes out of your mouth it is going to hurt somebody, and then that hurt will come back to you twice. If you connect yourself to quick thought, that will take you someplace you'll never find your way back from. This was told many generations ago. So it was handed down. So when you have that Chanunpa, you have to be humble and sincere. You ask for *health* and *help*. These are the two key words that the Chanunpa carries.

That Chanunpa will serve you many times—not just one time, but many times. So that is why the Chanunpa is *wakan*. The spirit will come and tell you the Chanunpa is *wakan*. You had better start praying because that is a warning. That doesn't mean that it's a cure-all or you have a safety insurance. It's not that way. It's a warning. Then you have to pray. So I began to wonder about that,

and I asked Tunkashila, "How come the spirit comes in and tells us that Chanunpa is *wakan*?" I asked the spirit that question. Then I learned the answer. When a person prays, that power goes back to the Creator. Even if you misinterpret or mistranslate something that doesn't belong to you, or it doesn't belong to the Chanunpa, or it doesn't belong to the Creator or Grandmother, then some unknown power will destroy that. The way he said it was, "If a bad thought or word comes, you pray, and that bad thought or word will turn around. It will go back to the mouth where it came out from. It will go back to the mouth, and it will go back to earth along with the robe, the body. Then, the shadow of that man will be standing there. So then that bad thought or word will return to earth. Then there will be nothing; so the body will deteriorate."

So one of my people had a question. "If we carry this Chanunpa, what will happen if we drink alcohol and take drugs?" The spirit answered. He mentioned a cloth. He said your robe [body] is like a piece of cloth. So when you put alcohol and drugs in there it will go back to earth again, because this medicine is sacred. So when that person takes it, he'll go back to earth. So here is your robe. If you pour it on this cloth, it will seep right through and will return to earth. That cloth will start to fall apart, and it will be back to earth. So when you drink and take all those pills, your body will deteriorate, and it will go back to earth.

Then your shadow will be standing there, wandering and floating around. "What happened to my robe? It's dirt." Then you will see the wonders and mysteries of Tunkashila. You are going to see that *black light*. You are going to see all those creatures around you. We don't see them, but they see us. You see your people here, but they can't see you. So you go back to the breath of spirit. It remains here, because the wisdom [from Tunkashila] and knowledge [from Grandmother] were placed here. It doesn't go anywhere; it just stays right here.

So we were told that way. So the spirit that we are talking about, it is a great mystery. Like this air. It is here. You can see it moving the grass and leaves around. You can feel it, but you can't see it with your naked eyes. But it's here, and we are all breathing it, whether it's a black man or red man or yellow man or white man or winged, four-legged, creeping-crawler, mammal, or fish-people. We are all breathing the same air. So that's just an example of how spirit goes back to spirit. This is the way it was told. So I pray this wind will blow away piece by piece those bad thoughts coming our way.

So you could pray to this wind. Maybe you have a problem in your head because, like they say in the medical science, a virus is going around. So you take an aspirin. But aspirin doesn't purify the air. It removes your headache, but it doesn't clear the virus away. But those creatures over there, every day they nibble and drink water. So they are still able to communicate with those powers. They are here twenty-four hours around the clock. They are much closer than us two-leggeds, because we lost that communication. So what we do is to ask for help from one of those creatures, like the deer, through this Chanunpa. We have a deer medicine. Each creature has a medicine, so there are many medicines. Because they are so close to the Creator, they are able to communicate that medicine. Then they bring help and health.

Our minds are contaminated. So the Earth and its creatures are also contaminated. When a deer gets a headache, well, he goes to that medicine, and he prays. He nibbles on that green and drinks water. When he lies down, that medicine

goes all the way around and clears out all the virus. So all those little guys [fawns] jumping around there, they also benefit because one deer prayed. So we borrow that medicine from the deer. So he brings that medicine. Then it clears our head. It not only clears the headache, it also clears the virus causing the headache so it doesn't go around in my family. Then it doesn't come to us. It goes away. So that's just one medicine. That's just an example of what we call deer medicine.

So it is a spirit. So they bring those powers in a certain way. Through the Chanunpa, tobacco ties, and robes, you call them. Then they come in and wear those robes. They're standing there watching you. So when those stone-people become alive again, they come in [to the stone-people-lodge]. Then you visit with them and tell them your problems. Then the power that pollutes our mind is released. That fire will come in and destroy bad thoughts and words. Only good thoughts and words will remain. To that the spirit adds power and returns it to us. That's what the spirit does—the stone-people, fire, rock, and water.

So there is a ritual you have to follow. Never do it on your own. You always have to have a spirit guide. When you go there, when you have the fire and the stone-people, you offer a little green and water to them. Then, through this Chanunpa, somebody is listening to you, somebody is watching you. When you go there you have to have *courage, patience, endurance, and alertness*. These four you have to have. If you are missing one of them, that's your weak spot. So you have to have all four of them to be an Earth Man. So you are going to develop. You are going to educate yourself. You are going to exercise and develop this power in yourself. So if you're not really sure, then test yourself through spring, summer, fall, and winter.

So you might go all four seasons around. Then you might try another round. You might go around four times before you reaffirm, rededicate yourself. Then you go in a humble way. Then Tunkashila will pity you. He'll come, but he is going to test you first. He might even test you three or four times.

FRIEDRICH NIETZSCHE

from Thus Spoke Zarathustra, The Antichrist, and The Gay Science

Friedrich Nietzsche was a German nineteenth-century philosopher who wrote many works on the nature of morality and religion that were highly critical of the morality of his day and of religion, especially Christianity. In more than one place Nietzsche explicitly reflected on the sources of and motives for religious belief. Nietzsche believed that "we" had outgrown our need for belief in God, and he famously announced that "God is dead" and that "we have killed him." Our reading consists of three selections from three of Nietzsche's books.

The first is "On the Afterworldly" from *Thus Spoke Zarathustra*. In *Thus Spoke Zarathustra* Nietzsche uses Zarathustra as an alter-ego to express in aphoristic form many of his thoughts about morality, religion, and the requirements of personal growth. In this selection from *Thus Spoke Zarathustra* Zarathustra says that "weariness" is the source of "all gods and afterworlds."

The second selection is a chapter from *The Antichrist*. (In German *Der Antichrist* can mean simply "the anti-Christian" or it can mean "the Antichrist" in reference to the figure referred to in the New Testament.) In this work Nietzsche is critical of all religion, but he concentrates his most severe criticism on Christianity. In this reading from *The Antichrist* Nietzsche sees those with religious faith, or Christians, as blinding themselves to their own natural instincts to be strong and have power—and yet acting on them while condemning them in others. Nietzsche goes on to speak of the "instinctive hatred of reality" as the "motivating force at the root of Christianity."

The third selection is "The Madman" from *The Gay Science*. (Nietzsche's title, *Die Fröhliche Wissenschaft*, is usually translated as *The Gay Science*. The German *fröhliche* means "merry, gay, cheerful.") In our reading a "madman" goes to the market place and cries "I seek God." His apparent belief in God is mocked by the people in the market place, but when he tells them that they, and he, have killed God they fall silent. They are unbelievers, but they are not yet ready to "become gods" themselves. For Nietzsche they still have need of God or the heritage of their belief as the source of their values.

Nietzsche in these selections does not disprove the existence of God. In fact, strictly, even if Nietzsche were right that weariness is what creates all gods and afterworlds and that a denial of natural instincts is the "motivating force" behind Christian belief, it could still be true that God exists. However, if Nietzsche were right about the source of motive of belief in god, that would call into question whether God's presence was ever *discovered*.*

from Thus Spoke Zarathustra

ON THE AFTERWORLDLY

At one time Zarathustra too cast his delusion beyond man, like all the afterworldly. The work of a suffering and tortured god, the world then seemed to me. A dream the world then seemed to me, and the fiction of a god: colored smoke before the eyes of a dissatisfied deity. Good and evil and joy and pain and I and you—colored smoke this seemed to me before creative eyes. The creator wanted to look away from himself; so he created the world.

Drunken joy it is for the sufferer to look away from his suffering and to lose himself. Drunken joy and loss of self the world once seemed to me. This world, eternally imperfect, the image of an eternal contradiction, an imperfect image—a drunken joy for its imperfect creator: thus the world once appeared to me.

Thus I too once cast my delusion beyond man, like all the afterworldly. Beyond man indeed?

Alas, my brothers, this god whom I created was man-made and madness, like all gods! Man he was, and only a poor specimen of man and ego: out of my own ashes and fire this ghost came to me, and, verily, it did not come to me from beyond. What happened, my brothers? I overcame myself, the sufferer; I carried my own ashes to the mountains; I invented a brighter flame for myself. And behold, then this ghost *fled* from me. Now it would be suffering for me

and agony for the recovered to believe in such ghosts: now it would be suffering for me and humiliation. Thus I speak to the afterworldly.

It was suffering and incapacity that created all afterworlds—this and that brief madness of bliss which is experienced only by those who suffer most deeply.

Weariness that wants to reach the ultimate with one leap, with one fatal leap, a poor ignorant weariness that does not want to want any more: this created all gods and afterworlds.

Believe me, my brothers: it was the body that despaired of the body and touched the ultimate walls with the fingers of a deluded spirit. Believe me, my brothers: it was the body that despaired of the earth and heard the belly of being speak to it. It wanted to crash through these ultimate walls with its head, and not only with its head—over there to "that world." But "that world" is well concealed from humans—that dehumanized inhuman world which is a heavenly nothing; and the belly of being does not speak to humans at all, except as a human.

Verily, all being is hard to prove and hard to induce to speak. Tell me, my brothers, is not the strangest of all things proved most nearly?

Indeed, this ego and the ego's contradiction and confusion still speak most honestly of its being—this creating, willing, valuing ego, which is the measure and value of things. And this most honest being, the ego, speaks of the body and still wants the body, even when it poetizes and raves and flutters with broken wings. It learns to speak ever more honestly, this ego: and the more it learns, the more words and honors it finds for body and earth.

A new pride my ego taught me, and this I teach men: no longer to bury one's head in the sand of heavenly things, but to bear it freely, an earthly head, which creates a meaning for the earth.

A new will I teach men: to *will* this way which man has walked blindly, and to affirm it, and no longer to sneak away from it like the sick and decaying.

It was the sick and decaying who despised body and earth and invented the heavenly realm and the redemptive drops of blood: but they took even these sweet and gloomy poisons from body and earth. They wanted to escape their own misery, and the stars were too far for them. So they sighed: "Would that there were heavenly ways to sneak into another state of being and happiness!" Thus they invented their sneaky ruses and bloody potions. Ungrateful, these people deemed themselves transported from their bodies and this earth. But to whom did they owe the convulsions and raptures of their transport? To their bodies and this earth.

Zarathustra is gentle with the sick. Verily, he is not angry with their kinds of comfort and ingratitude. May they become convalescents, men of overcoming, and create a higher body for themselves! Nor is Zarathustra angry with the convalescent who eyes his delusion tenderly and, at midnight, sneaks around the grave of his god: but even so his tears still betray sickness and a sick body to me.

Many sick people have always been among the poetizers and God-cravers; furiously they hate the lover of knowledge and that youngest among the virtues, which is called "honesty." They always look backward toward dark ages; then, indeed, delusion and faith were another matter: the rage of reason was godlikeness, and doubt was sin.

I know these godlike men all too well: they want one to have faith in them, and doubt to be sin. All too well I also know what it is in which they have most faith. Verily, it is not in afterworlds and redemptive drops of blood, but in the body, that they too have most faith; and their body is to them their thing-in-itself. But a sick thing it is to them, and gladly would they shed their skins. Therefore they listen to the preachers of death and themselves preach afterworlds.

Listen rather, my brothers, to the voice of the healthy body: that is a more honest and purer voice. More honestly and purely speaks the healthy body that is perfect and perpendicular: and it speaks of the meaning of the earth.

Thus spoke Zarathustra.

From The Antichrist

39

I go back, I tell the *genuine* history of Christianity. The very word "Christianity" is a misunderstanding: in truth, there was only *one* Christian, and he died on the cross. The "evangel" *died* on the cross. What has been called "evangel" from that moment was actually the opposite of that which *he* had lived: "*ill* tidings," a *dysangel*. It is false to the point of nonsense to find the mark of the

Christian in a "faith," for instance, in the faith in redemption through Christ: only Christian *practice*, a life such as he *lived* who died on the cross, is Christian.

Such a life is still possible today, for certain people even necessary: genuine, original Christianity will be possible at all times.

Not a faith, but a doing; above all, a *not* doing of many things, another state of *being*. States of consciousness, any faith, considering something true, for example— every psychologist knows this—are fifth-rank matters of complete indifference compared to the value of the instincts: speaking more strictly, the whole concept of spiritual causality is false. To reduce being a Christian, Christianism, to a matter of considering something true, to a mere phenomenon of consciousness, is to negate Christianism. *In fact, there have been no Christians at all.* The "Christian," that which for the last two thousand years has been called a Christian, is merely a psychological self-misunderstanding. If one looks more closely, it was, in spite of all "faith," only the instincts that ruled in him—and *what instincts!*

"Faith" was at all times, for example, in Luther, only a cloak, a pretext, a *screen* behind which the instincts played their game—a shrewd *blindness* about the dominance of *certain* instincts. "Faith"—I have already called it the characteristic Christian shrewdness—one always *spoke* of faith, but one always *acted* from instinct alone.

In the Christian world of ideas there is nothing that has the least contact with reality—and it is in the instinctive hatred of reality that we have recognized the only motivating force at the root of Christianity. What follows from this? That *in psychologicis* too, the error here is radical, that it is that which determines the very essence, that it is the *substance*. One concept less, one single reality in its place—and the whole of Christianity hurtles down into nothing.

Viewed from high above, this strangest of all facts—a religion which is not only dependent on errors but which has its inventiveness and even its genius *only* in harmful errors, *only* in errors which poison life and the heart—is really a *spectacle for gods*, for those gods who are at the same time philosophers and whom I have encountered, for example, at those famous dialogues on Naxos. The moment *nausea* leaves them (*and* us!), they become grateful for the spectacle of the Christian: perhaps the miserable little star that is called earth deserves a divine glance, a divine sympathy, just because of *this* curious case. For let us not underestimate the Christian: the Christian, false *to the point of innocence*, is far above the ape—regarding Christians, a well-known theory of descent becomes a mere compliment.

from The Gay Science

[125]

T he Madman. Have you not heard of that madman who lit a lantern in the bright morning hours, ran to the market place, and cried incessantly, "I seek God! I seek God!" As many of those who do not believe in God were standing around just then, he provoked much laughter. Why, did he get lost? said one. Did he lose his way like a child? said another. Or is he hiding? Is he afraid of us? Has he gone on a voyage? or emigrated? Thus they yelled and laughed. The madman jumped into their midst and pierced them with his glances.

"Whither is God" he cried. "I shall tell you. *We have killed him*—you and I. All of us are his murderers. But how have we done this? How were we able to drink up the sea? Who gave us the sponge to wipe away the entire horizon? What did we do when we unchained this earth from its sun? Whither is it moving now? Whither are we moving now? Away from all suns? Are we not plunging continually? Backward, sideward, forward, in all directions? Is there any up or down left? Are we not straying as through an infinite nothing? Do we not feel the breath of empty space? Has it not become colder? Is not night and more night coming on all the while? Must not lanterns be lit in the morning? Do we not hear anything yet of the noise of the gravediggers who are burying God? Do we not smell anything yet of God's decomposition? Gods too decompose. God is dead. God remains dead. And we have killed him. How shall we, the murderers of all murderers, comfort ourselves? What was holiest and most powerful of all that the world has yet owned has bled to death under our knives. Who will wipe this blood off us? What water is there for us to clean ourselves? What festivals of atonement, what sacred games shall we have to invent? Is not the greatness of this deed too great for us?

Must not we ourselves become gods simply to seem worthy of it? There has never been a greater deed; and whoever will be born after us—for the sake of this deed he will be part of a higher history than all history hitherto."

Here the madman fell silent and looked again at his listeners; and they too were silent and stared at him in astonishment. At last he threw his lantern on the ground, and it broke and went out. "I come too early," he said then; "my time has not come yet. This tremendous event is still on its way, still wandering—it has not yet reached the ears of man. Lightning and thunder require time, the light of the stars requires time, deeds require time even after they are done, before they can be seen and heard. This deed is still more distant from them than the most distant stars—*and yet they have done it themselves.*"

It has been related further that on that same day the madman entered divers churches and there sang his *requiem aeternam deo.* Led out and called to account, he is said to have replied each time, "What are these churches now if they are not the tombs and sepulchers of God?"

SIGMUND FREUD

from The Future of an Illusion

Sigmund Freud, the father of psychoanalysis, developed his thinking about psychoanalysis and religion in the early part of the twentieth century. In his view religion is "the universal obsessional neurosis of humanity." That is, religion is a disfunction (neurosis) that involves an irresistible idea (obsession) that affects all of humanity (is universal). For Freud religious belief is motivated by wish-fulfilment arising from a deep need to be secure. What leads people to believe in God, and to believe they feel God's presence, is not a realization of God's presence but the psychological working of their need and wish for security. The motive that Freud says leads to religious belief is close to one that

Nietzsche names—weariness (or the wish for relief from weariness)—although Freud gives a special place to a Father image.

Freud said that religion is an "illusion," by which he meant that it is a belief formed in a nonrational way, by wish-fulfilment. He appreciated that "illusions" could in theory turn out to be true. But if that were to happen in the case of religious belief in God, it would be a sheer accident, and, if Freud is right, religious belief is never supported by a discovery of God. Our reading consists of Chapters 4, and 6 from *The Future of an Illusion*.*

IV

An enquiry which proceeds like a monologue, without interruption, is not altogether free from danger. One is too easily tempted into pushing aside thoughts which threaten to break into it, and in exchange one is left with a feeling of uncertainty which in the end one tries to keep down by over-decisiveness. I shall therefore imagine that I have an opponent who follows my arguments with mistrust, and here and there I shall allow him to interject some remarks.[1]

I hear him say: 'You have repeatedly used the expressions "civilization creates these religious ideas", "civilization places them at the disposal of its participants". There is something about this that sounds strange to me. I cannot myself say why, but it does not sound so natural as it does to say that civilization has made rules about distributing the products of labour or about rights concerning women and children.'

I think, all the same, that I am justified in expressing myself in this way. I have tried to show that religious ideas have arisen from the same need as have all the other achievements of civilization: from the necessity of defending one-self against the crushingly superior force of nature. To this a second motive was added—the urge to rectify the shortcomings of civilization which made themselves painfully felt. Moreover, it is especially apposite to say that civilization gives the individual these ideas, for he finds them there already; they are presented to him ready-made, and he would not be able to discover them for himself. What he is entering into is the heritage of many generations, and he takes it over as he does the multiplication table, geometry, and similar things. There is indeed a difference in this, but that difference lies elsewhere and I cannot examine it yet. The feeling of strangeness that you mention may be partly due to the fact that this body of religious ideas is usually put forward as a divine revelation. But this presentation of it is itself a part of the religious system, and it entirely ignores the known historical development of these ideas and their differences in different epochs and civilizations.

[1] [Freud had adopted the same method of presentation in his recent discussion of lay analysis (1926e) and also, though in somewhat different circumstances, a quarter of a century earlier in his paper on 'Screen Memories' (1899a).]

'Here is another point, which seems to me to be more important. You argue that the humanization of nature is derived from the need to put an end to man's perplexity and helplessness in the face of its dreaded forces, to get into a relation with them and finally to influence them. But a motive of this kind seems superfluous. Primitive man has no choice, he has no other way of thinking. It is natural to him, something innate, as it were, to project his existence outwards into the world and to regard every event which he observes as the manifestation of beings who at bottom are like himself. It is his only method of comprehension. And it is by no means self-evident, on the contrary it is a remarkable coincidence, if by thus indulging his natural disposition he succeeds in satisfying one of his greatest needs.'

I do not find that so striking. Do you suppose that human thought has no practical motives, that it is simply the expression of a disinterested curiosity? That is surely very improbable. I believe rather that when man personifies the forces of nature he is again following an infantile model. He has learnt from the persons in his earliest environment that the way to influence them is to establish a relation with them; and so, later on, with the same end in view, he treats everything else that he comes across in the same way as he treated those persons. Thus I do not contradict your descriptive observation; it is in fact natural to man to personify everything that he wants to understand in order later to control it (psychical mastering as a preparation for physical mastering); but I provide in addition a motive and a genesis for this peculiarity of human thinking.

'And now here is yet a third point. You have dealt with the origin of religion once before, in your book *Totem and Taboo* [1912–13]. But there it appeared in a different light. Everything was the son-father relationship. God was the exalted father, and the longing for the father was the root of the need for religion. Since then, it seems, you have discovered the factor of human weakness and helplessness, to which indeed the chief role in the formation of religion is generally assigned, and now you transpose everything that was once the father complex into terms of helplessness. May I ask you to explain this transformation?'

With pleasure. I was only waiting for this invitation. But is it really a transformation? In *Totem and Taboo* it was not my purpose to explain the origin of religions but only of totemism. Can you, from any of the views known to you, explain the fact that the first shape in which the protecting deity revealed itself to men should have been that of an animal, that there was a prohibition against killing and eating this animal and that nevertheless the solemn custom was to kill and eat it communally once a year? This is precisely what happens in totemism. And it is hardly to the purpose to argue about whether totemism ought to be called a religion. It has intimate connections with the later god-religions. The totem animals become the sacred animals of the gods; and the earliest, but most fundamental moral restrictions—the prohibitions against murder and incest—originate in totemism. Whether or not you accept the conclusions of *Totem and Taboo*, I hope you will admit that a number of very remarkable, disconnected facts are brought together in it into a consistent whole.

The question of why in the long run the animal god did not suffice, and was replaced by a human one, was hardly touched on in *Totem and Taboo*, and other problems concerning the formation of religion were not mentioned in the book at all. Do you regard a limitation of that kind as the same thing as a denial? My work is a good example of the strict isolation of the particular contribution which psycho-analytic discussion can make to the solution of the problem of religion. If I am now trying to add the other, less deeply concealed part, you should not accuse me of contradicting myself, just as before you accused me of being one-sided. It is, of course, my duty to point out the connecting links between what I said earlier and what I put forward now, between the deeper and the manifest motives, between the father-complex and man's helplessness and need for protection.

These connections are not hard to find. They consist in the relation of the child's helplessness to the helplessness of the adult which continues it. So that, as was to be expected, the motives for the formation of religion which psychoanalysis revealed now turn out to be the same as the infantile contribution to the *manifest* motives. Let us transport ourselves into the mental life of a child. You remember the choice of object according to the anaclitic [attachment] type, which psycho-analysis talks of?[2] The libido there follows the paths of narcissistic needs and attaches itself to the objects which ensure the satisfaction of those needs. In this way the mother, who satisfies the child's hunger, becomes its first love-object and certainly also its first protection against all the undefined dangers which threaten it in the external world— its first protection against anxiety, we may say.

In this function [of protection] the mother is soon replaced by the stronger father, who retains that position for the rest of childhood. But the child's attitude to its father is coloured by a peculiar ambivalence. The father himself constitutes a danger for the child, perhaps because of its earlier relation to its mother. Thus it fears him no less than it longs for him and admires him. The indications of this ambivalence in the attitude to the father are deeply imprinted in every religion, as was shown in *Totem and Taboo*. When the growing individual finds that he is destined to remain a child for ever, that he can never do without protection against strange superior powers, he lends those powers the features belonging to the figure of his father; he creates for himself the gods whom he dreads, whom he seeks to propitiate, and whom he nevertheless entrusts with his own protection. Thus his longing for a father is a motive identical with his need for protection against the consequences of his human weakness. The defence against childish helplessness is what lends its characteristic features to the adult's reaction to the helplessness which *he* has to acknowledge—a reaction which is precisely the formation of religion. But it is not my intention to enquire any further into the development of the idea of God; what we are concerned with here is the finished body of religious ideas as it is transmitted by civilization to the individual.

VI

I think we have prepared the way sufficiently for an answer to both these questions. It will be found if we turn our attention to the psychical origin of religious ideas. These, which are given out as teachings, are not precipitates of experience or end-results of thinking: they are illusions, fulfilments of the oldest, strongest and most urgent wishes of mankind. The secret of their strength lies

---

[2] [See Freud's paper on narcissism (1914c), *Standard Ed.*, 14, 87.]

in the strength of those wishes. As we already know, the terrifying impression of helplessness in childhood aroused the need for protection—for protection through love—which was provided by the father; and the recognition that this helplessness lasts throughout life made it necessary to cling to the existence of a father, but this time a more powerful one. Thus the benevolent rule of a divine Providence allays our fear of the dangers of life; the establishment of a moral world-order ensures the fulfilment of the demands of justice, which have so often remained unfulfilled in human civilization; and the prolongation of earthly existence in a future life provides the local and temporal framework in which these wish-fulfilments shall take place. Answers to the riddles that tempt the curiosity of man, such as how the universe began or what the relation is between body and mind, are developed in conformity with the underlying assumptions of this system. It is an enormous relief to the individual psyche if the conflicts of its childhood arising from the father-complex—conflicts which it has never wholly overcome—are removed from it and brought to a solution which is universally accepted.

When I say that these things are all illusions, I must define the meaning of the word. An illusion is not the same thing as an error; nor is it necessarily an error. Aristotle's belief that vermin are developed out of dung (a belief to which ignorant people still cling) was an error; so was the belief of a former generation of doctors that *tabes dorsalis* is the result of sexual excess. It would be incorrect to call these errors illusions. On the other hand, it was an illusion of Columbus's that he had discovered a new sea-route to the Indies. The part played by his wish in this error is very clear. One may describe as an illusion the assertion made by certain nationalists that the Indo-Germanic race is the only one capable of civilization; or the belief, which was only destroyed by psycho-analysis, that children are creatures without sexuality. What is characteristic of illusions is that they are derived from human wishes. In this respect they come near to psychiatric delusions. But they differ from them, too, apart from the more complicated structure of delusions. In the case of delusions, we emphasize as essential their being in contradiction with reality. Illusions need not necessarily be false—that is to say, unrealizable or in contradiction to reality. For instance, a middle-class girl may have the illusion that a prince will come and marry her. This is possible; and a few such cases have occurred. That the Messiah will come and found a golden age is much less likely. Whether one classifies this belief as an illusion or as something analogous to a delusion will depend on one's personal attitude. Examples of illusions which have proved true are not easy to find, but the illusion of the alchemists that all metals can be turned into gold might be one of them. The wish to have a great deal of gold, as much gold as possible, has, it is true, been a good deal damped by our present-day knowledge of the determinants of wealth, but chemistry no longer regards the transmutation of metals into gold as impossible. Thus we call a belief an illusion when a wish-fulfilment is a prominent factor in its motivation, and in doing so we disregard its relations to reality, just as the illusion itself sets no store by verification.

Having thus taken our bearings, let us return once more to the question of religious doctrines. We can now repeat that all of them are illusions and insusceptible of proof. No one can be compelled to think them true, to believe in them. Some of them are so improbable, so incompatible with everything we have laboriously discovered about the reality of the world, that we may compare them—if we pay proper regard to the psychological differences—to delusions. Of the reality value of most of them we cannot judge; just as they cannot be proved, so they cannot be refuted. We still know too little to make a critical approach to them. The riddles of the universe reveal themselves only slowly to our investigation; there are many questions to which science to-day can give no answer. But scientific work is the only road which can lead us to a knowledge of reality outside ourselves. It is once again merely an illusion to expect anything from intuition and introspection; they can give us nothing but particulars about our own mental life, which are hard to interpret, never any information about the questions which religious doctrine finds it so easy to answer. It would be insolent to let one's own arbitrary will step into the breach and, according to one's personal estimate, declare this or that part of the religious system to be less or more acceptable. Such questions are too momentous for that; they might be called too sacred.

At this point one must expect to meet with an objection. 'Well then, if even obdurate sceptics admit that the assertions of religion cannot be refuted by reason, why should I not believe in them, since they have so much on their side— tradition, the agreement of mankind, and all the consolations they offer?' Why not, indeed? Just as no one can be forced to believe, so no one can be forced to disbelieve. But do not let us be satisfied with deceiving ourselves that arguments like these take us along the road of correct thinking. If ever there was a case of a lame excuse we have it here. Ignorance is ignorance; no right to believe anything can be derived from it. In other matters no sensible person will behave so irresponsibly or rest content with such feeble grounds for his opinions and for the line he takes. It is only in the highest and most sacred things that he allows himself to do so. In reality these are only attempts at pretending to oneself or to other people that one is still firmly attached to religion, when one has long since cut oneself loose from it. Where questions of religion are concerned, people are guilty of every possible sort of dishonesty and intellectual misdemeanour. Philosophers stretch the meaning of words until they retain scarcely anything of their original sense. They give the name of 'God' to some vague abstraction which they have created for themselves; having done so they can pose before all the world as deists, as believers in God, and they can even boast that they have recognized a higher, purer concept of God, notwithstanding that their God is now nothing more than an insubstantial shadow and no longer the mighty personality of religious doctrines. Critics persist in describing as 'deeply religious' anyone who admits to a sense of man's insignificance or impotence in the face of the universe, although what constitutes the essence of the religious attitude is not this feeling but only the next step after it, the reaction to it which seeks a remedy for it. The man who goes no further, but humbly acquiesces in the small part which human beings play in the great world—such a man is, on the contrary, irreligious in the truest sense of the word.

To assess the truth-value of religious doctrines does not lie within the scope of the present enquiry. It is enough for us that we have recognized them as being, in their psychological nature, illusions. But we do not have to conceal the fact that this discovery also strongly influences our attitude to the question which must appear to many to be the most important of all. We know approximately at what periods and by what kind of men religious doctrines were created. If in addition we discover the motives which led to this, our attitude to the problem of religion will undergo a marked displacement. We shall tell ourselves that it would be very nice if there were a God who created the world and was a benevolent Providence, and if there were a moral order in the universe and an after-life; but it is a very striking fact that all this is exactly as we are bound to wish it to be. And it would be more remarkable still if our wretched, ignorant and downtrodden ancestors had succeeded in solving all these difficult riddles of the universe.

Chapter **6**

The Religious Problem of Evil

There is more than one problem of evil. Perhaps the most pressing problem of evil is: How can we lessen the evil there is in the world? How can we lessen the evil of disease and the evil of famine, and what if anything can we do to lessen the oppression and injustice that there is in the world? This problem may be called the practical problem of evil. Important as it is, it is not the religious problem of evil. The religious problem of evil relates to traditional religious belief in God. It arises, or can arise, when a religious believer in God comes to experience evil in her or his life. When a religious believer in God experiences the loss of her child to disease or finds that he himself has a terminal disease or faces the loss of family and friends in such a great evil as the holocaust, then the religious believer may ask "Why? Why did God allow this to happen?" In such an instance the religious problem of evil arises as a personal problem and may become a crisis of faith.

This personal religious problem of evil can take a more general form for religious believers, and it has. When it does the question is not "Why has this evil happened to me (or to my child or to my family)?" but "Why is there any evil in the world, why is there any suffering of any children?" Though a more general problem, it is still concrete in that it is focused on flesh-and-blood instances of suffering.

In a chapter of Fyodor Dostoyevsky's great novel, *The Brothers Karamazov*, Ivan Karamazov presents to his deeply religious brother, Alyosha, a catalogue of evils done to children. His catalogue is not that long, but it consists of flesh-and-blood cases, complete with terrible details. The children in Ivan's catalogue are not his own, but the problem of evil he presents is not the less concrete for that reason, and it is easy to see how, as Ivan feels for the suffering inflicted on the children that he recounts, we can go on to feel for the suffering of other children, and men and women, throughout the world. In this way the general and concrete problem can be extended to include any human being, or any sentient being (for beings other than humans suffer pain). The religious problem of evil then becomes: Why does God allow such suffering to be inflicted on others and why does God allow human beings and other sentient beings to suffer so?

The religious problem of evil arises in faith-traditions where there is faith in God and God is believed to be good and to be all-powerful as the creator and master of the universe. These beliefs are in the background of the mother's crisis of faith when her child dies of a disease. We can see they are by noticing that it is no answer to her question "Why did God allow this to happen?" for her to try to explain her child's dying of a disease by saying either "God is not good after all" or "God did not have the power to prevent the death of my child." If she were to say either of these, she would abandon her faith in God. If she says "God is not good after all", she ceases to trust in God and God's goodness. If she says "God did not have the power to prevent the death of my child," then she accepts it that God does not have the power to bring about what is good, and in this way ceases to trust in and have faith in God.

There are three propositions which taken together can lead to the religious problem of evil: the first two are central beliefs about God in the great theistic traditions and are locked into faith in God:

1. *God is good.* God is believed to be good or all-good. God's goodness is unfaltering and unending, in the biblical tradition. This belief closely connects to continuing trust and faith in God.
2. *God is all-powerful.* God is the creator of the universe, and the universe is subject to God's will and power. As God can part the waters of the Red Sea or raise one who is dead, so God has the power to change any natural event. This religious belief about God connects to believers' trust in God's loving ability to give them in their lives what is good.
3. *Evil exists in the world.* This proposition arises from what the religious and nonreligious alike see about them in the world: the suffering from diseases like malaria and AIDS, natural disasters and famines (such evils are called *natural evils*, or, sometimes, physical evils); and the evil things people do ranging from the many small ungenerous and mean things people do without thinking to planned and deliberate genocide (such evils are called *moral evils*).

The tension between these three propositions is between any one and the other two. It can be expressed in the following reasoning. If there is evil in the world, and God wishes to remove it but cannot remove it, then God is not all-powerful. (Propositions 1 and 3 rule out Proposition 2). If there is evil in the world and God can remove it but does not wish to remove it, then God is not all-good. (Propositions 2 and 3 rule out Proposition 1) If God wishes to remove evil and can remove evil, then there should be no evil (Propositions 1 and 2 rule out Proposition 3). Since the existence of evil is hard to deny, the problem is one of reconciling God's being both all-good and all-powerful with the existence of evil. (Sometimes God's being all-knowing is also brought into the problem, but we can leave this attribute out of the equation with the observation that of course God in any traditional religious conception of God would know about the existence of evil.)

Religious thinkers or theologians have for centuries sought a way of understanding how there can both be the God of religious belief and evil in the world. They have sought a reason that explains why God allows evil and justifies God's allowing evil. Such a reason is offered by a *theodicy*, an effort to explain evil and vindicate God.

The readings in this chapter cover a range of perspectives. The first reading, from Dostoyevsky's *The Brothers Karamazov*, includes the chapter entitled

"Rebellion" in which Ivan Karamazov catalogues to his brother Alyosha horrendous evils done to children, and it also includes some sections from Bk. 10 and the Epilogue of the novel in which Dostoyevsky presents the reaction of Alyosha to the evils in the lives of young boys, especially in the life of one boy, Kolya. Second, there are Parts 10 and 11 of David Hume's *Dialogues Concerning Natural Religion*, in which Hume argues that evil is inconsistent with God's existence, or at least strong evidence that there is no God. The third reading is an article by John Hick, "An Irenaean Theodicy," in which Hick presents what he sees as a strong contender for an adequate theodicy. In the fourth reading, "God and Evil," H. J. McCloskey argues that all proposed theodicies fail. And in the last reading, "God's Goodness and God's Evil," James Kellenberger argues that for certain religious believers in God, though there is an experience of evil in their lives, there may be no religious problem of evil.

FYODOR DOSTOYEVSKY

from Rebellion and Other Selections from The Brothers Karamazov

Dostoyevsky's novel *The Brothers Karamazov* is on the surface a murder mystery, but at a deeper level it is a psychological novel that explores religious and moral themes. One of the three brothers of the title is Ivan Karamazov, who, as he says, has returned to God his "ticket of admission." In the chapter entitled "Rebellion" Ivan explains to his religious brother Alyosha why he has done so. The other selections from *The Brothers Karamazov* in this reading are from Book 10 and the Epilogue. In these pages from the novel we see Alyosha's reaction to evil, which is very different from his brother's.*

Rebellion

'I must make a confession to you,' Ivan began. 'I never could understand how one can love one's neighbours. In my view, it is one's neighbours that one can't possibly love, but only perhaps these who live far away. I read somewhere about "John the Merciful" (some saint) who, when a hungry and frozen stranger came to him and begged him to warm him, lay down with him in his bed and, putting his arms round him, began breathing into his mouth, which was festering and fetid

---

* From *The Brothers Karamazov* by Fyodor Dostoyevsky, translated with an introduction by David Magarshack (Penguin Classics, 1958). Copyright © David Magarshack, 1958.

from some awful disease. I'm convinced that he did so from heartache, from heartache that originated in a lie, for the sake of love arising from a sense of duty, for the sake of a penance he had imposed upon himself. To love a man, it's necessary that he should be hidden, for as soon as he shows his face, love is gone.'

'The elder Zossima has talked about it more than once,' observed Alyosha. 'He, too, declared that a man's face often prevented many people who were inexperienced in love from loving him. But then there's a great deal of love in mankind, almost Christ-like love, as I know myself, Ivan. . . .'

'Well, I'm afraid I don't know anything about it yet and I can't understand it, and an innumerable multitude of people are with me there. You see, the question is whether that is due to men's bad qualities or whether that is their nature. In my opinion, Christ's love for men is in a way a miracle that is impossible on earth. It is true he was a god. But we are no gods. Suppose, for instance, that I am capable of profound suffering, but no one else could ever know how much I suffer, because he is someone else and not I. Moreover, a man is rarely ready to admit that another man is suffering (as if it were some honour). Why doesn't he admit it, do you think? Because, I suppose, I have a bad smell or a stupid face, or because I once trod on his foot. Besides, there is suffering and suffering: there is humiliating suffering, which degrades me; a benefactor of mine, for instance, would not object to my being hungry, but he would not often tolerate some higher kind of suffering in me, for an idea, for instance. That he would only tolerate in exceptional cases, and even then he might look at me and, suddenly realize that I haven't got the kind of face which, according to some fantastic notion of his, a man suffering for some idea ought to have. So he at

once deprives me of all his benefactions, and not from an evil heart, either. Beggars, especially honourable beggars, should never show themselves in the streets, but ask for charity through the newspapers. Theoretically it is still possible to love one's neighbours, and sometimes even from a distance, but at close quarters almost never. If everything had been as on the stage, in the ballet, where, if beggars come in, they wear silken rags and tattered lace and beg for alms dancing gracefully, then it would still be possible to look at them with pleasure. But even then we might admire them but not love them. But enough of this. All I wanted is to make you see my point of view. I wanted to discuss the suffering of humanity in general, but perhaps we'd better confine ourselves to the sufferings of children. This will reduce the scope of my argument by a tenth, but I think we'd better confine our argument to the children. It's all the worse for me, of course. For, to begin with, one can love children even at close quarters and even with dirty and ugly faces (though I can't help feeling that children's faces are never ugly). Secondly, I won't talk about grown-ups because, besides being disgusting and undeserving of love, they have something to compensate them for it: they have eaten the apple and know good and evil and have become "like gods". They go on eating it still. But little children haven't eaten anything and so far are not guilty of anything. Do you love little children, Alyosha? I know you do and you will understand why I want to talk only about them now. If they, too, suffer terribly on earth, they do so, of course, for their fathers. They are punished for their fathers who have eaten the apple, but this is an argument from another world, an argument that is incomprehensible to the human heart here on earth. No innocent must suffer for another, and such innocents, too! You may be surprised at me, Alyosha, for I too love little children terribly. And note, please, that cruel men, passionate and carnal men, Karamazovs, are sometimes very fond of children. Children, while they are children, up to seven years, for instance, are very different from grown-up people: they seem to be quite different creatures with quite different natures. I knew a murderer in prison: in the course of his career he had murdered whole families in the houses he had broken into at night for the purpose of robbery, and while about it he had also murdered several children. But when he was in prison he showed a very peculiar affection for them. He used to stand by the window of his cell for hours watching the children playing in the prison yard. He trained one little boy to come up to his window and made great friends with him. You don't know why I'm telling you this, Alyosha? I'm afraid I have a headache and I'm feeling sad.'

'You speak with a strange air,' Alyosha observed uneasily, 'as though you were not quite yourself.'

'By the way, not so long ago a Bulgarian in Moscow told me,' Ivan went on, as though not bothering to listen to his brother, 'of the terrible atrocities committed all over Bulgaria by the Turks and Circassians who were afraid of a general uprising of the Slav population. They burn, kill, violate women and children, nail their prisoners' ears to fences and leave them like that till next morning when they hang them, and so on—it's impossible to imagine it all. And, indeed, people sometimes speak of man's "bestial" cruelty, but this is very unfair and insulting to the beasts: a beast can never be so cruel as a man, so ingeniously, so artistically cruel. A tiger merely gnaws and tears to pieces, that's all he knows. It would never occur to him to nail men's ears to a fence and leave them like that overnight, even if he were able to do it.

These Turks, incidentally, seemed to derive a voluptuous pleasure from torturing children, cutting a child out of its mother's womb with a dagger and tossing babies up in the air and catching them on a bayonet before the eyes of their mothers. It was doing it before the eyes of their mothers that made it so enjoyable. But one incident I found particularly interesting. Imagine a baby in the arms of a trembling mother, surrounded by Turks who had just entered her house. They are having great fun: they fondle the baby, they laugh to make it laugh and they are successful: the baby laughs. At that moment the Turk points a pistol four inches from the baby's face. The boy laughs happily, stretches out his little hands to grab the pistol, when suddenly the artist pulls the trigger in the baby's face and blows his brains out. . . . Artistic, isn't it? Incidentally, I'm told the Turks are very fond of sweets.'

'Why are you telling me all this, Ivan?' asked Alyosha.

'I can't help thinking that if the devil doesn't exist and, therefore, man has created him, he has created him in his own image and likeness.'

'Just as he did God, you mean.'

'Oh, you're marvellous at "cracking the wind of the poor phrase", as Polonius says in *Hamlet*,' laughed Ivan. 'You've caught me there. All right. I'm glad. Your God is a fine one, if man created him in his own image and likeness. You asked me just now why I was telling you all this: you see, I'm a collector of certain interesting little facts and, you know, I'm jotting down and collecting from newspapers and books, from anywhere, in fact, certain jolly little anecdotes, and I've already a good collection of them. The Turks, of course, have gone into my collection, but they are, after all, foreigners. I've also got lovely stories from home. Even better than the Turkish ones. We like corporal punishment, you know. The birch and the lash mostly. It's a national custom. With us nailed ears are unthinkable, for we are Europeans, after all. But the birch and the lash are something that is our own and cannot be taken away from us. Abroad they don't seem to have corporal punishment at all now. Whether they have reformed their habits or whether they've passed special legislation prohibiting flogging—I don't know, but they've made up for it by something else, something as purely national as ours. Indeed, it's so national that it seems to be quite impossible in our country, though I believe it is taking root here too, especially since the spread of the religious movement among our aristocracy. I have a very charming brochure, translated from the French, about the execution quite recently, only five years ago, of a murderer in Geneva. The murderer, Richard, a young fellow of three and twenty, I believe, repented and was converted to the Christian faith before his execution. This Richard fellow was an illegitimate child who at the age of six was given by his parents *as a present* to some shepherds in the Swiss mountains. The shepherds brought him up to work for them. He grew up among them like a little wild animal. The shepherds taught him nothing. On the contrary, when he was seven they sent him to take the cattle out to graze in the cold and wet, hungry and in rags. And it goes without saying that they never thought about it or felt remorse, being convinced that they had every right to treat him like that, for Richard had been given to them just as a chattel and they didn't even think it necessary to feed him. Richard himself testified how in those years, like the prodigal son in the Gospel, he was so hungry that he wished he could eat the mash given to the pigs, which were fattened for sale. But he wasn't given even that and he was beaten when he stole from the pigs. And

that was how he spent all his childhood and his youth, till he grew up and, having grown strong, he himself went to steal. The savage began to earn his living as a day labourer in Geneva, and what he earned he spent on drink. He lived like a brute and finished up by killing and robbing an old man. He was caught, tried, and sentenced to death. There are no sentimentalists there, you see. In prison he was immediately surrounded by pastors and members of different Christian sects, philanthropic ladies, and so on. They taught him to read and write in prison, expounded the Gospel to him, exhorted him, tried their best to persuade him, wheedled, coaxed, and pressed him till he himself at last solemnly confessed his crime. He was converted and wrote to the court himself that he was a monster and that at last it had been vouchsafed to him by God to see the light and obtain grace. Everyone in Geneva was excited about him—the whole of philanthropic and religious Geneva. Everyone who was well-bred and belonged to the higher circles of Geneva society rushed to the prison to see him. They embraced and kissed Richard: "You are our brother! Grace has descended upon you!" Richard himself just wept with emotion: "Yes, grace has descended upon me! Before in my childhood and youth I was glad of pigs' food, but now grace has descended upon me, too, and I'm dying in the Lord!" "Yes, yes, Richard, die in the Lord. You've shed blood and you must die in the Lord. Though it was not your fault that you knew not the Lord when you coveted the pigs' food and when you were beaten for stealing it (what you did was very wrong, for it is forbidden to steal), You've shed blood and you must die." And now the last day comes. Richard, weak and feeble, does nothing but cry and repeat every minute: "This is the happiest day of my life. I'm going to the Lord!" "Yes," cry the pastors, the judges, and the philanthropic ladies, "this is the happiest day of your life, for you are going to the Lord!" They all walked and drove in carriages behind the cart on which Richard was being taken to the scaffold. At last they arrived at the scaffold: "Die, brother," they cried to Richard, "die in the Lord, for His grace has descended upon you!" And so, covered with the kisses of his brothers, they dragged brother Richard on to the scaffold, placed him on the guillotine, and chopped off his head in a most brotherly fashion because grace had descended upon him too. Yes, that's characteristic. That brochure has been translated into Russian by some aristocratic Russian philanthropists of the Lutheran persuasion and sent gratis to the newspapers and other editorial offices for the enlightenment of the Russian people. The incident with Richard is so interesting because it's national. Though we may consider it absurd to cut off the head of a brother of ours because he has become our brother and because grace has descended upon him, we have, I repeat, our own national customs which are not much better. The most direct and spontaneous historic pastime we have is the infliction of pain by beating. Nekrassov has a poem about a peasant who flogs a horse about its eyes, "its gentle eyes". Who hasn't seen that? That is a truly Russian characteristic. He describes how a feeble nag, which has been pulling too heavy a load, sticks in the mud with its cart and cannot move. The peasant beats it, beats it savagely and, in the end, without realizing why he is doing it and intoxicated by the very act of beating, goes on showering heavy blows upon it. "Weak as you are, pull you must! I don't care if you die so long as you go on pulling!" The nag pulls hard but without avail, and he begins lashing the poor defenceless creature across its weeping, "gentle eyes". Beside itself with pain, it

gives one tremendous pull, pulls out the cart, and off it goes, trembling all over and gasping for breath, moving sideways, with a curious sort of skipping motion, unnaturally and shamefully—it's horrible in Nekrassov. But it's only a horse and God has given us horses to be flogged. So the Tartars taught us and left us the whip as a present. But men, too, can be flogged. And there you have an educated and well-brought-up gentleman and his wife who birch their own little daughter, a child of seven—I have a full account of it. Daddy is glad that the twigs have knots, for, as he says, "it will sting more" and so he begins "stinging" his own daughter. I know for a fact that there are people who get so excited that they derive a sensual pleasure from every blow, literally a sensual pleasure, which grows progressively with every subsequent blow. They beat for a minute, five minutes, ten minutes. The more it goes on the more "stinging" do the blows become. The child screams, at last it can scream no more, it is gasping for breath. "Daddy, Daddy, dear Daddy!" The case, by some devilishly indecent chance, is finally brought to court. Counsel is engaged. The Russian people have long called an advocate—"a hired conscience". Counsel shouts in his client's defence: "It's such a simple thing, an ordinary domestic incident. A father has given a hiding to his daughter and, to our shame, it's been brought to court!" Convinced by him, the jurymen retire and bring in a verdict of not guilty. The public roars with delight that the torturer has been acquitted. Oh, what a pity I wasn't there! I'd have bawled out a proposal to found a scholarship in the name of the torturer! . . . Charming pictures. But I have still better ones about children. I've collected a great deal of facts about Russian children, Alyosha. A father and mother, "most respectable people of high social position, of good education and breeding", hated their little five-year-old daughter. You see, I repeat again most emphatically that this love of torturing children and only children is a peculiar characteristic of a great many people. All other individuals of the human species these torturers treat benevolently and mildly like educated and humane Europeans, but they are very fond of torturing children and, in a sense, this is their way of loving children. It's just the defencelessness of these little ones that tempts the torturers, the angelic trustfulness of the child, who has nowhere to go and no one to run to for protection—it is this that inflames the evil blood of the torturer. In every man, of course, a wild beast is hidden—the wild beast of irascibility, the wild beast of sensuous intoxication from the screams of the tortured victim. The wild beast let off the chain and allowed to roam free. The wild beast of diseases contracted in vice, gout, bad liver, and so on. This poor five-year-old girl was subjected to every possible torture by those educated parents. They beat her, birched her, kicked her, without themselves knowing why, till her body was covered with bruises; at last they reached the height of refinement: they shut her up all night, in the cold and frost, in the privy and because she didn't ask to get up at night (as though a child of five, sleeping its angelic, sound sleep, could be trained at her age to ask for such a thing), they smeared her face with excrement and made her eat it, and it was her mother, her mother who made her! And that mother could sleep at night, hearing the groans of the poor child locked up in that vile place! Do you realize what it means when a little creature like that, who's quite unable to understand what is happening to her, beats her little aching chest in that vile place, in the dark and cold, with her tiny fist and weeps searing, unresentful and gentle tears to "dear, kind God" to protect

her? Can you understand all this absurd and horrible business, my friend and brother, you meek and humble novice? Can you understand why all this absurd and horrible business is so necessary and has been brought to pass? They tell me that without it man could not even have existed on earth, for he would not have known good and evil. But why must we know that confounded good and evil when it costs so much? Why, the whole world of knowledge isn't worth that child's tears to her "dear and kind God"! I'm not talking of the sufferings of grown-up people, for they have eaten the apple and to hell with them—let them all go to hell, but these little ones, these little ones! I'm sorry I'm torturing you, Alyosha. You're not yourself. I'll stop if you like.'

'Never mind, I want to suffer too,' murmured Alyosha.

'One more, only one more picture, and that, too; because it's so curious, so very characteristic, but mostly because I've only just read about it in some collection of Russian antiquities, in the *Archives* or *Antiquity*. I'll have to look it up, I'm afraid I've forgotten where I read it. It happened in the darkest days of serfdom, at the beginning of this century—and long live the liberator of the people! There was at the beginning of the century a General, a very rich landowner with the highest aristocratic connexions, but one of those (even then, it is true, rather an exception) who, after retiring from the army, are almost convinced that their service to the State has given them the power of life and death over their "subjects". There were such people in those days. Well, so the General went to live on his estate with its two thousand serfs, imagining himself to be God knows how big a fellow and treating his poorer neighbours as though they were his hangers-on and clowns. He had hundreds of hounds in his kennels and nearly a hundred whips—all mounted and wearing uniforms. One day, a serf-boy, a little boy of eight, threw a stone in play and hurt the paw of the General's favourite hound. "Why is my favourite dog lame?" He was told that the boy had thrown a stone at it and hurt its paw. "Oh, so it's you, is it?" said the General, looking him up and down. "Take him!" They took him. They took him away from his mother, and he spent the night in the lock-up. Early next morning the General, in full dress, went out hunting. He mounted his horse, surrounded by his hangers-on, his whips, and his huntsmen, all mounted. His house-serfs were all mustered to teach them a lesson, and in front of them all stood the child's mother. The boy was brought out of the lock-up. It was a bleak, cold, misty autumn day, a perfect day for hunting. The General ordered the boy to be undressed. The little boy was stripped naked. He shivered, panic-stricken and not daring to utter a sound. "Make him run!" ordered the General. "Run, run!" the whips shouted at him. The boy ran. "Sick him!" bawled the General, and set the whole pack of borzoi hounds on him. They hunted the child down before the eyes of his mother, and the hounds tore him to pieces! I believe the General was afterwards deprived of the right to administer his estates. Well, what was one to do with him? Shoot him? Shoot him for the satisfaction of our moral feelings? Tell me, Alyosha!'

'Shoot him!' Alyosha said softly, raising his eyes to his brother with a pale, twisted sort of smile.

'Bravo!' yelled Ivan with something like rapture. 'If you say so, then—you're a fine hermit! So that's the sort of little demon dwelling in your heart, Alyosha Karamazov!'

'What I said was absurd, but—'

'Yes, but—that's the trouble, isn't it?' cried Ivan. 'Let me tell you, novice, that absurdities are only too necessary on earth. The world is founded on absurdities and perhaps without them nothing would come to pass in it. We know a thing or two!'

'What do you know?'

'I understand nothing,' Ivan went on as though in delirium, 'and I don't want to understand anything now. I want to stick to facts. I made up my mind long ago not to understand. For if I should want to understand something, I'd instantly alter the facts and I've made up my mind to stick to the facts. . . .'

'Why are you putting me to the test?' exclaimed Alyosha, heart-brokenly. 'Will you tell me at last?'

'Of course I will tell you. That's what I was leading up to. You're dear to me. I don't want to let you go and I won't give you up to your Zossima.'

Ivan was silent for a minute and his face suddenly became very sad.

'Listen to me: I took only children to make my case clearer. I don't say anything about the other human tears with which the earth is saturated from its crust to its centre—I have narrowed my subject on purpose. I am a bug and I acknowledge in all humility that I can't understand why everything has been arranged as it is. I suppose men themselves are to blame: they were given paradise, they wanted freedom and they stole the fire from heaven, knowing perfectly well that they would become unhappy, so why should we pity them? Oh, all that my pitiful earthly Euclidean mind can grasp is that suffering exists, that no one is to blame, that effect follows cause, simply and directly, that everything flows and finds its level—but then this is only Euclidean nonsense. I know that and I refuse to live by it! What do I care that no one is to blame, that effect follows cause simply and directly and that I know it—I must have retribution or I shall destroy myself. And retribution not somewhere in the infinity of space and time, but here on earth, and so that I could see it myself. I was a believer, and I want to see for myself. And if I'm dead by that time, let them resurrect me, for if it all happens without me, it will be too unfair. Surely the reason for my suffering was not that I as well as my evil deeds and sufferings may serve as manure for some future harmony for someone else. I want to see with my own eyes the lion lie down with the lamb and the murdered man rise up and embrace his murderer. I want to be there when everyone suddenly finds out what it has all been for. All religions on earth are based on this desire, and I am a believer. But then there are the children, and what am I to do with them? That is the question I cannot answer. I repeat for the hundredth time—there are lots of questions, but I've only taken the children, for in their case it is clear beyond the shadow of a doubt what I have to say. Listen: if all have to suffer so as to buy eternal harmony by their suffering, what have the children to do with it—tell me, please? It is entirely incomprehensible why they, too, should have to suffer and why they should have to buy harmony by their sufferings. Why should they, too, be used as dung for someone's future harmony? I understand solidarity in sin among men, I understand solidarity in retribution, too, but, surely, there can be no solidarity in sin with children, and if it is really true that they share their fathers' responsibility for all their fathers' crimes, then that truth is not, of course, of this world and it's incomprehensible to me. Some humorous fellow may say that it makes no difference since a child is bound to grow up and sin, but, then, he didn't grow up: he was torn to pieces by dogs at the age of eight. Oh, Alyosha, I'm not blaspheming! I understand, of course, what a cataclysm of the universe it will be

when everything in heaven and on earth blends in one hymn of praise and everything that lives and has lived cries aloud: "Thou art just, O Lord, for thy ways are revealed!" Then, indeed, the mother will embrace the torturer who had her child torn to pieces by his dogs, and all three will cry aloud: "Thou art just, O Lord!", and then, of course, the crown of knowledge will have been attained and everything will be explained. But there's the rub: for it is that I cannot accept. And while I'm on earth, I hasten to take my own measures. For, you see, Alyosha, it may really happen that if I live to that moment, or rise again to see it, I shall perhaps myself cry aloud with the rest, as I look at the mother embracing her child's torturer: "Thou art just, O Lord!" But I do not want to cry aloud then. While there's still time, I make haste to arm myself against it, and that is why I renounce higher harmony altogether. It is not worth one little tear of that tortured little girl who beat herself on the breast and prayed to her "dear, kind Lord" in the stinking privy with her unexpiated tears! It is not worth it, because her tears remained unexpiated. They must be expiated, for otherwise there can be no harmony. But how, how are you to expiate them? Is it possible? Not, surely, by their being avenged? But what do I want them avenged for? What do I want a hell for torturers for? What good can hell do if they have already been tortured to death? And what sort of harmony is it, if there is a hell? I want to forgive. I want to embrace? I don't want any more suffering. And if the sufferings of children go to make up the sum of sufferings which is necessary for the purchase of truth, then I say beforehand that the entire truth is not worth such a price. And, finally, I do not want a mother to embrace the torturer who had her child torn to pieces by his dogs! She has no right to forgive him! If she likes, she can forgive him for herself, she can forgive the torturer for the immeasurable suffering he has inflicted upon her as a mother; but she has no right to forgive him for the sufferings of her tortured child. She has no right to forgive the torturer for that, even if her child were to forgive him! And if that is so, if they have no right to forgive him, what becomes of the harmony? Is there in the whole world a being who could or would have the right to forgive? I don't want harmony. I don't want it, out of the love I bear to mankind. I want to remain with my suffering unavenged. I'd rather remain with my suffering unavenged and my indignation unappeased, *even if I were wrong*. Besides, too high a price has been placed on harmony. We cannot afford to pay so much for admission. And therefore I hasten to return my ticket of admission. And indeed, if I am an honest man, I'm bound to hand it back as soon as possible. This I am doing. It is not God that I do not accept, Alyosha. I merely most respectfully return him the ticket.'

'This is rebellion,' Alyosha said softly, dropping his eyes.

'Rebellion? I'm sorry to hear you say that,' Ivan said with feeling. 'One can't go on living in a state of rebellion, and I want to live. Tell me frankly, I appeal to you—answer me: imagine that it is you yourself who are erecting the edifice of human destiny with the aim of making men happy in the end, of giving them peace and contentment at last, but that to do that it is absolutely necessary, and indeed quite inevitable, to torture to death only one tiny creature, the little girl who beat her breast with her little fist, and to found the edifice on her unavenged tears—would you consent to be the architect on those conditions? Tell me and do not lie!'

'No, I wouldn't,' Alyosha said softly.

Book Ten: The Boys

I

Kolya Krasotkin

Early november. there had been eleven degrees of frost in our town and the ground was crusted with ice. A little dry snow had fallen on the frozen ground during the night, and a 'dry, sharp' wind was lifting and blowing it along the dreary streets of our little town and especially along the market square. It was a dull morning, but the snow had ceased. Not far from the square, close to Plotnikov's shop, there stood a small house, very clean inside and out, belonging to the widow of the civil servant Krasotkin. The provincial secretary Krasotkin himself had been dead a long time, almost fourteen years, but his widow, a rather comely lady in her early thirties, was living 'on her capital' in her clean little house. She led a quiet and exemplary life and she was of an affectionate but rather gay disposition. She was about eighteen when her husband died, having lived with him for only a year and borne him one son. Since then, from the day of his death, she had devoted herself entirely to the upbringing of her darling boy Kolya, and though she had loved him dearly during those fourteen years, she had, of course, far more trouble than joy from him, trembling and dying with fear almost every day, afraid that he might fall ill, catch cold, be naughty, climb on a chair and fall off, and so on. When Kolya began going to school and then to our grammar school, the mother began studying all the subjects with him, in order to help him do his homework, began making the acquaintance of his teachers and their wives, was nice to Kolya's schoolmates and made up to them so that they shouldn't touch Kolya, or make fun of him or beat him. She went so far that the boys really began making fun of him on her account and began teasing him with being 'a mother's darling'. But the boy knew how to stand up for himself. He was a brave little boy, 'terribly strong', as was rumoured and soon confirmed in his class; he was nimble, stubborn, daring, and resourceful. He was good at his lessons, and it was even said that he could beat his teacher, Dardanelov, at arithmetic and world history. But though the boy looked down upon everyone, his nose in the air, he was a good comrade and was not really conceited. He accepted the respect of his schoolmates as his due, but behaved in a friendly way to them. Above all, he knew where to stop, he could restrain himself when necessary and never overstepped a certain inviolate and sacred line beyond which every offence becomes a riot, a rebellion, and a breach of the law, and cannot be tolerated. And yet he certainly never missed a chance of playing some mischievous prank at any favourable opportunity like the wildest street urchin, and not so much to do something he shouldn't as to excel himself in doing something strange and wonderful, something 'extra-special', to dazzle, to show off. Above all, he was very vain. He knew how to make even his mother submit to

him and he treated her almost despotically. She submitted to him, oh, she had submitted to him long ago, and the one thought she could not bear was that her boy did not 'love her enough'. It always seemed to her that Kolya was 'unfeeling' to her and there were times when, weeping hysterically, she began reproaching him with his coldness. The boy did not like it, and the more heartfelt effusions she demanded from him, the more unyielding he deliberately became. But all this was not so much deliberate as involuntary—such was his character. His mother was wrong: he loved her very much, he merely disliked her 'sloppy sentimentality', as he put it in his schoolboy language. There was a bookcase left in the house after his father's death, which contained a few books; Kolya was fond of reading and he had read several of them by himself. It did not worry his mother, though she could not help wondering sometimes why, instead of running out to play, her boy spent hours by the bookcase poring over some book. In that way Kolya read some things which he should not have been given to read at his age. However, more recently the boy, though he took care not to overstep a certain limit in his pranks, began to do things which frightened his mother in good earnest; it is true they were not immoral, but certainly wild and reckless. It just happened that summer, in July, during the school holidays, that the mother and son went to another district, about forty-five miles away, to spend a week with a distant relative whose husband was an official at the railway station (the same station, the nearest one to our town, from which a month later Ivan Karamazov left for Moscow). There Kolya began by a thorough examination of the railway, making a study of the rules and regulations, in the hope of impressing his schoolmates with his newly acquired knowledge on his return. But there happened to be other boys there at the time with whom he made friends. Some of them lived at the station and others in the neighbourhood—boys between twelve and fifteen, altogether about six or seven of them, two of whom happened to be from our town. The boys played games together, and on the fourth or fifth day of Kolya's visit they made a quite absurd bet of two roubles: Kolya, who was almost the youngest among them and therefore rather looked down upon by the others, out of vanity and inexcusable recklessness, volunteered to lie down between the rails when the eleven o'clock train was due to arrive at the station and lie without moving while the train passed over him at full speed. It is true, they made a preliminary investigation which showed that it was indeed possible to lie flat between the rails in a way that the train would go over without touching, but all the same it would take some courage to lie there! Kolya insisted stoutly that he would. The other boys at first laughed at him, called him a little liar and boaster, but made him even more determined to carry on with his bet. What incensed him most was the way the fifteen-year-old boys turned up their noses at him and at first even treated him as 'a little boy' and refused to play with him, which he felt to be a quite intolerable insult. And so it was decided that they should go in the evening to a spot about half a mile from the station, so that the train might have time to gather full speed after leaving the station. The boys assembled. It was a moonless night, not just dark but almost pitch-black. At the fixed time Kolya lay down between the rails. The other five, who had accepted his bet, waited in the bushes below the embankment with sinking hearts and, finally, overcome with fear and remorse. At last there came in the distance the rumble of the train leaving the station. Two red lights gleamed out of the darkness and they could hear the roar of the approaching monster. 'Run, run away from the rails!' the terror-stricken boys shouted to Kolya from the bushes, but it was too late: the train rolled over him and thundered past. The boys rushed up to Kolya: he lay motionless. They began pulling at him and tried to lift him up. Kolya suddenly got up and went down the embankment in silence. He then declared that he had lain there as though unconscious on purpose so as to frighten them, but the fact was that he really had lost consciousness, as he confessed long after to his mother. Thus it was that his reputation as 'a desperate character' stuck to him forever. He returned home to the station white as a sheet. Next day he had a slight attack of a nervous fever, but he was in high spirits, happy, and pleased with himself. The incident became known, though not immediately, but after their return to our town; it became known throughout the school and reached the ears of the authorities. But his fond mother at once went to beseech the school authorities on her boy's behalf and succeeded in persuading Dardanelov, one of the most respected and influential masters, to take his part and intercede for him, and the affair was hushed up. Dardanelov, a middle-aged bachelor, had been passionately in love with Mrs Krasotkin for many years, and about a year before, faint with fear and the delicacy of his sentiments, very respectfully ventured to offer his hand; but she refused him point-blank, considering that her consent would have been a betrayal of her boy, though from certain mysterious signs Dardanelov might perhaps have had some right to entertain the hope that he was not entirely objectionable to the charming but a little too virtuous and fond young widow. Kolya's mad prank seemed to have broken the ice, and as a reward for his intercession

Dardanelov had been given a hint that there might still be some hope for him; the hint was rather vague, but for Dardanelov, who was a paragon of purity and delicacy, that was for the time being sufficient to make him perfectly happy. He was fond of Kolya, though he would have considered it humiliating to curry favour with him. He therefore treated him sternly and exactingly in class. But Kolya kept him at a respectful distance himself, he did his lessons well, was second in his class, treated Dardanelov coldly, and the whole class firmly believed that Kolya was so good at world history that he could easily 'beat' Dardanelov himself. And, indeed, when Kolya one day asked Dardanelov who had founded Troy, the master replied in general terms about the movements and migrations of different peoples, the remoteness of the times, the legendary stories, but the question who had founded Troy, that is, what persons, he could not answer, and for some reason even found the question to be idle and of no importance. But the boys remained convinced that Dardanelov did not know who had founded Troy. Kolya had read about the founders of Troy in Smaragdov, whose history was among the books in his father's bookcase. In the end everyone, even the boys, became interested in the question who it was that had founded Troy, but Kolya would not tell his secret and his reputation for learning remained unshaken.

After the incident on the railway a certain change took place in Kolya's relations with his mother. When Mrs Krasotkin learnt of her son's exploit she nearly went out of her mind with horror. She had such terrible attacks of hysterics, lasting with intervals for several days, that Kolya, frightened in good earnest, gave her his solemn promise that he would never engage in such pranks again. He swore on his knees before the icon

and by the memory of his father, at the demand of Mrs Krasotkin herself, and, overcome by his 'feelings', the 'manly' Kolya himself burst into tears like a six-year-old boy, and mother and son spent the whole of that day throwing themselves into each other's arms and sobbing their hearts out. Next morning Kolya woke up as 'unfeeling' as ever, but he became more silent, more modest, more sedate, and more thoughtful. It is true that a month later he got himself into trouble again and his name even reached the ears of our Justice of the Peace, but it was quite another kind of trouble, foolish and ridiculous, and it would seem that he was not responsible for it, but only got mixed up in it. But of that later. His mother continued to be worried and to tremble for him, and the more troubled she became, the more did Dardanelov's hopes increase. It must be noted that Kolya understood and was aware of Dardanelov's hopes, and, quite naturally, despised him greatly for his 'feelings'. Before, he had even been indelicate enough to reveal his contempt to his mother, hinting vaguely that he understood very well what Dardanelov was up to. But after the incident on the railway he changed his behaviour in this respect, too: he did not permit himself any more hints, even of the vaguest kind, and began speaking more respectfully of Dardanelov in the presence of his mother, which the sensitive Mrs Krasotkin at once appreciated with infinite gratitude in her heart; but at the slightest and quite inadvertent mention of Dardanelov by some visitor in Kolya's presence she would blush like a rose with shame. At such moments Kolya either stared, frowning, out of the window, or became absorbed in looking for holes in his boots, or began shouting fiercely for Perezvon, the rather big, shaggy, and mangy dog which he had acquired somewhere a month before, brought home and kept for some reason secretly indoors, not showing it to any of his friends. He bullied him terribly, teaching him all sorts of tricks, and reduced him to such a state that he howled whenever he was away at school and squealed with delight when he came home, rushed about like mad, begged, lay down on the ground and pretended to be dead, and so on, in fact, showed all the tricks he had been taught, no longer at a word of command but solely from the ardour of his rapturous feelings and his grateful heart.

Incidentally, I forgot to mention that Kolya Krasotkin was the boy whom Ilyusha, the son of the retired captain Snegiryov, already known to the reader, had stabbed with a penknife, in defending his father, whom the schoolboys had taunted with the name of 'bast-sponge'.

* * * * * * * * * * * * * * * * * * *

6

Precocious Development

'What do you think the doctor will say to him?' Kolya asked rapidly.

'What a disgusting face, though, don't you agree? I can't bear medicine!'

'Ilyusha's going to die,' Alyosha replied sadly. 'It seems to me beyond doubt.'

'The frauds! Medicine's a fraud. I'm glad, though, to have met you, Karamazov. I've wanted to meet you for a long time. I'm only sorry we had to meet in such sad circumstances.'

Kolya would have very much liked to say something warmer and more effusive, but something about Alyosha seemed to stop him. Alyosha noticed it, smiled, and pressed his hand.

'I've long learned to respect you as a rare person,' Kolya murmured again, hesitantly and confusedly. 'I've heard you are a mystic and that you've been in a monastery. I know you are a mystic but—that hasn't put me off. Contact with reality will cure you. It's always like that with natures like yours.'

'What do you call a mystic? What will it cure me of?' Alyosha asked, looking a little surprised.

'Well—God and the rest of it.'

'Why, don't you believe in God?'

'On the contrary, I've nothing against God. Of course, God is only a hypothesis but—I admit that he is necessary for—for order—for world order and so on, and that if there were no God he'd have to be invented,' Kolya added, beginning to blush.

He suddenly fancied that Alyosha might think that he wished to show off his knowledge and let him see that he was 'grown up'. 'And I don't want to show off my knowledge to him at all!' Kolya thought indignantly. And he suddenly felt very annoyed.

'I must confess I hate entering into all these discussions,' he blurted out. 'One can love humanity without believing in God—don't you think so? Voltaire did not believe in God but he loved mankind, didn't he?' ('Again! Again!' he thought to himself.)

'Voltaire believed in God, but not, I suppose, very much, and I can't help thinking that he didn't love mankind very much, either,' Alyosha said, quietly, res-trainedly and quite naturally, as though talking to someone of his own age, or, indeed, to someone much older than himself.

Kolya was at once struck by Alyosha's apparent diffidence about Voltaire's views and by the fact that he seemed to be leaving the question for him, little Kolya, to settle.

'Have you read Voltaire?' asked Alyosha, in conclusion.

'Well, not really.... I've read *Candide*, though, in a Russian translation, in an old, bad translation, a ridiculous translation.' ('Again! Again!')

'And did you understand it?'

'Oh yes, everything—that is ... why do you suppose I shouldn't understand it? There are, of course, lots of obscenities in it. I'm, of course, quite capable of understanding that it is a philosophical novel, and written to propagate an idea,' Kolya had got thoroughly muddled by now. 'I'm a socialist, Karamazov, I'm an incorrigible socialist,' he broke off suddenly for no obvious reason.

'A socialist?' Alyosha laughed. 'But when have you had time to become one? You're only thirteen, aren't you?'

Kolya winced.

'First of all, I'm not thirteen, but fourteen, I shall be fourteen in a fortnight,' he declared, flushing. 'And, secondly, I completely fail to understand what my age has got to do with it? What matters are my convictions and not how old I am. Don't you agree?'

'When you're older, you'll understand how important age is for a man's convictions. It also seemed to me that you were not expressing your own ideas,' Alyosha replied quietly and modestly, but Kolya interrupted him hotly.

'Why, you want obedience and mysticism. You must admit that Christianity, for instance, has been useful only to the rich and powerful to keep the lower classes in slavery. Isn't that so?'

'Oh, I know where you read that,' exclaimed Alyosha. 'And I'm sure someone must have told you that!'

'Good Lord, why must I have read it? And no one told me anything. I can think for myself. And, if you like, I'm not against Christ. He was a very humane person, and if he were alive today, he would most certainly have joined the revolutionaries and would, perhaps, play a conspicuous part. I'm quite sure of that.'

'Good heavens, where did you get all that from? What fool have you had to do with?'

'You can't hide the truth, you know. It's true that I often talk to Mr Rakitin in connection with a certain affair, but, I'm told, old Belinsky used to say that too.'

'Belinsky? I don't remember. He hasn't written that anywhere.'

'If he didn't write it, I'm told he said it. I heard it from a—however, it doesn't matter.'

'And have you read Belinsky?'

'Well, you see, as a matter of fact, I haven't read him at all, but I did read the passage about Tatyana—why she didn't go off with Onegin.'

'Didn't go off with Onegin? Why, do you already understand—such things?'

'Good Lord, you must take me for that little boy Smurov,' Kolya grinned, irritably. 'Still, you mustn't think I'm such a terrible revolutionary. I often disagree with Mr Rakitin. If I mentioned Tatyana, it was not because I'm in favour of the emancipation of women. I'm of the opinion that a woman is a subordinate creature and must obey. *Les femmes tricottent*, as Napoleon said,' Kolya grinned for some reason, 'and in that at least I fully share the opinion of that pseudo-great man. I furthermore believe, for instance, that to run away to America from your own country is mean, and even worse than mean—stupid. Why go to America when we can do a great deal of good for humanity in our country, too? Especially now. A whole mass of fruitful activity. That's what I replied.'

'Who did you reply to? What do you mean? Has anyone already asked you to go to America?'

'I admit, they've tried to persuade me, but I refused. That's, of course, between you and me, Karamazov. Don't say a word to anyone about it, do you hear? I'm telling this to you alone. I certainly do not intend to fall into the clutches of the Secret Police and take lessons at the Chain Bridge.'

You will ever remember,
The house at the Chain Bridge.

'Remember? Excellent! What are you laughing at? You don't think I've been telling you lies?' ('And what if he finds out that there's only one copy of *The Bell* in father's bookcase and that I haven't read anything more of it?' Kolya thought with a shudder.)

'Good heavens, no! I'm not laughing and I don't think you've been telling me lies. That's the trouble, you see, that I don't think so, because all of it is, alas, only too true! But tell me, have you read Pushkin, I mean, *Onegin*? You spoke of Tatyana just now. . . .'

'No, I haven't read it yet, but I want to read it. I have no prejudices, Karamazov. I want to hear both sides. Why did you ask?'

'Oh, I just wondered.'

'Tell me, Karamazov, do you despise me very much?' Kolya asked abruptly, drawing himself up to his full height before Alyosha, as though taking up a position to meet any attack. 'Do me a favour, tell me frankly.'

'Despise you?' said Alyosha, looking at him with surprise. 'Why should I? I'm only sorry that a charming nature such as yours should have been perverted by all this crude nonsense before you've begun to live.'

'Don't worry about my nature,' Kolya interrupted not without self-satisfaction,

'but it's quite true that I'm very sensitive. Stupidly sensitive. Crudely sensitive. You smiled just now and I imagined that you. . .'

'Oh, I smiled at something quite different. You see what I smiled at was this: I recently read the opinion of a German who had lived in Russia about our schoolboys today. "Show a Russian schoolboy," he writes, "a map of the stars, of which he had no idea before, and he'll return it to you corrected next day." No knowledge and utter self-conceit—that's what the German meant to say about the Russian schoolboy.'

'Oh, but that's perfectly true!' Kolya suddenly burst out laughing. '*Verissimo!* Exactly so! Bravo, German! But the damned foreigner failed to notice the good side, eh? What do you think? Self-conceit—I admit. That's a sign of youth, that will be corrected, if it has to be corrected, but, on the other hand, there's also an independent spirit almost from early childhood, and boldness of thought and convictions, and not their spirit of cringing servility before authority. . . . But, all the same, the German put it well! Bravo, German! Though Germans ought to be strangled for all that. They may be good at science, but they ought to be strangled. . . .'

'But why on earth strangle them?' smiled Alyosha.

'Oh well, I've been talking nonsense. Sorry, I agree. I'm a perfect child sometimes, and when something pleases me I can't control myself and talk a lot of nonsense. Look here, we're talking about all sorts of silly things here, while that doctor has been a very long time there. However, he may be examining Mrs Snegiryov and that poor cripple Nina. You know, I liked that Nina. She whispered to me suddenly as I walked past her: "Why didn't you come before?" And in such a reproachful voice! I think she's awfully good and so pathetic.'

'Yes, yes! When you come again, you'll realize what a nice girl she is. It'll do you a lot of good to know such people, for it will teach you to value many things you can find out from knowing them,' Alyosha observed heatedly. 'That more than anything will make you a different person.'

'Oh, I'm so sorry and I curse myself for not having come earlier!' cried Kolya, with bitter feeling.

'Yes, it's a great pity. You saw for yourself how glad the poor child was to see you! He was so upset because you did not come!'

'Don't tell me! You make me feel awful. Still, it serves me right: I didn't come, out of vanity, out of egoistical vanity and a beastly desire to lord it over people, which I can never get rid of, though I've been doing my best all my life to be different. I can see now that I've been a cad in lots of ways, Karamazov!'

'No, you've a charming nature, though it's been perverted, and I quite understand why You've had such an influence on this generous and morbidly sensitive boy!' Alyosha retorted warmly.

'And you say that to me!' cried Kolya, 'and, you know, I have thought several times—I've thought it just now—that you despise me! If only you knew how highly I think of your opinion!'

'But are you really so sensitive? At your age! You know, that was exactly my impression when I watched you telling your story in there. I couldn't help thinking that you must be very sensitive.'

'Did you? You see what an eye You've got! I bet it was when I was telling about the goose. It was just then that I fancied that you must despise me greatly for being in such a hurry to show what a fine fellow I was, and I even hated you for it and talked a lot of rot. Then I fancied (it was just now, here) that when I said that if there were no God he had to be invented, that I was too much in a hurry to show

how well educated I was, particularly as I had got that phrase out of a book. But I swear I was in such a hurry to show off not out of vanity but—well, I really don't know why. . . . Out of joy, perhaps. Yes, I do believe it was out of joy, though I admit it's a highly disgraceful thing for a man to hurl himself at the heads of people out of joy. I know that. But I'm quite convinced now that you don't despise me and that I'm imagining it all. Oh, Karamazov, I'm terribly unhappy. I sometimes imagine goodness knows what, that everyone is laughing at me, the whole world, and then—then I'm simply ready to destroy the whole order of things.'

'And you are horrid to everyone,' Alyosha smiled.

'And I'm horrid to everyone, to Mother especially. Tell me, Karamazov, am I making myself very ridiculous now?'

'Don't think about it, don't think about it at all!' cried Alyosha. 'And what does ridiculous mean? Does it matter how many times a man is or seems to be ridiculous? Besides, today almost all people of ability are terribly afraid of making themselves ridiculous and that makes them unhappy. The only thing that surprises me is that you should be feeling this so early, though I've noticed it for some time now and not only in you. Today even those who are little more than children have begun to suffer from it. It's almost a kind of insanity. It's the devil who has taken the form of this vanity and entered into the whole generation—yes, the devil,' added Alyosha, without smiling, as Kolya, who was staring at him, thought he would. 'You're just like everyone clsc,' Alyosha concluded, 'that is, like many others. Except that one ought not to be like everyone else. That's the important thing.'

'Even if everyone's like that?'

'Yes, even if everyone's like that. You ought to be the only one who isn't like that. And as a matter of fact you are not like everyone else: you weren't ashamed to confess a moment ago to something bad and even ridiculous. And who confesses to that nowadays? No one. People do not any longer even feel the need of admitting that they're wrong. So don't be like everyone else, even if you are the only one who is not.'

'Excellent! I was not mistaken in you. You have the gift of comforting people. Oh, I was so anxious to know you! I have wished to meet you for such a long time! Have you really thought about me too? You did say just now that you had thought about me, too, didn't you?'

'Yes, I've heard about you and thought about you and—and if it's to a certain extent vanity that makes you ask, it doesn't matter.'

'You know, Karamazov, our talk has been like a declaration of love,' said Kolya in a sort of nervous and bashful voice. 'This isn't ridiculous, is it?'

'Of course not, and even if it were, it wouldn't matter a bit, because it's so splendid,' Alyosha smiled brightly.

'But, you know, Karamazov, you must admit that you feel a little ashamed yourself now. I can see it from your eyes,' Kolya smiled slyly, but also with undisguised happiness.

'What is there to be ashamed of?'

'Well, why are you blushing?'

'Why, it's you who made me blush!' laughed Alyosha and, indeed, he blushed all over. 'Well, yes, I am a little ashamed. Goodness knows why. I'm sure I don't,' he muttered, almost embarrassed.

'Oh, I love and admire you at this moment just because for some reason you feel ashamed. Because you're just like me!' Kolya exclaimed with genuine delight. His cheeks were burning, his eyes sparkled.

'Listen, Kolya, I can't help feeling that you'll be very unhappy in life,' said Alyosha suddenly without really knowing what made him say that.

'I know, I know. How you do know it all beforehand!' Kolya at once agreed.

'But on the whole you will bless life all the same.'

'Yes, indeed. Hurrah! You're a prophet. Oh, we shall be good friends, Karamazov. You know, what I like so much about you is that you treat me just as if I were your equal. And we are not equals, are we? No, we're not. You're higher than I. But we shall be friends. You know, during the past month I've been saying to myself: "We shall either be friends at once and for ever or we shall part enemies to the grave after our first meeting"!'

'And, of course, saying that, you loved me already!' Alyosha laughed gaily.

'Yes, I did. I loved you terribly. I've been loving you and dreaming about you! And how do you know everything beforehand? Ah, here's the doctor. Good Lord, what will he say, I wonder. Look at him!'

* * * * * * * * * * * * * * * *

Epilogue

Meanwhile they were all walking slowly along the path, and suddenly Smurov exclaimed:

'Here's the stone under which he wanted to bury Ilyusha!'

They all stopped in silence at the big stone. Alyosha looked at it and the picture suddenly came back to him of what Snegiryov had told him the other day of how Ilyusha, crying and embracing his father, exclaimed, 'Daddy, Daddy, how he has humiliated you!' Something seemed to give way in his soul. He looked round with a serious and grave expression at the sweet bright faces of the schoolboys, Ilyusha's friends, and suddenly said to them:

'Boys, I should like to say something to you here, at this place.'

The boys crowded round him and at once bent their eager, expectant glances upon him.

'Boys, we shall soon part. I'm staying here at present with my two brothers, one of whom is going to Siberia and the other is dangerously ill. But soon I shall leave this town, perhaps for a long time. So we may not see each other again. Let us, therefore, agree here, at Ilyusha's stone, never to forget, first, Ilyusha, and, secondly, one another. And whatever may befall us in life afterwards, even if we do not meet again for twenty years, we shall always remember how we buried the poor boy at whom we threw stones before at that little bridge—remember?— and how we all loved him so much afterwards. He was a nice boy, a good and brave boy. He was deeply conscious of his father's honour and the cruel insult to him, against which he had fought so stoutly. So, first of all, boys, let us remember him all our life. And though we may be occupied with most important things, win honours or fall upon evil days, yet let us never forget how happy we were here, when we were all of us together, united by such a good and kind feeling, which made us, too, while we loved the poor boy, better men, perhaps, than we are. My little doves—let me call you my little doves, for you are very like them, very like those pretty, bluish-grey birds, now, at this moment as I look at your kind, dear faces. My dear children, perhaps you will not understand what I'm going to say to you now, for I often speak very incomprehensibly, but, I'm sure, you will remember that there's nothing higher, stronger, more wholesome and more useful in life than some good memory, especially when it goes back to the days of your childhood, to the days of your life at home. You are told a lot about your education, but some beautiful, sacred memory, preserved since childhood, is perhaps the best education of all. If a man carries many such memories into life with him, he is saved for the rest of his days. And even if only one good memory is left in our hearts, it may also be the instrument of our salvation one day. Perhaps we may become wicked afterwards and be unable to resist a bad action, may laugh at men's tears and at those who say, as Kolya has just said: "I want to suffer for all mankind"—we may even jeer spitefully at such people. And yet, however wicked we may become, which God forbid, when we remember how we buried Ilyusha, how we loved him during these last days, and how we have been talking like friends together just now at this stone, the most cruel and the most cynical of us—if we do become so—will not dare to laugh inwardly at having been so good and kind at this moment! What's more, perhaps this memory alone will keep him from great evil, and he will change his mind and say, "Yes, I was good and brave and honest then." Let him laugh at himself—never mind, a man often laughs at what is good and kind; that is only from thoughtlessness; but I assure you that as soon as he laughs, he will at once say in his heart: "No, I did wrong to laugh, for one should not laugh at such a thing!"'

'It will certainly be so, Karamazov!' Kolya exclaimed with flashing eyes. 'I understand you, Karamazov!'

The boys were excited and also wanted to say something, but they restrained themselves and looked intently and with emotion at the speaker.

'I am referring to our fear of becoming bad,' Alyosha went on, 'but why should we become bad—isn't that so, boys? Let us be, first and above all, kind, then honest, and then—don't let us ever forget each other. I say that again. I give you my word, boys, that I will never forget any one of you. I shall remember every face that is looking at me now, even after thirty years. Kolya said to Kartashov a moment ago that we did not care whether he existed or not. But how can I forget that Kartashov exists and that he doesn't blush now as when he discovered Troy, but is looking at me with his dear, kind, happy little eyes? Boys, my dear boys, let us all be generous and brave like Ilyusha, intelligent, brave, and generous like Kolya, who, I'm sure, will be much cleverer when he grows up, and let us be modest but also clever and kind like Kartashov. But why am I talking only about the two of them? You're all dear to me from now on, boys. I will find a place for you all in my heart and I beg you to find a place for me in your hearts also! Well, and who has united us in this good and kind feeling which we shall remember and intend to remember all our lives? Who did it, if not Ilyusha, the good boy, the dear boy, dear to us for ever and ever! Don't let us, then, ever forget him, may his memory live in our hearts for ever and ever!'

'Yes, yes, for ever and ever!' all the boys cried in their ringing voices, looking deeply moved.

'Let us remember his face and his clothes and his poor little boots, and his coffin, and his unhappy and sinful father, and how bravely he stood up for him alone against his whole class!'

'We will, we will remember!' the boys cried again. 'He was brave, he was kind!'

'Oh, how I loved him!' exclaimed Kolya.

'Oh, my dear children, my dear friends, do not be afraid of life! How good life is when you do something that is good and just!'

'Yes, yes,' the boys repeated enthusiastically.

'Karamazov, we love you!' a voice, probably Kartashov's, cried impulsively.

'We love you, we love you,' the other boys echoed.

There were tears in the eyes of many of them.

'Hurrah for Karamazov!' Kolya shouted enthusiastically.

'And may the dead boy's memory live for ever!' Alyosha added again with feeling.

'May it live for ever!' the boys echoed again.

'Karamazov,' cried Kolya, 'is it really true that, as our religion tells us, we shall all rise from the dead and come to life and see one another again, all, and Ilyusha?'

'Certainly we shall rise again, certainly we shall see one another, and shall tell one another gladly and joyfully all that has been,' Alyosha replied, half laughing, half rapturously.

'Oh, how wonderful it will be!' Kolya cried.

'Well, now let us make an end of talking and go to his wake. Don't let it worry you that we shall be eating pancakes. It is a very old custom and there's something nice about that,' Alyosha laughed. 'Well, come along! And now we do go hand in hand.'

'And always so, all our life hand in hand! Hurrah for Karamazov!' Kolya cried again with enthusiasm, and once more all the boys cheered.

DAVID HUME

from Dialogues Concerning Natural Religion

This selection consists of Parts X and XI of Hume's *Dialogues Concerning Natural Religion*. In Part X Philo, speaking for Hume, argues that the existence of evil, or pain and misery, is *incompatible* with the existence of a God who has infinite power and goodness, which means that *if* there is pain and misery in the world (as we have to say there is), *then* God cannot exist. At the end of Part X Philo "retire[s]" from this position, and in Part XI he argues that even if it is allowed that evil and God's existence are compatible, we should conclude from the preponderance of evil in the world, evil that an all-powerful God could have eliminated, that goodness in any human understanding of that term cannot apply to God.*

PART X

It is my opinion, I own, replied *Demea*, that each man feels, in a manner, the truth of religion within his own breast; and from a consciousness of his imbecility and misery, rather than from any reasoning, is led to seek protection from that being, on whom he and all nature is dependent. So anxious or so tedious are even the best scenes of life, that futurity is still the object of all our hopes and fears. We incessantly look forward, and endeavour, by prayers, adoration, and sacrifice, to appease those unknown powers, whom we find, by experience, so able to afflict and oppress us. Wretched creatures that we are! What resource for us amidst the innumerable ills of life, did not religion suggest some methods of atonement, and appease those terrors, with which we are incessantly agitated and tormented?

I am indeed persuaded, said *Philo*, that the best and indeed the only method of bringing everyone to a due sense of religion is by just representations of the misery and wickedness of men. And for that purpose a talent of eloquence and strong imagery is more requisite than that of reasoning and argument. For is it necessary to prove, what everyone feels within himself? It is only necessary to make us feel it, if possible, more intimately and sensibly.

The people, indeed, replied *Demea*, are sufficiently convinced of this great and melancholy truth. The miseries of life, the unhappiness of man, the general corruptions of our nature, the unsatisfactory enjoyment of pleasures, riches, honours; these phrases have become almost proverbial in all languages. And who can doubt of what all men declare from their own immediate feeling and experience?

In this point, said *Philo*, the learned are perfectly agreed with the vulgar; and in all letters, *sacred* and *profane*, the topic of human misery has been insisted on with the most pathetic eloquence, that sorrow and melancholy could inspire. The poets, who speak from sentiment, without a system, and whose testimony has therefore the more authority, abound in images of

---

* From David Hume, *Dialogues Concerning Natural Religion*, 1779.

this nature. From *Homer* down to *Dr Young*, the whole inspired tribe have ever been sensible, that no other representation of things would suit the feeling and observation of each individual.

As to authorities, replied *Demea*, you need not seek them. Look round this library of *Cleanthes*. I shall venture to affirm, that, except authors of particular sciences, such as chemistry or botany, who have no occasion to treat of human life, there scarce is one of those innumerable writers, from whom the sense of human misery has not, in some passages or other, extorted a complaint and confession of it. At least, the chance is entirely on that side; and no one author has ever, so far as I can recollect, been so extravagant as to deny it.

There you must excuse me, said *Philo: Leibniz* has denied it; and is perhaps the first,* who ventured upon so bold and paradoxical an opinion; at least, the first, who made it essential to his philosophical system.

And by being the first, replied *Demea*, might he not have been sensible of his error? For is this a subject, in which philosophers can propose to make discoveries, especially in so late an age? And can any man hope by a simple denial (for the subject scarcely admits of reasoning) to bear down the united testimony of mankind, founded on sense and consciousness?

And why should man, added he, pretend to an exemption from the lot of all other animals? The whole earth, believe me, *Philo*, is cursed and polluted. A perpetual war is kindled amongst all living creatures. Necessity, hunger, want stimulate the strong and courageous: fear, anxiety, terror agitate the weak and infirm. The first entrance into life gives anguish to the new-born infant and to its wretched parent: Weakness, impotence, distress attend each stage of that life: And it is at last finished in agony and horror.

Observe, too, says *Philo*, the curious artifices of nature, in order to embitter the life of every living being. The stronger prey upon the weaker, and keep them in perpetual terror and anxiety. The weaker too, in their turn, often prey upon the stronger, and vex and molest them without relaxation. Consider that innumerable race of insects, which either are bred on the body of each animal, or flying about infix their stings in him. These insects have others still less than themselves, which torment them. And thus on each hand, before and behind, above and below, every animal is surrounded with enemies, which incessantly seek his misery and destruction.

Man alone, said *Demea*, seems to be, in part, an exception to this rule. For by combination in society, he can easily master lions, tigers, and bears, whose greater strength and agility naturally enable them to prey upon him.

On the contrary, it is here chiefly, cried *Philo*, that the uniform and equal maxims of nature are most apparent. Man, it is true, can, by combination, surmount all his *real* enemies, and become master of the whole animal creation: But does he not immediately raise up to himself *imaginary* enemies, the demons of his fancy, who haunt him with superstitious terrors and blast every enjoyment of life? His pleasure, as he imagines, becomes, in their eyes, a crime: His food and repose give them umbrage and offence: His very sleep and dreams furnish new materials to anxious fear: And even death, his refuge from every other ill, presents only

---

* That sentiment had been maintained by Dr King and some few others before *Leibniz*; though by none of so great a fame as that German philosopher.

the dread of endless and innumerable woes. Nor does the wolf molest more the timid flock, than superstition does the anxious breast of wretched mortals.

Besides, consider, *Demea*: this very society, by which we surmount those wild beasts, our natural enemies; what new enemies does it not raise to us? What woe and misery does it not occasion? Man is the greatest enemy of man. Oppression, injustice, contempt, contumely, violence, sedition, war, calumny, treachery, fraud; by these they mutually torment each other: And they would soon dissolve that society which they had formed, were it not for the dread of still greater ills, which must attend their separation.

But though these external insults, said *Demea*, from animals, from men, from all the elements which assault us, form a frightful catalogue of woes, they are nothing in comparison of those, which arise within ourselves, from the distempered condition of our mind and body. How many lie under the lingering torment of diseases. Hear the pathetic enumeration of the great poet.

Intestine stone and ulcer, colic pangs,
Daemoniac frenzy, moping melancholy,
And moon-struck madness, pining atrophy,
Marasmus and wide wasting pestilence.
Dire was the tossing, deep the groans:
   DESPAIR
Tended the sick, busiest from couch to
   couch.
And over them triumphant DEATH his dart
Shook, but delayed to strike, though oft
   invoked
With vows, as their chief good and final
   hope.

The disorders of the mind, continued *Demea*, though more secret, are not perhaps less dismal and vexatious. Remorse, shame, anguish, rage, disappointment, anxiety, fear, dejection, despair: who has ever passed through life without cruel inroads from these tormentors? How many have scarcely ever felt any better sensations? Labour and poverty, so abhorred by everyone, are the certain lot of the far greater number: And those few privileged persons, who enjoy ease and opulence, never reach contentment or true felicity. All the goods of life united would not make a very happy man: But all the ills united would make a wretch indeed; and any one of them almost (and who can be free from every one) nay often the absence of one good (and who can possess all) is sufficient to render life ineligible.

Were a stranger to drop, on a sudden, into this world, I would show him, as a specimen of its ills, a hospital full of diseases, a prison crowded with malefactors and debtors, a field of battle strewed with carcasses, a fleet foundering in the ocean, a nation languishing under tyranny, famine, or pestilence. To turn the gay side of life to him, and give him a notion of its pleasures; whither should I conduct him? to a ball, to an opera, to court? He might justly think, that I was only showing him a diversity of distress and sorrow.

There is no evading such striking instances, said *Philo*, but by apologies, which still farther aggravate the charge. Why have all men, I ask, in all ages, complained incessantly of the miseries of life?—They have no just reason, says one: These complaints proceed only from their discontented, repining, anxious disposition—And can there possibly, I reply, be a more certain foundation of misery, than such a wretched temper?

But if they were really as unhappy as they pretend, says my antagonist, why do they remain in life?—

Not satisfied with life, afraid of death.

This is the secret chain, say I, that holds us. We are terrified, not bribed to the continuance of our existence.

It is only a false delicacy, he may insist, which a few refined spirits indulge, and which has spread these complaints among the whole race of mankind—And what is this delicacy, I ask, which you blame? Is it anything but a greater sensibility to all the pleasures and pains of life? And if the man of a delicate, refined temper, by being so much more alive than the rest of the world, is only so much more unhappy; what judgement must we form in general of human life?

Let men remain at rest, says our adversary; and they will be easy. They are willing artificers of their own misery—No! reply I: An anxious languor follows their repose: Disappointment, vexation, trouble, their activity and ambition.

I can observe something like what you mention in some others, replied *Cleanthes*: But I confess, I feel little or nothing of it in myself; and hope that it is not so common as you represent it.

If you feel not human misery yourself, cried *Demea*, I congratulate you on so happy a singularity. Others, seemingly the most prosperous, have not been ashamed to vent their complaints in the most melancholy strains. Let us attend to the great, the fortunate emperor, *Charles* the fifth, when, tired with human grandeur, he resigned all his extensive dominions into the hands of his son. In the last harangue, which he made on that memorable occasion, he publicly avowed, *that the greatest prosperities which he had ever enjoyed, had been mixed with so many adversities, that he might truly say he had never enjoyed any satisfaction or contentment.* But did the retired life, in which he sought for shelter, afford him any greater happiness? If we may credit his son's account, his repentance commenced the very day of his resignation.

Cicero's fortune, from small beginnings, rose to the greatest lustre and renown; yet what pathetic complaints of the ills of life do his familiar letters, as well as his philosophical discourses, contain? And suitably to his own experience, he introduces *Cato*, the great, the fortunate *Cato*, protesting in his old age, that, had he a new life in his offer, he would reject the present.

Ask yourself, ask any of your acquaintance, whether they would live over again the last ten or twenty years of their life. No! But the next twenty, they say, will be better.

And from the dregs of life, hope to receive
What the first sprightly running could
    not give.

Thus at last they find (such is the greatness of human misery; it reconciles even contradictions) that they complain, at once, of the shortness of life, and of its vanity and sorrow.

And is it possible, *Cleanthes*, said *Philo*, that after all these reflections, and infinitely more, which might be suggested, you can still persevere in your anthropomorphism, and assert the moral attributes of the deity, his justice, benevolence, mercy, and rectitude, to be of the same nature with these virtues in human creatures? His power we allow is infinite: Whatever he wills is executed: But neither man nor any other animal is happy: Therefore he does not will their happiness. His wisdom is infinite: He is never mistaken in choosing the means to any end: But the course of nature tends not to human or animal felicity: Therefore it is not established for that purpose. Through the whole compass of human knowledge, there are no inferences more certain and infallible than these. In what respect, then, do his benevolence and mercy resemble the benevolence and mercy of men?

Epicurus's old questions are yet unanswered. Is he willing to prevent evil, but not able? then is he impotent. Is he able, but not willing? then is he malevolent. Is he both able and willing? whence then is evil?

You ascribe *Cleanthes*, (and I believe justly), a purpose and intention to nature. But what, I beseech you, is the object of that curious artifice and machinery, which she has displayed in all animals? The preservation alone of individuals and propagation of the species. It seems enough for her purpose, if such a rank be barely upheld in the universe, without any care or concern for the happiness of the members that compose it. No resource for this purpose: No machinery, in order merely to give pleasure or ease: No fund of pure joy and contentment: No indulgence without some want or necessity, accompanying it. At least, the few phenomena of this nature are overbalanced by opposite phenomena of still greater importance.

Our sense of music, harmony, and indeed beauty of all kinds gives satisfaction, without being absolutely necessary to the preservation and propagation of the species. But what racking pains, on the other hand, arise from gouts, gravels, megrims, toothaches, rheumatisms, where the injury to the animal-machinery is either small or incurable? Mirth, laughter, play, frolic seem gratuitous satisfactions, which have no further tendency: Spleen, melancholy, discontent, superstition are pains of the same nature. How then does the divine benevolence display itself, in the sense of you anthropomorphites? None but we mystics, as you were pleased to call us, can account for this strange mixture of phenomena, by deriving it from attributes, infinitely perfect, but incomprehensible.

And have you, at last, said *Cleanthes* smiling, betrayed your intentions, *Philo*? Your long agreement with *Demea* did indeed a little surprise me; but I find you were all the while erecting a concealed battery against me. And I must confess, that you have now fallen upon a subject, worthy of your noble spirit of opposition and controversy. If you can make out the present point, and prove mankind to be unhappy or corrupted, there is an end at once of all religion. For to what purpose establish the natural attributes of the deity, while the moral are still doubtful and uncertain?

You take umbrage very easily, replied *Demea*, at opinions the most innocent, and the most generally received even amongst the religious and devout themselves: And nothing can be more surprising than to find a topic like this, concerning the wickedness and misery of man, charged with no less than atheism and profaneness. Have not all pious divines and preachers, who have indulged their rhetoric on so fertile a subject; have they not easily, I say, given a solution of any difficulties, which may attend it? This world is but a point in comparison of the universe: This life but a moment in comparison of eternity. The present evil phenomena, therefore, are rectified in other regions, and in some future period of existence. And the eyes of men, being then opened to larger views of things, see the whole connection of general laws, and trace, with adoration, the benevolence and rectitude of the deity, through all the mazes and intricacies of his providence.

No! replied *Cleanthes*, No! These arbitrary suppositions can never be admitted contrary to matter of fact, visible and uncontroverted. Whence can any cause be known but from its known effects? Whence can any hypothesis be proved but from the apparent phenomena? To establish one hypothesis upon another is building entirely in the air; and the utmost we ever attain, by these conjectures and fictions, is to ascertain the bare possibility of our opinion; but never can we, upon such terms, establish its reality.

The only method of supporting divine benevolence (and it is what I willingly embrace) is to deny absolutely the misery and wickedness of man. Your representations are exaggerated: Your melancholy views mostly fictitious: Your inferences contrary to fact and experience. Health is more common than sickness: Pleasure than pain: Happiness than misery. And for one vexation which we meet with, we attain, upon computation, a hundred enjoyments.

Admitting your position, replied *Philo*, which yet is extremely doubtful; you must, at the same time, allow, that, if pain be less frequent than pleasure, it is infinitely more violent and durable. One hour of it is often able to outweigh a day, a week, a month of our common insipid enjoyments: And how many days, weeks, and months are passed by several in the most acute torments? Pleasure, scarcely in one instance, is ever able to reach ecstasy and rapture: And in no one instance can it continue for any time at its highest pitch and altitude. The spirits evaporate; the nerves relax; the fabric is disordered; and the enjoyment quickly degenerates into fatigue and uneasiness. But pain often, good God, how often! rises to torture and agony; and the longer it continues, it becomes still more genuine agony and torture. Patience is exhausted; courage languishes; melancholy seizes us; and nothing terminates our misery but the removal of its cause, or another event, which is the sole cure of all evil, but which, from our natural folly, we regard with still greater horror and consternation.

But not to insist upon these topics, continued *Philo*, though most obvious, certain, and important; I must use the freedom to admonish you, *Cleanthes*, that you have put this controversy upon a most dangerous issue, and are unawares introducing a total scepticism into the most essential articles of natural and revealed theology. What! no method of fixing a just foundation for religion, unless we allow the happiness of human life, and maintain a continued existence even in this world, with all our present pains, infirmities, vexations, and follies, to be eligible and desirable! But this is contrary to every one's feeling and experience: It is contrary to an authority so established as nothing can subvert: No decisive proofs can ever be produced against this authority; nor is it possible for you to compute, estimate, and compare all the pains and all the pleasures in the lives of all men and of all animals: And thus by your resting the whole system of religion on a point, which, from its very nature, must forever be uncertain, you tacitly confess, that that system is equally uncertain.

But allowing you, what never will be believed; at least, what you never possibly can prove, that animal, or at least, human happiness in this life exceeds its misery; you have yet done nothing: For this is not, by any means, what we expect from infinite power, infinite wisdom, and infinite goodness. Why is there any misery at all in the world? Not by chance, surely. From some cause then. Is it from the intention of the deity? But he is perfectly benevolent. Is it contrary to his intention? But he is almighty. Nothing can shake the solidity of this reasoning, so short, so clear, so decisive; except we assert, that these subjects exceed all human capacity, and that our common measures of truth and falsehood are not applicable to them; a topic, which I have all along insisted on, but which you have, from the beginning, rejected with scorn and indignation.

But I will be contented to retire still from this retrenchment: For I deny that you can ever force me in it: I will allow, that pain or misery in man is *compatible* with infinite power and goodness in the deity, even in your sense of these attributes: What are you advanced by all these concessions? A mere possible compatibility is not sufficient. You must *prove* these pure, unmixed, and uncontrollable attributes from the present mixed and confused phenomena, and from these alone. A hopeful undertaking! Were the phenomena ever so pure and unmixed, yet, being finite, they would be insufficient for that purpose. How much more, where they are also so jarring and discordant? Here, *Cleanthes*, I find myself at ease in my argument. Here I triumph. Formerly, when we argued concerning the natural attributes of intelligence and design, I needed all my sceptical and metaphysical subtlety to elude your grasp. In many views of the universe, and of its parts, particularly the latter, the beauty and fitness of final causes strike us with such irresistible force that all objections appear (what I believe they really are) mere cavils and sophisms; nor can we then imagine how it was ever possible for us to repose any weight on them. But there is no view of human life or of the condition of mankind, from which, without the greatest violence, we can infer the moral attributes, or learn that infinite benevolence, conjoined with infinite power and infinite wisdom, which we must discover by the eyes of faith alone. It is your turn now to tug the labouring oar, and to support your philosophical subtleties against the dictates of plain reason and experience.

PART XI

I SCRUPLE not to allow, said *Cleanthes*, that I have been apt to suspect the frequent repetition of the word, infinite, which we meet with in all theological writers, to savour more of panegyric than of philosophy, and that any purposes of reasoning, and even of religion, would be better served, were we to rest contented with more accurate and more moderate expressions. The terms, *admirable, excellent, superlatively great, wise*, and *holy*; these sufficiently fill the imaginations of men; and anything beyond, besides that it leads into absurdities, has no influence on the affections or sentiments. Thus, in the present subject, if we abandon all human analogy, as seems your intention, *Demea*, I am afraid we abandon all religion and retain no conception of the great object of our adoration. If we preserve human analogy, we must for ever find it impossible to reconcile any mixture of evil in the universe with infinite attributes; much less, can we ever prove the latter from the former. But supposing the author of nature to be finitely perfect, though far exceeding mankind; a satisfactory account may then be given of natural and moral evil, and every untoward phenomenon be explained and adjusted. A less evil may then be chosen, in order to avoid a greater: Inconveniences be submitted to, in order to reach a desirable end: And in a word, benevolence, regulated by wisdom, and limited by necessity, may produce just such a world as the present. You, *Philo*, who are so prompt at starring views, and reflections, and analogies; I would gladly hear, at length, without interruption, your opinion of this new theory; and if it deserves our attention, we may afterwards, at more leisure, reduce it into form.

My sentiments, replied *Philo*, are not worth being made a mystery of; and therefore, without any ceremony, I shall deliver what occurs to me, with regard to the present subject. It must, I think, be allowed, that, if a very limited intelligence, whom we shall suppose utterly unacquainted with the universe, were assured, that it were the production of a very good, wise, and powerful being, however finite, he would, from his conjectures, form *beforehand* a different notion of it from what we find it to be by experience; nor would he ever imagine, merely from these attributes of the cause of which he is informed, that the effect could be so full of vice and misery and disorder, as it appears in this life. Supposing now, that this person were brought into the world, still assured, that it was the workmanship of such a sublime and benevolent being; he might, perhaps, be surprised at the disappointment; but would never retract his former belief, if founded on any very solid argument; since such a limited intelligence must be sensible of his own blindness and ignorance, and must allow that there may be many solutions of these phenomena, which will for ever escape his comprehension. But supposing, which is the real case with regard to man, that this creature is not antecedently convinced of a supreme intelligence, benevolent, and powerful, but is left to gather such a belief from the appearances of things; this entirely alters the case, nor will he ever find any reason for such a conclusion. He may be fully convinced of the narrow limits of his understanding, but this will not help him in forming an inference concerning the goodness of superior powers, since he must form that inference from what he knows, not from what he is ignorant of. The more you exaggerate his weakness and ignorance; the more diffident you render him, and give him the greater suspicion, that such subjects are beyond the reach of his faculties. You are obliged, therefore, to reason with him merely from the known phenomena, and to drop every arbitrary supposition or conjecture.

Did I show you a house or palace, where there was not one apartment convenient or agreeable; where the windows, doors, fires, passages, stairs, and the whole economy of the building were the source of noise, confusion, fatigue, darkness, and the extremes of heat and cold; you would certainly blame the contrivance, without any farther examination. The architect would in vain display his subtlety, and prove to you, that if this door or that window were altered, greater ills would ensue. What he says, may be strictly true: The alteration of one particular, while the other parts of the building remain, may only augment the inconveniences. But still you would assert in general, that, if the architect had had skill and good intentions, he might have formed such a plan of the whole, and might have adjusted the parts in such a manner, as would have remedied all or most of these inconveniences. His ignorance or even your own ignorance of such a plan, will never convince you of the impossibility of it. If you find many inconveniences and deformities in the building, you will always, without entering into any detail, condemn the architect.

In short, I repeat the question: Is the world, considered in general, and as it appears to us in this life, different from what a man or such a limited being would, *beforehand*, expect from a very powerful, wise, and benevolent deity? It must be strange prejudice to assert the contrary. And from thence I conclude, that, however consistent the world may be, allowing certain suppositions and conjectures, with the idea of such a deity, it can never afford us an inference concerning his existence. The consistency is not absolutely denied, only the inference. Conjectures, especially where infinity is excluded from the divine attributes, may, perhaps, be sufficient to prove a consistency; but can never be foundations for any inference.

There seem to be *four* circumstances, on which depend all, or the greatest part of the ills, that molest sensible creatures; and it is not impossible but all these circumstances may be necessary and unavoidable. We know so little beyond common life, or even of common life, that, with regard to the economy of a universe, there is no conjecture, however wild, which may not be just; nor any one, however plausible, which may not be erroneous. All that belongs to human understanding, in this deep ignorance and obscurity, is to be sceptical, or at least cautious; and not to admit of any hypothesis, whatever; much less, of any which is supported by no appearance of probability. Now this I assert to be the case with regard to all the causes of evil, and the circumstances, on which it depends. None of them appear to human reason, in the least degree, necessary or unavoidable; nor can we suppose them such, without the utmost license of imagination.

The *first* circumstance, which introduces evil, is that contrivance or economy of the animal creation, by which pains, as well as pleasures, are employed to excite all creatures to action, and make them vigilant in the great work of self-preservation. Now pleasure alone, in its various degrees, seems to human understanding sufficient for this purpose. All animals might be constantly in a state of enjoyment; but when urged by any of the necessities of nature, such as thirst, hunger, weariness; instead of pain, they might feel a diminution of pleasure, by which they might be prompted to seek that object, which is necessary to their subsistence. Men pursue pleasure as eagerly as they avoid pain; at least, might have been so constituted. It seems, therefore, plainly possible to carry on the business of life without any pain. Why then is any animal ever rendered susceptible of such a sensation? If animals can be free from it an hour, they might enjoy a perpetual exemption from it; and it required as particular a contrivance of their organs to produce that feeling, as to endow them with sight, hearing, or any of the senses. Shall we conjecture, that such a contrivance was necessary, without any appearance of reason? And shall we build on that conjecture as on the most certain truth?

But a capacity of pain would not alone produce pain, were it not for the *second* circumstance, viz., the conducting of the world by general laws; and this seems no wise necessary to a very perfect being. It is true; if everything were conducted by particular volitions, the course of nature would be perpetually broken, and no man could employ his reason in the conduct of life. But might not other particular volitions remedy this inconvenience? In short, might not the deity exterminate all ill, wherever it were to be found; and produce all good, without any preparation or long progress of causes and effects?

Besides, we must consider, that, according to the present economy of the world, the course of nature, though supposed exactly regular, yet to us appears not so, and many events are uncertain, and many disappoint our expectations. Health and sickness, calm and tempest, with an infinite number of other accidents, whose causes are unknown and variable, have a great influence both on the fortunes of particular persons and on the prosperity of public societies: And indeed all human life, in a manner, depends on such accidents. A being, therefore, who knows the secret springs of the universe, might easily, by particular volitions, turn all these accidents to the good of mankind, and render the whole world happy, without discovering himself in any operation. A fleet, whose purposes were salutary to society, might always meet with a fair wind: Good princes enjoy sound health and long life: Persons, born to power and authority, be framed with good tempers and virtuous dispositions. A few such events as these, regularly and wisely conducted, would change the face of the world; and yet would no more seem to disturb the course of nature or confound human conduct, than the present economy of things, where the causes are secret, and variable, and compounded. Some small touches, given to *Caligula's* brain in his infancy, might have converted him into a *Trajan*: One wave, a little higher than the rest, by burying *Caesar* and his fortune in the bottom of the ocean, might have restored liberty to a considerable part of mankind. There may, for aught we know, be good reasons, why Providence interposes not in this manner; but they are unknown to us: And though the mere supposition, that such reasons exist, may be sufficient to *save* the conclusion concerning the divine attributes, yet surely it can never be sufficient to *establish* that conclusion.

If everything in the universe be conducted by general laws, and if animals be rendered susceptible of pain, it scarcely seems possible but some ill must arise in the various shocks of matter, and the various concurrence and opposition of general laws: But this ill would be very rare, were it not for the *third* circumstance which I proposed to mention, *viz.*, the great frugality, with which all powers and faculties are distributed to every particular being. So well adjusted are the organs and capacities of all animals, and so well fitted to their preservation, that, as far as history or tradition reaches, there appears not to be any single species, which has yet been extinguished in the universe. Every animal has the requisite endowments; but these endowments are bestowed with so scrupulous an economy, that any considerable diminution must entirely destroy the creature. Wherever one power is increased, there is a proportional abatement in the others. Animals, which excel in swiftness are commonly defective in force. Those, which possess both, are either imperfect in some of their senses, or are oppressed with the most craving

wants. The human species, whose chief excellence is reason and sagacity, is of all others the most necessitous, and the most deficient in bodily advantages; without clothes, without arms, without food, without lodging, without any convenience of life, except what they owe to their own skill and industry. In short, nature seems to have formed an exact calculation of the necessities of her creatures; and like a *rigid master*, has afforded them little more powers and endowments, than what are strictly sufficient to supply those necessities. An *indulgent parent* would have bestowed a large stock, in order to guard against accidents, and secure the happiness and welfare of the creature, in the most unfortunate concurrence of circumstances. Every course of life would not have been so surrounded with precipices, that the least departure from the true path, by mistake or necessity, must involve us in misery and ruin. Some reserve, some fund would have been provided to ensure happiness; nor would the powers and the necessities have been adjusted with so rigid an economy. The author of nature is inconceivably powerful: His force is supposed great, if not altogether inexhaustible; Nor is there any reason, as far as we can judge, to make him observe this strict frugality in his dealings with his creatures. It would have been better, were his power extremely limited, to have created fewer animals, and to have endowed these with more faculties for their happiness and preservation. A builder is never esteemed prudent, who undertakes a plan, beyond what his stock will enable him to finish.

In order to cure most of the ills of human life, I require not that man should have the wings of the eagle, the swiftness of the stag, the force of the ox, the arms of the lion, the scales of the crocodile or rhinoceros; much less do I demand the sagacity of an angel or cherubim. I am contented to take an increase in one single power or faculty of his soul. Let him be endowed with a greater propensity to industry and labour; a more vigorous spring and activity of mind; a more constant bent to business and application. Let the whole species possess naturally an equal diligence with that which many individuals are able to attain by habit and reflection; and the most beneficial consequences, without any allay of ill, is the immediate and necessary result of this endowment. Almost all the moral, as well as natural evils of human life arise from idleness; and were our species, by the original constitution of their frame, exempt from this vice or infirmity, the perfect cultivation of land, the improvement of arts and manufactures, the exact execution of every office and duty, immediately follow; and men at once may fully reach that state of society which is so imperfectly attained by the best regulated government. But as industry is a power, and the most valuable of any, nature seems determined, suitably to her usual maxims, to bestow it on men with a very sparing hand; and rather to punish him severely for his deficiency in it, than to reward him for his attainments. She has so contrived his frame, that nothing but the most violent necessity can oblige him to labour, and she employs all his other wants to overcome, at least in part, the want of diligence, and to endow him with some share of a faculty, of which she has thought fit naturally to bereave him. Here our demands may be allowed very humble, and therefore the more reasonable. If we required the endowments of superior penetration and judgement, of a more delicate taste of beauty, of a nicer sensibility to benevolence and friendship; we might be told, that we impiously pretend to break the order of nature, that we want to exalt ourselves into a higher rank of being, that the presents which we require, not being suitable to our state and condition, would only be pernicious to us. But it is hard; I dare to repeat it, it is hard, that being placed in a world so full of wants and necessities; where almost every being and element is either our foe or refuses us their assistance; we should also have our own temper to struggle with, and should be deprived of that faculty, which can alone fence against these multiplied evils.

The *fourth* circumstance, whence arises the misery and ill of the universe, is the inaccurate workmanship of all the springs and principles of the great machine of nature. It must be acknowledged, that there are few parts of the universe, which seem not to serve some purpose, and whose removal would not produce a visible defect and disorder in the whole. The parts hang all together; nor can one be touched without affecting the rest, in a greater or less degree. But at the same time, it must be observed, that none of these parts or principles, however useful, are so accurately adjusted, as to keep precisely within those bounds, in which their utility consists; but they are, all of them, apt, on every occasion, to run into the one extreme or the other. One would imagine, that this grand production had not received the last hand of the maker; so little finished is every part, and so coarse are the strokes, with which it is executed. Thus, the winds are requisite to convey the vapours along the surface of the globe, and to assist men in navigation: But how oft, rising up to tempests and hurricanes, do they become pernicious? Rains are necessary to nourish all the plants and animals of the earth: But how often are they defective? how often excessive? Heat is requisite to all life and vegetation; but is not always found in the due proportion. On the mixture and secretion of the humours and juices of the body depend the health and prosperity of the animal: But the parts perform not regularly their proper function. What more useful than all the passions of the mind, ambition, vanity, love, anger? But how oft do they break their bounds, and cause the greatest convulsions in society? There is nothing so advantageous in the universe, but what frequently becomes pernicious, by its excess or defect; nor has nature guarded, with the requisite accuracy, against all disorder or confusion. The irregularity is never, perhaps, so great as to destroy any species; but it is often sufficient to involve the individuals in ruin and misery.

On the concurrence, then, of these *four* circumstances does all, or the greatest part of natural evil depend. Were all living creatures incapable of pain, or were the world administered by particular volitions, evil never could have found access into the universe: And were animals endowed with a large stock of powers and faculties, beyond what strict necessity requires; or were the several springs and principles of the universe so accurately framed as to preserve always the just temperament and medium; there must have been very little ill in comparison of what we feel at present. What then shall we pronounce on this occasion? Shall we say, that these circumstances are not necessary, and that they might easily have been altered in the contrivance of the universe? This decision seems too presumptuous for creatures, so blind and ignorant. Let us be more modest in our conclusions. Let us allow, that, if the goodness of the deity (I mean a goodness like the human) could be established on any tolerable reasons *a priori*, these phenomena, however untoward, would not be sufficient to subvert that principle, but might easily, in some unknown manner, be reconcilable to it. But let us still assert, that as this goodness is not antecedently established, but must be inferred from

the phenomena, there can be no grounds for such an inference, while there are so many ills in the universe, and while these ills might so easily have been remedied, as far as human understanding can be allowed to judge on such a subject. I am sceptic enough to allow, that the bad appearances, notwithstanding all my reasonings, may be compatible with such attributes as you suppose: But surely they can never prove these attributes. Such a conclusion cannot result from scepticism; but must arise from the phenomena, and from our confidence in the reasonings, which we deduce from these phenomena.

Look round this universe. What an immense profusion of beings, animated and organized, sensible and active! You admire this prodigious variety and fecundity. But inspect a little more narrowly these living existences, the only beings worth regarding. How hostile and destructive to each other! How insufficient all of them for their own happiness! How contemptible or odious to the spectator! The whole presents nothing but the idea of a blind nature, impregnated by a great vivifying principle, and pouring forth from her lap, without discernment or parental care, her maimed and abortive children!

Here the Manichaean system occurs as a proper hypothesis to solve the difficulty. And no doubt, in some respects, it is very specious, and has more probability than the common hypothesis, by giving a plausible account of the strange mixture of good and ill which appears in this life. But if we consider, on the other hand, the perfect uniformity and agreement of the parts of the universe, we shall not discover in it any marks of the combat of a malevolent with a benevolent being. There is indeed an opposition of pains and pleasures in the feelings of sensible creatures: But are not all the operations of nature carried on by an opposition of principles, of hot and cold, moist and dry, light and heavy? The true conclusion is, that the original source of all things is entirely indifferent to all these principles, and has no more regard to good above ill than to heat above cold, or to drought above moisture, or to light above heavy.

There may *four* hypotheses be framed concerning the first causes of the universe: *that* they are endowed with perfect goodness, *that* they have perfect malice, *that* they are opposite and have both goodness and malice, *that* they have neither goodness nor malice. Mixed phenomena can never prove the two former unmixed principles. And the uniformity and steadiness of general laws seem to oppose the third. The fourth, therefore, seems by far the most probable.

What I have said concerning natural evil will apply to moral, with little or no variation; and we have no more reason to infer, that the rectitude of the supreme being resembles human rectitude than that his benevolence resembles the human. Nay, it will be thought, that we have still greater cause to exclude from him moral sentiments, such as we feel them; since moral evil, in the opinion of many, is much more predominant above moral good than natural evil above natural good.

But even though this should not be allowed, and though the virtue, which is in mankind, should be acknowledged much superior to the vice; yet so long as there is any vice at all in the universe, it will very much puzzle you anthropomorphites, how to account for it. You must assign a cause for it, without having recourse to the first cause. But as every effect must have a cause, and that cause another, you must either carry on the progression *in infinitum*, or rest on that original principle, who is the ultimate cause of all things.

Hold! hold! cried *Demea*: Whither does your imagination hurry you? I joined in alliance with you, in order to prove the incomprehensible nature of the divine being, and refute the principles of *Cleanthes*, who would measure everything by human rule and standard. But I now find you running into all the topics of the greatest libertines and infidels; and betraying that holy cause, which you seemingly espoused. Are you secretly, then, a more dangerous enemy than *Cleanthes* himself?

And are you so late in perceiving it? replied *Cleanthes*. Believe me, *Demea*; your friend, *Philo*, from the beginning, has been amusing himself at both our expense; and it must be confessed, that the injudicious reasoning of our vulgar theology has given him but too just a handle of ridicule. The total infirmity of human reason, the absolute incomprehensibility of the divine nature, the great and universal misery and still greater wickedness of man; these are strange topics surely to be so fondly cherished by orthodox divines and doctors. In ages of stupidity and ignorance, indeed, these principles may safely be espoused; and perhaps, no views of things are more proper to promote superstition, than such as encourage the blind amazement, the diffidence, and melancholy of mankind. But at present—

Blame not so much, interposed *Philo*, the ignorance of these reverend gentlemen. They know how to change their style with the times. Formerly it was a most popular theological topic to maintain, that human life was vanity and misery, and to exaggerate all the ills and pains, which are incident to men. But of late years, divines, we find, begin to retract this position, and maintain, though still with some hesitation, that there are more goods than evils, more pleasures than pains, even in this life. When religion stood entirely upon temper and education, it was thought proper to encourage melancholy; as, indeed, mankind never have recourse to superior powers so readily as in that disposition. But as men have now learned to form principles, and to draw consequences, it is necessary to change the batteries, and to make use of such arguments as will endure, at least, some scrutiny and examination. This variation is the same (and from the same causes) with that which I formerly remarked with regard to scepticism.

Thus *Philo* continued to the last his spirit of opposition, and his censure of established opinions. But I could observe, that *Demea* did not at all relish the latter part of the discourse; and he took the occasion soon after, on some pretence or other, to leave the company.

JOHN HICK
An Irenaean Theodicy

In this reading John Hick develops a theodicy that in seminal form was suggested by Irenaeus in the second century of the Common Era. For this theodicy, human beings are created in a spiritually immature state, though it is possible for them to strive toward moral and spiritual perfection and final fellowship with God. The basic idea of this theodicy is that we human beings live in a "soul-making" world, or as Hick puts it in this article, a "person-making world," in which both moral and natural evils are necessary for the spiritual growth of human beings. In order for human beings to grow spiritually they must have free will, and free will allows the entry of moral evil. Natural evils and their suffering are required as obstacles for human beings to overcome in their moral and spiritual development, so that they may grow toward the final end of spiritual fellowship with God.

In this way the Irenaean theodicy accounts for, or addresses, both moral evil and natural evil. Both are needed for the moral and spiritual development of human beings. If it is asked why God did not create human beings with full moral and spiritual development, ready for fellowship with God, the reply offered by this theodicy is that spiritual perfection requires choices and striving. Logically, it cannot be "built in."*

An Irenaean Theodicy

Can a world in which sadistic cruelty often has its way, in which selfish lovelessness is so rife, in which there are debilitating diseases, crippling accidents, bodily and mental decay, insanity, and all manner of natural disasters be regarded as

* From *Encountering Evil.* © 1981 Stephen T. Davis. Used with permission from Westminster John Knox Press.

the expression of infinite creative goodness? Certainly all this could never by itself lead anyone to believe in the existence of a limitlessly powerful God. And yet even in a world which contains these things innumerable men and women have believed and do believe in the reality of an infinite creative goodness, which they call God. The theodicy project starts at this point, with an already operating belief in God, embodied in human living, and attempts to show that this belief is not rendered irrational by the fact of evil. It attempts to explain how it is that the universe, assumed to be created and ultimately ruled by a limitlessly good and limitlessly powerful Being, is as it is, including all the pain and suffering and all the wickedness and folly that we find around us and within us. The theodicy project is thus an exercise in metaphysical construction, in the sense that it consists in the formation and criticism of large-scale hypotheses concerning the nature and process of the universe.

Since a theodicy both starts from and tests belief in the reality of God, it naturally takes different forms in relation to different concepts of God. In this paper I shall be discussing the project of a specifically Christian theodicy; I shall not be attempting the further and even more difficult work of comparative theodicy, leading in turn to the question of a global theodicy.

The two main demands upon a theodicy-hypothesis are (1) that it be internally coherent, and (2) that it be consistent with the data both of the religious tradition on which it is based, and of the world, in respect both of the latter's general character as revealed by scientific enquiry and of the specific facts of moral and natural evil. These two criteria demand, respectively, possibility and plausibility.

Traditionally, Christian theology has centered upon the concept of God as both limitlessly powerful and limitlessly good and loving; and it is this concept of deity that gives rise to the problem of evil as a threat to theistic faith. The threat was definitively expressed in Stendhal's bombshell, "The only excuse for God is that he does not exist!" The theodicy project is the attempt to offer a different view of the universe which is both possible and plausible and which does not ignite Stendhal's bombshell.

Christian thought has always included a certain range of variety, and in the area of theodicy it offers two broad types of approach. The Augustinian approach, representing until fairly recently the majority report of the Christian mind, hinges upon the idea of the fall, which has in turn brought about the disharmony of nature. This type of theodicy is developed today as "the free will defense." The Irenaean approach, representing in the past a minority report, hinges upon the creation of humankind through the evolutionary process as an immature creature living in a challenging and therefore person-making world. I shall indicate very briefly why I do not find the first type of theodicy satisfactory, and then spend the remainder of this paper in exploring the second type.

In recent years the philosophical discussion of the problem of evil has been dominated by the free-will defense. A major effort has been made by Alvin Plantinga and a number of other Christian philosophers to show that it is logically possible that a limitlessly powerful and limitlessly good God is responsible for the existence of this world. For all evil may ultimately be due to misuses of creaturely freedom. But it may nevertheless be better for God to have created free than unfree beings; and it is logically possible that any and all free beings whom God might create would, as a matter of contingent fact, misuse their freedom by falling into sin.

In that case it would be logically impossible for God to have created a world containing free beings and yet not containing sin and the suffering which sin brings with it. Thus it is logically possible, despite the fact of evil, that the existing universe is the work of a limitlessly good creator.

These writers are in effect arguing that the traditional Augustinian type of theodicy, based upon the fall from grace of free finite creatures—first angels and then human beings—and a consequent going wrong of the physical world, is not logically impossible. I am in fact doubtful whether their argument is sound, and will return to the question later. But even if it should be sound, I suggest that their argument wins only a Pyrrhic victory, since the logical possibility that it would establish is one which, for very many people today, is fatally lacking in plausibility. For most educated inhabitants of the modern world regard the biblical story of Adam and Eve, and their temptation by the devil, as myth rather than as history; and they believe that so far from having been created finitely perfect and then falling, humanity evolved out of lower forms of life, emerging in a morally, spiritually, and culturally primitive state. Further, they reject as incredible the idea that earthquake and flood, disease, decay, and death are consequences either of a human fall, or of a prior fall of angelic beings who are now exerting an evil influence upon the earth. They see all this as part of a prescientific world view, along with the stories of the world having been created in six days and of the sun standing still for twenty-four hours at Joshua's command. One cannot, strictly speaking, disprove any of these ancient biblical myths and sagas, or refute their confident elaboration in the medieval Christian picture of the universe. But those of us for whom the resulting theodicy, even if logically possible, is radically implausible, must look elsewhere for light on the problem of evil.

I believe that we find the light that we need in the main alternative strand of Christian thinking, which goes back to important constructive suggestions by the early Hellenistic Fathers of the Church, particularly St. Irenaeus (A.D. 120–202). Irenaeus himself did not develop a theodicy, but he did—together with other Greek-speaking Christian writers of that period, such as Clement of Alexandria—build a framework of thought within which a theodicy became possible which does not depend upon the idea of the fall, and which is consonant with modern knowledge concerning the origins of the human race. This theodicy cannot, as such, be attributed to Irenaeus. We should rather speak of a type of theodicy, presented in varying ways by different subsequent thinkers (the greatest of whom has been Friedrich Schleiermacher), of which Irenaeus can properly be regarded as the patron saint.

The central theme out of which this Irenaean type of theodicy has arisen is the two-stage conception of the creation of humankind, first in the "image" and then in the "likeness" of God. Re-expressing this in modern terms, the first stage was the gradual production of *homo sapiens*, through the long evolutionary process, as intelligent ethical and religious animals. The human being is an animal, one of the varied forms of earthly life and continuous as such with the whole realm of animal existence. But the human being is uniquely intelligent, having evolved a large and immensely complex brain. Further, the human being is ethical—that is, a gregarious as well as an intelligent animal, able to realize and respond to the complex demands of social life. And the human being is a religious animal, with an innate tendency to experience the world in terms of the presence and activity of supernatural beings and powers. This then is early *homo sapien*, the intelligent social animal capable of awareness of the divine. But early *homo sapien* is not the Adam and Eve of Augustinian theology, living in perfect harmony with self, with nature, and with God. On the contrary, the life of this being must have been a constant struggle against a hostile environment, and capable of savage violence against one's fellow human beings, particularly outside one's own immediate group; and this being's concepts of the divine were primitive and often blood-thirsty. Thus existence "in the image of God" was a potentiality for knowledge of and relationship with one's Maker rather than such knowledge and relationship as a fully realized state. In other words, people were created as spiritually and morally immature creatures, at the beginning of a long process of further growth and development, which constitutes the second stage of God's creative work. In this second stage, of which we are a part, the intelligent, ethical, and religious animal is being brought through one's own free responses into what Irenaeus called the divine "likeness." The human animal is being created into a child of God. Irenaeus' own terminology (*eikon, homoiosis; imago, similitudo*) has no particular merit, based as it is on a misunderstanding of the Hebrew parallelism in Genesis 1:26; but his conception of a two-stage creation of the human, with perfection lying in the future rather than in the past, is of fundamental importance. The notion of the fall was not basic to this picture, although it was to become basic to the great drama of salvation depicted by St. Augustine and accepted within western Christendom, including the churches stemming from the Reformation, until well into the nineteenth century. Irenaeus himself however could not, in the historical knowledge of his time, question the fact of the fall; though he treated it as a relatively minor lapse, a youthful error, rather than as the infinite crime and cosmic disaster which has ruined the whole creation. But today we can acknowledge that there is no evidence at all of a period in the distant past when humankind was in the ideal state of a fully realized "child of God." We can accept that, so far as actual events in time are concerned, there never was a fall from an original righteousness and grace. If we want to continue to use the term fall, because of its hallowed place in the Christian tradition, we must use it to refer to the immense gap between what we actually are and what in the divine intention is eventually to be. But we must not blur our awareness that the ideal state is not something already enjoyed and lost, but is a future and as yet unrealized goal. The reality is not a perfect creation which has gone tragically wrong, but a still continuing creative process whose completion lies in the eschaton.

Let us now try to formulate a contemporary version of the Irenaean type of theodicy, based on this suggestion of the initial creation of humankind, not as a finitely perfect, but as an immature creature at the beginning of a long process of further growth and development. We may begin by asking why one should have been created as an imperfect and developing creature rather than as the perfect being whom God is presumably intending to create? The answer, I think, consists in two considerations which converge in their practical implications, one concerned with the human's relationship to God and the other with the relationship to other human beings. As to the first, we could have the picture of God creating finite beings, whether angels or persons, directly in his own presence, so that in being conscious of that which is other than one's self the creature is automatically conscious of God, the limitless divine reality and power, goodness and love, knowledge and wisdom, towering above one's self. In such a situation the disproportion between Creator and creatures would be so great that the latter would have no freedom in relation to God; they would indeed not exist as independent autonomous persons. For what freedom could finite beings have in an immediate consciousness of the presence of the one who has created them, who knows them through and through, who is limitlessly powerful as well as limitlessly loving and good, and who claims their total obedience? In order to be a person, exercising some measure of genuine freedom, the creature must be brought into existence, not in the immediate divine presence, but at a "distance" from God. This "distance" cannot of course be spatial; for God is omnipresent. It must be an epistemic distance, a distance in the cognitive dimension. And the Irenaean hypothesis is that this "distance" consists, in the case of humans, in their existence within and as part of a world which functions as an autonomous system and from within which God is not overwhelmingly evident. It is a world, in Bonhoeffer's phrase, *etsi deus non daretur*, as if there were no God. Or rather, it is religiously ambiguous, capable both of being seen as a purely natural phenomenon and of being seen as God's creation and experienced as mediating his presence. In such a world one can exist as a person over against the Creator. One has space to exist as a finite being, a space created by the epistemic distance from God and protected by one's basic cognitive freedom, one's freedom to open or close oneself to the dawning awareness of God which is experienced naturally by a religious animal. This Irenaean picture corresponds, I suggest, to our actual human situation. Emerging within the evolutionary process as part of the continuum of animal life, in a universe which functions in accordance

with its own laws and whose workings can be investigated and described without reference to a creator, the human being has a genuine, even awesome, freedom in relation to one's Maker. The human being is free to acknowledge and worship God; and is free—particularly since the emergence of human individuality and the beginnings of critical consciousness during the first millennium BC—to doubt the reality of God.

Within such a situation there is the possibility of the human being coming freely to know and love one's Maker. Indeed, if the end-state which God is seeking to bring about is one in which finite persons have come in their own freedom to know and love him, this requires creating them initially in a state which is not that of their already knowing and loving him. For it is logically impossible to create beings already in a state of having come into that state by their own free choices.

The other consideration, which converges with this in pointing to something like the human situation as we experience it, concerns our human moral nature. We can approach it by asking why humans should not have been created at this epistemic distance from God, and yet at the same time as morally perfect beings? That persons could have been created morally perfect and yet free, so that they would always in fact choose rightly, has been argued by such critics of the free-will defense in theodicy as Antony Flew and J. L. Mackie, and argued against by Alvin Plantinga and other upholders of that form of theodicy. On the specific issue defined in the debate between them, it appears to me that the criticism of the freewill defense stands. It appears to me that a perfectly good being, although formally free to sin, would in fact never do so. If we imagine such a being in a morally frictionless environment, involving no stresses or temptation, then we must assume that one would exemplify the ethical equivalent of Newton's first law of motion, which states that a moving body will continue in uniform motion until interfered with by some outside force. By analogy, a perfectly good being would continue in the same moral course forever, there being nothing in the environment to throw one off it. But even if we suppose the morally perfect being to exist in an imperfect world, in which one is subject to temptations, it still follows that, in virtue of moral perfection, one will always overcome those temptations—as in the case, according to orthodox Christian belief, of Jesus Christ. It is, to be sure, logically possible, as Plantinga and others argue, that a free being, simply as such, may at any time contingently decide to sin. However, a responsible free being does not act randomly, but on the basis of moral nature. And a free being whose nature is wholly and unqualifiedly good will accordingly never in fact sin.

But if God could, without logical contradiction, have created humans as wholly good free beings, why did he not do so? Why was humanity not initially created in possession of all the virtues, instead of having to acquire them through the long hard struggle of life as we know it? The answer, I suggest, appeals to the principle that virtues which have been formed within the agent as a hard won deposit of his own right decisions in situations of challenge and temptation, are intrinsically more valuable than virtues created within him ready made and without any effort on his own part. This principle expresses a basic value-judgment, which cannot be established by argument but which one can only present, in the hope that it will be as morally plausible, and indeed compelling, to others as to oneself. It is, to repeat, the judgement that a moral goodness which exists as the

agent's initial given nature, without ever having been chosen by him in the face of temptations to the contrary, is intrinsically less valuable than a moral goodness which has been built up through the agent's own responsible choices through time in the face of alternative possibilities.

If, then, God's purpose was to create finite persons embodying the most valuable kind of moral goodness, he would have to create them, not as already perfect beings but rather as imperfect creatures who can then attain to the more valuable kind of goodness through their own free choices as in the course of their personal and social history new responses prompt new insights, opening up new moral possibilities, and providing a milieu in which the most valuable kind of moral nature can be developed.

We have thus far, then, the hypothesis that one is created at an epistemic distance from God in order to come freely to know and love the Maker; and that one is at the same time created as a morally immature and imperfect being in order to attain through freedom the most valuable quality of goodness. The end sought, according to this hypothesis, is the full realization of the human potentialities in a unitary spiritual and moral perfection in the divine kingdom. And the question we have to ask is whether humans as we know them, and the world as we know it, are compatible with this hypothesis.

Clearly we cannot expect to be able to deduce our actual world in its concrete character, and our actual human nature as part of it, from the general concept of spiritually and morally immature creatures developing ethically in an appropriate environment. No doubt there is an immense range of possible worlds, any one of which, if actualized, would exemplify this concept. All that we can hope to do is to show that our actual world is one of these. And when we look at our human situation as part of the evolving life of this planet we can, I think, see that it fits this specification. As animal organisms, integral to the whole ecology of life, we are programmed for survival. In pursuit of survival, primitives not only killed other animals for food but fought other human beings when their vital interests conflicted. The life of prehistoric persons must indeed have been a constant struggle to stay alive, prolonging an existence which was, in Hobbes' phrase, "poor, nasty, brutish and short." And in his basic animal self-regardingness humankind was, and is, morally imperfect. In saying this I am assuming that the essence of moral evil is selfishness, the sacrificing of others to one's own interests. It consists, in Kantian terminology, in treating others, not as ends in themselves, but as means to one's own ends. This is what the survival instinct demands. And yet we are also capable of love, of self-giving in a common cause, of a conscience which responds to others in their needs and dangers. And with the development of civilization we see the growth of moral insight, the glimpsing and gradual assimilation of higher ideals, and tension between our animality and our ethical values. But that the human being has a lower as well as a higher nature, that one is an animal as well as a potential child of God, and that one's moral goodness is won from a struggle with one's own innate selfishness, is inevitable given one's continuity with the other forms of animal life. Further, the human animal is not responsible for having come into existence as an animal. The ultimate responsibility for humankind's existence, as a morally imperfect creature, can only rest with the Creator. The human does not, in one's own degree of freedom and responsibility, choose one's origin, but rather one's destiny.

This then, in brief outline, is the answer of the Irenaean type of theodicy to the question of the origin of moral

evil: the general fact of humankind's basic self-regarding animality is an aspect of creation as part of the realm of organic life; and this basic self-regardingness has been expressed over the centuries both in sins of individual selfishness and in the much more massive sins of corporate selfishness, institutionalized in slavery and exploitation and all the many and complex forms of social injustice.

But nevertheless our sinful nature in a sinful world is the matrix within which God is gradually creating children for himself out of human animals. For it is as men and women freely respond to the claim of God upon their lives, transmuting their animality into the structure of divine worship, that the creation of humanity is taking place. And in its concrete character this response consists in every form of moral goodness, from unselfish love in individual personal relationships to the dedicated and selfless striving to end exploitation and to create justice within and between societies.

But one cannot discuss moral evil without at the same time discussing the non-moral evil of pain and suffering. (I propose to mean by "pain" physical pain, including the pains of hunger and thirst; and by "suffering" the mental and emotional pain of loneliness, anxiety, remorse, lack of love, fear, grief, envy, etc.). For what constitutes moral evil as evil is the fact that it causes pain and suffering. It is impossible to conceive of an instance of moral evil, or sin, which is not productive of pain or suffering to anyone at any time. But in addition to moral evil there is another source of pain and suffering in the structure of the physical world, which produces storms, earthquakes, and floods and which afflicts the human body with diseases— cholera, epilepsy, cancer, malaria, arthritis, rickets, meningitis, etc.—as well as with broken bones and other outcomes of physical accident. It is true that a great deal both of pain and of suffering is humanly caused, not only by the inhumanity of man to man but also by the stresses of our individual and corporate life-styles, causing many disorders—not only lung cancer and cirrhosis of the liver but many cases of heart disease, stomach and other ulcers, strokes, etc.—as well as accidents. But there remain nevertheless, in the natural world itself, permanent causes of human pain and suffering. And we have to ask why an unlimitedly good and unlimitedly powerful God should have created so dangerous a world, both as regards its purely natural hazards of earthquake and flood etc., and as regards the liability of the human body to so many ills, both psychosomatic and purely somatic.

The answer offered by the Irenaean type of theodicy follows from and is indeed integrally bound up with its account of the origin of moral evil. We have the hypothesis of humankind being brought into being within the evolutionary process as a spiritually and morally immature creature, and then growing and developing through the exercise of freedom in this religiously ambiguous world. We can now ask what sort of a world would constitute an appropriate environment for this second stage of creation? The development of human personality—moral, spiritual, and intellectual—is a product of challenge and response. It does not occur in a static situation demanding no exertion and no choices. So far as intellectual development is concerned, this is a well-established principle which underlies the whole modern educational process, from pre-school nurseries designed to

provide a rich and stimulating environment, to all forms of higher education designed to challenge the intellect. At a basic level the essential part played in learning by the learner's own active response to environment was strikingly demonstrated by the Held and Heim experiment with kittens.[1] Of two littermate kittens in the same artificial environment one was free to exercise its own freedom and intelligence in exploring the environment, whilst the other was suspended in a kind of "gondola" which moved whenever and wherever the free kitten moved. Thus the second kitten had a similar succession of visual experiences as the first, but did not exert itself or make any choices in obtaining them. And whereas the first kitten learned in the normal way to conduct itself safely within its environment, the second did not. With no interaction with a challenging environment there was no development in its behavioral patterns. And I think we can safely say that the intellectual development of humanity has been due to interaction with an objective environment functioning in accordance with its own laws, an environment which we have had actively to explore and to co-operate with in order to escape its perils and exploit its benefits. In a world devoid both of dangers to be avoided and rewards to be won we may assume that there would have been virtually no development of the human intellect and imagination, and hence of either the sciences or the arts, and hence of human civilization or culture.

The fact of an objective world within which one has to learn to live, on penalty of pain or death, is also basic to the development of one's moral nature. For it

---

[1] R. Held and A. Hein, "Movement-produced stimulation in the development of visually guided behaviour", *Journal of Comparative and Physiological Psychology*, Vol. 56 (1963), pp. 872–876.

is because the world is one in which men and women can suffer harm—by violence, disease, accident, starvation, etc.,—that our actions affecting one another have moral significance. A morally wrong act is, basically, one which harms some part of the human community; whilst a morally right action is, on the contrary, one which prevents or neutralizes harm or which preserves or increases human well being. Now we can imagine a paradise in which no one can ever come to any harm. It could be a world which, instead of having its own fixed structure, would be plastic to human wishes. Or it could be a world with a fixed structure, and hence the possibility of damage and pain, but whose structure is suspended or adjusted by special divine action whenever necessary to avoid human pain. Thus, for example, in such a miraculously pain-free world one who falls accidentally off a high building would presumably float unharmed to the ground; bullets would become insubstantial when fired at a human body; poisons would cease to poison; water to drown, and so on. We can at least begin to imagine such a world. And a good deal of the older discussion of the problem of evil—for example in Part xi of Hume's *Dialogues Concerning Natural Religion*—assumed that it must be the intention of a limitlessly good and powerful Creator to make for human creatures a pain-free environment; so that the very existence of pain is evidence against the existence of God. But such an assumption overlooks the fact that a world in which there can be no pain or suffering would also be one in which there can be no moral choices and hence no possibility of moral growth and development. For in a situation in which no one can ever suffer injury or be liable to pain or suffering there would be no distinction between right and wrong action. No action would be morally

wrong, because no action could have harmful consequences; and likewise no action would be morally right in contrast to wrong. Whatever the values of such a world, it clearly could not serve a purpose of the development of its inhabitants from self-regarding animality to self-giving love.

Thus the hypothesis of a divine purpose in which finite persons are created at an epistemic distance from God, in order that they may gradually become children of God through their own moral and spiritual choices, requires that their environment, instead of being a pain-free and stress-free paradise, be broadly the kind of world of which we find ourselves to be a part. It requires that it be such as to provoke the theological problem of evil. For it requires that it be an environment which offers challenges to be met, problems to be solved, dangers to be faced, and which accordingly involves real possibilities of hardship, disaster, failure, defeat, and misery as well as of delight and happiness, success, triumph and achievement. For it is by grappling with the real problems of a real environment, in which a person is one form of life among many, and which is not designed to minister exclusively to one's well-being, that one can develop in intelligence and in such qualities as courage and determination. And it is in the relationships of human beings with one another, in the context of this struggle to survive and flourish, that they can develop the higher values of mutual love and care, of self-sacrifice for others, and of commitment to a common good.

To summarize thus far:

(1) The divine intention in relation to humankind, according to our hypothesis, is to create perfect finite personal beings in filial relationship with their Maker.

(2) It is logically impossible for humans to be created already in this perfect state,

because in its spiritual aspect it involves coming freely to an uncoerced consciousness of God from a situation of epistemic distance, and in its moral aspect, freely choosing the good in preference to evil.

(3) Accordingly the human being was initially created through the evolutionary process, as a spiritually and morally immature creature, and as part of a world which is both religiously ambiguous and ethically demanding.

(4) Thus that one is morally imperfect (i.e., that there is moral evil), and that the world is a challenging and even dangerous environment (i.e., that there is natural evil), are necessary aspects of the present stage of the process through which God is gradually creating perfected finite persons.

In terms of this hypothesis, as we have developed it thus far, then, both the basic moral evil in the human heart and the natural evils of the world are compatible with the existence of a Creator who is unlimited in both goodness and power. But is the hypothesis plausible as well as possible? The principal threat to its plausibility comes, I think, from the sheer amount and intensity of both moral and natural evil. One can accept the principle that in order to arrive at a freely chosen goodness one must start out in a state of moral immaturity and imperfection. But is it necessary that there should be the depths of demonic malice and cruelty which each generation has experienced, and which we have seen above all in recent history in the Nazi attempt to exterminate the Jewish population of Europe? Can any future fulfillment be worth such horrors? This was Dostoevski's haunting question: "Imagine that you are creating a fabric of human destiny with the object of making men happy in the end, giving them peace and rest at last, but that it was essential and inevitable to torture to death only one tiny creature—that baby beating its breast with its fist, for instance—and to found that edifice on its unavenged tears, would you consent to be the architect on those conditions?"[2] The theistic answer is one which may be true but which takes so large a view that it baffles the imagination. Intellectually one may be able to see, but emotionally one cannot be expected to feel, its truth; and in that sense it cannot satisfy us. For the theistic answer is that if we take with full seriousness the value of human freedom and responsibility, as essential to the eventual creation of perfected children of God, then we cannot consistently want God to revoke that freedom when its wrong exercise becomes intolerable to us. From our vantage point within the historical process we may indeed cry out to God to revoke his gift of freedom, or to overrule it by some secret or open intervention. Such a cry must have come from millions caught in the Jewish Holocaust, or in the yet more recent laying waste of Korea and Vietnam, or from the victims of racism in many parts of the world. And the thought that humankind's moral freedom is indivisible, and can lead eventually to a consummation of limitless value which could never be attained without that freedom, and which is worth any finite suffering in the course of its creation, can be of no comfort to those who are now in the midst of that suffering. But whilst fully acknowledging this, I nevertheless want to insist that this eschatological answer

---

[2] Fyodor Dostoyevsky, *The Brothers Karamazov*, trans. by Constance Garnett (New York: Modern Library, n.d.), Bk. V, chap. 4, p. 254.

may well be true. Expressed in religious language it tells us to trust in God even in the midst of deep suffering, for in the end we shall participate in his glorious kingdom.

Again, we may grant that a world which is to be a person-making environment cannot be a pain-free paradise but must contain challenges and dangers, with real possibilities of many kinds of accident and disaster, and the pain and suffering which they bring. But need it contain the worst forms of disease and catastrophe? And need misfortune fall upon us with such heartbreaking indiscriminateness? Once again there are answers, which may well be true, and yet once again the truth in this area may offer little in the way of pastoral balm. Concerning the intensity of natural evil, the truth is probably that our judgments of intensity are relative. We might identify some form of natural evil as the worst that there is—say the agony that can be caused by death from cancer—and claim that a loving God would not have allowed this to exist. But in a world in which there was no cancer, something else would then rank as the worst form of natural evil. If we then eliminate this, something else; and so on. And the process would continue until the world was free of all natural evil. For whatever form of evil for the time being remained would be intolerable to the inhabitants of that world. But in removing all occasions of pain and suffering, and hence all challenge and all need for mutual care, we should have converted the world from a person-making into a static environment, which could not elicit moral growth. In short, having accepted that a person-making world must have its dangers and therefore also its tragedies, we must accept that whatever form these take will be intolerable to the inhabitants of that world. There could not be a person-making

world devoid of what we call evil; and evils are never tolerable—except for the sake of greater goods which may come out of them.

But accepting that a person-making environment must contain causes of pain and suffering, and that no pain or suffering is going to be acceptable, one of the most daunting and even terrifying features of the world is that calamity strikes indiscriminately. There is no justice in the incidence of disease, accident, disaster and tragedy. The righteous as well as the unrighteous are struck down by illness and afflicted by misfortune. There is no security in goodness, but the good are as likely as the wicked to suffer "the slings and arrows of outrageous fortune." From the time of Job this fact has set a glaring question mark against the goodness of God. But let us suppose that things were otherwise. Let us suppose that misfortune came upon humankind, not haphazardly and therefore unjustly, but justly and therefore not haphazardly. Let us suppose that instead of coming without regard to moral considerations, it was proportioned to desert, so that the sinner was punished and the virtuous rewarded. Would such a dispensation serve a person-making purpose? Surely not. For it would be evident that wrong deeds bring disaster upon the agent whilst good deeds bring health and prosperity; and in such a world truly moral action, action done because it is right, would be impossible. The fact that natural evil is not morally directed, but is a hazard which comes by chance, is thus an intrinsic feature of a person-making world.

In other words, the very mystery of natural evil, the very fact that disasters afflict human beings in contingent, undirected and haphazard ways, is itself a necessary feature of a world that calls forth mutual aid and builds up mutual caring and love. Thus on the one hand it would be completely wrong to say that God sends misfortune upon individuals, so that their death, maiming, starvation or ruin is God's will for them. But on the other hand God has set us in a world containing unpredictable contingencies and dangers, in which unexpected and undeserved calamities may occur to anyone; because only in such a world can mutual caring and love be elicited. As an abstract philosophical hypothesis this may offer little comfort. But translated into religious language it tells us that God's good purpose enfolds the entire process of this world, with all its good and bad contingencies, and that even amidst tragic calamity and suffering we are still within the sphere of his love and are moving towards his kingdom.

But there is one further all-important aspect of the Irenaean type of theodicy, without which all the foregoing would lose its plausibility. This is the eschatological aspect. Our hypothesis depicts persons as still in course of creation towards an end-state of perfected personal community in the divine kingdom. This end-state is conceived of as one in which individual egoity has been transcended in communal unity before God. And in the present phase of that creative process the naturally self-centered human animal has the opportunity freely to respond to God's non-coercive self-disclosures, through the work of prophets and saints, through the resulting religious traditions, and through the individual's religious experience. Such response always has an ethical aspect; for the growing awareness of God is at the same time a growing awareness of the moral claim which God's presence makes upon the way in which we live.

But it is very evident that this person-making process, leading eventually to

perfect human community, is not completed on this earth. It is not completed in the life of the individual—or at best only in the few who have attained to sanctification, or moksha, or nirvana on this earth. Clearly the enormous majority of men and women die without having attained to this. As Eric Fromm has said, "The tragedy in the life of most of us is that we die before we are fully born."[3] And therefore if we are ever to reach the full realization of the potentialities of our human nature, this can only be in a continuation of our lives in another sphere of existence after bodily death. And it is equally evident that the perfect all-embracing human community, in which self-regarding concern has been transcended in mutual love, not only has not been realized in this world, but never can be, since hundreds of generations of human beings have already lived and died and accordingly could not be part of any ideal community established at some future moment of earthly history. Thus if the unity of humankind in God's presence is ever to be realized it will have to be in some sphere of existence other than our earth. In short, the fulfillment of the divine purpose, as it is postulated in the Irenaean type of theodicy, presupposes each person's survival, in some form of bodily death, and further living and growing towards that end-state. Without such an eschatological fulfillment, this theodicy would collapse.

A theodicy which presupposes and requires an eschatology will thereby be rendered implausible in the minds of many today. I nevertheless do not see how any coherent theodicy can avoid dependence upon an eschatology. Indeed I would go further and say that the belief in the reality of a limitlessly loving and

---

[3] Erich Fromm, "Values, Psychology, and Human Existence," in *New Knowledge of Human Values*, ed. A. H. Maslow (New York: Harper, 1959), p. 156.

powerful deity must incorporate some kind of eschatology according to which God holds in being the creatures whom he has made for fellowship with himself, beyond bodily death, and brings them into the eternal fellowship which he has intended for them. I have tried elsewhere to argue that such an eschatology is a necessary corollary of ethical monotheism; to argue for the realistic possibility of an after-life or lives, despite the philosophical and empirical arguments against this; and even to spell out some of the general features which human life after death may possibly have.[4] Since all this is a very large task, which would far exceed the bounds of this paper, I shall not attempt to repeat it here but must refer the reader to my existing discussion of it. It is that extended discussion that constitutes my answer to the question whether an Irenaean theodicy, with its eschatology, may not be as implausible as an Augustinian theodicy, with its human or angelic fall. (If it is, then the latter is doubly implausible; for it also involves an eschatology!)

There is however one particular aspect of eschatology which must receive some treatment here, however brief and inadequate. This is the issue of "universal salvation" versus "heaven and hell" (or perhaps annihilation instead of hell). If the justification of evil within the creative process lies in the limitless and eternal good of the end-state to which it leads, then the completeness of the justification must depend upon the completeness, or universality, of the salvation achieved. Only if it includes the entire human race can it justify the sins and sufferings of the entire human race throughout all history. But, having given human beings cognitive freedom, which in turn makes possible moral freedom, can the Creator bring it about that in the end all his human creatures freely turn to him in love and trust? The issue is a very difficult one; but I believe that it is in fact possible to reconcile a full affirmation of human freedom with a belief in the ultimate universal success of God's creative work. We have to accept that creaturely freedom always occurs within the limits of a basic nature that we did not ourselves choose; for this is entailed by the fact of having been created. If then a real though limited freedom does not preclude our being endowed with a certain nature, it does not preclude our being endowed with a basic Godward bias, so that, quoting from another side of St. Augustine's thought, "our hearts are restless until they find their rest in Thee."[5] If this is so, it can be predicted that sooner or later, in our own time and in our own way, we shall all freely come to God; and universal salvation can be affirmed, not as a logical necessity but as the contingent but predictable outcome of the process of the universe, interpreted theistically. Once again, I have tried to present this argument more fully elsewhere, and to consider various objections to it.[6]

On this view the human, endowed with a real though limited freedom, is basically formed for relationship with God and destined ultimately to find the fulfillment of his or her nature in that relationship. This does not seem to me excessively paradoxical. On the contrary, given the theistic postulate, it seems to

[4] John Hick, *Death and Eternal Life* (New York: Harper & Row, and London: Collins, 1976).
[5] *The Confessions of St. Augustine*, trans. by F. J. Sheed (New York: Sheed and Ward, 1942), Bk. 1, Chap. 1, p. 3.
[6] Hick, *Death and Eternal Life*, chap. 13.

me to offer a very probable account of our human situation. If so, it is a situation in which we can rejoice; for it gives meaning to our temporal existence as the long process through which we are being created, by our own free responses to life's mixture of good and evil, into "children of God" who "inherit eternal life."

H. J. MCCLOSKEY

God and Evil

H. J. McCloskey in "God and Evil" divides the religious problem of evil into two problems: the problem of physical (or natural) evil and the problem of moral evil. He then considers proposed "solutions" to each of these two problems of evil, each solution in effect being a theodicy or partial theodicy. Each proposed solution, he argues, is unsuccessful. McCloskey concludes that there is "unnecessary" or "superfluous" evil and this shows that an all-powerful and perfectly good God cannot exist.*

God and Evil

A. The Problem Stated:

Evil is a problem for the theist in that a contradiction is involved in the fact of evil on the one hand, and the belief in the omnipotence and perfection of God on the other. God cannot be both all-powerful and perfectly good if evil is real. This contradiction is well set out in its detail by Mackie in his discussion of the problem.[1] In his discussion Mackie seeks to show that this contradiction cannot be resolved in terms of man's free will. In arguing in this way Mackie neglects a large number of important points, and concedes far too much to the theist. He implicitly allows that whilst physical evil creates a problem, this problem is reducible to the problem of moral evil and that therefore the satisfactoriness of solutions of the problem of evil turns on the compatibility of free will and absolute goodness. In fact physical evils create a number of distinct problems which are not reducible to the problem of moral evil. Further, the proposed solution of the problem of moral evil in terms of free will renders the attempt to account for physical evil in terms of moral good, and the attempt thereby to reduce the problem of evil to the problem of moral evil, completely

* H.J. McCloskey, "God and Evil," in *The Philosophical Quarterly*, vol. 10 (1960): 97–114. Published by Blackwell. Reprinted by permission of Blackwell Publishing.
[1] "Evil and Omnipotence", *Mind*, 1955.

untenable. Moreover, the account of moral evil in terms of free will breaks down on more obvious and less disputable grounds than those indicated by Mackie. Moral evil can be shown to remain a problem whether or not free will is compatible with absolute goodness. I therefore propose in this paper to reopen the discussion of "the problem of evil", by approaching it from a more general standpoint, examining a wider variety of solutions than those considered by Mackie and his critics.

The fact of evil creates a problem for the theist; but there are a number of simple solutions available to a theist who is content seriously to modify his theism. He can either admit a limit to God's power, or he can deny God's moral perfection. He can assert either (1) that God is not powerful enough to make a world that does not contain evil, or (2) that God created only the good in the universe and that some other power created the evil, or (3) that God is all-powerful but morally imperfect, and chose to create an imperfect universe. Few Christians accept these solutions, and this is no doubt partly because such 'solutions' ignore the real inspiration of religious beliefs, and partly because they introduce embarrassing complications for the theist in his attempts to deal with other serious problems. However, if any one of these 'solutions' is accepted, then the problem of evil is avoided, and a weakened version of theism is made secure from attacks based upon the fact of the occurrence of evil.

For more orthodox theism, according to which God is both omnipotent and perfectly good, evil creates a real problem; and this problem is well-stated by the Jesuit, Father G. H. Joyce. Joyce writes:

"The existence of evil in the world must at all times be the greatest of all problems which the mind encounters when it reflects on God and His relation to the world. If He is, indeed, all-good and all-powerful, how has evil any place in the world which He has made? Whence came it? Why is it here? If He is all-good why did He allow it to arise? If all-powerful why does He not deliver us from the burden? Alike in the physical and moral order creation seems so grievously marred that we find it hard to understand how it can derive in its entirety from God".[2]

The facts which give rise to the problem are of two general kinds, and give rise to two distinct types of problem. These two general kinds of evil are usually referred to as 'physical' and as 'moral' evil. These terms are by no means apt—suffering for instance is not strictly physical evil—and they conceal significant differences. However, this terminology is too widely-accepted, and too convenient to be dispensed with here, the more especially as the various kinds of evil, whilst important as distinct kinds, need not for our purposes be designated by separate names.

Physical evil and moral evil then are the two general forms of evil which independently and jointly constitute conclusive grounds for denying the existence of God in the sense defined, namely as an all-powerful, perfect Being. The acuteness of these two general problems is evident

---

[2] Joyce: *Principles of Natural Theology*, ch. XVII. All subsequent quotations from Joyce in this paper are from this chapter of this work.

when we consider the nature and extent of the evils of which account must be given. To take physical evils, looking first at the less important of these.

(*a*) *Physical evils:* Physical evils are involved in the very constitution of the earth and animal kingdom. There are deserts and icebound areas; there are dangerous animals of prey, as well as creatures such as scorpions and snakes. There are also pests such as flies and fleas and the hosts of other insect pests, as well as the multitude of lower parasites such as tapeworms, hookworms and the like. Secondly, there are the various natural calamities and the immense human suffering that follows in their wake—fires, floods, tempests, tidalwaves, volcanoes, earthquakes, droughts and famines. Thirdly, there are the vast numbers of diseases that torment and ravage man. Diseases such as leprosy, cancer, poliomyelitis, appear *prima facie* not to be creations which are to be expected of a benevolent Creator. Fourthly, there are the evils with which so many are born—the various physical deformities and defects such as misshapen limbs, blindness, deafness, dumbness, mental deficiency and insanity. Most of these evils contribute towards increasing human pain and suffering; but not all physical evils are reducible simply to pain. Many of these evils are evils whether or not they result in pain. This is important, for it means that, unless there is one solution to such diverse evils, it is both inaccurate and positively misleading to speak of *the* problem of physical evil. Shortly I shall be arguing that no one 'solution' covers all these evils, so we shall have to conclude that physical evils create not one problem but a number of distinct problems for the theist.

The nature of the various difficulties referred to by the theist as the problem of physical evil is indicated by Joyce in a way not untypical among the more honest, philosophical theists, as follows:

"The actual amount of suffering which the human race endures is immense. Disease has store and to spare of torments for the body: and disease and death are the lot to which we must all look forward. At all times, too, great numbers of the race are pinched by want. Nor is the world ever free for very long from the terrible sufferings which follow in the track of war. If we concentrate our attention on human woes, to the exclusion of the joys of life, we gain an appalling picture of the ills to which the flesh is heir. So too if we fasten our attention on the sterner side of nature, on the pains which men endure from natural forces—on the storms which wreck their ships, the cold which freezes them to death, the fire which consumes them—if we contemplate this aspect of nature alone we may be led to wonder how God came to deal so harshly with His Creatures as to provide them with such a home."

Many such statements of the problem proceed by suggesting, if not by stating, that the problem arises at least in part by concentrating one's attention too exclusively on one aspect of the world. This is quite contrary to the facts. The problem is not one that results from looking at only one aspect of the universe. It may be the case that over-all pleasure predominates over pain, and that physical goods in general predominate over physical evils, but the opposite may equally well be the case. It is both practically impossible and logically impossible for this question to be resolved. However, it is not an unreasonable presumption, with the large bulk of mankind inadequately fed and housed and without adequate medical and health services, to suppose that physical evils at present predominate over physical goods. In the light of the facts at our disposal, this would seem to be a much more reasonable conclusion than the conclusion hinted at by Joyce and openly advanced by less cautious theists, namely, that physical goods in fact outweigh physical evils in the world.

However, the question is not, Which predominates, physical good or physical evil? The problem of physical evil remains a problem whether the balance in the universe is on the side of physical good or not, because the problem is that of accounting for the fact that physical evil occurs at all.

(*b*) *Moral evil:* Physical evils create one of the groups of problems referred to by the theist as 'the problem of evil'. Moral evil creates quite a distinct problem. Moral evil is simply immorality—evils such as selfishness, envy, greed, deceit, cruelty, callousness, cowardice and the larger scale evils such as wars and the atrocities they involve.

Moral evil is commonly regarded as constituting an even more serious problem than physical evil. Joyce so regards it, observing:

> "The man who sins thereby offends God. . . . We are called on to explain how God came to create an order of things in which rebellion and even final rejection have such a place. Since a choice from among an infinite number of possible worlds lay open to God, how came He to choose one in which these occur? Is not such a choice in flagrant opposition to the Divine Goodness?"

Some theists seek a solution by denying the reality of evil or by describing it as a 'privation' or absence of good. They hope thereby to explain it away as not needing a solution. This, in the case of most of the evils which require explanation, seems to amount to little more than an attempt to sidestep the problem simply by changing the name of that which has to be explained. It can be exposed for what it is simply by describing some of the evils which have to be explained. That is why a survey of the data to be accounted for is a most important part of the discussion of the problem of evil.

In *The Brothers Karamazov*, Dostoievsky introduces a discussion of the problem of evil by reference to some then recently committed atrocities. Ivan states the problem:

> " 'By the way, a Bulgarian I met lately in Moscow', Ivan went on . . . 'told me about the crimes committed by Turks in all parts of Bulgaria through fear of a general rising of the Slavs. They burn villages, murder, outrage women and children, and nail their prisoners by the ears to the fences, leave them till morning, and in the morning hang them—all sorts of things you can't imagine. People talk sometimes of bestial cruelty, but that's a great injustice and insult to the beasts; a beast can never be so cruel as a man, so artistically cruel. The tiger only tears and gnaws and that's all he can do. He would never think of nailing people by the ears, even if he were able to do it. These Turks took a pleasure in torturing children too; cutting the unborn child from the mother's womb, and tossing babies up in the air and catching them on the points of their bayonets before their mothers' eyes. Doing it before the mother's eyes was what gave zest to the amusement. Here is another scene that I thought very interesting. Imagine a trembling mother with her baby in her arms, a circle of invading Turks around her. They've planned a diversion: they pet the baby to make

it laugh. They succeed; the baby laughs. At that moment, a Turk points a pistol four inches from the baby's face. The baby laughs with glee, holds out its little hands to the pistol, and he pulls the trigger in the baby's face and blows out its brains. Artistic, wasn't it?' ".[3]

Ivan's statement of the problem was based on historical events. Such happenings did not cease in the nineteenth century. *The Scourge of the Swastika* by Lord Russell of Liverpool contains little else than descriptions of such atrocities; and it is simply one of a host of writings giving documented lists of instances of evils, both physical and moral.

Thus the problem of evil is both real and acute. There is a clear *prima facie* case that evil and God are incompatible—both cannot exist. Most theists admit this, and that the onus is on them to show that the conflict is not fatal to theism; but a consequence is that a host of proposed solutions are advanced.

The mere fact of such a multiplicity of proposed solutions, and the widespread repudiation of each other's solutions by theists, in itself suggests that the fact of evil is an insuperable obstacle to theism as defined here. It also makes it impossible to treat of all proposed solutions, and all that can be attempted here is an examination of those proposed solutions which are most commonly invoked and most generally thought to be important by theists.

Some theists admit the reality of the problem of evil, and then seek to sidestep it, declaring it to be a great mystery which we poor humans cannot hope to comprehend. Other theists adopt a rational approach and advance rational arguments to show that evil, properly understood, is compatible with, and even a consequence of God's goodness. The arguments to be advanced in this paper are directed against the arguments of the latter theists; but in so far as these arguments are successful against the rational theists, to that extent they are also effective in showing that the non-rational approach in terms of great mysteries is positively irrational.

B. Proposed Solutions to the Problem of Physical Evil:

Of the large variety of arguments advanced by theists as solutions to the problem of physical evil, five popularly used and philosophically significant solutions will be examined. They are, in brief: (i) Physical good (pleasure) requires physical evil (pain) to exist at all; (ii) Physical evil is God's punishment of sinners; (iii) Physical evil is God's warning and reminder to man; (iv) Physical evil is the result of the natural laws, the operations of which are on the whole good; (v) Physical evil increases the total good.

(i) *Physical Good is Impossible without Physical Evil*: Pleasure is possible only by way of contrast with pain. Here the analogy of colour is used. If everything were blue we should, it is argued, understand neither what colour is nor what blue is. So with pleasure and pain.

The most obvious defect of such an argument is that it does not cover all physical goods and evils. It is an argument commonly invoked by those who think of physical evil as creating only one problem, namely the problem of human pain. However, the problems of physical evils are not reducible to the one problem, the problem of pain; hence the argument is simply irrelevant to much physical evil. Disease and insanity are evils, but health

---

[3] P. 244, Garnett translation, Heinemann.

and sanity are possible in the total absence of disease and insanity. Further, if the argument were in any way valid even in respect of pain, it would imply the existence of only a speck of pain, and not the immense amount of pain in the universe. A speck of yellow is all that is needed for an appreciation of blueness and of colour generally. The argument is therefore seen to be seriously defective on two counts even if its underlying principle is left unquestioned. If its underlying principle is questioned, the argument is seen to be essentially invalid. Can it seriously be maintained that if an individual were born crippled and deformed and never in his life experienced pleasure, that he could not experience pain, not even if he were severely injured? It is clear that pain is possible in the absence of pleasure. It is true that it might not be distinguished by a special name and called 'pain', but the state we now describe as a painful state would nonetheless be possible in the total absence of pleasure. So too the converse would seem to apply. Plato brings this out very clearly in Book 9 of the *Republic* in respect of the pleasures of taste and smell. These pleasures seem not to depend for their existence on any prior experience of pain. Thus the argument is unsound in respect of its main contention; and in being unsound in this respect, it is at the same time ascribing a serious limitation to God's power. It maintains that God cannot create pleasure without creating pain, although as we have seen, pleasure and pain are not correlatives.

(ii) *Physical Evil is God's Punishment for Sin*: This kind of explanation was advanced to explain the terrible Lisbon earthquake in the 18th century, in which 40,000 people were killed. There are many replies to this argument, for instance Voltaire's. Voltaire asked: "Did God in this earthquake select the 40,000 least virtuous of the Portuguese citizens?" The distribution of disease and pain is in no obvious way related to the virtue of the persons afflicted, and popular saying has it that the distribution is slanted in the opposite direction. The only way of meeting the fact that evils are not distributed proportionately to the evil of the sufferer is by suggesting that all human beings, including children, are such miserable sinners, that our offences are of such enormity, that God would be justified in punishing all of us as severely as it is possible for humans to be punished; but even then, God's apparent caprice in the selection of His victims requires explanation. In any case it is by no means clear that young children who very often suffer severely are guilty of sin of such an enormity as would be necessary to justify their sufferings as punishment.

Further, many physical evils are simultaneous with birth—insanity, mental defectiveness, blindness, deformities, as well as much disease. No crime or sin of *the child* can explain and justify these physical evils as punishment; and, for a parent's sin to be punished in the child is injustice or evil of another kind.

Similarly, the sufferings of animals cannot be accounted for as punishment. For these various reasons, therefore, this argument must be rejected. In fact it has dropped out of favour in philosophical and theological circles, but it continues to be invoked at the popular level.

(iii) *Physical Evil is God's Warning to Men*: It is argued, for instance of physical calamities, that "they serve a moral end which compensates the physical evil which they cause. The awful nature of these phenomena, the overwhelming power of the forces at work, and man's utter helplessness before them, rouse him from the religious indifference to which he is so prone. They inspire a reverential awe of the Creator who made them, and controls them, and a salutary fear of violating the laws which He has imposed". (Joyce). This is where immortality is often alluded to as justifying evil.

This argument proceeds from a proposition that is plainly false; and that the proposition from which it proceeds is false is conceded implicitly by most theologians. Natural calamities do not necessarily turn people to God, but rather present the problem of evil in an acute form; and the problem of evil is said to account for more defections from religion than any other cause. Thus if God's object in bringing about natural calamities is to inspire reverence and awe, He is a bungler. There are many more reliable methods of achieving this end. Equally important, the use of physical evil to achieve this object is hardly the course one would expect a benevolent God to adopt when other, more effective, less evil methods are available to Him. for example, miracles, special revelation, etc.

(iv) *Evils are the Results of the Operation of Laws of Nature*: This fourth argument relates to most physical evil, but it is more usually used to account for animal suffering and physical calamities. These evils are said to result from the operation of the natural laws which govern these objects, the relevant natural laws being the various causal laws, the law of pleasure-pain as a law governing sentient beings, etc. The theist argues that the non-occurrence of these evils would involve either the constant intervention by God in a miraculous way, and contrary to his own natural laws, or else the construction of a universe with different components subject to different laws of nature; for God, in creating a certain kind of being, must create it subject to its appropriate law; He cannot create it and subject it to any law of His own choosing. Hence He creates a world which has components and laws good in their total effect, although calamitous in some particular effects.

Against this argument three objections are to be urged. First, it does not cover all physical evil. Clearly not all disease can be accounted for along these lines. Secondly, it is not to give a reason against God's miraculous intervention simply to assert that it would be unreasonable for Him constantly to intervene in the operation of His own laws. Yet this is the only reason that theists seem to offer here. If, by intervening in respect to the operation of His laws, God could thereby eliminate an evil, it would seem to be unreasonable and evil of Him not to do so. Some theists seek a way out of this difficulty by denying that God has the power miraculously to intervene; but this is to ascribe a severe limitation to His power. It amounts to asserting that when His Creation has been effected, God can do nothing else except contemplate it. The third objection is related to this, and is to the effect that it is already to ascribe a serious limitation to God's omnipotence to suggest that He could not make sentient beings which did not experience pain, nor sentient beings without deformities and deficiencies, nor natural phenomena with different laws of nature governing them. There is no reason why better laws of nature governing the existing objects are not possible on the divine hypothesis. Surely, if God is all-powerful, He could have made a better universe in the first place, or one with better laws of nature governing it, so that the operation of its laws did not produce calamities and pain. To maintain this is not to suggest that an omnipotent God should be capable of achieving what is logically impossible. All that has been indicated here is logically possible, and therefore not beyond the powers of a being Who is really omnipotent.

This fourth argument seeks to exonerate God by explaining that He created a universe sound on the whole, but such that He had no direct control over the laws governing His creations, and had control only in His selection of His creations. The previous two arguments attribute the detailed results of the operations of these laws directly to God's will. Theists commonly use all three arguments. It is not without significance that they betray such uncertainty as to whether God is to be *commended* or *exonerated*.

(v) *The Universe is Better with Evil in it*: This is the important argument. One version of it runs:

> "Just as the human artist has in view the beauty of his composition as a whole, not making it his aim to give to each several part the highest degree of brilliancy, but that measure of adornment which most contributes to the combined effect, so it is with God."
>
> (Joyce)

Another version of this general type of argument explains evil not so much as *a component* of a good whole, seen out of its context as a mere component, but rather as *a means* to a greater good. Different as these versions are, they may be treated here as one general type of argument, for the same criticisms are fatal to both versions.

This kind of argument if valid simply shows that some evil may enrich the Universe; it tells us nothing about *how much* evil will enrich this particular universe, and how much will be too much. So, even if valid in principle—and shortly I shall argue that it is not valid—such an argument does not in itself provide a justification for the evil in the universe. It shows simply that the evil which occurs might have a justification. In view of the immense amount of evil the probabilities are against it.

This is the main point made by Wisdom in his discussion of this argument. Wisdom sums up his criticism as follows:

> "It remains to add that, unless there are independent arguments in favour of this world's being the best logically possible world, it is probable that some of the evils in it are not logically necessary to a compensating good; it is probable because there are so many evils".[4]

Wisdom's reply brings out that the person who relies upon this argument as a conclusive and complete argument is seriously mistaken. The argument, if valid, justifies only some evil. A belief that it justifies all the evil that occurs in the world is mistaken, for a second argument, by way of a supplement to it, is needed. This supplementary argument would make the form of a proof that all the evil that occurs is *in fact* valuable and necessary as a means to greater good. Such a supplementary proof is in principle impossible; so, at best, this fifth argument can be taken to show only that some evil *may be* necessary for the production of good, and that the evil in the world may perhaps have a justification on this account. This is not to justify a physical evil, but simply to suggest that physical evil might nonetheless have a justification, although we may never come to know this justification.

Thus the argument even if it is valid as a general form of reasoning is unsatisfactory because inconclusive. It is, however, also unsatisfactory in that it follows on the principle of the argument that, just as it is possible that evil in the total context contributes to increasing the total ultimate good, so equally, it will hold that good in the total context may increase the ultimate evil. Thus if the principle of the argument were sound, we could never know whether evil is really evil, or good really good. (Aesthetic analogies may be used to illustrate this point.) By implication it follows that it would be dangerous to eliminate evil because we may thereby introduce a discordant element into the divine symphony of the universe; and, conversely, it may be wrong to condemn the elimination of what is good, because the latter may result in the production of more, higher goods.

So it follows that, even if the general principle of the argument is not questioned, it is still seen to be a defective argument. On the one hand, it proves too little—it justifies only some evil and not necessarily all the evil in the universe; on the other hand it proves too much because it creates doubts about the goodness of apparent goods. These criticisms in themselves are fatal to the argument as a solution to the problem of physical evil. However, because this is one of the most popular and plausible accounts of physical evil, it is worthwhile considering whether it can properly be claimed to establish even the very weak conclusion indicated above.

Why, and in what way, is it supposed that physical evils such as pain and misery, disease and deformity, will heighten the total effect and add to the value of the moral whole? The answer given is that physical evil enriches the whole by giving rise to moral goodness. Disease, insanity, physical suffering and the like are said to bring into being the noble moral virtues—courage, endurance, benevolence, sympathy and the like. This is what the talk about the enriched whole comes to. W. D. Niven makes this explicit in his version of the argument:

> "Physical evil has been the goad which has impelled men to most of those achievements which made the history of man so wonderful. Hardship is a stern but fecund parent of invention. Where life is easy because physical ills are at a minimum we find man degenerating in body, mind, and character".

And Niven concludes by asking:

> "Which is preferable—a grim fight with the possibility of splendid triumph; or no battle at all?"[5]

---

[5] W. D. Niven, *Encyclopedia of Religion and Ethics*.
Joyce's corresponding argument runs:
    "Pain is the great stimulant to action. Man no less than animals is impelled to work by the sense of hunger. Experience shows that, were it not for this motive the majority of men would be content to live in indolent ease. Man must earn his bread".
    "One reason plainly why God permits suffering is that man may rise to a height of heroism which would otherwise have been beyond his scope. Nor are these the only benefits which it confers. That sympathy for others which is one of the most precious parts of our experience, and one of the most fruitful sources of well-doing, has its origin in the fellow-feeling engendered by endurance of similar trials. Furthermore, were it not for these trials, man would think little enough of a future existence, and of the need of striving after his last end. He would be perfectly content with his existence, and would reck little of any higher good. These considerations here briefly advanced suffice at least to show how important is the office filled by pain in human life, and with what little reason it is asserted that the existence of so much suffering is irreconcilable with the wisdom of the Creator".
And:
    "It may be asked whether the Creator could not have brought man to perfection without the use of suffering. Most certainly He could have conferred upon him a similar degree of virtue with

The argument is: Physical evil brings moral good into being, and in fact is an essential precondition for the existence of some moral goods. Further, it is sometimes argued in this context that those moral goods which are possible in the total absence of physical evils are more valuable in themselves if they are achieved as a result of a struggle. Hence physical evil is said to be justified on the grounds that moral good plus physical evil is better than the absence of physical evil.

A common reply, and an obvious one, is that urged by Mackie.[6] Mackie argues that whilst it is true that moral good plus physical evil together are better than physical good alone, the issue is not as simple as that, for physical evil also gives rise to and makes possible many moral evils that would not or could not occur in the absence of physical evil. It is then urged that it is not clear that physical evils (for example, disease and pain) plus some moral goods (for example courage) plus some moral evil (for example, brutality) are better than physical good and those moral goods which are possible and which would occur in the absence of physical evil.

This sort of reply, however, is not completely satisfactory. The objection it raises is a sound one, but it proceeds by conceding too much to the theist, and by overlooking two more basic defects of the argument. It allows implicitly that the problem of physical evil may be reduced to the problem of moral evil; and it neglects the two objections which show that the problem of physical evil cannot be so reduced.

The theist therefore happily accepts this kind of reply, and argues that, if he can give a satisfactory account of moral evil he will then have accounted for both physical and moral evil. He then goes on to account for moral evil in terms of the value of free will and/or its goods. This general argument is deceptively plausible. It breaks down for the two reasons indicated here, but it breaks down at another point as well. If free will alone is used to justify moral evil, then even if no moral good occurred, moral evil would still be said to be justified; but physical evil would have no justification. Physical evil is not essential to free will; it is only justified if moral good actually occurs, and if the moral good which results from physical evils outweighs the moral evils. This means that the argument from free will cannot alone justify physical evil along these lines; and it means that the argument from free will and its goods does not justify physical evil, because such an argument is incomplete, and necessarily incomplete. It needs to be supplemented by factual evidence that it is logically and practically impossible to obtain.

The correct reply, therefore, is first that the argument is irrelevant to many instances of physical evil, and secondly that it is not true that physical evil plus the moral good it produces is better than physical good and its moral goods. Much pain and suffering, in fact much physical

out requiring any effort on his part. Yet it is easy to see that there is a special value attaching to a conquest of difficulties such as man's actual demands, and that in God's eyes this may well be an adequate reason for assigning this life to us in preference to another. . . . Pain has value in respect to the next life, but also in respect to this. The advance of scientific discovery, the gradual improvement of the organization of the community, the growth of material civilization are due in no small degree to the stimulus afforded by pain".
[6] Mackie, "Evil and Omnipotence", *Mind*, 1955.

evil generally, for example in children who die in infancy, animals and the insane passes unnoticed; it therefore has no morally uplifting effects upon others, and cannot by virtue of the examples chosen have such effects on the sufferers. Further, there are physical evils such as insanity and much disease to which the argument is inapplicable. So there is a large group of significant cases not covered by the argument. And where the argument is relevant, its premiss is plainly false. It can be shown to be false by exposing its implications in the following way.

We either have obligations to lessen physical evil or we have not. If we have obligations to lessen physical evil then we are thereby reducing the total good in the universe. If, on the other hand, our obligation is to increase the total good in the universe it is our duty to prevent the reduction of physical evil and possibly even to increase the total amount of physical evil. Theists usually hold that we are obliged to reduce the physical evil in the universe; but in maintaining this, the theist is, in terms of this account of physical evil, maintaining that it is his duty to reduce the total amount of real good in the universe, and thereby to make the universe worse. Conversely, if by eliminating the physical evil he is not making the universe worse, then that amount of evil which he eliminates was unnecessary and in need of justification. It is relevant to notice here that evil is not always eliminated for morally praiseworthy reasons. Some discoveries have been due to positively unworthy motives, and many other discoveries which have resulted in a lessening of the sufferings of mankind have been due to no higher a motive than a scientist's desire to earn a reasonable living wage.

This reply to the theist's argument brings out its untenability. The theist's argument is seen to imply that war plus courage plus the many other moral virtues war brings into play are better than peace and its virtues; that famine and its moral virtues are better than plenty; that disease and its moral virtues are better than health. Some Christians in the past, in consistency with this mode of reasoning, opposed the use of anaesthetics to leave scope for the virtues of endurance and courage, and they opposed state aid to the sick and needy to leave scope for the virtues of charity and sympathy. Some have even contended that war is a good in disguise, again in consistency with this argument. Similarly the theist should, in terms of this fifth argument, in his heart if not aloud regret the discovery of the Salk polio vaccine because Dr. Salk has in one blow destroyed infinite possibilities of moral good.

There are three important points that need to be made concerning this kind of account of physical evil. (*a*) We are told, as by Niven, Joyce and others, that pain is a goad to action and that part of its justification lies in this fact. This claim is empirically false as a generalization about all people and all pain. Much pain frustrates action and wrecks people and personalities. On the other hand many men work and work well without being goaded by pain or discomfort. Further, to assert that men need goading is to ascribe another evil to God, for it is to claim that God made men naturally lazy. There, is no reason why God should not have made men naturally industrious; the one is no more incompatible with free will than the other. Thus the argument from physical evil being a goad to man breaks down on three distinct counts. Pain often frustrates human endeavour, pain is not essential as a goad with many men, and where pain is a goad to higher endeavours, it is clear that less evil means to this same end are available to an omnipotent God. (*b*) The real fallacy in the argument is in the assumption that all or the highest moral excellence results from physical evil. As we have already seen, this assumption is completely false. Neither all moral goodness nor the highest moral goodness is triumph in the face of adversity or benevolence towards others in suffering. Christ Himself stressed this when He observed that the two great commandments were commandments to love. Love does not depend for its possibility on the existence and conquest of evil. (c) The 'negative' moral virtues which are brought into play by the various evils—courage, endurance, charity, sympathy and the like—besides not representing the highest forms of moral virtue, are in fact commonly supposed by the theist and atheist alike not to have the value this fifth argument ascribes to them. We—theists and atheists alike—reveal our comparative valuations of these virtues and of physical evil when we insist on state aid for the needy; when we strive for peace, for plenty, and for harmony within the state.

In brief, the good man, the morally admirable man, is he who loves what is good knowing that it is good and preferring it because it is good. He does not need to be torn by suffering or by the spectacle of another's sufferings to be morally admirable. Fortitude in his own sufferings, and sympathetic kindness in others' may reveal to us his goodness; but his goodness is not necessarily increased by such things.

Five arguments concerning physical evil have now been examined. We have seen that the problem of physical evil is a problem in its own right, and one that cannot be reduced to the problem of moral evil; and further, we have seen that physical evil creates not one but a number of problems to which no one nor any combination of the arguments examined offers a solution.

C. Proposed Solutions to the Problem of Moral Evil:

The problem of moral evil is commonly regarded as being the greater of the problems concerning evil. As we shall see, it does create what appears to be insuperable difficulties for the theist; but so too, apparently, do physical evils.

For the theist moral evil must be interpreted as a breach of God's law and as a rejection of God Himself. It may involve the eternal damnation of the sinner, and in many of its forms it involves the infliction of suffering on other persons. Thus it aggravates the problem of physical evil, but its own peculiar character consists in the fact of sin. How could a morally perfect, all-powerful God create a universe in which occur such moral evils as cruelty, cowardice and hatred, the more especially as these evils constitute a rejection of God Himself by His creations, and as such involve them in eternal damnation?

The two main solutions advanced relate to free will and to the fact that moral evil is a consequence of free will. There is a third kind of solution more often invoked implicitly than as an explicit and serious argument, which need not be examined here as its weaknesses are plainly evident. This third solution is to the effect that moral evils and even the most brutal atrocities have their justification in the moral goodness they make possible or bring into being.

(i) *Free will alone provides a justification for moral evil:* This is perhaps the more popular of the serious attempts to explain moral evil. The argument in brief runs: men have free will; moral evil is a consequence of free will; a universe in which men exercise free will even with lapses into moral evil is better than a universe in which men become *automata* doing good always because predestined to do so. Thus on this argument it is the mere fact of the supreme value of free will itself that is taken to provide a justification for its corollary moral evil.

(ii) *The goods made possible by free will provide a basis for accounting for moral evil:* According to this second argument, it is not the mere fact of free will that is claimed to be of such value as to provide a justification of moral evil, but the fact that free will makes certain goods possible. Some indicate the various moral virtues as the goods that free will makes possible, whilst others point to beatitude, and others again to beatitude achieved by man's own efforts or the virtues achieved as a result of one's own efforts. What all these have in common is the claim that the good consequences of free will provide a justification of the bad consequences of free will, namely moral evil.

Each of these two proposed solutions encounters two specific criticisms, which are fatal to their claims to be real solutions.

(i) To consider first the difficulties to which the former proposed solution is exposed. (*a*) A difficulty for the first argument—that it is free will alone that provides a justification for moral evil—lies in the fact that the theist who argues in this way has to allow that it is logically possible on the free will hypothesis that all men should always will what is evil, and that even so, a universe of completely evil men possessing free will is better than one in which men are predestined to virtuous living. It has to be contended that the value of free will itself is so immense that it more than outweighs the total moral evil, the eternal punishment of the wicked, and the sufferings inflicted on others by the sinners in their evilness. It is this paradox that leads to the formulation of the second argument; and it is to be noted that the explanation of moral evil switches to the second argument or to a combination of the first

and second argument, immediately the theist refuses to face the logical possibility of complete wickedness, and insists instead that in fact men do not always choose what is evil.

(*b*) The second difficulty encountered by the first argument relates to the possibility that free will is compatible with less evil, and even with no evil, that is, with absolute goodness. If it could be shown that free will is compatible with absolute goodness, or even with less moral evil than actually occurs, then all or at least some evil will be left unexplained by free will alone.

Mackie, in his recent paper, and Joyce, in his discussion of this argument, both contend that free will is compatible with absolute goodness. Mackie argues that if it is not possible for God to confer free-will on men and at the same time ensure that no moral evil is committed He cannot really be omnipotent. Joyce directs his argument rather to fellow-theists, and it is more of an *ad hominem* argument addressed to them. He writes:

"Free will need not (as is often assumed) involve the power to choose wrong. Our ability to misuse the gift is due to the conditions under which it is exercised here. In our present state we are able to reject what is truly good, and exercise our power of preference in favour of some baser attraction. Yet it is not necessary that it should be so. And all who accept Christian revelation admit that those who attain their final beatitude exercise freedom of will, and yet cannot choose aught but what is truly good. They possess the knowledge of Essential Goodness; and to it, not simply to good in general, they refer every choice. Moreover, even in our present condition it is open to omnipotence so to order our circumstances and to confer on the will such instinctive impul-ses that we should in every election adopt the right course and not the wrong one".

To this objection, that free will is compatible with absolute goodness and that therefore a benevolent, omnipotent God would have given man free will and ensured his absolute virtue, it is replied that God is being required to perform what is logically impossible. It is logically impossible, so it is argued, for free will and absolute goodness to be combined, and hence, if God lacks omnipotence only in this respect, He cannot be claimed to lack omnipotence in any sense in which serious theists have ascribed it to Him.

Quite clearly, if free will and absolute goodness are logically incompatible, then God, in not being able to confer both on man does not lack omnipotence in any important sense of the term. However, it is not clear that free will and absolute goodness are logically opposed; and Joyce does point to considerations which suggest that they are not logical incompatibles. For my own part I am uncertain on this point; but my uncertainty is not a factual one but one concerning a point of usage. It is clear that an omnipotent God could create rational agents predestined always to make virtuous 'decisions'; what is not clear is whether we should describe such agents as having free will. The considerations to which Joyce points have something of the status of test cases, and they would suggest that we should describe such agents as having free will. However, no matter how we resolve the linguistic point, the question remains— Which is more desirable, free will and moral evil and the physical evil to which free will gives rise, or this special free will or pseudo-free will which goes with absolute goodness? I suggest that the latter is clearly preferable. Later I shall

endeavour to defend this conclusion; for the moment I am content to indicate the nature of the value judgement on which the question turns at this point.

The second objection to the proposed solution of the problem of moral evil in terms of free will alone, related to the contention that free will is compatible with less moral evil than occurs, and possibly with no moral evil. We have seen what is involved in the latter contention. We may now consider what is involved in the former. It may be argued that free will is compatible with less moral evil than in fact occurs on various grounds.

1. God, if He were all-powerful, could miraculously intervene to prevent some or perhaps all moral evil; and He is said to do so on occasions in answer to prayers, (for example, to prevent wars) or of His own initiative (for instance, by producing calamities which serve as warnings, or by working miracles, etc.).

2. God has made man with a certain nature. This nature is often interpreted by theologians as having a bias to evil. Clearly God could have created man with a strong bias to good, whilst still leaving scope for a decision to act evilly. Such a bias to good would be compatible with freedom of the will. 3. An omnipotent God could so have ordered the world that it was less conducive to the practice of evil.

These are all considerations advanced by Joyce, and separately and jointly, they establish that God could have conferred free will upon us, and at least very considerably *reduced* the amount of moral evil that would have resulted from the exercise of free will. This is sufficient to show that *not all* the moral evil that exists can be justified by reference to free will alone. This conclusion is fatal to the account of moral evil in terms of free will alone. The more extreme conclusion that Mackie seeks to establish—that absolute goodness is compatible with free will—is not essential as a basis for refuting the free will argument. The difficulty is as fatal to the claims of theism whether all moral evil or only some moral evil is unaccountable. However, whether Mackie's contentions are sound is still a matter of logical interest, although not of any real moment in the context of the case against theism, once the fact that less moral evil is compatible with free will has been established.

(ii) The second free will argument arises out of an attempt to circumvent these objections. It is not free will, but the value of the goods achieved through free will that is said to be so great as to provide a justification for moral evil.

(*a*) This second argument meets a difficulty in that it is now necessary for it to be supplemented by a proof that the number of people who practise moral virtue or who attain beatitude or who attain beatitude and/or virtue after a struggle is sufficient to outweigh the evilness of moral evil, the evilness of their eternal damnation and the physical evil they cause to others. This is a serious defect in the argument, because it means that the argument can at best show that moral evil *may have* a justification, and not that it has a justification. It is both logically and practically impossible to supplement and complete the argument. It is necessarily incomplete and inconclusive even if its general principle is sound.

(*b*) This second argument is designed also to avoid the other difficulty of the first argument—that free will may be compatible with no evil and certainly with less evil. It is argued that even if free will is compatible with absolute goodness it is still better that virtue and beatitude be attained after a genuine personal struggle; and this, it is said, would not occur if God in conferring free will nonetheless prevented moral evil or reduced the risk of it. Joyce argues in this way:

"To receive our final beatitude as the fruit of our labours, and as the recompense of a hard-worn victory, is an incomparably higher destiny than to receive it without any effort on our part. And since God in His wisdom has seen fit to give us such a lot as this, it was inevitable that man should have the power to choose wrong. We could not be called to merit the reward due to victory without being exposed to the possibility of defeat".

There are various objections which may be urged here. First, this argument implies that the more intense the struggle, the greater is the triumph and resultant good, and the better the world; hence we should apparently, on this argument, court temptation and moral struggles to attain greater virtue and to be more worthy of our reward. Secondly, it may be urged that God is being said to be demanding too high a price for the goods produced. He is omniscient. He knows that many will sin and not attain the goods or the Good free will is said to make possible. He creates men with free will, with the natures men have, in the world as it is constituted, knowing that in His doing so He is committing many to moral evil and eternal damnation. He could avoid all this evil by creating men with rational wills predestined to virtue, or He could eliminate much of it by making men's natures and the conditions in the world more conducive to the practice of virtue. He is said not to choose to do this. Instead, at the cost of the sacrifice of the many, He is said to have ordered things so as to allow fewer men to attain this higher virtue and higher beatitude that result from the more intense struggle.

In attributing such behaviour to God, and in attempting to account for moral evil along these lines, theists are, I suggest, attributing to God immoral behaviour of a serious kind—of a kind we should all unhesitatingly condemn in a fellow human being.

We do not commend people for putting temptation in the way of others. On the contrary, anyone who today advocated, or even allowed where he could prevent it, the occurrence of evil and the sacrifice of the many—even as a result of their own freely chosen actions—for the sake of the higher virtue of the few, would be condemned as an immoralist. To put severe temptation in the way of the many, knowing that many and perhaps even most will succumb to the temptation, for the sake of the higher virtue of the few, would be blatant immorality; and it would be immoral whether or not those who yielded to the temptation possessed free will. This point can be brought out by considering how a conscientious moral agent would answer the question: Which should I choose for other people, a world in which there are intense moral struggles and the possibility of magnificent triumphs and the certainty of many defeats, or a world in which there are less intense struggles, less magnificent triumphs but more triumphs and fewer defeats, or a world in which there are no struggles, no triumphs and no defeats? We are constantly answering less easy questions than this in a way that conflicts with the theist's contentions. If by modifying our own behaviour we can save someone else from an intense moral struggle and almost certain moral evil, for example if by refraining from gambling or excessive drinking ourselves we can help a weaker person not to become a confirmed gambler or an alcoholic, or if by locking our car and not leaving it

unlocked and with the key in it we can prevent people yielding to the temptation to become car thieves, we feel obliged to act accordingly, even though the persons concerned would freely choose the evil course of conduct. How much clearer is the decision with which God is said to be faced—the choice between the higher virtue of some and the evil of others, or the higher but less high virtue of many more, and the evil of many fewer. Neither alternative denies free will to men.

These various difficulties dispose of each of the main arguments relating to moral evil. There are in addition to these difficulties two other objections that might be urged.

If it could be shown that man has not free will both arguments collapse; and even if it could be shown that God's omniscience is incompatible with free will they would still break down. The issues raised here are too great to be pursued in this paper; and they can simply be noted as possible additional grounds from which criticisms of the main proposed solutions of the problem of moral evil may be advanced.

The other general objection is by way of a follow-up to points made in objections (*b*) to both arguments (i) and (ii). It concerns the relative value of free will and its goods and evils and the value of the best of the alternatives to free will and its goods. Are free will and its goods so much more valuable than the next best alternatives that their superior value can really justify the immense amount of evil that is introduced into the world by free will?

Theologians who discuss this issue ask, Which is better—men with free will striving to work out their own destinies, or automata-machine-like creatures, who never make mistakes because they never make decisions? When put in this form we naturally doubt whether free will plus moral evil plus the possibility of the eternal damnation of the many and the physical evil of untold billions are quite so unjustified after all; but the fact of the matter is that the question has not been fairly put. The real alternative is, on the one hand, rational agents with free wills making many bad and some good decisions on rational and non-rational grounds, and 'rational' agents predestined always 'to choose' the right things for the right reasons—that is, if the language of automata must be used, rational automata. Predestination does not imply the absence of rationality in all senses of that term. God, were He omnipotent, could preordain the decisions and the reasons upon which they were based; and such a mode of existence would seem to be in itself a worthy mode of existence, and one preferable to an existence with free will, irrationality and evil.

D. Conclusion

In this paper it has been maintained that God, were He all-powerful and perfectly good, would have created a world in which there was no unnecessary evil. It has not been argued that God ought to have created a perfect world, nor that He should have made one that is in any way logically impossible. It has simply been argued that a benevolent God could, and would, have created a world devoid of superfluous evil. It has been contended that there is evil in this world—unnecessary evil— and that the more popular and philosophically more significant of the many attempts to explain this evil are completely unsatisfactory. Hence we must conclude from the existence of evil that there cannot be an omnipotent, benevolent God.

JAMES KELLENBERGER

God's Goodness and God's Evil

In "God's Goodness and God's Evil" James Kellenberger argues that certain believers that he calls "Job-like believers" would not have the religious problem of evil, even though they recognized and experienced evil in the world. Such believers, if they are as they understand themselves to be, would have experienced and become truly aware of God's goodness. Being in this position, Kellenberger argues, they would not and should not see evil as any evidence against God's goodness.

From *Religious Studies*, vol 41, 2005. Reprinted by permission of Cambridge University Press.

God's Goodness and God's Evil

Abstract: Starting with Job's reaction to evil, I identify three elements of Job-like belief. They are: (1) the recognition of evil in the world; (2) the conviction that God and God's creation are good; and (3) the sense of beholding God's goodness in the world. The interconnection of these three elements is examined along with a possible way of understanding Job-like believers beholding and becoming experientially aware of God's goodness. It is brought out why, given that they are as they understand themselves to be, Job-like believers properly do not see evil as evidence against God's goodness. Finally, Job-like belief is related to the different reactions to evil by Ivan and Aloysha in *The Brothers Karamazov*.

Introduction

It is hard to deny that evil is real. Natural evils, such as earthquakes, storms, and disease, and moral evils, consisting of the morally wrong or evil things that humans do to one another, directly or indirectly, confront us daily. Some have seen the evil of the world, or its 'superfluous evil', as contradictory to, and so a conclusive argument against, the existence of God.[1] Others have seen evil as requiring some reason for its existence, in the light of which we can, in John Milton's phrase, 'justify the ways of God to men', a theodicy of some sort.[2] There is another reaction to the evils of the world, however. When Job loses his riches and his sons and daughters, and then is himself afflicted with disease, his wife, in her despair, addresses him in his loss and suffering and advises him to 'Curse God and die'. Job replies with a rhetorical question: 'Shall we receive good at the hand of God, and shall we not receive evil?' In saying this, in acknowledging that evils are a part of God's domain or creation, we are told, Job does not sin with his lips (Job 1.9-10).[3]

[1] J. L. Mackie 'Evil and omnipotence', and H. J. McCloskey 'God and evil', both reprinted in Nelson Pike (ed.) *God and Evil* (Englewood Cliffs NJ: Prentice-Hall, 1964). McCloskey allows that it is 'superfluous evil' that forces us to conclude that there cannot be an omnipotent, benevolent God.

[2] A theodicy, as an effort to 'justify God's way to men', offers an answer to the traditional religious problem of evil: 'If God is all-good, all-powerful, all-knowing, why is there evil in the world?' Some, like McCloskey, would distinguish between the problem of physical, or natural, evil (natural evils being earthquakes, disease, and the like) and the problem of moral evil (moral evils being the morally wrong or evil things done by human beings). Any thoroughly adequate theodicy would have to account for both types of evil.

In more recent discussions some, addressing the 'logical problem of evil', arising from the claim that the existence of evil is logically inconsistent with God's existence (the claim made by Mackie and McCloskey), have offered a 'defence' designed to show that God could consistently allow evil, as Alvin Plantinga has done in *God and Other Minds* (Ithaca NY: Cornell University Press, 1967), 131ff. A theodicy tries to identify and argue for God's reason for evil, while a defence tries to identify a *possible* reason that God consistently could have for evil, thus showing that evil is compatible with God's existence; the same consideration, e.g. human free will, can be offered as a theodicy or as a defence.

[3] All biblical quotations are from the Revised Standard Version.

In what follows, I will explore Job's position, or better, Job's self-understanding vis-à-vis evil. There are, to be sure, several interpretations of the Book of Job, and of Job. Job may be understood as one seeking from God a reason for his suffering and for there being evil in the world. He may be seen as the personification of innocent suffering in an indifferent universe, or as an argument against a caring or just God. I will explore the internal logic of Job's position or self-understanding, on a particular reading of the Book of Job. My concern is not to defend the exegesis I will draw upon. It is to explore the structure of Job's position or self-understanding vis-à-vis evil, given that exegesis. More accurately, I want to examine the internal logic of a Job-like believer's position vis-à-vis evil. To do so I will need to fill out the Joban position and in doing this I will go beyond the Book of Job, but not beyond the broader biblical tradition.

In that broader tradition, or the strain of it that I will follow, I find three main elements in Job-like belief: first, the concession, even the insistence, that there is great evil in the world, natural and moral evil; second, the acknowledgment and utter conviction that God and God's creation are good. These two elements are embodied in the reading of the Book of Job that informs my exploration, even if they—especially the second—are not embodied in other readings of the Book of Job. The third element is the sense that God's goodness, love, and righteousness can be experienced or beheld in God's creation. This element, though not evident in the Book of Job, is alive and well in a strain of the broader biblical tradition. In the following discussion, I will try to bring into relief the logic of a Joban self-understanding, or rather, the logic of a Job-like believer's self-understanding, by clarifying the interconnectedness of these three elements.

Job's Suffering

Job suffers natural or physical evil, but also moral evil. Both are included in the Joban recognition of the reality of evil. Job, in his acceptance of the evil that he and his family have endured at the hand of God, is referring to the natural evils of the fire that consumed his sheep and servants, the great wind that destroyed the house of his eldest son and killed all his sons and daughters, and the disease that afflicts his own body. He is, as well, referring to the moral evil of the raiders who slew his servants and stole his herds (Job 1 and 2). Job, in the prologue, speaks out of his personal suffering caused by these natural and moral evils. However, the sufferings of his children and of his wife also are evils, and as the rest of the Book of Job makes clear, Job is aware that evils of both kinds are visited upon human beings generally. Subsequent Job-like believers have been aware of natural evils half a world away in the form of famines and disease, and of moral evils in the form of genocide, ethnic cleansing, and as expressed in great and small acts of malice.

While it is true that Job would 'fill [his] mouth with arguments' and make his case to God (Job 23.4), on the understanding of the Book of Job that I am following, he does not seek God's reason for allowing evil. He does not seek to establish a theodicy.[4] Rather, he tries to defend himself against the charge that his suffering is deserved as punishment for his sinful and wrongful actions in the hope that he 'should be acquitted for ever by

---

[4] Nor of course does he try to establish a 'defence'.

[his] judge' (Job 23.7). The view here, as Elihu puts it, is that 'according to the work of a man [the Almighty] will requite him' (Job 34.11).[5] This is the view of Job's condition put forward by Elihu and Job's three friends and 'comforters', whose dialogue with Job makes up most of the Book of Job. In speaking to their charge and arguing for his innocence Job accepts their assumption. In the long run, only the guilty are made to suffer. So Job argues for his innocence (Job 31). But this view of suffering is mistaken: the innocent also suffer.[6] When God speaks out of the whirlwind and rebukes Job for speaking without understanding, on my reading, He is rebuking Job for taking up his interlocutors' view of suffering as punishment. Here Job has erred, for, along with his interlocutors, he has wrongly, if not arrogantly, assumed that he understood the ways of God. But, on my reading, Job never doubts the goodness of God or His creation (the second element of the tradition of Job-like believers). If Job had doubted God's goodness, his faith would have failed, for his trust in God and in His goodness would have failed.

Though Job's soul is bitter (Job 27.2), and his heart is in turmoil (Job 30.27), Job's faith in God never falters. His faith does not falter even though he does not understand God's reason for allowing, if not creating, evil, in particular the great evil that the Lord has brought upon him. In the Book of Job, certainly in the prologue, and throughout, if the exegesis I am following is correct, Job maintains his faith in God. Though he has received evil from God, Job continues to believe in God's goodness, in particular His goodness toward him. Job's faith, thus understood, fits with a traditional biblical understanding of God: God is good and His creation is good (Genesis 1). Job does not know why he has been afflicted with evil, but as long as he trusts in God, he believes, and must believe, that God is good. He, in fact, affirms that he *knows* that his Redeemer lives (Job 19.25), and in this utterance we have Job's expression of absolute faith in God and His goodness. Job does not seek a theodicy, then, because he does not have the religious problem of evil. He does not feel the need to find God's reason for the evil He allows or creates in order to continue to believe in God's goodness. It is not that he already has a theodicy. He does not, nor does God, speaking out of the whirlwind, provide Job with his reason for evil. Job does not even have what we may call a 'theological interest' in the religious problem of evil. He is not among those who have sought to justify God's ways to men, to defend God, or to show that God's existence, as an all-good, all-knowing, and all-powerful Being, is compatible with the existence of evil, not necessarily for the

---

[5] John T. Wilcox calls this the 'orthodox' or 'traditional' view or doctrine in his *The Bitterness of Job* (Ann Arbor MI: University of Michigan Press, 1989), 10–11.

[6] Cf. Wesley Morriston 'God's answer to Job', *Religious Studies*, 32 (1996). On 340 he lists four 'mutually inconsistent propositions' that constitute 'the problem of Job'. They are:

1. God is making Job suffer.
2. A just God would not cause an innocent person [to] suffer as Job has suffered.
3. God is just.
4. Job is innocent of any wrong-doing serious enough to justify the punishment he has received.

On my interpretation all four are true—if we make (2) read 'A just God would not cause an innocent person *to be punished as it appears Job is being punished*'. Notice how Morriston shifts from 'suffer' in (2) to 'punishment' in (4).

sake of their own faith, but to buttress the faith of others or simply to try to resolve the theological problem.

The Third Element of Job-Like Belief

For Job to continue to have faith in God he must trust in God, and his continuing trust in God requires his belief in God's goodness. His belief in God's goodness does not require an understanding of God's reason for allowing or creating evil. It is, however, essential that Job unfalteringly believes in God's goodness and the goodness of God's creation (the second element in Job-like belief). But whence this conviction? Job *knows* his Redeemer lives. Whence this knowledge? These questions bring us to the third element of Job-like belief. In order to pursue these questions, and to address the third element, we need now to bring into our purview more of the biblical tradition as it relates to Job-like belief. In particular we need to look at a strain of the biblical tradition that I find well represented in the Psalms.

In the Psalms and elsewhere, for this tradition, there is a beholding of God and God's goodness in what is majestic and quotidian in creation. The Psalmist is aware of God's presence in all of his life: the heavens tell of the glory of the Lord, but God is also present in the Psalmist's going out and coming in (Psalms 19.1 and 121.8).[7] The Psalmist could not

escape God's presence should he want to: '[W]hither shall I flee from thy presence?' the Psalmist asks; even in Sheol, God is there, and even though the Psalmist should 'take the wings of the morning and dwell in the uttermost parts of the sea', God is there to lead him (Psalms 139.7-9). But the Psalmist's experience of God is also an experience of the goodness of God. 'O taste and see that the LORD is good!' he cries (Psalms 34.8). 'The heavens proclaim his righteousness' (Psalms 97.6); '[T]he LORD is good; his steadfast love endures for ever' (Psalms 100.5); 'Thy steadfast love, O LORD, extends to the heavens, thy faithfulness to the clouds' (Psalms 36.5). In various Psalms the Psalmist speaks of God's goodness, love, righteousness, and mercy.

This strain of religious sensibility, evident in the Psalms, does not begin or end with the Psalms. Here is a twentieth-century expression of this sensibility: 'Walking in a garden, or through the fields, a man of sensitive spirit may suddenly become livingly aware, through the contemplation of the beauty and richness and orderly reliability of nature, of the steadfast goodness of God toward man—including himself—in all his weakness and dependency.'[8] It is a part of the self-understanding of the Job-like believer that she/he is *aware* of God's goodness in the things of life, in God's creation. This, again, is not to be aware of God's reason for allowing or creating evil, but to be

[7] While the Psalms may have several authors, I will follow tradition and speak of 'the Psalmist' as their author. I have discussed the experience of God's presence as a discovery or beholding of God's presence, along with the epistemological issues that attend it, in my *The Cognitivity of Religion: Three Perspectives* (London: Macmillan, and Berkeley and Los Angeles CA: University of California Press, 1985), 104ff.

[8] H. H. Farmer *The World and God*, 2nd edn (London: James Nisbet and Co. Ltd; New York NY: Harper and Row, 1936), 118 of ch. 7. Pages 107–127 of ch. 7 are repr. in John Hick (ed.) *Classical and Contemporary Readings in the Philosophy of Religion* (Englewood Cliffs NJ: Prentice-Hall, 1964), 352.

aware of God's effulgent goodness and, in particular, of God's goodness toward oneself. The analogy here is believing in, or knowing, the goodness of another person, in particular her/his goodness toward oneself, which is the soul of trust in another. The Job-like believer, in believing in and in experiencing the goodness of God, finds her/himself in a relationship to God, a relationship of trust or faith in God and in God's goodness.

The particularly revealing instantiation of the analogy is a child's trust of a parent. In a happy parent–child relationship, the child is aware of the loving parent's goodness toward her/him and trusts the parent, even if the reasons for the parent's decisions are often not understood. In this way, in the strain of biblical tradition I am drawing upon, God is thought of as a loving father, a heavenly father, or, just as appropriately, as a mother. Julian of Norwich, in her *Showings*, says,

> The mother may sometimes suffer the child to fall and to be distressed in various ways, for its own benefit, but she can never suffer any kind of peril to come to her child, because of her love. And though our earthly mother may suffer her child to perish our heavenly Mother Jesus may never suffer us who are his children to perish. . . .[9]

Eleonore Stump in her quasi-autobiographical essay, 'The mirror of evil', also uses the image of God as a loving mother, and she says that Job ' in seeing the face of a loving God . . . has an answer to his question about why God afflicted him . . . a general answer [that] lets Job see that God allows his suffering for his own spiritual or psychological good, out of love for him'.[10] Stump is close to Julian in the reason for suffering that she puts forward: suffering is for one's own benefit or one's own spiritual good. To offer such a reason is to offer a proto-theodicy, and I have suggested that we do not find a theodicy in the Book of Job. On my reading, Job's trust in God does not fail, and so we may say, using a phrase used by Julian that is a variant of a phrase found in the Psalms, that Job, believing in God's goodness, believes that all will be well.[11] But to believe that all will be well is not to offer a reason for evil; it is simply to affirm one's trust in an all-powerful God's goodness. To the extent that the Job-like believer is aware of God's goodness and love, she/he is aware that all will be well, even in the absence of an understood reason for one's suffering and for evil generally.

There is another valuable element of Stump's essay that we should notice at this point. In the passage just quoted, Stump allows that Job 'see[s] the face of a loving God'. She is aware that when we humans recognize one another it is by means of a 'cognitive facult[y] that we don't understand much about but regularly and appropriately rely upon'.[12] Our intuitive recognition of evil, and of goodness, she suggests, is similar in its reliance on cognitive faculties not well

[9] Julian of Norwich *Showings* (long text) in Edmund Colledge, OSA and James Walsh, SJ (tr. and eds) *Julian of Norwich: Showings* (New York NY: Ramsey, and Toronto: Paulist Press, 1978), 300–301.
[10] Eleonore Stump 'The mirror of evil', in Thomas V. Morris (ed.) *God and the Philosophers: The Reconciliation of Faith and Reason* (New York NY and Oxford: Oxford University Press, 1994), 242, 246, n. 10.
[11] Julian of Norwich *Showings* (long text), 225; Psalms 128.2.
[12] Stump 'The mirror of evil', 239.

understood. So, seeing the face of God will involve this kind of intuitive recognition. Her point is useful, I think. I would observe, however, that the category of experience in the Psalms is not seeing the face of God; it is coming into the presence of God, and, often, coming into the presence of a loving and righteous God. Experiencing the presence of God, of a loving God, in creation, though, would be like recognizing the face of someone in that it would not be by means of a definitive feature we can specify. If so, such a beholding of God's loving presence would be very different from reasoning to God's existence or love on the basis of design. It would be like a child's being aware of a parent's caring love though the general presentation of the parent's loving presence. As in the quotation above, one may become aware of God's goodness through the general 'contemplation' of the beauty and richness of nature.

God's Goodness

For the Job-like believer, then, there is the sense that she/he is aware of God's goodness; and if Job-like believers are as they understand themselves to be, they are indeed aware of God's goodness. Allowing this much leaves open the character of God's goodness and of the goodness of God's creation; and some have suggested that the goodness of God or of God's creation should not be understood as *moral* goodness. Marilyn McCord Adams and John Wilcox see divine goodness as a form of *aesthetic* goodness. For Adams, divine incommensurate goodness is to be understood aesthetically, and for

Wilcox, in the Book of Job, nature's goodness is its beauty.

Adams is concerned with 'horrendous evils', which she understands as great evils, 'the participation in which . . . constitutes prima facie reason to doubt whether the participant's life could . . . be a great good to him/her on the whole'.[13] Examples of horrendous evil include the Holocaust, other mass exterminations and genocides, and, at the individual level, rape and child abuse. While Adams argues that horrendous evils and the existence of God's goodness are possible together, she does not offer a divine morally sufficient reason for allowing such evils. She believes that seeking such a 'global' morally sufficient reason that God might have is misguided, and that such proffered reasons are ultimately unsatisfying.[14] Rather, she seeks to show that horrendous evils are compossible with the existence of an omniscient, omnipotent, perfectly good God by turning attention to the aesthetic dimension of individual lives.

She does not argue that God allows horrendous evils because such evils, though negatively valued in isolation, are necessary for the final beauty of the whole.[15] Her focus is on individual persons and their experience of or participation in horrendous evil. For Adams, individual human lives have an important aesthetic dimension in which 'life narratives' are constructed, and horrendous evils operate in that dimension in that they interrupt the effort of individual human persons to fashion 'the materials of their lives into wholes of positive significance'. For Adams, what is 'criterial for solving the problem of horrendous

[13] Marilyn McCord Adams *Horrendous Evils and the Goodness of God* (Ithaca NY and London: Cornell University Press, 1999), 26.
[14] *Ibid.*, 54.
[15] *Ibid.*, 149.

evils [is] the idea that God guarantee to created persons lives that are great goods to them on the whole'. God must '*beautify* the person'. This would be done by God's giving individual persons what is needed to 'recognize and appropriate meanings sufficient to render [her/his life] worth living' in the face of experienced horrendous evil.[16] God must give the individual the imaginative power to weave horrendous evils into a narrative that creates a life narrative of positive meaning.

Wilcox's approach is different. Wilcox, heeding God's speeches toward the end of the Book of Job, argues that God does not establish the justice of His ways (which is in accord with our earlier observation). Rather, God shows Job the smallness of human understanding and beyond that, Wilcox argues, God brings Job to see 'the goodness, or beauty, or awesomeness of the created world of nature', but it is a beauty in 'some amoral and often harsh sense'.[17] Wilcox seems to be very much aware that one might come to see the awesomeness of nature—in the presence of lightning and thunder, storms, the great beasts of nature, and the movements of the heavens—and have no sense of God's moral presence.[18]

The suggestion I find in the biblical tradition I am following is that we humans are such that when we are allowed to lift up our eyes and to behold God's creation, we will behold God's goodness, righteousness, and love in it, so that, in addition to our standing in awe before the transcendent majesty of creation, we might well be moved to bless the name of the Lord and

to be joyful. In the same way, in this biblical tradition, upon being given the capacity to find positive meaning in our lives in the face of horrendous evil we might thank God for His goodness toward us. Beholding God's goodness, we trust God and thereby enter into, or revivify, a trusting relationship to God: we have faith in God and believe, in the Psalmist's phrase, that all will be well. Is this beheld goodness God's *moral* goodness reflected in the moral goodness of creation? I think that it includes a moral dimension. In the strain of religious tradition I am drawing upon, God's unfaltering goodness, love, and righteousness are never in doubt. A Job-like believer feels aware of God's goodness, love, and righteousness. If we become aware of the beneficent love or concern that another person has toward us, surely we become aware of something of moral significance in her/his attitude toward us. So too with the job-like believer's becoming aware of God's love toward her or him, and God's righteousness toward all: God's goodness in this tradition must be in significant part moral goodness.

On the other hand, beholding God's goodness and love in creation is not to discover God's moral reason for allowing or creating evil, and this means that there is a gap in our understanding of God's goodness, given the way we most often think of moral goodness. If a person is morally good, then if she/he does not prevent evil, she/he must have a morally sufficient reason for not doing so. Furthermore, if we enter the judgement

---

[16] *Ibid.*, 189, 148, 149 (Adams's emphasis), and 156.

[17] Wilcox *The Bitterness of Job*, 212, 217.

[18] Morriston says, 'The book of Job moves back and forth between these two poles: between the idea of a God who cares about the doings of particular men like Job, and the idea of a God who is almost too big, too mysterious, too wholly other, for anything like that to make sense', 'God's answer to Job', 356. Morriston suggests that the Book of Job does not perfectly reconcile these two poles. Wilcox in effect rejects the first for the second.

that a person has such a reason for not preventing some evil, great or small, we should be able to cite this reason.

Now, even if we could somehow propose a morally sufficient reason for God's allowing or creating evil, in embracing any such divine morally sufficient reason, we may feel the kind of moral repugnance that Alyosha in *The Brothers Karamazov* felt at the prospect of God's making human happiness rest on the suffering of a tortured child. When Alyosha's brother Ivan asks him if *he* would consent to being the architect of such a world order, Alyosha says that he would not.[19] The sort of reason that God might have for the evils done to children, and all the other moral and natural evils of the world, defies our moral imagination—a point that Marilyn McCord Adams sees with great clarity.[20]

Still, *if* we have come to know that God is good and is loving, then we can be confident that God's goodness will prevail, and all will be well, even if we cannot speak of God's reasons for evil.

The Cognitive Position of Job-Like Believers

If we allow that Job-like believers are aware of God's goodness, and so are as they understand themselves to be, then we should allow that they have a particular cognitive standing regarding evil that determines their logical attitude toward

evil as being no evidence whatsoever against God's existence. In fact, they *properly* would not regard evil as evidence of any sort or degree against God's goodness or existence. For if they know there is a God whose goodness shines through creation, then whatever might seem to others to be evidence against God's goodness cannot really be that. The logic here is general. If someone, S, knows something, P, then what appears to others to be evidence against P will not appear to S to be evidence against P, and, moreover, it will not be evidence against P if S really knows P to be true. If I know that I have just put three oranges in the bowl before me on the table, I will not take it as evidence that there are only two if someone says from across the room that she can see only two or if I see an image of the bowl in a mirror that shows only two. Of course in a case like this there is always a possibility (in a weak sense of 'possibility') that one is mistaken in the initial judgement, and so does not really know—I might have put only two oranges in the bowl, thinking I handled three, perhaps due to distraction.

So let us consider another case where the possibility of initial error is eliminated or reduced to an utter minimum. Let us say that I, a house guest in a wealthy home, one night, after all are asleep, steal the jewels of my hostess. In order to cover my tracks I frame the butler. I plant evidence that will

[19] Fyoder Dostoyevsky *The Brothers Karamazov*, bk 5, ch. 4 'Rebellion'; David Magarshack (tr.) *The Brothers Karamazov* (Baltimore MD: Penguin Books, 1958), vol. 1, 287–288. 'Rebellion' is reprinted in Pike *God and Evil*, see 16.
[20] Adams *Horrendous Evils and the Goodness of God*, 54. Others have appreciated that a proposed morally sufficient reason, given to God by a theodicy to justify such evils as those presented by Ivan Karamazov, would register on our moral sense as repugnant and insensitive. See Stewart R. Sutherland *God, Jesus and Belief* (Oxford: Blackwell, 1984), 23–25, and D. Z. Phillips 'The problem of evil', in Stuart C. Brown (ed.) *Reason and Religion* (Ithaca, NY and London: Cornell University Press, 1977), 115–116. Peter Byrne cites Phillips and Sutherland and critically discusses their views in his *The Moral Interpretation of Religion* (Grand Rapids M1 and Cambridge: Eerdmans, 1998), 139–148.

incriminate him. I leave his glove by the jewel cabinet. I lift his fingerprints from a drinking glass and transfer them to the glass of the cabinet. I use the key to the jewel cabinet issued to him and leave it in the cabinet lock. The police are called and dutifully investigate. As I planned, they find the evidence I planted: the glove, the fingerprints, the key. As they collect these items of evidence (as the police take them to be), the police, quite properly, begin to think that the butler did it. But should I, along with the police, begin to think that, after all, perhaps the butler did it? Clearly not. Notice that it does not really matter whether I planted the evidence. Say that the butler had just happened to leave his glove at the scene, his fingerprints on the cabinet glass, and his key in the lock. Still I would be quite irrational to take these items as evidence that the butler had stolen the jewels when I know full well that I took them. These items, I could allow, are *seeming* evidence that the butler did it, which, from my standpoint, are fortuitously taken to be real evidence by the police. But I would be quite irrational if I took them to be any real evidence at all that the butler had committed the crime. The same holds in other cases of knowing. Thus, given that the Job-like believer *knows* that God is good and that God's goodness shines through creation, she/he would not, and should not, see evil as any evidence against God's goodness.

While we may have a question about whether Job-like believers are truly aware of God's goodness, they have no such question; and thus it is not surprising if they, like Job in the prologue when he replies to his wife, do not see evil as evidence against God's goodness. Moreover, if they are as they see themselves, they are right in not regarding evil as evidence against God's goodness. Job-like believers, if they wished, could of course pursue the problem of evil out of what I earlier called a 'theological interest'. If they did so, then the problem of evil would be for them, in Nelson Pike's words, a 'non-crucial perplexity of relatively minor importance'.[21] Pike suggests that this is the case for those who accept God's existence as an 'item of faith' and for those who hold God's existence on the 'basis of an a priori argument'. Those with either of these positions do not approach the subject of God's existence as a 'quasi-scientific subject', arguing for the existence of God on the basis of observed facts. It is only for this latter approach, taken by Cleanthes in Hume's *Dialogues Concerning Natural Religion*, Pike argues, that evil can weigh against other observations and take on the import of negative evidence.

I believe that Pike makes an important point here, but we should appreciate that the cognitive status of Job-like believers is distinguishable from the status of those who accept God's existence on faith and distinguishable from the status of those who rely upon an a priori argument. Those who accept it as an item of faith that God exists (whose faith does not have a provenance and grounding in an experience of God, as it does for Job-like believers), would seem to have to give some evidential weight to evil, even if they have not formed their belief in God through a 'quasi-scientific' weighing of evidence for and against; for the existence of evil would seem to be some indication that their belief in an all-good and all-powerful God is false. At least they could not regard evil as evidentially irrelevant because they *know* God is good, as Job-like believers

[21] Nelson Pike 'Hume on evil', reprinted in *idem God and Evil*, 102.

can do.[22] Those who accept the existence of God on the basis of an a priori argument will have knowledge of God's existence only if the argument they depend on is logically sound. Their discounting evil as evidence, then, is contingent on the logical soundness of an argument, while this is not the case with Job-like believers, who behold God's existence and goodness in creation.

Seeing God's Goodness through Evil

The scope and penetration of the Job-like believer's perception of God's goodness can hardly be overestimated. Eleonore Stump in 'The mirror of evil' says this:

> . . . in an odd sort of way, the mirror of evil can also lead us to God. A loathing focus on the evils of our world and ourselves prepares us to be the more startled by the taste of true goodness when we find it and the

more determined to follow that taste until we see where it leads. And where it leads is to the truest goodness of all. . . . The mirror of evil becomes translucent, and we can see through it to the goodness of God.[23]

There are, I believe, two associated ideas here. One is that our perception of evils can *lead to* an awareness of God and God's goodness: focusing on evil we can, in the terms of the Psalms, come to taste more keenly goodness when we find it in human affairs and then come to see—become aware of—God's ultimate goodness. The other idea is that we can come to see God's goodness *through* experiencing evil. Both ideas are at home in the tradition of Job-like belief, but the second idea is, in particular. In that tradition, evil is not evidence against God's goodness, and evil, being from God, can only be an expression of and 'mirror' God's goodness.[24]

Job-like believers do not seek a theodicy as something relevant to their

---

[22] I will leave to one side the position of Aquinas that faith itself gives us a kind of knowledge: *ST*, II–II q. 2, a. 4.

[23] Srump 'The mirror of evil',242.

[24] In 'The mirror of evil', Stump, it seems to me, is close to the religious sensibility of Job-like belief. Elsewhere she has defended a theodicy offered by Aquinas, that pain and suffering can lead to the greatest spiritual benefit and happiness, to be united with God in heaven: 'Aquinas on the sufferings of Job' in Daniel Howard-Snyder (ed.) *The Evidential Argument from Evil* (Bloomington IN: Indiana University Press, 1996). The proto-theodicy that Stump offers in 'The mirror of evil', to which I referred earlier, is essentially a form of Aquinas' theodicy with unspecified spiritual benefits.

In a more recent article Stump develops the category of second-person experience: 'Second-person accounts and the problem of evil' in Tommi Lehtonen and Timo Koistinen (eds) *Perspectives in Contemporary Philosophy of Religion* (Helsinki: Luther-Agricola-Society, 2000). In second-person experience 'you interact consciously and directly with another person' (90). In an example she uses, a sick child, 'who has a shared history of loving relations with his mother [may] know that she allows him to suffer only because she loves him. But an outsider [with] no relation to her may well want to know what the connection between the suffering and the child's well-being is, before he is willing to grant that the mother is justified in allowing the child to suffer' (112). Stump in this article keeps in place her proto-theodicy (or, here, a theodicy). Setting that aside, in this article too she draws our attention to the religious significance of an experience of God's goodness. However, for her, the experience of Job that is relevant is his face-to-face conversation with God at the end of the Book of Job. The experience that I find internal to a Job-like believer's self-understanding is an experience of God's goodness in God's creation, in accord with the sensibility of the Psalms, that Job, understood as a Job-like believer, would have had before the prologue.

faith because they do not have the problem of evil that seeks a theodicy. It is a part of God's goodness that we should receive evil from God. If, however, the evil becomes unendurable so that it comes to seem to such a believer that God, if God is good, would not allow such things to happen, then doubt enters and the believer no longer sees her/himself as knowing. She/he ceases to be aware of God's goodness and, no longer beholding God's goodness, no longer knows God to be good. There is a loss of Job-like faith. Now evil takes on evidential import against the goodness of God, and now a theodicy becomes something that is religiously relevant to her/his position. But now such a believer has ceased to be a Job-like believer.

The Practical Problem of Evil

What would lead to the loss of Job-like faith or belief is not the recognition of evil per se, but the rising sense that God, if good, would not allow the evil one now confronts. It must be kept in mind that Job-like believers do not deny the existence of moral and natural evil. They may be acutely aware of it, and this means that they are in a position to recognize the practical problem of evil. Marilyn McCord Adams writes: 'Evil is a problem for everyone regardless of religious or philosophical orientation—the problem of how to cope in some way as to survive and, if possible, flourish (hence a practical problem), of how—despite all—to win lives filled with positive meaning (and so an existential problem).'[25] If the existential problem is how to find again meaning in our personal lives when we experience horrendous evil (Adams's central concern), the practical problem is how to address, mitigate, and prevent natural and moral evil in our lives and in the lives of others. Adams is of course right that evil is a problem—a practical problem—for everyone 'regardless of religious or philosophical orientation'. John Kekes, who rejects the religious idea 'that the scheme of things is good', addresses what he calls 'the secular problem of evil', which is simply 'the prevalence of evil'.[26] Often those who oppose and seek to mitigate the evils of the world address natural evils such as famine and the rampage of AIDS. One may think here of such nongovernmental organizations (NGOs) as Oxfam and Doctors Without Borders. Sometimes the effort is to oppose moral evil, as with Amnesty International. There is, I think, informing all such efforts a sense that evil is objectively evil, that is, evil irrespective of individual judgement or cultural discernment. Certainly there are gross evils, ranging from famine to the sexual enslavement of children, that are recognized as evils nearly universally, even if there is not universal agreement on the subtler forms of psychological evil.

While Job in the epilogue of the Book of Job does not recognize the practical problem of evil and does not set himself to remedy and oppose evils in the world, this reaction to evil is hardly closed to Job-like believers. In fact, on religious and moral grounds, Job-like believers should recognize and address the practical problem of evil, although this does not say how evil is to be opposed or which evils are to be focused upon. Let me end by returning to Dostoyevsky's Alyosha and his

[25] Adams *Horrendous Evils and the Goodness of God*, 181.
[26] John Kekes *Facing Evil* (Princeton NJ: Princeton University Press, 1990), 4.

reaction to evil. In most discussions of the problem of evil, if some part of *The Brothers Karamazov* is referred to, it is the chapter entitled 'Rebellion', in which Ivan catalogues evils done to children. I myself referred to it earlier. It is at the end of this chapter that Alyosha confesses to his brother that, if he were the architect of the world order, he would not found human happiness on the torture of a single child. In effect, Alyosha is rejecting that kind of theodicy that seeks a justification of suffering in the creation of a greater good. No better theodicy is offered by Alyosha or Dostoyevsky. The problem of evil, the theological problem, drops from view. However the practical problem of evil does not.

In book 10 of the novel Dostoyevsky introduces a number of schoolboys, prominent among whom is thirteen-year-old Kolya. Kolya is an only child, and his mother, a young widow, is overly protective. Kolya is taunted by the boys with being a mother's darling, and Kolya reacts with a kind of aloofness toward his mother, which causes her grief. At the same time he impresses his schoolfellows with a feat of derring-do—he lies down between the rails and lets a train pass over him. He thus gains the reputation of being a 'desperate character'[27] among the schoolboys, who now start to look up to him. As a part of his role, in the streets Kolya lies to and treats disrespectfully peasants and tradespeople. As a further part of his role, he nurtures a growing coldness toward his mother—with some lapses—and toward the other boys. When a younger student, Ilyusha, joins the school and seeks to attach himself to Kolya, Kolya responds with ever more coldness the more Ilyusha expresses fondness for him. Ilyusha comes to suffer greatly at the hands of the boys, once it is clear to them that he is not under Kolya's protection. Ilyusha's father is a drunkard, and the boys use this fact to taunt him. They get into fights, and Kolya does nothing. One day, after school, Ilyusha rushes at his tormentors and Kolya does nothing to prevent the fighting. He just stands and watches from a short distance. Ilyusha, in desperation, takes out his penknife and, rushing up to Kolya, stabs him in the thigh. Kolya, after the event, tells Alyosha about all this, and says he is sorry. He says that he is a 'sworn enemy of all sloppy sentiments' and that he wanted 'to train him [Ilyusha] to be a man'.[28]

Alyosha comes into the boys' lives because one of the boys has told him about Ilyusha.[29] Ilyusha has become ill, apparently with consumption, and though it is the time of Dmitry's trial, with which Alyosha is preoccupied, he goes regularly to visit Ilyusha. It is on such a visit that Alyosha meets Kolya. Alyosha's role with the boys is that of a mentor, especially for Kolya. In some ways Alyosha is, for the schoolboys, what a contemporary interactive role model is for today's urban gangs. However, there are differences. Alyosha needs to make no effort to keep Kolya and the other boys in school. The boys are not dropouts or in danger of dropping out. In fact Kolya loves to read. He has read Voltaire, and is proud to proclaim himself a socialist. In his notebooks for *The Brothers Karamazov*, Dostoyevsky refers to a variety of incidents that did not make their way into the novel: the torture of a

---

[27] Dostoyevsky *The Brothers Karamazov*, bk 10, ch. 1; *The Brothers Karamazov*, David Magarshack (tr.), vol. 2, 606.

[28] *Ibid.*, bk 10, ch. 4; *The Brothers Karamazov*, David Magarshack (tr.), vol. 2, 626.

[29] *Ibid.*, bk 10, ch. 3; *The Brothers Karamazov*, David Magarshack (tr.), vol. 2, 615.

four-year-old boy, the suicide of a small boy, a shot fired from a window, the theft by boys of money from a trunk.[30] If these actions had been included—depending on how they were developed—the boys, under Kolya's leadership, could have taken on more of the character of young criminals. As the novel is, however, the evils addressed are the psychological evils of coldness, vanity, and aloof pride, especially as found in Kolya. While some may not see these traits as evils, but rather as aspects of personal independence and strength (as Kolya tends to),[31] for Dostoyevsky these are certainly evils, evils of the soul or psychological evils. In Dostoyevsky's presentation, these elements affect even Kolya's expression of generosity.

Before Kolya met Alyosha he wanted to meet him, for there is something 'sympathetic and attractive' in the stories he has heard about Alyosha. In fact, though, Kolya is deeply ambivalent toward Alyosha. He has hitherto 'assumed an air of contemptuous indifference' when Alyosha was spoken of by the boys. He does not want to 'disgrace' himself. He wants to be friends with Alyosha but does not want to show how anxious he is to be his friend.[32] It is as though good and bad aspects of Kolya's soul were struggling with one another. Without putting too fine a point on it, Alyosha counteracts these psychological evils and encourages the goodness in Kolya's character, and in the character of the other boys. In the third and final chapter of the Epilogue—the very end of the novel—Alyosha speaks to the boys. The occasion of their gathering is the death of Ilyusha, who has succumbed to his consumptive condition. Alyosha does not speak of the evil of little Ilyusha dying of consumption, but of how he should be remembered as a good boy and as dear to them. 'Oh, how I loved him!' exclaims Kolya.[33] He has found in himself what before he would call a 'sloppy sentiment'. Alyosha does not name evil or speak to it; he interacts with and speaks to the boys—not with righteous denunciation, but with communicative love—and thereby mitigates evil.

Allowing that evils of the soul are evils, we may well feel that the evils that Alyosha remedies—the vanity and coldness of young boys—are not that serious, compared to the terrible suffering inflicted on children that Ivan brings forward. Another author might put his protagonist against a greater evil, as when Camus enlisted Rieux to oppose the plague. Rieux, of course, is not a religious believer in God, but one need not be a Rieux to oppose the natural and moral plagues of the world. A contemporary Alyosha might address the banal evils near to hand, or he might be active in Oxfam or Amnesty International, or be a hospital worker in Lambaréné or Calcutta. Yet, as he is in the novel, Alyosha *is* addressing the practical problem of evil and seeking to remedy evil as he finds it.

Alyosha does not react to the evil of the world by rejecting or defying God, as does his brother, or by holding his religious faith in abeyance until he can find an adequate theodicy. Alyosha has no theodicy to offer and, like Ivan, rejects a

[30] *The Notebooks for* The Brothers Karamazov, Edward Wasiolek (ed. and tr.) (Chicago IL and London: University of Chicago Press, 1971), 183.
[31] Dostoyevsky *The Brothers Karamazov*, bk 10, ch. 4; *The Brothers Karamazov*, David Magarshack (tr.), vol. 2, 623.
[32] *Ibid.*
[33] *Ibid.*, 912.

theodicy that would justify evils done to children by citing an ultimate good that requires such evils. In this sense Alyosha has no answer to the religious problem of evil, which he does not address. Yet he is aware of evil. He engages evil and seeks to lessen it in the lives of the boys he helps. Both Ivan and Alyosha, it is to be noted, react to the evil in the lives of children, but their reactions are utterly different. Ivan's reaction is to indict God. Alysosha's reaction is to help children themselves. Alyosha does so with a vigour of spirit equal to his brother's defiance. The religious problem of evil, then, he neither has nor addresses, even though he is invited to the problem by Ivan, while the practical problem of evil he both has and addresses. He addresses evil as an expression of his religious commitment to God and neighbour, and in answer to the moral and religious demands that apply to us all.[34] In this sense, in *The Brothers Karamazov*, Alysoha transmutes the one problem of evil into the other.

Alyosha, we should allow, may or may not embody all the elements of Job-like belief. Dostoyevsky makes it clear that Father Zossima, Alyosha's religious mentor, has had the experience of beholding God's goodness in the world, but it is less clear that Alyosha has had such an experience.[35] What is clear is that Alyosha believes in God and accepts life in the world as good—and that he seeks to remedy evil as it confronts him. Following Alyosha, or the religious sensibility he expresses, with its appreciation of our moral and religious reposnsibility to stand up to evil, Job-like believers would face evil and seek to mitigate it. In doing so they would transmute the problem of evil that others have into the practical problem of evil.

[34] The general moral obligations to prevent harm where we can and to do good where we can are widely recognized, and of course the religious obligation to love our neighbours is recognized by Christian believers, Job-like or not.

[35] Zossima's experience, had when he was a young man, is recalled by him in *The Brothers Karamazov*, bk 6, ch. 2; *The Brothers Karamazov*, David Magarshack (tr.), vol. 1, 352. Alysoha's rapturous experience beneath the starry heavens the night he leaves the cell in which Father Zossima's coffin lay is, it seems, unclear in this regard; *The Brothers Karamazov*, bk 7, ch. 4; *The Brothers Karamazov*, David Magarshack (tr.), vol. 2, 426–427.

Chapter 7

Miracles

In popular discourse we quite properly use the term "miracle" in several ways or senses. The term can be used, for instance, in reference to an occurrence that was very unlikely or unexpected. A forest fire burns up the canyon toward our house. It is unstoppable, but at the last minute the wind shifts and our house is saved. Or we might use the term to describe a natural but wonderful event, as when we speak of the "miracle of birth." Sometimes we apply the term to an event that goes counter to the natural order of things, as we would do if we called an instance of levitation a miracle. Such events as these may be referred to as "miracles" by the religious and the nonreligious alike, for such events may not be regarded as having any *religious* significance.

When we look at what is meant by "miracle" in religious traditions, we again find some variety. For instance events in this last sense we identified— an event that goes counter to the natural order of things or against the "laws of nature"—are often regarded as having religious significance in different traditions, but they may not be attributed to God. They may be attributed to a religious founder, a saint, or to a prophet, as when in Buddhism miracles are attributed to the Buddha and in Christianity miracles are attributed to saints.

The basic religious meaning of *miracle* that is addressed by the readings in this chapter is an event, often unlikely, always wonderful in some way, that was caused by God. In this meaning, miracles have religious significance and— if they have occurred—are acts of God. Within the three main Western monotheistic traditions, miracles in this basic sense are caused by the one God. In other polytheistic traditions, such as Hinduism, miracles in this sense may be caused by one god or another. This is the basic meaning that forms the focus of this chapter, although, there are three significant variations on this basic meaning.

The first variation on this basic meaning of miracle is *intervention miracle*. An intervention miracle is an act of God by which God *intervenes in the natural order* and causes an event that goes against and so "violates" a natural law. Intervention miracles are *physically impossible* (because they go counter to the natural order that defines what is physically possible), although they are not *logically impossible* (for their descriptions do not contain any logical contradiction). Often when we think of a religious miracle we think of a miracle in this sense. In each of the three Western monotheistic traditions several examples of miracles in this sense are widely recognized and accepted by believers. Here are some examples. In Judaism: Moses hearing God speak out of the bush that burns without being consumed (Exodus 3.2-6) and the parting of the Red Sea (Exodus 14.21). In Christianity: Jesus' turning water to wine at the wedding in Cana (John 2.7-9) and raising Lazarus from the dead (John 11.43-44). In Islam: God's revealing, through Gabriel, the Qur'an to Muhammad and Muhammad's ascension to paradise, where he talked with the Prophets that preceded him.

The second variation is what may be called *contingency miracle*. The name of this category is from R.F. Holland's essay "The Miraculous," where he coins the term "the contingency concept" of miracle, in contrast to "the violation concept." Holland argues that the underlying idea of a miracle is that it is something for which God may be thanked by the religious, and sometimes this may be an event that is a violation of natural law, but sometimes it is not. Sometimes it is a coincidence that does not violate natural law. For Holland, however, it would have to be the right kind of coincidence to qualify. It would have to have religious significance and invite a religious believer to thank God for its occurrence, as when a coincidence results in someone's life being saved.

The third variation in the basic concept of *miracle*, according to which a miracle is an event, often unlikely, always wonderful, that in some way is caused by God, is what we may call *natural miracle*. This category or sense of the miraculous is implicit in those forms of religious sensibility that find it appropriate to thank God for many of the ordinary things of life, such as, the bread on the table.

In this chapter we have four readings. The first reading is Section 10, "Of Miracles," from David Hume's *An Enquiry Concerning Human Understanding*, in which Hume first argues against the reasonableness of believing in intervention miracles and then argues against their possible occurrence. The second reading consists of a chapter, and sections of chapters, from Richard Swinburne's *The Concept of Miracle*, in which he examines the question of whether evidence could establish the occurrence of an intervention miracle. In the third reading, from "The Miraculous," R.F. Holland argues that the idea that a miracle violates a natural law is too narrow, and he introduces the "contingency concept" of miracle. In the last reading, a section from "Miracles," James Kellenberger describes and defends the category of natural miracle.

DAVID HUME

Of Miracles

David Hume's "Of Miracles," Section 10 of his *An Enquiry Concerning Human Understanding*, is perhaps the most influential philosophical critique of miracles ever written. Since the publication of *An Enquiry Concerning Human Understanding* in 1748, "Of Miracles" has become a classic to be acknowledged and contended with by subsequent writers on miracles. While "Of Miracles" is open to interpretation to some extent, on one straightforward reading Hume is arguing against intervention miracles, or miracles that violate natural laws, in two ways. First he argues that it is never reasonable to believe a report that a violation of a law of nature has occurred, for any such report must go counter to the "uniform experience" of humanity that establishes the law of nature. He argues, secondly, that the very idea of a violation of the laws of nature is confused. Say that an abundance of testimony established that an extraordinary event, a candidate for a violation of a natural law, occurred. Then, Hume says, we ought to "search for the causes whence it might be derived." That is, Hume is saying, we ought to look for the *natural explanation* for the event. Hume's argument is that if it is established that the unusual event really took place, this is sufficient for the conclusion that it is in accord with natural laws and our previous conception of the natural law involved was deficient. Thus whenever an event is established as having occurred, it is established that it is *not* a violation of a natural law, but at most only unusual.*

SECTION X

Of Miracles

PART I

There is, in Dr. Tillotson's writings, an argument against the *real presence*, which is as concise, and elegant, and strong as any argument can possibly be supposed against a doctrine, so little worthy of a serious refutation. It is acknowledged on all hands, says that learned prelate, that the authority, either of the scripture or of tradition, is founded merely in the testimony of the apostles, who were eye-witnesses to those miracles of our Saviour, by which he proved his divine mission. Our evidence, then, for the truth of the *Christian* religion is less than the evidence for the truth of our senses; because, even in the first authors of our religion, it was no greater; and it is evident it must diminish in passing from them to their disciples; nor can any one rest such confidence in their testimony, as in the immediate object of his senses. But a weaker evidence can never destroy a stronger; and therefore, were the doctrine of the real presence ever so clearly revealed in scripture, it were directly contrary to the rules of just reasoning to give our assent to it. It contradicts sense, though both the scripture and tradition, on which it is supposed to be built, carry not such evidence with them as sense; when they are considered merely as external evidences, and are not brought home to every one's breast, by the immediate operation of the Holy Spirit.

Nothing is so convenient as a decisive argument of this kind, which must at least *silence* the most arrogant bigotry and superstition, and free us from their impertinent solicitations. I flatter myself, that I have discovered an argument of a like nature, which, if just, will, with the wise and learned, be an everlasting check to all kinds of superstitious delusion, and consequently, will be useful as long as the world endures. For so long, I presume, will the accounts of miracles and prodigies be found in all history, sacred and profane.

---

* From David Hume, *An Enquiry Concerning Human Understanding.*

Though experience be our only guide in reasoning concerning matters of fact; it must be acknowledged, that this guide is not altogether infallible, but in some cases is apt to lead us into errors. One, who in our climate, should expect better weather in any week of June than in one of December, would reason justly, and conformably to experience; but it is certain, that he may happen, in the event, to find himself mistaken. However, we may observe, that, in such a case, he would have no cause to complain of experience; because it commonly informs us beforehand of the uncertainty, by that contrariety of events, which we may learn from a diligent observation. All effects follow not with like certainty from their supposed causes. Some events are found, in all countries and all ages, to have been constantly conjoined together: Others are found to have been more variable, and sometimes to disappoint our expectations; so that, in our reasonings concerning matter of fact, there are all imaginable degrees of assurance, from the highest certainty to the lowest species of moral evidence.

A wise man, therefore, proportions his belief to the evidence. In such conclusions as are founded on an infallible experience, he expects the event with the last degree of assurance, and regards his past experience as a full *proof* of the future existence of that event. In other cases, he proceeds with more caution: He weighs the opposite experiments: He considers which side is supported by the greater number of experiments: to that side he inclines, with doubt and hesitation; and when at last he fixes his judgement, the evidence exceeds not what we properly call *probability*. All probability, then, supposes an opposition of experiments and observations, where the one side is found to overbalance the other, and to

produce a degree of evidence, proportioned to the superiority. A hundred instances or experiments on one side, and fifty on another, afford a doubtful expectation of any event; though a hundred uniform experiments, with only one that is contradictory, reasonably beget a pretty strong degree of assurance. In all cases, we must balance the opposite experiments, where they are opposite, and deduct the smaller number from the greater, in order to know the exact force of the superior evidence.

To apply these principles to a particular instance; we may observe, that there is no species of reasoning more common, more useful, and even necessary to human life, than that which is derived from the testimony of men, and the reports of eye-witnesses and spectators. This species of reasoning, perhaps, one may deny to be founded on the relation of cause and effect. I shall not dispute about a word. It will be sufficient to observe that our assurance in any argument of this kind is derived from no other principle than our observation of the veracity of human testimony, and of the usual conformity of facts to the reports of witnesses. It being a general maxim, that no objects have any discoverable connexion together, and that all the inferences, which we can draw from one to another, are founded merely on our experience of their constant and regular conjunction; it is evident, that we ought not to make an exception to this maxim in favour of human testimony, whose connexion with any event seems, in itself, as little necessary as any other. Were not the memory tenacious to a certain degree, had not men commonly an inclination to truth and a principle of probity; were they not sensible to shame, when detected in a falsehood: Were not these, I say, discovered by *experience* to be qualities, inherent in human nature, we should never repose the least confidence in human testimony. A man delirious, or noted for falsehood and villany, has no manner of authority with us.

And as the evidence, derived from witnesses and human testimony, is founded on past experience, so it varies with the experience, and is regarded either as a *proof* or a *probability*, according as the conjunction between any particular kind of report and any kind of object has been found to be constant or variable. There are a number of circumstances to be taken into consideration in all judgements of this kind; and the ultimate standard, by which we determine all disputes, that may arise concerning them, is always derived from experience and observation. Where this experience is not entirely uniform on any side, it is attended with an unavoidable contrariety in our judgements, and with the same opposition and mutual destruction of argument as in every other kind of evidence. We frequently hesitate concerning the reports of others. We balance the opposite circumstances, which cause any doubt or uncertainty; and when we discover a superiority on any side, we incline to it; but still with a diminution of assurance, in proportion to the force of its antagonist.

This contrariety of evidence, in the present case, may be derived from several different causes; from the opposition of contrary testimony; from the character or number of the witnesses; from the manner of their delivering their testimony; or from the union of all these circumstances. We entertain a suspicion concerning any matter of fact, when the witnesses contradict each other; when they are but few, or of a doubtful character; when they have an interest in what they affirm; when they deliver their testimony with hesitation, or on the contrary, with too violent asseverations. There are many other particulars of the same kind, which may diminish or destroy the force of any argument, derived from human testimony.

Suppose, for instance, that the fact, which the testimony endeavours to establish, partakes of the extraordinary and the marvellous; in that case, the evidence, resulting from the testimony, admits of a diminution, greater or less, in proportion as the fact is more or less unusual. The reason why we place any credit in witnesses and historians, is not derived from any *connexion*, which we perceive *a priori*, between testimony and reality, but because we are accustomed to find a conformity between them. But when the fact attested is such a one as has seldom fallen under our observation, here is a contest of two opposite experiences; of which the one destroys the other, as far as its force goes, and the superior can only operate on the mind by the force, which remains. The very same principle of experience, which gives us a certain degree of assurance in the testimony of witnesses, gives us also, in this case, another degree of assurance against the fact, which they endeavour to establish; from which contradition there necessarily arises a counterpoize, and mutual destruction of belief and authority.

I should not believe such a story were it told me by Cato, was a proverbial saying in Rome, even during the lifetime of that philosophical patriot[1]. The incredibility

---

[1] Plutarch, in vita Catonis.

of a fact, it was allowed, might invalidate so great an authority.

The Indian prince, who refused to believe the first relations concerning the effects of frost, reasoned justly; and it naturally required very strong testimony to engage his assent to facts, that arose from a state of nature, with which he was unacquainted, and which bore so little analogy to those events, of which he had had constant and uniform experience. Though they were not contrary to his experience, they were not conformable to it[1].

But in order to encrease the probability against the testimony of witnesses, let us suppose, that the fact, which they affirm, instead of being only marvellous, is really miraculous; and suppose also, that the testimony considered apart and in itself, amounts to an entire proof; in that case, there is proof against proof, of which the strongest must prevail, but still with a diminution of its force, in proportion to that of its antagonist.

A miracle is a violation of the laws of nature; and as a firm and unalterable experience has established these laws, the proof against a miracle, from the very nature of the fact, is as entire as any argument from experience can possibly be imagined. Why is it more than probable, that all men must die; that lead cannot, of itself, remain suspended in the air; that fire consumes wood, and is extinguished by water; unless it be, that these events are found agreeable to the laws of nature, and there is required a violation of these laws, or in other words, a miracle to prevent them? Nothing is esteemed a miracle, if it ever happen in the common course of nature. It is no miracle that a man, seemingly in good health, should die on a sudden: because such a kind of death, though more unusual than any other, has yet been frequently observed to happen. But it is a miracle, that a dead man should come to life; because that has never been observed in any age or country. There must, therefore, be a uniform experience against every miraculous event, otherwise the event would not merit that appellation. And as a uniform experience amounts to a proof, there is here a direct and full *proof*, from the nature of the fact, against the existence of any miracle; nor can such a proof be destroyed, or the miracle rendered

---

[1] No Indian, it is evident, could have experience that water did not freeze in cold climates. This is placing nature in a situation quite unknown to him; and it is impossible for him to tell *a priori* what will result from it. It is making a new experiment, the consequence of which is always uncertain. One may sometimes conjecture from analogy what will follow; but still this is but conjecture. And it must be confessed, that, in the present case of freezing, the event follows contrary to the rules of analogy, and is such as a rational Indian would not look for. The operations of cold upon water are not gradual, according to the degrees of cold; but whenever it comes to the freezing point, the water passes in a moment, from the utmost liquidity to perfect hardness. Such an event, therefore, may be denominated *extraordinary*, and requires a pretty strong testimony, to render it credible to people in a warm climate: But still it is not *miraculous*, nor contrary to uniform experience of the course of nature in cases where all the circumstances are the same. The inhabitants of Sumatra have always seen water fluid in their own climate, and the freezing of their rivers ought to be deemed a prodigy: But they never saw water in Muscovy during the winter; and therefore they cannot reasonably be positive what would there be the consequence.

credible, but by an opposite proof, which is superior[1].

The plain consequence is (and it is a general maxim worthy of our attention), 'That no testimony is sufficient to establish a miracle, unless the testimony be of such a kind, that its falsehood would be more miraculous, than the fact, which it endeavours to establish; and even in that case there is a mutual destruction of arguments, and the superior only gives us an assurance suitable to that degree of force, which remains, after deducting the inferior.' When anyone tells me, that he saw a dead man restored to life, I immediately consider with myself, whether it be more probable, that this person should either deceive or be deceived, or that the fact, which he relates, should really have happened. I weigh the one miracle against the other; and according to the superiority, which I discover, I pronounce my decision, and always reject the greater miracle, If the falsehood of his testimony would be more miraculous, than the event which he relates; then, and not till then, can he pretend to command my belief or opinion.

PART II

In the foregoing reasoning we have supposed, that the testimony, upon which a miracle is founded, may possibly amount to an entire proof, and that the falsehood of that testimony would be a real prodigy: But it is easy to shew, that we have been a great deal too liberal in our concession, and that there never was a miraculous event established on so full an evidence.

For *first*, there is not to be found, in all history, any miracle attested by a sufficient number of men, of such unquestioned good-sense, education, and learning, as to secure us against all delusion in themselves; of such undoubted integrity, as to place them beyond all suspicion of any design to deceive others; of such credit and reputation in the eyes of mankind, as to have a great deal to lose in case of their being detected in any falsehood; and at the same time, attesting facts performed in such a public manner and in so celebrated a part of the world, as to render the detection unavoidable: All which circumstances are requisite to give us a full assurance in the testimony of men.

---

[1] Sometimes an event may not, *in itself, seem* to be contrary to the laws of nature, and yet, if it were real, it might, by reason of some circumstances, be denominated a miracle; because, in *fact*, it is contrary to these laws. Thus if a person, claiming a divine authority, should command a sick person to be well, a healthful man to fall down dead, the clouds to pour rain, the winds to blow, in short, should order many natural events, which immediately follow upon his command; these might justly be esteemed miracles, because they are really, in this case, contrary to the laws of nature. For if any suspicion remain, that the event and command concurred by accident, there is no miracle and no transgression of the laws of nature. If this suspicion be removed, there is evidently a miracle, and a transgression of these laws; because nothing can be more contrary to nature than that the voice or command of a man should have such an influence. A miracle may be accurately defined, *a transgression of a law of nature by a particular volition of the Deity, or by the interposition of some invisible agent.* A miracle may either be discoverable by men or not. This alters not its nature and essence. The raising of a house or ship into the air is a visible miracle. The raising of a feather, when the wind wants ever so little of a force requisite for that purpose, is as real a miracle, though not so sensible with regard to us.

Secondly. We may observe in human nature a principle which, if strictly examined, will be found to diminish extremely the assurance, which we might, from human testimony, have, in any kind of prodigy. The maxim, by which we commonly conduct ourselves in our reasonings, is, that the objects, of which we have no experience, resembles those, of which we have; that what we have found to be most usual is always most probable; and that where there is an opposition of arguments, we ought to give the preference to such as are founded on the greatest number of past observations. But though, in proceeding by this rule, we readily reject any fact which is unusual and incredible in an ordinary degree; yet in advancing farther, the mind observes not always the same rule; but when anything is affirmed utterly absurd and miraculous, it rather the more readily admits of such a fact, upon account of that very circumstance, which ought to destroy all its authority. The passion of *surprise* and *wonder*, arising from miracles, being an agreeable emotion, gives a sensible tendency towards the belief of those events, from which it is derived. And this goes so far, that even those who cannot enjoy this pleasure immediately, nor can believe those miraculous events, of which they are informed, yet love to partake of the satisfaction at second-hand or by rebound, and place a pride and delight in exciting the admiration of others.

With what greediness are the miraculous accounts of travellers received, their descriptions of sea and land monsters, their relations of wonderful adventures, strange men, and uncouth manners? But if the spirit of religion join itself to the love of wonder, there is an end of common sense; and human testimony, in these circumstances, loses all pretensions to authority. A religionist may be an enthusiast, and imagine he sees what has no reality: he may know his narrative to be false, and yet persevere in it, with the best intentions in the world, for the sake of promoting so holy a cause: or even where this delusion has not place, vanity, excited by so strong a temptation, operates on him more powerfully than on the rest of mankind in any other circumstances; and self-interest with equal force. His auditors may not have, and commonly have not, sufficient judgement to canvass his evidence: what judgement they have, they renounce by principle, in these sublime and mysterious subjects: or if they were ever so willing to employ it, passion and a heated imagination disturb the regularity of its operations. Their credulity increases his impudence: and his impudence overpowers their credulity.

Eloquence, when at its highest pitch, leaves little room for reason or reflection; but addressing itself entirely to the fancy or the affections, captivates the willing hearers, and subdues their understanding. Happily, this pitch it seldom attains. But what a Tully or a Demosthenes could scarcely effect over a Roman or Athenian audience, every *Capuchin*, every itinerant or stationary teacher can perform over the generality of mankind, and in a higher degree, by touching such gross and vulgar passions.

The many instances of forged miracles, and prophecies, and supernatural events, which, in all ages, have either been detected by contrary evidence, or which detect themselves by their absurdity, prove sufficiently the strong propensity of mankind to the extraordinary and the marvellous, and ought reasonably to beget a suspicion against all relations of this kind. This is our natural way of thinking, even with regard to the most common and most credible events. For instance: There is no kind of report which rises so easily, and spreads so quickly, especially in country places and provincial towns, as those concerning marriages; insomuch that two young persons of equal condition never see each other twice, but the whole neighbourhood immediately join them together. The pleasure of telling a piece of news so interesting, of propagating it, and of being the first reporters of it, spreads the intelligence. And this is so well known, that no man of sense gives attention to these reports, till he find them confirmed by some greater evidence. Do not the same passions, and others still stronger, incline the generality of mankind to believe and report, with the greatest vehemence and assurance, all religious miracles?

Thirdly. It forms a strong presumption against all supernatural and miraculous relations, that they are observed chiefly to abound among ignorant and barbarous nations; or if a civilized people has ever given admission to any of them, that people will be found to have received them from ignorant and barbarous ancestors, who transmitted them with that inviolable sanction and authority, which always attend received opinions. When we peruse the first histories of all nations, we are apt to imagine ourselves transported into some new world; where the whole frame of nature is disjointed, and every element performs its operations in a different manner, from what it does at present. Battles, revolutions, pestilence, famine and death, are never the effect of those natural causes, which we experience. Prodigies, omens, oracles, judgements, quite obscure the few natural events, that are intermingled with them. But as the former grow thinner every page, in proportion as we advance nearer the enlightened ages, we soon learn, that there is nothing mysterious or supernatural in the case, but that all proceeds from the usual propensity of mankind towards the marvellous, and that, though this inclination may at intervals receive a check from sense and learning, it can never be thoroughly extirpated from human nature.

It is strange, a judicious reader is apt to say, upon the perusal of these wonderful historians, *that such prodigious events never happen in our days*. But it is nothing strange, I hope, that men should lie in all ages. You must surely have seen instances enough of that frailty. You have yourself heard many such marvellous relations started, which, being treated with scorn by all the wise and judicious, have at last been abandoned even by the vulgar. Be assured, that those renowned lies, which have spread and flourished to such a monstrous height, arose from like beginnings; but being sown in a more proper soil, shot up at last into prodigies almost equal to those which they relate.

It was a wise policy in that false prophet, Alexander, who though now forgotten, was once so famous, to lay the first scene of his impostures in Paphlagonia, where, as Lucian tells us, the people were extremely ignorant and stupid, and ready to swallow even the grossest delusion. People at a distance, who are weak enough to think the matter at all worth enquiry, have no opportunity of receiving better information. The stories come magnified to them by a hundred circumstances. Fools are industrious in propagating the imposture; while the wise and learned are contented, in general, to deride its absurdity, without informing themselves of the particular facts, by which it may be distinctly refuted. And thus the impostor above mentioned was enabled to proceed, from his ignorant Paphlagonians, to the enlisting of votaries, even among the Grecian philosophers, and men of the most eminent rank and distinction in Rome: nay, could engage the attention of that sage emperor Marcus Aurelius; so far as to make him trust the success of a military expedition to his delusive prophecies.

The advantages are so great, of starting an imposture among an ignorant people, that, even though the delusion should be too gross to impose on the generality of them (*which, though seldom, is sometimes the case*) it has a much better chance for succeeding in remote countries, than if the first scene had been laid in a city renowned for arts and knowledge. The most ignorant and barbarous of these barbarians carry the report abroad. None of their countrymen have a large correspondence, or sufficient credit and authority to contradict and beat down the delusion. Men's inclination to the marvellous has full opportunity to display itself. And thus a story, which is universally exploded in the place where it was first started, shall pass for certain at a thousand miles distance. But had Alexander fixed his residence at Athens, the philosophers of that renowned mart of learning had immediately spread, throughout the whole Roman empire, their sense of the matter; which, being supported by so great authority, and displayed by all the force of reason and eloquence, had entirely opened the eyes of mankind. It is true; Lucian, passing by chance through Paphlagonia, had an opportunity of performing this good office. But, though much to be wished, it does not always happen, that every Alexander meets with a Lucian, ready to expose and detect his impostures.

I may add as a *fourth* reason, which diminishes the authority of prodigies, that there is no testimony for any, even those which have not been expressly detected, that is not opposed by an infinite number of witnesses; so that not only the miracle destroys the credit of testimony, but the testimony destroys itself. To make this the better understood, let us consider, that, in matters of religion, whatever is different is contrary; and that it is impossible the religions of ancient Rome, of Turkey, of Siam, and of China should, all of them, be established on any solid foundation. Every miracle, therefore, pretended to have been wrought in any of these religions (and all of them abound in miracles), as its direct scope is to establish the particular system to which it is attributed; so has it the same force, though more indirectly, to overthrow every other system. In destroying a rival system, it likewise destroys the credit of those miracles, on which that system was established; so that all the prodigies of different religions are to be regarded as contrary facts, and the evidences of these prodigies, whether weak or strong, as opposite to each other. According to this method of reasoning, when we believe any miracle of Mahomet or his successors, we have for our warrant the testimony of a few barbarous Arabians: And on the other hand, we are to regard the authority of Titus Livius, Plutarch, Tacitus, and, in short, of all the authors and witnesses, Grecian, Chinese, and Roman Catholic, who have related any miracle in their particular religion; I say, we are to regard their testimony in the same light as if they had mentioned that Mahometan miracle, and had in express terms contradicted it, with the same certainty as they have for the miracle they relate. This argument may appear over subtile and refined; but is not in reality different from the reasoning of a judge, who supposes, that the credit of two witnesses, maintaining a crime against any one, is destroyed by the testimony of two others, who affirm him to have been two hundred leagues distant, at the same instant when the crime is said to have been committed.

One of the best attested miracles in all profane history, is that which Tacitus reports of Vespasian, who cured a blind man in Alexandria, by means of his spittle, and a lame man by the mere touch of his foot; in obedience to a vision of the god Serapis, who had enjoined them to have recourse to the Emperor, for these miraculous cures. The story may be seen in that fine historian[1]; where every circumstance seems to add weight to the testimony, and might be displayed at large with all the force of argument and eloquence, if any one were now concerned to enforce the evidence of that exploded and idolatrous superstition. The gravity, solidity, age, and probity of so great an emperor, who, through the whole course of his life, conversed in a familiar manner with his friends and courtiers, and never affected those extraordinary airs of divinity assumed by Alexander and Demetrius. The historian, a cotemporary writer, noted for candour and veracity, and withal, the greatest and most penetrating genius, perhaps, of all antiquity; and so free from any tendency to credulity, that he even lies under the contrary imputation, of atheism and profaneness: The persons, from whose authority he related the miracle, of established character for judgement and veracity, as we may well presume; eye-witnesses of the fact, and confirming their testimony, after the Flavian family was despoiled of the empire, and could no longer give any reward, as the price of a lie. *Utrumque, qui interfuere, nunc quoque memorant, postquam nullum mendacio pretium.* To which if we add the public nature of the facts, as related, it will appear, that no evidence can well be supposed stronger for so gross and so palpable a falsehood.

There is also a memorable story related by Cardinal de Retz, which may well deserve our consideration. When that intriguing politician fled into Spain, to avoid the persecution of his enemies, he passed through Saragossa, the capital of Arragon, where he was shewn, in the cathedral, a man, who had served seven years as a doorkeeper, and was well known to every body in town, that had ever paid his devotions at that church. He had been seen, for so long a time, wanting a leg; but recovered that limb by the rubbing of holy oil upon the stump; and the cardinal assures us that he saw him with two legs. This miracle was vouched by all the canons of the church; and the whole company in town were appealed to for a confirmation of the fact; whom the cardinal found, by their zealous devotion, to be thorough believers of the miracle. Here the relater was also cotemporary to the supposed prodigy, of an incredulous and libertine character, as well as of great genius; the miracle of so *singular* a nature as could scarcely admit of a counterfeit, and the witnesses very numerous, and all of them, in a manner, spectators of the fact, to which they gave their testimony. And what adds mightily to the force of the evidence, and may double our surprise on this occasion, is, that the cardinal himself, who relates the story, seems not to give any credit to it, and consequently cannot be suspected of any concurrence in the holy fraud. He considered justly, that it was not requisite, in order to reject a fact of this nature, to be able accurately to disprove the testimony, and to trace its falsehood, through all the circumstances of knavery and credulity which produced it. He knew, that, as this was commonly altogether impossible at any small distance of time and place; so was it extremely

[1] Hist. lib. iv. cap. 81. Suetonius gives nearly the same account *in vita* Vesp.

difficult, even where one was immediately present, by reason of the bigotry, ignorance, cunning, and roguery of a great part of mankind. He therefore concluded, like a just reasoner, that such an evidence carried falsehood upon the very face of it, and that a miracle, supported by any human testimony, was more properly a subject of derision than of argument.

There surely never was a greater number of miracles ascribed to one person, than those, which were lately said to have been wrought in France upon the tomb of Abbé Paris, the famous Jansenist, with whose sanctity the people were so long deluded. The curing of the sick, giving hearing to the deaf, and sight to the blind, were every where talked of as the usual effects of that holy sepulchre. But what is more extraordinary; many of the miracles were immediately proved upon the spot, before judges of unquestioned integrity, attested by witnesses of credit and distinction, in a learned age, and on the most eminent theatre that is now in the world. Nor is this all: a relation of them was published and dispersed every where; nor were the *Jesuits*, though a learned body, supported by the civil magistrate, and determined enemies to those opinions, in whose favour the miracles were said to have been wrought, ever able distinctly to refute or detect them. Where shall we find such a number of circumstances, agreeing to the corroboration of one fact? And what have we to oppose to such a cloud of witnesses, but the absolute impossibility or miraculous nature of the events, which they relate? And this surely, in the eyes of all reasonable people, will alone be regarded as a sufficient refutation.

Is the consequence just, because some human testimony has the utmost force and authority in some cases, when it relates the battle of Philippi or Pharsalia for instance; that therefore all kinds of testimony must, in all cases, have equal force and authority? Suppose that the Cæsarean and Pompeian factions had, each of them, claimed the victory in these battles, and that the historians of each party had uniformly ascribed the advantage to their own side; how could mankind, at this distance, have been able to determine between them? The contrariety is equally strong between the miracles related by Herodotus or Plutarch, and those delivered by Mariana, Bede, or any monkish historian.

The wise lend a very academic faith to every report which favours the passion of the reporter; whether it magnifies his country, his family, or himself, or in any other way strikes in with his natural inclinations and propensities. But what greater temptation than to appear a missionary, a prophet, an ambassador from heaven? Who would not encounter many dangers and difficulties, in order to attain so sublime a character? Or if, by the help of vanity and a heated imagination, a man has first made a convert of himself, and entered seriously into the delusion; who ever scruples to make use of pious frauds, in support of so holy and meritorious a cause?

The smallest spark may here kindle into the greatest flame; because the materials are always prepared for it. The *avidum genus auricularum*[1], the gazing populace, receive greedily, without examination, whatever sooths superstition, and promotes wonder.

How many stories of this nature have, in all ages, been detected and exploded in their infancy? How many more have been celebrated for a time, and have afterwards sunk into neglect and oblivion? Where such reports, therefore, fly about, the solution of the

[1] Lucret.

phenomenon is obvious; and we judge in conformity to regular experience and observation, when we account for it by the known and natural principles of credulity and delusion. And shall we, rather than have a recourse to so natural a solution, allow of a miraculous violation of the most established laws of nature?

I need not mention the difficulty of detecting a falsehood in any private or even public history, at the place, where it is said to happen; much more when the scene is removed to ever so small a distance. Even a court of judicature, with all the authority, accuracy, and judgement, which they can employ, find themselves often at a loss to distinguish between truth and falsehood in the most recent actions. But the matter never comes to any issue, if trusted to the common method of altercations and debate and flying rumours; especially when men's passions have taken part on either side.

In the infancy of new religions, the wise and learned commonly esteem the matter too inconsiderable to deserve their attention or regard. And when afterwards they would willingly detect the cheat, in order to undeceive the deluded multitude, the season is now past, and the records and witnesses, which might clear up the matter, have perished beyond recovery.

No means of detection remain, but those which must be drawn from the very testimony itself of the reporters: and these, though always sufficient with the judicious and knowing, are commonly too fine to fall under the comprehension of the vulgar.

Upon the whole, then, it appears, that no testimony for any kind of miracle has ever amounted to a probability, much less to a proof; and that, even supposing it amounted to a proof, it would be opposed by another proof; derived from the very nature of the fact, which it would endeavour to establish. It is experience only, which gives authority to human testimony; and it is the same experience, which assures us of the laws of nature. When, therefore, these two kinds of experience are contrary, we have nothing to do but substract the one from the other, and embrace an opinion, either on one side or the other, with that assurance which arises from the remainder. But according to the principle here explained, this substraction, with regard to all popular religions, amounts to an entire annihilation; and therefore we may establish it as a maxim, that no human testimony can have such force as to prove a miracle, and make it a just foundation for any such system of religion.

I beg the limitations here made may be remarked, when I say, that a miracle can never be proved, so as to be the foundation of a system of religion. For I own, that otherwise, there may possibly be miracles, or violations of the usual course of nature, of such a kind as to admit of proof from human testimony; though, perhaps, it will be impossible to find any such in all the records of history. Thus, suppose, all authors, in all languages, agree, that, from the first of January 1600, there was a total darkness over the whole earth for eight days: suppose that the tradition of this extraordinary event is still strong and lively among the people: that all travellers, who return from foreign countries, bring us accounts of the same tradition, without the least variation or contradiction: it is evident, that our present philosophers, instead of doubting the fact, ought to receive it as certain, and ought to search for the causes whence it might be derived. The decay, corruption, and dissolution of nature, is an event rendered probable by so many analogies, that any phenomenon, which seems to have a tendency towards that catastrophe, comes within the reach of human testimony, if that testimony be very extensive and uniform.

But suppose, that all the historians who treat of England, should agree, that, on the first of January 1600, Queen Elizabeth died; that both before and after her death she was seen by her physicians and the whole court, as is usual with persons of her rank; that her successor was acknowledged and proclaimed by the parliament; and that, after being interred a month, she again appeared, resumed the throne, and governed England for three years: I must confess that I should be surprised at the concurrence of so many odd circumstances, but should not have the least inclination to believe so miraculous an event. I should not doubt of her pretended death, and of those other public circumstances that followed it: I should only assert it to have been pretended, and that it neither was, nor possibly could be real. You would in vain object to me the difficulty, and almost impossibility of deceiving the world in an affair of such consequence; the wisdom and solid judgement of that renowned queen; with the little or no advantage which she could reap from so poor an artifice: All this might astonish me; but I would still reply, that the knavery and folly of men are such common phenomena, that I should rather believe the most extraordinary events to arise from their concurrence, than admit of so signal a violation of the laws of nature.

But should this miracle be ascribed to any new system of religion; men, in all ages, have been so much imposed on by ridiculous stories of that kind, that this very circumstance would be a full proof of a cheat, and sufficient, with all men of sense, not only to make them reject the fact, but even reject it without farther examination. Though the Being to whom the miracle is ascribed, be, in this case, Almighty, it does not, upon that account, become a whit more probable; since it is impossible for us to know the attributes or actions of such a Being, otherwise than from the experience which we have of his productions, in the usual course of nature. This still reduces us to past observation, and obliges us to compare the instances of the violation of truth in the testimony of men, with those of the violation of the laws of nature by miracles, in order to judge which of them is most likely and probable. As the violations of truth are more common in the testimony concerning religious miracles, than in that concerning any other matter of fact; this must diminish very much the authority of the former testimony, and make us form a general resolution, never to lend any attention to it, with whatever specious pretence it may be covered.

Lord Bacon seems to have embraced the same principles of reasoning. 'We ought,' says he, 'to make a collection or particular history of all monsters and prodigious births or productions, and in a word of every thing new, rare, and extraordinary in nature. But this must be done with the most severe scrutiny, lest we depart from truth. Above all, every relation must be considered as suspicious, which depends in any degree upon religion, as the prodigies of Livy: And no less so, every thing that is to be found in the writers of natural magic or alchimy, or such authors, who seem, all of them, to have an unconquerable appetite for falsehood and fable[1].'

I am the better pleased with the method of reasoning here delivered, as I think it may serve to confound those dangerous friends or disguised enemies to the *Christian Religion*, who have undertaken to defend it by the principles of human reason. Our most holy religion is founded on Faith, not on reason; and it is a sure method of exposing it to put it to such a trial as it is, by no means, fitted to

[1] Nov. Org. lib. ii. aph. 29.

endure. To make this more evident, let us examine those miracles, related in scripture; and not to lose ourselves in too wide a field, let us confine ourselves to such as we find in the *Pentateuch*, which we shall examine, according to the principles of these pretended Christians, not as the word or testimony of God himself, but as the production of a mere human writer and historian. Here then we are first to consider a book, presented to us by a barbarous and ignorant people, written in an age when they were still more barbarous, and in all probability long after the facts which it relates, corroborated by no concurring testimony, and resembling those fabulous accounts, which every nation gives of its origin. Upon reading this book, we find it full of prodigies and miracles. It gives an account of a state of the world and of human nature entirely different from the present: Of our fall from that state: Of the age of man, extended to near a thousand years: Of the destruction of the world by a deluge: Of the arbitrary choice of one people, as the favourites of heaven; and that people the countrymen of the author: Of their deliverance from bondage by prodigies the most astonishing imaginable: I desire any one to lay his hand upon his heart, and after a serious consideration declare, whether he thinks that the falsehood of such a book, supported by such a testimony, would be more extraordinary and miraculous than all the miracles it relates; which is, however, necessary to make it be received, according to the measures of probability above established.

What we have said of miracles may be applied, without any variation, to prophecies; and indeed, all prophecies are real miracles, and as such only, can be admitted as proofs of any revelation. If it did not exceed the capacity of human nature to foretell future events, it would be absurd to employ any prophecy as an argument for a divine mission or authority from heaven. So that, upon the whole, we may conclude, that the *Christian Religion* not only was at first attended with miracles, but even at this day cannot be believed by any reasonable person without one. Mere reason is insufficient to convince us of its veracity: And whoever is moved by *Faith* to assent to it, is conscious of a continued miracle in his own person, which subverts all the principles of his understanding, and gives him a determination to believe what is most contrary to custom and experience.

RICHARD SWINBURNE

from The Concept of Miracle

In the selections from his *The Concept of Miracle* that make up this reading Richard Swinburne examines the concept of a *violation of a law of nature*. He goes on to classify different types of evidence that might in theory be evidence for the occurrence of a miracle and to consider what might be evidence that a violation of a natural law was caused by a god. In his concluding pages Swinburne suggests that the evidence "for or against" the occurrence of a particular miracle is "extremely widespread."

From Richard Swinburne, *The Concept of Miracle*. London: Macmillan and New York: St Martin's, 1970. Reproduced with permission of Palgrave Macmillan.

Violation of a Law of Nature

Laws of Nature

The task of the theoretical scientist is to set forth the laws of nature (which may be physical, chemical, biological or psychological laws, or laws of any other science). In any field he will have a number of observational results. He seeks the most natural generalisation or extrapolation of those results, or, as I shall put it, the simplest formula from which the past results can be deduced.

In a primitive way ordinary people generalise their observations in the most natural or simple way to obtain general statements about how things behave, from which they can deduce how things will behave in future. Thus, to take a well-worn example, suppose that swans had not previously been observed and then we observe in different parts of England a number of swans and find them all to be white. We might set forward a hypothesis 'all swans are white'. This allows us to infer of each past swan observed that it was white, and predicts of each future swan which will be observed that it will be white. Another formula equally compatible with observations to date, but making different predictions is 'all swans in England are white, but elsewhere are black'. Yet this would never be seriously proposed because it is so obviously less simple than, a less natural extrapolation from the data than, the alternative formula.

The task of the scientist may thus be compared to that of a man finding a formula governing the occurrence of points on a graph. Compatible with any finite set of data, there will always be an infinite number of possible formulae from which the data can be predicted. We can rule out many by further tests, but however many tests we make we shall still have only a finite number of data and hence an infinite number of formulae compatible with them. Yet some of these formulae will be highly complex relative to the data so that no scientist would consider that the data provided evidence that those formulae were laws of nature. Others are very simple formulae such that the data can be said to provide evidence that they are laws of nature. Thus suppose the scientist finds marks at (1,1), (2,2), (3,3), and (4,4), the first number of each pair being the x-coordinate and the second the y-coordinate. One formula which would predict these marks is $x - y$. Another one is $(x - 1)(x - 2)(x - 3)(x - 4) + x = y$. But clearly we would not regard the data as supporting the second formula. It is too clumsy a formula to explain four observations. Among simple formulae supported by the data, the simplest is the best supported and regarded, provisionally, as correct. If the formula survives further tests, that increases the evidence in its favour as a law.

What counts as a formula of sufficient simplicity to be adopted as a law and so used for prediction in the absence of simpler formulae is a matter of the quantity and variety of the data on the basis of which it is constructed. While

$$(x - 1)(x - 2)(x - 3)(x - 4) + x = y$$

would not do if supported only by the four cited data, it could reasonably be put forward on the basis of four hundred data. Einstein's field equations of General Relativity could hardly be put forward solely on the basis of observations of the movement of Mercury's perihelion (observations compatible with those equations) but could be put forward on the basis of an enormous number of terrestrial and planetary motions and of optical phenomena, previously accounted for by Newtonian mechanics or the Special Theory of Relativity, and of certain further phenomena (such as the movement of Mercury's perihelion) not compatible with the latter theories.

Often, unlike in my two initial examples, a number or different formulae of similar simplicity (no one clearly simpler than the rest) are equally compatible with past data, yet, being different formulae, make different predictions for the future. An artificial example of this would be if we had a number of points on a graph which could be fitted on to hyperbolic curves of different eccentricity but not on to any simpler curves (e.g. a straight line). More complicated real-life examples are provided by current cosmological theories, e.g. 'big bang' and 'steady state' theories. They all take account of the same data of astronomy and mechanics, yet integrate these in different ways so as to get different predictions. Yet many of them seem equally simple, no one a more natural extrapolation from the data than the others. In such cases, in so far as he can, a scientist will test between conflicting predictions and reject those formulae which yield incorrect predictions. If he can do this and is left with only one formula compatible with the data of observation, then he will adopt that.

Sometimes the scientist will be able to see no simple formula, that is formula of sufficient simplicity, compatible with a collection of data in some field, and in that case will not feel justified in adopting any one formula and making predictions on the basis of it. If in our studies of swans we had observed in England several white, several black, and several red ones with no obvious pattern of geographical distribution, we would not be able to produce any simple formula covering these data which would enable us to

predict the colours of future swans. In so far as a formula is simple and the simplest known formula compatible with observations, we regard it—provisionally—as a law of nature. Any proposed law of nature will be corrigible—that is, future observations could show the proposed law not to be a true law. But in so far as a formula survives further tests, that increases the evidence in its favour as a true law.

Another example of these points is provided by Kepler's work on planetary motion. Studying the positions of planets observed during the previous thirty years, Kepler sought formulae from which those results could be deduced. But not any formulae would do; the formulae would have to be formulae of fairly simple curves, describing each planet as having travelled along a curve of that type, in order for us to be justified in supposing that the formulae described the future as well as the past behaviour of planets. If the formulae were simply records of past positions with unrelated predictions attached, we would not, despite the fact that they accurately recorded past positions, think ourselves justified in believing the future predictions yielded by them. Only if they were the formulae of simple curves which fitted the past positions would we think that we could predict from them. Kepler eventually fitted the positions of each planet on to an ellipse, having the Sun at one focus. The neat fit of the past positions on to this curve justified men in supposing that planets in future would travel in elliptical paths.

The general points of the last few pages would, I believe—with qualifications and additions—be accepted by most philosophers of science. Philosophers of science today are very concerned to bring out clearly and explicitly the criteria for choosing between alternative theories equally compatible with observations obtained so far, criteria which, in common with many philosophers of science, I have termed criteria of simplicity. But although philosophers may still disagree about exactly what those criteria are, they agree that such criteria operate, and they agree in many particular cases when two different theories equally compatible with observations obtained to date are constructed which of the two is to be preferred.

The upshot of all this is that—against McKinnon[16]—laws of nature do not just describe what happens ('the actual course of events'). They describe what happens in a regular and predictable way. When what happens is entirely irregular and unpredictable, its occurrence is not something describable by natural laws.

Meaning of 'Violation of a Law of Nature'

Given this understanding of a law of nature, what is meant by a violation of a law of nature? I think that those who, like Hume, have used this or a similar expression have intended to mean by it an occurence of a non-repeatable counter-instance to a law of nature (this useful definition is provided by Professor Ninian Smart in his discussion of Hume's account of miracles[17]). The use of the definiens and of the definiendum, violation of a law of nature, both assume that the operation of a law of nature is logically compatible with the occurrence of an exception to its operation. This point will be developed below.

Clearly, as we have noted, events contrary to predictions of formulae which we had good reason to believe to be laws of nature often occur. But if we have good reason to believe that they have occurred and good reason to believe that similar events would occur in similar circumstances, then undoubtedly we have good reason to believe that the formulae which we previously believed to be the laws of nature were not in fact such laws. For then the real laws of nature will, we can best suppose, be the old purported laws with a modification for the circumstances in question. There cannot be repeatable counter-instances to genuine laws of nature, that is, counter-instances which would be repeated in similar circumstances. Repeatable counter-instances to purported laws only show those purported laws not to be genuine laws.

But what are we to say if we have good reason to believe that an event E has occurred contrary to predictions of a formula L which otherwise we have good reason to believe to be a law of nature, and we have good reason to believe that events similar to E would not occur in circumstances as similar as we like in any respect to those of the occurrence of E? E would then be a non-repeatable counter-instance to L. In this case we could say *either* (as before) that L cannot be the law of nature operative in the field, since an exception to its operation has occurred, *or* that L is the law of nature operative in the field, but that an exceptional non-repeatable counter-instance to its occurrence has occurred. The advantage of saying the former is particularly obvious where universal laws are involved. As a universal law has the form 'so-and-sos always do such and such', it seems formally incompatible with a counter-instance reported by 'this is a so-and-so, and did not do such-and-such'.

[16] Alastair McKinnon, '"Miracle" and "Paradox"', in 'American Philosophical Quarterly', iv (1967) 308–14.
[17] Ninian Smart, 'Philosophers and religious Truth' (S.C.M. Press, London, 1964) ch. ii: 'Miracles and David Hume'.

Both statements cannot be true together, the argument goes; evidence in favour of the exception is evidence against the purported law. The advantage of saying the latter is however this. The evidence shows that we cannot replace L by a more successful law allowing us to predict E as well as other phenomena supporting L. For any modified formula which allowed us to predict E would allow us to predict similar events in similar circumstances and hence, *ex hypothesi*, we have good reason to believe, would give false predictions. Whereas if we leave the formula L unmodified, it will, we have good reason to believe, give correct predictions in all other conceivable circumstances. Hence if we are to say that any law of nature is operative in the field in question we must say that it is L. The only alternative is to say that no law of nature operates in the field. Yet saying this does not seem to do justice to the (in general) enormous success of L in predicting occurrences in the field.

For these latter reasons it seems not unnatural to describe E as a non-repeatable counter-instance to a law of nature L. If we do say this we have to understand the operation of a universal law of the form 'so-and-so's always do such-and-such' as logically compatible with 'this is a so-and-so and does not do such-and-such'. To say that a certain such formula is a law is to say that in general its predictions are true and that any exceptions to its operation cannot be accounted for by another formula which could be taken as a law (by the criteria discussed earlier). One must thus distinguish between a formula being a law *and* a formula being (universally) true or being a law which holds without exception.

I believe this second account of the way to describe the relation between a formula which otherwise we have good reason to believe to be a law of nature, and an isolated exception to it, to be more natural than the first, that is, to do more justice to the way in which most of us ordinarily talk about these matters. However that may be, it is clearly a coherent way of talking, and it is the way adopted by those who talk of violations of natural laws. For if any exception to its operation was incompatible with a law being a true law, there appears to be no ready sense which could be given to 'a violation of a law of nature'. Hence I shall in future presuppose the second account. Since the second account is a possible account, the concept of a violation of a law of nature is coherent, and we must reject the views of McKinnon and others who claim that it is not logically possible that a law of nature be violated.

If, as seems natural, we understand by the physically impossible what is ruled out by a law of nature, then our account of laws of nature suggests that it makes sense to suppose that on occasion the physically impossible occurs. (If this seems too paradoxical a thing to say we shall have to give a different sense to the 'physically impossible'.) Substantially the same conclusion is reached by Holland.[18] For Holland a violation of a law of nature is a 'conceptual impossibility'. He terms it this because the supposition that there is an object behaving in a way other than that laid down by laws of nature is the supposition that there is an object behaving in ways other than the ways embodied in our normal understanding of it, and so, in wide senses of 'involved' and 'concept', involved in our ordinary concept of it. Therefore, having shown that it makes sense to suppose a law of nature violated, Holland argues that in such a case the conceptually impossible

[18] R. F. Holland, 'The Miraculous', in 'American Philosophical Quarterly', ii (1965) 43–51.

would occur. That being so, he concludes, one cannot deduce from a thing having happened that it is a possible occurrence—*ab esse ad posse non valet consequentia*. (When assessing Holland's conclusion, we should remember what he means by 'conceptual impossibility'. He does not mean what most philosophers mean by that expression—viz. something the description of which involves a self-contradiction—but merely something the occurrence of which is ruled out by our ordinary (and with this exception basically correct) understanding of the way objects behave.)

Evidence as to Which Events, if they Occurred, Would Be Violations of Laws of Nature

The crucial question however is what would be good reason for believing that an event E, if it occurred, was a non-repeatable as opposed to a repeatable counter-instance to a formula L which we have on all other evidence good reason to believe to be a law of nature. The evidence that E is a repeatable counter-instance would be that a new formula L^1 better confirmed than L as a law of nature can be set up, which, unlike L, predicted E. A formula is confirmed by data, it will be recalled, in so far as the data obtained so far are predicted by the formula, new predictions are successful, and the formula is a simple one relative to the collection of data (viz. a natural extrapolation from the data). Now L^1 will be better confirmed than L if it, like L, predicts the data so far obtained, other than E; unlike L, predicts E; and is no more complex than L. If it is considerably more complex than L, that counts against it and might perhaps balance the fact that it, unlike L, predicts E. And if it is so much more complicated than L that it is not of sufficient simplicity relative to

the data (see our earlier discussion) to be a law of nature, it will clearly have to be rejected. In so far as there is a doubt whether any proposed law L^1 is more satisfactory than L, clearly the scientist will, if he can, test between the further predictions of the two laws. If, for matters where they make conflicting predictions, L^1 predicts successfully and L unsuccessfully, L^1 will be preferred, and vice versa. It follows from all this that L will have to be retained as a law of nature and E regarded as a non-repeatable counter-instance to it, if any proposed rival formula L^1 were too much more complicated than L without giving better new predictions, or predicted new phenomena unsuccessfully where L predicted successfully. L^1 would certainly be too much more complicated if it were not of sufficient simplicity relative to the data to be a law of nature at all (see our earlier discussion). L would have to be abandoned if some proposed rival formula L^1 which predicted E were not much more complicated than L, or predicted new phenomena successfully where L predicted unsuccessfully.

Here is an example. Suppose E to be the levitation (i.e. rising into the air and remaining floating on it, in circumstances where no known forces other than gravity (e.g. magnetism) are acting) of a certain holy person. E is thus a counter-instance to otherwise well-substituted laws of nature L (viz. the laws of mechanics, electro-magnetism etc.) which together purport to give an account of all the forces operating in nature. We could show E to be a repeatable counter-instance if we could construct a formula L^1 which predicted E and also successfully predicted other divergencies from L, as well as all other tested predictions of L; *or* if we could construct L^1 which was comparatively simple relative to the data and predicted E and all the other tested predictions of L, but predicted divergencies from L which had not yet been tested. L^1 might differ from L in postulating the operation of an entirely new kind of force, e.g. that under certain circumstances bodies exercise a gravitational repulsion on each other, and those circumstances would include the circumstances in which E occurred. If L^1 satisfied either of the above two conditions, we would adopt it, and we would then say that under certain circumstances people do levitate and so E was not a counter-instance to a law of nature. However it might be that any modification which we made to the laws of nature to allow them to predict E might not yield any more successful predictions than L and they might be so clumsy that there was no reason to believe that their predictions not yet tested would be successful. Under these circumstances we would have good reason to believe that the levitation of the holy person violated the laws of nature.

If the laws of nature are statistical and not universal, as

Quantum Theory suggests, it is not in all cases so clear what counts as a counter-instance to them. A universal law is a law of the form 'all so-and-sos do such-and-such', and a counter-instance is therefore a so-and-so which does not do such-and-such. The occurrence of such a counter-instance is the occurrence of an exception to the law. A statistical law is a law of the form 'n% of so-and-sos do such-and-such'. But here however many so-and-sos are observed which do not do such-and-such, their occurrence is not completely ruled out by the theory. The theory tells us the proportion of so-and-sos which do such-and-such in an infinite class, and however many so-and-sos are found not to do such-and-such in a finite class, this finite class may be just an unrepresentative selection from the infinite class. It *may* be. But if something

occurs which, given the truth of the law, is highly unlikely, that counts against the law, is counter-evidence to it, even if not formally ruled out by it. If the proportion of so-and-sos which do such-and-such in one of the very few, albeit large, finite classes studied is vastly different from that stated to hold in the law, that is counter-evidence to the law. Such an event is therefore not unnaturally described as an exception to a statistical law and the question can therefore be discussed whether it is a repeatable or a non-repeatable exception. It is formally compatible with the currently accepted statistical version of the second law of thermodynamics that a kettle of water put on a fire freeze instead of boiling. But it is vastly improbable that such an event will ever happen within human experience. Hence if it does happen, it is not unnaturally described as an exception to the law. If the evidence does not lead to our adopting a rival law, the event can then be described as a violation of the second law of thermodynamics. Any who speak of a violation of statistical laws would presumably mean the occurrence of a non-repeatable counter-instance to such laws, in the above sense of counter-instance.

All claims about what are the laws of nature are corrigible. However much support any purported law has at the moment, one day it may prove to be no true law. So likewise will be all claims about what does or does not violate the laws of nature. When an event apparently violates such laws, the appearance may arise simply because no one has thought of the true law which could explain the event, or, while they have thought of it, it is so complex relative to the data as rightly to be dismissed before even being tested, or too complex to be adopted without further testing and the tests too difficult in practice to carry out. New scientific knowledge may later turn up which forces us to revise any such claims about what violates laws of nature. But then all claims to knowledge about the physical world are corrigible, and we must reach provisional conclusions about them on the evidence available to us. We have to some extent good evidence about what are the laws of nature, and some of them are so well established and account for so many data that any modifications to them which we could suggest to account for the odd counter-instance would be so clumsy and *ad hoc* as to upset the whole structure of science. In such cases the evidence is strong that if the purported counter-instance occurred it was a violation of the law of nature. There is good reason to believe that the following events, if they occurred, would be violations of the laws of nature: levitation; resurrection from the dead in full health of a man whose heart has not been beating for twenty-four hours and who was dead also by other currently used criteria; water turning into wine without the assistance of chemical apparatus or catalysts; a man getting better from polio in a minute. We know quite enough about how things behave to be reasonably certain that, in the sense earlier delineated, these events are physically impossible.

Historical Evidence

The claim of the last chapter was that we could have good reason to suppose that an event E, if it occurred, was a violation of a law of nature L. But could one have good evidence that such an event E occurred ? At this point we must face the force of Hume's own argument. This, it will be remembered, runs as follows. The evidence, which *ex hypothesi* is good evidence, that L is a law of nature is evidence that E did not occur. We have certain other evidence that E did occur. In such circumstances, writes Hume, the wise man 'weighs the opposite experiments. He considers which side is supported by the greater number of experiments'[11]. Since he supposes that the evidence that E occurred would be that of testimony, Hume concludes 'that no testimony is sufficient to establish a miracle, unless the testimony be of such a kind, that its falsehood would be more miraculous, than the fact which it endeavours to establish'. . . .

Four Kinds of Historical Evidence

We have four kinds of evidence about what happened at some past instant—our own apparent memories of our past experiences, the testimony of others about their past experiences, physical traces and our contemporary understanding of what things are physically impossible or improbable. (The fourth is only a corrective to the other three, not an independent source of detailed information.) A piece of evidence gives grounds for believing that some past event occurred, except in so far as it conflicts with other pieces of evidence. In so far as pieces of evidence conflict, they have to be weighed against each other.

---

[11] David Hume, 'An enquiry Concerning Human Understanding', section x: 'Of Miracles' (first published 1748; 2nd ed., ed. L. A. Selby-Bigge, Oxford University Press, 1902) 111.

Let us consider more fully the kinds of evidence. Firstly we have our own apparent memories. I remember, in my opinion, to some extent what I was doing yesterday or last year, what happened to me, and what was going on in the neighbourhood. True, though I may think that I remember these things I may be mistaken, and evidence of other types about what happened may convince me that I am mistaken. However in the usual use of 'remember', if I remember that p, then of logical necessity it was the case that p. Hence the memory evidence for what happened to be weighed against other evidence is best described as evidence of apparent memory. While I may be mistaken about what happened (my claims to memory may be wrong), I can be certain about my apparent memories. Secondly we have the testimony of others—what they say that they did and saw and what happened to them. This may be testimony spoken to us personally or written down long ago. Thirdly we have physical traces of what happened—footprints, fingerprints, ashes, bomb craters. Such physical states are evidence for us that certain past events probably happened, of which events they may be termed traces. A particular present state or event, that is change of state, A_1 is a trace for us of a particular past state or event B_1 if the two events are members of classes of events A's and B's, when the occurrence of A's is highly correlated in our experience with prior occurrence of B's. (1) This correlation (unless—which is highly unlikely—it is coincidental) will arise either because B's cause A's (and A's are seldom caused by anything else) or because C's cause both B's and A's, first B's and then later A's (and A's are seldom caused by anything else). Thus a particular human footprint (in the sense of a mark in the shape of a human foot) in the sand is for us a trace that someone with a foot of that size has walked there recently, because we have observed that men walking on sand produce footprints, and that these are seldom produced by any other cause. Fourthly we have our contemporary understanding of what things are physically impossible or improbable, that is, ruled out or rendered improbable by the laws of nature or generalisations of what usually happens. This scientific knowledge serves as a check on the evidence of apparent memory, testimony and traces. Evidence as to what is physically impossible is, as Hume emphasised, a very strong check on other evidence. If a witness says that he saw a man recover within a minute from polio, or a man walk on air, we, with our contemporary scientific knowledge, have reason to believe that such things are not physically possible, and so have strong evidence against that testimony. Evidence about what is physically improbable is a check, but a less strong one, on other evidence. It counts against evidence that Smith was dealt all thirteen cards of a suit one Friday night at bridge that only extremely rarely are all thirteen cards of a suit dealt at bridge to one player's hand, i.e. that such an event is highly improbable.

My classification of kinds of evidence is, I believe, exhaustive (viz. there are no other kinds), but the classes do to some extent overlap. Thus testimony to the occurrence of X may also be a trace of an event Y. If Jones tells the police that Smith did the robbery, then this event is testimony to Smith having done the robbery. But if we know that on past occasions Jones has only betrayed men to the police when Mrs Jones has persuaded him to do so, then on this occasion his telling the police is also a trace of Mrs Jones having persuaded him to do so.

Now it will be evident from the account which I gave in Chapter 2 of Hume's discussion of miracles that Hume says a great deal about evidence of the second and fourth kinds, but nothing at all about evidence of the first and third kinds. Hume supposes that the conflict about what happens is a conflict between testimony and scientific knowledge. And so no doubt were most conflicts known to Hume—e.g. conflicts about whether the biblical miracles took place. But sometimes the evidence available to an inquirer consists not merely of the testimony of others but of one's own apparently remembered observations. Some men have the evidence of their own eyes, not merely the testimony of others. What, one wonders, would Hume say, if he himself apparently saw a man walk on water? And Hume says nothing at all about traces, fingerprints, footprints and cigarette ash, the impersonal kind of evidence on which detectives like to rely a great deal. But then Hume lived before the era of scientific criminology, and so would hardly be likely to be aware of what could be established by such methods.

However, the evidence of traces could be of considerable importance in assessing whether some event E occurred which if it occurred would have violated a law of nature. Thus if E consists in a state X being followed by a state Y, and we have a trace of the state X and an observed later state Y, or a trace thereof, then we have evidence of traces that E occurred. Thus we might have evidence of footprints in soft mud that Jones was on one side of a broad river one minute ago, and evidence of Jones on the other side now not in the least wet, with not the slightest indication of water having touched his body or clothes (viz. no traces of his having swum across the river), and no bridge, boats, aeroplanes or rope by which he could have crossed. Hence the evidence indicates that he must have walked or flown across. Traces alone, unsupported by testimony, could thus provide evidence that such an event occurred.

It must, however, be admitted that traces are of more use in inquiring into alleged recent miracles than into alleged miracles of long ago. For it is a sad fact which detectives bemoan that many traces become obliterated in the course of time. Foorprints in the sand and cigarette ash still warm are useful indications of what happened a minute or two ago—but footprints get smudged out, and ash gets cold and scattered, and they do not serve as indications of what happened centuries ago. Yet there are many traces which do not become obliterated and which historians are now learning to use—C_{14} dating to determine the age of artefacts, errors of transcription to determine the history of documents, peculiarities of style to determine authorship etc. Science is continually discovering new kinds of traces which reveal facets of ancient history. Who knows how much detail about the past the science of the future will be able to infer from then current remains?

So much for the kinds of evidence which we have about the past and their sources. Clearly one piece of evidence will often conflict with another. The testimony of Jones may conflict with what I appear to remember, or with the testimony of Smith. Jones says that he stayed with Robinson at home all day yesterday, while I 'distinctly remember' having seen him at the Pig and Whistle, and Smith claims to have seen him at the Horse and Hounds. Testimony may conflict with traces. Jones has a scar of a certain type normally caused by a knife wound, but denies having been slashed. Or traces may conflict with each other. A bomb crater may indicate a recent explosion, but the healthy state of the surrounding vegetation count against this. And our contemporary understanding of the physically possible may count against the evidence of particular traces, testimony or apparent memory. I appear to remember having seen the conjurer take the rabbit out of the hat, but he cannot have done so, because the laws of light are such that, had the rabbit been in the hat, I would have seen it.

* * * * * * * * * * * * * * * * * * * *

The Weight of Apparent Memory

The argument of the preceding pages is that we can assess any testimony or trace of the past on evidence of the reliability of testimony or traces of similar kind. It suggests that we can assess our own apparent memory, or claims to knowledge of our own past experience, by similar tests. It suggests also that any apparent memory of having observed some event E has to be weighed against any other evidence that E did not occur, and that sufficient of the latter could always outweigh the former.

There is an argument against all this by Holland who proposes another principle for assessing evidence, the adoption of which would mean that evidence could on balance easily be favourable to the occurrence of a violation of a law of nature. This is the principle that sometimes evidence of apparent memory is strong enough (quite apart from evidence of its reliability) to outweigh any rival evidence, for sometimes, according to Holland, we can know incorrigibly (viz. in such a way that nothing could count against our claim to knowledge) what we observed on a particular occasion. Holland does not give any rules for distinguishing occasions where we know incorrigibly what happens (whatever science etc. may tell us about what can or cannot happen)—e.g. how long ago our incorrigible knowledge can extend, how familiar we have to be with the subject matter etc. He would

probably say that sometimes we just do know and realise that we know incorrigibly and that is all there is to it. Holland claims that unless we do say this, 'a distinction gets blurred which is at least as important as the distinction between a law and a hypothesis—namely the distinction between a hypothesis and a fact. The distinction between my saying when I come across an infant who is screaming and writhing and holding his ear 'he's got an abscess' and my making this statement after looking into the ear, whether by means of an instrument or without, and actually seeing, coming across the abscess'.

The only argument that I know of to support the claim that we know some truths about the physical world incorrigibly, that some judgements of observations which we report cannot possibly be mistaken, is that given by Holland, that 'if there were not things of this kind of which we can be certain we wouldn't be able to be uncertain of anything either'. This argument is given more fully by Norman Malcolm in his 'Knowledge and Certainty' (Prentice-Hall, Englewood Cliffs, N.J., 1963) pp. 66–72. Malcolm claims (p. 69) that 'in order for it to be possible that any statements about physical things should *turn out to be false* it is necessary that some statements about physical things *cannot* turn out to be false'. By 'statements about physical things' Malcolm means empirical statements, statements about the world (as opposed to e.g. statements of mathematics) other than statements about mental states (e.g. the statement that I am now experiencing a pain). I can only consider, he claims, e.g. who did a murder, if there are some physical things about which I cannot be mistaken, e.g. that Jones had blood on his hands. The latter is a fact, the former an hypothesis. Only if there are facts, the argument goes, can I consider hypotheses.

This argument seems mistaken. Certainly for argument, discussion, inference to take place about physical things, there must be some statements about physical things of which we are at present with reason highly confident, and other statements about physical things of which we are more doubtful. Then using the former as premises, we can discuss the truth of the latter. In this context we treat the former statements as statements of facts and the latter as hypotheses. But all this is quite compatible with the claim that anything taken for granted in one discussion could be seriously questioned in another discussion. In a new discussion what was previously not open to question could be treated as an hypothesis and evidence could be adduced for and against it. A historian may take it for granted in general in discussing ancient history that Trajan became emperor in A.D. 98 but if another historian presents arguments against this assertion, then it in its turn could be discussed. The argument that argument can only take place about physical things and hypotheses about them be rejected if we know some physical things incorrigibly is mistaken.

Given that this particular argument fails, the question remains whether I can ever rightly treat something as a fact if I alone claim to have observed it, its occurrence is apparently physically impossible, and there is no evidence to show the reliability of my memory. My own view is that our standards of evidence are unclear here, that some people would certainly stand by some of their apparent memories despite any amount of counter-evidence and that other people would not and that there are no relevant commonly accepted standards to which members of the two groups can appeal to decide who

is right. Thus consider an example of Holland's:

Suppose that a horse, which has been normally born and reared, and is now deprived of all nourishment (we could be completely certain of this)—suppose that, instead of dying this horse goes on thriving (which is again something we could be completely certain about). A series of thorough examinations reveals no abnormality in the horse's condition: its digestive system is always found to be working and to be at every moment in more or less the state it would have been if the horse had eaten a meal an hour or two before.[12]

Now if only one observer is involved, can he really be certain (even without evidence on the reliability of his own memory) that the horse is not being surreptitiously fed? It is not clear, nor is it clear how we can settle whether he can be certain. But if the testimony of others comes in as well as apparent memory (many others claim to have watched the horse in turn day and night), then surely a man can be sure that the horse has not been fed, and so that a law of nature has been violated. (This latter may be Holland's claim in the particular example. Whether he is considering only one observer or many observers who give testimony to each other is unclear from his paper.)

So I conclude that although standards for weighing evidence are not always clear, apparent memory, testimony and traces could sometimes outweigh the evidence of physical impossibility. It is just a question of how much evidence of the former kind we have and how reliable we can show it to have been. However Hume's general point must be admitted,

[12] R.F. Holland, 'The Miracutous' 48.

that we should accept the historical evidence, viz. a man's apparent memory, the testimony of others and traces, only if the falsity of the latter would be 'more miraculous', i.e. more improbable 'than the event which he relates'. Subject to a crucial qualification to be considered in Chapter 6, I share Hume's conviction that the balance of evidence is unlikely to be very often of this kind, but the considerations of this chapter indicate, I suggest, that the balance is much more likely to be of this kind than Hume suggests.

* * * * * * * * * * * * * * * * * * *

Evidence that a Violation is Caused by a God

But, on Hume's definition, miracles are wrought by gods, not men. What would be grounds for attributing a violation of a natural law E to the agency of a god? We will continue to suppose that we have no good reason to suppose that there exist (or do not exist) any gods, apart from evidence provided by the occurrence of violations of natural laws. Now we cannot attribute E to the agency of a god on the grounds of having seen his body bring E about, for gods (by our definition) do not in general have bodies. But suppose that E occurs in ways and circumstances otherwise strongly analogous to those in which occur events brought about intentionally by human agents, and that other violations occur in such circumstances. We would then be justified in claiming that E and other such violations are, like effects of human actions, brought about by agents, but agents unlike men in not being material objects. This inference would be justified because, if an analogy between effects is strong enough, we are always justified in postulating slight difference in causes to account for slight difference in effects. Thus if because of its other observable

behaviour we say that light is a disturbance in a medium, then the fact that the medium, if it exists, does not, like other media, slow down material bodies passing through it, is not by itself (viz. if there are no other disanalogies) a reason for saying that light is not a disturbance in a medium but only for saying that the medium in which light is a disturbance has the peculiar property of not resisting the passage of material bodies. So if because of very strong similarity between the ways and circumstances of the occurrence of E and other violations of laws of nature to the ways and circumstances in which effects are produced by human agents, we postulate a similar cause—a rational agent—the fact that there are certain disanalogies (viz. we cannot point to the agent, say where his body is) does not mean that our explanation is wrong. It only means that the agent is unlike humans in not having a body. But this move is only justified if the similarities are otherwise strong. Nineteenth-century scientists eventually concluded that for light the similarities were not strong enough to outweigh the dissimilarities and justify postulating the medium with the peculiar property.

Now what similarities in the ways and circumstances of their occurrence could there be between E (and other violations of laws of nature) and the effects of intentional human actions to justify the postulation of similar causes?

Our description of the other grounds for attributing the production of events to the intentional actions of agents suggests grounds of the following kind for postulating similar causes. E occurs in answer to a request (a prayer) addressed to a named individual (e.g. a prayer addressed 'O Apollo' or 'O Allah'). Other such requests are also sometimes granted by the occurrence of violations of laws of nature, but otherwise violations are far less frequent. The making of a request of this kind is often followed by a voice, not being the voice of an embodied agent, giving reasons for granting or refusing the request. These reasons together with the kinds of events produced show a common pattern of character. Thus requests for the relief of suffering might generally be successful, whereas requests for the punishment of enemies might not be. The voice would say to those who asked for the relief of suffering that they had asked wisely, and to those who asked for the punishment of enemies that they were being malicious, and that it was no part of divine providence to forward their malice. All of this would, I urge, suggest a god with a certain character tampering with the world. Normally however the evidence claimed by theists for the occurrence of miracles is not as strong as I have indicated that very strong evidence would be. Violations are sometimes reported as occurring subsequent to prayer for them to occur, and seldom otherwise; but voices giving reasons for answering such a request are rarely reported. Whether in cases where voices are not heard but the occurrence of violations following prayers for their occurrence were well confirmed we would be justified in concluding the existence of a god who brought E about is a matter of whether the analogy is strong enough as it stands. The question of exactly when an analogy is strong enough to render a conclusion based on it sufficiently probable to be believed is always a difficult one and it is hard to give general rules. Yet it is always possible to describe cases where it clearly is and cases where it clearly is not strong enough to render a conclusion credible. I claim to have described a case where the analogy would clearly be strong enough to render credible the conclusion that a god brought about a violation of a law of nature.

* * * * * * * * * * * * * * * * * * * *

Fitting our Account to Other Definitions of 'Miracle'

So far we have conducted our inquiry into the evidence which can be adduced for or against the occurrence of miracles in terms of the Humean definition of a miracle as a violation of a law of nature by the act of a god. But we saw in Chapter 1 the inadequacies of this definition, and it is now time to fit the account given so far to other definitions.

Firstly, we may wish to widen the Humean definition to allow the agent of a miracle to be not a god but a man. We have described in this chapter the grounds for saying that a man had produced an effect.

Secondly we saw that in order to be a miracle an event has to be in some sense of an extraordinary kind. But this need not, we saw, be a violation of a law of nature; it could be an extraordinary coincidence. If it were such, and occurred entirely in accordance with natural processes, the evidence that a god was responsible for it must be rather different from evidence that a god was responsible for a violation of a law of nature. For a violation of a law of nature is an event separate from other surrounding events, which does not occur in accord with the scientific pattern. Scientifically it is inexplicable. It is to be judged the act of a god according to the circumstances of its occurrence. But an event which occurs in accordance with natural processes already has another explanation. It is explained by natural laws acting on precedent events. Hence if its occurrence is to be explained by something else in a way compatible with that explanation, this can only be because the something else is responsible for the natural laws and the precedent events. The scientific explanation is, *ex hypothesi*, correct. Consequently the explanation by the act of a god is not a rival to this explanation; it can only be true if it is a more fundamental explanation of the scientific explanation. The extraordinary coincidence has the same kind of natural explanation as other natural events, viz. the scientific explanation. Hence the action of a god is only to be accepted as an explanation of the extraordinary coincidence if it is to be accepted as an explanation of all regular natural processes. The action of a god can only explain an extraordinary coincidence within history if it can explain the whole of history as well. The arguments for the existence of a god are almost all arguments for the existence of a god who controls the natural order. Thus the argument from design (or teleological argument) purports to show that the order and succession of things in the world shows a designer and controller. In so far as arguments for the existence of a god together give sufficient support to make credible the claim that there exists a god who controls the natural order, they thereby give sufficient support to make credible the claim that a god was responsible for the extraordinary coincidence. The worth of many arguments, other than the argument from violations of natural laws, to the existence of a god will be considered in other volumes in this series.

Thirdly we noted that the Humean definition was inadequate in not making its religious significance part of the definition of a miracle. We saw in Chapter 1 that there were wider and narrower understandings of religious significance, and we illustrated briefly what these were.

So on the other and more adequate definitions of 'miracle' considerations additional to those involved in the Humean definition have to be taken into account in assessing evidence for or against the occurrence of a miracle. However the major philosophical problems about miracles seem to arise with the notion, involved in most definitions of 'miracle,' of a violation of a law of nature by a god, which is in effect Hume's definition. For this reason I have worked for most of this book with the Humean definition. Now that I have drawn attention to the way in which other considerations are relevant to assessing evidence about miracles in other senses of the term, I shall again work with the Humean definition for the argument of the final chapter. But the considerations which I shall adduce there will be seen to be crucially relevant to the assessment of evidence for or against the occurrence of a miracle on most definitions.

* * * * * * * * * * * * * * * * * * * *

Thus suppose a faithful blind Christian is suddenly cured in a way that violates natural laws. Then if we have other evidence for the existence of the Christian God (e.g. that provided, if it is provided, by the traditional proofs) and evidence from his other behaviour (viz. what other effects he brought about in the world) that he is a compassionate God and so liable to intervene in the natural order to help the afflicted, particularly the Christian afflicted, then this event can reasonably be ascribed to his intervention whether or not the blind man or other Christians had ever prayed for that result.

However the external evidence might not favour Paley's conclusion. Firstly, it might not lend any support to the claim that there exists at least one god. The traditional arguments for the existence of God might be shown to be worthless, and other arguments produced against the existence of any gods. Secondly, even if the external evidence favoured the existence of at least one god, it might show him to be of a non-interventionist character. More radical Christians have often claimed that God is not the sort to tamper with his divine order. Summarising the views of many such persons (with whom he disagreed), C. S. Lewis wrote that it will 'be felt (and justly) that miracles interrupt the orderly march of events, the steady development of nature according to her own interest, genius or character. That regular march seems to such critics as I have in mind more impressive than any miracle. Looking up (like Lucifer in Meredith's sonnet) at the night sky they feel it almost impious to suppose that God should sometimes unsay what he has once said with such magnificence'[8]. Tillich has expressed theological objections of this kind to miracles in the Humean sense:

> Miracles cannot be interpreted in terms of a super-natural interference in natural processes. If such an interpretation were true, the manifestation of the ground of being would destroy the structure of being; God would be split within himself, as religious dualism has asserted.[9]

Such evidence of the non-existence of any interventionist god would, in advance of any internal evidence, render highly improbable the occurrence of any miracle. Much stronger internal evidence in favour of the occurrence of a miracle than that earlier sketched would be needed to overcome such evidence.

It should by now be apparent that the evidence for or against the occurrence of some particular miracle is extremely widespread. With one *Weltanschauung* ('world-view') one rightly does not ask much in the way of detailed historical evidence for a miracle since miracles are the kind of events which one expects to occur in many or certain specific circumstances. The testimony of one witness to an occurrence of the kind of miracle which in its circumstances one would expect to happen should be sufficient to carry conviction, just as we accept the testimony of one witness to a claim that when he let go of a book which he was holding it fell to the ground. With another *Weltanschauung* one rightly asks for a large amount of historical evidence, because of one's general conviction that the world is a certain sort of world, a world without a god and so a world in which miracles do not happen. Which *Weltanschauung* is right is a matter for long argument on matters towards the solution of some of which the other studies of this series offer some suggestions. What we have been assessing in this study is the value of the historical and scientific evidence about particular alleged miracles to the claim that a miracle has occurred, against the background of the different *Weltanschauungen*. As we have seen, such particular historical and scientific evidence makes its small contribution to supporting or opposing the different *Weltanschauungen*.

R.F. HOLLAND

from The Miraculous

I n "The Miraculous" R.F. Holland argues that the idea that a miracle violates a natural law is too narrow, for, while there may be some miracles that violate a natural law, there are other candidates for miracles that are unlikely coincidences,

[8] C. S. Lewis, 'Miracles' (Bles, London, 1947) 115.
[9] Paul Tillich, 'Systematic Theology', Vol. i (Nisbet, London, 1953) 129.

but do not violate any natural law. The latter sort Holland puts under the "contingency concept" of miracle. For Holland the unifying idea underlying both the "contingency concept" and the "violation concept" of miracle is that miracles have religious significance. And they have religious significance in that they are seen by the religious as events for which God may be thanked, events that might be prayed for, that are regarded with awe, that might elicit a religious vow.*

The Miraculous

Most people think of a miracle as a violation of natural law; and a good many of those who regard the miraculous in this way incline to the idea that miracles are impossible and that "science" tells us this (the more sophisticated might say that what tells us this is an unconfused *conception* of science). I shall argue that the conception of the miraculous as a violation of natural law is an inadequate conception because it is unduly restrictive, though there is also a sense in which it is not restrictive enough. To qualify for being accounted a miracle an occurrence does not have to be characterizable as a violation of natural law. However, though I do not take the conception of miracles as violations of natural law to be an adequate conception of the miraculous, I shall maintain that occurrences are conceivable in respect to which it could be said that some law or laws of nature had been violated—or it could be said equally that there was a contradiction in our experience: and if the surrounding circumstances were appropriate it would be possible for such occurrences to have a kind of human significance and hence intelligible for them to be hailed as miracles. I see no philosophical reason against this.

But consider first the following example. A child riding his toy motor-car strays on to an unguarded railway crossing near his house and a wheel of his car gets stuck down the side of one of the rails. An express train is due to pass with the signals in its favor and a curve in the track makes it impossible for the driver to stop his train in time to avoid any obstruction he might encounter on the crossing. The mother coming out of the house to look for her child sees him on the crossing and hears the train approaching. She runs forward shouting and waving. The little boy remains seated in his car looking downward, engrossed in the task of pedaling it free. The brakes of the train are applied and it comes to rest a few feet from the child. The mother thanks God for the miracle; which she never ceases to think of as such although, as she in due course learns, there was nothing supernatural about the manner in which the brakes of the train came to be applied. The driver had fainted, for a reason that had nothing to do with the presence of the child on the line, and the brakes were applied automatically as his hand ceased to exert pressure on the control lever. He fainted on this particular afternoon because his blood pressure had risen after an exceptionally heavy lunch during which he had quarrelled with a colleague, and the change in blood pressure caused a clot of blood to be dislodged and circulate. He fainted at the time when he did on the afternoon in

* From the *American Philosophical Quarterly*, vol. 2, 1965. Reprinted with permission.

question because this was the time at which the coagulation in his blood stream reached the brain.

Thus the stopping of the train and the fact that it stopped when it did have a natural explanation. I do not say a *scientific* explanation, for it does not seem to me that the explanation here as a whole is of this kind (in order for something to be unsusceptible of scientific explanation it does not have to be anything so queer and grandiose as a miracle). The form of explanation in the present case, I would say, is *historical*; and the considerations that enter into it are various. They include medical factors, for instance, and had these constituted the whole extent of the matter the explanation could have been called scientific. But as it is, the medical considerations, though obviously important, are only one aspect of a complex story, alongside other considerations of a practical and social kind; and in addition there is a reference to mechanical considerations. All of these enter into the explanation of, or story behind, the stopping of the train. And just as there is an explanatory story behind the train's stopping when and where it did, so there is an explanatory story behind the presence of the child on the line at the time when, and in the place where, he was. But these two explanations or histories are independent of each other. They are about as disconnected as the history of the steam loom is from the history of the Ming dynasty. The spacio-temporal coincidence, I mean the fact that the child was on the line at the time when the train approached and the train stopped a few feet short of the place where he was, is exactly what I have just called it, a coincidence—something which a chronicle of events can merely record, like the fact that the Ming dynasty was in power at the same time as the house of Lancaster.

But unlike the coincidence between the rise of the Ming dynasty and the arrival of the dynasty of Lancaster, the coincidence of the child's presence on the line with the arrival and then the stopping of the train is impressive, significant; not because it is very unusual for trains to be halted in the way this one was, but because the life of a child was imperiled and then, against expectation, preserved. The significance of some coincidences as opposed to others arises from their relation to human needs and hopes and fears, their effects for good or ill upon our lives. So we speak of our luck (fortune, fate, etc.). And the kind of thing that, outside religion, we call luck is in religious parlance the grace of God or a miracle of God. But while the reference here is the same, the meaning is different. The meaning is different in that whatever happens by God's grace or by a miracle is something for which God is thanked or thankable, something which has been or could have been prayed for, something which can be regarded with awe and be taken as a sign or made the subject of a vow (e.g., to go on a pilgrimage), all of which can only take place against the background of a religious tradition. Whereas what happens by a stroke of luck is something in regard to which one just seizes one's opportunity or feels glad about or feels relieved about, something for which one may thank one's lucky stars. To say that one thanks one's lucky stars is simply to express one's relief or to emphasize the intensity of the relief: if it signifies anything more than this it signifies a superstition (*cf.* touching wood).

But although a coincidence can be taken religiously as a sign and called a miracle and made the subject of a vow, it cannot without confusion be taken as a sign of divine interference with the natural order. If someone protests that it is no part of the natural order that an express train should stop for a child on the line whom the driver cannot see then in *protesting* this he misses the point. What he says has been agreed to be perfectly true in the sense that there is no natural order relating the train's motion to the child which could be either preserved or interfered with. The concept of the miraculous which we have so far been considering is distinct therefore from the concept exemplified in the biblical stories of the turning of water into wine and the feeding of five thousand people on a very few loaves and fishes. Let us call the former the contingency concept and the latter the violation concept.

To establish the contingency concept of the miraculous as a possible concept it seems to me enough to point out (1) that *pace* Spinoza, Leibniz, and others, there are genuine contingencies in the world, and (2) that certain of these contingencies can be, and are in fact, regarded religiously in the manner I have indicated. If you assent to this and still express a doubt— "But are they really miracles?"—then you must now be questioning whether people are right to react to contingencies in this way, questioning whether you ought yourself to go along with them. Why not just stick to talking of luck? When you think this you are somewhat in the position of one who watches others fall in love and as an outsider thinks it unreasonable, hyperbolical, ridiculous (surely friendship should suffice).

JAMES KELLENBERGER

from Miracles

I n the section from "Miracles" in this reading James Kellenberger describes and argues for the category of "natural miracle," defending it against the criticism that a natural event cannot be considered an act of God without loss of "content."*

Natural Miracles

I n the eyes of the religious person it may be that most if not all events are due to God's agency. He will give thanks to God for the beginning of a new day, for bread being on his table, and for the birth of his child. In doing so he attributes to God some form of responsibility for these events, but he may profess ignorance regarding the mode of God's agency. At the same time, like the atheist, he will pay the baker for his bread, whom he will hold responsible if the bread is stale; and he will employ the services of an obstetrician to attend his wife's delivery, whom he will hold responsible if there are complications arising from the delivery. But while he will blame the baker if the bread is stale and blame the

* From James Kellenberger, "Miracles," in the *International Journal for Philosophy of Religion*, vol. 10 (1979): 145–62. Reprinted with kind permission of Springer Science and Business Media.

obstetrician if his wife has an avoidable hemorrhage, and not blame God, if the bread is wholesome and if his child is born, he will thank God. How can we understand such an apparently confused attribution of Divine responsibility, one that allows God praise but not blame?

We can, I think, come to some understanding of it through reflection on a certain model of human agency and responsibility. Natural miracles occur *through* God's agency; they are not instances of God's *direct action*. There is no intervention by God, but God, as creator, is deemed thankable for establishing the ground for natural events. In an analogous way a father who establishes an education fund for his son can be thanked by him, and others, for making his college education possible. The father is thankable even though he exerts no direct influence on his son's college career: the fund may have been established in the boy's infancy. In such cases there is a dual responsibility. When the son earns his degree he will be congratulated, and rightly so, for the degree was earned though his efforts; but the father remains thankable for making it possible for his son to attend college in the first place. If, on the other hand, the son fails to earn his degree, other things being equal, he alone of the two is responsible.

The analogy is not perfect, however. The father did not create his son's intellectual powers and so is not responsible for his failure. But God did create the baker and the obstetrician and their abilities. And so, one might think, God is responsible for their failures. Here we are on the outskirts of the problem of evil. For one consistently to blame the obstetrician, and not God, for an avoidable hemorrhage, one must, I believe, see men as beings with "free will" or at least with responsibility for what are indeed *their* failures and oversights. Also, what of

unavoidable hemorrhaging, which is not caused by the obstetrician's failure? Is God responsible? Yes, but He cannot be blameworthy. In the eyes of the believer God's purpose must remain good, though unseen. God cannot be blamed in the sense that a live man cannot die. That is blameworthiness can be attributed to God, but only at the cost of denying that there is a God. A person who blames God no longer sees God as all-good, and God necessarily is all-good. There is an even deeper-running religious implication here than the denial of God's existence. A religious person who comes to blame God would cease to trust in God, which is to say that he would cease to religiously have faith *in* God, even if, *per impossible*, he could continue consistently to believe *that* God exists. Job suffered at the hands of God, but continued to have faith in God, for he continued to trust that His purposes was good. Ivan Karamazov, who could not believe in God's goodness in the face of evil done to children, but who continued to speak of God as though there were a God, had nevertheless ceased to trust and have faith in God.

I do not want to argue that these comments resolve the problem of evil discussed by contemporary philosophers. To say that men have "free will" or are themselves responsible for what are in fact their failures is to begin a discussion of the problem of evil, not to end one. And to affirm that God has a purpose for suffering as believers see it, is, again, to settle nothing. My point here is that there is a model of agency, applicable to both human and Divine agency, admittedly with implications for the problem of evil, that gives us a purchase on God's responsibility and thankability for natural events.

Still there are problems. Terence Penelhum, in his book *Survival and Disembodied Existence*, asks this question: "What is the difference between saying of some natural event . . . that it is also an act of God?"[13] In Penelhum's language, what is the difference in *"content"* between "This event is a natural event" and "This event is a miracle" or "This event is a natural miracle"? As he points out, the difference cannot be simply the claim that the event contributes to the betterment of man. If it where, then saying that all or most natural events are due to God's agency would only be a misleading way of saying that the world is constantly improving, or some such thing. However, Penelhum himself goes wrong, I believe, when he tries to say what would be required to give content to the claim that an event is a Divine act.

As Penelhum sees it, there must be something "in" God to give content to the claim that natural events are acts of God. The concept of Divine agency requires the postulation of a Divine mental life, he says, and the claim that natural events are acts of God logically requires that God should *choose*. Yet, at the same time, he feels we must admit total agnosticism about the character of God's mental life, or say He chooses and wishes timelessly (which fail to yield content for the claim) or embrace the notion of Divine disembodied existence (which is fraught with confusion, he believes).

Can we answer Penelhum's question? Can we say what the difference in content is between "This event is a natural event" and "This event is a miracle," and between "This event is a natural event" and "This event is a natural miracle"? Yes, I think that we can. But first we need to remind ourselves that "content" means meaning. The concern with the difference between saying that an event is a natural event and saying that an

event is a miracle, or a natural miracle, is a concern with meaning. Or, at any rate, it should be, for we can explicate the differences here in terms of meaning. To affirm that an event is a miracle *simpliciter* is to affirm that God in some manner has responsibility for that event, and so is thankable. To affirm that an event is a *natural* miracle is to affirm that God is responsible for that event, not through His intervention, but by making it possible through His creation for that event to occur. The meaning of "This event is a natural event," on the other hand, is, roughly, that the event in question is not a violation of natural laws a content consistent with either affirming or denying God's thankability and responsibility.

But, some philosophers might insist, "content" means *empirical* content. Is there a difference in empirical content between the claim that an event is a natural event and the claim that an event is a natural miracle? I think that there may well not be. Certainly there is no public test that can be conducted to determine if a natural event is an act of God. Penelhum, I believe, was equating content with empirical content when he reasoned that total agnosticism regarding the Divine "mental life" would entail that God's choosing could not provide the needed content: total agnosticism about the nature of God's choices would mean no definite, empirical test and hence no empirical content. But while content can be equated with meaning, empirical content cannot be. And it would remain that the difference between saying that an event is a natural event and saying that an event is a miracle, or specifically a natural miracle, could be given in terms of

[13] Terence Penelhum, *Survival and Disembodied Existence* (London: Routledge & Kegan Paul; New York: Humanities Press, 1970), p. 106.

meaning; thus a difference would remain. Nor is the difference insignificant. The man who says and believes that an event is a natural miracle will in his heart be thankful to God; the man who sees the event as only a natural event will not be. Nor should we think that there being no difference in empirical content entails that there is no way to discover that a natural event is an act of God. It is true that such a discovery could not be experimental, or hypothetical, for there would be no empirical test or verification procedure by which it could be made. Put another way, whether an event is a natural miracle would not be a *scientific question*. But this is far from saying that there is no way for one to discover that a natural event is indeed due to God's agency.

Our primary concern, though, is not whether an event could be discovered to be a natural miracle. Rather it remains the coherence of the concept of natural miracle. I would argue that there is indeed a viable possibility that natural events can be discovered to be due to God's agency. But we concede too much, I believe, if we concede that the coherence of the notion depends upon the possibility of discovery. And, once again, we shall have enough to understand a transcendent God's presence in the world if there is some coherent notion of miracle.

4. Miracles and God's Presence in the World

At this point, it may be hoped, the concept of the miraculous has been seen to be coherent. In fact, I would hope that three concepts of miracle have now emerged as coherent and understandable: the violation concept, the contingency concept and the concept of natural miracle.

This is not to say that there have been such miracles, only that these notions make sense, that we can coherently speak of such miracles and begin to ponder whether the events of the world are miraculous. God's presence in the world, then, is similarly coherent, for He may be said to have a presence in the world in as much as He acts in the world.

To be sure, however, it must be acknowledged that miracles cannot provide a proof that a transcendent God has a presence in the world or that there is a God. That is, they cannot if a proof is something accessible to all rational men, as it surely is. The only "proof" that miracles allow is:

There are miracles (acts of God). Therefore there is a God.

While this argument is valid, the conclusion is doubtful because the premise is, at least to many rational men. However, we should not think that, therefore, no man can come to a discovery of God through the miraculous. Only those who already believe in God will speak of miracles (as occurrent). But one need not already believe in God in order to come to see that an event is a miracle.

A Final Comment

Often religious thinkers, including some religious philosophers, feel that philosophy departs from what is of greatest concern to them. One might feel that a concern with how God can be a nonspatial, transcendent Being still involved in the world is, in just this way, far from a religious concern—a philosophical speculation devoid of religious significance. And here, perhaps, we are reminded of Tillich's strictures of those who see God as "*a* being" and those who see the point of miracle stories as the violation of natural laws.[14]

The religious concern, expressed in Christian terms, is said to be to participate in the "mystical body of Christ," or, in Judaeo-Christian terms, it is to live according to God's law. This, we are told, we do in fellowship with our brothers and through charitable works. Surely this is a religious concern, perhaps the religious concern. Clearly, also, this participation involves the way we live. But let us ask this question: Does participation in the mystical body of Christ, or living according to God's law, exactly equal living a good and charitable life for others? Or does it require living such a life as part of what is seen as a relationship to God? The former is possible without a belief in God; the latter is not. The former is religious in the way humanism is; the latter is religious in the way traditional Judaeo-Christian belief is. Let us grant that humanism is a religion or, rather, recognize it since it is a fact. At the same time

let us be aware that participation in what is seen as a realized relationship to God has been, and is now, more than leading a good life in association with others and for others. It involves a belief in God. More specifically, it involves a belief relating to those acts of charity and love so important for participation. God is the God "through whom all blessings flow." An act of charity or love is a blessing for the one who receives and for the one who gives. It is a part of this belief in participation that we believe men are granted the spirituality to act out of love. We act in love through the mercy of God's allowing us to act. In this way every act of love is God's acting in the world, albeit indirectly. That is, every act of love is a natural miracle. Consequently when we focus on living a life of love and what that means in the traditional religious sense, we do not turn away from the miraculous but towards what is in its essence conceived to be miraculous and to involve God's presence in the world.

[14] Paul Tillich, *Systematic Theology* (Chicago: The University of Chicago Press, 1951), 1, 237 and 117–18.

Chapter **8**

Religion and Morality

Many within the various religious traditions, and many outside religion, have asked: What is the relationship between religion and morality? This question can be understood in different ways. It might be taken to be asking if individual *persons* can be moral—morally good—without being religious, or if individual *persons* can be religious without being moral. These questions can be readily answered, it seems. While many who are religious have led exemplary moral lives, not all who are moral have been committed religiously. Conversely it appears that not all who are religious have been morally upright. While we have religious leaders like Martin Luther King, Jr. and Mahatma Ghandi who have led efforts to obtain moral justice, we have also seen slavery defended in the name of religion. A better way to understand the question is as a question about morality itself and religion itself. How is morality connected to religion? Is religion in some way the foundation of morality? Is morality independent of religion?

Taking our question to be the question about the relationship between morality itself and religion itself, we can distinguish three views, each with its different answer:

 I. Morality is independent of religion because human beings can appeal to their moral sense of right and wrong without any appeal to God or Religious Reality.
 II. Morality is strongly dependent on religion because what makes something morally wrong is its being contrary to God's commands, as what makes something a moral obligation is its being commanded by God.
III. Morality is connected to religion because divine action or Religious Reality is the foundation of morality, but not because God's commands make actions right or wrong.

In this chapter we have readings relating to these three views and to two preliminary questions. One preliminary question is about the relationship between religious morality and non-religious or secular morality, and the second is the question of whether religious morality is the same from religion to religion. The first reading is "Moral and Religious Conceptions of Duty: An Analysis" by D. Z. Phillips. Phillips, writing from a theistic and specifically Christian perspective, explores the difference between religious and non-religious morality.

The second reading is "The Ideal of Generous Goodwill, Love, Compassion," by John Hick. It addresses the question of whether religious morality is the same from religion to religion and argues that within all the great religious traditions there is "the moral ideal of generous goodwill, love, compassion."

The third, fourth, and fifth readings in this chapter relate to the three views of the relationship between religion and morality that we identified above. The third reading is a Socratic dialogue, the *Euthyphro*. It is at once an argument against the idea that what *makes* right actions right is the gods loving them or, in monotheisitic terms, God's commanding them (View II) and for the independence of morality from religion (View I). The fourth reading is Robert Merrihew Adams' "A Modified Divine Command Theory of Ethical Wrongness," in which Adams argues for the view that actions that are contrary to God's commands are morally wrong (View II). The last reading in this chapter consists of three selections from St. Thomas Aquinas' *Summa Theologica*, in which he expounds a natural law view of God's moral order and the relationship between religion and morality (View III).

D. Z. PHILLIPS

Moral and Religious Conceptions of Duty: An Analysis

D. Z. Phillips writes from a theistic and specifically Christian perspective. In "Moral and Religious Conceptions of Duty: An Analysis" Phillips reflects on what he identifies as five differences between "moral duties" and religious "duties to God."*

X

Moral and Religious Conceptions of Duty: An Analysis[1]

D. Z. PHILLIPS

What would it mean if I said that duties to God are given, whereas moral duties are not? Religious *and* moral duties seem to be given. We do not choose a religion in the sense of deciding that it should be the kind of thing it is, any more than we decide what our moral duties shall be. What morality

---

* D.Z. Phillips, "Moral and Religious Conceptions of Duty: An Analysis, "From *Mind*, vol. 73 (1964): 406–12. Reprinted by permission of Oxford University Press.
[1] I am indebted to Mr. Rush Rhees for the many discussions I have had with him on this topic.

is and what religion is does not depend on the individual will. All sorts of forces and influences have played a part in shaping our morality, most of which do not depend on any specific person. Similarly, an account could be given of the development of religious ideas, showing that there were contributory factors, not themselves religious, which played an important part in the development of religion. So it seems untrue to say that the duties we owe to God are given and that moral duties are not. Both it seems are given, in so far as they arc not dependent on individual choices. On the other hand, this argument does not take us very far in the attempt to understand the concept of duty in the respective spheres. To do this one must view the matter from the inside. What must be considered is the grammar of these concepts. It is from the point of view of the grammar of the concepts that I suggest that there is some sense in saying that whereas duties to God are given, moral duties are not.

Moral duties are not given in the sense in which military orders are given. Despite the fact that one could give a justification of military commands in terms of discipline or strategy, and despite the fact that in war-time, for the sake of morale, the soldier is allowed an elementary glimpse of the importance of the order—the success of this mission is all important for our campaign—Britain depends on every man to do his duty—despite all this, the ideal characterization of military orders is, Do as you are told. Military orders seem to provide the most literal example of duties being given.

Moral duties are not given in this way. Military commands are important for the soldier not because of what is said, but because what is said is an order. The mere fact that it is an order makes it a duty irrespective of what the order may

be. In morality, however, it is the content of the duties which make them important.

Religious duties are more akin to military duties than moral duties are. I do not wish to press an analogy which has obvious limitations, but there is a similarity between the soldier's saying in reply to a question why he must perform an action, 'Because these are my superior's orders', and the religious believer's answering the same question, 'Because this is the will of God'. One might object to this by pointing out that the believer who has any insight at all into his Faith could proceed to say something of why he thinks it important to obey God's commands; he could distinguish between a life with God and a life without God. The believer and the unbeliever who is concerned with moral questions can give an account of the duties they obey, but there are important differences to be noted. When the unbeliever expounds the importance of moral duties, what he refers to is the importance of doing *this* action rather than *that* one. This is not what the believer does. When he says that it is important to do the will of God, he is not expounding the contents of God's commands, and as it were, their importance in human relationships, but rather, he is expounding the meaning of submission to the authority of the commands. The unbeliever is saying something about the role of the duties themselves; the believer is talking about *the role of the Giver of the duties*. In religious duties one has a distinction between the content of the duty and the authority of the duty which is absent in moral duties. The radical difference between doing one's duty in and outside religion rests, to a large extent, on the religious identification of duty with the will of God. This difference is illustrated in the following ways:

First, moral duties are not always present; we do not spend even the greater part of our time thinking about duty. On the other hand, the more one meditates on the law of God and disciplines oneself to it, the nearer one is said to be to God: 'But his delight is in the law of the Lord; and in his law doth he meditate day and night' (Psalm i. 2). If anyone talked of meditating on his duty day and night he would be an unbearable person and morally reprehensible. The moral life is not ruled by duty in the way in which the religious life is ruled by the will of God. One of the differences between the average believer and the saint is that the life of the latter is governed more by meditation and obedience than the life of the former. In morality, on the other hand, the admirable person would be the person who acted admirably in given situations. The characteristic of thinking constantly about duty should be absent in such a man.

Secondly, what is to be done in the performance of one's moral duty is usually quite specific. In the profounder kinds of moral perplexity, the question is not, 'How much shall I do?' but 'What ought I to do?' Many moral problems do bring in the former question. One often says, 'I could have done more had I been prepared to sacrifice'. There are always levels of achievement in this respect beyond the level attained by the individual. There are other situations, however, usually involving more intimate human relationships, where the person involved does not know what he ought to do. Sometimes the situation is such that whatever one does one will hurt someone. There is no question here of attaining higher and higher ends, since the person involved says, 'I wish I knew the answer', or in other words, 'I wish I knew what my duty was here'.

In religion, on the other hand, apart from the negative duties of 'thou shalt not . . .', almost all the duties do present one with this indefinite area of achievement. In the command to love and to forgive

one's neighbour, one is not given a limit at which to stop. In morality, whether the question is 'How much shall I do?' or 'What ought I to do?' it makes sense to say at some stage, 'I have done enough'. We say of a third person, 'He has done his duty admirably'. One cannot say of someone in religion, 'He has done his duty' and mean by this, 'He has done enough'.

The two differences between moral and religious conceptions of duty which we have considered are based on a third, more fundamental, difference, namely, that moral duties, unlike religious duties, are often thought of in relation to needs. I recognize that it is my moral duty to do something in face of a need for that particular action to be done which makes up my duty. If a duty is done in relation to needs it at least makes sense to suppose that the need can be met. In so far as the people who benefit from the performance of religious duties get what they needed, it makes sense to talk of answering needs in the performance of religious duties. Yet, the *meaning* of the religious conception of duty resides in the fact that the deed was not done as a duty towards these people, but as a duty towards God, and as a duty to God the divine requirement is never met. The reason for this difference is that religious duties are not done because God needs them. What would it mean for the believer to say that he had helped him on whom he believed himself to be utterly dependent? Or as Kierkegaard has it,

> . . . God needs no man. It would otherwise be a highly embarrassing thing to be a creator, if the result was that the creator came to depend on the creature (*Concluding Unscientific Postscript*, Book II, part ii, chap. i, p. 122).

Many people would want to say that God does need the fulfilment of duties. They want to say that it makes sense to attribute specific needs and emotions to God. Disobedience offends God; obedience pleases him. Biblical covenants seem to take the form of conditional agreements: 'If you'll do this, I'll do that.' This makes the promises of God less profound than human loyalty which endures irrespective of whether it is deserved or not. This argument assumes that human promises and divine promises are essentially the same. But is this so? In answering this question we come to a fourth difference between moral and religious conceptions of duty.

Failure to keep one's promise to another person often leads to an injury to that person. If one fails to do the will of God does one injure God in some way? The sorrow that a thoughtless act can cause is inextricable from the kind of life that human beings live; we do misunderstand one another, and by so doing cause pain and sorrow. But God does not exist in this way. God does not have ups and downs! If one injures another person seriously enough, one can never, despite being forgiven, begin again as if nothing had happened. As a result of God's forgiveness complete reconciliation is said to be possible. What was lost between the sinner and God can be found again, whereas in morality, what was lost through injury can often never be restored.

Again, the ignoring of moral duty can lead to an accentuation of distress. A person's distress could be increased by his discovering that those who could help would not. Disobedience as an offence against God cannot be understood in this way. The fulfilment of religious duties is an expression of the believer's love of God. The horror of sin consists not in any injury done to God, but in the sinner's realization of his rejection and violation of the love which God has shown to him.

The idea of religious duties as expressions of love of God might suggest an analogy with certain human relationships where, although duties are involved, one would not normally speak of duty as a motive for action. I refer to relationships such as those which exist between husband and wife, child and parent, friend and friend. The fulfilment of the marriage vow seems akin to religious duties, since this too is an expression of love. There are, however, important differences to take account of. The love found in marriage, in friendship, and in the family, is essentially particular. By this I mean that it is the separation of these people from everyone else, which to a large extent, makes these relationships what they are. In marriage it is the taking of *this* man and *this* woman which is the source of much of its importance. Again, if everyone were one's friend, friendship would not be the kind of thing it is. The love which exists between the believer and God is not of this order, since it does not depend on the particularity of the individual relationship to God. Love of the child for the parent does depend on the particularity of the relationship, since if we were all children of the same parents, the love of the child for the parent would be radically different. But all men are said to be the children of God.

Having a relationship with God is very different from having a relationship with another human being. The fulfilment of duties in morality often makes possible a participation in certain relationships, and the answering of specific needs. The fulfilment of religious duties makes possible a relationship with God, but what such a relationship entails is a certain attitude to life, and seeing what one's life ought to be. One important aspect of such a relationship is the possibility of giving thanks for one's existence. In morality there need not be anything like an attitude to one's existence as a whole. There would be no contradiction

in holding that moral values are important, while believing that life is a hopeless
mess. One could not believe in God and
assert that life is devoid of hope.

To understand, then, what is meant
by the religious conception of duty, one
must understand what it means to believe
in God. This must be recognized in any
analysis of religious conceptions of duty,
and it brings one to perhaps the most
important difference between them and
moral conceptions of duty.

In morality, adherence to certain values often involves a recognition of why
these values are important. True, moral
standards are often observed without any
particular insight into their importance.
Moral perplexity, however, usually calls
for moral and psychological insight. One
cannot possess such insight unless one
has thought one's way through to an
appreciation of a moral analysis of various situations. If God is important to the
believer, and if it is all-important that
God's will is done, this is not because the
believer has somehow thought his way
through to God. That is why St. John of
the Cross makes such radical assertions
as the following:

> '. . . if any among you seemeth to be
> wise let him become ignorant that he
> may be wise; for the wisdom of this
> world is foolishness with God.' So
> that, in order to come to union with
> the wisdom of God, the soul has to
> proceed by unknowing rather than
> by knowing (*Ascent of Mount Carmel*,
> Book I, chap. iv, p. 19).

The idea of 'the way of unknowing' is
important for our analysis and for philosophy of religion generally. Morality is part
of the way of knowing; it involves an
appreciation of values. The profound
believer does not arrive at his belief in a
way akin to the unbeliever's arrival at a

moral decision. It is only when he realizes
that he does not know the answers that the
believer finds the grace of God. In finding
God the believer has not thought his way
through to a meaning in his life or in life in
general, but has accepted, without reservation, the will of God. What Job came to
know was that he did not know the answers
about himself or about the world.

The above argument which contrasts
religious acceptance with moral understanding should be understood as a corrective, rather than as an independent
thesis. I am anxious-to avoid a position in
which religious language seems to be a
special language cut off from other forms
of human discourse. Religion would not
have the kind of importance it has were
it not connected with the rest of life.
Religious discourse has much in common
with moral discourse. The naked are
clothed and the starving are fed whether
the motive is moral or religious.
Religion, in the form of prayer, can often
help to resolve moral difficulties. More
important is the fact that we say that the
later stages of a religion are *deeper* than
the earlier stages; we say too that one
person's faith is deeper than the faith of
another person. These judgements can
be made by non-believers, which suggests that religious concepts are not inaccessible to non-religious understanding.

On the other hand, I also want to avoid
the view that religious concepts can be
accounted for in moral terms. My emphasis
on the differences between moral and religious conceptions of duty was meant to
combat such a view, an example of which is
seen in Gilbert Murray's position:

> . . . the various bodies who have
> accepted or put into articulate shape
> these moral ideals always have some
> difficulty in accounting for them.
> Man has known that he wished to be
> good and do good, but has never

quite found a satisfactory answer to the question why he wished it. He nearly always had to invent what I will venture to call a mythology (*Myths and Ethics*, p. 18).

The concept of God must be central in an analysis of religious conceptions of duty. This centrality is illustrated by the way in which the analogy between military duties and religious duties breaks down. Military commands or commands of the state can be challenged. Other obligations may be thought to be more important; for example, obligations to one's family (cf. Antigone). It does not make sense to assume that in certain situations other duties might be more important than one's duty to God. God's

commands cannot become of secondary importance without being abandoned.

The distinction between the moral and religious conceptions of duty is not one of degree. As Kierkegaard says,

> Concerning the spiritual relation one cannot—if he wishes to avoid speaking foolishly—talk like a shop-keeper who has a best quality of goods, but also an intermediate quality which he also ventures to recommend as very good, as almost equally good (*Works of Love*, p. 38).

The distinction between the concepts is one of grammar; that is to say, what it makes sense to say of one, it often does not make sense to say of the other. This is no trivial matter.

JOHN HICK

The Ideal of Generous Goodwill, Love, Compassion

In the third reading John Hick offers reflections that address the second preliminary question. Hick argues that within all the great religious traditions there is "the moral ideal of generous goodwill, love, compassion." This is the ideal contained in the Golden Rule, but, examining the sacred texts of the world religions, Hick finds this moral ideal in some expression to be universal among the world religions, including Judaism, Christianity, Islam, and Buddhism. Selections from several of the sacred texts cited by Hick are in Chapter 1.*

The Ethical Criterion

Thou shalt love thy neighbour as thyself.
(*Jesus the Christ, Matthew 22:39*)

As a mother cares for her son, all her days, so towards all living things a man's mind should be all-embracing.
(*Gautama the Buddha*, Sutta Nipata, *149*)

1. The Ideal Of Generous Goodwill, Love, Compassion

That all the great traditions teach the moral ideal of generous goodwill, love, compassion epitomised in the Golden

* From John Hick, *An Interpretation of Religion*, Chap. 18. New Haven and London: Yale University Press, 1989. Reproduced with permission of Palgrave Macmillan.

Rule must now be confirmed by pointing to it more fully in their scriptures. It should be emphasised that I am not here trying to expound the entire ethical teachings of these traditions, nor to describe the actual behaviour of their adherents through the centuries, but to show that love, compassion, generous concern for and commitment to the welfare of others is a central ideal for each of them.

Within the many-sided and many-levelled complex of Indian traditions known to the modern West as Hinduism the basis for universal compassion lies in a belief in the hidden unity of all life. As we have already noted, there is no one universally accepted system of Hindu ideas, and the scriptures use both personal and non-personal language in speaking of the ultimate reality, Brahman. But this difference does not affect the sense of the oneness of life and hence the 'compassion', the feeling with and for others, which it produces. Both the advaitic view that all selves are ultimately identical and the vishishtadvaitist view that they are all individually part of the one divine being point to a human unity: 'Thus one Universal Inner Self of all beings becomes one separate self for each form' (*Katha* Up., II:2:10—cf. Radhakrishnan 1969, 639). The liberated person 'sees himself in all beings, and all beings in himself' (*Bhagavad Gita*, vi:29—Bolle 1979, 77); 'And he who sees all beings in his own self and his own self in all beings, he does not feel any revulsion' (*Īśa* Up., 6—Radhakrishnan 1969, 572).[1] Accordingly, 'One should look upon all creatures as one's own self' (*Mahabharata*, 12:29—Roy 1891; cf. 310, 5:33f). Or as

Gandhi expressed it, 'I believe in the absolute oneness of God and therefore also of humanity. What though we have many bodies? We have but one soul' (Mahatma Gandhi 1924, 313).[2] And in the *Bhagavad Gita* (also part of the *Mahabharata*) we read this description of the good person:

He is generous and shows self-restraint ...
Practices austerity
    and honesty.
He is gentle, truthful, not given to anger,
    able to give up possesions.
He has peace
    and does not slander anyone.
He has compassion toward all creatures
    and no greed.
He knows mildness and humility,
    and is not fickle in his behavior.
There is majesty in him.
He is forbearing, firm, and pure,
Free from all treachery
    and conceit.
        (xvi:1–3—Bolle 1979, 179)

Spelled out in explicitly ethical terms this requires the three '*da*'s': *damyata*, self-control; *datta*, giving; *dayadhvam*, compassion (*Brhadāranyaka* Up., V:2:2–3). Again, 'Confidence, modesty, forgiveness, liberality, purity, freedom from laziness, absence of cruelty, freedom from delusion, compassion to all creatures, absence of backbiting, joy, contentment, joviality, humility, good behaviour, purity in all action' are enjoined (*Anugītā*, xxiii—Müller [1884] 1908a, 326). The *Mahabharata*, by which so many generations of Indians have been nurtured, presents the same ideal: 'He who ... benefits persons of all orders, who

---

[1] Radhakrishnan comments, 'He shrinks from nothing as he knows that the one Self is manifested in the multiple forms' (Radhakrishnan 1969, 572).
[2] The Hindu philosopher Ramchandra Gandhi (a grandson of the Mahatma) has written a book entitled *I am Thou* (1984).

is always devoted to the good of all beings, who does not feel aversion for anybody . . . succeeds in ascending to Heaven' (Anushana parva, 145:24—Roy 1893, 659). Again, 'Abstention from injury, truth, absence of wrath, and liberality of gifts . . . these constitute eternal Righteousness' (Anushana parva, 142:22—Roy 1983, 760). Or again, 'Not having done any injury to anyone, such a man lives fearlessly and with a pure heart' (Shanti parva, 259:13— Roy 1891, 344).

Basically similar injunctions occur in the Jewish Torah, expressed here as concrete *mitzvot* for the daily life of the people:

> When you reap the harvest of your land, you shall not reap your field to its very border, neither shall you gather the gleanings after your harvest. And you shall not strip your vineyard bare, neither shall you gather the fallen grapes of your vineyard; you shall leave them for the poor and the sojourner; I am the Lord your God.
>
> You shall not oppress your neighbour or rob him. The wages of a hired servant shall not remain with you all night until the morning. You shall not curse the deaf or put a stumbling block before the blind, but you shall fear your God: I am the Lord.
>
> You shall do no injustice in judgment; you shall not be partial to the poor or defer to the great, but in righteousness shall you judge your neighbour. You shall not go up and down as a slanderer among your people, and you shall not stand forth against the life of your neighbour: I am the Lord.
>
> You shall not hate your brother in your heart, but you shall reason with your neighbour, lest you bear sin because of him. You shall not take vengeance or bear any grudge against the sons of your own people, but you shall love (*ahabta*) your neighbour (*re'a*) as yourself:[3] I am the Lord.
>
> When a stranger sojourns with you in your land, you shall not do him wrong. The stranger who sojourns with you shall be to you as the native among you, and you shall love him as yourself; for you were strangers in the land of Egypt: I am the Lord your God.
>
> (Leviticus, 19:9–10, 11–18)

The fact that awareness of the Real, known to the Jewish people as the God of Abraham, sets human beings under a profound moral claim was likewise the powerfully reiterated message of the great Hebrew prophets:

> Woe to those who decree iniquitous decrees,
> and the writers who keep writing oppression,

---

[3] There has been considerable discussion as to who the *re'a*, neighbour, is who is to be loved. A widely held view (expressed, e.g., by Ernst Simon 1975) is that throughout most of the rabbinic period the injunction was generally understood to refer to fellow children of Israel and thus to apply only to relationships between Jews, but that it has been opened out in many modern treatments to apply universally—as by Martin Buber (1951, 69–70). It is however important to add (see Norman Solomon 1985, 6, 16) that the Jew's ethical relationship with gentiles is governed, in rabbinic thought, by certain broad principles—'*tiqqun olam* ('establishing the world aright'), *darkhe shalom* ('the ways of peace') and '*qiddush Hashem* ('sanctifying God's name')—which lead to essentially the same sort of behaviour as to one's neighbour within the Jewish community of faith.

to turn aside the needy from justice
and to rob the poor of my people of their
    right,
that widows may be their spoil,
and that they may make the fatherless
    their prey!

(Isaiah 10:1–2)

For Jews, to know the Holy One, blessed be he, is to live according to God's law, which is, fundamentally, to 'do justice, to love kindness, and to walk humbly with your God' (*Micah* 6:8).[4]

When we turn to the Buddhist tradition we move outside the sphere of divine commands. The motivation to live rightly is neither fear of punishment nor hope of reward, except in the sense that 'All we are is the result of what we have thought: it is founded on our thoughts, and is made up of our thoughts. If a man speaks or acts with a pure thought, happiness follows him, like a shadow that never leaves him' (*Dhammapada*, 1). For the way of the Dharma is not only intrinsically connected with inner happiness but is at the same time the way to final liberation. This is the Noble Eightfold Path, some of the steps in which are directly ethical:

> Verily it is this Ariyan eightfold way, to wit: Right view (*ditthi*), right aim (*sankappa*), right speech (*vaca*), right action (*kammanta*), right living or livelihood, *ajiva*), right effort (*vayama*), right mindfulness (*sati*), and right concentration (*samādhi*). This, monks, is that middle path which giveth vision, which giveth knowledge, which causeth calm, special knowledge, enlightenment, Nibbana.
>
> (*Saṃyutta Nikāya*, V:421—
> Woodward 1956, 357)

Right speech, action and livelihood involve abstention from lying, backbiting, slander, abuse and idle gossip; from destroying life, stealing, dishonesty and illegitimate sexual intercourse; and from making one's living in ways that harm others, such as dealing in weapons and dangerous drugs and poisons, defrauding people or slaughtering animals.

This moral outlook, expressed in the Pali scriptures, developed in due course into the ideal of the bodhisattva: one who has attained to the verge of Nirvana and thus to the end of the process of rebirth but who out of limitless compassion (*karunā*) renounces final nirvanisation until the whole human race has been raised to the same level. The vow of the bodhisattva is one of self-sacrifice for the salvation of many:

> All creatures are in pain, all suffer from bad and hindering karma . . . so that they cannot see the Buddhas or hear the Law of Righteousness or know the Order . . . All that mass of pain and evil karma I take in my own body . . . I take upon myself the burden of sorrow . . . Assuredly I must bear the burdens of all beings . . . for I have resolved to save them all. I must set them all free, I must save the whole world from the forest of birth, old age, disease, and rebirth, from misfortune and sin, from the round of birth and death, from the toils of heresy . . . For all beings are caught in the net of craving, encompassed by ignorance, held by the desire for existence . . . I work to establish the kingdom of perfect wisdom for all beings . . .
>
> (*Śikṣāsamuccaya*, 278f—de Bary
> 1972, 84–5)

---

[4] See also Nelson Glueck 1975 and the article on *hesed* in Botterweck & Ringrenn 1986, vol. 5.

Returning to the Pali scriptures, the four cardinal virtues extolled in them are friendliness (*mettā*), compassion (*karuṇā*), sympathetic joy (*muditā*) and serenity (*samatha*). The following passage conveys the flavour of this Buddhist outlook:

May all be happy and safe!
May all beings gain inner joy—
All living beings whatever...
Seen or unseen,
Dwelling afar or near,
Born or yet unborn—
May all beings gain inner joy.
May no being deceive another,
Nor in any way scorn another,
Nor, in anger or ill-will,
Desire another's sorrow.
As a mother cares for her son,
Her only son, all her days,
So towards all things living
A man's mind should be all-embracing.

Friendliness for the whole world,
All-embracing, he should raise in his
mind,
Above, below, and across,
Unhindered, free from hate and ill-will.
(*Sutta Nipata*, 143f—de Bary 1972, 37–8)

Essentially the same ideal of universal compassion or love (*agape*)[5] is central to Christianity. When Jesus was asked, Which is the greatest commandment? he answered by bringing together two texts from the Torah: 'Thou shalt love the Lord thy God with all thy heart, and with all thy soul, and with all thy mind. This is the first and great commandment. And the second is like unto it. Thou shalt love thy neighbour as thyself' (Matthew 22:36–9). The New Testament collection of Jesus' sayings known as the Sermon on the Mount begins with a series of beatitudes, several of which are ethical in content:

Blessed are the meek, for they shall inherit the earth.
Blessed are those who hunger and thirst for righteousness, for they shall be filled.
Blessed are the merciful, for they shall obtain mercy.
Blessed are the peacemakers, for they shall be called sons of God.
(Matthew 5:5–7, 9)

The Sermon then teaches the personal love commandment and its implication of non-violence:

Ye have heard that it hath been said, An eye for an eye, and a tooth for a tooth: but I say unto you, That ye resist not evil: but whosoever shall smite thee on thy right cheek, turn to him the other also. And if any man will sue thee at law, and take away thy coat, let him have thy cloak also. And whosoever shall compel thee to go a mile, go with him twain. Give to him that asketh thee, and from him that would borrow of thee turn not thou away.

Ye have heard that it hath been said, Thou shalt love thy neighbour, and hate thine enemy. But I say unto you, Love your enemies, bless them that curse you, do good to them that hate you, and pray for them that despitefully use you, and persecute you; that ye may be the children of your Father which is in heaven: for he maketh his sun to rise on the evil and on the good, and sendeth rain on the just and on the unjust. For if ye love

[5] In all the following quotations from the New Testament 'love' translates *agape* and its cognates. On the word *agape* see Victor Paul Furnish 1973, Appendix.

them which love you, what reward have ye? Do not even the publicans the same? And if ye salute your brethren only, what do ye more than others? Do not even the publicans so? Be ye therefore perfect, even as your Father which is in heaven is perfect.

(Matthew 5:38–48)

The love commandment is echoed in the letters of St John and St Paul. The former writes, 'Beloved, let us love one another: for love is of God; and every one that loveth is born of God, and knoweth God. He that loveth not knoweth not God; for God is love ... If a man say, I love God, and hateth his brother, he is a liar: for he that loveth not his brother whom he hath seen, how can he love God whom he hath not seen?' (I John 4:7–8, 20). And St Paul writes to the Galatians that 'the fruit of the Spirit is love, joy, peace, longsuffering, gentleness, goodness, faith, meekness, temperance: against such there is no law' (Galatians 5:22–3). But the most eloquent celebration of love in the New Testament is St Paul's 'hymn':

> Though I speak with the tongues of men and of angels, and have not love, I am become as sounding brass, or a tinkling cymbal. And though I have the gift of prophecy, and understand all mysteries, and all knowledge; and though I have all faith, so that I could remove mountains, and have not love, I am nothing. And though I bestow all my goods to feed the poor, and though I give my body to be burned, and have not love, it profiteth me nothing. Love suffereth long, and is kind; love envieth not: love vaunteth not itself, is not puffed up, doth not behave itself unseemly, seeketh not her own, is not easily provoked, thinketh no evil; rejoiceth not in iniquity,

> but rejoiceth in the truth; beareth all things, believeth all things, hopeth all things, endureth all things. Love never faileth: but whether there be prophecies, they shall fail; whether there be tongues, they shall cease; whether there be knowledge, it shall vanish away ... And now abideth faith, hope, love, these three; but the greatest of these is love.

(I Corinthians 13:1–8, 13)

In the neighbouring Islamic tradition the moral ideal is expressed in the Qur'an and illustrated in the *hadith* reports of the sayings of Muhammad and stories of his life. The Muslim knows him or herself to be a slave of God, the Merciful, the Compassionate. This central relationship is to be lived out in a spirit of mercy and forgiveness toward others, compassion toward parents and orphans, travellers and the poor, in honesty and just dealing, faithfulness in marriage, kindness to children, cheerful courtesy and humility of bearing. For example, in Sura 17 of the Qur'an we read these injunctions, addressed to a sixth-century CE Arabian society living under harsh conditions in which the weak—widows and orphans, the poor, the old, slaves—were pitifully vulnerable, in which travel was dangerous, and in which infanticide was practised because female children were seen as an economic burden:

> Thy Lord hath decreed
> That ye worship none but Him.
> And that ye be kind
> To parents. Whether one
> Or both of them attain
> Old age in thy life,
> Say not to them a word
> Of contempt, nor repel them,
> But address them
> In terms of honour.
> And, out of kindness,
> Lower to them the wing

Of humility, and say 'My Lord! bestow
on them
Thy Mercy even as they
Cherished me in childhood.' (23–4)
And render to the kindred
Their due rights, as (also)
To those in want,
And to the wayfarer. (26)
Kill not your children
For fear of want: We shall
Provide sustenance for them
As well as for you.
Verily the killing of them
Is a great sin. (31)
Nor come nigh to adultery:
For it is a shameful (deed)
And an evil, opening the road
(To other evils). (32)
Come not nigh
To the orphan's property
Except to improve it,
Until he attains the age
Of full strength; and fulfil
(Every) engagement,
For (every) engagement
Will be inquired into
(On the Day of Reckoning).
Give full measure when ye
Measure, and weigh
with a balance that is straight. (34–5)
Nor walk on the earth
With insolence: for thou
Canst not rend the earth
Asunder, nor reach
The mountains in height. (37)
                    (Trans. Yusuf Ali, 1977)

Elsewhere there is this account of true
religion:

It is not righteousness
That ye turn your faces
Towards East or West;
But it is righteousness—
To believe in God
And the Last Day,
And the Angels,

And the Book,
And the Messengers;
To spend of your substance,
Out of love for Him,
For your kin,
For orphans,
For the needy,
For the wayfarer,
For those who ask,
And for the ransom of slaves;
To be steadfast in prayer,
And practise regular charity;
To fulfil the contracts
Which ye have made.
        (Qur'an 2:177, trans. Yusuf Ali, 1977)

And at various places in the Qur'an we read such verses as these: 'Do thou good, as God has been good to thee' (28:77); 'Whoever submits his whole self to God and is a doer of good, he will get his reward with his Lord' (2:112).

In the *hadith* many sayings of the Prophet call for generous kindness, love, compassion for one's fellows. For example, 'It is one form of faith (*iman*) that one loves (*hub*) his brother as one loves oneself' (*Bukhari*, ch. on *iman*, 7). To take other examples from the *Al-Hadis of Miskat-ul-Masibih* (Karim 1960–4): 'Verily Allah is kind. He loves kindness; and He bestows over kindness what He bestows not over harshness' (1:253); 'He who is devoid of kindness is devoid of all good' (1:252); 'You shall not enter Paradise until you believe; and you will not believe till you love one another' (1:226); 'The main part of wisdom after religion is love for men and doing good to everyone, pious or sinner' (1:248); 'Feed the hungry, visit the sick, and free the captive' (1:220); 'The best home of Muslims is a home wherein there is an orphan who is treated well' (1:202); 'Pay trust to one who has entrusted you, and be not treacherous to one who was treacherous to you' (1:347); 'The strong man is not one who can wrestle, but the strong man is one who can control himself in the time of anger' (1:351). And concerning Muhammad himself we read that 'Forgiveness was a chief jewel in the Prophet's character. So broad was his heart that the spirit of revenge was absolutely absent from it' (IV:283); 'the Holy Prophet used always to invoke blessings on his enemies instead of taking revenge on them for the wrongs done to him' (IV:286); 'Abu Hurairah reported that it was questioned: O Messenger of Allah! curse against the polytheists. He replied: Verily I have been sent not to curse, but verily I have been raised up as mercy' (1:247).

Works Cited in Text and Notes

Bolle, Kees
1979: *The Bahagavadgita: A New Translation* (Berkeley and London: University of California Press).
Botterweck, G., and H. Ringrenn (eds)
1986: *Theological Dictionary of the Old Testament*, vol. 5, trans. David Green (Grand Rapids, MI: Wm B. Eerdmans).
Buber, Martin
1951: *Two Types of Faith*, trans. Norman Goldhawk (London: Routledge & Kegan Paul).
de Bary, William Theodore, (ed.)
1972: *The Buddhist Tradition in India, China and Japan* [1969] (New York: Vintage Books).
Furnish, Victor Paul
1973: *The Love Command in the New Testament* (London: SCM Press).
Glueck, Nelson
1975: *Hesed in the Bible*, trans. Alfred Gottschalk (New York: KTAV).
Müller, Max
1908a: *The Sacred Books of the East* [1884], vol. 8 (*Anugīuā*), 2nd edition (Oxford: Clarendon Press).
Radhakrishnan, S., (trans.)
1969: *The Principal Upanishads* [1953] (London: George Allen & Unwin, and New York: Humanities Press).
Roy, Pratapa Chandra (trans.)
1891: *The Mahabharata*, Shanti parva (Calcutta: Bhārata Press).
1893: *The Mahabharata*, Anushana parva (Calcutta: Bhārata Press).
Simon, Ernst
1975: 'The Neighbour (*Re'a*) Whom We Shall Love', in Fox (ed.) 1975.
Solomon, Norman
1985: 'Judaism and World Religions' (Birmingham: Centre for the Study of Judaism and Jewish/Christian Relations).

PLATO

from Euthyphro

In the *Euthyphro*, a dialogue written by Plato, Socrates' student, Socrates questions Euthyphro about the nature of piety or holiness. Euthyphro at one point near the end of our reading says that what all the gods love is pious or holy, and the opposite, which they all hate, impious. This evokes from Socrates the question: Is the pious or holy beloved by the gods because it is holy, or is it holy because it is beloved by the gods? Euthyphro must say that it is the second, but Socrates argues that it is the first. Socrates argues that what is loved by the gods (the god-beloved) has one nature, but the holy or pious has a different nature. The god-beloved is what it is *because the gods love it*. But the holy or pious has a nature *to be loved*—there is something in its nature that makes it worthy of love before the gods love it. So it cannot be that the gods' loving it *makes it* holy or pious. In the dialogue Euthyphro defines piety in terms of the then flourishing polytheistic belief in the Greek gods. However the challenge to the monotheistic view that God's commands make actions wrong or right (in the sense of obligatory)—that is, View II—posed by the dialogue and Socrates' question is apparent when Socrates' question is rephrased as "Does God command what God does because it is right, or is it right because God commands it?" Those who hold View II must say that it is the second, while those who oppose View II would say that it the first. Socrates reasoning, appropriately rephrased, would still apply. What God commands is what it is *because God commands it*. But the morally right has a nature *to be commanded*—there is something in its nature that makes it worthy of being commanded before God commands it. So it cannot be that God's commanding it *makes it* morally right.

Our reading consists of a little more than the first two-thirds of the dialogue.*

Euthyphro

PERSONS OF THE DIALOGUE

SOCRATES.
EUTHYPHRO.

SCENE: The porch of the King Archon.

EUTHYPHRO. Why have you left the lyceum, Socrates: and what are you doing in the porch of the King Archon? Surely you cannot be concerned in a suit before the king, like myself?

SOCRATES. Not in a suit, Euthyphro; impeachment is the word which the Athenians use.

EUTH. What! I suppose that some one has been prosecuting you, for I cannot believe that you are the prosecutor of another.

SOC. Certainly not.

EUTH. Then some one else has been prosecuting you?

SOC. Yes.

EUTH. And who is he?

SOC. A young man who is little known, Euthyphro; and I hardly know

him: his name is Meletus, and he is one of the deme of Pitthis. Perhaps you may remember his appearance; he has a beak, and long straight hair, and a beard which is ill grown.

EUTH. No, I do not remember him, Socrates. But what is the charge which he brings against you?

SOC. What is the charge? Well, a very serious charge, which shows a good deal of character in the young man, and for which he is certainly not to be despised. He says he knows how the youth are corrupted and who are their corrupters. I fancy that he must be a wise man, and seeing that I am the reverse of a wise man, he has found me out, and is going to accuse me of corrupting his young friends. And of this our mother the State is to be the judge. Of all our political men he is the only one who seems to me to begin in the right way, with the cultivation of virtue in youth; like a good husbandman, he makes the young shoots his first care, and clears away us who are the destroyers of them. This is only the first step; he will

* From Plato's *Euthyphro, translated by Benjamin Jowett.*

afterwards attend to the elder branches; and if he goes on as he has begun, he will be a very great public benefactor.

EUTH. I hope that he may; but I rather fear, Socrates, that the opposite will turn out to be the truth. My opinion is that in attacking you he is simply aiming a blow at the foundation of the State. But in what way does he say that you corrupt the young?

SOC. He brings a wonderful accusation against me, which at first hearing excites surprise: he says that I am a poet or maker of gods, and that I invent new gods and deny the existence of old ones; this is the ground of his indictment.

EUTH. I understand, Socrates; he means to attack you about the familiar sign which occasionally, as you say, comes to you. He thinks that you are a neologian, and he is going to have you up before the court for this. He knows that such a charge is readily received by the world, as I myself know too well; for when I speak in the assembly about divine things, and foretell the future to them, they laugh at me and think me a madman. Yet every word that I say is true. But they are jealous of us all; and we must be brave and go at them.

SOC. Their laughter, friend Euthyphro, is not a matter of much consequence. For a man may be thought wise; but the Athenians, I suspect, do not much trouble themselves about him until he begins to impart his wisdom to others; and then for some reason or other, perhaps, as you say from jealousy, they are angry.

EUTH. I am never likely to try their temper in this way.

SOC. I dare say not, for you are reserved in your behaviour, and seldom impart your wisdom. But I have a benevolent habit of pouring out myself to everybody, and would even pay for a listener, and I am afraid that the Athenians may think me too talkative. Now if, as I

was saying, they would only laugh at me, as you say that they laugh at you, the time might pass gaily enough in the court; but perhaps they may be in earnest, and then what the end will be you soothsayers only can predict.

EUTH. I dare say that the affair will end in nothing, Socrates, and that you will win your cause; and I think that I shall win my own.

SOC. And what is your suit, Euthyphro? are you the pursuer or the defendant?

EUTH. I am the pursuer.

SOC. Of whom?

EUTH. You will think me mad when I tell you.

SOC. Why, has the fugitive wings?

Euth. Nay, he is not very volatile at his time of life.

SOC. Who is he?

EUTH. My father.

SOC. Your father! my good man?

EUTH. Yes.

SOC. And of what is he accused?

EUTH. Of murder, Socrates.

SOC. By the powers, Euthyphro! how little does the common herd know of the nature of right and truth. A man must be an extraordinary man, and have made great strides in wisdom, before he could have seen his way to bring such an action.

EUTH. Indeed, Socrates, he must.

SOC. I suppose that the man whom your father murdered was one of your relatives—clearly he was; for if he had been a stranger you would never have thought of prosecuting him.

EUTH. I am amused, Socrates, at your making a distinction between one who is a relation and one who is not a relation; for surely the pollution is the same in either case, if you knowingly associate with the murderer when you ought to clear yourself and him by proceeding against him. The real question is whether the murdered man has been justly slain. If justly, then your duty is to let the matter alone; but if unjustly, then, even if the murderer lives under the same roof with you and eats at the same table, proceed against him. Now, the man who is dead was a poor dependent of mine who worked for us as a field labourer on our farm in Naxos, and one day in a fit of drunken passion he got into a quarrel with one of our domestic servants and slew him. My father bound him hand and foot and threw him into a ditch, and then sent to Athens to ask of a diviner what he should do with him. Meanwhile he never attended to him and took no care about him, for he regarded him as a murderer; and thought that no great harm would be done even if he did die. Now this was just what happened. For such was the effect of cold and hunger and chains upon him, that before the messenger returned from the diviner, he was dead. And my father and family are angry with me for taking the part of the murderer and prosecuting my father. They say that he did not kill him, and that if he did, the dead man was but a murderer, and I ought not to take any notice, for that a son is impious who prosecutes a father. Which shows, Socrates, how little they know what the gods think about piety and impiety.

Soc. Good heavens, Euthyphro! and is your knowledge of religion and of things pious and impious so very exact, that, supposing the circumstances to be as you state them, you are not afraid lest you too may be doing an impious thing in bringing an action against your father?

Euth. The best of Euthyphro, and that which distinguishes him, Socrates, from other men, is his exact knowledge of all such matters. What should I be good for without it?

Soc. Rare friend! I think that I cannot do better than be your disciple. Then before the trial with Meletus comes on I shall challenge him, and say that I have always had a great interest in religious questions, and now, as he charges me with rash imaginations and innovations in religion, I have become your disciple. You, Meletus, as I shall say to him, acknowledge Euthyphro to be a great theologian, and sound in his opinions; and if you approve of him you ought to approve of me, and not have me into court; but if you disapprove, you should begin by indicting him who is my teacher, and who will be the ruin, not of the young, but of the old; that is to say, of myself whom he instructs, and of his old father whom he admonishes and chastises. And if Meletus refuses to listen to me, but will go on, and will not shift the indictment from me to you, I cannot do better than repeat this challenge in the court.

Euth. Yes, indeed, Socrates; and if he attempts to indict me I am mistaken if I do not find a flaw in him; the court shall have a great deal more to say to him than to me.

Soc. And I, my dear friend, knowing this, am desirous of becoming your disciple. For I observe that no one appears to notice you—not even this Meletus; but his sharp eyes have found me out at once, and he has indicted me for impiety. And therefore I adjure you to tell me the nature of piety and impiety, which you said that you knew so well, and of murder, and of other offences against the gods. What are they? Is not piety in every action always the same? and impiety, again—is it not always the opposite of piety, and also the same with itself, having, as impiety, one notion which includes whatever is impious?

Euth. To be sure, Socrates.

Soc. And what is piety, and what is impiety?

Euth. Piety is doing as I am doing; that is to say, prosecuting any one who is guilty of murder, sacrilege, or of any similar crime—whether he be your father or mother, or whoever he may be—that makes no difference; and not to prosecute them is impiety. And please to consider, Socrates, what a notable proof I will give you of the truth of my words, a proof which I have already given to others:—of the principle, I mean, that the impious, whoever he may be, ought not to go unpunished. For do not men regard Zeus as the best and most righteous of the gods?—and yet they admit that he bound his father (Cronos) because he wickedly devoured his sons, and that he too had punished his own father (Uranus) for a similar reason, in a nameless manner. And yet when I proceed against my father, they are angry with me. So inconsistent are they in their way of talking when the gods are concerned, and when I am concerned.

Soc. May not this be the reason, Euthyphro, why I am charged with impiety—that I cannot away with these stories about the gods? and therefore I suppose that people think me wrong. But, as you who are well informed about them approve of them, I cannot do better than assent to your superior wisdom. What else can I say, confessing as I do, that I know nothing about them? Tell me, for the love of Zeus, whether you really believe that they are true.

Euth. Yes, Socrates; and things more wonderful still, of which the world is in ignorance.

Soc. And do you really believe that the gods fought with one another, and had dire quarrels, battles, and the like, as the poets say, and as you may see represented in the works of great artists? The temples are full of them; and notably the robe of Athene, which is carried up to the Acropolis at the great Panathenaea, is embroidered with them. Are all these tales of the gods true, Euthyphro?

Euth. Yes, Socrates; and, as I was saying, I can tell you, if you would like to hear them, many other things about the gods which would quite amaze you.

Soc. I dare say; and you shall tell me them at some other time when I have leisure. But just at present I would rather hear from you a more precise answer, which you have not as yet given, my friend, to the question, What is "piety"? When asked, you only replied, Doing as you do, charging your father with murder.

Euth. And what I said was true, Socrates.

Soc. No doubt, Euthyphro; but you would admit that there are many other pious acts?

Euth. There are.

Soc. Remember that I did not ask you to give me two or three examples of piety, but to explain the general idea which makes all pious things to be pious. Do you not recollect that there was one idea which made the impious impious, and the pious pious?

Euth. I remember.

Soc. Tell me what is the nature of this idea, and then I shall have a standard to which I may look, and by which I may measure actions, whether yours or those of any one else, and then I shall be able to say that such and such an action is pious, such another impious.

Euth. I will tell you, if you like.

Soc. I should very much like.

Euth. Piety, then, is that which is dear to the gods, and impiety is that which is not dear to them.

Soc. Very good, Euthyphro; you have now given me the sort of answer which I wanted. But whether what you say is true or not I cannot as yet tell, although I make no doubt that you will prove the truth of your words.

Euth. Of course.

Soc. Come, then, and let us examine what we are saying. That thing or person which is dear to the gods is pious, and that thing or person which is hateful to the gods is impious, these two being the extreme opposites of one another. Was not that said?

EUTH. It was.

SOC. And well said?

EUTH. Yes, Socrates, I thought so; it was certainly said.

SOC. And further, Euthyphro, the gods were admitted to have enmities and hatreds and differences?

EUTH. Yes, that was also said.

SOC. And what sort of difference creates enmity and anger? Suppose, for example, that you and I, my good friend, differ about a number; do differences of this sort make us enemies and set us at variance with one another? Do we not go at once to arithmetic, and put an end to them by a sum?

EUTH. True.

SOC. Or suppose that we differ about magnitudes, do we not quickly end the difference by measuring?

EUTH. Very true.

SOC. And we end a controversy about heavy and light by resorting to a weighing machine?

EUTH. To be sure.

SOC. But what differences are there which cannot be thus decided, and which therefore make us angry and set us at enmity with one another? I dare say the answer does not occur to you at the moment, and therefore I will suggest that these enmities arise when the matters of difference are the just and unjust, good and evil, honourable and dishonourable. Are not these the points about which men differ, and about which when we are unable satisfactorily to decide our differences, you and I and all of us quarrel, when we do quarrel?

EUTH. Yes, Socrates, the nature of the differences about which we quarrel is such as you describe.

SOC. And the quarrels of the gods, noble Euthyphro, when they occur, are of a like nature?

EUTH. Certainly they are.

SOC. They have differences of opinion, as you say, about good and evil, just and unjust, honourable and dishonourable: there would have been no quarrels among them, if there had been no such differences—would there now?

EUTH. You are quite right.

SOC. Does not every man love that which he deems noble and just and good, and hate the opposite of them?

EUTH. Very true.

SOC. But, as you say, people regard the same things, some as just and others as unjust,—about these they dispute; and so there arise wars and fightings among them.

EUTH. Very true.

SOC. Then the same things are hated by the gods and loved by the gods, and are both hateful and dear to them?

EUTH. True.

SOC. And upon this view the same things, Euthyphro, will be pious and also impious?

EUTH. So I should suppose.

SOC. Then, my friend, I remark with surprise that you have not answered the question which I asked. For I certainly did not ask you to tell me what action is both pious and impious: but now it would seem that what is loved by the gods is also hated by them. And therefore, Euthyphro, in thus chastising your father you may very likely be doing what is agreeable to Zeus but disagreeable to Cronos or Uranus, and what is acceptable to Hephaestus but unacceptable to Here, and there may be other gods who have similar differences of opinion.

EUTH. But I believe, Socrates, that all the gods would be agreed as to the propriety of punishing a murderer: there would be no difference of opinion about that.

SOC. Well, but speaking of men, Euthyphro, did you ever hear any one arguing that a murderer or any sort of evildoer ought to be let off?

EUTH. I should rather say that these are the questions which they are always arguing, especially in courts of law: they commit all sorts of crimes, and there is nothing which they will not do or say in their own defence.

SOC. But do they admit their guilt, Euthyphro, and yet say that they ought not to be punished?

EUTH. No; they do not.

SOC. Then there are some things which they do not venture to say or do: for they do not venture to argue that the guilty are to be unpunished, but they deny their guilt, do they not?

EUTH. Yes.

SOC. Then they do not argue that the evildoer should not be punished, but they argue about the fact of who the evildoer is, and what he did and when?

EUTH. True.

SOC. And the gods are in the same case, if as you assert they quarrel about just and unjust, and some of them say while others deny that injustice is done among them. For surely neither God nor man will ever venture to say that the doer of injustice is not to be punished?

EUTH. That is true, Socrates, in the main.

SOC. But they join issue about the particulars—gods and men alike; and, if they dispute at all, they dispute about some act which is called in question, and which by some is affirmed to be just, by others to be unjust. Is not that true?

EUTH. Quite true.

SOC. Well, then, my dear friend Euthyphro, do tell me, for my better instruction and information, what proof have you that in the opinion of all the gods a servant who is guilty of murder, and is put in chains by the master of the dead man, and dies because he is put in chains before he who bound him can learn from the interpreters of the gods what he ought to do with him, dies unjustly; and that on behalf of such an one a son ought to proceed against his father and accuse him of murder? How would you show that all the gods absolutely agree in approving of his act? Prove to me that they do, and I will applaud your wisdom as long as I live.

EUTH. It will be a difficult task; but I could make the matter very clear indeed to you.

SOC. I understand; you mean to say that I am not so quick of apprehension as the judges: for to them you will be sure to prove that the act is unjust, and hateful to the gods.

EUTH. Yes, indeed, Socrates; at least if they will listen to me.

SOC. But they will be sure to listen if they find that you are a good speaker. There was a notion that came into my mind while you were speaking; I said to myself: "Well, and what if Euthyphro does prove to me that all the gods regarded the death of the serf as unjust, how do I know anything more of the nature of piety and impiety? for granting that this action may be hateful to the gods, still piety and impiety are not adequately defined by these distinctions, for that which is hateful to the gods has been shown to be also pleasing and dear to them." And therefore, Euthyphro, I do not ask you to prove this; I will suppose, if you like, that all the gods condemn and abominate such an action. But I will amend the definition so far as to say that what all the gods hate is impious, and what they love pious or holy; and what some of them love and others hate is both or neither. Shall this be our definition of piety and impiety?

EUTH. Why not, Socrates?

SOC. Why not! certainly, as far as I am concerned, Euthyphro, there is no reason why not. But whether this admission will greatly assist you in the task of instructing me as you promised, is a matter for you to consider.

EUTH. Yes, I should say that what all the gods love is pious and holy, and the opposite which they all hate, impious.

SOC. Ought we to enquire into the truth of this, Euthyphro, or simply to accept the mere statement on our own authority and that of others? What do you say?

EUTH. We should enquire; and I believe that the statement will stand the test of enquiry.

SOC. We shall know better, my good friend, in a little while. The point which I should first wish to understand is whether the pious or holy is beloved by the gods because it is holy, or holy because it is beloved of the gods.

EUTH. I do not understand your meaning, Socrates.

SOC. I will endeavour to explain: we speak of carrying and we speak of being carried, of leading and being led, seeing and being seen. You know that in all such cases there is a difference and you know also in what the difference lies?

EUTH. I think that I understand.

SOC. And is not that which is beloved distinct from that which loves?

EUTH. Certainly.

SOC. Well; and now tell me, is that which is carried in this state of carrying because it is carried, or for some other reason?

EUTH. No; that is the reason.

SOC. And the same is true of what is led and of what is seen?

EUTH. True.

SOC. And a thing is not seen because it is visible, but conversely, visible because it is seen; nor is a thing led because it is in the state of being led, or

carried because it is in the state of being carried, but the converse of this. And now I think, Euthyphro, that my meaning will be intelligible; and my meaning is, that any state of action or passion implies previous action or passion. It does not become because it is becoming, but it is in a state of becoming because it becomes; neither does it suffer because it is in a state of suffering, but it is in a state of suffering because it suffers. Do you not agree?

EUTH. Yes.

SOC. Is not that which is loved in some state either of becoming or suffering?

EUTH. Yes.

SOC. And the same holds as in the previous instances; the state of being loved follows the act of being loved, and not the act the state.

EUTH. Certainly.

SOC. And what do you say of piety, Euthyphro: is not piety, according to your definition, loved by all the gods?

EUTH. Yes.

SOC. Because it is pious or holy, or for some other reason?

EUTH. No, that is the reason.

SOC. It is loved because it is holy, not holy because it is loved?

EUTH. Yes.

SOC. And that which is dear to the gods is loved by them, and is in a state to be loved of them because it is loved of them?

EUTH. Certainly.

SOC. Then that which is dear to the gods, Euthyphro, is not holy, nor is that which is holy loved of God, as you affirm; but they are two different things.

EUTH. How do you mean, Socrates?

SOC. I mean to say that the holy has been acknowledged by us to be loved of God because it is holy, not to be holy because it is loved.

EUTH. Yes.

SOC. But that which is dear to the gods is dear to them because it is loved by them, not loved by them because it is dear to them.

EUTH. True.

SOC. But, friend Euthyphro, if that which is holy is the same with that which is dear to God, and is loved because it is holy, then that which is dear to God would have been loved as being dear to God; but if that which is dear to God is dear to him because loved by him, then that which is holy would have been holy because loved by him. But now you see that the reverse is the case, and that they are quite different from one another. For one (θεοφιλὲζ) is of a kind to be loved because it is loved, and the other (δσιον) is loved because it is a kind to be loved. Thus you appear to me, Euthyphro, when I ask you what is the essence of holiness, to offer an attribute only, and not the essence—the attribute of being loved by all the gods. But you still refuse to explain to me the nature of holiness. And therefore, if you please, I will ask you not to hide your treasure, but to tell me once more what holiness or piety really is, whether dear to the gods or not (for that is a matter about which we will not quarrel); and what is impiety?

ROBERT MERRIHEW ADAMS

from A Modified Divine Command Theory Of Ethical Wrongness

View II—the view that what makes something morally right in the sense of being a moral obligation is its being commanded by God (and what makes something morally wrong is its being contrary to God's commands)—is called the Divine Command Theory or Divine Command Morality. One criticism of this view is that, if it were true, then if God commanded us to be cruel to one another it would be wrong for us act contrary to God's command by not practicing cruelty. With this criticism in mind, Robert Merrihew Adams formulates what he calls a "modified" Divine Command Theory. In his modified theory Adams endeavors to explain moral or ethical rightness and wrongness in terms of God's will or commands. But Adams' Divine Command Theory is a modified theory because he does not accept the implication that if God commanded cruelty, then it would be wrong to disobey and not practice cruelty. What Adams says is that if God commanded cruelty, then his concept of ethical wrongness would "break down." If God commanded cruelty, then, Adams explains, he would not hold that it would be either wrong or permitted to disobey, nor would he hold that it would be wrong or permitted to obey. His concept of moral wrongness (and permittedness) understood in terms of God's commands would "break down" in that they would cease to be applicable. For Adams, though a *part* of what "the believer" means by "X is wrong" is "X is contrary to God's will or commands," a believer may feel in certain extreme cases (for instance, if God commanded cruelly) that she is *not* committed to following God's command.

From *Religion and Morality*, edited by Gene Outka and John P. Reeder, Jr. Garden City, NY: Doubleday, 1973. Reprinted with permission.

A Modified Divine Command Theory of Ethical Wrongness

I

It is widely held that all those theories are indefensible which attempt to explain in terms of the will or commands of God what it is for an act to be ethically right or wrong. In this paper I shall state such a theory, which I believe to be defensible; and I shall try to defend it against what seem to me to be the most important and interesting objections to it. I call my theory a *modified* divine command theory because in it I renounce certain claims that are commonly made in divine command analyses of ethical terms. (I should add that it is *my* theory only in that I shall state it, and that I believe it is defensible—not that I am sure it is correct.) I present it as a theory of ethical *wrongness* partly for convenience. It could also be presented as a theory of the nature of ethical obligatoriness or of ethical permittedness. Indeed, I will have occasion to make some remarks about the concept of ethical permittedness. But as we shall see (in Section IV) I am not prepared to claim that the theory can be extended to all ethical terms; and it is therefore important that it not be presented as a theory about ethical terms in general.

It will be helpful to begin with the statement of a simple, *un*-modified divine command theory of ethical wrongness. This is the theory that ethical wrongness *consists in* being contrary to God's commands, or that the word "wrong" in ethical contexts *means* "contrary to God's commands." It implies that the following two statement forms are logically equivalent.

(1) It is wrong (for A) to do X.
(2) It is contrary to God's commands (for A) to do X.

Of course that is not all that the theory implies. It also implies that (2) is conceptually prior to (1), so that the meaning of (1) is to be explained in terms of (2), and not the other way round. It might prove fairly difficult to state or explain in what that conceptual priority consists, but I shall not go into that here. I do not wish ultimately to defend the theory in its unmodified form, and I think I have stated it fully enough for my present purposes.

I have stated it as a theory about the meaning of the word "wrong" in ethical contexts. The most obvious objection to the theory is that the word "wrong" is used in ethical contexts by many people who cannot mean by it what the theory says they must mean, since they do not believe that there exists a God. This objection seems to me sufficient to refute the theory if it is presented as an analysis of what *everybody* means by "wrong" in ethical contexts. The theory cannot reasonably be offered except as a theory about what the word "wrong" means as used by *some but not all* people in ethical contexts. Let us say that the theory offers an analysis of the meaning of "wrong" in Judeo-Christian religious ethical discourse. This restriction of scope will apply to my modified divine command theory too. This restriction obviously gives rise to a possible objection. Isn't it more plausible to suppose that Judeo-Christian believers use "wrong" with the same meaning as other people do? This problem will be discussed in Section VI.

In Section II, I will discuss what seems to me the most important objection to the unmodified divine command theory, and suggest how the theory can be modified to meet it. Section III will be devoted to a brief but fairly comprehensive account of the use of "wrong" in Judeo-Christian ethical discourse, from the point of view of the modified divine command theory. The theory will be further elaborated in dealing with objections in Sections IV to VI. In a seventh and final section, I will note some problems arising from unresolved issues in the general theory of analysis and meaning, and briefly discuss their bearing on the modified divine command theory.

II

The following seems to me to be the gravest objection to the divine command theory of ethical wrongness, in the form in which I have stated it. Suppose God should command me to make it my chief end in life to inflict suffering on other human beings, for no other reason than that He commanded it. (For convenience I shall abbreviate this hypothesis to "Suppose God should command cruelty for its own sake.") Will it seriously be claimed that in that case it would be wrong for me not to practice cruelty for its own sake? I see three possible answers to this question.

(1) It might be claimed that it is logically impossible for God to command cruelty for its own sake. In that case, of course, we need not worry about whether it would be wrong to disobey if He did command it. It is senseless to agonize about what one should do in a logically impossible situation. This solution to the problem seems unlikely to be available to the divine command theorist, however. For why would he hold that it is logically impossible for God to command cruelty for its own sake? Some theologians (for instance, Thomas Aquinas) have believed (a) that what is right and wrong is independent of God's will, *and* (b) that God always does right by the necessity of His nature. Such theologians, if they believe that it would be wrong for God to command cruelty for its own sake, have reason to believe that it is logically impossible for Him to do so. But the divine command theorist, who does not agree that what is right and wrong is independent of God's will, does not seem to have such a reason to deny that it is logically possible for God to command cruelty for its own sake.

(2) Let us assume that it is logically possible for God to command cruelty for its own sake. In that case the divine command theory seems to imply that it would be wrong not to practice cruelty for its own sake. There have been at least a few adherents of divine command ethics who have been prepared to accept this consequence. William Ockham held that those acts which we call "theft," "adultery," and "hatred of God" would be meritorious if God had commanded them.[1] He would surely have said the same about what I have been calling the practice of "cruelty for its own sake."

---

[1] Guillelmus de Occam, *Super 4 libros sententiarum*, bk. II, qu. 19, O, in Vol. IV of his *Opera plurima* (Lyon, 1494–96; réimpression en fac-similé, Farnborough, Hants., England: Gregg Press, 1962). I am not claiming that Ockham held a divine command theory of exactly the same sort that I have been discussing.

This position is one which I suspect most of us are likely to find somewhat shocking, even repulsive. We should therefore be particularly careful not to misunderstand it. We need not imagine that Ockham disciplined himself to be ready to practice cruelty for its own sake if God should command it. It was doubtless an article of faith for him that God is unalterably opposed to any such practice. The mere logical possibility that theft, adultery, and cruelty might have been commanded by God (and therefore meritorious) doubtless did not represent in Ockham's view any real possibility.

(3) Nonetheless, the view that if God commanded cruelty for its own sake it would be wrong not to practice it seems unacceptable to me; and I think many, perhaps most, other Jewish and Christian believers would find it unacceptable too. I must make clear the sense in which I find it unsatisfactory. It is not that I find an internal inconsistency in it. And I would not deny that it may reflect, accurately enough, the way in which some believers use the word "wrong." I might as well frankly avow that I am looking for a divine command theory which at least might possibly be a correct account of how I use the word "wrong." I do not use the word "wrong" in such a way that I would say that it would be wrong not to practice cruelty if God commanded it, and I am sure that many other believers agree with me on this point.

But now have I not rejected the divine command theory? I have assumed that it would be logically possible for God to command cruelty for its own sake. And I have rejected the view that if God commanded cruelty for its own sake, it would be wrong not to obey. It seems to follow that I am committed to the view that in certain logically possible circumstances it would not be wrong to disobey God. This position seems to be inconsistent with the theory that "wrong" means "contrary to God's commands."

I want to argue, however, that it is still open to me to accept a modified form of the divine command theory of ethical wrongness. According to the modified divine command theory, when I say, "It is wrong to do X," (at least part of) what I *mean* is that it is contrary to God's commands to do X. "It is wrong to do X" *implies* "It is contrary to God's commands to do X." But "It is contrary to God's commands to do X" implies "It is wrong to do X" only if certain conditions are assumed—namely, only if it is assumed that God has the character which I believe Him to have, of loving His human creatures. If God were really to command us to make cruelty our goal, then He would not have that character of loving us, and I would not say it would be wrong to disobey Him.

But do I say that it would be wrong to obey Him in such a case? This is the point at which I am in danger of abandoning the divine command theory completely. I do abandon it completely if I say both of the following things.

(A) It would be wrong to obey God if He commanded cruelty for its own sake.

(B) In (A), "wrong" is used in what is for me its normal ethical sense.

If I assert both (A) and (B), it is clear that I cannot consistently maintain that "wrong" in its normal ethical sense for me means or implies "contrary to God's commands."

But from the fact that I deny that it would be wrong to disobey God if He commanded cruelty for its own sake, it does not follow that I must accept (A) and (B). Of course someone might claim that obedience and disobedience would both be ethically permitted in such a case; but that is not the view that I am suggesting. If I adopt the modified divine command theory as an analysis of my present concept of ethical wrongness (and if I adopt a similar analysis of my concept of ethical permittedness), I will not hold either that it would be wrong to disobey, or that it would be ethically permitted to disobey, or that it would be wrong to obey, or that it would be ethically permitted to obey, if God commanded cruelty for its own sake. For I will say that my concept of ethical wrongness (and my concept of ethical permittedness) would "break down" if I really believed that God commanded cruelty for its own sake. Or to put the matter somewhat more prosaically, I will say that my concepts of ethical wrongness and permittedness could not serve the functions they now serve, because using those concepts I could not call any action ethically wrong or ethically permitted, if I believed that God's will was so unloving. This position can be explained or developed in either of two ways, each of which has its advantages.

I could say that by "X is ethically wrong" I mean "X is contrary to the commands of a *loving* God" (i.e., "There is a *loving* God and X is contrary to His commands") and by "X is ethically permitted" I mean "X is in accord with the commands of a *loving* God" (i.e., "There is a *loving* God and X is not contrary to His commands"). On this analysis we can reason as follows. If there is only one God and He commands cruelty for its own sake, then presumably there is not a *loving* God. If there is not a loving God then neither "X is ethically wrong" nor "X is ethically permitted" is true of any X. Using my present concepts of ethical wrongness and permittedness, therefore, I could not (consistently) call any action ethically wrong or permitted if I believed that God commanded cruelty for its own sake. This way of developing the modified divine

command theory is the simpler and neater of the two, and that might reasonably lead one to choose it for the construction of a theological ethical theory. On the other hand, I think it is also simpler and neater than ordinary religious ethical discourse, in which (for example) it may be felt that the statement that a certain act is wrong is *about* the will or commands of God in a way in which it is not about His love.

In this essay I shall prefer a second, rather similar, but somewhat untidier, understanding of the modified divine command theory, because I think it may lead us into some insights about the complexities of actual religious ethical discourse. According to this second version of the theory, the statement that something is ethically wrong (or permitted) says something about the will or commands of God, but not about His love. Every such statement, however, *presupposes* that certain conditions for the applicability of the believer's concepts of ethical right and wrong are satisfied. Among these conditions is that God does not command cruelty for its own sake—or, more generally, that God loves His human creatures. It need not be assumed that God's love is the only such condition.

The modified divine command theorist can say that the possibility of God commanding cruelty for its own sake is not provided for in the Judeo-Christian religious ethical system as he understands it. The possibility is not provided for, in the sense that the concepts of right and wrong have not been developed in such a way that actions could be correctly said to be right or wrong if God were believed to command cruelty for its own sake. The modified divine command theorist agrees that it is logically possible[2] that God

---

[2] Perhaps he will even think it is causally possible, but I do not regard any view on that issue as an integral part of the theory. The question whether it is causally possible for God to act "out of character" is a difficult one which we need not go into here.

should command cruelty for its own sake; but he holds that it is unthinkable that God should do so. To have *faith* in God is not just to believe that He exists, but also to trust in His love for mankind. The believer's concepts of ethical wrongness and permittedness are developed within the framework of his (or the religious community's) religious life, and therefore within the framework of the assumption that God loves us. The concept of the will or commands of God has a certain function in the believer's life, and the use of the words "right" (in the sense of "ethically permitted") and "wrong" is tied to that function of that concept. But one of the reasons why the concept of the will of God can function as it does is that the love which God is believed to have toward men arouses in the believer certain attitudes of love toward God and devotion to His will. If the believer thinks about the unthinkable but logically possible situation in which God commands cruelty for its own sake, he finds that in relation to that kind of command of God he cannot take up the same attitude, and that the concept of the will or commands of God could not then have the same function in his life. For this reason he will not say that it would be wrong to disobey God, or right to obey Him, in that situation. At the same time he will not say that it would be wrong to obey God in that situation, because he is accustomed to use the word "wrong" to say that something is contrary to the will of God, and it does not seem to him to be the right word to use to express his own personal revulsion toward an act against which there would be no divine authority. Similarly, he will not say that it would be "right," in the sense of "ethically permitted," to disobey God's command of cruelty; for that does not seem to him to be the right way to express his own personal attitude toward an act which would not be in accord with a divine authority. In this way the believer's concepts of ethical rightness and wrongness would break down in the situation in which he believed that God commanded cruelty for its own sake—that is, they would not function as they now do, because he would not be prepared to use them to say that any action was right or wrong.

* *

IV

The modified divine command theory clearly conceives of believers as valuing some things independently of their relation to God's commands. If the believer will not say that it would be wrong not to practice cruelty for its own sake if God commanded it, that is because he values kindness, and has a revulsion for cruelty, in a way that is at least to some extent independent of his belief that God commands kindness and forbids cruelty. This point may be made the basis of both philosophical and theological objections to the modified divine command theory, but I think the objections can be answered.

The philosophical objection is, roughly, that if there are some things I value independently of their relation to God's commands, then my value concepts cannot rightly be analyzed in terms of God's commands. According to the modified divine command theory, the acceptability of divine command ethics depends in part on the believer's independent positive valuation of the sorts of things that God is believed to command. But then, the philosophical critic objects, the believer must have a prior, nontheological conception of ethical right and wrong, in terms of which he judges God's commandments to be acceptable—and to admit that the believer has a prior, nontheological conception of ethical right and wrong is to abandon the divine command theory.

The weakness of this philosophical objection is that it fails to note the distinctions that can be drawn among various value concepts. From the fact that the believer values some things independently of his beliefs about God's commands, the objector concludes, illegitimately, that the believer must have a conception of ethical right and wrong that is independent of his beliefs about God's commands. This inference is illegitimate because there can be valuations which do not imply or presuppose a judgment of ethical right or wrong. For instance, I may simply like something, or want something, or feel a revulsion at something.

What the modified divine command theorist will hold, then, is that the believer values some things independently of their relation to God's commands, but that these valuations are not judgments of ethical right and wrong and do not of themselves imply judgments of ethical right and wrong. He will maintain, on the other

hand, that such independent valuations are involved in, or even necessary for, judgments of ethical right and wrong which also involve beliefs about God's will or commands. The adherent of a divine command ethics will normally be able to give reasons for his adherence. Such reasons might include: "Because I am grateful to God for His love"; "Because I find it the most satisfying form of ethical life"; "Because there's got to be an objective moral law if life isn't to fall to pieces, and I can't understand what it would be if not the will of God."[4] As we have already noted, the modified divine command theorist also has reasons why he would not accept a divine command ethics in certain logically possible situations which he believes not to be actual. All of these reasons seem to me to involve valuations that are independent of divine command ethics. The person who has such reasons wants certain things—happiness, certain satisfactions—for himself and others; he hates cruelty and loves kindness; he has perhaps a certain unique and "numinous" awe of God. And these are not attitudes which he has simply because of his beliefs about God's commands.[5] They are not attitudes, however, which presuppose judgments of moral right and wrong.

* * * * * * * * * * * * * * * * * * *

V

The ascription of moral qualities to God is commonly thought to cause problems for divine command theories of ethics. It is doubted that God, as an agent, can properly be called "good" in the moral sense if He is not subject to a moral

[4] The mention of moral law in the last of these reasons may presuppose the ability to *mention* concepts of moral right and wrong, which may or may not be theological and which may or may not be concepts one uses oneself to make judgments of right and wrong. So far as I can see, it does not *presuppose* the *use* of such concepts to make judgments of right and wrong, or one's adoption of them for such use, which is the crucial point here.
[5] The independence ascribed to these attitudes is not a *genetic* independence. It may be that the person would not have come to have some of them had it not been for his religious beliefs. The point is that he has come to hold them in such a way that his holding them does not now depend entirely on his beliefs about God's commands.

law that is not of His own making. For if He is morally good, mustn't He do what is right *because* it is right? And how can He do that, if what's right is right because He wills it? Or it may be charged that divine command theories trivialize the claim that God is good. If "X is (morally) good" means roughly "X does what God wills," then "God is (morally) good" means only that God does what He wills—which is surely much less than people are normally taken to mean when they say that God is (morally) good. In this section I will suggest an answer to these objections.

Surely no analysis of Judeo-Christian ethical discourse can be regarded as adequate which does not provide for a sense in which the believer can seriously assert that God is good. Indeed an adequate analysis should provide a plausible account of what believers do in fact mean when they say, "God is good." I believe that a divine command theory of ethical (rightness and) wrongness can include such an account. I will try to indicate its chief features.

(1) In saying "God is good" one is normally expressing a favorable emotional attitude toward God. I shall not try to determine whether or not this is part of the meaning of "God is good"; but it is normally, perhaps almost always, at least one of the things one is doing if one says that God is good. If we were to try to be more precise about the type of favorable emotional attitude normally expressed by "God is good," I suspect we would find that the attitude expressed is most commonly one of *gratitude*.

(2) This leads to a second point, which is that when God is called "good" it is very often meant that He is *good to us*, or *good to* the speaker. "Good" is sometimes virtually a synonym for "kind." And for the modified divine command theorist it is not a trivial truth that God is kind. In saying that God is good in the sense of "kind," one presupposes, of

course, that there are some things which the beneficiaries of God's goodness value. We need not discuss here whether the beneficiaries must value them independently of their beliefs about God's will. For the modified divine command theorist does admit that there are some things which believers value independently of their beliefs about God's commands. Nothing that the modified divine command theorist says about the meaning of ("right" and) "wrong" implies that it is a trivial truth that God bestows on His creatures things that they value.

(3) I would not suggest that the descriptive force of "good" as applied to God is exhausted by the notion of kindness. "God is good" must be taken in many contexts as ascribing to God, rather generally, qualities of character which the believing speaker regards as virtues in human beings. Among such qualities might be faithfulness, ethical consistency, a forgiving disposition, and, in general, various aspects of love, as well as kindness. Not that there is some definite list of qualities, the ascription of which to God is clearly implied by the claim that God is good. But saying that God is good normally commits one to the position that God has some important set of qualities which one regards as virtues in human beings.

(4) It will not be thought that God has *all* the qualities which are virtues in human beings. Some such qualities are logically inapplicable to a being such as God is supposed to be. For example, aside from certain complications arising from the doctrine of the incarnation, it would be logically inappropriate to speak of God as controlling His sexual desires. (He doesn't have any.) And given some widely held conceptions of God and His relation to the world, it would hardly make sense to speak of Him as *courageous*. For if He is impassible and has predetermined absolutely everything that happens, He has no risks to

face and cannot endure (because He cannot suffer) pain or displeasure.[12]

Believers in God's goodness also typically think He lacks some human virtues which would *not* be logically inapplicable to a being like Him. A virtuous man, for instance, does not intentionally cause the death of other human beings, except under exceptional circumstances. But God has intentionally brought it about that all men die. There are agonizing forms of the problem of evil; but I think that for most Judeo-Christian believers (especially those who believe in life after death), this is not one of them. They believe that God's making men mortal and His commanding them not to kill each other, fit together in a larger pattern of harmonious purposes. How then can one distinguish between human virtues which God must have if He is good and human virtues which God may lack and still be good? This is an interesting and important question, but I will not attempt here to formulate a precise or adequate criterion for making the distinction. I fear it would require a lengthy digression from the issues with which we are principally concerned.

(5) If we accept a divine command theory of ethical rightness and wrongness, I think we shall have to say that *dutifulness* is a human virtue which, like sexual chastity, is logically inapplicable to God. God cannot either do or fail to do His duty, since He does not have a duty— at least not in the most important sense in which human beings have a duty. For He is not subject to a moral law not of His own making. Dutifulness is one virtuous disposition which men can have that God cannot have. But there are other virtuous dispositions which God can have as well as men. Love, for instance. It hardly makes sense to say that God does what He does *because* it is right. But it does not follow that God cannot have any reason for doing what He does. It does not even follow that He cannot have reasons of a type on which it would be morally virtuous for a man to act. For example, He might do something because He knew it would make His creatures happier.

(6) The modified divine command theorist must deny that in calling God "good" one presupposes a standard of moral rightness and wrongness superior to the will of God, by reference to which it is determined whether God's character is virtuous or not. And I think he can consistently deny that. He can say that morally virtuous and vicious qualities of character are those which agree and conflict, respectively, with God's commands, and that it is their agreement or disagreement with God's commands that makes them virtuous or vicious. But the believer normally thinks he has at least a general idea of what qualities of character are in fact virtuous and vicious (approved and disapproved by God). Having such an idea, he can apply the word "good" descriptively to God, meaning that (with some exceptions, as I have noted) God has the qualities which the believer regards as virtues, such as faithfulness and kindness.

I will sum up by contrasting what the believer can mean when he says, "Moses is good," with what he can mean when he says, "God is good," according to the modified divine command theory. When the believer says,

---

[12] The argument here is similar to one which is used for another purpose by Ninian Smart in "Omnipotence, Evil, and Superman," *Philosophy*, XXXVI (1961), reprinted in Nelson Pike, ed., *God and Evil* (Englewood Cliffs, N.J.: Prentice-Hall, 1964), pp. 103–12.

I do not mean to endorse the doctrines of divine impassibility and theological determinism.

"Moses is good," (a) he normally is expressing a favorable emotional attitude toward Moses—normally, though perhaps not always. (Sometimes a person's moral goodness displeases us.) (b) He normally implies that Moses possesses a large proportion of those qualities of character which are recognized in the religious-ethical community as virtues, and few if any of those which are regarded as vices. (c) He normally implies that the qualities of Moses' character on the basis of which he describes Moses as good are qualities approved by God.

When the believer says, "God is good," (a) he normally is expressing a favorable emotional attitude toward God—and I think exceptions on this point would be rarer than in the case of statements that a man is good. (b) He normally is ascribing to God certain qualities of character. He may mean primarily that God is kind or benevolent, that He is *good to* human beings or certain ones of them. Or he may mean that God possesses (with some exceptions) those qualities of character which are regarded as virtues in the religious-ethical community. (c) Whereas in saying, "Moses is good," the believer was stating or implying that the qualities of character which he was ascribing to Moses conform to a standard of ethical rightness which is independent of the will of Moses, he is not stating or implying that the qualities of character which he ascribes to God conform to a standard of ethical rightness which is independent of the will of God.

VI

As I noted at the outset, the divine command theory of ethical wrongness, even in its modified form, has the consequence that believers and nonbelievers use the word "wrong" with different meanings in ethical contexts, since it will hardly be thought that nonbelievers mean by "wrong" what the theory says believers mean by it. This consequence gives rise to an objection. For the phenomena of common moral discourse between believers and nonbelievers suggest that they mean the same thing by "wrong" in ethical contexts. In the present section I shall try to explain how the modified divine command theorist can account for the facts of common ethical discourse.

I will first indicate what I think the troublesome facts are. Judeo-Christian believers enter into ethical discussions with people whose religious or anti-religious beliefs they do not know. It seems to be possible to conduct quite a lot of ethical discourse, with apparent understanding, without knowing one's partner's views on religious issues. Believers also discuss ethical questions with persons who are known to them to be nonbelievers. They agree with such persons, disagree with them, and try to persuade them, about what acts are morally wrong. (Or at least it is normally *said*, by the participants and others, that they agree and disagree about such issues.) Believers ascribe, to people who are known not to believe in God, beliefs that certain acts are morally wrong. Yet surely believers do not suppose that nonbelievers, in calling acts wrong, mean that they are contrary to the will or commandments of God. Under these circumstances how can the believer really mean "contrary to the will or commandments of God" when he says "wrong"? If he agrees and disagrees with nonbelievers about what is wrong, if he ascribes to them beliefs that certain acts are wrong, must he not be using "wrong" in a nontheological sense?

What I shall argue is that in some ordinary (and I fear imprecise) sense of "mean," what believers and nonbelievers mean by "wrong" in ethical contexts may well be partly the same and partly different. There are agreements between believers and nonbelievers which make common moral discourse between them possible. But these agreements do not show that the two groups mean exactly the same thing by "wrong." They do not show that "contrary to God's will or commands" is not part of what believers mean by "wrong."

* * * * * * * * * * * * * * * * * * * *

Let us sum up these observations about the conditions which make common moral discourse between believers and nonbelievers possible. (1) They use many of the same ethical terms, such as "wrong." (2) They treat those terms as having the same basic grammatical and logical status, and many of the same logical connections with other expressions. (3) They agree to a large extent about what types of action are to be called "wrong." To call an action "wrong" is, among other things, to classify it with certain other actions, and there is considerable agreement between believers and nonbelievers as to what actions those are. (4) The emotional and volitional attitudes which believers and nonbelievers normally express in saying that something is "wrong" are similar, and (5) saying that something is "wrong" has much the same social functions for believers and nonbelievers.

So far as I can see, none of this is inconsistent with the modified divine command theory of ethical wrongness. According to that theory there are several things which are true of the believer's use of "wrong" which cannot plausibly be supposed to be true of the nonbeliever's. In saying, "X is wrong," the believer commits himself (subjectively, at least, and publicly if he is known to be a believer) to the claim that X is contrary to God's will or commandments. The believer will not say that anything would be wrong, under any possible circumstances, if it were not contrary to God's will or commandments. In many contexts he uses the term "wrong" interchangeably with "against the will of God" or "against the commandments of God." The heart of the modified divine command theory, I have suggested, is the claim that when the believer says, "X is wrong," one thing he means to be doing is stating a nonnatural objective fact about X, and the nonnatural objective fact he means to be stating is that X is contrary to the will or commandments of God. This claim may be true even though the uses of "wrong" by believers and nonbelievers are similar in all five of the ways pointed out above.

Suppose these contentions of the modified divine command theory are correct. (I think they are very plausible as claims about the ethical discourse of at least some religious believers.) In that case believers and nonbelievers surely do not mean exactly the same thing by "X is wrong" in ethical contexts. But neither is it plausible to suppose that they mean entirely different things, given the phenomena of common moral discourse. We must suppose, then, that their meaning is partly the same and partly different. "Contrary to God's will or commands" must be taken as expressing only part of the meaning with which the believer uses "wrong." Some of the similarities between believers' and nonbelievers' use of "wrong" must also be taken as expressing parts of the meaning with which the believer uses "wrong." This view of the matter agrees with the account of the modified divine command theory in Section III above, where I pointed out that the modified divine command theorist cannot mean exactly the same thing by "wrong" that he means by "contrary to God's commands."

We have here a situation which commonly arises when some people hold, and others do not hold, a given theory about the nature of something which everyone talks about. The chemist, who believes that water is a compound of hydrogen and oxygen, and the man who knows nothing of chemistry, surely do not use the word "water" in entirely different senses; but neither is it very plausible to suppose that they use it with exactly the same meaning. I am inclined to say that in some fairly ordinary sense of "mean," a phenomenalist, and a philosopher who holds some conflicting theory about what it is for a physical object to exist, do not mean exactly the same thing by "There is a bottle of milk in the refrigerator." But they certainly do not mean entirely different things, and they can agree that there is a bottle of milk in the refrigerator.

ST. THOMAS AQUINAS

from On The Various Kinds of Law and The Natural Law (Summa Theologica I-II, q. 91, a. 2 and q. 94, aa. 2 and 4)

Natural law theory regards normative moral laws (which till us how we ought to behave) as discoverable in nature. For religious thinkers following natural law theory God is the source of moral natural law. In the *Summa Theologica* Aquinas sought to clarify and defend natural law thinking. The natural law, for Aquinas, is the "participation of the eternal law in the rational creature." The eternal law is the basic moral law of the universe, not subject to time, emanating from God's divine reason, and by "rational creature" Aquinas means human beings. It is by the natural law that human beings "participate" in God's eternal law. The natural law, for Aquinas, is *in us*. Aquinas takes it to be "the first principle" of practical (action oriented) reason that *good is that which all things seek after*. The fundamental "precept" (or rule) of the natural law, then, is that *good is to be done and promoted, and evil is to be avoided*. For Aquinas, the natural law is seen in human beings' "inclinations," what they naturally apprehend by their reason as good and are naturally inclined to do. There are three levels of this natural inclination in human beings toward their good, for Aquinas. First, there is an inclination toward the good in accord with the nature human beings have in common with all substances—the inclination toward self preservation is an example. Second, there is an inclination toward the good in accord with the nature human beings have in common with other animals—the inclinations toward sexual intercourse and the education of offspring are examples. Third there is an inclination toward the good in accord with the nature of human beings' reason, which is the nature "proper to him [human beings]"—and so, using Aquinas' examples, human beings have a natural inclination to know the truth about God and to live in society.

Within the natural law, Aquinas allows, there are many "precepts." There are "first common principles" and they are the same for all. Also, however, there are "secondary principles" or "detailed proximate conclusions drawn from first principles." These can be influenced by "conditions," so much so that proper action is *not* to follow the first principle. Aquinas provides an example of this: reason teaches us that it is proper to restore goods entrusted to us to their owner; but if the owner plans to use those goods to do injury to others then that condition makes it unreasonable and wrong to restore the goods. In general it is right to restore goods but in such specific circumstances the "rectitude" of the principle fails. Aquinas also appreciates that the "knowledge" of a principle may fail. Though a principle has "rectitude" (and so is right), some persons may fail to acknowledge the principle. This can happen because "passion" or "evil habit[s]" may "pervert" reason, and in such a case some human beings may fail to acknowledge a common principle. Aquinas offers an example that he takes from Julius Caesar's commentaries on the Gallic Wars: Julius Caesar relates that theft was not considered wrong by the Germans (who in the time of Julius Caesar, the first century B.C.E, were given to marauding). While reason teaches us that it is wrong to take the property of others, passion or evil habits perverted the reason of the Germans encountered by Julius Caesar and they could not acknowledge this common principle of the natural law.

In Aquinas' elaboration of the natural law we see his explanation of (1) how human beings can discern which regularities in nature express the precepts of the natural law, (2) how human beings can determine when a "common principle" requires a special application, and (3) why some human beings fail to recognize some of the precepts of the natural law. In all these cases what is crucial is the role of reason—the rational nature that Aquinas believes God has given human beings.

Our reading consists of three articles from the *Summa Theologica* I-II (First Part of the Second Part), in which Aquinas addresses questions relating to natural law and its divine origin.*

Q. 91 On The Various Kinds of Law

Second Article

WHETHER THERE IS IN US A NATURAL LAW?

We proceed thus to the Second Article:
Objection 1. It would seem that there is no natural law in us. For man is governed sufficiently by the eternal law, since Augustine says that *the eternal law is that by which it is right that all things should be most orderly*.[4] But nature does not abound in superfluities as neither does she fail in necessaries. Therefore man has no natural law.

* From *Basic Writings of St. Thomas Aquinas*, vol. 2, edited by Anton C. Pegis. New York: Random House, 1945. Copyright, 1945 by Random House, Inc. Reprinted by permission of Hackett Publishing Company, Inc. All rights reserved.
[4] *De Lib. Arb.*, I, 6 (PL 32, 1229).

Obj. 2. Further, by the law man is directed, in his acts, to the end, as was stated above.[5] But the directing of human acts to their end is not a function of nature, as is the case in irrational creatures, which act for an end solely by their natural appetite; whereas man acts for an end by his reason and will. Therefore man has no natural law.

Obj. 3. Further, the more a man is free, the less is he under the law. But man is freer than all the animals because of his free choice, with which he is endowed in distinction from all other animals. Since, therefore, other animals are not subject to a natural law, neither is man subject to a natural law.

On the contrary, the *Gloss* on *Rom.* ii. 14 (*When the Gentiles, who have not the law, do by nature those things that are of the law*) comments as follows: *Although they have no written law, yet they have the natural law, whereby each one knows, and is conscious of, what is good and what is evil.*[6]

I answer that, As we have stated above,[7] law, being a rule and measure, can be in a person in two ways: in one way, as in him that rules and measures; in another way, as in that which is ruled and measured, since a thing is ruled and measured in so far as it partakes of the rule or measure. Therefore, since all things subject to divine providence are ruled and measured by the eternal law, as was stated above, it is evident that all things partake in some way in the eternal law, in so far as, namely, from its being imprinted on them, they derive their respective inclinations to their proper acts and ends. Now among all others, the rational creature is subject to divine providence in a more excellent way, in so far as it itself partakes of a share of providence, by being provident both for itself and for others. Therefore it has a share of the eternal reason, whereby it has a natural inclination to its proper act and end; and this participation of the eternal law in the rational creature is called the natural law. Hence the Psalmist, after saying (*Ps.* iv. 6): *Offer up the sacrifice of justice*, as though someone asked what the works of justice are, adds: *Many say, Who showeth us good things?* in answer to which question he says: *The light of Thy countenance, O Lord, is signed upon us.* He thus implies that the light of natural reason, whereby we discern what is good and what is evil, which is the function of the natural law, is nothing else than an imprint on us of the divine light. It is therefore evident that the natural law is nothing else than the rational creature's participation of the eternal law.

Reply Obj. 1. This argument would hold if the natural law were something different from the eternal law; whereas it is nothing but a participation thereof, as we have stated above.

Reply Obj. 2. Every act of reason and will in us is based on that which is according to nature, as was stated above.[8] For every act of reasoning is based on principles that are known naturally, and every act of appetite in respect of the means is derived from the natural appetite in respect of the last end. Accordingly, the first direction of our acts to their end must needs be through the natural law.

Reply Obj. 3. Even irrational animals partake in their own way of the eternal reason, just as the rational creature does. But because the rational creature partakes thereof in an intellectual and rational

[5] Q. 90, a. 2.
[6] *Glossa ordin.* (VI, 7E); Peter Lombard, *In Rom.*, super II, 14 (PL 191, 1345).
[7] Q. 90, a. 1, ad 1.   [8] Q. 10, a. 1.

manner, therefore the participation of the eternal law in the rational creature is properly called a law, since a law is something pertaining to reason, as was stated above.[9] Irrational creatures, however, do not partake thereof in a rational manner, and therefore there is no participation of the eternal law in them, except by way of likeness.

Q. 94 The Natural Law

Second Article

WHETHER THE NATURAL LAW CONTAINS SEVERAL PRECEPTS, OR ONLY ONE?

We proceed thus to the Second Article:—

Objection 1. It would seem that the natural law contains, not several precepts, but only one. For law is a kind of precept, as was stated above.[7] If therefore there were many precepts of the natural law, it would follow that there are also many natural laws.

Obj. 2. Further, the natural law is consequent upon human nature. But human nature, as a whole, is one, though, as to its parts, it is manifold. Therefore, either there is but one precept of the law of nature because of the unity of nature as a whole, or there are many by reason of the number of parts of human nature. The result would be that even things relating to the inclination of the concupiscible power would belong to the natural law.

Obj. 3. Further, law is something pertaining to reason, as was stated above.[8] Now reason is but one in man. Therefore there is only one precept of the natural law.

On the contrary, The precepts of the natural law in man stand in relation to operable matters as first principles do to matters of demonstration. But there are several first indemonstrable principles. Therefore there are also several precepts of the natural law.

I answer that, As was stated above, the precepts of the natural law are to the practical reason what the first principles of demonstrations are to the speculative reason, because both are self-evident principles.[9] Now a thing is said to be self-evident in two ways: first, in itself; secondly, in relation to us. Any proposition is said to be self-evident in itself, if its predicate is contained in the notion of the subject; even though it may happen that to one who does not know the definition of the subject, such a proposition is not self-evident. For instance, this proposition, *Man is a rational being*, is, in its very nature, self-evident, since he who says *man*, says *a rational being*; and yet to one who does not know what a man is, this proposition is not self-evident. Hence it is that, as Boethius says,[10] certain axioms or propositions are universally self-evident to all; and such are the

[9] Q. 90, a. 1.
[7] Q. 92, a. 2.   [8] Q. 90, a. 1.   [9] Q. 91, a. 3.   [10] *De Hebdom.* (PL 64, 1311).

propositions whose terms are known to all, as, *Every whole is greater than its part,* and, *Things equal to one and the same are equal to one another.* But some propositions are self-evident only to the wise, who understand the meaning of the terms of such propositions. Thus to one who understands that an angel is not a body, it is self-evident that an angel is not circumscriptively in a place. But this is not evident to the unlearned, for they cannot grasp it.

Now a certain order is to be found in those things that are apprehended by men. For that which first falls under apprehension is *being,* the understanding of which is included in all things whatsoever a man apprehends. Therefore the first indemonstrable principle is that *the same thing cannot be affirmed and denied at the same time,* which is based on the notion of *being* and *not-being*: and on this principle all others are based, as is stated in *Metaph.* iv.[11] Now as *being* is the first thing that falls under the apprehension absolutely, so *good* is the first thing that falls under the apprehension of the practical reason, which is directed to action (since every agent acts for an end, which has the nature of good). Consequently, the first principle in the practical reason is one founded on the nature of good, viz., that *good is that which all things seek after.* Hence this is the first precept of law, that *good is to be done and promoted, and evil is to be avoided.* All other precepts of the natural law are based upon this; so that all the things which the practical reason naturally apprehends as man's good belong to the precepts of the natural law under the form of things to be done or avoided.

Since, however, good has the nature of an end, and evil, the nature of the contrary, hence it is that all those things to which man has a natural inclination are naturally apprehended by reason as being good, and consequently as objects of pursuit, and their contraries as evil, and objects of avoidance. Therefore, the order of the precepts of the natural law is according to the order of natural inclinations. For there is in man, first of all, an inclination to good in accordance with the nature which he has in common with all substances, inasmuch, namely, as every substance seeks the preservation of its own being, according to its nature; and by reason of this inclination, whatever is a means of preserving human life, and of warding off its obstacles, belongs to the natural law. Secondly, there is in man an inclination to things that pertain to him more specially, according to that nature which he has in common with other animals; and in virtue of this inclination, those things are said to belong to the natural law *which nature has taught to all animals,*[12] such as sexual intercourse, the education of offspring and so forth. Thirdly, there is in man an inclination to good according to the nature of his reason, which nature is proper to him. Thus man has a natural inclination to know the truth about God, and to live in society; and in this respect, whatever pertains to this inclination belongs to the natural law: *e.g.,* to shun ignorance, to avoid offending those among whom one has to live, and other such things regarding the above inclination.

Reply Obj. 1. All these precepts of the law of nature have the character of one natural law, inasmuch as they flow from one first precept.

Reply Obj. 2. All the inclinations of any parts whatsoever of human nature, *e.g.,* of the concupiscible and irascible

---

[11] Aristotle, *Metaph.*, III, 3 (1005b 29).
[12] *Dig.*, I, i, 1 (I, 29a).—Cf. O. Lottin, *Le droit naturel,* pp. 34, 78.

parts, in so far as they are ruled by reason, belong to the natural law, and are reduced to one first precept, as was stated above. And thus the precepts of the natural law are many in themselves, but they are based on one common foundation.

Reply Obj. 3. Although reason is one in itself, yet it directs all things regarding man; so that whatever can be ruled by reason is contained under the law of reason.

Fourth Article

WHETHER THE NATURAL LAW IS THE SAME IN ALL MEN?

We proceed thus to the Fourth Article:—
Objection 1. It would seem that the natural law is not the same in all. For it is stated in the *Decretals* that *the natural law is that which is contained in the Law and the Gospel.*[16] But this is not common to all men, because, as it is written (*Rom.* x. 16), *all do not obey the gospel.* Therefore the natural law is not the same in all men.

Obj. 2. Further, *Things which are according to the law are said to be just,* as is stated in *Ethics* v.[17] But it is stated in the same book that nothing is so just for all as not to be subject to change in regard to some men.[18] Therefore even the natural law is not the same in all men.

Obj. 3. Further, as was stated above, to the natural law belongs everything to which a man is inclined according to his nature. Now different men are naturally inclined to different things,—some to the desire of pleasures, others to the desire of honors, and other men to other things. Therefore, there is not one natural law for all.

On the contrary, Isidore says: *The natural law is common to all nations.*[19]

I answer that, As we have stated above, to the natural law belong those things to which a man is inclined naturally; and among these it is proper to man to be inclined to act according to reason. Now it belongs to the reason to proceed from what is common to what is proper, as is stated in *Physics* i.[20] The speculative reason, however, is differently situated, in this matter, from the practical reason. For, since the speculative reason is concerned chiefly with necessary things, which cannot be otherwise than they are, its proper conclusions, like the universal principles, contain the truth without fail. The practical reason, on the other hand, is concerned with contingent matters, which is the domain of human actions; and, consequently, although there is necessity in the common principles, the more we descend towards the particular, the more frequently we encounter defects. Accordingly, then, in speculative matters truth is the same in all men, both as to principles and as to conclusions; although the truth is not known to all as regards the conclusions, but only as regards the principles which are called *common notions.*[21] But in matters of action, truth or practical rectitude is not the same for all as to what is particular, but only as to the common principles; and where there is the same rectitude in relation to particulars, it is not equally known to all.

It is therefore evident that, as regards the common principles whether of speculative or of practical reason, truth or rectitude is the same for all, and is equally known by all. But as to the proper conclusions of the speculative reason, the

---

[16] Gratian, *Decretum*, I, i. prol. (I, 1).   [17] Aristotle, *Eth.*, V, 1 (1129b 12).
[18] *Op. cit.*, V, 7 (1134b 32).   [19] *Etymol.*, V, 4 (PL 82, 199).
[20] Aristotle, *Phys.*, I, 1 (184a 16).   [21] Boethius, *De Hebdom.* (PL 64, 1311).

truth is the same for all, but it is not equally known to all. Thus, it is true for all that the three angles of a triangle are together equal to two right angles, although it is not known to all. But as to the proper conclusions of the practical reason, neither is the truth or rectitude the same for all, nor, where it is the same, is it equally known by all. Thus, it is right and true for all to act according to reason, and from this principle it follows, as a proper conclusion, that goods entrusted to another should be restored to their owner. Now this is true for the majority of cases. But it may happen in a particular case that it would be injurious, and therefore unreasonable, to restore goods held in trust; for instance, if they are claimed for the purpose of fighting against one's country. And this principle will be found to fail the more, according as we descend further towards the particular, e.g., if one were to say that goods held in trust should be restored with such and such a guarantee, or in such and such a way; because the greater the number of conditions added, the greater the number of ways in which the principle may fail, so that it be not right to restore or not to restore.

Consequently, we must say that the natural law, as to the first common principles, is the same for all, both as to rectitude and as to knowledge. But as to certain more particular aspects, which are conclusions, as it were, of those common principles, it is the same for all in the majority of cases, both as to rectitude and as to knowledge; and yet in some few cases it may fail, both as to rectitude, by reason of certain obstacles (just as natures subject to generation and corruption fail in some few cases because of some obstacle), and as to knowledge, since in some the reason is perverted by passion, or evil habit, or an evil disposition of nature. Thus at one time theft, although it is expressly contrary to the natural law, was not considered wrong among the Germans, as Julius Cæsar relates.[22]

Reply Obj. 1. The meaning of the sentence quoted is not that whatever is contained in the Law and the Gospel belongs to the natural law, since they contain many things that are above nature; but that whatever belongs to the natural law is fully contained in them. Therefore Gratian, after saying that *the natural law is what is contained in the Law and the Gospel*, adds at once, by way of example, *by which everyone is commanded to do to others as he would be done by*.[23]

Reply Obj. 2. The saying of the Philosopher is to be understood of things that are naturally just, not as common principles, but as conclusions drawn from them, having rectitude in the majority of cases, but failing in a few.[24]

Reply Obj. 3: Just as in man reason rules and commands the other powers, so all the natural inclinations belonging to the other powers must needs be directed according to reason. Therefore it is universally right for all men that all their inclinations should be directed according to reason.

---

[22] Caesar, *De Bello. Gallico*, VI, 23 (I, 348).   [23] *Decretum*, I, i, prol. (I, 1).   [24] *Eth*., V, 1 (1129b 12).

Chapter **9**

Religious Language, Metaphor, and Gender

Issues of Religious Language

Questions about religious language, particularly the language used to speak about God, have been raised from a number of standpoints. In one strain of religious sensibility, going back to well before the Middle Ages, it has been felt that human language and conceptions are inadequate in their application to God. It has been felt that strictly it cannot be said of God that God "knows" or "is good" or "is loving." These terms apply to human beings, but not to God. Another strain of religious sensibility, however, has stressed the importance for faith in God that God *is*, or at least can be believed to be, good and loving. The issue here is to what extent these and other terms crucial to religious belief apply *literally* or only *figuratively* to God.

Related to this issue is the gender issue. Often in the Western theistic traditions God is spoken of using male gender terms. In Christianity Jesus spoke of a heavenly *Father*, and in the Bible and the Qur'an the masculine pronoun "he" is used to refer to God. Does this mean that God is male? Could God just as well be referred to as "she"? This issue has been brought to prominence in recent years by feminist theologians, but this issue too goes back many centuries.

Another kind of issue relating to language about God has been raised from a scientific standpoint, or, more accurately, from a philosophical standpoint that has been greatly influenced by the procedures and standards of science. The sense that there is a tension between *reason* and *faith* has a long heritage in the Western theistic traditions. In the age of science, though, there developed a concern about the *meaning* of religious beliefs, or "religious statements," like "There is a God" or "God is merciful." Unlike scientific statements, some philosophers argued, such religious statements lack "factual meaning."

In this chapter we have readings that relate to the issues of metaphor, gender, and factual meaning. The chapter begins with readings that relate to the issue of factual meaning.

Does Religious Language have Factual Meaning?

In this section we have readings that relate to the question of whether "religious statements" about God have "factual meaning." The concern is whether they actually say or assert anything at all. The concern is whether they have only the appearance of being real assertions or statements. Scientific statements clearly make claims about what is the case, but they can be tested by our experience. We know in principle how to verify a zoologist's claim that certain species of mammals can survive without ingesting water or the claim that a water molecule consists of one atom of oxygen and two atoms of hydrogen. In principle we know how to verify whether there is water on the moons of Jupiter. In the same way we know how to verify our everyday statements like "The keys are on the table." But religious statements like "God has given us the ten commandments" or even "God exists" do not seem to have any such means of verification, or falsification. It seems that there is no condition they deny that would show them to be false if it should occur. This being the case some philosophers have concluded that religious statements are not genuine statements at all. They do not really *state* that anything is the case. They lack "factual meaning."

Our first reading is from the last section of David Hume's *An Enquiry Concerning Human Understanding*, in which Hume draws an important and influential distinction between "abstract reasoning concerning quantity or number" and "experimental reasoning concerning matter of fact and existence." The second reading is from a discussion paper by Antony Flew, who, writing in the spirit of Hume, issues a challenge to religious believers: if your religious belief is really saying something is true, tell us what it denies. The third reading is from the writings of John Wisdom. Wisdom considers the question of God's existence to be a meaningful question that can be addressed with reasons for and against, even if not in the two ways of reasoning that Hume identified.

DAVID HUME

from An Enquiry Concerning Human Understanding

Hume identified two kinds of reasoning: "abstract reasoning concerning quantity and number" and "experimental reasoning concerning matter of fact and existence." We use the first when we reason that "if a is bigger than b and b is bigger than c, than a is bigger than c," and we use the second when we "reason" that "there is a fig on the table" because we can see it there. For the first kind of reasoning the meanings of terms supply the conclusion (the meaning of "bigger" in our example), and for the second kind of reasoning an "experiment," or our experience, supplies the conclusion. Hume said that if anything we read does not contain one of these kinds of reasoning or the other, it is "sophistry," or nonsense, and we should "Commit it to the flames." Hume is speaking of "reasoning," but his thinking clearly extends to the meaningfulness of claims or statements. Our reading consists of Sec. XII, Pt. III of Hume's *Enquiry*, the last pages of the *Enquiry*.

From David Hume, *An Enquiry Concerning Human Understanding*.

PART III

There is, indeed, a more *mitigated* scepticism or *academical* philosophy, which may be both durable and useful, and which may, in part, be the result of this Pyrrhonism, or *excessive* scepticism, when its undistinguished doubts are, in some measure, corrected by common sense and reflection. The greater part of mankind are naturally apt to be affirmative and dogmatical in their opinions; and while they see objects only on one side, and have no idea of any counterpoising argument, they throw themselves precipitately into the principles, to which they are inclined; nor have they any indulgence for those who entertain opposite sentiments. To hesitate or balance perplexes their understanding, checks their passion, and suspends their action. They are, therefore, impatient till they escape from a state, which to them is so uneasy: and they think, that they could never remove themselves far enough from it, by the violence of their affirmations and obstinacy of their belief. But could such dogmatical reasoners become sensible of the strange infirmities of human understanding, even in its most perfect state, and when most accurate and cautious in its determinations; such a reflection would naturally inspire them with more modesty and reserve, and diminish their fond opinion of themselves, and their prejudice against antagonists. The illiterate may reflect on the disposition of the learned, who, amidst all the advantages of study and reflection, are commonly still diffident in their determinations: and if any of the learned be inclined, from their natural temper, to haughtiness and obstinacy, a small tincture of Pyrrhonism might abate their pride, by showing them, that the few advantages, which they may have attained over their fellows, are but inconsiderable, if compared with the universal perplexity and confusion, which is inherent in human nature. In general, there is a degree of doubt, and caution, and modesty, which, in all kinds of scrutiny and decision, ought for ever to accompany a just reasoner.

Another species of *mitigated* scepticism which may be of advantage to mankind, and which may be the natural result of the Pyrrhonian doubts and scruples, is the limitation of our enquiries to such subjects as are best adapted to the narrow capacity of human understanding. The *imagination* of man is naturally sublime, delighted with whatever is remote and extraordinary, and running, without control, into the most distant parts of space and time in order to avoid the objects, which custom has rendered too familiar to it. A correct *Judgement* observes a contrary method, and avoiding all distant and high enquiries, confines itself to common life, and to such subjects as fall under daily practice and experience; leaving the more sublime topics to the embellishment of poets and orators, or to the arts of priests and politicians. To bring us to so salutary a determination, nothing can be more serviceable, than to be once thoroughly convinced of the force of the Pyrrhonian doubt, and of the impossibility, that anything, but the strong power of natural instinct, could free us from it. Those who have a propensity to philosophy, will still continue their researches; because they reflect, that, besides the immediate pleasure, attending such an occupation, philosophical decisions are nothing but the reflections of common life, methodized and corrected. But they will never be tempted to go beyond common life, so long as they consider the imperfection of those faculties which they employ, their narrow reach, and their inaccurate operations. While we cannot give a satisfactory reason, why we believe, after a thousand experiments, that a stone will fall, or fire burn; can we ever satisfy ourselves concerning any determination, which we may form, with regard to the origin of worlds, and the situation of nature, from, and to eternity?

This narrow limitation, indeed, of our enquiries, is, in every respect, so reasonable, that it suffices to make the slightest examination into the natural powers of the human mind and to compare them with their objects, in order to recommend it to us. We shall then find what are the proper subjects of science and enquiry.

It seems to me, that the only objects of the abstract science or of demonstration are quantity and number, and that all attempts to extend this more perfect species of knowledge beyond these bounds are mere sophistry and illusion. As the component parts of quantity and number are entirely similar, their relations become intricate and involved; and nothing can be more curious, as well as useful, than to trace, by a variety of mediums, their equality or inequality, through their different appearances. But as all other ideas are clearly distinct and different from each other, we can never advance farther, by our utmost scrutiny, than to observe this diversity, and, by an obvious reflection, pronounce one thing not to be another. Or if there be any difficulty in these decisions, it proceeds entirely from the undeterminate meaning of words, which is corrected by juster definitions. That *the square of the hypothenuse is equal to the squares of the other two sides*, cannot be known, let the terms be ever so exactly defined, without a train of reasoning and enquiry. But to convince us of this proposition, *that where there is no property, there can be no injustice*, it is only necessary to define the terms, and explain injustice to be a violation of property. This proposition

is, indeed, nothing but a more imperfect definition. It is the same case with all those pretended syllogistical reasonings, which may be found in every other branch of learning, except the sciences of quantity and number; and these may safely, I think, be pronounced the only proper objects of knowledge and demonstration.

All other enquiries of men regard only matter of fact and existence; and these are evidently incapable of demonstration. Whatever *is* may *not be*. No negation of a fact can involve a contradiction. The non-existence of any being, without exception, is as clear and distinct an idea as its existence. The proposition, which affirms it not to be, however false, is no less conceivable and intelligible, than that which affirms it to be. The case is different with the sciences, properly so called. Every proposition, which is not true, is there confused and unintelligible. That the cube root of 64 is equal to the half of 10, is a false proposition, and can never be distinctly conceived. But that Cæsar, or the angel Gabriel, or any being never existed, may be a false proposition, but still is perfectly conceivable, and implies no contradiction.

The existence, therefore, of any being can only be proved by arguments from its cause or its effect; and these arguments are founded entirely on experience. If we reason *a priori*, anything may appear able to produce anything. The falling of a pebble may, for aught we know, extinguish the sun; or the wish of a man control the planets in their orbits. It is only experience, which teaches us the nature and bounds of cause and effect, and enables us to infer the existence of one object from that of another[1]. Such is the foundation of moral

[1] That impious maxim of the ancient philosophy, *Ex nihilo, nihil fit*, by which the creation of matter was excluded, ceases to be a maxim, according to this philosophy. Not only the will of the supreme Being may create matter; but, for aught we know *a priori*, the will of any other being might create it, or any other cause, that the most whimsical imagination can assign.

reasoning, which forms the greater part of human knowledge, and is the source of all human action and behaviour.

Moral reasonings are either concerning particular or general facts. All deliberations in life regard the former; as also all disquisitions in history, chronology, geography, and astronomy.

The sciences, which treat of general facts, are politics, natural philosophy, physic, chemistry, &c. where the qualities, causes and effects of a whole species of objects are enquired into.

Divinity or Theology, as it proves the existence of a Deity, and the immortality of souls, is composed partly of reasonings concerning particular, partly concerning general facts. It has a foundation in *reason*, so far as it is supported by experience. But its best and most solid foundation is *faith* and divine revelation.

Morals and criticism are not so properly objects of the understanding as of taste and sentiment. Beauty, whether moral or natural, is felt, more properly than perceived. Or if we reason concerning it, and endeavour to fix its standard, we regard a new fact, to wit, the general tastes of mankind, or some such fact, which may be the object of reasoning and enquiry.

When we run over libraries, persuaded of these principles, what havoc must we make? If we take in our hand any volume; of divinity or school metaphysics, for instance; let us ask, *Does it contain any abstract reasoning concerning quantity or number?* No. *Does it contain any experimental reasoning concerning matter of fact and existence?* No. Commit it then to the flames: for it can contain nothing but sophistry and illusion.

ANTONY FLEW

from Theology and Falsification

Antony Flew in our reading maintains that whenever we assert that something is true or the case, our doing so is equivalent to denying that that something is not the case. So to assert that it is raining is to deny that there is no water falling from the sky. This means that when we assert anything, if our assertion is genuine, we must also be denying something. So Flew reasons. Thus if religious believers are making genuine assertions when they say that God exists or say other things about God, their alleged assertions should deny some state of affairs, which if it occurred would falsify or disprove their assertion. Flew starts with a "parable," the parable of the garden. He uses it to argue implicitly that when religious believers say that God exists, or that God loves us or other things about God, they are not really denying anything. His implied conclusion is that religious "assertions" are not genuine assertions and really do not say anything factual at all. He ends by issuing a challenge to religious believers to say what would have to occur to disprove God's existence or God's love.

Our reading consists of Flew's contribution to a discussion of "Theology and Falsification," that is, a discussion of theological or religious statements or assertions about God and falsification.

Theology and Falsification

Let us begin with a parable. It is a parable developed from a tale told by John Wisdom in his haunting and revelatory article 'Gods'.[1] Once upon a time two explorers came upon a clearing in the jungle. In the clearing were growing many flowers and many weeds. One explorer says, 'Some gardener must tend this plot'. The other disagrees, 'There is no gardener'. So they pitch their tents and set a watch. No gardener is ever seen. 'But perhaps he is an invisible gardener.' So they set up a barbed-wire fence. They electrify it. They patrol with blood-hounds. (For they remember how H. G. Wells's *The Invisible Man* could be both smelt and touched though he could not be seen.) But no shrieks ever suggest that some intruder has received a shock. No movements of the wire ever betray an invisible climber. The bloodhounds never give cry. Yet still the Believer is not convinced. 'But there is a gardener, invisible, intangible, insensible to electric shocks, a gardener who has no scent and makes no sound, a gardener who comes secretly to look after the garden which he loves.' At last the Sceptic despairs, 'But what remains of your original assertion? Just how does what you call an invisible, intangible, eternally elusive gardener differ from an imaginary gardener or even from no gardener at all'?

In this parable we can see how what starts as an assertion, that something exists or that there is some analogy between certain complexes of phenomena, may be reduced step by step to an altogether different status, to an expression perhaps of a 'picture preference'.[2] The Sceptic says there is no gardener. The Believer says there is a gardener (but invisible, etc.). One man talks about sexual behaviour. Another man prefers to talk of Aphrodite (but knows that there is not really a superhuman person additional to, and somehow responsible for, all sexual phenomena).[3] The process of qualification may be checked at any point before the original assertion is completely withdrawn and something of that first assertion will remain (Tautology). Mr. Wells's invisible man could not, admittedly, be seen, but in all other respects he was a man like the rest of us. But though the process of qualification may be, and of course usually is, checked in time, it is not always judiciously so halted. Someone may dissipate his assertion completely without noticing that he

---

[1] *P.A.S.*, 1944–5, reprinted as Ch. X of *Logic and Language*, Vol I (Blackwell, 1951), and in his *Philosophy and Psychoanalysis* (Blackwell, 1953).

[2] Cf. J. Wisdom, 'Other Minds', *Mind*, 1940; reprinted in his *Other Minds* (Blackwell, 1952).

[3] Cf. Lucretius, *De Rerum Natura*, II, 655–60,

> Hic siquis mare Neptunum Cereremque vocare
> Constituet fruges et Bacchi nomine abuti
> Mavolat quam laticis proprium proferre vocamen
> Concedamus ut hic terrarum dictitet orbem
> Esse deum matrem dum vera re tamen ipse
> Religione animum turpi contingere parcat.

has done so. A fine brash hypothesis may thus be killed by inches, the death by a thousand qualifications.

And in this, it seems to me, lies the peculiar danger, the endemic evil, of theological utterance. Take such utterances as 'God has a plan', 'God created the world', 'God loves us as a father loves his children'. They look at first sight very much like assertions, vast cosmological assertions. Of course, this is no sure sign that they either are, or are intended to be, assertions. But let us confine ourselves to the cases where those who utter such sentences intend them to express assertions. (Merely remarking parenthetically that those who intend or interpret such utterances as crypto-commands, expressions of wishes, disguised ejaculations, concealed ethics, or as anything else but assertions, are unlikely to succeed in making them either properly orthodox or practically effective).

Now to assert that such and such is the case is necessarily equivalent to denying that such and such is not the case.[4] Suppose then that we are in doubt as to what someone who gives vent to an utterance is asserting, or suppose that, more radically, we are sceptical as to whether he is really asserting anything at all, one way of trying to understand (or perhaps it will be to expose) his utterance is to attempt to find what he would regard as counting against, or as being incompatible with, its truth. For if the utterance is indeed an assertion, it will necessarily be equivalent to a denial of the negation of that assertion. And anything which would count against the assertion, or which would induce the speaker to withdraw it

and to admit that it had been mistaken, must be part of (or the whole of) the meaning of the negation of that assertion. And to know the meaning of the negation of an assertion, is as near as makes no matter, to know the meaning of that assertion.[5] And if there is nothing which a putative assertion denies then there is nothing which it asserts either: and so it is not really an assertion. When the Sceptic in the parable asked the Believer, 'Just how does what you call an invisible, intangible, eternally elusive gardener differ from an imaginary gardener or even from no gardener at all?' he was suggesting that the Believer's earlier statement had been so eroded by qualification that it was no longer an assertion at all.

Now it often seems to people who are not religious as if there was no conceivable event or series of events the occurrence of which would be admitted by sophisticated religious people to be a sufficient reason for conceding 'There wasn't a God after all' or 'God does not really love us then'. Someone tells us that God loves us as a father loves his children. We are reassured. But then we see a child dying of inoperable cancer of the throat. His earthly father is driven frantic in his efforts to help, but his Heavenly Father reveals no obvious sign of concern. Some qualification is made—God's love is 'not a merely human love' or it is 'an inscrutable love', perhaps—and we realize that such sufferings are quite compatible with the truth of the assertion that 'God loves us as a father (but, of course, . . .)'. We are reassured again. But then perhaps we ask: what is this assurance of God's (appropriately qualified)

[4] For those who prefer symbolism: $p \equiv \sim\sim p$. [5] For by simply negating $\sim p$ we get $p: \sim\sim p \equiv p$.

love worth, what is this apparent guarantee really a guarantee against? Just what would have to happen not merely (morally and wrongly) to tempt but also (logically and rightly) to entitle us to say 'God does not love us' or even 'God does not exist'? I therefore put to the succeeding symposiasts the simple central questions, 'What would have to occur or to have occurred to constitute for you a disproof of the love of, or of the existence of, God?'

JOHN WISDOM

from Gods

John Wisdom in "Gods" says that the question of God's existence is no longer an "experimental issue" in the way that it was. Still he feels that it is a question that can be reasonably addressed. Wisdom, like Hume, is concerned with the range of the issues that reason can address and which in this sense can be meaningfully pursued. Unlike Hume, however, he maintains that there can be meaningful issues that do not fall into either of Hume's two categories.

Wisdom uses a "story," or parable, about two people returning to a neglected garden to try to show how "the existence of God" may not be an "experimental issue" (one of Hume's two categories) and how—though it clearly is not an "abstract" issue about "quantity and number" (Hume's other category)—it may yet be a meaningful issue, regarding which "reasons for and against may be offered"—but not "scientific reasons."*

Gods

1. *The existence of God is not an experimental issue in the way it was.* An atheist or agnostic might say to a theist 'You still think there are spirits in the trees, nymphs in the streams, a God of the world.' He might say this because he noticed the theist in time of drought pray for rain and make a sacrifice and in the morning look for rain.

But disagreement about whether there are gods is now less of this experimental or betting sort than it used to be. This is due in part, if not wholly, to our better knowledge of why things happen as they do.

It is true that even in these days it is seldom that one who believes in God has no hopes or fears which an atheist has not.

* John Wisdom, "Gods" from *Proceedings of the Aristotelian Society*, 1944. Published by Blackwell. Reprinted by permission of Blackwell Publishing.

Few believers now expect prayer to still the waves, but some think it makes a difference to people and not merely in ways the atheist would admit. Of course with people, as opposed to waves and machines, one never knows what they won't do next, so that expecting prayer to make a difference to them is not so definite a thing as believing in its mechanical efficacy. Still, just as primitive people pray in a business-like way for rain so some people still pray for others with a real feeling of doing something to help. However, in spite of this persistence of an experimental element in some theistic belief, it remains true that Elijah's method on Mount Carmel of settling the matter of what god or gods exist would be far less appropriate to-day than it was then.

2. *Belief in gods is not merely a matter of expectation of a world to come.* Someone may say 'The fact that a theist no more than an atheist expects prayer to bring down fire from heaven or cure the sick does not mean that there is no difference between them as to the facts, it does not mean that the theist has no expectations different from the atheist's. For very often those who believe in God believe in another world and believe that God is there and that we shall go to that world when we die.'

This is true, but I do not want to consider here expectations as to what one will see and feel after death nor what sort of reasons these logically unique expectations could have. So I want to consider those theists who do not believe in a future life, or rather, I want to consider the differences between atheists and theists in so far as these differences are not a matter of belief in a future life.

3. *What are these differences? And is it that theists are superstitious or that atheists are blind?* A child may wish to sit a while with his father and he may, when he has done what his father dislikes, fear punishment and feel distress at causing vexation, and while his father is alive he may feel sure of help when danger threatens and feel that there is sympathy for him when disaster has come. When his father is dead he will no longer expect punishment or help. Maybe for a moment an old fear will come or a cry for help escape him, but he will at once remember that this is no good now. He may feel that his father is no more until perhaps someone says to him that his father is still alive though he lives now in another world and one so far away that there is no hope of seeing him or hearing his voice again. The child may be told that nevertheless his father can see him and hear all he says. When he has been told this the child will still fear no punishment nor expect any sign of his father, but now, even more than he did when his father was alive, he will feel that his father sees him all the time and will dread distressing him and when he has done something wrong he will feel separated from his father until he has felt sorry for what he has done. Maybe when he himself comes to die he will be like a man who expects to find a friend in the strange country where he is going, but even when this is so, it is by no means all of what makes the difference between a child who believes that his father lives still in another world and one who does not.

Likewise one who believes in God may face death differently from one who does not, but there is another difference between them besides this. This other difference may still be described as belief in another world, only this belief is not a matter of expecting one thing rather than another here or hereafter, it is not a matter of a world to come but of a world that now is, though beyond our senses.

We are at once reminded of those other unseen worlds which some philosophers 'believe in' and others 'deny', while non-philosophers unconsciously 'accept' them by using them as models with which to 'get the hang of' the patterns in the flux of experience. We recall the timeless entities whose changeless connections we seek to represent in symbols, and the values which stand firm[1] amidst our flickering satisfaction and remorse, and the physical things which, though not beyond the corruption of moth and rust, are yet more permanent than the shadows they throw upon the screen before our minds. We recall, too, our talk of souls and of what lies in their depths and is manifested to us partially and intermittently in our own feelings and the behaviour of others. The hypothesis of mind, of other human minds and of animal minds, is reasonable because it explains for each of us why certain things behave so cunningly all by themselves unlike even the most ingenious machines. Is the hypothesis of minds in flowers and trees reasonable for like reasons? Is the hypothesis of a world mind reasonable for like reasons—someone who adjusts the blossom to the bees, someone whose presence may at times be felt—in a garden in high summer, in the hills when clouds are gathering, but not, perhaps, in a cholera epidemic?

4. *The question 'Is belief in gods reasonable?' has more than one source.* It is clear now that in order to grasp fully the logic of belief in divine minds we need to examine the logic of belief in animal and human minds. But we cannot do that here and so for the purposes of this discussion about divine minds let us acknowledge the reasonableness of our belief in human minds without troubling ourselves about its logic. The question of the reasonableness of belief in divine minds then becomes a matter of whether there are facts in nature which support

claims about divine minds in the way facts in nature support our claims about human minds.

* * * * * * * * * * * * * * * * * * *

6.1. *How it is that an explanatory hypothesis, such as the existence of God, may start by being experimental and gradually become something quite different can be seen from the following story*:

Two people return to their long neglected garden and find among the weeds a few of the old plants surprisingly vigorous. One says to the other 'It must be that a gardener has been coming and doing something about these plants'. Upon inquiry they find that no neighbour has ever seen anyone at work in their garden. The first man says to the other 'He must have worked while people slept'. The other says 'No, someone would have heard him and besides, anybody who cared about the plants would have kept down these weeds'. The first man says 'Look at the way these are arranged. There is purpose and a feeling for beauty here. I believe that someone comes, someone invisible to mortal eyes. I believe that the more carefully we look the more we shall find confirmation of this.' They examine the garden ever so carefully and sometimes they come on new things suggesting that a gardener comes and sometimes they come on new things suggesting the contrary and even that a malicious person has been at work. Besides examining the garden carefully they also study what happens to gardens left without attention. Each learns all the other learns about this and about the garden. Consequently, when after all this, one says 'I still believe a gardener comes' while the other says 'I don't' their different words now reflect no difference as to what they

---

[1] In another world, Dr. Joad says in the *New Statesman* recently.

have found in the garden, no difference as to what they would find in the garden if they looked further and no difference about how fast untended gardens fall into disorder. At this stage, in this context, the gardener hypothesis has ceased to be experimental, the difference between one who accepts and one who rejects it is now not a matter of the one expecting something the other does not expect. What is the difference between them? The one says 'A gardener comes unseen and unheard. He is manifested only in his works with which we are all familiar', the other says 'There is no gardener' and with this difference in what they say about the gardener goes a difference in how they feel towards the garden, in spite of the fact that neither expects anything of it which the other does not expect.

But is this the whole difference between them—that the one calls the garden by one name and feels one way towards it, while the other calls it by another name and feels in another way towards it? And if this is what the difference has become then is it any longer appropriate to ask 'Which is right?' or 'Which is reasonable?'

And yet surely such questions *are* appropriate when one person says to another 'You still think the world's a garden and not a wilderness, and that the gardener has not forsaken it' or 'You still think there are nymphs of the streams, a presence in the hills, a spirit of the world'. Perhaps when a man sings 'God's in His heaven' we need not take this as more than an expression of how he feels. But when Bishop Gore or Dr. Joad write about belief in God and young men read them in order to settle their religious doubts the impression is not simply that of persons choosing exclamations with which to face nature and the 'changes and chances of this mortal life'. The disputants speak as if they are concerned with a matter of scientific fact, or of trans-sensual, trans-scientific and metaphysical fact, but still of fact and still a matter about which reasons for and *against* may be offered, although no scientific reasons in the sense of field surveys for fossils or experiments on delinquents are to the point.

Metaphor

A metaphor is a figure of speech in which a word or term that literally denotes or means one thing is applied to another thing so that an implied comparison between the two things is made. An example is "an idea *dawned* upon her." No literal dawn is referred to; the sun is not coming up in the morning. But the implied comparison is with the sun's coming up.

A question that arises within and about religion is: To what extent is religious language literal and to what extent is it metaphorical or figurative? As it applies to theistic religions, it relates primarily to language about or describing God. To what extent is it figurative to speak of God as a Heavenly Father, as is done in Christianity? To what extent is it literally true of God that God is loving, just, and merciful? Almost all religious believers in God would allow that there are some metaphorical descriptions of God. Certainly most Jews and Christians would allow this. In the poetry of the Psalms several metaphors are used to present God and the believer's relationship to God. The Psalmist says of those in the shelter of God that God will cover them "with his pinions," or feathers, and "under his wings [they] will find refuge" (Ps. 94.4). God is their "refuge and . . . fortress" (Ps. 91.2). The Psalmist says that God is the "Rock of my salvation" (Ps. 89.26). While these metaphors underline the steadfastness of God's support and caring protection, clearly it would be misguided for religious believers to think that God has feathers or wings or is a Rock.

Fairly clearly, in the traditions of Judaism and Christianity God is spoken of metaphorically, but is there anything that can be said of God literally, or do believers have only metaphors? It is a metaphor to say God has protective wings or is a Rock, but is it a metaphor when we say that God's love is steadfast, as we find in the Psalms (Ps 36.5) or that God is our Father, as we find in the Psalms (Ps. 89.26), or our heavenly Father, as we find in the New Testament (in Matthew 6.9)? Closely related to this question is the question whether we can say of human beings and God that they are loving, wise, merciful *in the same sense*.

There are several related reasons why some who are religious think that what we say about God (the descriptive adjectives or what we "predicate" of God) should not be understood in the same sense we use when speaking of human beings. For one thing, there is the religious sense that God is so far above human understanding that we cannot have an adequate conceptual understanding of God. The sensibility here is that God is so far beyond us and our rational understanding that God cannot be captured by our concepts. Nothing can be said about the true nature of God, except that it is beyond our concepts and inexpressible. It is in this sense *ineffable*. This idea is at home in *mysticism*, which is a strain of religious expression found in several religions.

Within religion, specifically within theistic traditions, there are two kinds of religious sensibilities in tension with one another. On the one hand, there is the just noted religious sensibility, that God, or God's true nature, is the wholly other, that which transcends our understanding, of which we cannot speak with our ordinary concepts—except perhaps to say what God is not. On the other hand, religious believers need to believe that God is concerned, loving, and merciful *in a way they can understand* in order for there to be comfort or reassurance in trusting in God, and in believing that God is concerned, loving, and merciful. What point is there is believing that God is "loving" and "merciful" if these terms applied to God mean something different from what we understand them to mean? What point is there in believing that God is a forgiving God if "forgiving" doesn't mean what we mean when we forgive one another?

St. Thomas Aquinas in the *Summa Theologica* wrestled with the problem of how we should understand the predicates we apply to God. Aquinas argued that God is *literally*, not figuratively, good and wise (and more). But at the same time, he argued, God is not good and wise in the *same sense* that human beings are good and wise (when they are). This does not mean that the sense in which these predicates apply to God is utterly different from the sense in which we apply them to human beings. These terms, "good" and "wise," and other predicates apply to God and to human being neither in the same sense (*univocally*) nor in a different sense (*equivocally*). Rather, Aquinas argued, they are *analogically predicated* of God. The concept of *analogical predication* is Aquinas' distinctive contribution to an understanding of how God's goodness and wisdom (and more) can be beyond what we ordinarily mean by these terms and yet God can be literally good and wise (and more).

In this section we have two readings from Christian mystics, Meister Eckhart and Dionysius. A third reading from the Jewish mystical tradition of Kabbalah, from the *Zohar*, is in Chapter 1. The fourth reading is from Rudolf Otto's *The Idea of the Holy*. The fifth reading is from Part I of Aquinas's *Summa Theologica*. It consists of three articles from Question 13, The Names of God.

MEISTER ECKHART
Sermon: Now I Know

M eister Eckhart, a medieval Christian mystic, said in his sermon "Now I Know" that "God's being" (God's true nature) is "beyond all knowledge" and cannot be named; though in experience we can "taste" God (as the Psalms say—Ps. 34.8) and the soul can "know with the purest knowledge," but it is not a knowledge that allows us to apply "names" to God or to say anything about God.*

Now I know

NUNC SCIO VERE, QUIA MISIT DOMINUS ANGELUM SUUM, ET ERIPUIT ME DE MANU HERODIS, ET DE OMNE EXSPECTATIONE PLEBUS IUDAEORUM
(*Acts 12:11*)

W hen Peter was set free from the bonds of his captivity, by the power of the supreme God, he said: "Now I know of a surety that the Lord hath sent his angel and delivered me out of the power of Herod and out of the hand of the enemy."

We shall turn this expression around and say: "When God has sent his angel to me, then I know of a surety." Let Peter stand for knowledge. On other occasions I have said that knowledge and intellect unite the soul to God. Intellect falls within [the category of] pure Being, but knowledge precedes it—precedes it and breaks out the way—so that God's only begotten Son can be born. Our Lord says in the Gospel of St. Matthew, that no one knows the Father but the Son. The authorities declare that knowledge is limited [by the requirement of] likeness. For that reason, some of them say that the soul is composite of everything,

* Sermon 9: "Now I Know" (pp. 140–2) from MEISTER ECKHART: A MODERN TRANSLATION by RAYMOND BERNARD BLAKNEY. Copyright 1941 by Harper & Brothers. Reprinted by permission of HarperCollins Publishers.

---

because it can understand everything. This sounds foolish but it is true. They say that what I am to know must be present in me already and like what I know. Moreover, the saints say that the Father has power, the Son, likeness, and the Holy Spirit, unity; so that if the Father is completely represented by the Son and the Son is always like him, no one can possibly know the Father but the Son.

"Now I know of a surety," exclaims St. Peter. How does anyone know with certainty? Because there is a divine light that deceives nobody, and in that light things are seen clearly, without coatings, and undisguised. St. Paul says that "God lives in a light to which there is no approach." The authorities again assert that the wisdom we acquire here we shall keep in heaven; but Paul says that "it shall vanish away." One authority says: "Pure knowledge, even in this present body, is so pleasant that all the delights of creation are as nothing to the pleasure it unfolds." And yet, noble as our knowledge may be, it is still contingent, and compared to the uncoated, pure Truth; all the wisdom one may acquire here is as insignificant as one small word would be against the whole world. Thus Paul says: "It shall vanish away." And even if it did not, it would become like foolish vanity when compared to that pure, uncoated Truth which is yet to be known.

The third reason why we shall know with certainty up yonder is that those things which are here seen to be so changeable and changing are known there as changeless and perceived at a given time as undivided and almost as if they were one. Things that are widely separate here are near together there, where everything is present at once. What happened on the first day, and shall happen at the latter day, happen all together in one present there.

"Now I know of a surety that the Lord hath sent his angel to me." When God sends his angel to the soul, it becomes the one who knows for sure. Not for nothing did God give the keys into St. Peter's keeping, for Peter stands for knowledge, and knowledge has the key that unlocks the door, presses forward and breaks in, to discover God as he is. Then it tells its partner, the will, what it has taken possession of, for it had already taken charge of the will. For what I will, that I seek after, but knowledge goes before. It is like a princess seeking to rule in the prince's place, in that virgin realm which she proclaims to the soul, and the soul to the nature and the nature to the physical senses. Still, at its highest and best, the soul's rank is such that no scholar can find a name for it. They call it the "soul," since it gives being to the body.

The authorities teach that next to the first emanation, which is the Son coming out of the Father, the angels are most like God. And it may well be true, for the soul at its highest is formed like God, but an angel gives a closer idea of him. That is all an angel is: an idea of God. For this reason the angel was sent to the soul, so that the soul might be re-formed by it, to be the divine idea by which it was first conceived. Knowledge comes through likeness. And so, because the soul may know everything, it is never at rest until it comes to the original idea, in which all things are one. And there it comes to rest in God. No creature is more respected than another by God.

The authorities say that being and knowing are identical, because if a thing does not exist no one knows it, but that whatever has most being is most known. Because God's being is transcendent, he is beyond all knowledge, as I said the day before yesterday in my former sermon. There, where the soul is informed with the primal purity, stamped with the seal of pure being, where it tastes God himself as he was before he ever took upon himself the forms of truth and knowledge, where everything that can be named is sloughed off—there the soul knows with its purest knowledge and takes on Being in its most perfect similitude. St. Paul says of the matter: "God dwells in the light no man can approach unto." God is one and lives within his own pure being, which contains nothing else. All alloy must be done away. He himself is a pure presence in which there is neither this nor that, because what is in God is God!

One heathen says: "The agents of the soul which are under God's suasion, belong in God, for however freely they may exist, their inner connection is with that which has neither beginning nor end and nothing alien may intrude in God." Heaven is an example of this. Heaven will receive nothing alien, as an alien. Thus, by the same token, whatever comes to God is changed. However mean it may be, let it be brought to God and it will no longer be what it was. Take, for example: I may have wisdom, but I am not wisdom myself. I can acquire wisdom and also lose it. But what is of God is God! And it can never fall away from him. It is implanted in the divine nature and the divine nature is so stable that whatever gets into it is part of it forever—either that, or it stays out altogether. Then listen, and be astonished! If God so changes little things, what do you think he will do with the soul, which he has already fashioned so gloriously in his own likeness? . . .

DIONYSIUS

from The Divine Names and from The Mystical Theology

The Christian mystic Dionysius, who lived around 500 C.E., expressed the theme of ineffability about God, when he said that while we can call God "wise" and "benevolent" these are "symbols" "drawn from the world of sense" and do not apply to God in God's true being, which is above all knowledge. However, Dionysius thought that we might be able to say what God is *not*, using the *via negativa*, or "negative way," so that we can say God is not darkness nor is God light, and God does not belong to the category of non-existence nor to the category of existence.

Our reading consists of Chap. I, Secs. 4 and 5, from *The Divine Names* and Chaps. IV and V from *The Mystical Theology*.*

* From Dionysius, *The Divine Names* and *The Mystical Theology*, both in *Dionysius the Areopagite*, translated by C. E. Roit, London: SPCK, 1940. Reprinted by permission of Kessinger Publishing, LLC.

The Divine Names

4. These mysteries we learn from the Divine Scriptures, and thou wilt find that in well-nigh all the utterances of the Sacred Writers the Divine Names refer in a Symbolical Revelation[2] to Its beneficent Emanations.[3] Wherefore, in almost all consideration of Divine things we see the Supreme Godhead celebrated with holy praises as One and an Unity, through the simplicity and unity of Its supernatural indivisibility, from whence (as from an unifying power) we attain to unity, and through the supernal conjunction of our diverse and separate qualities are knit together each into a Godlike Oneness, and all together into a mutual Godly union.[4] And It is called the Trinity because Its supernatural fecundity is revealed in a Threefold Personality,[5] wherefrom all Fatherhood in heaven and on earth exists and draws Its name. And It is called the Universal Cause[6] since all things came into being through Its bounty, whence all being springs; and It is called Wise and Fair because all things which keep their own nature uncorrupted are full of all Divine harmony and holy Beauty;[1] and especially It is called Benevolent[2] because, in one of Its Persons, It verily and wholly shared in our human lot, calling unto Itself and uplifting the low estate of man, wherefrom, in an ineffable manner, the simple Being of Jesus assumed a compound state,[3] and the Eternal hath taken a temporal existence, and He who supernaturally transcends all the order of all the natural world was born in our Human Nature without any change or confusion of His ultimate properties. And in all the other Divine enlightenments which the occult Tradition of our inspired teachers hath, by mystic Interpretation, accordant with the Scriptures, bestowed upon us, we also have been initiated: apprehending these things in the present life (according to our powers), through the sacred veils of that loving kindness which in the Scriptures and the Hierarchical Traditions,[4] enwrappeth spiritual truths in terms drawn from the world of sense, and super-essential truths

[2] ἐκφαντορικῶς καὶ ὑμνητικῶς

[3] i. e. God's differentiated activities. Since the ultimate Godhead is ineffable, Scripture can only hint at Its Nature by speaking of Its manifestations in the relative sphere.

[4] God is ineffable and transcends unity. But, since His presence in man produces an unity in each individual (and in human society), Scripture calls Him "One."

[5] The ineffable Godhead transcends our conception of the Trinity. But we call Him a Trinity because we experience His trinal working—as our ultimate Home, as an Individual Personality Who was once Incarnate, and as a Power within our hearts.

[6] God is not a First Cause, for a cause is one event in a temporal series, and God is beyond Time and beyond the whole creation. Yet in so far as He acts on the relative plane He may, by virtue of this manifestation of Himself in the creation, be spoken of as a Cause.

[1] Beauty is a sacrament and only truly itself when it points to something beyond itself. That is why "Art for Art's sake" degrades art. Beauty reveals God, but God is more than Beauty. Hence Beauty has its true being *outside* itself in Him. Cf. Intr., p. 31.

[2] Love is the most perfect manifestation of God. Yet God is in a sense beyond even love as we know it. For love, as we know it, implies the distinction between "me" and "thee," and God is ultimately beyond such distinction. See Intr., p. 35.

[3] ὁ ἁπλοῦς Ἰησοῦς συνετέθη. Cf. *Myst. Theol.* III., "Super-Essential Jesus."

[4] ἱεραρχικῶν παραδόσεων, i.e. Ecclesiastical Tradition.

in terms drawn from Being, clothing with shapes and forms things which are shapeless and formless, and by a variety of separable symbols, fashioning manifold attributes of the imageless and supernatural Simplicity. But hereafter, when we are corruptible and immortal and attain the blessed lot of being like unto Christ, then (as the Scripture saith), we shall be for ever with the Lord,[1] fulfilled with His visible Theophany in holy contemplations, the which shall shine about us with radiant beams of glory (even as once of old it shone around the Disciples at the Divine Transfiguration); and so shall we, with our mind made passionless and spiritual, participate in a spiritual illumination from Him, and in an union transcending our mental faculties, and there, amidst the blinding blissful impulsions of His dazzling rays, we shall, in a diviner manner than at present, be like unto the heavenly Intelligences.[2] For, as the infallible Scripture saith, we shall be equal to the angels and shall be the Sons of God, being Sons of the Resurrection.[3] But at present we employ (so far as in us lies), appropriate symbols for things Divine; and then from these we press on upwards according to our powers to behold in simple unity the Truth perceived by spiritual contemplations, and leaving behind us all human notions of godlike things, we still the activities of our minds, and reach (so far as this may be) into the Super-Essential Ray,[4] wherein all kinds of knowledge so have

their pre-existent limits (in a transcendently inexpressible manner), that we cannot conceive nor utter It, nor in any wise contemplate the same, seeing that It surpasseth all things, and wholly exceeds our knowledge, and super-essentially contains beforehand (all conjoined within Itself) the bounds of all natural sciences and forces (while yet Its force is not circumscribed by any), and so possesses, beyond the celestial Intelligences,[1] Its firmly fixed abode. For if all the branches of knowledge belong to things that have being, and if their limits have reference to the existing world, then that which is beyond all Being must also be transcendent above all knowledge.[2]

5. But if It is greater than all Reason and all knowledge, and hath Its firm abode altogether beyond Mind and Being, and circumscribes, compacts, embraces and anticipates all things[3] while Itself is altogether beyond the grasp of them all, and cannot be reached by any perception, imagination, conjecture, name, discourse, apprehension, or understanding, how then is our Discourse concerning the Divine Names to be accomplished, since we see that the Super-Essential Godhead is unutterable and nameless? Now, as we said when setting forth our Outlines of Divinity, the One, the Unknowable, the Super-Essential, the Absolute Good (I mean the Trinal Unity of Persons possessing the same Deity and Goodness), 'tis impossible to

---

[1] I Thess. iv. 16.
[2] ἐν θεοιτέρᾳ μιμήσει τῶν ὑφερουρανίων νοῶν—i.e, the angels.
[3] Luke xx. 36.
[4] Meditation leads on to Contemplation; and the higher kind of Contemplation is performed by the *Via Negativa*.
[1] *i.e.* The Angels. I have throughout translated ὑπερουράνιος "celestial" instead of "super-celestial." Presumably the meaning is "beyond the *material* sky," or "celestial in a *transcendent* sense."
[2] The whole of this passage shows that there is a positive element in Unknowing.
[3] πάντων . . . προληπτική—i.e. contains them eternally before their creation.

describe or to conceive in Its ultimate Nature; nay, even the angelical communions of the heavenly Powers Therewith which we describe as either Impulsions or Derivations[4] from the Unknowable and blinding Goodness are themselves beyond utterance and knowledge, and belong to none but those angels who, in a manner beyond angelic knowledge, have been counted worthy thereof. And godlike Minds,[1] angelically[2] entering (according to their powers) unto such states of union and being deified and united, through the ceasing of their natural activities, unto the Light Which surpasseth Deity, can find no more fitting method to celebrate its praises than to deny It every manner of Attribute.[3] For by a true and supernatural illumination from their blessed union Therewith, they learn that It is the Cause of all things and yet Itself is nothing, because It super-essentially transcends them all. Thus, as for the Super-Essence of the Supreme Godhead (if we would define the Transcendence of its Transcendent Goodness[4]) it is not lawful to any lover of that Truth which is above all truth to celebrate It as Reason or Power or Mind or Life or Being, but rather as most utterly surpassing all condition, movement, life, imagination, conjecture, name, discourse, thought, conception, being, rest, dwelling, union,[5] limit, infinity, everything that exists. And yet since, as the Subsistence[6] of goodness, It, by the very fact of Its existence, is the Cause of all things, in celebrating the bountiful Providence of the Supreme Godhead we must draw upon the whole creation. For It is both the central Force of all things, and also their final Purpose, and *is* Itself before them all, and they all subsist in It; and through the fact of Its existence the world is brought into being and maintained; and It is that which all things desire—those which have intuitive or discursive Reason seeking It through knowledge, the next rank of beings through perception, and the rest through vital movement or the property of mere existence belonging to their state.[1] Conscious of this, the Sacred Writers celebrate It by every Name while yet they call It Nameless.[2]

---

[4] ἂς εἶτε ἐπιβολὰς εἶτε παραδοχὰς χρῆ φάναι—*i.e*, according as we describe the act from above or below. God sends the impulse, the angels receive it.

[1] οἱ θεοειδεῖς . . . νόες—*i.e.* human minds.

[2] ἀγγελομιμητῶς. "In a manner which imitates the angels." Cf. Wordsworth, *Prelude*, xiv. 108, 102: "Like angels stopped upon the wing by sound of harmony from heaven's remotest spheres."

[3] This shows that the *Via Negativa* is based on an experience and not on a mere speculation.

[4] δ τι ποτέ ἐστιν ἡ τῆς ὑπεραγαθότητος ὑπερύπαρξις.

[5] "Union" (ἔνωσις). This word has more than one meaning in D., and hence occasional ambiguity. It may = (1) Unity (*i.e.* that which makes an individual thing to be one thing); (2) Mental or Spiritual intercourse; (3) Physical intercourse; (4) Sense perception. Here it = either (1) or (2), probably (1).

[6] ἀγαθότητος ὑπαρξι s—*i.e.* the ultimate Essence in which goodness consists.

[1] Man—Animal—Vegetable—Inorganic Matter. For the thought of this whole passage, cf. Shelley, *Adonais*: "That Light whose smile kindles the universe." "The property of mere existence" = οὐσιώδη καὶ ἑκτικὴν ἐπιτηδειότητα. οὐσία = an individual existence. Its highest meaning is a "personality," its lowest a "thing." οὐσιώδης refers generally to its lowest meaning and = "possessing mere existence," *i.e.* "belonging to the realm of inorganic matter."

[2] This shows that there is a *positive* element in D.'s *Via Negativa*.

The Mystical Theology

CHAPTER 4

That He Who is the Pre-eminent Cause of everything sensibly perceived is not Himself any one of the things sensibly perceived.

We therefore maintain[2] that the universal Cause transcending all things is neither impersonal nor lifeless, nor irrational nor without understanding: in short, that It is not a material body, and therefore does not possess outward shape or intelligible form, or quality, or quantity, or solid weight; nor has It any local existence which can be perceived by sight or touch; nor has It the power of perceiving or being perceived; nor does It suffer any vexation or disorder through the disturbance of earthly passions, or any feebleness through the tyranny of material chances, or any want of light; nor any change, or decay, or division, or deprivation, or ebb and flow, or anything else which the senses can perceive. None of these things can be either identified with it or attributed unto It.

CHAPTER 5

That He Who is the Pre-eminent Cause of everything intelligibly perceived is not Himself any one of the things intelligibly perceived.

Once more, ascending yet higher we maintain[1] that It is not soul, or mind, or endowed with the faculty of imagination, conjecture, reason, or understanding; nor is It any act of reason or understanding; nor can It be described by the reason or perceived by the understanding, since It is not number, or order, or greatness, or littleness, or equality, or inequality, and since It is not immovable nor in motion, or at rest, and has no power, and is not power or light, and does not live, and is not life; nor is It personal essence, or eternity, or time; nor can It be grasped by the understanding, since It is not knowledge or truth; nor is It kingship or wisdom; nor is It one, nor is It unity, nor is It Godhead[2] or Goodness; nor is It a Spirit, as we understand the term, since It is not Sonship or Fatherhood; nor is It any other thing such as we or any other being can have knowledge of; nor does It belong to the category of non-existence or to that of existence; nor do existent beings know It as it actually is, nor does It know them as they actually are;[3] nor can the reason attain to It to name It or to know It; nor is it darkness, nor is It light, or error, or truth;[4] nor can any affirmation or negation[1] apply to it; for

[2] Being about to explain, in these two last chapters, that no material or mental qualities are *present* in the Godhead, D. safeguards the position against pure negativity by explaining that they are not *absent* either. The rest of this chapter deals with the qualities (1) of inanimate matter; (2) of material life.
[1] It is not (1) a Thinking Subject; nor (2) an Act or Faculty of Thought; nor (3) an Object of Thought.
[2] *Divine Names*, II. 7. Godhead is regarded as the property of Deified men, and so belongs to relativity.
[3] It knows only Itself, and there knows all things in their Super-Essence—*sub specie aeternitatis*.
[4] Truth is an Object of Thought. Therefore, being beyond objectivity, the ultimate Reality is not Truth. But still less is It Error.
[1] Cf. p. 199, n. 2.

while applying affirmations or negations to those orders of being that come next to It, we apply not unto It either affirmation or negation, inasmuch as It transcends all affirmation by being the perfect and unique Cause of all things, and transcends all negation by the pre-eminence of Its simple and absolute nature—free from every limitation and beyond them all.[2]

ZOHAR

The Creation of Elohim *and The Hidden Light*

The *Zohar* is a vast mystical work in Kabbalah, a Jewish mystical tradition. It was written by or is attributed to Moses de Leon, a thirteenth century Spanish kabbalist. Two sections from the *Zohar* are "The Creation of *Elohim*" and "The Hidden Light." Elohim is one of the names by which God was known by the early writers of the Bible. In "The Creation of *Elohim*" Moses de Leon speaks of "the Concealed One who is not known," that is, the *Ein Sof* (the Infinite or ultimate reality of God beyond all differentiation). These two sections of the *Zohar* are in Chapter 1 in the section on Judaism.

RUDOLF OTTO

from The Idea of the Holy

Rudolf Otto, who lived from 1869 to 1937, was a German theologian. He insisted that theistic religion, and Christianity in particular, had a rational side in that it conceptualizes God with such attributes as reason, purpose, good will, and unity—all of which can be rationally reflected upon. But also, he insisted, religion has a feeling side that is nonrational. In *The Idea of the Holy*, Otto presents these nonrational "numinous" feelings, with which God or the divine can be experienced by the religious as the "wholly other," something experienced as real and outside of ourselves, but something utterly mysterious and awe-evoking, felt to be ineffable.

Our reading consists of Chap. II of *The Idea of the Holy*, in which Otto presents his category of the "numinous."*

[2] It is (1) *richer* than all concrete forms of positive existence; (2) more *simple* than the barest abstraction.
* From Rudolf Otto, *The Idea of the Holy*, 2nd edition, translated by John W. Harvey. London and New York: Oxford University Press, 1950. Reprinted by permission of Oxford University Press.

CHAPTER 2

'Numen' and the 'Numinous'

'Holiness'— 'the holy'—is a category of interpretation and valuation peculiar to the sphere of religion. It is, indeed, applied by transference to another sphere— that of ethics—but it is not itself derived from this. While it is complex, it contains a quite specific element or 'moment', which sets it apart from 'the rational' in the meaning we gave to that word above, and which remains inexpressible—an ἄρρητον or *ineffabile*—in the sense that it completely eludes apprehension in terms of concepts. The same thing is true (to take a quite different region of experience) of the category of the beautiful.

Now these statements would be untrue from the outset if 'the holy' were merely what is meant by the word, not only in common parlance, but in philosophical, and generally even in theological usage. The fact is we have come to use the words 'holy', 'sacred' (*heilig*) in an entirely derivative sense, quite different from that which they originally bore. We generally take 'holy' as meaning 'completely good'; it is the absolute moral attribute, denoting the consummation of moral goodness. In this sense Kant calls the will which remains unwaveringly obedient to the moral law from the motive of duty a 'holy' will; here clearly we have simply the *perfectly moral* will. In the same way we may speak of the holiness or sanctity of duty or law, meaning merely that they are imperative upon conduct and universally obligatory.

But this common usage of the term is inaccurate. It is true that all this moral significance is contained in the word 'holy', but it includes in addition—as even we cannot but feel—a clear overplus of meaning, and this it is now our task to isolate. Nor is this merely a later or acquired meaning; rather, 'holy', or at least the equivalent words in Latin and Greek, in Semitic and other ancient languages, denoted first and foremost *only* this overplus: if the ethical element was present at all, at any rate it was not original and never constituted the whole meaning of the word. Any one who uses it to-day does undoubtedly always feel 'the morally good' to be implied in 'holy'; and accordingly in our inquiry into that element which is separate and peculiar to the idea of the holy it will be useful, at least for the temporary purpose of the investigation, to invent a special term to stand for 'the holy' *minus* its moral factor or 'moment', and, as we can now add, minus its 'rational' aspect altogether.

It will be our endeavour to suggest this unnamed Something to the reader as far as we may, so that he may himself feel it. There is no religion in which it does not live as the real innermost core, and without it no religion would be worthy of the name. It is pre-eminently a living force in the Semitic religions, and of these again in none has it such vigour as in that of the Bible. Here, too, it has a name of its own, viz. the Hebrew *qādôsh*, to which the Greek ἅγιοǎ and the Latin *sanctus*, and, more accurately still, *sacer*, are the corresponding terms. It is not, of course, disputed that these terms in all three languages connote, as part of their meaning, *good, absolute goodness*, when, that is, the notion has ripened and reached the highest stage in its development. And we then use the word 'holy' to translate them. But this 'holy' then represents the gradual shaping and filling in with ethical meaning, or what we shall call the 'schematization', of what was a unique original feeling-response, which can be in itself ethically neutral and claims consideration in its own right. And when this moment or element first emerges and begins its long development, all those expressions (*qādôsh*, ἅγιος, *sacer*, &c.) mean beyond all question something quite other than 'the good'. This is universally agreed by contemporary criticism, which rightly explains the rendering of *qā dôsh* by 'good' as a mistranslation and unwarranted 'rationalization' or 'moralization' of the term.

Accordingly, it is worth while, as we have said, to find a word to stand for this element in isolation, this 'extra' in the meaning of 'holy' above and beyond the meaning of goodness. By means of a special term we shall the better be able, first, to keep the meaning clearly apart and distinct, and second, to apprehend and classify connectedly whatever subordinate forms or stages of development it may show. For this purpose I adopt a word coined from the Latin *numen*. *Omen* has given us 'ominous', and there is no reason why from *numen* we should not similarly form a word 'numinous'. I shall speak, then, of a unique 'numinous'

category of value and of a definitely 'numinous' state of mind, which is always found wherever the category is applied. This mental state is perfectly *sui generis* and irreducible to any other; and therefore, like every absolutely primary and elementary datum, while it admits of being discussed, it cannot be strictly defined. There is only one way to help another to an understanding of it. He must be guided and led on by consideration and discussion of the matter through the ways of his own mind, until he reach the point at which 'the numinous' in him perforce begins to stir, to start into life and into consciousness. We can co-operate in this process by bringing before his notice all that can be found in other regions of the mind, already known and familiar, to resemble, or again to afford some special contrast to, the particular experience we wish to elucidate. Then we must add: 'This *X* of ours is not precisely *this* experience, but akin to this one and the opposite of that other. Cannot you now realize for yourself what it is?' In other words our *X* cannot, strictly speaking, be taught, it can only be evoked, awakened in the mind; as everything; that comes 'of the spirit' must be awakened.

ST. THOMAS AQUINAS

from The Names of God (Summa Theologica I, q. 13, aa. 3, 5, and 6)

Aquinas recognized that some "names," or things said of God, can be applied to God only metaphorically. He gives as an example "stone" (which is like "rock" in "the Rock of my salvation" in the Psalms, and Aquinas no doubt had this passage in mind). Since "stone" (or "rock") signifies a material thing, and God is not material, Aquinas says that it can be applied to God only in a metaphorical sense. On the other hand, for Aquinas several things said of God can be applied to God "properly," or literally. This is so of the "perfections"— "goodness, life, being and the like"—for God is their source and they are in God "in a more eminent way" (more fully, in a greater degree) than in "creatures" (human beings and other things that God has created). So it is said of God literally, not metaphorically, that God is good or has being or is wise, for Aquinas. But Aquinas did not think that God is good or wise in the *same sense* that human beings are wise.

Aquinas distinguished three kinds of predication in which "names" may be predicated of or applied to things. First, there is *univocal* predication. In univocal predication a name or term is applied to two things in the same sense. When we say of two large pieces of iron that each is heavy, "heavy" is applied to each piece of iron in the same sense. Second, there is *equivocal* predication. In equivocal predication a name or term is applied to two things in different senses. When we say that a man dresses smartly and we say that another man hit a ball smartly, "smartly" is used in two distinct senses. The third kind of predication is *analogical* predication. Aquinas says there are two kinds of analogical predication, but the kind that is important for God predication is when a name or term is predicated of two things according as the one thing is "proportioned" to the other.

It is this kind of predication that is used in saying that God is wise and that human beings are wise. God is properly or literally said to be wise, but when it is said that God and human beings are wise, it is according to a relation between God and human beings by which God's wisdom is the "principle and cause" of human wisdom.

For Aquinas, however, it is not merely that God is the cause of human wisdom. Wisdom and goodness exist in God in a "more excellent way" so that "these perfections flow from God" to human beings. For Aquinas "wise" and "good" apply to God *primarily*. This makes analogical predication applied to God different from metaphors, for Aquinas. Metaphors, like "rock," apply to "creatures" primarily. When we say that God is the Rock of our salvation, we are saying God is *like* a rock, a thing that we experience in the world, to which "rock" applies primarily. But when we say God is good or wise we are not saying God is like a good or wise person. Rather, we are saying God *is* good and wise, and we are using predicates that apply primarily to God, for God has these perfections more eminently or in a more excellent way. So, for Aquinas, the ideas of wisdom and goodness applied to God and the ideas applied to human beings are not one and the same, but also they are not utterly different. The one is related "proportionately" to the other. For Aquinas, the same is to be said of the other perfections of God.

Our reading is taken from the the first part of the *Summa Theologica*. It consists of three articles from Question 13 The Names of God, in which Aquinas presents his view of analogical predication.

Question XIII

The Names of God

Third Article

WHETHER ANY NAME CAN BE APPLIED TO GOD PROPERLY?

We proceed thus to the Third Article:—

Objection 1. It seems that no name is applied properly to God. For all names which we apply to God are taken from creatures; as was explained above. But the names of creatures are applied to God metaphorically, as when we say, God is a stone, or a lion, or the like. Therefore names are applied to God in a metaphorical sense.

Obj. 2. Further, no name can be applied properly to anything if it should be more truly denied of it than given to it. But all such names as *good, wise,* and the like, are more truly denied of God than given to Him; as appears from what Dionysius says.[13] Therefore none of these names is said of God properly.

Obj. 3. Further, corporeal names are applied to God in a metaphorical sense only, since He is incorporeal. But all such names imply some kind of corporeal condition; for their meaning is bound up with time and composition and like corporeal conditions. Therefore all these names are applied to God in a metaphorical sense.

On the contrary, Ambrose says, *Some names there are which express evidently the property of the divinity, and some which express the clear truth of the divine majesty; but others there are which are said of God metaphorically by way of similitude.*[14] Therefore not all names are applied to God in a metaphorical sense, but there are some which are said of Him properly.

I answer that, According to the preceding article, our knowledge of God is derived from the perfections which flow from Him to creatures; which perfections are in God in a more eminent way than in creatures. Now our intellect apprehends them as they are in creatures, and as it apprehends them thus does it signify them by names. Therefore, as to the names applied to God, there are two things to be considered—viz., the perfections themselves which they signify, such as goodness, life, and the like, and their mode of signification. As regards what is signified by these names, they belong properly to God, and more properly than they belong to creatures, and are applied primarily to Him. But as regards their mode of signification, they do not properly and strictly apply to God; for their mode of signification befits creatures.

Reply Obj. 1. There are some names which signify these perfections flowing from God to creatures in such a way that the imperfect way in which creatures receive the divine perfection is part of the very signification of the name itself, as *stone* signifies a material being; and names of this kind can be applied to God only in a metaphorical sense. Other names, however, express the perfections themselves absolutely, without any such mode of participation being part of their signification, as the words *being, good, living,* and the like; and such names can be applied to God properly.

---

[13] *De Cael. Hier.,* II, 3 (PG 3, 141).   [14] *De Fide,* II, Prol. (PL 16, 583).

Reply Obj. 2. Such names as these, as Dionysius shows, are denied of God for the reason that what the name signifies does not belong to Him in the ordinary sense of its signification, but in a more eminent way. Hence Dionysius says also that God is above all substance and all life.[15]

Reply Obj. 3. These names which are applied to God properly imply corporeal conditions, not in the thing signified, but as regards their mode of signification; whereas those which are applied to God metaphorically imply and mean a corporeal condition in the thing signified.

* * * * * * * * * * * * * * * * * * * *

Fifth Article

WHETHER WHAT IS SAID OF GOD AND OF CREATURES IS UNIVOCALLY PREDICATED OF THEM?

We proceed thus to the Fifth Article:—
Objection 1. It seems that the things attributed to God and creatures are univocal. For every equivocal term is reduced to the univocal, as many are reduced to one: for if the name *dog* be said equivocally of the barking dog and of the dogfish, it must be said of some univocally—viz., of all barking dogs; otherwise we proceed to infinitude. Now there are some univocal agents which agree with their effects in name and definition, as man generates man; and there are some agents which are equivocal, as the sun which causes heat, although the sun is hot only in an equivocal sense. Therefore it seems that the first agent, to which all other agents are

reduced, is a univocal agent: and thus what is said of God and creatures is predicated univocally.

Obj. 2. Further, no likeness is understood through equivocal names. Therefore, as creatures have a certain likeness to God, according to the text of *Genesis* (i. 26), *Let us make man to our image and likeness*, it seems that something can be said of God and creatures univocally.

Obj. 3. Further, measure is homogeneous with the thing measured, as is said in *Metaph.* x.[16] But God is the first measure of all beings. Therefore God is homogeneous with creatures; and thus a name may be applied univocally to God and to creatures.

On the contrary, Whatever is predicated of various things under the same name but not in the same sense is predicated equivocally. But no name belongs to God in the same sense that it belongs to creatures; for instance, wisdom in creatures is a quality, but not in God. Now a change in genus changes an essence, since the genus is part of the definition; and the same applies to other things. Therefore whatever is said of God and of creatures is predicated equivocally.

Further, God is more distant from creatures than any creatures are from each other. But the distance of some creatures makes any univocal predication of them impossible, as in the case of those things which are not in the same genus. Therefore much less can anything be predicated univocally of God and creatures; and so only equivocal predication can be applied to them.

I answer that, Univocal predication is impossible between God and creatures. The reason of this is that every effect which is not a proportioned result of the power of the efficient cause receives the

---

[15] *De Cael. Hier.*, II, 3 (PG3, 141).　[16] Aristotle, *Metaph.*, IX, 1 (1053a 24).

similitude of the agent not in its full degree, but in a measure that falls short; so that what is divided and multiplied in the effects resides in the agent simply, and in an unvaried manner. For example, the sun by the exercise of its one power produces manifold and various forms in these sublunary things. In the same way, as was said above, all perfections existing in creatures divided and multiplied pre-exist in God unitedly. Hence, when any name expressing perfection is applied to a creature, it signifies that perfection as distinct from the others according to the nature of its definition; as, for instance, by this term *wise* applied to a man, we signify some perfection distinct from a man's essence, and distinct from his power and his being, and from all similar things. But when we apply *wise* to God, we do not mean to signify anything distinct from His essence or power or being. And thus when this term *wise* is applied to man, in some degree it circumscribes and comprehends the thing signified; whereas this is not the case when it is applied to God, but it leaves the thing signified as uncomprehended and as exceeding the signification of the name. Hence it is evident that this term *wise* is not applied in the same way to God and to man. The same applies to other terms. Hence, no name is predicated univocally of God and of creatures.

Neither, on the other hand, are names applied to God and creatures in a purely equivocal sense, as some have said.[17] Because if that were so, it follows that from creatures nothing at all could be known or demonstrated about God; for the reasoning would always be exposed to the fallacy of equivocation. Such a view is against the Philosopher, who proves many things about God, and also against what the Apostle says: *The invisible things of* God *are clearly seen being understood by the things that are made* (*Rom.* i. 20). Therefore it must be said that these names are said of God and creatures in an *analogous* sense, that is, according to proportion.

This can happen in two ways: either according as many things are proportioned to one (thus, for example *healthy* is predicated of medicine and urine in relation and in proportion to health of body, of which the latter is the sign and the former the cause), or according as one thing is proportioned to another (thus, *healthy* is said of medicine and an animal, since medicine is the cause of health in the animal body). And in this way some things are said of God and creatures analogically, and not in a purely equivocal nor in a purely univocal sense. For we can name God only from creatures. Hence, whatever is said of God and creatures is said according as there is some relation of the creature to God as to its principle and cause, wherein all the perfections of things pre-exist excellently. Now this mode of community is a mean between pure equivocation and simple univocation. For in analogies the idea is not, as it is in univocals, one and the same; yet it is not totally diverse as in equivocals; but the name which is thus used in a multiple sense signifies various proportions to some one thing: *e.g.*, *healthy*, applied to urine, signifies the sign of animal health; but applied to medicine, it signifies the cause of the same health.

Reply Obj. 1. Although in predications all equivocals must be reduced to univocals, still in actions the non-univocal agent must precede the univocal agent. For the non-univocal agent is the universal cause of the whole species, as the sun is the cause of the generation of

[17] Maimonides, *Guide*, I, 59 (p. 84); Averroes, *In Metaph*, XII. comm. 51 (VIII, 158r).

all men. But the univocal agent is not the universal efficient cause of the whole species (otherwise it would be the cause of itself, since it is contained in the species), but is a particular cause of this individual which it places under the species by way of participation. Therefore the universal cause of the whole species is not a univocal agent: and the universal cause comes before the particular cause. But this universal agent, while not univocal, nevertheless is not altogether equivocal (otherwise it could not produce its own likeness); but it can be called an analogical agent, just as in predications all univocal names are reduced to one first non-univocal analogical name, which is *being*.

Reply Obj. 2. The likeness of the creature to God is imperfect, for it does not represent the same thing even generically.[18]

Reply Obj. 3. God is not a measure proportioned to the things measured; hence it is not necessary that God and creatures should be in the same genus.

The arguments adduced in the contrary sense prove indeed that these names are not predicated univocally of God and creatures; yet they do not prove that they are predicated equivocally.

Sixth Article

WHETHER NAMES PREDICATED OF GOD ARE PREDICATED PRIMARILY OF CREATURES?

We proceed thus to the Sixth Article:—
Objection 1. It seems that names are predicated primarily of creatures rather than of God. For we name anything accordingly as we know it, since *names*, as the Philosopher says,[19] *are signs of ideas*. But we know creatures before we know God. Therefore the names imposed by us are predicated primarily of creatures rather than of God.

Obj. 2. Further, Dionysius says that we name God from creatures.[20] But names transferred from creatures to God are said primarily of creatures rather than of God; as *lion*, *stone*, and the like. Therefore all names applied to God and creatures are applied primarily to creatures rather than to God.

Obj. 3. Further, all names applied to God and creatures in common *are applied to God as the cause of all creatures*, as Dionysius says.[21] But what is applied to anything through its cause is applied to it secondarily; for *healthy* is primarily predicated of animal rather than of medicine, which is the cause of health. Therefore these names are said primarily of creatures rather than of God.

On the contrary, It is written, *I bow my knees to the Father of our Lord Jesus Christ, of Whom all paternity in heaven and earth is named* (Ephes. iii. 14,15); and the same holds of the other names applied to God and creatures. Therefore these names are applied primarily to God rather than to creatures.

I answer that, In names predicated of many in an analogical sense, all are predicated through a relation to some one thing; and this one thing must be placed in the definition of them all. And since *the essence expressed by the name is the definition*, as the Philosopher says,[22] such a name must be applied primarily to that which is put in the definition of the other things, and secondarily to these others

---

[18] Q. 4, a. 3.   [19] *Perih.*, I (16a 3).   [20] *De Div. Nom.*, I, 6 (PG 3, 596).
[21] *De Myst. Theol.*, I, 2 (PG 3, 1000).   [22] Aristotle, *Metaph.*, III, 7 (1012a 23).

according as they approach more or less to the first. Thus, for instance, *healthy* applied to animals comes into the definition of *healthy* applied to medicine, which is called healthy as being the cause of health in the animal; and also into the definition of *healthy* which is applied to urine, which is called healthy in so far as it is the sign of the animal's health.

So it is that all names applied metaphorically to God are applied to creatures primarily rather than to God, because when said of God they mean only similitudes to such creatures. For as *smiling* applied to a field means only that the field in the beauty of its flowering is like to the beauty of the human smile by proportionate likeness, so the name of *lion* applied to God means only that God manifests strength in His works, as a lion in his. Thus it is clear that applied to God the signification of these names can be defined only from what is said of creatures.

But to other names not applied to God in a metaphorical sense, the same rule would apply if they were spoken of God as the cause only, as some have supposed.[23] For when it is said, *God is good*, it would then only mean, *God is the cause of the creature's goodness*; and thus the name

good applied to God would include in its meaning the creature's goodness. Hence *good* would apply primarily to creatures rather than God. But, as was shown above, these names are applied to God not as the cause only, but also essentially. For the words, *God is good*, or *wise*, signify not only that He is the cause of wisdom or goodness, but that these exist in Him in a more excellent way. Hence as regards what the name signifies, these names are applied primarily to God rather than to creatures, because these perfections flow from God to creatures; but as regards the imposition of the names, they are primarily applied by us to creatures which we know first. Hence they have a mode of signification which belongs to creatures, as was said above.

Reply Obj. 1. This objection refers to the imposition of the name: to that extent it is true.

Reply Obj. 2. The same rule does not apply to metaphorical and to other names, as was said above.

Reply Obj. 3. This objection would be valid if these names were applied to God only as cause, and not also essentially, for instance, as *healthy* is applied to medicine.

The Gender Issue

In traditional forms of Judaism, Christianity, and Islam, there is a God who is believed in and who is believed to exist. What is required of the traditional concept of God? In the general traditional core concept of God, God is the supreme being and creator of the world, and in these main theistic traditions other traditional attributes are included: merciful, all-knowing, all-powerful, eternal and more. Anselm thought that the supreme being contains all the perfections, which are those attributes it is better to have than not to have. In the

---

[23] Allain of Lille, *Theol. Reg.*, XXI; XXVI (PL 210, 631; 633).

Christian tradition when Anselm and Aquinas speak of the "perfections" of God, or of God's attributes, they do not include being masculine. God in the Christian tradition, as in Judaism and Islam, is differently conceived from how, say, the gods of the Greek pantheon (the collection of all the gods and goddesses in the polytheistic belief of the ancient Greeks) may be conceived. Many of the stories associated with Zeus require that he be masculine. But in the core concept of the monotheistic traditions of Judaism, Christianity, and Islam God is not so conceived. However there are two issues involved in the gender issue. One relates to how God should be *conceived*, and the other relates to how God should be *imaged*.

Granting that God is not to be conceived as masculine, the greater part of the gender issue is how God should be *imaged*. How should God be presented religiously? As a father? As a mother? This issue persists after we appreciate that images are metaphors. While images do not literally describe God, as predication does or ostensibly does, they may communicate something religiously important about God: God's love or guidance, God's knowing our hearts, or God's steadfastness. While the role of images is different from literal description, they offer a way to the religious of metaphorically presenting God to themselves. In doing so they have the practical effect of facilitating the religious life.

Some religious thinkers, especially some feminist theologians, seek a feminine imagery of the divine. They perceive a male bias or patriarchy (domination by men) in the exclusive use of the masculine imagery of God as Father. They recall Julian of Norwich, who in the fourteenth century used the image of a heavenly Mother to refer to God and overtly referred to "Mother Jesus." Though an earthly mother may allow her child to perish, "our heavenly Mother Jesus," Julian said, will not allow his children to perish, "for he is almighty, all wisdom and all love." The primary feminist objection is to the *dominance* of the imagery or model of God as Father, as Sallie McFague puts it; the objection is not to imaging God as Father in itself. Rosemary Ruether says something similar. She draws attention to what strikes her as the "peculiarity of imaging God solely through one gender."

Within the gender issue, several stances regarding imaging God with gender images can be distinguished. One is that in worship services or liturgy it is necessary to have feminine images to balance masculine images, especially the image of God as Father. Religious believers should not use either feminine or masculine images to the exclusion of the other. *Both* should be used. Another stance is that some religious believers or congregations may use masculine images exclusively *and* some religious believers and congregations may use feminine images exclusively, depending on what "facilitates their growth in the Faith." A third stance is that believers should only use *genderless* images, such as, Almighty God or Merciful God and so avoid the gender issue altogether. A fourth is that religious believers in the various dimensions of their religious lives may use various images: shepherd, fortress, and others, in addition to Father and Mother, but they should be aware that all these images are metaphors.

The readings in this section begin with three short chapters from *Revelations of Divine Love*, written by Julian of Norwich more than six hundred years ago. The second reading is by a contemporary feminist theologian, Rosemary

Radford Ruether, from her *Sexism and God-Talk*, and the third reading is from *Metaphorical Theology*, written by Sallie McFague, another contemporary feminist theologian. The last two readings are by two contemporary philosophers. William Harper argues that it is at least permissible to "refer to God exclusively in male terms." George F. Isham, replying to Harper, argues against Harper's position.

JULIAN OF NORWICH

from Revelations of Divine Love

Julian of Norwich wrote *Revelations of Divine Love* in the fourteenth century. She wrote in Chapter 2 of having received her revelations or "showings" in 1373 (an alternative title is *Showings*). Little is known about Julian's life, although it is known that she was a recluse who lived in a cell adjoining a church in Norwich, England. In our selection of three chapters from *Revelations of Divine Love* Julian speaks of God's mercy and love and evokes God's love as the love of "our true mother, Jesus."*

59

In the chosen, wickedness is turned into blessedness through mercy and grace, for the nature of God is to do good for evil, through Jesus, our mother in kind grace; and the soul which is highest in virtue is the meekest, that being the ground from which we gain other virtues.

And we have all this blessedness through mercy and grace; a kind of blessedness which we might never have known if the quality of goodness which is God had not been opposed. It is by this means that we gain this blessedness; for wickedness has been allowed to rise and oppose goodness, and the goodness of mercy and grace has opposed wickedness and turned it all to goodness and glory for all those who shall be saved; for it is the nature of God to do good for evil.

Thus Jesus Christ who does good for evil is our true mother; we have our being from him where the ground of motherhood begins, with all the sweet protection of love which follows eternally. God is our mother as truly as he is our father; and he showed this in everything, and especially in the sweet words where he says, 'It is I', that is to say, 'It is I: the power and goodness of fatherhood. It is I: the wisdom of motherhood. It is I: the light and the grace which is all blessed

* From *Revelations of Divine Love* by Julian of Norwich, translated by Elizabeth Spearing, introduction and notes by A. C. Spearing (Penguin Classics, 1998). Translation copyright © Elizabeth Spearing, 1998. Introduction and Notes © A. C. Spearing, 1998.

love. It is I: the Trinity. It is I: the unity. I am the sovereign goodness of all manner of things. It is I that make you love. It is I that make you long. It is I: the eternal fulfilment of all true desires.'

For the soul is highest, noblest and worthiest when it is lowest, humblest and gentlest; and from this essential ground we all have our virtues and our sensory being by gift of nature and with the help and assistance of grace, without which we could gain nothing. Our great father, God almighty, who is Being, knew and loved us from before the beginning of time. And from his knowledge, in his marvellously deep love and through the eternal foreseeing counsel of the whole blessed Trinity, he wanted the second Person to become our mother, our brother, our saviour. From this it follows that God is our mother as truly as God is our father. Our Father wills, our Mother works, our good lord the Holy Ghost confirms. And therefore it behoves us to love our God in whom we have our being, reverently thanking and praising him for our creation, praying hard to our Mother for mercy and pity, and to our lord the Holy Ghost for help and grace; for our whole life is in these three— nature, mercy and grace; from them we have humility, gentleness, patience and pity, and hatred of sin and wickedness; for it is a natural attribute of virtues to hate sin and wickedness. And so Jesus is our true mother by nature, at our first creation, and he is our true mother in grace by taking on our created nature. All the fair work and all the sweet, kind service of beloved motherhood is made proper to the second Person; for in him this godly will is kept safe and whole everlastingly, both in nature and in grace, out of his very own goodness.

I understood three ways of seeing motherhood in God: the first is that he is the ground of our natural creation, the second is the taking on of our nature (and there the motherhood of grace begins), the third is the motherhood of works, and in this there is, by the same grace, an enlargement of length and breadth and of height and deepness without end, and all is his own love.

60

How we are redeemed and enlarged by the mercy and grace of our sweet, kind and ever-loving mother Jesus; and of the properties of motherhood; but Jesus is our true mother, feeding us not with milk, but with himself, opening his side for us and claiming all our love.

But now it is necessary to say a little more about this enlargement, as I understand it in our Lord's meaning, how we are redeemed by the motherhood of mercy and grace and brought back into our natural dwelling where we were made by the motherhood of natural love; a natural love which never leaves us. Our natural Mother, our gracious Mother (for he wanted to become our mother completely in every way), undertook to begin his work very humbly and very gently in the Virgin's womb. And he showed this in the first revelation, where he brought that humble maiden before my mind's eye in the girlish form she had when she conceived; that is to say, our great God, the most sovereign wisdom of all, was raised in this humble place and dressed himself in our poor flesh to do the service and duties of motherhood in every way. The mother's service is the closest, the most helpful and the most sure, for it is the most faithful. No one ever might, nor could, nor has performed this service fully but he alone. We know that our mothers only bring us into the world to suffer and die, but our true mother, Jesus, he who is all love, bears us into joy and eternal life; blessed may he be! So he sustains us within himself in love and was in labour for the full time until he suffered the sharpest pangs and the most grievous sufferings that ever were or shall be, and at the last he died. And when it was finished and he had born us to bliss, even this could not fully satisfy his marvellous love; and that he showed in these high surpassing words of love, 'If I could suffer more, I would suffer more.'

He could not die any more, but he would not stop working. So next he had to feed us, for a mother's dear love has made him our debtor. The mother can give her child her milk to suck, but our dear mother Jesus can feed us with himself, and he does so most generously and most tenderly with the holy sacrament which is the precious food of life itself. And with all the sweet sacraments he sustains us most mercifully and most graciously. And this is what he meant in those blessed words when he said, 'It is I that Holy Church preaches and teaches to you'; that is to say, 'All the health and life of the sacraments, all the power and grace of my word, all the goodness which is ordained in Holy Church for you, it is I.'

The mother can lay the child tenderly to her breast, but our tender mother Jesus, he can familiarly lead us into his blessed breast through his sweet open side, and

show within part of the Godhead and the joys of heaven, with spiritual certainty of endless bliss; and that was shown in the tenth revelation, giving the same understanding in the sweet words where he says, 'Look how I love you', looking into his side and rejoicing. This fair, lovely word 'mother', it is so sweet and so tender in itself that it cannot truly be said of any but of him, and of her who is the true mother of him and of everyone. To the nature of motherhood belong tender love, wisdom and knowledge, and it is good, for although the birth of our body is only low, humble and modest compared with the birth of our soul, yet it is he who does it in the beings by whom it is done. The kind, loving mother who knows and recognizes the need of her child, she watches over it most tenderly, as the nature and condition of motherhood demands. And as it grows in age her actions change, although her love does not. And as it grows older still, she allows it to be beaten to break down vices so that the child may gain in virtue and grace. These actions, with all that is fair and good, our Lord performs them through those by whom they are done. Thus he is our natural mother through the work of grace in the lower part, for love of the higher part. And he wants us to know it; for he wants all our love to be bound to him. And in this I saw that all the debt we owe, at God's bidding, for his fatherhood and motherhood, is fulfilled by loving God truly; a blessed love which Christ arouses in us. And this was shown in everything, and especially in the great, generous words where he says, 'It is I that you love.'

61

Jesus behaves more tenderly in giving us spiritual birth; though he allows us to fall so that we may recognize our sinfulness,

he quickly raises us, not withdrawing his love because of our transgression, for he cannot allow his child to perish; he wants us to have the nature of a child, always rushing to him in our need.

And in our spiritual birth he behaves with incomparably more tenderness, in as much as our soul is of greater value in his eyes. He fires our understanding, he directs our ways, he eases our conscience, he comforts our soul, he enlightens our heart and gives us some degree of knowledge and love of his blessed Godhead, with awareness through grace of his precious Manhood and his blessed Passion, and with courteous wonder at his great and surpassing goodness; and he makes us love all that he loves, for his love's sake, and makes us take pleasure in him and all his works. If we fall, he quickly raises us by calling us tenderly and touching us with grace. And when we have been strengthened like this by his dear actions, then we choose him willingly, through his precious grace, we choose to serve him and to love him for ever and ever. And after this he allows some of us to fall harder and more painfully than we ever did before, or so it seems to us. And those of us who are not very wise think that all our earlier effort has gone for nothing. But it is not so; for we need to fall, and we need to be aware of it; for if we did not fall, we should not know how weak and wretched we are of ourselves, nor should we know our Maker's marvellous love so fully; for in heaven we shall see truly and everlastingly that we have sinned grievously in this life, and we shall see that in spite of this his love for us remained unharmed, and we were never less valuable to him. And by experiencing this failure, we shall gain a great and marvellous knowledge of love in God for all eternity; for that love which cannot and will not be broken by sin is strong and marvellous. And this is one aspect of the benefit we gain. Another is the humility and gentleness

we shall gain from seeing our fall; for by this we shall be raised up high in heaven, a rise which we might never have known without that humility. And therefore we need to see it, and if we do not see it, though we should fall, it would not profit us. Usually, we fall first, then we see it, and both through the mercy of God. The mother may allow the child to fall sometimes and to be hurt for its own benefit, but her love does not allow the child ever to be in any real danger. And though our earthly mother may allow her child to perish, our heavenly mother Jesus cannot allow us who are his children to perish; for he and none but he is almighty, all wisdom and all love. Blessed may he be!

But often when our falling and our wretched sin is shown to us, we are so terrified and so very ashamed that we hardly know where to put ourselves. But then our kind Mother does not want us to run from him, there is nothing he wants less. But he wants us to behave like a child; for when it is hurt or frightened it runs to its mother for help as fast as it can; and he wants us to do the same, like a humble child, saying, 'My kind Mother, my gracious Mother, my dearest Mother, take pity on me. I have made myself dirty and unlike you and I neither may nor can remedy this without your special help and grace.' And if we do not feel that we are immediately given help, we can be sure that he is behaving like a wise mother, for if he sees that it would be more beneficial for us to grieve and weep, with sorrow and pity he allows it to continue until the right moment, and all for love. So then he wants us to take on the nature of a child which always naturally trusts the love of its mother in weal and woe.

And he wants us to cling strongly to the faith of Holy Church and find our dearest Mother there in the comfort of true understanding with the whole blessed community; for a single person may often feel broken, but the whole body of Holy

Church has never been broken, nor ever shall be, for all eternity. And therefore it is a safe, good and gracious thing to wish humbly and strongly to be supported by and united to our mother, Holy Church, that is Christ Jesus; for there is plenty of the food of mercy which is his dearest blood and precious water to make us clean and pure. The blessed wounds of our Saviour are open and rejoice to heal us; the sweet, gracious hands of our Mother are ready and carefully surround us; for in all this he does the work of a kind nurse who has nothing to do but occupy herself with the salvation of her child. His task is to save us, and it is his glory to do so, and it is his wish that we know it; for he wants us to love him tenderly, and trust him humbly and strongly. And he showed this in these gracious words, 'I hold you quite safely.'

ROSEMARY RADFORD RUETHER

from Sexism and God-Language: Male and Female Images of the Divine

Rosemary Ruether is among those feminist theologians who have seen a religious need for various images of God, including feminine and masculine images. She recounts how in ancient times there was a belief in a Mother Goddess and in the time of Judaism's early development there were in various cultures in the Near East belief in both God and Goddess. Even in the "male monotheism" of Judaism and Christianity she finds feminine elements that echo the Goddess theme, as in the feminine persona of Wisdom.

In our reading Ruether presents four "Biblical traditions" and goes on to explore different parables told by Jesus in the New Testament so that she can show how two parables may be "parallel" though one uses a male image and one uses a female image. Two she compares are the parable of the shepherd who leaves his flock of ninety-nine sheep to find the one that is lost and the parable of the woman who has ten silver coins and, when she has lost one coin, lights a lamp and sweeps her house until she has found it (Lk. 15.3-10). In each case when the lost is found there is rejoicing—as God rejoices when one who is lost is found. In these parables the images of male and female are "equivalent images for God," Ruether says. They both stand for the same thing, as "paired images." In these parables where the images are equivalent, inclusiveness and drawing upon the experiences of the two genders would provide a reason for using both images to express the divine attitude toward those who are lost religiously. It should be noted, furthermore, Ruether points out, that in these two parables the male and female images are not parental. They do not image God as father or mother, but as finder of the lost (as Redeemer).

Our reading consists of the last section of Chapter 2 of Rosemary Ruether's *Sexism and God-Talk*.

God-Language beyond Patriarchy in the Biblical Tradition

The Prophetic God

Although the predominantly male images and roles of God make Yahwism an agent in the sacralization of patriarchy, there are critical elements in Biblical theology that contradict this view of God. By patriarchy we mean not only the subordination of females to males, but the whole structure of Father-ruled society: aristocracy over serfs, masters over slaves, king over subjects, racial overlords over colonized people. Religions that reinforce hierarchical stratification use the Divine as the apex of this system of privilege and control. The religions of the ancient Near East link the Gods and Goddesses with the kings and queens, the priests and priestesses, the warrior and temple aristocracy of a stratified society. The Gods and Goddesses mirror this ruling class and form its heavenly counterpart. The divinities also show mercy and favor to the distressed, but in the manner of noblesse oblige.

Yahweh, as tribal God of Israel, shows many characteristics similar to those of the Near Eastern deities, as mighty king, warrior, and one who shows mercy and vindicates justice. But these characteristics are put in a new and distinct context: Yahweh is unique as the God of a tribal confederation that identifies itself as liberated slaves. The basic identity of Yahweh as God of this confederation lies in "his" historical action as the divine power that liberated these slaves from bondage and led them to a new land. This confederation is not an ethnic people, but a bonding of groups of distinct backgrounds. A core group experienced the escape from bondage in Egypt that formed the primary identity of Israel. They were joined by nomadic groups from the desert and hill peoples in Canaan in revolt against the feudal power of the city-states of the plains. Norman Gottwald reconstructs the premonarchical formation of this tribal confederation (1250–1050 B.C.). The identification of Yahweh with liberation from bondage allowed this diverse group to unite in a new egalitarian society and to revolt against the stratified feudal society of the city-states that oppressed the peasant peoples of the hills with taxes and forced labor.[21]

The Davidic monarchy represents a capitulation of Judaic leadership to the city-state model of power, but the prophets of Israel continue the tradition of protest against the hierarchical, urban, landowning society that deprives and oppresses the rural peasantry. This established at the heart of Biblical religion a motif of protest against the status quo of ruling-class privilege and the deprivation of the poor. God is seen as a critic of this society, a champion of the social victims. Salvation is envisioned as deliverance from systems of social oppression and as restoration of an egalitarian peasant society of equals, "where each have their own vine and fig tree and none need be afraid" (Mic. 4:4).

Although Yahwism dissents against class hierarchy, it issues no similar protest against gender discrimination. There are several reasons (not to be seen as "excuses")

---

[21] Norman K. Gottwald, *The Tribes of Yahweh: A Sociology of the Religion of Liberated Israel, 1250–1050 B.C.* (Maryknoll, N.Y.: Orbis Press, 1979), pp. 210–219, 489–587, 692–709.

for this. First, there is always a sociology of knowledge in social ideology, even in liberation ideology. Those male prophets who were aware of oppression by rich urbanites or dominating empires were not similarly conscious of their own oppression of dependents—women and slaves—in the patriarchal family. Only the emergence of women conscious of their oppression could have applied the categories of protest to women. This did not happen in Yahwism. Second, although Hebrew religion was to shape systems of patriarchal law that emphasize gender dualism and hierarchy, in its protest against Canaanite urban society it would have known powerful females, queens, priestesses, and wealthy landowners who functioned as oppressors. It would have been difficult to recognize women as an oppressed gender group when the primary social stratification integrated some women into roles of power. Indeed, perhaps it was not until the early modern period that the perception of women as marginalized by gender became stronger than the perception of women as divided by class. Only then could a feminist movement arise that protested the subjugation of women as a group.

The New Testament contains a renewal and radicalization of prophetic consciousness, now applied to marginalized groups in a universal, nontribal context. Consequently, it is possible to recognize as liberated by God social groups overlooked in Old Testament prophecy. Class, ethnicity, and gender are now specifically singled out as the divisions overcome by redemption in Christ. In the New Testament stories, gender is recognized as an additional oppression within oppressed classes and ethnic groups.[22] Women, the doubly oppressed within marginalized groups, manifest God's iconoclastic, liberating action in making "the last first and the first last." All women are not doubly oppressed; there are also queens and wealthy women. But women's experience of oppression has begun to become visible and to be addressed by prophetic consciousness (very likely because of the participation of women in the early Christian movement).

The Liberating Sovereign

A second antipatriarchal use of God-language occurs in the Old and New Testaments when divine sovereignty and fatherhood are used to break the ties of bondage under human kings and fathers. Abraham is called into an adoptive or covenanted relation with God only by breaking his ties with his family, leaving behind the graves of his ancestors.[23] The God of Exodus establishes a relationship with the people that breaks their ties with the ruling overlords. As the people flee from the land of bondage, Pharaoh and his horsemen are drowned. God's kingship liberates Israel from human kings. The antimonarchical tradition inveighs against Israel's capitulation to the customs of the surrounding people by adopting kingship.

These Old Testament traditions are developed in Jesus' teaching. It has been often pointed out that Jesus uses a unique word for God. By adopting the word *Abba* for God, he affirms a primary relationship to God based on love and trust; *Abba* was the intimate word used by children in the family for their fathers. It is not fully conveyed by English terms such as *Daddy*, for

[22] See, for example, Matt. 15:21–28; Mark 5:25–33; Luke 7:11–17, 7:36–50, 10:38–42, 13:10–17.
[23] Robert Hamerton-Kelly, *God the Father: Theology and Patriarchy in the Teachings of Jesus* (Philadelphia: Fortress, 1979), pp. 21–28.

it was also a term an adult could use of an older man to signify a combination of respect and affection.[24] But is it enough to conclude from this use of *Abba* that Jesus transforms the patriarchal concept of divine fatherhood into what might be called a maternal or nurturing concept of God as loving, trustworthy parent?

The early Jesus movement characteristically uses this concept of God as *Abba* to liberate the community from human dominance-dependence relationships based on kinship ties or master-servant relationships. In the Gospel tradition, joining the new community of Jesus creates a rupture with traditional family ties and loyalties. In order to follow Jesus one must "hate" (that is, put aside one's loyalty to) father and mother, sisters and brothers (Luke 14:26; Matt. 10:37-38). The patriarchal family is replaced by a new community of brothers and sisters (Matt. 12:46-50; Mark 3:31-35; Luke 8:19-21). This new community is a community of equals, not of master and servants, father and children. Matthew 23:1-10 states that the relationship to God as *Abba* abolishes all father-child, master-servant relations between people within the Jesus community: "You are to call no man father, master or Lord." The relationship between Christians is to be one of mutual service and not of mastery and servitude. At the end of the Gospel of John, Jesus tells the disciples that their relationship has now become one of equals. They now have the same *Abba* relation to God as he does and

can act out of the same principles: "No longer do I call you servants, . . . but I have called you friends" (John 15:15). These traditions reverse the symbolic relation between divine fatherhood and sovereignty and the sacralization of patriarchy. Because God is our king, we need obey no human kings. Because God is our parent, we are liberated from dependence on patriarchal authority.

But the language used in this tradition creates an obvious ambivalence. It works to establish a new liberated relationship to a new community of equals for those in revolt against established authorities. This is true not only in the formation of Israel and in the rise of the Jesus movement; again and again throughout Christian history this antipatriarchal use of God-language has been rediscovered by dissenting groups. The call to "obey God rather than men" has perhaps been the most continuous theological basis for dissent in the Christian tradition. Throughout Christian history women discovered this concept of direct relation to God as a way to affirm their own authority and autonomy against patriarchal authority. God's call to them to preach, to teach, to form a new community where women's gifts were fully actualized overruled the patriarchal authority that told them to remain at home as dutiful daughters or wives.[25]

But once the new community becomes a part of the dominant society,

[24] Ibid., pp. 70–81.

[25] The revolt of women against the patriarchal authority of fathers, husbands, or fiancés, as well as political authority, is found continuously in Christian popular literature of the second and third centuries, particularly in martyrologies and apocryphal Acts. See Stevan Davies, *The Revolt of the Widows: The Social World of the Apocryphal Acts* (Carbondale: Southern Illinois University Press, 1980), pp. 50–69. This theme is continued in medieval lives of female saints. See Eleanor McLaughlin, "Women, Power and the Pursuit of Holiness in Medieval Christianity," in *Women of Spirit: Female Leadership in the Jewish and Christian Traditions*, ed. R. Ruether and E. McLaughlin (New York: Simon and Schuster, 1979), pp. 108–111. The theme is also typical in conversion stories of nineteenth-century Evangelical women. A dramatic example is found in the diary of the black Shaker Rebecca Jackson. See Jean McMahon Humez, *Gifts of Power: The Writings of Rebecca Jackson* (Amherst: University of Massachusetts Press, 1981), pp. 18–23 and passim.

God as father and king can be assimilated back into the traditional patriarchal relationships and used to sacralize the authority of human lordship and patriarchy. The radical meaning of *Abba* for God is lost in translation and interpretation. Instead, a host of new ecclesiastical and imperial "holy fathers" arises, claiming the fatherhood and kingship of God as the basis of their power over others. In order to preserve the prophetic social relationships, we need to find a new language that cannot be as easily co-opted by the systems of domination.

The Proscription of Idolatry

A third Biblical tradition that is important to a feminist theology is the proscription of idolatry. Israel is to make no picture or graven image of God; no pictorial or verbal representation of God can be taken literally. By contrast, Christian sculpture and painting represents God as a powerful old man with a white beard, even crowned and robed in the insignia of human kings or the triple tiara of the Pope. The message created by such images is that God is both similar to and represented by the patriarchal leadership, the monarchs and the Pope. Such imaging of God should be judged for what it is—as idolatry, as the setting up of certain human figures as the privileged images and representations of God. To the extent that such political and ecclesiastical patriarchy incarnates unjust and oppressive relationships, such images of God become sanctions of evil.

The proscription of idolatry must also be extended to verbal pictures. When the word *Father* is taken literally to mean that God is male and not female, represented by males and not females, then this word becomes idolatrous. The Israelite tradition is circumspect about the verbal image,

printing it without vowel signs. The revelation to Moses in the burning bush gives as the name of God only the enigmatic "I am what I shall be." God is person without being imaged by existing social roles. God's being is open-ended, pointing both to what is and to what can be.

Classical Christian theology teaches that all names for God are analogies. The tradition of negative or *apophatic* theology emphasizes the unlikeness between God and human words for God. That tradition corrects the tendency to take verbal images literally; God is like but also unlike any verbal analogy. Does this not mean that male words for God are not in any way superior to or more appropriate than female analogies? God is both male and female and neither male nor female. One needs inclusive language for God that draws on the images and experiences of both genders. This inclusiveness should not become more abstract. Abstractions often conceal androcentric assumptions and prevent the shattering of the male monopoly on God-language, as in "God is not male. He is Spirit." Inclusiveness can happen only by naming God/ess in female as well as male metaphors.

Equivalent Images for God as Male and Female

Are there any Biblical examples of such naming of God/ess in female as well as male metaphors that are truly equivalent images, that is, not "feminine" aspects of a male God? The synoptic Gospels offer some examples of this in the parallel parables, which seem to have been shaped in the early Christian catechetical community. They reflect the innovation of the early Christian movement of including women equally in those called to study the Torah of Jesus. Jesus justifies this practice in the Mary-Martha story, where he defends Mary's right to study in the circle of disciples around Rabbi Jesus in the words "Mary has chosen the better part which shall not be taken from her" (Luke 10:38-42).

In the parables of the mustard seed and the leaven the explosive power of the Kingdom, which God, through Jesus, is sowing in history through small signs and deeds, is compared to a farmer sowing the tiny mustard seed that produces a great tree or a woman folding the tiny bit of leaven in three measures of flour which then causes the whole to rise (Luke 13:18-21; Matt. 13:31-33). The parables of the lost sheep and the lost coin portray God seeking the sinners despised by the "righteous" of Israel. God is compared to a shepherd who leaves his ninety-nine sheep to seek the one that is lost or to a woman with ten coins who loses one and sweeps her house diligently until she finds it. Having found it, she rejoices and throws a party for her friends. This rejoicing is compared to God's rejoicing with the angels in heaven over the repentance of one sinner (Luke 15:1-10).

These metaphors for divine activity are so humble that their significance has been easily overlooked in exegesis, but we should note several important points. First, the images of male and female in these parables are equivalent. They both stand for the same things, as paired images. One is in no way inferior to the other. Second, the images are not drawn from the social roles of the mighty, but from the activities of Galilean peasants. It might be objected that the roles of the women are stereotypical and enforce the concept of woman as housekeeper. But it is interesting that the women are never described as related to or dependent on men. The small treasure of the old

woman is her own. Presumably she is an independent householder. Finally, and most significantly, the parallel male and female images do not picture divine action in parental terms. The old woman seeking the lost coin and the woman leavening the flour image God not as mother or father (Creator), but as seeker of the lost and transformer of history (Redeemer).

TOWARD A FEMINIST UNDERSTANDING OF GOD/ESS

The four preceding Biblical traditions may not be adequate for a feminist reconstruction of God/ess, but they are suggestive. If all language for God/ess is analogy, if taking a particular human image literally is idolatry, then male language for the divine must lose its privileged place. If God/ess is not the creator and validator of the existing hierarchical social order, but rather the one who liberates us from it, who opens up a new community of equals, then language about God/ess drawn from kingship and hierarchical power must lose its privileged place. Images of God/ess must include female roles and experience. Images of God/ess must be drawn from the activities of peasants and working people, people at the bottom of society. Most of all, images of God/ess must be transformative, pointing us back to our authentic potential and forward to new redeemed possibilities. God/ess-language cannot validate roles of men or women in stereotypic ways that justify male dominance and female subordination. Adding an image of God/ess as loving, nurturing mother, mediating the power of the strong, sovereign father, is insufficient.

Feminists must question the overreliance of Christianity, especially modern bourgeois Christianity, on the model of

God/ess as parent. Obviously any symbol of God/ess as parent should include mother as well as father. Mary Baker Eddy's inclusive term, *Mother-Father God*, already did this one hundred years ago. Mother-Father God has the virtue of concreteness, evoking both parental images rather than moving to an abstraction (Parent), which loses effective resonance. Mother and father image God/ess as creator, as the source of our being. They point back from our own historical existence to those upon whom our existence depends. Parents are a symbol of roots, the sense of being grounded in the universe in those who have gone before, who underlie our own existence.

But the parent model for the divine has negative resonance as well. It suggests a kind of permanent parent-child relationship to God. God becomes a neurotic parent who does not want us to grow up. To become autonomous and responsible for our own lives is the gravest sin against God. Patriarchal theology uses the parent image for God to prolong spiritual infantilism as virtue and to make autonomy and assertion of free will a sin. Parenting in patriarchal society also becomes the way of enculturating us to the stereotypic male and female roles. The family becomes the nucleus and model of patriarchal relations in society. To that extent parenting language for God reinforces patriarchal power rather than liberating us from it. We need to start with language for the Divine as redeemer, as liberator, as one who fosters full personhood and, in that context, speak of God/ess as creator, as source of being.

Patriarchal theologies of "hope" or liberation affirm the God of Exodus, the God who uproots us from present historical systems and puts us on the road to new possibilities. But they typically do this in negation of God/ess as Matrix, as source and ground of our being. They make the fundamental mistake of identifying the ground of creation with the foundations of existing social systems. Being, matter, and nature become the ontocratic base for the evil system of what is. Liberation is liberation out of or against nature into spirit. The identification of matter, nature, and being with mother makes such patriarchal theology hostile to women as symbols of all that "drags us down" from freedom. The hostility of males to any symbol of God/ess as female is rooted in this identification of mother with the negation of liberated spirit. God/ess as Matrix is thought of as "static" immanence. A static, devouring, death-dealing matter is imaged, with horror, as extinguishing the free flight of transcendent consciousness. The dualism of nature and transcendence, matter and spirit as female against male is basic to male theology.

Feminist theology must fundamentally reject this dualism of nature and spirit. It must reject both sides of the dualism: both the image of mother-matter-matrix as "static immanence" and as the ontological foundation of existing, oppressive social systems and also the concept of spirit and transcendence as rootless, antinatural, originating in an "other world" beyond the cosmos, ever repudiating and fleeing from nature, body, and the visible world. Feminist theology needs to affirm the God of Exodus, of liberation and new being, but as rooted in the foundations of being rather than as its antithesis. The God/ess who is the foundation (at one and the same time) of our being and our new being embraces both the roots of the material substratum of our existence (matter) and also the endlessly new creative potential (spirit). The God/ess who is the foundation of our being-new being does not lead us back to a stifled, dependent self or uproot us in a spirit-trip outside the earth. Rather it leads us to the converted center, the harmonization of self and body, self and other, self and world. It is the *Shalom* of our being.

God/ess as once and future *Shalom* of being, however, is *not* the creator, founder, or sanctioner of patriarchal-hierarchical society. This world arises in revolt against God/ess and in alienation from nature. It erects a false system of alienated dualisms modeled on its distorted and oppressive social relationships. God/ess liberates us from this false and alienated world, not by an endless continuation of the same trajectory of alienation but as a constant breakthrough that points us to new possibilities that are, at the same time, the regrounding of ourselves in the primordial matrix, the original harmony. The liberating encounter with God/ess is always an encounter with our authentic selves resurrected from underneath the alienated self. It is not experienced against, but in and through relationships, healing our broken relations with our bodies, with other people, with nature. We have no adequate name for the true God/ess, the "I am who I shall become." Intimations of Her/His name will appear as we emerge from false naming of God/ess modeled on patriarchal alienation.

SALLIE McFAGUE

from God the Father: Model or Idol?

Sallie McFague in our reading examines the status of the image of the divine as God the Father. Is it a "model" or an idol? she asks. Models, for McFague, are images of God, or those central images, or metaphors, that can have a significant impact on believers' religious lives. They give concreteness to the believer's spiritual relationship to God as the believer experiences it. For McFague several images of the divine are needed, and she points to several models. As she sees it, we need to balance maternal and paternal models with "non-familial and non-gender-related" models. One such model is the impersonal model of Being Itself. Another is the model of friend, and McFague examines the strengths and limitations of this model. Her final conclusion is that the "root-metaphor of Christianity" is not any one model. Rather, several are needed to express the relationship between God and human beings.

Our reading consists of selections from Chap 5. of Sallie McFague's *Metaphorical Theology*.

From Sallie McFague, *Metaphorical Theology*. Philadelphia: Fortress Press, 1982. Reprinted by permission of Augsburg Fortress Press.

5

God the Father: Model or Idol?

Among the criteria advanced for theological models are two of special significance for the issues of idolatry and irrelevance. The first is the necessity for many complementary models to intimate the richness and complexity of the divine-human relationship. If this criterion is not accepted, idolatry results. The second is the ability of the major models of a tradition to cope with anomalies. If this criterion cannot be met, irrelevance occurs. The issues of idolatry and irrelevance come together in the image of God as father, for more than any other dominant model in Christianity, this one has been both absolutized by some and, in recent times, found meaningless by others. The feminist critique of God as father centers on the *dominance* of this one model to the exclusion of others, and on the *failure* of this model to deal with the anomaly presented by those whose experience is not included by this model. It is, therefore, an excellent test case for a metaphorical theology, since its task is to envision ways of talking about the divine-human relationship which, in continuity with the parables and Jesus as parable, are nonidolatrous but

relevant. A metaphorical theology, guided by the Protestant sensibility, insists that we will not relinquish our idolatry in religious language unless we are freed from the myth that in order for images to be true they must be literal. It also insists that we will not find religious language relevant unless we are freed from the myth that in order for images to be meaningful they must be traditional.

Much has been written on this model in recent years and it is not our intention to repeat that material here;[1] rather, we wish to assess both the power and the limitations of the model from the perspective of a metaphorical theology as an example of a good model gone astray. In the feminist critique of the model of God as father an anomaly has entered the Christian paradigm, a serious rupture has appeared, and the question is posed whether the paradigm can weather the storm. As we recall, a change in the root-metaphor of a paradigm is a basic change; in a religious tradition such a change, David Tracy suggests, means a new religion.[2] Is the feminist critique of this sort? Does it reach to the root-metaphor of

---

[1] The literature criticizing the model of God as father is large and growing. A few well-known and readily available studies include the following: Carol P. Christ and Judith Plaskow, eds., *Womanspirit Rising: A Feminist Reader in Religion* (New York: Harper & Row, 1979); Sheila D. Collins, *A Different Heaven and Earth: A Feminist Perspective on Religion* (Valley Forge, Pa.: Judson Press, 1974); Mary Daly, *Beyond God the Father: Toward A Philosophy of Women's Liberation* (Boston: Beacon Press, 1973) and idem, *Gyn/Ecology: The Metaphysics of Radical Feminism* (Boston: Beacon Press, 1978); Naomi R. Goldenberg, *Changing of the Gods: Feminism and the End of Traditional Religions* (Boston: Beacon Press, 1979); Rita Gross, ed., *Beyond Androcentrism: New Essays on Women and Religion* (Missoula, Mont.: Scholars Press, 1977); Robert Hamerton-Kelly, *God the Father: Theology and Patriarchy in the Teaching of Jesus*, Overtures to Biblical Theology (Philadelphia: Fortress Press, 1979); Rosemary Ruether, ed., *Religion and Sexism: Images of Women in the Jewish and Christian Traditions* (New York: Simon & Schuster, 1974) and idem, *New Woman-New Earth: Sexist Ideologies and Human Liberation* (New York: Crossroad, 1975); Phyllis Trible, *God and the Rhetoric of Sexuality*, Overtures to Biblical Theology (Philadelphia: Fortress Press, 1978).
[2] David Tracy, "Metaphor and Religion: The Test Case of Christian Texts," in *On Metaphor*, ed. Sheldon Sacks (Chicago: Univ. of Chicago Press, 1978). p. 106.

Christianity? Or is the root-metaphor of Christianity not the model of God the father, and are there resources within the Christian paradigm both for limiting that model and for permitting complementary models? These questions will be central ones as we look at the possibilities within Christianity for dealing with one of the most serious and far-reaching criticisms of a dominant model in the history of Christianity. Whether there is revolution or reformation—a new paradigm or a change in the existing paradigm—depends both on the profundity of the basic models of a tradition and a tradition's flexibility in admitting limitations and new options.

It has been the contention of this essay that the root-metaphor of Christianity is not God the father but the kingdom or rule of God, a relationship between the divine and the human that *no* model can encompass. The divine-human relationship, therefore, demands both the limitation of the fatherhood model and the introduction of other models.

* * * * * * * * * * * * * * * * * * *

Therefore, I advance the thesis that by attending to the relationship between God and human beings rather than to descriptions of God, it is possible to find sources within the Christian paradigm for religious models liberating to women. A similar possibility, of course, is open to other groups of persons—racial, cultural, economic—who have also felt excluded by the patriarchal model. While we will be focusing mainly on one kind of imagery—the imagery emerging from experiencing the relationship with God in feminine terms—this focus should be understood illustratively rather than restrictively. The case can certainly be made that just as "father" is a natural dominant model in religion and especially in Christianity, so "mother" is as well, but it should be obvious that a relational

perspective cannot absolutize any model, whether it be feminine, masculine, parental, personal, or impersonal.

As we turn to the Christian tradition to support this thesis, we will rely on the work of reformist feminist theologians, those who have found, in biblical texts and other sources, support for feminine metaphors for the divine-human relationship. The point of this exercise is not to suggest that since feminine imagery can be found in the Bible and the tradition, it is therefore legitimate; such an approach would be contrary to the basic openness and relativity of a metaphorical theology. Even if the Christian tradition gave no support for images from women's experience, they might still be appropriate. The critical criterion is not whether the Bible and the tradition contain such metaphors, but whether they are appropriate ones in which to suggest dimensions of the new divine-human relationship intrinsic to this religious tradition. Since women have been excluded *as women* from that tradition, it comes as no surprise that feminine imagery is not central. The fact, however, that it is present at all in spite of patriarchalism is witness to its importance for expressing experiences of the new way of being in the world which other metaphors are unable to express as well. The goal of our analysis of Christian sources, therefore, is to show both that feminine images are not only there but also have been suppressed. More importantly, we will show that feminine images are highly desirable and necessary in order to express certain profound dimensions of the experiences of relating to God as the gracious giver of a new way of being in the world. As we shall also see, feminine images for God are important to men as well as to women, as both attempt to express the depths of what this new relationship means to them.

* * * * * * * * * * * * * * * * * * *

God the Friend

Parental models alone, however, whether maternal or paternal, are obviously insufficient. They screen out certain critical aspects of the divine-human relationship. For instance, by their elevation and absolutizing of divine compassion, guidance, and security for the individual, they neglect the public and political dimensions of that relationship, those dimensions concerned with what one critic of parental imagery calls "the contemporary world-wide struggle for the humanisation and self-assertion of the masses."[79] Thus, parental images need to be balanced, as the medieval mystics clearly illustrate, by many other metaphors. Certainly our time of desecration of the natural environment desperately needs immanental, natural metaphors which will help to address the imbalance that centuries of the Judeo-Christian emphasis on humanity's "dominion over the earth" have brought about. This is not the place to engage in a diatribe against Western religion's contribution to the pollution of the atmosphere, the decline of natural resources, the proliferation of nuclear weapons, and so forth. At the very least, however, it must be mentioned that an open and appreciative attitude toward Eastern models, which portray the divine presence as immanent not only in human beings but also in nature, is mandatory.

In addition, maternal and paternal models need to be balanced by nonfamilial, non-gender-related ones. One such metaphor, although by no means the only one, is God as "friend," a metaphor with potential for becoming a model. It is found here and there in the Bible: in the sweeping inclusion of all Israel as friends of God in Isaiah—"But you, Israel my servant, you Jacob whom I have chosen, race of Abraham my friend" (Isa. 41:18); in Jesus' saying that there is no greater love than laying down one's life for one's friends (John 15:13); in Jesus' reference to the Son of man as the friend of tax collectors and sinners (Matt. 11:19). Friendship with God is also suggested in biblical passages referring to companionship or fellowship with God (Josh. 1:5, 1 John 1:3, John 17:21) and partnership with God (Hos. 2:23, 1 Cor. 3:9). It is found in the tradition, though sparingly: in Irenaeus of Lyons for whom the friendship of God for humanity is a powerful metaphor; in the medieval mystics; and a variation of it in A. N. Whitehead's metaphor for God as "fellow-sufferer."

As a balance to parental models, the model of friendship has much to offer. First, female and male experience is not exhausted by parenthood; many people are not parents today, have no intention of becoming parents, and rightfully resent femininity and masculinity being linked to the ability or desire to produce children. In our society, parent-child relationships are not as central as they have been in former times, and it is unnecessarily restrictive to interpret personal models only in parental terms. Second, parental images stress the characteristics of compassion

[79] A theology (and this is something that political theology understands) located in the family situation, which nowadays is characterized by need-satisfaction and wish-fulfilment, must necessarily unilaterally favour the illusionary natue of belief to the disadvantage of its concern to banish political repression and economic exploitation. . . . Only if theological research succeeds in incorporating family symbolism into the contemporary world-wide struggle for the humanisation and self-assertion of the masses, is it possible for the religious symbolism of the family to become a truly guiding image ("God the Father in a Fatherless Society," in *God as Father?*, ed. Metz and Schillebeeckx, pp. 8–9).

and acceptance as well as guidance and discipline, but they cannot express mutuality, maturity, cooperation, responsibility, or reciprocity. The metaphor of friendship is ideally suited to express certain dimensions of a mature relationship with God. Third, in a time such as ours when at both the personal and political levels all kinds of people are working together for common causes, friendship expresses that ideal of relationship among peoples of all ages, both sexes, and whatever color or religion. It is an increasingly important metaphor for us on the human level. Hence, following the logic of all religious imagery that what matters most to us is the way to model our relationship with God, it is also an appropriate religious model.

By "friendship" we do not of course mean easy empathy for one's own kind to be found in clubs, secret societies, and unfortunately, churches all over the world. Genuine friendship does not negate differences but can thrive on them, as the old adage, "opposites attract," suggests. But even beyond the personal level, the ideal of friendship to the stranger, to the alien both as individual and as nation or culture, suggests a model. Like Dante's vision of the harmony in paradise where the saints hold hands and dance in a circle, the friendship model is one for the future on our increasingly small and beleaguered planet, where, if people do not become friends, they will not survive. Rosemary Ruether suggests a similar model when she writes: "Women seek a re-construction of relationships for which we have neither words nor models. . . . We seek a new concept of relationships

between persons, groups, life systems, a relationship which is not competitive or hierarchical but mutually enhancing."[80] She calls this new concept "communal personhood"; I prefer the model of friendship, for it is as old as human beings are, and it runs deep in our history and in our blood, and now, after centuries of hierarchical, polarized models, it is especially appropriate for us.

In Ursula LeGuin's fantasy of two people separated by all that can separate human beings—not only the usual matters of race, culture, religion, and sex, but the extraordinary one of being citizens of different planets—it is *friendship* that describes the relationship developing between them. In notes on *The Left Hand of Darkness*, LeGuin says that the real subject of the book is not gender or sexual difference but betrayal and fidelity. And it is for this reason, she says, that the dominant image in the book is an extended metaphor of a winter journey through ice, cold, and snow.[81] Her two characters, opposed in so many ways, are put to the test of achieving friendship through the trials of an incredible journey, the success of which depends entirely on their fidelity to each other. Their sexual difference is a metaphor for all their differences, differences which might have led to betrayal, but instead lead to friendship. Genly Ali says: "For it seemed to me, and I think to him, that it was from that sexual tension between us, admitted now and understood, but not assuaged, that the great and sudden assurance of friendship between us arose: a friendship so much needed by us both in our exile, and already so well proved in the days and nights of our bitter

---

[80] Ruether, *New Woman-New Earth*, p. 26.   [81] LeGuin, *The Language of the Night*, p. 162.
[82] LeGuin, *The Left Hand of Darkness*, p. 235.

journey, that it might as well be called, now as later, love.'"[82]

The model of friendship for our relationship with God and its ramifications for our relationship with other human beings, however, suggest more than the overcoming of differences. If one of the most meaningful contemporary understandings of the atonement is the suffering of God for and with the pain and oppression of the world, then the model of God as friend takes on special significance. Jesus, in his identification with the sufferings of others throughout his life and especially at his death, is a parable of God's friendship with us at the most profound level.

We see this identification in parables such as the Lost Sheep, the Prodigal Son, the Good Samaritan, and the Great Supper where the outcasts are welcomed and the conventionally righteous turned aside. We see it also in the Beatitudes and in Jesus' reading in Luke 4 from Isaiah 61:1-2 proclaiming good news to the poor, release to the captives, and liberty for the oppressed. But we see it even more dramatically, as many New Testament scholars have suggested, in Jesus' table-fellowship with "sinners and tax collectors." Joachim Jeremias, Günther Bornkamm, and Norman Perrin, for instance, agree that Jesus' practice of eating with the outcasts of his society was both the central feature and the central scandal of his ministry.[83] The passage in Matthew— "the Son of man came eating and drinking, and they say, 'Behold, a glutton and a drunkard, a friend of tax collectors and sinners'" (11:19)—is not only one of the best-authenticated sayings in the New Testament but also what could be called "an enacted parable." Bornkamm states this directly when he writes, "what the parables say actually happens in Jesus' fellowship with other people" and Perrin claims that Jesus' table-fellowship "is not a proclamation in words at all, but an acted parable."[84] Jesus' table-fellowship both shocked his enemies and impressed his followers because eating with others was the closest form of intimacy for Jews of that time and conveyed honor to those chosen. One did not eat with the ritually unclean, with Gentiles, with those in despised trades; hence, for Jesus to eat with such peoples, to be called the "friend" of such people, was a scandal to most people as well as a form of radical acceptance for his friends at table. Jeremias and Perrin agree that such a practice alone was sufficient cause for his being put to death on a cross, for it shattered the Jews' attempt to close ranks against the Roman enemy by keeping the community pure. Jeremias states: "For the offence after Easter was Jesus' accursed death on the cross— his table-fellowship with sinners was the pre-Easter scandal."[85]

The acceptance of the outcasts and the oppressed at table is a concrete enactment of forgiveness of sins. Here Jesus is not just expressing God's love but, as Bornkamm says, doing what God alone

---

[83] See Joachim Jeremias, *New Testament Theology* (New York: Charles Scribner's Sons, 1971), vol. 1, pp. 115–16, 121; Günther Bornkamm, *Jesus of Nazareth*, Eng. trans. Irene and Fraser McLuskey with James Robinson (New York: Harper & Row, 1960), pp. 80–81; Norman Perrin, *Rediscovering the Teaching of Jesus* (New York: Harper & Row, 1967), pp. 102, 107. I am indebted to Mary Ann Tolbert for directing me to this material.

[84] Bornkamm, *Jesus of Nazareth*, p. 81; Perrin, *Rediscovering the Teaching of Jesus*, p. 102.

[85] Jeremias, *New Testament Theology*, p. 121; see also Perrin, *Rediscovering the Teaching of Jesus*, p. 102.

can do—forgiving sins, extending salvation to the outcasts.[86] If, as seems to be generally agreed by New Testament scholars, the fellowship of the table for the early Christian community is a symbol of the messianic banquet (as well as a precursor of the Eucharist),[87] then Jesus, in his friendship with outcasts and sinners, is a model of friendship with God. Jesus as parable enacts God's friendship with humanity. The God of Jesus is the One who invites us to table to eat together as friends.

If Jesus is the friend who identifies with the sufferings of the oppressed in his table-fellowship against all expectations and conventions, so also is he the one who in his death, as John says, lays down his life for his friends (15:12-15). The Johannine passage is of a piece with the table-fellowship, although no claims have been advanced for its authenticity as it is probably a postresurrection tradition. What is critical, however, as Raymond Brown points out, is that "the model of the disciples' love is Jesus' supreme act of love, his laying down his life."[88] His way of expressing his love for his friends also must be our way of expressing gratitude for such love—we too must lay down our lives. Thus, we are no longer called "servants" but "friends," doing for others what our friend did for us.

The life and death of Jesus as friend, are, then, of a piece: as parable of God they reveal, as Jürgen Moltmann says, a God who suffers for us and, by so doing, invites us into a fellowship of suffering with God and for others. Such a relationship, says Moltmann, is "friendship with

God": "The friend of God does not live any longer 'under God', but with and in God." Such a person shares in the grief and the joy of God; such a person has become "one" with God.[89]

The model of friend for God, as is evident from the foregoing analysis, moves away from hierarchism and toward egalitarianism. It also has strong immanental tendencies: we are no longer under but with and in God. Initially, many people in the Western religious tradition may be wary of such a model for it raises difficult questions: What is the authority of God as friend? Can such a God protect and save individuals and the world? How do we worship a God who is our friend? These are large and important questions that cannot be fully answered here. But some attempt can be made.

* * * * * * * * * * * * * * * * * * *

Worshiping God as Friend

The thought of praying to a friend probably seems odd if not inappropriate to most of us. As Ruth Page says, one may proliferate many models of God which are theologically fruitful, but unless they work in practice—unless they mediate God—they will be seriously inadequate. Her comment on prayer to God as companion is therefore an interesting one.

> Prayer as a session with a companion has changed the felt quality of the practice. Confession, for instance, becomes startlingly existential precisely because I can imagine what it is

[86] Bornkamm, *Jesus of Nazareth*, p. 81.

[87] Jeremias, *New Testament Theology*, pp. 115–16; Bornkamm, *Jesus of Nazareth*, p. 81; Perrin, *Rediscovering the Teaching of Jesus*, p. 107.

[88] Raymond E. Brown, *The Gospel of John*, Anchor Bible Commentaries (New York: Doubleday & Co., 1970), vol. 29a, p. 682.

[89] Moltmann, "The Motherly Father," in *God as Father?*, ed. Metz and Schillebeeckx, p. 55.

to confess to companions or colleagues. God as Companion therefore does not simply underwrite complacent personhood.[96]

The comment is especially pertinent in that it underscores again the adult quality of the friend model. Once we pass childhood most of us more often ask forgiveness and acceptance from colleagues and friends than from parents. The vast majority of people today, women as well as men, work outside the home; hence many of the tensions, conflicts, and failures in our lives occur with companions and colleagues.

More than confession, however, is involved in worship. How intimate can one be with God as friend? Can one feel thankful to God as friend? Can one ask God as friend for aid and support? The friend model appears especially suggestive in regard to feeling close to God, thanking God, and asking for help. It is no accident that the friendship model appears in the immanental tradition within Christianity—in the Gospel of John, in Irenaeus, in the medieval mystics. This tradition stresses our union with God through Jesus Christ and as a consequence the oneness of all people with each other. A powerful model for expressing this sense of union has been friendship, for as a nonfamilial, non-gender-related image, it crosses the boundaries separating people of different classes, sexes, races, ages, and religions. One *can* be friends with *anyone*, including, in mystical thought, God.[97] The friendship model is in part eschatological: it projects a possibility of a time when all

peoples *shall* be one with God and with each other. It models not only what we are now in part but what we hope to be. As an eschatological model, it offers us a standard or perspective from which to see our present alienation more clearly and to criticize, in prophetic fashion, that alienation more perceptively. It suggests that the adequate and appropriate worship of God is not a solitary affair between the soul and God but, as Dante envisioned in the *Paradisio*, a dance in which all will join together accompanied by the music of the spheres. Friendship is an intimation of the unification of all that is, the natural as well as the human, joined together in harmony with God.

In addition, the intimacy intrinsic to friendship makes the model a good one for worship. Friends are deeply thankful to one another for all the gifts, both material and spiritual, that pass between them. They feel free to ask for help when it is needed and take pleasure in supporting each other. Thankfulness and requests for help between friends do not carry the notes of duty or expectation conventionally found in parent/child relationships. While parents and children are expected to give gifts to one another and to help when needed, a gift from a friend or an offer of aid is suggestive of grace, of unworthiness, of surprise. Hence, the friend model balances the parental model: our experiences of relating to God include both comforting expectation of acceptance as well as amazement for the many gifts and aid we receive.

The intimacy with God intrinsic to the friendship model is not, however, one

---

[96] Page, "Human Liberation and Divine Transcendence," p. 190.

[97] "The reader of medieval piety is constantly assailed with images of God and God's relationship to the soul which break out of the sexual/familial range of experiences. A most obvious category is friendship with God: God as Friend to the soul and vice versa is a recurring theme, especially in the later middle ages" (McLaughlin, "Christ My Mother," p. 381).

of cozy relaxation. The mystical tradition, which more than any other has emphasized *oneness* with God, also insists on *distance* from God. The closer one becomes to a friend the more one realizes the mystery of the other. Acquaintances do not seem particularly mysterious, but friends, who have shared much over a long time, seldom feel they know the other completely. The mystics witness to this paradox of intimacy and distance—the dark night of the soul comes not to those who do *not* know God but to those who *do*. Because of the blood ties in families, this sense of distance is often less pronounced. Parents can see their children as extensions of themselves, and children can imagine they have grown beyond their parents' more simple worlds. Friends rarely reduce each other in such fashion, for differences in backgrounds and experience create a sense of otherness between them. To be friends with God is to be friends with ultimate mystery—the paradox remains.

The Limitations of the Model of God as Friend

No one model is adequate and indeed, all models together are not adequate to express our experiences of relating to God. We have attempted a "thought experiment" with the model of God as friend, but like any model, it has its limitations. Friendship and its associated commonplaces—mutual respect, listening, sharing of joy and suffering, reciprocity, forgiveness, solidarity, reconciliation, sacrifice, fidelity—are all appropriate motifs for modeling certain aspects of the parabolic understanding of life with God. The model of friendship does not, it seems to me, have the potential for becoming a root-metaphor in the way that the patriarchal model presumably has, but so much the better, for the basic problem with the patriarchal model has been its expansion, its inclusiveness, its hegemony, its elevation to an idol. The root-metaphor of Christianity is not *any one* model but a relationship that occurs between God and human beings. Many models are needed to intimate what that relationship is like; none can capture it.[98] "Friendship" is but one suggestion; a model perhaps particularly relevant to women in their relations with each other and with men, but to all people as well, a model for a common humanity in which differences will be the occasion, not for alienation, but for that love based on mutual respect, on reciprocity, on shared suffering and joy. Since we model God in

---

[98] A good source for other contemporary nonsexist models is the article, "Changing Language and the Church," by Letty M. Russell in her edited book, *The Liberating Word: A Guide to Non-Sexist Interpretation of the Bible* (Philadelphia: Westminster Press, 1976). Many Protestant denominations have issued statements on language about God. The one by the United Presbyterian Church, U.S.A. has a fine paragraph:

> Given that God does act in our (Israel's) midst, the whole realm of language and association, feminine as well as masculine, is available for the describing and confessing of God's activity, though the tradition has made little use of the full range. This is the crux: as metaphor, everything is admissible which does not demean or confine. Nevertheless, as long as the female and the feminine are assumed in our culture to be limiting, defective or evil, feminine language for the naming of God's acts is excluded. The theological problem of language about God derives from anthropological assumptions about human possibility—in Old Testament times as well as today (UPCUSA. "Language About God: 'Opening the Door,' " adopted by the 187th General Assembly, 1975).

the significant images of our time, the friendship we seek in the human community causes us also to look at God as our friend.

The model of God as friend, however, needs to be balanced by other models, for friendship is deficient in several respects. First, it can appear to be too individualistic. Letty Russell prefers the model of "partner," for it is a social image suggesting commitment to a common struggle: "Partnership may be described as a new focus of relationship in which there is continuing commitment and common struggle in interaction with a wider community context."[99] Just as the trinitarian God is a *relationship*—a partnership of mutual love between the persons and toward creation—so we too are partners with God.[100] We share in the work of the economic trinity—"the work of caring for creation, setting the captives free, and standing as witness for and with those who need an advocate."[101] The model of partner, as a variation and expansion of the model of friend, is appropriate. To me, however, it has connotations of contracts, of business affairs, of casual relations. It lacks the ancient, deep roots in human experience of "friend" and has less personally significant associations. "Friend" is comparable in depth to "father," "mother," and "lover" as basic bonds in the experience of all peoples from our beginnings. Therefore, I did not choose "partner" as the model for my experiment, although I accept its socializing associations as a necessary balance to friendship.

Second, the model of God as friend needs to be complemented by models which differentiate between the status of the friends. These need not be hierarchical models such as father, king, lord, and master, but should be ones intimating guidance, leadership, protection, governance, preeminence. It is difficult in a democratic society to suggest models which possess these characteristics intrinsically, since democracies choose officials to *function* in these ways. Thus, president, prime minister, or governor are too extrinsic to serve as models of God's preeminent status as guide and protector. It seems to me that the search for models of *intrinsic* leadership is one of the most difficult issues of our time. We do not trust our leaders and have few contemporary models of guidance with integrity and wide-spread acceptance. It may simply have to be acknowledged that *we do not know* how to model God in this respect in terms of current images from our society and will not know until our own patterns of governance prove more viable and successful. Yet, it would be a mistake, I believe, to revert to anachronistic models or to return to hierarchical models which give all power to a determining, controlling God who alone is in charge of human affairs. The *via negativa* is an old tradition when one does not know *how* to speak to God and perhaps the most honest response is to evoke it on the issue of divine guidance.

Third, the model of God as friend is unable to express experiences of awe, ecstasy, fear, and silence in relating to God. In fact, none of the anthropocentric images can convey these experiences. Again, the mystics are instructive for not only have they produced novel anthropocentric images but they are also rich in images from nature suggestive of the emotional heights and depths of relating to the cosmic God. Such images need not be abstract or impersonal, for as Eleanor McLaughlin points out, many were

---

[99] Letty M. Russell, *The Future of Partnership* (Philadelphia: Westminster Press, 1979), p. 18.
[100] Ibid., p. 35.   [101] Ibid., pp. 34–35.

extraordinarily intimate.[102] One medieval mystic speaks of God as follows:

> Thou art an immense ocean of all sweetness . . . lose myself in the flood of thy living love as a drop of sea water . . . let me die in the torrent of thy infinite compassion as a burning spark dies in the rushing current of the river. Let the rain of thy boundless love fall round about me.[103]

The nature imagery of the mystics is, of course, hardly new for one recalls the rich natural imagery of the Hebrew Psalms. The variety and depth of such imagery should undercut any pretensions to idolatry of the major anthropocentric models. God cannot be imaged in any *one* model, for the whole cosmos is God's "body." "The world is charged with the glory of God," says Gerard Manley Hopkins, and God is imaged in "all things counter, original, spare, strange."[104] The Christian tradition has narrowed its metaphors and models of God, excluding natural images and focusing on hierarchical, authoritarian, anthropocentric ones. Primitive religions as well as Eastern religions support the mystics and the writers of the Psalms by insisting that experiences of God cannot be so limited, for much of what we feel in worship demands them. Ecstasy and awe cannot be contained in models of God as parent or friend—the ocean, the sky, and the earth express them more fully.

Finally, impersonal models are necessary not only as safeguards against the limits of all images but also as expressions of the depths of our dependence on God. Paul Tillich was right to say that God is "Being-Itself,"[105] for even though, once again, the only kind of "being" we know is creaturely existence and hence "Being-Itself" is a metaphor, still, the phrase points to God as the source and depth of our being. We have no words for this sense of radical and absolute dependence on Another for life itself. We know it is not of our making or doing, that all that is derives from "not itself," that we are something but come from nothing.

WILLIAM HARPER

On Calling God "Mother"

William Harper in "On Calling God 'Mother' " argues for the view that it is religiously permissible for believers to refer to God using only "male terms" by referring to God exclusively as God the Father. He argues that feminist conceptions of maleness are stereotypical and that the feminist arguments for using a feminine image for the divine are unconvincing. He concludes that

---

[102] McLaughlin, "Christ My Mother," p. 381.   [103] Ibid.
[104] *Poems and Prose of Gerard Manley Hopkins*, ed. W. H. Gardner (Harmondsworth, Eng.: Penguin Bks., 1953), pp. 27, 31.
[105] Paul Tillich, *Systematic Theology*, (Chicago: Univ. of Chicago Press, 1959), vol. 1, pp. 238–39.

some religious believers or congregations may use masculine images exclusively *and* some religious believers and congregations may use feminine images exclusively, depending on what "facilitates their growth in the Faith."*

On Calling God 'Mother'

Patricia Altenbernd Johnson argues that referring to God in female terms is desirable in that it would help overcome patriarchy, bring to our image of God positive qualities missing when God is referred to in male terms, and would be more inclusive. I find that Johnson's notion of patriarchy is such that overcoming it involves introducing pantheistic elements into Christian belief. Also, Johnson's arguments assume an objectionable stereotype of maleness. The argument from inclusiveness is not supported by observation. Concluding that Johnson's arguments fail, I suggest that Biblical example is sufficient permission for referring to God exclusively in male terms.

I n her article "Feminist Christian Philosophy?," Patricia Altenbernd Johnson argues in favor of referring to God in female terms, at least as mixed with male terms.[1] Johnson's advocacy of the use of female terms for God is based on assertions that certain advantages would result from the practice. One alleged advantage is that the use of female terms for God would emphasize positive traits that are de-emphasized by the use of male terms, thus allowing our awareness of God to be more positive and emotionally complete. In support of this claim Johnson presents at length the claims of Sara Ruddick that the notions of preservation, growth, and social acceptability are especially tied to maternal activity.[2] Johnson then claims that each of these attributes is expressed, for example, by the term 'Mother-God.' The term 'Mother-God' expresses the idea that God's power is not so much "total control" but a preserving love, "a hopeful and supportive presence to help us face and cope with our lives."[3] 'Mother-God' stands for "ways of thinking that help the mother and child grow and change." This specifically includes the practice of story-telling.[4] 'Mother-God' also supposedly calls to mind the training of children "to be the kind of person others can accept and whom the mothers themselves can actively appreciate."[5]

The main problem with this claim is that there is nothing especially maternal about any of these practices. Consider the "preserving love" Johnson mentions. For millennia, fathers have protected their children while teaching them how to take

---

* From *Faith and Philosophy*, vol. 11 (1994). Reprinted by permission.
[1] Patricia Altenbernd Johnson, "Feminist Christian Philosophy?" *Faith and Philosophy*, 9 (1992), 320–34.
[2] Sara Ruddick, *Maternal Thinking: Toward a Politics of Peace* (Boston: Beacon Press, 1989).
[3] Johnson, p. 330.   [4] Johnson, pp. 330–31.   [5] Johnson, p. 331.

care of themselves, warning them against dangers, and teaching them how to confront and deal with unavoidable dangers in appropriate ways. Johnson ignores this role completely. Instead, she makes these characteristics primarily maternal, and contrasts them against the supposedly paternal notion of power as "total control." She argues similarly with regard to the notions of psychological growth and training in social acceptability, as though the paternal role had little to do with socialization or psychological growth. In turn, Johnson's paternal God is cold and impersonal, and relates to us through power and control, not love. Johnson's view of the paternal God seems to be based on a deficient and arid view of fatherhood.

If Ruddick is, indeed, the origin of these views, we can trace Johnson's mistake. For Ruddick, 'mother' and 'Father' are not gender indexed terms.[6] In fact, Ruddick advocates that males become mothers, that all parents be mothers.

> Fathers, historically, are meant to provide material support for child care and to defend mothers and their children from external threat. They are supposed to represent the world—its language, culture, work, and rule—and to be the arbiters of the child's acceptability in the world they represent . . . . The point about—or against—Fathers is that their authority is not earned by care and indeed undermines the maternal authority that is so earned. . . . Fatherhood is more a role determined by cultural demands than a kind of work determined by children's needs. . . . The point against

Fatherhood is that it offers unrealistic hopes and burdens to women and men who take up the caring labor of maternity. . . . Male (or female) parents who have enjoyed or been burdened by the ideology of Fatherhood can and should take up the work of mothering instead.[7]

In contrast, motherhood is characterized by Ruddick as a rich, emotionally nuanced institution. In fact, it becomes clear in her text that motherhood includes providing for the material well-being of the child and raising the child to be adapted to a demanding world— actions appropriate to Fatherhood as Ruddick characterizes it. Now, any author has leeway to define terms as he or she wishes. If we accept Ruddick's characterizations of Fatherhood and motherhood as definitions of those roles, then *of course* we would want all parents to be mothers. We would hope no parent is so emotionally vacant as to limit himself or herself to a role as arid as the Fatherhood described by Ruddick. Ruddick goes on in her book to make many excellent and subtle points about parenting (she calls it 'mothering'). However, outside the context of the book we should revert to using terms in their accustomed senses, and in the real world 'fatherhood' refers to the roles played by real fathers in all their rich diversity. It is true that fatherhood has traditionally involved a responsibility to be the primary bread-winner, but to define 'fatherhood' as being limited to this and a few other functions would be no better than to define 'motherhood' as being limited to changing diapers and cooking food.

---

[6] While discussing Ruddick, I will follow her practice of capitalizing 'father' and 'fatherhood' while leaving 'mother' and 'motherhood' in lower case. See Ruddick, p. 42.

[7] Ruddick, p. 42.

In this context Johnson also cites Sallie McFague's assertion that referring to God as 'Mother' "could facilitate the experience of god [sic] as intimate and caring."[8] Of course, referring to God as 'Mother' could not enhance our experience of these qualities unless referring to God as 'Father' had somehow failed to include these qualities. Such a view is simply a distorted caricature of the paternal role. There is no need to begin using female terms for God if the sole purpose of doing so is to import such positive notions as preserving love, growth, and socialization. All of these qualities are fully expressed in the term 'father.' To deny that is simply to resort to a narrow stereotype of male parenthood. If paternity were what Johnson thinks it is, we would have a reason in favor of supplementing it with maternal notions. But the problem is with Johnson's perception of fatherhood, not with the genuine connotations of the word 'father.'

Another benefit Johnson sees in the adoption of female terms for God is the assistance it would lend to the destruction of patriarchy. 'Patriarchy' can mean, 'domination by men,' and that seems to be Johnson's use of the term. Evidently, the use of female terms for God would advance a non-dualistic eco-holism—the view that the integrity of nature is the supreme ethical value—which would in turn involve the demise of patriarchy. Here Johnson cites Rosemary Ruether: "Ruether suggests that using the name 'God/ess' would help us overcome the dualism of nature and spirit."[9] Ruether's program for overcoming this dualism is to combine the transcendence of God with a full measure of immanence. This importation of the divine into nature should, she thinks, result in an elevated valuation of nature and the adoption of the belief that humans must subordinate their interests to nature. According to Ruether, we must see our possession of intelligence as laying upon us "the responsibility and necessity to convert our intelligence to the earth."[10] Ruether implies in her work that nature is good and that human influence is typically detrimental.

> There is virtually no place on the planet where one can go to find "nature untouched by human hands." Even if humans have not been there before, their influence has been carried by wind, water, and soil, birds, insects, and animals who bear within their beings the poisoning effects of human rapine of the globe. Nature, in this sense, can be seen as "fallen," not that it is evil itself but in that it has been marred and distorted by human misdevelopment.[11]

In the same vein, Johnson refers us to the work of Elizabeth Dodson Gray. Gray claims in her book *Green Paradise Lost* that humans are no more important than any other species. Speciesism is seen as one type of hierarchical thinking. In turn, hierarchical thinking is seen as characteristically male and as the source of many social ills. Gray says that a first step in correcting such a system would be to assign rights for

---

[8] Johnson, p. 328. See Sallie McFague, "God as Mother," in *Weaving the Visions*, eds. Judith Plaskow and Carol P. Christ (San Francisco: Harper and Row, 1989).

[9] Johnson, p. 327.

[10] Rosemary Radford Ruether, *Sexism and God-Talk* (Boston: Beacon Press, 1983), p. 89.

[11] Ruether, p. 91.

natural objects. In the chapter "We Must Re-Myth Genesis" she implies that humans do not have any greater intrinsic value than any other aspect of nature whatever.[12]

McFague, too, holds views which are in line with this thinking. I will quote her at some length.

> The feminist theologians who have given attention to the nonhuman world have been, for the most part, those involved in Goddess traditions and witch-craft, for whom the body, the earth, and nature's cycles are of critical importance. Those of us within the Christian tradition have much to learn from these sources, but even these feminists have not, I believe, focused primarily on the intrinsic value of the nonhuman in a way sufficient to bring about the needed change of consciousness. . . . The principal insight of liberation theologies—that redemption is not the rescue of certain individuals for eternal life in another world but the fulfillment of all humanity in the political and social realities of this world—must be further deprivatized to include the well-being of all life. . . . An ecological perspective recognizing human dependence on its environment . . . is the dominant paradigm of our time and theology that is not done in conversation with this paradigm is not theology *for our time*.[13]

Of course, it is a truism that human life is dependent upon its environment, but McFague and the other authors cited are talking about something distinct from this. They claim that we have an ethical obligation to care for the environment for its own sake. McFague explicitly wants to replace the I-it relationship with an I-Thou relationship.[14]

To make sense of such talk we must inspirit nature. Otherwise, nature would have to be seen as totally indifferent to change of any kind, and the notions of harming or destroying nature would make no sense. To an indifferent nature, volcanic eruptions, ice ages, and the collisions of continents are not destruction; they are business as usual. Terms like 'destruction' and 'harm' are relative to values and interests. Historically, cultivated land, land changed to better serve human needs, was regarded for that reason as improved land.[15] Damaging the Earth meant altering it so that it was less useful to people. Inspiriting the Earth, on the other hand, gives the Earth interests. Making the Earth a part of God makes us accountable to the Earth for God's own sake. In the latter case, harm to the Earth is no longer understood relative to human interests but relative to God's interests. Presumably, God, immanent in the world, has as interests the stability, equilibrium, and species diversity of the eco-system,[16] but different prophets might give us different agendas.

In the Judeo-Christian tradition, God is not the Earth. The Earth is cursed

---

[12] Elizabeth Dodson Gray, *Green Paradise Lost* (Wellesley, MA: Roundtable Press, 1981).

[13] Sallie McFague, *Models of God: Theology for an Ecological, Nuclear Age* (Philadelphia: Fortress Press, 1987), p. 7.

[14] McFague, p. 11.

[15] See, for example, John Locke, *Second Treatise of Government*, Ch. 5, § 37.

[16] See William Aiken, "Ethical Issues in Agriculture," in *Earthbound: New Introductory Essays in Environmental Ethics*, ed. Tom Regan (New York: Random House, 1984), p. 268, where 'ecocentrism' roughly corresponds to my use of 'eco-holism.'

(Gen. 3.17). Christian ethics does not encourage us to act naturally. Acting naturally is what separates us from God. Christianity demands that we act supra-naturally. God transcends the Earth, and we seek communion with God, not the Earth. Denying the reality of this bifurcation effectively denies original sin and vitiates any need for a Christ. The immanence of God in the world would seem to be inconsistent with the Gospel message, and claims of God's immanence would thus be no proper motivation for anything, including referring to God as female.

What is more important here, is that there is no essential or practical connection between monotheism and environmental disruption. The essential transcendence of God is not a reason to lay waste to the planet. God said to subdue the Earth, not to make it uninhabitable. A conservationist attitude follows from an awareness that we have an obligation not to put people arbitrarily at risk and that the ecosystem cannot continue to support people if it is stressed without limit. There is no need to resort to pantheism for adequate motivation to protect the environment.

Johnson's argument presupposes that maleness, patriarchy and dualism are linked in some essential or causal way, not only to each other but to a number of other disdained qualities and practices. This view is shared by the authors Johnson cites for support. Gray is the most advanced of these authors. Male hierarchical thinking is seen by Gray as the common denominator of sexism, classism, racism, speciesism, dualism, scientific reductionism, patriarchy, and inequality in general.

Ruether, in turn, simply *defines* 'patriarchy' as hierarchy, explicitly including in the notion of 'patriarchy' master-slave relationships and "racial over-lords over colonized people."[17] Modes of reasoning are seen as gender typed, as when she claims that the elimination of gender bias will require a "new form of human intelligence," since the present one is "white Western male" rationality.[18]

One problem with this conceptual approach is that, while decrying dualism and reductionism of one sort, it is in its own way reductionist and rigidly dualistic. We are offered a virtually undifferentiated complex—male/logical/hierarchical/rational/linear/human-centered/oppressive/exploitive/capitalistic/patriarchal/individualistic/imperialistic/dualistic. This complex is reductionist in the sense that all these qualities reduce to maleness. It is rounded out by occasional references to whiteness, Westernness, and heterosexuality. It is balanced by a corresponding complex of allegedly female qualities so that we end up with a dualism whose complements are male/female, hierarchical/communal, capitalist/socialist,exploitive/non-exploitive, etc. All of the "male" traits are valued negatively, the "female" traits positively. Paradoxically, the complements include dualistic/holistic and reductionist/non-reductionist, with dualism and reductionism supposedly being traits characteristic of male thinking. The evident logical deficiencies of this kind of conflation, and the one-sided valuations of its metaphysic, require no further comment.

Suppose, though, that the gender-dualist picture of reality is correct. Then God Himself would surely be aware of this dichotomy, and we would have to begin asking in earnest why God revealed Himself exclusively in male terms, why Jesus deliberately called God 'Father' and

[17] Ruether, p. 61.   [18] Ruether, p. 89.

not 'Mother.' If the authors quoted above are correct in the gender-dualistic view of society implicit in their arguments, then Christian women become radically estranged from God in a way no conservative theologian has ever dared allege. On the other hand, if we deny such gender dualism we leave open the possibility that male references to God in the Bible signify nothing essentially non-female about God.

I conclude that Johnson's argument is unconvincing. Johnson's advocacy of the use of female terms for God rests on a demeaning, false stereotype of maleness, a stereotype which does not deserve our support. Her argument also appeals to an alleged ecological imperative to radically revalue the Christian faith. The support for this imperative is lacking in that ecological destruction is not entailed by transcendental views of God, and the pantheism involved in the proposed revaluation is objectionable. As well, Johnson's argument rests upon a conflation of several concepts, including 'patriarchy' and 'spirit-matter dualism,' that have no obvious connection. A realistic view of maleness, together with a more careful, non-reductionist use of terms, would shatter the gender-dualist paradigm presupposed in Johnson's argument.

Although Johnson fails to provide support for a societal imperative to refer to God using female terms, there might be other causal links between the use of female terms for God and improved social conditions. However, consider the Kogi of the Colombian Sierra Nevada. They refer to the Creator of the Universe exclusively in females terms, yet their society is a rigid patriarchy, the all-male priesthood dictating even the most minute aspects of Kogi life.[19] Consider also the social structures of ancient Egypt and other societies with strong goddess traditions. Historically, there seems to be no correlation whatever between the gender of a supreme Deity and social conditions. The case for a causal connection between the perceived gender of God and social conditions is tenuous at best. Therefore, it is not at all clear that a referentially hermaphroditic supreme Deity (God/ess), or an alternately male and female supreme Deity, would be causally efficacious on social conditions.[20]

Does there remain an adequate reason for breaking with tradition and Biblical example, and for referring to God as female? Johnson implies in her paper that the exclusive use of male terms for God alienates women from the Church, making them "invisible." This is a serious matter. The Gospel is for everyone, and we should not engage in practices that suggest otherwise. But experience indicates that the alleged alienation is more a matter of interpretation than a matter of reality. For example, in the United States, the fastest growing churches are mostly conservative, and most of their new membership is women. Women hold fewer

[19] See G. Reichel-Dolmatoff, *The Sacred Mountain of Colombia's Kogi Indians* (Leiden: E. J. Brill, 1990). The Kogi also reject Cartesian-style spirit-matter dualism, and live according to an extremely eco-holistic ethic, practices Johnson claims are conducive to the demise of patriarchy.

[20] It has been suggested that a goddess may be of a sort that serves only to reflect and reinforce existing gender roles. (See Jane Mary Trau, "Exclusively Male Imagery in Religious Language," *Worship* 66, No. 4 (1992), 314–15.) It is not clear that goddesses can actually be efficacious in this way, but if so, and if Johnson's contention is correct that male and female terms for God would have different connotations corresponding to contemporary gender roles (whatever those roles actually are), then no societal changes would be effected by referring to God as female. Rather, present social attitudes would only be reinforced.

positions of authority in the more conservative churches, but women are aware of that when they join, and they are joining conservative churches anyway and in numbers that significantly exceed men.[21] This suggests that Johnson's allegation is a victory of theory over observation. Christianity is already inclusive. We are not all Semitic, or Jewish, or male, but all who accept Christ are children of Abraham, are God's chosen people—and sons, in the sense of full inheritors in the Kingdom of God.

It may be that certain individuals, for whatever reasons, feel alienated from God when they refer to God exclusively in male terms. If this is the case, and if referring to God in female terms facilitates their growth as Christians, then that would be a reason in favor of their so referring to God. This does not imply that those who refer to God in exclusively male terms are wrong to do so. Rather, it is a principle that admits of personal differences in how people best relate to their Creator. It states that individuals and individual churches should do what best facilitates their growth in the Faith, and that possibly no one practice will be best for all people.

I have spoken with some people who seem to take the liberalism of the above paragraph as an affront to equality. The objection seems to be ideological, requiring that references to God should include female terms not because doing so is instrumentally good (Johnson's approach) but because using a single gender is intrinsically wrong. Even assuming that such a principle holds at all, additional premises would be required to establish it as an *overriding* principle. In any case, it does not seem tenable for anyone subscribing to the perfection of Christ. While we do not have a record of Jesus specifically denouncing every form of evil, he surely never took part in wrongdoing, and Jesus referred to God exclusively in male terms. It would seem, then, that there is nothing intrinsically wrong in doing so.

As for God the Father, He is, as always, flowing with just those positive qualities that Johnson wants to say are gynocentric and in opposition to maleness. God, Abba, is loving, supportive, gracious, charitable, forgiving and encouraging, and He is patiently training us to be likewise.[22]

GEORGE F. ISHAM

Is God Exclusively a Father

George Isham in addressing Harper's argument finds that Harper depends upon five reasons to support his position. Each is open to criticism, Isham argues. For instance, in reply to Harper's point that referring to the divine with

[21] Tony Walter, "Why Are Most Churchgoers Women?," *Vox Evangelica* 20 (1990), 73–80.
[22] An earlier version of this paper was read at Berry College at the 1993 Eastern Regional Meeting of the Society of Christian philosophers. I thank those taking part in the discussion for their helpful comments.

female terms, or Goddess worship, does not necessarily bring about social improvement, Isham observes, that there may still be "a need for a deity with which women can relate and identify." Although women may be able to relate to God imaged as a Father, women cannot *identify* with God so imaged.*

Is God Exclusively a Father?

William Harper presents five reasons for concluding that God should be referred to exclusively in male terms. To the contrary, I argue that: (1) by devaluating the feminine gender, Harper is guilty of the same reductionist and dichotomous thinking as his [opponents]., (2) Harper's view of God is contrary to "the Biblical example," and (3) Harper's position rests on a number of logical confusions. I conclude that Harper's view should be rejected by both men and women of Christian convictions.

In his article "On Calling God 'Mother'," William Harper argues against feminists who depict God in female terms, or "at least as mixed with male terms."[1] He uses five reasons to demonstrate that Christian philosophers should refer to God exclusively with male attributes:

(1) Some feminists assume an objectionable view of maleness.

(2) Some feminists connect their interests with an ecological imperative, thereby introducing pantheistic elements into Christian belief.

(3) Some feminists assume a "gender-dualistic paradigm" which falls prey to the fallacies of reductionism and false dichotomy.

(4) Empirical evidence does not support the contention that Goddess worship will lead to improved social conditions for women.

(5) The Biblical example gives sufficient grounds for referring to God exclusively in male terms.

My response to Harper will maintain a moderate position between his views and those of the feminists whom he critiques.

The issues raised by Harper are very important. According to Genesis 1:27, God fashioned the human race in His own image, and in so doing, He created both the male and female genders. It would seem to follow that both men and women possess significant characteristics that somehow retain a likeness to the divine, even if presently marred by sin. However, Harper informs us that "God reveals Himself exclusively in male terms . . .".[2] Thus, although both genders are made in the divine image, Harper's God manifests Himself in such a manner that only one gender (namely, the male) could ever come to some awareness of what its divine likeness entails. Presumably the other sex (namely, the female) is destined forever to be deprived of such knowledge, or at least to receive its awareness from sources other than Harper's God.

* From *Faith and Philosophy*, vol. 13 (1996). Reprinted by permission.
[1] William Harper, "On Calling God 'Mother'," *Faith and Philosophy*, 11 (1994), 290.
[2] *Ibid.*, p. 294.

Both I and Harper would disagree with a Goddess worshipper like Carol P. Christ, but she at least compels us to view this situation from a feminine perspective:

> A woman ... can never have the experience that is freely available to every man and boy in her culture, of having her full sexual identity affirmed in the image and likeness of God.[3]

Christ is not discussing some alleged inability on the part of women to relate to an all-male deity. Women have been relating to men from the beginning of the human race, and they are more than capable of sustaining relationships with an all-male God. The (supposed) deprivation of women does not reside in a relationship, but rather in a perceived identity or likeness. Women (as women) can relate to, but never be like, an all-male God. Men, on the other hand, can both relate to, and experience similarities with, such a deity. Thus, if Christ is correct, Harper's God effectively disenfranchises half of the human race from certain aspects of religious experience. Given the possibility of such a conclusion, the issues raised by Harper are certainly important and worthy of further investigation.

I

Harper's first reason may assume an objectionable view of fatherhood. He cites Sara Ruddick and Sallie McFague as examples of feminists who assign positive qualities to motherhood, supposedly at the expense of affirming these qualities for fathers. Protesting that fatherhood also entails positive attributes, Harper draws a zealous conclusion:

> There is no need to begin using female terms for God if the sole purpose of doing so is to import such positive notions as preserving love, growth, and socialization. All of these qualities are fully expressed in the term 'father.' To deny that is simply to resort to a narrow stereotype of male parenthood.[4]

I agree that fathers are capable of expressing such positive attributes as love, growth, and socialization. However, if these qualities are *fully* expressed in the term 'father,' can we infer that other terms (like 'mother,' for example) have nothing of significance to add to these properties? By using the terms 'fully expressed,' Harper may be guilty of the same tactic as his [opponents]. He assigns positive attributes to one gender at the expense of the other.

I believe that a more moderate view would see both fathers and mothers as capable of expressing significant aspects of love, growth, and socialization. Since neither gender can "fully express" such properties, each needs the other for purposes of enhancement and completion. Thus, denying "full expression" to fathers does not necessarily entail "a narrow stereotype of male parenthood." It is simply admitting that both men and women

---

[3] Carol P. Christ and Judith Plaskow, eds., *WomanSpirit Rising* (San Francisco: Harper-Collins, 1992), p. 275.
[4] Harper, *op. cit.*, p. 292.

have significant parts to play in the "full expression" of positive attributes.

Similar remarks can be made about Harper's third reason. He accuses feminists like Elizabeth Dodson Gray of reductionist and dichotomous thinking, since they propose "a virtually undifferentiated complex" of "male/female, hierarchial/communal, capitalist/socialist, exploitive/non-exploitive, etc."[5] If Harper assumes that "full expression" must belong to one gender at the expense of the other, then he engages in the same type of thinking. It is both dichotomous and reductionist to think that only one gender is capable of "full expression."

Some feminists have set forth historical reasons to justify their formation of "undifferentiated complexes." Perhaps the original source for this line of reasoning is Simone de Beauvoir's *The Second Sex*. Writing in 1949, de Beauvoir declares:

> It amounts to this: just as for the ancients there was an absolute vertical with reference to which the oblique was defined, so there is an absolute human type, the masculine. . . . "The female is a female by virtue of a certain lack of qualities," said Aristotle; "we should regard the female nature as afflicted with a natural defectiveness." And St. Thomas for his part pronounced woman to be an "imperfect man," an "incidental" being. This is symbolized in Genesis where Eve is depicted as made from what Bossuet called "a supernumerary bone" of Adam. Thus humanity is male and

man defines woman not in herself but as relative to him; she is not regarded as an autonomous being.[6]

In more recent years, Caroline Whitbeck and Marilyn Pearsall have expressed similar views.[7] From the formation of the ancient Chinese philosophy of yin and yang, to the creation of modern Jungian psychology, men have tended to evaluate positively the properties of their own nature. Insofar as women were perceived as being different, they became the opposing (or negative) gender, a "defective" creation, or (in de Beauvoir's terms) the second (other) sex.

Apparently some modern feminists believe in the old adage: "turnabout is fair play." Since "male philosophers" have supposedly engaged in "undifferentiated complexes" that devalue women, some feminists apparently feel justified in reversing the situation. It is not my present purpose to judge whether de Beauvoir or Whitbeck have given a fair treatment of "male philosophy." Instead, it should be sufficient to point out that, from the standpoint of Christian ethics, all such gender devaluation is wrong. This conclusion holds true regardless of who is doing the devaluation: Aristotle, St. Thomas Aquinas, Sara Ruddick, or even William Harper. If God created both human genders, blessed them and pronounced them "very good" (Gen. 1:26-31), then it is highly improper to grant "full expression" to one sex at the expense of the other.

---

[5] Harper, *op. cit.*, p. 294.
[6] Simone de Beauvoir, *The Second Sex* (New York: Alfred A. Knopf, 1989), pp. xv–xvi.
[7] Caroline Whitbeck, "Theories of Sex Difference," *The Philosophical Forum*, Vol. V, Nos. 1–2 (Fall/Winter 1973–74), pp. 54–80. Marilyn Pearsall, ed., *Women and Values* (Belmont, California: Wadsworth Publishing Company, 1994), p. 32.

II

Harper also reasons that we should follow the Biblical example of depicting God exclusively in male terms. Nowhere does Harper explain or define what he means by "the Biblical example." If he intends these words to refer to the preserved texts of the Old and New Testaments, then his argument rests on a false premise. Although Harper might prove that the Bible depicts God *predominantly* with male attributes, he cannot demonstrate that the Scriptures refer to God *exclusively* in masculine terms. This is true because the Bible sometimes uses feminine imagery to describe features of God's love and wisdom. The Old Testament Psalmist, for example, declares that the believer's hope in God has a calming effect, "like a child quieted at its mother's breast" (Ps. 131:1-2). The Book of Isaiah states that the possibility of God forgetting Israel is like the chances of a mother forgetting her suckling infant (Is. 49:15). The Lord comforts Jerusalem, just like a mother soothes her children (Is. 66:13). In the Book of Proverbs, God's wisdom is personified as a woman who calls in the marketplace to all who will follow her advice (Prov. 1:20-21; 8:1-2). Given such feminine imagery, Harper cannot prove that the Biblical God is manifested exclusively in male terms.

Perhaps Harper intends "Biblical example" to refer to the Scriptural record of Jesus' life and teachings, rather than the preserved texts of the entire Bible. If so, then Harper's article maintains an inadequate view of the New Testament Christ. According to Harper, "Jesus deliberately called God 'Father' and not 'Mother'."[8] I leave aside the complex, epistemological questions of how Harper knows Jesus' language was deliberate, and if so, what intentions were accomplished by such references. Instead, I will simply note that, by the end of his article, Harper uses this allegation as a premise in a longer argument:

> Jesus . . . surely never took part in wrongdoing, and Jesus referred to God exclusively in male terms. It would seem, then, that there is nothing intrinsically wrong in doing so.[9]

This would be a compelling argument were it not for one, minor drawback: Jesus does not refer to God exclusively in male terms.

According to the authors of the New Testament, Jesus referred to himself as God. In fact, the identity between his nature and the divine was so complete that Jesus "did not count equality with God a thing to be grasped" (Phil. 2:6, RSV). On at least one occasion, Jesus also referred to himself in clearly feminine terms (Mt. 23:37; Lu. 13:34). Now, if 'being Jesus' is logically equivalent to 'being God', and if 'being Jesus' entails 'the possession of some feminine attributes,' then it follows that 'being God' also entails 'the possession of some feminine attributes.' While it is true that Jesus calls God his Father, it is equally true that, by identifying himself with deity and by ascribing feminine attributes to his own nature, Jesus thereby assigns some feminine properties to God. Thus, he does not refer to deity in exclusively male terms.

---

[8] Harper, *op. cit.*, p. 294.   [9] Harper, *op. cit.*, p. 296.

After the New Testament era, there was a persistent (albeit at times, underground) tradition in Christianity which continued to assign feminine properties to the Second Person of the Trinity. A saying attributed alternatively to the Montanist prophets, Priscilla and Quintilla, declared: "Christ came to me in the form of a woman in shining garments and taught me wisdom . . ."[10] Perhaps this tradition reached its zenith in the writings of the Late Medieval mystic and philosopher, Dame Julian of Norwich. She argued that the Second Person of the Trinity can be properly addressed as Mother, since that term best describes the nurturing love and mercy of Jesus.[11] From Luther onward, Protestants have generally repudiated this tradition, but in light of the modern feminist movement, perhaps it is time for Protestant Christians to re-examine the historical resources within Christianity for assigning feminine properties to God.[12]

III

Harper's second and fourth reasons rest on a number of confusions. Among the items which he confuses, are the following:

(1) Ascribing feminine properties to God, versus personifying these attributes as a distinct Goddess. The Bible assigns feminine characteristics to God, but it firmly condemns the worship of Goddesses (Ex. 34:13; Dt. 7:5; Ac. 19:23-41; etc.).

(2) Believing that nature possesses a derived moral value because God originally pronounced it as "good" (Gen. 1:31), versus worshipping the earth as a Goddess who possesses absolute, underived moral worth. Although nature is presently corrupted by human sin (Gen. 2:17; Ro. 8:22), it is not as "indifferent" as Harper maintains. I believe that a moderate position would view nature as possessing a secondary, derived value, as opposed to absolute or little worth. Thus, the basis for an ecological ethics is not simply human self-interest, but also the value which God originally conferred on creation (Ro. 1:20).

(3) Believing that God is (or can be) immanent, versus believing in pantheism. Harper rejects pantheism, but in the process, he also concludes that "the immanence of God in the world would seem to be inconsistent with the Gospel message . . ."[13] To the contrary, I wonder how Jesus could have preached the Gospel message other than by coming into the world and being immanent (Jn. 1:14).

(4) Perceiving that Goddess worship does not necessarily lead to improved social conditions for women, versus maintaining that worship of an all-male God is somehow beneficial for the feminine gender. Some feminists are well

---

[10] Epiphanius, *Panarion* XLIX. 1. See Arthur Cushman McGiffert, *A History of Christian Thought* (New York: Charles Scribner's Sons, 1960), vol. 1, p. 168.

[11] Julian of Norwich, *Revelations of Divine Love*, (Roger L. Roberts, ed.), Ridgefield, Connecticutt: Morehouse Publishers, 1982.

[12] For feminist treatments of Luther's views, see Ann Loades, ed., *Feminist Theology: A Reader* (Louisville: John Knox Press, 1991), pp. 120–148.

[13] Harper, *op. cit.*, p. 293.

aware of the fact that Goddess worship is often practiced in rigidly patriarchal societies.[14] However, this fact does not abrogate the need for a deity with which women can both relate and identify. I believe that the Biblical God can meet such needs, whereas Harper's all-male (but somehow, at the same time, Totally Transcendent) God cannot.

I conclude that a "loving, supportive, gracious, charitable, forgiving and encouraging" deity would not deprive half of the human race from experiencing significant aspects of the divine nature.[15] The Biblical God, a deity who is revealed in both masculine and feminine terms, does not so deprive women. However, Harper's all-male deity does not allow women to affirm their gender as being created in the image of God. For that and the other reasons discussed above, Harper's position should be rejected by both men and women of Christian convictions.

---

[14] Consult, for example, Serry B. Ortner, "Is Female to Male as Nature Is to Culture?" in Michelle Zimbalist, et. al., eds., *Woman, Culture, and Society* (Stanford: Stanford University Press, 1974), pp. 67–87.

[15] Harper, *op. cit.*, p. 296.

Chapter **10**

Religious Realism and the Meaning of God

It is possible to ask religious believers in the three great monotheistic traditions "What do you mean by 'God'?" A traditional reply to this question would in some way cite the core concept of these traditions, according to which God is the supreme being and the creator of all that is. Sometimes when religious believers try to say what they mean by "God" they do not say much more than this. However, there is more to the core concept of God shared by Judaism, Christianity, and Islam. God in all of these traditions is transcendent, and God is self-subsistent, depending on nothing, while everything depends on God for its being. God is not just one more thing or being. God is *the* supreme being. Moreover, God in all of these traditions is merciful, compassionate, and just, to name a few of the attributes or "perfections" in the shared core concept. In these traditions God is a personal God. God knows, wills, asks, punishes, forgives, and loves. God is omniscient or all-knowing. God is omnibenevolent or all-good. God is omnipresent, so that God's presence may be found everywhere.

For most or many traditional believers in these three traditions, it is a part of the core concept of God that God interacts with believers and others. That is, God in some way provides revelations to special prophets or to messengers or provides guidance to believers or in some other way performs miracles. At the same time, in the core concept of God, there is much that is beyond human comprehension regarding God's ways and the manifestations of God's love and goodness.

To be sure a full reply to the question "What do you mean by 'God'?" by a traditional Christian would in a number of significant respects be different from a full reply given by a traditional Jew or Muslim. For the traditional Christian part of what she or he means by "God" would include there being "God the Father" and "God the Son," while this would not be so for Jews and Muslims. In the same way a full reply by a traditional Jew or Muslim would differ from that of the Christian and from one another in certain respects. In this way traditional believers can say, or begin to say, what they mean by "God," even if not all traditional believers in the three traditions would give identical full replies.

There is, however, another question that may be raised *after* religious believers have answered the question "What do you mean by 'God'"? This second question has been phrased as "What is the *meaning* of God?" This question is not "What do believers *mean by* 'God'?" It is "What does *God mean* for believers?" Some would put the issue as "What is the best understanding of *God* in a religious life?" When we ask this question we are asking about the deepest religious significance of God. We are asking what understanding of God connects most deeply to religious practice and sensibility.

The issue of religious realism is precisely the issue that has arisen within religion and religious thought about the *meaning* of God. It relates to the theistic or monotheistic religions, where belief in God is central. The issue of religious realism consists of two main concerns: how to understand the meaning of God; and, arising from the first concern, whether theistic religion and spirituality, or religiousness, require a belief in a real, transcendent God, existing independently of religious practice. For *realism* religious belief in God and a religious life rooted in religious belief require a belief in a transcendent realist God, while for *non-realism* religious commitment and spirituality do not require belief in a transcendent realist God. At times in their everyday life the issue of religious realism can arise for the religious and for those who have a religious background in one of the theistic traditions. It may arise when one hears a person say, "I am religious, but I do not believe in God" or "I believe in God, but not a God up there somewhere."

In contemporary reflection, the issue of religious realism has arisen specifically within and for Christianity. As an issue about the meaning of God, in a superficial way it is like the issue about factual meaning and beliefs about God (on which there were readings in the last chapter), but it is different. The older issue is about the meaning of claims about God, about their factual meaning, and was inspired by a scientific standard. Often this older issue was raised as a challenge that was put to religion, and often it came from those standing outside religion. The issue of religious realism is between those within religion to a great extent. But the issue is about the meaning of God, not the factual meaning of statements about God.

There are three readings in this chapter. In the first Don Cupitt elaborates and defends his non-realist understanding of the meaning of God. In the second D. Z. Phillips develops his own non-realist position from a slightly different perspective. And in the third reading John Hick finds significant points of agreement between non-realism and realism but goes on to argue against the adequacy of religious non-realism on the basis of its flawed position on the "ultimate issue" between non-realism and realism.

DON CUPITT

The Meaning of God

Several contemporary religious thinkers have defended non-realism as a way of understanding God and spiritual commitment. Prominent among them is the religious thinker Don Cupitt, writing out of the Christian tradition. Cupitt is aware of the traditional core concept, but he calls it "metaphysical or realist." (Metaphysics is the area of philosophy that is concerned with the nature of ultimate reality.) Cupitt regards the traditional concept of a transcendent God metaphysical or realist because it postulates a "supernatural" God (above nature) with an "objective" existence (an existence independent of religious practice).

Along with a belief in a realist supernatural God go further metaphysical beliefs about supernatural events, intervention miracles, such as the belief that God parted the Red Sea or the belief that Jesus raised Lazarus from the dead. Such a realist understanding of God misrepresents the very meaning of God, as Cupitt sees it. Cupitt's thesis is that we should "break with" the realist view of God, and with "the old 'literal' personal theism." We should, in his words, "take leave of God" where God is understood as a supernatural personal being "objectively" existing over and above the requirement and the goal of a religious life. However, this does not mean there is no role for God in Cupitt's non-realism. "God is," Cupitt says, "the unifying symbol of the religious life." God is not to be understood as an independently existing being, but as a *symbol* that unifies the religious life, or the religious life of theistic believers. Our reading is a chapter from Cupitt's book *Taking Leave of God*, and the God from whom Cupitt is taking leave is the God of religious realism. In our reading Cupitt develops and defends his non-realist understanding of God.*

The Meaning of God

So what is wrong with the position I have just described as Christian Buddhism? Not much. It shows intellectual virtue in refraining from making unnecessary and unprovable doctrinal claims. But it is incomplete, and I shall certainly be expected to provide a much more detailed and clearer explanation of what 'God' is and the part God plays in the spiritual life than has yet been given. People do feel dissatisfied and cheated when presented with anything other than the metaphysical view of God that comes ultimately from Philo of Alexandria, who lived from about 20 BC to AD 50. Nevertheless, as we have seen, there are various reasons for trying to break with this realist or metaphysical view of God. It seems that we do not have sufficiently good grounds for thinking that such a being exists, there are some doubts about whether he even can exist, he threatens human spiritual and moral autonomy, he threatens the principle of the autonomy of religion, and in any case scripture—the teaching of men like the prophets and Jesus—is pre-philosophical and is by no means unambiguously committed to any one particular view as to the kind of reality that God has. It is sometimes forgotten by philosophers who denounce anti-metaphysical theologies that people contrived to believe in God before the God of the philosophers was invented, people who were quite innocent of platonism or any other species of metaphysics. So maybe some alternative to the realist view of God is possible, and maybe behind the philosophical ways of thinking about God there are more archaic religious ways which can help us in the task of grasping the post-metaphysical meaning of God.

The new religious meaning of God will however not be the same as the old, even though it will learn from it. We said earlier that the original prophetic type of experience of God is today no longer

* From Don Cupitt, *Taking Leave of God*. London: SCM Press, 1980. Reprinted by permission of SCM-Canterbury Press.

available to us. The modern concern for the autonomy of the individual human spirit, and the closely-related concern for the autonomy of purely religious values and claims, make it no longer possible for us to have quite the original prophetic experience of being summoned by an alien almighty and commanding will. The awesome theophany of pure commanding authority seems not to occur now. For us God is no longer a distinct person over against us who authoritatively and by his *ipse dixit* imposes the religious demand upon us. If he did so present himself we would have to reject him. The moral law similarly no longer depends, and cannot depend, upon a divine command for its authority. We recognize it as autonomously authoritative and freely choose to impose it upon ourselves. That is what it is, nowadays, to be a moral agent. Similarly, the religious requirement, that we must become spirit, is no longer now laid upon us by another but is autonomously authoritative. *God* is not an almighty individual other than the religious requirement whose will creates the religious requirement, makes it authoritative and binds it upon us. Rather, God *is* the religious requirement personified, and his attributes are a kind of projection of its main features as we experience them.

For example, to be religious means that one's whole life is as it were subject to a constant scrutiny and under assessment from an absolute point of view that silently records everything and misses nothing. The religious requirement extends to one's whole life and to every detail of one's life. It does not allow one to keep any secret compartments or locked doors. It searches the

heart. And it is of course this feature of the religious demand that has given rise to the traditional affirmation of the omniscience of God.

In metaphysical theology the divine omniscience is understood as if there were a super-intelligence of infinite capacity, its memory stocked with all true propositions: 'The doctrine of omniscience is easy to formulate precisely: it is the doctrine that, for all *p*, if *p*, then God knows that *p*.'[1] But the same writer who so defines God's omniscience is also obliged to admit that this infinite memory-bank (an utterly non-religious idea, obviously) is not God's omniscience as described in the Bible: 'The Old and New Testament passages describing God's omniscience are too poetical and rhetorical for it to be possible to decide how literally their writers intended the idea that God knows everything.'[2]

This still misses the point. The Bible is inexact metaphysics because it is quite unconcerned with metaphysics, but as religion there is nothing wrong with it, for it is always very clear and precise. It makes two points about God's knowledge. First, biblical knowledge is always intensely practical and ethical; it is knowledge of good and evil and knowledge of what to do. God is not interested in accumulating information for its own sake. God's business is with sifting, discerning, weighing in the balance, searching out and discriminating, because God is judge, and judges have to know the whole truth in order to pass just judgment. God is only interested in religiously-relevant knowledge, not knowledge in general. So secondly, God's knowledge is always, and above all, knowledge of mysteries and secrets. It is always knowledge of things

---

[1] Anthony Kenny, *The God of the Philosophers*, Oxford University Press 1979, p. 10.
[2] Ibid., p. 6.

men do not know, do not want to know, do not want to become publicly known, or do not yet know.

We can grasp the point here if we ask ourselves why the Bible never represents God as knowing what everybody knows, or what is manifestly and publicly obvious. Why is God interested only in what is hidden? To a theological realist this must surely convey a rather quaint impression of a snooper or busybody; but no, that is not the point. The point is that the religious requirement is for complete spiritual integrity, for purity of heart and for an entire change of life. Nothing can be kept secret or withheld from it. It is precisely what I have most carefully hidden and have kept most deeply buried that the religious requirement insists on bringing to light. I do not begin to be truly religious until I have faced things that I have hidden even from myself and quite forgotten; and in that sense the religious requirement seems to be omniscient, for it searches the heart and knows me better than I know myself. It breaks down barriers to self-knowledge that I have erected as internal defences within myself. For what the religious requirement exposes and brings to light is always bad news. Hence it is spoken of as judging us and condemning us.

How does this happen? I am capable of being religious and recognizing the authority of the religious requirement insofar as I have attained some modest degree of self-awareness. The natural man's self-awareness, self-criticism and self-mastery are very imperfect indeed, but even such as they are they give him some small measure of transcendence of his fate. He is no longer merely as one of the beasts that perish. He can begin to think himself and his relation to his own existence, and this very modest power to know, criticize and change himself enables him to recognize the religious

requirement as demanding and promising a complete and final knowledge, criticism and transformation of himself through which alone he can attain complete emancipation from fate—in a word, salvation. But the modest measure of self-knowledge that he has already got has been deeply influenced by his wishes. It is highly selective and, worse than that, distorted. It is a kind of idealized, propagandist and self-deceiving self-image, a false ego with a good deal of wounded vanity, resentment, fear and so on built into it. Into my natural self-understanding I build, for example, a theory of why it is that other people do not yet recognize my merits as they ought to do.

Given all this, which is disagreeably familiar and upon which it would be superfluous to dwell at present, the religious requirement must be experienced as condemnation before it can be experienced as salvation; it has to take us apart before it can remake us. So I have as it were to cast myself upon its mercy. Is this a reprehensible surrender of autonomy, a case of grovelling before something on no better grounds than that it is bigger, more knowledgeable and more powerful than I am? No, for the religious requirement is not an objectively-existing individual being quite distinct from myself. It is a judgment upon myself and a way to salvation that I have freely invoked upon myself and for myself. In one of its more demythologizing moments, the Fourth Gospel itself recognizes that we bring judgment upon ourselves. That is true, and more so than most people think.

The religious requirement is not heteronomy, in the sense of being an odious subjection to the will of another such as is incompatible with the dignity of a conscious rational self. It is true that I cast myself on God's mercy, knowing that the false self I have made of myself must die before I can attain my spiritual destiny. But I do not suppose God to be an objective individual over and above the religious requirement. The religious requirement has been radically internalized and made my own, so that *I* will its judgment upon myself.

But if the religious requirement is not heteronomy, neither is it a way of vulgar self-affirmation. On the contrary, it is the way of the cross and demands the surrender of everything. It is true that I know I can achieve my spiritual destiny just because I am *capax dei*, that is, capable of recognizing and laying upon myself the religious demand. But there is no vulgar self-affirmation here, for my spiritual destiny is precisely to achieve perfect disinterestedness, and a kind of selfhood so different from my present natural ego that by present standards it seems almost like egolessness, for it is perfectly non-acquisitive, non-defensive, self-communicating and free. Such a spiritual objective is neither heteronomous nor vulgarly egoistic and man-centred.

And God is not only the requirement personified, but also the goal personified. When we choose God we choose a demand upon ourselves which is *a priori* and overriding, namely the demand that we shall become fully individuated, free, responsive and purely-spiritual subjects. God is that, and when we have become what is demanded of us we are united with God. Then we are spirit as God is spirit.

What does it mean to say that God is spirit? Originally spirit was a power or activity. It was thought of somewhat as a totally unscientific person might think of wind or electricity. It was an invisible pervasive sacred force that might enter people and cause them to act, for good or ill, in ways outside their ordinary range of behaviour. So spirit was thought of as supernatural because people under

its influence surpass themselves, and in connection with its presence words like inspiration, grace, possession and charisma were used. The metaphors are physical: spirit enters people rather as air enters their lungs or water goes down their throats, and those who are filled with spirit are much more than usually roused, active, excitable, energetic, talented and commanding.

Two things follow from this. The first is that it is not quite correct to speak of spirit merely as a capacity, for one ought to add that it is an *extraordinary* capacity of persons. Because it is extraordinary it is portrayed mythologically as a force or energy that is poured into a person from outside him. It is not 'literally' that, for spirit is not any empirically-detectable physical energy. I have briefly defined it elsewhere as 'the power of transcendence'. More fully, spirit is the capacity to exceed one's natural capacities, the power of self-knowledge and self-transcendence. Spirit is that we can wholly surpass ourselves, which is why Kierkegaard can call spirit a relation, a way in which the self relates itself to itself. What this means is perhaps best shown by contrasting it with the way an animal lives, for an animal lives immersed in its own nature and acts out its own nature; it simply is itself and is not at any remove from itself. It is soulish and it does have intra-natural freedom to explore, to learn and so on; but it does not have freedom from nature and so it does not transcend nature through self-transcendence, for it just is identical with itself. It has intra-natural freedom to act within the limits of its own natural capacities, but it does not have supernatural freedom, the capacity to exceed its natural capacities, for only a person, a being that can become spirit, has that.

Secondly, if spirit is a supernatural capacity (namely the capacity entirely to exceed one's natural capacities, the power of self-transcendence) are there any beings who are purely spirits—just spiritual, so that their being spirit is their essence?

It is very difficult to see how this can be so. The difficulty is rather like that which one feels over Aristotle's God, who was supposed to be purely self-absorbed self-thinking thought. There is nothing for such a being to think, nothing indeed for such a being to be, for how can a being be nothing but its own—inevitably contentless—thought of itself? The idea is surely as empty as St Thomas' doctrine that God is his own existence because what God is is merely that God is. Similarly, how can an individual being be nothing but its own relation of transcendence to itself? There is nothing for it to transcend. Surely only a being that is already something else, that already has a nature, can have superadded to it the power of self-transcendence? So the idea of an individual pure spirit appears to be an empty idea. There cannot be a free-floating pure spirit. There can only be something's becoming spirit. So spirit exists only in persons who have become spirit. In them it is self-transcendence, but it is not a transcendent being apart from them.

Yet most of mankind in the past have certainly supposed that there were such things as individual spirit-beings. How could they think such a thing if, as I have suggested, the idea of an individual spirit-being is empty? It seems that when they experienced spiritual powers within themselves they naturally supposed themselves to have been entered by spirit-beings. They personified the new capacities they had acquired. We still have a great many idioms describing states in which one seems to oneself to have an intruding alien personality within oneself. For example:

I don't know what's come over me.
The devil's in me tonight!
I don't know what made me do it.
He fought like a man possessed.

And it is still exceedingly common for people to speak of inspiration, influence, the Muse, grace, possession and so forth. C. G. Jung has described in detail how readily elements in the psyche can take on the aspect of distinct personalities. The literary form of allegory reflects this fact, for allegory personifies forces, virtues and motives that are in dialogue or conflict with each other within the self; though it is noticeable that we today are much less inclined than were our ancestors to think in such ways.

The reason why most of mankind in the past have believed in individual spirits seems then to be that if I am in an unusual mood or feel I am in possession of unusual powers I very readily personify as an intruder or visitant from outside this unusual element within myself. The human mind simply works like that, so much so that many preliterate cultures believed in a plurality of souls in everybody. Today, since the Enlightenment, we are generally less inclined to think in animistic ways, and in particular we are much less inclined to perceive strange elements within ourselves as intrusive spirits, foreign or visitant personal beings possessing us.

With this very important cultural change has come an increased awareness of an ancient difficulty: how can one tell spirits apart? Suppose we grant that there are spirits, that spirits are known by what they do, and that we are justified in blaming evil spirits for unpleasant happenings. Still, so far as anyone can tell, all evil spirits presumably get up to much the same sorts of unpleasant tricks, and nobody I think claims that you can learn to distinguish the handiwork of individual evil spirits. So how could we ever hope to be able to tell one spirit from another? Is there, for example, one big Devil or can we discriminate many little demons? One old answer was to the effect that spirits have names, and you can identify an individual spirit by pronouncing the correct name, that is, the one that you find gives you power over that individual demon, or wins you the favour of that individual deity. But I think no one will seriously propose that solution now, and the general problem of identifying spirits applies to all classes of disembodied persons or quasi-personal beings whether they be angels, demons, the souls of the dead or gods. To complete this argument, if we cannot see how we could ever reliably tell them apart, how can we be justified in claiming that there actually are distinct individual spirit-beings? We are making a claim that we can never substantiate nor put to practical use.

We have been discussing the meaning of spirit and what it might mean to say that God is spirit, and we have reached the apparently paradoxical and disappointing conclusion that spirit is only a capacity of persons (a capacity to exceed one's capacities, a capacity of complete self-knowledge and self-transcendence) and that—at least, so far as we are concerned—it does not seem to make sense to suppose that there can exist a being that is pure spirit and nothing else. For how can there be a pure subsistent relation of transcending without any 'matter' or nature that is transcended? It seems not to make sense to say that the transcending *is* the nature. So it appears that we are forced back to the point from which we began, namely that for us there is no god but the religious requirement: the imperative *Become spirit!* is the presence of God within us, and for us it is God, it is the goal as well as the requirement. For the requirement, as it bears upon us, awakens divine spirituality within us and so brings about the indwelling of the divine spirit—not as a distinct substance but as a metaphorical way of speaking about those supernatural capacities.

This is not as strange as it may seem, for it is after all the teaching of the prophets. They held that to know the divine requirement and to have internalized it *is* to know God. For us human beings there is no knowledge of God but the knowledge of the requirement, and for the prophets it was a blessed, longed-for state of affairs that one should have the divine requirement written within one's heart as an immanent or internalized commandment. Thus to have the divine law written within one's heart, they declared, would be to have the divine spirit poured out within oneself, it would be to have God living within one's heart. For them the radical internalization of religious realities and of the religious demand which I have been describing—and which the reader has doubtless been thinking to be some sort of reductionism, some sort of diminished version of religious realities—for them all this was the goal of religious development, because only along these lines can heteronomy or alienation between God and man be overcome. The objectified law written on tablets of stone had proved a failure and must be replaced by a new mode of knowledge of the divine will in which the way the divine requirement constrains us becomes so fully internalized that it becomes a demand that we make upon ourselves. My will and God's will coincide.

Now we run into the familiar paradox which has become such a feature of the religious debate in modern times, and I shall state it in the baldest form:

Preacher: You must internalize!
Philosopher: Internalization is atheism!

In a word, religion moves by its own inner momentum towards a condition which the philosophers consider to be atheism. In this way it seems to some shrewd outsiders that religion's inner logic is suicidal.

For at the heart of any great religious tradition will be found the insistence that the self can only attain its fullest emancipation and spiritual liberation by radically internalizing religious objects and themes. To use Christian language, it will be said that, merely as objective historical data, Christ's birth and death have no saving power and are of no religious interest. They become divine and saving only in their subjective appropriation, as Christ is born in me, dies in me, rises in me. Subjectivity is the only true divinity, for only as I take religious realities to heart and make them wholly my own do I discover what religious truth is. And the specifically religious requirement is just this demand, that I shall achieve spiritual liberation by wholly internalizing religious objects such as God, Christ, the spirit and so on. It is only by internalizing religious ideals that I can attain them.

Although this theme has been expressed with the most outstanding force by Luther, Kierkegaard and some of their modern followers, it has always been present in the tradition. It is implicit in the Jewish prophets' hope, explicit in Paul's Christ-mysticism, and a constant topic of devotional writers. If theology takes it seriously, then theology must shift from an objective to a subjective and internalized interpretation of Christian doctrines. Then it is that complaints of reductionism and atheism begin to be made.

There is no way of avoiding this vulnerable position. It is too deeply rooted in scripture and the tradition. For the law, the prophets and the psalmist tells us not to worship idols and not to rely upon any objective expression or sign of God's reality and fidelity. One of the worst heresies was considered to be the belief that there can be theoretical knowledge of God. In opposition to it the mainstream of tradition said that faith in God is a cleaving to the impenetrable divine mystery in non-cognitive practical obedience. The only way to know God was to decide for God and to obey God.

So in our argument we have run pretty close to the old doctrine. 'So far as you are concerned', the prophets said, 'there is no knowledge of God but the doing of the will of God.' They had faintly absurd ideas of how to ascertain God's will—you inquired of Yahweh by means of an ephod, or Urim and Thummim, or an entranced holy man—and I have replaced the expression 'the will of God' by 'the religious requirement'. But the teaching comes out much the same. There is so far as we are concerned no God but the religious requirement, the choice of it, the acceptance of its demand and the liberating self-transcendence it brings about in us.

Is that atheism? How does it differ from the old doctrine? I think it will be said that there is a crucial difference over the question of the personality of God, the grace of God, the divine initiative and the divine love. For often in the old 'literal' personal theism God's will was disclosed, God's judgment fell and God's blessing was bestowed *ad hoc*. You could almost say God improvised, made up his own mind on the spur of the moment and was subject to fits of moodiness, savagery and tender mercy. Such a God was not dull to live with. He was exuberantly and outrageously 'personal'. By contrast, the religious requirement is an impersonal categorically-binding unconditional principle against which we bounce ourselves, and which breaks and remakes us simply by being itself so utterly unyielding. It is the immutability of God, his eternal silent waiting without batting an eyelid, that forces us to confess everything. What an interrogator! He does not lift a finger and yet he gets everything he wants.

Yes, there *is* considerable change here, and it is of course the changeover from a descriptive to an expressive use of religious language. I am religious, I have freely chosen to live under the religious requirement, and it is in fact highly dramatic so to live, but the drama has become internalized. In the Old Testament it was God who appeared to be posturing dramatically, and the believer hid in the cleft of the rock, kept his head down, remained very still and hoped that the divine storm would soon blow itself out. Today God keeps still—and I jump. For as we have seen in the course of the discussion, when I bind the religious requirement unconditionally upon myself it so affects me that I quite properly and meaningfully describe it as waiting, as searching me out, as judging and condemning me, as restoring me, freeing me, and as filling me with divine spirit. So the relation to the religious requirement is personal, in that it generates a highly dramatic religious life in the believer. But I do not anthropomorphically project the personal characteristics into the requirement itself, for to do so would be to fall into the pathetic fallacy. So far as we can tell, there is no objective personal God. The old language is still used, but the modern believer should use it expressively rather than descriptively. Again, the modern form of faith has deep roots in the tradition. For it was always said first that God is immutable and impassible and secondly that he cannot be spoken of or known directly but only in terms of his effects. We have taken full account of both these points. So again, if you judge my view atheistic please acknowledge also that it has an approximately equal

claim to be judged orthodox and I shall be satisfied. Meanwhile I maintain that we have no way of judging that there is a god who is a person, who takes the initiative and so forth, for the personal language that we use is expressive of the effect of the religious requirement upon us, and it is mere sentimentality to project it upon that silent, unconditional, unchanging demand. For it seems that the religious requirement in itself is not a personal being but a categorical imperative principle.

Many people claim that God acts. But talk of God's action belongs only within the context of religious language and imagery. Nowadays not even the most conservative believers can claim to be able to deploy the idea of divine action effectively in the fields of natural and social science, politics and economics. Tacitly, the point has been conceded that talk of divine action belongs to the expressive language of religion. For what is the evidence that God acts? People refer to the witness of sacred writings, and to a 'feeling of givenness', that is, the fact that in the drama of the religious life it feels as if we are acted upon by, and as if we find ourselves responding to, the action of Another. That is undoubtedly true, for monotheists at least, but we have seen how this 'feeling' is generated. The religious requirement is itself unconditional, categorical and immutable. It acts only in the pickwickian sense that it produces a whole spectrum of remarkable effects in us just by being itself so unbending. Struggling with its silent unyielding demand—'You must change your whole life. That is the only way to spiritual integrity and freedom from this false and ugly self that you are, for at present your very selfhood is a pack of lies!'—confronted with such a demand and accepting it, we find that it is utterly searching, condemning, reviving, forgiving and gracious. We may well find ourselves using the rich expressive vocabulary of religion in order to tell what is happening to us. We speak of the judgment and mercy of God, and we are right to do so—provided we accept the expressive character of the language. It does not show nothing, as is sometimes mistakenly supposed; but what it shows is not what God is like, but what the human response to God is like. It expresses the structure of the human religious life. God acts only in the sense that he produces effects in us—by being immutable.

We can now summarize the view of God we have arrived at—a view which aims to be non-metaphysical and adequate to religious reality.

God is the central, unifying symbol of the religious life. The unconditional religious requirement ('the will of God') is an autonomous inner imperative that urges us to fulfil our highest possible destiny as spiritual, self-conscious beings emerging from nature. The requirement is *not* purely immanent, because it is not merely a demand that we fulfil the immanent teleology of our own present natures; on the contrary, it requires self-transcendence and victory over nature. Hence the appropriateness of the symbol of a transcendent being who imposes it; and he not only imposes it but also represents the goal towards which it directs us, for God is pictured as being already sovereign over nature ('the creator of the world'), with the highest degree of spirituality and self-awareness ('life, spirit'), freedom and love.

Thus God is both the beginning and the end of the religious life, and the various things that are said of and to God by believers are all rooted in various phases or moments of the inner life. This traditional expression, 'the inner life', is in truth rather misleading; what is meant is that when the religious requirement

imposes upon us its own unconditional authority it plunges us into a kind of mythic drama of considerable violence. That mythic drama is the so-called inner life, and religious language is founded in it. For example, the religious requirement demands an entire change in our whole way of life. Nothing is allowed to escape it. It searches out everything. From this experience is derived talk about the eye of God, and about the omniscience of God.

But much of what the requirement searches out and brings to light is just the material that we would have preferred to keep hidden (God sifts, weighs in the balance and judges). And the call to become spirit, the call to intensified individuality, self-awareness and self-transcendence on the way to perfect emancipation from natural necessity and perfectly disinterested spirituality—this call requires a death and a loss of the old false self. God is experienced as judging and condemning us before he is experienced as bringing us to new life. So the religious demand pushes believers through the ancient psychodrama of the descent into the underworld, the passage through darkness to light, through death to life. Our typical language about God is simply the script for this drama, as the Hebrew psalter makes so clear.

Thus for a monotheist God is that about which the religious life revolves and—to put it another way—the phrase 'the relation to God' encompasses all the vast and turbulent emotional range of the religious life. The religious requirement itself is simply a principle, very like a Kantian categorically-imperative principle, which we are able to recognize in virtue of our capacity for self-transcendence and liberation from natural necessity. It commands us to seek the full completion of something which ordinarily is ours only in a very small and partial way; a completion which in the language of religion is given such names as salvation, eternal life, beatitude and so forth. We use the word 'God' as a comprehensive symbol that incorporates the way the religious demand presents itself to us (God's will), its ideal fulfilment by us (God's essence), and the mythic psychodrama that envelops us on the way (God's action).

Inevitably the question will be put, 'Does God exist outside faith's relation to God, or is the concept of God just a convenient heuristic fiction that regulates the religious life?' The crucial point about this often-asked question[3] is that it is of no religious interest. There cannot be any religious interest in any supposed extra-religious reality of God, and I have argued all along that the religious requirement's authority is autonomous and does not depend upon any external imponent. The authority of the religious requirement has to be autonomous and intrinsic in order that it may be fully internalized, imposed by us freely upon ourselves and made our own.

Why?—Because it is a contradiction to suppose that my highest spiritual freedom could be determined for me from without, and by the act of another. It must be actualized within me through the operation of an autonomous and intrinsically-authoritative principle that commands me to seek it, a principle that I make my own, that I confess as Lord and make the governing principle of my own life. If my salvation is my highest spiritual liberation then the God who gives it and the 'I' who receive it must coincide in the act of realizing it.

So it would seem that religion forbids that there should be any extra-religious reality of God. The most we can say is that it is religiously appropriate to think that there may be beyond the God of religion a transcendent divine mystery witnessed to in various ways by the faith of mankind. But we cannot say anything about it. Any possibility of a non-religious knowledge of this mystery would weaken the stringency and the saving power of the religious requirement. The religious requirement is for the transformation of the. self and not for theoretical or speculative illumination. So no more than the merest chink of openness to the possibility of objective theism is permissible. The traditional emphasis on the negative way, on *agnōsia* or unknowing, was at its best an attempt to inhibit the development of a metaphysical theology and to safeguard the primacy of religion. Today we do not have a well-established metaphysical theology and cannot create one, so we should be glad to be spared the temptation to do so. In practice we have to make do with the use of the word 'God' as an incorporating or unifying symbol connoting the whole of what we are up against in the spiritual life.

D. Z. PHILLIPS

Faith, Scepticism, and Religious Understanding

D. Z. Phillips, a contemporary philosopher who has written extensively about the issues of philosophy of religion, argues in defense of non-realism in "Faith, Scepticism, and Religious Understanding" that religious belief does not involve

---

[3] See Alan Keightley, *Wittgenstein, Grammar and God*, Epworth Press 1976, especially pp. 122ff.

accepting the truth of "there is a God," understood as an existence-claim about an object or being in the universe, that is, a realist God. For Phillips, religious belief does not involve a claim like the claim that there is one more star or planet than we thought. As Phillips says, in accord with Cupitt, "Coming to see that there is a God involves seeing a new meaning in one's life, and being given a new understanding." Taking up religious belief, for Phillips, as for the earlier philosopher, Ludwig Wittgenstein, is taking up a belief that regulates in one's life, affecting one's actions and affections. It is to enter into a form of life, to use Wittgenstein's term, but it is not to make an existence-claim about God. Phillips is not offering a new understanding of the meaning of God, as Cupitt sometimes says he is. Phillips is offering an understanding of ordinary or traditional religious belief in God, or at least of one of its main forms. Whether religious belief is now, as it stands, really non-realist, as Phillips suggests, or alternatively religious believers must "break with" realist belief, as Cupitt says, Phillips would agree with Cupitt that so far as religion is realistic it ceases to be religious. For Cupitt, and for Phillips, spirituality and religious maturity *require* no longer believing in a realist transcendent God.*

Faith, Scepticism, and Religious Understanding

The relation between religion and philosophical reflection needs to be reconsidered. For the most part, in recent philosophy of religion, philosophers, believers, and non-believers alike, have been concerned with discovering *the grounds* of religious belief. Philosophy, they claim, is concerned with reasons; it considers what is to count as good evidence for a belief. In the case of religious beliefs, the philosopher ought to enquire into the reasons anyone could have for believing in the existence of God, for believing that life is a gift from God, or for believing that an action is the will of God. Where can such reasons be found? One class of reasons comes readily to mind. Religious believers, when asked why they believe in God, may reply in a variety of ways. They may say, 'I have

had an experience of the living God', 'I believe on the Lord Jesus Christ', 'God saved me while I was a sinner', or, 'I just can't help believing'. Philosophers have not given such reasons very much attention. The so-called trouble is not so much with the content of the replies as with the fact that the replies are made by believers. The answers come from *within* religion, they presuppose the framework of Faith, and therefore cannot be treated as *evidence* for religious belief. Many philosophers who argue in this way seem to be searching for evidence or reasons for religious beliefs *external* to belief itself. It is assumed that such evidence and reasons would, if found, constitute the grounds of religious belief.

The philosophical assumption behind the ignoring of religious testimony as

* D. Z. Phillips, "Faith, Scepticism, and Religious understanding," from *Faith and Philosophical Enquiry*, edited by D. Z. Phillips. Oxford: Blackwell, 1967. Reprinted by permission of Blackwell Publishing.

begging the question, and the search for external reasons for believing in God, is that one could settle the question of whether there is a God or not without referring to the form of life of which belief in God is a fundamental part. What would it be like for a philosopher to settle the question of the existence of God? Could a philosopher say that he believed that God exists and yet never pray to Him, rebel against Him, lament the fact that he could no longer pray, aspire to deepen his devotion, seek His will, try to hide from Him, or fear and tremble before Him? In short, could a man believe that God exists without his life being touched *at all* by the belief? Norman Malcolm asks with good reason, 'Would a belief that he exists, if it were completely non-affective, really be a belief that he exists? Would it be anything at all? What is "the form of life" into which it would enter? What difference would it make whether anyone did or did not have this belief?'[1]

Yet many philosophers who search for the grounds of religious belief, claim, to their own satisfaction at least, to understand what a purely theoretical belief in the existence of God would be. But the accounts these philosophers give of what religious believers seem to be saying are often at variance with what many believers say, at least, when *they* are not philosophizing. Every student of the philosophy of religion will have been struck by the amount of talking at cross purposes within the subject. A philosopher may say that there is no God, but a believer may reply, 'You are creating and then attacking a fiction. The god whose existence you deny is not the God I believe in.' Another philosopher may say that religion is meaningless, but another believer may reply, 'You say that when applied to God, words such as "exists", "love", "will", etc., do not mean what they signify in certain non-religious contexts. I agree. You conclude from this that religion is meaningless, whereas the truth is that you are failing to grasp the meaning religion has.' Why is there this lack of contact between many philosophers and religious believers? One reason is that many philosophers who do not believe that God exists assume that they know what it means to say that there is a God. Norman Kemp Smith made a penetrating analysis of this fact when commenting on the widespread belief among American philosophers in his day of the uselessness of philosophy of religion.

> . . . those who are of this way of thinking, however they may have thrown over the religious beliefs of the communities in which they have been nurtured, still continue to be influenced by the phraseology of religious devotion—a phraseology which, in its endeavour to be concrete and universally intelligible, is at little pains to guard against the misunderstandings to which it may so easily give rise. As they insist upon, and even exaggerate, the merely literal meaning of this phraseology, the God in whom they have ceased to believe is a Being whom they picture in an utterly anthropomorphic fashion. . . .[2]

The distinction between religious believers and atheistical philosophers is not, of course, as clear-cut as I have suggested. It

[1] 'Is it a Religious Belief that "God Exists"?' in *Faith and the Philosophers*, ed. John Hick, London, 1964, 107.
[2] 'Is Divine Existence Credible?' in *Religion and Understanding*, ed. D. Z. Phillips, Blackwell, 1967, 105–6.

is all too evident in contemporary philosophy of religion that many philosophers who *do* believe in God philosophize about religion in the way which Kemp Smith found to be true of philosophical non-believers. Here, one can say either that their philosophy reflects their belief, in which case they believe in superstition but not in God, or, taking the more charitable view, that they are failing to give a good philosophical account of what they really believe.

Insufficient attention has been paid to the question of what kind of philosophical enquiry the concept of divine reality calls for. Many philosophers assume that everyone knows *what* it means to say that there is a God, and that the only outstanding question is *whether* there is a God. Similarly, it might be thought, everyone knows what it means to say that there are unicorns, although people may disagree over whether in fact there are any unicorns. If there were an analogy between the existence of God and the existence of unicorns, then coming to see that there is a God would be like coming to see that an additional being exists. 'I know what people are doing when they worship,' a philosopher might say. 'They praise, they confess, they thank, and they ask for things. The only difference between myself and religious believers is that I do not believe that there is a being who receives their worship.' The assumption, here, is that the meaning of worship is contingently related to the question whether there is a God or not. The assumption might be justified by saying that there need be no consequences of existential beliefs. Just as one can say, 'There is a planet Mars, but I couldn't care less,' so one can say, 'There is a God, but I couldn't care less.' But

what is one *saying* here when one says that there is a God? Despite the fact that one need take no interest in the existence of a planet, an account could be given of the kind of difference the existence of the planet makes, and of how one could find out whether the planet exists or not. But all this is foreign to the question whether there is a God. That is not something anyone could *find out*. It has been far too readily assumed that the dispute between the believer and the unbeliever is over a *matter of fact*. Philosophical reflection on the reality of God then becomes the philosophical reflection appropriate to an assertion of a matter of fact. I have tried to show that this is a misrepresentation of the religious concept, and that philosophy can claim justifiably to show what is meaningful in religion only if it is prepared to examine religious concepts in the contexts from which they derive their meaning.[3]

A failure to take account of the above context has led some philosophers to ask religious language to satisfy criteria of meaningfulness alien to it. They say that religion must be rational if it is to be intelligible. Certainly, the distinction between the rational and the irrational must be central in any account one gives of meaning. But this is not to say that there is a paradigm of rationality to which all modes of discourse conform. A necessary prolegomenon to the philosophy of religion, then, is to show the diversity of criteria of rationality; to show that the distinction between the real and the unreal does not come to the same thing in every context. If this were observed, one would no longer wish to construe God's reality as being that of an existent among existents, an object among objects.

---

[3] See pages 1–5 of the previous chapter.

Coming to see that there is a God is not like coming to see that an additional being exists. If it were, there would be an extension of one's knowledge of facts, but no extension of one's understanding. Coming to see that there is a God involves seeing a new meaning in one's life, and being given a new understanding. The Hebrew-Christian conception of God is not a conception of a being among beings. Kierkegaard emphasized the point when he said bluntly, 'God does not exist. He is eternal.'[4]

The distinction between eternity and existence has been ignored by many philosophers of religion, and as a result they have singled out particular religious beliefs for discussion, divorcing them from the context of belief in God. Alasdair MacIntyre has pointed out the importance of recognizing the need, not simply to discuss specific religious utterances, but to ask why such utterances are called religious in the first place.

Those linguistic analysts who have turned their attention to theology have begun to examine in detail particular religious utterances and theological concepts. This examination of the logic of religious language has gone with a great variety of religious attitudes on the part of the philosophers concerned. Some have been sceptics, others believers. But what their enterprise has had in common is an examination of *particular* religious forms of speech and utterance, whether such examination has been presented as part of an argument for

or as part of an argument against belief. What such examinations may omit is a general consideration of what it means to call a particular assertion or utterance part of a religious belief as distinct from a moral code or a scientific theory.[5]

In his more recent work in the philosophy of religion, MacIntyre has said that the above distinction buys a position at the price of emptiness,[6] but I think his earlier view is the correct one. It stresses the artificiality of separating the love, mercy, or forgiveness of God from His nature. One cannot understand what praising, confessing, thanking, or asking mean in worship apart from belief in an eternal God. The eternity of the Being addressed determines the meaning of all these activities. One implication of this fact is that philosophers who do not see anything in belief in God can no longer think of their rejection as the denial of something *with which they are familiar*. Discovering that belief in God is meaningful is not like establishing that something is the case within a universe of discourse with which we are already familiar. On the contrary, it is to discover that there *is* a universe of discourse we had been unaware of. The flattering picture that the academic philosopher may have of himself as possessing the key to reality has to be abandoned. The philosopher, like anyone else, may fail to understand what it means to believe in an eternal God.

In saying that one must take account of the concept of the eternal if one wishes

---

[4] *Concluding Unscientific Postscript*, 296.
[5] 'The Logical Status of Religious Belief', in *Metaphysical Beliefs*, ed. A. MacIntyre, London, 1957, 172.
[6] See 'Is Understanding Religion Compatible with Believing?' in *Faith and the Philosophers*, ed. John Hick, London, 1964.

to understand various religious activities, I realize that I am laying myself open to all kinds of misunderstandings. Some religious believers, when they have wanted to turn aside the philosopher's questions, have said, 'Finite understanding cannot understand the eternal,' or something similar. This is not what I am saying. There is a proper place to say such things, that God is the inexpressible, for example, but that place is within religious belief. These are religious utterances whose meaning is seen in the role they play in the lives of believers. Sometimes, however, the utterances are used as a form of protectionism against intellectual enquiry. They began as religious utterances, but end up as pseudo-epistemological theories.[7] When this happens, the philosopher's censure is deserved. In saying that human understanding cannot fathom the eternal, the believer is claiming that there is some higher order of things that transcends all human discourse, that religion expresses 'the nature of things'. In saying this, the believer falsifies the facts. Such a position involves upholding what John Anderson calls 'a hierarchical doctrine of reality'. Anderson has a powerful argument against this brand of religious apologetics. He says that to speak in this way

> . . . is to speak on behalf of the principle of authority—and so again (whatever the actual power may be that is thus metaphysically bolstered up) to support a low way of living. It is low, in particular, because it is anti-intellectual, because it is necessarily dogmatic. Some account can be given of the relation of a particular

'rule' or way of behaving to a certain way of life, but it can have no demonstrable relation to 'the nature of things'. To say that something is required by the nature of things is just to say that it is required—to say, without reason, that it 'is to be done'; and, as soon as any specification is attempted, the whole structure breaks down. If, for example, we are told to do something because God commands us to do so, we can immediately ask why we should do what God commands—and any intelligible answer brings us back to *human* relationships, to the struggle between opposing movements.[8]

I should like to make it quite clear that I agree with Anderson in the above criticism. In speaking of religion as turning away from the temporal towards the eternal, I am not putting forward any kind of epistemological thesis. On the contrary, I am referring to the way in which the concept of the eternal does play a role in very many human relationships. I am anxious to show that religion is not some kind of technical discourse or esoteric pursuit cut off from the ordinary problems and perplexities, hopes, and joys which most of us experience at some time or other. If it were, it would not have the importance it does have for so many people. By considering one example in detail—namely, eternal love or the love of God—I shall try to show what significance it has in human experience, the kind of circumstances which occasion it, and the kind of human predicament it answers. By so doing I hope to illustrate how seeing that there is a God

[7] See ch. V.

[8] 'Art and Morality', *Australasian Journal of Psychology and Philosophy*, XIX (December, 1941), 256–7.

in this context is synonymous with seeing the possibility of eternal love.[9]

Let me begin by speaking of a distinction with which we are all familiar: the distinction between *mine* and *yours*. The distinction is relevant to the concept of justice. If I take what is yours, or if you take what is mine, justice is thereby transgressed against. Our relationships with other people are pervaded by a wide range of rights and obligations, many of which serve to emphasize the distinction between *mine* and *yours*. But all human relationships are not like this. In erotic love and in friendship, the distinction between *mine* and *yours* is broken down. The lovers or the friends may say, 'All I have is his, and what is his is mine.' Kierkegaard says that the distinction between *mine* and *yours* has been transformed by a relationship in which the key term is *ours*. Nevertheless, he goes on to show that the *mine/yours* distinction is not completely transformed by such relationships, since the *ours* now functions as a new *mine* for the partners in the relationships. The distinguishing factor in the *mine/yours* distinction is now the relation of erotic love or friendship as opposed to the self-love which prevailed previously. *Mine* and *yours* now refer to those who are within and to those who are outside the specific relationship.

Now, Christianity wishes to speak of a kind of love which is such that no man is excluded from it. It calls this love 'love of one's neighbour'. What is more, it claims that this love is internally related to the love of God; that is, that without knowing what this love is, one cannot know what the love of God is either. An attempt to elucidate what is meant by love of the neighbour will therefore be an attempt to elucidate what is meant by the love of God.

If one considers self-love in its simplest form—namely, as the desire to possess the maximum of what one considers to be good for oneself—it is easy enough to imagine conditions in which such love could be thwarted. War, famine, or some other natural disaster might upset the normal conditions in which rights and obligations operate. Even given such conditions, the self-lover's ambitions may be thwarted by the greater ingenuity of his competitors. Sooner or later he may be forced to realize that the minimum rather than the maximum is going to be his lot. Self-love might be called temporal love in so far as it depends on states of affairs contingently related to itself. If a man's life revolves around self-love, it is obvious that he is forever dependent on the way things go, since it is the way things go that determines whether his self-love is satisfied or not.

It might be thought that erotic love and friendship avoid the predicament of self-love outlined above. The lovers or the friends may say to one another, 'Come what may, we still have each other.' Yet, such reliance shows that this love too is temporal; it depends on certain states of affairs being realized. To begin with, the point of such love depends on the existence of *the other*. Often, when the lovers or the friends love each other very much, the death of the beloved can rob life of its meaning; for what is love without the beloved? Again, erotic love and friendship depend on the unchangeability of the beloved. But the beloved may change. Friendship can cool, and love can fade. If the relationship is such that it depended on reciprocation,

[9] Anyone acquainted with Kierkegaard's *Works of Love* will recognize in what follows how dependent I am on the second part of that work.

then a change in the beloved or in the friend may rob it of its point. So although erotic love and friendship are far removed from self-love, they too are forms of temporal love in so far as they are dependent on how things go.

Temporal love, then, is marked by certain characteristics: it depends on how things go, it may change, and it may end in failure. Eternal love, it is said, is not dependent on how things go, it cannot change, and it cannot suffer defeat. One must not think that this contrast presents the believer with an either/or. He is not asked to choose between loving God on the one hand and loving the loved one on the other. What he is asked to do is not to love the loved one in such a way that the love of God becomes impossible. The death of the beloved must not rob life of its meaning, since for the believer the meaning of life is found in God. The believer claims that there is a love that will not let one go whatever happens. This is the love of God, the independence of which from what happens is closely bound up with the point of calling it eternal.

The object of Christian love is the neighbour. But who is the neighbour? The neighbour is every man. The obligation to love the neighbour does not depend on the particularity of the relationship, as in the case of the love which exists between parents and children, lovers or friends. The neighbour is not loved because of his being a parent, lover, or friend, but simply because of his being. In relation to the agent, the love takes the form of self-renunciation. In this self-renunciation, man discovers the Spirit of God. Consider how love of the neighbour exhibits the three characteristics I mentioned earlier: independence of the

way things go, unchangeability, and immunity from defeat. Kierkegaard brings out the contrast between love of one's neighbour on the one hand, and erotic love and friendship on the other, in these terms.

The beloved can treat you in such a way that he is lost to you, and you can lose a friend, but whatever a neighbour does to you, you can never lose him. To be sure, you can also continue to love your beloved and your friend no matter how they treat you, but you cannot truthfully continue to call them beloved and friend when they, sorry to say, have really changed. No change, however, can take your neighbour from you, for it is not your neighbour who holds you fast—it is your love which holds your neighbour fast.[10]

For someone with eyes only for the prudential, and common-sense considerations, the love which Kierkegaard is talking about seems to lead inevitably to self-deception, and to a kind of foolishness. On the contrary, Kierkegaard argues, eternal love is precisely the only kind of love which can never deceive one. After a certain stage of unrequited love, no one could be blamed for saying, 'The lover has deceived me.' It becomes intelligible and justifiable to say this because the love in question does not have much point without some degree of reciprocation. At first sight it looks as if the same conclusions apply to love of one's neighbour. But eternal love believes all things, and yet is never deceived! Ordinarily speaking, we say that only a fool believes all things; only a man who ignores the odds could be so stupid. Yet, Christianity

[10] *Op. cit.*, 76.

says that eternal love cannot be deceived, for if a believer is wrong about a man but continues to love him, in what sense is he deceived? True, one can enumerate all the ways in which obvious deceptions have taken place: loans unreturned, promises broken, trusts betrayed, etc., but the believer continues to love the neighbour despite all this. Those who see little in the love of the neighbour will say, especially if the believer is reduced to a state which many would call ruin, that the believer has lost all. On the contrary, Kierkegaard tells us, the believer, in the act of self-renunciation, possesses all; he possesses love. To possess this love is to possess God. Indeed, the only way in which the believer can be deceived is by ceasing to love. Ordinarily, when we say, 'I shall show no more love towards him,' we envisage the loss as suffered by the person who is the object of one's love. But if the believer says, 'I shall love the neighbour no longer,' he is the victim of deception, since the loss of loving is his loss too. Kierkegaard brings this point out very clearly:

> When someone says, 'I have given up my love for this man,' he thinks that it is this person who loses, this person who was the object of his love. The speaker thinks that he himself possesses his love in the same sense as when one who has supported another financially says, 'I have quit giving assistance to him.' In this case the giver keeps for himself the money which the other previously received, he who is the loser, for the giver is certainly far from losing by this financial shift. But it is not like this with love; perhaps the one who was the object of love does lose, but he who 'has given up his love for this man' is the loser. Maybe he does not detect this himself; perhaps he does not detect that the language mocks him, for he says explicitly, 'I have given up my love.' But if he has given up his love, he has then ceased to be loving. True enough, he adds 'my love for this man', but this does not help when love is involved, although in money matters one can manage things this way without loss to oneself. The adjective *loving* does not apply to me when I have given up my love 'for this man'—alas, even though I perhaps imagined that he was the one who lost. It is the same with despairing over another person; it is oneself who is in despair.[11]

In this way, Kierkegaard illustrates the truth that for the believer, love itself is the real object of the relationship between himself and another person. This love is the Spirit of God, and to possess it is to walk with God. Once this is realized, one can see how love and understanding are equated in Christianity. To know God is to love Him. There is no theoretical understanding of the reality of God.

> If anyone thinks he is a Christian and yet is indifferent towards his being a Christian, then he really is not one at all. What would we think of a man who affirmed that he was in love and also that it was a matter of indifference to him?[12]

'But, so far,' the non-believer might complain, 'you have simply concealed the advantage entailed in religion, namely,

[11] *Ibid.*, 239–40.   [12] *Ibid.*, 42.

God's love for the sinner. Is not this the reason for love of the neighbour? Unless one loves the neighbour, God will not love one.' There is truth in this *unless*, but not as conceived in the above objection. The love of the neighbour is not the means whereby a further end is realized— namely, one's own forgiveness. On the contrary, there is an internal relation between forgiving another and being forgiven oneself. I cannot hope to emulate Kierkegaard's analysis of this religious truth, so I must ask the reader to forgive a final quotation of two passages where his analysis is particularly forceful:

> When we say, 'Love saves from death,' there is straightway a reduplication in thought: the lover saves another human being from death, and in entirely the same or yet in a different sense he saves himself from death. This he does at the same time; it is one and the same; he does not save the other at one moment and at another save himself, but in the moment he saves the other he saves himself from death. Only love never thinks about the latter, about saving oneself, about acquiring confidence itself; the lover in love thinks only about giving confidence and saving another from death. But the lover is not thereby forgotten. No, he who in love forgets himself, forgets his sufferings in order to think of another's, forgets all his wretchedness in order to think of another's, forgets what he himself loses in order lovingly to consider another's loss, forgets his advantage in order lovingly to look after another's advantage: truly, such a person is not forgotten. There is one who thinks of him, God in

heaven; or love thinks of him. God is love, and when a human being because of love forgets himself, how then should God forget him! No, while the lover forgets himself and thinks of the other person, God thinks of the lover. The self-lover is busy; he shouts and complains and insists on his rights in order to make sure he is not forgotten—and yet he is forgotten. But the lover, who forgets himself, is remembered by love. There is one who thinks of him, and in this way it comes about that the lover gets what he gives.[13]

And again:

> '*Forgive, and you will also be forgiven.*' Meanwhile, one might nevertheless manage to understand these words in such a way that he imagined it possible to receive forgiveness without his forgiving. Truly this is a misunderstanding. Christianity's view is: forgiveness *is* forgiveness: your forgiveness is your forgiveness; your forgiveness of another is your own forgiveness: the forgiveness which you give you receive, not contrariwise that you give the forgiveness which you receive. It is as if Christianity would say: pray to God humbly and believing in your forgiveness, for he really is compassionate in such a way as no human being is; but if you will test how it is with respect to the forgiveness, then observe yourself. If honestly before God you wholeheartedly forgive your enemy (but remember that if you do, God sees it), then you dare hope also for your forgiveness, for it is one and the same. God forgives you neither more nor less nor otherwise than *as* you forgive

13 *Ibid.*, 262.

your trespassers. It is only an illusion to imagine that one himself has forgiveness, although one is slack in forgiving others.[14]

My purpose in discussing the Christian concept of love was to show how coming to see the possibility of such love amounts to the same thing as coming to see the possibility of belief in God. As I said earlier, to know God is to love Him, and the understanding which such knowledge brings is the understanding of love. Belief, understanding, and love can all be equated with each other in this context. There are, however, certain objections which can be made against this conclusion. Before ending, I want to consider one of the strongest of these made recently by Alasdair MacIntyre:

> And if the believer wishes to he can always claim that we can only disagree with him because we do not understand him. But the implications of this defence of belief are more fatal to it than any attack could be.[15]

One of the fatal implications of identifying understanding and believing, according to MacIntyre, is that one can no longer give an intelligible account of a rejection of religious belief. MacIntyre says that the Protestant who claims that grace is necessary before one can possess religious understanding is soon convicted of paradox.

> For the Protestant will elsewhere deny what is entailed by his position, namely that nobody ever rejects Christianity (since anyone who thinks he has rejected it must have

lacked saving grace and so did not understand Christianity and so in fact rejected something else).[16]

Does MacIntyre's point hold for any identification of understanding and believing? I suggest not. To begin with, there is a perfectly natural use of the word *rejection* which is connected with the inability of the person who rejects to make any sense of what is rejected. I can see no objection to saying that the man who says that religion means nothing to him rejects the claims of religion on his life. Apparently, when Oscar Wilde was accused of blasphemy during his trial, he replied 'Sir, blasphemy is a word I never use.' Wilde is rejecting a certain way of talking. Similarly, the man who says, 'Religion is mumbo-jumbo as far as I am concerned,' is making a wholesale rejection of a way of talking or a way of life. That way of talking and that way of life mean nothing to him, but this does not mean that he cannot reject them.

On the other hand, I agree with MacIntyre that there are difficulties involved in the view I wish to maintain if the rejection of religion in question is not the rejection of the meaningless, but rebellion against God. Camus says of the rebel:

> The rebel defies more than he denies. Originally, at least, he does not deny God, he simply talks to Him as an equal. But it is not a polite dialogue. It is a polemic animated by the desire to conquer.[17]

But if the rebel knows God and yet defies Him, how can one say that to know God is to love Him? Clearly, some kind

[14] *Ibid.*, 351–2.
[15] 'Is Understanding Religion Compatible with Believing?', *Faith and the Philosophers*, 133.
[16] *Ibid.*, 116.   [17] *The Rebel*, Peregrine Book edn., trans. by Anthony Bower, 31.

of modification of my thesis is called for. I agree. But what is not called for is a denial of the identification of belief and understanding in religion. The fact of rebellion makes one think otherwise because of a false and unnecessary assimilation of 'I believe in God' to 'I believe in John'. Belief in God has a wider range of application than belief in another person. This point has been made very clearly by Norman Malcolm:

> Belief in a person primarily connotes trust or faith: but this is not so of belief in God. A man could properly be said to believe in God whose chief attitude towards God was *fear*. ('A sword is sent upon you, and who may turn it back?') But if you were enormously afraid of another human being you could not be said to believe in him. At least you would not believe in him *in so far* as you were afraid of him: whereas the fear of God is one form of belief in Him.
>
> I am suggesting that *belief-in* has a wider meaning when God is the object of it than when a human being is. Belief in God encompasses not only trust but also awe, dread, dismay, resentment, and perhaps even hatred. Belief in God will involve some affective state or attitude, having God as its object, and those attitudes could vary from reverential love to rebellious rejection.[18]

I should still want to argue, however, that the love of God is the primary form of belief in God if only because the intelligibility of all the other attitudes Malcolm mentions is logically dependent on it. The rebel must see the kind of relationship God asks of the believer

before he can reject and defy it. He sees the story from the inside, but it is not a story that captivates him. The love of God is active in his life, but in him it evokes hatred. To say that he does not believe in God is absurd, for whom does he hate if not God?

Similar difficulties to those mentioned by MacIntyre might be thought to arise in giving an account of seeking for God. If one must believe before one can know God, how can one know that it is God one is seeking for? The answer to this difficulty has been given by Pascal: 'Comfort yourself, you would not seek me if you had not found me.' One must not think of belief in God as an all-or-nothing affair. Whether the love of God means anything in a man's life can be assessed, not simply by his attainments, but also by his aspirations. So even if a man does not actually love God, his understanding of what it means to love God can be shown by his aspirations towards such love.

On the other hand, it would be a mistake to conclude that in the absence of religious attainments only religious aspirations could be the sign that religion held some meaning for a person. We have seen already in the case of the rebel that belief in God need not entail a worshipful attitude on the part of the believer. Neither need the believer aspire to attain love of God. On the contrary, he may want to flee from it. Instead of feeling sad because he spurns God's love, he may hate the fact that he cannot rid his life of God. If someone were to say to him, 'You do not believe in God', he might reply, 'How can you say that when God will not leave me alone?'

What, then, are our conclusions? The assertion that to know God is to love Him

---

[18] *Op. cit.*, 106–7.

is false if it is taken to imply that everyone who believes in God loves Him. What it stresses, quite correctly, is that there is no theoretical knowledge of God. As Malcolm said, 'belief in God involves some affective state or attitude'. I think that love of God is fundamental in religion, since all other attitudes can be explained by reference to it. I believe that Kierkegaard says somewhere that in relation to God there are only lovers—happy or unhappy—but lovers. The unhappy or unruly lover has an understanding of what it means to believe in God as well as the happy lover. The man who construes religious belief as a theoretical affair distorts it. Kierkegaard emphasizes that there is no understanding of religion without passion. And when the philosopher understands that, *his* understanding of religion is incompatible with scepticism.

JOHN HICK

from Contemporary Non-Realist Religion

Perhaps the most prominent defender of the realist perspective is John Hick. Hick allows that realism and non-realism can agree on several significant points, but finally, he argues, non-realism is deeply flawed. In Hick's view, the "ultimate issue" between non-realism and realism is about nothing less than the nature of our universe. For non-realism, the physical universe is not created by any more ultimate divine power, religious values originate with human beings and do not reflect an objective structure of the universe, and no supernatural beings exist except as ideas in our minds. If non-realism is correct about these points, however, as Hick sees it, it is "bad news" religiously for most of humanity. It is because, while salvation as spiritual attainment will be possible for some, salvation will be denied to most. Salvation in non-realist terms will be attainable to those who, as Cupitt would say, internalize the religious requirement, and so strive toward spiritual transformation. But this will be only an elite few, Hick points out. At the same time, if non-realism is the right view, salvation will not be attained by those who are incapable of following the religious requirement in this life, and it will be denied to all those who have lived and died without attaining this spiritual goal. The message of the great religious traditions is very different, Hick maintains. Their message is profoundly optimistic, for it holds out the hope of spiritual attainment for all human beings in a life to come if not in this life. However, Hick argues, this optimism of the great religious traditions rests upon the realist belief that the universe has an objective structure that allows this final attainment for humanity in general. While the specific realist belief varies from tradition to tradition, for the monotheistic traditions it is the belief in an objectively existing God who is caring, loving, and compassionate, and whose mercy extends to all.

Our reading consists of three sections from a chapter of *An Interpretation of Religion*.

From John Hick, "Contemporary Non-Realist Religion," Chap. 12 of *An Interpretation of Religion*. New Haven and London: Yale University Press, 1989. Reproduced with permission of Palgrave Macmillan.

III

Phillips and Cupitt

D. Z. Phillips' main philosophical inspiration comes from the later writings of Wittgenstein. Whether Wittgenstein's own intention, in his occasional non-systematic references to religion, was non-realist can be and has been argued both ways;[4] and since this is an historical question which does not affect the issue before us I shall not attempt to settle it. Regardless, then, of whether one thinks that Wittgenstein would have endorsed his proposals[5] Phillips has provided a clear and eloquent version of a non-realist interpretation of religious discourse.[6] I shall use as a representative sample his analysis of language about death and immortality. '[It] would be foolishness', he says, 'to speak of eternal life as some kind of appendage to human existence, something that happens *after* human life on earth is over.' For 'Eternal life is the reality of goodness, that in terms of which human life is to be assessed' (Phillips 1970, 48). Again, 'Eternity is not *more* life, but this life seen under certain moral and religious modes of thought' (49). Thus 'Questions about the immortality of the soul are seen not to be questions concerning the extent of a man's life . . . but questions concerning the kind of life a man is living' (49).[7]

Phillips amplifies this theme in ways which we need not pursue here, even finding a use for the notions of prayers for the dead (57) and—a *tour de force* indeed—of prayers by the dead for the living (58). We are concerned here with his central view that language which appears to be about unending life is really a coded language about our present spiritual states. Here two questions have to be distinguished. One is the factual question whether human personality does or does not survive bodily death; and the other concerns the meaning of such religious terms as 'eternal life'.

Given this distinction, one possible 'scenario' is that there is in fact continued consciousness after death, but that 'eternal life' does not refer to this but rather to a limitlessly better quality of existence which may begin now and may have unlimited scope after death. From this point of view the issue is not an eternal quality of life *versus* survival of bodily death. On the contrary it might be that the latter opens up the possibility of eternal life to that majority of human beings who do not seem to have attained it in the present life. However this is not Phillips' own position. He has previously argued (1970, ch. 1) that all conceptions of a continued post-mortem existence are either meaningless or patently false. Accordingly eternal life has to be defined in exclusively this-worldly terms, namely as 'living and dying in a way which could not be rendered pointless by death' (50). Phillips extends his non-realist interpretation to every aspect of religious language, including talk about God. Thus, concerning the love of God and receiving everything as a gift of God, Phillips says, 'In learning by contemplation, attention, renunciation, what forgiving, thanking, loving, etc. mean in these contexts, the believer is participating in the reality of God: *this is what we mean by God's reality*' (Phillips 1970, 55; his italics).

---

[4] See Joseph M. Incandela 1985.   [5] For the negative view see Faghoury and Armour 1984.
[6] Another contemporary neo-Wittgensteinian philosopher who has expressed similar views, and to whom Phillips often refers, is Peter Winch. See, e.g., Winch 1977.
[7] Cf. Cupitt 1985, 54.

We have here, then, a philosophy of religion which respects and supports the use of traditional religious language, with all its emotional depths and reverberations, but which understands it throughout as referring, not to realities alleged to exist independently of ourselves, but to our own moral and spiritual states. Thus to say that God exists is not to affirm the reality of, in Richard Swinburne's definition, 'a person without a body (i.e. a spirit) who is eternal, is perfectly free, omnipotent, omniscient, perfectly good, and the creator of all things' (Swinburne 1979, 8). That 'God exists' means that there are human beings who use the concept of God and for whom it is the presiding idea in their form of life.

Phillips does not argue that the classical users of God-talk—for example, the biblical figures, or indeed ordinary believers through the centuries—consciously accepted or were even aware of this kind of non-realist interpretation. They doubtless normally believed in a real and powerful divine Person and in a literal conscious existence after death in heaven or hell. Phillips' contention is rather that in the light of twentieth-century philosophy, and particularly the revolutionary work of Wittgenstein, we are now in a position to analyse this language correctly and to distinguish between its merely literal and its authentically religious meaning.

But the positive claim that all that is important in religious forms of life and belief can continue, and indeed be enhanced, when the language is deliberately construed in a non-realist way, is perhaps most impressively made today by Don Cupitt. Like Braithwaite and Phillips, Cupitt holds that religious beliefs, understood as involving 'various supernatural beings, powers and events' (Cupitt 1980, 1), are manifestly false. It is impossible any longer, in the modern world, to believe in an 'objective' God who is 'there' independently of human believing. 'If . . .

belief in God has to take that very objectified form then the religious consciousness must be obsolete' (xii). However religious belief expresses something of immense importance and can retain, or regain, a central place in human life by becoming autonomous. 'The main requirements . . . are a break with our habitual theological realism, a full internalization of all religious doctrines and themes, and a recognition that it is possible autonomously to adopt religious principles and practices as intrinsically valuable' (xii).

Cupitt argues that in the modern period human consciousness has finally become individualised and autonomous. Accordingly we now see morality as 'standing on its own feet': the rightness of right action and the wrongness of wrong action do not depend upon an external authority. Justice and love, for example, are intrinsically good and injustice and cruelty intrinsically evil and are recognised as such by our own rational nature. This has been widely accepted since it was asserted by Kant at the end of the eighteenth century. Cupitt argues that we must now recognise the autonomy of religion also. Like ethics, religion must be allowed to come of age, as the practice of a spirituality which is not dependent for its validity upon any outside authority and whose claim upon us is grounded in our own nature. The 'religious requirement' to rise to unselfish compassion and detached serenity expresses a possibility within us whose fulfilment is its own reward. From this 'objectively atheous' (Cupitt 1980, 13) point of view the term 'God' does not refer to an 'immense cosmic or supracosmic Creator-Mind' (8). Rather, 'God is a personal religious ideal, internal to the spiritual self' (Cupitt 1985, 136). Again, 'God *is* the religious requirement personified, and his attributes are a kind of projection of its main features as we experience them' (Cupitt 1980, 85); 'God is, quite simply, what the religious requirement comes to mean to us as we respond to it' (88). And so 'the doctrine of God is an encoded set of spiritual directives' (107).

Given this non-realist hermeneutic, Cupitt's religious vocabulary is virtually indistinguishable from that of a religious realist. He frequently says such things as that 'God indwells the believer, enlightening his understanding, kindling his affections and enabling his will' (5), or that authentic love is pure and disinterested and 'When one loves in that way then one is in the love of God' (68). He is thus able to use all the familiar biblical and liturgical language. It is only the invisible brackets that turn the worship of God into 'an expression of allegiance to a particular set of values' (69). For

> The journey has taken us from an old world in which faith was experienced as a supernaturally prescribed and guided response to objective supernatural realities, to a new world in which faith is instead seen as a creative and freely-undertaken commitment to a life-path guided by rituals, myths, symbols and ideals; rituals, myths and so forth which, moreover, are fully and consciously acknowledged as such without even the most secret and residual attempt at self-deception.
>
> (Cupitt 1982, 1)

IV

Penultimate Issues

This growing movement of the non-realist construal of religious language raises both an ultimate issue and a series of penultimate issues. I want to argue that on many of the penultimate issues its advocates are right, and stand on common ground with many religious realists; but that on the ultimate issues there is a decisive difference.[8] Let us begin with matters penultimate.

First, it is surely right to emphasise strongly the fruits of faith in human life—both in the moral life and in what Cupitt (following a long tradition) calls the spiritual life. Religious realist and non-realist alike can agree that growth in love or compassion, the transcending of the self-centred point of view, purity of heart, are intrinsically good. They commend themselves to the deepest aspect of our nature. From a realist as well as from a non-realist point of view we can say that they are good whether or not there is a divine reality to which they may be a response. However, according to the realist, there is such a reality and these self-transcending qualities constitute the difference made within us by our conscious or unconscious awareness of it. The non-realist, of course, does not see self-transcendence in this way, as a response to a greater reality which draws us out of our enclosed egos, but simply as an achievement of human nature itself. But as to the central importance of self-transcendence, and the value of its moral and spiritual fruits, the religious realist and non-realist can be at one.

Second, realist and non-realist can today agree that the forms of religious belief, experience and practice have always been culturally conditioned. For example, the maleness of God as thought and experienced within the Semitic traditions reflects and validates the patriarchal human societies whose traditions they are; the hierarchical character of medieval

---

[8] Cf. John Bowker 1987.

Christendom was reflected in and validated by a hierarchical—monarchial theology; and so on. The relativity of religion to human cultures is today common knowledge—though like many other aspects of modern knowledge it has had to push its way to general consciousness against the weight of pre-modern dogmas. The epistemology of religion advocated in this book arises within this contemporary awareness. It understands that the postulated Real is thought and experienced by us in the ways made possible by the structures of our own minds, which in turn reflect cultural variations within the basic human form. Thus to affirm a reality to which our religious concepts ultimately refer is not to claim that that reality is accurately defined by those concepts, or that the Real in its unlimited ultimacy is identical with the personae and impersonae which its presence generates within our human consciousness. The cultural relativity of religious thought and experience can thus be fully acknowledged by both religious realist and non-realist.

Third, Randall's analogy between religious and aesthetic perception parallels a good deal of traditional realist discourse concerning the new appreciation of the natural and human world which faith can evoke. This kind of transformation of consciousness is exemplified in a number of the classic reports of conversions. George Fox, for example, the founder of the Quaker movement, recorded in his Journal that 'All things were new; and all the creation gave another smell unto me than before, beyond what words can utter . . .' (Fox [1694] 1924, 17). Jonathan Edwards (quoted by William James) tells how 'The appearance of everything was

altered; there seemed to be, as it were, a calm, sweet cast, or appearance of divine glory, in almost everything. God's excellency, his wisdom, his purity and love, seemed to appear in everything; in the sun, moon and stars; in the clouds and blue sky; in the grass, flowers, and trees; in the water and all nature; which used greatly to fix my mind . . .' (James [1902] 1960, 248). James also quotes a simple convert: 'I remember this, that everything looked new to me, the people, the fields, the cattle, the trees. I was like a new man in a new world . . .' (James [1902] 1960, 248). Such a transformation of consciousness is also characteristic of many of the mystics.[9] It is also startlingly exemplified by the Mahayana Buddhist experience of enlightenment in which Samsara, the ever-changing flow of ordinary life, is discovered to be Nirvana, glowing with the 'wondrous being' of all things. And without elaborating further it is, I think, evident that the religiously transformed mind is frequently able to discern new dimensions of meaning and value in the natural world and in human life; and that this is something which can be fully acknowledged and appreciated by religious realist and non-realist alike.

Fourth, Phillips (1970, ch. 2) and Cupitt (1980, ch. 6) as well as others emphasise strongly the autonomy of the moral life. The rightness of loving actions which benefit or avert harm from others, and the wrongness of acts of cruelty, malice and injustice, do not depend upon external divine commandments or prohibitions. On the contrary, a divine command to be selfish, cruel and unjust would itself be a morally wrong command and a divine prohibition against love, compassion, honesty and justice

[9] See Evelyn Underhill [1911] 1955, ch. 4, section 2, 'The illuminated Vision of the World'.

would be a morally wrong prohibition. Further, good deeds done to win a heavenly reward or to avoid punishment in hell are, by that very fact, not done from a moral motive. This is not however a new or a distinctively non-realist insight. It was the Muslim mystic Rabia who prayed, 'O God! if I worship Thee for fear of Hell, burn me in Hell; and if I worship Thee in hope of Paradise, exclude me from Paradise; but if I worship Thee for Thine own sake, withhold not Thine everlasting beauty!'[10] And it was Immanuel Kant who classically asserted that ethics is autonomous because it is based upon the universal or rational aspect of our nature.[11]

To see morality as based in the structure of human nature (as I have presented it in Chapter 9.1) is as possible to a religious realist as to a non-realist—although there are of course also religious realists, of the literalist kind, who reject this.[12] From a modern realist point of view our ethical nature, which makes possible moral judgment and moral obligation, is an aspect of our existence 'in the image of God', or as servants of God, or as temporarily separate egos seeking to realise our true nature as the universal *ātman* or the eternal Buddha-nature. Thus from a religious point of view morality is independent of external support or sanctions because it already rests on the foundation of a religiously constituted human existence. Accordingly the autonomy of ethics is not an issue between advocates of a non-realist use of religious language and of the realist use that I am recommending.

V

The Ultimate Issue

What then is the real issue? It concerns the nature of the universe—using this term in its most comprehensive sense—and our place within it. On a non-realist interpretation of religious language the situation within which we find ourselves is essentially as follows:

(a) The physical universe (including the consciousness generated by physical brains) is itself the only reality: it is not a creation or emanation of any more ultimate divine power, or a teleological process embodying a creative purpose or leading to some kind of nirvanic fulfilment, or reabsorption of the illusorily separate many in the ultimate One.

(b) The human species is a form of animal existence, part of the evolution of life on this earth. As such, humans are destined individually to perish like all other animals and plants; and the species itself is also likely to perish as the earth gradually ceases to sustain life—if not earlier, as a result of some sudden catastrophe. However whilst we humans exist we are the most cerebrally complex form of life on earth, capable not only of intelligent reflection and action but also of conceiving and being grasped and shaped by moral, aesthetic and religious ideals. We are animals to whom certain emotions and certain modes of behaviour are intrinsically valuable in ways which have led to the development of ethical language; and to whom certain characteristics of the

---

[10] R. A. Nicholson 1963, 115. The same prayer is sometimes attributed to St Francis Xavier. Cf. also Gregory of Nyssa, *The Life of Moses*, II:320 (1978, 137). Long before, Plotinus had said, 'If a man desires the good life except for itself, it is not the good life that he desires'.
[11] Immanuel Kant [1785] 1947, ch. 2.
[12] Thus Archdeacon William Paley declared that virtue is 'the doing good to mankind, in obedience to the will of God, and for the sake of everlasting happiness' (Paley [1786] 1817, 36).

surrounding world and of our own artistic creations are intrinsically valuable in ways that have led to the development of aesthetic language. In addition to this we possess a capacity for imaginative self-transcendence in virtue of which we have projected our values—particularly our moral values—onto the cosmos as personal gods and non-personal absolutes and in ideas of eternal life and of an ultimate existence beyond egoity.

(c) The supernatural beings and states of which the religious traditions speak exist only as ideas in our minds. Having realised this, however, we can move to a new point of view—the non-realist religious standpoint—from which we accept that the values which were formerly expressed in objective religious terms retain their intrinsic validity after this apparent foundation has dissolved. Indeed religious language, and the institutions whose discourse it is, can take on new life in a post-realist religious age as guides to spirituality, pointing us to ever greater possibilities of self-transcendence.

Non-realist religion can thus have a strong appeal, particularly in an age in which our natural human religiousness is increasingly unsatisfied by traditional forms.[13] It seems to offer everything that is of indubitable value in religion—the quest for inner peace and purity of heart, the development of love and compassion, the outgrowing of the natural ego with its obsessive cupidity and corrosive anxieties—without the encumbrance of a system of supernatural beliefs which has lost its plausibility for many modern minds.[14]

There is, however, a fundamental anomaly in this non-realist position: namely that whereas the central core of religious discourse interpreted in a realist way constitutes, if true, good news to all humankind, on a non-realist interpretation it constitutes bad news for all except a fortunate minority. This is a major and disturbing anomaly, for the non-realist interpretation professes to express the permanently valuable meaning of our traditional religious language. That language presents a picture which, whilst often grimly pessimistic in the short run—acknowledging fully the structural inevitability of suffering and the universality of moral wickedness—is nevertheless on the long view profoundly optimistic. For it looks beyond death to resurrection, beyond sin and suffering to an eternal heavenly life, beyond the pain-ridden wheel of Samsara through the gateway of enlightenment to Moksha or to the 'further shore' of Nirvana.

It is true that in the Semitic faiths there are also threats of eternal torment, and that there have even been theologians who could think of God as creating some human beings in order that they be damned. But discounting this latter aberration, the doctrine of hell leaves us with the choice between a life leading to fulfilment and a life leading to disaster, and permits the hope that the latter possibility will never in fact be realised.[15] Thus the idea of hell need not negate

---

[13] Although it is not completely clear whether they intend a full naturalistic reduction of the concept of God, a number of contemporary Christian thinkers write as though they do. For example Gordon Kaufman says, 'Though we understand ourselves to have been brought into being by a complex configuration of factors, powers and processes (physical, vital and historico-cultural), it is appropriate to symbolize and hold all this together in the single symbol or concept, *God*' (Kaufman 1985, 42). See also Kaufman 1981. Again, Charles Birch and John Cobb equate God with Life in Birch and Cobb 1981, ch. 6.

[14] For a sympathetic Jewish response see Dan Cohn-Sherbok 1985. See also Harold Schulweis 1983.

[15] I have developed this thought more fully in Hick 1985b, ch. 13.

our interpretation of post-axial religion as an ultimate optimism concerning the character of the universe in which we find ourselves. But however austere their sense of human sinfulness and however vivid their awareness of human pain and suffering, the religions proclaim the good news that, in the haunting words once again of Julian of Norwich, in the end 'all shall be well, and all shall be well, and all manner of thing shall be well'. Indeed they proclaim that the final fulfilment is already present to those whose minds and hearts are open to it: Nirvana and Samsara are one; eternal life can be experienced now, in each moment of time.

But in order for the religious message, that the universe is from our human point of view ultimately such as to be rejoiced in, to be good news for all and not only for those few who can realise Moksha, Nirvana, an eternal quality of existence in this life, the structure of the universe must be such as to make this possible. There are conceivable cosmic structures within which an eventual universal human fulfilment would be possible and others within which it would not. And the universe as described by the non-realist users of religious language is clearly of the latter kind. For if God/Brahman/the Dharmakaya are human ideas, existing only *in mente*, and if life terminates definitively at bodily death, then the universe is good only for a small minority of men and women. It does *not* sustain a religious message that is good news for all.

It is good news *in principle* for all, in that no one is theoretically debarred from attaining to Moksha, Nirvana, the eternal quality of life at each present moment. But this permissiveness is analogous to the fact that in a desperately poor country with great social and economic inequalities no one is in principle debarred from becoming a millionaire!

Likewise it is logically possible for anyone and everyone to become in this life jivanmukti, a bodhisattva, a saint. But this logical possibility falls far short of being good news for all. For the actuality of human existence in history, as also—so far as we know—throughout pre-history, has been that the relentless struggle to survive, the continual battle against natural dangers and human and animal predators, the restrictions and pressures and often pathetic brevity of life, have prevented the great majority of human beings from making more than a small beginning towards the fulfilment of which the religions speak. If that potential is ever to be realised—and that it is to be realised is the meaning for human life of the ultimate goodness of the universe—then reality must be structured accordingly. But to believe that it is indeed so structured is to construe religious language in a basically realist way.

The kind of non-realist religiousness advocated by such contemporaries as D. Z. Phillips and Don Cupitt offers, then, welcome news for the few which is at the same time grim news for the many. It is for this reason that it has to face the charge of an unintended elitism. This charge is not avoided by saying that the non-realist religious person, having found his or her own salvation, is called actively to spread the message, and also to work politically to change the social structures which make it virtually impossible for so many to respond. For, first, even if the human situation should presently change markedly for the better, so that a much greater proportion of people are able to find inner peace and fulfilment, it would still be true that thousands of millions have already lived and died, their highest potentialities unfulfilled—and, if the non-realists are right, permanently and irrevocably unfulfilled. This would negate any notion of the ultimate goodness of the universe. And second, non-realist missionary activity could only mitigate the bad news in so far as the mission succeeds. But the hope that the world is about to be dramatically transformed for the better, although entertained periodically throughout history, has so far always proved delusory. There would be little plausibility, in the circumstances of the world today, in a religious message whose validity depends upon that hitherto deceptive utopian vision.

There are analogies in past religious thinking to this elitism. They are not however flattering. In western thought the one which comes most readily to mind is the strand of Augustinian and Calvinist theology which consigned the large majority of human beings to a predestined eternal damnation whilst a minority were recipients of an arbitrary and unmerited divine grace. In this doctrine the distinction between the fortunate few and the unfortunate many was drawn by divine decree, whereas for contemporary non-realist religion it is drawn by the accidents of nature and history, and does not extend into eternity. But in each case the structure of the universe is such that this division occurs, and is such that most human beings have been its unhappy victims whilst a small minority have been its fortunate beneficiaries. Another difference is that whereas the Augustinian-Calvinist doctrine was developed explicitly, and its horrifying implications frankly accepted, the advocates of non-realist spirituality seem not yet to have noticed the harsh implication of their own teaching.

Needless to say, the fact that a religious doctrine constitutes bad news for ordinary struggling humanity—though at the same time good news for a fortunate few—does not show that it is false. It is possible that the fundamentally unwelcome situation which it depicts actually obtains. My argument, then, is not that a basically pessimistic creed is necessarily false. It is rather that it cannot credibly claim to represent the message of the great spiritual traditions. For it proposes such a reversal of their faith, from a cosmic optimism to a cosmic pessimism, as to offer a radically different vision. The positive argument for going beyond a non-realist understanding of religion will accordingly be an argument for accepting an account of the universe based upon the witness of the religious traditions interpreted in a basically realist manner; and this will be the task of the next chapter.

Works Cited in the Text

Cupitt, Don
1980: *Taking Leave of God* (London: SCM Press, and New York: Crossroad [1981]).
1982: *The World to Come* (London: SCM Press).
1985: *Only Human* (London: SCM Press).
Fox, George
1924: *The Journal of George Fox* [1694], Everyman's Library (London: J. M. Dent, and New York: E. P. Dutton).
James, William
1960: *Varieties of Religious Experience* [1902] (London: Collins, and New York: Mentor Books).
Phillips, D. Z.
1970: *Death and Immortality* (London: Macmillan, and New York: St. Martin's Press).
Swinburne, Richard
1979: *The Existence of God* (Oxford: Clarendon Press, and New York: Oxford University Press).

Chapter 11

Religious Plurality: The Mutual-Opposition View, Exclusivism, Inclusivism, and Pluralism

There are in the world many religions. In other words there is in the world a religious plurality. Sometimes, in order to emphasize that the world's religions are significantly different from one another, this plurality is spoken of as a diversity of religions. That there are in the world different religions has been appreciated for centuries. In the West since the Middle Ages, and before, Jews, Christians, and Muslims have been aware of one another's religions. In ancient India Jainism, Hinduism, and Buddhism existed together. Today in the various countries of Asia Buddhism, Hinduism, Islam, and Christianity coexist. In the twenty-first century all of the religions I have mentioned, and others too, are represented on all or many continents and thus are world religions.

Moreover, as modern anthropology has made us aware, there is in addition a great multiplicity of geographically limited religions that are not world religions, although they may have many followers. While it is clear that the fact of religious plurality was not discovered in the twenty-first century, or even in the twentieth century, what has happened in the late twentieth century and is continuing to happen in the twenty-first century is that different world religions have more and more come to coexist in single cultures around the world. In Asia this religious coexistence within a single culture has visibly been the case for centuries; now it is to be found in the cultures of Europe and the Americas. In the twenty-first century many of us on various continents live in communities where, within the radius of a few miles, there are synagogues, churches, mosques, Hindu temples, and Buddhist temples. Many in today's world know people or have friends in religions other than our own. Religious plurality for many has in this way come to be something in their own experience, not just something they read about. Many others have come to experience religious plurality at least indirectly through television reports and documentaries that make us aware of different religious traditions and of the encounters between religious traditions. For these reasons the fact of religious plurality is now more acutely felt as something real.

The underlying question here is: How should we understand this undeniable religious plurality in the world? This question addresses both the religious and those who are not religious, for both live in the same world of religious plurality. Whether we ourselves are or are not religious we can appreciate that an individual's religion can be significant in that individual's life. A religion presents a picture of life and its meaning; it can guide our actions and shape our feelings. So, if I am religious how should I understand the relationship of my religion to other religions, and if I am not religious how should I understand the relationship between the various religions of the world? If I notice that lots of people have different kinds of cars, I can say, "Well, different people have different tastes and like different things in cars." But I cannot say this about different religions. Religions are not just a matter of taste. For one thing there is no conflict between my having a Honda and your having a Ford. But different religions say different things about the deepest meaning of the world. How then should we understand different religions and the relationship between them?

Several different answers have been proposed to the question of how we should understand the religious plurality we find in the world. This chapter and the next contains readings that present a range of answers to this question. Important among these answers are *exclusivism*, *inclusivism*, and *pluralism*. Exclusivism, inclusivism, and pluralism come from serious thinkers within some religious tradition, but not all answers to the question of how to understand religious plurality come from within religion. An answer that does not come from within religion is provided by a view that may be called the *mutual-opposition view* of religious plurality. The chapter begins with the mutual-opposition view, which David Hume presented in "Of Miracles," Part 2. Parts 1 and 2 of Hume's "Of Miracles" are the first reading in Chapter 7. The first reading in the pages of this chapter is Alvin Plantinga's "Pluralism: A Defense of Religious Exclusivism," which is a defense of exclusivism against pluralism. It is followed by Karl Rahner's "Christianity and the Non-Christian Religions", which is an exposition of inclusivism. John Hick presents his case for pluralism in the chapter's third reading, "Religious Pluralism and Salvation," and in the fourth reading, "The Ideal of Generous Goodwill, Love, Compassion," already in Chap. 8, Hick endeavors to show that the "moral ideal . . . epitomised in the Golden Rule" is found in the scriptures of the various world religions. The last reading, "Divine Ineffability" by Keith Ward, contains a version of religious pluralism different from Hick's.

DAVID HUME

Of Miracles, Part 2

T he mutual-opposition view holds that *religious plurality shows that no religion is right or at least that there is no reason to accept one religion over any other*. The viewpoint of this answer to the question of religious plurality is that of someone who is aware of the diversity of religions in the world but who stands apart from them all. Some offering this answer may be anti-religious and opposed to religion in all its forms, while others may not be anti-religious but can see no reason to adopt any religion.

Among those who not only stand apart from religion but stand opposed to religion some have the sense that the various religions cancel each other out in that what supports one tells against the others. For them the best view of the plurality of religions in the world is that, while they are mutually opposed, they are more than mutually opposed; they mutually refute each other. Those with this more extreme view—the *mutual-cancellation view*, we may call it—may realize that religions differ significantly in what they hold as orthodox belief. For Islam, Muhammad is "the Seal of the prophets," the final and greatest Prophet of God, while Muhammad is not given this position by Judaism or Christianity. For Christianity, Jesus Christ is the Son of God, while Jesus is not given this position by Judaism or Islam. For Hinduism, there is a cycle of rebirth or being born over and over in a series of lives, determined by one's actions in prior lives, called karmic rebirth, while this is not so for the Western religions. In all these cases, it would be reasoned from this viewpoint, whatever supports the orthodox beliefs of one religion would count against the beliefs of the others.

In the eighteenth century David Hume in "Of Miracles" in *An Enquiry Concerning Human Understanding* reasoned in a similar way about the different religions of the world. He said "Of Miracles." Part 2, that "in matters of religions, whatever is different is contrary." That is, the different beliefs of different religions should be understood as contrary to each other so that if one is right the others are wrong. And so, he thought, it is impossible that all the religions of the world should "be established on any solid foundation." Hume reasoned that everything that supports one religion, as its proclaimed miracles are meant to do, has "the same force, though more indirectly, to overthrow every other system" of religion. Thus every "miracle" cited in support of one religion, he reasoned, would tell against every other religion, "and," Hume observed, "all of them abound in miracles." "Of Miracles," Part 2 is in Chapter 7.

ALVIN PLANTINGA

Pluralism: A Defense of Religious Exclusivism

Exclusivism is the view that *my religion alone is right and other religions that differ from mine are excluded from being right*. Many who belong to a particular religion and feel deeply committed to that particular religion may feel this way. Often exclusivism is associated with Christianity, and it is true that the underlying idea has been advanced in Christian circles as a way of viewing Christianity. Still, while many Christians in the past have been exclusivists, and many Christians are today, not all Christians have been or are exclusivists, and, viewing exclusivism broadly, it is possible for there to be exclusivists in other religions as well. In the broad sense that we will use those are exclusivists who hold that their religion is right and all other religions that differ from it are not right.

In this reading Alvin Plantinga, a contemporary American philosopher, defends a form or religious exclusivism against both moral and epistemic objections that may be brought against it. He argues that objections of both kinds can be answered.*

Pluralism: A Defense of Religious Exclusivism

When I was a graduate student at Yale, the philosophy department prided itself on diversity: and it was indeed diverse. There were idealists, pragmatists, phenomenologists, existentialists, Whiteheadians, historians of philosophy, a token positivist, and what could only be described as observers of the passing intellectual scene. In some ways, this was indeed something to take pride in; a student could behold and encounter real live representatives of many of the main traditions in philosophy. It also had an unintended and unhappy side effect, however. If anyone raised a philosophical question inside, but particularly outside, class, the typical response would be a catalog of some of the various different answers the world has seen: there is the Aristotelian answer, the existentialist answer, the Cartesian answer, Heidegger's answer, perhaps the Buddhist answer, and so on. But the question 'what is the truth about this matter?' was often greeted with disdain as unduly naive. There are all these different answers, all endorsed by people of great intellectual power and great dedication to philosophy; for every argument *for* one of these positions, there is another *against* it; would it not be excessively naive, or perhaps arbitrary, to suppose that one of these

is in fact *true*, the others being false? Or, if there really is a truth of the matter, so that one of them is true and conflicting ones false, wouldn't it be merely arbitrary, in the face of this embarrassment of riches, to *endorse* one of them as the truth, consigning the others to falsehood? How could you possibly know which was true?

Some urge a similar attitude with respect to the impressive variety of religions the world displays. There are theistic religions but also at least some nontheistic religions (or perhaps nontheistic strands of religion) among the enormous variety of religions going under the names 'Hinduism' and 'Buddhism'; among the theistic religions, there are strands of Hinduism and Buddhism and American Indian religion as well as Islam, Judaism, and Christianity; and all these differ significantly from one another. Isn't it somehow arbitrary, or irrational, or unjustified, or unwarranted, or even oppressive and imperialistic to endorse one of these as opposed to all the others? According to Jean Bodin, "each is refuted by all";[1] must we not agree? It is in this neighborhood that the so-called problem of pluralism arises. Of course, many concerns and problems can come under this rubric; the specific problem I mean to discuss can be

---

* Reprinted Alvin Plantinga: "Pluralism: A Defense of Religious Exclusivism" from *The Rationality of Belief and the Plurality of Faith*, edited by Thomas D. Senor. Copyright © 1995 by Cornell University. Used by permission of the publisher, Cornell University Press.
[1] *Colloquium Heptaplomeres de rerum sublimium arcanis abditis*, written by 1593 but first published in 1857. English translation by Marion Kuntz (Princeton: Princeton University Press, 1975). The quotation is from the Kuntz translation, p. 256.

thought of as follows. To put it in an internal and personal way, I find myself with religious beliefs, and religious beliefs that I realize aren't shared by nearly everyone else. For example, I believe both

(1) The world was created by God, an almighty, all-knowing, and perfectly good personal being (one that holds beliefs; has aims, plans, and intentions; and can act to accomplish these aims)

and

(2) Human beings require salvation, and God has provided a unique way of salvation through the incarnation, life, sacrificial death, and resurrection of his divine son.

Now there are many who do not believe these things. First, there are those who agree with me on (1) but not (2): there are non-Christian theistic religions. Second, there are those who don't accept either (1) or (2) but nonetheless do believe that there is something beyond the natural world, a something such that human well-being and salvation depend upon standing in a right relation to it. And third, in the West and since the Enlightenment, anyway, there are people—*naturalists*, we may call them—who don't believe any of these three things. And my problem is this: when I become really aware of these other ways of looking at the world, these other ways of

responding religiously to the world, what must or should I do? What is the right sort of attitude to take? What sort of impact should this awareness have on the beliefs I hold and the strength with which I hold them? My question is this: how should I think about the great religious diversity the world in fact displays? Can I sensibly remain an adherent of just one of these religions, rejecting the others? And here I am thinking specifically of *beliefs*. Of course, there is a great deal more to any religion or religious practice than just belief, and I don't for a moment mean to deny it. But belief is a crucially important part of most religions; it is a crucially important part of *my* religion; and the question I mean to ask here is what the awareness of religious diversity means or should mean for my religious beliefs.

Some speak here of a *new* awareness of religious diversity, and speak of this new awareness as constituting (for us in the West) a crisis, a revolution, an intellectual development of the same magnitude as the Copernican revolution of the sixteenth century and the alleged discovery of evolution and our animal origins in the nineteenth.[2] No doubt there is at least some truth to this. Of course, the fact is all along many Western Christians and Jews have known that there are other religions and that not nearly everyone shares *their* religion.[3] The ancient Israelites—some of the prophets, say—were clearly aware of Canaanitish religion; and the apostle Paul said that he preached "Christ crucified, a

---

[2] Thus Joseph Runzo: "Today, the impressive piety and evident rationality of the belief systems of other religious traditions inescapably confronts Christians with a crisis—and a potential revolution." "God, Commitment, and Other Faiths: Pluralism vs. Relativism," *Faith and Philosophy* 5 (October 1988), 343.

[3] As explained in detail in Robert Wilken, "Religious Pluralism and Early Christian Thought," so far unpublished. Wilken focuses on the third century; he explores Origen's response to Celsus and concludes that there are striking parallels between Origen's historical situation and ours. What is different today, I suspect, is not that Christianity has to confront other religions but that we now call this situation 'religious pluralism'.

stumbling block to Jews and folly to the Greeks" (I Cor. 1:23). Other early Christians, the Christian martyrs, say, must have suspected that not everyone believed as they did. The church fathers, in offering defenses of Christianity, were certainly apprised of this fact; Origen, indeed, wrote an eight-volume reply to Celsus, who urged an argument similar to those put forward by contemporary pluralists. Aquinas, again, was clearly aware of those to whom he addressed the *Summa contra gentiles*, and the fact that there are non-Christian religions would have come as no surprise to the Jesuit missionaries of the sixteenth and seventeenth centuries or to the Methodist missionaries of the nineteenth. In more recent times, when I was a child, *The Banner*, the official publication of the Christian Reformed Church, contained a small column for children; it was written by 'Uncle Dick', who exhorted us to save our nickels and send them to our Indian cousins at the Navaho mission in New Mexico. Both we and our elders knew that the Navahos had or had had a religion different from Christianity, and part of the point of sending the nickels was to try to rectify that situation.

Still, in recent years probably more of us Western Christians have become aware of the world's religious diversity; we have probably learned more about people of other religious persuasions, and we have come to see more clearly that they display what looks like real piety, devoutness, and spirituality. What is new, perhaps, is a more widespread sympathy for other religions, a tendency to see them as more valuable, as containing more by way of truth, and a new feeling of solidarity with their practitioners.

There are several possible reactions to awareness of religious diversity. One is to continue to believe what you have all along believed; you learn about this diversity but continue to believe, that is, take to be true, such propositions as (1) and (2) above, consequently taking to be false any beliefs, religious or otherwise, that are incompatible with (1) and (2). Following current practice, I call this *exclusivism;* the exclusivist holds that the tenets or some of the tenets of *one* religion—Christianity, let's say—are in fact true; he adds, naturally enough, that any propositions, including other religious beliefs, that are incompatible with those tenets are false. Now there is a fairly widespread belief that there is something seriously wrong with exclusivism. It is irrational, or egotistical and unjustified,[4] or intellectually arrogant,[5] or elitist,[6] or a manifestation of

---

[4] Thus Gary Gutting: "Applying these considerations to religious belief, we seem led to the conclusion that, because believers have many epistemic peers who do not share their belief in God . . . , they have no right to maintain their belief without a justification. If they do so, they are guilty of epistemological egoism." *Religious Belief and Religious Skepticism* (Notre Dame: University of Notre Dame Press, 1982), p. 90 (but see the following pages for an important qualification).
[5] "Here my submission is that on this front the traditional doctrinal position of the Church has in fact militated against its traditional moral position, and has in fact encouraged Christians to approach other men immorally. Christ has taught us humility, but we have approached them with arrogance. . . . This charge of arrogance is a serious one." Wilfred Cantwell Smith, *Religious Diversity* (New York: Harper and Row, 1976), p. 13.
[6] Runzo, "Ethically, Religious Exclusivism has the morally repugnant result of making those who have privileged knowledge, or who are intellectually astute, a religious elite, while penalizing those who happen to have no access to the putatively correct religious view, or who are incapable of advanced understanding." "God, Commitment, and Other Faiths," p. 348.

harmful pride,[7] or even oppressive and imperialistic.[8] The claim is that exclusivism as such is or involves a vice of some sort: it is wrong or deplorable; and it is this claim I want to examine. I propose to argue that exclusivism need not involve either epistemic or moral failure and that furthermore something like it is wholly unavoidable, given our human condition.

These objections are not to the *truth* of (1) or (2) or any other proposition someone might accept in this exclusivist way (although, of course, objections of that sort are also put forward); they are instead directed to the *propriety* or *rightness* of exclusivism. And there are initially two different kinds of indictments of exclusivism: broadly moral or ethical indictments and broadly

intellectual or epistemic indictments. These overlap in interesting ways, as we shall see below. But initially, anyway, we can take some of the complaints about exclusivism as *intellectual* criticisms: it is *irrational* or *unjustified* to think in an exclusivistic way. And the other large body of complaint is moral: there is something *morally* suspect about exclusivism: it is arbitrary, or intellectually arrogant, or imperialistic. As Joseph Runzo suggests, exclusivism is "neither tolerable nor any longer intellectually honest in the context of our contemporary knowledge of other faiths."[9] I want to consider both kinds of claims or criticisms; I propose to argue that the exclusivist is not as such necessarily guilty of any of these charges.

Moral Objections to Exclusivism

I first turn to the moral complaints: that the exclusivist is intellectually arrogant, or egotistical, or self-servingly arbitrary, or dishonest, or imperialistic, or oppressive. But first three qualifications. An exclusivist, like anyone else, will probably be guilty of some or all of these things to at least some degree, perhaps particularly the first two; the question is, however, whether she is guilty of these things just by virtue of being an exclusivist. Second, I shall use the term 'exclusivism' in such a way that you don't count

as an exclusivist unless you are rather fully aware of other faiths, have had their existence and their claims called to your attention with some force and perhaps fairly frequently, and have to some degree reflected on the problem of pluralism, asking yourself such questions as whether it is or could be really true that the Lord has revealed himself and his programs to us Christians, say, in a way in which he hasn't revealed himself to those of other faiths. Thus my grandmother, for example, would not have counted as

[7] "But natural pride, despite its positive contribution to human life, becomes harmful when it is elevated to the level of dogma and is built into the belief system of a religious community. This happens when its sense of its own validity and worth is expressed in doctrines implying an exclusive or a decisively superior access to the truth or the power to save." John Hick, "Religious Pluralism and Absolute Claims," in Leroy Rouner, ed. *Religious Pluralism* (Notre Dame: University of Notre Dame Press, 1984), p. 197.
[8] Thus John Cobb: "I agree with the liberal theists that even in Pannenberg's case, the quest for an absolute as a basis for understanding reflects the long tradition of Christian imperialism and triumphalism rather than the pluralistic spirit." "The Meaning of Pluralism for Christian Self-Understanding," in Rouner, *Religious Pluralism*, p. 171.
[9] "God, Commitment, and Other Faiths," p. 357.

an exclusivist. She had, of course, *heard* of the heathen, as she called them, but the idea that perhaps Christians could learn from them, and learn from them with respect to religious matters, had not so much as entered her head; and the fact that it *hadn't* entered her head, I take it, was not a matter of moral dereliction on her part. The same would go for a Buddhist or Hindu peasant. These people are not, I think, plausibly charged with arrogance or other moral flaws in believing as they do.

Third, suppose I am an exclusivist with respect to (1), for example, but nonculpably believe, like Thomas Aquinas, say, that I have a knock-down, drag-out argument, a demonstration or conclusive proof of the proposition that there is such a person as God; and suppose I think further (and nonculpably) that if those who don't believe (1) were to be apprised of this argument (and had the ability and training necessary to grasp it, and were to think about the argument fairly and reflectively), they too would come to believe (1). Then I could hardly be charged with these moral faults. My condition would be like that of Gödel, let's say, upon having recognized that he had a proof for the incompleteness of arithmetic. True, many of his colleagues and peers didn't believe that arithmetic was incomplete, and some believed that it *was* complete; but presumably Gödel wasn't arbitrary or egotistical in believing that arithmetic is in fact incomplete. Furthermore, he would not have been at fault had he nonculpably but *mistakenly* believed that he had found such a proof. Accordingly, I shall use the term 'exclusivist' in such a way that you don't count as an exclusivist if you nonculpably think you know of a demonstration or conclusive argument for the beliefs with respect to which you are an exclusivist, or even if you nonculpably think you know of

an argument that would convince all or most intelligent and honest people of the truth of that proposition. So an exclusivist, as I use the term, not only believes something like (1) or (2) and thinks false any proposition incompatible with it; she also meets a further condition C that is hard to state precisely and in detail (and in fact any attempt to do so would involve a long and at present irrelevant discussion of ceteris paribus clauses). Suffice it to say that C includes (1) being rather fully aware of other religions, (2) knowing that there is much that at the least looks like genuine piety and devoutness in them, and (3) believing that you know of no arguments that would necessarily convince all or most honest and intelligent dissenters of your own religious allegiances.

Given these qualifications, then, why should we think that an exclusivist is properly charged with these moral faults? I shall deal first and most briefly with charges of oppression and imperialism: I think we must say that they are on the face of it wholly implausible. I daresay there are some among you who reject some of the things I believe; I do not believe that you are thereby oppressing me, even if you do not believe you have an argument that would convince me. It is conceivable that exclusivism might in some way *contribute to* oppression, but it isn't in itself oppressive.

The important moral charge is that there is a sort of self-serving arbitrariness, an arrogance or egotism, in accepting such propositions as (1) or (2) under condition C; exclusivism is guilty of some serious moral fault or flaw. According to Wilfred Cantwell Smith, "except at the cost of insensitivity or delinquency, it is morally not possible actually to go out into the world and say to devout, intelligent, fellow human beings: '. . . we believe that we know

God and we are right; you believe that you know God, and you are totally wrong'."[10]

So what can the exclusivist have to say for herself? Well, it must be conceded immediately that if she believes (1) or (2), then she must also believe that those who believe something incompatible with them are mistaken and believe what is false. That's no more than simple logic. Furthermore, she must also believe that those who do not believe as she does—those who believe neither (1) nor (2), whether or not they believe their negations—*fail* to believe something that is true, deep, and important, and that she *does* believe. She must therefore see herself as *privileged* with respect to those others—those others of both kinds. There is something of great value, she must think, that *she* has and *they* lack. They are ignorant of something—something of great importance—of which she has knowledge. But does this make her properly subject to the above censure?

I think the answer must be no. Or if the answer is yes, then I think we have here a genuine moral dilemma; for in our earthly life here below, as my Sunday School teacher used to say, there is no real alternative; there is no reflective attitude that is not open to the same strictures. These charges of arrogance are a philosophical tar baby: get close enough to them to use them against the exclusivist, and you are likely to find them stuck fast to yourself. How so? Well, as an exclusivist, I realize I can't convince others that they should believe as I do, but I nonetheless continue to believe as I do: and the charge is that I am as a result arrogant or egotistical, arbitrarily preferring my way of doing things to other ways.[11] But what are my alternatives with respect to a proposition like (1)? There seem to be three choices.[12] I can continue to hold it; I can withhold it, in Roderick Chisholm's sense, believing neither it nor its denial; and I can accept its denial. Consider the third way, a way taken by those pluralists who, like John Hick, hold that such propositions as (1) and (2) and their colleagues from other faiths are literally false although in some way still valid responses to the Real. This seems to me to be no advance at all with respect to

---

[10] Smith, *Religious Diversity*, p. 14. A similar statement: "Nor can we reasonably claim that our own form of religious experience, together with that of the tradition of which we are a part, is veridical whilst others are not. We can of course claim this; and indeed virtually every religious tradition has done so, regarding alternative forms of religion either as false or as confused and inferior versions of itself. . . . Persons living within other traditions, then, are equally justified in trusting their own distinctive religious experience and in forming their beliefs on the basis of it. . . . let us avoid the implausibly arbitrary dogma that religious experience is all delusory with the single exception of the particular form enjoyed by the one who is speaking." John Hick, *An Interpretation of Religion* (New Haven, Yale University Press, 1989), p. 235.

[11] "The only reason for treating one's tradition differently from others is the very human but not very cogent reason that it is one's own!" Hick, *Interpretation of Religion*, p. 235.

[12] To speak of choice here suggests that I can simply choose which of these three attitudes to adopt; but is that at all realistic? Are my beliefs to that degree within my control? Here I shall set aside the question whether and to what degree my beliefs are subject to my control and within my power. Perhaps we have very little control over them; then the moral critic of exclusivism can't properly accuse the exclusivist of dereliction of moral duty, but he could still argue that the exclusivist's stance is unhappy, bad, a miserable state of affairs. Even if I can't help it that I am overbearing and conceited, my being that way is a bad state of affairs.

the arrogance or egotism problem; this is not a way out. For if I do this, I will then be in the very same condition as I am now: I will believe many propositions others don't believe and will be in condition C with respect to those propositions. For I will then believe the denials of (1) and (2) (as well as the denials of many other propositions explicitly accepted by those of other faiths). Many others, of course, do not believe the denials of (1) and (2), and in fact believe (1) and (2). Further, I will not know of any arguments that can be counted on to persuade those who do believe (1) or (2) (or propositions accepted by the adherents of other religions). I am therefore in the condition of believing propositions that many others do not believe and furthermore am in condition C. If, in the case of those who believe (1) and (2), that is sufficient for intellectual arrogance or egotism, the same goes for those who believe their denials.

So consider the second option: I can instead *withhold* the proposition in question. I can say to myself; "the right course here, given that I can't or couldn't convince these others of what *I* believe, is to believe neither these propositions nor their denials." The pluralist objector to exclusivism can say that the right course under condition C, is to *abstain* from believing the offending proposition and also abstain from believing its denial; call him, therefore, 'the abstemious pluralist'. But does he thus really avoid the condition that, on the part of the exclusivist, leads to the charges of egotism and arrogance? Think, for a moment, about disagreement. Disagreement, fundamentally, is a matter of adopting conflicting propositional attitudes with respect to a given proposition. In the simplest and most familiar case, I disagree with you if there is some proposition p such that I believe p and you believe -p. But that's just the simplest case: there are also others. The one that is at present of interest is this: I believe p and you withhold it, fail to believe it. Call the first kind of disagreement 'contradicting'; call the second 'dissenting'.

My claim is that if contradicting others (under the condition C spelled out above) is arrogant and egotistical, so is dissenting (under that same condition). For suppose you believe some proposition p but I don't: perhaps you believe it is wrong to discriminate against people simply on the grounds of race, but I, recognizing that there are many people who disagree with you, do not believe this proposition. I don't disbelieve it either, of course, but in the circumstances I think the right thing to do is to abstain from belief. Then am I not implicitly condemning your attitude, your *believing* the proposition, as somehow improper— naive, perhaps, or unjustified, or in some other way less than optimal? I am implicitly saying that my attitude is the superior one; I think my course of action here is the right one and yours somehow wrong, inadequate, improper, in the circumstances at best second-rate. Also, I realize that there is no questions, here, of *showing* you that your attitude is wrong or improper or naive; so am I not guilty of intellectual arrogance? Of a sort of egotism, thinking I know better than you, arrogating to myself a privileged status with respect to you? The problem for the exclusivist was that she was obliged to think she possessed a truth missed by many others; the problem for the abstemious pluralist is that he is obliged to think he possesses a virtue others don't, or acts rightly where others don't. If, in conditions C, one is arrogant by way of believing a proposition others don't, isn't one equally, under those reflective conditions, arrogant by way of withholding a proposition others don't?

Perhaps you will respond by saying that the abstemious pluralist gets into trouble, falls into arrogance, by way of implicitly saying or believing that his way of proceeding is *better* or *wiser* than other ways pursued by other people, and perhaps he can escape by abstaining from *that* view as well. Can't he escape the problem by refraining from believing that racial bigotry is wrong, and also refraining from holding the view that it is *better*, under the conditions that obtain, to withhold that proposition than to assert and believe it? Well, yes, he can; then he has no *reason* for his abstention; he doesn't believe that abstention is better or more appropriate; he simply does abstain. Does this get him off the egotistical hook? Perhaps. But then, of course, he can't, in consistency, also hold that there is something wrong with *not* abstaining, with coming right out and *believing* that bigotry is wrong; he loses his objection to the exclusivist. Accordingly, this way out is not available for the abstemious pluralist who accuses the exclusivist of arrogance and egotism.

Indeed, I think we can show that the abstemious pluralist who brings charges of intellectual arrogance against exclusivism is hoist with his own petard, holds a position that in a certain way is self-referentially inconsistent in the circumstances. For he believes

(3) If S knows that others don't believe p and that he is in condition C with respect to p, then S should not believe p;

this or something like it is the ground of the charges he brings against the exclusivist. But, the abstemious pluralist realizes that many do not accept (3); and I suppose he also realizes that it is unlikely that he can find arguments for (3) that will convince them; hence he knows that

he is in condition C. Given his acceptance of (3), therefore, the right course for him is to abstain from believing (3). Under the conditions that do in fact obtain—namely, his knowledge that others don't accept it and that condition C obtains—he can't properly accept it.

I am therefore inclined to think that one can't, in the circumstances, properly hold (3) or any other proposition that will do the job. One can't find here some principle on the basis of which to hold that the exclusivist is doing the wrong thing, suffers from some moral fault—that is, one can't find such a principle that doesn't, as we might put it, fall victim to itself.

So the abstemious pluralist is hoist with his own petard; but even apart from this dialectical argument (which in any event some will think unduly cute), aren't the charges unconvincing and implausible? I must concede that there are a variety of ways in which I can be and have been intellectually arrogant and egotistic; I have certainly fallen into this vice in the past and no doubt am not free of it now. But am I really arrogant and egotistic just by virtue of believing what I know others don't believe, where I can't show them that I am right? Suppose I think the matter over, consider the objections as carefully as I can, realize that I am finite and furthermore a sinner, certainly no better than those with whom I disagree, and indeed inferior both morally and intellectually to many who do not believe what I do; but suppose it *still* seems clear to me that the proposition in question is true: can I really be behaving immorally in continuing to believe it? I am dead sure that it is wrong to try to advance my career by telling lies about my colleagues; I realize there are those who disagree; I also realize that in all likelihood there is no way I can find to show them that they are wrong; nonetheless, I think they *are* wrong. If I think this after careful reflection—if

I consider the claims of those who disagree as sympathetically as I can, if I try level best to ascertain the truth here—and it *still* seems to me sleazy, wrong, and despicable to lie about my colleagues to advance my career, could I really be doing something immoral in continuing to believe as before? I can't see how. If, after careful reflection and thought, you find yourself convinced that the right propositional attitude to take to (1) and (2) in the face of the facts of religious pluralism is abstention from belief, how could you properly be taxed with egotism, either for so believing or for so abstaining? Even if you knew others did not agree with you? So I can't see how the moral charge against exclusivism can be sustained.

Epistemic Objections to Exclusivism

I turn now to *epistemic* objections to exclusivism. There are many different specifically epistemic virtues, and a corresponding plethora of epistemic vices; the ones with which the exclusivist is most frequently charged, however, are *irrationality* and *lack of justification* in holding his exclusivist beliefs. The claim is that as an exclusivist, he holds unjustified beliefs and/or irrational beliefs. Better, *he is* unjustified or irrational in holding these beliefs. I shall therefore consider those two claims, and I shall argue that the exclusivistic views need not be either unjustified or irrational. I shall then turn to the question whether his beliefs could have *warrant*: that property, whatever precisely it is, that distinguishes knowledge from mere true belief, and whether they could have enough warrant for knowledge.

Justification

The pluralist objector sometimes claims that to hold exclusivist views, in condition C, is *unjustified—epistemically* unjustified. Is this true? And what does he mean when he makes this claim? As even a brief glance at the contemporary epistemological literature shows, justification is a protean and multifarious notion.[13] There are, I think, substantially two possibilities as to what he means. The central core of the notion, its beating heart, the paradigmatic center to which most of the myriad contemporary variations are related by way of analogical extension and family resemblance, is the notion of *being within one's intellectual rights*, having violated no intellectual or cognitive duties or obligations in the formation and sustenance of the belief in question. This is the palimpsest, going back to Descartes and especially Locke, that underlies the multitudinous battery of contemporary inscriptions. There is no space to argue that point here; but chances are when the pluralist objector to exclusivism claims that the latter is unjustified, it is some notion lying in this neighborhood that he has in mind. (And, here we should note the very close connection between the moral objections to exclusivism and the objection that exclusivism is epistemically unjustified.)

The duties involved, naturally enough, would be specifically *epistemic* duties: perhaps a duty to proportion degree of belief to (propositional) evidence from what is *certain*, that is, self-evident or incorrigible,

---

[13] See my "Justification in the Twentieth Century," *Philosophy and Phenomenological Research* 50, supplement (Fall 1990), 45 ff., and see chap. 1 of my *Warrant: The Current Debate* (New York: Oxford University Press, 1993).

as with Locke, or perhaps to try one's best to get into and stay in the right relation to the truth, as with Roderick Chisholm,[14] the leading contemporary champion of the justificationist tradition with respect to knowledge. But at present there is widespread (and, as I see it, correct) agreement that there is no duty of the Lockean kind. Perhaps there is one of the Chisholmian kind;[15] but isn't the exclusivist conforming to that duty if, after the sort of careful, indeed prayerful, consideration I mentioned in the response to the moral objection, it still seems to him strongly that (1), say, is true and he accordingly still believes it? It is therefore hard to see that the exclusivist is necessarily unjustified in this way.

The second possibility for understanding the charge—the charge that exclusivism is epistemically unjustified—has to do with the oft-repeated claim that exclusivism is intellectually *arbitrary*. Perhaps the idea is that there is an intellectual duty to treat similar cases similarly; the exclusivist violates this duty by arbitrarily choosing to believe (for the moment going along with the fiction that we *choose* beliefs of this sort) (1) and (2) in the face of the plurality of conflicting religious beliefs the world presents. But suppose there is such a duty. Clearly, you do not violate it if you nonculpably think the beliefs in question are *not* on a par. And, as an exclusivist, I *do* think (nonculpably, I hope) that they are not on a par: I think (1) and (2) *true* and those incompatible with either of them *false*.

The rejoinder, of course, will be that it is not *alethic* parity (their having the same truth value) that is at issue: it is *epistemic* parity that counts. What kind of epistemic parity? What would be relevant here, I should think, would be *internal* or internalist epistemic parity: parity with respect to what is internally available to the believer. What is internally available to the believer includes, for example, detectable relationships between the belief in question and other beliefs you hold; so internal parity would include parity of propositional evidence. What is internally available to the believer also includes the *phenomenology* that goes with the beliefs in question: the *sensuous* phenomenology, but also the nonsensuous phenomenology involved, for example, in the belief's just having the feel of being *right*. But once more, then, (1) and (2) are not on an internal par, for the exclusivist, with beliefs that are incompatible with them. (1) and (2), after all, seem to me to be true; they have for me the phenomenology that accompanies that seeming. The same cannot be said for propositions incompatible with them. If, furthermore, John Calvin is right in thinking that there is such a thing as the Sensus Divinitatis and the Internal Testimony of the Holy Spirit, then perhaps (1) and (2) are produced in me by those belief-producing processes, and have for me the phenomenology that goes with them; the same is not true for propositions incompatible with them.

But then the next rejoinder: isn't it probably true that those who reject

[14] See the three editions of *Theory of Knowledge* referred to in note 23.
[15] Some people think there is, and also think that withholding belief, abstaining from belief, is always and automatically the safe course to take with respect to this duty, whenever any question arises as to what to believe and withhold. But that isn't so. One can go wrong by withholding as well as by believing: there is no safe haven here, not even abstention. If there is a duty of the Chisholmian kind, and if I, out of epistemic pride and excessive scrupulosity, succeed in training myself not to accept ordinary perceptual judgments in ordinary perceptual circumstances, I am not performing works of epistemic supererogation; I am epistemically culpable.

(1) and (2) in favor of other beliefs have propositional evidence for their beliefs that is on a par with mine for my beliefs; and isn't it also probably true that the same or similar phenomenology accompanies their beliefs as accompanies mine? So that those beliefs really are epistemically and internally on a par with (1) and (2), and the exclusivist is still treating like cases differently? I don't think so: I think there really are arguments available for (1), at least, that are not available for its competitors. And as for similar phenomenology, this is not easy to say; it is not easy to look into the breast of another; the secrets of the human heart are hard to fathom; it is hard indeed to discover this sort of thing even with respect to someone you know really well. But I am prepared to stipulate both sorts of parity. Let's agree for purposes of argument that these beliefs are on an epistemic par in the sense that those of a different religious tradition have the same sort of internally available markers—evidence, phenomenology, and the like—for their beliefs as I have for (1) and (2). What follows?

Return to the case of moral belief. King David took Bathsheba, made her pregnant, and then, after the failure of various stratagems to get her husband Uriah to think the baby was his, arranged for Uriah to be killed. The prophet Nathan came to David and told him a story about a rich man and a poor man. The rich man had many flocks and herds; the poor man had only a single ewe lamb, which grew up with his children, "ate at his table, drank from his cup, lay in his bosom, and was like a daughter to him." The rich man had unexpected guests. Instead of slaughtering one of his own sheep, he took the poor man's single ewe lamb, slaughtered it, and served it to his guests. David exploded in anger: "The man who did this deserves to die!" Then,

in one of the most riveting passages in all the Bible, Nathan turns to David, stretches out his arm and points to him, and declares, "*You are that man!*" And David sees what he has done.

My interest here is in David's reaction to the story. I agree with David: such injustice is utterly and despicably wrong; there are really no words for it. I believe that such an action is wrong, and I believe that the proposition that it *isn't* wrong—either because really *nothing* is wrong, or because even if *some* things are wrong, *this* isn't—is false. As a matter of fact, there isn't a lot I believe more strongly. I recognize, however, that there are those who disagree with me; and once more, I doubt that I could find an argument to show them that I am right and they wrong. Further, for all I know, their conflicting beliefs have for them the same internally available epistemic markers, the same phenomenology, as mine have for me. Am I then being arbitrary, treating similar cases differently in continuing to hold, as I do, that in fact that kind of behavior *is* dreadfully wrong? I don't think so. Am I wrong in thinking racial bigotry despicable, even though I know there are others who disagree, and even if I think they have the same internal markers for their beliefs as I have for mine? I don't think so. I believe in Serious Actualism, the view that no objects have properties in worlds in which they do not exist, not even nonexistence. Others do not believe this, and perhaps the internal markers of their dissenting views have for them the same quality as my views have for me. Am I being arbitrary in continuing to think as I do? I can't see how.

And the reason here is this: in each of these cases, the believer in question doesn't really think the beliefs in question *are* on a relevant epistemic par. She may agree that she and those who dissent are equally convinced of the truth of their belief, and even that they are internally on a par, that the internally available markers are similar, or relevantly similar. But she must still think that there is an important epistemic difference: she thinks that somehow the other person has *made a mistake*, or *has a blind spot*, or hasn't been wholly attentive, or hasn't received some grace she has, or is in some way epistemically less fortunate. And, of course, the pluralist critic is in no better case. He thinks the thing to do when there is internal epistemic parity is to withhold judgment; he knows there are others who don't think so, and for all he knows, that belief has internal parity with his; if he continues in that belief, therefore, he will be in the same condition as the exclusivist; and if he doesn't continue in this belief, he no longer has an objection to the exclusivist.

But couldn't I be wrong? Of course I could! But I don't avoid that risk by withholding all religious (or philosophical or moral) beliefs; I can go wrong that way as well as any other, treating all religions, or all philosophical thoughts, or all moral views, as on a par. Again, there is no safe haven here, no way to avoid risk. In particular, you won't reach safe haven by trying to take the same attitude toward all the historically available patterns of belief and withholding: for in so doing, you adopt a particular pattern of belief and withholding, one incompatible with some adopted by others. You pays your money and you takes your choice, realizing that you, like anyone else, can be desperately wrong. But what else can you do? You don't really have an alternative. And how can you do better than believe and withhold according to what, after serious and responsible consideration, seems to you to be the right pattern of belief and withholding?

Irrationality

I therefore can't see how it can be sensibly maintained that the exclusivist is unjustified in his exclusivistic views; but perhaps, as is sometimes claimed, he or his view is *irrational*. Irrationality, however, is many things to many people; so there is a prior question: what is it to be irrational? More exactly: precisely what quality is it that the objector is attributing to the exclusivist (in condition C) when the former says the latter's exclusivist beliefs are irrational? Since the charge is never developed at all fully, it isn't easy to say. So suppose we simply consider the main varieties of irrationality (or, if you prefer, the main senses of 'irrational') and ask whether any of them attach to the exclusivist just by virtue of being an exclusivist. I believe there are substantially five varieties of rationality, five distinct but analogically[16] connected senses of the term 'rational'; fortunately, not all of them require detailed consideration.

(1) *Aristotelian Rationality*. This is the sense in which man is a rational animal, one that has *ratio*, one that can look before and after, can hold beliefs, make inferences, and is capable of knowledge. This is perhaps the basic sense, the one of which the others are analogical extensions. It is also, presumably, irrelevant in the present context; at any rate, I hope the objector does not mean to hold that an exclusivist will by that token no longer be a rational animal.

(2) *The Deliverances of Reason*. To be rational in the Aristotelian sense is to possess reason: the power of thinking, believing, inferring, reasoning, knowing. Aristotelian rationality is thus *generic*. But there is an important more specific sense

---

[16] In Aquinas's sense, so that analogy may include causality, proportionality, resemblance, and the like.

lurking in the neighborhood; this is the sense that goes with reason taken more narrowly, as the source of a priori knowledge and belief.[17] An important use of 'rational' analogically connected with the first has to do with reason taken in this more narrow way. It is by reason thus construed that we know *self-evident* beliefs—beliefs so obvious that you can't so much as grasp them without seeing that they couldn't be false. These are among the *deliverances of reason*. Of course, there are other beliefs—*38 × 39 = 1482*, for example—that are not self-evident but are a consequence of self-evident beliefs by way of arguments that are self-evidently valid; these too are among the deliverances of reason. So say that the deliverances of reason is the set of those propositions that are self-evident for us human beings, closed under self-evident consequence. This yields another sense of rationality: a belief is *rational* if it is among the deliverances of reason and *irrational* if it is contrary to the deliverances of reason. (A belief can therefore be neither rational nor irrational, in this sense.) This sense of 'rational' is an analogical extension of the fundamental sense, but it is itself extended by analogy to still other senses. Thus we can broaden the category of reason to include memory, experience, induction, probability,

and whatever else goes into science; this is the sense of the term when reason is sometimes contrasted with faith. And we can also soften the requirement for self-evidence, recognizing both that self-evidence or a priori warrant is a matter of degree, and that there are many propositions that have a priori warrant but are not such that no one who understands them can fail to believe them.[18]

Is the exclusivist irrational in *these* senses? I think not; or at any rate the question whether he is isn't the question at issue. For his exclusivist beliefs are irrational in these senses only if there is a good argument from the deliverances of reason (taken broadly) to the denials of what he believes. I myself do not believe there are any such arguments. Presumably, the same goes for the pluralist objector; at any rate his objection is not that (1) and (2) are demonstrably false or even that there are good arguments against them from the deliverances of reason; his objection is instead that there is something wrong or subpar with believing them in condition C. This sense too, then, is irrelevant to our present concerns.

(3) *The Deontological Sense.* This sense of the term has to do with intellectual *requirement*, or *duty*, or *obligation*: a person's belief is irrational in this sense

---

[17] But then (because of the Russell paradoxes) we can no longer take it that the deliverances of reason are closed under self-evident consequence. See my *Warrant and Proper Function* (New York: Oxford University Press, 1993), chap. 6.

[18] See my *Warrant and Proper Function*, chap. 6. Still another analogical extension: a *person* can be said to be irrational if he won't listen to or pay attention to the deliverances of reason. He may be blinded by lust, or inflamed by passion, or deceived by pride: he might then act contrary to reason—*act* irrationally but also *believe* irrationally. Thus Locke: "Let never so much probability land on one side of a covetous man's reasoning, and money on the other, it is easy to foresee which will outweigh. Tell a man, passionately in love, that he is jilted; bring a score of witnesses of the falsehood of his mistress, 'tis ten to one but three kind words of hers, shall invalidate all their testimonies. . . . and though men cannot always openly gain-say, or resist the force of manifest probabilities, that make against them; yet yield they not to the argument." *An Essay Concerning Human Understanding*, ed. A. D. Woozley (New York: World Publishing Co., 1963), bk. IV, sec. xx, p. 439.

if in forming or holding it she violates such a duty. This is the sense of 'irrational' in which, according to many contemporary evidentialist objectors to theistic belief, those who believe in God without propositional evidence are irrational.[19] Irrationality in this sense is a matter of failing to conform to intellectual or epistemic duties; and the analogical connection with the first, Aristotelian sense is that these duties are thought to be among the deliverances of reason (and hence among the deliverances of the power by virtue of which human beings are rational in the Aristotelian sense). But we have already considered whether the exclusivist is flouting duties; we need say no more about the matter here. As we saw, the exclusivist is not necessarily irrational in this sense either.

(4) *Zweckrationalität*. A common and very important notion of rationality is *means-end* rationality—what our Continental cousins, following Max Weber, sometimes call *Zweckrationalität*, the sort of rationality displayed by your actions if they are well calculated to achieve your goals. (Again, the analogical connection with the first sense is clear: the calculation in question requires the power by virtue of which we are rational in Aristotle's sense.) Clearly, there is a whole constellation of notions lurking in the nearby bushes: what would *in fact* contribute to your goals, what you *take* it would contribute to your goals, what you *would* take it would contribute to your goals if you were sufficiently acute, or knew enough, or weren't distracted by lust, greed, pride, ambition, and the like,

what you would take it would contribute to your goals if you weren't thus distracted and were also to reflect sufficiently, and so on. This notion of rationality has assumed enormous importance in the last one hundred fifty years or so. (Among its laurels, for example, is the complete domination of the development of the discipline of economics.) Rationality thus construed is a matter of knowing how to get what you want; it is the cunning of reason. Is the exclusivist properly charged with irrationality in this sense? Does his believing in the way he does interfere with his attaining some of his goals, or is it a markedly inferior way of attaining those goals?

An initial caveat: it isn't clear that this notion of rationality applies to belief at all. It isn't clear that in *believing* something, I am acting to achieve some goal. If believing is an action at all, it is very far from being the paradigmatic kind of action taken to achieve some end; we don't have a choice as to whether to have beliefs, and we don't have a lot of choice with respect to which beliefs we have. But suppose we set this caveat aside and stipulate for purposes of argument that we have sufficient control over our beliefs for them to qualify as actions: would the exclusivist's beliefs then be irrational in this sense? Well, that depends upon what his goals *are*; if among his goals for religious belief is, for example, not believing anything not believed by someone else, then indeed it would be. But, of course, he needn't have *that* goal. If I do have an end or goal in holding such beliefs as (1) and (2), it would presumably be that of

[19] Among those who offer this objection to theistic belief are Brand Blanshard, *Reason and Belief* (London: Allen and Unwin, 1974), pp. 400 ff.; Antony Flew, *The Presumption of Atheism* (London: Pemberton, 1976), pp. 22 ff; and Michael Scriven, *Primary Philosophy* (New York: McGraw-Hill, 1966), pp. 102 ff. See my "Reason and Belief in God," in Alvin Plantinga and Nicholas Wolterstorff, eds., *Faith and Rationality*: (Notre Dame: University of Notre Dame Press, 1983), pp. 17 ff.

believing the truth on this exceedingly important matter, or perhaps that of trying to get in touch as adequately as possible with God, or more broadly with the deepest reality. And if (1) and (2) are *true*, believing them will be a way of doing exactly that. It is only if they are *not* true, then, that believing them could sensibly be thought to be irrational in this means-ends sense. Since the objector does not propose to take as a premise the proposition that (1) and (2) are false—he holds only that there is some flaw involved in *believing* them—this also is presumably not what he means.

(5) *Rationality as Sanity and Proper Function.* One in the grip of pathological confusion, or flight of ideas, or certain kinds of agnosia, or the manic phase of manic-depressive psychosis will often be said to be irrational; the episode may pass, after which he regains rationality. Here 'rationality' means absence of dysfunction, disorder, impairment, pathology with respect to rational faculties. So this variety of rationality is again analogically related to Aristotelian rationality; a person is rational in this sense when no malfunction obstructs her use of the faculties by virtue of the possession of which she is rational in the Aristotelian sense. Rationality as sanity does not require possession of particularly exalted rational faculties; it requires only normality (in the nonstatistical sense), or health, or proper function. This use of the term, naturally enough, is prominent in psychiatric discussions— Oliver Sacks's man who mistook his wife for a hat,[20] for example, was thus irrational.[21] This fifth and final sense of rationality is itself a family of analogically related senses. The fundamental sense here is that of sanity and proper function, but there are other closely related senses. Thus we may say that a belief (in certain circumstances) is irrational not because no sane person would hold it, but because no person who was sane and had also undergone a certain course of education would hold it, or because no person who was sane and furthermore was as intelligent as we and our friends would hold it; alternatively and more briefly, the idea is not merely that no one who was functioning properly in those circumstances would hold it but rather no one who was functioning *optimally*, as well or nearly as well as human beings ordinarily do (leaving aside the occasional great genius) would hold it. And this sense of rationality leads directly to the notion of *warrant*; I turn now to that notion; in treating it we also treat *ambulando* this fifth kind of irrationality.

Warrant

So the third version of the epistemic objection: that at any rate the exclusivist doesn't have warrant, or anyway *much* warrant (enough warrant for knowledge), for his exclusivistic views. Many pluralists—for

---

[20] Oliver Sacks, *The Man Who Mistook His Wife for a Hat* (New York: Harper and Row, 1987).

[21] In this sense of the term, what is properly called an 'irrational impulse' may be perfectly rational: an irrational impulse is really one that goes contrary to the deliverances of reason; but undergoing such impulses need not be in any way dysfunctional or a result of the impairment of cognitive faculties. To go back to some of William James's examples, that I will survive my serious illness might be unlikely, given the statistics I know and my evidence generally; perhaps we are so constructed, however, that when our faculties function properly in extreme situations, we are more optimistic than the evidence warrants. This belief, then, is irrational in the sense that it goes contrary to the deliverances of reason; it is rational in the sense that it doesn't involve dysfunction.

example, Hick, Runzo, and Wilfred Cantwell Smith—unite in declaring that at any rate the exclusivist certainly can't *know* that his exclusivistic views are true.[22] But is this really true? I shall argue briefly that it is not. At any rate from the perspective of each of the major contemporary accounts of knowledge, it may very well be that the exclusivist knows (1) or (2) or both. First, consider the two main internalistic accounts of knowledge: the justified true belief account(s) and the coherentist account(s). As I have already argued, it seems clear that a theist, a believer in (1), could certainly be *justified* (in the primary sense) in believing as she does: she could be flouting no intellectual or cognitive duties or obligations. But then on the most straightforward justified true belief account of knowledge, she can also *know* that it is true—if, that is, it *can* be true. More exactly, what must be possible is that both the exclusivist is justified in believing (1) and/or (2) and they be true. Presumably, the pluralist does not mean to dispute this possibility.

For concreteness, consider the account of justification given by the classical Chisholm.[23] On this view, a belief has warrant for me to the extent that accepting it is apt for the fulfillment of my epistemic duty, which (roughly speaking) is that of trying to get and remain in the right relation to the truth. But if after the most careful, thorough, thoughtful, open, and prayerful consideration, it still seems to me—perhaps more strongly than ever—that (1) and (2) are true, then clearly accepting them has great aptness for the fulfillment of that duty.[24]

A similarly brief argument can be given with respect to coherentism, the view that what constitutes warrant is coherence with some body of belief. We must distinguish two varieties of coherentism. On the one hand, it might be held that what is required is coherence with some or all of the other beliefs I actually hold; on the other, that what is required is coherence with my *verific* noetic structure (Keith Lehrer's term): the set of beliefs that remains when all

---

[22] Hick, *An Interpretation of Religion*, p. 234; Runzo, "God, Commitment, and Other Faiths," p. 348; Smith, *Religious Diversity*, p. 16.

[23] See his *Perceiving: A Philosophical Study* (Ithaca: Cornell University Press, 1957), the three editions of *Theory of Knowledge* (New York: Prentice-Hall, 1st ed., 1966; 2d ed., 1977; 3d ed., 1989), and *The Foundations of Knowing* (Minneapolis: University of Minnesota Press, 1982); and see my "Chisholmian Internalism," in David Austin, ed., *Philosophical Analysis: A Defense by Example* (Dordrecht: D. Reidel, 1988), and chap. 2 of *Warrant: The Current Debate*.

[24] Of course, there are many variations on this internalist theme. Consider briefly the postclassical Chisholm (see his "The Place of Epistemic Justification," in Roberta Klein, ed., *Philosophical Topics* 14, no. 1 (1986), 85, and the intellectual autobiography in *Roderick M. Chisholm*, ed. Radu Bogdan [Dordrecht: D. Reidel, 1986], pp. 52 ff.), who bears a startling resemblance to Brentano. According to this view, justification is not *deontological* but *axiological*. To put it another way, warrant is not really a matter of justification, of fulfilling duty and obligation; it is instead a question whether a certain relation of fittingness holds between one's evidential base (very roughly, the totality of one's present experiences and other beliefs) and the belief in question. (This relationship's holding, of course, is a valuable state of affairs; hence the axiology.) Can the exclusivist have warrant from this perspective? Well, without more knowledge about what this relation is, it isn't easy to tell. But here at the least the postclassical Chisholmian pluralist would owe us an explanation why he thinks the exclusivist's beliefs could not stand in this relation to his evidence base.

the false ones are deleted or replaced by their contradictories. But surely a coherent set of beliefs could include both (1) and (2) together with the beliefs involved in being in condition C; what would be required, perhaps, would be that the set of beliefs contain some explanation of why it is that others do not believe as I do. And if (1) and (2) *are* true, then surely (and a fortiori) there can be coherent verific noetic structures that include them. Hence neither of these versions of coherentism rules out the possibility that the exclusivist in condition C could know (1) and/or (2).

And now consider the main externalist accounts. The most popular externalist account at present would be one or another version of *reliabilism*. And there is an oft-repeated pluralistic argument (an argument that goes back at least to John Stuart Mill's *On Liberty* and possibly all the way back to the third century) that seems to be designed to appeal to reliabilist intuitions. The conclusion of this argument is not always clear, but here is its premise, in John Hick's words:

> For it is evident that in some ninety-nine percent of cases the religion which an individual professes and to which he or she adheres depends upon the accidents of birth. Someone born to Buddhist parents in Thailand is very likely to be a Buddhist, someone born to Muslim parents in Saudi Arabia to be a Muslim, someone born to Christian parents in Mexico to be a Christian, and so on.[25]

As a matter of sociological fact, this may be right. Furthermore, it can certainly produce a sense of intellectual vertigo. But what is one to do with this fact, if fact it is, and what follows from it? Does it follow, for example, that I ought not to accept the religious views that I have been brought up to accept, or the ones that I find myself inclined to accept, or the ones that seem to me to be true? Or that the belief-producing processes that have produced those beliefs in me are unreliable? Surely not. Furthermore, self-referential problems once more loom; this argument is another philosophical tar baby.

For suppose we concede that if I had been born in Madagascar rather than Michigan, my beliefs would have been quite different.[26] (For one thing, I probably wouldn't believe that I was born in Michigan.) But, of course, the same goes for the pluralist. Pluralism isn't and hasn't been widely popular in the world at large; if the pluralist had been born in Madagascar, or medieval France, he probably wouldn't have been a pluralist. Does it follow that he shouldn't be a pluralist or that his pluralistic beliefs are produced in him by an unreliable belief-producing process? I doubt it. Suppose I hold

(4) If S's religious or philosophical beliefs are such that if S had been born elsewhere and elsewhen, she wouldn't have held them, then those beliefs are produced by unreliable belief-producing mechanisms and hence have no warrant;

or something similar: then once more I will be hoist with my own petard. For in all probability, someone born in Mexico to Christian parents wouldn't believe (4)

---

[25] *Interpretation of Religion*, p. 2.
[26] Actually, this conditional as it stands is probably not true; the point must be stated with more care. Given my parents and their proclivities, if I had been born in Madagascar, it would probably have been because my parents were (Christian) missionaries there.

itself. No matter what philosophical and religious beliefs we hold and withhold (so it seems), there are places and times such that if we had been born there and then, then we would not have displayed the pattern of holding and withholding of religious and philosophical beliefs we *do* display. As I said, this can indeed be vertiginous; but what can we make of it? What can we infer from it about what has warrant and how we should conduct our intellectual lives? That's not easy to say. Can we infer *anything at all* about what has warrant or how we should conduct our intellectual lives? Not obviously.

To return to reliabilism, then: for simplicity, let's take the version of reliabilism according to which S knows p iff the belief that p is produced in S by a reliable belief-producing mechanism or process. I don't have the space, here, to go into this matter in sufficient detail: but it seems pretty clear that if (1) and (2) are true, then it *could be* that the beliefs that (1) and (2) be produced in me by a reliable belief-producing process. For either we are thinking of *concrete* belief-producing processes, like your memory or John's powers of a priori reasoning (*tokens* as opposed to types), or else we are thinking of *types* of belief-producing processes (type reliabilism). The problem with the latter is that there are an enormous number of *different* types of belief-producing processes for any given belief, some of which are reliable and some of which are not; the problem (and a horrifying problem it is[27]) is to say which of these is the type the reliability of which determines whether the belief in question has warrant. So the first (token reliabilism) is the better way of stating

reliabilism. But then, clearly enough, if (1) or (2) *is* true, it could be produced in me by a reliable belief-producing process. Calvin's Sensus Divinitatis, for example, could be working in the exclusivist in such a way as reliably to produce the belief that (1); Calvin's Internal Testimony of the Holy Spirit could do the same for (2). If (1) and (2) are true, therefore, then from a reliabilist perspective there is no reason whatever to think that the exclusivist might not know that they are true.

There is another brand of externalism that seems to me to be closer to the truth than reliabilism: call it (faute de mieux) 'proper functionalism'. This view can be stated to a first approximation as follows: S knows p iff (1) the belief that p is produced in S by cognitive faculties that are functioning properly (working as they ought to work, suffering from no dysfunction), (2) the cognitive environment in which p is produced is appropriate for those faculties, (3) the purpose of the module of the epistemic faculties producing the belief in question is to produce true beliefs (alternatively: the module of the design plan governing the production of p is aimed at the production of true beliefs), and (4) the objective probability of a belief's being true, given that it is produced under those conditions, is high.[28] All this needs explanation, of course; for present purposes, perhaps, we can collapse the account into the first condition. But then clearly it *could* be, if (1) and (2) are true, that they are produced in me by cognitive faculties functioning properly under condition C. For suppose (1) is true. Then it is surely possible that God has created us human

---

[27] See Richard Feldman, "Reliability and Justification," *The Monist* 68 (1986), 159–74, and chap. 9 of my *Warrant and Proper Function*.
[28] See chap. 10 of my *Warrant: The Current Debate* and the first two chapters of my *Warrant and Proper Function* for exposition and defense of this way of thinking about warrant.

beings with something like Calvin's Sensus Divinitatis, a belief-producing process that in a wide variety of circumstances functions properly to produce (1) or some very similar belief. Furthermore, it is also possible that in response to the human condition of sin and misery, God has provided for us human beings a means of salvation, which he has revealed in the Bible. Still further, perhaps he has arranged for us to come to believe what he means to teach there by way of the operation of something like the Internal Testimony of the Holy Spirit of which Calvin speaks. So on this view, too, if (1) and (2) are true, it is certainly possible that the exclusivist *know* that they are. We can be sure that the exclusivist's views lack warrant and are irrational in this sense, then, only if they are false; but the pluralist objector does not mean to claim that they *are* false; this version of the objection, therefore, also fails. The exclusivist isn't necessarily irrational, and indeed might *know* that (1) and (2) are true, if indeed they *are* true.

All this seems right. But don't the realities of religious pluralism count for anything at all? Is there nothing at all to the claims of the pluralists?[29] Could that really be right? Of course not. For many or most exclusivists, I think, an awareness of the enormous variety of human religious response serves as a *defeater* for such beliefs as (1) and (2)—an *undercutting* defeater, as opposed to a *rebutting* defeater. It calls into question, to some degree or other, the sources of one's belief in (1) or (2). It doesn't or needn't do so by way of an *argument*; and indeed, there isn't a very powerful argument from the proposition that many apparently devout people around the world dissent from (1) and

(2) to the conclusion that (1) and (2) are false. Instead, it works more directly; it directly reduces the level of confidence or degree of belief in the proposition in question. From a Christian perspective, this situation of religious pluralism and our awareness of it is itself a manifestation of our miserable human condition; and it may deprive us of some of the comfort and peace the Lord has promised his followers. It can also deprive the exclusivist of the *knowledge* that (1) and (2) are true, even if they *are* true and he *believes* that they are. Since degree of warrant depends in part on degree of belief, it is possible, though not necessary, that knowledge of the facts of religious pluralism should reduce an exclusivist's degree of belief and hence of warrant for (1) and (2) in such a way as to deprive him of knowledge of (1) and (2). He might be such that if he *hadn't* known the facts of pluralism, then he would have known (1) and (2), but now that he *does* know those facts, he doesn't know (1) and (2). In this way he may come to know less by knowing more.

Things *could* go this way with the exclusivist. On the other hand, they *needn't* go this way. Consider once more the moral parallel. Perhaps you have always believed it deeply wrong for a counselor to use his position of trust to seduce a client. Perhaps you discover that others disagree; they think it more like a minor peccadillo, like running a red light when there's no traffic; and you realize that possibly these people have the same internal markers for their beliefs that you have for yours. You think the matter over more fully, imaginatively recreate and rehearse such situations, become more aware of just what is involved in such a

[29] See William P. Alston, "Religious Diversity and Perceptual Knowledge of God," *Faith and Philosophy* 5 (October 1988), 433 ff.

situation (the breach of trust, the breaking of implied promises, the injustice and unfairness, the nasty irony of a situation in which someone comes to a counselor seeking help but receives only hurt) and come to believe even more firmly the belief that such an action is wrong—which belief, indeed, can in this way acquire more warrant for you. But something similar can happen in the case of religious beliefs. A fresh or heightened awareness of the facts of religious pluralism could bring about a reappraisal of one's religious life, a reawakening, a new or renewed and deepened grasp and apprehension of (1) and (2). From Calvin's perspective, it could serve as an occasion for a renewed and more powerful working of the belief-producing processes by which we come to apprehend (1) and (2). In that way knowledge of the facts of pluralism could initially serve as a defeater, but in the long run have precisely the opposite effect.

KARL RAHNER

Christianity and the Non-Christian Religions

Inclusivism is the view that *my religion alone is right but other religions may participate in its rightness and so are included*. Karl Rahner was a Catholic theologian who developed a form of inclusivism that would not deny that Christianity, or more specifically Catholicism, is the one true way to salvation, and yet would include those in other, non-Christian religions. Rahner's chief contribution to Christian inclusivism is his category of the "anonymous Christian." For Rahner, it is best to suppose that every human being is exposed to the influence of supernatural grace by which God communicates himself whether the individual accepts or refuses this grace. Nevertheless, for Rahner, salvation remains *Christian* and all salvation is through Christianity and Christ.

In "Christianity and the Non-Christian Religions" Rahner advances four theses. First, "Christianity understands itself as the absolute religion, intended for all men." Second, "a non-Christian religion . . . does not merely contain elements of a natural knowledge of God. . . . It contains also supernatural elements. . . ." Third, Christianity confronts a non-Christian "as someone who can and must already be regarded . . . as an anonymous Christian." Fourth, regarding the "religious pluralism"—that is, the plurality of religions—in the world, it is "permissible for the Christian . . . to interpret this non-Christianity as Christianity of an anonymous kind" and to meet it as a missionary to bring it to "the explicit consciousness" of what already belongs to it as "a divine offer" or "as a divine gift of grace accepted unreflectedly and implicitly."

From Karl Rahner, *Theological Investigations*, vol. 5. London: Darton, Longman, and Todd; Baltimore: Helicon Press, 1966. Reprinted by permission of Crossroad Publishing.

Christianity and the Non-Christian Religions

'Open Catholicism' involves two things. It signifies the fact that the Catholic Church is opposed by historical forces which she herself cannot disregard as if they were purely 'worldly' forces and a matter of indifference to her but which, on the contrary, although they do not stand in a positive relationship of peace and mutual recognition to the Church, do have a significance for her. 'Open Catholicism' means also the task of becoming related to these forces in order to understand their existence (since this cannot be simply acknowledged), in order to bear with and overcome the annoyance of their opposition and in order to form the Church in such a way that she will be able to overcome as much of this pluralism as should not exist, by understanding herself as the higher unity of this opposition. 'Open Catholicism' means therefore a certain attitude towards the present-day pluralism of powers with different outlooks on the world. We do not, of course, refer to pluralism merely as a fact which one simply acknowledges without explaining it. Pluralism is meant here as a fact which ought to be thought about and one which, without denying that—in part at least—it should not exist at all, should be incorporated once more from a more elevated viewpoint into the totality and unity of the Christian understanding of human existence. For Christianity, one of the gravest elements of this pluralism in which we live and with which we must come to terms, and indeed the element most difficult to incorporate, is the pluralism of religions. We do not refer by this to the pluralism of Christian denominations. This pluralism too is a fact, and a challenge and task for Christians. But we are not concerned with it here.

Our subject is the more serious problem, at least in its ultimate and basic form, of the different religions which still exist even in Christian times, and this after a history and mission of Christianity which has already lasted two thousand years. It is true, certainly, that all these religions together, including Christianity, are faced today with an enemy which did not exist for them in the past. We refer to the decided lack of religion and the denial of religion in general. This denial, in a sense, takes the stage with the ardour of a religion and of an absolute and sacred system which is the basis and the yard-stick of all further thought. This denial, organized on the basis of a State, represents itself as *the* religion of the future—as the decided, absolute secularization of human existence excluding all mystery. No matter how paradoxical this may sound, it does remain true that precisely this state of siege in which religion in general finds itself, finds one of its most important weapons and opportunities for success in the fact that humanity is so torn in its religious adherence. But quite apart from this, this pluralism is a greater threat and a reason for greater unrest for Christianity than for any other religion. For no other religion—not even Islam—maintains so absolutely that it is *the* religion, the one and only valid revelation of the one living God, as does the Christian religion.

The fact of the pluralism of religions, which endures and still from time to time becomes virulent anew even after a history of two thousand years, must therefore be the greatest scandal and the greatest vexation for Christianity. And the threat of this vexation is also greater for the individual Christian today than ever before. For in the past, the other religion was in practice the religion of a completely different cultural environment. It belonged to a history with which the individual only communicated very much on the periphery of his own history; it was the religion of those who were even in every other respect alien to oneself. It is not surprising, therefore, that people did not wonder at the fact that these 'others' and 'strangers' had also a different religion. No wonder that in general people could not seriously consider these other religions as a challenge posed to themselves or even as a possibility for themselves. Today things have changed. The West is no longer shut up in itself; it can no longer regard itself simply as the centre of the history of this world and as the centre of culture, with a religion which even from this point of view (i.e. from a point of view which has really nothing to do with a decision of faith but which simply carries the weight of something quite self-evident) could appear as the obvious and indeed sole way of honouring God to be thought of for a European. Today everybody is the next-door neighbour and spiritual neighbour of everyone else in the world. And so everybody today is determined by the inter-communication of all those situations of life which affect the whole world. Every religion which exists in the world is—just like all cultural possibilities and actualities of other people—a question posed, and a possibility offered, to every person. And just as one experiences someone else's culture in practice as something relative to one's own and as something existentially demanding, so it is also involuntarily with alien religions. They have become part of one's own existential situation—no longer merely theoretically but in the concrete—and we experience them therefore as something which puts the absolute claim of our own Christian faith into question. Hence, the question

about the understanding of and the continuing existence of religious pluralism as a factor of our immediate Christian existence is an urgent one and part of the question as to how we are to deal with today's pluralism.

This problem could be tackled from different angles. In the present context we simply wish to try to describe a few of those basic traits of a Catholic dogmatic interpretation of the non-Christian religions which may help us to come closer to a solution of the question about the Christian position in regard to the religious pluralism in the world of today. Since it cannot be said, unfortunately, that Catholic theology—as practised in more recent times—has really paid sufficient attention to the questions to be posed here, it will also be impossible to maintain that what we will have to say here can be taken as the common thought of Catholic theology. What we have to say carries, therefore, only as much weight as the reasons we can adduce, which reasons can again only be briefly indicated. Whenever the propositions to be mentioned carry a greater weight than this in theology, anyone trained in theology will realize it quite clearly from what is said. When we say that it is necessarily a question also of theories controverted among Christians themselves. It simply means that we will not be able to enter explicitly into the question as to whether the theses to be stated here can also hope to prove acceptable to Protestant theology. We say too that we are going to give a dogmatic interpretation, since we will pose our question not as empirical historians of religion but out of the self-understanding of Christianity itself, i.e. as dogmatic theologians.

1st Thesis: We must begin with the thesis which follows, because it certainly represents the basis in the Christian faith of the theological understanding of other religions. This thesis states that Christianity understands itself as the absolute religion, intended for all men, which cannot recognize any other religion beside itself as of equal right. This proposition is self-evident and basic for Christianity's understanding of itself. There is no need here to prove it or to develop its meaning. After all, Christianity does not take valid and lawful religion to mean primarily that relationship of man to God which man himself institutes on his own authority. Valid and lawful religion does not mean man's own interpretation of human existence. It is not the reflection and objectification of the experience which man has of himself and by himself.

Valid and lawful religion for Christianity is rather God's action on men, God's free self-revelation by communicating himself to man. It is God's relationship to men, freely instituted by God himself and revealed by God in this institution. *This* relationship of God to man is basically the same for all men, because it rests on the Incarnation, death and resurrection of the one Word of God become flesh. Christianity is God's own interpretation in his Word of this relationship of God to man founded in Christ by God himself. And so Christianity can recognize itself as the true and lawful religion for all men only where and when it enters with existential power and demanding force into the realm of another religion and—judging it by itself—puts it in question. Since the time of Christ's coming—ever since he came in the flesh as the Word of God in absoluteness and reconciled, i.e. united the world with God by his death and resurrection, not merely theoretically but really—Christ and his continuing historical presence in the world (which we call

'Church') is *the* religion which binds man to God.

Already we must, however, make one point clear as regards this first thesis (which cannot be further developed and proved here). It is true that the Christian religion itself has its own pre-history which traces this religion back to the beginning of the history of humanity— even though it does this by many basic steps. It is also true that this fact of having a pre-history is of much greater importance, according to the evidence of the New Testament, for the theoretical and practical proof of the claim to absolute truth made by the Christian religion than our current fundamental theology is aware of. Nevertheless, the Christian religion as such has a beginning in history; it did not always exist but began at some point in time. It has not always and everywhere been *the* way of salvation for men— at least not in its historically tangible ecclesio-sociological constitution and in the reflex fruition of God's saving activity in, and in view of, Christ. As a historical quantity Christianity has, therefore, a temporal and spatial starting point in Jesus of Nazareth and in the saving event of the unique Cross and the empty tomb in Jerusalem. It follows from this, however, that this absolute religion—even when it begins to be this for practically all men—must come in a historical way to men, facing them as the only legitimate and demanding religion for them. It is therefore a question of whether this moment, when the existentially real demand is made by the absolute religion in its historically tangible form, takes place really at the same chronological moment for all people, or whether the occurrence of this moment has itself a history and thus is not chronologically simultaneous for all people, cultures and spaces of history. (This is a question which up until now Catholic theology has not thought through with sufficient clarity and reflection by really confronting it with the length and intricacy of real human time and history.) Normally the beginning of the objective obligation of the Christian message for all men—in other words, the abolition of the validity of the Mosaic religion *and* of all other religions which (as we will see later) may also have a period of validity and of being-willed-by-God—is thought to occur in the apostolic age. Normally, therefore, one regards the time between this beginning and the actual acceptance of the personally guilty refusal of Christianity in a non-Jewish world and history as the span between the already given promulgation of the law and the moment when the one to whom the law refers takes cognizance of it.

It is not just an idle academic question to ask whether such a conception is correct or whether, as we maintain, there could be a different opinion in this matter, i.e. whether one could hold that the beginning of Christianity for actual periods of history, for cultures and religions, could be postponed to those moments in time when Christianity became a real historical factor in an individual history and culture—a real historical moment in a particular culture. For instance, one concludes from the first, usual answer that *everywhere* in the world, since the first Pentecost, baptism of children dying before reaching the use of reason is necessary for their supernatural salvation, although this was not necessary before that time. For other questions, too, a correct and considered solution of the present question could be of great importance, as for instance for the avoidance of immature conversions, for the justification and importance of 'indirect' missionary

work, etc. One will have to ask oneself whether one can still agree today with the first opinion mentioned above, in view of the history of the missions which has already lasted two thousand years and yet is still to a great extent in its beginnings—for even Suarez himself, for instance, had already seen (at least with regard to the *Jews*) that the *promulgatio* and *obligatio* of the Christian religion, and not merely the *divulgatio* and *notitia promulgationis*, take place in historical sequence. We cannot really answer this question here, but it may at least be pointed out as an open question; in practice, the correctness of the second theory may be presupposed since it alone corresponds to the real historicity of Christianity and salvation-history.

From this there follows a delicately differentiated understanding of our first thesis: we maintain positively only that, as regards destination, Christianity is the absolute and hence the only religion for all men. We leave it, however, an open question (at least in principle) at what exact point in time the absolute obligation of the Christian religion has in fact come into effect for every man and culture, even in the sense of the *objective* obligation of such a demand. Nevertheless—and this leaves the thesis formulated still sufficiently exciting—wherever in practice Christianity reaches man in the real urgency and rigour of his actual existence, Christianity—once understood—presents itself as the only still valid religion for this man, a necessary means for his salvation and not merely an obligation with the necessity of a precept. It should be noted that this is a question of the necessity of a *social* form for salvation. Even though this is Christianity and not some other religion, it may surely still be said without hesitation that this thesis contains implicitly another thesis which states that in concrete human existence as such, the nature of religion itself must include a social constitution—which means that religion can exist only in a social form. This means, therefore, that man, who is commanded to have a religion, is also commanded to seek and accept a social form of religion. It will soon become clear what this reflection implies for the estimation of non-Christian religions.

Finally, we may mention one further point in this connection. What is vital in the *notion of paganism* and hence also of the non-Christian pagan religions (taking 'pagan' here as a theological concept without any disparaging intent) is not the actual refusal to accept the Christian religion but the absence of any sufficient historical encounter with Christianity which would have enough historical power to render the Christian religion really present in this pagan society and in the history of the people concerned. If this is so, then paganism ceases to exist in this sense by reason of what is happening today. For the Western world is opening out into a universal world history in which every people and every cultural sector becomes an inner factor of every other people and every other cultural sector. Or rather, paganism is slowly entering a new phase: there is *one* history of the world, and in this *one* history both the Christians and the non-Christians (i.e. the old and new pagans together) live in one and the same situation and face each other in dialogue, and thus the question of the theological meaning of the other religions arises once more and with even greater urgency.

2nd Thesis: Until the moment when the Gospel really enters into the historical situation of an individual, a non-Christian religion (even outside the Mosaic religion) does not merely contain elements of a natural knowledge of God, elements, moreover, mixed up with human depravity which is the result of original sin and later aberrations. It contains also supernatural elements arising out of the grace which is given to men as a gratuitous gift on account of Christ. For this reason a non-Christian religion can be recognized as a *lawful* religion (although only in different degrees) without thereby denying the error and depravity contained in it. This thesis requires a more extensive explanation.

We must first of all note the point up to which this evaluation of the non-Christian religions is valid. This is the point in time when the Christian religion becomes a historically real factor for those who are of this religion. Whether this point is the same, theologically speaking, as the first Pentecost, or whether it is different in chronological time for individual peoples and religions, is something which even at this point will have to be left to a certain extent an open question. We have, however, chosen our formulation in such a way that it points more in the direction of the opinion which seems to us the more correct one in the matter although the *criteria* for a more exact determination of this moment in time must again be left an open question.

The thesis itself is divided into two parts. It means first of all that it is *a priori* quite possible to suppose that there are supernatural, grace-filled elements in non-Christian religions. Let us first of all deal with this statement. It does not mean, of course, that all the elements of a polytheistic conception of the divine, and all the other religious, ethical and metaphysical aberrations contained in the non-Christian religions, are to be or may be treated as harmless either in theory or in practice. There have been constant protests against such elements throughout the history of Christianity and throughout the history of the Christian interpretation of the non-Christian religions, starting with the Epistle to the Romans and following on the Old Testament polemics against the religion of the 'heathens'. Every one of these protests is still valid in what was really meant and expressed by them. Every such protest remains a part of the message which Christianity and the Church has to give to the peoples who profess such religions. Furthermore, we are not concerned here with an *a posteriori* history of religions. Consequently, we also cannot describe empirically what should not exist and what is opposed to God's will in these non-Christian religions, nor can we represent these things in their many forms and degrees. We are here concerned with dogmatic theology and so can merely repeat the universal and unqualified verdict as to the unlawfulness of the non-Christian religions right from the moment when they came into real and historically powerful contact with Christianity (and at first only thus!). It is clear, however, that this condemnation does not mean to deny the very basic differences within the non-Christian religions especially since the pious, God-pleasing pagan was already a theme of the Old Testament, and especially since this God-pleasing pagan cannot simply be thought of as living absolutely outside the concrete socially constituted religion and constructing his own religion on his native foundations—just as St Paul in his speech on the Areopagus did not simply exclude a positive and basic view of the pagan religion.

The decisive reason for the first part of our thesis is basically a theological consideration. This consideration (prescinding from certain more precise qualifications) rests ultimately on the fact that, if we wish to be Christians, we must profess belief in the universal and serious salvific purpose of God towards all men which is true even within the post-paradisean phase of salvation dominated by original sin. We know, to be sure, that this proposition of faith does not say anything certain about the *individual* salvation of man understood as something which has in fact been reached. But God desires the salvation of everyone. And this salvation willed by God is the salvation won by Christ, the salvation of supernatural grace which divinizes man, the salvation of the beatific vision. It is a salvation really intended for all those millions upon millions of people who lived perhaps a million years before Christ—and also for those who have lived after Christ—in nations, cultures and epochs of a very wide range which were still completely shut off from the viewpoint of those living in the light of the New Testament. If, on the one hand, we conceive salvation as something specifically *Christian*, if there is no salvation apart from Christ, if according to Catholic teaching the supernatural divinization of mankind can never be replaced merely by good will on the part of man but is necessary as something itself given in this earthly life; and if, on the other hand, God has really, truly and seriously intended this salvation for all men—then these two aspects cannot be reconciled in any other way than by stating that every human being is really and truly exposed to the influence of divine, supernatural grace which offers an interior union with God and by means of which God communicates himself whether the individual takes up an attitude of acceptance or of refusal towards this grace. It is senseless to suppose cruelly—and without any hope of acceptance by the man of today, in view of the enormous extent of the extra-Christian history of salvation and damnation—that nearly all men living outside the official and public Christianity are so evil and stubborn that the offer of supernatural grace ought not even to be made in fact in most cases, since these individuals have already rendered themselves unworthy of such an offer by previous, subjectively grave offences against the natural moral law.

If one gives more exact theological thought to this matter, then one cannot regard nature and grace as two phases in the life of the individual which follow each other in time. It is furthermore impossible to think that this offer of supernatural, divinizing grace made to all men on account of the universal salvific purpose of God, should in general (prescinding from the relatively few exceptions) remain ineffective in most cases on account of the personal guilt of the individual. For, as far as the Gospel is concerned, we have no really conclusive reason for thinking so pessimistically of men. On the other hand, and contrary to every merely human experience, we do have every reason for thinking optimistically of God and his salvific will which is more powerful than the extremely limited stupidity and evil-mindedness of men. However little we can say with certitude about the final lot of an individual inside or outside the officially constituted Christian religion, we have every reason to think optimistically—i.e. truly hopefully and confidently in a Christian sense—of God who has certainly the last word and who has revealed to us that he has spoken his powerful word of reconciliation and forgiveness into the world. If it is true that the eternal Word of God has become flesh and has died the death of sin for the sake of our salvation and in spite of our guilt, then the Christian has no right to suppose that the fate of the world—having regard to the whole of the world—takes the same course on account of man's refusal as it would have

taken if Christ had not come. Christ and his salvation are not simply one of two possibilities offering themselves to man's free choice; they are the need of God which bursts open and redeems the false choice of man by overtaking it. In Christ God not only gives the *possibility* of salvation, which in that case would still have to be effected by man himself, but the actual salvation itself, however much this includes also the right decision of human freedom which is itself a gift from God. Where sin already existed, grace came in superabundance. And hence we have every right to suppose that grace has not only been offered even outside the Christian Church (to deny this would be the error of Jansenism) but also that, in a great many cases at least, grace gains the victory in man's free acceptance of it, this being again the result of grace.

Of course, we would have to show more explicitly than the shortness of time permits that the empirical picture of human beings, their life, their religion and their individual and universal history does not disprove this optimism of a faith which knows the whole world to be subjected to the salvation won by Christ. But we must remember that the theoretical and ritualistic factors in good and evil are only a very inadequate expression of what man actually accomplishes in practice. We must remember that the same transcendence of man (even the transcendence elevated and liberated by God's grace) can be exercised in many different ways and under the most varied labels. We must take into consideration that whenever the religious person acts really religiously, he makes use of, or omits unthinkingly, the manifold forms of religious institutions by making a consciously critical choice among and between them. We must consider the immeasurable difference—which it seems right to suppose to exist even in the Christian sphere—between what is objectively wrong in moral life and the extent to which this is really realized with subjectively grave guilt. Once we take all this into consideration, we will not hold it to be impossible that grace is at work, and is even being accepted, in the spiritual, personal life of the individual, no matter how primitive, unenlightened, apathetic and earth-bound such a life may at first sight appear to be. We can say quite simply that, wherever, and in so far as, the individual makes a moral decision in his life (and where could this be declared to be in any way absolutely impossible—except in precisely 'pathological' cases?), this moral decision can also be thought to measure up to the character of a supernaturally elevated, believing and thus saving act, and hence to be more in actual fact than merely 'natural morality'. Hence, if one believes seriously in the universal salvific purpose of God towards all men in Christ, it need not and cannot really be doubted that gratuitous influences of properly Christian supernatural grace are conceivable in the life of all men (provided they are first of all regarded as individuals) and that these influences can be presumed to be accepted in spite of the sinful state of men and in spite of their apparent estrangement from God.

Our second thesis goes even further than this, however, and states in its second part that, from what has been said, the actual religions of 'pre-Christian' humanity too must not be regarded as simply illegitimate from the very start, but must be seen as quite capable of having a positive significance. This statement must naturally be taken in a very different sense which we cannot examine here for the various particular religions. This means that the different religions will be able to lay claim to being lawful

religions only in very different senses and to very different degrees. But precisely this variability is not at all excluded by the notion of a 'lawful religion', as we will have to show in a moment. A lawful religion means here an institutional religion whose 'use' by man at a certain period can be regarded on the whole as a positive means of gaining the right relationship to God and thus for the attaining of salvation, a means which is therefore positively included in God's plan of salvation.

That such a notion and the reality to which it refers can exist even where such a religion shows many theoretical and practical errors in its concrete form becomes clear in a theological analysis of the structure of the Old Covenant. We must first of all remember in this connection that only in the New Testament—in the Church of Christ understood as something which is eschatologically final and *hence* (and only for this reason) 'indefectible' and infallible—is there realized the notion of a Church which, because it is instituted by God in some way or other, already contains the permanent norm of differentiation between what is right (i.e. willed by God) and what is wrong in the religious sphere, and contains it both as a permanent institution and as an intrinsic element of this religion. There was nothing like this in the Old Testament, although it must undoubtedly be recognized as a lawful religion. The Old Covenant—understood as a concrete, historical and religious manifestation—contained what is right, willed by God, *and* what is false, erroneous, wrongly developed and depraved. But there was no permanent, continuing and institutional court of appeal in the Old Covenant which could have differentiated authoritatively, always and with certainty for the conscience of the individual between what was willed by God and what was due to human corruption in the actual religion. Of course, there were the prophets. They were not a permanent institution, however, but a conscience which had always to assert itself anew on behalf of the people in order to protest against the corruption of the religion as it existed at the time, thus—incidentally—confirming the existence of this corruption. The official, institutional forms known as the 'kingdom' and the priesthood were so little proof against this God-offending corruption that they could bring about the ruin of the Israelitic religion itself. And since there were also pseudo-prophets, and no infallible 'institutional' court of appeal for distinguishing genuine and false prophecy, it was—in the last analysis—left to the conscience of the individual Israelite himself to differentiate between what in the concrete appearance of the Israelitic religion was the true covenant with God and what was a humanly free, and so in certain cases falsifying, interpretation and corruption of this God-instituted religion. There might have been objective criteria for such a distinction of spirits, but their application could not simply be left to an 'ecclesiastical' court—not even in the most decisive questions—since official judgements could be wrong even about these questions and in fact were completely wrong about them.

This and nothing more—complete with its distinction between what was willed by God and what was human, all too human, a distinction which was ultimately left to be decided by the individual—was the concrete Israelitic religion. The Holy Scriptures do indeed give us the official and valid deposit to help us differentiate among the spirits which moved the history of the Old Testament religion. But since the infallible delimitation of the canon of the Old Testament is

again to be found only in the New Testament, the exact and final differentiation between the lawful and the unlawful in the Old Testament religion is again possible only by making use of the New Testament as something eschatologically final. The unity of the concrete religion of the Old Testament, which (ultimately) could be distinguished only gropingly and at one's own risk, was however the unity willed by God, providential for the Israelites in the order of salvation and indeed the lawful religion for them. In this connection it must furthermore be taken into consideration that it was meant to be this only for the Israelites and for no one else; the institution of those belonging to the Jewish religion without being of the Jewish race (i.e. of the proselytes), was a very much later phenomenon. Hence it cannot be a part of the notion of a lawful religion in the above sense that it should be free from corruption, error and objective moral wrong in the concrete form of its appearance, or that it should contain a clear objective and permanent final court of appeal for the conscience of the individual to enable the individual to differentiate clearly and with certainty between the elements willed and instituted by God and those which are merely human and corrupt.

We must therefore rid ourselves of the prejudice that we can face a non-Christian religion with the dilemma that it must either come from God in everything it contains and thus correspond to God's will and positive providence, or be simply a purely human construction. If man is under God's grace even in these religions—and to deny this is certainly absolutely wrong—then the possession of this supernatural grace cannot but show itself, and cannot but become a formative factor of life in the concrete, even where (though not only where) this life turns the relationship to the absolute into an explicit theme, viz. in religion. It would perhaps be possible to say in theory that where a certain religion is not only accompanied in its concrete appearance by something false and humanly corrupted but also makes this an explicitly and consciously adopted element—an explicitly declared condition of its *nature*—this religion is wrong in its deepest and most specific being and hence can no longer be regarded as a lawful religion—not even in the widest sense of the word. This may be quite correct in theory. But we must surely go on to ask whether there is any religion apart from the Christian religion (meaning here even only the Catholic religion) with an authority which could elevate falsehood into one of its really essential parts and which could thus face man with an alternative of either accepting this falsehood as the most real and decisive factor of the religion or leaving this religion. Even if one could perhaps say something like this of Islam as such, it would have to be denied of the majority of religions. It would have to be asked in every case to what extent the followers of such religions would actually agree with such an interpretation of their particular religion. If one considers furthermore how easily a concrete, originally religious act can be always directed in its intention towards one and the same absolute, even when it manifests itself in the most varied forms, then it will not even be possible to say that theoretical polytheism, however deplorable and objectionable it may be objectively, must always and everywhere be an absolute obstacle to the performance in such a religion of genuinely religious acts directed to the one true God. This is particularly true since it cannot be proved that the practical religious life of the ancient Israelites, in so far as it manifested itself in popular theory, was always more than mere henotheism.

Furthermore, it must be borne in mind that the individual ought to and must have the possibility in his life of partaking in a genuine saving relationship to God, and this at all times and in all situations of the history of the human race. Otherwise there could be no question of a serious and also actually effective salvific design of God for all men, in all ages and places. In view of the social nature of man and the previously even more radical social solidarity of men, however, it is quite unthinkable that man, being what he is, could actually achieve this relationship to God—which he must have and which if he is to be saved, is and must be made possible for him by God—in an absolutely private interior reality and this outside of the actual religious bodies which offer themselves to him in the environment in which he lives. If man had to be and could always and everywhere be a *homo religiosus* in order to be able to save himself as such, then he was this *homo religiosus* in the concrete religion in which 'people' lived and had to live at that time. He could not escape this religion, however much he may have and did take up a critical and selective attitude towards this religion on individual matters, and however much he may have and did put different stresses in practice on certain things which were at variance with the official theory of this religion. If, however, man can always have a positive, saving relationship to God, and if he always had to have it, then he has always had it within *that* religion which in practice was at his disposal by being a factor in his sphere of existence. As already stated above, the inherence of the individual exercise of religion in a social religious order is one of the essential traits of true religion as it exists in practice. Hence, if one were to expect from someone who lives outside the Christian religion that he should have exercised his genuine, saving relationship to God absolutely outside the religion which society offered him, then such a conception would turn religion into something intangibly interior, into something which is always and everywhere performed only indirectly, a merely transcendental religion without anything which could become tangible in categories. Such a conception would annul the above-mentioned principle regarding the necessarily social nature of all religion in the concrete, so that even the Christian Church would then no longer have the necessary presupposition of general human and natural law as proof of her necessity. And since it does not at all belong to the notion of a lawful religion intended by God for man as something positively salvific that it should be pure and positively willed by God in all its elements, such a religion can be called an absolutely legitimate religion for the person concerned. That which God has intended as salvation for him reached him, in accordance with God's will and by his permission (no longer adequately separable in practice), in the *concrete* religion of his actual realm of existence and historical condition, but this fact did not deprive him of the right and the limited possibility to criticize and to heed impulses of religious reform which by God's providence kept on recurring within such a religion. For a still better and simpler understanding of this, one has only to think of the natural and socially constituted morality of a people and culture. Such a morality is never pure but is always also corrupted, as Jesus confirmed even in the case of the Old Testament. It can always be disputed and corrected, therefore, by the individual in accordance with his conscience. Yet, taken in its totality, it is *the* way in which the individual encounters the natural divine law according to

God's will, and the way in which the natural law is given real, actual power in the life of the individual who cannot reconstruct these tablets of the divine law anew on his own responsibility and as a private metaphysician.

The morality of a people and of an age, taken in its totality, is therefore the legitimate and concrete form of the divine law (even though, of course, it can and may have to be corrected), so that it was not until the New Testament that the institution guaranteeing the purity of this form became (with the necessary reservations) an element of this form itself. Hence, if there existed a divine moral law and religion in the life of man *before* this moment, then its absolute purity (i.e. its constitution by divinely willed elements alone) must not be made the condition of the lawfulness of its existence. In fact, if every man who comes into the world is pursued by God's grace—and if one of the effects of this grace, even in its supernatural and salvifically elevating form, is to cause changes in consciousness (as is maintained by the better theory in Catholic theology) even though it cannot be simply *as* such a direct object of certain reflection—then it cannot be true that the actually existing religions do not bear any trace of the fact that all men are in some way affected by grace. These traces may be difficult to distinguish even to the enlightened eye of the Christian. But they must be there. And perhaps we may only have looked too superficially and with too little love at the non-Christian religions and so have not really seen them. In any case it is certainly not right to regard them as new conglomerates of natural theistic metaphysics and as a humanly incorrect interpretation and institutionalization of this 'natural religion'. The religions existing in the concrete must contain supernatural, gratuitous elements, and in using *these* elements the pre-Christian was able to attain God's grace: presumably, too, the pre-Christian exists even to this day, even though the possibility is gradually disappearing *today*. If we say that there were lawful religions in pre-Christian ages even outside the realm of the Old Testament, this does not mean that these religions were lawful in *all* their elements—to maintain this would be absurd. Nor does it mean that *every* religion was lawful; for in certain cases several forms, systems and institutions of a religious kind offered themselves within the historically concrete situation of the particular member of a certain people, culture, period of history, etc., so that the person concerned had to decide as to *which* of them was here and now, and on the whole, the more correct way (and hence for him *in concreto* the only correct way) of finding God.

This thesis is not meant to imply that the lawfulness of the Old Testament religion was of exactly the same kind as that which we are prepared to grant in a certain measure to the extra-Christian religions. For in the Old Testament the prophets saw to it (even though not by way of a permanent institution) that there existed a possibility of distinguishing in public salvation-history between what was lawful and what was unlawful in the history of the religion of the Israelites. This cannot be held to be true to the same extent outside this history, although this again does not mean that outside the Old Testament there could be no question of any kind of divinely guided salvation-history in the realm of public history and institutions.

The main difference between such a salvation-history and that of the Old Testament will presumably lie in the fact that the historical, factual nature of the New Testament has *its* immediate pre-history in the *Old Testament* (which pre-history, in parenthesis, is insignificantly brief in comparison with the general salvation-history which counts perhaps a million years—for the former can be known with any certainty only from the time of Abraham or of Moses). Hence, the New Testament unveils *this* short span of salvation-history distinguishing its divinely willed elements and those which are contrary to God's will. It does this by a distinction which we cannot make in the same way in the history of any other religion. The second part of this second thesis, however, states two things positively. It states that even religions other than the Christian and the Old Testament religions contain quite certainly elements of a supernatural influence by grace which must make itself felt even in these objectifications. And it also states that by the fact that in practice man as he really is can live his proffered relationship to God only in society, man must have had the right and indeed the duty to live this his relationship to God within the religious and social realities offered to him in his particular historical situation.

3rd Thesis: If the second thesis is correct, then Christianity does not simply confront the member of an extra-Christian religion as a mere non-Christian but as someone who can and must already be regarded in this or that respect as an anonymous Christian. It would be wrong to regard the pagan as someone who has not yet been touched in any way by God's grace and truth. If, however, he has experienced the grace of God—if, in certain circumstances, he has already accepted this grace as the ultimate, unfathomable entelechy of his existence by accepting the immeasurableness of his dying existence as opening out into infinity—then he has already been given revelation in a true sense even before he has been affected by missionary preaching from without. For this grace, understood as the *a priori* horizon of all his spiritual acts, accompanies his consciousness subjectively, even though it is not known objectively. And the revelation which comes to him from without is not in such a case the proclamation of something as yet absolutely unknown, in the sense in which one tells a child here in Bavaria, for the first time in school, that there is a continent called Australia. Such a revelation is then the expression in objective concepts of something which this person has already attained or could already have attained in the depth of his rational existence. It is not possible here to prove more exactly that this *fides implicita* is something which dogmatically speaking can occur in a so-called pagan. We can do no more here than to state our thesis and to indicate the direction in which the proof of this thesis might be found. But if it is true that a person who becomes the object of the Church's missionary efforts is or may be already someone on the way towards his salvation, and someone who in certain circumstances finds it, without being reached by the proclamation of the Church's message—and if it is at the same time true that this salvation which reaches him in this way is Christ's salvation, since there is no other salvation—then it must be possible to be not only an anonymous theist but also an anonymous Christian. And then it is quite true that in the last analysis, the proclamation of the Gospel does not simply turn someone absolutely abandoned by God and Christ into a Christian, but turns an anonymous Christian into someone who now also knows about his Christian belief in the depths of his grace-endowed being by objective reflection and in the profession of faith which is given a social form in the Church.

It is not thereby denied, but on the contrary implied, that this explicit self-realization of his previously anonymous Christianity is itself part of the development of this Christianity itself—a higher stage of development of this Christianity demanded by his being—and that it is therefore intended by God in the same way as everything else about salvation. Hence, it will not be possible in any way to draw the conclusion from this conception that, since man is already an anonymous Christian even without it, this explicit preaching of Christianity is superfluous. Such a conclusion would be just as false (and for the same reasons) as to conclude that the sacraments of baptism and penance could be dispensed with because a person can be justified by his subjective acts of faith and contrition even before the reception of these sacraments.

The reflex self-realization of a previously anonymous Christianity is demanded (1) by the incarnational and social structure of grace and of Christianity, and (2) because the individual who grasps Christianity in a clearer, purer and more reflective way has, other things being equal, a still greater chance of salvation than someone who is merely an anonymous Christian. If, however, the message of the Church is directed to someone who is a 'non-Christian' only in the sense of living by an anonymous Christianity not as yet fully conscious of itself, then her missionary work must take this fact into account and must draw the necessary conclusions when deciding on its missionary strategy and tactics. We may say at a guess that this is still not the case in sufficient measure. The exact meaning of all this, however, cannot be developed further here.

4th Thesis: It is possibly too much to hope, on the one hand, that the religious pluralism which exists in the concrete situation of Christians will disappear in the foreseeable future. On the other hand, it is nevertheless absolutely permissible for the Christian himself to interpret this non-Christianity as Christianity of an anonymous kind which he does always still go out to meet as a missionary, seeing it as a world which is to be brought to the explicit consciousness of what already belongs to it as a divine offer or already pertains to it also over and above this as a divine gift of grace accepted unreflectedly and implicitly. If both these statements are true, then the Church will not so much regard herself today as the exclusive community of those who have a claim to salvation but rather as the historically tangible vanguard and the historically and socially constituted explicit expression of what the Christian hopes is present as a hidden reality even outside the visible Church.

To begin with, however much we must always work, suffer and pray anew and indefatigably for the unification of the whole human race, in the one Church of Christ, we must nevertheless expect, for theological reasons and not merely by reason of a profane historical analysis, that the religious pluralism existing in the world and in our own historical sphere of existence will not disappear in the foreseeable future. We know from the gospel that the opposition to Christ and to the Church will not disappear until the end of time. If anything, we must even be prepared for a heightening of this antagonism to Christian existence. If, however, this opposition to the Church cannot confine itself merely to the purely private sphere of the individual but must also be of a public, historical character, and if this opposition is said to be present in a history which today, in contrast to previous ages, possesses a worldwide unity, then the continuing opposition to the Church can no longer exist merely locally and outside a certain

limited sector of history such as that of the West. It must be found in our vicinity and everywhere else. And this is part of what the Christian must expect and must learn to endure. The Church, which is at the same time the homogenous characterization of an in itself homogeneous culture (i.e. the medieval Church), will no longer exist if history can no longer find any way to escape from or go back on the period of its planetary unity. In a unified world history in which everything enters into the life of everyone, the 'necessary' public opposition to Christianity is a factor in the existential sphere of all Christianity. If this Christianity, thus always faced with opposition and unable to expect seriously that this will ever cease, nevertheless believes in God's universal salvific will—in other words, believes that God can be victorious by his secret grace even where the Church does not win the victory but is contradicted— then this Church cannot feel herself to be just *one* dialectic moment in the whole of history but has already overcome this opposition by her faith, hope and charity. In other words, the others who oppose her are merely those who have not yet recognized what they nevertheless really already are (or can be) even when, on the surface of existence, they are in opposition; they are already anonymous Christians, and the Church is not the communion of those who possess God's grace as opposed to those who lack it, but is the communion of those who can explicitly confess what they *and* the others hope to be. Non-Christians may think it presumption for the Christian to judge everything which is sound or restored (by being sanctified) to be the fruit in every man of the grace of his Christ, and to interpret it as anonymous Christianity; they may think it presumption for the Christian to regard the non-Christian as a Christian who has not yet come to himself reflectively. But the Christian cannot renounce this 'presumption' which is really the source of the greatest humility both for himself and for the Church. For it is a profound admission of the fact that God is greater than man and the Church. The Church will go out to meet the non-Christian of tomorrow with the attitude expressed by St Paul when he said: What therefore you do not know and yet worship [and yet *worship*!] that I proclaim to you (Acts 17:23). On such a basis one can be tolerant, humble and yet firm towards all non-Christian religions.

JOHN HICK

Religious Pluralism and Salvation

Pluralism in its barest form is the view that *all the great religions of the world are right*. John Hick is the foremost proponent of pluralism and has done most to develop this view in recent years. As Hick has developed his pluralism it has two central elements. First, Hick's pluralism advances the idea that the different religions of the world embody different responses to the one ultimate transcendent reality, which Hick calls the Real. Elaborating this idea, Hick explains that what he means by the Real is a Religious Reality that is beyond human conception and experience *as it is in itself*. The Real-in-itself is experienced and conceived of in the various religions of the world, but it is not experienced or conceived as it is in itself. Thus Christians will experience the Real as God or the Holy Trinity, while Buddhists will experience the Real as Dharmakaya (the transcendent or primordial Buddha-nature). The second main element of Hick's pluralism is the claim that the movement toward salvation is taking place equally in the various religious traditions as far as we can tell. Hick characterizes salvation as the transformation of human existence from self-centeredness to Reality-centeredness—a transformation variously called liberation, enlightenment, salvation, or fulfilment in different religious traditions. Put in other words the second main element of Hick's pluralism is the idea that the movement toward saintliness or spiritual development or religious attainment is taking place equally in the world's religions. Hick advances his pluralism as the best "hypothesis" to explain the plurality of religions in the world.

In this reading Hick presents both of these main elements of his pluralism. He also discusses different kinds or levels of doctrinal differences (differences in religious beliefs) that divide the different religions. The first doctrinal difference is over different conceptions of the Real, which Hick explains in terms of the first main element of his pluralism. The other two are differences in metaphysical and historical belief. Hick's article concludes with comments on exclusivism and inclusivism.

From *Faith and Philosophy* vol. 5, 1988. Reprinted by permission.

Religious Pluralism and Salvation

Let us approach the problems of religious pluralism through the claims of the different traditions to offer salvation— generically, the transformation of human existence from self-centeredness to Reality-centeredness. This approach leads to a recognition of the great world faiths as spheres of salvation; and so far as we can tell, more or less equally so. Their different truth-claims express (a) their differing perceptions, through different religio-cultural 'lenses,' of the one ultimate divine Reality; (b) their different answers to the boundary questions of origin and destiny, true answers to which are however not necessary for salvation, and (c) their different historical memories.

I

The fact that there is a plurality of religious traditions, each with its own distinctive beliefs, spiritual practices, ethical outlook, art forms and cultural ethos, creates an obvious problem for those of us who see them, not simply as human phenomena, but as responses to the Divine. For each presents itself, implicitly or explicitly, as in some important sense absolute and unsurpassable and as rightly claiming a total allegiance. The problem of the relationship between these different streams of religious life has often been posed in terms of their divergent belief-systems. For whilst there are various overlaps between their teachings there are also radical differences: is the divine reality (let us refer to it as the Real) personal or non-personal; if personal, is it unitary or triune; is the universe created, or emanated, or itself eternal; do we live only once on this earth or are we repeatedly reborn? and so

on and so on. When the problem of understanding religious plurality is approached through these rival truth-claims it appears particularly intractable.

I want to suggest, however, that it may more profitably be approached from a different direction, in terms of the claims of the various traditions to provide, or to be effective contexts of, salvation. 'Salvation' is primarily a Christian term, though I shall use it here to include its functional analogues in the other major world traditions. In this broader sense we can say that both Christianity and these other faiths are paths of salvation. For whereas pre-axial religion was (and is) centrally concerned to keep life going on an even keel, the post-axial traditions, originating or rooted in the 'axial age' of the first millenium B.C.E.—principally Hinduism, Judaism, Buddhism, Christianity, Islam—are centrally concerned with a radical transformation of the human situation.

It is of course possible, in an alternative approach, to define salvation in such a way that it becomes a necessary truth that only one particular tradition can provide it. If, for example, from within Christianity we define salvation as being forgiven by God because of Jesus' atoning death, and so becoming part of God's redeemed community, the church, then salvation is by definition Christian salvation. If on the other hand, from within Mahayana Buddhism, we define it as the attainment of *satori* or awakening, and so becoming an ego-free manifestation of the eternal Dharmakaya, then salvation is by definition Buddhist liberation. And so on. But if we stand back from these different conceptions to compare them we can, I think, very naturally and properly see them as different forms of the more fundamental conception of a radical change from a profoundly unsatisfactory state to one that is limitlessly better because rightly related to the Real. Each tradition conceptualizes in its own way the wrongness of ordinary human existence—as a state of fallenness from paradisal virtue and happiness, or as a condition of moral weakness and alienation from God, or as the fragmentation of the infinite One into false individualities, or as a self-centeredness which pervasively poisons our involvement in the world process, making it to us an experience of anxious, unhappy unfulfillment. But each at the same time proclaims a limitlessly better possibility, again conceptualized in different ways—as the joy of conforming one's life to God's law; as giving oneself to God in Christ, so that 'it is no longer I who live, but Christ who lives in me' (Galatians 2:20), leading to eternal life in God's presence; as a complete surrender (*islam*) to God, and hence peace with God, leading to the bliss of paradise; as transcending the ego and realizing oneness with the limitless being-consciousness-bliss (*satchitananda*) of Brahman; as overcoming the ego point of view and entering into the serene selflessness of nirvana. I suggest that these different conceptions of salvation are specifications of what, in a generic formula, is the transformation of human existence from self-centeredness to a new orientation, centered in the divine Reality. And in each case the good news that is proclaimed is that this limitlessly better possibility is actually available and can be entered upon, or begin to be entered upon, here and now. Each tradition sets forth the way to attain this great good: faithfulness to the Torah, discipleship to Jesus, obedient living out of the Qur'anic way of life, the Eightfold Path of the Buddhist dharma, or the three great Hindu *margas* of mystical insight, activity in the world, and self-giving devotion to God.

II

The great world religions, then, are ways of salvation. Each claims to constitute an effective context within which the transformation of human existence can and does take place from self-centeredness to Reality-centeredness. How are we to judge such claims? We cannot directly observe the inner spiritual quality of a human relationship to the Real; but we can observe how that relationship, as one's deepest and most pervasive orientation, affects the moral and spiritual quality of a human personality and of a man's or woman's relationship to others. It would seem, then, that we can only assess these salvation-projects insofar as we are able to observe their fruits in human life. The inquiry has to be, in a broad sense, empirical. For the issue is one of fact, even though hard to define and difficult to measure fact, rather than being settleable by *a priori* stipulation.

The word 'spiritual' which occurs above is notoriously vague; but I am using it to refer to a quality or, better, an orientation which we can discern in those individuals whom we call saints—a Christian term which I use here to cover such analogues as arahat, bodhisattva, jivanmukti, mahatma. In these cases the human self is variously described as becoming part of the life of God, being 'to the Eternal Goodness what his own hand is to a man'; or being permeated from within by the infinite reality of Brahman; or becoming one with the eternal Buddha nature. There is a change in their deepest orientation from centeredness in the ego to a new centering in the Real as manifested in their own tradition. One is conscious in the presence of such a person that he or she is, to a startling extent, open to the transcendent, so as to be largely free from self-centered concerns and anxieties and empowered to live as an instrument of God/Truth/Reality.

It is to be noted that there are two main patterns of such a transformation. There are saints who withdraw from the world into prayer or meditation and saints who seek to change the world—in the medieval period a contemplative Julian of Norwich and a political Joan of Arc, or in our own century a mystical Sri Aurobindo and a political Mahatma Gandhi. In our present age of sociological consciousness, when we are aware that our inherited political and economic structures can be analyzed and purposefully changed, saintliness is more likely than in earlier times to take social and political forms. But, of whichever type, the saints are not a different species from the rest of us; they are simply much more advanced in the salvific transformation.

The ethical aspect of this salvific transformation consists in observable modes of behavior. But how do we identify the kind of behavior which, to the degree that it characterizes a life, reflects a corresponding degree of reorientation to the divine Reality? Should we use Christian ethical criteria, or Buddhist, or Muslim . . . ? The answer, I suggest, is that at the level of their most basic moral insights the great traditions use a common criterion. For they agree in giving a central and normative role to the unselfish regard for others that we call love or compassion. This is commonly expressed in the principle of valuing others as we value ourselves, and treating them accordingly. Thus in the ancient Hindu *Mahabharata* we read that 'One should never do to another that which one would regard as injurious to oneself. This, in brief, is the rule of Righteousness' (*Anushana parva*, 113:7). Again, 'He who . . . benefits persons of all orders, who is always devoted to the good of all beings, who does not feel aversion to anybody . . . succeeds in ascending to Heaven' (*Anushana parva*, 145:24). In the Buddhist *Sutta Nipata* we read, 'As a

mother cares for her son, all her days, so towards all living things a man's mind should be all-embracing' (149). In the Jain scriptures we are told that one should go about 'treating all creatures in the world as he himself would be treated' (*Kitanga Sutra*, I.ii.33). Confucius, expounding humaneness (*jen*), said, 'Do not do to others what you would not like yourself' (*Analects*, xxi, 2). In a Taoist scripture we read that the good man will 'regard [others'] gains as if they were his own, and their losses in the same way' (*Thai Shang*, 3). The Zoroastrian scriptures declare, 'That nature only is good when it shall not do unto another whatever is not good for its own self' (*Dadistan-i-dinik*, 94:5). We are all familiar with Jesus' teaching, 'As ye would that men should do to you, do ye also to them likewise' (Luke 6:31). In the Jewish Talmud we read 'What is hateful to yourself do not do to your fellow man. That is the whole of the Torah' (*Babylonian Talmud*, Shabbath 31a). And in the Hadith of Islam we read Muhammad's words, 'No man is a true believer unless he desires for his brother that which he desires for himself' (*Ibn Madja*, Intro. 9). Clearly, if everyone acted on this basic principle, taught by all the major faiths, there would be no injustice, no avoidable suffering, and the human family would everywhere live in peace.

When we turn from this general principle of love/compassion to the actual behavior of people within the different traditions, wondering to what extent they live in this way, we realize how little research has been done on so important a question. We do not have much more to go on than general impressions, supplemented by travellers tales and anecdotal reports. We observe among our neighbors within our own community a great deal of practical loving-kindness; and we are told, for example, that a remarkable degree of self-giving love is to be found among the Hindu fishing families in the mud huts along the Madras shore; and we hear various other similar accounts from other lands. We read biographies, social histories and novels of Muslim village life in Africa, Buddhist life in Thailand, Hindu life in India, Jewish life in New York, as well as Christian life around the world, both in the past and today, and we get the impression that the personal virtues (as well as vices) are basically much the same within these very different religio-cultural settings and that in all of them unselfish concern for others occurs and is highly valued. And, needless to say, as well as love and compassion we also see all-too-abundantly, and apparently spread more or less equally in every society, cruelty, greed, hatred, selfishness and malice.

All this constitutes a haphazard and impressionistic body of data. Indeed I want to stress, not how easy it is, but on the contrary how difficult it is, to make responsible judgments in this area. For not only do we lack full information, but the fragmentary information that we have has to be interpreted in the light of the varying natural conditions of human life in different periods of history and in different economic and political circumstances. And I suggest that all that we can presently arrive at is the cautious and negative conclusion that we have no good reason to believe that any one of the great religious traditions has proved itself to be more productive of love/compassion than another.

The same is true when we turn to the large-scale social outworkings of the different salvation-projects. Here the units are not individual human lives, spanning a period of decades, but religious cultures spanning many centuries. For we can no more judge a civilization than a human life by confining our attention to a single temporal cross-section. Each of the great streams of religious life has had its times of flourishing and its times of deterioration.

Each has produced its own distinctive kinds of good and its own distinctive kinds of evil. But to assess either the goods or the evils cross-culturally is difficult to say the least. How do we weigh, for example, the lack of economic progress, and consequent widespread poverty, in traditional Hindu and Buddhist cultures against the endemic violence and racism of Christian civilization, culminating in the twentieth century Holocaust? How do we weigh what the west regards as the hollowness of arranged marriages against what the east regards as the hollowness of a marriage system that leads to such a high proportion of divorces and broken families? From within each culture one can see clearly enough the defects of the others. But an objective ethical comparison of such vast and complex totalities is at present an unattainable ideal. And the result is that we are not in a position to claim an over-all moral superiority for any one of the great living religious traditions.

Let us now see where we have arrived. I have suggested that if we identify the central claim of each of the great religious traditions as the claim to provide, or to be an effective context of, salvation; and if we see salvation as an actual change in human beings from self-centeredness to a new orientation centered in the ultimate divine Reality; and if this new orientation has both a more elusive 'spiritual' character and a more readily observable moral aspect—then we arrive at the modest and largely negative conclusion that, so far as we can tell, no one of the great world religions is salvifically superior to the rest.

III

If this is so, what are we to make of the often contradictory doctrines of the different traditions? In order to make progress at this point, we must distinguish various kinds and levels of doctrinal conflict.

There are, first, conceptions of the ultimate as Jahweh, or the Holy Trinity, or Allah, or Shiva, or Vishnu, or as Brahman, or the Dharmakaya, the Tao, and so on.

If salvation is taking place, and taking place to about the same extent, within the religious systems presided over by these various deities and absolutes, this suggests that they are different manifestations to humanity of a yet more ultimate ground of all salvific transformation. Let us then consider the possibility that an infinite transcendent divine reality is being differently conceived, and therefore differently experienced, and therefore differently responded to from within our different religio-cultural ways of being human. This hypothesis makes sense of the fact that the salvific transformation seems to have been occurring in all the great traditions. Such a conception is, further, readily open to philosophical support. For we are familiar today with the ways in which human experience is partly formed by the conceptual and linguistic frameworks within which it occurs. The basically Kantian insight that the mind is active in perception, and that we are always aware of our environment as it appears to a consciousness operating with our particular conceptual resources and habits, has been amply confirmed by work in cognitive psychology and the sociology of knowledge and can now be extended with some confidence to the analysis of religious awareness. If, then, we proceed inductively from the phenomenon of religious experience around the world, adopting a religious as distinguished from a naturalistic interpretation of it, we are likely to find ourselves making two moves. The first is to postulate an ultimate transcendent divine reality (which I have been referring to as the Real) which, being beyond the scope of our human concepts, cannot be directly experienced by us as it is in itself but only as it appears through our various human thought-forms. And the second is to identify the thought-and-experienced deities and absolutes as different manifestations of the Real within different historical forms of human consciousness. In Kantian terms, the divine noumenon, the Real *an sich*, is experienced through different human receptivities as a range of divine phenomena, in the formation of which religious concepts have played an essential part.

These different 'receptivities' consist of conceptual schemas within which various personal, communal and historical factors have produced yet further variations. The most basic concepts in terms of which the Real is humanly thought-and-experienced are those of (personal) deity and of the (non-personal) absolute. But the Real is not actually experienced either as deity in general or as the absolute in general. Each basic concept becomes (in Kantian terminology) schematized in more concrete form. It is at this point that individual and cultural factors enter the process. The religious tradition of which we are a part, with its history and ethos and its great exemplars, its scriptures feeding our thoughts and emotions, and perhaps above all its devotional or meditative practices, constitutes an uniquely shaped and coloured 'lens' through which we are concretely aware of the Real specifically as the personal Adonai, or as the Heavenly Father, or as Allah, or Vishnu, or Shiva . . . or again as the non-personal Brahman, or Dharmakaya, or the Void or the Ground . . . Thus, one who uses the forms of Christian prayer and sacrament is thereby led to experience the Real as the divine Thou, whereas one who practices advaitic yoga or Buddhist zazen is thereby brought to experience the Real as the infinite being-consciousness-bliss of Brahman, or as the limitless emptiness of *sunyata* which is at the same time the infinite fullness of immediate reality as 'wondrous being.'

Three explanatory comments at this point before turning to the next level of doctrinal disagreement. First, to suppose that the experienced deities and absolutes which are the intentional objects of worship or content of religious meditation, are appearances or manifestations of the Real, rather than each being itself the Real *an sich*, is not to suppose that they are illusions—any more than the varying ways in which a mountain may appear to a plurality of differently placed observers are illusory. That the same reality may be variously experienced and described is true even of physical objects. But in the case of the infinite, transcendent divine reality there may well be much greater scope for the use of varying human conceptual schemas producing varying modes of phenomenal experience. Whereas the concepts in terms of which we are aware of mountains and rivers and houses are largely (though by no means entirely) standard throughout the human race, the religious concepts in terms of which we become aware of the Real have developed in widely different ways within the different cultures of the earth.

As a second comment, to say that the Real is beyond the range of our human concepts is not intended to mean that it is beyond the scope of purely formal, logically generated concepts—such as the concept of being beyond the range of (other than purely formal) concepts. We would not be able to refer at all to that which cannot be conceptualized in any way, not even by the concept of being unconceptualizable! But the other than purely formal concepts by which our

experience is structured must be presumed not to apply to its noumenal ground. The characteristics mapped in thought and language are those that are constitutive of human experience. We have no warrant to apply them to the noumenal ground of the phenomenal, i.e., experienced, realm. We should therefore not think of the Real *an sich* as singular or plural, substance or process, personal or non-personal, good or bad, purposive or non-purpose. This has long been a basic theme of religious thought. For example, within Christianity, Gregory of Nyssa declared that:

> The simplicity of the True Faith assumes God to be that which He is, namely, incapable of being grasped by any term, or any idea, or any other device of our apprehension, remaining beyond the reach not only of the human but of the angelic and all supramundane intelligence, unthinkable, unutterable, above all expression in words, having but one name that can represent His proper nature, the single name being "Above Every Name" (*Against Eunomius*, I, 42).

Augustine, continuing this tradition, said that 'God transcends even the mind' (*True Religion*, 36:67), and Aquinas that 'by its immensity, the divine substance surpasses every form that our intellect reaches' (*Contra Gentiles*, I, 14, 3). In Islam the Qur'an affirms that God is 'beyond what they describe' (6:101). The Upanishads declare of Brahman, 'There the eye goes not, speech goes not, nor the mind' (*Kena Up.*, 1, 3), and Shankara wrote that Brahman is that 'before which words recoil, and to which no understanding has ever attained' (Otto, *Mysticism East and West*, E. T. 1932, p. 28).

But, third, we might well ask, why postulate an ineffable and unobservable divine-reality-in-itself? If we can say virtually nothing about it, why affirm its existence? The answer is that the reality or non-reality of the postulated noumenal ground of the experienced religious phenomena constitutes the difference between a religious and a naturalistic interpretation of religion. If there is no such transcendent ground, the various forms of religious experience have to be categorized as purely human projections. If on the other hand there is such a transcendent ground, then these phenomena may be joint products of the universal presence of the Real and of the varying sets of concepts and images that have crystallized within the religious traditions of the earth. To affirm the transcendent is thus to affirm that religious experience is not solely a construction of the human imagination but is a response—though always culturally conditioned—to the Real.

Those doctrinal conflicts, then, that embody different conceptions of the ultimate arise, according to the hypothesis I am presenting, from the variations between different sets of human conceptual schema and spiritual practice. And it seems that each of these varying ways of thinking-and-experiencing the Real has been able to mediate its transforming presence to human life. For the different major concepts of the ultimate do not seem—so far as we can tell—to result in one religious totality being soteriologically more effective than another.

IV

The second level of doctrinal difference consists of metaphysical beliefs which cohere with although they are not exclusively linked to a particular conception of the ultimate. These are beliefs about the relation of the material universe to the

Real: creation *ex nihilo*, emanation, an eternal universe, an unknown form of dependency . . .? And about human destiny: reincarnation or a single life, eternal identity, or transcendence of the self . . .? Again, there are questions about the existence of heavens and hells and purgatories and angels and devils and many other subsidiary states and entities. Out of this mass of disputed religious issues let me pick two major examples: is the universe created *ex nihilo*, and do human beings reincarnate?

I suggest that we would do well to apply to such questions a principle that was taught by the Buddha two and a half millennia ago. He listed a series of 'undetermined questions' (*avyakata*)—whether the universe is eternal, whether it is spatially infinite, whether (putting it in modern terms) mind and brain are identical, and what the state is of a completed project of human existence (a Tathagata) after bodily death. He refused to answer these questions, saying that we do not need to have knowledge of these things in order to attain liberation or awakening (nirvana); and indeed that to regard such information as soteriologically essential would only divert us from the single-minded quest for liberation. I think that we can at this point profitable learn from the Buddha, even extending his conception of the undetermined questions further than he did—for together with almost everyone else in his own culture he regarded one of our examples, reincarnation, as a matter of assured knowledge. Let us, then, accept that we do not *know* whether, e.g., the universe was created *ex nihilo*, nor whether human beings are reincarnated; and, further, that it is not necessary for salvation to hold a correct opinion on either matter.

I am not suggesting that such issues are unimportant. On their own level they are extremely important, being both of great interest to us and also having widely ramifying implications within our belief-systems and hence for our lives. The thought of being created out of nothing can nourish a salutary sense of absolute dependence. (But other conceptions can also nurture that sense.) The idea of reincarnation can offer the hope of future spiritual progress; though, combined with the principle of karma, it can also serve to validate the present inequalities of human circumstances. (But other eschatologies also have their problems, both theoretical and practical). Thus these—and other—disputed issues do have a genuine importance. Further, it is possible that some of them may one day be settled by empirical evidence. It might become established, for example, that the 'big bang' of some fifteen billion years ago was an absolute beginning, thus ruling out the possibility that the universe is eternal. And again, it might become established, by an accumulation of evidence, that reincarnation does indeed occur in either some or all cases. On the other hand it is possible that we shall never achieve agreed knowledge in these areas. Certainly, at the present time, whilst we have theories, preferences, hunches, inherited convictions, we cannot honestly claim to have secure knowledge. And the same is true, I suggest, of the entire range of metaphysical issues about which the religions dispute. They are of intense interest, properly the subject of continuing research and discussion, but are not matters concerning which absolute dogmas are appropriate. Still less is it appropriate to maintain that salvation depends upon accepting some one particular opinion or dogma. We have seen that the transformation of human existence from self-centeredness to Reality-centeredness seems to be taking place within each of the great traditions despite their very different answers

to these debated questions. It follows that a correct opinion concerning them is not required for salvation.

V

The third level of doctrinal disagreement concerns historical questions. Each of the great traditions includes a larger or smaller body of historical beliefs. In the case of Judaism these include at least the main features of the history described in the Hebrew scriptures; in the case of Christianity, these plus the main features of the life, death and resurrection of Jesus as described in the New Testament; in the case of Islam, the main features of the history described in the Qur'an; in the case of Vaishnavite Hinduism, the historicity of Krishna; in the case of Buddhism, the historicity of Guatama and his enlightenment at Bodh Gaya; and so on. But although each tradition thus has its own records of the past, there are rather few instances of direct disagreement between these. For the strands of history that are cherished in these different historical memories do not generally overlap; and where they do overlap they do not generally involve significant differences. The overlaps are mainly within the thread of ancient near eastern history that is common to the Jewish, Christian and Muslim scriptures; and within this I can only locate two points of direct disagreement—the Torah's statement that Abraham nearly sacrificed his son Isaac at Mount Moriah (Genesis 22) versus the Muslim interpretation of the Qur'anic version (in Sura 37) that it was his other son Ishmael; and the New Testament witness that Jesus died on the cross versus the Qur'anic teaching that 'they did not slay him, neither crucified him, only a likeness of that was shown them' (Sura 4:156). (This latter however would seem to be a conflict between an historical report, in the New Testament, and a theological inference—that God would not allow so great a prophet to be killed—in the Qur'an.)

All that one can say in general about such disagreements, whether between two traditions or between any one of them and the secular historians, is that they could only properly be settled by the weight of historical evidence. However, the events in question are usually so remote in time, and the evidence so slight or so uncertain, that the question cannot be definitively settled. We have to be content with different communal memories, enriched as they are by the mythic halo that surrounds all long-lived human memories of events of transcendent significance. Once again, then, I suggest that differences of historical judgment, although having their own proper importance, do not prevent the different traditions from being effective, and so far as we can tell equally effective, contexts of salvation. It is evidently not necessary for salvation to have correct historical information. (It is likewise not necessary for salvation, we may add, to have correct scientific information.)

VI

Putting all this together, the picture that I am suggesting can be outlined as follows: our human religious experience, variously shaped as it is by our sets of religious concepts, is a cognitive response to the universal presence of the ultimate divine Reality that, in itself, exceeds human conceptuality. This Reality is however manifested to us in ways formed by a variety of human concepts, as the range of divine personae and metaphysical impersonae witnessed to in the history of religions. Each major tradition,

built around its own distinctive way of thinking-and-experiencing the Real, has developed its own answers to the perennial questions of our origin and destiny, constituting more or less comprehensive and coherent cosmologies and eschatologies. These are human creations which have, by their association with living streams of religious experience, become invested with a sacred authority. However they cannot all be wholly true; quite possibly none is wholly true; perhaps all are partly true. But since the salvific process has been going on through the centuries despite this unknown distribution of truth and falsity in our cosmologies and eschatologies, it follows that it is not necessary for salvation to adopt any one of them. We would therefore do well to learn to tolerate unresolved, and at present unresolvable, differences concerning these ultimate mysteries.

One element, however, to be found in the belief-systems of most of the traditions raises a special problem, namely that which asserts the sole salvific efficacy of that tradition. I shall discuss this problem in terms of Christianity because it is particularly acute for those of us who are Christians. We are all familiar with such New Testament texts as 'There is salvation in no one else [than Jesus Christ], for there is no other name under heaven given among men by which we must be saved' (Acts 4:12), and with the Catholic dogma *Extra ecclesiam nulla salus* (No salvation outside the church) and its Protestant equivalent—never formulated as an official dogma but nevertheless implicit within the 18th and 19th century Protestant missionary expansion,—no salvation outside Christianity. Such a dogma differs from other elements of Christian belief in that it is not only a statement about the potential relationship of Christians to God but at the same time about the actual relationship of non-Christians to God. It says that the latter, in virtue of being non-Christians, lack salvation. Clearly such a dogma is incompatible with the insight that the salvific transformation of human existence is going on, and so far as we can tell going on to a more or less equal extent, within all the great traditions. Insofar, then, as we accept that salvation is not confined to Christianity we must reject the old exclusivist dogma.

This has in fact now been done by most thinking Christians, though exceptions remain, mostly within the extreme Protestant fundamentalist constituencies. The *Extra ecclesiam* dogma, although not explicitly repealed, has been outflanked by the work of such influential Catholic theologians as Karl Rahner, whose new approach was in effect endorsed by Vatican II. Rahner expressed his more inclusivist outlook by suggesting that devout people of other faiths are 'anonymous Christians,' within the invisible church even without knowing it, and thus within the sphere of salvation. The present Pope, in his Encyclical *Redemptor Hominis* (1979) has expressed this thought even more comprehensively by saying that 'every man without exception has been redeemed by Christ' and 'with every man without any exception whatever Christ is in a way united, even when man in unaware of it' (para. 14). And a number of Protestant theologians have advocated a comparable position.

The feature that particularly commends this kind of inclusivism to many Christians today is that it recognizes the spiritual values of other religions, and the occurrence of salvation within them, and yet at the same time preserves their conviction of the ultimate superiority of their own religion over all others. For it maintains that salvation, wherever it occurs, is Christian salvation; and Christians are accordingly those who alone know and preach the source of salvation, namely in the atoning death of Christ.

This again, like the old exclusivism, is a statement not only about the ground of salvation for Christians but also for Jews, Muslims, Hindus, Buddhists and everyone else. But we have seen that it has to be acknowledged that the immediate ground of their transformation is the particular spiritual path along which they move. It is by living in accordance with the Torah or with the Qur'anic revelation that Jews and Muslims find a transforming peace with God; it is by one or other of their great *margas* that Hindus attain to *moksha*; it is by the Eightfold Path that Theravada Buddhists come to *nirvana*; it is by *zazen* that Zen Buddhists attain to *satori*; and so on. The Christian inclusivist is, then, by implication, declaring that these various spiritual paths are efficacious, and constitute authentic contexts of salvation, because Jesus died on the cross; and, by further implication, that if he had not died on the cross they would not be efficacious.

This is a novel and somewhat astonishing doctrine. How are we to make sense of the idea that the salvific power of the dharma taught five hundred years earlier by the Buddha is a consequence of the death of Jesus in approximately 30 C.E.? Such an apparently bizarre conception should only be affirmed for some very good reason. It was certainly not taught by Jesus or his apostles. It has emerged only in the thought of twentieth century Christians who have come to recognize that Jews are being salvifically transformed through the spirituality of Judaism, Muslims through that of Islam, Hindus and Buddhists through the paths mapped out by their respective traditions, and so on, but who nevertheless wish to retain their inherited sense of the unique superiority of Christianity. The only outlet left for this sense, when one has acknowledged the salvific efficacy of the various great spiritual ways, is the arbitrary and contrived notion of their metaphysical dependency upon the death of Christ. But the theologian who undertakes to spell out this invisible causality is not to be envied. The problem is not one of logical possibility—it only requires logical agility to cope with that—but one of religious or spiritual plausibility. It would be a better use of theological time and energy, in my opinion, to develop forms of trinitarian, christological and soteriological doctrine which are compatible with our awareness of the independent salvific authenticity of the other great world faiths. Such forms are already available in principle in conceptions of the Trinity, not as ontologically three but as three ways in which the one God is humanly thought and experienced; conceptions of Christ as a man so fully open to and inspired by God as to be, in the ancient Hebrew metaphor, a 'son of God'; and conceptions of salvation as an actual human transformation which has been powerfully elicited and shaped, among his disciples, by the influence of Jesus.

There may indeed well be a variety of ways in which Christian thought can develop in response to our acute late twentieth century awareness of the other world religions, as there were of responding to the nineteenth century awareness of the evolution of the forms of life and the historical character of the holy scriptures. And likewise there will no doubt be a variety of ways in which each of the other great traditions can rethink its inherited assumption of its own unique superiority. But it is not for us to tell people of other traditions how to do their own business. Rather, we should attend to our own.

Notes

This paper was originally delivered as the second Kegley Lecture at California State University, Bakersfield, on February 10th, 1988. For a fuller account of its proposals the reader is invited to see my *An Interpretation of Religion* (New Haven: Yale University Press and London: Macmillan, 1988).

JOHN HICK

The Ideal of Generous Goodwill, Love, Compassion

Hick suggests that, broadly speaking, there are two main patterns of religious transformation to Reality-centeredness in the world's religions: in one pattern there is a focus on prayer and meditation and withdrawal from the world, as in a monastic life; in the other there is a focus on changing the world for the better, as in medical missionary work. In the different religious traditions of the world there have been individuals greatly advanced in religious transformation in both patterns. Such individuals Hick calls "saints." In "Religious Pluralism and Salvation" he mentions Julian of Norwich, whom he counts as a more contemplative saint, and Mahatma Gandhi, who is a more active and political saint. We could as well mention Mother Teresa of Calcutta as another saintly person following the active pattern.

For Hick there is an "ethical criterion" that applies to both patterns of transformation from self-centeredness to Reality-centeredness. It is not a criterion that belongs uniquely to Islam or to Buddhism or to any one religion, but is a common criterion in the world religions, Hick claims. It is the criterion of love/compassion. It is by virtue of this common criterion and the ideal it expresses that saints can be identified in all the great religious traditions. The ideal of "generous goodwill, love, compassion" is embodied in the Golden Rule that "it is good to benefit others and evil to harm them," which Hick finds in some form to be universal among the world religions. And in applying this criterion to the religions of the world Hick comes to the tentative judgment that, while vicious and evil behavior is found among the religious in all the world religions, it appears that all the great religious traditions are equally productive of love/compassion, and this holds both at the personal level and at the level of large scale religious efforts. In this way Hick concludes that, as far as we can tell, no one religious tradition is superior to the others in transforming human consciousness from self-centeredness to Reality-centeredness.

In this reading Hick endeavors to show that if we look at the scriptures and religious writings of the great religious traditions, we will find that each tradition teaches the moral ideal of generous goodwill, love, compassion. "The Ideal of Generous Goodwill, Love, Compassion" is in Chap. 8, where it was included to show how Hick finds the moral ideal of "generous goodwill, love, compassion," in some expression, to be universal among the world religions.

KEITH WARD

Divine Ineffability

Keith Ward is the author of many books in theology and philosophy of religion. In "Divine Ineffability" Ward agrees with John Hick in rejecting both exclusivism and inclusivism, but he disagrees with Hick's pluralism on a point of some importance. For Hick the Real, or the Real-in-itself, cannot be experienced or conceived. This means that the Real is "ineffable" in the strong sense that human concepts and language do not apply to it. The Real may be experienced by Christians *as* a loving God, but it is not the Real-in-itself that is loving or is experienced as loving, for Hick. Ward's criticism of Hick's pluralism is on this point of ineffability.

Ward offers an alternative form of pluralism. In Ward's pluralism the Real or the ultimate *is* a reality of compassion and bliss, "a supreme reality of value, love, and power," which is "one, perfect, the cause of all." For Ward's form of pluralism there are "genuine experiences of the Real," but they are not confined to any one religious tradition, and the "interaction of many traditions is desirable to attain a more adequate grasp of [religious] reality."

From *God, Truth, and Reality: Essays in Honour of John Hick*, edited by Arvind Sharma. London: Macmillan and New York: St. Martin's, 1993. Reproduced with permission of Palgrave Macmillan.

Divine Ineffability

'We know our God from his operations (*energeia*), but do not undertake to approach near to his essence (*ousia*)' (Basil, Epistle 234). There is a strong tradition in Christianity of the ineffability of God, the utter transcendence of the Divine nature to any human thought. John Hick, in his recent work, uses what seems to be a similar doctrine of the distinction between the noumenal nature of the Real and the phenomenal appearances which are known to human beings. He uses it, however, to suggest that the noumenal reality may appear in many different ways to different observers, depending upon their conceptual equipment, culture and temperament. Thus many of the great world faiths may be responding to the same Real, as it appears to them in various ways. We might indeed put this by saying that we know the Real from its appearances (phenomena), but do not undertake to approach near to its noumenal essence. It could be, then, that Professor Hick's use of the noumenal/phenomenal distinction simply restates the classical Christian doctrine of Divine ineffability. I want to explore the extent to which this may be the case.

It is difficult to know exactly what the Cappadocian Fathers had in mind when they distinguished the nature from the operations of God. But since a question about the *ousia* of something is often a request to be told the sort of thing it is, one may take the Divine essence to be that which is definitive of God as God really is, that which makes this entity God and not something else. When one asks about the operations of God, however, one is asking about the things God does, or about how God relates to the world, about the actions in the world of a being of a certain nature.

Obviously, the actions of a being express its nature to some extent. Some philosophers would hold that it is my actions which define my nature, what I am. But it is quite conceivable that a being might conceal its nature or act in ways which reveal, at best, only a small part of what it is. Suppose, for example, we meet a being from another galaxy which appears to us only as a blob of light. It causes systematic changes in its environment, which we conceive as actions, since they seem to exhibit purpose and design. Yet we may have no idea of what is going on in its 'mind'; whether it has thoughts and feelings like ours, or how much about it there is that is invisible to us and that we cannot understand. All we see are the apparently purposive changes in the world around it. We might say that these changes do show how that being wishes to relate to us. In one sense, then, they do show something of the nature of the being; they show that the being can and wishes to relate to us in these ways. But they may not show what that being is like 'from the inside', or when it is not relating to us. Its inner processes may remain quite mysterious to us.

It does not seem to be an absurd supposition that there may be something which human concepts simply cannot describe at all, if it is so different from anything we know that we are at a loss to know how to describe it. However, even in saying, if we do, that it is a 'thing' and that it is different from all other things, we are saying something about it. Basil was not supposing that the essence of God was unknowable, in the sense that it might be blind energy or a malevolent committee of demons for all we know. If God is indescribable by us, it is because God is a reality of greater, not lesser, intelligibility, beauty and bliss than any we can imagine.

We get to the notion of Divine ineffability by starting with the power and wisdom of a personal creator, as seen in the world; or by starting with personal experience of a presence which seems to be both awe-inspiring and mysterious. Only when we qualify these initial concepts by successively denying all limitations on the creator and denying the adequacy of all specific descriptive terms to characterise the object of our experience do we come to say that God is ineffable. In other words, the idea of 'the ineffable God' is not simply the idea of something totally unknowable. Since it is necessarily true that whatever is unknowable is unknown, this would entail that such a God is quite unknown. But it is essential to theism to claim that one *knows* the ineffable God; one is acquainted with what is beyond understanding. One can put this by stressing that this idea of the ineffable is not just of some ineffable thing or other; it is the idea of an ineffable *God*; that is, of a creator truly known to us in experience, yet whose essential nature transcends our understanding. Certain statements, for Basil and for all orthodox Christians, are unequivocally true of God—that God is more perfect than human beings; that God is one; and that God is Trinitarian in being. It is just that we cannot comprehend what such a being is really like, in the fullness of its reality. It is wholly misleading, therefore, to say that, according to Basil the Great, we have a purely negative knowledge of God.

Immanuel Kant perhaps came closest to having such a doctrine of negative knowledge in the *Critique of Pure Reason*, when he argued that, because of the Antinomies of Reason, we can know that the real world is not as we suppose it to be; but we can be certain that there is a real world. The 'proof', repeated in various forms by many later Idealist philosophers, shows that this world is contradictory (that we can prove contradictory propositions to be true of it); therefore we can know it is not real. In Kant's case, one can resolve the antinomies of space and time by positing that they are not objective realities, but forms of intuition; from which it follows that reality must be positively unlike them—but, of course, we cannot know in what way.

It is rather unsatisfactory to say merely that reality is completely indescribable, since it seems to get one no further towards knowing what reality is. At that point, the antinomies of freedom and necessity, and of contingency and necessity, suggested to Kant that, though one could *know* nothing of the real world, one was forced to think of it in a specific way, as a necessary demand of Reason. One had to postulate God, freedom and immortality for practical purposes to do with the regulative employment of the Understanding in respect of the phenomenal world. So Reason compels one to think the unknowable in a specific manner. One has no knowledge of it, theoretically speaking; but one has a thought of it, which one must adopt for practical purposes. The justification for thinking of the unknowable in a specific way is that Reason compels us to do so as a condition of the possibility of scientific investigation into and moral action in the world.

For this argument to succeed, one must show both that phenomenal reality, as ordinarily conceived, is contradictory; and that some urgently practical and totally unavoidable necessity compels one to think of reality in a specific way. It has to be said that few have been convinced that Kant succeeded in either of these tasks; and it seems likely that his concept of a noumenal or intelligible world, as the very name implies, is a hangover from the pre-Critical philosophy which permitted real and indeed certain knowledge of the intelligible realm, which was in no doubt that reality was 'intelligible' or noumenal, and saw the phenomenal world as a sort of confused appearance of what only pure Reason could truly discern. Divorced from that full-blooded metaphysic, Kant's demythologising of the noumenal is likely to seem rather like the Cheshire Cat's smile—no longer fully appealing once the cat itself has gone.

Professor Hick has a rather similar two-stage argument, which may seem rather more convincing than Kant's. For the first stage, religious experience is seen to be contradictory, in the sense that various religions, all with a *prima facie* claim to truth, present contradictory views of the nature of reality. This suggests either that all are false, which just has too many wise and saintly people suffering from delusions; or that one is correct and all the rest are false, which is not much better; or that all are genuine encounters with reality, not with reality as it is but with phenomenal appearances of reality. As with Kant, the implication is that in fact none of our knowledge is of the Real as it really is; it is largely if not entirely a product of our minds. In the second stage of the argument, what compels us to think of reality in a specific way is not some universal demand of Reason, but the claim of religious experience to objective validity. The idea of a noumenal Real is a postulate for asserting that such experiences can be both contradictory and veridical—for they are of appearances only, and not of the Real in itself; yet they are appearances *of* the Real.

The problem that is at once glaringly apparent is to decide how anyone can be sure that appearances are of the Real, that they are 'authentic manifestations' of the Real, rather than pure inventions of the mind. I think Professor Hick simply wants us to *postulate* that they are, to accept that all widely-accepted experiences that seem to be of the Real are what they seem to be. But there is a major paradox in this position, which can be briefly set out as follows:

1. When it seems to me that X, then probably X. (This 'principle of credulity' is one that Hick applies to religious experiences.)
2. It seems to some that X, to some that Y, to some that Z. . . .
3. So probably X, Y and Z (from 1, 2).
4. X, Y and Z are inconsistent.
5. Reality cannot be inconsistent.
6. So X, Y and Z are not true of Reality (from 4, 5).
7. What is true of appearances need not be true of Reality.
8. So X, Y and Z are true of appearances, not of Reality (from 3, 6, 7).

This is all satisfactory, until it seems to someone, *P*, that X is true of Reality in itself, but it seems to *Q* that it is not. Then, it is probably true that X is true of Reality in itself (by 1); but X cannot be true of Reality (by 6). Therefore if P's belief that X is true of Reality is probably true, it can only be so if it is true of appearance, not of Reality (by 8). In other words, it can only be true if it is false. X is both true of Reality and not, at the same time. Since a contradiction is unacceptable (as 5 states), some of the premises of this argument must be modified.

The obvious premise to modify is 1, which is highly dubious in any case, and to admit that many people are mistaken in claims as to what they apprehend. Professor Hick himself does not hesitate to do this in the case of the dispute between realism and non-realism in religion. Here, while he insists on the epistemic right of differing individuals to hold conflicting beliefs, he also insists that one of them must be mistaken (*An Interpretation of Religion* (Macmillan, 1989), p. 13). I am simply pointing out that the same must be true of many religious disputes, when I must admit that someone is mistaken, and I am clearly not going to think it is me! But, of course, this is not a matter of 'all or nothing'. I need not say that all my truth-claims are valid and none of anyone else's is. I can easily say that some of my claims will be false (though I do not now know which); and many of your claims may be true (though I doubt all of them are). So I do not have to say that either all experience claims in religion are false, or only my claims are true. Nor need I get into the self-refuting position that all claims about objects of worship or devotion are veridical. If there is an ineffable God (not a wholly unknowable noumenon), there will plainly be many truths about God I have not perceived, and I may well have misconstrued some of the things I think are true about God. Yet I do at least claim that there is a being whose nature is ineffable, but some of whose causal manifestations in the world I take myself to have true beliefs about.

I therefore doubt whether a Kantian philosophy can provide an adequate construal of Divine ineffability. According to Kant's way of resolving the contradictions of experience, the transcendental ideality of space and time means that space and time are not objectively real at all; they are forms of human perception, contributed by the perceiving mind. But it would not satisfy many religious believers to be told that their gods are not objectively real; that they are contributed by human imagination; and whatever it is that underlies them is totally unknowable.

One does not wish to discard the experiences of others and claim sole validity for one's own; that does seem arbitrary and arrogant. An obvious move is then to see all such experiences as subject to conceptual interpretation, which may qualify the character of the experience. The validity of the experience will then depend on the accuracy of the interpretation. And it may be true that no interpretation is adequate to the richness and complexity of the religious object. What one will have is a range of more or less adequate interpretations, caused in part by an object which probably transcends any of them.

This, I think, is the situation Professor Hick has well illuminated by his writings. But does the introduction of a noumenal/phenomenal distinction help, or does it introduce needless confusion? What seems wrong with it is, first, that it leads us to regard all objects of religious experience as illusory or subjective in some sense; whereas believers want to make claims to objectivity, however inadequate. Second, it leads us to renounce all claims to knowledge of noumenal reality; whereas most believers wish to claim some knowledge of ultimate reality— again, even if inadequately conceived. In other words, the Kantian distinction turns disputes about the relative adequacy of interpretations of reality into wholly unresolvable claims about a completely unknowable reality. In fact, if reality is completely unknowable, no cognitive claims can be made about it at all; so religion inevitably becomes a wholly subjective matter of personal attitudes.

Kant was not speaking of a diverse set of inadequate and partial interpretations of an experienced, very complex reality. He was speaking of a universal and necessary phenomenal reality which left noumenal reality both unexperienced and unknowable. But Professor Hick does claim to know some things about the Real—that it is a supremely valuable reality; that it is one cause of everything other than itself; that it manifests to human experience in a number of ways which are not wholly misleading. And he does wish to rule out some experiences as inadequate—experiences of the Real as malevolent, as having no causal effects on the future, or as entailing no ontological claims about how the world is. So he does work with a criterion of adequacy, embodying ideas of moral demand and promise for the future; and with a concept of the Real as one supreme cause. Bluntly, he is a theist who is concerned to show how God may be experienced in many traditions, which partially show aspects of the Divine being. Some of these ways are more adequate than others, though one might be unwise to claim that one was wholly adequate and all the others quite inadequate by comparison. It is, however, quite clear that Professor Hick believes there is one supremely valuable reality which can bring us into conscious relationship with itself, a relationship which will realise human hopes for a fulfilled and happy existence. His complete rejection of non-realism in religion in favour of some form of 'cosmic optimism' shows his commitment to ontological realism, and against the view that we can know nothing of what is truly real.

Since Professor Hick is a religious realist, he does not really believe in a noumenal reality at all, as something of which one can say absolutely nothing. He rather believes that there is a reality of supreme value, love and power (for it can and will bring us all to final happiness by knowing and loving it in the end). This is a definite claim to knowledge of the Real. It is quite consistent to go on to say that our knowledge of the Real is very inadequate and may well be mistaken in many

details. It will be affected by our culture, our background knowledge and temperament. Now we see in a glass darkly; though we hope to see face to face; and we claim to know there is a face, however dimly discerned, to be seen.

Consequently, we do not need Kant's complex doctrine of a regulative use of concepts, in accordance with which we think of a reality which is theoretically completely unknown to us. That is just as well, since the reasons Kant gave for thinking that the regulative idea of God was practically necessary are generally adjudged to be almost wholly unconvincing. He thought we needed to postulate a God in order to view the natural world as an ordered systematic whole; but physicists can apparently dispense with God without too much regret. He thought we needed to postulate God in order to reinforce our moral commitment; but moralists tend to think of such an appeal to God as an abandonment of morality for the sake of long-term prudence. We do not need to postulate God to back up any of our independent practical commitments. We do not even need God to be happy, altruistic and psychologically well-balanced, as any Freudian analyst will testify. Once a claim to the objective truth of theism is given up, any attempted pragmatic justification for a religious way of life will be shattered by the hatred, violence and bigotry of its adherents. Only if one believed it to be true could one possibly accept a form of belief which is so often and so clearly destructive of human good.

Professor Hick's underlying argument is that, if there is a reality of supreme power, love and value, it will not confine its saving activity (its efforts to bring humans to fulfilment in conscious loving relation to it) to one part of the human race or one culture. Thus one will expect to find traces of its actions everywhere and at all times. This seems to me a most persuasive point. The moral world we are moving in here is very different from, say, the fifth-century Augustinian view that all humans are born in sin and deserve eternal damnation; so that it is unmerited grace if God saves anyone at all; and who he saves is entirely up to him. On the contrary, humans should not be damned unless they really knowingly choose to be; and such a conscious choice is almost unthinkable; so that God is seen more as a universal persuader towards love and away from selfishness, than as the Judge who will be merciful to whom he wills. And if God is such a universal persuader, his persuasion must naturally be seen universally; that is, presumably, in most religious traditions, and even, in however hidden a form, in non-religious traditions too.

In contrasting the Augustinian view with Professor Hick's, it is immediately clear that there are real religious conflicts, and that no one can regard Augustine and Hick as having an equally adequate view of the Real. One gives a more adequate view than the other, because it has reflected more deeply on the nature of Divine love and human freedom. It does not follow that Augustine had no veridical experiences of God. All that follows is that some interpretations of some of his experiences were inadequate to the reality of God. By parity of reasoning, one might expect that all of us will be prey to some inadequacy of interpretation; but we cannot accept that our view is no more adequate than that of others. At points of conflict we must claim the exclusive correctness of our perception. If one believes as Professor Hick does, in the universal persuasiveness of the Divine love, one must accept that this is just one view of religion and of the Real among others; and that it would be rejected by those who do not believe there is a Divine love (e.g.

Buddhists) or that, if there is, it is universally persuasive (e.g. Calvinists).

How pluralistic is this view, in fact? It is not pluralist in the sense that all competing views are in some sense correct. It claims exclusive truth for the propositions that the Divine love is universally persuasive. We must look at all religions, then, to see in them the persuasive self-disclosure of the love of God. Such love will be active and finally effective in all religions; and that is a form of pluralism (it might be called 'soft pluralism'). However, it does not follow that all religions will present God in equally adequate ways. If that were so, it would not matter which religion one adopted, or which form of which religion. Yet there are both moral and rational choices to be made in religion; and Professor Hick himself is clear that some religious beliefs are immoral (substitutionary atonement, for example), and that some are irrational (seven-day creation, perhaps). One must seek the most intellectually, morally and spiritually adequate view one can find (one that is consistent with well-established scientific and historical knowledge; that enshrines a sensitive concern for the good of all human lives; and that contains a sustainable concept of individual human perfection).

Now as one looks at the religious traditions of humanity, one can discern a development from pre-scientific cosmologies, restricted tribal moralities and ritualistic concepts of piety towards a more experimental attitude to the world, a more universal approach to morality and a more inward idea of faith. Christianity itself shows a development from early apocalyptic expectations of the end of the world to a vision of a God of universal self-giving love, discerned in the Christ-event. Once one treats the Christian tradition in this way, not as a preservation of literal and definitive truths about the life and status of Jesus but as a matrix for developing theological reflection, it is possible or even obligatory to treat other traditions in a similar way. The pluralistic hypothesis now becomes the view that virtually all serious religious traditions will contain matrices of myth which implicitly contain a disclosure of a reality of compassion and bliss which calls human beings to union with itself. This is not the view that all traditions are true or even compatible; rather, they contain the possibility of evoking more adequate insights into the Real as time goes by. The committed pluralist will now call members of all traditions to explore their own paradigm myths and develop them to find a more adequate disclosure of the Real in them. In so far as such an exploration is expected to disclose one supremely valuable reality calling humans to union with itself, it may be termed 'convergent pluralism'.

But the essential presupposition of this form of pluralism is that religious traditions contain myths which manifest a supreme reality of value, love and power, perceived in many names and forms. This is an exclusive truth-claim, though it does not belong to only one tradition. It entails that any traditions which explicitly make this claim are, in that respect, more adequate than traditions which do not (though they may make many false claims in other respects—about life after death, for example; so that one may hesitate to call them 'more adequate' traditions *per se*). The full truth of religion does not lie in the past, in some completed and final revelation. It lies ahead, in the continuing exploration of that infinite Divine nature which requires a dialectic of conflict and convergence between many traditions to disclose the richness of its being more adequately.

This is not most helpfully put by saying that there is a noumenal reality the nature of which is wholly unknowable. That entails that no one will ever know it or have any idea of its true nature; and that therefore no one can be in any position to see whether or not it is being truly expressed to any extent at all in human concepts. Nor is it helpful to say that all religions are, as they stand, authentic expressions of this reality. For certain views are plain wrong, and truth would be a casualty on any such view. What needs to be said, to capture the position most adequately, is that there is a spiritual reality of supreme power and value; but we are unlikely to have a very adequate conception of it. However, there are many ways in which it may be disclosed to human beings; and all of them are likely to exhibit defects of human conception and limitation of vision. In particular, the claims of any tradition to have an exclusively true grasp of it must be denied. This is one possible interpretation of the pluralistic hypothesis. It says that religious truth is not confined to one tradition (exclusivism); nor does one tradition contain in a more adequate form all the truths that others contain (inclusivism).

However, it does not suppose that all traditions are equally adequate expressions of the Real or that they will lead with approximately equal efficacy to one common goal or salvation. Nor does it imply any noumenal/phenomenal distinction. On the contrary, it requires that there are genuine experiences of the Real, however difficult it is for us to distinguish the real from the illusory; and thus that the Real is truly expressed in the phenomenal, even if its nature far transcends what we can grasp. We can still truly say that it is one, perfect, the cause of all. We can agree with Basil that its operations are truly known, but that its essential being lies beyond our complete comprehension, even though we know some true facts about it. One can agree with John Hick that God is partially known in many traditions and that God can be expected to operate in all. It then does seem plausible to think that one cannot claim a complete and final apprehension of God in any tradition, and thus that the interaction of many traditions is desirable to attain a more adequate grasp of its reality. In face of this degree of agreement, it may seem a small cavil to protest at the terminology of noumenon and phenomenon.

Its importance, however, is this: once all knowledge of the noumenal is renounced, all criteria of the adequacy of religious beliefs must operate simply on a pragmatic basis, of what best suits our human needs and purposes. Truth then becomes a means to an end, whether of happiness, morality or human perfection. It seems to me that religion must continue to make claims to truth, and indeed only define what salvation is in terms of its perception of the truth about what is ultimately the case about the world, human nature and destiny. Religion must be fundamentally realist; and realists can have nothing to do with the noumenal. In the end, Basil the Great has little in common with Immanuel Kant. Orthodox theists can, however, coherently claim that God's essence is ineffable; meaning, not that they know nothing at all about it, but that they admit that in its perfection, its value and its power it transcends our understanding. Professor Hick's exciting and visionary theology takes this insight, adds the Christian belief that God is a God of universal love, and presses home the implications of this for a global view of revelation and salvation. Where he leads I am happy to follow—until he begins to walk towards the unknown country of the noumenal, at which point I feel constrained to tell him that there is simply nothing there.

Chapter 12

Other Ways of Understanding Religious Plurality

The last chapter contains readings on four different ways of understanding religious plurality. Three of those ways—exclusivism, inclusivism, and pluralism—are open to those committed to a particular religion. Only pluralism, however, accepts it that all religions or all the major religions are right. John Hick, who has developed a distinctive form of pluralism, maintains that exclusivism, inclusivism, and pluralism exhaust the possible views on the relationship between religions (at least for "Christian theologies of religion"). This may be correct. However, if it is, then it must be allowed that there can be different forms of pluralism taken as the view that all major religions are right. The last chapter contains readings by John Hick and Keith Ward that present two forms of pluralism so taken. This chapter contains readings on four other ways of understanding the relationship between different religions that will sustain the view that all major religions are right. These four ways are the *different aspects approach*, the *common core approach* in both its *belief* and *practice* forms, the *indeterminacy approach*, and the *relationships approach*.

The previous chapter contains discussions that present and argue for or defend a thesis about the best way to understand religious plurality. In this chapter we have various readings. Some, like those in the previous chapter, make a reasoned case for a thesis or present reasoned criticisms of a thesis. Others, however, are stories that amount to parables about the best way to understand religious plurality. The first reading in this chapter is Leo Tolstoy's short story *The Coffee-House of Surat*, which contains an expression of both the different aspects approach and the common core approach. The second reading is John Hick's "The Ideal of Generous Goodwill, Love, Compassion," which is in Chap. 8 and is also a reading in the last chapter in its connection to Hick's pluralism. It is included in this chapter because it offers support for the common core approach. The third reading is from Ninian Smart's "Truth and Religions." In this essay, in a way that is pertinent to the common core approach, Ninian Smart reflects critically on whether the truth-claims of different religions can be reconciled, let alone shared, and on whether religious "fruits" or practice are the same in different traditions. The fourth reading is from two chapters of John H. Whittaker's *Matters of Faith and Matters of Principle*. In our reading he develops a version of the indeterminacy approach. In the fifth reading "To What God?" Shivesh Thakur presents other considerations that recommend an indeterminacy approach. The sixth reading, already in Chapter Three, is Søren Kierkegaard's "parable of the idol-worshipper," as we may call it. It is pertinent here as it applies to the relationships approach. The seventh reading, "The Way of Relationships" from James Kellenberger's *God-Relationships With and Without God*, also applies to the relationships approach.

LEO TOLSTOY

The Coffee-House of Surat

The basic idea that all the different major religions are right, and that all the major religions are in some way paths to God, or to the same Religious Reality, has a long history. It can take different forms. In one form or another it has often been expressed in popular thought in stories and parables, as opposed to fully developed philosophical or theological views. One form of this idea is expressed in a parable that is attributed to the Buddha, the parable of the blind men. In this parable a number of blind men encounter an elephant for the first time. Each touches a different part of the elephant—an ear, a leg, a tusk. The one who feels the ear says that an elephant is flexible, like canvass. The one who touches the elephant's leg says that an elephant is a rigid column, like a tree trunk. And the one who feels the elephant's tusk says that an elephant is sharp and pointed, like a sword blade. As the blind men cannot see the elephant in its entirety so the various religious cannot "see" all of Religious Reality, yet each religion is in touch with part of the truth about that Reality, as each blind man can feel part of the elephant. Religions go wrong, however, if they think they have the whole religious truth. So runs the lesson of the parable.

We find the same underlying idea in a story by the well-known Russian author Leo Tolstoy. Tolstoy is perhaps best known for his novels, one of which is *War and Peace*. But he also wrote stories or tales. One of his stories, adapted from a French author's story, is *The Coffee-House of Surat*. Surat is a city in India and in Tolstoy's story travellers from different parts of the world, who are followers of different religions, find themselves together in Surat's coffee-house. A religious discussion develops, involving a Hindu, a Jew, a Catholic, a Protestant, a Muslim, and others, who disagree about the nature of God and the way to salvation. When the discussion becomes heated, an appeal is made to a Chinese man, who has remained quiet and out of the fray. He is asked for his judgment. His response takes the form of a parable. While the moral of Tolstoy's story, as he draws it, is complex, with a little pressure the moral could be construed as being that there is no absolute religious perspective. There are only the perspectives of Hinduism, Judaism, Catholicism, Protestantism, Islam, and other religions, from which one sees only one aspect of God or Religious Reality. Understood this way Tolstoy's story contains an expression of the *different aspects approach*.

Tolstoy's story, of course, is not a theological or philosophical essay arguing for the different aspects approach. As a story it contains no explicit argument for any particular approach to understanding religious plurality. Rather, it contains a parable with a moral open to interpretation. It is not surprising, then, that

The Coffee-House of Surat may also be understood as expressing other approaches besides or in addition to the different aspects approach. In particular it can be interpreted as expressing the common core approach to understanding religious plurality.

The *common core approach* looks for what the different religious traditions share, what they hold in common. If all the major religions share a core, then they will not be in conflict over that core and can all be right by virtue of the core they share. This approach can take several forms. In one form the approach looks for a common core of belief. In another it looks for a common core of practice. The *common core of belief approach* seeks to find a common core of mutually held beliefs among the world's religions, an undisturbed eye of agreed-upon beliefs at the center of divergent and perhaps incompatible truth-claims. The *common core of practice approach* seeks to find a common core of religious practice among the world's religions. The practice of a religion expresses itself in what the followers of that religion *do*, in the actions of the religion's followers. The religious actions that are of concern to this approach, however, are not the ritualistic actions of religions (praying facing Mecca, crossing oneself with holy water). This approach focuses on the *moral* behavior and action required or encouraged by the different major religious traditions. It is in the area of religious moral practice that this approach finds a common core.

Part of the moral of *The Coffee-House of Surat*, as Tolstoy presents it, is that "the better [a person] knows God the nearer will he draw to Him, imitating His goodness, His mercy, and His love of man," and in this spirit he will not blame or despise those who believe differently from him. This part of Tolstoy's moral points toward the common core of practice approach. As Tolstoy presents his moral, it is theistic in characterizing the core of practice in terms of imitating God's goodness, mercy and love. But the common core of practice view can be understood in such a way that it includes both theistic and non-theistic religions.*

After Bernardin De Saint-Pierre

The Coffeehouse of Surat

In the town of Surat, in India, was a coffeehouse where many travellers and foreigners from all parts of the world met and conversed.

One day a learned Persian theologian visited this coffeehouse. He was a man who had spent his life studying the nature of the Deity, and reading and writing books upon the subject. He had thought, read, and written so much about God, that eventually he lost his wits, became quite confused, and ceased even to believe in the existence of a God. The Shah, hearing of this, had banished him from Persia.

* From *Twenty-Three Tales*, Oxford world's classics, by Leo Tolstoy, edited and translated by Louise and Alymer Maude. Reprinted by permission of Oxford University Press.

After having argued all his life about the First Cause, this unfortunate theologian had ended by quite perplexing himself, and instead of understanding that he had lost his own reason, he began to think that there was no higher Reason controlling the universe.

This man had an African slave who followed him everywhere. When the theologian entered the coffeehouse, the slave remained outside, near the door sitting on a stone in the glare of the sun, and driving away the flies that buzzed around him. The Persian having settled down on a divan in the coffeehouse, ordered himself a cup of opium. When he had drunk it and the opium had begun to quicken the workings of his brain, he addressed his slave through the open door:

"Tell me, wretched slave," said he, "do you think there is a God, or not?"

"Of course there is," said the slave, and immediately drew from under his girdle a small idol of wood.

"There," said he, "that is the God who has guarded me from the day of my birth. Every one in our country worships the fetish tree, from the wood of which this God was made."

This conversation between the theologian and his slave was listened to with surprise by the other guests in the coffeehouse. They were astonished at the master's question, and yet more so at the slave's reply.

One of them, a Brahmin, on hearing the words spoken by the slave, turned to him and said:

"Miserable fool! Is it possible you believe that God can be carried under a man's girdle? There is one God—Brahma, and he is greater than the whole world, for he created it. Brahma is the One, the mighty God, and in His honor are built the temples on the Ganges' banks, where his true priests, the Brahmins, worship

him. They know the true God, and none but they. A thousand score of years have passed, and yet through revolution after revolution these priests have held their sway, because Brahma, the one true God, has protected them."

So spoke the Brahmin, thinking to convince every one; but a Jewish broker who was present replied to him, and said:

"No! the temple of the true God is not in India. Neither does God protect the Brahmin caste. The true God is not the God of the Brahmins, but of Abraham, Isaac, and Jacob. None does He protect but His chosen people, the Israelites. From the commencement of the world, our nation has been beloved of Him, and ours alone. If we are now scattered over the whole earth it is but to try us; for God has promised that He will one day gather His people together in Jerusalem. Then, with the Temple of Jerusalem—the wonder of the ancient world—restored to its splendor, shall Israel be established a ruler over all nations."

So spoke the Jew, and burst into tears. He wished to say more, but an Italian missionary who was there interrupted him.

"What you are saying is untrue," said he to the Jew. "You attribute injustice to God. He cannot love your nation above the rest. Nay rather, even if it be true that of old He favored the Israelites, it is now nineteen hundred years since they angered Him, and caused Him to destroy their nation and scatter them over the earth, so that their faith makes no converts and has died out except here and there. God shows preference to no nation, but calls all who wish to be saved to the bosom of the Catholic Church of Rome, the one outside whose borders no salvation can be found."

So spoke the Italian. But a Protestant minister who happened to be present, growing pale, turned to the Catholic missionary and exclaimed:

"How can you say that salvation belongs to your religion? Those only will be saved, who serve God according to the Gospel, in spirit and in truth, as bidden by the word of Christ."

Then a Turk, an officeholder in the customhouse at Surat, who was sitting in the coffeehouse smoking a pipe, turned with an air of superiority to both the Christians.

"Your belief in your Roman religion is vain," said he. "It was superseded twelve hundred years ago by the true faith: that of Mohammed! You cannot but observe how the true Mohammedan faith continues to spread both in Europe and Asia, and even in the enlightened country of China. You say yourselves that God has rejected the Jews; and, as a proof, you quote the fact that the Jews are humiliated and their faith does not spread. Confess then the truth of Mohammedanism, for it is triumphant and spreads far and wide. None will be saved but the followers of Mohammed, God's latest prophet; and of them, only the followers of Omar, and not of Ali, for the latter are false to the faith."

To this the Persian theologian, who was of the sect of Ali, wished to reply; but by this time a great dispute had arisen among all the strangers of different faiths and creeds present. There were Abyssinian Christians, Lamas from Tibet, Ismailians and Fire-worshippers. They all argued about the nature of God, and how He should be worshipped. Each of them asserted that in his country alone was the true God known and rightly worshipped.

Every one argued and shouted, except a Chinaman, a student of Confucius, who sat quietly in one corner of the coffeehouse, not joining in the dispute. He sat there drinking tea and listening to what the others said, but did not speak himself.

The Turk noticed him sitting there, and appealed to him, saying:

"You can confirm what I say, my good Chinaman. You hold your peace, but if you spoke I know you would uphold my opinion. Traders from your country, who come to me for assistance, tell me that though many religions have been introduced into China, you Chinese consider Mohammedanism the best of all, and adopt it willingly. Confirm, then, my words, and tell us your opinion of the true God and of His prophet."

"Yes, yes," said the rest, turning to the Chinaman, "let us hear what you think on the subject."

The Chinaman, the student of Confucius, closed his eyes, and thought a while. Then he opened them again, and drawing his hands out of the wide sleeves of his garment, and folding them on his breast, he spoke as follows, in a calm and quiet voice.

Sirs, it seems to me that it is chiefly pride that prevents men agreeing with one another on matters of faith. If you care to listen to me, I will tell you a story which will explain this by an example.

I came here from China on an English steamer which had been round the world. We stopped for fresh water, and landed on the east coast of the island of Sumatra. It was midday, and some of us, having landed, sat in the shade of some coconut palms by the seashore, not far from a native village. We were a party of men of different nationalities.

As we sat there, a blind man approached us. We learnt afterwards that he had gone blind from gazing too long and too persistently at the sun, trying to find out what it is, in order to seize its light.

He strove a long time to accomplish this, constantly looking at the sun; but the only result was that his eyes were injured by its brightness, and he became blind.

Then he said to himself:

"The light of the sun is not a liquid; for if it were a liquid it would be possible to pour it from one vessel into another, and it would be moved, like water, by the wind. Neither is it fire; for if it were fire, water would extinguish it. Neither is light a spirit, for it is seen by the eye, nor is it matter, for it cannot be moved. Therefore, as the light of the sun is neither liquid, nor fire, nor spirit, nor matter, it is—nothing!"

So he argued, and, as a result of always looking at the sun and always thinking about it, he lost both his sight and his reason. And when he went quite blind, he became fully convinced that the sun did not exist.

With this blind man came a slave, who after placing his master in the shade of a coconut tree, picked up a coconut from the ground, and began making it into a night-light. He twisted a wick from the fibre of the coconut: squeezed oil from the nut into the shell, and soaked the wick in it.

As the slave sat doing this, the blind man sighed and said to him:

"Well, slave, was I not right when I told you there is no sun? Do you not see how dark it is? Yet people say there is a sun . . . But if so, what is it?"

"I do not know what the sun is," said the slave "That is no business of mine. But I know what light is. Here, I have made a night-light, by the help of which I can serve you and find anything I want in the hut."

And the slave picked up the coconut shell, saying:

"This is my sun."

A lame man with crutches, who was sitting near by heard these words, and laughed:

"You have evidently been blind all your life," said he to the blind man, "not to know what the sun is, I will tell you what it is. The sun is a ball of fire, which rises every morning out of the sea and goes down again among the mountains of our island each evening. We have all seen this, and if you had had your eyesight you too would have seen it."

A fisherman, who had been listening to the conversation, said:

"It is plain enough that you have never been beyond your own island. If you were not lame, and if you had been out as I have in a fishing boat, you would know that the sun does not set among the mountains of our island, but as it rises from the ocean every morning so it sets again in the sea every night. What I am telling you is true, for I see it every day with my own eyes."

Then an Indian who was of our party, interrupted him by saying:

"I am astonished that a reasonable man should talk such nonsense. How can a ball of fire possibly descend into the water and not be extinguished? The sun is not a ball of fire at all, it is the Deity named Deva who rides for ever in a chariot round the golden mountain, Meru. Sometimes the evil serpents Ragu and Ketu attack Deva and swallow him: and then the earth is dark. But our priests pray that the Deity may be released, and then he is set free. Only such ignorant men as you, who have never been beyond their own island, can imagine that the sun shines for their country alone."

Then the master of an Egyptian vessel, who was present, spoke in his turn.

"No," said he, "you also are wrong. The sun is not a Deity, and does not move only round India and its golden mountain. I have sailed much on the Black Sea, and along the coasts of Arabia, and have been to Madagascar and to the Philippines. The sun lights the whole earth, and not India alone. It does not circle round one mountain, but rises far in the east, beyond the Isles of Japan, and sets far, far away in the west, beyond the islands of England. That is why the Japanese call their country 'Nippon,' that is 'the birth of the sun.' I know this well, for I have myself seen much, and heard more from my grandfather, who sailed to the very ends of the sea."

He would have gone on, but an English sailor from our ship interrupted him.

"There is no country," he said, "where people know so much about the sun's movements as in England. The sun, as every one in England knows, rises nowhere and sets nowhere. It is always moving round the earth. We can be sure of this for we have just been round the world ourselves, and nowhere knocked up against the sun. Wherever we went, the sun showed itself in the morning and hid itself at night, just as it does here."

And the Englishman took a stick and, drawing circles on the sand, tried to explain how the sun moves in the heavens and goes round the world. But he was unable to explain it clearly, and pointing to the ship's pilot said:

"This man knows more about it than I do. He can explain it properly."

The pilot, who was an intelligent man, had listened in silence to the talk till he was asked to speak. Now every one turned to him, and he said:

"You are all misleading one another, and are yourselves deceived. The sun does not go round the earth, but the earth goes round the sun, revolving as it goes and turning towards the sun in the course of each twenty-four hours, not only Japan, and the Philippines and Sumatra where we now are, but Africa, and Europe and America, and many lands besides. The sun does not shine for some one mountain, or for some one island, or for some one sea, nor even for one earth alone, but for other planets as well as our earth. If you would only look up at the heavens, instead of at the ground beneath your own feet, you might all understand this, and would then no longer suppose that the sun shines for you, or for your country alone."

Thus spoke the wise pilot, who had voyaged much about the world, and had gazed much upon the heavens above.

"So on matters of faith," continued the Chinaman, the student of Confucius, "it is pride that causes error and discord among men. As with the sun, so it is with God. Each man wants to have a special God of his own, or at least a special God for his native land. Each nation wishes to confine in its own temples Him, whom the world cannot contain.

"Can any temple compare with that which God Himself has built to unite all men in one faith and one religion?

"All human temples are built on the model of this temple, which is God's own world. Every temple has its fonts, its vaulted roof, its lamps, its pictures or sculptures, its inscriptions, its books of the law, its offerings, its altars and its priests. But in what temple is there such a font as the ocean; such a vault as that of the heavens; such lamps as the sun, moon, and stars; or any figures to be compared with living, loving, mutually helpful men? Where are there any records of God's goodness so easy to understand as the blessings which God has strewn abroad for man's happiness? Where is there any book of the law so clear to each man as that written in his heart? What sacrifices equal the self-denials which loving men and women make for one another? And what altar can be compared with the heart of a good man, on which God Himself accepts the sacrifice?

"The higher a man's conception of God, the better will he know Him. And the better he knows God, the nearer will he draw to Him, imitating His goodness, His mercy, and His love of man.

"Therefore, let him who sees the sun's whole light filling the world, refrain from blaming or despising the superstitious man, who in his own idol sees one ray of that same light. Let him not despise even the unbeliever who is blind and cannot see the sun at all."

So spoke the Chinaman, the student of Confucius; and all who were present in the coffeehouse were silent, and disputed no more as to whose faith was the best.

JOHN HICK

The Ideal of Generous Goodwill, Love, Compassion

John Hick claims that there is a common "ethical criterion" that applies to the world religions. It is the criterion of love/compassion. By virtue of this common criterion and the ideal it expresses saints can be identified in all the great religious traditions, Hick maintains. It is by applying this criterion to the religions of the world that Hick comes to the tentative judgment that all the great religious traditions are equally productive of love/compassion. To do so is not to apply a foreign criterion to any of the religions of the world, Hick believes. For the ideal of "generous goodwill, love, compassion" that Hick finds embodied in the Golden Rule he finds to be universally recognized by the world religions. If we look at the scriptures and religious writings of the great religious traditions, Hick believes that we will find that each tradition teaches the moral ideal of generous goodwill, love, compassion.

The ethical criterion of "generous goodwill, love, compassion," then, is both a criterion by which religions can be judged ethically *and* a shared ideal of religious practice. In this way, to the extent that the different scriptures and religious writings of the different religious traditions teach the same ideal, as Hick endeavors to show they do in this reading, we find a common core of practice among the theistic and non-theistic religions of the world. "The Ideal of Generous Goodwill, Love, Compassion" is in Chapter 8.

NINIAN SMART

from Truth and Religions

I n this reading Ninian Smart presents considerations that are relevant to both
the common core of belief approach and the common core of practice
approach. Smart reflects critically on whether the truth-claims of different religions can be reconciled and on whether religious "fruits" or practices are the
same in different traditions. Smart makes the point that Christian theology
changes over time and it is difficult to predict what changes it will undergo. He
observes that if it changes enough in its understanding of Christian beliefs then
what are at present incompatible truth-claims between Christianity and other
religions may through new understanding and construction be "synthesized" or
brought together as compatible beliefs. While two compatible beliefs would still
be two different beliefs, if they are "synthesized" enough they might become
indistinguishable. Smart also reflects on the "practice-claims" of different religions, that is, on the moral practices religions enjoin or encourage. Though different religions may encourage practice in accord with love/compassion there
may yet be differences between the specific actions different religions would
encourage or approve of.

Toward the end of the reading Smart raises an issue that is relevant to the
relationships approach when he turns to the question of "What justifies one in
saying that the Christian and Muslim worship the same God?"*

*Is there a Problem about how the Truth-
Claims of Christianity can be Reconciled with
those of other Religions?*

T he first question about the question
is about truth-claims. Not just *truth-
claims*, surely? There can be imperatival
incompatibilities Religions appear to recommend or command different paths.
For the Christian pacifist, 'Turn the other
cheek' is vitally right; for the Muslim, it is
better to say something like 'Act honourably, but there is no need to turn the
other cheek.' Again, different rituals are
commended or commanded. For the
Catholic, the Mass; for the Muslim, daily
prayers and the pilgrimage to Mecca.

So we are not merely concerned with
possible incompatibilities as to truth-
claims; but also with possible incompatibilities in *practice*-claims.

The next problem about the question has to do with the *identification* of
truth-claims and practice-claims as being
Christian. The Christian tradition is variegated, as we all know; and we need no
reminding that in this age as in many previous epochs Christianity is in flux. It is
highly fluctuating in regard to theology,
as it, happens. How then do we identify
the core of Christian truth-claims?

We sometimes operate on the assumption that though there are many Chris-
tianities there is only one Christian faith.

* From "Truth and Religions" in *Truth and Dialogue*, edited by John Hick. London: Sheldon Press, 1974.
Reprinted by permission of Sheldon Press.

Thus the great task of theology is to penetrate to this one faith and articulate it and express it. This assumption of the single faith is unaffected by the recognition that there are changing cultural circumstances—that modern man, for instance, may find some elements of traditional expression of the faith (miracle stories, for instance) unacceptable. The programme of demythologization itself is a phase in the never-ending supposed task of relating the one faith to the changing cultural milieu. It is a case of adapting the one to the many. Different times, different theologies—but always the one faith. Different climes, different theologies—but always the one faith. This is the pervasive model at the back of our minds, when we ask about the compatibility or otherwise of Christian truth-claims and those of other faiths. Similar remarks apply, perhaps, to the practice-claims: there is, so to say, a single divine imperative, could we but find it.

The model of a single faith is reinforced by the historical accident (or is it an accident?) that the churches recognize in the New Testament the single platform upon which they all stand. The task of the theologian then becomes importantly to extract the single faith from its pages. Paul here stands as a looming figure, for the more the historicity of the Gospels is called in question (and a century and a half of scientific history is bound to plaster the text with queries), the greater the significance of the great theologian of the risen Christ.

Naturally, there is a similar question about other faiths. Is there a single substance of the Buddhist dharma, for instance? Even in Islam, pegged to the glorious revelation of the Qur'ān, there are variations, developments. Is there then a single Islam?

The question of identifying the one faith in Christianity is made harder by a feeling that often accompanies the model of the one faith—namely that necessarily the focus of faith transcends the concepts which we use to try to express it. If it were not so, the task of identifying the one faith might not be too hard. For one could ask: If Augustine, Aquinas, Luther, and Barth each expressed, in differing cultural milieus, the one faith, then let us state that faith and see the correlation. But it seems that each new theology takes a given core of faith and then elaborates it; rather each new theology is an expression of the theology-transcending X. There is, so to say, no going behind each theology to discover what it is about. It tells you what it is about; it is so to say the glass through which we see the X, and the X can only be seen through one glass or another. If this is so, then the 'one faith' is very much a construct, and one without content. In this respect, the quest of the historical Jesus has been a way of trying to get back to a content, round the glasses which filter our vision.

If what I have said on this score is correct, it presents us with one way of talking about Christian truth- and practice-claims, namely to take the whole exhibition of coloured windows through which the Christian tradition has looked out and back on the theology-transcending focus of faith. Or if it be not possible to treat seriously the whole gallery of theologies, then at least a selection of them. However, the very fact (if it is so) that the focus of faith transcends theologies means that the theological traditions can never be fixed. What is to preclude a new theology being devised, to set alongside the others? In this case, though, there is one sort of identification question which can profitably be asked, namely what is the norm whereby some new theology is adjudged to be *Christian*? Some resemblance, presumably, to earlier theologies. But how much? These things seem to be settled by an informal method of acceptance in the community. For example, Paul van Buren's *The Secular Meaning of the Gospel* expresses an atheistic Christology; but a number of Christians took this with sufficient seriousness to deem it as genuinely a *Christian* theology, despite its formal atheism.

Since new theologies await us over the horizon, it is also necessary to recall that the very situation of interplay between religions, which so markedly characterizes contemporary religious culture, may itself have an impact on theologizing: so that a new theology now beyond the horizon might in theory dissolve some of the incompatibilities between earlier theologies and received non-Christian theologies. For instance, there seems to be a conflict of *Weltanschauung* between theistic Christianity and non-theistic Buddhism; but the incompatibility is less obvious the more Existentialist Christian theology becomes. So new syntheses may await us over the horizon; and they cannot be ruled out *a priori*.

However, there is another check upon indiscriminate synthesizing; this arises from the relation between truth-claims and practice-claims (to put it crudely). It is very obvious that the ritual, experiential and institutional aspects of a religion, and its ethical prescriptions, are not always well co-ordinated to the theologies being purveyed within it. For example, the meaning of the Eucharist, in Anglicanism, is shaped by the milieu of liturgy, architecture, custom, style of life of those engaged: it is not merely determined theologically, still less by the most *avant garde* theology. Attitudes to the Buddha in Theravāda Buddhism are not simply determined by doctrines, but by the whole temple-cultus, etc. Thus there is always the possibility of a lack of co-ordination between truth-claims, and actual practice-claims. In one way, this is doubtless a good thing, for it might be held to be the task of the

theologian to criticize, where necessary, the actual practices of the church. But how is this legitimate critical tension to be preserved while at the same time theology is to escape the charge of disingenuousness? For it is a cheat if the theologian does not relate the ideal church to the actual church—if he recommends a faith that has no purchase on the received tradition.

For these and other reasons, the question of incompatibilities between one faith and another is a complex matter. In a way we are concerned with the elasticity of a faith—whether certain kinds of stretching the concepts and practices result in a snap. Let us try out a thought-experiment here, by considering what is to be said about Hindu attitudes to Christianity.

The modern Hindu ideology, if one may so dub it, consists in a neo-Śankaran theology in which all religions, albeit existing at different levels, ultimately point to the one truth. This is an appealing doctrine to many; for it suggests that religions are held apart by externals, institutional narrownesses, rather than by any essential conflict. It is the obverse of the conclusion sometimes drawn from conflicts of revelations and teachings, namely that they are all false; the modern Hindu ideology declares that they are all true. The best religion, however, is one which is explicitly synthesizing, all-embracing (this being the merit of Hinduism). It follows from the modern Hindu ideology that there is no incompatibility between Hinduism and Christianity: they both ultimately have the same focus, though symbolized and concretized differently (Christ and Krishna, for example, are different manifestations of the one God). Should Christianity resist this synthesis? Not just on the ground that the Christian tradition is unique—for every tradition is. Let us consider some of the reasons for resisting the synthesis that might be advanced.

'The Hindu conception of deity is different from that revealed to the Christian tradition.' *Comment*: it is true that God in the main Christian tradition is conceived in a more personal way than is the neo-Advaitin *Brahman*; but in *this* respect the ultimate reality of Tillich and John Robinson is similarly 'impersonal' (compare also pseudo-Dionysius, Meister Eckhart, Dean Mansel). The anti-synthesis argument thus becomes a means of shutting off certain kinds of theological development within Christianity.

'Christ is uniquely Son of God: there are no other incarnations.' *Comment*: this point can be stated if there is a prior monotheism and an identification of sorts of Christ with the one God; but the anti-synthesis argument here will not work in the following conditions: (i) if Christ is seen as a 'window on ultimate reality' (for there can be many windows); (ii) if Christ is seen, liberal theology-wise, as an examplar of moral values (for there could be other exemplars, such as the Buddha); (iii) if Christ is simply the preached Christ—the historical anchor of an imperatival *kerygma* (for there could be a variety of other historical and mystical anchors of existential challenge). In brief, the appeal to the uniqueness of the incarnation implies a rather conservative ontology. But can't it somehow be done by making a practice-claim? Thus:

'Christ alone is to be worshipped.' The Hindu synthesis here seems to be rejected (unless secretly Krishna and others can be *identified* with Christ: to this sort of identification theme we shall return). *Comment*: the practice-claim could simply be a surd imperative, like a surd revelation. But it is usual in the Christian tradition to advance some grounds for the claim—that the risen Christ provides the key to liberation; that it is through sacramental participation in the death and resurrection of Christ that

sin and death are overcome; and negatively that other gods do not have liberating power, are phantasms leading men astray, do not exist. It is thus difficult to give grounds for the practice-claim which does not imply some ontology: some account of the human predicament and of the way in which it is overcome. Historically, moreover, the worship of Christ in part arises from the background of worship of the one God. Here is another respect in which the Christian rejection of synthesis rests upon a particular theism. But as I said earlier, there is no knowing what the future may bring: yet at the present time it seems that Christianity, to maintain its incompatibility with Hinduism, would have to appeal to a particular theism as constituting part of its essence. I shall return to this point after a brief excursus on the paradox of a situation in which incompatibility is regarded as a good thing.

Why should there be a motive for standing out against the noble Hindu synthesis? It is partly a matter of having a *raison d'être*. A movement, religious or otherwise, which does not have a distinctive message tends (rightly) to wither. Still, couldn't Christianity have a more modest *raison d'être*—to nurture those within it and those who find that it chimes in with their spiritual and moral condition? It could be, so to speak, a loosely knit tribal religion, but where the tribe is a new Israel, not ethnically determined (although well rooted in certain, mainly western cultures). One must here, however, understand the logical and cultural predicament of a tribal religion in an intercultural situation (this too will cast light upon the reason for the evolution of the new Hindu ideology).

A tribal religion, like other religions, contains a doctrinal element, woven into the whole practical side: a certain picture of the world and of spirit is drawn.

Consider the predicament of the tribal folk when it is faced with a new culture, with a transethnic religion. Is it possible for the tribal folk long to maintain that their world-picture is for them, the other world-picture for others? It is hard to say (from a logical point of view) that P is true for one group and not-P for another, unless all that is meant is that the one group *believes* P and the other believes not-P. Various devices have to be employed if the tribal picture is to remain itself at all. One option is hard—to claim that the tribal picture is of universal validity, for it was always meant for those initiated into tribal lore, and wasn't meant at all for other tribes. This secretive non-universalism could be carried with equanimity when the tribe constituted the real world, the values of other men being a mere shadowy penumbra. Even very big groups have felt like this: for the Chinese, barbarian values were shadowy until Buddhism crept in and destroyed the illusion; for expansionist Europe, the beliefs of colonized folk tended to be curiosities, oddities; in India over a long period the real world was the subcontinent, until Buddhism began to flicker outwards. So then our tribal folk will find the universalist option hard to maintain, because of the tight connection between the picture of the world and the secret sacraments of the tribe. Another option it may not want to face—namely to abandon entirely its own picture and assimilate that of the new culture, though even here unconsciously the old gods can be smuggled in. A *via media* is called for: one in which an adjusted world-picture is seen as a contribution to the store of myths and insights which point towards transcendent. We may call this option: unity through conscious pluralism, or in short 'the pluralistic solution'.

We can now return to the question of whether Christianity can regard itself modestly as a loosely-knit tribal religion, nurturing those who participate in its sacraments. Faced with other transcultural faiths, it would be essentially in the tribal predicament, if so; and truth is no respecter of groups. To retain its modesty, without losing its *raison d'être*, it would have itself to adopt the pluralistic solution, and this would be virtually to accept the Hindu synthesis. In the context of the variety of faiths and of the virtual certainty that they will continue substantially in a plural world, the pluralistic solution seems sound common sense. Hence its appeal (a wide appeal, even among many Christians, who express this pluralism through a scepticism about missions, though not about hospitals in alien climes).

I have made something in this argument of the tightness of the connection between the tribal world-picture and their secret sacraments. This point is highly relevant to problems of meaning and understanding. Crudely one can distinguish between an initiatory and a non-initiatory view of understanding religious concepts. From the initiatory point of view, understanding God can only be approached via the sacramental or analogous activities, or can only be gained by the initiation constituted by the experience of grace. Full-bloodedly, the initiatory view is a sort of conceptual fideism: only those who can say 'I know that my redeemer liveth' know what 'redeemer' means. A thin-blooded view would be that we can imaginatively enter into initiations (hence the possibility of coming to understand something of other faiths). Those espousing a hardheaded natural theology would hold that at least some key concepts in religion could be understood metaphysically, without specific religious initiation.

There is a tension here. The more conceptually initiatory a religion is, the more it takes on the character of a tribal religion, except that it may be the religion of an open rather than a closed tribe, adding new members as it can. But though it could be thus universal evangelically, in the sense that any man or all men might join the faith-community, it could, if thus conceptually initiatory, give no reasons why men should join, save 'Come and see', maybe. In *practice*, of course, men who join use reasons: the fruits are good—you can see peace on their faces, and so forth. This is a kind of practical natural theology, adding some rationality to the otherwise surd initiation. But by contrast, if a religion seems to be hardly initiatory at all, for the understanding of its concepts, it takes on the guise of a metaphysics, and the link between belief and sacrament is ruptured.

Extreme conceptual fideism as an account of the Christian faith does, I think, have to be rejected, if the aim at any rate is to avoid the pluralistic solution. For paradoxically conceptual fideism can give no account of what other faiths mean (e.g. the Hindu synthesis): for it is implied that initiation is necessary for understanding. Given the further premiss that one cannot be initiated properly into more than one faith (*pace* Ramakrishna), then the Christian conceptual fideist can have no ground for rejecting any other faith. All faiths have this rather negative equal status. This being so, there can be no reason to reject the Hindu claim that all faiths point to the same Truth. Initiatory conceptual fideism slides in to acceptance of a polytheism, or rather a polyfideism, if one may coin so barbarous a hybrid.

But *should* the extra premiss, that one cannot be properly initiated into more than one faith, be accepted? Is it that no man can serve two masters? But how are we to know that they *are* two masters? Is it that a person cannot be converted from

one faith to another? We know that this happens empirically, so to speak; but could he really have had his earlier faith if he were converted? These are questions which extreme conceptual fideism is not in a position to answer.

As a postscript to the discussion of extreme conceptual fideism, it is worth noting that whereas truth and falsity do not admit, in any straightforward way, at least, of degrees, understanding does. One person can show greater, deeper, etc., understanding than another. It may be that a very deep understanding of the concepts of a given faith is not accessible to the adherent of another faith; but this does not at all show that *some* level of understanding is impossible for him; and it can of course well be that the adherent of a faith has a less profound understanding of it than some person of another faith.

The pluralistic solution, as we have outlined it, is not absolute pluralism: there is at least the notion that there is a single truth towards which different religions point—in line with the modern Hindu ideology, which itself constitutes the response of a sophisticated, variegated cultural tradition faced by an incoming transethnic faith, accompanied by aggressive European values. This attempt at making differing traditions compatible by postulating a single focus of aspiration does, however, depend on identifications—identifying one divine focus of faith with another. Can such identifications be justified?

Let us begin with a relatively simple example. What justifies one in saying that the Christian and Muslim worship the same God? As far as the concepts and practices go, the two foci of faith are different. Among other things, the Christian worships Christ as a person of the Trinity: the Christian concept of God is thus organically related to God's manifestation in history and to his representation of himself in the sacraments. These are elements not present in the Muslim's conception of Allah. Thus conceptually the Christian God and Allah are different. This does not entail that the concepts do not refer to the same Being: far from it, a major point about identity statements is that the concepts are different (not all identity statements, but many, e.g. 'Tomorrow is Friday'). The statement 'The Christian and the Muslim worship the same God' is not just to be interpreted intentionally, with phenomenological brackets as it were: rather, it is itself a theological statement, assuming the existence of a single God for both Christians and Muslims to worship. But if it is a theological claim, then from within which tradition? Or does it stand outside both? It could do, e.g., if it is part of the expression of the modern Hindu ideology. But let us consider more narrowly the reasons that a *Christian* theologian might give for the assertion. Let us assume too that he here as elsewhere is presenting a glass through which one can look on the focus of faith— there being no independent access to that focus. The only ground, one supposes, for the identification is that there is a sufficient degree of resemblance between the Christian and Muslim conceptions of God. Since, however, there is a certain degree of elasticity in Christian theology itself, for the focus of faith is theology-transcending, it is unlikely that it would take very strict account of what constitutes a sufficient degree of resemblance.

However, this way of discussing the issue might seem overly conceptual. After all, is it not largely upon the practical side of religion that the theologian feeds? Does his concept of God not articulate what is given in experience, ritual, history? Not surprisingly, those who espouse the pluralistic solution tend to stress the unity of religious *experience*.

Thus an important part of the task of trying to establish a sufficient degree of resemblance is the attempt to evaluate the existential and experiential impact of different foci of faith. Strictly, there are two things to do: first, to arrive at a sensible and sensitive phenomenology of religious experience (basically a descriptive task this, though not without its conceptual pitfalls); and second, to see whether the results contribute to the judgement that there is a sufficient degree of resemblance to justify the identification of one focus of faith with another.

The phenomenological judgement as to whether there is a basic common core of religious experience must be based on the facts, and not determined *a priori* by theology. I do not wish to argue the point here: but my own view is that there is no such common core, but rather that there are different sorts of religious experience which recur in different traditions, though not universally. From a phenomenological point of view it is not possible to base the judgement that all religions point to the same truth upon religious *experience*. Nor is it reasonable to think that there is sufficient conceptual resemblance between God and nirvāṇā (as conceived in Theravāda Buddhism) to aver that the Theravādin and the Christian are worshipping the same God (for one thing, the Theravādin is not basically *worshipping*). Thus it is hard to justify the pluralistic solution, at least as elaborated in the modern Hindu ideology—save by saying that Christians and Buddhists are really aspiring towards the same focus of faith, even though they cannot know that they are. But what then are the criteria of identity of aspiration? Is there a conceptual baptism of desire?

In brief, there are problems about the pluralistic solution, mainly problems of identification of the religious ultimate. It still remains, however, that there is something to commend the solution: to put the matter in a nasty nutshell, the more evangelical Christianity is, the more it approximates to an open tribal faith, for the truth has to be experienced through the forms of Christian faith; but by the same token there is less ground for dismissing the truth of other initiations. On the other hand, the less evangelical Christianity becomes, the less motive it will have for resisting the pluralistic solution.

But *still* the argument may be over-conceptual, over-theological. Can the practical natural theology mentioned earlier come in to provide the test? It would be something of an irony if human fruits were invoked to decide the interpretation of divinity. But this is not a simple affair, as can be imagined; for what counts as fruits is in part determined by the theologies and the institutions. For example, a Christian might bring sustenance to villagers by getting things done, notably by getting folk to hunt birds; but the fruits of Christian dynamism have to be judged by attitudes to animal life. The Buddhist might not be unqualified in his praise of the dynamism. This indicates that the problem of compatibility is not just to do with the religious ultimate, but with the diagnosis of the worldly situation, including importantly the human situation.

The pluralistic situation is attractive, but it is doubtful whether it could work in the present state of religious traditions, because it is phenomenologically unsound. In an important way, then, there is incompatibility (at present) between religious truth-claims. There is also divergence in practice-claims. It is a further question as to the *criteria* for resolving questions of truth and practice. There are, however, certainly grounds for arguing both for and against the monotheism which makes sense of Christ's exclusive claim as liberator. As I have attempted to argue elsewhere, these criteria importantly have to do with religious experience and cultus. For the rest, we must accept that every religion has a given starting point, each unique. The pictures in the gallery are different, have different atmospheres and messages; they cannot be aligned in the same pictorial perspective. And for most men only one picture can be a real focus of loyalty.

JOHN H. WHITTAKER

from Matters of Faith and Matters of Principle

The *indeterminacy approach* accepts it that different religions make different truth-claims, that they have different propositional beliefs-that-somthing-is-true, or truth-beliefs (as we may call them). This approach, furthermore, accepts it that these different truth-beliefs are religiously important. However this approach regards the different beliefs of different religious traditions as *indeterminately* related. This means that the beliefs of different traditions are *incommensurable* (that is, they cannot be compared; they are like apples and oranges). In this way the truth of a belief in one religion will not necessitate the falsity of an apparently opposing belief in another religion. And so the various major religions can all be right in the sense that their beliefs do not conflict. One exponent of the indeterminacy approach is John Whittaker.

He recounts a story about Spinoza, the seventeenth century philosopher and religious thinker. Spinoza was asked by his landlady if she could be saved in the religion she professed (which was probably some form of Christianity). Spinoza, who had been born in the Jewish tradition but was at odds with the Jewish community in Amsterdam where he lived, replied, "Your religion is a very good one; you need not look for another, nor doubt that you may be saved in it, provided, whilst you apply yourself to piety, you live at the same time a peaceable and quiet life." As Whittaker reads this story, the lesson is that as long as a person follows the "demands of right living, while applying himself [or herself] to piety, [he or she] stands fast in God's truth no matter what his [or her] beliefs may be." So read, the story, like one reading of Tolstoy's tale, recommends the common core of practice approach.

But for Whittaker such a view of religion is not correct, for it leaves out the essential role of religious truth-beliefs. Whittaker appreciates that traditional religion needs a "cognitive" element; that is, it needs beliefs that something is *true*, such as, that Abraham had a covenant with God or that Jesus is the Son of God and our savior or that Muhammad is the last and greatest prophet. In other words Whittaker acknowledges that religions importantly make truth-claims. They importantly have propositional beliefs-that-something-is-true, or truth-beliefs, such as the Jewish, Christian, and Islamic beliefs just cited. In his words, "one cannot do justice to religious belief by entirely severing it from propositions." Whittaker calls the basic truth-beliefs of a religion religious *principles*.

Whittaker wants us to appreciate that being religious is not *simply* an allegiance to a creed or a set of beliefs. But for Whittaker there is an undeniable place in religion for truth-beliefs. Presumably, then, Whittaker observes, "to believe that one's religion is true, one must believe that every other religion is false." It is this presumption that Whittaker attacks with his indeterminacy approach.

Our reading is taken from "The Exclusiveness of Religious Conviction," Chapter VI of Whittaker's *Matters of Faith and Matters of Principle*.*

6

The Exclusiveness of Religious Conviction

According to his biographer, Spinoza's landlady once asked him if he thought that she could be saved in the religion she professed, and Spinoza gave her the following gently moving answer: "Your religion is a very good one; you need not look for another, nor doubt that you may be saved in it, provided, whilst

* From John H. Whittaker, *Matters of Faith and Matters of Principle*, Chap. VI. San Antonio: Trinity University Press, 1981. Reprinted by permission of the author.

you apply yourself to piety, you live at the same time a peaceable and quiet life."[1] The woman was probably a Christian of some kind, but it makes little difference, as Spinoza regarded any religion which promotes a virtuous life a "very good one" in which a devout person may be "saved." The point of believing is not to possess more knowledge but to live more truly, for the saving blessings of religion attend the quality of one's life and not the correctness of one's opinions. *True* faith is not a matter of knowledge at all, but of obedience; and so the simple believer who bends his will to the demands of right living, while applying himself to piety, stands fast in God's truth no matter what his beliefs may be.[2]

This easy acceptance of other religions made Spinoza a radical and dangerous thinker in his day. In our day a similar perspective has become almost a requirement of philosophical analysis, as if any *other* account would summon forth all the horrors of militant, dogmatic religion. All but the most conservative theologians have thrown away the old assumption that only one religion can be true, lest their indemonstrable affirmations be presumptuously converted into denials of another person's faith. To avoid this problem some people would rather avoid religious controversies altogether. Others, who are more sympathetic to religion, would rather make their affirmations so broad that no one's religious views are implicitly denied. That way, if there is any truth or happiness to be found in religion, one can cast a net widely enough to cover it.

* * * * * * * * * * * * * * * * * * * *

I see no escape from denying the truth of every belief which is incompatible with one's own beliefs. To give up this kind of exclusiveness would be to sacrifice one's beliefs as truth claims. Yet this does not mean that we have to develop our religious convictions by passing judgment on every alternative. In matters of faith there is a certain asymmetry which leaves one in a better position to affirm one's own beliefs than to deny those of another. Every believer must in his own mind reject incompatible doctrines, but it is not always possible to tell how compatible or incompatible other religious beliefs are with one's own. Nor is it necessary to decide these questions in order to develop one's belief in a reasonable way. The alien beliefs of other religious cultures do not have to be affirmed or denied; often they can simply be ignored.

The peculiar asymmetry of religious judgment, and the benign neglect which goes with it, result from the fact that principles are at stake in matters of faith. The affirmation of principles depends on certain conditions which are not always filled as the believer turns his attention from one set of religious claims to another. Before he can adopt them, the believer must understand the point which these beliefs acquire as regulative claims; and before he can resolve his doubts about them, he must appreciate their force in framing a new dimension of reflection. Yet a potential believer generally has this kind of familiarity with only a few religious traditions, sometimes only one. Thus he can deal responsibly only with those for which he has a working understanding. The others he must ignore until he is in a position to evaluate.

[1] From Johannes Colerus in the introduction to *The Chief Works of Benedict de Spinoza*, trans. R. H. M. Elwes (New York: Dover, 1951), vol. I, xix.
[2] Spinoza, *Theological-Political Treaties*, in *Chief Works*, vol. I, 9–10 *passim*.

To show how different this is from an easy relativism or a harsh dogmatism, Spinoza's reply to his landlady can be compared with a story from Kierkegaard. In a passage in his *Journals*, Kierkegaard considers the objections which a Christian's commitment to only one means of salvation is likely to provoke. To one who has found new happiness in Christ, he says, "the only possible objection would be: but you might possibly have been saved in another way." Yet to this objection there is no answer. "It is as though one were to say to someone in love, yes, but you might have fallen in love with another girl; to which he would have to answer: there is no answer to that, for I only know that she is my love."[4] Kierkegaard thought that this is how it is for the devout believer, too. Inasmuch as the believer has found through faith the understanding which he seeks—and inasmuch as he has no *other* reason to doubt the teachings which have brought him to this understanding—he need not know or care whether he might have made sense of his life in some other way.

This analogy between faith and love is not perfect (why should it be if it is only an analogy?), but one can press it a long way before having to give it up. One who is in love need not pass judgment on every other person whom he might have loved, not because finding a mate is such a relative thing that anyone will do, but because finding a mate is not something one can do in the abstract.

* * * * * * * * * * * * * * * * * * * *

To take religious teachings seriously and to judge them appropriately, one must concentrate his interest in a more or less exclusive manner, centering his thoughts on those whose point and promise he understands. One might have a working understanding of more than one religion, just as one might be intimate with more than one lover. Yet one still has to "test" his principles by following them, much as a lover must test his love by relying on it. Then, if the believer finds that the principles which he chooses hold up, that they enable him to reduce more and more of the anomalies of his experience to some sort of ordered understanding, he may be able to dismiss his other live options as incompatible possibilities. His dead options, those whose point he never understood, will remain outside the proper scope of his judgments. Thus the built-in exclusivity of religious commitment does not come about as the result of choosing one option and ruling out all the others in the same series of comparative tests. It comes from having to limit one's thinking to those beliefs which one can understand well enough to judge in practice.

2

The only trouble with this analogy between faith and love is that the lover only has to decide what is right *for him*, whereas the believer needs to determine what is right *for anyone*. In affirming his principles as *truths*, the believer holds his beliefs for any and all persons, but the lover never supposes that everyone else should choose one and the same person to love. Thus, if we liken the "truth" of the believer's convictions to the "rightness" of the lover's choice, we may find it

[4] Søren Kierkegaard, *The Journals of Søren Kierkegaard*, trans. Alexander Dru (Oxford: Oxford University Press, 1938), entry number 922.

hard to resist a purely subjective account of faith. What is "true" for one person may not be "true" for another. Yet if we insist that truth is at stake in matters of faith, and that error is a possibility, then we may have to give up the analogy between faith and love.

In defense of the analogy, it may be said that matters of the heart are not entirely subjective. Love, at least, is not self-certifying. When it is tempted and begins to fade, the troubled lover cannot always allay his doubts simply by strengthening his commitment. As he knows very well, he can have made a poor choice. Merely thinking that he has made the right one does not make it so. Nevertheless, the fact remains that the lover's judgments are qualified by the need to determine only what is right for him, whereas the believer's judgments, being truth claims, represent unqualified claims about what is the case and ought (ideally) to be believed by anyone. Here the analogy does break down, but we do not have to revoke anything we have said so far about the asymmetry of religious conviction to acknowledge this difference. We simply need to supplement the analogy with some further analysis.

Presumably, to believe that one's own religion is true, one must believe that every other religion is false. Since this is the objection which seems to destroy the analogy between love and faith, this is the assumption which must be challenged. It may seem safe enough at first, but it turns out to be far more debatable than one might think. For one thing, it is not clear just what the source of such exclusivity is supposed to be. This exclusivity could be ascribed to the peculiar demands of *religious* conviction, or it could be attributed to the *generic* features of belief. The first alternative is highly dubious, since the devotees of some religions make it a point of faith to repudiate other religions, while other believers explicitly hold out a place for the truth contained in other religions. In the Athanasian Creed, for example, one finds the Christian faith proclaimed as the only true faith. In Hinduism, by contrast, one finds the view that all great religions share in the one truth which includes all partial truths and all particular faiths. Here there is no *avowed* exclusivity, and so it obviously will not do to say that religious belief is bound to be exclusive because every religion teaches the falsity of every other religion. Religions differ on this point.

Yet even if every religion did include explicit denunciations of other faiths, individual believers would not have to share in these denunciations. To suppose that they could not be Christians, for example, without endorsing the rejection of other religions would be to confuse religious belief with party affiliation. Becoming religious is primarily a matter of having one's thoughts and one's passions informed by a new set of concepts and principles, not a matter of joining one particular group in preference to another. Religious organizations are undoubtedly necessary to preserve and to nurture religious understanding, and these organizations may very well need to define themselves in contrast to one another. The believer who best exemplifies and upholds his traditions, however, is not the one who has a passion for religious institutions but the one who keeps his moral struggles and his existential concerns in the perspective afforded by his principles. Most believers, in fact, do not even know all the official dogmas of their churches or their traditions, and many do not understand some of the teachings which they do know. So if one had to understand and to accept all the doctrines of a religion to be a believer, few ordinary believers would qualify.

The point here is not to criticize institutional religion but to show that the exclusiveness which religions accrue theologically in their institutionalized forms is not entailed by the nature of *faith*. Party disputes in religious matters are bound to arise, and the history of religion is to a large extent a history of perpetual disagreement and conflict. Yet one can be religious *without taking sides on every issue*. The idea that one must affiliate with a particular religious party to become a religious believer rests on the mistaken idea that we must compare and contrast whole sets of doctrines if we are to affirm any religious teachings. We do not have to do that—indeed, we cannot do that without treating religious principles as hypotheses and thereby obscuring their point. The understanding we need comes from the intensification of possibilities, not from their multiplication. We need depth more than breadth to avoid prejudging religious principles. Thus we do not have to develop every potential contrast between our beliefs and the beliefs of others. Battles enough are already raging, and new ones can doubtlessly be joined; but the would-be believer does not have to fight them all to conform his thoughts to religious ideals.

In view of the widespread antipathy toward all forms of exclusiveness, and in view of the debilitating relativism which usually accompanies this antipathy, the last point seems well worth emphasizing. One does not have to be a relativist to avoid presumptuous denials of other religions; one need only give up the false ideal of comparing every religious claim with all its rivals, for we have no adequate list of independent criteria by which to judge them. Faith develops by fulfilling a (cognitive) *need*, not by fulfilling an abstract list of rational criteria.

Nevertheless, sooner or later we have to face the more serious objection that the exclusivity of religious belief belongs to the *generic* features of belief. The believer who does not want to adopt a negative stance toward other religious teachings cannot avoid doing so as long as he wishes to affirm his beliefs as truth claims. Elementary logic tells us that the affirmation of a proposition is equivalent to the denial of its contradictory, and this is such a rudimentary point of logic that we cannot abandon it without passing beyond the logic of truth claims altogether. As long as we continue to advance and espouse our religious beliefs as truth claims, how can we avoid the implicit denial of other religious claims? Clearly there must be *some* exclusivity built into religious belief, since believing that those who do not agree with us are *wrong* is simply the other side of affirming the *truth* of our own convictions. In this respect Hindus are no more tolerant than the most militant Christians, for a Hindu cannot affirm his own inclusive conception of faith without at the same time denying every other incompatible point of view. To all those who say, for example, that there is only one means of salvation, Hindus must say (or at least think), "you are wrong, there are many roads to the mountaintop." This is not inconsistency on their part; it is a logical necessity.

One cannot affirm a truth claim of any sort without denying every other incompatible assertion, whether one means to or not. This applies to religious assertions as well as to any other assertions. In fact, it is one of the strongest reasons we have for thinking that religious beliefs are truth claims. Religious believers refuse to admit the contradictories of what they say, something which they need not do if they are not asserting truth claims. Yet this elementary observation about truth claims is not as telling as it seems; for despite appearances, the doctrines of two different religions may be compatible (or even equivalent) in meaning, in which case the affirmation of one will obviously not entail a denial of the other. In other cases, religious claims will conflict; and then the believer who wishes to affirm one *will* have to deny the other once he sees their incompatibility. These two possibilities, however, do not exhaust the alternatives. There is a third possibility which is much more interesting. Instead of being compatible or incompatible, two different religious principles may stand in an indeterminate logical relationship, in which case the implicit exclusivity of religious belief becomes impossible to trace.

Instances of this third sort are more numerous than one might think. As missionaries come across various native beliefs, for example, they must often find themselves unable to say whether these native beliefs are compatible with their own. Admittedly, they may be uncertain because they do not understand the native beliefs well enough, or because they do not understand their own beliefs well enough. Yet the same uncertainty might also arise because the beliefs in question are too ill-defined to permit any *definitive* pronouncement. The concepts which they involve may have an "open texture," a sense which is clear enough for normal usages but not sufficiently clear for cross-cultural comparisons.

Consider miracle claims, for example. David Hume thought that the miracle stories of different religions mutually contradicted one another, so that a believer who accepted the miracle claims of his own tradition was thereby bound to reject those of another. Perhaps he assumed too much. Must a Christian deny every faith healing not conducted in the name of Christ? Must he ascribe such healings to the work of the devil, or must he turn to some psychological explanation? Does he know that God never

intervenes in other contexts, perhaps even on other planets? Christian teachings just are not that clear, so there may not be an answer to be *discovered* at all. Instead of discovering the compatibility or incompatibility of certain miracle claims, believers may have to make a *ruling* on this point, thereby sharpening the sense of the claims which they wish to make. Prior to such rulings, the question of the compatibility of two religious assertions may be indeterminable. Indeed, why else should theologians have to *add* various teachings about what is to count as a miracle?— Only because on this and on other points of doctrine religions can be initially too ill-defined to settle the full range of their compatibility and incompatibility.

Perhaps it is the responsibility of theologians to clarify continually the teachings of their own traditions vis-a-vis those of other traditions. Certainly it is the responsibility of people engaged in the comparative study of religion, but that is not the point. The point is that these comparisons are bound to be difficult owing to the under-determination of the beliefs and concepts involved. The would-be *believer*, however, does not have to resolve these questions in order to adopt some religious principles. And to that extent he need not *presumptuously* deny every other religious claim.

One can easily become confused about this. Almost irresistibly the law of excluded middle tempts us to say that there cannot be indeterminate logical relationships between propositions. Either something is the case or it is not the case; this much seems certain, and so we have only to apply this law of logic to conclude of any two beliefs that they are either compatible or incompatible. Yet there is, in fact, another possibility, since the law of excluded middle does not *always* apply. In effect, this law says that we cannot simultaneously ascribe and deny a predicate to the same subject (e.g., that we cannot say of any two propositions that they are compatible and incompatible at the same time). With some subjects and some predicates, however, we cannot make any ascriptions *or* denials. This can happen for any one of several reasons: (1) because any use of the predicate would involve a "category mistake" (Arthur is either metrical or nonmetrical), (2) because the standards for applying the predicate are unclear (Arthur is either great or not great), or (3) because the subject itself is not sufficiently defined or developed to permit a confident judgment (young Arthur is a saint).

Although it is a bit more complicated, the attempt to compare two religious beliefs may run into difficulties of the third variety: the beliefs themselves and hence the relationship between them may be insufficiently developed to permit a confident judgment of their compatibility. They may be like two adolescents whose parents are trying to arrange a marriage—are the adolescents suited to each other or not? There may not be any answer to this question, not because the parents do not know their children well enough but because their children have not yet assumed sufficiently definite personalities. I see no reason why the same thing may not *at times* be said of religious beliefs. They too may not have assumed fully definite senses, so that comparative judgments might have to be postponed.

The only serious objection to this would be to argue that truth claims must always have fully determinate senses, so that propositions which can be said to be true or false must also be definitely compatible or incompatible. This objection, however, sounds more powerful than it is. It makes more sense if hypotheses are being compared than it does if principles are being examined, for the meaning of hypotheses is more determinate than the meaning of principles. Inasmuch as hypotheses have independently specifiable truth conditions, the meanings of an obscure hypothesis can be spelled out in a more definitive way by being restated in terms of these conditions. What it would take to confirm a hypothesis tells us, in effect, what it would mean for it to be true. Consequently, the same thing which makes an assertion a hypothesis—i.e., independent truth conditions—also makes it comparable to other hypotheses. The data needed to confirm two different hypotheses provide the means of determining their compatibility or incompatibility. Indeed, the positivists could have (and perhaps should have) advanced their verification principle as a means of showing when two ostensibly different hypotheses are actually equivalent in meaning. If these hypotheses have the same truth conditions, then they have the same meaning. Alternatively, if they have incompatible truth conditions, then they are genuine rivals.

SHIVESH THAKUR

from To What God . . . ?

In his discussion Whittaker acknowledges that a problem arises for the application of indeterminacy to beliefs. It arises in the light of a basic rule of reasoning and logic called "the law of excluded middle." The law of excluded middle says that any proposition is either true or false (there is no middle ground). But this appears to require us to reject the idea that two truth-beliefs can be indeterminately related. For it requires that the predicate "compatible" either fits two beliefs or it does not. Either it is true that two beliefs are compatible or it is false (and they are incompatible). So in regard to the belief that Jesus is the Son of God and the belief that the Buddha attained Enlightenment, the proposition "They are compatible" is either true or false, according to the law of excluded middle. Whittaker argues, however, that it is a mistake to think that the law of excluded middle always applies.

Shivesh Thakur in "To What God . . .?" also comments on the law of excluded middle as it applies to relationships between religious beliefs. Unlike Whittaker, Thakur suggests that there may be other "values" (or "truth-values") besides true and false that can be given to propositions. For instance, it may be that a proposition (or a truth-belief) is "partly true" or "largely false" or it may be that it is is some degree "probable," as opposed to simply true or false.

If Thakur is right, then in some modes of discourse the law of excluded middle will not apply. His view relates to religious belief in that it would allow individuals to accept their religions as true without being required to regard other religions as false. Other religions could consistently be regarded as, say, more or less true or partly true. While Thakur's thinking here is close to Whittaker's, it is different in two respects. First, Thakur is reflecting on the "truth" and incompatibility of religions *in their entirety*, as opposed to the incompatibility of particular religious beliefs or "principles," which is Whittaker's concern. Second, Thakur's thinking leads to the conclusion that different religions are *not* incompatible, as opposed to the conclusion that the predicate "incompatible" does not apply, which is Whittaker's conclusion. While for Whittaker religious "principles"—basic and formative religious beliefs—are indeterminately related, and indeterminately related "principles" are not comparable, for Thakur religions are comparable, at least comparable enough for us to make the judgment that the truth of one does not entail the falsity of the others. For both thinkers, however, the law of excluded middle is escaped—escaped by religions for Thakur, and escaped by religious "principles" for Whittaker.*

To What God. . . ?

It is perfectly safe to assert, I think, that no religious tradition has yet propagated or found a proper philosophical framework, a recipe, for coming to terms with the existence of other religions. This is hardly surprising, for until relatively recently no religion could be said to have even confronted the question, explicitly;

* From Shivesh Thakur, "To What God . . . ?" in *The Experience of Religious Diversity*, edited by John Hick and Hasan Askari. Aldershot, England and Brookfield, Vermont: Gower, 1985. Reprinted by permission of the author.

and not many could be said to have tackled it obliquely either. *Hinduism*, however, could be regarded as one religion which has had to come to grips with the issue, although in a very different guise. Faced with the plurality of gods and goddesses, all vying with each other for special honors, the *Rig Veda*, the most ancient of Hindu scriptures, addressed one of its most celebrated hymns to the question, 'To what God shall we offer our oblations?'[1] The answer given in the final verse of the hymn is that it must, of course, be Prajapati, for he was, as earlier in the hymn he had been declared to be, the 'one God above the gods.' This 'answer' however masks what might be most interesting about it, namely, what Hindu tradition actually made of the answer. And this was the Hindu's conclusion that *any* god (and not just Prajapati) could, on a given occasion, be considered the proper recipient of our honors, as long as he (or she) was seen to be the 'one God above the gods.' Hindus from the very outset actually adopted this very 'egalitarian' approach towards their deities, thus forcing Max *Muller* to concoct a new term, 'henotheism' or 'kathenotheism,' to designate this peculiar Hindu cocktail of polytheism and monotheism.

That such a device might actually 'contaminate' their monotheism does not seem to have worried Hindus themselves unduly although it has worried, even dismayed, others. It is possible to see this device merely as one of the more blatant examples of the notorious Hindu propensity for wanting to eat one's cake and have it as well. But there may be good reason for thinking that there might be more than that involved. Another famous hymn from the *Rig Veda* could be said to

furnish the larger, more pertinent insight operating in the background. 'To what is one, sages give many a name: they call it Agni, Yama, Matarishvan,'[2] not to mention Prajapati, Indra and a host of others. It should not be difficult to see that an adaptation of the 'device' and the 'insight' to the context of the diversity of religions, would serve the Hindu well, and easily, as a guide to his/or her response to other faiths. It is not in the least surprising, nor accidental, that historical Hinduism has embraced within it a bewildering variety of beliefs and practices, rituals and forms of worship, perceptions of the ultimate religious goal and of paths leading to these goals. It is, after all, with good reason that observers and commentators have often wondered whether 'Hinduism' represented one religion or was merely an umbrella-term for many different ones. This is not to say that every aspect of Hinduism encourages this tolerance; nor that there are no bigots among Hindus. Far from it, in fact. All that can be said safely, I think, is that for those Hindus who are temperamentally inclined to be tolerant of other faiths there is powerful justification in their scripture and tradition and (by and large) in their practice, for the attitude in question. It certainly should not be heretical for a Hindu to be respectful of other religions.

But even for the Hindu, and undoubtedly for followers of most other faiths—more credal or doctrinal in their approaches—there are genuine, and serious, philosophical difficulties in reconciling their adherence to their own faith, and accepting, if that is what they wish to do, that the existence of other religions is a good thing. If they accept their own

[1] *Rig Veda*, X, 121. [2] *Ibid.*, I, 164.

faith, they must in so doing accept the truth, in some sense, of the doctrines, dogmas and points of view of that faith. On the face of it, at least, if not as a matter of fact also, this would seem to entail that other religions and their teachings must be false. And if so, they cannot, without being hypocritical, actually believe that other religions are also valuable, except perhaps as relics of humanity's mistakes. The question, then, is: is it really possible, i.e., does it make sense, for a believer in one faith to accept that religious diversity is valuable, from any important point of view? Or must it inevitably remain a pious platitude, a mere lip service?

Sadly, for the evergrowing numbers of individuals genuinely interested in any constructive dialogue between religions, the intensity of the problem posed above would seem to be directly proportional to the degree of commitment one has—to one's own religion, on the one hand and to the value of religious diversity on the other. For a person 'lukewarm' in one or both respects, the problem, while not nonexistent, is not serious: no problem *could* be, in that setting. But strong personal commitment would, on the fact of it, seem to preclude the simultaneous acceptance of both options. *Either* one's own faith *or* some other, *not both*. It is possible to go so far as to say that the profession of genuine respect for all religions is only possible from a nonreligious, or secular, point of view. A person with no specific religious commitments of his/or her own—it may even be argued that *only* such a person—can truly, and without inconsistency, profess regard for all religions, either simply as interesting manifestations of human cultural diversity or, more importantly, as possible sources of *truth* and values. A committed believer of any given religion, on the other hand, can only do so, it seems, on pain of having the authenticity of his *faith* questioned. It may

be that the only effective answer to this dilemma, in the end, is to acknowledge that human beings, even the most thoughtful, do as a matter of fact do strange things, such as entertaining incompatible views; and that's all there is to it! But this solution may not appeal to those who do subscribe to a specific faith and who at the same time wish to profess the value of religious diversity without leaving themselves wide open to the charge of blatant inconsistency. So, can more be said about the dilemma? What, if anything, can be done, philosophically that is, which may either eliminate this inconsistency or show it to be less crude than it appears to be? In the following pages we will discuss some of the possibilities.

Since the acceptance of truth of one's own faith only entails the falsity of another on the presupposed validity of the so-called Law of Excluded Middle, it may seem desirable to challenge, or reject, this Law. If, for example, one were to accept some form of 'many-valued' logic (as against the logic incorporating Excluded Middle, which allows only two values, i.e., true/false, to propositions), then the dilemma of the believer who also thinks that the existence of other religions is a good thing either disappears or looks less stark. He/or she may then quite consistently hold his/her own religious beliefs to be true without being forced to reject at the outset the possibility of truth, in *some* sense or to *some* degree, of other religions. This is not the place to attempt either an exposition or defense of the philosophical idea of 'many-valued' logics. So one or two examples of what might be meant will have to do. If I were to point to a rubic cube's red surface and make the claim, either polemically or perversely, that the cube was red, would my claim be true or false? Since one of its surfaces was red, the claim that the cube was red was obviously *partly* true. Equally, since the five other surfaces are not red, the claim about the redness of the cube itself was partly—one might say, largely!—false. But if I still insisted on having the claim declared *simply* as either true or false, I would be quite properly judged to be behaving in an irrational, silly, fashion; for the claim is partly true, partly false, both true and false, or neither true nor false, *depending on the point of view*. No Excluded Middle here. It might be claimed that, for all practical purposes, all nonformal propositions present, in varying degrees perhaps, a similar picture of complexity in respect of their truth/falsity, as indeed in most other respects. As will be evident, a case for many-valued logics has already got off the ground. Let us move to another example, away from mere common sense and towards natural science. As is well known, propositions (and theories) in natural science are not, typically, judged to be true or false; they are assigned different degrees of probability depending on the evidence. Since no empirical proposition can have a hundred percent probability (for future evidence, or the possible rejection in future of the theory supporting the proposition, may make it false), it is, for all practical purposes and at any given time, only more or less true. This applies to common sense examples, such as 'The sun will rise tomorrow,' as well as to more sophisticated scientific propositions, such as 'Quarks exist.' The probability in respect of truth that any propositon could have would normally be some decimal point between 0 and 1. So, once again, there seems to be no simple 'true *or* false' value to be assigned to a proposition; and hence the Law of Excluded Middle does not seem to operate.

What would be the consequences of adopting a suitable variant of this position in our present context? It should be clear that there will no longer be a problem of incompatibility between commitment to one's own faith and the belief that other religions might be of value too, even in respect of truth. For no longer does the assumption of the truth of my religion oblige me to regard every other religion as false, as a requirement of logical consistency: something about another religion, or even the whole of it, may be true, although perhaps in a different sense, to a different degree, or from a different point of view. It should now be possible for, say, a Christian or a Muslim happily to declare that 'God is at work, or true reality known, within other traditions as well as our own.' And this might not be an insubstantial gain from the sacrifice of the Law of Excluded Middle, considering especially that most religions themselves have often been guilty of sacrificing much more worthwhile entities, such as human lives, for scant gains or no gains at all!

However, what I suspect would appear to make this option less palatable, even to the ardent admirer of religious diversity, might possibly be its tendency to open the door to relativism. To many, relativism in such important matters as truth and morals may seem to be not only intellectually but also morally reprehensible. To introduce any variables, such as degrees, senses, or points of view into a discussion of matters concerning the truth or falsity of propositions or the rightness or wrongness of actions, would seem to them to be tantamount to abandonment of any serious interest in upholding the ideals of truth and morality in human transactions. I must say forthwith, without here offering a defense of what I have to say, that such fears are at best highly exaggerated and at worst without any foundation in logic. The very least that can be pertinently added here is that there are degrees of relativism as well; and of these only that of the extreme kind may be said to lead to the feared consequences. Relativism of a moderate kind, or degree, on the other hand, may not only be intellectually defensible but also positively beneficial for one's intellectual and moral health; and would certainly serve as a valuable antidote to dogmatism, that progenitor of bigotry, not infrequently found among religious people although by no means exclusively among them. Nor should it be thought that relativisim is of necessity a doctrine propounded by the nonreligious for antireligious purposes. Jainism, I believe, is one of the most compassionate of religions and yet it advocates a relativist logic and epistemology founded in its particular insight about how best to approach the question about what is real. But more on that later. For the moment all I wish to add is that the very fact of many actual religions helps to introduce relativism, although only as a descriptive, and not a normative, premise into questions about truth and morals; and whoever else may wish, or choose, to ignore it, anyone with the slightest interest in serious interreligious 'dialogue' cannot afford to do so.

* * * * * * * * * * * * * * * * * * * *

SØREN KIERKEGAARD

from "Subjective Truth, Inwardness; Truth is Subjectivity"

The "parable of the idol-worshipper" from Kierkegaard's *Concluding Unscientific Postscript* was included in Chapter 3 as a reading pertinent to the idea that "Proofs for the existence of God are irrelevant to religious faith and can be distracting to the religious." Here it is pertinent to the relationships approach.

In his "parable" Kierkegaard asks us to consider two individuals. One is an individual who has the "true conception of God" and goes to the "house of God, the house of the true God" but "prays in a false spirit." The second individual does not have the true conception of God and does not go to "the house of the true God," but prays in the right spirit. Where is there "most truth," Kierkegaard asks? His implicit answer is that "most truth" is with the one who prays in the right spirit, despite a wrong conception of God, and the one who prays falsely, despite having the "true conception of God," "worships in fact an idol." (Notice that Kierkegaard's parable does not require us to say *what* the "true conception" of God is. Kierkegaard was a Christian and thought that the Christian conception of God was the true one, but a Muslim or an Orthodox Jew could just as well present Kierkegaard's parable.)

While Kierkegaard was greatly concerned with the requirements of faith, he did not focus on *faith in* as a distinctive form of faith. In the parable of the idol worshipper, then, he is not trying to tell us something about religious *faith in God* as such, but still his parable can be used to bring out an important point about *faith in God*. Even though Kierkegaard does not put it this way, the first individual who prays in a false spirit does not have faith *in* God; the commitment of passion and trust are lacking. And the second individual, who prays with commitment and trust, does have faith *in* God even though she/he has the wrong conception of God. The important point that Kierkegaard brings to our attention is that a person can have true faith in God without having the right conception of God (just as one can have the true conception of God without having true faith in God). Faith in God does not absolutely require having the true conception of God. In this way, if this lesson of Kierkegaard's parable is right, two individuals in different thistic religious traditions with different conceptions of God can both have *faith in* God and so both can have a faith relationship to God.

The "parable of the idol-worshipper" is in Chapter 3 in the first of the two readings taken from "Subjective Truth, Inwardness; Truth is Subjectivity."

JAMES KELLENBERGER
The Way of Relationships

In "The Way of Relationships" James Kellenberger elaborates a way of understanding how all the great religions of the world can be right in terms of possible relationships to Religious Reality. For the *relationships approach* the major religions of the world can all be right in that they allow and encourage a right relationship to God or Religious Reality. Two distinguishable kinds of relationships to God or Religious Reality are important for this approach: *faith relationships* and *abiding relationships*.

A *faith relationship* is the relationship to God that believers are in (or see themselves as being in) by virtue of having *faith in God*. It is essentially a trust relationship to God. The other half of the relationships approach makes use of the idea of *abiding relationships* to God or Religious Reality. In the New Testament, in his first letter, John says that "he who abides in love abides in God, and God abides in him." Through "abiding" in love of others, through dwelling in love and being loving, John is saying, one abides in or dwells with God. Through loving others one enters into a kind of relationship to God, an abiding relationship, one not defined by faith in God but by living a life of love. In the Jewish Bible, the Tanakh, in the Book of Micah, we are told that what God requires of us is "to do justice and to love goodness and to walk modestly with your God." Here the image is not dwelling with God but walking with God, which again is done by a kind of doing, as opposed to having faith in God.

What is significant about abiding relationships is that individuals enter them through what they *do*, not through their *faith*. One enters an abiding relationship through walking modestly with God and following his way and his law or through imitating the life of Jesus or through the love or compassion one shows for others. One does not enter an abiding relationship through belief or faith. For this reason individuals in non-theistic religions, like Buddhism and advaitist Hinduism, can be recognized by theistic believers as being in an abiding relationship to God by virtue of their way of living, and, moreover, Kellenberger argues, individuals in theistic religions can be recognized by those in non-theistic religions as being in an abiding relationship to Reality conceived in non-theistic terms.

In this reading, taken from his *God-Relationships With and Without God*, Kellenberger refers to the "Way of Relationships" as "the sixth way" because he has previously discussed another five ways of understanding religious plurality.*

VI The Way of Relationships

To appreciate fully the import of the sixth way one must distinguish between types of God-relationships, or relationships to Divine Reality, and heed their distinct logics. In particular one must distinguish between faith relationships and abiding relationships. Without recapitulating our discussion in Chapter 3 we should, just here, note again several of the salient features of these two types of relationships. Faith relationships are defined by *faith in* (or *belief in* where this term is used synonymously). Faith in God, or in Divine Reality, we have recognized, requires the belief that God, or Divine Reality, exists. And, I have argued, *faith in* is or involves trust and certain beliefs associated with trust. Beyond these it seems to me that in various traditions, and in particular relationships, there may be other requirements, such as obedience. However, importantly, faith in God, or Divine Reality, does not require a specific conception of God or Divine Reality. That this is so has nothing to do with the nature of God or of Divine Reality. It follows from the general concept of *faith in* alone—quite independently of the character of the object of faith. Thus different persons may have different, even incompatible conceptions of God or Divine Reality and yet have faith in God or Divine Reality. And so, despite their different conceptions of God, Muslims, Jews, and Christians may all have faith in—have a faith relationship to—the same God. Abiding relationships are unlike faith relationships in that they are not defined in terms of faith. Accordingly they do not require even the minimal belief that faith relationships require. Specifically they do not require the belief that there exists a Divine Reality or any beliefs about Divine Reality. Indeed, as we have seen . . . many who explicitly renounce all religious belief may be in an abiding relationship by virtue of selfless commitment to Justice or Peace or love of neighbor. Belief in and beliefs about Divine Reality are allowed of course, and I would suppose that many in abiding relationships to Divine Reality believe in the existence of Divine Reality and hold beliefs about It. Nevertheless they do not do so as part of their abiding relationship to Divine

---

* From James Kellenberger, *God-Relationships With and Without God*. New York: St. Martin's Press, 1989. Reproduced with permission of Palgrave Macmillan.

Reality. Since abiding relationships do not require faith they are not limited to theistic religions or to those religions or variants that conceive of Divine Reality as a *persona*. One abides with God or Divine Reality, not by virtue of belief or faith, but by virtue of commitment or practice, by virtue of, say, love of neighbor or compassion for sentient creatures.

The view of the way of relationships, in a fuller expression than our initial formulation, is the view that many, even all, individuals in the various religious traditions and cultures of the world are, or may be, in a faith relationship or an abiding relationship to Divine Reality. (The disjunction of course is not exclusive.) The irenic force of the sixth way should be evident: it allows that Muslims, Jews, Christians, devotional visistadvaitist Hindus, Jodo and Shin Sect Buddists, and those in other traditions that conceive of Divine Reality as personal, may be at one through being in a faith relationship to Divine Reality; and, in a greater embrace, it allows that all those in religions that conceive of Divine Reality as personal, such as Islam, Judaism, and other traditions, and, as well, all those in traditions that conceive of Divine Reality as a nonpersonal Absolute, such as Taoism, advaita Vedanta, and Zen Buddhism, may be at one through being in some abiding relationship to Divine Reality.

Moreover the way of relationships allows that many who subscribe to nonreligious world views, such as Marxism or secular humanism, may be in abiding relationships to Divine Reality by virtue of their practice. But I note this essentially in passing, not because the point is unimportant, but because our concern is with *religious* plurality and the concept of religion does not in any clear way include Marxism and secular humanism. This is so despite the fact that these world views have certain analogies with the religions they oppose, as Ninian Smart points out.[102] Again, it may be significant that Hick, as we have seen, at times suggests that his religious pluralism can be extended to Marxism and secular humanism. The focus of the sixth way, the way of relationships, as I am developing it here, however, is on religious plurality.

Let me now proceed to bring out what I take to be the various virtues of the sixth way. To an extent I shall do this by contrasting it with the other five approaches we have considered, which I believe will show that it does not suffer from some of the perhaps untoward implications of these other approaches.

First, let us note that faith relationships and abiding relationships are complete as they are: they are not incomplete versions of something else, such as an explicit acceptance of a particular religion. This of course is a point of contrast between the sixth way and the way of implicit belief (or acceptance or desire), according to which implicit belief is made complete only by the ultimate explicit acceptance of Christianity. For the sixth way Hindus, Jews, Muslims, Buddhists, and others *as they are* may be rightly related to Divine Reality by virtue of their individual faith relationships or abiding relationships. Also the way of relationships, unlike, say, the common-core-of-belief approach, is prepared to find religious rightness or truth, in its personal dimension, in the depth or character of an individual relationship to Reality, which, it understands, does not arise merely from holding true (propositional) beliefs about

---

[102] Ninian Smart, *The Religious Experience of Mankind* (3rd edn; Charles Scribner's Sons, 1984) pp. 5–6.

Divine Reality. It is alive, then, to that dimension of truth that Cantwell Smith calls a 'truth of persons'. It is alive as well to the related Kierkegaardian point that impeccable objective belief is consistent with a meager subjectivity, or (as I shall put it) that one may hold only true theological beliefs about God and His nature with a ravishing subtlety of discernment and yet lack a right relationship to God, while another may have a right relationship to God and be theologically unsophisticated, even to the point of significant theological error (as in Tolstoy's short story, *The Three Hermits*, in which the hermits, who are holy men, pray with the words, 'You are three, we are three, have mercy upon us', in innocent ignorance of the doctrine of the Trinity).

But, we should be clear, the way of relationships does not deny that religions make cognitive claims, propositional truth-claims, which are either true or false. It can allow that there are, as Hugo Meynell says, 'real cognitive differences between religious doctrines', and that he is right when he says:

> However much the Muslim admits that he has positively to learn from the Christian or the Buddhist, he has, so long as he remains a Muslim at all, to insist that they are in error so long as they do not believe these crucial facts [e.g., that the Qur'an is the culminating revelation of God]; which, of course they cannot come to believe without thereby ceasing to be a Christian or a Buddhist.[103]

The logic of the sixth way's approach allows it to agree that there are such real incompatibilities of belief between religions, but it is not required to agree to this. The sixth way could alternatively allow that the Islamic belief that the Qur'an is the culminating revelation of God, while it makes a cognitive claim, is indeterminately related to, say, the Christian's claim that Christ is the Son of God. Why this latitude? Because the presence, or absence, of incompatible beliefs does not affect one way or the other the existence of relationships to Divine Reality in the various religious traditions. Thus, while the sixth way does not deny that religions make truth-claims, and, moreover, is itself committed to the claim that there is a Divine Reality to which individuals may be related, its view, in contrast both to the way of logical indeterminacy and to Meynell's counterview, entails no specific stand on the logical relationship that obtains between the claims of various religions.

This means, further, that the sixth way need not deny or urge the removal of those central and distinctive claims made by religions that assert, or imply, their superiority to all other religions. Granted, in themselves such assertions (Hick calls them 'absolute claims' in one essay[104]) do not ease the problem of religious diversity, and perhaps they bear implications for some of the other ways we have discussed, such as the way of the common core of belief. Nevertheless the fact that Muslims claim the Qur'an to be God's final revelation, that Jews claim they are God's chosen people, and that Christians claim Christ is God does not say anything about the existence or the non-existence of individual God-relationships, or relationships to Divine Reality, within and without each of these religions. The sixth way, so far as its own logic is concerned, can consistently say: 'Let these differences remain; and, if any

103 Hugo Meynell, 'The Idea of a World Theology', *Modern Theology*, 1 (1985) pp. 159 and 154.
104 John Hick, 'Religious Pluralism and Absolute Claims', *Problems of Religious Pluralism*, pp. 46 ff.

care to make them, let even overt claims to uniqueness and superiority flourish among the religions'. When such claims are made they, in accord with a remark made by Hick, seem analogous to expressions of national pride.[105] Nevertheless, even if they are true (or rather, even if one of them is true), this would not rule out either faith relationships or abiding relationships in other traditions. It would not rule out faith relationships in what, under this assumption, would be 'inferior' traditions with a false understanding of Divine Reality because one's being in a faith relationship to Divine Reality does not pre-suppose one's having a correct conception of Divine Reality. And it would not rule out abiding relationships in these other traditions because one's being in an abiding relationship to Divine Reality does not presuppose one's having any beliefs, true or false, about Divine Reality, or even the belief that there is a Divine Reality.

* * * * * * * * * * * * * * * * * * * *

The way of relationships, in its understanding of religious diversity, does not deny the place of truth—propositional truth—in religion, but for the sixth way, regarding the interrelatedness of religions (as opposed to the question of the correctness of their respective claims), it recedes in importance; and incompatible beliefs between religions, which may remain, become less divisive in the sense that, in spite of them, we can see how different religions can support the same or similar relationships to Divine Reality. The sixth way recognizes that cognitive truth is claimed by religions and so . . . it recognizes that relationships to Divine Reality, or God-relationships, can be described in terms specific to any of the various religious

traditions; it allows that God-relationships can be described in Christian-specific terms, but it also recognizes that they can be described in, say, Buddhist-specific terms as *Dharmakaya*-relationships, as well as neutrally as relationships to Divine Reality. Since it recognizes that religions make truth-claims, the sixth way avoids non-cognitivism and its paradoxes, such as the paradox that, given a non-cognitivist construction of religion, religious persons do not, or should not, understand their deepest religious beliefs to be true by virtue of a correspondence to an independent Divine Reality, and the paradox, identified by John Hick, that if Christianity's truth consists in there being true (sincere) Christians and Islam's truth consists in there being true (sincere) Muslims, and so on, then, not only will there be no religious knowledge, but 'in this personalistic and subjective sense Nazism [is] also a true faith, as is warlock worship, and faith in witchcraft and in astrology'.[110] In fact, as I have noted, cognitive truth is necessary for the sixth way in that it posits a Divine Reality and the (possible) existence of individual relationships to Divine Reality. Nevertheless for the sixth way cognitivity and cognitive differences cease to form the ground on which the various religions meet or fail to meet. They meet on the ground of relationships, shared or similar relationships to Divine Reality, identified in terms of faith or commitment to Divine Reality, or—for abiding relationships—in terms of practice informed by, for instance, love of neighbor in one of its expressions or by compassion. And, though Nazism and warlock worship may be false because their truth-claims are false, more significantly for the sixth way those who follow their practices will fail to be in abiding

---

[105] Hick, 'Religious Pluralism and Absolute Claims', *Problems of Religious Pluralism*, p. 49.
[110] Hick, 'The Outcome: Dialogue into Truth', *Truth and Dialogue* pp. 147–8.

relationships to Divine Reality by virtue of the nature of their practices.

This element of the sixth way—its recognizing the cognitivity of religion, while allowing cognitivity to recede in importance so far as the interrelatedness of religions is concerned—I take to be a signal virtue of the approach, and so let me offer an analogy that may help to remove any lingering suspicions regarding it. The analogy is in a way homely and in presenting it I shall once more draw upon human relations. Many husbands may say of their wives, 'She is the best wife in the world'. Perhaps when we hear such a comment we smile and understand it as hyperbole, endearing and appropriate, but still hyperbole. We may, but we need not. We may also understand it as a literal truth-claim. If so, however, and if one makes the same claim about one's own wife, then, logically, one must regard all the claims of all the other husbands as not quite right, in fact as false as they stand. It is this unpleasant implication, with its suggestion that perhaps honesty requires us explicitly to state our disagreement, that recommends the construction of hyperbole. If hyperbole is at work, then there is really no disagreement among the husbands. But if literal truth-claims are being made, then it appears that they must disagree. And, yes, they must *logically* disagree—that is, the truth of the claim of each entails the falsity of the claim of every other—but this does not mean that there is a point to their stating their disagreement, not if the intent of each claim is taken into consideration. Each husband, in making his claim, is proclaiming the depth and rightness of the relationship between himself and his wife. And there is no logical tension created by many, even all, husbands proclaiming, and having, right individual relationships to their respective wives. The purely logical tension between the claims themselves recedes into the background as not important so far as the interrelatedness of one marriage relation to all the others goes.[111]

The analogy is not perfect, of course, for (in the monogamous cases I have in mind) no two husbands are married to the same wife, while all the religions are, or may be, 'married' to the same Divine Reality. And the (possibly) incompatible claims of the various religions are many and diverse. Yet the underlying point of analogy remains: just as there may be

---

[111] Paul Knitter, in reflecting on the exclusivist language about Jesus in the New Testament (the 'one and only' language about Jesus), suggests that it is best understood as confession or testimony; and he uses an analogy, somewhat like the one I have offered, to make his point. He observes that the second-person 'You are the most beautiful woman in the world . . . you are the only woman for me', spoken by a husband, is an instance of confession or testimony. This is surely right. Knitter goes on to say that while such statements are true in the 'context of the marital relationship' they are not true in such a way as to require the husband in a larger context to take an oath as to their truth. Certainly this is one way to understand what the husband says, but—especially with examples of husbandly expressions more like the one I offer—not the only way. And the sixth way need not understand religious claims on Knitter's model. Knitter, *No Other Name?* p. 185.

By the way, these exclusivist claims—that one's wife is the best or the most beautiful or that Jesus was the one and only saviour—should not be confused with certain uniqueness claims, such as the claim that Jesus was unique in various ways. Often uniqueness claims from different religious traditions are compatible. For instance one can with consistency allow that both Jesus and the Buddha were unique liberators. Cf. Knitter's 'Catholic Theology at the Crossroads', *Concilium* 183 (February 1986) p. 106 and my 'The Slippery Slope of Religious Relativism', *Religious Studies* 21 (1985) p. 46.

many husbands with incompatible claims who may be rightly related to their wives, and who may even use their conflicting claims to express their relationships, so there may be many religions with (possibly) incompatible claims which may be rightly related to Divine Reality, and which may even use their multifarious and perhaps often conflicting claims to express their relationships.

* * * * * * * * * * * * * * * * * * * *

Let me go somewhat further. We have just observed that the sixth way posits relationships, possible relationships, to Divine Reality. So it does. But it does not require that these relationships, beyond their being faith relationships or abiding relationships, be precisely the same in all the religious traditions of the world. This much should be evident since, for one thing, there can be different abiding relationships. Moreover the sixth way can allow that not even all faith relationships are the same. Faith relationships are by definition relationships of *faith in* God or Divine Reality, and I argued earlier (in Chapter 3) that *faith in* is or involves trust. I believe that this point is correct. Certainly in the Judaeo-Christian tradition the role of trust within faith—faith in God—is well recognized, as it is by both John Calvin and Martin Buber, for instance.[112] In fact it could be argued that the very meaning of 'faith in' in English includes trust in both religious and non-religious uses ('I have faith in my doctor' means 'I trust my doctor'). Still, let us say that *faith in* is not,

and does not involve, trust in some religious traditions, or that for some individuals their faith relationships are defined only by, say, obedience to God or commitment to God or holding God dear—as opposed to these elements filling out an individual faith relationship in addition to what on my view is faith's essential trust. Even if we grant this, the primary point regarding faith relationships made by the sixth way would remain: individuals need not conceive of God or Divine Reality correctly, and different individuals need not conceive of God or Divine Reality in the same way, in order for them to have faith in God or Divine Reality. For, as with trust, one can be obedient to, committed to, and hold another dear while having a wrong conception of another. In this way, then, the sixth way is not wedded to my analysis of *faith in* and can leave it open whether faith itself is the same from religion to religion.

A similar latitude may be noted regarding abiding relationships. It should be clear that not all abiding relationships are the same: one person may have an abiding relationship to God or Divine Reality by virtue of an absolute and selfless commitment to, say, gaining justice for the oppressed, another by virtue of such a commitment to the pursuit of world peace. However there is a point about distinguishing more closely similar abiding relationships that merits our attention. In Chapter 3, in discussing abiding relationships, I suggested that as a Christian may be in an abiding relationship to Divine

---

[112] Both Calvin and Buber distinguish between two 'kinds' or 'types' of faith: a propositional *belief that* something is so and *faith in*, Pistis and Emunah respectively for Buber. For both, *belief that* need not, and *faith in* must involve trust. John Calvin, *The Institutes*, Chapter 2 of the 1535 edition; John Dillenberger (ed.), *John Calvin: Selections from His Writings* (Garden City, N.Y.: Anchor Books, 1971) p. 274. Martin Buber, *Two Types of Faith*, translated by Norman P. Goldhawk (Harper Torchbook, 1961) pp. 7, 26, 28, 43–4 and *passim*.

Reality by virtue of his or her love of neighbor so a Buddhist may be in an abiding relationship to Divine Reality by virtue of his or her compassion for sentient beings. I went on to raise the question whether they would be in the same abiding relationship. They would be, I suggested, to the extent that their *practice* is the same, although I did not try to reach a judgment on that matter. Nor do I intend to do so now. Earlier in this chapter, in connection with Hick's common-core view regarding the soteriological function of religions, we briefly explored what is involved in assessing whether religious practices are the same. It is not always an easy matter, it emerges. The point I want to stress here is that one following the sixth way need not make a judgment about whether the Christian and the Buddhist, or any two individuals, are in the *same* abiding relationship in order to judge that they are both in *some* abiding relationship. In this way the application of the sixth way to a large extent can avoid the comparison-of-practices problems we identified. It can merely leave it open whether hard-to-compare practices, as well as such practice-defining virtues as, say, love and compassion, or humility and overcoming desire, are the same in different religious traditions.

Let me recapitulate some of the strengths of the sixth way that we have just seen, for we have identified what I take to be a number of strengths or virtues of the way of relationships. In each case the virtue accrues because options are left open or, what amounts to the same thing, requirements are kept to a minimum. This means that if we follow the sixth way in seeking an irenic understanding of the interrelatedness of the world's religions we shall leave open a variety of issues, which if pronounced upon could themselves invite disagreement. So it is that the logic of the way of relationships does not entail or deny that one religion is superior to the others. Also the sixth way allows those who follow it to regard the beliefs of their religion as either probable or certain, as either logically incompatible with or indeterminately related to the beliefs of other religions, and to regard the distinctive beliefs of their religion, or of others, as either literally true or mythical. In this way, while for the sixth way religious belief is cognitive, no specific judgment is entailed regarding the exact logical relationship between the beliefs of different traditions. This is a virtue of the sixth way in that its adoption does not require one to assume a position on this complex and thorny matter. Of course one may want to come to a judgment on the logical relationship between the beliefs of the different religious traditions, and there may be positive reasons for doing so, but the sixth way in the absence of such reasons does not require one to do so. Again the sixth way can leave fairly open what will count as faith in the various religious traditions, and, as we have seen, despite what might be called a slight predisposition, it does not entail that the Divine Reality it posits be One and can allow that Divine Reality is Many. In the same way it can to a great extent avoid making judgments about the sameness of hard-to-compare religious practices in different traditions.

The sixth way, then, may fairly be said to have its virtues or strengths. It also has its problems. One in particular is both quickly apparent and deep-running in that it relates to the essential role the view must give to relationships. The problem is this: The way of relationships is committed to giving a central place to relationships to Divine Reality in considering the interrelatedness of the world's religions, but some religions, or variants, such as, for instance, Zen Buddhism and advaitist Hinduism, do not readily lend themselves to the category of *relationship*. *Nirvana* is not a relationship to anything, it seems, but rather a state that is attained. For non-devotional advaitist Hinduism the atman is identical with Brahman, not related to it as an individual may be to God in the thinking of theistic traditions. Earlier, in fact, in discussing the second part of John Hick's pluralism, we saw that he was open to criticism for speaking of a 'right relationship' in connection with Buddhism— a problem that must remain for him, despite judicious terminology, to the extent that he views salvation, liberation, and fulfilment as species of a relationship to Reality. In any case, however great the problem is for Hick, clearly there is a problem for the sixth way regarding the central place it gives to relationships to Divine Reality.

The problem for the sixth way relates particularly to those forms of religion that are non-theistic and do not conceive of Divine Reality as being ultimately personal, such as Zen Buddhism or advaitist Hinduism, and to those forms of religion whose ultimate is not conceived as a transcendent Reality, such as Theravada Buddhism.[113] Such traditions of course offer no opportunity for a faith relationship to Divine Reality, but, I would maintain, they do accommodate abiding relationships to Divine Reality. Earlier I argued that a (Mahayana) Buddhist may be said to be in an abiding relationship by virtue of his or her compassion for sentient beings. The question before us is whether in speaking of even abiding relationships the sixth way violates the categories and self-understanding of these

traditions. I think it can be argued that, finally, the sixth way is compatible with the categories of these traditions. Recall that sometimes these traditions have terms that in some manner designate Divine Reality. In Mahayana Buddhism 'Dharmakaya' designates the Dharma Body of the Buddha, or *sunyata*, the ultimate Divine Reality for Mahayana Buddhism, and in advaitist Hinduism 'Brahman' designates the final all-embracing Divine Reality. But, one might say, Brahman *is* atman, and *moksha* is the realization at the deepest level of this identity: it is not entering a new relationship with Brahman. This, I think, must be acknowledged, just as it must be acknowledged that attaining *nirvana* in Mahayana and Theravada Buddhism is coming to a realization or new state. However relationships to Divine Reality are not thereby ruled out. In fact the lack of enlightenment or realization—ignorance—is a kind of relationship to the truth of things, a wrong epistemic relationship; and, accordingly, enlightenment or realization is a species of right relationship. True, it is not a faith relationship, nor is it an abiding relationship of the sort I have discussed. It is a kind of epistemic relationship, perhaps unique to certain non-theistic traditions, which is defined in terms of realization. This much shows us that the category of *relationship* is not incompatible with the conceptual frameworks of these traditions. But is the category of *abiding relationship* compatible with them?

For Mahayana Buddhism and advaitist Hinduism the question comes down to this: Can Buddhists and advaitist Hindus consistently allow that individuals may

[113] For some Theravda Buddhists *nirvana* is not a transcendent spiritual reality but a positive psychological state in which the arhat escapes *samsara*, attains egolessness and at death becomes extinct. John Hick calls this view the 'minimal theraveda interpretation of nirvana'. *Death and Eternal Life*, pp. 436–7.

have an abiding relationship to *Dharmakaya* or Brahman by virtue of their embodied lives, even though those individuals live in and participate in other religious cultures? This question must not be confused with the question whether the category of *abiding relationships* is foreign to these traditions. The answer to the latter question may be affirmative (as I suppose it is) and yet the category of *abiding relationship* can be compatible with their conceptual frameworks. We should recall that, while this category may be quite foreign to the thinking of many Jews and Christians, nevertheless it is residually present in the Old and New Testaments and hence compatible with the Judaic and Christian conceptual frameworks. The crucial question is not whether the category is familiar to those in the Mahayana Buddhist and advaitist Hindu traditions, but whether it can be used within these traditions without contradiction. And, just as I see no conceptual reason why Jews, Christians, and Muslims cannot without contradiction speak of abiding relationships, so I do not see why Mahayana Buddhists and advaitist Hindus cannot without contradiction speak of abiding relationships. Accordingly, as within Mahayana Buddhism it is allowable for Buddhists to speak of Buddhists and others as being in an abiding relationship to *Dharmakaya*, so within advaitist Hinduism a Hindu may speak of Hindus and others as being in an abiding relationship to *Brahman*. A more difficult case perhaps is that of Theravada Buddhism. However, even in that form of Theravada Buddhism in which there is no transcendent Reality, there is the Eightfold Path to arhatship, the Buddhist moral rule, which involves right action, right thought and more. And, accordingly, when Theravada Buddhists encounter those in their own tradition or in other

religious traditions who in a significant degree live the external and internal life of a Buddhist, they may speak of them as being in an abiding relationship to the Eightfold Path to arhatship by virtue of their life-practice. The category of *abiding relationship* is not wedded or limited to theistic traditions and ultimately, I believe, could be utilized by the various religious traditions of the world. It may not be without significance that among the religious thinkers from various traditions I cite at the end of Chapter 3, who it seems to me anticipate the category of *abiding relationship*, one (Shivesh Thakur) is from the Hindu tradition.

A second problem that faces the sixth way may be put in the form of a reservation. The sixth way concentrates exclusively on individual relationships to Divine Reality, and, some may be concerned with the inattention to religious practice, belief, worship, ritual, the sacraments, and more that are important for every religious community. Practice of course plays a great role in defining abiding relationships, and the other elements mentioned—belief, worship, ritual, and the sacraments—where they are distinctive, are not promising as a basis for accommodating religious diversity. Still it must be allowed that the way of relationships has a focus that simply leaves aside much that is a part of communal religious life and much that vivifies individual religious lives. In reply, though, it can be said that the sixth way need not be relied upon to the exclusion of the other ways in a search for an understanding of the interrelatedness of the world's religious traditions. If the way of relationships is adopted, it can still be used in conjunction with other ways. For, with the exception of the way of non-cognitivism, it is, I think, compatible with each of the other ways we have discussed. Consider the way of implicit belief. This way makes one religion, Christianity, superior; and the sixth way has no such implication. On the other hand the sixth way does not deny it—just as it does not deny that, say, Hinduism is superior. Regarding the way of differential experience, the sixth way is not at odds with the idea that all religions experience the same Divine Reality or different aspects of the same Divine Reality. This way and the sixth way, which says nothing about religious experience, might work out to be supplements to one another. Again, the common-core approach, in both its belief form and its soteriological-function form, seems quite compatible with the sixth way. And since the sixth way says nothing about the compatibility or incompatibility of the religious claims made by the various traditions, it is compatible with the way of logical indeterminacy. Perhaps, with suitable adjustments, all of these ways, including the sixth way, can be used in conjunction in a common effort to find an irenic understanding of the interrelatedness of the world's religious traditions.

Index

ObjectWindows Reference

Borland®
ObjectWindows®

Borland International, Inc., 100 Borland Way
P.O. Box 660001, Scotts Valley, CA 95067-0001

1E0R0196   WBC1350WW21774
9697989900-9 8 7 6 5 4 3 2 1
D2
ISBN 0-672-30927-0

Contents

Part II
ObjectComponents programmer's reference   783

Part III
Windows System classes reference   933

Chapter 12
Windows system classes   935

Introduction

This *Reference* can be used to help you perform the following tasks in ObjectWindows:

- Look up the overall purpose for each class.

- Learn the details about how to use a particular ObjectWindows class and its members and functions.

- View the virtual and nonvirtual multiple inheritance relationships among ObjectWindows classes.

- Learn which classes introduce or redefine functions.

- Determine which ancestor of a class introduced a data member or member function.

- Learn how data members and member functions are declared.

- Create OLE2 applications easily by using ObjectComponents classes.

- Use event-handling functions to respond to messages.

- Use dispatch functions to crack Windows messages.

How this book is organized

This book is divided into the following parts.

Part I, "ObjectWindows programmer's reference," provides an overview of the ObjectWindows classes, libraries, and header files. It organizes the classes according to their functional groups and explains their purpose within that group. All the standard ObjectWindows classes, constants, enumerators, event handlers, functions, macros, type definitions, and dispatch functions are grouped into separate chapters and presented in alphabetical order.

Part II, "ObjectComponents programmer's reference," provides an overview of the ObjectComponents classes, libraries, and header files. It organizes classes according to their functional groups and explains their purpose within that group. All the standard ObjectComponents classes are presented in alphabetical order in a reference chapter that includes explanations of their purpose, usage, and members, as well as describes the nonobject elements such as structures, constants, variables, and macros that classes use.

Part III, "Windows system classes reference," describes in detail the Windows System classes, structures, and typedefs alphabetically.

Conventions used in this book

This book uses the following special fonts:

`Monospace`	This type represents text that you type or text as it appears onscreen.
Italics	These are used to emphasize and introduce words, and to indicate variable names (identifiers), function names, class names, and structure names.
Bold	This type indicates reserved keywords words, format specifiers, and command-line options.
Keycap	This type represents a particular key you should press on your keyboard. For example, "Press *Del* to erase the character."
Key1+Key2	This indicates a command that requires you to press *Key1* with *Key2*. For example, *Shift+a* (although not a command) indicates the uppercase letter "A."
ALL CAPS	This type represents disk directories, file names, and application names. (However, header file names are presented in lowercase to be consistent with how these files are usually written in source code.)
Menu ǀ Choice	This represents menu commands. Rather than use the phrase "choose the Save command from the File menu," Borland manuals use the convention "choose File ǀ Save."

Note   This icon indicates material that you should take special notice of.

Cross-referenced entries to ObjectWindows functions include the class name, the scope resolution operator, and the function name. For example,

See also   TApplication::PumpWaitingMessages

C++ data types that are keywords (such as **int** and **long**) are in lowercase bold. Predefined Windows types (such as HWND) are in capital letters; for example,

```
bool TrackPopupMenu(uint flags, int x, int y, int rsvd, HWND wnd, TRect* rect=0);
```

ObjectWindows programmer's reference

Part I is the programmer's reference for ObjectWindows and is organized into the following chapters:

- **Chapter 1, "Overview of ObjectWindows,"** provides an overview of the ObjectWindows classes, libraries, and header files. It organizes the classes according to functional groups and explains the purpose of each class within that group.

- **Chapter 2, "ObjectWindows class reference,"** is an alphabetical listing of all the standard ObjectWindows classes, including explanations of their purpose, usage, and members. It also describes the nonobject elements such as structures, constants, variables, and macros that classes use.

- Chapter 3, "ObjectWindows constants," presents all the ObjectWindows constants.

- **Chapter 4, "ObjectWindows enumerated types,"** presents all the ObjectWindows enumerators.

- **Chapter 5, "ObjectWindows event handlers,"** presents the ObjectWindows functions and notification codes that crack Windows messages.

- **Chapter 6, "ObjectWindows global functions,"** presents all the ObjectWindows functions.

- **Chapter 7, "ObjectWindows macros,"** presents all the ObjectWindows macros.

- **Chapter 8, "ObjectWindows type definitions,"** presents all the ObjectWindows type definitions.

- **Chapter 9, "ObjectWindows dispatch functions,"** lists all of the ObjectWindows functions that dispatch Windows messages.

1

Overview of ObjectWindows

This chapter presents an overview of the ObjectWindows classes, libraries, and header files. It describes the classes according to the functional groups represented on the ObjectWindows hierarchy diagram shown in Figures 1.1 and 1.2.

It covers the following topics:

- ObjectWindows classes
- ObjectWindows libraries
- ObjectWindows header files
- ObjectWindows resource files
- ObjectWindows data types
- ObjectWindows scoped types

The hierarchy diagram groups classes according to functional categories, and all related classes are in one shaded unit. A rectangle surrounds the name of the class. A class is enclosed in dashed lines if it is a parent class for a multiply-inherited class. For example, *TListBox* is the parent class for *TListView*, which is derived from both *TView* and *TListBox*. Base classes are placed above inherited classes and are connected to inherited classes by straight lines. The triangle on the connecting lines indicates the type of inheritance association that exists between the classes. A solid black triangle indicates virtual inheritance between the parent and its derived classes; an unfilled triangle illustrates nonvirtual inheritance.

Figure 1.1 ObjectWindows hierarchy

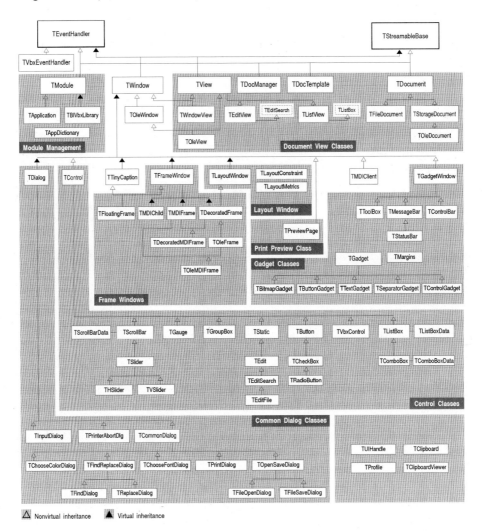

Nonvirtual inheritance   Virtual inheritance

Figure 1.2 ObjectWindows hierarchy

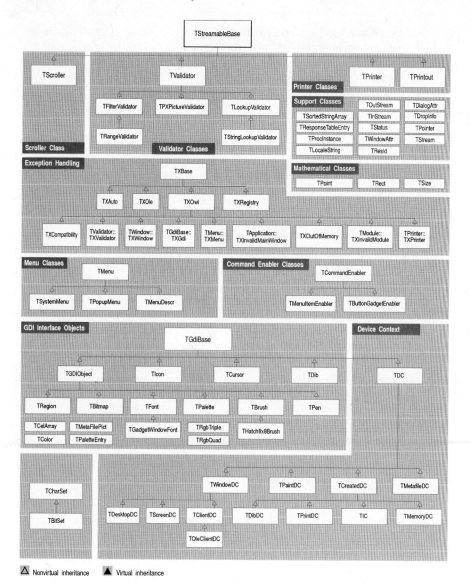

ObjectWindows classes

The ObjectWindows hierarchy includes a forest of classes that you can use, modify, or derive from in order to create your own application. This section describes these groups of classes and how you can use them to build your application. These classes can be divided into the following groups:

- Base classes
- Window management classes
- Module and application management classes
- Graphics classes
- Validator classes
- Exception handling classes

Base classes

TEventHandler, *TStreamableBase*, and *TGdiBase* are important base classes. All ObjectWindows classes are derived from one or more of these classes. Classes that inherit from *TEventHandler* are able to respond to window messages. Classes that inherit from *TStreamableBase* support streaming; that is, their objects can write to and read from streams. Almost all of the ObjectWindows classes are derived from *TStreamableBase*. You can use multiple inheritance to derive a class from both *TEventHandler* and *TStreamableBase*. Classes that inherit from *TGDIBase*, a private base class, support GDI drawing objects such as pens, brushes, fonts, and bitmaps.

- *TEventHandler* sends messages to the appropriate message handler.

- *TStreamableBase* provides support for C++ streaming and persistence.

- *TGdiBase* is the root class for all derived GDI classes that support Windows' GDI library.

Window management classes

Derived from *TEventHandler* and *TStreamableBase*, *TWindow* is the parent class for all window classes. It represents the functionality common to all windows, whether they are dialog boxes, controls, multiple document interface (MDI) windows, or layout windows. One of the fundamental ObjectWindows classes that implements OLE functionality, *TOleWindow*, provides support for embedding objects in a compound document application.

- Frame windows
- Decorated windows
- Common dialogs
- Controls
- Gadgets
- Menus

Frame windows

A frame window, which is actually an application's main window, has the ability to contain other client windows and also support UI elements such as menus and icons. Serving as main windows of MDI-compliant applications, MDI frame windows manage multiple documents or windows in a single document (SDI) application. ObjectWindows also provides OLE support for both SDI and MDI applications. A floating frame window provides the same functionality but lets you position the window anywhere within the parent window.

- *TFrameWindow* adds special functionality designed to simplify the managment of main windows.
- *TFloatingFrame*, derived from *TFloatingFrame* and *TTinyCaption*, provides the functionality of a frame window enhanced with a tiny caption bar.
- *TMDIChild* defines the behavior of MDI child windows.
- *TMDIFrame* provides support for frame windows designed to be used as MDI windows.
- *TOleFrame* provides OLE support for the main window of an SDI application.
- *TOleMDIFrame* provides OLE support for the main window of an MDI application.

Mix-in window classes such as *TLayoutWindow* and *TClipboardViewer* add the special functionality of layout capabilities and Clipboards to the main window classes. Use *TLayoutWindow* to design the placement of a window on the screen and *TClipboardViewer* to view the data shared between applications.

Decorated windows

Multiply inherited from *TFrameWindow* and *TLayoutWindow*, decorated window classes let you add decorated control bars and status bars to the frame of a window and adjust the child window to accommodate the placement of these decorations.

- *TDecoratedFrame* is basically a frame window with added decorations.
- *TDecoratedMDIFrame* is an MDI frame window that supports decorations.

Common dialogs

TDialog lets you create specialized windows referred to as dialog boxes. Dialog boxes typically ask users for information about fonts, colors, files, printing options, or searching and replacing text. Depending on their purpose, dialog boxes can be either modal, those which prevent a user from selecting other windows, or modeless, those which permit a user to select other windows.

You can create your own customized dialog boxes or use one of the ObjectWindows classes that encapsulates Windows' common dialog boxes. The following common dialog classes are derived from *TCommonDialog* which is itself derived from *TDialog*, the base dialog box class.

- *TChooseFontDialog* objects represent modal dialog boxes that allow font selection, style, point size, and color.

- *TChooseColorDialog* objects represent modal dialog boxes that allow color selection and custom color adjustment.

- *TOpenSaveDialog* is the base class for modal dialog boxes that let you open and save a file under a specified name.

- *TPrintDialog* displays a modal print or a printer setup dialog box.

- *TFindReplaceDialog* is the base class for modeless dialog boxes that let you search for and replace text.

Controls

The control classes support standard Windows controls such as list boxes, combo boxes, group boxes, check boxes, scroll bars, buttons, radio buttons, edit controls, and static controls.

Although most windows come with scroll bars already installed, you can use *TScrollBar* to create a standalone vertical or horizontal scroll bar; for example, as a dialog box control.

Unlike standard Windows controls, ObjectWindows supports widgets, specialized controls written entirely in C++. The widget classes ObjectWindows provides include support for sliders, controls that are used for providing nonscrolling position information, and gauges, controls that provide duration or analog information about a particular process.

- *TSlider* defines the basic behavior of sliders.
- *THSlider* implements horizontal sliders.
- *TVSlider* implements vertical sliders.
- *TGauge* defines the basic behavior of gauge controls.

Gadgets

TGadget is the base class for several derived classes that support gadget objects that belong to a gadget window, have borders and margins, and their own style attributes. Derived from *TWindow*, *TGadgetWindow* maintains a list of gadgets, controls the display of the gadgets, and sends the necessary messages to the gadgets.

Additional gadget classes derived from *TGadgetWindow* such as *TToolBox*, *TMessageBar*, *TStatusBar*, and *TControlBar* manipulate gadgets in different ways so that you can enhance a bar or tool box attached to a frame window.

- *TToolBox* lets you place a set of gadgets in a matrix of columns and rows.

- *TMessageBar* implements a message bar with one text gadget.

- *TStatusBar* lets you include multiple text gadgets and different border styles in a status bar.

- *TControlBar* implements a control bar that provides a set of buttons on a bar in a frame window.

Menus

TMenu and its derived classes let you construct, modify, and create menu objects. The classes derived from *TMenu* include the following:

- *TPopupMenu* lets you add a pop-up menu to an existing window or pop-up menu.
- *TSystemMenu* creates a system menu object.

Module management classes

Derived from *TModule*, *TApplication* supplies functionality common to all ObjectWindows applications. Classes derived from *TApplication* have the ability to create instances of a class, create main windows, and process messages. *TModule* defines behavior shared by both library (DLL) and application modules. Virtually derived from *TModule*, *TBiVbxLibrary* lets you add Visual Basic (VBX) controls to your application.

- Command enabling
- Doc/view
- Print and print/preview

Command enabling classes

Although several ObjectWindows classes process commands, there are three classes specifically devoted to enabling and disabling the commands available to an application.

- *TCommandEnabler* is the base class from which *TButtonGadgetEnabler* and *TMenuItemEnabler* are derived.

- *TButtonGadgetEnabler* enables and disables button gadgets.

- *TMenuItemEnabler* enables and disables menu options and places check marks by menu options.

Doc/View classes

Doc/View classes support the Doc/View model, a system in which data is contained in and accessed through a document object, and displayed and manipulated through a view object. Any number of views can be associated with a particular document type. Various classes control the flow of information within this system. Several classes also provide support for OLE's compound document and compound file structure within the Doc/View model.

TDocManager is the base class designed to handle documents, templates, messages and so on.

- *TDocument* is an abstract base class that serves as an interface between the document, its views, and its document manager.

- *TStorageDocument* supports OLE's compound file structure and lets you create compound documents with embedded objects.

- *TOleDocument* implements the document half of an OLE-enabled Doc/View application.

- *TView* is the base class that displays the document's data and gets user input.

- *TListView* supports views for list boxes.

- *TOleView* supports the view half of an OLE-enabled Doc/View application.

Printer classes

TPrinter, *TPrintout*, and *TPreviewPage* provide various functions that make it easy for you to set up a printer dialog box, view a document in a print preview window, and print a document.

- *TPrinter* represents the physical printer device.
- *TPrintout* represents the physical printed document sent to the printer.
- *TPreviewPage* displays a page of a document in a print preview window.

Graphics classes

ObjectWindows GDI classes encapsulate Windows' Graphics Device Interface (GDI) to make it easier to use device context (DC) classes and GDI objects. The GDI library supports device independent drawing operations using DIBS (device independent bitmaps).

- GDI objects
- Device contexts

GDI classes

ObjectWindows graphics library contains several classes that you can use to create DIBS, brushes, palettes, pens, and other drawing tools.

- *TGdiBase* is the private base class from which *TGDIObject*, *TIcon*, *TCursor*, and *TDib* are derived.

- *TGDIObject* is a base class for several other GDI classes that support drawing tools.

- *TDib* encapsulates the creation of structures containing format and palette information.

- *TCursor* encapsulates GDI cursor objects.

Device context (DC) classes

Instead of drawing directly on a device (like the screen or a printer), you can use GDI classes to draw on a bitmap using a device context (DC). A device context is a structure that contains information about the drawing attributes (pens, brushes, text color, and so on) of a particular device. DC classes support a variety of device context operations.

- *TDC* is the root class for GDI DC wrapper classes.

- *TWindowDC* and its derived classes such as *TClientDC* and *TScreenDC* provide access to the area owned by a window.

- *TCreatedDC* and its derived classes provide access to various DCs that are created and deleted such as memory and print DCs.

Validator classes

TValidator forms the base class for several ObjectWindows classes that encapsulate validation objects. The following derived classes make it easy for you to add data validation to your applications.

- *TFilterValidator* and its derived class, *TRangeValidator*, check an input field as the user types data into the field in order to determine the validity of the entered data.

- *TPXPictureValidator* compares user input with a picture of a data format.

- *TLookupValidator* compares a string typed by a user with a list of acceptable values.

Exception handling classes

Exception handling classes provide various functions that help you write error-free ObjectWindows applications. *TXBase* is the base class for all ObjectWindows and ObjectComponents classes. Derived from the *TXBase* class, *TXOwl* is the base class for the following ObjectWindows exception classes:

- *TXCompatibility* is included for backward compatibility with ObjectWindows 1.0 code.

- *TXOutOfMemory* describes exceptions that arise from out of memory conditions.

- Nested exception classes such as *TXInvalidMainWindow*, *TXInvalidModule*, *TXWIndow*, *TXMenu*, *TXValidator*, *TXGdi*, and *TXPrinter* describe specific error conditions such as those that occur when a main window, a module, a menu object, a validator object, a GDI object, or a printer device context is invalid.

ObjectWindows libraries

This section covers the following topics:

- Compiler options
- Building ObjectWindows libraries
- Using ObjectWindows libraries

The following tables list the ObjectWindows static and dynamic libraries, their uses, and the operating system under which the library is available. These files are in your library directory.

The name of the OWLWx.LIB file varies, depending on several factors—whether you are building a medium or large memory model application or a Win16 or Win32 application. For example, if the application is built for a 16-bit, large memory model, the name of the library file is OWLWL.LIB. If you're building a flat model Win32 application, the name of the library file is OWLWF.LIB where "F" indicates a flat model application. If run-time diagnostics are enabled, ObjectWindows adds "D" to the name of the library. If you are building a multi-threaded application, ObjectWindows adds "T" to the name of the library.

Different versions of these files are included on your installation disk. If the diagnostic files are not shipped, you can build these files by adding the switch –DDIAGS to the ObjectWindows makefile located in your ..\EXAMPLES subdirectory.

Table 1.1   Summary of static libraries

File name	Application	Use
OWLWM.LIB	Win16	16-bit medium model
OWLWL.LIB	Win16	16-bit large model
OWLWI.LIB	Win16	16-bit import library for OWL50.DLL
OWLDWM.LIB	Win16	16-bit diagnostic medium model
OWLDWL.LIB	Win16	16-bit diagnostic large model
OWLDWI.LIB	Win16	16-bit diagnostic import library
OWLWLU.LIB	Win16	16-bit large static for user .DLL
OWLWIU.LIB	Win16	16-bit import static for user .DLL
OWLDWLU.LIB	Win16	16-bit diagnostic large static for user .DLL
OWLDWIU.LIB	Win16	16-bit diagnostic import static for user .DLL
OWLWF.LIB	Win32	32-bit library
OWLWFI.LIB	Win32	32-bit import library for OWL50F.DLL
OWLDWF.LIB	Win32	32-bit diagnostic library
OWLDWFI.LIB	Win32	32-bit diagnostic import library
OWLWT.LIB	Win32	32-bit static multi-threaded
OWLWTI.LIB	Win32	32-bit import multi-threaded
OWLDWT.LIB	Win32	32-bit diagnostic static multi-threaded
OWLDWTI.LIB	Win32	32-bit diagnostic import multi-threaded

The dynamic-link library (DLL) versions of ObjectWindows are contained in the \BIN subdirectory of the installation. The following table lists the DLL names and uses, and the operating system under which each library is available.

File name	Application	Use
OWL50.DLL	Win16	16-bit dynamic library
OWL50F.DLL	Win32	32-bit dynamic library
OWL50D.DLL	Win16	Diagnostic version of 16-bit dynamic library
OWL50DF.DLL	Win32	Diagnostic version of 32-bit dynamic library
OWL50T.DLL	Win32	32-bit multi-threaded dynamic library
OWL50DT.DLL	Win32	Diagnostic version of 32-bit multi-threaded dyanmic library

Compiler options for building and using ObjectWindows libraries

You need to use different compiler options depending on whether you are building or using ObjectWindows DLLs or static libraries. Unless you specify otherwise, ObjectWindows makes several assumptions about the default values for system platforms and memory models. That is, ObjectWindows assumes that the platform is Win16 unless MODEL is explicitly set to "f"; in which case, ObjectWindows assumes that the platform is Win32. The default MODEL setting is "d," where "d" indicates that you are building the DLL version of an library.

The following table lists the combinations of SYSTEM and MODEL settings you can use to build the specified target applications.

For this target application:	Use SYSTEM=	Use MODEL=
16-bit Windows medium model static version	WIN16	m
16-bit Windows large model static version	WIN16	l
16-bit Windows large model DLL	WIN16	d
32-bit Windows static version	WIN32	f
32-bit Windows DLL	WIN32	d
32-bit Windows multi-threaded DLL	WIN32	t

Building ObjectWindows libraries

If you are building ObjectWindows DLLs and libraries, you need to use several predefined macros. For example, defining the make macro USERDLL builds ObjectWindows for use in a user DLL and adds the suffix, "U" to the name of the library. The preprocessor macro _BUILDOWLDLL, which must be defined to build the ObjectWindows DLL, sets the values for the _OWLCLASS, _OWLDATA, _OWLFUNC macros.

You can specify the system model as either s (small), m (medium), l (large), f (flat), or d (DLL). The make options you set are then responsible for generating the specified preprocessor macro, which, in turn, generates the indicated values for the

_OWLCLASS, _OWLDATA, and _OWLFUNC macros and builds the appropriate library. For an example of how these settings are used, see the makefile in the \SOURCE\OWL directory or defs.h in the INCLUDE\OWL directory.

The following table lists the make options you need to use if you are building either 16- or 32-bit ObjectWindows.

If you are building:	Use these make options:	Preprocessor macro	_OWLCLASS _OWLDATA _OWLFUNC	Libraries
ObjectWindows DLL				
16-bit EXE	MODEL = d	_BUILDOWLDLL	All defined as __export	OWLWI.LIB
32-bit EXE or DLL	MODEL = d –DWIN32	_BUILDOWLDLL	All defined as _export	OWLWF.LIB
16-bit DLL	MODEL = d –D USERDLL	_BUILDOWLDLL	All defined as __export	OWLWIU.LIB
ObjectWindows static library				
16-bit EXE	MODEL = m or l	Nothing	Nothing	OWLWS.LIB OWLWM.LIB OWLWL.LIB
32-bit EXE or DLL	MODEL = f –DWIN32	Nothing	Nothing	OWLWF.LIB
16-bit DLL	MODEL = l –D USERDLL	Nothing	Nothing	OWLWLU.LIB
32-bit EXE (multi-thread)	WIN32 = 1 MT = 1	Nothing	Nothing	OWLWT.LIB
32-bit DLL (multi-thread)	WIN32 = 1 MT = 1 DLL = 1	Nothing	Nothing	OWLWTI.LIB

Using ObjectWindows libraries

You can specify the memory model as either m (medium), l (large), f (flat), or d (DLL). Keep in mind that the make options SYSTEM=WIN32 and –DWIN32 are the same. The make options you set are then responsible for generating the specified preprocessor macro, which, in turn, generates the indicated values for the _OWLCLASS, _OWLDATA, and _OWLFUNC macros and builds the appropriate library. For an example of how these settings are used, see MAKEFILE.GEN in the \OWL\ EXAMPLES directory.

The following table lists the make options you need to specify if you are using either 16- or 32-bit ObjectWindows applications.

If you are building:	Use these make options:	Preprocessor macro	_OWLCLASS _OWLDATA _OWLFUNC	Libraries
ObjectWindows DLL				
16-bit EXE	MODEL = d	_OWLDLL	All defined as __import	OWLWI.LIB
32-bit DLL	MODEL = d –DWIN32	_OWLDLL	All defined as __import	OWLWF.LIB
16-bit DLL	MODEL = d	_OWLDLL	All defined as __import	OWLWIULIB
ObjectWindows static library				
16-bit EXE	MODEL = s or m or l	Nothing	Nothing	OWLWS.LIB OWLWM.LIB OWLWL.LIB
32-bit EXE or DLL	MODEL = f –DWIN32	Nothing	Nothing	OWLWF.LIB
16-bit DLL	MODEL = l	Nothing	Nothing	OWLWLU.LIB

The following table lists the makefile and compiler options for the _OWLFARVTABLE macro, which moves ObjectWindows virtual function tables (vtables) out of the DGROUP of the data segment and stores them in the code segment.

Use this compile option:	Define in your makefile:	With this result:
_OWLFARVTABLE _BIDSFARVTABLE _RTLFARVTABLE	OWLFARVTABLE	Adds _huge to the OWLCLASS class modifier when static models are used.
_FASTTHIS	Doesn't apply	Adds _fastthis to the _OWLCLASS macro.

The ObjectWindows header files

Header files contain prototype declarations for class functions, and definitions for data types and symbolic constants.

File name	Class definition	Use
animctrl.h	TAnimateCtrl	Creates an animation control in a window.
appdict.h	TAppDictionary	Contains a set of associations between an application using the DLL version of ObjectWindows and a process ID.
applicat.h	TApplication	Controls the basic behavior of all ObjectWindows applications.

File name	Class definition	Use
	TBwccDll	
	TCommCtrlDll	
	TCtl3dDll	
	TWinG	
	TXInvalidMainWindow	
bitmapga.h	TBitmapGadget	A set including but no more than 256 items managed by bits.
bitset.h	TBitSet	Sets or clears one or more bits.
	TCharSet	A set of characters.
button.h	TButton	Creates different types of button controls.
buttonga.h	TButtonGadget	Creates button gadgets that can be clicked on or off.
celarray.h	TCelArray	Creates an array of bitmap cels.
checkbox.h	TCheckbox	Represents a check box control.
checklst.h	TCheckList	
	TCheckListItem	
chooseco.h	TChooseColorDialog	Represents modal dialog boxes that allow color selection.
choosefo.h	TChooseFontDialog	Represents modal dialog boxes that allow font selection.
clipboar.h	TClipboard	Contains functions that control how Clipboard data is handled.
	TClipboardFormatIterator	
	TXClipboard	
clipview.h	TClipboardViewer	Registers a TClipboardViewer as a Clipboard viewer.
colmnhdr.h	TColumnHeader	Displays labels above columnar lists. Also accepts user input to control column widths and sorting order.
	THdrItem	Holds information about an item of a column header control.
	THdrNotify	
combobox.h	TComboBox	Creates combo boxes or combo box controls in a window.
	TComboBoxData	Used to transfer data between combo boxes.
commctrl.h	TNotify	
	TXCommCtrl	
commdial.h	TCommonDialog	Abstract base class for TCommonDialog objects.
compat.h		Defines functions and constants used internally by ObjectWindows.
contain.h	TCollection - wait	
	TInt	
	TIntArray	
	TIntArrayIterator	
	TStringArray	
	TStringArrayIterator	
	TUint32Array	
	TUint32ArrayIterator	
control.h	TControl	Used to create control objects in derived classes.
controlb.h	TControlBar	Implements a control bar that provides mnemonic access for its button gadgets.

File name	Class definition	Use
controlg.h	TControlGadget	Allows controls to be placed in a gadget window.
dc.h	TClientDC	GDI DC wrapper classes that create DC objects.
	TCreatedDC	
	TDC	Root class for GDI DC wrappers.
	TDeskTopDC	Provides access to the desktop window's client area.
	TDibDC	Provides access to device-independent bitmaps (DIBs).
	TEnhMetaFilePict	
	TIC	Provides a constructor for creating a DC object from explicit driver, device, and port names.
	TMemoryDC	Provides access to a memory DC.
	TMetaFileDC	Provides access to a device context with a metafile selected for drawing.
	TPaintDC	Wraps begin and end paint calls for use in a WM_PAINT response function.
	TPrintDC	Provides access to a printer.
	TScreenDC	Provides direct access to the screen bitmap.
	TWindowDC	Provides access to the entire area owned by a window.
decframe.h	TDecoratedFrame	Creates a client window into which decorations can be placed.
decmdifr.h	TDecoratedMDIFrame	Creates a frame object that supports decorated child windows.
dialog.h	TControlEnabler	
	TDialog	Creates modal and modeless dialog box interface elements.
dibitmap.h	TDiBitmap	
	THalftonePalette	
	TIdentityPalette	
dispatch.h		Defines dispatch functions designed to crack Windows messages.
dockable.h	TDockableControlBar	Creates a dockable control bar.
docking.h	TDockable	An abstract base class for either fixed or floating docking windows.
	TDockableGadgetWindow	Creates a dockable gadget window.
	TDockingSlip	An abstract base class for windows which accept and hold dockable windows.
	TEdgeSlip	Creates the actual docking slips along the decorated frame's client's edges.
	TFastList - wait	
	TFloatingSlip	Creates a floating frame which can hold a dockable window.
	THarbor	The object that holds all the docking slips and performs the actual docking insertion and coordination.
docmanag.h	TDocManager	Creates a document manager object that manages the documents and templates.
	TDvFileOpenDialog	
	TDvFileSaveDialog	
	TDvOpenSaveData	

File name	Class definition	Use
	TDvOpenSaveOwner	
doctpl.h	TDocTemplate	Creates the templates.
	TDocTemplateT<D,V>	Registers the associated document and view classes.
docview.h	TDocument	Creates, destroys, and sends messages about TWindowView, TStream, document views.
	TInStream	Defines streams for documents.
	TOutStream	Defines streams for documents.
	TStream	Defines streams for documents.
	TView	Defines the interface presented to a document so it can access its client views.
	TWindowView	A streamable base class that can be used for deriving window-based views.
draglist.h	TDragList	Creates an augmented list box that lets the user rearrange items with a mouse.
	TDragListEventHandler	
edit.h	TEdit	Creates an edit control interface element.
editfile.h	TEditFile	Creates a file editing window.
editsear.h	TEditSearch	Creates an edit control that responds to search and replace commands.
editview.h	TEditView	View wrapper for TEdit.
eventhan.h	TEventHandler	Used to derive class capable of handling messages.
	TResponseTableEntry	A template class that lets you define a pattern for entries into a response table.
except.h	TStatus	Describes a status exception.
	TXBase	Base exception-handling class for ObjectWindows and ObjectComponents classes.
	TXCompatibility	Included for backward compatibility.
	TXOutOfMemory	Describes an out-of-memory exception.
	TXOwl	Base exception-handling class for ObjectWindows classes.
filedoc.h	TFileDocument	Opens and closes document views.
findrepl.h	TFindDialog	These classes create and define the attributes of
	TFindReplaceDialog	modeless dialog boxes that respond to search and replace
	TReplaceDialog	commands.
floatfra.h	TFloatingFrame	Implements a floating frame within a parent window.
framewin.h	TFrameWindow	Controls window-specific behavior such as keyboard navigation and command processing.
	TMenuItemEnabler	Enables and disables menu options and places check marks by menu options.
gadget.h	TGadget	Creates gadget objects that belong to a gadget window and have specified attributes.
	TSeparatorGadget	Creates a separator between gadgets.
	TSizeGripGadget	
gadgetwi.h	TGadgetControl	
	TGadgetList	
	TGadgetWindow	Maintains a list of tiled gadgets for a window.
	TGadgetWindowFont	Defines the font used in gadget windows.

File name	Class definition	Use
gauge.h	TGauge	Establishes the behavior of gauge controls.
gdibase.h	TGdiBase	Abstract base class for all GDI classes.
	TXGdi	Constructs a TXGdi object with a default IDS_GDIFAILURE message.
gdiobjec.h	TBitmap	Constructs a bitmap from many sources.
	TBrush	Creates solid, styled, or patterned brushes from explicit information.
	TCursor	Creates a cursor object from a resource or from explicit information.
	TDib	Creates a device independent bitmap (DIB) object.
	TFont	Creates font objects from explicit information or indirectly.
	TGDIObject	Pseudo-abstract base class for GDI (Graphics Device Interface) wrappers.
	THatch8x8Brush	Defines a small, 8x8, monochrome, configurable hatch brush.
	TIcon	Creates icon objects from a resource or from explicit information.
	TPalette	Creates palettes from explicit information or indirectly from various color table types that are used by DIBs.
	TPen	Encapsulates the GDI pen tool.
	TRegion	Creates GDI abstract shapes or regions objects with various shapes.
	TSystemFont	
glyphbtn.h	TBtnBitmap	
	TGlyphButton	Creates a button with a bitmap in addition to text.
groupbox.h	TGroupBox	Creates a group box object that represents a group box element in Windows.
hlpmanag.h	THelpContext	
	THelpFileManager	
hotkey.h	THotKey	Creates a simple edit-like control for accepting hot-key strokes from the user.
imagelst.h	TImageInfo	A structure that describes an image within an image list.
	TImageList	A wrapper class for the ImageList common control.
inputdia.h	TInputDialog	Creates a generic dialog box that accepts text.
layoutco.h	TEdgeConstraint struct	Allows manipulation of edge constraints.
	TEdgeOrHeightConstraint	
	TEdgeOrSizeConstraint	A template class that supports size constraints in addition to all the operations that TEdgeConstraint provides.
	TEdgeOrWidthConstraint	
	TLayoutConstraint	Creates layout constraints.
layoutwi.h	TLayoutMetrics	Contains the layout constraints used to define the layout metrics for a window.
	TLayoutWindow	Provides layout options for a window.
listbox.h	TListBox	Creates a list box object.
	TListBoxData	Used to transfer the contents of a list box.
listview.h	TListView	Provides views for list boxes.

File name	Class definition	Use
listwind.h	TListWindColumn	A column within a list window.
	TListWindItem	An item within a list window.
	TListWindow	Displays items in four ways: large (regular) icons, small icons, as a list, or as a report.
	TLwComparer	A base class for comparisons to sort items.
	TLwDispInfoNotify	A list window notification to repaint an item.
	TLwFindInfo	A structure to find an item in a list window.
	TLwHitTestInfo	Determines whether or not a point is somewhere on an item.
	TLwKeyDownNotify	A list window notification that a key has been pressed.
	TLwNotify	A basic list window notification.
mailer.h	TMailer	Provides mail enabling.
mci.h	TMci	
	TMciHiddenWindow	
	TMciWaveAudio	
mdi.h	TMdiClient	Manages MDI child windows.
	TMdiFrame	The main window of MDI-compliant applications.
mdichild.h	TMdiChild	Defines the behavior of MDI child windows.
menu.h	TMenu	Creates menu objects.
	TMenuDescr	A menu bar with groups.
	TPopupMenu	Creates menu objects.
	TSystemMenu	Base menu class.
	TXMenu	Describes a menu exception.
menugadg.h	TMenuGadget	
messageb.h	TMessageBar	Implements a message bar.
metafile.h	TMetaFilePict	A wrapper class used with TMetaFileDC.
modegad.h	TModeGadget	A mode-tracking text gadget class.
module.h	TDllLoader	
	TErrorMode	
	TModule	Defines the basic behavior for ObjectWindows libraries and applications.
	TModuleProc	
	TModuleVersionInfo	Provides access to a TModule's VERSIONINFO resource.
	TXInvalidModule	Describes an exception that results from an invalid module.
notetab.h	TNoteTab	
	TNoteTabItem	
oledialg.h	TOleDialog	
	TRegisterOcxWnd	
oledoc.h	TOleDocument	Implements the Document half of the Doc/View pair.
olefacto.h	TAutoFactory	Template class that supports component create callbacks for automated OLE-enabled applications.
	TOleFactory	Template class that supports component create callbacks for Doc/View and non-Doc/View OLE-enabled applications.

File name	Class definition	Use
	TOleAutoFactory	
	TOleDocViewAutoFactory	
	TOleDocViewFactory	
	TOleFactoryAuto	
	TOleFactoryBase	Template class that creates callback code for ObjectWindows classes.
	TOleFactoryDocView	
	TOleFactoryNoAuto	
	TOleFactoryNoDocView	
oleframe.h	TOleFrame	Supports OLE-enabled main windows for SDI applications.
olemdifr.h	TOleMdiFrame	Supports OLE-enabled main windows for MDI applications.
oleview.h	TOleLinkView	Provides embedding and linking support for a portion of a document instead of an entire document.
	TOleView	Supports the View half of the Doc/View pair.
olewindo.h	TOleClientDC	Translates between two different coordinate systems.
olewindo.h	TOleWindow	Provides support for embedding objects in a compound document and serves as the client of a frame window.
opensave.h	TFileOpenDialog	Creates a modal dialog box that lets you specify the name of a file to open.
	TFileSaveDialog	Creates a modal dialog box that lets you specify the name of a file to save.
	TOpenSaveDialog	Base class for modal open and save dialog boxes.
owldc.h	TBandInfo	Used to pass information to a printer driver that supports banding.
picklist.h	TPickListDialog	Allows selection of an item from a list in a dialog with OK and Cancel buttons.
	TPickListPopup	
pictwind.h	TPictureWindow	
preview.h	TPreviewDCBase	
	TPreviewPage	Displays a document page in a print preview window.
	TPrintPreviewDC	Maps printer device coordinates to screen coordinates.
prevwin.h	TPreviewWin	
printdia.h	TPrintDialog	Displays a modal print or print setup dialog box.
printer.h	TPrinter	Represents the printer device.
	TPrinterAbortDialog	Represents the printer-abort dialog box.
	TPrintout	Represents the printed document.
	TXPrinter	Describes an exception that results from an invalid printer object.
propsht.h	TPropertyPage	Represents a dialog box found within a property sheet.
	TPropertySheet	Creates a multipage window with pages that can be navigated using a built-in tab control.
	TResource	
radiobut.h	TRadioButton	Create a radio button control.
rcntfile.h	TRecentFiles	

File name	Class definition	Use
richedit.h	TCharFormat	
	TCharRange	
	TEditStream	
	TEnDropFiles	
	TEnProtected	
	TFindText	
	TFormatRange	
	TMsgFilter	
	TParaFormat	
	TReqResize	
	TRichEdit	Creates a full-featured rich text format (RTF) editor.
	TSelChange	
	TTextRange	
richedpr.h	TDynArray	
	TRichEditPagePreview	
	TRichEditPreviewFrame	
	TRichEditPrintout	
rolldial.h	TRollDialog	
scrollba.h	TScrollBar	Represents a vertical or horizontal scroll bar control.
scroller.h	TScroller	Implements automatic window scrolling.
serialze.h	TSerializer	
	TSerializeReceiver	
shellitm.h	TContextMenu	
	TDataObject	
	TDropTarget	
	TExtractIcon	
	TPidl	An item identifier list class.
	TShellItem	Creates an item in the shell's name space.
	TShellItemIterator	An interator for walking through the contents of a folder.
	TShellMalloc	
	TXShell	
slider.h	THSlider	A horizontal slider.
	TSlider	Defines the basic behavior of sliders.
	TVSlider	A vertical slider.
splashwi.h	TSplashWindow	Creates a layout window that contains a TPictureWindow and optionally, a TStatic and a TGauge.
splitter.h	TPaneSplitter	
static.h	TStatic	Create a static control in a window.
statusba.h	TStatusBar	Constructs a status bar.
stgdoc.h	TStorageDocument	Supports compound file structure mechanisms.
tabctrl.h	TTabControl	Creates a window that provides a UI similar to dividers in a notebook.
	TTabEntryInternal	

File name	Class definition	Use
	TTabHitTestInfo	
	TTabItem	Represents a single tab within a tab control.
	TTabKeyDown	
textgadg.h	TTextGadget	Constructs a text gadget object.
timegadg.h	TTimeGadget	Constructs a time gadget object.
tinycapt.h	TTinyCaption	Produces a smaller caption bar for a window.
toolbox.h	TToolBox	Creates a toolbox object with a specified number of rows and columns.
tooltip.h	TToolEntryInternal	
	TToolInfo	Contains information about a particular tool.
	TTooltip	Creates a small popup window that displays a single line of descriptive test giving the purpose of the item underneath the current cursor location.
	TTooltipEnabler	
	TTooltipHitTestInfo	
	TTooltipText	Identifies a tool for which text is to be displayed.
treewind.h	TTreeItem	Represents the data to be stored in the tree window.
	TTreeNode	
	TTreeWindow	Provides a hierarchical tree display in a list.
	TTwComparer	Base class for comparisons of sort items.
	TTwDispInfoNotify	A tree window notification to repaint an item.
	TTwHitTestInfo	A tree window notification for hit-testing.
	TTwKeyDownNotify	A tree window notification that a key has been pressed.
	TTwNotify	A basic tree window notification.
uihelper.h	TUIHandle	Defines and draws UI handles.
	TUIBorder	Assists in drawing borders of many styles.
	TUIFace	Assists in painting UI elements in various states.
	TUIPart	
updown.h	TUpDown	Creates an up/down control which is a pair of arrow buttons that can be used to increment or decrement a value.
	TUpDownNotify	
validate.h	TFilterValidator	Filter validator.
	TLookupValidator	Lookup validation.
	TPXPictureValidator	Picture validator.
	TRangeValidator	Range validatator.
	TSortedStringArray	Creates a sorted array of elements that are string objects.
	TStringLookupValidator	String validation.
	TValidator	Base validator class.
	TXValidator	Describes an exception that results from an invalid validator object.
vbxctl.h	TVbxControl	Provides an interface for VBX controls.
	TVbxEventHandler	Handles events from VBX controls.
	TXVbxLibrary	
	TBIVbxLibrary	Loads and initializes BIVBXxx.DLL.

File name	Class definition	Use
window.h	TCommandEnabler	An abstract base class used for automatic enabling and disabling of commands.
	TWindow	Provides window-specific behavior and encapsulates many of the Windows API functions.
	TWindowsAttr	Contains the attributes of a window.
	TXWindow	Describes an exception that results from trying to create an invalid window.
winsock.h	TWinSockDll	
wskaddr.h	TINetSocketAddress	
	TSocketAddress	
wskerr.h	TSocketError	
wskhostm.h	THostEntry	
	THostInfoManager	
	THostInfoWindow	
wskservm.h	TServiceEntry	
	TServiceManager	
	TServiceWindow	
wsksock.h	TSocket	
	TStreamSocket	
	TQueueItem	
wsksockd.h	TDatagramSocket	
wsksockm.h	TSocketInfo	
	TSocketManager	

ObjectWindows resource files

The ObjectWindows resource files (\INCLUDE\OWL) define resource and command IDs.

File name	Use
docview.rh	Defines resource and command IDs to use with docview.h and docview.rc.
edit.rh	Defines command IDs to use with edit.h.
editfile.rh	Defines resource and command IDs to use in editfile.rc and editfile.h.
editsear.rh	Defines resource and command IDs to use in editsear.rc and editsear.h.
editview.rh	Defines accelerator and menu IDs to use with TEditView.
except.rh	Defines string resource IDs to use with except.h and except.rc.
inputdia.rh	Defines resource IDs to use with inputdia.rc and inputdia.h.
listview.rh	Defines resource and command IDs to use with listview.h.
locale.rh	Defines localization resource Ids.
mdi.rh	Defines resource and command IDs to use with mdi.h.
oleview.rh	Defines resource IDs to use with OLE-enabled views.

File name	Use
panespli.rh	
picklist.rh	
prevwin.rh	
printer.rh	Defines resource IDs to use with printer.rc and printer.h.
shellitm.rh	
slider.rh	Defines resource IDs to use with slider.h.
statusba.rh	Defines resource IDs to use with statusba.h.
validate.rh	Defines resources to use with TValidator and derived classes.
window.rh	Defines command IDs to use with window.h.
winsock.rh	

ObjectWindows data types

ObjectWindows data types have been updated to use more portable type names. To ensure that these new types are used correctly, be sure to include the ObjectWindows header files before any Windows files, such as windows.h, in your application files. The new C++ type, which maps a nonzero value to TRUE, lets you assign an integer to a **bool** type. You can then compare this Boolean value to TRUE.

The following table lists the Windows API type names, the underlying C type definitions, and the new ObjectWindows type names.

Windows	C/C++ definition	New type	Description
	char	int8	Used when 8-bit signed value is needed
BYTE	unsigned char	uint8	Always 8 bits
WORD	unsigned short	uint16	Always 16 bits
int	int	int	16 or 32 bits depending on the platform
UINT	unsigned int	uint	16 or 32 bits depending on the platform
LONG	long	long, int32	Long (Could be 64 bits on some platforms)
WPARAM	TParam1	TParam1	Type of first message parameter (uint)
LPARAM	TParam2	TParam1	Type of second message parameter (uint32)
LRESULT	TResult	TResult	Returned result of a message
ULONG	unsigned long	ulong, int32	Long (Could be 64 bits on some platforms)
	long	int32	Always 32 bits
DWORD	unsigned long	uint32	Always 32 bits
BOOL	int	bool	New C++ type if available; otherwise, emulated using an enum
TRUE	1	true	
FALSE	0	false	

ObjectWindows scoped types

The following table lists the Windows API type names, the underlying class scope, and the new ObjectWindows type names.

Windows	Class scope	New type	Description
HANDLE	THandle	THandle	Number that uniquely identifies a handle.
HBITMAP	TBitmap	THandle	Number that uniquely identifies a bitmap.
HBRUSH	TBrush	THandle	Number that uniquely identifies a brush.
HCURSOR	TCursor	THandle	Number that uniquely identifies a cursor.
HFONT	TFont	THandle	Number that uniquely identifies a font.
HGDIOBJ	TGdiObject	THandle	Number that uniquely identifies a GDI object.
HICON	TIcon	THandle	Number that uniquely identifies an icon.
HINSTANCE	TInstance	THandle	Number that uniquely identifies a instance.
HPALETTE	TPalette	THandle	Number that uniquely identifies a palette.
HPEN	TPen	THandle	Number that uniquely identifies a pen.
HRGN	TRegion	THandle	Number that uniquely identifies a region.
HWND	TWindow	THandle	Number that uniquely identifies a window.

2

ObjectWindows library reference

This chapter alphabetically lists the ObjectWindows classes. The header file that defines each entry is listed opposite the entry name. Class members are grouped according to their access specifiers, either public or protected. Within these categories, data members, then constructors (and the destructor, if one exists), and member functions are listed alphabetically.

Because many of the properties of the classes in the hierarchy are inherited from base classes, only data members and member functions that are *new* or *redefined* for a particular class are listed. Private members are not listed. If any response table entries exist, they are also listed. The cross-referenced entries provide additional information about how to use the specified entry. The first sample entry illustrates this format.

For a list of all the inherited as well as overridden virtual functions, see the online Help.

TBird class [sample]   bird.h

Type definitions

This section alphabetically lists all typedefs and enums defined within a class.

typedef unsigned short TOwlId
typedef unsigned short TOwlId;
This text explains what this typdef contains, and how you use it.

See also   Related damembers, member functions, classes, constants, and types

Public data members

This section alphabetically lists all public data members and their declarations, and explains how they are used.

anOwlBeak
anOwlType anOwlBeak;
anOwlBeak is a data member that holds information about this sample class. This text explains what *anOwlBeak* contains, and how you use it.

See also   Related data members, member functions, classes, constants, and types

anOwlWing
anOwlType anOwlWing;
anOwlWing is another public data member.

Public constructor and destructor

This section lists any public constructors and destructor for this class. Classes can have more than one constructor; they never have more than one destructor.

Constructor
TBird(anOwlType aParameter);
Constructor for a new sample class; sets the *anOwlBeak* data member to *aParameter*.

Destructor
~TBird;
Destructor for a new sample class; destroys the *TBird* object.

Public member functions

This section alphabetically lists all public member functions that are either newly defined for this class or that are redefined inherited member functions. The description includes the purpose of each parameter and the return value of the function. If a function overrides a virtual base class function, the text specifies this:

The inline keyword isn't provided because it doesn't affect usage.

EvGetDlgCode
UINT OwlHoot();
Responds to WM_GETDLGCODE messages.

OwlHoot
void OwlHoot();
The *OwlHoot* member function causes the sample class to perform some action. This function overrides the function *OwlHoot* in its base class, *TParent*.

See also   *TParent::OwlHoot*

OwlSleep
virtual int OwlSleep(int index);
The *OwlSleep* function performs another action and overrides the function *OwlSleep* in its base class, *TParent*.

See also   TParent::OwlSleep

Protected data members

This section alphabetically lists all protected data members and their declarations, and explains how they are used.

anOwlFeather
anOwlType anOwlFeather;
anOwlFeather is a protected data member that holds information about this sample class.

See also   Related data members, member functions, classes, constants, and types

Protected constructors

Constructor
TBird(anOwlType bParameter);
If the class has a protected constructor, it is listed here.

Protected member functions

This section lists all protected member functions.

OwlCry
BOOLEAN OwlCry;
The *OwlCry* member function causes the sample class to perform some action.

See also   TSomethingElse::OwlCry

ZatsIt
virtual int ZatsIt(int index);
The *ZatsIt* function performs a particular function in class *TBird*.

Response table entries

The *TBird* response table contains this predefined macro for the EV_xxxx messages and calls this member function:

Response table entry	Member function
EV_WM_GETDLGCODE	EVGetDlgCode

Factory template classes (ObjectWindows)   olefacto.h

The factory template classes create callback code for both automated and non-automated Doc/View and non-Doc/View ObjectWindows applications. Use these factory template classes to make objects for embedding and linking. (That is, when an application object needs to be embedded within another container, the callback function is responsible for creating the embedded object.) Depending on the template arguments passed to the factory class, you obtain different kinds of factories designed to create the object you need. All the templetized classes, however, assume that the application is using a global *AppDictionary* (the application's dictionary), and a global *Registrar* (the TOcRegistrar pointer that manages registering the application in the database).

ObjectWindows includes several factory template classes, divided into two main categories: those designed for Doc/View applications and those designed for non-Doc/View applications. Although all these classes contain the same functions, they are designed to create different types of objects.

The factory class hierarchy chart illustrates the inheritance relationship among these classes.

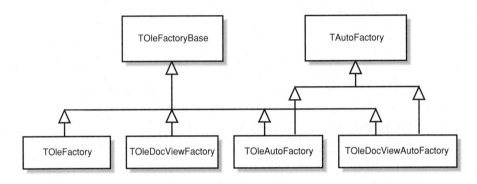

△ Nonvirtual inheritance

Each class takes three arguments: the application class, the automation class, and the Doc/View class. The arguments indicate whether or not the application is a Doc/View application and whether or not the application is automated. The factory classes and their definitions include the following four classes.

TOleDocViewFactory class for Doc/View, non-automated, OLE components
```
template <class T> class TOleDocViewFactory
: public TOleFactoryBase<T, TOleFactoryDocView<T,
  TOleFactoryNoAuto<T>>>{};
```

TOleDocViewAutoFactory class for Doc/View, automated OLE components
```
template <class T> class TOleDocViewAutoFactory
: public TOleFactoryBase<T, TOleFactoryDocView<T,
  TOleFactoryAuto<T>>>{};
```

TOleFactory class for non-Doc/View, non-automated, OLE components
```
template <class T> class TOleFactory
: public TOleFactoryBase<T, TOleFactoryNoDocView<T,
  TOleFactoryNoAuto<T>>>{};
```

TOleAutoFactory class for non-Doc/View, automated OLE components
```
template <class T> class TOleAutoFactory
: public TOleFactoryBase<T, TOleFactoryNoDocView<T,
  TOleFactoryAuto<T>>>{};
```

For either a Doc/View or a non-Doc/View application, you need to register your application in your *OwlMain* function. The argument to *TOcRegistrar* (in this case,

TOleFactory<TDrawApp>) constructs an object and converts it to a *TComponentFactory* ype, using the operator *TComponentFactory* to create a function pointer. In reality, the object is never created because all the factory class's functions are static.

Pass your application object derived from *TApplication* as the parameter to *TOleFactory*, as the following code from STEP15.CPP illustrates:

```
int
OwlMain(int /*argc*/, char* /*argv*/ [])
{
  try {
    Registrar = new TOcRegistrar(AppReg, TOleFactory<TDrawApp>(),
                          TApplication::GetCmdLine());
    if (Registrar->IsOptionSet(TOcCmdLine::AnyRegOption))
       return 0;
//If this is a normal exe server, run the application now; otherwise,
// wait until the factory is called.
    return Registrar->Run();
}
```

In general, the following steps, illustrated in the Factory Class Callback Flowchart, show the steps each factory class follows in the default callback code:

1 The factory gets the application. This is the application object derived from *TApplication*. For a DLL server, there can be several instances of the object. Using *TAppDictionary::GetApplication*, the factory verifies whether or not there is an entry in the application dictionary for an application object for the current process.

2 If the application does not exist, the factory creates the application object and tests to see if the application was created successfully before creating its corresponding *TOcApp* object. If the shutdown option flag is set, it then exits. (If the application has already been destroyed, the shutdown flag is set.)

3 If the factory is passed a shutdown option flag (one of the *TOcAppMode* enum values), it then shuts down the application and calls the factory's *DestroyApp* function to destroy the application.

4 If the application is automated, the factory creates a corresponding automation object.

5 If the object ID is not zero, the factory creates the object and gets the OLE interface. Otherwise, it gets the application's OLE interface. At this point, the Doc/View and non-Doc/View processes differ because they need to create different types of objects. If the application is automated, the factory creates an automated helper object.

6 The factory checks to see if the option flag *amRun* (one of the *TOcAppMode* enum values) is set, and, if so, it runs the application. This occurs if the application either was built as an .EXE or is a DLL running as an .EXE. If the *amRun* flag is not set and the application is an in-proc DLL server and should not be running, the factory just starts the application.

7 The factory returns either the OLE interface for the object or 0 if no interface was requested or if an error occurred.

The following diagram illustrates this process.

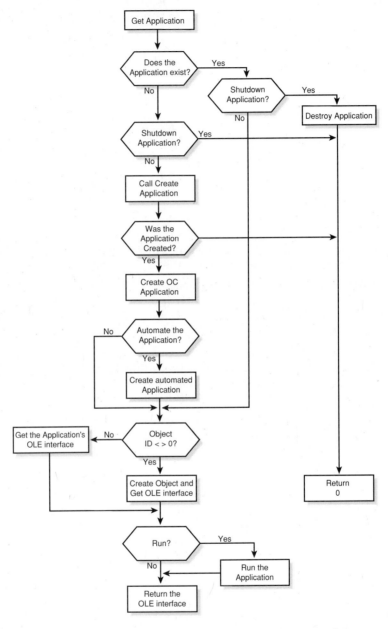

The factory can be called back to walk through this process several times:

1 On the first callback, the factory creates the application, and if the *amRun* flag is set, it enters a message loop.

2 On the second callback, OLE calls the factory to automate or embed or link an object. In the case of an embedded and/or linked object, this pass can occur one or more

times. (In the case of an automation object, however, this second pass occurs only once because any subsequent requests pass through the automated application itself.)

3 On the final callback, the factory shuts down the application.

See also   TAutoFactory class, TAutoFactory::DestroyApp, TComponentFactory typedef, TOcAppMode enum, TOcRegistrar class, TOleFactoryBase class, TOleFactoryBase::DestroyApp, TOleFactoryBase::TComponentFactory

Mix-in classes

These are classes designed to be used in conjunction with other classes to provide special functionality or behavior. Mix-in classes are designed not to stand alone, but to be combined with other bases when declaring a new class. The new class is derived through multiple inheritance from the mix-in and other base classes.

For example, if you are building a frame window, you can derive your frame window class from both the base class *TFrameWindow* and the mix-in class *TLayoutWindow* to get the additional functionality of layout windows.

See also   TClipboardViewer, TEventHandler enum, TOcModule, TTinyCaption

TAnimateCtrl class   animctrl.h

TAnimateCtrl encapsulates a class that plays an .AVI file.

Public constructors

AnimateCtrl
Form 1   TAnimateCtrl(TWindow* parent, int id, int x, int y, int w, int h, TModule* module = 0);
Constructor for a *TAnimateCtrl* to be associated with a new underlying control.

Form 2   TAnimateCtrl(TWindow* parent, int resourceId, TModule* module = 0);
Constructor to alias a control defined in a dialog resource.

Public member functions

Open
bool Open(char far* fileOrRes);
Opens an .AVI file and displays the first frame. The *res* parameter may be a resourceId if the .AVI is from a resource. It may also be a full path of an .AVI file. Use NULL (0) as *res* to close any previously opened .AVI file.

Play
bool Play(uint16 start = 0, uint16 end = -1, uint repeat = 1);
Plays the .AVI file from frame index *start* to frame index *end*. The *repeat* parameter is the number of times to play the frames. Use -1 for *repeat* to play indefinitely.

Note The control plays the clip in the backgroud while the current thread continues executing.

Seek

bool Seek(uint16 frame);

Seek to frame index *frame*. The value is zero-based and must not exceed 65,536.

Stop

void Stop();

Stops playing the current AVI file.

Protected member functions

GetClassName

char far* GetClassName();

Returns the predefined class registered by the Common Control library for the Animation control.

TAppDictionary class   appdict.h

A *TAppDictionary* is a dictionary of associations between a process ID and an application object. A process ID identifies a process: a program (including all its affiliated code, data, and system resources) that is loaded into memory and ready to execute. A *TAppDictionary* object supports global application lookups using the global *GetApplicationObject* function or *TAppDictionary*'s *GetApplication* function. If you do not define an application dictionary, ObjectWindows provides a default, global application dictionary that is exported. In fact, for .EXEs, this global application dictionary is automatically used.

TAppDictionary includes a *TEntry* struct, which stores a process ID and the corresponding application object associated with the ID. The public member functions add, find, and remove the entries in the application dictionary.

If you are statically linking ObjectWindows, you do not have to explicitly create an application dictionary because the default global ObjectWindows application dictionary is used. However, when writing a DLL component that is using ObjectWindows in a DLL, you do need to create your own dictionary. To make it easier to define an application dictionary, ObjectWindows includes a macro DEFINE_APP_DICTIONARY, which automatically creates or references the correct dictionary for your application.

Although this class is transparent to most users building .EXEs, component DLLs need to create an instance of a *TApplication* class for each task that they service. This kind of application differs from an .EXE application in that it never runs a message loop. (All the other application services are available, however.)

Although a component may consist of several DLLs, each with its own *TModule*, the component as a whole has only one *TApplication* for each task. A *TAppDictionary*, which is used for all servers (including DLL servers) and components, lets users produce a complete, self-contained application or component. By using a *TAppDictionary*, these components can share application objects.

When 16-bit ObjectWindows is statically linked with an .EXE or under Win32, with per-instance data, the *TAppDictionary* class is implemented as a wrapper to a single application pointer. In this case, there is only one *TApplication* that the component ever sees.

To build a component DLL using the ObjectWindows DLL, a new *TAppDictionary* object must be constructed for that DLL. These are the steps an application must follow in order to associate the component DLL with the *TAppDictionary*, the application, and the window class hierarchy:

1 Use the DEFINE_APP_DICTIONARY macro to construct an instance of *TAppDictionary*. Typically, this will be a static global in one of the application's modules (referred to as "AppDictionary"). The DEFINE_DICTIONARY macro allows the same code to be used for .EXEs and DLLs.

```
DEFINE_APP_DICTIONARY(AppDictionary);
```

2 Construct a generic *TModule* and assign it to the global *::Module*. This is the default provided in the ObjectWindows' *LibMain* function.

```
LibMain(...)
   ::Module  = new TModule(0, hInstance);
```

3 When each *TApplication* instance is constructed, pass a pointer to the *TAppDictionary* as the last argument to ensure that the application will insert itself into this dictionary. In addition, for 16-bit DLLs, the *gModule* argument needs to be supplied with a placeholder value because the *Module* construction has already been completed at this point, as a result of the process performed in step 2 above.

```
TApplication* app = new TMyApp(..., app, AppDictionary);
```

4 If the Doc/View model is used, supply the application pointer when constructing the *TDocManager* object.

```
SetDocManager(new TDocManager(mode, this));
```

5 When a non-parented window (for example, the main window) is being constructed, pass the application as the module.

```
SetMainWindow(new TFrameWindow(0, "", false, this));
```

See also   TApplication::GetWindowPtr, TWindow::GetWindowPtr, DEFINE_APP_DICTIONARY macro

Type definitions

TEntry struct
struct TEntry {
 unsigned Pid;
 TApplication* App;
};
An application dictionary entry that associates a process ID (*Pid*) with an application (*App*). The dictionary is indexed by *Pid* and can have only 1 entry per process ID.

See also   TAppDictionary::TEntryIterator typedef

TEntryIterator
typedef void(*TEntryIterator)(TEntry&);
A dictionary iterator function pointer type that receives a reference to an entry. You can supply a function of this type to the *Iterate* function to iterate through the entries in the dictionary.

See also   TAppDictionary::TEntry struct, TAppDictionary::Iterate

Public constructor and destructor

Constructor
TAppDictionary();
Constructs a *TAppDictionary* object.

Destructor
~TAppDictionary();
Destroys the *TAppDictionary* object and calls *DeleteCondemned* to clean up the condemned applications.

Public member functions

Add
void Add(TApplication* app, unsigned pid = 0);
Adds an application object (*app*) and corresponding process ID to this dictionary. The default ID is the current process's ID.

See also   TAppDictionary::Remove

Condemn
void Condemn(TApplication* app);
Marks an application in this dictionary as condemned by zeroing its process ID so that the application can be deleted later when *DeleteCondemned* is called.

DeleteCondemned
bool DeleteCondemned();
Deletes all condemned applications from the dictionary. If no applications remain in the dictionary, *DeleteCondemned* returns **true**.

See also   TAppDictionary::Condemn

GetApplication
TApplication* GetApplication(unsigned pid = 0);
Looks up and returns the application associated with a given process ID. The default ID is the ID of the current process. If no application is associated with the process ID, *GetApplication* returns 0.

Iterate
void Iterate(TEntryIterator iter);
Iterates through the entries in the application dictionary, calling the *iter* callback function for each entry.

See also   TAppDictionary::TEntryIterator

Remove

Form 1   void Remove(TApplication* app);

Searches for the dictionary entry using the specified application (*app*). Then removes a given application and process ID entry from this dictionary, but does not delete the application object.

Form 2   void Remove(uint pid);

Searches for the dictionary entry using the specified process ID (*pid*). Then removes a given application and its associated process ID entry from this dictionary, but does not delete the application.

See also   TAppDictionary::Add

TApplication class   applicat.h

Derived from *TModule*, *TApplication* acts as an object-oriented stand-in for an application module. *TApplication* and *TModule* supply the basic behavior required of an application. *TApplication* member functions create instances of a class, create main windows, and process messages.

To create an OLE-enabled Doc/View application, you need to derive your application from both *TApplication* and *TOcModule*.

Public data members

AccTable

HACCEL HAccTable;

Included to provide backward compatibility, *HAccTable* holds a handle to the current accelerator table being used by the application. New applications should instead use the accelerator table handle *TWindowAttr::AccelTable* for each window object in the application.

See also   TWindow::LoadAcceleratorTable, TWindowAttr struct

hPrevInstance

HINSTANCE hPrevInstance;

Contains the handle of the previously executing instance of the Windows application. If *hPrevInstance* is 0, there was no previously executing instance when this instance began execution. Under Win32, this value is always 0.

nCmdShow

int nCmdShow;

Indicates how the main window is to be displayed (either maximized or as an icon). These correspond to the *WinMain* parameter *nCmdShow*. *nCmdShow* can contain one of the following constants:

Constant	Meaning
SW_SHOWDEFAULT	Shows the default SW_xxxx command.
SW_HIDE	Hides the window.

Constant	Meaning
SW_MINIMIZE	Minimizes the specified window.
SW_SHOW	Activates a window using current size and position.
SW_SHOWMAXIMIZED	Displays a maximized window.
SW_SHOWMINIMIZED	Displays a minimized window.
SW_SHOWNA	Displays window in its current state.
SW_SHOWNOACTIVATE	Displays the window as an icon.
SW_SHOWNORMAL	Displays a window in its original size and position.
SW_SHOWSMOOTH	Shows a window by updating it in a bitmap and then copying the bits to the screen.

Public constructors and destructor

Constructors

Form 1   TApplication(const char far* name = 0, TModule*& gModule = ::Module, TAppDictionary* appDict = 0);
Creates a new *TApplication* object named *name*. You can use *gModule* to specify the global module pointer that points to this application. The *appDict* parameter specifies which dictionary this application will insert itself into. To override the default ObjectWindows *TAppDictionary* object, pass a pointer to a user-supplied *appDict* object.

Form 2   TApplication(const char far* name, HINSTANCE hInstance, HINSTANCE hPrevInstance,
          const char far* cmdLine, int cmdShow, TModule*& gModule = ::Module, TAppDictionary* appDict = 0);
Creates a *TApplication* object with the application name (*name*), the application instance handle (*instance*), the previous application instance handle (*prevInstance*), the command line invoked (*cmdLine*), and the main window show flag (*cmdShow*). The *appDict* parameter specifies which dictionary this application will insert itself into. To override the default ObjectWindows *TAppDictionary* object, pass a pointer to a user-supplied *appDict* object.

If you want to create your own *WinMain*, use this constructor because it provides access to the various arguments provided by *WinMain*. You can use *gModule* to to specify the global module pointer that points to this application.

Destructor
~TApplication();
~TApplication destroys the *TApplication* object.

See also   TApplication::nCmdShow, TModule

Public member functions

BeginModal
int BeginModal(TWindow* window, int flags = MB_APPLMODAL);
Called to begin a modal window's modal message loop. After determining which window to disable, *BeginModal* saves the current status of the window, disables the window, calls MessageLoop, and then reenables the window when the message loop is

finished. The flags determine how *BeginModal* treats the window. *flags* can be one of the following values:

Constant	Meaning
MB_APPLMODAL	The window to be disabled (which is usually an ancestor of the modal window) is identified by *window*. If *window* is 0, no window is disabled.
MB_SYSTEMMODAL	The window to become system modal is identified by *window*.
MB_TASKMODAL	All top-level windows are disabled, and *window* is ignored. *BeginModal* returns -1 if an error occurs.

See also   TWindow

BWCCEnabled
bool BWCCEnabled();
Indicates if the Borland Custom Controls library (BWCC) is enabled. Returns **true** if BWCC is enabled and **false** if BWCC is disabled.

CanClose
virtual bool CanClose();
Returns **true** if it is OK for the application to close. By default, *CanClose* calls the *CanClose* member function of its main window and returns **true** if both the main window and the document manager (*TDocManager*) can be closed. If any of the *CanClose* functions return **false**, the application does not close.

This member function is seldom redefined; closing behavior is usually redefined in the main window's *CanClose* member function, if needed.

See also   TWindow::CanClose

Condemn
void Condemn(TWindow* win);
Performs window cleanup.

Ctl3dEnabled
bool Ctl3dEnabled() const;
Returns **true** if the Microsoft 3-D Controls Library DLL is enabled. This DLL gives controls a three-dimensional look and feel.

See also   TApplication::EnableCtl3d, TApplication::EnableCtl3dAutosubclass

Dispatch
virtual TResult Dispatch(TEventInfo& info, TParam1 wp, TParam2 lp = 0);
Overrides *TEventHandler::Dispatch()* to handle multi-thread synchonization.

EnableBWCC
void EnableBWCC(bool enable = true, uint Language = 0);
Loads and registers either BWCC.DLL if you are running 16-bit applications or BWCC32.DLL if you are running 32-bit applications. By default, BWCC is enabled. To disable BWCC, set *enable* to **false**.

See also   TDialog

EnableCtl3d
void EnableCtl3d(bool enable = true);
Enables or disables the use of the CTL3D DLL. If *enable* is **true**, *EnableCtl3d* loads and registers the CTL3D.DLL if it is not already enabled.

See also   TApplication::Ctl3dEnabled, TApplication::EnableCtl3dAutosubclass

EnableCtl3dAutosubclass
void EnableCtl3dAutosubclass(bool enable);
Enables or disables CTL3D's use of autosubclassing if CTL3D is already enabled using *Ctl3dEnabled*. If autosubclassing is enabled, any non-ObjectWindows dialog boxes have a 3-D effect. The common dialog classes and *TDocManager* use this function both to turn on autosubclassing before creating a non-ObjectWindows dialog box to make it three-dimensional and to turn off autosubclassing immediately after the dialog box is destroyed.

See also   TDialog::EvCtlColor, TApplication::EnableCtl3d, TApplication::Ctl3dEnabled

EndModal
void EndModal(int result);
Called to end a modal window's modal message loop. Sets *result* to -1 if an error occurs.

Find
bool Find(TEventInfo &, TEqualOperator = 0);
Because *TApplication* has no event table itself, it defers event handling to the DocManager. If a DocManager has been installed, *Find* calls *TDocManager* to handle events.

See also   TEventHandler::TEventInfo

GetBWCCModule
TModule* GetBWCCModule() const;
Returns a pointer to the enabled Borland Windows Custom Controls library (BWCC) module.

GetCmdLine
static string& GetCmdLine();
Returns the command line of the application. Most programs do not need to call this because *OwlMain* has the parameters already parsed.

GetCmdShow
int GetCmdShow() const;
Retrieves the initial state of the main window.

GetCtl3dModule
TModule* GetCtl3dModule() const;
Returns a pointer to the enabled Ctl3d module.

GetCurrentEvent
TCurrentEvent& GetCurrentEvent();
Returns the current event from the message queue.

GetDocManager
TDocManager* GetDocManager();
Returns a pointer to the document manager object that invoked the application.

See also   TApplication::SetDocManager, TDocManager

GetMainWindow
TFrameWindow* GetMainWindow();
Returns a pointer to the application's main window.

See also   TApplication::SetMainWindow, TFrameWindow

GetPrevInstance
HINSTANCE GetPrevInstance() const;
Returns the HINSTANCE of the previous running instance.

GetWindowPtr
TWindow* GetWindowPtr(HWND hWnd) const;
Retrieves a *TWindow* pointer associated with the handle to a window (*hWnd*), allowing more than one application to share the same HWND.

See also   TWindow::GetWindowPtr

GetWinMainParams
void GetWinMainParams();
Initializes a static instance of an application. ObjectWindows *OwlMain* uses this function to support static application instances.

See also   TApplication::SetWinMainParams

MessageLoop
virtual int MessageLoop();
Operates the application's message loop, which runs during the lifetime of the application. *MessageLoop* queries for messages. If one is received, it processes it by calling *ProcessAppMsg*. If the query returns without a message, *MessageLoop* calls *IdleAction* to perform some processing during the idle time. *MessageLoop* calls *PumpWaitingMessages* to get and dispatch waiting messages. *MessageLoop* can be broken if *BreakMessageLoop* is set by *EndModal*.

PostDispatchAction
void PostDispatchAction();
If *TApplication*'s message loop is not used, this function should be called after each message is dispatched.

PreProcessMenu
virtual void PreProcessMenu(HMENU hmenu);
Your application can call *PreProcessMenu* to process the main window's menu before it is displayed.

See also   TDocmanager::EvPreProcessMenu, TMenu::TMenu

ProcessAppMsg
virtual bool ProcessAppMsg(MSG& msg);

Checks for any special processing that is required for modeless dialog box, accelerator, and MDI accelerator messages. Calls the virtual *TWindow::PreProcessMsg* function of the window receiving the message. If your application does not create modeless dialog boxes, does not respond to accelerators, and is not an MDI application, you can improve performance by overriding this member function to return **false**.

See also   MSG struct

PumpWaitingMessages
bool PumpWaitingMessages();

Called by *MessageLoop*, *PumpWaitingMessages* processes and dispatches all waiting messages until the queue is empty. It also sets *BreakMessageLoop* when a WM_QUIT message is received.

QueryThrow
int QueryThrow();

Tests to see if an exception is suspended and returns one or more of the bit flags in the xs exception status enum.

ResumeThrow
void ResumeThrow();

Checks and rethrows suspended exceptions. Call this function any time you reenter ObjectWindows code from exception-unsafe code where an exception could have been thrown.

Run
virtual int Run();

Initializes the instance, calling *InitApplication* for the first executing instance and *InitInstance* for all instances. If the initialization is successful, *Run* calls *MessageLoop* and runs the application. If exceptions are thrown outside the message loop, *Run* catches these exceptions.

If an error occurs in the creation of a window, *Run* throws a *TXWindow* exception. If *Status* is assigned a nonzero value (which ObjectWindows uses to identify an error), a *TXCompatibility* exception is thrown.

SetCmdShow
void SetCmdShow(int cmdshow);

Sets the initial state of the main window. Typically passed by the operating system.

SetPrevInstance
void SetPrevInstance(HINSTANCE pi);

Sets the previous instance. This should not be called by normal programs.

SetWinMainParams
static void SetWinMainParams(HINSTANCE hInstance, HINSTANCE hPrevInstance, const char far* cmdLine, int cmdShow);

The ObjectWindows default *WinMain* function calls *SetMainWinParams* so that *TApplication* can store the parameters for future use. To construct an application instance, *WinMain* calls the *OwlMain* function that is in the user's code. As it is being constructed, the application instance can fill in the parameters using those set earlier by *SetMainWinParams*.

See also TApplication::GetWinMainParams

Start
virtual int Start();
Starts this application and returns immediately. Used for component DLLs. Initializes instances, creating and displaying their main window. (Calls *InitApplication* for the first executing instance and *InitInstance* for all other instances). Each of the virtual functions called are expected to throw an exception if there is an error. Does not run a message loop.

SuspendThrow
Form 1 void SuspendThrow(xalloc& x);
Saves *xalloc* exception information.

Form 2 void SuspendThrow(xmsg& x);
Saves *xmsg* exception information.

Form 3 void SuspendThrow(TXOwl& x);
Saves a copy of a *TXOwl* exception.

Form 4 void SuspendThrow(int);
Sets the xs exception status enum bit flags to the specified exception (for example, *Bad_cast* or *Bad_typeid*).

Uncondemn
void Uncondemn (TWindow* win);
Removes condemned children from the list of condemned windows.

See also TWindow

Protected data members

BreakMessageLoop
bool BreakMessageLoop;
Causes the current modal message loop to break and terminate. If the current modal message loop is the main application, and your program sets *BreakMessageLoop*, your main application terminates.

See also TApplication::EndModal, TApplication::MessageLoop, TApplication::PumpWaitingMessages

CmdLine
string CmdLine;
String object copy of command line.

MessageLoopResult
int MessageLoopResult;
Set by a call to *EndModal*, *MessageLoopResult* contains the value that is returned by *MessageLoop* and *BeginModal*.

Protected member functions

IdleAction
virtual bool IdleAction(long idleCount);
ObjectWindows calls *IdleAction* when no messages are waiting in the queue to be processed. You can override *IdleAction* to do background processing. However, the default action is to give the main window a chance to do idle processing as long as *IdleAction* returns **true**. *idleCount* specifies the number of times *IdleAction* has been called between messages.

See also　TFrameWindow::IdleAction

InitApplication
virtual void InitApplication();
ObjectWindows calls *InitApplication* to initialize the first instance of the application. For subsequent instances, this member function is not called.

The following sample program calls *InitApplication* the first time an instance of the program begins.

```
class TTestApp : public TApplication {
  public:
    TTestApp(): TApplication("Instance Tester")
      {strcpy(WindowTitle, "Additional Instance");}
  protected:
    char WindowTitle[20];
    void InitApplication() {strcpy(WindowTitle, "First Instance");}
    void InitMainWindow() {MainWindow = new TFrameWindow(0, WindowTitle);}
};
static TTestApp App;
```

InitInstance
virtual void InitInstance();
Performs each instance initialization necessary for the application. Unlike *InitApplication*, which is called for the first instance of an application, *InitInstance* is called whether or not there are other executing instances of the application. *InitInstance* calls *InitMainWindow*, and then creates and shows the main window element by *TWindow::Create* and *TWindow::Show*. If the main window cannot be created, a *TXInvalidMainWindow* exception is thrown.

If you redefine this member function, be sure to explicitly call *TApplication::InitInstance*.

See also　TApplication::Run, TModule::MakeWindow

InitMainWindow
virtual void InitMainWindow();
By default, *InitMainWindow* constructs a generic *TFrameWindow* object with the name of the application as its caption. You can redefine *InitMainWindow* to construct a useful main window object of *TFrameWindow* (or a class derived from *TFrameWindow*) and store it in *MainWindow*. The main window must be a top-level window; that is, it must be derived from *TFrameWindow*. A typical use is

```
virtual void TMyApp_InitMainWindow(){
  SetMainWindow(TMyWindow(NULL, Caption));
}
```

InitMainWindow can be overridden to create your own custom window.

SetDocManager
TFrameWindow* SetDocManager(TDocManager* docManager);
Sets a pointer to the document manager object that invoked the application.

See also   TApplication::GetDocManager, TDocManager, TFrameWindow

SetMainWindow
TFrameWindow* SetMainWindow(TFrameWindow* window);
Sets up a new main window and sets the window's WM_MAINWINDOW flag.

See also   TApplication::GetMainWindow, TFrameWindow

TermInstance
virtual int TermInstance(int status);
Handles the termination of each executing instance of an ObjectWindows application.

TAutoFactory< > class   olefacto.h

A template class, *TAutoFactory<>* creates callback code for ObjectWindows classes. The application class is passed as the argument to the template. By itself, *TAutoFactory<>* does not provide linking or embedding support for ObjectWindows automated applications.

Although *TAutoFactory<>* simplifies the process of creating the callback function, you can write your own callback function or provide alternate implementation for any or all of *TAutoFactory<>*'s functions.

See also   TComponentFactory typedef, TOcRegistrar class, Factory Template Classes, TOleFactoryBase class

Public member functions

TComponentFactory
operator TComponentFactory() {return Create;};
Converts the object into a pointer to the factory. ObjectComponents uses this pointer to create the automated object.

CreateApp
static T* CreateApp(uint32 options);
CreateApp creates a new automated application. By default, it creates a new application of template type *T* with no arguments. The *options* argument is one of the *TOcAppMode* enum values, for example, *amRun*, *amAutomation*, and so on that indicate the application's mode when running.

See also   TAutoFactory::DestroyApp, TOcAppMode enum

DestroyApp
static void DestroyApp(T* app);
Destroys the previously created application referred to in *app*.

See also   TAutoFactory::CreateApp

Create

static IUnknown* Create(IUnknown* outer, uint32 options, uint32 id);

Create is a *TComponentFactory* callback function that creates or destroys the application or creates objects. If an application object does not already exist, *Create* creates a new one. The *outer* argument points to the OLE 2 *IUnknown* interface with which this object aggregates itself. If *outer* is 0, the new object is not aggregated, or it will become the main object.

The *options* argument indicates the application's mode while it is running. The values for *options* are either set from the command line or set by ObjectComponents. They are passed in by the "Registrar" to this callback. The application looks at these flags to know how to operate, and the factory callback looks at them to know what to do. For example, a value of *amExeMode* indicates that the server is running as an .EXE either because it was built as an .EXE or because it is a DLL that was launched by an .EXE stub and is now running as an executable program. See *TOcAppMode* enum for a description of the possible values for the *options* argument.

If the application already exists, *Create* returns the application's OLE interface and registers the options from *TOcAppMode* enum which contains OLE-related flags used in the application's command line. For example, the *amAutomation flag* tells the server to register itself as a single-user application. (In general, these flags tell the application whether it has been run as a server, whether it needs to register itself, and so on.)

The *id* argument, which is not used for *TAutoFactory*, is always 0.

See also   TAutoFactory::DestroyApp, TOcAppMode enum

TBandInfo struct   dc.h

An ObjectWindows struct, *TBandInfo* is used to pass information to a printer driver that supports banding. *TBandInfo* is declared as follows:

```
struct TBandInfo {
bool HasText;
TRect GraphicsRect;
```

HasGraphics is true if graphics are (or are expected to be) on the page or in the band; otherwise, it is false.

HasText is true if text is (or is expected to be) on the page or in the band; otherwise, it is false.

GraphicsRect defines the bounding region for all graphics on the page.

See also   TPrintDC::BandInfo, TPrintDC::NextBand

TBitmap class

TBitmap is the GDI bitmap class derived from *TGdiObject*. *TBitMap* can construct a bitmap from many sources. *TBitmap* objects are DDBs (device-dependent bitmaps), which are different from the DIBs (device-independent bitmaps) represented by *TDib* objects. This bitmap is the lowest level object that is actually selected into a DC.

Public constructors

Form 1   TBitmap(HBITMAP handle, TAutoDelete autoDelete = NoAutoDelete);
Creates a *TBitmap* object and sets the *Handle* data member to the given borrowed *handle*. The *ShouldDelete* data member defaults to false, ensuring that the borrowed handle will not be deleted when the C++ object is destroyed.

Form 2   TBitmap(const TClipboard& clipboard);
Creates a *TBitmap* object with values from the given Clipboard.

Form 3   TBitmap(const TBitmap& bitmap);
Creates a copy of the given *bitmap* object.

Form 4   TBitmap(int width, int height, uint8 planes=1, uint8 bitCount=1, void far* bits=0);
Creates a bitmap object from *bitCount* bits in the *bits* buffer with the given *width, height,* and *planes* argument values.

Form 5   TBitmap(const BITMAP far* bitmap);
Creates a bitmap object with the values found in the given *bitmap* structure.

Form 6   TBitmap(const TDC& Dc, int width, int height, bool discardable = false);
Creates a bitmap object for the given device context with the given argument values.

Form 7   TBitmap(const TDC& Dc, const TDib& dib, uint32 usage=CBM_INIT);
Creates a bitmap object for the given device context with the given *dib* and *usage* argument values.

Form 8   TBitmap(const TMetaFilePict& metaFile, TPalette& palette, const TSize& size);
Creates a bitmap object from the given *metaFile* using the given *palette* and *size* arguments.

Form 9   TBitmap(const TDib& dib, const TPalette* palette = 0);
Creates a bitmap object from the given *dib* and *palette* arguments. A working palette constructed from the DIB's color table is used if no palette is supplied. The default system palette can also be passed using *&TPalette::GetStock(TPalette::Default);*

Form 10   TBitmap(HINSTANCE instance, TResID resID);
Creates a bitmap object for the given application instance from the given resource.

See also   TClipBoard::GetClipboardData, TDC, TDib, TGdiObject::Handle, TGdiObject::ShouldDelete, TPalette, BITMAP struct

Public member functions

BitsPixel
uint8 BitsPixel() const;
Returns the number of bits per pixel in this bitmap.

See also   TBitmap::GetObject

GetBitmapBits
uint32 GetBitmapBits(uint32 count, void far* bits) const;
Copies up to *count* bits of this bitmap to the buffer *bits*.

GetBitmapDimension
bool GetBitmapDimension(TSize& size) const;
Retrieves the size of this bitmap (width and height, measured in tenths of millimeters) and sets it in the *size* argument. Returns true if the call is successful; otherwise returns false.

See also   TSize

GetHandle
THandle GetHandle() const;
Returns the handle of the bitmap of type BITMAP.

GetObject
bool GetObject(BITMAP far& bitmap) const;
Retrieves data (width, height, and color format) for this bitmap and sets it in the given BITMAP structure. To retrieve the bit pattern, use *GetBitmapBits*.

See also   TBitMap::GetBitmapBits, BITMAP struct

Height
int Height() const;
Returns the height of this bitmap.

See also   TBitmap::GetObject

operator <<
TClipboard& operator <<(TClipboard& clipboard, TBitmap& bitmap);
Copies the given *bitmap* to the given *clipboard* argument. Returns a reference to the resulting Clipboard, which allows normal chaining of <<.

See also   TClipboard

operator HBITMAP()
operator HBITMAP() const;
Typecasting operator. Converts this bitmap's *Handle* to type *HBITMAP* (the data type representing the handle to a physical bitmap).

operator THandle
operator THandle() const;
Type accessor.

Planes
uint8 Planes() const;
Returns the number of planes in this bitmap.

See also TBitmap::GetObject

SetBitmapBits
uint32 SetBitmapBits(uint32 count, const void far* bits);
Copies up to *count* bits from the *bits* buffer to this bitmap.

SetBitmapDimension
bool SetBitmapDimension(const TSize& size, TSize far* oldSize=0);
Sets the size of this bitmap from the given *size* argument (width and height, measured in tenths of millimeters). The previous size is set in the *oldSize* argument. Returns true if the call is successful; otherwise returns false.

See also TSize

Size
TSize Size() const;
The width and height of the bitmap in pixels.

ToClipboard
void ToClipboard(TClipboard& clipboard);
Copies this bitmap to the given Clipboard.

See also TClipboard::SetClipboardData

Width
int Width() const;
Returns the width of this bitmap.

See also TBitmap::GetObject

Protected constructor

TBitmap
TBitMap();
Protected constructor for a *TBitmap* object.

Protected member functions

Create
Form 1   void Create(const TBitmap &src);

Form 2   void Create(const TDib& dib, const TPalette &palette);
Creates a bitmap handle from the given argument objects.

See also TDib, TPalette

TBitmapGadget class   bitmapga.h

Derived from *TGadget*, *TBitmapGadget* is a simple gadget that can display an array of bitmap images one at a time.

See also   TGadget, TBitmap

Public constructor and destructor

Constructor
TBitmapGadget(TResId imageResIdOrIndex, int id, TBorderStyle borderStyle, int numImages, int startImage = 0,
    bool sharedCels = false);
Constructs a *TBitmapGadget* and sets the current image to the beginning image (*startImage*) in the array of images. Then, sets the border style to the current *TGadget* border style and *numImages* to the number of images in the array.

Destructor
~TBitmapGadget();
Deletes the array of images.

Public member functions

GetImage
int GetImage() const;

SelectImage
int SelectImage(int imageNum, bool immediate);
Determines the current image and repaints the client area if the image has changed. Updates the client area if the image has changed.

SysColorChange
void SysColorChange();
When the system colors have been changed, *SysColorChange* is called by the gadget window's *EvSysColorChange* so that bitmap gadgets can be rebuilt and repainted.

Protected member functions

GetDesiredSize
void GetDesiredSize(TSize& size);
Calls *TGadget::GetDesiredSize*, which determines how big the bitmap gadget can be. The gadget window sends this message to query the gadget's size. If shrink-wrapping is requested, *GetDesiredSize* returns the size needed to accommodate the borders and margins. If shrink-wrapping is not requested, it returns the gadget's current width and height. *TGadgetWindow* needs this information to determine how big the gadget needs to be, but it can adjust these dimensions if necessary. If *WideAsPossible* is true, then the width parameter (*size.cx*) is ignored.

Paint
void Paint(TDC& dc);
Paints the gadget's border and the contents of the bitmap.

See also   TGadget::Paint

SetBounds
void SetBounds(const TRect& boundRect);
Calls *TGadget::SetBounds* and passes the dimensions of the bitmap gadget. *SetBounds* informs the control gadget of a change in its bounding rectangle.

See also   TGadget::SetBounds

TBitSet class   bitset.h

TBitSet sets or clears a single bit or a group of bits. You can use this class to set and clear option flags and to retrieve information about a set of bits. The class *TCharSet* performs similar operations for a string of characters.

Constructors

Form 1   TBitSet();
Constructs a *TBitSet* object.

Form 2   TBitSet(const TBitSet& src);
Constructs a *TBitSet* object as a copy of another *TBitSet*.

Public member functions

DisableItem
Form 1   void DisableItem(uint8 item);
Clears a single bit at *item*.

Form 2   void DisableItem(const TBitSet& bs);
Clears the set of bits enabled in *bs*.

EnableItem
Form 1   void EnableItem(uint8 item);
Sets a single bit at *item*.

Form 2   void EnableItem(const TBitSet& bs);
Sets the set of bits enabled in *bs*.

Has
int Has(uint8 item);
Is nonzero if *item* is in the set of bits.

IsEmpty
int TBitSet::IsEmpty() const;
Is nonzero if the set is empty; otherwise, is 0.

operator !=
friend int operator !=(const TBitSet& bs1, const TBitSet& bs2);
Returns true if the two bitsets are not identical.

operator &
friend TBitSet operator &(const TBitSet& bs1, const TBitSet& bs2);
Logically ANDs each individual bit.

operator +=

Form 1   TBitSet& operator +=(uint8 item);
Calls *EnableItem* to set a bit in the copied set. Returns a reference to the copied *TBitSet* object.

Form 2   TBitSet& operator +=(const TBitSet& bs);
Calls *EnableItem* to set the bits enabled in *bs*. Returns a reference to the copied *TBitSet* object.

operator -=

Form 1   TBitSet& operator -=(uint8 item);
Calls *DisableItem* to clear a bit in the set. Returns a reference to the copied *TBitSet* object.

Form 2   TBitSet& operator -=(const TBitSet& bs);
Calls *DisableItem* to clear the bits enabled in *bs*. Returns a reference to the copied *TBitSet* object.

operator &=
TBitSet& operator &=(const TBitSet&);
ANDs all the bits in the copied set and returns a reference to the copied *TBitSet* object.

operator <<
friend opstream& operator <<(opstream& out, const TBitSet& bs);
Inserts the bitset into a persistent output stream.

operator ==
friend int operator ==(const TBitSet& bs1, const TBitSet& bs2);
Returns true if the two bitsets are indentical.

operator >>
friend ipstream& operator >>(ipstream& in, TBitSet& bs);
Extracts the bitset from a persistent input stream.

operator |
friend TBitSet operator |(const TBitSet& bs1, const TBitSet& bs2);
Returns the OR of two bitsets.

operator |=
TBitSet& operator |=(const TBitSet& bs);
ORs all of the bits in the copied set and returns a reference to the copied *TBitSet* object.

operator ~
TBitSet operator ~() const;
Returns the set of bits that is the opposite of a specified set of bits. For example, if the set of bits is 01010101, the returned set is 10101010. Returns a reference to the copied *TBitSet* object.

TBIVbxLibrary class

vxbctl.h

Virtually derived from TModule, *TBIVbxLibrary* handles loading and initializing of BIVBX10.DLL. If you want to use VBX controls, construct a *TBIVbxLibrary* object with the same scope as your application. For example,

```
int OwlMain(int, char**)
{
  TBIVbxLibrary vbxLib;
  return TTestApp().Run();
}
```

Public constructor and destructor

Constructor
TBIVbxLibrary();
Constructs a *TBIVbxLibrary* object.

Destructor
~TBIVbxLibrary();
Destroys a *TBIVbxLibrary* object.

TBrush class

gdiobjec.h

The GDI Brush class is derived from *TGdiObject*. *TBrush* provides constructors for creating solid, styled, or patterned brushes from explicit information. It can also create a brush indirectly from a borrowed handle.

Public constructors

Form 1　TBrush(HBRUSH handle, TAutoDelete autoDelete = NoAutoDelete);
Creates a *TBrush* object and sets the *Handle* data member to the given borrowed *handle*. The *ShouldDelete* data member defaults to false, ensuring that the borrowed handle will not be deleted when the C++ object is destroyed.

Form 2　TBrush(const TColor& color);
Creates a solid *TBrush* object with the given color. To save a brush creation this constructor uses a cache that can detect any color that matches a stock color.

Form 3　TBrush(TColor color, int style);
Creates a hatched *TBrush* object with the given style and color.

Form 4　TBrush(const TBitmap& pattern);
Creates a patterned *TBrush* object with the given pattern.

Form 5　TBrush(const TDib& pattern);
Creates a patterned *TBrush* object with the given DIB pattern.

Form 6　TBrush(const LOGBRUSH far* logBrush);
Creates a *TBrush* object with values from the given *logBrush*.

Form 7   TBrush(const TBrush& src);
Constructs a copy of an existing brush. Contructed brush will share the handle unless NO_GDI_SHARE_HANDLES is defined, in which case a new handle is created.

See also   TBitmap, TColor, TDib, TGdiObject::Handle, TGdiObject::ShouldDelete, LOGBRUSH struct

Public member functions

GetHandle
THandle GetHandle() const;
Returns the handle of the brush with type HBRUSH.

GetObject
bool GetObject(LOGBRUSH far& logBrush) const;
Retrieves information about this brush object and places it in the given LOGBRUSH structure. Returns true if the call is successful; otherwise returns false.

See also   TGdiObject::GetObject, LOGBRUSH struct

operator HBRUSH()
operator HBRUSH() const;
Typecasting operator. Converts this brush's *Handle* to type HBRUSH (the data type representing the handle to a physical brush).

THandle
operator THandle() const;
Returns the handle of the brush with type HBRUSH.

UnrealizeObject
bool UnrealizeObject();
Directs the GDI to reset the origin of this brush the next time it is selected. Returns true if call is successful; otherwise returns false.

TBtnBitmap class   glyphbtn.h

TBtnBitmap is an enhanced version of *TBitmap* with the ability to update the face color of a bitmap to match the current system BTNFACE color.

Public constructors

Form 1   TBtnBitmap(HINSTANCE hInstance, TResId resId, const TColor& faceColor = TColor(192, 192, 192));
Constructor of BtnBitmap—loads the specified bitmap and updates the face color if necessary.

Form 2   TBtnBitmap(HBITMAP hBitmap, const TColor& faceColor = TColor(192, 192, 192),
          TAutoDelete autoDelete = NoAutoDelete);
Constructor of BtnBitmap—aliases the specified bitmap handle and updates the face color if necessary.

Public member functions

MapColor
static void MapColor(TDC& dc, TDC& srcDC, const TColor& toColor, const TColor& fromColor,
    int width, int height);
Helper routine used to map the face color of the underlying bitmap.

UpdateFaceColor
void UpdateFaceColor();
Updates the face color of the associated bitmap if the current face color does not match the 3DFACE system color.

Protected member function

FaceColor
TColor FaceColor;
Current face color of bitmap.

TButton class   button.h

TButton is an interface class that represents a push button interface element. You must use a *TButton* to create a button control in a parent *TWindow* object. You can also use a *TButton* to facilitate communication between your application and the button controls of a *TDialog* object. This class is streamable.

There are two types of pushbuttons: regular and default. Regular buttons have a thin border. Default buttons (which represent the default action of the window) have a thick border.

Public data member

IsDefPB
bool IsDefPB;
Indicates whether the button is to be considered the default push button. Used for owner-drawn buttons, *IsDefPB* is set by a *TButton* constructor based on BS_DEFPUSHBUTTON style setting.

Public constructors

Form 1   TButton(Window *parent, int Id, const char far* text, int X, int Y, int W, int H, bool isDefault = false,
        TModule* module = 0);
Constructs a button object with the supplied parent window (*parent*), control ID (*Id*), associated text (*text*), position (*X,Y*) relative to the origin of the parent window's client area, width (*W*), and height (*H*). If *IsDefault* is **true**, the constructor adds BS_DEFPUSHBUTTON to the default styles set for the *TButton* (in *Attr.Style*). Otherwise, it adds BS_PUSHBUTTON.

Form 2   TButton(TWindow* parent, int resourceID, TModule* module = 0);
Constructs a *TButton* object to be associated with a button control of a *TDialog* object. Calls *DisableTransfer* to exclude the button from the transfer mechanism because there is no data to be transferred.

The *resId* parameter must correspond to a button resource that you define.

Form 3   ~TButton();
Outputs a debug message if the diagnostic libraries are being used.

See also   TControl::TControl

Public member functions

GetIsCurrentDefPB
bool GetIsCurrentDefPB() const;
Returns true if this button is the current default pushbutton.

GetIsDefPB
bool GetIsDefPB() const;
Returns true if this button is the default pushbutton.

SetIsCurrentDefPB
void SetIsCurrentDefPB(bool is);
Sets this button as the current default pushbutton.

SetIsDefPB
void SetIsDefPB(bool isdefpb);
Sets this button as the default pushbutton.

Protected data members

IsCurrentDefPB
bool IsCurrentDefPB;
Indicates whether the current button is the default push button.

Protected member functions

BMSetStyle
TResult BMSetStyle(TParam1, TParam2);
Because a button can't have both owner-drawn and push button styles, *BMSetStyle* keeps track of the style if the button is owner-drawn and the system tries to set the style to BS_DEFPUSHBUTTON. *BMSetStyle* sets *IsCurrentDefPB* to **true** if the button style is BS_DEFPUSHBUTTON.

EvGetDlgCode
uint EvGetDlgCode(MSG far*);
Responds to WM_GETDLGCODE messages that are sent to a dialog box associated with a control. *EvGetDlgCode* allows the dialog manager to intercept a message that would normally go to a control and then ask the control if it wants to process this

message. If not, the dialog manager processes the message. The *msg* parameter indicates the kind of message (for example, a control, command, or button message) sent to the dialog box manager.

EvGetDlgCode returns a code that indicates how the button is to be treated. If this is the currently used push button, *EvGetDlgCode* returns either DLGC_DEFPUSHBUTTON or DLGC_UNDEFPUSHBUTTON.

See also   DLGC_xxxx Dialog Control Message Constants

GetClassName
char far* GetClassName();
Overrides *TWindow*'s *GetClassName* function. If Borland Windows Custom Controls (BWCC) is enabled, returns the name of *TButton*'s registration class, "BUTTON_CLASS". If BWCC isn't enabled, returns the name "BUTTON".

SetupWindow
void SetupWindow();
Overrides *TWindow*'s *SetupWindow* function. If the button is the default push button and an owner-drawn button, *SetupWindow* sends a DM_SETDEFID message to the parent window.

Response table entries

Response table entry	Member function
EV_WM_GETDLGCODE	EVGetDlgCode
EV_MESSAGE (BM_SETSTYLE, BMSetStyle)	BMSetStyle

TButtonGadget class   buttonga.h

Derived from *TGadget*, *TButtonGadgets* represent buttons that you can click on or off. You can also apply attributes such as color, style, and shape (notched or unnotched) to your button gadgets.

In general, button gadgets are classified as either command or attribute buttons. Attribute buttons include radio buttons (which are considered exclusive), or check boxes (which are nonexclusive). The public data member, *TType*, enumerates these button types.

TButtonGadget contains several functions that let you change the style of a button. Use *SetAntialiasEdges* to turn antialiasing on and off, *SetNotchCorners* to control corner notching, and *SetShadowStyle* to change the style of the button shadow.

TButtonGadget objects respond to mouse events in the following manner: when a mouse button is pressed, the button is pressed; when the mouse button is released, the button is released. Commands can be entered only when the mouse button is in the "up" state. When the mouse is pressed, *TButtonGadget* objects capture the mouse and reserve all mouse messages for the current window. When the mouse button is up, button gadgets release the capture for the current window. The public data member, *TState*, enumerates the three button states.

Type definitions

TGlyphType enum

Header File
buttonga.h

enum TGlyphType {CelNormal, CelDisabled, CelIndeterm, CelDown, CelPressed};
TGlyphType contains values that allow a glyph button to display different glyphs when its state changes. For example, the *CelPressed* constant could be used to toggle a glyph button between a happy face and a sad face when it is pressed.

Table 2.1   Glyph type constants

Constant	Meaning if set
CelNormal	Displayed under normal circumstances.
CelDisabled	Displayed when the button is disabled (grayed).
CelIndeterm	Displayed when an ambiguous or indeterminate state is encountered.
CelDown	Displayed when the button is down or checked.
CelPressed	Displayed when the button is pressed.

TShadowStyle enum
enum TShadowStyle{SingleShadow = 1, DoubleShadow = 2};
Enumerates button shadow styles—either single (1) or double (2) shadow borders.

TState enum
enum TState{Up, Down, Indeterminate};
TState enumerates the three button positions during which the button can be pressed: up (0), down (1), and an indeterminate state (2). A nonzero value indicates a highlighted button.

TType enum
enum TType{Command, Exclusive, NonExclusive, SemiExclusive, RepeatCmd};
Enumerates the types of button gadgets. An exclusive button is one that works in conjunction with other buttons such that one button is activated at a time.

Table 2.2   Button type constants

Constant	Meaning if pressed
Command	Sends a command when pressed.
Exclusive	Stays down when pressed and causes other buttons in the group to pop back up.
NonExclusive	Toggles its state when pressed and ignores other buttons.
SemiExclusive	Same as exclusive, except that it also pops back up if pressed while it is down.
RepeatCmd	Auto-repeating command button.

Public constructor and destructor

Constructor
TButtonGadget(TResId bmpResId, int id, TType type = Command, bool enabled = false, TState state = Up,
    bool repeat = false);

Constructs a *TButtonGadget* object using the specified bitmap ID, button gadget ID, and type, with *enabled* set to false and in a button-up state. The button isn't enabled—its initial state before command enabling occurs.

Destructor
~TButtonGadget();

Deconstructs a *TButtonGadget* object.

See also   TButtonGadget::TState

Public member functions

CommandEnable
void CommandEnable();

Enables the button gadget to capture messages. Calls *SendMessage* to send a WM_COMMAND_ENABLE message to the gadget window's parent, passing a *TCommandEnable: EvCommandEnable* message for this button.

GetAntialiasEdges
bool GetAntialiasEdges() const;

Returns true if the border edges are antialiased.

GetButtonState
TState GetButtonState();

Returns the state of the button. If 0, the button is up, if 1, the button is down, if 2, the state is indeterminate.

See also   TButtonGadget::TState

GetButtonType
TType GetButtonType();

Returns the button type as 1 if the button is a command, 2 if exclusive, or 3 if nonexclusive.

GetDesiredSize
void GetDesiredSize(TSize& size);

Stores the width and height (measured in pixels) of the button gadget in size. Calls *TGadget's GetDesiredSize* to calculate the relationship between one rectangle and another.

GetNotchCorners
bool GetNotchCorners() const;

Returns true if the button has rounded corners.

GetShadowStyle
TShadowStyle GetShadowStyle() const;

Return the current shadow style of the button.

SetAntialiasEdges
SetAntialiasEdges(bool anti = true);
Turns the antialiasing of the button bevels on or off. By default, antialiasing is on.

SetBounds
void SetBounds(TRect& r);
Gets the size of the bitmap, calls *TGadget::SetBounds* to set the boundary of the rectangle, and centers the bitmap within the button's rectangle.

SetButtonState
void SetButtonState(TState);
Sets the state of the button. If the state has changed, the button is exclusive, and is in the down state, checks that the button is exclusive, sets *State*, and calls *Invalidate* to mark the changed area of the gadget for repainting.

See also   TButtonGadget::TState

SetNotchCorners
void SetNotchCorners(bool notchCorners = true);
By default, *SetNotchCorners* implements notched corners for buttons. To repaint the frame of the button if the window has already been created, call *InvalidateRect* with the *Bounds* rectangle.

See also   TButtonGadget::Invalidate, TGadget::InvalidateRect, TGadget::Paint

SetShadowStyle
void SetShadowStyle(TShadowStyle);
Sets the button style to a shadow style which, by default, is DoubleShadow. Sets the left and top borders to 2 and the right and bottom borders to ShadowStyle + 1.

SysColorChange
void SysColorChange();
SysColorChange responds to an *EvSysColorChange* message forwarded by the owning *TGadgetWindow* by setting the dither brush to zero. If a user-interface bitmap exists, *SysColorChange* deletes and rebuilds it to get the new button colors.

Protected data members

AntialiasEdges
bool AntialiasEdges;
Is true if antialiasing is turned on.

BitmapOrigin
TPoint BitmapOrigin;
Points to the x and y coordinates of the bitmap used for this button gadget.

CelArray
TCelArray* CelArray;
The array of cels used by this button gadget.

GlyphIndex
int GlyphIndex;
The base index for the glyph bitmap.

NotchCorners
bool NotchCorners;
Initialized to 1, *NotchCorners* is 1 if the button gadget has notched corners or 0 if it doesn't have notched corners.

Pressed
bool Pressed;
Initialized to 1, *Pressed* is 1 if the button is released or 0 if it isn't released.

See also   TButtonGadget::Activate, TButtonGadget::BeginPressed, TButtonGadget::CancelPressed

Repeat
bool Repeat;
Initialized to 1, *Repeat* stores the repeat count for keyboard events.

ResId
TResId ResId;
Holds the resource ID for this button gadget's bitmap.

ShadowStyle
TShadowStyle ShadowStyle;
Holds the shadow style for the button—1 for single and 2 for double.

SharingGlyph
bool SharingGlyph;
Flag for whether the button should share glyphs with its gadget window.

State
TState State;
Holds the state of the button—either up, down, or indeterminate.

Type
TType Type;
Holds the type of the button—either command, exclusive, or nonexclusive.

Protected member functions

Activate
virtual void Activate(TPoint& p);
Invoked when the mouse is in the "up" state, *Activate* sets *Pressed* to false, changes the state for attribute buttons, and paints the button in its current state. To do this, it calls *CancelPressed*, posts a WM_COMMAND message to the gadget window's parent, and sends menu messages to the gadget window's parent.

See also   TButtonGadget::Pressed

BeginPressed
virtual void BeginPressed(TPoint& p);

When the mouse button is pressed, *BeginPressed* sets *Pressed* to true, paints the pressed button, and sends menu messages to the gadget window's parent.

See also   TButtonGadget::Pressed

BuildCelArray
virtual void BuildCelArray();

Builds a cel array using the resource bitmap as the base glyph. Any existing cel array should be deleted if a replacement is built.

See also   TCelArray

CancelPressed
virtual void CancelPressed(TPoint& p);

When the mouse button is released, *CancelPressed* sets *Pressed* to false, paints the button, and sends menu messages to the gadget window's parent.

See also   TButtonGadget::Pressed

GetGlyphDib
virtual TDib* GetGlyphDib();

Supplies the glyphdib. You can override this function to get a different *dib*, or to change the attributes of the *dib*, such as the colors, and so on.

Invalidate
void Invalidate();

If a button is pressed or the state of the button is changed, *Invalidate* invalidates (marks for repainting) the changed area of the gadget. *Invalidate* only invalidates the area that changes. To repaint the entire gadget, call *TGadget::InvalidateRect* and pass the rectangle's boundaries.

See also   TButtonGadget::TState, TGadget::InvalidateRect

LButtonDown
void LButtonDown(uint modKeys, TPoint& p);

Overrides *TGadget* member function and responds to a left mouse button click by calling *BeginPressed*.

See also   TButtonGadget::BeginPressed

LButtonUp
void LButtonUp(uint modKeys, TPoint& p);

Overrides *TGadget* member functions and responds to a release of the left mouse button by calling *Activate*.

See also   TButtonGadget::Activate

MouseEnter
void MouseEnter(uint modKeys, TPoint& p);

Called when the mouse enters the boundary of the button gadget. *modKeys* indicates the virtual key information and can be any combination of the following values: MK_CONTROL, MK_LBUTTON, MK_MBUTTON, MK_RBUTTON, or MK_SHIFT. *p* indicates where the mouse entered the button gadget.

MouseLeave

void MouseLeave(uint modKeys, TPoint& p);

Called when the mouse leaves the boundary of the button gadget. *modKeys* indicates the virtual key information and can be any combination of the following values: MK_CONTROL, MK_LBUTTON, MK_MBUTTON, MK_RBUTTON, or MK_SHIFT. *p* indicates the place where the mouse left the button gadget.

MouseMove

void MouseMove(uint modKeys, TPoint& p);

Calls *TGadget::MouseMove* in response to the mouse being dragged. If the mouse moves off the button, *MouseMove* calls *CancelPressed*. If the mouse moves back onto the button, *MouseMove* calls *BeginPressed*.

See also   TButtonGadget::BeginPressed, TButtonGadget::CancelPressed

Paint

void Paint(TDC& dc);

Gets the width and height of the window frame (in pixels), calls *GetImageSize* to retrieve the size of the bitmap, and sets the inner rectangle to the specified dimensions. Calls *TGadget::PaintBorder* to perform the actual painting of the border of the control. Before painting the control, *Paint* determines whether the corners of the control are notched, and then calls *GetSysColor* to see if highlighting or shadow colors are used. *Paint* assumes the border style is plain. Then, *Paint* draws the top, left, right, and bottom of the control, adjusts the position of the bitmap, and finishes drawing the control using the specified embossing, fading, and dithering.

ReleaseGlyphDib

virtual void ReleaseGlyphDib(TDib* glyph);

Releases the *glyph dib* depending on how it was obtained by *GetGlyphDib*.

SetButtonType

void SetButtonType(TType newType);

Sets the type of the button.

See also   TGadget::SetBounds

TButtonGadgetEnabler class   buttonga.cpp

Derived from *TCommandEnabler*, *TButtonGadgetEnabler* serves as a command enabler for button gadgets. The functions in this class modify the text, check state, and appearance of a button gadget.

Public constructor

Constructor

TButtonGadgetEnabler(HWND hWndReceiver, TButtonGadget* g)

Constructs a *TButtonGadgetEnabler* for the specified gadget. *hWndReceiver* is the window receiving the message.

Protected data member

gadget
TButtonGadget* gadget;
The button gadget being enabled or disabled.

Public member functions

Enable
void Enable(bool enable);
Overrides *TCommandEnable::Enable*. Enables or disables the keyboard, mouse input and appearance of the corresponding button gadget.

SetCheck
void SetCheck(int state)
Overrides *TCommandEnable::SetCheck*. Changes the check state of the corresponding button gadget.

SetText
void SetText(const char far*)
Overrides *TCommandEnable::SetText*. Changes the text of the corresponding button gadget.

TBwccDll class   applicat.h

The *TBwccDll* class encapsulates the Borland Windows Custom Control (BWCC) DLL (BWCC[32].DLL). It provides an easy method to dynamically test for the availability of the DLL and bind to its exported functions at runtime. By using the *TBwccDll* class instead of direct calls to the BWCC DLL, ObjectWindows applications can provide the appropriate behavior when running in an environment where the DLL is not available.

Each data member of the *TBwccDll* class corresponds to the API with a similar name exposed by the BWCC DLL. For example, *TBwccDll::MessageBox* corresponds to the BWCCMessageBox API exported by the BWCC DLL.

The following is a list of the members of the *TBwccDll* class corresponding to functions exposed by the DLL. For more information about these members, consult the documentation about the corresponding API exposed by the BWCC DLL.

TBwccDll::TBwccDll
DefDlgProc
DefGrayDlgProc
DefMDIChildProc
DefWindowProc
GetPattern
GetVersion

IntlInit
IntlTerm
MangleDialog
MessageBox
Register
SpecialLoadDialog

TCelArray class   celarray.h

TCelArray is a horizontal array of cels (a unit of animation) created by slicing a portion of or an entire bitmap into evenly sized shapes. Gadgets such as buttons can use a *TCelArray* to save resource space. *TCelArray's* functions let you control the dimensions of each cel and determine if the cel can delete the bitmap.

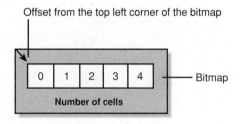

Public constructors and destructor

Constructors

Form 1   TCelArray(TBitmap* bmp, int numCels, TSize celSize = 0, TPoint Offset = 0, TAutoDelete = AutoDelete);
Constructs a *TCelArray* from a bitmap by slicing the bitmap into a horizontal array of cels of a specified size. If *autoDelete* is true, *TCelArray* can automatically delete the bitmap. The *ShouldDelete* data member defaults to true, ensuring that the handle will be deleted when the bitmap is destroyed.

Form 2   TCelArray(const TDib& dib, int numCels);
Constructs a *TCelArray* from a device independent bitmap (DIB) by slicing the DIB into a horizontal array of evenly sized cels.

Form 3   TCelArray(const TCelArray& src);
Constructs a *TCelArray* as a copy of an existing one. If the original *TCelArray* owned its bitmap, the constructor copies this bitmap; otherwise, it keeps a reference to the bitmap.

Form 4   TCelArray(const TSize& size, uint flags, int init, int grow);
Constructs an empty *CelArray* of a given size.

Destructor
virtual ~TCelArray();
If *ShouldDelete* is true (the default value), the bitmap is deleted. If *ShouldDelete* is false, no action is taken.

Public member functions

Add

Form 1   int Add(const TCelArray& src, int index);

Adds a cel from another *CelArray* to this *CelArray*.

Form 2   int Add(const TBitmap& image);

Adds new cels to the *CelArray*—returns the index of the new addition. No mask bitmap is added.

BitBlt

Form 1   bool BitBlt(int index, TDC&, int x, int y, int dx, int dy, const TColor& bgClr, const TColor& fgClr);

Draws the image of the cel onto the DC.

Form 2   bool BitBlt(int index, TDC& dc, int x, int y);

Draws the cel at index onto the DC at position *x* and *y*.

CelOffset

TPoint CelOffset(int cel) const;

Returns the position of the upper left corner of a given cel relative to the upper left corner of the bitmap.

CelRect

TRect CelRect(int cel) const;

Returns the upper left and lower right corner of a given cell relative to the upper left corner of the bitmap.

CelSize

TSize CelSize() const;

Returns the size in pixels of each cell.

GetBkColor

TColor GetBkColor() const;

Get the current background color for this *CelArray*.

NumCels

int NumCels() const;

Returns the number of cels in the array.

Offset

TPoint Offset() const;

Returns the offset of the entire *CelArray*.

operator [ ]

TRect operator [](int cel) const;

Returns *CelRect*.

operator =

TCelArray& operator =(const TCelArray&);

Returns *TCelArray*.

Remove
bool Remove(int index = -1);
Removes a cel from this *CelArray*.

RemoveAll
bool RemoveAll();
Removes all the cels from the array.

Replace
bool Replace(int index, const TBitmap& image);
Replaces a cel in this *CelArray*.

SetBkColor
TColor SetBkColor(const TColor&);
Sets the current background color for this *CelArray*, returning the previous color.

SetCelSize
void SetCelSize(TSize size);
Sets the size of each cel in the array.

SetNumCels
void SetNumCels(int numCels);
Sets the number of cels in the array.

SetOffset
void SetOffset(TPoint offs);
Sets the offset for the cels in the array.

operator TBitmap&
operator TBitmap&();
Returns a reference to the bitmap.

Protected data members

Bitmap
TBitmap* Bitmap;
Points to the bitmap.

BkColor
TColor BkColor;
The background color used when the image is smaller than the cell size.

CSize
TSize CSize;
The size of a cell in the array.

NCels
int NCels;
The number of cells in the cel array.

NCelsUsed
int NCelsUsed;
The number of cels currently in use.

NGrowBy
int NGrowBy;
How much to grow the array by when full.

Offs
TPoint Offs;
Holds the offset of the upper left corner of the cel array from the upper left corner of the bitmap.

ShouldDelete
bool ShouldDelete;
Is true if the Destructor needs to delete the bitmap associated with the cel array.

TCharFormat class   richedit.h

TCharFormat encapsulates the CHARFORMAT structure, which contains information about character formatting in a rich edit control.

Public constructor

TCharFormat(const TRichEdit& edit, bool selection, ulong mask);
Constructs a CharacterFormat structure from the current character attributes of a RICHEDIT control.

Note   Specifying true for selection returns the attribute of the character at the current location if there are no blocks of data selected in the control.

Public member functions

EnableBold
void EnableBold(bool = true);
Toggles the bold character attribute according to the Boolean parameter specified.

EnableItalic
void EnableItalic(bool = true);
Toggles italic character attribute based on the Boolean parameter specified.

EnableProtected
void EnableProtected(bool = true);
Toggles the protected character attribute based on the Boolean parameter specified.

EnableStrikeOut
void EnableStrikeOut(bool = true);
Toggles the strike-out character attribute based on the Boolean parameter specified.

EnableUnderline

void EnableUnderline(bool = true);

Toggles the underline character attribute based on the Boolean parameter specified.

GetFontInfo

void GetFontInfo(const LOGFONT& lf);

Initializes the underlying CHARFORMAT structure using the information stored in a LOGFONT structure.

GetTextColor

TColor GetTextColor() const;

Retrieves the character color stored in the CHARFORMAT structure.

Note   Default to system text color of no explicit color was set in the CHARFORMAT structure.

SetCharSet

void SetCharSet(uint8);

Sets the character set of the font. Valid values include the following: ANSI_CHARSET, OEM_CHARSET, and SYMBOL_CHARSET.

SetFaceName

void SetFaceName(const char far*);

Sets the face name of the font.

SetFontInfo

void SetFontInfo(LOGFONT& lf) const;

Transfers the information currently in the underlying CHARFORMAT structure to a LOGFONT structure. This is useful when changing the editor's font, as initialized LOGFONT structure can subsequently be used when invoking the FONT Common Dialog (i.e., *TChooseFontDialog*).

SetHeight

void SetHeight(long);

Sets the character height.

SetOffset

void SetOffset(long);

Sets the character offset from the baseline. If the parameter is positive, the character is a superscript; if it is negative, the character is a subscript.

SetPitchAndFamily

void SetPitchAndFamily(uint8);

Sets the pitch and family of the font. The two lower-bits specify the pitch of the font and can be one of the following values: DEFAULT_PITCH, FIXED_PITCH, VARIABLE_PITCH.

Bits 4 through 7 of the member specify the font family and can be one of the following values: FF_DECORATIVE, FF_DONTCARE, FF_MODERN, FF_ROMAN, FF_SCRIPT, FF_SWISS.

SetTextColor

void SetTextColor(const TColor& = TColor::None);

Updates the CHARFORMAT structure with the specified color.

Note If *TColor::None* is specified, enable the flag specifying that the color should default to the system text color.

ToggleEffectsBit
void ToggleEffectsBit(ulong flag);
Toggles the effect bits specified in the *flag* parameter.

ToggleMaskBit
void ToggleMaskBit(ulong flag);
Toggles the mask bits specified in the *flag* parameter.

TCharRange class   richedit.h

TCharRange encapsulates the CHARRANGE structure, which specifies a range of characters in a rich edit control.

Public constructor

TCharRange(long min = 0, long max = -1);
Constructs a *TCharRange* structure initialized with the specified *min* and *max* parameters.

TCharSet class   bitset.h

Derived from *TBitSet*, *TCharSet* sets and clears bytes for a group of characters. You can use this class to set or clear bits in a group of characters, such as the capital letters from "A" through "Z" or the lowercase letters from "a" through "z". The class *TBitSet* performs similar operations for a group of bits.

Public constructors

Form 1   TCharSet();
Constructs a *TCharSet* object.

Form 2   TCharSet(const TCharSet&);
Copy constructor for a *TCharSet* object.

Form 3   TCharSet(const char far* str);
Constructs a string of characters.

Public member function

operator !=
int operator !=(const TBitSet& bs1, const TBitSet& bs2);
ORs all the bits in the copied string and returns a reference to the copied *TCharSet* object.

TCheckBox class

TCheckBox is a streamable interface class that represents a check box control. Use *TCheckBox* to create a check box control in a parent window. You can also use *TCheckBox* objects to more easily manipulate check boxes you created in a dialog box resource. Two-state check boxes can be *checked* or *unchecked*; three-state check boxes have an additional *grayed* state. *TCheckBox* member functions let you easily control the check box's state. A check box can be in a group box (a *TGroupBox* object) that groups related controls.

Public data member

Group

TGroupBox* Group;

If the check box belongs to a group box (a *TGroupBox* object), *Group* points to that object. If the check box is not part of a group, *Group* is zero.

Public constructors

Form 1 TCheckBox(TWindow* parent, int Id, const char far* title, int x, int y, int w, int h, TGroupBox* group = 0, TModule* module = 0);

Constructs a check box object with the specified parent window (*parent*), control ID (*Id*), associated text (*title*), position relative to the origin of the parent window's client area (*x, y*), width (*w*), height (*h*), associated group box (*group*), and owning module (*module*). Invokes the *TButton* constructor with similar parameters. Sets the check box's style to WS_CHILD | WS_VISIBLE | WS_TABSTOP | BS_AUTOCHECKBOX.

Form 2 TCheckBox(TWindow* parent, int resourceId, TGroupBox* group = 0, TModule* module = 0);

Constructs an associated *TCheckBox* object for the check box control with a resource ID of *resourceId* in the parent dialog box. Sets *Group* to *group* then enables the data transfer mechanism by calling *TWindow::EnableTransfer*.

Public member functions

Check

void Check();

Forces the check box to be checked by calling *SetCheck* with the value BF_CHECKED. Notifies the associated group box, if there is one, that the state was changed.

See also   TCheckBox::GetCheck, TCheckBox::Toggle, TCheckBox::Uncheck, TGroupBox::SelectionChanged

GetCheck

uint GetCheck() const;

Returns the state of the check box.

Table 2.3   TCheckBox Check States

Check box state	Return value
Checked	BF_CHECKED
Unchecked	BF_UNCHECKED
Grayed	BF_GRAYED

See also   TCheckBox::SetCheck

GetGroup
TGroupBox* GetGroup() const;
Returns the group with which the check box is associated.

GetState
uint GetState() const;
Returns the check, focus, and highlight state of the check box.

See also   TCheckBox::SetState

SetCheck
void SetCheck(uint check);
Forces the check box into the state specified by *check*.

See also   TCheckBox::GetCheck

SetGroup
void SetGroup(TGroupBox* group);
Sets the group with which the check box is associated.

SetState
void SetState(uint state);
Sets the check, focus, and highlight state of the check box.

See also   TCheckBox::GetState

SetStyle
void SetStyle(uint style, bool redraw);
Changes the style of the check box.

Toggle
void Toggle();
Toggles the check box between checked and unchecked if it is a two-state check box; toggles it between checked, unchecked, and gray if it is a three-state check box.

See also   TCheckBox::SetCheck

Transfer
uint Transfer(void* buffer, TTransferDirection direction);
Overrides *TWindow::Transfer*. Transfers the check state of the check box to or from *buffer*, using the values specified in the table in GetCheck. If *direction* is *tdGetDate*, the check box state is transferred into the buffer. If *direction* is *tdSetData*, the check box state is changed to the settings in the transfer *buffer*.

Transfer returns the size of the transfer data in bytes. To get the size without actually transferring the check box, use *tdSizeData* as the *direction* argument.

Uncheck

void Uncheck();

Forces the check box to be unchecked by calling *SetCheck* with a value of BF_UNCHECKED. Notifies the associated group box, if there is one, that the state has changed.

See also   TCheckBox::Check, TCheckBox::SetCheck, TCheckBox::Toggle

Protected member functions

BNClicked

void BNClicked();

Responds to notification message BN_CLICKED, indicating that the user clicked the check box. If *Group* isn't 0, *BNClicked* calls the group box's *SelectionChanged* member function to notify the group box that the state has changed.

EvGetDlgCode

uint EvGetDlgCode(MSG far* msg);

Overrides *TButton*'s response to the WM_GETDLGCODE message, an input procedure associated with a control that is not a check box, by calling *DefaultProcessing*. The *msg* parameter indicates the kind of message sent to the dialog box manager, such as a control message, a command message, or a check box message.

EvGetDlgCode returns a code that indicates how the check box is to be treated.

See also   TButton::EvGetDlgCode, TWindow::DefaultProcessing, DLGC_xxxxdialogcontrolmessageconstants

GetClassName

char far* GetClassName();

If BWCC is enabled, returns CHECK_CLASS. If BWCC is not enabled, returns "BUTTON."

Response table entries

Response table entry	Member function
EV_NOTIFY_AT_CHILD (BN_CLICKED, BNClicked)	BNClicked
EV_WM_GETDLGCODE	EVGetDlgCode

TCheckList class   checklst.h

TCheckList is an owner-drawn list box to select multiple items.

Public constructors and destructor

Constructors

Form 1   TCheckList(TWindow* parent, int id, int x, int y, int w, int h, TCheckListItem* items, int numItems,
            TModule* module = 0);
Constructor to create a window.

Form 2   TCheckList(TWindow* parent, int resourceId, TCheckListItem* items, int numItems, TModule* module = 0);
Constructor used for resources.

Destructor
~TCheckList();
Destructor for this class.

Protected member functions

EvChar
void EvChar(uint key, uint repeatCount, uint flags);
Toggles the "checked" state when the spacebar is pressed.

EvLButtonDown
void EvLButtonDown(uint modKeys, TPoint& point);
Toggles the "checked" state when the mouse is clicked in the check box.

GetItemAtIndex
TCheckListItem* GetItemAtIndex(int index);
Returns the item at the specified index.

ODADrawEntire
void ODADrawEntire(DRAWITEMSTRUCT far& drawInfo);
Repaints the item entirely.

ODAFocus
void ODAFocus(DRAWITEMSTRUCT far& drawInfo);
Repaints the item entirely.

ODASelect
void ODASelect(DRAWITEMSTRUCT far& drawInfo);
Repaints the item entirely.

PaintItem
void PaintItem(DRAWITEMSTRUCT far& drawInfo);
Paints the item entirely.

SetupWindow
void SetupWindow();
Adds the strings into the list box.

Update
void Update();
Refreshes the window.

TCheckListItem class

TCheckListItem is each item displayed and manipulated by *TCheckList*.

Public constructors and destructor

Constructors

Form 1   TCheckListItem();
Initializes the state of *TCheckListItem*.

Form 2   TCheckListItem(const char far* text, uint state = BF_UNCHECKED);
Constructs the object with a text string and a starting state.

Destructor
~TCheckListItem();
Deletes the allocated copied text.

Public member functions

Check
void Check();
Programmatically checks the item.

GetText
void GetText(char far* buffer, int len);
Returns the text of the item.

IsChecked
bool IsChecked() const;
Returns true if the item has been checked.

IsIndeterminate
bool IsIndeterminate() const;
Returns true if the item is in the indeterminate state.

SetIndeterminate
void SetIndeterminate();
Programmatically makes the item indeterminate.

SetText
void SetText(const char far* text);
Copies the text string.

SetThreeStates
void SetThreeStates(bool);
Sets the three-state property.

Toggle
void Toggle();
Toggles the state of the item. If the item has three states, the cycle goes from unchecked to checked to indeterminate and back to unchecked. Otherwise, the state toggles between unchecked and checked.

Uncheck
void Uncheck();
Programmatically unchecks the item.

TChooseColorDialog class   chooseco.h

TChooseColorDialog objects represent modal dialog box interface elements that allow color selection and custom color adjustment. *TChooseColorDialog* can be made to appear modeless to the user by creating the dialog's parent as an invisible pop-up window and making the pop-up window a child of the main application window. *TChooseColorDialog* uses the *TChooseColor::TData* struct to initialize the dialog box with the user's color selection.

Public constructor

TChooseColorDialog(TWindow* parent, TData& data, TResId templateID = 0, const char far* title = 0,
    TModule* module = 0);
Constructs a dialog box with specified parent window, data, resource identifier, window caption, and module ID. Sets the attributes of the dialog box based on info in the *TChooseColor::TData* structure.

See also   TChooseColorDialog::TData

Public member function

SetRGBColor
void SetRGBColor(TColor color);
Sets the current RGB color for the open dialog box by sending a *SetRGBMsgId*. You can use *SetRGBColor* to send a message to change the current color selection.

Public data members

cc
CHOOSECOLOR cc;
Stores the length of the *TChooseColorDialog* structure, the window that owns the dialog box, and the data block that contains the dialog template. It also points to an array of 16 RGB values for the custom color boxes in the dialog box, and specifies the dialog-box initialization flags.

See also   TChooseColorDialog::TData

Protected data member

Data
TData& Data;
Data is a reference to the *TData* object passed in the constructor.

See also   TChooseColorDialog::TData

Protected member functions

DialogFunction
bool DialogFunction(uint message, WPARAM, LPARAM);
Returns true if a message is handled.

See also   TDialog::DialogFunction

DoExecute
int DoExecute();
If no error occurs, *DoExecute* copies flags and colors into *Data* and returns zero. If an error occurs, *DoExecute* returns the IDCANCEL with *Data.Error* set to the value returned from *CommDlgExtendedError*.

EvSetRGBColor
LPARAM EvSetRGBColor(WPARAM, LPARAM);
Responds to the message sent by *SetRGBColor* by forwarding to the original class. This event handler is not in the response table.

GetCC
CHOOSECOLOR& GetCC();
Returns the CHOOSECOLOR data structure for this dialog.

GetData
TData& GetData();
Returns the data object for this common dialog.

SetCC
void SetCC(const CHOOSECOLOR& cc);
Sets the CHOOSECOLOR data structure for this dialog. Use this function with caution!

SetData
void SetData(TData& data);
Sets the data for this common dialog. Use this function with caution!

SetRGBMsgId
static uint SetRGBMsgId;
Contains the ID of the registered message sent by *SetRGBColor*.

TChooseColorDialog::TData class

chooseco.h

Defines information necessary to initialize the dialog box with the user's color selection.

Public data members

TData::Color
TColor Color;
Specifies the color that is initially selected when the dialog box is created. Contains the user's color selection when the dialog box is closed.

TData::CustColors
TColor* CustColors;
Points to an array of 16 colors.

TData::Error
uint32 Error;
If the dialog box is successfully executed, *Error* is 0. Otherwise, it contains one of the following codes:

Constant	Meaning
CDERR_DIALOGFAILURE	Failed to create a dialog box.
CDERR_FINDRESFAILURE	Failed to find a specified resource.
CDERR_LOADRESFAILURE	Failed to load a specified resource.
CDERR_LOCKRESOURCEFAILURE	Failed to lock a specified resource.
CDERR_LOADSTRFAILURE	Failed to load a specified string.

TData::Flags
uint32 Flags;
Flags can be a combination of the following values that control the appearance and functionality of the dialog box:

Constant	Meaning
CC_FULLOPEN	Causes the entire dialog box to appear when the dialog box is created.
CC_PREVENTFULLOPEN	Disables the "Define Custom Colors" push button.
CC_RGBINIT	Causes the dialog box to use the color specified in *rgbResult* as the initial color selection.
CC_SHOWHELP	Causes the dialog box to show the Help push button.

See also   TChooseColorDialog::Data

TChooseFontDialog class

choosefo.h

A *TChooseFontDialog* represents modal dialog-box interface elements that create a system-defined dialog box from which the user can select a font, a font style (such as bold or italic), a point size, an effect (such as strikeout or underline), and a color.

TChooseFontDialog can be made to appear modeless by creating the dialog's parent as an invisible pop-up window and making the pop-up window a child of the main application window. *TChooseFontDialog* uses the *TChooseFontDialog::TData* structure to initialize the dialog box with the user-selected font styles.

Public constructor

TChooseFontDialog(TWindow* parent, TData& data, TResID templateID = 0, const char far* title = 0,
    TModule* module = 0);

Constructs a dialog box with specified data, parent window, resource identifier, window caption, and module ID. Sets the attributes of the dialog box based on the font information in the *TChooseFontDialog::TData* structure.

See also   TChooseFontDialog::TData

Protected data members

cf
CHOOSEFONT cf;

Contains font attributes. *cf* is initialized using fields in the *TChooseFontDialog::TData* structure. It stores the length of the structure, the window that owns the dialog box and the data block that contains the dialog template. It also specifies the dialog-box initialization flags.

See also   TChooseFontDialog::TData

Data
TData& Data;

Data is a reference to the *TData* object passed in the constructor.

See also   TChooseFontDialog::TData

Protected member functions

CmFontApply
void CmFontApply();

Default handler for the third push button (the Apply button) in the dialog box.

DialogFunction
bool DialogFunction(uint message, WPARAM, LPARAM);

Returns true if a dialog box message is handled.

See also   TDialog::DialogFunction

DoExecute
int DoExecute();

If no error occurs, *DoExecute* copies the flag values and font information into *Ddata*, and returns IDOK or IDCANCEL. If an error occurs, *DoExecute* returns an error code from *TChooseFontDialog::TData* structure's *Error* data member.

See also   TChooseFontDialog::TData

GetCF
CHOOSEFONT& GetCF();
Returns the CHOOSEFONT data structure for this dialog.

GetData
TData& GetData();
Returns the data associated with this dialog.

SetCF
void SetCF(const CHOOSEFONT& cf);
Sets the CHOOSEFONT data structure for this dialog.

SetData
void SetData(TData& data);
Sets the data associated with this dialog. Use this function with caution!

TChooseFontDialog::TData class

choosefo.h

Defines information necessary to initialize the dialog box with the user's font selection.

Public data members

TData::Color
TColor Color;
Indicates the font color that is initially selected when the dialog box is created; contains the user's font color selection when the dialog box is closed.

TData::DC
HDC DC;
Handle to the device context from which fonts are obtained.

TData::Error
uint32 Error;
If the dialog box is successfully executed, *Error* returns 0. Otherwise, it contains one of the following codes:

Constant	Meaning
CDERR_DIALOGFAILURE	Failed to create a dialog box.
CDERR_FINDRESFAILURE	Failed to find a specified resource.
CDERR_LOCKRESOURCEFAILURE	Failed to lock a specified resource.
CDERR_LOADRESFAILURE	Failed to load a specified resource.
CDERR_LOADSTRFAILURE	Failed to load a specified string.
CFERR_MAXLESSTHANMIN	The size specified in *SizeMax* is less than the size in *SizeMin*.
CFERR_NOFONTS	No fonts exist.

TData::Flags
uint32 Flags;

Flags can be a combination of the following constants that control the appearance and functionality of the dialog box:

Constant	Meaning
CF_APPLY	Enables the display and use of the Apply button.
CF_ANSIONLY	Specifies that the *ChooseFontDialog* structure allows only the selection of fonts that use the ANSI character set.
CF_BOTH	Causes the dialog box to list both the available printer and screen fonts.
CF_EFFECTS	Enables strikeout, underline, and color effects.
CF_FIXEDPITCHONLY	Enables fixed-pitch fonts only.
CF_FORCEFONTEXIST	Indicates an error if the user selects a nonexistent font or style.
CF_INITTOLOGFONTSTRUCT	Uses the LOGFONT structure at which *LogFont* points to initialize the dialog controls.
CF_LIMITSIZE	Limits font selection to those between *SizeMin* and *SizeMax*.
CF_NOSIMULATIONS	Does not allow GDI font simulations.
CF_PRINTERFONTS	Causes the dialog box to list only the fonts supported by the printer that is associated with the device context.
CF_SCALABLEONLY	Allows only the selection of scalable fonts.
CF_SCREENFONTS	Causes the dialog box to list only the system-supported screen fonts.
CF_SHOWHELP	Causes the dialog box to show the Help button.
CF_TTONLY	Enumerates and allows the selection of TrueType fonts only.
CF_USESTYLE	Specifies that *Style* points to a buffer containing the style attributes used to initialize the selection of font styles.
CF_WYSIWYG	Allows only the selection of fonts available on both the printer and the screen.

TData::FontType
uint16 FontType;

Font type or name.

TData::LogFont
LOGFONT LogFont;

Attributes of the font.

TData::PointSize
int PointSize;

Point size of the font.

TData::SizeMax
int SizeMax;

Maximum size of the font.

TData::SizeMin
int SizeMin;

Minimum size of the font.

TData::Style
char far* Style;
Style of the font such as bold, italic, underline, or strikeout.

TClientDC class

A device context class derived from *TWindowDC*, *TClientDC* provides access to the client area owned by a window.

See also   TOleClientDC

Public constructor

TClientDC(HWND wnd);
Creates a *TClientDC* object with the given owned window. The data member *Wnd* is set to *wnd*.

See also   TWindowDC::Wnd, TDC::TDC

TClipboard class

TClipboard encapsulates and manipulates Clipboard data. You can open, close, empty, and paste data in a variety of data formats between the Clipboard and the open window. An object on the Clipboard can exist in a variety of Clipboard formats, which range from bitmaps to text.

Usually, the window is in charge of manipulating Clipboard interactions between the window and the Clipboard. It does this by responding to messages sent between the Clipboard owner and the application. The following ObjectWindows event-handling functions encapsulate these Clipboard messages:

- *EvRenderFormat*—Responds to a WM_RENDERFORMAT message sent to the Clipboard owner if a specific Clipboard format that an application has requested hasn't been rendered. After the Clipboard owner renders the data in the requested format, it calls *SetClipboardData* to place the data on the Clipboard.

- *EvRenderAllFormats*—Responds to a message sent to the Clipboard owner if the Clipboard owner has delayed rendering a Clipboard format. After the Clipboard owner renders data in all of possible formats, it calls *SetClipboardData*.

The following example tests to see if there is a palette on the Clipboard. If one exists, *TClipboard* retrieves the palette, realizes it, and then closes the Clipboard.

```
if (clipboard.IsClipboardFormatAvailable(CF_PALETTE)) {
  newPal = new TPalette(TPalette(clipboard));  // make a copy
  UpdatePalette(true);
}
// Try DIB format first
if (clipboard.IsClipboardFormatAvailable(CF_DIB)) {
  newDib = new TDib(TDib(clipboard));          // make a copy
  newBitmap = new TBitmap(*newDib, newPal);  // newPal==0 is OK
```

```
        // try metafile Second
        //
    } else if (clipboard.IsClipboardFormatAvailable(CF_METAFILEPICT)) {
        if (!newPal)
            newPal = new TPalette((HPALETTE)GetStockObject(DEFAULT_PALETTE));
        newBitmap = new TBitmap(TMetaFilePict(clipboard), *newPal,
                            GetClientRect().Size());
...
    // Gets a bitmap , keeps it, and sets up data on the clipboard.
    //
    delete Bitmap;
    Bitmap = newBitmap;

    if (!newDib)
        newDib = new TDib(*newBitmap, newPal);
#endif
    delete Dib;
    Dib = newDib;

    delete Palette;
    Palette = newPal ? newPal : new TPalette(*newDib);
    Palette->GetObject(Colors);

    PixelWidth  = Dib->Width();
    PixelHeight = Dib->Height();
    AdjustScroller();
    SetCaption("(Clipboard)");

    clipboard.CloseClipboard();
```

Public destructor

~TClipboard();
Destroys the *TClipboard* object.

Public data member

DefaultProtocol
static const char* DefaultProtocol;
Points to a string that specifies the name of the protocol the client needs. The default protocol is "StdFileEditing," which is the name of the object linking and embedding protocol.

See also   TClipboard::QueryCreate

Public member functions

operator bool
operator bool() const;
Checks handle. Should use *IsOk* instead.

CloseClipboard
void CloseClipboard()
If the Clipboard is closed (*IsOpen* is false), closes the Clipboard. Closing the Clipboard allows other applications to access the Clipboard.

See also TClipboard::OpenClipboard

CountClipboardFormats
int CountClipboardFormats() const;
Returns a count of the number of types of data formats that the Clipboard can use.

See also TClipboard::RegisterClipboardFormat

EmptyClipboard
bool EmptyClipboard();
Clears the Clipboard and frees any handles to the Clipboard's data. Returns true if the Clipboard is empty, or false if an error occurs.

GetClipboard
static TClipboard& GetClipboard()
Returns a reference to the *TClipboard* object.

GetClipboardData
HANDLE GetClipboardData(uint format) const;
Retrieves data from the Clipboard in the format specified by *format*. The following formats are supported:

Value	Meaning
CF_BITMAP	Data is in a bitmap format
CF_DIB	Data is memory
CF_DIF	Data is in a Data Interchange Format (DIF).
CF_DSPMETAFILEPICT	Data is in a metafile format.
CF_DSPTEXT	Data is in a text format.
CF_METAFILEPICT	Data is in a metafile structure.
CF_OEMTEXT	Data is an array of text characters in OEM character set.
CF_OWNERDISPLAT	Data is in a special format that the application must display.
CF_PALETTE	Data is in a color palette format.
CF_PENDATA	Data is used for pen format.
CF_RIFF	Data is in Resource Interchange File Format (RIFF).
CF_SYLK	Data is in symbolic Link format (SYLK).
CF_TEXT	Data is stored as an array of text characters.
CF_TIFF	Data is in Tag Image File Format (TIFF).
CF_WAVE	Data is in a sound wave format.

See also TClipboard::SetClipboardData

GetClipboardFormatName

int GetClipboardFormatName(uint format, char far* formatName, int maxCount) const;

Retrieves the name of the registered format specified by *format* and copies the format to the buffer pointed to by *formatName*. *maxCount* specifies the maximum length of the name of the format. If the name is longer than *maxCount*, it is truncated.

See also   TClipboard::CountClipboardFormats

GetClipboardOwner

HWND GetClipboardOwner() const;

Retrieves the handle of the window that currently owns the Clipboard, otherwise returns NULL.

GetClipboardViewer

HWND GetClipboardViewer() const;

Retrieves the handle of the first window in the Clipboard-view chain. Returns NULL if there is no viewer.

See also   TClipboard::SetClipboardViewer

GetOpenClipboardWindow

HWND GetOpenClipboardWindow() const;

Retrieves the handle of the window that currently has the Clipboard open. If the Clipboard is not open, the return value is false. Once the Clipboard is opened, applications cannot modify the data.

GetPriorityClipboardFormat

int GetPriorityClipboardFormat(uint FAR * priorityList, int count) const;

Returns the first Clipboard format in a list. *priorityList* points to an array that contains a list of the Clipboard formats arranged in order of priority. See *GetClipboardData* for the Clipboard formats.

See also   TClipboard::GetClipboardData

IsClipboardFormatAvailable

bool IsClipboardFormatAvailable(uint format) const;

Indicates if the format specified in *format* exists for use in the Clipboard. See *GetClipBoardData* for a description of Clipboard data formats.

The following code tests if the Clipboard can support the specified formats:

```
void
TBmpViewWindow::CePaste(TCommandEnabler& ce)
{
  TClipboard& clipboard = OpenClipboard();
  ce.Enable(
    clipboard && (
      clipboard.IsClipboardFormatAvailable(CF_METAFILEPICT) ||
      clipboard.IsClipboardFormatAvailable(CF_DIB) ||
      clipboard.IsClipboardFormatAvailable(CF_BITMAP)
    )
  );
  clipboard.CloseClipboard();
```

See also   TClipboard::GetClipboardData

OpenClipboard

bool OpenClipboard(HWND Wnd);

Opens the Clipboard and associates it with the window specified in *Wnd*. Other applications cannot change the Clipboard data until the Clipboard is closed. Returns true if successful; otherwise, returns false.

See also TClipboard::CloseClipboard

QueryCreate

bool QueryCreate(const char far* protocol = DefaultProtocol, OLEOPT_RENDER renderopt = olerender_draw,
      OLECLIPFORMAT format = 0);

QueryCreate determines if the object on the Clipboard supports the specified protocol and rendering options. *DefaultProtocol* points to a string specifying the name of the protocol the client application needs to use. *renderopt* specifies the client application's display and printing preference for the Clipboard object. *renderopt* is set to *olerender_draw*, which tells the client library to obtain and manage the data presentation. *format* specifies the Clipboard format the client application requests. The macros _OLE_H or _INC_OLE must be defined before this function can be used.

See also TClipboard::QueryLink

QueryLink

bool QueryLink(const char far* protocol = DefaultProtocol, OLEOPT_RENDER renderopt = olerender_draw,
      OLECLIPFORMAT format = 0);

QueryLink determines if a client application can use the Clipboard data to produce a linked object that uses the specified protocol and rendering options. See *TClipboard::QueryCreate* for a description of the parameters. The macros _OLE_H or _INC_OLE must be defined before this function can be used.

See also TClipboard::QueryCreate

RegisterClipboardFormat

uint RegisterClipboardFormat(const char far* formatName) const;

Registers a new Clipboard format. *formatName* points to a character string that identifies the new format. If the format can be registered, the return value indicates the registered format. If the format can't be registered, the return value is 0. Once the format is registered, it can be used as a valid format in which to render the data.

See also TClipboard::CountClipboardFormats, TClipboard::GetClipboardFormatName

SetClipboardData

HANDLE SetClipboardData(uint format, HANDLE handle);

Sets a handle to the block of data at the location indicated by *handle*. *format* specifies the format of the data block. The Clipboard must have been opened before the data handle is set. *format* can be any one of the valid Clipboard formats (for example, CF_BITMAP or CF_DIB). See *GetClipboardData* for a list of these formats. *handle* is a handle to the memory location where the data data is stored. If successful, the return value is a handle to the data; if an error occurs, the return value is 0. Before the window is updated with the Clipboard data, the Clipboard must be closed.

See also TClipboard::GetClipboardData

SetClipboardViewer
HWND SetClipboardViewer(HWND Wnd) const;
Adds the window specified by *Wnd* to the chain of windows that
WM_DRAWCLIPBOARD notifies whenever the contents of the Clipboard change.

See also   TClipboard::GetClipboardViewer

Protected data members

IsOpen
bool IsOpen;
Returns true if the Clipboard is open.

TheClipboard
static TClipboard TheClipboard;
Holds the current Clipboard.

Protected constructor

TClipboard
TClipboard();
Constructs a *TClipboard* object.

TClipboardViewer class   clipview.h

TClipboardViewer is a mix-in class that registers a *TClipboardViewer* as a Clipboard viewer
when the user interface element is created, and removes itself from the Clipboard-
viewer chain when it is destroyed.

Protected data member

HWndNext
HWND HWndNext;
Specifies the next window in the Clipboard-viewer chain.

Protected constructors

Form 1   TClipboardViewer();
Constructs a *TClipboardViewer* object.

Form 2   TClipboardViewer(HWND hWnd, TModule* module = 0);
Constructs a *TClipboardViewer* object with a handle (*hWnd*) to the windows that will
receive notification when the Clipboard's contents are changed.

Protected member functions

DoChangeCBChain
TEventStatus DoChangeCBChain(HWND hWndRemoved, HWND hWndNext);
Tests to see if the Clipboard has changed and, if so, *DoChangeCBChain* forwards this message.

DoDestroy
TEventStatus DoDestroy();
Removes the window from the Clipboard-viewer chain.

DoDrawClipboard
TEventStatus DoDrawClipboard();
Handles *EvDrawClipboard* messages.

EvChangeCBChain
void EvChangeCBChain(HWND hWndRemoved, HWND hWndNext);
Responds to a WM_CHANGECBCHAIN message. *hWndRemoved* is a handle to the window that's being removed. *hWndNext* is the window following the removed window.

EvDestroy
void EvDestroy();
Responds to a WM_DESTROY message when a window is removed from the Clipboard-viewer chain.

EvDrawClipboard
void EvDrawClipboard();
Responds to a WM_DRAWCLIPBOARD message sent to the window in the Clipboard-viewer chain when the contents of the Clipboard change.

GetNextWindow
HWND GetNextWindow() const;
Return the next window in the viewer chain.

SetNextWindow
void SetNextWindow(HWND hwndnext);
Set the next window in the viewer chain.

SetupWindow
void SetupWindow();
Adds a window to the Clipboard-viewer chain.

See also   TWindow::SetupWindow

Response table entries

Response table entry	Member function
EV_WM_CHANGECBCHAIN	EvChangeCbChain
EV_WM_DESTROY	EvDestroy
EV_WM_DRAWCLIPBOARD	EvDrawClipBoard

TColumnHeader class
colmnhdr.h

TColumnHeader encapsulates the 'header control', a window usually positioned above columns of text or numbers.

Public constructors

Form 1
TColumnHeader(TWindow* parent, int id, int x, int y, int w, int h, TModule* module = 0);

Constructor for *TColumnHeader*. Initializes its data fields using parameters passed and default values. By default, a *ColumnHeader* associated with the *TColumnHeader* will:

- be visible upon creation
- have a border, divider tracks
- be a horizontal header window

Form 2
TColumnHeader(TWindow* parent, int resourceId, TModule* module = 0);

Constructor of a *ColumnHeader* object that aliases a control found within a dialog.

Public member functions

Add
int Add(const THdrItem& item);

Adds a new item to the column header. The following illustrates a typical use of the *Add* method:

```
THdrItem hdrItem("&Employee Names");
hdr.Add(hdrItem);
```

Delete
bool Delete(int index);

Deletes the item at the specified *index* from the header control.

GetCount
int GetCount() const;

If successful, returns the number of items in the header control. If unsuccessful, it returns -1.

GetItem
bool GetItem(THdrItem&, int index, uint mask = 0);

Retrieves information about the item at the specified index by filling out the *itemInfo* structure passed in. The *msk* contains one or more HDI_xxxx constants and can be used to specify which information should be copied.

Insert

int Insert(const THdrItem& item, int index);

Inserts a new item at the specified location, *index*, in the *ColumnHeader* control. The following illustrates a typical use of the *Insert* method:

```
THdrItem hdrItem(GetModule().LoadBitmap(IDB_COMPANYLOGO));
hdr.Insert(hdrItem, 0);
```

Layout

Form 1   bool Layout(uint swpFlags = 0);

This method repositions the *ColumnHeader* control within the client area of its parent window by taking advantage of the *ColumnHeader*'s ability to specify its desired / appropriate position from a specified bounding rectangle. This method assumes that the control will occupy the full width of the client area of its parent.

Form 2   bool Layout(TRect& boundingRect, WINDOWPOS& winPos);

This method retrieves the size and position of a header control within a given rectangle. It determines the appropriate dimensions of a new header control that is to occupy the given rectangle.

Upon entry, the *boundingRect* parameter specifies the rectangle within which the *ColumnHeader* must lie. The control then updates the WINDOWPOS structure to contain the desired / appropriate dimensions for the control to occupy within the specified rectangle.

SetItem

bool SetItem(const THdrItem& itemInfo, int index);

Updates the attribute(s) of the item at the specified *index*.

Transfer

uint Transfer(void* buffer, TTransferDirection direction);

Transfers are not implemented for *ColumnHeaders*. They simply return 0.

Protected member functions

GetClassName

char far* GetClassName();

Returns the header control's classname.

TComboBox class   combobox.h

You can use *TComboBox* to create a combo box or a combo box control in a parent *TWindow,* or to facilitate communication between your application and the combo box controls of *TDialog. TComboBox* objects inherit most of their behavior from *TListBox.* This class is streamable.

There are three types of combo boxes: simple, drop down, and drop down list. These types are governed by the style constants CBS_SIMPLE, CBS_DROPDOWN, and CBS_DROPDOWNLIST. These constants, supplied to the constructor of a *TComboBox*, indicate the type of combo box element to create.

See also   TWindow::SetupWindow

Public data members

TextLen
uint TextLen;
Contains the length of the text in the combo box's associated edit control.

Public constructors

TComboBox
Form 1   TComboBox(TWindow* parent, int id, int x, int y, int w, int h, uint32 style, uint textLimit, TModule* module = 0);
Constructs a combo box object with the specified parent window (*parent*), control ID (*Id*), position (*x, y*) relative to the origin of the parent window's client area, width (*w*), height (*h*), style (*style*), and text length (*textLimit*).

Invokes the *TListBox* constructor with similar parameters. Then sets *Attr.Style* as follows:

```
Attr.Style = WS_CHILD | WS_VISIBLE | WS_GROUP | WS_TABSTOP |
             CBS_SORT | CBS_AUTOHSCROLL | WS_VSCROLL | style;
```

One of the following combo box style constants must be among the styles set in *style*: CBS_SIMPLE, CBS_DROPDOWN, CBS_DROPDOWNLIST, CBS_OWNERDRAWFIXED, or CBS_OWNERDRAWVARIABLE.

Form 2   TComboBox(TWindow* parent, int ResourceId, uint textLen = 0, TModule* module = 0);
Constructs a default combo box with the given parent window control ID text length.

See also   TComboBox::GetTextLen, TListBox::TListBox

Public member functions

AddString
virtual int AddString(const char far* string);
Adds a string to an associated list part of a combo box. Returns the index of the string in the list. The first entry is at index zero. Returns a negative value if an error occurs.

Clear
void Clear();
Clears the text of the associated edit control.

ClearList
virtual void ClearList();
Clears out all associated entries in the associated list.

DeleteString
virtual int DeleteString(int index);

Deletes the string at the passed index in the associated list part of a combo box. Returns a count of the entries remaining in the list or a negative value if an error occurs.

DirectoryList
virtual int DirectoryList(uint attrs, const char far* fileSpec);

Fills the combo box with file names from a specified directory.

FindString
virtual int FindString(const char far* find, int indexStart) const;

Searches for a match beginning at the passed Index. If a match is not found after the last string has been compared, the search continues from the beginning of the list until a match is found or until the list has been completely traversed. Returns the index of the first string in the associated list part of a combo box or a negative value if an error occurs.

GetCount
virtual int GetCount() const;

Returns the number of entries in the associated list part of the combo box or a negative value if an error occurs.

GetDroppedControlRect
void GetDroppedControlRect(TRect& Rect) const;

For combo boxes, gets the screen coordinates of the dropped down list box.

GetDroppedState
bool GetDroppedState() const;

For drop down combo boxes, determines if a list box is visible.

GetEditSel
int GetEditSel(int &startPos, int &endPos);

Returns the starting and ending positions of the text selected in the associated edit control. Returns CB_ERR if the combo box has no edit control.

GetExtendedUI
bool GetExtendedUI() const;

Determines if the combo box has the extended user interface, which differs from the default user interface in the following ways:

- Displays the list box if the user clicks the static text field.
- Displays the list box if the user presses the *Down* key.
- Disables scrolling in the static text field if the item list is not visible.

Returns true if the combo box has the extended user interface; otherwise returns false.

See also   TComboBox::SetExtendedUI

GetItemData
virtual uint32 GetItemData(int index) const;

Returns the 32-bit value associated with the combo box's item.

See also   TListBox::GetItemData

GetItemHeight
int GetItemHeight(int index) const;

Returns the height in pixels of the combo box's list items. If an error occurs, returns a negative value.

See also   TComboBox::GetItemData, TListBox::GetItemData

GetSelIndex
virtual int GetSelIndex() const;

Returns the index of the list selection or a negative value if none exists.

GetString
virtual int GetString(char far* str, int index) const;

Retrieves the contents of the string at the position supplied in *index* and returns it in *string*. *GetString* returns the string length or a negative value if an error occurs. The buffer must be large enough for the string and the terminating zero.

See also   TListBox::GetString

GetStringLen
virtual int GetStringLen(int index) const;

Returns the string length (excluding the terminating zero) of the item at the position index supplied in *index*. Returns a negative value if an error occurs.

See also   TListBox::GetStringLen

GetText
int GetText(char far* str, int maxChars) const;

Retrieves the number of characters in the edit or static portion of the combo box.

GetTextLen
int GetTextLen() const;

Returns the text length (excluding the terminating zero) of the edit control or static portion of the combo box.

GetTextLimit
uint GetTextLimit();

Returns the limit of new characters that can be entered into the edit control portion of the combo box.

HideList
void HideList();

Hides the drop down list of a drop down or drop down list combo box.

InsertString
virtual int InsertString(const char far* str, int index);

Inserts a string in the associated list part of a combo box at the position supplied in *Index*. Returns the index of the string in the list or a negative value if an error occurs.

See also   TListBox::InsertString

SetEditSel
int SetEditSel(int startPos, int endPos);

Selects characters that are between *startPos* and *endPos* in the edit control of the combo box. Returns CB_ERR if the combo box does not have an edit control.

SetExtendedUI
int SetExtendedUI(bool extended);

If the combo box has the extended user interface, sets the extended user interface.

See also   TComboBox::GetExtendedUI

SetItemData
virtual int SetItemData(int index, uint32 itemData);

Sets the 32-bit value associated with the *TComboBox's* item. If an error occurs, returns a negative value.

SetItemHeight
int SetItemHeight(int index, int height);

Sets the height of the list items or the edit control portion in a combo box. If the index or height is invalid, returns a negative value.

See also   TComboBox::GetItemHeight

SetSelIndex
virtual int SetSelIndex(int index);

Selects a string of characters in a combo box. *index* specifies the index of the string of characters in the list box to select. If the index is 0, the first line in the list box is selected. If the index is -1, the current selection is removed. If an error occurs, a negative value is returned.

See also   TComboBox::GetSelIndex

SetSelString
virtual int SetSelString(const char far* findStr, int indexStart);

Selects a string of characters in the associated list box and sets the contents of the associated edit control to the supplied string.

SetText
void SetText(const char far* string);

Selects the first string in the associated list box that begins with the supplied *string*. If there is no match, *SetText* sets the contents of the associated edit control to the supplied string and selects it.

SetTextLimit
void SetTextLimit(uint textlimit);

Sets the text length limit member and associated control.

ShowList
Form 1   void ShowList();

Shows the list of a drop down or drop down list combo box.

Form 2   void ShowList(bool show = true);
Shows or hides the drop down or drop down list combo box depending on the value of show. If show is true, shows the list; if show is false, hides the list.

See also   TComboBox::HideList

Transfer
uint Transfer(void* buffer, TTransferDirection direction);
Transfers the items and selection of the combo box to or from a transfer buffer if *tdSetData* or *tdGetData*, respectively, is passed as the *direction*. *buffer* is expected to point to a *TComboBoxData* structure.

Transfer returns the size of a pointer to a *TComboBoxData*. To retrieve the size without transferring data, your application must pass *tdSizeData* as the *direction*.

You must use a pointer in your transfer buffer to these structures. You cannot embed copies of the structures in your transfer buffer, and you cannot use these structures as transfer buffers.

See also   TComboBoxData, TWindow::Transfer

Protected member functions

CleanupWindow
void CleanupWindow();
Cleans up aliases created in *SetupWindow*.

GetClassName
char far* GetClassName();
Returns the name of *TComboBox's* registration class, *ComboBox*.

SetupWindow
void SetupWindow();
Sets up the window and limits the amount of text the user can enter in the combo box's edit control to the value of *TextLen* minus 1.

TComboBoxData class   combobox.h

An interface object that represents a transfer buffer for a *TComboBox*.

Public constructor and destructor

Constructor
TComboBoxData();
Constructs a *TComboBoxData* object, initializes *Strings* and *ItemDatas* to empty arrays, and initializes *Selection* and *SelIndex* to 0.

Destructor
~TComboBoxData();
Destructor for *TComboBoxData*. Deletes *Strings*, *ItemDatas*, and *Selection*.

Public member functions

AddString
void AddString(const char *str, bool isSelected = false);
Adds the specified string to the array of *Strings*. If *IsSelected* is true, *AddString* deletes *Selection* and copies *string* into *Selection*.

AddStringItem
void AddStringItem(const char* str, uint32 itemData, bool isSelected = false);
Adds a given string and uint32 item to the *Strings* and *ItemDatas* array and copies the string into *Selection* if *isSelected* is true.

Clear
void Clear();
Flushes the *Strings* and *ItemDatas* members. Resets the index and selected string values.

GetItemDatas
TDwordArray& GetItemDatas();
Returns the array of DWORDs to transfer to or from a combo box's associated list box.

GetSelCount
int GetSelCount() const;
Returns the number of items selected, either 0 or 1.

GetSelection
string& GetSelection();
Returns the currently selected string (the *Selection* data member) to transfer to or from a combo box.

GetSelIndex
int GetSelIndex();
Returns the index (the *SelIndex* data member) of the selected item in the strings array.

GetSelString
void GetSelString(char far* buffer, int bufferSize) const;
Copies the selected string into a buffer of the specified size. *bufferSize* includes the terminating 0.

GetSelStringLength
int GetSelStringLength() const;
Returns length of the currently selected string excluding the terminating 0.

GetStrings
TStringArray& GetStrings();

Returns the array of strings (the *Strings* data member) to transfer to or from a combo box's associated list box.

ResetSelections
void ResetSelections();
Resets the index of the selected item and the currently selected string.

Select
void Select(int index);
Selects the item at the given index.

SelectString
void SelectString(const char far* str);
Selects the selection string (*str*) and makes the matching *String* entry (if one exists) as selected.

Protected data members

ItemDatas
TDwordArray ItemDatas;
Array of DWORDs to transfer to or from a combo box's associated list box.

Selection
string Selection;
The currently selected string to transfer to or from a combo box.

Strings
TStringArray Strings;
Array of class string to transfer to or from a combo box's associated list box.

TCommandEnabler class   window.h

An abstract base class used for automatic enabling and disabling of commands, *TCommandEnabler* is a class from which you can derive other classes, each one having its own command enabler. For example, *TButtonGadgetEnabler* is a derived class that's a command enabler for button gadgets, and *TMenuItemEnabler* is a derived class that's a command enabler for menu items. Although your derived classes are likely to use only the functions *Enable*, *SetCheck*, and *GetHandled*, all of *TCommandEnabler*'s functions are described so that you can better understand how ObjectWindows uses command processing. The following paragraphs explain the dynamics of command processing.

Handling command messages

Commands are messages of the windowsWM_COMMAND type that have associated command identifiers (for example, CM_FILEMENU). When the user selects an item from a menu or a toolbar, when a control sends a notification message to its parent window, or when an accelerator keystroke is translated, a WM_COMMAND message is sent to a window.

Responding to command messages

A command is handled differently depending on which type of command a window receives. Menu items and accelerator commands are handled by adding a command entry to a message response table using the EV_COMMAND macro. The entry requires two arguments:

- A command identifier (for example, CM_LISTUNDO)
- A member function (for example, *CMEditUndo*)

Child ID notifications, messages that a child window sends to its parent window, are handling by using one of the notification macros defined in the header file windowev.h.

It is also possible to handle a child ID notification at the child window by adding an entry to the child's message response table using the EV_NOTIFY_AT_CHILD macro. This entry requires the following arguments:

- A notification message (for example, LBN_DBLCLK)
- A member function (for example, *CmEditItem*)

TWindow command processing

One of the classes designed to handle command processing, *TWindow* performs basic command processing according to these steps;

1 The member function *WindowProc* calls the virtual member function *EvCommand*.

2 *EvCommand* checks to see if the window has requested handling the command by looking up the command in the message response table.

3 If the window has requested handling the command identifier by using the EV_COMMAND macro, the command is dispatched.

TWindow also handles Child ID notifications at the child window level.

TFrameWindow command processing

TFrameWindow provides specialized command processing by overriding its member function *EvCommand* and sending the command down the command chain (that is, the chain of windows from the focus window back up to the frame itself, the original receiver of the command message).

If no window in the command chain handles the command, *TFrameWindow* delegates the command to the application object. Although this last step is theoretically performed by the frame window, it is actually done by *TWindow*'s member function, *DefaultProcessing*.

Invoking EvCommand

When *TFrameWindow* sends a command down the command chain, it does not directly dispatch the command; instead, it invokes the window's *EvCommand* member function. This procedure gives the windows in the command chain the flexibility to handle a command by overriding the member function *EvCommand* instead of being limited to handling only the commands requested by the EV_COMMAND macro.

Handling command enable messages

Most applications expend considerable energy updating menu items and tool bar buttons to provide the necessary feedback indicating that a command has been enabled. In order to simplify this procedure, ObjectWindows lets the event handler that is going to handle the command make the decision about whether or not to enable or disable a command.

Although the WM_COMMAND_ENABLE message is sent down the same command chain as the WM_COMMAND event; exactly when the WM_COMMAND_ENABLE message is sent depends on the type of command enabling that needs to be processed.

Command enabling for menu items

TFrameWindow performs this type of command enabling when it receives a WM_INITMENUPOPUP message. It sends this message before a menu list appears. ObjectWindows then identifies the menu commands using the command IDs and sends requests for the commands to be enabled.

Note that because ObjectWindows actively maintains toolbars and menu items, any changes made to the variables involved in the command enabling functions are implemented dynamically and not just when a window is activated.

Command enabling for toolbar buttons

This type of command enabling is performed during idle processing (in the *IdleAction* function). The Default Message-Processing Flowchart that accompanies *TWindow::DefaultProcessing* is a graphical illustration of this process.

Creating specialized command enablers

Associated with the WM_COMMAND_ENABLE message is an object of the *TCommandEnabler* type. This family of command enablers includes specialized command enablers for menu items and toolbar buttons.

As you can see from *TCommandEnabler*'s class declaration, you can do considerably more than simply enable or disable a command using the command enabler. For example, you have the ability to change the text associated with the command as well as the state of the command.

Using the EV_COMMAND_ENABLE macro

You can use the EV_COMMAND_ENABLE macro to handle WM_COMMAND_ENABLE messages. Just as you do with the EV_COMMAND macro, you specify the command identifier that you want to handle and the member function you want to invoke to handle the message.

Automatically enabling and disabling commands

ObjectWindows simplifies enabling and disabling of commands by automatically disabling commands for which there are no associated handlers. *TFrameWindow*'s member function *EvCommandEnable* performs this operation, which involves completing a two-pass algorithm.

1 The first pass sends a WM_COMMAND_ENABLE message down the command chain giving each window an explicit opportunity to do the command enabling.

2 If no window handles the command enabling request, then ObjectWindows checks to see whether any windows in the command chain are going to handle the command through any associated EV_COMMAND entries in their response tables. If there is a command handler in one of the response tables, then the command is enabled; otherwise it is disabled.

Because of this implicit command enabling or disabling, you do not need to (and actually should not) do explicit command enabling unless you want to change the command text, change the command state, or conditionally enable or disable the command.

If you handle commands indirectly by overriding the member function *EvCommand* instead of using the EV_COMMAND macro to add a response table entry, then ObjectWindows will not be aware that you are handling the command. Consequently, the command may be automatically disabled. Should this occur, the appropriate action to take is to also override the member function *EvCommandEnable* and explicitly enable the command.

See also   Command enabling overview

Type definitions

TCommandState enum
enum CheckState{Unchecked, Checked, Indeterminate};

Enumerates the values for the check state of the command sender. This state applies to buttons, such as those used for tool bars, or to control bar gadgets.

Table 2.4   Command State Constants

Constant	Meaning if set
Unchecked	Command is not enabled
Checked	Command is enabled
Indeterminate	Command is unavaiable

TCommandStatus enum
enum TCommandStatus {WasHandled = 1, NonSender = 2};

TCommandStatus is used to describe whether the associated command has been enabled or disabled, and whether the command generates WM_COMMAND messages.

Table 2.5   Command Status Constants

Constant	Meaning if set
WasHandled	Command was enabled or disabled
NonSender	Command does not generate WM_COMMAND messages

Public data member

Id
const uint Id;

Command ID for the enabled command.

Public constructor

TCommandEnabler
TCommandEnabler(uint id, HWND hWndReceiver = 0);

Constructs the *TCommandEnabler* object with the specified command ID. Sets the message responder (*hWndReceiver*) to zero.

Public member functions

Enable
virtual void Enable(bool enable = true);

Enables or disables the command sender. When *Enable* is called, it sets the *Handled* flag.

GetHandled
bool GetHandled();

Returns *Handled*, a flag value that shows if this command enabler has been handled, in which case *Handled* is **true**.

GetId
uint GetId() const;

Retrieves the ID of the command.

GetReceiver
HWND GetReceiver() const;

Returns the handle of the window that this enabler was destined for.

IsReceiver
bool IsReceiver(HWND hReceiver);

Returns **true** if *receiver* is the same as the message responder originally set up in the constructor.

SendsCommand
bool SendsCommand() const;

Returns **true** if this command enabler sends a command message.

SetCheck
virtual void SetCheck(int check) = 0;

Changes the *check* state of the command sender to either *unchecked*, *checked*, or *indeterminate*. This state applies to buttons, such as those used for tool bars, or to control bar gadgets.

SetReceiver
void SetReceiver(HWND hReceiver);

Sets the receiver for the enabler.

SetText
virtual void SetText(const char far* text) = 0;

Changes the text associated with a command sender; for example, text associated with a menu item or text on a button.

Protected data members

Handled
bool Handled;

Is **true** if the command enabler has been handled.

HWndReceiver
const HWND HWndReceiver;

The message responder (the window) that receives the command.

Protected member function

SetHandled
void SetHandled();

Marks that the enabler has been handled.

TCommCtrlDll class   commctrl.h

The *TCommCtrlDll* class encapsulates the Common Control DLL (COMCTL32.DLL). It provides an easy method to dynamically test for the availability of the DLL and bind to its exported functions at runtime. By using the *TCommCtrlDll* class instead of direct calls to the Common Control DLL, ObjectWindows applications can provide the appropriate behavior when running in an environment where the DLL is not available.

Each data member of the *TCommCtrlDll* class corresponds to the API with a similar name exposed by the Common Control DLL. For example, *TCommCtrlDll::InitCommonControls* corresponds to the *InitCommonControls* API exported by the Common Control DLL.

The following is a list of the members of the *TCommCtrlDll* class corresponding to functions exposed by the DLL. For more information about these members, consult the documentation about the corresponding API exposed by the Common Control DLL.

TCommCtrlDll::TCommCtrlDll
AddMasked
BeginDrag
CreateMappedBitmap
CreatePropertySheetPage
CreatePropertySheetPageA
CreateStatusWindow
DragEnter
DragLeave
DragMove
DragShowNolock
DrawEx
EndDrag
GetDragImage
GetIcon
GetIconSize
GetImageInfo
InitCommonControls
LoadImage
Merge
Remove
Replace
SetDragCursorImage
SetIconSize

TCommonDialog class

commdial.h

Derived from *TDialog*, *TCommonDialog* is the abstract base class for *TCommonDialog* objects. It provides the basic functionality for creating dialog boxes using the common dialog DLL. The ObjectWindows classes that inherit this common dialog functionality include

- *TChooseColorDialog*: a modal dialog box that lets a user select colors for an application.

- *TChooseFontDialog*: a modal dialog box that lets a user select fonts for an application.

- *TReplaceDialog*: a modeless dialog box that lets a user specify a text selection to replace.

- *TFindDialog*: a modeless dialog box that lets a user specify a text selection to find.

- *TFileOpenDialog*: a modal dialog box that lets a user specify a file to open.

- *TFileSaveDialog*: a modal dialog box that lets a user specify a file to save.

- *TPrintDialog*: a modal dialog box that lets a user specify printer options.

Each common dialog class uses a nested class, *TData*, that stores the attributes and user-specified data. For example, the *TChooseColorDialog::TData* class stores the color attributes the user selects in response to a prompt in a common dialog box. In fact, to create a common dialog box, you construct a *TData* object first, then fill in the data members of the *TData* object before you even construct the common dialog box object. Finally, you either execute a modal dialog box or create a modeless dialog box.

Public constructor

TCommonDialog(TWindow* parent, const char far* title = 0, TModule* module = 0);

Invokes a *TWindow* constructor, passing the parent window *parent*, and constructs a common dialog box that you can modify to suit your specifications. You can indicate the module ID (*module*) and window caption (*title*), which otherwise default to 0.

Public member functions

DoCreate
HWND DoCreate();
Called by *Create*, *DoCreate* creates a modeless dialog box. It returns 0 if unsuccessful.

DoExecute
int DoExecute();
Called by *Execute*, *DoExecute* executes a modal dialog box. If the dialog box execution is canceled or unsuccessful, *DoExecute* returns IDCANCEL.

Protected data member

CDTitle
const char far* CDTitle;
CDTitle stores the optional caption displayed in the common dialog box.

See also   TDialog::SetCaption

Protected member functions

CmHelp
void CmHelp();
Default handler for the *pshHelp* push button (the Help button in the dialog box).

CmOkCancel
void CmOkCancel();
Responds to a click on the dialog box's OK or Cancel button by calling *DefaultProcessing* to let the common dialog DLL process the command.

See also   TDialog::CmCancel, TDialog::CmOk

EvClose
void EvClose();

Responds to a WM_CLOSE message by calling *DefaultProcessing* to let the common dialog DLL process the command.

See also   TDialog::EvClose

GetCDTitle
const char far* GetCDTitle() const;
Returns the title from the common dialog.

SetupWindow
void SetupWindow();
Assigns the caption of the dialog box to *CDTitle* if *CDTitle* is nonzero.

See also   TDialog::SetupWindow

Response table entries

Response table entry	Member function
EV_COMMAND(IDCANCEL, CmOkCancel)	CmOkCancel
EV_COMMAND(IDOK, CmOkCancel)	CmOkCancel
EV_WM_CLOSE	EvClose
EV_WM_CTLCOLOR	EvCtlColor

TContextMenu class   shellitm.h

TContextMenu wraps the *IContextMenu* interface (currently lightweight). A *TContextMenu* is returned by *TShellItem::GetContextMenu* Default, *TComRef<IContextMenu>*, and copy constructors supplied. *TComRef<IContextMenu>* and *TContextMenu* assignment operators are also supplied.

Public constructors

Form 1   TContextMenu(IContextMenu* iface = 0);
Default constructor for *TContextMenu*.

Form 2   TContextMenu(const TComRef<IContextMenu>& source);
TContextMenu constructor to construct from *TComRef<IContextMenu>*.

Form 3   TContextMenu(const TContextMenu& source);
TContextMenu copy constructor.

Public member functions

operator=
Form 1   TContextMenu& operator= (const TContextMenu& source);
TContextMenu assignment operator (from another *TContextMenu*).

Form 2   TContextMenu& operator= (const TComRef<IContextMenu>& source);
TContextMenu assignment operator (from *TComRef<IContextMenu>*).

TControl class   control.h

TControl unifies its derived control classes, such as *TScrollBar*, *TControlGadget*, and *TButton*. Control objects of derived classes are used to represent control interface elements. A control object must be used to create a control in a parent *TWindow* object or a derived window. A control object can be used to facilitate communication between your application and the controls of a *TDialog* object. *TControl* is a streamable class.

Public constructors

Form 1   TControl(TWindow* parent, int id, const char far* title, int x, int y, int w, int h, TModule* module = 0);
Invokes *TWindow's* constructor, passing it *parent* (parent window), *title* (caption text), and *module*. Sets the control attributes using the supplied library ID (*Id*), position (*x*, *y*) relative to the origin of the parent window's client area, width (*w*), and height (*h*) parameters. It sets the control style to WS_CHILD | WS_VISIBLE | WS_GROUP | WS_TABSTOP.

Form 2   TControl(TWindow* parent, int resourceId, TModule* module = 0);
Constructs an object to be associated with an interface control of a *TDialog* object. Invokes the *TWindow* constructor, then enables the data transfer mechanism by calling *TWindow::EnableTransfer*.

The *id* parameter must correspond to a control interface resource that you define.

Protected member functions

CompareItem
virtual int CompareItem (COMPAREITEMSTRUCT far& compareInfo);
Also used with owner-draw buttons and list boxes, *CompareItem* compares two items. The derived class supplies the compare logic.
See also   COMPAREITEMSTRUCT struct

DeleteItem
virtual void DeleteItem (DELETEITEMSTRUCT far& deleteInfo);
Used with owner-drawn buttons and list boxes. In such cases, the derived class supplies the delete logic.
See also   DELETEITEMSTRUCT struct

DrawItem
virtual void DrawItem(DRAWITEMSTRUCT far& drawInfo);
Responds to a message forwarded by *TWindow* to a drawable control when the control needs to be drawn. *DrawItem* calls one of the following: *ODADrawEntire* if the entire control needs to be drawn, *ODASelect* if the selection state of the control has changed, or *ODAFocus* if the focus has been shifted to or from the control.

See also   DRAWITEMSTRUCT struct

EvCompareItem
LRESULT EvCompareItem(uint ctrlId, COMPAREITEMSTRUCT far& comp);
Handles a WM_COMPAREITEM message for owner-drawn controls.

See also   COMPAREITEMSTRUCT struct

EvDeleteItem
void EvDeleteItem(uint ctrlId, DELETEITEMSTRUCT far& del);
Handles a WM_DELETEITEM message for owner-drawn controls.

See also   DELETEITEMSTRUCT struct

EvDrawItem
void EvDrawItem(uint ctrlId, DRAWITEMSTRUCT far& draw);
Handles a WM_DRAWITEM message.

See also   DRAWITEMSTRUCT struct

EvMeasureItem
void EvMeasureItem(uint ctrlId, MEASUREITEMSTRUCT far& meas);
Handles a WM_MEASUREITEM message.

See also   MEASUREITEMSTRUCT struct

EvPaint
void EvPaint();
If the control has a predefined class, *EvPaint* calls *TWindow::DefaultProcessing* for painting. Otherwise, it calls *TWindow::EvPaint*.

See also   TWindow::Paint

GetNativeUse
TNativeUse GetNativeUse() const;
Returns whether or not OWL is using the native common control.

MeasureItem
virtual void MeasureItem (MEASUREITEMSTRUCT far& measureInfo);
Used by owner-drawn controls to set the dimensions of the specified item. For list boxes and control boxes, this function applies to specific items; for other owner-drawn controls, this function is used to set the total size of the control.

See also   MEASUREITEMSTRUCT struct

ODADrawEntire
virtual void ODADrawEntire(DRAWITEMSTRUCT far& drawInfo);
Responds to a notification message sent to a drawable control when the control needs to be drawn. *ODADrawEntire* can be redefined by a drawable control to specify the manner in which it is to be drawn.

See also   TControl::DrawItem, DRAWITEMSTRUCT struct

ODAFocus

virtual void ODAFocus(DRAWITEMSTRUCT far& drawInfo);

Responds to a notification sent to a drawable control when the focus has shifted to or from the control. *ODAFocus* can be redefined by a drawable control to specify the manner in which it is to be drawn when losing or gaining the focus.

See also   TControl::DrawItem, DRAWITEMSTRUCT struct

ODASelect

virtual void ODASelect(DRAWITEMSTRUCT far& drawInfo);

Responds to a notification sent to a drawable control when the selection state of the control changes. *ODASelect* can be redefined by a drawable control to specify the manner in which it is drawn when its selection state changes.

See also   TControl::DrawItem, DRAWITEMSTRUCT struct

TControl

TControl(HWND hWnd, TModule* module = 0);

Constructor to alias a non-OWL control.

Response table entries

Response table entry	Member function
EV_WM_PAINT	EvPaint
EV_WM_COMPAREITEM	EvCompareItem
EV_WM_DELETEITEM	EvDeleteItem
EV_WM_DRAWITEM	EvDrawItem
EV_WM_MEASUREITEM	EvMeasureItem

TControlBar class   controlb.h

Derived from *TGadgetWindow*, *TControlBar* implements a control bar that provides mnemonic access for its button gadgets. The sample MDIFILE.CPP ObjectWindows program on your distribution disk displays the following example of a control bar:

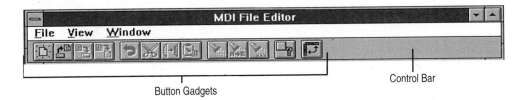

Button Gadgets

Control Bar

To construct, build, and insert a control bar into a frame window, you can first define the following response table:

```
DEFINE_RESPONSE_TABLE1(TMDIFileApp, TApplication)
    EV_COMMAND(CM_FILENEW, CmFileNew),
    EV_COMMAND(CM_FILEOPEN, CmFileOpen),
```

```
          EV_COMMAND(CM_SAVESTATE, CmSaveState),
          EV_COMMAND(CM_RESTORESTATE, CmRestoreState),
     END_RESPONSE_TABLE;
```

Next, add statements that will construct a main window and load its menu, accelerator table, and icon. Then, to construct, build and insert a control bar into the frame window, insert these statements:

```
TControlBar* cb = new TControlBar(frame);
cb->Insert(*new TButtonGadget(CM_FILENEW, CM_FILENEW));
cb->Insert(*new TButtonGadget(CM_FILEOPEN, CM_FILEOPEN));
cb->Insert(*new TButtonGadget(CM_FILESAVE, CM_FILESAVE));
cb->Insert(*new TSeparatorGadget(6));
cb->Insert(*new TButtonGadget(CM_EDITCUT, CM_EDITCUT));
cb->Insert(*new TButtonGadget(CM_EDITCOPY, CM_EDITCOPY));
cb->Insert(*new TButtonGadget(CM_EDITPASTE, CM_EDITPASTE));
cb->Insert(*new TSeparatorGadget(6));
cb->Insert(*new TButtonGadget(CM_EDITUNDO, CM_EDITUNDO));
frame->Insert(*cb, TDecoratedFrame::Top);
```

Public constructor

TControlBar
TControlBar(TWindow* parent = 0, TTileDirection direction = Horizontal,
     TFont* font = new TGadgetWindowFont, TModule* module = 0);
Constructs a *TControlBar* interface object with the specified direction (either horizontal or vertical) and window font.

Public member function

PreProcessMsg
bool PreProcessMsg(MSG& msg);
Preprocesses messages. Because *PreProcessMsg* does not translate any accelerator keys for *TControlBar*, it returns false.

Protected member function

PositionGadget
void PositionGadget(TGadget* previous, TGadget* next, TPoint& p);
Gets the border style, determines the direction of the gadget, and positions the button gadget on either a horizontal or vertical border if any overlapping is required.

TControlEnabler class
dialog.h

TControlEnabler is a *TCommandEnabler* for child controls in a dialog.

Public constructor

TControlEnabler
TControlEnabler(uint id, HWND hWndReceiver = 0);
Constructor. Initializes the base class.

Public member functions

Enable
void Enable(bool enable = true);
Enables the control.

SetCheck
void SetCheck(int check);
Use this method only with buttons.

SetText
void SetText(const char far* text);
Sets the text of the control.

TControlGadget class   controlg.h

TControlGadget serves as a surrogate for *TControl* so that you can place *TControl* objects such as edit controls, buttons, sliders, gauges, or third-party controls, into a gadget window. If necessary, *TControlGadget* sets a parent window and creates the control gadget. See *TGadget* for more information about gadget objects.

See also   TGadget

Public constructor and destructor

Constructor
TControlGadget(TWindow& control, TBorderStyle = None);
Creates a *TControlGadget* object associated with the specified *TControl* window.

Destructor
~TControlGadget();
Destroys a *TControlGadget* object and removes it from the associated window.

Protected data members

Control
TWindow* Control;
Points to the control window that is managed by this *TControlGadget*.

Protected member functions

GetControl
TWindow* GetControl() const;

Returns the control that is simulating a gadget.

GetDesiredSize
void GetDesiredSize(TSize& size);

Calls *TGadget::GetDesiredSize* and passes the size of the control gadget. Use *GetDesiredSize* to find the size the control gadget needs to be in order to accommodate the borders and margins as well as the highest and widest control gadget.

See also   TGadget::GetDesiredSize

GetInnerRect
void GetInnerRect(TRect&);

Computes the area of the control gadget's rectangle excluding the borders and margins.

Inserted
void Inserted();

Called when the control gadget is inserted in the parent window. Displays the window in its current size and position.

Invalidate
void Invalidate(bool erase = true);

Used to invalidate the active (usually nonborder) portion of the control gadget, *Invalidate* calls *InvalidateRect* and passes the boundary width and height of the area to erase.

InvalidateRect
void InvalidateRect(const TRect&, bool erase = true);

Invalidates the control gadget rectangle in the parent window.

Removed
void Removed();

Called when the control gadget is removed from the parent window.

SetBounds
void SetBounds(TRect& rect);

Calls *TGadget::SetBounds* and passes the dimensions of the control gadget's rectangle. *SetBounds* informs the control gadget of a change in its bounding rectangle.

See also   TGadget::SetBounds

SetControl
void SetControl(TWindow* control);

Sets the control that is simulating a gadget.

Update
void Update();

Updates the client area of the specified window by immediately sending a WM_PAINT message.

TCreatedDC class

An abstract *TDC* class, *TCreatedDC* serves as the base for *DCs* that are created and deleted.

See *TDC* for more information about *DC* objects.

Public constructors and destructor

Constructors

Form 1   TCreatedDC(const char far* driver, const char far* device, const char far* output,
            const DEVMODE far* initData=0);

Creates a device context (DC) object for the device specified by *driver* (driver name), *device* (device name), and *output* (the name of the file or device [port] for the physical output medium). The optional *initData* argument provides a DEVMODE structure containing device-specific initialization data for this DC. *initData* must be 0 (the default) if the device is to use any default initializations specified by the user.

Form 2   TCreatedDC(HDC handle TAutoDelete autoDelete);
Creates a DC object using an existing DC.

Destructor

~TCreatedDC();
Calls *RestoreObjects* clears any nonzero *OrgXXX* data members. If *ShouldDelete* is true the destructor deletes this DC.

See also   enum TDC::TAutoDelete, TDC::RestoreObjects, TDC::ShouldDelete, DEVMODE struct

Protected constructors

TCreatedDC

TCreatedDC();
Creates a device context (DC) for the given device. DC objects can be constructed either by borrowing an existing HDC handle or by supplying device and driver information.

TCtl3dDll class

The *TCtl3dDll* class encapsulates the Control 3D DLL (CTL3D[V2|32].DLL). It provides an easy method to dynamically test for the availability of the DLL and bind to its exported functions at runtime. By using the *TCtl3dDll* class instead of direct calls to the Control 3D DLL, ObjectWindows applications can provide the appropriate behavior when running in an environment where the DLL is not available.

Each data member of the *TCtl3dDll* class corresponds to the API with a similar name exposed by the Control 3D DLL. For example, *TCtl3dDll::AutoSubclass* corresponds to the *Ctl3dAutoSubclass* API exported by the Control 3D DLL.

The following is a list of the members of the *TCtl3dDll* class corresponding to functions exposed by the DLL. For more information about these members, consult the documentation about the corresponding API exposed by the Control 3D DLL.

TCtl3dDll::TCtl3dDll
AutoSubclass
ColorChange
CtlColorEx
DlgFramePaint
Enabled
GetVer
Register
SubclassCtl
SubclassDlg
SubclassDlgEx
Unregister
WinIniChange

TCursor class

gdiobjec.h

TCursor, derived from *TGdiBase*, represents the GDI cursor object class. *TCursor* constructors can create cursors from a resource or from explicit information. Because cursors are not real GDI objects, the *TCursor* destructor overrides the base destructor, *~TGdiBase*.

Public constructors and destructor

Constructors

Form 1   TCursor(HCURSOR handle, TAutoDelete autoDelete = NoAutoDelete);

Creates a *TCursor* object and sets the *Handle* data member to the given borrowed handle. The *ShouldDelete* data member defaults to false, ensuring that the borrowed handle will not be deleted when the C++ object is destroyed.

Form 2   TCursor(HINSTANCE, const TCursor& cursor);

Creates a copy of the given *cursor* object. The 32bit version (for compiling a Win32 application) uses *CopyIcon*() and does a cast to get to HICON.

Form 3   TCursor(HINSTANCE, TResId);

Constructs a *cursor* object from the specified resource ID.

Form 4   TCursor(HINSTANCE, const TPoint& hotSpot, const TSize& size, void far* andBits, void far* xorBits);

Constructs a *TCursor* object of the specified size at the specified point.

Form 5   TCursor(const void* resBits, uint32 resSize);

(32 bit only) Constructs a *TCursor* object from the specified resource.

Form 6   TCursor(const ICONINFO* iconInfo);
(32 bit only) Creates a *TCursor* object from the specified ICONINFO structure information.

Destructor
~TCursor();
Destroys a *TCursor* object.

See also   ~TGdiObject, TGdiObject::Handle, TGdiObject::ShouldDelete, TPoint, TSize, ICONINFO struct

Public member functions

GetHandle
THandle GetHandle() const;
Returns the handle of the cursor with type HCURSOR.

GetIconInfo
bool GetIconInfo(ICONINFO* iconInfo) const;
(32-bit only) Retrieves information about this icon and copies it in the given ICONINFO structure. Returns true if the call is successful; otherwise returns false.

See also   ICONINFO struct

operator HCURSOR()
operator HCURSOR() const;
An inline typecasting operator. Converts this cursor's *Handle* to type HCURSOR (the data type representing the handle to a cursor resource).

operator ==
bool operator ==(const TCursor& other) const;
Returns true if this cursor equals *other*; otherwise returns false.

THandle
operator THandle() const;
Returns the handle of the cursor with type HCURSOR.

TDatagramSocket class   wsksockd.h

TDatagramSocket encapsulates a Windows Sockets datagram (non-reliable, packet-based) socket.

Public constructors

Form 1   TDatagramSocket();
This function does nothing. It relies on *TSocket* to do all the work.

Form 2   TDatagramSocket(SOCKET& src);
This function does nothing. It relies on *TSocket* to do all the work.

Form 3   TDatagramSocket(TSocketAddress& newSocketAddress, int addressFormat=PF_INET, int type=SOCK_DGRAM,
int protocol=0);
This function does nothing. It relies on *TSocket* to do all the work.

Public member functions

operator =
TDatagramSocket& operator =(TDatagramSocket& newDatagramSocket1);
This function copies the datagram socket connection information.

Read
int Read(char* data, int& charsToRead, TSocketAddress& sAddress);
This function reads the chars into the *chData* buffer, and removes the data from the queue. *chData* is a pointer to a destination buffer for the data. *nCharsToRead* should be set to the maximum desired read size, which needs to be equal or less to the size of *chData*.

The *sAddress* parameter is filled with the address of the sender. It returns WINSOCK_ERROR if there was an error, WINSOCK_NOERROR otherwise. This Read will get the data from the next buffered packet and delete the packet from memory when finished. Thus if this function is called with a *nCharsToRead* that is smaller than the next packet, only part of the packet will be read and the rest will be lost.

Upon return, *nCharsToRead* is set to the actual number of characters read. If *nCharsToRead* returns 0, no data was read. If the function return value is WINSOCK_ERROR, there was a Windows Sockets error. Otherwise, the call was successful, even though no data may have been read.

SetMaxPacketSendSize
void SetMaxPacketSendSize(int size);
This function sets the maximum size of the send packet buffer.

Write
Form 1   int Write(char* data, int& charsToWrite, bool becomeOwnerOfData=true, bool copyData=true);
Simply calls the other *Write()* function with the latest address. Arguments and return values are the same.

Form 2   int Write(char* data, int& charsToWrite, TSocketAddress& outSocketAddress, bool becomeOwnerOfData=1,
bool copyData=1);
This function puts the data in the queue and attempts to write the first item in the queue. At the end of the function, an attempt to write the queue is made. If it fails, the data is sent later, after the system has given notification that it is ready. This function returns WINSOCK_ERROR or WINSOCK_NOERROR.

Protected data members

MaxPacketSendSize
static int MaxPacketSendSize;
512 is the absolute guaranteed minimum value. The *WSAData* structure has the actual value (greater than or equal to 512).

Protected member functions

DoReadNotification
DoReadNotification(const SOCKET& s, int error);
This function is called whenever the socket receives a read notification. This means that data on the port is ready to be read. This function doesn't do much with the error parameter. It simply doesn't do the read if there is an error value.

DoWriteNotification
DoWriteNotification(const SOCKET& s, int error);
This function is called whenever the socket receives a write notification.

TDataObject class   shellitm.h

TDataObject wraps the *IDataObject* interface (currently lightweight). A *TDataObject* is returned by *TShellItem::GetDataObject* Default, *TComRef<IDataObject>* and copy constructors supplied. *TComRef<IDataObject>* and *TDataObject* assignment operators are also supplied

Public constructors

Form 1   TDataObject(IDataObject* iface = 0);
Default constructor for *TDataObject*.

Form 2   TDataObject(const TComRef<IDataObject>& source);
TDataObject constructor to construct from *TComRef<IDataObject>*.

Form 3   TDataObject(const TDataObject& source);
TDataObject copy constructor.

Public member functions

operator=
Form 1   TDataObject& operator= (const TDataObject& source);
TDataObject assignment operator (from another *TDataObject*).

Form 2   TDataObject& operator= (const TComRef<IDataObject>& source);
TDataObject assignment operator (from *TComRef<IDataObject>*).

TDC class

TDC is the root class for GDI DC wrappers. DC objects can be created directly with *TDC* constructors, or via the constructors of specialized subclasses (such as *TWindowDC*, *TMemoryDC*, *TMetaFileDC*, *TDibDC*, and *TPrintDC*) to get specific behavior. DC objects can be constructed with an already existing and borrowed HDC handle or from scratch by supplying device driver information, as with *::CreateDC*. The class *TCreateDC* takes over much of the creation and deletion work from *TDC*.

TDC has four handles as protected data members: *OrgBrush*, *OrgPen*, *OrgFont*, and *OrgPalette*. These handles keep track of the stock GDI objects selected into each DC. As new GDI objects are selected with *SelectObject* or *SelectPalette*, these data members store the previous objects. The latter can be restored individually with *RestoreBrush*, *RestorePen*, and so on, or they can all be restored with *RestoreObjects*. When a *TDC* object is destroyed (via ~TDC::TDC), all the originally selected objects are restored. The data member *TDC::ShouldDelete* controls the deletion of the TDC object.

Public constructor and destructor

Constructor
TDC(HDC handle);
Creates a DC object "borrowing" the handle of an existing DC. The *Handle* data member is set to the given *handle* argument.

Destructor
virtual ~TDC();
Calls *RestoreObjects*.

See also   TCreatedDC, TDC::RestoreObjects, TDC::ShouldDelete

Public member functions

AngleArc
Form 1   bool AngleArc(int x, int y, uint32 radius, float startAngle, float sweepAngle);

Form 2   bool AngleArc(const TPoint& center, uint32 radius, float startAngle, float sweepAngle);
32-bit only. Draws a line segment and an arc on this DC using the currently selected pen object. The line is drawn from the current position to the beginning of the arc. The arc is that part of the circle (with the center at logical coordinates (x, y) and positive radius, *radius*) starting at *startAngle* and ending at (*startAngle* + *sweepAngle*). Both angles are measured in degrees, counterclockwise from the x-axis (the default arc direction). The arc might appear to be elliptical, depending on the current transformation and mapping mode. *AngleArc* returns true if the figure is drawn successfully; otherwise, it returns false. If successful, the current position is moved to the end point of the arc.

See also   TDC::Arc, TPoint

Arc

Form 1   bool Arc(int x1, int y1, int x2, int y2, int x3, int y3, int x4, int y4);

Form 2   bool Arc(const TRect& r, const TPoint& start, const TPoint& end);
Draws an elliptical arc on this DC using the currently selected pen object. The center of the arc is the center of the bounding rectangle, specified either by $(x1, y1)/(x2, y2)$ or by the rectangle r. The starting/ending points of the arc are specified either by $(x3, y3)/(x4, y4)$ or by the points *start* and *end*. All points are specified in logical coordinates. *Arc* returns true if the arc is drawn successfully; otherwise, it returns false. The current position is neither used nor altered by this call. The drawing direction default is counterclockwise.

See also   TDC::AngleArc, TPoint, TRect

BeginPath
bool BeginPath();
32-bit only. Opens a new path bracket for this DC and discards any previous paths from this DC. Once a path bracket is open, an application can start calling draw functions on this DC to define the points that lie within that path. The draw functions that define points in a path are the following *TDC* members: *AngleArc, Arc, Chord, CloseFigure, Ellipse, ExtTextOut, LineTo, MoveToEx, Pie, PolyBezier, PolyBezierTo, PolyDraw, Polygon, Polyline, PolylineTo, PolyPolygon, PolyPolyline, Rectangle, RoundRect,* and *TextOut.*

A path bracket can be closed by calling *TDC::EndPath.*

BeginPath returns true if the call is successful; otherwise, it returns false.

See also   TDC::FillPath, TDC::EndPath, TDC::PathToRegion, TDC::StrokePath, TDC::StrokeandFillPath, TDC::WidenPath

BitBlt

Form 1   bool BitBlt(int dstX, int dstY, int w, int h, const TDC& srcDC, int srcX, int srcY, uint32 rop=SRCCOPY);

Form 2   bool BitBlt(const TRect& dst, const TDC& srcDC, const TPoint& src, uint32 rop=SRCCOPY);
Performs a bit-block transfer from *srcDc* (the given source DC) to this DC (the destination DC). Color bits are copied from a source rectangle to a destination rectangle. The location of the source rectangle is specified either by its upper left-corner logical coordinates (*srcX, srcY*), or by the *TPoint* object, *src*. The destination rectangle can be specified either by its upper left-corner logical coordinates (*dstX, dstY*), width *w*, and height *h*, or by the *TRect* object, *dst*. The destination rectangle has the same width and height as the source. The *rop* argument specifies the raster operation used to combine the color data for each pixel. See *TDC::MaskBlt* for a detailed list of *rop* codes.

When recording an enhanced metafile, an error occurs if the source DC identifies the enhanced metafile DC.

See also   TPoint, TRect

Chord

Form 1   bool Chord(int x1, int y1, int x2, int y2, int x3, int y3, int x4, int y4);

Form 2   bool Chord(const TRect& r, const TPoint& start, const TPoint& end);
Draws and fills a chord (a region bounded by the intersection of an ellipse and a line segment) on this DC using the currently selected pen and brush objects. The ellipse is

specified by a bounding rectangle given either by $(x1, y1)/(x2, y2)$ or by the rectangle R. The starting/ending points of the chord are specified either by $(x3, y3)/(x4, y4)$ or by the points *Start* and *End*. *Chord* returns true if the call is successful; otherwise, it returns false. The current position is neither used nor altered by this call.

See also   TDC::Arc, TPoint, TRect

CloseFigure

bool CloseFigure();

32-bit only. Closes an open figure in this DC's open path bracket by drawing a line from the current position to the first point of the figure (usually the point specified by the most recent *TDC::MoveTo* call), and connecting the lines using the current join style for this DC. If you close a figure with *TDC::LineTo* instead of with *CloseFigure*, end caps (instead of a join) are used to create the corner. The call fails if there is no open path bracket on this DC. Any line or curve added to the path after a *CloseFigure* call starts a new figure. A figure in a path remains open until it is explicitly closed with *CloseFigure* even if its current position and start point happen to coincide.

CloseFigure returns true if the call is successful; otherwise, it returns false.

See also   TDC::BeginPath, TDC::EndPath

CreateDIBSection

HBITMAP CreateDIBSection(const BITMAPINFO& info, uint usage, void** bits, HANDLE section=0,
     uint32 offset=0);

Creates a fast DIB under Win32.

DPtoLP

bool DPtoLP(TPoint* points, int count = 1) const;

Converts each of the *count* points in the *points* array from device points to logical points. The conversion depends on this DC's current mapping mode and the settings of its window and viewport origins and extents. *DPtoLP* returns true if the call is successful; otherwise, it returns false.

See also   TDC::LPtoDP, TPoint

DrawFocusRect

Form 1   bool DrawFocusRect(int x1, int x2, int y1, int y2);

Form 2   bool DrawFocusRect(const TRect& rect);

Draws the given rectangle on this DC in the style used to indicate focus. Calling the function a second time with the same *rect* argument will remove the rectangle from the display. A rectangle drawn with *DrawFocusRect* cannot be scrolled. *DrawFocusRect* returns true if the call is successful; otherwise, it returns false.

See also   TRect

DrawIcon

Form 1   bool DrawIcon(int x, int y, const TIcon& icon);

Form 2   bool DrawIcon(const TPoint& point, const TIcon& icon);

Draws the given *icon* on this DC. The upper left corner of the drawn icon can be specified by x- and y-coordinates or by the *point* argument. *DrawIcon* returns true if the call is successful; otherwise, it returns false.

See also   TIcon

DrawText

virtual bool DrawText(const char far* string, int count, const TRect& r, uint16 format = 0);

Formats and draws in the given rectangle, *r*, up to *count* characters of the null-terminated *string* using the current font for this DC. If *count* is -1, the whole string is written. The rectangle must be specified in logical units. Formatting is controlled with the *format* argument, which can be various combinations of the following values:

Value	Meaning
DT_BOTTOM	Specifies bottom-justified text. This value must be combined (bitwise OR'd) with DT_SINGLELINE.
DT_CALCRECT	Determines the width and height of the rectangle. If there are multiple lines of text, *DrawText* uses the width of *r* (the rectangle argument) and extends the base of the rectangle to bound the last line of text. If there is only one line of text, *DrawText* uses a modified value for the right side of *r* so that it bounds the last character in the line. In both cases, *DrawText* returns the height of the formatted text but does not draw the text.
DT_CENTER	Centers text horizontally.
DT_EXPANDTABS	Expands tab characters. The default number of characters per tab is eight.
DT_EXTERNALLEADING	Includes the font external leading in line height. Normally, external leading is not included in the height of a line of text.
DT_LEFT	Aligns text flush-left.
DT_NOCLIP	Draws without clipping. *DrawText* is somewhat faster when DT_NOCLIP is used.
DT_NOPREFIX	Turns off processing of prefix characters. Normally, *DrawText* interprets the prefix character **&** as a directive to underscore the character that follows, and the prefix characters **&&** as a directive to print a single **&**. By specifying DT_NOPREFIX, this processing is turned off.
DT_RIGHT	Aligns text flush-right.
DT_SINGLELINE	Specifies single line only. Carriage returns and linefeeds do not break the line.
DT_TABSTOP	Sets tab stops. Bits 15-8 (the high-order byte of the low-order word) of the *format* argument are the number of characters for each tab. The default number of characters per tab is eight.
DT_TOP	Specifies top-justified text (single line only).
DT_VCENTER	Specifies vertically centered text (single line only).
DT_WORDBREAK	Specifies word breaking. Lines are automatically broken between words if a word would extend past the edge of the rectangle specified by *r*. A carriage return/line sequence will also break the line.

Note that the DT_CALCRECT, DT_EXTERNALLEADING, DT_INTERNAL, DT_NOCLIP, and DT_NOPREFIX values cannot be used with the DT_TABSTOP value.

DrawText uses this DC's currently selected font, text color, and background color to draw the text. Unless the DT_NOCLIP format is used, *DrawText* clips the text so that it does not appear outside the given rectangle. All formatting is assumed to have multiple lines unless the DT_SINGLELINE format is given.

If the selected font is too large for the specified rectangle, *DrawText* does not attempt to substitute a smaller font.

If successful, *DrawText* returns TRUE; otherwise, returns FALSE.

See also TDC::GrayString, TDC::TabbedTextOut, TDC::TextOut, TRect

Ellipse

Form 1 bool Ellipse(int x1, int y1, int x2, int y2);

Form 2 bool Ellipse(const TPoint& p1, const TPoint& p2);

Form 3 bool Ellipse(const TPoint& point, const TSize& size);

Form 4 bool Ellipse(const TRect& rect);

Draws and fills an ellipse on this DC using the currently selected pen and brush objects. The center of the ellipse is the center of the bounding rectangle specified either by $(x1, y1)/(x2, y2)$ or by the *rect* argument. *Ellipse* returns true if the call is successful; otherwise, it returns false. The current position is neither used nor altered by this call.

See also TDC::Arc, TPoint, TRect, TSize

EndPath

bool EndPath();

32-bit only. Closes the path bracket and selects the path it defines into this DC. Returns true if the call is successful; otherwise, returns false.

See also TDC::BeginPath, TDC::CloseFigure

EnumEnhMetaFile

int EnumEnhMetaFile(const TEnhMetaFilePict& metaFile, ENHMFENUMPROC callback, void* data, const TRect* rect) const;

Enumerates through the enhanced metafile records.

EnumFontFamilies

int EnumFontFamilies(const char far* family, FONTENUMPROC proc, void far* data) const;

Enumerates the fonts available to this DC in the font family specified by *family*. The given application-defined callback *proc* is called for each font in the family or until *proc* returns 0, and is defined as:

```
typedef int (CALLBACK* FONTENUMPROC)(CONST LOGFONT *, CONST TEXTMETRIC *, DWORD,
        LPARAM);
```

data lets you pass both application-specific data and font data to *proc*. If successful, the call returns the last value returned by *proc*.

See also TDC::EnumFonts, LOGFONT struct, TEXTMETRIC struct

EnumFonts

int EnumFonts(const char far* faceName, OLDFONTENUMPROC callback, void far* data) const;

Enumerates the fonts available on this DC for the given *faceName*. The font type, LOGFONT, and TEXTMETRIC data retrieved for each available font is passed to the user-defined *callback* function together with any optional, user-supplied data placed in the *data* buffer. The *callback* function can process this data in any way desired. Enumeration continues until there are no more fonts or until the *callback* function returns 0. If *faceName* is 0, *EnumFonts* randomly selects and enumerates one font of each available typeface. *EnumFonts* returns the last value returned by the *callback* function. Note that OLDFONTENUMPROC is defined as FONTENUMPROC for Win32 only.

FONTENUMPROC is a pointer to a user-defined function and has the following prototype:

```
int CALLBACK EnumFontsProc(LOGFONT *lplf, TEXTMETRIC *lptm, uint32 dwType,
                           LPARAM lpData);
```

where *dwType* specifies one of the following font types: DEVICE_FONTTYPE, RASTER_FONTTYPE, or TRUETYPE_FONTTYPE.

See also   TDC::EnumFontFamilies, LOGFONT struct, TEXTMETRIC struct

EnumMetaFile
int EnumMetaFile(const TMetaFilePict& metaFile, MFENUMPROC callback, void* data) const;
Enumerates the GDI calls within the given *metaFile*. Each such call is retrieved and passed to the given *callback* function, together with any client data from *data*, until all calls have been processed or a callback function returns 0. *MFENUMPROC* is defined as:

```
typedef int (CALLBACK* MFENUMPROC)(HDC, HANDLETABLE FAR*, METARECORD FAR*, int,
                                   LPARAM);
```

See also   TDC::PlayMetaFile, METARECORD struct

EnumObjects
int EnumObjects(uint objectType, GOBJENUMPROC proc, void far* data) const;
Enumerates the pen or brush objects available for this DC. The parameter *objectType* can be either OBJ_BRUSH or OBJ_PEN. For each pen or brush found, *proc*, a user-defined *callback* function, is called until there are no more objects found or the callback function returns 0. *proc* is defined as:

```
typedef int (CALLBACK* GOBJENUMPROC)(LPVOID, LPARAM);
```

Parameter *data* specifies an application-defined value that is passed to *proc*.

ExcludeClipRect
int ExcludeClipRect(const TRect& rect);
Creates a new clipping region for this DC. This new region consists of the current clipping region minus the given rectangle, *rect*. The return value indicates the new clipping region's type as follows:

Region	Meaning
COMPLEXREGION	Clipping region has overlapping borders.
ERROR	Invalid DC.
NULLREGION	Clipping region is empty.
SIMPLEREGION	Clipping region has no overlapping borders.

See also   TDC::GetClipBox, TRect

ExcludeUpdateRgn
int ExcludeUpdateRgn(HWND wnd);

Prevents drawing within invalid areas of a window by excluding an updated region of this DC's window from its clipping region. The return value indicates the resulting clipping region's type as follows:

Region	Meaning
COMPLEXREGION	Clipping region has overlapping borders.
ERROR	Invalid DC.
NULLREGION	Clipping region is empty.
SIMPLEREGION	Clipping region has no overlapping borders.

ExtFloodFill
bool ExtFloodFill(const TPoint& point, TColor color, uint16 fillType);
Fills an area on this DC starting at *point* and using the currently selected brush object. The *color* argument specifies the color of the boundary or of the region to be filled. The *fillType* argument specifies the type of fill, as follows:

FLOODFILLBORDER   The fill region is bounded by the given *color*. This style coincides with the filling method used by *FloodFill*.

FLOODFILLSURFACE   The fill region is defined by the given *color*. Filling continues outward in all directions as long as this color is encountered. Use this style when filling regions with multicolored borders.

Not every device supports *ExtFloodFill*, so applications should test first with *TDC::GetDeviceCaps*.

ExtFloodFill returns true if the call is successful; otherwise, it returns false.

See also   TDC::FloodFill, TDC::GetDeviceCaps, TColor, TPoint

ExtTextOut
Form 1   virtual bool ExtTextOut(int x, int y, uint16 options, const TRect* r, const char far* string, int count, const int far* dx = 0);

Form 2   bool ExtTextOut(const TPoint& p, uint16 options, const TRect* r, const char far* string, int count, const int far* dx = 0);
Draws up to *count* characters of the given null-terminated *string* in the current font on this DC. If *count* is -1, the whole string is written.

An optional rectangle *r* can be specified for clipping, opaquing, or both, as determined by the *options* value. If *options* is set to ETO_CLIPPED, the rectangle is used for clipping the drawn text. If *options* is set to ETO_OPAQUE, the current background color is used to fill the rectangle. Both options can be used if ETO_CLIPPED is OR'd with ETO_OPAQUE.

The (*x*, *y*) or *p* arguments specify the logical coordinates of the reference point that is used to align the first character. The current text-alignment mode can be inspected with *TDC::GetTextAlign* and changed with *TDC::SetTextAlign*. By default, the current position is neither used nor altered by *ExtTextOut*. However, if the align mode is set to TA_UPDATECP, *ExtTextOut* ignores the reference point argument(s) and uses or updates the current position as the reference point.

The *dx* argument is an optional array of values used to set the distances between the origins (upper left corners) of adjacent character cells. For example, *dx[i]* represents the number of logical units separating the origins of character cells *i* and *i+1*. If *dx* is 0, *ExtTextOut* uses the default inter-character spacings.

ExtTextOut returns true if the call is successful; otherwise, it returns false.

See also   TDC::TextOut, TDC::GetTextAlign, TDC::TabbedTextOut, TPoint, TRect

FillPath
bool FillPath();
32-bit only. Closes any open figures in the current path of this DC and fills the path's interior using the current brush and polygon fill mode. After filling the interior, *FillPath* discards the path from this DC.

FillPath returns true if the call is successful; otherwise, it returns false.

See also   TDC::BeginPath, TDC::CloseFigure, TDC::StrokePath, TDC::StrokeAndFillPath, TDC::SetPolyFillMode

FillRect
Form 1   bool FillRect(int x1, int y1, int x2, int y2, const TBrush& brush);

Form 2   bool FillRect(const TRect& rect, const TBrush& brush);
Fills the given rectangle on this DC using the specified brush. The fill covers the left and top borders but excludes the right and bottom borders. *FillRect* returns true if the call is successful; otherwise, it returns false.

See also   TBrush, TRect

FillRgn
bool FillRgn(const TRegion& region, const TBrush& brush);
Fills the given *region* on this DC using the specified *brush*. *FillRgn* returns true if the call is successful; otherwise, it returns false.

See also   TDC::InvertRgn, TDC::PaintRgn, TBrush, TRegion

FlattenPath
bool FlattenPath();
32-bit only. Transforms any curves in the currently selected path of this DC. All such curves are changed to sequences of linear segments. Returns true if the call is successful; otherwise, returns false.

See also   TDC::WidenPath, TDC::BeginPath

FloodFill
bool FloodFill(const TPoint& point, TColor color);
Fills an area on this DC starting at *point* and using the currently selected brush object. The *color* argument specifies the color of the boundary or of the area to be filled. Returns true if the call is successful; otherwise, returns false. *FloodFill* is maintained in the WIN32 API for compatibility with earlier APIs. New WIN32 applications should use *TDC::ExtFloodFill*.

See also   TDC::ExtFloodFill, TColor, TPoint

FrameRect

Form 1   bool FrameRect(int x1, int x2, int y1, int y2, const TBrush& brush);

Form 2   bool FrameRect(const TRect& rect, const TBrush& brush);
Draws a border on this DC around the given rectangle, *rect*, using the given brush, *brush*. The height and width of the border is one logical unit. Returns true if the call is successful; otherwise, it returns false.

See also   TBrush, TRect

FrameRgn

bool FrameRgn(const TRegion& region, const TBrush& brush, const TPoint& p);
Draws a border on this DC around the given region, *region*, using the given brush, *brush*. The width and height of the border is specified by the *p* argument. Returns true if the call is successful; otherwise, returns false.

See also   TBrush, TRegion

GetAspectRatioFilter

bool GetAspectRatioFilter(TSize& size) const;
Retrieves the setting of the current aspect-ratio filter for this DC.

See also   TSize

GetAttributeHDC

virtual HDC GetAttributeHDC() const;
Returns the attributes of the DC object.

See also   TPrintPreviewDC::GetAttributeHDC

GetBkColor

TColor GetBkColor() const;
Returns the current background color of this DC.

See also   TDC::SetBkColor, TColor

GetBkMode

int GetBkMode() const;
Returns the background mode of this DC, either OPAQUE or TRANSPARENT.

See also   TDC::SetBkMode

GetBoundsRect

bool GetBoundsRect(TRect& bounds, uint16 flags) const;
Reports in *bounds* the current accumulated bounding rectangle of this DC or of the Windows manager, depending on the value of *flags*. Returns true if the call is successful; otherwise, returns false.

The *flags* argument can be DCB_RESET or DCB_WINDOWMGR or both. The *flags* value work as follows:

DCB_RESET   Forces the bounding rectangle to be cleared after being set in bounds.

DCB_WINDOWMGR   Reports the Windows current bounding rectangle rather than that of this DC.

There are two bounding-rectangle accumulations, one for Windows and one for the application. *GetBoundsRect* returns screen coordinates for the Windows bounds, and logical units for the application bounds. The Windows accumulated bounds can be queried by an application but not altered. The application can both query and alter the DC's accumulated bounds.

See also   TDC::SetBoundsRect, TRect

GetBrushOrg
bool GetBrushOrg(TPoint& point) const;
Places in *point* the current brush origin of this DC. Returns true if successful; otherwise, returns false.

See also   TPoint

GetCharABCWidths
bool GetCharABCWidths(uint firstChar, uint lastChar, ABC* abc);
Retrieves the widths of consecutive characters in the range *firstChar* to *lastChar* from the current TrueType font of this DC. The widths are reported in the array *abc* of *ABC* structures. Returns true if the call is successful; otherwise, returns false.

See also   TDC::GetCharWidth, ABC struct

GetCharWidth
bool GetCharWidth(uint firstChar, uint lastChar, int* buffer);
Retrieves the widths in logical units for a consecutive sequence of characters in the current font for this DC. The sequence is specified by the inclusive range, *firstChar* to *lastChar*, and the widths are copied to the given *buffer*. If a character in the range is not represented in the current font, the width of the default character is assigned. Returns true if the call is successful; otherwise, returns false.

See also   TDC::GetCharABCWidths

GetClipBox
Form 1   int GetClipBox(TRect& rect) const;

Form 2   TRect GetClipBox() const;
Places the current clip box size of this DC in *rect*. The clip box is defined as the smallest rectangle bounding the current clipping boundary. The return value indicates the clipping region's type as follows:

Region	Meaning
COMPLEXREGION	Clipping region has overlapping borders.
ERROR	Invalid DC.

Region	Meaning
NULLREGION	Clipping region is empty.
SIMPLEREGION	Clipping region has no overlapping borders.

See also   TDC::ExcludeClipRect, TRect

GetClipRgn
bool GetClipRgn(TRegion& region) const;
Retrieves this DC's current clip-region and, if successful, places a copy of it in the *region* argument. You can alter this copy without affecting the current clip-region. Returns true if the call is successful; otherwise, returns false.

See also   TRegion

GetCurrentObject
HANDLE GetCurrentObject(uint objectType) const;
Returns a handle to the currently selected object of the given *objectType* associated with this DC. Returns 0 if the call fails. *objectType* can be OBJ_PEN, OBJ_BRUSH, OBJ_PAL, OBJ_FONT, or OBJ_BITMAP.

GetCurrentPosition
bool GetCurrentPosition(TPoint& point) const;
Reports in *point* the logical coordinates of this DC's current position. Returns true if the call is successful; otherwise, returns false.

See also   TPoint

GetDCOrg
bool GetDCOrg(TPoint& point) const;
Obtains the final translation origin for this device context and places the value in *point*. This value specifies the offset used to translate device coordinates to client coordinates for points in an application window. Returns true if the call is successful; otherwise, returns false.

See also   TPoint

GetDeviceCaps
virtual int GetDeviceCaps(int index) const;
Used under WIN3.1 or later, *GetDeviceCaps* returns capability information about this DC. The *index* argument specifies the type of information required.

GetDIBits
Form 1   bool GetDIBits(const TBitmap& bitmap, uint16 startScan, uint16 numScans, void HUGE* bits,
        const BITMAPINFO far& info, uint16 usage);

Form 2   bool GetDIBits(const TBitmap& bitmap, TDib& dib);
The first version retrieves some or all of the bits from the given *bitmap* on this DC and copies them to the *bits* buffer using the DIB (device-independent bitmap) format specified by the BITMAPINFO argument, *info*. *numScan* scanlines of the bitmap are

retrieved, starting at scan line *startScan*. The *usage* argument determines the format of the *bmiColors* member of the BITMAPINFO structure, according to the following table:

Value	Meaning
DIB_PAL_COLORS	The color table is an array of 16-bit indexes into the current logical palette.
DIB_RGB_COLORS	The color table contains literal RGB values.
DIB_PAL_INDICES	There is no color table for this bitmap. The DIB bits consist of indexes into the system palette. No color translation occurs. Only the BITMAPINFOHEADER portion of BITMAPINFO is filled in.

In the second version of *GetDIBits*, the bits are retrieved from *bitmap* and placed in the *dib.Bits* data member of the given *TDib* argument. The BITMAPINFO argument is supplied from *dib.info*.

GetDIBits returns true if the call is successful; otherwise, it returns false.

See also   TDC::SetDIBits, TBitmap, TDib, BITMAPINFO struct

GetFontData
uint32 GetFontData(uint32 table, uint32 offset, void* buffer, long data);

Retrieves font-metric information from a scalable TrueType font file (specified by *table* and starting at *offset* into this table) and places it in the given *buffer*. *data* specifies the size in bytes of the data to be retrieved. If the call is successful, it returns the number of bytes set in *buffer*; otherwise, -1 is returned.

GetGlyphOutline
uint32 GetGlyphOutline (uint chr, uint format, GLYPHMETRICS far& gm, uint32 buffSize, voidfar* buffer, const MAT2 far& mat2);

Retrieves TrueType metric and other data for the given character, *chr*, on this DC and places it in *gm* and *buffer*. The *format* argument specifies the format of the retrieved data as indicated in the following table. (A value of 0 simply fills in the GLYPHMETRICS structure but does not return glyph-outline data.)

Value	Meaning
1	Retrieves the glyph bitmap.
2	Retrieves the curve data points in the rasterizer's native format and uses the font's design units. With this value of format, the *mat2* transformation argument is ignored.

The *gm* argument specifies the GLYPHMETRICS structure that describes the placement of the glyph in the character cell. *buffSize* specifies the size of buffer that receives data about the outline character. If either *buffSize* or *buffer* is 0, *GetGlyphOutline* returns the required buffer size. Applications can rotate characters retrieved in bitmap format (format = 1) by specifying a 2 x 2 transformation matrix via the *mat2* argument.

GetGlyphOutline returns a positive number if the call is successful; otherwise, it returns GDI_ERROR.

See also   TDC::GetOutlineTextMetrics, GLYPHMETRICS struct

GetHDC
HDC GetHDC() const;

Returns a handle to the DC.

GetKerningPairs

int GetKerningPairs(int pairs, KERNINGPAIR far* krnPair);

Retrieves kerning pairs for the current font of this DC up to the number specified in *pairs* and copies them into the *krnPair* array of KERNINGPAIR structures. If successful, the function returns the actual number of pairs retrieved. If the font has more than *pairs* kerning pairs, the call fails and returns 0. The *krnPair* array must allow for at least *pairs* KERNINGPAIR structures. If *krnPair* is set to 0, *GetKerningPairs* returns the total number of kerning pairs for the current font.

See also   KERNINGPAIR struct

GetMapMode

int GetMapMode() const;

If successful, returns the current window mapping mode of this DC; otherwise, returns 0. The mapping mode defines how logical coordinates are mapped to device coordinates. It also controls the orientation of the device's x- and y-axes. The mode values are shown in the following table:

Value	Meaning
MM_ANISOTROPIC	Logical units are mapped to arbitrary units with arbitrarily scaled axes. *SetWindowExtEx* and *SetViewportExtEx* must be used to specify the desired units, orientation, and scaling.
MM_HIENGLISH	Each logical unit is mapped to 0.001 inch. Positive x is to the right; positive y is at the top.
MM_HIMETRIC	Each logical unit is mapped to 0.01 millimeter. Positive x is to the right; positive y is at the top.
MM_ISOTROPIC	Logical units are mapped to arbitrary units with equally scaled axes; that is, one unit along the x-axis is equal to one unit along the y-axis. *SetWindowExtEx* and *SetViewportExtEx* must be used to specify the desired units and the orientation of the axes. GDI makes adjustments as necessary to ensure that the x and y units remain the same size (e.g., if you set the window extent, the viewport is adjusted to keep the units isotropic).
MM_LOENGLISH	Each logical unit is mapped to 0.01 inch. Positive x is to the right; positive y is at the top.
MM_LOMETRIC	Each logical unit is mapped to 0.1 millimeter. Positive x is to the right; positive y is at the top.
MM_TEXT	Each logical unit is mapped to one device pixel. Positive x is to the right; positive y is at the bottom.
MM_TWIPS	Each logical unit is mapped to one twentieth of a printer's point (1/1440 inch). Positive x is to the right; positive y is at the top.

See also   TDC::SetMapMode

GetNearestColor

TColor GetNearestColor(TColor Color) const;

Returns the color nearest to the given *Color* argument for the current palette of this DC.

See also   TColor

GetOutlineTextMetrics

Form 1   uint32 GetOutlineTextMetrics(uint data, OUTLINETEXTMETRIC far& otm);

Form 2   uint16 GetOutlineTextMetrics(uint data, OUTLINETEXTMETRIC far& otm);

Retrieves metric information for TrueType fonts on this DC and copies it to the given array of OUTLINETEXTMETRIC structures, *otm*. This structure contains a TEXTMETRIC and several other metric members, as well as four string-pointer members for holding family, face, style, and full font names. Since memory must be allocated for these variable-length strings in addition to the font metric data, you must pass (with the *data* argument) the total number of bytes required for the retrieved data. If *GetOutlineTextMetrics* is called with *otm* = 0, the function returns the total buffer size required. You can then assign this value to *data* in subsequent calls.

Returns nonzero if the call is successful; otherwise, returns 0.

See also   TDC::GetTextMetrics, OUTLINETEXTMETRIC struct, TEXTMETRIC struct

GetPixel
Form 1   TColor GetPixel(int x, int y) const;

Form 2   TColor GetPixel(const TPoint& point) const;
Returns the color of the pixel at the given location.

See also   TDC::SetPixel, TPoint

GetPolyFillMode
int GetPolyFillMode() const;
Returns the current polygon-filling mode for this DC, either ALTERNATE or WINDING.

See also   TDC::SetPolyFillMode

GetROP2()
int GetROP2() const;
Returns the current drawing (raster operation) mode of this DC.

See also   TDC::SetROP2

GetStretchBltMode
int GetStretchBltMode() const;
Returns the current stretching mode for this DC: BLACKONWHITE, COLORONCOLOR, or WHITEONBLACK. The stretching mode determines how bitmaps are stretched or compressed by the *StretchBlt* function.

See also   TDC::SetStretchBltMode, TDC::StretchBlt

GetSystemPaletteEntries
uint GetSystemPaletteEntries(int start, int num, PALETTEENTRY far* entries) const;
Retrieves a range of up to *num* palette entries, starting at *start*, from the system palette to the *entries* array of PALETTEENTRY structures. Returns the actual number of entries transferred.

See also   PALETTEENTRY struct

GetSystemPaletteUse
uint GetSystemPaletteUse() const;
Determines whether this DC has access to the full system palette. Returns SYSPAL_NOSTATIC or SYSPAL_STATIC.

See also   TDC::SetSystemPaletteUse

GetTabbedTextExtent
Form 1   bool GetTabbedTextExtent(const char far* string, int stringLen, int numPositions, const int far* positions,
            TSize& size) const;

Form 2   TSize GetTabbedTextExtent(const char far* string, int stringLen, int numPositions, const int far* positions) const;
Computes the extent (width and height) in logical units of the text line consisting of *stringLen* characters from the null-terminated *string*. The extent is calculated from the metrics of the current font or this DC, but ignores the current clipping region. In the first version of *GetTabbedTextExtent*, the extent is returned in *size*; in the second version, the extent is the returned *TSize* object. Width is *size.x* and width is *size.y*.

The width calculation includes the spaces implied by any tab codes in the string. Such tab codes are interpreted using the *numPositions* and *positions* arguments. The *positions* array specifies *numPositions* tab stops given in device units. The tab stops must have strictly increasing values in the array. If *numPositions* and *positions* are both 0, tabs are expanded to eight times the average character width. If *numPositions* is 1, all tab stops are taken to be *positions*[0] apart.

If kerning is being applied, the sum of the extents of the characters in a string might not equal the extent of the string.

See also   TDC::TabbedTextOut, TDC::GetTextExtent, TSize

GetTextAlign
uint GetTextAlign() const;
If successful, returns the current text-alignment flags for this DC; otherwise, returns the value GDI_ERROR. The text-alignment flags determine how *TDC::TextOut* and *TDC::ExtTextOut* align text strings in relation to the first character's screen position. *GetTextAlign* returns certain combinations of the flags listed in the following table:

Value	Meaning
TA_BASELINE	The reference point will be on the baseline of the text.
TA_BOTTOM	The reference point will be on the bottom edge of the bounding rectangle.
TA_TOP	The reference point will be on the top edge of the bounding rectangle.
TA_CENTER	The reference point will be aligned horizontally with the center of the bounding rectangle.
TA_LEFT	The reference point will be on the left edge of the bounding rectangle.
TA_RIGHT	The reference point will be on the right edge of the bounding rectangle.
TA_NOUPDATECP	The current position is not updated after each text output call.
TA_UPDATECP	The current position is updated after each text output call.
	When the current font has a vertical default baseline (as with Kanji) the following values replace TA_BASELINE and TA_CENTER:
	VTA_BASELINE: The reference point will be on the baseline of the text.
	VTA_CENTER: The reference point will be aligned vertically with the center of the bounding rectangle.

The text-alignment flags are not necessarily single bit-flags and might be equal to 0. The flags must be examined in groups of the following related flags:

- TA_LEFT, TA_RIGHT, and TA_CENTER
- TA_BOTTOM, TA_TOP, and TA_BASELINE
- TA_NOUPDATECP and TA_UPDATECP

If the current font has a vertical default baseline (as with Kanji), these are groups of related flags:

- TA_LEFT, TA_RIGHT, and VTA_BASELINE
- TA_BOTTOM, TA_TOP, and VTA_CENTER
- TA_NOUPDATECP and TA_UPDATECP

To verify that a particular flag is set in the return value of this function, the application must perform the following steps:

1 Apply the bitwise OR operator to the flag and its related flags.

2 Apply the bitwise AND operator to the result and the return value.

3 Test for the equality of this result and the flag.

The following example shows a method for determining which horizontal alignment flag is set:

```
switch ((TA_LEFT | TA_RIGHT | TA_CENTER) & dc.GetTextAlign()) {
  case TA_LEFT:
  ...
  case TA_RIGHT:
  ...
  case TA_CENTER:
  ...
}
```

See also   TDC::SetTextAlign, TDC::TextOut, TDC::ExtTextOut

GetTextCharacterExtra
int GetTextCharacterExtra() const;
If successful, returns the current intercharacter spacing, in logical units, for this DC; otherwise, returns INVALID_WIDTH.

See also   TDC::SetTextCharacterExtra

GetTextColor
TColor GetTextColor() const;
Returns the current text color of this DC. The text color determines the color displayed by *TDC::TextOut* and *TDC::ExtTextOut*.

See also   TDC::SetTextColor, TDC::TextOut, TDC::ExtTextOut, TColor

GetTextExtent
Form 1   bool GetTextExtent(const char far* string, int stringLen, TSize& size);

Form 2   TSize GetTextExtent(const char far* string, int stringLen);
Computes the extent (width and height) in logical units of the text line consisting of *stringLen* characters from the null-terminated *string*. The extent is calculated from the metrics of the current font or this DC, but ignores the current clipping region. In the first

version of *GetTextExtent* the extent is returned in *size*; in the second version, the extent is the returned *TSize* object. Width is *size.cx* and height is *size.cy*.

If kerning is being applied, the sum of the extents of the characters in a string might not equal the extent of the string.

See also   TSize

GetTextFace
int GetTextFace(int count, char far* facename) const;
Retrieves the typeface name for the current font on this DC. Up to *count* characters of this name are copied to *facename*. If successful, *GetTextFace* returns the number of characters actually copied; otherwise, it returns 0.

See also   TDC::GetTextAlign, TDC::GetTextMetrics

GetTextMetrics
bool GetTextMetrics(TEXTMETRIC far& metrics) const;
Fills the *metrics* structure with metrics data for the current font on this DC. Returns true if the call is successful; otherwise, returns false.

See also   TEXTMETRIC struct

GetViewportExt
Form 1   bool GetViewportExt(TSize& extent) const;

Form 2   TSize GetViewportExt() const;
The first version retrieves this DC's current viewport's x- and y-extents (in device units) and places the values in *extent*. This version returns true if the call is successful; otherwise, it returns false. The second version returns only these x- and y-extents.

The *extent* value determines the amount of stretching or compression needed in the logical coordinate system to fit the device coordinate system. *extent* also determines the relative orientation of the two coordinate systems.

See also   TDC::SetViewportExt, TSize

GetViewportOrg
Form 1   bool GetViewportOrg(TPoint& point) const;

Form 2   TPoint GetViewportOrg() const;
The first version sets in the *point* argument the x- and y-extents (in device-units) of this DC's viewport. It returns true if the call is successful; otherwise, it returns false. The second version returns the x- and y-extents (in device-units) of this DC's viewport.

See also   TDC::SetViewportOrg, TDC::OffsetViewportOrg, TPoint

GetWindowExt
Form 1   bool GetWindowExt(TSize& extent) const;

Form 2   TSize GetWindowExt() const;
Retrieves this DC's window current x- and y-extents (in device units). The first version places the values in *extent* and returns true if the call is successful; otherwise, it returns false. The second version returns the current extent values. The *extent* value determines the amount of stretching or compression needed in the logical coordinate system to fit

the device coordinate system. *extent* also determines the relative orientation of the two coordinate systems.

See also   TDC::SetWindowExt, TSize

GetWindowOrg
Form 1   bool GetWindowOrg(TPoint& point) const;

Form 2   TPoint GetWindowOrg() const;
Places in *point* the x- and y-coordinates of the origin of the window associated with this DC. Returns true if the call is successful; otherwise, returns false.

See also   TDC::SetWindowOrg, TDC::OffsetWindowOrg, TPoint

GrayString
virtual bool GrayString(const TBrush& brush, GRAYSTRINGPROC outputFunc, const char far* string,
    int count, const TRect& r);
Draws in the given rectangle (*r*) up to *count* characters of gray text from *string* using the given brush, *brush,* and the current font for this DC. If *count* is -1 and *string* is null-terminated, the whole string is written. The rectangle must be specified in logical units. If *brush* is 0, the text is grayed with the same brush used to draw window text on this DC. Gray text is primarily used to indicate disabled commands and menu items.

GrayString writes the selected text to a memory bitmap, grays the bitmap, then displays the result. The graying is performed regardless of the current brush and background color.

The *outputFunc* pointer to a function can specify the procedure instance of an application-supplied drawing function and is defined as

```
typedef BOOL (CALLBACK* GRAYSTRINGPROC)(HDC, LPARAM, int);
```

If *outputFunc* is 0, *GrayString* uses *TextOut* and *string* is assumed to be a normal, null-terminated character string. If *string* cannot be handled by *TextOut* (for example, the string is stored as a bitmap), you must provide a suitable drawing function via *outputFunc.*

If the device supports a solid gray color, it is possible to draw gray strings directly without using *GrayString.* Call *GetSysColor* to find the color value; for example, *G* of COLOR_GRAYTEXT. If *G* is nonzero (non-black), you can set the text color with *SetTextColor(G)* and then use any convenient text-drawing function.

GrayString returns true if the call is successful; otherwise, it returns false. Failure can result if *TextOut* or *outputFunc* return false, or if there is insufficient memory to create the bitmap.

See also   TDC::TextOut, TBrush, TRect

operator HDC()
operator HDC() const{return Handle;}
Typecasting operator. Converts a pointer to type HDC (the data type representing the handle to a DC).

IntersectClipRect

int IntersectClipRect(const TRect& rect);

Creates a new clipping region for this DC's window by forming the intersection of the current region with the rectangle specified by *rect*. The return value indicates the resulting clipping region's type as follows:

Region	Meaning
COMPLEXREGION	Clipping region has overlapping borders.
ERROR	Invalid DC.
NULLREGION	Clipping region is empty.
SIMPLEREGION	Clipping region has no overlapping borders.

See also   TDC::GetClipBox, TRect

InvertRect

Form 1   bool InvertRect(int x1, int x2, int y1, int y2);

Form 2   bool InvertRect(const TRect& rect);

Inverts the given rectangle, *rect*, on this DC. On monochrome displays, black-and-white pixels are interchanged. On color displays, inversion depends on how the colors are generated for particular displays. Calling *InvertRect* an even number of times restores the original colors. *InvertRect* returns true if the call is successful; otherwise, it returns false.

See also   TRect

InvertRgn

bool InvertRgn(const TRegion& region);

Inverts the given *region*, on this DC. On monochrome displays, black-and-white pixels are interchanged. On color displays, inversion depends on how the colors are generated for particular displays. Calling *InvertRegion* an even number (n>=2) of times restores the original colors. Returns true if the call is successful; otherwise, it returns false.

See also   TDC::PaintRgn, TDC::FillRgn, TRegion

LineTo

Form 1   bool LineTo(int x, int y);

Form 2   bool LineTo(const TPoint& point);

Draws a line on this DC using the current pen object. The line is drawn from the current position up to, but not including, the given end point, which is specified by (x, y) or by *point*. If the call is successful, *LineTo* returns true and the current point is reset to *point*; otherwise, it returns false.

See also   TPoint

LPtoDP

bool LPtoDP(TPoint* points, int count = 1) const;

Converts each of the *count* points in the *points* array from logical points to device points. The conversion depends on this DC's current mapping mode and the settings of its window and viewport origins and extents. Returns true if the call is successful; otherwise, it returns false.

See also   TDC::DPtoLP, TPoint

MaskBlt

bool MaskBlt(const TRect& dst, const TDC& srcDC, const TPoint& src, const TBitmap& maskBm,
    const TPoint& maskPos, uint32 rop=SRCCOPY);

Copies a bitmap from the given source DC to this DC. *MaskBlt* combines the color data from source and destination bitmaps using the given mask and raster operation. The *srcDC* argument specifies the DC from which the source bitmap will be copied. The destination bitmap is given by the rectangle, *dst*. The source bitmap has the same width and height as *dst*. The *src* argument specifies the logical coordinates of the upper left corner of the source bitmap. The *maskBm* argument specifies a monochrome mask bitmap. An error will occur if *maskBm* is not monochrome. The *maskPos* argument gives the upper left corner coordinates of the mask. The raster-operation code, *rop*, specifies how the source, mask, and destination bitmaps combine to produce the new destination bitmap. The raster-operation codes are as follows:

Value of rop	Meaning
BLACKNESS	Fill *dst* with index-0 color of physical palette (default is black).
DSTINVERT	Invert *dst*.
MERGECOPY	Merge the colors of source with mask with Boolean AND.
MERGEPAINT	Merge the colors of inverted-source with the colors of *dst* using Boolean OR.
NOTSRCCOPY	Copy inverted-source to *dst*.
NOTSRCERASE	Combine the colors of source and *dst* using Boolean OR, then invert result.
PATCOPY	Copy mask to *dst*.
PATINVERT	Combine the colors of mask with the colors of *dst* using Boolean XOR.
PATPAINT	Combine the colors of mask with the colors of inverted-source using Boolean OR, then combine the result with the colors of *dst* using Boolean OR.
SRCAND	Combine the colors of source and *dst* using the Boolean AND.
SRCCOPY	Copy source directly to *dst*.
SRCERASE	Combine the inverted colors of *dst* with the colors of source using Boolean AND.
SRCPAINT	Combine the colors of source and *dst* using Boolean OR.
WHITENESS	Fill *dst* with index-1 color of physical palette (default is white).

If *rop* indicates an operation that excludes the source bitmap, the *srcDC* argument must be 0. A value of 1 in the mask indicates that the destination and source pixel colors should be combined using the high-order word of *rop*. A value of 0 in the mask indicates that the destination and source pixel colors should be combined using the low-order word of *rop*. If the mask rectangle is smaller than *dst*, the mask pattern will be suitably duplicated.

When recording an enhanced metafile, an error occurs if the source DC identifies the enhanced metafile DC.

If a rotation or shear transformation is in effect for the source DC when *MaskBlt* is called, an error occurs. Other transformations are allowed. If necessary, *MaskBlt* will adjust the destination and mask color formats to match that of the source bitmaps. Before using *MaskBlt*, an application should call *GetDeviceCaps* to determine if the source and destination DCs support *MaskBlt*.

MaskBlt returns true if the call is successful; otherwise, it returns false.

See also   TDC::BitBlt, TDC::PlgBlt, TDC::GetDeviceCaps, TBitmap, TPoint, TRect

ModifyWorldTransform
bool ModifyWorldTransform(XFORM far& xform, uint32 mode);

Changes the current world transformation for this DC using the given *xform* and *mode* arguments. *mode* determines how the given XFORM structure is applied, as listed below:

Value	Meaning
MWT_IDENTITY	Resets the current world transformation using the identity matrix. If this mode is specified, the XFORM structure pointed to by *lpXform* is ignored.
MWT_LEFTMULTIPLY	Multiplies the current transformation by the data in the XFORM structure. (The data in the XFORM structure becomes the left multiplicand, and the data for the current transformation becomes the right multiplicand.)
MWT_RIGHTMULTIPLY	Multiplies the current transformation by the data in the XFORM structure. (The data in the XFORM structure becomes the right multiplicand, and the data for the current transformation becomes the left multiplicand.) *ModifyWorldTransform* returns true if the call is successful; otherwise, it returns false.

See also   TDC::SetWorldTransform, XFORM struct

MoveTo
Form 1   bool MoveTo(int x, int y);

Form 2   bool MoveTo(const TPoint& point);

Form 3   bool MoveTo(const TPoint& point, TPoint& oldPoint);

Moves the current position of this DC to the given x- and y-coordinates or to the given *point*. The third version sets the previous current position in *oldPoint*. Returns true if the call is successful; otherwise, returns false.

See also   TPoint

OffsetClipRgn
int OffsetClipRgn(const TPoint& delta);

Moves the clipping region of this DC by the x- and y-offsets specified in *delta*. The return value indicates the resulting clipping region's type as follows:

Region	Meaning
COMPLEXREGION	Clipping region has overlapping borders.
ERROR	Invalid DC.
NULLREGION	Clipping region is empty.
SIMPLEREGION	Clipping region has no overlapping borders.

See also   TDC::GetClipBox, TPoint

OffsetViewportOrg
virtual bool OffsetViewportOrg(const TPoint& delta, TPoint* oldOrg = 0);

Modifies this DC's viewport origin relative to the current values. The *delta* x- and y-components are added to the previous origin and the resulting point becomes the new viewport origin. The previous origin is saved in *oldOrg*. Returns true if the call is successful; otherwise, returns false.

See also   TDC::SetViewportOrg, TDC::GetViewportOrg, TPoint

OffsetWindowOrg
bool OffsetWindowOrg(const TPoint& delta, TPoint* oldOrg = 0);
Modifies this DC's window origin relative to the current values. The *delta* x- and y-components are added to the previous origin and the resulting point becomes the new window origin. The previous origin is saved in *oldOrg*. Returns true if the call is successful; otherwise, returns false.

See also   TDC::GetWindowOrg, TDC::SetWindowOrg, TPoint

OWLFastWindowFrame
void OWLFastWindowFrame(TBrush& brush, TRect& rect, int xWidth, int yWidth)
Draws a frame of the specified size and thickness with the given brush. The old brush is restored after completion.

See also   TBrush, TRect

PaintRgn
bool PaintRgn(const TRegion& region);
Paints (fills) the given *region* on this DC using the currently selected brush. Returns true if the call is successful; otherwise, returns, false.

See also   TDC::FillRgn, TDC::SelectObject, TRegion

PatBlt
Form 1   bool PatBlt(int x, int y, int w, int h, uint32 rop=PATCOPY);

Form 2   bool PatBlt(const TRect& dst, uint32 rop=PATCOPY);
Paints the given rectangle using the currently selected brush for this DC. The rectangle can be specified by its upper left coordinates (x, y), width w, and height h, or by a single *TRect* argument. The raster-operation code, *rop*, determines how the brush and surface color(s) are combined, as explained in the following table:

Value	Meaning
PATCOPY	Copies pattern to destination bitmap.
PATINVERT	Combines destination bitmap with pattern using the Boolean OR operator.
DSTINVERT	Inverts the destination bitmap.
BLACKNESS	Turns all output to binary 0s.
WHITENESS	Turns all output to binary 1s.

The allowed values of *rop* for this function are a limited subset of the full 256 ternary raster-operation codes; in particular, an operation code that refers to a source cannot be used with *PatBlt*.

Not all devices support the *PatBlt* function, so applications should call *TDC::GetDeviceCaps* to check the features supported by this DC.

PatBlt returns true if the call is successful; otherwise, returns false.

See also   TDC::GetDeviceCaps, TRect

PathToRegion
HRGN PathToRegion();
If successful, returns a region created from the closed path in this DC; otherwise, returns 0.

Pie
Form 1   bool Pie(int x1, int y1, int x2, int y2, int x3, int y3, int x4, int y4);

Form 2   bool Pie(const TRect& rect, const TPoint& start, const TPoint& end);
Using the currently selected pen and brush objects, draws and fills a pie-shaped wedge by drawing an elliptical arc whose center and end points are joined by lines. The center of the ellipse is the center of the rectangle specified either by $(x1, y1)/(x2, y2)$ or by the *rect* argument. The starting/ending points of pie are specified either by $(x3, y3)/(x4, y4)$ or by the points *Start* and *End*. Returns true if the call is successful; otherwise, returns false. The current position is neither used nor altered by this call.

See also   TDC::Chord, TDC::Arc, TPoint, TRegion, TRect

PlayEnhMetaFile
bool PlayEnhMetaFile(const TEnhMetaFilePict& metaFile, const TRect* rect);
Plays the enhanced metafile onto this device context.

PlayEnhMetaFileRecord
void PlayEnhMetaFileRecord(HANDLETABLE& handletable, ENHMETARECORD& metaRecord, uint count);
Plays one record from the enhanced metafile onto this DC.

PlayMetaFile
bool PlayMetaFile(const TMetaFilePict& metaFile);
Plays the contents of the given *metaFile* on this DC. The metafile can be played any number of times. Returns true if the call is successful; otherwise, returns false.

See also   TDC::EnumMetaFile, TDC::PlayMetaFileRecord, TMetaFilePict

PlayMetaFileRecord
void PlayMetaFileRecord(HANDLETABLE far& Handletable, METARECORD far& metaRecord, int count);
Plays the metafile record given in *metaRecord* to this DC by executing the GDI function call contained in that record. *Handletable* specifies the object handle table to be used. *count* specifies the number of handles in the table.

See also   TDC::PlayMetaFile, TDC::EnumMetaFile, HANDLETABLE struct, METARECORD struct

PlgBlt
bool PlgBlt(const TPoint& dst, const TDC& srcDC, const TRect& src, const TBitmap& maskBm,
        const TPoint& maskPos, uint32 rop=SRCCOPY);
32-bit only. Performs a bit-block transfer from the given source DC to this DC. Color bits are copied from the *src* rectangle on *srcDC*, the source DC, to the parallelogram *dst* on this DC. The *dst* array specifies three points A,B, and C as the corners of the destination parallelogram. The fourth point D is generated internally from the vector equation D = B + C - A. The upper left corner of *src* is mapped to A, the upper right corner to B, the lower left corner to C, and the lower right corner to D. An optional monochrome bitmap

can be specified by the *maskBm* argument. (If *maskBm* specifies a valid monochrome bitmap, *PlgBlt* uses it to mask the colorbits in the source rectangle. An error occurs if *maskBm* is not a monochrome bitmap.) *maskPos* specifies the upper left corner coordinates of the mask bitmap. With a valid *maskBm*, a value of 1 in the mask causes the source color pixel to be copied to *dst*; a value of 0 in the mask indicates that the corresponding color pixel in *dst* will not be changed. If the mask rectangle is smaller than *dst*, the mask pattern will be suitably duplicated.

The destination coordinates are transformed according to this DC (the destination DC). The source coordinates are transformed according to the source DC. If a rotation or shear transformation is in effect for the source DC when *PlgBlt* is called, an error occurs. Other transformations, such as scaling, translation, and reflection are allowed. The stretching mode of this DC (the destination DC) determines how *PlgBlt* will stretch or compress the pixels if necessary. When recording an enhanced metafile, an error occurs if the source DC identifies the enhanced metafile DC.

If necessary, *PlgBlt* adjusts the source color formats to match that of the destination. An error occurs if the source and destination DCs are incompatible. Before using *PlgBlt*, an application should call *GetDeviceCaps* to determine if the source and destination DCs are compatible.

PlgBlt returns true if the call is successful; otherwise, it returns false.

See also TDC::GetDeviceCaps, TDC::MaskBlt, TDC::SetStretchBltMode, TDC::StretchBlt, TBitmap, TPoint, TRect

PolyBezier
bool PolyBezier(const TPoint* points, int count);
Draws one or more connected cubic Bezier splines through the points specified in the *points* array using the currently selected pen object. The first spline is drawn from the first to the fourth point of the array using the second and third points as controls. Subsequent splines, if any, each require three additional points in the array, since the previous end point is taken as the next spline's start point. The *count* argument (>= 4) specifies the total number of points needed to specify the complete drawing. To draw *n* splines, *count* must be set to (3n + 1). Returns true if the call is successful; otherwise, returns false. The current position is neither used nor altered by this call. The resulting figure is not filled.

See also TDC::PolyBezierTo, TPoint

PolyBezierTo
bool PolyBezierTo(const TPoint* points, int count);
Draws one or more connected cubic Beziers splines through the points specified in the *points* array using the currently selected pen object. The first spline is drawn from the current position to the third point of the array using the first and second points as controls. Subsequent splines, if any, each require three additional points in the array, since the previous end point is taken as the next spline's start point. The *count* argument (>= 4) specifies the total number of points needed to specify the complete drawing. To draw *n* splines, *count* must be set to *3n*. Returns true if the call is successful; otherwise, returns false. The current position is moved to the end point of the final Bezier curve. The resulting figure is not filled.

See also TDC::PolyBezier, TPoint

PolyDraw

bool PolyDraw(const TPoint* points, uint8* types, int count);

Using the currently selected pen object, draws one or more possibly disjoint sets of line segments or Bezier splines or both on this DC. The *count* points in the *points* array provide the end points for each line segment or the end points and control points for each Bezier spline or both. The *count* BYTEs in the *types* array determine as follows how the corresponding point in *points* is to be interpreted:

Byte	Meaning
PT_BEZIERTO	This point is a control or end point for a Bezier spline. PT_BEZIERTO types must appear in sets of three: the current position is the Bezier start point; the first two PT_BEZIERTO points are the Bezier control points; and the third PT_BEZIERTO point is the Bezier end point, which becomes the new current point. An error occurs if the PT_BEZIERTO types do not appear in sets of three. An end-point PT_BEZIERTO can be bit-wise OR'd with PT_CLOSEFIGURE to indicate that the current figure is to be closed by drawing a spline from this end point to the start point of the most recent disjoint figure.
PT_CLOSEFIGURE	Optional flag that can be bit-wise OR'd with PT_LINETO or PT_BEZIERTO, as explained above. Closure updates the current point to the new end point.
PT_LINETO	A line is drawn from the current position to this point, which then becomes the new current point. PT_LINETO can be bit-wise OR'd with PT_CLOSEFIGURE to indicate that the current figure is to be closed by drawing a line segment from this point to the start point of the most recent disjoint figure.
PT_MOVETO	This point starts a new (disjoint) figure and becomes the new current point.

PolyDraw is an alternative to consecutive calls to *MoveTo, LineTo, Polyline, PolyBezier,* and *PolyBezierTo*. If there is an active path invoked via *BeginPath, PolyDraw* will add to this path.

Returns true if the call is successful; otherwise, returns false.

See also   TDC::MoveTo, TDC::LineTo, TDC::PolyBezier, TDC::PolyBezierTo, TDC::Polyline, TDC::BeginPath, TPoint

Polygon

bool Polygon(const TPoint* points, int count);

Using the current pen and polygon-filling mode, draws and fills on this DC a closed polygon with a number of line segments equal to *count* (which must be >= 2). The *points* array specifies the vertices of the polygon to be drawn. The polygon is automatically closed, if necessary, by drawing a line from the last to the first vertex. The current position is neither used nor altered by *Polygon*. Returns true if the call is successful; otherwise, returns false.

See also   TDC::Polyline, TDC::SetPolyFillMode, TDC::GetPolyFillMode, TPoint

Polyline

bool Polyline(const TPoint* points, int count);

Using the current pen object, draws on this DC a *count* of line segments (there must be at least 2). The *points* array specifies the sequence of points to be connected. The current position is neither used nor altered by *Polyline*. Returns true if the call is successful; otherwise, returns false.

See also   TDC::Polygon, TDC::PolyPolyline, TPoint

PolylineTo

bool PolylineTo(const TPoint* points, int count);

Draws one or more connected line segments on this DC using the currently selected pen object. The first line is drawn from the current position to the first of the *count* points in the *points* array. Subsequent lines, if any, connect the remaining points in the array, with each end point providing the start point of the next segment. The final end point becomes the new current point. No filling occurs even if a closed figure is drawn. Returns true if the call is successful; otherwise, returns false.

See also   TDC::PolyDraw, TDC::LineTo, TPoint

PolyPolygon

bool PolyPolygon(const TPoint* points, const int* PolyCounts, int count);

Using the current pen and polygon-filling mode, draws and fills on this DC the number of closed polygons indicated in *count* (which must be >= 2). The polygons can overlap. The *points* array specifies the vertices of the polygons to be drawn. *PolyCounts* is an array of *count* integers specifying the number of vertices in each polygon. Each polygon must be a closed polygon. The current position is neither used nor altered by *Polygon*. Returns true if the call is successful; otherwise, returns false.

See also   TDC::PolyPolyline, TDC::SetPolyFillMode, TDC::GetPolyFillMode, TPoint

PolyPolyline

bool PolyPolyline(const TPoint* points, const int* PolyCounts, int count);

Using the currently selected pen object, draws on this DC the number of polylines (connected line segments) indicated in *count*. The resulting figures are not filled. The *PolyCounts* array provides *count* integers specifying the number of points (>= 2) in each polyline. The *points* array provides, consecutively, each of the points to be connected. Returns true if the call is successful; otherwise, returns false. The current position is neither used nor altered by this call.

See also   TDC::Polyline, TDC::PolyPolygon, TPoint

PtVisible

bool PtVisible(const TPoint& point) const;

Returns true if the given *point* lies within the clipping region of this DC; otherwise, returns false.

See also   TDC::RectVisible, TPoint

RealizePalette

int RealizePalette();

Maps to the system palette the logical palette entries selected into this DC. Returns the number of entries in the logical palette that were mapped to the system palette.

See also   TPalette

Rectangle

Form 1   bool Rectangle(int x1, int y1, int x2, int y2);

Form 2   bool Rectangle(const TPoint& p1, const TPoint& p2);

Form 3   bool Rectangle(const TPoint& point, const TSize& s);

Form 4   bool Rectangle(const TRect& rect);
Draws and fills a rectangle of the given size on this DC with the current pen and brush objects. The current position is neither used nor altered by this call. Returns true if the call is successful; otherwise, returns false.

See also   TDC::RoundRect, TPoint, TRect, TSize

RectVisible
bool RectVisible(const TRect& rect) const;
Returns true if any part of the given rectangle, *rect*, lies within the clipping region of this DC; otherwise, returns false.

See also   TDC::PtVisible, TRect

ResetDC
virtual bool ResetDC(DEVMODE far& devMode);
Updates this DC using data in the given *devMode* structure. Returns true if the call is successful; otherwise, returns false.

See also   DEVMODE struct

RestoreBrush
void RestoreBrush();
Restores the original GDI brush object to this DC.

See also   TDC::OrgBrush, TBrush

RestoreDC
virtual bool RestoreDC(int savedDC = -1);
Restores the given *savedDC*. Returns true if the context is successfully restored; otherwise, returns false.

See also   TDC::SaveDC

RestoreFont
virtual void RestoreFont();
Restores the original GDI font object to this DC.

See also   TDC::OrgFont, TFont

RestoreObjects
void RestoreObjects();
Restores all the original GDI objects to this DC.

See also   TGdiObject

RestorePalette
void RestorePalette();
Restores the original GDI palette object to this DC.

See also   TDC::OrgPalette, TPalette

RestorePen
void RestorePen();
Restores the original GDI pen object to this DC.

See also   TDC::OrgPen, TPen

RestoreTextBrush
void RestoreTextBrush();
Restores the original GDI text brush object to this DC.

See also   TBrush

RoundRect
Form 1   bool RoundRect(int x1, int y1, int x2, int y2, int x3, int y3);

Form 2   bool RoundRect(const TPoint& p1, const TPoint& p2, const TPoint& rad);

Form 3   bool RoundRect(const TPoint& p, const TSize& s, const TPoint& rad);

Form 4   bool RoundRect(const TRect& rect, const TPoint& rad);
Draws and fills a rounded rectangle of the given size on this DC with the current pen and brush objects. The current position is neither used nor altered by this call. Returns true if the call is successful; otherwise, returns false.

See also   TDC::Rectangle, TPoint, TRect, TSize

SaveDC
virtual int SaveDC() const;
Saves the current state of this DC on a context stack. The saved state can be restored later with *RestoreDC*. Returns a value specifying the saved DC or 0 if the call fails.

See also   TDC::RestoreDC

ScaleViewportExt
virtual bool ScaleViewportExt(int xNum, int xDenom, int yNum, int yDenom, TSize* oldExtent = 0);
Modifies this DC's viewport extents relative to the current values. The new extents are derived as follows:

- $xNewVE = (xOldVE * xNum) / xDenom$
- $yNewVE = (I * yNum) / yDenom$

The previous extents are saved in *oldExtent*. Returns true if the call is successful; otherwise, returns false.

See also   TDC::SetViewportExt, TSize

ScaleWindowExt
virtual bool ScaleWindowExt(int xNum, int xDenom, int yNum, int yDenom, TSize* oldExtent = 0);
Modifies this DC's window extents relative to the current values. The new extents are derived as follows:

- $xNewWE = (xOldWE * xNum) / xDenom$
- $yNewWE = (yOldWE * yNum) / yDenom$

The previous extents are saved in *oldExtent*. Returns true if the call is successful; otherwise, returns false.

See also   TDC::SetWindowExt, TSize

ScrollDC

Form 1 bool ScrollDC(int x, int y, const TRect& scroll, const TRect& clip, TRegion& updateRgn, TRect& updateRect);

Form 2 bool ScrollDC(const TPoint& delta, const TRect& scroll, const TRect& clip, TRegion& updateRgn,
        TRect& updateRect);

Scrolls a rectangle of bits horizontally by *x* (or *delta.x* in the second version) device-units, and vertically by *y* (or *delta.y*) device-units on this DC. The scrolling and clipping rectangles are specified by *scroll* and *clip*. *ScrollDC* provides data in the *updateRgn* argument telling you the region (not necessarily rectangular) that was uncovered by the scroll. Similarly, *ScrollDC* reports in *updateRect* the rectangle (in client coordinates) that bounds the scrolling update region. This is the largest area that requires repainting.

Returns true if the call is successful; otherwise, returns false.

See also TPoint, TRect, TRegion

SelectClipPath

bool SelectClipPath(int mode);

Selects the current path on this DC as a clipping region, combining any existing clipping region using the specified *mode* as shown in the following table:

Mode	Meaning
RGN_AND	The new clipping region includes the overlapping areas of the current clipping region and the current path (intersection).
RGN_COPY	The new clipping region is the current path.
RGN_DIFF	The new clipping region includes the areas of the current clipping region with those of the current path excluded.
RGN_OR	The new clipping region includes the combined areas of the current clipping region and the current path (union).
RGN_XOR	The new clipping region includes the combined areas of the current clipping region and the current path but without the overlapping areas.

Returns true if the call is successful; otherwise, returns false.

SelectClipRgn

int SelectClipRgn(const TRegion& region);

Selects the given *region* as the current clipping region for this DC. A copy of the given *region* is used, letting you select the same region for other DC objects. The return value indicates the new clipping region's type as follows:

Region	Meaning
COMPLEXREGION	Clipping region has overlapping borders.
ERROR	Invalid DC.
NULLREGION	Clipping region is empty.
SIMPLEREGION	Clipping region has no overlapping borders.

See also TDC::OffsetClipRgn, TDC::GetClipBox, TRegion

SelectObject

Form 1 void SelectObject(const TBrush& brush);

Form 2   void SelectObject(const TPen& pen);

Form 3   virtual void SelectObject(const TFont& font);

Form 4   void SelectObject(const TPalette& palette, bool forceBackground = false);
Selects the given GDI object into this DC. The previously selected object is saved in the appropriate OrgXXX protected data member. For a palette argument, if *forceBackgound* is set false (the default), the selected logical palette is a foreground palette when the window has input focus. If *forceBackground* is true, the selected palette is always a background palette whether the window has focus or not.

See also   TDC::OrgBrush, TDC::OrgFont, TDC::OrgPalette, TDC::OrgPen, TDC::OrgTextBrush, TBrush, TFont, TPalette, TPen, TMemoryDC::SelectObject

SelectStockObject
virtual void SelectStockObject(int index);
Selects into the DC a predefined stock pen, brush, font, or palette.

See also   TPrintPreviewDC::SelectStockObject

SetBkColor
virtual TColor SetBkColor(TColor color);
Sets the current background color of this DC to the given *color* value or the nearest available. Returns 0x80000000 if the call fails.

See also   TDC::GetBkColor, TColor

SetBkMode
int SetBkMode(int mode);
Sets the background mode to the given *mode* argument, which can be either OPAQUE or TRANSPARENT. Returns the previous background mode.

See also   TDC::GetBkMode

SetBoundsRect
uint SetBoundsRect(TRect& bounds, uint flags);
Controls the accumulation of bounding rectangle information for this DC. Depending on the value of *flags*, the given *bounds* rectangle (possibly NULL) can combine with or replace the existing accumulated rectangle. *flags* can be any appropriate combination of the following values:

Constant	Meaning
DCB_ACCUMULATE	Add *bounds* (rectangular union) to the current accumulated rectangle.
DCB_DISABLE	Turn off bounds accumulation.
DCB_ENABLE	Turn on bounds accumulation (the default setting for bounds accumulation is disabled).
DCB_RESET	Set the bounding rectangle to empty.
DCB_SET	Set the bounding rectangle to *bounds*.

There are two bounding-rectangle accumulations, one for Windows and one for the application. The Windows-accumulated bounds can be queried by an application but not altered. The application can both query and alter the DC's accumulated bounds.

See also   TDC::GetBoundsRect, TRect

SetBrushOrg
bool SetBrushOrg(const TPoint& origin, TPoint* oldOrg = 0);
Sets the origin of the currently selected brush of this DC with the given *origin* value. The previous origin is passed to *oldOrg*. Returns true if successful; otherwise, returns false.

See also   TDC::GetBrushOrg, TPoint

SetDIBits
Form 1   bool SetDIBits(TBitmap& bitmap, uint16 startScan, uint16 numScans, const void HUGE* bits,
              const BITMAPINFO far& Info, uint16 usage);

Form 2   bool SetDIBits(TBitmap& Bitmap, const TDib& dib);
The first version sets the pixels in *bitmap* (the given destination bitmap on this DC) from the source DIB (device-independent bitmap) color data found in the byte array *bits* and the BITMAPINFO structure, *Info*. *numScan* scanlines are taken from the DIB, starting at scanline *startScan*. The *usage* argument specifies how the *bmiColors* member of BITMAPINFO is interpreted, as explained in *TDC::GetDIBits*.

In the second version of *SetDIBits*, the pixels are set in *bitmap* from the given source *TDib* argument.

SetDIBits returns true if the call is successful; otherwise, it returns false.

See also   TDC::GetDIBits, TDC::SetDIBitsToDevice, TBitmap, BITMAPINFO struct, TDib

SetDIBitsToDevice
Form 1   bool SetDIBitsToDevice(const TRect& dst, const TPoint& src, uint16 startScan, uint16 numScans,
              const void HUGE* bits, const BITMAPINFO far& bitsInfo, uint16 usage);

Form 2   bool SetDIBitsToDevice(const TRect& dst, const TPoint& src, const TDib& dib);
The first version sets the pixels in *dst* (the given destination rectangle on this DC) from the source DIB (device-independent bitmap) color data found in the byte array *bits* and the BITMAPINFO structure, *bitsInfo*. The DIB origin is specified by the point *src*. *numScan* scanlines are taken from the DIB, starting at scanline *startScan*. The *usage* argument determines how the *bmiColors* member of BITMAPINFO is interpreted, as explained in *TDC::GetDIBits*.

In the second version of *SetDIBitsToDevice*, the pixels are set in *dst* from *dib*, the given source *TDib* argument.

SetDIBitsToDevice returns true if the call is successful; otherwise, it returns false.

See also   TDC::GetDIBits, TDib, TPoint, TRect, BITMAPINFO struct

SetMapMode
virtual int SetMapMode(int mode);
Sets the current window mapping mode of this DC to *mode*. Returns the previous mapping mode value. The mapping mode defines how logical coordinates are mapped to device coordinates. It also controls the orientation of the device's x- and y-axes. See *TDC::GetMapMode* for a complete list of mapping modes.

See also   TDC::GetMapMode

SetMapperFlags

uint32 SetMapperFlags(uint32 flag);

Alters the algorithm used by the font mapper when mapping logical fonts to physical fonts on this DC. If successful, the function sets the current font-mapping flag to *flag* and returns the previous mapping flag; otherwise GDI_ERROR is returned. The mapping flag determines whether the font mapper will attempt to match a font's aspect ratio to this DC's aspect ratio. If bit 0 of *flag* is set to 1, the mapper selects only matching fonts. If no matching fonts exist, a new aspect ratio is chosen and a font is retrieved to match this ratio.

SetMiterLimit

bool SetMiterLimit(float newLimit, float* oldLimit = 0);

Sets the limit of miter joins to *newLimit* and puts the previous value in *oldLimit*. Returns true if successful; otherwise, returns false.

SetPixel

Form 1   TColor SetPixel(int x, int y, TColor color);

Form 2   TColor SetPixel(const TPoint& p, TColor color);

Sets the color of the pixel at the given location to the given *color* and returns the pixel's previous color.

See also   TDC::GetPixel, TColor, TPoint

SetPolyFillMode

int SetPolyFillMode(int mode);

Sets the polygon-filling mode for this DC to the given *mode* value, either ALTERNATE or WINDING. Returns the previous fill mode.

See also   TDC::GetPolyFillMode, TDC::Polygon

SetROP2

int SetROP2(int mode);

Sets the current foreground mix mode mode of this DC to the given *mode* value and returns the previous mode. The *mode* argument determines how the brush, pen, and existing screen image combine when filling and drawing. *mode* can be one of the following values:

Value	Meaning
R2_BLACK	Pixel is always binary 0.
R2_COPYPEN	Pixel is the pen color.
R2_MASKNOTPEN	Pixel is a combination of the colors common to both the display and the inverse of the pen.
R2_MASKPEN	Pixel is a combination of the colors common to both the pen and the display.
R2_MASKPENNOT	Pixel is a combination of the colors common to both the pen and the inverse of the display.
R2_MERGEPEN	Pixel is a combination of the pen color and the display color.
R2_MERGENOTPEN	Pixel is a combination of the display color and the inverse of the pen color.
R2_MERGEPENNOT	Pixel is a combination of the pen color and the inverse of the display color.
R2_NOP	Pixel remains unchanged.

Value	Meaning
R2_NOT	Pixel is the inverse of the display color.
R2_NOTCOPYPEN	Pixel is the inverse of the pen color.
R2_NOTMASKPEN	Pixel is the inverse of the R2_MASKPEN color.
R2_NOTMERGEPEN	Pixel is the inverse of the R2_MERGEPEN color.
R2_NOTXORPEN	Pixel is the inverse of the R2_XORPEN color.
R2_WHITE	Pixel is always binary 1.
R2_XORPEN	Pixel is a combination of the colors in the pen and in the display, but not in both.

See also   TDC::GetROP2, TDC::GetDeviceCaps

SetStretchBltMode
int SetStretchBltMode(int mode);
Sets the stretching mode of this DC to the given *mode* value and returns the previous mode. The *mode* argument (BLACKONWHITE, COLORONCOLOR, or WHITEONBLACK) defines what scan lines or columns or both are eliminated by *TDC::StretchBlt*.

See also   TDC::GetStretchBltMode, TDC::StretchBlt

SetSystemPaletteUse
int SetSystemPaletteUse(int usage);
Changes the usage of this DC's system palette. The *usage* argument can be SYSPAL_NOSTATIC or SYSPAL_STATIC. Returns the previous usage value.

See also   TDC::GetSystemPaletteUse

SetTextAlign
uint SetTextAlign(uint flags);
Sets the text-alignment flags for this DC. If successful, *SetTextAlign* returns the previous text-alignment flags; otherwise, it returns GDI_ERROR. The flag values are as listed for the *TDC::GetTextAlign* function. The text-alignment flags determine how *TDC::TextOut* and *TDC::ExtTextOut* align text strings in relation to the first character's screen position.

See also   TDC::GetTextAlign, TDC::TextOut, TDC::ExtTextOut

SetTextCharacterExtra
int SetTextCharacterExtra(int extra);
If successful, sets the current intercharacter spacing to *extra*, in logical units, for this DC, and returns the previous intercharacter spacing. Otherwise, returns 0. If the current mapping mode is not MM_TEXT, the *extra* value is transformed and rounded to the nearest pixel.

See also   TDC::GetTextCharacterExtra

SetTextColor
virtual TColor SetTextColor(TColor color);
Sets the current text color of this DC to the given *color* value. The text color determines the color displayed by *TDC::TextOut* and *TDC::ExtTextOut*.

See also   TDC::GetTextColor, TColor

SetTextJustification
bool SetTextJustification(int breakExtra, int breakCount);

When text strings are displayed using *TDC::TextOut* and *TDC::ExtTextOut*, sets the number of logical units specified in *breakExtra* as the total extra space to be added to the number of break characters specified in *breakCount*. The extra space is distributed evenly between the break characters. The break character is usually ASCII 32 (space), but some fonts define other characters. *TDC::GetTextMetrics* can be used to retrieve the value of the break character.

If the current mapping mode is not MM_TEXT, the extra value is transformed and rounded to the nearest pixel.

SetTextJustification returns true if the call is successful; otherwise, it returns false.

SetViewportExt
virtual bool SetViewportExt(const TSize& extent, TSize* oldExtent = 0);

Sets this DC's viewport x- and y-extents to the given *extent* values. The previous extents are saved in *oldExtent*. Returns true if the call is successful; otherwise, returns false. The *extent* value determines the amount of stretching or compression needed in the logical coordinate system to fit the device coordinate system. *extent* also determines the relative orientation of the two coordinate systems.

See also   TDC::GetViewportExt, TSize

SetViewportOrg
virtual bool SetViewportOrg(const TPoint& origin, TPoint* oldOrg = 0);

Sets this DC's viewport origin to the given *origin* value, and saves the previous origin in *oldOrg*. Returns true if the call is successful; otherwise, returns false.

See also   TDC::GetViewportOrg, TDC::OffsetViewportOrg, TPoint

SetWindowExt
virtual bool SetWindowExt(const TSize& extent, TSize* oldExtent = 0);

Sets this DC's window x- and y-extents to the given *extent* values. The previous extents are saved in *oldExtent*. Returns true if the call is successful; otherwise, returns false. The *extent* value determines the amount of stretching or compression needed in the logical coordinate system to fit the device coordinate system. *extent* also determines the relative orientation of the two coordinate systems.

See also   TDC::GetWindowExt, TDC::ScaleWindowExt, TSize

SetWindowOrg
bool SetWindowOrg(const TPoint& origin, TPoint* oldOrg = 0);

Sets the origin of the window associated with this DC to the given *origin* value, and saves the previous origin in *oldOrg*. Returns true if the call is successful; otherwise, returns false.

See also   TDC::GetWindowOrg, TDC::OffsetWindowOrg, TPoint

SetWorldTransform
bool SetWorldTransform(XFORM far& xform);

32-bit only. Sets a two-dimensional linear transformation, given by the *xform* structure, between world space and page space for this DC. Returns true if the call is successful; otherwise, returns false.

See also   TDC::ModifyWorldTransform, XFORM struct

StretchBlt

Form 1   bool StretchBlt(int dstX, int dstY, int dstW, int dstH, const TDC& srcDC, int srcX, int srcY, int srcW,
          int srcH, uint32 rop=SRCCOPY);

Form 2   bool StretchBlt(const TRect& dst, const TDC& srcDC, const TRect& src, uint32 rop=SRCCOPY);

Copies a bitmap from the source DC to a destination rectangle on this DC specified either by upper left-corner coordinates (*dstX*, *dstY*), width *dstW*, and height *dstH*, or (in the second version) by a *TRect* object, *dst*. The source bitmap is similarly specified with (*srcX*, *srcY*), *srcW*, and *srcH*, or by a *TRect* object, *src*. *StretchBlt* stretches or compresses the source according to the stretching mode currently set in this DC (the destination DC). The raster-operation code, *rop*, specifies how the colors are combined in output operations that involve a brush, a source bitmap, and a destination bitmap. The *rop* codes are described in the entry for *TDC::MaskBlt*.

See also   TDC::MaskBlt, TDC::SetStretchBltMode, TRect

StretchDIBits

Form 1   bool StretchDIBits(const TRect& dst, const TRect& src, const void HUGE* bits, const BITMAPINFO far& bitsInfo,
          uint16 usage, uint32 rop=SRCCOPY);

Form 2   bool StretchDIBits(const TRect& dst, const TRect& src, const TDib& dib, uint32 rop=SRCCOPY);

Copies the color data from *src*, the source rectangle of pixels in the given DIB (device-independent bitmap) on this DC, to *dst*, the destination rectangle. The DIB bits and color data are specified in either the byte array *bits* and the BITMAPINFO structure *bitsInfo* or in the *TDib* object, *dib*. The rows and columns of color data are stretched or compressed to match the size of the destination rectangle. The *usage* argument specifies how the *bmiColors* member of BITMAPINFO is interpreted, as explained in *TDC::GetDIBits* The raster operation code, *rop*, specifies how the source pixels, the current brush for this DC, and the destination pixels are combined to produce the new image. See *TDC::MaskBlt* for a detailed list of *rop* codes.

See also   TDC::GetDIBits, TDC::MaskBlt, TDib, TRect, BITMAPINFO struct

StrokeAndFillPath

bool StrokeAndFillPath();

32-bit only. Closes any open figures in the current path of this DC, strokes the outline of the path using the current pen, and fills its interior using the current brush and polygon fill mode. Returns true if the call is successful; otherwise, returns false.

See also   TDC::StrokePath, TDC::BeginPath, TDC::FillPath, TDC::EndPath, TDC::SetPolyFillMode, TBrush, TPen

StrokePath

bool StrokePath();

32-bit only. Renders the current, closed path on this DC and uses the DC's current pen.

See also   TDC::StrokeAndFillPath, TDC::BeginPath

TabbedTextOut

Form 1   bool TabbedTextOut(const TPoint& p, const char far* string, int count, int numPositions,
                const int far* positions, int tabOrigin);

Form 2   virtual bool TabbedTextOut(const TPoint& p, const char far* string, int count, int numPositions,
                const int far* positions, int tabOrigin, TSize& size);

Draws up to *count* characters of the given null-terminated *string* in the current font on this DC. If *count* is -1, the whole string is written.

Tabs are expanded according to the given arguments. The *positions* array specifies *numPositions* tab stops given in device units. The tab stops must have strictly increasing values in the array. If *numPositions* and *positions* are both 0, tabs are expanded to eight times the average character width. If *numPositions* is 1, all tab stops are taken to be *positions[0]* apart. *tabOrigin* specifies the x-coordinate in logical units from which tab expansion will start.

The *p* argument specifies the logical coordinates of the reference point that is used to align the first character depending on the current text-alignment mode. This mode can be inspected with *TDC::GetTextAlign* and changed with *TDC::SetTextAlign*. By default, the current position is neither used nor altered by *TabbedTextOut*. However, if the align mode is set to TA_UPDATECP, *TabbedTextOut* ignores the reference point argument(s) and uses/updates the current position as the reference point.

The *size* argument in the second version of *TabbedTextOut* reports the dimensions (*size.y* = height and *size.x* = width) of the string in logical units.

TabbedTextOut returns true if the call is successful; otherwise, it returns false.

See also   TDC::TextOut, TDC::GetTextAlign, TDC::SetTextAlign, TPoint, TSize

TextOut

Form 1   virtual bool TextOut(int x, int y, const char far* string, int count = -1);

Form 2   bool TextOut(const TPoint& p, const char far* string, int count = -1);

Draws up to *count* characters of the given null-terminated *string* in the current font on this DC. If *count* is -1 (the default), the entire string is written.

The (*x*, *y*) or *p* arguments specify the logical coordinates of the reference point that is used to align the first character, depending on the current text-alignment mode. This mode can be inspected with *TDC::GetTextAlign* and changed with *TDC::SetTextAlign*. By default, the current position is neither used nor altered by *TextOut*. However, the align mode can be set to TA_UPDATECP, which makes Windows use and update the current position. In this mode, *TextOut* ignores the reference point argument(s).

TextOut returns true if the call is successful; otherwise, it returns false.

See also   TDC::ExtTextOut, TDC::GetTextAlign, TDC::SetTextAlign, TPoint

TextRect

Form 1   bool TextRect(int x1, int y1, int x2, int y2);

Form 2   bool TextRect(const TRect& rect);

Form 3   bool TextRect(int x1, int y1, int x2, int y2, TColor color);

Form 4   bool TextRect(const TRect rect, TColor color);

Fills the given rectangle, clipping any text to the rectangle. If no *color* argument is supplied, the current backgound color is used. If a *color* argument is supplied, that color is set to the current background color which is then used for filling. *TextRect* returns true if the call is successful; otherwise, it returns false.

See also   TDC::SetBkColor, TColor, TRect

UpdateColors
void UpdateColors();
Updates the client area of this DC by matching the current colors in the client area to the system palette on a pixel-by-pixel basis.

WidenPath
bool WidenPath();
32-bit only. Redefines the current, closed path on this DC as the area that would be painted if the path were stroked with this DC's current pen. The current pen must have been created under the following conditions:

If the *TPen(int Style, int Width, TColor Color)* constructor, or the *TPen(const LOGPEN* LogPen)* constructor is used, the width of the pen in device units must be greater than 1.

If the *TPen(uint32 PenStyle, uint32 Width, const TBrush& Brush, uint32 StyleCount, LPDWORD pSTyle)* constructor, or the *TPen(uint32 PenStyle, uint32 Width, const LOGBRUSH& logBrush, uint32 StyleCount, LPDWORD pSTyle)* constructor is used, the pen must be a geometric pen.

Any Bezier curves in the path are converted to sequences of linear segments approximating the widened curves, so no Bezier curves remain in the path after a *WidenPath* call.

WidenPath returns true if the call is successful; otherwise, it returns false.

See also   TDC::FlattenPath, TDC::BeginPath, TPen

Protected constructors

Form 1   TDC();
For use by derived classes only. Calls *Init* to clear the *OrgXXX* data members and sets *ShouldDelete* to true.

Form 2   TDC(HDC handle, TAutoDelete AutoDelete);
For use by derived classes only. Constructs a TDC object using an existing DC handle. Calls *Init* to clear the *OrgXXX* data members.

See also   TDC::Init

Protected data members

Handle
TGdiBase::Handle;
The handle of this DC. Uses the base class's handle (*TGdiBase::Handle.*)

See also   TDC

OrgBrush
HBRUSH OrgBrush;
Handle to the original GDI brush object for this DC. Holds the previous brush object whenever a new brush is selected with *SelectObject(brush)*.

See also   TDC::SelectObject, TBrush

OrgFont
HFONT OrgFont;
Handle to the original GDI font object for this DC. Holds the previous font object whenever a new font is selected with *SelectObject(font)*.

See also   TDC::SelectObject, TFont

OrgPalette
HPALETTE OrgPalette;
Handle to the original GDI palette object for this DC. Holds the previous palette object whenever a new palette is selected with *SelectObject(palette)*.

See also   TDC::SelectObject, TPalette

OrgPen
HPEN OrgPen;
Handle to the original GDI pen object for this DC. Holds the previous pen object whenever a new pen is selected with *SelectObject(pen)*.

See also   TDC::SelectObject, TPen

OrgTextBrush
HBRUSH OrgTextBrush
32-bit only. The handle to the original GDI text brush object for this DC. Stores the previous text brush handle whenever a new brush is selected with *SelectObject(text_brush)*.

See also   TDC::SelectObject, TBrush

ShouldDelete
TGdiBase::ShouldDelete;
Set to true if the handle for this object should be deleted by the destructor; otherwise, set to false.

See also   ~TDC

Protected member functions

CheckValid
Form 1   TGdiBase::CheckValid(uint resId=IDS_GDIFAILURE)

Form 2   static void CheckValid(HANDLE handle, uint resId=IDS_GDIFAILURE)
Both versions of *CheckValid* check for a valid GDI object handle. If one is not found, a GDI exception is thrown for the given resource ID. Both versions use *TGdiBase::CheckValid*.

Init
void Init();

Sets *OrgBrush, OrgPen, OrgFont, OrgBitmap,* and *OrgPalette* to 0, and sets *ShouldDelete* to true. This function is for internal use by the *TDC* constructors.

See also   TDC constructors, TDC::SelectObject

TDecoratedFrame class

TDecoratedFrame automatically positions its client window (you must supply a client window) so that it is the same size as the client rectangle. You can add additional decorations like toolbars and status lines to a window. You can create a *TDecoratedFrame* without a caption bar by clearing all of the bits in the style data member of the *TWindowAttr* structure. *TDecoratedFrame* is a streamable class.

For OLE-enabled applications, use *TOleFrame*, which creates a decorated frame and manages decorations such as toolbars for the main window of an SDI (Single Document Interface) OLE application.

Type definitions

TLocation enum
enum TLocation (None = alNone, Top = alTop, Bottom = alBottom, Left = alLeft, Right = alRight);
TLocation enum describes *Top, Left, Bottom,* and *Right* positions where the decoration can be placed. *Insert* uses this enum to position the decoration.

Public constructor

TDecoratedFrame(TWindow* parent, const char far* title, TWindow* clientWnd, bool trackMenuSelection = false, TModule* module = 0);
Constructs a *TDecoratedFrame* object with the specified parent window (*parent*), window caption (*title*), and module ID. Sets *TWindow::Attr.Title* to the new title. Passes a pointer to the client window if one is specified. By default set to false, *trackMenuSelection* controls whether hint text appears at the bottom of the window when a menu item is highlighted.

Public member functions

Insert
void Insert (TWindow& decoration, TLocation = Top);
After you specify where the decoration should be placed, *Insert* adds it just above, below, left, or right of the client window. This process is especially important when there are multiple decorations. *Insert* looks at the decoration's *Attr.Style* member and checks the WS_VISIBLE flag to tell whether the decoration should initially be visible or hidden.

To position the decoration, *Insert* uses *TLocation* enum, which describes *Top*, *Left*, *Bottom*, and *Right* positions where the decoration can be placed.

PreProcessMsg
bool PreProcessMsg (MSG& msg);
Overrides the virtual function defined in *TFrameWindow* to give decorations an opportunity to perform mnemonic access preprocessing.

See also   TFrameWindow::PreProcessMsg, TWindow::PreProcessMsg

SetClientWindow
TWindow* SetClientWindow(TWindow* clientWnd);
Overrides *TFrameWindow's* virtual function. Sets the client window to the specified window. Users are responsible for destroying the old client window if they want to remove it.

Protected data members

MenuItemId
uint MenuItemID;
Specifies the menu item ID.

TrackMenuSelection
bool TrackMenuSelection;
Specifies whether you want menu selection and help status information visible.

Protected member functions

EvCommand
LRESULT EvCommand(uint Id, HWND hWndCtl, uint notifyCode);
Automates hiding and showing of decorations.

EvCommandEnable
void EvCommandEnable(TCommandEnabler& ce);
Handles checking and unchecking of menu items that are associated with decorations.

EvEnterIdle
void EvEnterIdle(uint source, HWND hWndDlg);
Responds to a window message that tells an application's main window that a dialog box or a menu is entering an idle state. *EvEnterIdle* also handles updating the status bar with the appropriate help message.

EvMenuSelect
void EvMenuSelect(uint MenuItemId, uint flags, HMENU hMenu);
Responds to user menu selection. If *MenuItemId* is blank, displays an empty help message; otherwise, it displays a help message with the specified string ID. See *EvEnterIdle* for a description of how the help message is loaded.

EvSize
void EvSize(uint sizeType, TSize& size);
Passes a WM_SIZE message to *TLayoutWindow*.

GetMenuItemId
uint GetMenuItemId() const;
Returns the cached id of the current menu item.

GetTrackMenuSelection
bool GetTrackMenuSelection() const;
Returns true if the decorated frame is tracking the menu selections. Sends a message to the status bar to display the hint text.

RemoveChild
void RemoveChild(TWindow* child);
Makes sure that both bases get a chance to see the child removed. *TWindow's* will be called twice, but the second call will be ignored. If the client is being removed and the client is not currently being set, then this function calls *SetClientWindow* to put in a placeholder.

SetMenuItemId
void SetMenuItemId(uint menuitemid);
Sets the cached id of the current menu item.

SetTrackMenuSelection
void SetTrackMenuSelection(bool tr=true);
Sets the flag for tracking menu selection.

SetupWindow
void SetupWindow();
Calls *TLayoutWindow::Layout* to size and position the decoration.

See also   TFrameWindow::SetUpWindow, TWindow::SetUpWindow, TLayoutWindow::Layout

Response table entries

Response table entry	Member function
EV_WM_ENTERIDLE	EvEnterIdle
EV_WM_MENUSELECT	EvMenuSelect
EV_WM_SIZE	EvSize

See also   TOleFrame

TDecoratedMDIFrame class   decmdifr.h

Derived from both *TMDIFrame* and *TDecoratedFrame*, *TDecoratedMDIFrame* is an MDI frame that supports decorated child windows.

TDecoratedMDIFrame supports custom toolbars. You can insert one set of decorations (for example, toolbars and rulers) into a decorated frame. When a different set of tools is needed, you can remove the previous set and reinsert another set of decorations.

However, be sure to remove all of the unwanted decorations from the adjusted sides (that is, the top, left, bottom, and right) before reinserting a new set.

TDecoratedMDIFrame is a streamable class.

Public constructor

TDecoratedMDIFrame(const char far* title, TResId menuResId, TMDIClient &clientWnd = *new TMDIClient,
 bool trackMenuSelection = false, TModule* module = 0);
Constructs a decorated MDI frame of the specified client window with the indicated menu resource ID. By default, menu hint text is not displayed.

Protected member function

DefWindowProc
LRESULT DefWindowProc(uint message, WPARAM wParam, LPARAM lParam);
Overrides *TWindow::DefWindowProc* . If the message parameter is WM_SIZE, *DefWindowProc* returns 0; otherwise, *DefWindowProc* returns the result of calling *TMDIFRame::DefWindowProc*.

See also   TMDIFrame::DefWindowProc

TDesktopDC class   dc.h

A DC class derived from *TWindowDC*, *TDesktopDC* provides access to the desktop window's client area, which is the screen behind all other windows.

Public constructor

TDesktopDC();
Default constructor for *TDesktopDC* objects.

TDialog class   dialog.h

Typically used to obtain information from a user, a dialog box is a window inside of which other controls such as buttons and scroll bars can appear. Unlike actual child windows which can only be displayed in the parent window's client area, dialog boxes can be moved anywhere on the screen. *TDialog* objects represent both modal and modeless dialog box interface elements. (A modal dialog box disables operations in its parent window while it is open, and, thus, lets you function in only one window "mode.")

A *TDialog* object has a corresponding resource definition that describes the placement and appearance of its controls. The identifier of this resource definition is supplied to the constructor of the *TDialog* object. A *TDialog* object is associated with a modal interface element by calling its *Execute* member function and with a modeless interface element by calling its *Create* member function.

You can use *TDialog* to build an application that uses a dialog as its main window by constructing your dialog as a *TDialog* and passing it as the client of a *TFrameWindow*. Your code might look something like this:

```
SetMainWindow(new TFrameWindow(0, "title" new TDialog(0, IDD_MYDIALOG)));
```

ObjectWindows also provides Borland Windows Custom Controls (BWCC) support for dialog boxes. Unless a custom template is specified, *TDialog* uses the BWCC templates. (By default, *TApplication's* member function *EnableBWCC* enables BWCC support.)

TDialog is a streamable class.

ObjectWindows also encapsulates common dialog boxes that let the user select font, file name, color, print options, and so on. *TCommonDialog* is the parent class for this group of common dialog box classes.

Type definitions

THow enum
enum THow {Next, Previous};
THow is used when invoking the *SetControlFocus* method. It specifies whether focus should be set to the next or the previous sibling of the current control with focus.

Table 2.6   Constants

Constant	Meaning if set
Next	Set focus to the next sibling
Previous	Set focus to the previous sibling

See also   TDialog::SetControlFocus

Public data members

Attr
TDialogAttr Attr;
Attr holds the creation attributes of the dialog box (for example, size and style).

See also   TDialogAttr

IsModal
bool IsModal;
IsModal is **true** if the dialog box is modal and **false** if it is modeless.

Public constructor and destructor

Constructor
TDialog(TWindow* parent, TResId resId, TModule* module = 0);

Invokes a *TWindow* constructor, passing *parent* and *module*, and calls *DisableAutoCreate* to prevent *TDialog* from being automatically created and displayed along with its parent. *TDialog* then initializes *Title* to -1 and sets *TDialogAttr.Name* using the dialog box's integer or string resource identifier, which must correspond to a dialog resource definition in the resource file. Finally, it initializes *TDialogAttr.Param* to 0 and sets *IsModal* to **false**.

Destructor
~TDialog();
If *Attr.Name* is a string and not an integer resource identifier, this destructor frees memory allocated to *Attr.Name*, which holds the name of the dialog box.

See also TApplication::EnableBWCC, TWindow::~TWindow, TWindow::DisableAutoCreate, TWindow::TWindow, TDialog::Attr

Public member functions

CloseWindow
void CloseWindow(int retValue = IDCANCEL);
Overrides the virtual function defined by *TWindow* and conditionally shuts down the dialog box. If the dialog box is modeless, it calls TWindow::CloseWindow. If the dialog box is modal, it calls *CanClose*. If *CanClose* returns **true**, *CloseWindow* calls *TransferData* to transfer dialog box data, passing it *retValue*. The default value of *retValue* is IDCANCEL.

See also TWindow::CloseWindow

CmCancel
void CmCancel();
Automatic response to a click on the Cancel button of the dialog box. Calls *Destroy*, passing IDCANCEL.

See also TDialog::CloseWindow

CmOk
void CmOk();
Responds to a click on the dialog box's OK button with the identifier IDOK. Calls *CloseWindow*, passing IDOK.

See also TDialog::CloseWindow

Create
virtual bool Create();
Creates a modeless dialog box interface element associated with the *TDialog* object. Registers all the dialog's child windows for custom control support. Calls *DoCreate* to perform the actual creation of the dialog box.

Create returns **true** if successful. If unsuccessful, *Create* throws a *TXInvalidWindow* exception.

See also TDialog::Execute, TModule::MakeWindow, TWindow::DisableAutoCreate

Destroy
virtual void Destroy(int retValue = IDCANCEL);

Destroys the interface element associated with the *TDialog* object. If the element is a modeless dialog box, *Destroy* calls *TWindow::Destroy*. If the element is a modal dialog box, *Destroy* calls *EnableAutoCreate* on all child windows. Then *Destroy* calls the Windows function *::EndDialog*, passing *retValue* as the value returned to indicate the result of the dialog's execution. The default *retValue* is IDCANCEL.

See also   TWindow::Destroy, TWindow::EnableAutoCreate

DialogFunction
virtual bool DialogFunction(uint message, WPARAM wParam, LPARAM lParam);
To process messages within the dialog function, your application must override this function. *DialogFunction* returns **true** if the message is handled and **false** if the message is not handled.

DoCreate
virtual HWND DoCreate();
DoCreate is called by *Create* to performs the actual creation of a modeless dialog box.

DoExecute
virtual int DoExecute();
DoExecute is called by *Execute* to perform the actual execution of a modal dialog box.

See also   TDialog::Execute

EvClose
void EvClose();
Responds to an incoming *EvClose* message by shutting down the window.

EvCtlColor
HBRUSH EvCtlColor(HDC hDC, HWND hWndChild, uint ctlType);
Passes the handle to the display context for the child window, the handle to the child window, and the default system colors to the parent window. The parent window then uses the display-context handle given in *hDC* to set the text and background colors of the child window.

If three-dimensional (3-D) support is enabled, *EvCtlColor* handles the EV_WM_CTLCOLOR message by allowing the CTL3D DLL to process the WM_CTLCOLOR message in order to set the background color and provide a background brush for the window.

See also   TApplication::EnableCtl3d

EvInitDialog
virtual bool EvInitDialog(HWND hWndFocus);
EvInitDialog is automatically called just before the dialog box is displayed. It calls *SetupWindow* to perform any setup required for the dialog box or its controls.

See also   TWindow::SetupWindow

EvPaint
void EvPaint();
EvPaint calls *TWindow's* general-purpose default processing function, *DefaultProcessing*, for Windows-supplied painting.

See also TWindow::DefaultProcessing

EvSetFont
virtual void EvSetFont(HFONT hfont, bool redraw);
Responds to a request to change a dialog's font.

Execute
virtual int Execute();
Creates and executes a modal dialog box interface element associated with the *TDialog* object. If the element is successfully associated, *Execute* does not return until the *TDialog* is closed.

Execute performs the following tasks:

- Registers this dialog's window class and all of the dialog's child windows.
- Calls *DoExecute* to execute the dialog box.
- Checks for exceptions and throws a *TXWindow* exception if an error occurs.

Execute returns an integer value that indicates how the user closed the modal dialog box. If the dialog box cannot be created, *Execute* returns -1.

See also TModule::ExecDialog, TWindow::DisableAutoCreate, TXWindow

GetDefaultId
uint GetDcommandsefaultId() const;
Gets the default resource ID.

GetDialogAttr
TDialogAttr& Format menu commandsGetDialogAttr();
Returns the attributes data member of *TDialog*.

GetIsModal
bool GetIsModal() const;
Returns true if the dialog is modal.

GetItemHandle
HWND GetItemHandle(int childId);
Returns the dialog box control's window handle identified by the supplied ID. Because *GetItemHandle* is now obsolete, new applications should use *TWindow::GetDlgItem*.

IdleAction
bool IdleAction(long idleCount);
Iterates over each child control and routes the command enabler. Does not rely on an OWL interface object to work.

MapDialogRect
void MapDialogRect(TRect& rect);
Converts the dialog units into screen coordinates.

PerformDlgInit
bool PerformDlgInit();

Initializes the dialog box controls with the contents of RT_DLGINIT, the dialog box resource identifier, which describes the appearance and location of the controls (buttons, group boxes, and so on). Returns **true** if successful; otherwise, returns **false**.

PreProcessMsg
bool PreProcessMsg(MSG& msg);

Overrides the virtual function defined by *TWindow* in order to perform preprocessing of window messages. If the child window has requested keyboard navigation, *PreProcessMsg* handles any accelerator key messages and then processes any other keyboard messages.

See also   TWindow::PreProcessMsg, MSG struct

SendDlgItemMsg
uint32 SendDlgItemMsg(int ChildId, uint16 Msg, uint16 WParam, uint32 LParam);

Sends a window control message, identified by *Msg*, to the dialog box's control identified by its supplied ID, *ChildID*. *WParam* and *LParam* become parameters in the control message. *SendDlgItemMsg* returns the value returned by the control, or 0 if the control ID is invalid. This function is obsolete.

SetCaption
void SetCaption(const char far* title);

Sets the caption of the dialog box to the value of the *title* parameter.

See also   TWindow::SetCaption

SetControlFocus
Form 1   void SetControlFocus(THow how);

Sets the focus to either the previous control with WS_TABSTOP, or the next control with WS_TABSTOP.

Form 2   void SetControlFocus(HWND hwnd);

Sets focus within a dialog to a specific control.

SetDefaultId
void SetDefaultId(uint Id);

Sets the default resource ID.

SetDialogAttr
void SetDialogAttr(TDialogAttr attr);

Sets the attributes of the dialog.

SetIsModal
void SetIsModal(bool ismodal);

Sets the modal data member of *TDialog*.

SetMsgResult
void SetMsgResult(uint32 result);

Sets the result of the message for the dialog's WndProc.

StdDlgProc
static int CALLBACK StdDlgProc(THandle, uint, TParam1, TParam2);

Handles messages that come from the window procedure of dialogs (WC_DIALOG's wndProc). If *DlgCreationWindow* is not 0, then msg is destined for *DlgCreationWindow*. When *StdDlgProc* first receives a message, it checks to see if it needs to associate the global C++ variable *DlgCreationWindow* with the one passed in HWND. If it needs to do that, it will then subclass the window procedure. It calls the virtual *DialogFunction()* to handle specific messages, mostly for the startup sequence.

Protected member functions

GetClassName
char far* GetClassName();
Overrides the virtual function defined in *TWindow* and returns the name of the dialog box's default Windows class, which must be used for a modal dialog box. For a modeless dialog box, *GetClassName* returns the name of the default *TWindow*. If BWCC is enabled, *GetClassName* returns BORDLGCLASS.

See also   TWindow::GetClassName

GetWindowClass
void GetWindowClass(WNDCLASS& wndClass);
Overrides the virtual function defined in *TWindow*. Fills *WndClass* with *TDialog* registration attributes obtained from an existing *TDialog* window or from Borland Windows Custom Controls (BWCC) if it is enabled.

If the class style is registered with CS_GLOBALCLASS, you must unregister the class style. You can do this by turning off the style bit. For example:

```
{
baseclass::GetWindowClass(wndClass);

...

WndClass.style &= ~CS_GLOBALCLASS:

...

}
```

See also   TWindow::GetWindowClass, TWindow, WNDCLASS struct

SetupWindow
void SetupWindow();
Overrides the virtual function defined in *TWindow*. Sets up the dialog box by calling *SetCaption* (sets *Title*) and *TWindow::SetupWindow*.

If three-dimensional (3-D) support is enabled, *SetupWindow* calls the CTL3D DLL to register the dialog box.

See also   TCommonDialog::SetupWindow

Response table entries

Response table entry	Member function
EV_COMMAND (IDCANCEL, CmCancel)	CmCancel
EV_COMMAND (IDOK, CmOk)	CmOk
EV_WM_CTLCOLOR	EvCtlColor
EV_WM_CLOSE	EvClose
EV_WM_PAINT	EvPaint

See also   TWindowFlags enum, TCommonDialog

TDialog class::TDialogAttr struct   dialog.h

struct TDialogAttr {char far* Name;uint32 Param};

Holds a *TDialog* object's creation attributes, which include the style, appearance, size, and types of controls associated with the dialog box. *TDialogAttr* contains two data members: *Name* (the resource id) and *Param*. These members contain user-defined data used for dialog box creation.

Public data members

TDialogAttr::Name

char far* Name;

Name holds the identifier, which can be either a string or an integer resource identifier, of the dialog resource.

TDialogAttr::Param

uint32 Param;

Param is used to pass initialization data to the dialog box when it is constructed. You can assign a value to this field in a derived class's constructor. Although any *Param*-type information passed to the dialog box can be saved as a data member, *Param* is especially useful if you want to create a dialog box that's implemented by non-ObjectWindows code.

After *Param* is accepted it is then available in the message response functions (for example, EvInitDialog) associated with WM_INITDIALOG.

TDib class   gdiobjec.h

The class *TDib*, derived from *TGdiObject*, represents GDI Device Independent Bitmap (DIB) objects. *TDibDC*s encapsulate the creation of DCs using DIB.DRV (a GDI driver provided with Windows MME and 3.1). DIBs have no Windows handle; they are just structures containing format and palette information and a collection of bits or pixels. *TDib* provides a convenient way to work with DIBs like any other GDI object. The memory for the DIB is in one *GlobalAlloc*'d unit so it can be passed to the Clipboard, OLE 2, and so on.

The *TDib* destructor overloads the base destructor because DIBs are not real GDI objects.

Type definitions

Map
enum Map{MapFace, MapText, MapShadow, MapHighlight, MapFrame};

Enumerates the values for the part of the window whose color is to be set. You can OR these together to control the colors used for face shading on push buttons, the color of a selected control button, the edge shading on push buttons, text on push buttons, the color of the window frame, and the background color of the various parts of a window. The function *MapUIColors* uses one of these values to map the colors of various parts of a window to a specified color.

See also   TDib::MapUIColors

Public constructors and destructor

Constructors

Form 1   TDib(HGLOBAL handle, TAutoDelete autoDelete = NoAutoDelete);
Creates a *TDib* object and sets the *Handle* data member to the given borrowed handle. The *ShouldDelete* data member defaults to false, ensuring that the borrowed handle will not be deleted when the C++ object is destroyed.

Form 2   TDib(const TClipboard& clipboard);
Constructs a *TDib* object with a handle borrowed from the given Clipboard.

Form 3   TDib(const TDib& src);
This public copy constructor creates a complete copy of the given *src* object as in:

```
TDib mySrc = yourSrc;
```

Form 4   TDib(int width, int height, int nColors, uint16 mode = DIB_RGB_COLORS);
Creates a DIB object with the given width, height, number of colors, mode values.

Form 5   TDib(HINSTANCE instance, TResID resID);
Creates a DIB object from the resource with the given ID.

Form 6   TDib(const char* name);
Creates a DIB object from the given resource file.

Form 7   TDib(TFile& file, bool readFileHeader = true);
Creates a DIB from the file.

Form 8   TDib(istream& is, bool readFileHeader = false);
Creates a DIB from the file stream.

Form 9   TDib(const TBitmap& bitmap, const TPalette* pal = 0);
Creates a DIB object from the given resource bitmap and palette. If *pal* is 0 (the default), the default palette is used.

Destructor

~TDib();

Overrides the base destructor.

See also ::GetClipboardData, ~TGdiObject, TDib::InfoFromHandle, TDib::LoadFile, TDib::LoadResource, TGdiObject::Handle, TGdiObject::ShouldDelete

Public member functions

operator BITMAPINFO()

Form 1   operator BITMAPINFO far*();

Form 2   operator const BITMAPINFO far*() const;

Typecasts this DIB by returning a pointer to its bitmap information structure (BITMAPINFO) which contains information about this DIB's color format and dimensions (size, width, height, resolution, and so on).

See also TDib::GetInfo, BITMAPINFO struct

operator BITMAPINFOHEADER()

Form 1   operator BITMAPINFOHEADER far*();

Form 2   operator const BITMAPINFOHEADER far*() const;

Typecasts this DIB by returning a pointer to its bitmap info header.

See also TDib::GetInfoHeader, BITMAPINFOHEADER struct

BitsPixel

int BitsPixel() const;

Bits per pixel: 2, 4, 8, 16, 24, or 32.

ChangeModeToPal

bool ChangeModeToPal(const TPalette& pal);

Converts the existing color table in place to use palette relative values. The palette that is passed is used as a reference. Returns true if the call is successful; otherwise returns false.

See also TDib::ChangeModeToRGB, TPalette::GetPaletteEntry

ChangeModeToRGB

bool ChangeModeToRGB(const TPalette& pal);

Converts the existing color table in place to use absolute RGB values. The palette that is passed is used as a reference. Returns true if the call is successful; otherwise returns false.

See also TDib::ChangeModetoPal, TPalette::GetPaletteEntry

Compression

uint32 Compression() const;

Compression and encoding flags.

CopyBlt

void CopyBlt(int dstX, int dstY, TDib& srcDib, int width=0, int height=0);

Copies the DIB by copying the bits.

FindColor

int FindColor(TColor color);

Returns the palette entry for the given color.

See also   TDib::GetColor, TColor, TDib::SetColor, TDib::MapColor

FindIndex

int FindIndex(uint16 index);

Returns the palette entry corresponding to the given index.

See also   TDib::GetIndex, TDib::SetIndex, TDib::MapIndex

FlippedY

int FlippedY(int y) const;

Returns the coordinate of y if the direction of the y-axis was reversed.

GetBits

Form 1   void HUGE* GetBits();

Form 2   const void HUGE* GetBits() const;

Returns the *Bits* data member for this DIB.

See also   TDib::Bits

GetColor

TColor GetColor(int entry) const;

Returns the color for the given palette entry.

See also   TDib::SetColor, TColor, TDib::FindColor, TDib::MapColor

GetColors

Form 1   TRgbQuad far* GetColors();

Form 2   const TRgbQuad far* GetColors() const;

Returns the *bmiColors* value of this DIB.

GetHandle

THandle GetHandle() const;

Returns the handle of the DIB with type HANDLE.

See also   TDib::Height, TDib::Size, TDib::NumScans

GetIndex

uint16 GetIndex(int entry) const;

Returns the color index for the given palette entry.

See also   TDib::SetIndex, TDib::FindIndex, TDib::MapIndex

GetIndices

Form 1   uint16 far* GetIndices();

Form 2   const uint16 far* GetIndices() const;

Returns the *bmiColors* indexes of this DIB.

See also   TDib::GetColors

GetInfo

Form 1   BITMAPINFO far* GetInfo();

Form 2   const BITMAPINFO far* GetInfo() const;

Returns this DIB's *Info* field. A DIB's BITMAPINFO structure contains information about the dimensions and color of the DIB and specifies an array of data types that define the colors in the bitmap.

See also   TDib::Info, TDib::GetInfoHeader

GetInfoHeader

Form 1   BITMAPINFOHEADER far* GetInfoHeader();

Form 2   const BITMAPINFOHEADER far* GetInfoHeader() const;

Returns this DIB's *bmiHeader* field of the BITMAPINFO structure contains information about the color and dimensions of this DIB.

See also   TDib::Info, TDib::GetInfo, BITMAPINFOHEADER struct

operator HANDLE()

operator HANDLE() const;

Typecasts this DIB by returning its *Handle*.

See also   TGdiObject::Handle

Height

int Height() const;

Returns *H*, this DIB's height.

See also   TDib::Info

IsOK

bool IsOK() const;

Returns false if *Info* is 0, otherwise returns true. If there is a problem with the construction of the DIB, memory is freed and *Info* is set to 0. Therefore, using *Info* is a reliable way to determine if the DIB is constructed correctly.

See also   TDib constructors, TDib::Info

IsPM

bool IsPM() const;

Returns true if *IsCore* is true; that is, if the DIB is an old-style PM DIB using core headers. Otherwise returns false.

See also   TDib::IsCore

LoadFile

bool LoadFile(const char* name);

Loads this DIB from the given file name. Returns true if the call is successful; otherwise returns false.

See also   TDib::LoadResource, TDib constructors

MapColor

int MapColor(const TColor& fromColor, const TColor& toColor, bool doAll = false);

Maps the *fromColor* to the *toColor* in the current palette of this DIB.

Returns the palette entry for the given color. Returns the palette entry for the *toColor* argument.

See also   TDib::GetColor, TColor, TDib::SetColor, TDib::FindColor

MapIndex

int MapIndex(uint16 fromIndex, Word toIndex, bool doAll = false);

Maps the *fromIndex* to the *toIndex* in the current palette of this DIB.

Returns the palette entry for the *toIndex* argument.

See also   TDib::FindIndex, TDib::SetIndex, TDib::GetIndex

MapToPalette

void MapToPalette(const TPalette& pal);

Modifies this DIB so that the pixels and color table coincide with a given palette.

MapUIColors

void MapUIColors(uint mapColors, const TColor* bkColor = 0); ˙

Maps the UI colors to the value specified in the parameter, *mapColors*, which is one of the values of the *Map* enum. Use this function to get the colors for the face shading on push buttons, the highlighting for a selected control button, the text on pushbuttons, the shade of the window frame and the background color.

See also   TDib::Map enum

NumColors

long NumColors() const;

Returns *NumClrs*, the number of colors in this DIB's palette.

See also   TDib::Info

NumScans

uint NumScans() const;

Returns the number of scans in this DIB.

See also   TDib::StartScan, TClipboard

operator ==

bool operator ==(const TDib& other) const;

Compares two handles and returns true if this DIB's handle equals the other (*other*) DIB's handle.

See also   Tdib::Handle

Pitch
int Pitch() const;
Width in bytes, or bytes per scan.

PixelPtr
void HUGE* PixelPtr(uint16 x, uint16 y);
Returns the byte of where the pixel is located.

SetColor
void SetColor(int entry, const TColor& color);
Sets the given color for the given palette entry.

See also   TDib::GetColor, TColor, TDib::MapColor, TDib::FindColor

SetIndex
void SetIndex(int entry, uint16 index);
Sets the given index for the given entry.

See also   TDib::GetIndex, TDib::FindIndex, TDib::MapIndex

Size
TSize Size() const;
Returns *TSize(W,H)*, the size of this DIB.

See also   TDib::Info, TSize

SizeColors
int32 SizeColors() const;
Size of the color table in bytes.

SizeDib
uint32 SizeDib() const;
Memory size of DIB in bytes.

SizeImage
uint32 SizeImage() const;
The size of the DIB image bits in bytes.

SpriteBlt
void SpriteBlt(int dstX, int dstY, TDib& srcDib, int width=0, int height=0, uint8 transparentColor=0);
Transparent bit the DIB.

StartScan
uint StartScan() const;
Returns the DIB's starting scan line.

See also   TDib::numScans

THandle
operator THandle() const;
Returns the handle of the DIB with type HANDLE. *TDib* encapsulates a memory HANDLE with a DIB.

ToClipboard
void ToClipboard(TClipboard& clipboard);
Puts this DIB onto the specified Clipboard.

See also TClipboard

operator TRgbQuad()
Form 1 operator TRgbQuad far*() const;

Form 2 operator const TRgbQuad far*() const;
Typecasts this DIB by returning a pointer to its colors structure.

See also TDib::GetColors, TRgbQuad

Usage
uint16 Usage() const;
Returns the *Mode* for this DIB. This value tells *GDI* how to treat the color table.

See also TDib::Mode

Width
int Width() const;
Returns *W*, the DIB width.

See also TDib::Info

Write
Form 1 bool Write(ostream& os, bool writeFileHeader = false);
Writes this DIB to an ostream.

Form 2 bool Write(TFile& file, bool writeFileHeader = false);
Write this DIB to a file object.

WriteFile
bool WriteFile(const char* filename);
Returns true if the call is successful; otherwise returns false.

XOffset
int XOffset(uint16 x) const;
Returns the byte offset from the start of the scan line to the xth pixel.

YOffset
int YOffset(uint16 y) const;
Returns the starting position of the scan line.

Protected data members

Bits
void HUGE* Bits;
Bits points into the block of memory pointed to by *Info*.

See also TDib::GetBits

Colors
TRgbQuad far* Colors;
Color table[NumClrs] for any bmp.

Info
BITMAPINFO far* Info;
Locked global allocated block.

See also   TDib::GetInfo, TDib::isPM

IsResHandle
bool IsResHandle;
Set true if this DIB is using a resource handle; otherwise, set false.

Mask
uint32 far* Mask;
Color mask[3] for 16 and 32 bpp bmps.

Mode
uint16 Mode;
If *Mode* is DIB_RGB_*Colors*, the color table contains 4-byte RGB entries. If *Mode* is *DIB_PAL_COLORS*, the color table contains 2-byte indexes into some other palette (such as the system palette). Because either of these two cases might exist, two versions of certain functions (such as *GetColors* and *GetIndices*) are required.

See also   TDib::GetColors, TDib::GetIndices, TDib::Usage

NumClrs
long NumClrs;
The number of colors associated with this DIB.

See also   TDib::NumColors, TDib::Width, TDib::Size

Protected constructor

TDib
TDib();
Constructs an empty DIB for use by derived classes.

Protected member functions

CheckValid
TGdiBase::CheckValid;
Makes this function available to derivatives.

CopyOnWrite
void CopyOnWrite();
Copies the DIB.

InfoFromHandle

void InfoFromHandle();

Locks this DIB's handle and extracts the remaining data member values from the DIB header.

See also   TDib::GetInfoHeader

InfoFromHeader

void InfoFromHeader(const BITMAPINFOHEADER& infoHeader);

Gets information and members from the handle.

LoadResource

bool LoadResource(HINSTANCE, TResId);

Loads this DIB from the given resource and returns true if successful.

See also   TDib::LoadFile, TDib constructors

MultiBlt

void MultiBlt(int type, int dstX, int dstY, TDib& srcDib, int width, int height, uint8 transparentColor=0);

Blasts the image from a DIB onto this bitmap.

Read

Form 1   bool Read(IFileIn& in, bool readFileHeader = false);

Reads a Windows 3.0 or PM 1.X device independent bitmap. (.BMP) from an implementor of TDib's IFileIn interface. Checks header, read Info, palette and bitmap. PM DIBs are converted to Windows 3.x DIBs on the fly. Returns true if DIB was read OK.

Form 2   bool Read(istream& is, bool readFileHeader = false);

Reads a Windows 3.0 or PM 1.X device independent bitmap. (.BMP). Checks header, read Info, palette and bitmap. PM DIBs can be converted to Win 3.x DIBs on the fly. Return true if DIB was read OK.

Form 3   bool Read(TFile& file, bool readFileHeader = false);

Reads a Windows 3.x or PM 1.x device independent bitmap from a Tfile. Returns true if DIB was read OK.

Form 4   bool Read(TFile& file, long offBits = 0);

Reads data to this DIB, starting at offset *offBits*, from any file, BMP, or resource. Returns true if the call is successful; otherwise returns false.

See also   TDib::LoadFile

ReadFile

bool ReadFile(const char* name);

Tests if the passed file is a Windows 3.x (or PM 1.x) DIB and if so reads it. Returns true if Dib was read OK.

ResToMemHandle

void ResToMemHandle();

Performs a read-only copy from res handle to mem handle.

ScanBytes
static int ScanBytes(long w, int bpp);

Returns the number of bytes used to store a scanline for the DIB. Rounded up to the nearest 32-bit boundary.

Write
bool Write(IFileOut& out, bool writeFileHeader = false);

Writes the DIB into a file stream.

TDibDC class

dc.h

A DC class derived from *TDC*, *TDibDC* provides access to device-independent bitmaps (DIBs).

Public constructors

Form 1 TDibDC();

Constructs a DC that can be used with DI Bitmaps. Under Win32 bitmaps selected must be DIBSections, under Win16 they must be WinG bitmaps.

Form 2 TDibDC(const TBitmap& bitmap);

Constructs a DC that can be used with DI Bitmaps, then auto-select the given bitmap in. Under Win32 bitmaps selected must be DIBSections, under Win16 they must be WinG bitmaps.

Form 3 TDibDC(const TDib& dib);

Creates a *TDibDC* object with the data provided by the given *TDib* object.

See also   classTDib, TDC::TDC

Public member functions

BitBltToScreen
Form 1 bool BitBltToScreen(TDC& dstDC, int dstX, int dstY, int dstW, int dstH, int srcX=0, int srcY=0) const;

BitBlts from this DIB onto the destination DC.

Form 2 bool BitBltToScreen(TDC& dstDC, const TRect& dst, const TPoint& src) const;

Dib Screen Update BitBlt's. A screen DC must be the destination.

BitBlts from this DIB onto the destination DC.

GetDIBColorTable
uint GetDIBColorTable(uint start, uint entries, RGBQUAD far* colors);

Gets the color table of the currently selected bitmap.

SetDIBColorTable
uint SetDIBColorTable(uint start, uint entries, const RGBQUAD far* colors);

Sets the color table of the currently selected bitmap.

StretchBltToScreen

Form 1   bool StretchBltToScreen(TDC& dstDC, int dstX, int dstY, int dstW, int dstH, int srcX, int srcY, int srcW, int srcH) const;
Stretches the DIB onto the destination DC.

Form 2   bool StretchBltToScreen(TDC& dstDC, const TRect& dst, const TRect& src) const;
Stretches the DIB onto the destination DC.

TDiBitmap class   dibitmap.h

TDiBitmap class is a combination of a TDib and a TBitmap. It can be constructed and manipulated like a *TDib*, but it can also be selected into a device context (DC) and manipulated with GDI. To guarantee functionality on all platforms, the *TDibDC* should be used as the memory DC to hold a *TDiBitmap*.

Public constructors

Form 1   TDiBitmap(HGLOBAL handle, TAutoDelete autoDelete = NoAutoDelete);
Constructs from existing bitmap handle.

Form 2   TDiBitmap(const TClipboard& clipboard);
Constructs from bitmap stored in clipboard.

Form 3   TDiBitmap(const TDib& src);
Constructs a copy from existing *TDib*.

Form 4   TDiBitmap(int width, int height, int nColors, uint16 mode=DIB_RGB_COLORS);
Constructs a new bitmap with the passed-in parameters.

Form 5   TDiBitmap(HINSTANCE module, TResId resid);
Constructs a bitmap stored as a resource.

Form 6   TDiBitmap(const char* name);
Constructs from DIB stored as a file.

Form 7   TDiBitmap(TFile& file, bool readFileHeader = true);
Constructs from a *TFile*.

Form 8   TDiBitmap(istream& is, bool readFileHeader = false);
Constructs from input stream.

Form 9   TDiBitmap(const TBitmap& bitmap, const TPalette* pal = 0);
Constructs from a bitmap and palette information.

Form 10   ~TDiBitmap();
Restores *Bits* data member to 0.

Public member functions

BitsPixel
int BitsPixel() const;
Returns the number of bits to hold each pixel.

Height
int Height() const;
Returns the height of the DIB.

Size
TSize Size() const;
Returns the size of the DIB.

Width
int Width() const;
Returns the width of the DIB.

Protected member function

InitBitmap
void InitBitmap();
Initializes our bitmap side from the DIB side. *TDib::Bits* gets setup to point to the new DIBSection/WinG-managed DIB buffer.

TDllLoader class
module.h

TDllLoader<> provides an easy way to load one instance of a DLL on demand.

Public constructors

Form 1   TDllLoader();
Deletes the DLL object and releases the DLL from memory.

Form 2   ~TDllLoader();
Deletes the DLL object and releases the DLL from memory.

Public member function

IsAvailable
static bool IsAvailable();
Loads the DLL on demand, returning true if it was loaded properly.

TDockable class

TDockable is an abstract base class for fixed or floating docking windows that want to be dockable into docking slips.

Public member functions

ComputeSize
virtual TSize ComputeSize(TAbsLocation loc, TSize* dim) = 0;

Returns the rectangle of the dockable window in the given location. The dockable chooses its layout (horizontal, vertical or rectangle) in that position.

GetRect
virtual void GetRect(TRect& rect) = 0;

Return the rectangle of the dockable window in the given location. The dockable chooses its layout (horizontal, vertical or rectangle) in that position.

GetWindow
virtual TWindow* GetWindow() = 0;

Gets dockable's window and hides it, in case we have to toss it around a bit.

Layout
virtual void Layout(TAbsLocation loc, TSize* dim=0) = 0;

Changes the window to be equal to the size returned from *ComputeNNNNN*.

ShouldBeginDrag
virtual bool ShouldBeginDrag(TPoint& pt) = 0;

This is overriden for any window that wants to be docked. This routine is called from an LButtonDown to determine if the mouse down should move the window or perform an action within the docked window. For example, if a gadget window is docked, this routine would decide if the mousedown is on an enabled gadget; if so, the control is not to be moved. Instead, the action of the gadget being depressed is performed. Otherwise, the gadget window is moved within the docking window.

TDockableControlBar class

TDockableControlBar is a control bar class that is dockable.

Public constructor

TDockableControlBar(TWindow* parent = 0, TTileDirection direction= Horizontal,
    TFont* font = new TGadgetWindowFont, TModule* module = 0);
Constructs a dockable control bar.

TDockableGadgetWindow class

A dockable version of *TGadgetWindow*.

Public constructor

TDockableGadgetWindow
TDockableGadgetWindow(TWindow* parent = 0, TTileDirection direction = Horizontal,
 TFont* font = new TGadgetWindowFont, TModule* module = 0);
This constructor creates a dockable gadget window and sets the appropriate styles for
the window.

Public member functions

ComputeSize
TSize ComputeSize(TAbsLocation loc, TSize* dim);
Finds out how big this dockable would be in a given location, and with a given optional
size hint.

GetHarbor
THarbor* GetHarbor();
Returns the harbor containing the dockable object.

GetRect
void GetRect(TRect& rect);
Gets this dockable's screen rectangle.

GetWindow
TWindow* GetWindow();
Returns the *TWindow* part of this dockable object. In this case, it is just this window.

Layout
void Layout(TAbsLocation loc, TSize* dim=0);
Causes this dockable to lay itself out vertically, horizontally, or rectangularly.

LayoutSession
virtual void LayoutSession();
If the gadget window changes size when laying out a dockable gadget window, this
function tells the dock about it so the dock can resize too.

ShouldBeginDrag
bool ShouldBeginDrag(TPoint& pt);
Returns true if the mouse click point is in a spot that should move this dockable around.

Protected member functions

EvLButtonDown
void EvLButtonDown(uint modKeys, TPoint& point);
Forwards event to slip to allow movement of gadget within the slip.

GetDirectionForLocation
virtual TTileDirection GetDirectionForLocation(TAbsLocation loc);
Returns a gadget window tile direction code, given a docking absolute location code.

TDockingSlip class   docking.h

TDockingSlip is an abstract base class for windows which accepts and holds dockable windows.

Public member functions

DockableInsert
virtual void DockableInsert(TDockable& dockable, const TPoint* topLeft=0, TRelPosition position=rpNone,
    TDockable* relDockable=0) = 0;
Inserts the dockable into the slip, based on arguments given.

DockableMove
virtual void DockableMove(TDockable& dockable, const TPoint* topLeft=0, TRelPosition position=rpNone,
    TDockable* relDockable=0) = 0;

DockableRemoved
virtual void DockableRemoved(const TRect& orgRect) = 0;

GetHarbor
THarbor* GetHarbor() const;

GetLocation
virtual TAbsLocation GetLocation() const = 0;

SetHarbor
void SetHarbor(THarbor* harbor);
Called by *Harbor* to initialize back pointer.

Protected member function

Harbor
THarbor* Harbor;

TDocManager class

docmanag.h

TDocManager creates a document manager object that manages the list of current documents and registered templates, handles standard file menu commands, and displays the user-interface for file and view selection boxes. To provide support for documents and views, an instance of *TDocManager* must be created by the application and attached to the application.

The document manager normally handles events on behalf of the documents by using a response table to process the standard CM_FILENEW, CM_FILEOPEN, CM_FILECLOSE, CM_FILESAVE, CM_FILESAVEAS, CM_FILEREVERT, CM_FILEPRINT, CM_FILEPRINTERSETUP, and CM_VIEWCREATE File menu commands. In response to a CM_FILENEW or a CM_FILEOPEN command, the document manager creates the appropriate document based on the user's selections. In response to the other commands, the document manager determines which of the open documents contains the view associated with the window that has focus. The menu commands are first sent to the window that is in focus and then through the parent window chain to the main window and finally to the application, which forwards the commands to the document manager.

When you create a *TDocManager* or a derived class, you must specify that it has either a multi-document *(dmMDI)* or single-document *(dmSDI)* interface. In addition, if you want the document manager to handle the standard file commands, you must **OR** *dmMDI* or *dmSDI* with *dmMenu*.

You can also enable or disable the document manager menu options by passing *dmSaveEnable* or *dmNoRevert* in the constructor. If you want to enable the File I Save menu option if the document is unmodified, pass the *dmSaveEnable* flag in the constructor. To disable the "Revert to Saved" menu option, pass *dmNoRevert* in the constructor.

When the application directly creates a new document and view, it can attach the view to its frame window, create MDI children, float the window, or create a splitter. However, when the document manager creates a new document and view from the File I Open or File I New menu selection, the application doesn't control the process. To give the application control, the document manager sends messages after the new document and view are successfully created. Then, the application can use the information contained in the template to determine how to install the new document or view object.

Public data members

DocList
TDocument::List DocList;
Holds the list of attached documents, or 0 if no documents exist.

Public constructors and destructor

Constructors

Form 1   TDocManager(int mode, TDocTemplate*& templateHead = DocTemplateStaticHead);

Constructs a *TDocManager* object that supports either single (SDI) or multiple (MDI) open documents depending on the application. The *mode* parameter is set to one of the following: *dmMenu, dmMDI, dmSDI, dmSaveEnable,* or *dmNoRevert*. To install the standard *TDocManager* File menu commands, you must **OR** *dmMDI* or *dmSDI* with *dmMenu*. For example,

```
DocManager = new TDocManager(DocMode | dmMenu);
```

The document manager can then use its menu and response table to handle these events. If you do not specify the *dmMenu* parameter, you must provide the menu and functions to handle these commands. However, you can still use your application object's *DocManager* data member to access the document manager's functions.

Form 2   TDocManager(int mode, TApplication* app, TDocTemplate*& templateHead = DocTemplateStaticHead);
The constructor performs the same operations as the first constructor. The additional *app* parameter, however, points to the application associated with this document.

Destructor

virtual ~TDocManager();

Destroys a *TDocManager* object removes attached documents templates. The constructor resets *TDocTemplate::DocTemplateStaticHead* to point to the head of the static template list.

See also   dmxxxx document manager mode constants

Public member functions

AttachTemplate

void AttachTemplate(TDocTemplate&);
Inserts a template into the chain of templates.

CmFileClose

virtual void CmFileClose();
Responds to a file close message. Tests to see if the document has been changed since it was last saved, and if not, prompts the user to confirm the save operation.

CmFileNew

virtual void CmFileNew();
Calls *CreateAnyDoc* with no path specified.

See also   dtxxxx document template constants

CmFileOpen

virtual void CmFileOpen();
Lets the user select a registered template from the list displayed in the dialog box. Calls *CreateAnyDoc*.

CmFileRevert

virtual void CmFileRevert();

Reverts to the previously saved document. Does not revert if the document has not been changed since last save; that is, if the document's *IsDirty* function returns **false**.

CmFileSave

virtual void CmFileSave();

Responds to a file save message. Sets *doc* to the current document. *CmFileSave* checks *IsDirty* only if the *dmSaveEnable flag* was not specified. Calls *PostDocError* with IDS_NOTCHANGED if *dmSaveEnable* was NOT specified and *IsDirty* returns **false**.

See also   IDS_xxxx Document String ID constants

CmFileSaveAs

virtual void CmFileSaveAs();

Prompts the user to enter a new name for the document and saves the document to that file.

CmViewCreate

virtual void CmViewCreate();

Creates a document view based on the view name of the current document. If more than one template exists for the document, *CmViewCreate* allows the user to select the type of view from the template list.

CreateAnyDoc

virtual TDocument* CreateAnyDoc(const char far* path, long flags= 0);

Creates a document based on the directory path and the specified template. The parameter *flags*, one of the document template constants, determines how the document template is created. If *path* is 0 and this is not a new document (the flag *dtNewDoc* is not set), it displays a dialog box. If *path* is 0 and *dtNewDoc* is not set and more than one template exists, *CreateAnyDoc* displays a dialog box and a list of templates.

See also   TDocTemplate::CreateDoc, dtxxxx document template constants

CreateAnyView

virtual TView* CreateAnyView(TDocument& doc, long flags= 0);

Creates a document view based on the directory path and specified template. The parameter *flags*, one of the document template constants, determines how the document template is created.

See also   TDocument, TDocTemplate::CreateView, dtxxxx document template constants

CreateDoc

TDocument* CreateDoc(TDocTemplate* tpl, const char far *, TDocument* parent, long flags = 0);

CreateDoc creates a document based on the directory path and the specified template. The *flags* parameter contains one of the document template constants that determines how the document is created.

See also   TDocument, TDocTemplate::CreateView, dtxxxx document template constants

CreateView

TView* CreateView(TDocument* doc);

Creates a view of the specified document.

See also   TDocTemplate::CreateView, dtxxxx document template constants

DeleteTemplate

void DeleteTemplate(TDocTemplate&);

Removes a template from the list of templates attached to the document.

See also   TDocManager::RefTemplate

EvCanClose

bool EvCanClose();

Checks to see if all child documents can be closed before closing the current document. If any child returns **false**, returns **false** and aborts the process. If all children return **true**, *EvCanClose* calls *TDocManager::FlushDoc* for each document. If *FlushDoc* finds that the document is dirty, it displays a message asking the user to save the document, discard any changes, or cancel the operation. If the document is not dirty and *CanClose* returns **true**, *EvCanClose* returns **true**.

EvPreProcessMenu

void EvPreProcessMenu(HMENU hmenu);

Called from *MainWindow*, *EvPreProcessMenu* loads and deletes a menu at the position specified by MF_POSITION or MF_POPUP. Your application can call *EvPreProcessMenu* to process the main window's menu before it is displayed.

See also   TApplication::PreProcessMenu

EvWakeUp

void EvWakeUp();

Used only after streaming in the doc manager, *EvWakeUp* allows for the windows to be created after the streaming has occurred.

FindDocument

TDocTemplate* FindDocument(const char far* path);

Returns the first document whose pattern matches the given file name. If no document is compatible with the supplied file name, or if the document is open already, it returns 0.

See also   TDocTemplate

FlushDoc

virtual bool FlushDoc(TDocument& doc);

Updates the document with any changes and prompts the user for confirmation of updates.

See also   TDocument

GetApplication

TApplication* GetApplication();

Returns the current application.

See also   TApplication

GetCurrentDoc

virtual TDocument* GetCurrentDoc();

Calls *TWindow::GetFocus* to determine the window with the focus. Searches the list of documents and returns the document that contains the view with the focus. Returns 0 if no document has a view with focus.

See also   TDocument

GetNextTemplate

TDocTemplate* GetNextTemplate(TDocTemplate* tpl);

Returns the next document template.

See also   TDocTemplate

InitDoc

TDocument* InitDoc(TDocument* doc, const char far* path, long flags)

Initializes the documents, the directory path for the document, and the *dtxxxx* document flag values (such as *dtNewDoc*) used to create document templates.

See also   TDocTemplate, dt Document View Constants

IsFlagSet

bool IsFlagSet(int Flag);

Returns **true** if the *dtxxxx* document template constant specified in *Flag* is set.

See also   dt Document View Constants

MatchTemplate

TDocTemplate* MatchTemplate(const char far* path);

Returns the first registered template whose pattern matches the given file name. If no template is compatible with the supplied file name, or if the template is open already, it returns 0.

See also   TDocTemplate

PostDocError

virtual uint PostDocError(TDocument& doc, uint sid, uint choice = MB_OK);

Displays a message box with the error message passed as a string resource ID in *sid*. By default, the message box contains either an OK push button or a question mark icon. If an error message can't be found, *PostDocError* displays a "Message not found" message. *choice* can be one or more of the *MB_Xxxx message* style constants. This function can be overridden.

See also   TDocument::PostError, MB_Xxxx Message Constants

PostEvent

Form 1 virtual void PostEvent(int id, TDocument& doc);

If the current document changes, posts a WM_OWLDOCUMENT message to indicate a change in the status of the document.

Form 2 virtual void PostEvent(int id, TView& view);

If the current view changes, posts a WM_OWLVIEW message to indicate a change in the status of the view.

See also TDocument, TView

RefTemplate

void RefTemplate(TDocTemplate&);

Adds a template to the list of templates attached to the document.

See also TDocManager::UnRefTemplate, TDocTemplate

SelectAnySave

virtual TDocTemplate* SelectAnySave(TDocument& doc, bool samedoc = true);

Selects a registered template to save with this document.

See also TDocTemplate, TDocument

SelectSave

bool SelectSave(TDocument& doc);

Prompts the user to select a file name for the document. Filters out read-only files.

See also TDocTemplate::SelectSave

UnRefTemplate

void UnRefTemplate(TDocTemplate&);

Removes a template from the list of templates attached to the document.

See also TDocManager::RefTemplate, TDocTemplate

Protected member functions

SelectDocPath

virtual int SelectDocPath(TDocTemplate** tpllist, int tplcount, char far* path, int buflen, long flags,
        bool save=false);

Prompts the user to select one of the templates to use for the file to be opened. Returns the template index used for the selection, or 0 if unsuccessful. For a file open operation, *save* is **false**. For a file save operation, *save* is **true**. This function can be overridden to provide a customized user interface.

See also TDocTemplate

SelectDocType

virtual int SelectDocType(TDocTemplate** tpllist, int tplcount);

Lets the user select a document type from a list of document templates. Returns the template index used for the selection, or 0 if unsuccessful. *SelectDocType* can be overridden.

See also   TDocTemplate

SelectViewType

virtual int SelectViewType(TDocTemplate** tpllist, int tplcount);

Lets the user select a view name for a new view from a list of view names. Returns the template index used for the selection or 0 if unsuccessful. *SelectViewType* can be overridden.

See also   TDocTemplate

Response table entries

Response table entry	Member function
EV_COMMAND(CM_FILECLOSE, CmFileClose)	CmFileClose
EV_COMMAND(CM_FILENEW, CmFileNew)	CmFileNew
EV_COMMAND(CM_FILEOPEN, CmFileOpen)	CmFileOpen
EV_COMMAND(CM_FILEREVERT, CmFileRevert)	CmFileRevert
EV_COMMAND(CM_FILESAVE, CmFileSave)	CmFileSave
EV_COMMAND(CM_FILESAVEAS, CmFileSaveAs)	CmFileSaveAs
EV_COMMAND(CM_VIEWCREATE, CmViewCreate)	CmViewCreate
EV_COMMAND_ENABLE(CM_FILECLOSE, CmEnableClose)	CmEnableClose
EV_COMMAND_ENABLE(CM_FILENEW, CmEnableNew)	CmEnableNew
EV_COMMAND_ENABLE(CM_FILEOPEN, CmEnableOpen)	CmEnableOpen
EV_COMMAND_ENABLE(CM_FILEREVERT, CmEnableRevert)	EmEnableRevert
EV_COMMAND_ENABLE(CM_FILESAVE, CmEnableSave)	CmEnableSave
EV_COMMAND_ENABLE(CM_FILESAVEAS, CmEnableSaveAs)	CmEnableSaveAs
EV_COMMAND_ENABLE(CM_VIEWCREATE, CmEnableCreate)	CmEnableCreate
EV_WM_CANCLOSE	EvCanClose
EV_WM_PREPROCMENU	EvPreProcessMenu
EV_WM_WAKEUP	EvWakeUp

TDocTemplate class   **doctpl.h**

TDocTemplate is an abstract base class that contains document template functionality. This document template class defines several functions that make it easier for you to use documents and their corresponding views. *TDocTemplate* classes create documents and views from resources and handle document naming and browsing. The document manager maintains a list of the current template objects. Each document type requires a separate document template.

Public member functions

ClearFlag
void ClearFlag(long flag);
Clears a document template constant.

See also   dt document template constants

Clone
virtual TDocTemplate* Clone(TModule* module, TDocTemplate*& phead=DocTemplateStaticHead)=0;
Makes a copy of a document template.

ConstructDoc
virtual TDocument* ConstructDoc(TDocument* parent = 0) = 0;
A pure virtual function that must be defined in a derived class, *ConstructDoc* creates a document specified by the document template class. Use this function in place of *CreateDoc*.

See also   TDocManager::CreateDoc

ConstructView
virtual TView* ConstructView(TDocument& doc = 0) = 0;
A pure virtual function that must be defined in a derived class, *ConstructView* creates the view specified by the document template class.

See also   TDocManager::CreateView

CreateDoc
virtual TDocument* CreateDoc(const char far* path, long flags = 0)= 0;
An obsolete pure virtual function that must be defined in a derived class, *CreateDoc* creates a document based on the directory path (*path*) and the specified template and *flags* value. If the *path* is 0 and the new flag (*dtNewDoc*) is not set, the dialog box is displayed. This function is obsolete: use *ConstructDoc* instead.

See also   TDocManager::CreateAnyDoc, TDocTemplate::ConstructDoc

CreateView

virtual TView* CreateView(TDocument& doc, long flags) = 0;

A pure virtual function that must be defined in a derived class, *CreateView* creates the view specified by the document template class. This function is obsolete: use *ConstructView* instead.

See also TDocManager::CreateAnyView, TDocTemplate::ConstructView

GetDefaultExt

const char far* GetDefaultExt() const;

Gets the default extension to use if the user has entered the name of a file without any extension. If there is no default extension, *GetDefaultExt* contains 0.

GetDescription

const char far* GetDescription() const;

Gets the template description to put in the file-selection list box or the File | New menu-selection list box.

GetDirectory

const char far* GetDirectory() const;

Gets the directory path to use when searching for matching files. This will get updated if a file is selected and the *dtUpdateDir* flag is set.

See also dt document template constants

GetDocManager

TDocManager* GetDocManager() const;

Points to the document manager.

GetFileFilter

const char far* GetFileFilter() const;

Gets any valid document matching pattern to use when searching for files.

GetFlags

long GetFlags() const;

Gets the document template constants, which indicate how the document is created and opened.

See also dt xxxx document template constants

GetModule

TModule*& GetModule();

Returns a module pointer.

GetNextTemplate

TDocTemplate* GetNextTemplate() const;

Gets the next template in the list of templates.

GetRefCount
int GetRefCount() const;

Returns the number of reference count of the template.

Note The reference count of static templates has the high bit set.

GetRegList
TRegList& GetRegList() const;

Gets the program's registration table, which contains the program's current program ID, class ID, executable path, as well as other attributes used to construct a *TDocTemplate* object. See the entry for Registration macros in this manual for information about how the registration macros generate registration information.

GetViewName
virtual const char far* GetViewName() = 0;

A pure virtual function that must be defined in a derived class, *GetViewName* gets the name of the view associated with the template.

InitDoc
TDocument* InitDoc(TDocument* doc, const char far* path, long flags);

InitDoc is called only from the subclass so that *CreateDoc* can continue its document processing.

See also TDocTemplate::CreateDoc

InitView
TView* InitView(TView* view);

Called only from the subclass to continue *CreateView* processing.

See also TDocTemplate::CreateView

IsFlagSet
bool IsFlagSet(long flag);

Returns nonzero if the document template flag is set.

See also dt xxxx document template constants

IsMyKindOfDoc
virtual TDocument* IsMyKindOfDoc(TDocument& doc)=0;

A pure virtual function that must be defined in a derived class, *IsMyKindOfDoc* tests if the template belongs to the same class as the document or to a derived class.

See also TDocTemplateT::IsMyKindOfDoc

IsMyKIndofView
virtual TView* IsMyKindOfView(TView& view) = 0;

A pure virtual function that must be defined in a derived class, *IsMyKindofView* tests if the template belongs to the same class as the view or to a derived class.

IsStatic
bool IsStatic();

Returns true if the template is statically constructed.

IsVisible
bool IsVisible();

Indicates whether the document can be displayed in the file selection dialog box. A document is visible if *dtHidden* isn't set and *Description* isn't 0.

SelectSave
bool SelectSave(TDocument& doc);

Prompts the user to select a file name for the document. Filters out read-only files.

SetDefaultExt
void SetDefaultExt(const char far*);

Sets the default extension to use if the user has entered the name of a file without any extension. If there is no default extension, *SetDefaultExt* contains 0.

SetDescription
void SetDescription(const char far*);

This function is maintained for backward compatability with code generated for versions prior to enhanced document templates.

SetDirectory
Form 1   void SetDirectory(const char far*);

Form 2   void SetDirectory(const char far*, int len);

Sets the directory path to use when searching for matching files. This will get updated if a file is selected and the *dtUpdateDir* flag is set.

See also   TDocTemplate::GetDirectory

SetDocManager
void SetDocManager(TDocManager* dm);

Sets the current document manager to the argument *dm*.

SetFileFilter
void SetFileFilter(const char far*);

Sets the valid document matching pattern to use when searching for files.

SetFlag
void SetFlag(long flag);

Sets the document template constants, which indicate how the document is created and opened.

See also   dtxxxx document template constants

SetModule
TModule*& SetModule();

Sets a module pointer.

Protected constructors and destructor

Constructors

Form 1   TDocTemplate(TRegList& regList, TModule*& module, TDocTemplate*& phead);

Uses the information in the registration table (*regList*) to construct a *TDocTemplate* with the specified file description, file filter pattern, search path for viewing the directory, default file extension, and flags representing the view and creation options from the registration list. Then, adds this template to the document manager's template list. If the document manager is not yet constructed, adds the template to a static list, which the document manager will later add to its template list.

The argument, *module*, specifies the *TModule* of the caller. *phead* specifies the template head for the caller's module. See the Registration macros entry in this manual for information about the registration macros that generate a *TRegList*, which contains the attributes used to create a *TDocTemplate* object.

Form 2   TDocTemplate(const char* desc, const char* filt, const char* dir, const char* ext, long flags, TModule*& module, TDocTemplate*& phead);

Constructs a Doc/View template from the description, filter, directory, file extension, '*dt*' flags, module and template head parameters. This constructor is primarily for backward compatibility with earlier implementation of ObjectWindows' Doc/View subsystem.

Destructor

~TDocTemplate();

Destroys a *TDocTemplate* object and frees the data members (*FileFilter, Description, Directory, and DefaultExt*). The Destructor is called only when no views or documents are associated with the template. Instead of calling this Destructor directly, use the *Delete* member function.

See also   dt xxxx document template constants

TDocTemplateT<D,V> class   doctpl.h

To register the associated document and view classes, a parameterized subclass, *TDocTemplateT<D,V>*, is used to construct a particular document and view, where *D* represents the document class and *V* represents the view class. The parameterized template classes are created using a macro, which also generates the associated streamable support. The document and view classes are provided through the use of a parameterized subclass. The template class name is used as a **typedef** for the parameterized class. For example,

```
DEFINE_DOC_TEMPLATE_CLASS(TFileDocument, TEditView, MyEditFile)
```

You can instantiate a document template using either a static member or an explicit construction. For example,

```
MyEditFile et1("Edit text files",
      "*.txt","D:\\doc",".TXT"",dtNoAutoView);
new MyEditFile(.....)
```

When a document template is created, the document manager (*TDocManager*) registers the template. When the document template's delete function is called to delete the template, it is no longer visible to the user. However, it remains in memory as long as any documents still use it.

Public constructors

Form 1   TDocTemplateT(const char far* filt, const char far* desc, const char far* dir, const char far* ext, long flags = 0,
          TModule*& module = ::Module, TDocTemplate*& phead = DocTemplateStaticHead);
Constructs a *TDocTemplateT* with the specified file description (*desc*), file filter pattern (*filt*), search path for viewing the directory (*dir*), default file extension (*ext*), and flags representing the view and creation options (*flags*). *module*, which is instantiated and exported directly from every executable module, can be used to access the current instance.

Form 2   TDocTemplateT(TRegList& regList, TModule*& module = ::Module,
          TDocTemplate*& phead = DocTemplateStaticHead);
Constructs a *TDocTemplateT* using the registration table to determine the file filter pattern, search path for viewing the directory, default file extension, and flag values. See the entry in this manual for registration macros for more information about how the registration tables are created. *module*, which is instantiated and exported directly from every executable module, can be used to access the current instance.

Public member functions

Clone
TDocTemplateT* Clone(TModule* module, TDocTemplate*& phead = DocTemplateStaticHead;
Makes a copy of the *TDocTemplateT* object.

ConstructDoc
D* ConstructDoc(TDocument* parent = 0);
Factory method to create a new document of type *D* using the specified parameter as the parent document.

ConstructView
V* ConstructView(TDocument& doc);
Factory method to create a new view of type *V* from the specified document parameter.

CreateDoc
D* CreateDoc(const char far* path, long flags = 0);
Creates a document of type *D* based on the directory path (*path*) and *flags* value.

See also   TDocTemplate::CreateDoc

CreateView
TView* CreateView(TDocument& doc, long flags = 0);
Creates the view specified by the document template class.

See also   TDocManager::CreateAnyView

GetViewName

virtual const char far* GetViewName();

Gets the name of the view associated with the template.

IsMyKindOfDoc

D* IsMyKindOfDoc(TDocument& doc);

Tests to see if the document (*doc*) is either the same class as the template's document class or a derived class. If the template can't use the document, *IsMyKIndOfDoc* returns 0.

See also   TDocTemplate::IsMyKindOfDoc

IsMyKindOfView

V* IsMyKindOfView(TView& view);

Tests to see if the view (*view*) is either the same class as the template's view class or a derived class. If the template can't use the view, *IsMyKIndOfView* returns 0.

TDocument class   docview.h

An abstract base class, *TDocument* is the base class for all document objects and serves as an interface between the document, its views, and the document manager (*TDocManager* class). *TDocument* creates, destroys, and sends messages about the view. For example, if the user changes a document, *TDocument* tells the view that the document has been updated. The DEFINE_DOC_TEMPLATE_CLASS macro associates a document with its views.

In order to send messages to its associated views, the document maintains a list of all the views existing for that document and communicates with the views using ObjectWindows event-handling mechanism. Rather than using the function *SendMessage*, the document accesses the view's event table. The views can update the document's data by calling the member functions of the particular document. Views can also request streams, which are constructed by the document.

Both documents and views have lists of properties for their applications to use. When documents and views are created or destroyed, messages are sent to the application, which can then query the properties to determine how to process the document or view. It is the document manager's responsibility to determine if a particular view is appropriate for the given document.

Because the property attribute functions are virtual, a derived class (which is called first) might override the properties defined in a base class. Each derived class must implement its own property attribute types of either string or binary data. If the derived class duplicates the property names of the parent class, it should provide the same behavior and data type as the parent.

In order to add persistence to documents, *TDocument* contains several virtual functions (for example, *InStream* and *OutStream*) that support streaming. Your derived classes need to override these functions in order to read and write data.

Although documents are usually associated with files, they do not necessarily have to be files; they can also consist of database tables, mail systems, fax or modem transmissions, disk directories, and so on.

Public data members

ChildDoc
List ChildDoc;

The list of child documents associated with this document.

Tag
void far* Tag;

Holds a pointer to the application-defined data. Typically, you can use *Tag* to install a pointer to your own application's associated data structure. *Tag*, which is initialized to 0 at the time a *TDocument* object is constructed, is not otherwise used by the document view classes.

Type definitions

TDocProp enum
enum TDocProp {PrevProperty = 0, DocumentClass, TemplateName, ViewCount, StoragePath, DocTitle, NextProperty};

These property values, which describe the basic properties of a document, are available in classes derived from *TDocument*. They can be used to update and query the attributes of a document. *PrevProperty* and *NextProperty* are delimiters for every document's property list.

Table 2.7   Document constants

Constant	Meaning if set
PrevProperty	Index of last property in base class
DocumentClass	Name of C++ class encapsulating document (text)
TemplateName	Name of template attached to document (text)
ViewCount	Number of views displaying this document (int)
StoragePath	Identifies object holding data of this document (text)
DocTitle	Caption of this document (text)
NextProperty	Next index to be used by derived class

See also   TDocument::GetProperty, TDocument::SetProperty

Public constructor and destructor

Constructor
TDocument(TDocument* parent = 0);

Although you do not create a *TDocument* object directly, you must call the constructor when you create a derived class. *parent* points to the parent of the new document. If no parent exists, *parent* is 0.

Destructor
virtual ~TDocument();

Deletes a *TDocument* object. Normally, *Close* is called first. *TDocument*'s destructor destroys all children and closes all open streams. If this is the last document that used the template, it closes the object's template and any associated views, deletes the object's stream, and removes itself from the parent's list of children if a parent exists. If there is no parent, it removes itself from the document manager's document list.

Public member functions

CanClose
virtual bool CanClose();

Checks to see if all child documents can be closed before closing the current document. If any child returns **false**, *CanClose* returns **false** and aborts the process. If all children return **true**, calls *TDocManager::FlushDoc*. If *FlushDoc* finds that the document has been changed but not saved, it displays a message asking the user to either save the document, discard any changes, or cancel the operation. If the document has not been changed and all children's *CanClose* functions return **true**, this *CanClose* function returns **true**.

Close
virtual bool Close();

Closes the document but does not delete or detach the document. Before closing the document, *Close* checks any child documents and tries to close them before closing the parent document. Even if you write your own *Close* function, call *TDocument*'s version to ensure that all child documents are checked before the parent document is closed.

Commit
virtual bool Commit(bool force = false);

Saves the current data to storage. When a file is closed, the document manager calls either *Commit* or *Revert*. If *force* is **true**, all data is written to storage. *Commit* checks any child documents and commits their changes to storage also. Before the current data is saved, all child documents must return **true**. If all child documents return **true**, *Commit* flushes the views for operations that occurred since the last time the view was checked. After all data for the document is updated and saved, *Commit* returns **true**.

DocWithFocus

virtual TDocument* DocWithFocus(HWND hwnd);

Return pointer to this document or one of its child documents if the spcecified window parameter is a view associated with the document.

Note Unlike *HasFocus*, this method allows you to distinguish whether the document with focus is a child document.

FindProperty

virtual int FindProperty(const char far* name);

Gets the property index, given the property name (*name*). Returns either the integer index number that corresponds to the name or 0 if the name isn't found in the list of properties.

See also pfxxxx property attribute constants, TDocument::PropertyName

GetDocManager

TDocManager& GetDocManager();

Returns a pointer to the current document manager.

GetDocPath

const char far* GetDocPath();

Returns the directory path for the document. This might change the SaveAs operation.

GetOpenMode

int GetOpenMode;

Gets the mode and protection flag values for the current document.

See also TDocument::SetOpenMode

GetParentDoc

TDocument* GetParentDoc();

Returns either the parent document of the current document or 0 if there is no parent document.

GetProperty

virtual int GetProperty(int index, void far* dest, int textlen=0);

Returns the total number of properties for this document, where *index* is the property index, *dest* contains the property data, and *textlen* is the size of the array. If *textlen* is 0, property data is returned as binary data; otherwise, property data is returned as text data.

See also pfxxxx property attribute constants, TDocument::SetProperty

GetStreamList

TStream* GetStreamList() const;

Returns head of the link list of streams associated with this document.

Note To iterate through all the streams, use the *NextStream* method with the pointer returned from this method.

GetTag

void far* GetTag() const;

Returns pointer to user-defined data [i.e. tag] attached to this document.

GetTemplate

TDocTemplate* GetTemplate();

Gets the template used for document creation. The template can be changed during a SaveAs operation.

GetTitle

CONST CHAR FAR* GetTitle();

Returns the title of the document.

GetViewList

TView* GetViewList() const;

Returns pointer to the head of the link list of views associated with this document.

Note   To iterate through all the views, use the *NextView* method with the pointer obtained from this method.

HasFocus

bool HasFocus(HWND hwnd);

Used by the document manager, *HasFocus* returns **true** if this document's view has focus. *hwnd* is a handle to the document. to determine if the document contains a view with a focus.

InitDoc

virtual bool InitDoc();

A virtual method that is overridden by *TOleDocument::InitDoc*. You can use this function to prepare the document before the view is constructed and before the *dnCreate* event, which indicates that the document has been created and is posted.

See also   dnxxxx Document Message enum

InitView

TView* InitView(TView* view);

InStream

virtual TInStream* InStream(int mode, const char far* strmId=0);

Generic input for the particular storage medium, *InStream* returns a pointer to a *TInStream*. *mode* is a combination of the *ios* bits defined in iostream.h. See the document open mode constants for a list of the open modes. Used for documents that support named streams, *strmId* is a pointer to the name of a stream. Override this function to provide streaming for your document class.

See also   TDocument::OutStream

IsDirty

virtual bool IsDirty();

Returns **true** if the document or one of its views has changed but has not been saved.

IsEmbedded

virtual bool IsEmbedded();

Returns **true** if the document is embedded in an OLE 2 container.

See also   TDocument::SetEmbedded

IsOpen

virtual bool IsOpen();

Checks to see if the document has any streams in its stream list. Returns **false** if no streams are open; otherwise, returns **true**.

NextStream

TStream* NextStream(const TStream* strm);

Gets the next entry in the stream. Holds 0 if none exists.

NextView

TView* NextView(const TView* view);

Gets the next view in the list of views. Holds 0 if none exists.

NotifyViews

bool NotifyViews(int event, long item=0, TView* exclude=0);

Notifies the views of the current document and the views of any child documents of a change. In contrast to QueryViews, *NotifyViews* sends notification of an event to all views and returns **true** if any views returned a **true** result. The event, EV_OWLNOTIFY, is sent with an event code, which is private to the particular document and view class, and a **long** argument, which can be cast appropriately to the actual type passed in the argument of the response function.

Open

virtual bool Open(int mode, const char far* path = 0);

Opens the document using the path specified by *DocPath*. Sets *OpenMode* to *mode*. *TDocument::Open* always returns **true** and actually performs no actions. Other classes override this function to open specified file documents and views.

See also   TFileDocument::Open

OutStream

virtual TOutStream* OutStream(int mode, const char far* strmId = 0);

Generic output for the particular storage medium, *OutStream* returns a pointer to a *TOutStream. mode* is a combination of the *ios* bits defined in iostream.h. Used for documents that support named streams, *strmId* points to the name of the stream. *TDocument::OutStream* version always returns 0. Override this function to provide streaming for your document class.

See also   TDocument::InStream

PostError

virtual uint PostError(uint sid, uint choice = MB_OK);

Posts the error message passed as a string resource ID in *sid. choice* is one or more of the MB_Xxxx style constants.

See also   TDocManager::PostDocError, MB_Xxxx message constants

PropertyCount
virtual int PropertyCount();

Gets the total number of properties for the *TDocument* object. Returns *NextProperty* -1.

See also   pfxxxx property attribute constants

PropertyFlags
virtual int PropertyFlags(int index);

Returns the attributes of a specified property given the index (*index*) of the property whose attributes you want to retrieve.

See also   pfxxxx property attribute constants, TDocument::FindProperty, TDocument::PropertyName

PropertyName
virtual const char* PropertyName(int index);

Returns the name of the property given the index value (*index*).

See also   pfxxxx property attribute constants, TDocument::FindProperty

QueryViews
TView* QueryViews(int event, long item=0, TView* exclude=0);

Queries the views of the current document and the views of any child documents about a specified event, but stops at the first view that returns **true**. In contrast to *NotifyViews*, *QueryViews* returns a pointer to the first view that responded to an event with a **true** result. The event, EV_OWLNOTIFY, is sent with an event code (which is private to the particular document and view class) and a **long** argument (which can be cast appropriately to the actual type passed in the argument of the response function).

Revert
virtual bool Revert(bool clear = false);

Performs the reverse of *Commit* and cancels any changes made to the document since the last commit. If *clear* is **true**, data is not reloaded for views. *Revert* also checks all child documents and cancels any changes if all children return **true**. When a file is closed, the document manager calls either *Commit* or *Revert*. Returns **true** if the operation is successful.

RootDocument
virtual TDocument& RootDocument();

Returns the **this** pointer as the root document.

SetDirty
void SetDirty(bool dirty = true);

Updates the document's dirty flag using the specified parameter.

SetDocManager
void SetDocManager(TDocManager& dm);

Sets the current document manager to the argument *dm*.

SetDocPath

virtual bool SetDocPath(const char far* path);

Sets the document path for Open and Save operations.

SetEmbedded

virtual bool SetEmbedded();

Marks the document as being embedded in an OLE 2 container. Typically, this happens when the server is created and when the factory template class creates the component.

See also   TDocument::IsEmbedded, Factory template classes

SetOpenMode

void SetOpenMode(int mode);

Sets the mode and protection flag values for the current document.

See also   TDocument::GetOpenMode

SetProperty

virtual bool SetProperty(int index, const void far* src);

Sets the value of the property, given *index*, the index value of the property, and *src*, the data type (either binary or text) to which the property must be set.

See also   pfxxxx property attribute constants, TDocument::GetProperty

SetTag

void SetTag(void* far* tag);

Attach an arbitrary (user-defined) pointer with this document.

Note   The *Tag* is a place-holder. It is not used by the Doc/View subsystem.

SetTemplate

bool SetTemplate(TDocTemplate* tpl);

Sets the document template. However, if the template type is incompatible with the file, the document manager will refuse to save the file as this template type.

SetTitle

virtual void SetTitle(const char far* title);

Sets the title of the document.

Protected data members

DirtyFlag

bool DirtyFlag;

Indicates that unsaved changes have been made to the document. Views can also independently maintain their local disk status.

Embedded

bool Embedded;

Indicates whether the document is embedded.

Protected member functions

AttachStream
virtual void AttachStream(TStream& strm);
Called from TStream's constructor, *AttachStream* attaches a stream to the current document.

DetachStream
virtual void DetachStream(TStream& strm);
Called from TStream's destructor, *DetachStream* detaches the stream from the current document.

TDocument::TList nested class   docview.h

The *TDocument::TList* nested class encapsulates the chain of documents. It allows addition, removal, and destruction of documents from the document list.

Public constructor and destructor

Constructor
TList() : DocList(0);
Constructs a *TDocument::TList* object.

Destructor
~TList();
Destroys a *TDocument::TList* object.

Public member functions

TList::Destroy
void Destroy();
Deletes all documents.

TList::Insert
bool Insert(TDocument* doc);
Inserts a new document into the document list. Fails if the document already exists.

TList::Next
TDocument* Next(const TDocument* doc);
If the *doc* parameter is 0, *Next* returns the first document in the list of documents.

TList::Remove
bool Remove(TDocument* doc);
Removes a document from the document list.

TDragListEventHandler class   draglist.h

TDragListEventHandler is a *TEventHandler mix-in*. This class is designed to handle the drag list notifications and forward the messages from the parent window to the *TDragList* class.

Public member function

DragNotify
TResult DragNotify(TParam1, TParam2);
Handles the DRAGLISTMSGSTRING notification by calling virtual functions based on the notification message.

TDragList class   draglist.h

TDragList is a draggable list box. A draggable list box is a list box which can be used to drag items to change their position. The program responds to drag events accordingly. Typical usage includes a list of fields that can be reordered.

Type definitions

TCursorType enum
enum TCursorType {dlStop = DL_STOPCURSOR, dlCopy = DL_COPYCURSOR,
    dlMove = DL_MOVECURSOR};
TCursorType returns the type of cursor to represent the allowable during a drag operation. The cursor provides feedback to the user about whether the object being dragged can be dropped and the operation resulting from the drop.

Table 2.8   Cursor type constants

Constant	Meaning if set
dlStop	The item cannot be dropped now (stop cursor)
dlCopy	The item dragged will be copied (copy cursor)
dlMove	The item dragged will be moved (move cursor)

Public constructors

TDragList
Form 1   TDragList(TWindow* parent, int id, int x, int y, int w, int h, TModule* module = 0);
Constructor for creating a drag list dynamically.

Form 2   TDragList(TWindow* parent, int resourceId, TModule* module = 0);
Constructor for creating a drag list from a resource.

Public member functions

BeginDrag
virtual bool BeginDrag(int item, const TPoint& point);

The drag UI has started. Return true to allow drag.

CancelDrag
virtual void CancelDrag(int item, const TPoint& point);

User has cancelled the drag.

Dragging
virtual TCursorType Dragging(int item, const TPoint& point);

User has moved the mouse. Return the type of cursor to represent the allowable action.

DrawInsert
void DrawInsert(int item);

Draws the drag cursor.

Dropped
virtual void Dropped(int item, const TPoint& point);

User has dropped the item.

ItemFromPoint
int ItemFromPoint(const TPoint& p, bool scroll = true);

Retrieve the item from the specified point. Return -1 if the point is not on an item. *scroll* determines whether the listbox will scroll if the point is above or below the listbox.

Protected member functions

SetupWindow
void SetupWindow();

SetupWindow for the drag listbox must call *MakeDragList()*.

TDropTarget class   shellitm.h

TDropTarget wraps the *IDropTarget* interface (currently lightweight). *A TDropTarget* is returned by *TShellItem::GetDropTarget Default, TComRef<IDropTarget>* and copy constructors supplied. *TComRef<IDropTarget>* and *TDropTarget* assignment operators are also supplied.

Public constructors

TDropTarget
Form 1   TDropTarget(IDropTarget* iface = 0);

Default constructor for *TDropTarget*.

Form 2   TDropTarget(const TComRef<IDropTarget>& source);
          TDropTarget constructor to construct from *TComRef<IDropTarget>*.

Form 3   TDropTarget(const TDropTarget& source);
          TDropTarget copy constructor.

Public member functions

operator =
Form 1   TDropTarget& operator= (const TDropTarget& source);
          TDropTarget assignment operator (from another *TDropTarget*).

Form 2   TDropTarget& operator= (const TComRef<IDropTarget>& source);
          TDropTarget assignment operator (from *TComRef<IDropTarget>*).

TDvFileOpenDialog class   docmanag.h

TDvFileOpenDialog encapsulates the FileOpen dialog used by the DocView manager. It enhances the standard ObjectWindows *TFileOpenDialog* by providing logic to update the dialog as the user switches between file types.

Public constructor

TDvFileOpenDialog
TDvFileOpenDialog(TWindow* parent, TDvOpenSaveData& data, const char* title = 0);
Constructor of the object encapsulating the Open File dialog used by the DocManager.

Protected member function

DialogFunction
bool DialogFunction(uint message, TParam1, TParam2);
Overriden virtual function of *TFileOpenDialog*. Allows detection of the user switching between file types (i.e., DocView templates).

TDvFileSaveDialog class   docmanag.h

TDvFileSaveDialog encapsulates the FileSave dialog used by the DocView manager. It enhances the standard ObjectWindows *TFileSaveDialog* by providing logic to update the dialog as the user switches between file types.

Public constructor

TDvFileSaveDialog
TDvFileSaveDialog(TWindow* parent, TDvOpenSaveData& data, const char* title = 0);
Constructor of the object encapsulating the FileSave dialog used by the DocManager.

Protected member function

DialogFunction
bool DialogFunction(uint message, TParam1, TParam2);
Overriden virtual function of *TFileOpenDialog*. Allows detection of the user switching between file types (i.e., DocView templates).

TDvOpenSaveData class   docmanag.h

TDvOpenSaveData encapsulates the information used to initialize the Open or Save As dialog box by ObjectWindows' DocView manager. Besides the typical *OPENFILENAME*-related information, it also provides methods to retrieve the template list and template count of the current Document Manager.

Public constructor

TDvOpenSaveData
TDvOpenSaveData(uint32 flags, char far* filter, const char far* initialDir, const char far* defExt, int filterIndex, TDocTemplate **tmplList, int tmplCount);
Constructor of the class representing the data to be displayed in the Open/Save dialogs used by the DocManager.

Public member functions

GetTmplCount
int GetTmplCount() const;
Returns the number of DocView templates currently displayed in the Open or Save dialogs used by the DocManager.

GetTmplList
TDocTemplate** GetTmplList() const;
Returns the list of templates displayed in the Open or Save dialogs used by the DocManager.

Protected member functions

TmplCount
int TmplCount;

Number of Doc/View templates in *TmplList*.

TmplIndex
int TmplIndex;

Index of the default template.

TmplList
TDocTemplate** TmplList;

List of Doc/View templates displayed in Common Dialog during a File | Open or File | SaveAs operation.

TEdgeConstraint struct

layoutco.h

TEdgeConstraint adds member functions that set edge (but not size) constraints. *TEdgeConstraint* always places your window one pixel above the other window and then adds margins.

For example, if the margin is 4, *TEdgeConstraint* places your window 5 pixels above the other window. The margin, which does not need to be measured in pixels, is defined using the units specified by the constraint. Therefore, if the margin is specified as 8 layout units (which are then converted to 12 pixels), your window would be placed 13 pixels above the other window.

See also   TLayoutConstraint struct, TEdgeOrSizeConstraint struct, TLayoutWindow (layout constraints example)

Public member functions

Above
void Above(TWindow* sibling, int margin = 0);

Positions your window above a sibling window. You must specify the sibling window and an optional margin between the two windows. If no margin is specified, *Above* sets the bottom of one window one pixel above the top of the other window.

See also   TEdgeConstraint::Below

Absolute
void Absolute(TEdge edge, int value);

Sets an edge of your window to a fixed value.

See also   TEdgeConstraint::PercentOf, TEdgeOrSizeConstraint::Absolute

AsIs
void AsIs(TEdge edge);

Below

void Below(TWindow* sibling, int margin = 0);

Positions your window with respect to a sibling window. You must specify the sibling window and an optional margin between the two windows. If no margin is specified, *Below* sets the top of one window one pixel below the bottom of the other window.

See also   TEdgeConstraint::Above

LeftOf

void LeftOf(TWindow* sibling, int margin = 0);

Positions one window with respect to a sibling window. You can specify the sibling window and an optional margin between the two windows.

See also   TEdgeConstraint::RightOf

PercentOf

void PercentOf(TWindow* otherWin, TEdge edge, int percent);

Specifies that the edge of one window indicated in *edge* should be a percentage of the corresponding edge of another window (*otherWin*).

See also   TEdgeConstraint::Absolute, TEdgeOrSizeConstraint::PercentOf

RightOf

void RightOf(TWindow* sibling, int margin = 0);

Positions one window with respect to a sibling window. You can specify the sibling window and an optional margin between the two windows.

See also   TEdgeConstraint::LeftOf

SameAs

void SameAs(TWindow* otherWin, TEdge edge);

Sets the edge of your window indicated by *edge* equivalent to the corresponding edge of the window in *otherWin*.

See also   TEdgeConstraint::Set, TEdgeOrSizeConstraint::SameAs

Set

void Set(TEdge edge, TRelationship rel, TWindow* otherWin, TEdge otherEdge, int value = 0);

Used for setting arbitrary edge constraints, *Set* specifies that your window's edge should be of a specified relationship to *otherWin's* specified edge.

See also   TEdgeOrSizeConstraint::SameAs

TEdgeOrSizeConstraint struct   layoutco.h

Derived from *TEdgeConstraint*, *TEdgeOrSizeConstraint* is a template class that supports size constraints in addition to all the operations that *TEdgeConstraint* provides. The width or height is specified in the template instantiation of this class. There are two versions of each member function: one sets both edge and size constraints; the other sets only edge constraints.

Public member functions

Absolute

Form 1   void Absolute (int value)

Sets the width or height of your window to a fixed value.

Form 2   void Absolute (TEdge edge, int value)

Used to determine edge constraints only, *Absolute* sets the edge of your window to a fixed value.

See also   TEdgeConstraint::Absolute

AsIs

Form 1   void AsIs(TWidthHeight edge);

Form 2   void AsIs(TEdge edge);

PercentOf

Form 1   void PercentOf(TWindow *otherWin, int percent, TWidthHeight otherWidthHeight = widthOrHeight);

Although a window's width or height defaults to being a percentage of the sibling or parent window's corresponding dimension, it can also be a percentage of the sibling or parent's opposite dimension. For example, one window's width can be 50% of the parent window's height.

Form 2   void PercentOf(TWindow* otherWin, TEdge edge, int percent);

Used to determine edge constraints only, *PercentOf* specifies that the edge of one window indicated in *edge* should be a percentage of the corresponding edge of another window (*otherWin*).

See also   TEdgeOrSizeConstraint::Absolute, TEdgeConstraint::PercentOf

SameAs

Form 1   void SameAs(TWindow* otherWin, TWidthHeight otherWidthHeight = widthOrHeight, int value = 0);

Although a window's width or height defaults to being the same as the sibling or parent window's corresponding dimension, it can be the same of the sibling's or parent's opposite dimension. For example, one window's width can be the same as the parent window's height.

Form 2   void SameAs(TWindow* otherWin, TEdge edge);

Used to determine edge constraints only, *SameAs* sets the edge of one window the same as the corresponding edge of the other window specified in *otherWin*.

See also   TEdgeOrSizeConstraint::PercentOf, TEdgeConstraint::SameAs

TEdgeSlip class   docking.h

TEdgeSlip is the class of windows used by *THarbor* as the actual docking slips along the decorated frame client's edges.

Public constructors

TEdgeSlip
TEdgeSlip(TDecoratedFrame& parent, TAbsLocation location, TModule* module = 0);
Constructs an edge slip, and sets the approriate styles for the window.

Public member functions

DockableInsert
void DockableInsert(TDockable& dockable, const TPoint* topLeft, TRelPosition position,
    TDockable* relDockable);
Overriden *TDockingSlip* virtual to insert a new dockable into this slip. Called by mouseup handler after a dockable is dropped into this docking window.

DockableMove
void DockableMove(TDockable& dockable, const TPoint* topLeft, TRelPosition position,
    TDockable* relDockable);
Overriden *TDockingSlip* virtual. Called by mouseup handler after a drag within this docking window.

DockableRemoved
void DockableRemoved(const TRect& orgRect);
Overriden *TDockingSlip* virtual. Called by mouseup handler after a dockable has been removed from this docking slip.

EvCommand
TResult EvCommand(uint id, THandle hWndCtl, uint notifyCode);
Changes the reciever to be the framewindow, not the docking window. The receiver window is normally set up in *Activate* upon the creation of *TButtonGadgetEnabler*.

EvCommandEnable
void EvCommandEnable(TCommandEnabler& commandEnabler);
Changes the receiver to be the framewindow, not the docking window. The receiver window is normally set up in *Activate* upon the creation of *TButtonGadgetEnabler*.

GetLocation
TAbsLocation GetLocation() const;
Retrieves the location of the slip.

ReLayout
void ReLayout(bool forcedLayout);
Changes the child metrics of this docking window within its decorated frame. Calls when the rectangle area of the docking area is different from the computed area of the dockable windows within the docking area.

SetupWindow
void SetupWindow();
Ensures that all decorations in the docking window are abutted against each other (both horizontally and vertically); there should be no gaping holes.

Protected data members

GridType
TGridType GridType;
Type of grid.

Location
TAbsLocation Location;
Location on the frame.

Protected member functions

CompressGridLines
void CompressGridLines();
Compresses or expands dockables perpendicular to the grid line.

CompressParallel
void CompressParallel(int width);
Compresses empty space along grid line if any dockables hang out past the end.

ComputeDockingArea
TSize ComputeDockingArea();
Computes the docking area size based on the dockables inside (total height if top/bottom docking area or total width if left/right docking area). Includes the non-client area etched borders or real window borders. Will return misleading *Size()* if dockables not 0 justified.

EvEraseBkgnd
bool EvEraseBkgnd(HDC);
Erases the background and draws in etched "borders" within the client area.

EvLButtonDblClk
void EvLButtonDblClk(uint modKeys, TPoint& point);
Handles WM_LBUTONDBLCLICK to tell the frame to edit a toolbar.

EvLButtonDown
void EvLButtonDown(uint modKeys, TPoint& point);
Forwards the left button down message to the dockable object.

EvNCCalcSize
uint EvNCCalcSize(bool calcValidRects, NCCALCSIZE_PARAMS far& calcSize);
Returns the size of the client area, leaving room for the etched separators.

EvNCPaint
void EvNCPaint();
Erases the background and draws in etched "borders" within the client area.

EvParentNotify
void EvParentNotify(uint event, uint childHandleOrX, uint childIDOrY);
Makes sure that the slip size is updated when a child changes size.

EvWindowPosChanging
void EvWindowPosChanging(WINDOWPOS far& windowPos);
When the slip shrinks, this function adjusts dockables where needed.

GridSize
int GridSize(int baseCoord);
Returns the perpendicular size of the grid line with the given base coordinates. Returns 0 if there are no dockables on the given grid line.

MoveAllOthers
void MoveAllOthers(TWindow* draggedWindow, TWindow* movedWindow);
Builds a list (sorted by left coordinate) of windows on the same horizontal (top/bottom docking) or vertical (left/right docking) of windows to the right of or below the dragged window. The function then slides all windows from the first one intersecting the dragged window to the last one in the list.

MoveDraggedWindow
TWindow* MoveDraggedWindow(TWindow* draggedWindow);
All terminology in this function is referenced to the following two windows: Drag and LeftEdge. The LeftEdge window is only valid if the Drag window's left side is intersecting the LeftEdge window's right side. The goal of this function is to anchor down the Drag window's left side. This is accomplished by one of three ways:

1 Leave the Drag window where it is if the Drag window's left side does not intersect with any other windows (no LeftEdge window).

2 Slide the Drag window to the right of the LeftEdge window being intersected. This is only done if the intersection is not beyond the midpoint (less than 50%) of the LeftEdge window.

3 Slide the Drag window to the left side position of the LeftEdge window (the Drag window's left side is equal to the LeftEdge window's left side). The LeftEdge window is then slid to the right side of the Drag window if the intersection is beyond the midpoint (more than 50%) of the LeftEdge window.

TEdit class   edit.h

A *TEdit* is an interface object that represents an edit control interface element. A *TEdit* object must be used to create an edit control in a parent *TWindow*. A *TEdit* can be used to facilitate communication between your application and the edit controls of a *TDialog*. This class is streamable.

There are two styles of edit control objects: single line and multiline. Multiline edit controls allow editing of multiple lines of text.

The position of the first character in an edit control is zero. For a multiline edit control, the position numbers continue sequentially from line to line; line breaks count as two characters.

Most of *TEdit's* member functions manage the edit control's text. *TEdit* also includes some automatic member response functions that respond to selections from the edit control's parent window menu, including cut, copy, and paste. Two important member functions inherited from *TEdit's* base class (*TStatic*) are *GetText* and *SetText*.

Public constructors

TEdit

Form 1   TEdit(TWindow* parent, int Id, const char far* text, int x, int y, int w, int h, uint textLimit = 0, bool multiline = false, TModule* module = 0);

Constructs an edit control object with a parent window (*parent*). Sets the creation attributes of the edit control and fills its *Attr* data members with the specified control ID (*Id*), position (*x, y*) relative to the origin of the parent window's client area, width (*w*), and height (*h*).

If text buffer length (*textLimit*) is 0 or 1, there is no explicit limit to the number of characters that can be entered. Otherwise *textLimit* - 1 characters can be entered. By default, initial text (*text*) in the edit control is left-justified and the edit control has a border. Multiline edit controls have horizontal and vertical scroll bars.

Form 2   TEdit(TWindow* parent, int resourceId, uint textLimit = 0, TModule* module = 0);

Constructs a *TEdit* object to be associated with an edit control of a *TDialog*. Invokes the *TStatic* constructor with identical parameters. The *resourceID* parameter must correspond to an edit resource that you define. Enables the data transfer mechanism by calling *EnableTransfer*.

See also   TStatic::TStatic

Public member functions

CanUndo

bool CanUndo();

Returns true if it is possible to undo the last edit.

See also   TEdit::Undo

Clear

void Clear();

Overrides *TStatic's* virtual member function and clears all text.

ClearModify
void ClearModify();

Resets the change flag of the edit control causing *IsModified* to return false. The flag is set when text is modified.

See also   TEdit::IsModified

Copy
void Copy();

Copies the currently selected text into the Clipboard.

Cut
void Cut();

Deletes the currently selected text and copies it into the Clipboard.

DeleteLine
bool DeleteLine(int lineNumber);

Deletes the text in the line specified by *lineNumber* in a multiline edit control. If -1 passed, deletes the current line. *DeleteLine* does not delete the line break and affects no other lines. Returns true if successful. Returns false if *lineNumber* is not -1 and is out of range or if an error occurs.

DeleteSelection
bool DeleteSelection();

Deletes the currently selected text, and returns false if no text is selected.

DeleteSubText
bool DeleteSubText(uint startPos, uint endPos);

Deletes the text between the starting and ending positions specified by *startPos* and *endPos*, respectively. *DeleteSubText* returns true if successful.

EmptyUndoBuffer
void EmptyUndoBuffer();

If an operation inside the edit control can be undone, the edit control undo flag is set. *EmptyUndoBuffer* resets or clears this flag.

FormatLines
void FormatLines(bool addEOL);

Indicates if the end-of-line characters (carriage return, linefeed) are to be added or removed from text lines that are wordwrapped in a multiline edit control. Returns true if these characters are placed at the end of wordwrapped lines or false if they are removed.

GetFirstVisibleLine
int GetFirstVisibleLine() const;

Indicates the topmost visible line in an edit control. For single-line edit controls, the return value is 0. For multiline edit controls, the return value is the index of the topmost visible line.

GetHandle

HLOCAL GetHandle() const;

Returns the data handle of the buffer that holds the contents of the control window.

This function is obsolete, and is not available under Presentation Manager.

See also   TEdit::SetHandle

GetLine

bool GetLine(char far* str, int strSize, int lineNumber);

Retrieves a line of text (whose line number is supplied) from the edit control and returns it in *str* (NULL-terminated). *strSize* indicates how many characters to retrieve. *GetLine* returns false if it is unable to retrieve the text or if the supplied buffer is too small.

See also   TStatic::GetText, TEdit::GetNumLines, TEdit::GetLineLength

GetLineFromPos

int GetLineFromPos(uint charPos);

From a multiline edit control, returns the line number on which the character position specified by *charPos* occurs. If *charPos* is greater than the position of the last character, the number of the last line is returned. If *charPos* is-1, the number of the line that contains the first selected character is returned. If there is no selection, the line containing the caret is returned.

GetLineIndex

uint GetLineIndex(int lineNumber);

In a multiline edit control, *GetLineIndex* returns the number of characters that appear before the line number specified by *lineNumber*. If *lineNumber* is -1, *GetLineIndex* returns the number of the line that contains the caret is returned.

GetLineLength

int GetLineLength(int lineNumber);

From a multiline edit control, *GetLineLength* returns the number of characters in the line specified by *lineNumber*. If it is -1, the following applies: if no text is selected, *GetLineLength* returns the length of the line where the caret is positioned; if text is selected on the line, *GetLineLength* returns the line length minus the number of selected characters; if selected text spans more than one line, *GetLineLength* returns the length of the lines minus the number of selected characters.

GetMemHandle

HLOCAL GetMemHandle() const;

Returns the memory handle for the edit control's buffer.

GetNumLines

int GetNumLines();

Returns the number of lines that have been entered in a multiline edit control: 1 if the edit control has no text (if it has one line with no text in it), or 0 if there is no text or if an error occurs.

GetPasswordChar
uint GetPasswordChar() const;

Returns the character to be displayed in place of a user-typed character. When the edit control is created with the ES_PASSWORD style specified, the default display character is an asterisk (*).

See also   TEdit::SetPasswordChar

GetRect
void GetRect(TRect& frmtRect) const;

Gets the formatting rectangle of a multiline edit control.

See also   TEdit::SetRect, TEdit::SetRectNP

GetSelection
void GetSelection(uint& startPos, uint& endPos);

Returns the starting (*startPos*) and ending (*endPos*) positions of the currently selected text. By using *GetSelection* in conjunction with *GetSubText*, you can get the currently selected text.

See also   TEdit::GetSubText

GetSubText
void GetSubText(char far* str, uint startPos, uint endPos);

Retrieves the text in an edit control from indexes *startPos* to *endPos* and returns it in *str*.

See also   TEdit::GetSelection

GetValidator
TValidator* GetValidator();

Returns the validator associated with this edit control.

GetWordBreakProc
EDITWORDBREAKPROC GetWordBreakProc() const;

Retrieves the current wordwrap function. Returns the address of the wordwrap function defined by the application or 0 if none exists.

See also   TEdit::SetWordBreakProc

Insert
void Insert(const char far* str);

Inserts the text supplied in *str* into the edit control at the current text insertion point (cursor position), and replaces any currently selected text. *Insert* is similar to *Paste*, but does not affect the Clipboard.

See also   TEdit::Paste

IsModified
bool IsModified();

Returns true if the user has changed the text in the edit control.

See also   TEdit::ClearModify

IsValid

bool IsValid(bool reportErr = false);

Returns true if the contents of the edit control are valid. *reportErr* is false so that, by default, *IsValid* doesn't bring up a system or custom message box with an error string created from the default string table.

LimitText

void LimitText(uint);

Limits the amount of new text that can be entered in the edit control.

LockBuffer

char far* LockBuffer(uint newsize=0);

Locks the edit control's buffer and returns a pointer to the buffer. Passing *newsize* greater than 0 causes the buffer to be resized to *newsize*. You must call *Unlock* when you are finished.

See also   TEdit::UnLockBuffer

Paste

void Paste();

Inserts text from the Clipboard into the edit control at the current text insertion point (cursor position).

See also   TEdit::CMEditPaste

Scroll

void Scroll(int horizontalUnit, int verticalUnit);

Scrolls a multiline edit control horizontally and vertically using the numbers of characters specified in *horizontalUnit* and *verticalUnit*. Positive values result in scrolling to the right or down in the edit control, and negative values result in scrolling to the left or up.

Search

int Search(uint startPos, const char far* text, bool caseSensitive=false, bool wholeWord=false, bool up=false);

Performs either a case-sensitive or case-insensitive search for the supplied text. If the text is found, the matching text is selected, and *Search* returns the position of the beginning of the matched text. If the text is not found in the edit control's text, *Search* returns -1. If -1 is passed as *startPos*, then the search starts from either the end or the beginning of the currently selected text, depending on the search direction.

SetHandle

void SetHandle(HLOCAL localMem);

Sets a handle to the text buffer used to hold the contents of a multiline edit control.

This function is obsolete, and is not available under Presentation Manager.

See also   TEdit::GetHandle

SetMemHandle

void SetMemHandle(HLOCAL localMem);

Sets the memory handle for the edit control's buffer.

SetPasswordChar
void SetPasswordChar(uint ch);

SetPasswordChar sets the character to be displayed in place of a user-typed character. When the ES_PASSWORD style is specified, the default display character is an asterisk (*).

See also   TEdit::GetPasswordChar

SetReadOnly
void SetReadOnly(bool readOnly);

Sets the edit control to be read-only or read-write.

SetRect
void SetRect(const TRect& frmtRect);

Sets the formatting rectangle for a multiline edit control.

See also   TEdit::GetRect, TEdit::SetRectNP

SetRectNP
void SetRectNP(const TRect& frmtRect);

Sets the formatting rectangle for a multiline edit control. Unlike *SetRect*, *SetRectNP* does not repaint the edit control.

See also   TEdit::GetRect, TEdit::SetRect

SetSelection
bool SetSelection(uint startPos, uint endPos);

Forces the selection of the text between the positions specified by *startPos* and *endPos*, but not including the character at *endPos*.

SetTabStops
void SetTabStops(int numTabs, const int far* tabs);

Sets the tab stop positions in a multiline edit control.

SetValidator
void SetValidator(TValidator* validator);

Establishes the validator object for the edit control.

SetWordBreakProc
void SetWordBreakProc(EDITWORDBREAKPROC proc);

In a multiline edit control, *SetWordBreakProc* indicates that an application-supplied word-break function has replaced the default word-break function. The application-supplied word-break function might break the words in the text buffer at a character other than the default blank character.

See also   TEdit::GetWordBreakProc

Transfer
uint Transfer(void* buffer TTransferDirection direction);

Transfers information for *TEdit* controls and sends information to the *Validator* if one exists, and if it has the transfer option set. Transfer can perform type conversion when validators are in place, for example, when *TRangeValidator* transfers integers. The return value is the size (in bytes) of the transfer data.

Undo
void Undo();
Undoes the last edit.

See also   TEdit::CanUndo, TEdit::CMEditUndo

UnlockBuffer
void UnlockBuffer(const char far* buffer, bool updateHandle=false);
Unlocks a locked edit control buffer. If the contents were changed, *updateHandle* should be true.

See also   TEdit::LockBuffer

ValidatorError
void ValidatorError();
Handles validation errors that occur as a result of validating the edit control.

Protected data members

Validator
TValidator* Validator;
Points to the validator object constructed in your derived class to validate input text. If no validator exists, *Validator* is zero.

Protected member functions

CanClose
bool CanClose();
Checks to see if all child windows can be closed before closing the current window. If any child window returns false, *CanClose* returns false and terminates the process. If all child windows can be closed, *CanClose* returns true.

CmCharsEnable
void CmCharsEnable(TCommandEnabler& commandHandler);
Determines whether the *Clear* menu item is enabled for the currently selected text.

CmEditClear
void CmEditClear();
Automatically responds to a menu selection with a menu ID of CM_EDITCLEAR by calling *Clear*.

See also   TStatic::Clear

CmEditCopy

void CmEditCopy();

Automatically responds to a menu selection with a menu ID of CM_EDITCOPY by calling *Copy*.

See also   TEdit::Copy

CmEditCut

void CmEditCut();

Automatically responds to a menu selection with a menu ID of CM_EDITCUT by calling *Cut*.

See also   TEdit::Cut

CmEditDelete

void CmEditDelete();

Automatically responds to a menu selection with a menu ID of CM_EDITDELETE by calling *DeleteSelection*.

See also   TEdit::DeleteSelection

CmEditPaste

void CmEditPaste();

Automatically responds to a menu selection with a menu ID of CM_EDITPASTE by calling *Paste*.

See also   TEdit::Paste

CmEditUndo

void CmEditUndo();

Automatically responds to a menu selection with a menu ID of CM_EDITUNDO by calling *Undo*.

See also   TEdit::Undo

CmModEnable

void CmModEnable(TCommandEnabler& commandHandler);

Determines whether the *Undo* menu item is enabled for the selected text.

CmPasteEnable

void CmPasteEnable(TCommandEnabler& commandHandler);

Determines whether the *Paste* menu item is enabled for the selected text.

CmSelectEnable

void CmSelectEnable(TCommandEnabler& commandHandler);

Determines whether the *Cut*, *Copy*, or *Delete* menu items are enabled for the selected text.

ENErrSpace

void ENErrSpace();

Sounds a beep in response to an error notification message that is sent when the edit control unsuccessfully attempts to allocate more memory.

EvChar

void EvChar(uint key, uint repeatCount, uint flags);

Validates the text entered into the edit control. If the input is incorrect, the original text is restored. Otherwise, the validated and modified text is placed back into the edit control, so the results of the auto-fill (if any) can be viewed. When *IsValidInput* is called, the *SupressFill* parameter defaults to False, so that the string can be modified.

EvChildInvalid

void EvChildInvalid(HWND);

Handles input validation message sent by parent.

EvGetDlgCode

uint EvGetDlgCode(MSG far* msg);

Responds to WM_GETDLGCODE messages that are sent to a dialog box associated with a control. *EvGetDlgCode* allows the dialog manager to intercept a message that would normally go to a control and then ask the control if it wants to process this message. If not, the dialog manager processes the message. The *msg* parameter indicates the kind of message, for example a control, command, or edit message, sent to the dialog box manager.

If the edit control contains valid input, then Tabs are allowed for changing focus and a DLGC_WANTTABS code is returned.

See also DLGC_xxxx dialog control message constants

EvKeyDown

void EvKeyDown(uint key, uint repeatCount, uint flags);

EvKeyDown translates the virtual key code into a movement. *key* indicates the virtual key code of the pressed key, *repeatCount* holds the number of times the same key is pressed, *flags* contains one of the messages that translates to a virtual key (VK) code for the mode indicators. If the Tab key is sent to the edit control, *EvKeyDown* checks the validity before allowing the focus to change.

EvKillFocus

void EvKillFocus(HWND hWndGetFocus);

In response to a WM_KILLFOCUS message sent to a window that is losing the keyboard, *EvKillFocus* hides and then destroys the caret. *EvKillFocus* validates text whenever the focus is about to be lost and holds onto the focus if the text is not valid. Doesn't kill the focus if another application, a Cancel button, or an OK button (in which case *CanClose* is called to validate text) has the focus.

EvSetFocus

void EvSetFocus(HWND hWndLostFocus);

Handles the set focus message and makes sure the anti-oscillation flag is cleared.

EvUpDown

void EvUpDown();

Handles up-down messages from an up-down control and adjusts contents if there is a validator to help.

GetClassName
char far* GetClassName();
Returns name of predefined Windows edit class.

See also   TWindow::GetClassName

SetupWindow
void SetupWindow();
If the textLimit data member is nonzero, *SetupWindow* limits the number of characters that can be entered into the edit control to *textLimit* -1.

See also   TStatic::TextLimit, TWindow::SetupWindow

Response table entries

Response table entry	Member function
EV_COMMAND (CM_EDITCLEAR, CmEditClear)	CmEditClear
EV_COMMAND (CM_EDITCOPY, CmEditCopy)	CmEditCopy
EV_COMMAND (CM_EDITCUT, CmEditCut)	CmEditCut
EV_COMMAND (CM_EDITDELETE, CmEditDelete)	CmEditClear
EV_COMMAND (CM_EDITPASTE, CmEditPaste)	CmEditPaste
EV_COMMAND (CM_EDITUNDO, CmEditUndo)	CmEditUndo
EV_COMMAND_ENABLE(CM_EDITCLEAR, CmCharsEnable)	CmCharsEnable
EV_COMMAND_ENABLE(CM_EDITCOPY, CmSelectEnable)	CmSelectEnable
EV_COMMAND_ENABLE(CM_EDITCUT, CmSelectEnable)	CmSelectEnable
EV_COMMAND_ENABLE(CM_EDITDELETE, CmSelectEnable)	CmSelectEnable
EV_COMMAND_ENABLE(CM_EDITPASTE, CmPasteEnable)	CmPasteEnable
EV_COMMAND_ENABLE(CM_EDITUNDO, CmModEnable)	CmModEnable
EV_NOTIFY_AT_CHILD (EN_ERRSPACE, ENErrSpace)	ENErrSpace
EV_WM_CHAR	EvChar
EV_WM_GETDLGCODE	EvGetdlgcode
EV_WM_KEYDOWN	EvKeydown
EV_WM_KILLFOCUS	EvKillFocus
EV_WM_CHILDINVALID	EvChildInvalid

TEditFile class

TEditFile is a file-editing window. *TEditFile*'s data members and member functions manage the file dialog box and automatic responses for file commands such as Open, Read, Write, Save, and SaveAs. *TEditFile* is streamable.

Public data members

FileData
TOpenSaveDialog::TData FileData;

Contains information about the user's file open or save selection.

See also   TOpenSaveDialog::TData struct

FileName
char far* FileName;

Contains the name of the file being edited.

Public constructor and destructor

Constructor
TEditFile(TWindow* ()t = 0, int Id = 0, const char far* text = 0, const char far* fileName = 0,
    TModule* module = 0);

Constructs a *TEditFile* window given the parent window, resource ID (*Id*), text, file name, and module ID. Sets *Filename* to *fileName*.

Destructor
~TEditFile();

Frees memory allocated to hold the name of the *TEditFile*.

Public member functions

CanClear
virtual bool CanClear();

Returns true if the text of the associated edit control can be cleared.

CanClose
virtual bool CanClose();

Returns true if the edit window can be closed.

GetFileData
TOpenSaveDialog::TData& GetFileData();

Returns the FileData data member used for the common dialogs.

GetFileName
const char far* GetFileName() const;

Returns the file name for this buffer.

NewFile
void NewFile();

Begins the edit of a new file after calling *CanClear* to determine that it is safe to clear the text of the editor.

See also   TEditFile::CanClear

Open
Open();

Opens a new file after determining that it is OK to clear the text of the *Editor*. Calls *CanClear*, and if true is returned, brings up a file dialog box to retrieve the name of a new file from the user. Calls *ReplaceWith* to pass the name of the new file.

See also   TEditFile::CanClear, TEditFile::ReplaceWith

Read
bool Read(const char far* fileName=0);

Reads the contents of a previously specified file into the *Editor*. Returns true if read operation is successful.

ReplaceWith
void ReplaceWith(const char far* fileName);

Calls *SetFileName* and *Read* to replace the file currently being edited with a file whose name is supplied.

See also   TEditFile::SetFileName, TEditFile::Read

Save
bool Save();

Saves changes to the contents of the *Editor* to a file. If *Editor->IsModified* returns false, *Save* returns true, indicating there have been no changes since the last open or save.

See also   TEditFile::SaveAs, TEditFile::Write

SaveAs
bool SaveAs();

Saves the contents of the *Editor* to a file whose name is retrieved from the user, through execution of a File Save dialog box. If the user selects OK, *SaveAs* calls *SetFileName* and *Write*. Returns true if the file was saved.

See also   TEditFile::SetFileName, TEditFile::Write

SetFileName
void SetFileName (const char far* fileName);

Sets *FileName* and updates the caption of the window.

Write

bool Write(const char far* fileName=0);

Saves the contents of the *Editor* to a file whose name is specified by *FileName*. Returns true if the write operation is successful.

Protected member functions

CmFileNew

void CmFileNew();

Calls *NewFile* in response to an incoming File New command with a CM_FILENEW command identifier.

See also   TEditFile::NewFile

CmFileOpen

void CmFileOpen();

Calls *Open* in response to an incoming File Open command with a CM_FILEOPEN command identifier.

See also   TEditFile::Open

CmFileSave

void CmFileSave();

Calls *Save* in response to an incoming File Save command with a CM_FILESAVE command identifier.

See also   TEditFile::Save

CmFileSaveAs

void CmFileSaveAs();

Calls *SaveAs* in response to an incoming File SaveAs command with a CM_FILESAVEAS command identifier.

See also   TEditFile::SaveAs

CmSaveEnable

void CmSaveEnable(TCommandEnabler& commandHandler);

Enables save command (only if text is modified).

SetupWindow

void SetupWindow();

Creates the edit window's *Editor* edit control by calling *TEditFile::SetupWindow*. Sets the window's caption to *FileName*, if available; otherwise sets the name to "Untitled."

See also   TEditFile::SetFileName, TEditFile::Read

Response table entries

Response table entry	Member function
EV_COMMAND (CM_FILENEW, CmFileNew)	CmFileNew
EV_COMMAND (CM_FILEOPEN, CmFileOpen)	CmFileOpen
EV_COMMAND (CM_FILESAVE, CmFileSave)	CmFileSave
EV_COMMAND (CM_FILESAVEAS, CmFileSaveAs)	CmFileSaveAs

TEditSearch class   editsear.h

TEditSearch is an edit control that responds to Find, Replace, and FindNext menu commands. This class is streamable.

Public data members

SearchCmd
uint SearchCmd;
Contains the search command identifier that opened the dialog box if one is open.

SearchData
TFindReplaceDialog::TData SearchData;
The *SearchData* structure defines the search text string, the replacement text string, and the size of the text buffer.

See also   TFindReplaceDialog::TData

SearchDialog
TFindReplaceDialog* SearchDialog;
Contains find or replace dialog-box information (such as the text to find and replace) and check box settings.

Public constructor

TEditSearch(TWindow* parent = 0, int Id = 0, const char far* text = 0, int x = 0, int y = 0, int w = 0, int h = 0,
   TModule* module = 0);
Constructs a *TEditSearch* object given the parent window, resource ID, and character string (*text*).

Public member functions

DoSearch
void DoSearch();
Performs a search or replace operation base on information in *SearchData*.

See also   TFindReplaceDialog::TData

GetSearchCmd

uint GetSearchCmd();

Returns the user selected command that brought up the search dialog.

GetSearchData

TFindReplaceDialog::TData& GetSearchData();

Returns the search data used for the common dialog.

GetSearchDialog

TFindReplaceDialog* GetSearchDialog();

Returns the common dialog pointer.

SetSearchCmd

void SetSearchCmd(uint searchcmd);

Remembers the command the user selected to bring up the search dialog.

SetSearchData

void SetSearchData(const TFindReplaceDialog::TData& searchdata);

Uses new search data.

SetSearchDialog

void SetSearchDialog(TFindReplaceDialog* searchdialog);

Uses new common dialog pointer.

SetupWindow

void SetupWindow();

Posts a CM_EDITFIND or a CM_EDITREPLACE message to re-open a find or replace modeless dialog box. Calls *TEdit::SetupWindow*.

See also   TEdit::SetupWindow

Protected member functions

CeEditFindNext

void CeEditFindNext(TCommandEnabler& ce);

Enables FindNext (only if there's data to search for).

CeEditFindReplace

void CeEditFindReplace(TCommandEnabler& ce);

Enables the find or replace option (only if no dialog is up).

CmEditFind

void CmEditFind();

Opens a *TFindDialog* in response to an incoming Find command with a CM_EDITFIND command.

CmEditFindNext

void CmEditFindNext();

Responds to an incoming FindNext command with a CM_EDITFINDNEXT command identifier by calling *DoSearch* to repeat the search operation.

See also   TEditSearch::DoSearch

CmEditReplace

void CmEditReplace();

Opens a *TReplaceDialog* in response to an incoming Replace command with a CM_EDITREPLACE command.

EvFindMsg

TResult EvFindMsg(TParam1, TParam2);

Responds to a message sent by the modeless find or replace dialog box. Calls *DoSearch* to continue searching if text is not found or the end of the document has not been reached.

See also   TEditSearch::DoSearch

Response table entries

Response table entry	Member function
EV_COMMAND(CM_EDITFIND, CmEditFind)	CmEditFind
EV_COMMAND(CM_EDITFINDNEXT, CmEditFindNext)	CmEditFindNext
EV_COMMAND(CM_EDITREPLACE, CmEditReplace)	CmEditReplace
EV_REGISTERED(FINDMSGSTRING, EvFindMsg)	EvFindMsg

TEditStream class   richedit.h

TEditStream encapsulates the *EDITSTREAM* structure, which contains information about a data stream used with a rich edit control.

Public constructors

Form 1   TEditStream();

Constructs a default *TEditStream* object. The members of the base *EDITSTREAM* object are initialized to zero.

Form 2   TEditStream(ulong cookie, EDITSTREAMCALLBACK);

Constructs a *TEditStream* object initializing the members with the specified parameter.

TEditView class

Derived from TView and TEditSearch, *TEditView* provides a view wrapper for the ObjectWindows text edit class (TEdit). A streamable class, *TEditView* includes several event-handling functions that handle messages between a document and its views.

Public constructor and destructor

Constructor
TEditView(TDocument& doc, TWindow* parent = 0);
Creates a *TEditView* object associated with the specified document and parent window. Sets *AttrAccelTable* to IDA_EDITVIEW to identify the edit view. Sets the *TView* private data member *ViewMenu* to the new TMenuDescr for this view.

Destructor
~TEditView()
Destroys a *TEditView* object.

Public member functions

CanClose
bool CanClose();
Returns a nonzero value if the view can be closed.

Create
bool Create()
Creates the view's window. Calls *GetDocPath* to determine if the file is new or if it already has data. If there is data, calls *LoadData* to add the data to the view. If the view's window cannot be created, *Create* indicates that the view is invalid.

GetViewName
const far char* GetViewName();
Overrides *TView::GetViewName* and returns the descriptive name of the class ("StaticName").

See also   TEditView::StaticName, TView::GetViewName

GetWindow
TWindow* GetWindow();
Overrides *TView::GetWindow* and returns **this** as a *TWindow*.

See also   TView::GetWindow

PerformCreate
void PerformCreate(int menuOrId);
Allocates memory as necessary so that *TEditView* can handle files up to and including 30,000 bytes.

SetDocTitle
bool SetDocTitle(const far char* docname, int index)
Overrides *TView::SetDocTitle* and forwards the title to its base class, *TEditSearch*. index is the number of the view displayed in the caption bar. docname is the name of the document displayed in the view window.

See also   TWindow::SetDocTitle, TView::SetDocTitle

StaticName
static const far char* StaticName();
Returns "Edit View", the descriptive name of the class for the ViewSelect menu.

Protected data member

Origin
long Origin;
Holds the file position at the beginning of the display.

Protected member functions

EvNCDestroy
void EvNCDestroy();
Used internally by *TEditView* to manage memory.

This member is not available under Presentation Manager.

GetOrigin
long GetOrigin() const;
Returns the position of the stream buffer at which the edit buffer is stored.

LoadData
bool LoadData();
Reads the view from the stream and closes the file. It returns a nonzero value if the view was successfully loaded. If the file cannot be read, *LoadData* posts an error and returns 0.

SetOrigin
void SetOrigin(long origin);
Sets the position of the stream buffer at which the edit buffer is stored.

VnCommit
bool VnCommit(bool force);
Commits changes made in the view to the document. If *force* is nonzero, all data, even if unchanged, is saved to the document.

See also   TEditView::vnRevert, vnxxxx view notification constants

VnDocClosed
bool VnDocClosed(int omode);

Indicates that the document has been closed. *mode* is one of the ofxxxx document open enum constants.

See also   vnxxxx view notification constants

VnIsDirty
bool VnIsDirty();

Returns a nonzero value if changes made to the data in the view have not been saved to the document; otherwise, it returns 0.

See also   vnxxxx view notification constants

VnIsWindow
bool VnIsWindow(HWND hWnd);

Returns a nonzero value if the window's handle passed in *hWnd* is the same as that of the view's display window.

VnRevert
bool VnRevert(bool clear);

Returns a nonzero value if changes made to the view should be erased and the data from the document should be restored to the view. If *clear* is nonzero, the data is cleared instead of restored to the view.

See also   TEditView::VnCommit

Response table entries

Response table entry	Member function
EV_VN_COMMIT	VnCommit
EV_VN_DOCCLOSED	VnDocClosed
EV_VN_ISDIRTY	VnIsDirty
EV_VN_ISWINDOW	VnIsWindow
EV_WM_NCDESTROY	EvNCDestroy
EV_VN_REVERT	VnRevert

TEnDropFiles class   commctrl.h

TEnDropFiles is a structure sent with EN_DROPFILES notification.

Public member function

operator NMHDR&
operator NMHDR&();

Allows the notification structure to be transparently treated as an NMHDR structure, thereby eliminating the need to explicitly refer to the NMHDR data member (which is always the first member of notification structures).

TEnhMetaFilePict class   metafile.h

TEnhMetaFilePict is a class that encapsulates the enhanced metafile.

Public constructors and destructor

Constructors

Form 1   TEnhMetaFilePict(HENHMETAFILE handle, TAutoDelete autoDelete);
Alias for an existing enhanced metafile handle.

Form 2   TEnhMetaFilePict(const char* filename);
Creates an enhanced metafile from an external file.

Form 3   TEnhMetaFilePict(const TEnhMetaFilePict& metafilepict, const char far* filename);
Copies a metafile.

Form 4   TEnhMetaFilePict(uint bytes, const void* buffer);
Creates metafile from buffer.

Destructor
~TEnhMetaFilePict();
Destroys the enhanced metafile picture.

Public member functions

GetBits
uint GetBits(uint bytes, void* buffer);
Returns the bits of the metafile.

GetDescription
uint GetDescription(uint bytes, void* buffer);
Retrieves the description of this enhanced metafile.

GetHeader
uint GetHeader(uint bytes, ENHMETAHEADER* record);
Retrieves the header information for the enhanced metafile.

GetPaletteEntries
uint GetPaletteEntries(uint count, PALETTEENTRY* entries);
Retrieves the palette entries of the enhanced metafile.

operator HENHMETAFILE
operator HENHMETAFILE() const;
Returns the associated handle of the enhanced metafile.

PlayOnto
bool PlayOnto(TDC& dc, const TRect* rect) const;
Plays this metafile onto a dc.

TEnProtected class   commctrl.h

TEnProtected is a structure sent with EN_PROTECTED notification.

Public member function

operator NMHDR&
operator NMHDR&();
Allows the notification structure to be transparently treated as an NMHDR structure, thereby eliminating the need to explicitly refer to the NMHDR data member (which is always the first member of notification structures).

TErrorMode class   module.h

TErrorMode is a simple encapsulation of the *SetErrorMode* call. It manages putting the error mode back to its previous state of destruction, and is thus exception-safe.

Public constructor and destructor

Constructor
TErrorMode(uint mode);
Constructs a *TErrorMode* object which invokes the *SetErrorMode* API function to control how/whether Windows handles interrupt 24h errors.

Destructor
~TErrorMode();
Destructor of *TErrorMode* object; restores the state of the error mode saved during construction of the object.

TEventHandler class

eventhan.h

TEventHandler is a base class from which you can derive classes that handle messages. Specifically, *TEventHandler* performs the following event-handling tasks:

1 Analyzes a window message.

2 Searches the class's response table entries for an appropriate event-handling function.

3 Dispatches the message to the designated event-handling function.

Most of ObjectWindows' classes are derived from *TEventHandler* and, therefore, inherit this event-handling behavior. In addition, any user-defined class derived from *TEventHandler* can handle message response functions that are associated with a particular window message.

Public member functions

Dispatch
TResult Dispatch(TEventInfo& info, TParam1 p1, TParam2 p2 = 0);

Takes the message data from *TEventInfo*'s *Msg* data member and dispatches it to the correct event-handling function.

DispatchMsg
TResult DispatchMsg(uint msg, uint id, TParam1 p1, TParam2 p2);

Dispatch a complete message, if found.

Find
virtual bool Find(TEventInfo&, TEqualOperator op = 0);

Searches the list of response table entries looking for a match. Because *TEventHandler* doesn't have any entries, *TEventHandler*'s implementation of this routine returns false.

Protected member function

SearchEntries
bool SearchEntries(TGenericTableEntry __RTFAR* entries, TEventInfo&, TEqualOperator op);

Searches the entries in the response table for an entry that matches *TEventInfo* or, if so designated, an entry that *TEqualOperator* specifies is a match.

See also   DECLARE_RESPONSE_TABLE macro

TEventHandler::TEventInfo class

eventhan.h

A nested class, *TEventInfo* provides specific information about the type of message sent, the class that contains the function to be handled, the corresponding response table entry, and the dispatch function that processes the message.

Public data members

TEventInfo::Entry
TGenericTableEntry __RTFAR* Entry;

Points to the response table entry (for example, *EvActivate*).

TEventInfo::Id
const uint Id;

Contains the menu or accelerator resource ID (CM_xxxx) for the message response member function.

TEventInfo::Msg
const uint Msg;

Contains the type of message sent. These can be command messages, child ID messages, notify-based messages such as LBN_SELCHANGE, or Windows messages such as LBUTTONDOWN.

TEventInfo::Object
GENERIC* Object;

Points to the object that contains the function to be handled.

Public constructor

TEventInfo::TEventInfo
TEventInfo(uint msg, uint id=0) : Msg(msg), Id(id);

Constructs a *TEventInfo* object with the specified ID and message type.

TExtractIcon class   shellitm.h

TExtractIcon wraps the *IExtractIcon* interface (currently lightweight). A *TExtractIcon* is returned by *TShellItem::GetExtractIcon Default, TComRef<IExtractIcon>* and copy constructors supplied. *TComRef<IExtractIcon>* and *TExtractIcon* assignment operators are also supplied.

Public constructors

Form 1   TExtractIcon(IExtractIcon* iface = 0);
           Default constructor for *TExtractIcon*.

Form 2   TExtractIcon(const TComRef<IExtractIcon>& source);
           TExtractIcon constructor to construct from *TComRef<IExtractIcon>*.

Form 3   TExtractIcon(const TExtractIcon& source);
           TExtractIcon copy constructor.

Public member functions

operator=

Form 1 TExtractIcon& operator= (const TExtractIcon& source);
TExtractIcon assignment operator (from another *TExtractIcon*).

Form 2 TExtractIcon& operator= (const TComRef<IExtractIcon>& source);
TExtractIcon assignment operator (from *TComRef<IExtractIcon>*).

TFileDocument class   filedoc.h

Derived from *TDocument*, *TFileDocument* opens and closes views and provides stream support for views. *TFileDocument* has member functions that continue to process FileNew and FileOpen messages after a view is constructed. You can add support for specialized file types by deriving classes from *TFileDocument*. *TFileDocument* makes this process easy by hiding the actual process of storing file types.

Type definitions

TFileDocProp enum
enum TFileDocProp {PrevProperty, CreateTime, ModifyTime, AccessTime, StorageSize, FileHandle, NextProperty};
Contains constants that define the following properties of the document:

Value	Description
PrevProperty	TDocument::NextProperty-1. This is the first value for view and document objects.
CreateTime	The time the view or document was created.
ModifyTime	The time the view or document was modified.
AccessTime	The time the view or document was last accessed.
StorageSize	An unsigned **long** containing the storage size.
FileHandle	The platform file handle.
NextProperty	The terminating value for the property.

Classes derived from *TDocument* and *TView* can use these generic file property values.

Public constructor and destructor

Constructor
TFileDocument(TDocument* parent = 0);
Constructs a *TFileDocument* object with the optional parent document.

Destructor
~TFileDocument();
Destroys a *TFileDocument* object.

Public member functions

Close
bool Close();

Closes the document but does not delete or detach any associated views. Before closing the document, *Close* calls *TDocument::Close* to make sure all child documents are closed. If any children are open, *Close* returns 0 and does not close the document. If all children are closed, *Close* checks to see if any associated streams are open, and if so, returns 0 and does not close the document. If there are no open streams, *Close* closes the file.

Commit
bool Commit(bool force = false);

Calls *TDocument::Commit* and clears *TDocument's DirtyFlag* data member, thus indicating that there are no unsaved changes made to the document.

FindProperty
int FindProperty(const char far* name);

Gets the property index, given the property name (*name*). Returns 0 if the name is not found.

See also   pfxxxx property attribute constants

GetProperty
int GetProperty(int index, void far* dest, int textlen=0);

Overrides *TDocument::GetProperty* and gets the property ID for the current file document.

See also   pfxxxx property attribute constants

InStream
TInStream* InStream(int mode, const char far* strmId = 0);

Overrides *TDocument::InStream* and provides generic input for the particular storage medium. *InStream* returns a pointer to a *TInStream. mode* is a combination of the *ios* bits defined in iostream.h. *strmId* is not used for file documents. The view reads data from the document as a stream or through stream functions.

See also   TFileDocument::OutStream

IsOpen
bool IsOpen();

Is nonzero if the document or any streams are open.

Open
Form 1   bool Open(HFILE fhdl);

Opens a file document using an existing file handle. Sets *TDocument::OpenMode* to PREV_OPEN and read/write. Sets the document path to 0. Sets FHdl to *fhdl*. Always returns a nonzero value.

Form 2   bool Open(int mode, const char far* path=0);

Overrides *TDocument::Open* and opens the file using the specified path. If the file is already open, returns 0. Calls *TDocument::SetDocPath* to set the directory path. If *mode* is not 0, sets *TDocument::OpenMode* to *mode*. If the file cannot be opened, returns 0.

See also   ofxxxx document open enum

OutStream

TOutStream* OutStream (int mode, const char far* strmId = 0);

Overrides *TDocument::OutStream* and provides generic input for the particular storage medium. *OutStream* returns a pointer to a *TOutStream. mode* is a combination of the *ios* bits defined in iostream.h. *strmId* is not used for file documents. Instead, the view reads data from the document through stream functions.

See also   TFileDocument::InStream

PropertyCount

int PropertyCount();

Return the number of property support by this document.

Note   The property count includes properties inherited from base document classes.

See also   pfxxxx property attribute constants

PropertyFlags

int PropertyFlags(int index);

Returns the property attribute constants (*pfGetText*, *pfHidden*, and so on).

See also   pfxxxx property attribute constants

PropertyName

const char* PropertyName(int index);

Returns the text name of the property given the index value.

See also   pfxxxx property attribute constants

Revert

bool Revert(bool clear = false);

Calls *TDocument::Revert* to notify the views to refresh their data. If *clear* is false, the data is restored instead of cleared.

See also   TFileDoc::Commit

SetProperty

bool SetProperty(int index, const void far* src);

Sets the property data, which must be in the native data type (either string or binary).

See also   pfxxxx property attribute constants

Protected data member

FHdl
HFILE FHdl;
Holds the file handle to an open file document.

Protected member functions

CloseThisFile
void CloseThisFile(HFILE fhdl, int omode);
Closes the file handle if the associated file was opened by *TFileDocument*. Calls TDocument::NotifyViews to notify all views that the file document has closed.

See also ofxxxx document open enum

OpenThisFile
HFILE OpenThisFile(int omode, const char far* name, streampos* pseekpos);
Opens the file document after checking the file sharing mode (*omode*). If a file mode is not specified as read, write, or read and write, *OpenThisFile* returns 0.

See also ofxxxx document open enum, shxxxx document sharing modes

TFileOpenDialog class   opensave.h

TFileOpenDialog is a modal dialog box that lets you specify the name of a file to open. Use this dialog box to respond to a CM_FILEOPEN command that's generated when a user selects File | Open from a menu. *TFileOpenDialog* uses the *TOpenSave::TData* structure to initialize the file open dialog box.

Public constructor

TFileOpenDialog
TFileOpenDialog(TWindow* parent, TData& data, TResID templateID = 0, const char far* title = 0,
    TModule* module = 0);
Constructs and initializes the *TFileOpen* object based on information in the *TOpenSaveDialog::TData* data structure. The *parent* argument points to the dialog box's parent window. *data* is a reference to the *TData* object. *templateID* is the ID for a custom template. *title* is an optional title. *module* points to the module instance.

See also TOpenSaveDialog::TData, TOpenSaveDialog, TResID, TModule

Public member function

DoExecute
int DoExecute();

Creates the *TFileOpenDialog* object.

See also   TDialog::DoExecute

TFileSaveDialog class

opensave.h

TFileSaveDialog is a modal dialog box that lets you enter the name of a file to save. Use *TFileSaveDialog* to respond to a CM_FILESAVEAS command generated when a user selects File | Save from a menu. *TFileSaveDialog* uses the *TOpenSave::TData* structure to initialize the file save dialog box.

Public constructor

TFileSaveDialog
TFileSaveDialog(TWindow* parent, TData& data, TResID templateID = 0, const char far* title = 0,
    TModule* module = 0);
Constructs and initializes the *TFileOpen* object based on the *TOpenSaveDialog::TData* structure, which contains information about the file name, file directory, and file name search filers.

See also   TOpenSaveDialog::TData structure, TModule, TResID, TWindow

Public member function

DoExecute
int DoExecute();
Creates the *TFileSaveDialog* object.

See also   TDialog::DoExecute, TOpenSaveDialog

TFilterValidator class

validate.h

A streamable class, *TFilterValidator* checks an input field as the user types into it. The validator holds a set of allowed characters. When the user enters a character, the filter validator indicates whether the character is valid or invalid.

See *TValidator* for an example of input validation.

Public constructor

TFilterValidator(const TCharSet& validChars);
Constructs a filter validator object by first calling the constructor inherited from *TValidator*, then setting *ValidChars* to *validChars*.

Public member functions

Error
void Error(TWindow* owner);

Error overrides *TValidator's* virtual function and displays a message box indicating that the text string contains an invalid character.

See also   TValidator::Error

IsValid
bool IsValid(const char far* str);

IsValid overrides *TValidator's* virtuals and returns true if all characters in *str* are in the set of allowed characters, *ValidChar*; otherwise, it returns false.

IsValidInput
bool IsValidInput(char far* str, bool suppressFill);

IsValidInput overrides *TValidator's* virtual function and checks each character in the string *str* to ensure it is in the set of allowed characters, *ValidChar*. *IsValidInput* returns true if all characters in *str* are valid; otherwise, it returns false.

See also   TValidator::IsValidInput

Protected data member

ValidChars
TCharSet ValidChars;

Contains the set of all characters the user can type. For example, to allow only numeric digits, set *ValidChars* to 0-9. *ValidChars* is set by the *validChars* parameter passed to the constructor.

Protected member functions

GetValidChars
const TCharSet& GetValidChars();

Returns the valid character set for the validator.

SetValidChars
void SetValidChars(const TCharSet& vc);

Sets the valid character set for the validator.

TFindDialog class   findrepl.h

TFindDialog objects represents modeless dialog box interface elements that let you specify text to find. *TFindDialog* communicates with the owner window using a registered message. Derived from *TFindReplaceDialog*, *TFindDialog* uses the

TFindReplaceDialog::TData structure to initialize the dialog box with user-entered values (such as the text string to find).

Public constructor

TFindDialog(TWindow* parent, TData& data, TResId templateId = 0, const char far* title = 0,
    TModule* module = 0);
Constructs a *TFindDialog* object with the given parent window, resource ID, and caption. Sets the attributes of the dialog box based on *TFindReplaceDialog::TData* structure, which contains information about the text string to search for.

See also   TFindReplaceDialog::TData

Protected member function

DoCreate
HWND DoCreate();
Creates the modeless interface element of a find dialog.

TFindReplaceDialog class   findrepl.h

TFindReplaceDialog is an abstract base class for a modeless dialog box that lets you search for and replace text. This base class contains functionality common to both derived classes, *TFindDialog* (lets you specify text to find) and *TReplaceDialog* (lets you specify replacement text). *TFindReplaceDialog* communicates with the owner window using a registered message.

Public constructor

TFindReplaceDialog
TFindReplaceDialog(TWindow* parent, TData& data, TResId templateId = 0, const char far* title = 0,
    TModule* module = 0);
Constructs a *TFindReplaceDialog* object with a parent window, resource ID, and caption. Sets the attributes of the dialog box with the specified data from the *TFindReplaceDialog::TData* structure.

See also   TFindReplaceDialog::TData struct, TModule, TResID, TWindow

Public member function

UpdateData
void UpdateData(TParam2 param = 0);
Updates the flags from the passed-in parameter. Assumes the parameters is a pointer to a FINDREPLACE structure.

Protected data members

CmCancel
void CmCancel();
Responds to a click of the Cancel button.

CmFindNext
void CmFindNext();
Responds to a click of the Find Next button.

CmReplace
void CmReplace();
Responds to a click of the Replace button.

CmReplaceAll
void CmReplaceAll();
Responds to a click of the Replace All button.

Data
TData& Data;
Data is a reference to the *TData* object passed in the constructor.

See also   TFindReplaceDialog::TData class

EvNCDestroy
void EvNCDestroy();
Calls *TWindow::EvNCDestroy*, which responds to an incoming EV_WM_NCDESTROY message which tells the owner window that is nonclient area is being destroyed.

fr
FINDREPLACE fr;
A **struct** that contains find-and-replace attributes, such as the size of the find buffer and pointers to search and replace strings, used for find-and-replace operations.

See also   FINDREPLACE class

Protected constructor

TFindReplaceDialog
TFindReplaceDialog(TWindow* parent, TResId templateId = 0, const char far* title = 0, TModule* module = 0);
Not used anywhere. Declared only for preventing users from using it accidentally.

Protected member functions

DoCreate
HWND DoCreate()=0;
DoCreate is a virtual function that is overridden in derived classes to create a modeless find or replace dialog box.

DialogFunction
bool DialogFunction(uint message, WPARAM, LPARAM);
Returns true if a message is handled.

See also   TDialog::DialogFunction

GetData
TData& GetData();
Returns the transfer data for the find and replace dialog.

GetFR
FINDREPLACE& GetFR();
Returns the underlying system structure for the find and replace dialog.

Init
void Init(TResId templateId);
Used by constructors in derived classes, *Init* initializes a *TFindReplaceDialog* object with the current resource ID and other members.

SetData
void SetData(TData& data);
Sets the transfer data for the dialog.

SetFR
void SetFR(const FINDREPLACE& _fr);
Sets the underlying system structure for the dialog.

Response table entries

Response table entry	Member function
EV_WM_NCDESTROY	EvNCDestroy

TFindReplaceDialog::TData class   findrepl.h

The *TFindReplaceDialog::TData* class encapsulates information necessary to initialize a *TFindReplace* dialog box. The *TFindDialog* and *TReplaceDialog* classes use the *TFindReplaceDialog::TData* class to initialize the dialog box and to accept user-entered options such as the search and replacement text strings.

Public constructor and destructor

Constructor
TFindReplaceDialog(uint32 flags = 0, int bufferSize = 81);
Constructs a *TData* object with the specified flag value that initializes the status of the dialog box control buttons and the buffer size for the find and replace search strings.

Destructor
~TData();
Destroys a *~TData* object.

Public data members

int BuffSize;
uint32 Error;
char* FindWhat;
uint32 Flags;
char* ReplaceWith;

TData::BuffSize
int BuffSize;
BuffSize contains the size of the text buffer.

TData::Error
uint32 Error;
If the dialog box is successfully created, *Error* is 0. Otherwise, it contains one or more of the following error codes:

Constant	Meaning
CDERR_LOCKRESOURCEFAILURE	Failed to lock a specified resource.
CDERR_LOADRESFAILURE	Failed to load a specified resource.
CDERR_LOADSTRFAILURE	Failed to load a specified string.
CDERR_REGISTERMSGFAIL	The window message (a value used to communicate between applications) cannot be registered. This message value is used when sending or posting window messages.

TData::FindWhat
char* FindWhat;
Contains the search string.

TData::Flags
uint32 Flags;

Flags, which indicates the state of the control buttons and the action that occurred in the dialog box, can be a combination of the following constants that indicate which command the user wants to select:

Constant	Meaning
FR_DOWN	The Down button in the Direction group of the Find dialog box is selected.
FR_HIDEMATCHCASE	The Match Case check box is hidden.
FR_HIDEWHOLEWORD	The Whole Word check box is hidden.
FR_HIDEUPDOWN	The Up and Down buttons are hidden.
FR_MATCHCASE	The Match Case check box is checked.
FR_NOMATCHCASE	The Match Case check box is disabled. This occurs when the dialog box is first initialized.
FR_NOUPDOWN	The Up and Down buttons are disabled. This occurs when the dialog box is first initialized.
FR_NOWHOLEWORD	The Whole Word check box is disabled. This occurs when the dialog box is first initialized.
FR_REPLACE	The Replace button was pressed in the Replace dialog box.
FR_REPLACEALL	The Replace All button was pressed in the Replace dialog box.
FR_WHOLEWORD	The Whole Word check box is checked.

TData::ReplaceWith
char* ReplaceWith;
ReplaceWith contains the replacement string.

See also   TEditSearch::SearchData, TFindReplaceDialog::Data

TFindText class   richedit.h

TFindText encapsulates the FINDTEXT structure, which contains information about text to search for in a rich edit control.

Public constructors

Form 1   TFindText(const TCharRange& range, const char far* text);
Constructs a *TFindText* describing the text to search for and the range of the search using the *text* and *range* parameters respectively.

Form 2   TFindText(long beg, long end, const char far* text);
Constructs a *TFindText* describing the text to search for via the *text* parameter, and the range to search for via the *beg* and *end* parameters, respectively.

TFloatingFrame class   floatfra.h

Derived from *TFrameWindow* and *TTinyCaption*, *TFloatingFrame* implements a floating frame that can be positioned anywhere in the parent window. Except for the addition of a tiny caption bar, the default behavior of *TFrameWindow* and *TFloatingFrame* is the same. Therefore, an application that uses *TFrameWindow* can easily gain the functionality of *TFloatingFrame* by just changing the name of the class to *TFloatingFrame*.

If there is a client window, the floating frame shrinks to fit the client window, leaving room for margins on the top, bottom, left, and right of the frame. Because the floating frame expects the client window to paint its own background, it does nothing in response to a WM_ERASEBKGND message. However, if there is no client window, the floating frame erases the client area background using COLOR_BTNFACE.

See PAINT.CPP, the sample program on your distribution disk, for an example of a floating frame.

Public constructor

TFloatingFrame(TWindow* parent, const char far* title = 0, TWindow* clientWnd = 0, bool shrinkToClient = false,
    int captionHeight = DefaultCaptionHeight, bool popupPalette = false, TModule* module = 0);

Constructs a *TFloatingFrame* object attached to the specified parent window. By default, the floating frame window doesn't shrink to fit the client window, and the floating palette style isn't enabled.

Set *popupPalette* to true if you want to enable a floating palette style for the window. The floating palette is a popup window with a tiny caption, a standard window border, and a close box instead of a system menu box. There are no maximize or minimize buttons. A one pixel border is added around the client area in case a toolbox is implemented. This style must be turned on before the window is created. After the window is created, its style can't be changed.

See also   TFrameWindow::TFrameWindow, TTinyCaption::TTinyCaption

Public member functions

SetDragFrame
void SetDragFrame(bool dragFrame);
Sets the flag for additional dragging area.

SetMargins
void SetMargins(const TSize& margin);
Sets the margins of the floating palette window to the size specified in *margin* and sets the height of the tiny caption bar.

See also   TTinyCaption::EnableTinyCaption

Protected member functions

DoNCHitTest
TEventStatus DoNCHitTest(TPoint& screenPt, uint& evRes);

If the floating palette is not enabled, returns *esPartial*. Otherwise, sends a message to the floating palette that the mouse or the cursor has moved, and returns *esComplete*.

EvCommand
TResult EvCommand(uint id, HWND hWndCtl, uint notifyCode);
Resolves ambiguous mixin reference by passing *EvCommand* first to the tiny caption and then to the frame bases.

EvNCCalcSize
uint EvNCCalcSize(bool calcValidRects, NCCALCSIZE_PARAMS far& calcSize);
Handles WM_NCCALCSIZE to possibly add in the drag frame margins.

EvNCHitTest
uint EvNCHitTest(TPoint& screenPt);
Returns where in the non-client area the mouse is. Delegates to tiny caption for the caption bar area, and when in DragFrame mode, makes the frame act like a caption for dragging.

EvNCPaint
void EvNCPaint();
Handles WM_NCPAINT to paint the non-client areas of this window.

Implementation: This function only needs to paint the drag frame margins. *TWindow* (via *DefWindowProc*) automatically paints the borders, and *TTinyCaption* automatically paints the caption.

EvSysCommand
void EvSysCommand(uint cmdType, TPoint& p);
This is an example of a mix-in that does partial event handling. This function calls the *do* function for the mixin instead of the *Ev* function, to avoid duplicate default processing.

Response table entries

Response table entry	Member function
EV_WM_SYSCOMMAND	EvSysCommand
EV_WM_NCCALCSIZE	EvNCCalcSize
EV_WM_NCPAINT	EvNCPaint
EV_WM_NCHITTEST	EvNcHitTest

TFloatingSlip class   docking.h

TFloatingSlip is a floating frame which can hold a dockable window. It is also dockable in order to act as a proxy for its held dockable when dragging.

Public constructor

TFloatingSlip
TFloatingSlip(TWindow* parent, int x, int y, TWindow* clientWnd = 0, bool shrinkToClient = true,
    int captionHeight = DefaultCaptionHeight, bool popupPalette = true, TModule* module = 0);
Constructs a floating slip and sets the appropriate style for the window.

Public member functions

ComputeSize
TSize ComputeSize(TAbsLocation loc, TSize* dim);
Forward the first four *TDockable* virtuals to the client dockable.

DockableInsert
void DockableInsert(TDockable& dockable, const TPoint* topLeft, TRelPosition position,
    TDockable* relDockable);
Overriden *TDockingSlip* virtual. Called by mouseup handler after a dockable is dropped
into this docking window.

DockableMove
void DockableMove(TDockable& dockable, const TPoint* topLeft, TRelPosition position,
    TDockable* relDockable);
Overriden *TDockingSlip* virtual. Called by lbutton up handler after a drag within this
docking window. This floating slip only moves itself.

DockableRemoved
void DockableRemoved(const TRect& orgRect);
Overriden *TDockingSlip* virtual. Called by lbutton up handler after a dockable has been
removed from this docking slip.

GetCommandTarget
HWND GetCommandTarget();
Floating slips never route commands down to their children; they just bubble them up
to the parent.

GetHarbor
THarbor* GetHarbor();
Returns the associated harbor.

GetLocation
TAbsLocation GetLocation() const;
Returns the location of the object.

GetRect
void GetRect(TRect& rect);
Gets this dockable's screen rect.

GetWindow
TWindow* GetWindow();

Returns the *TWindow* part of this dockable object. In this case it is actually the client window.

Layout
void Layout(TAbsLocation loc, TSize* dim=0);

Forwards the layout message over to the dockable object.

ShouldBeginDrag
bool ShouldBeginDrag(TPoint& pt);

A given mouse down should never begin a drag for this dockable.

Protected member functions

EvClose
void EvClose();

When closing the floating slip, removes any dockable first so that it is not destroyed. Dockables are owned by the harbor, not the slip, and must not be destroyed when the slip is destroyed.

EvCommandEnable
void EvCommandEnable(TCommandEnabler& commandEnabler);

Changes the receiver to be the framewindow, not the docking window. The receiver window is normally set up in Activate upon the creation of *TButtonGadgetEnabler*.

EvLButtonDown
void EvLButtonDown(uint hitTest, TPoint& point);

Handles lbutton down bubbled up from the client to begin a dockable drag operation.

EvNCLButtonDown
void EvNCLButtonDown(uint hitTest, TPoint& point);

Handles lbutton down bubbled up from the client to begin a dockable drag operation.

EvSizing
bool EvSizing(uint side, TRect& rect);

Handles the Windows 4.0 message for the best resize user feedback.

EvWindowPosChanged
void EvWindowPosChanged(WINDOWPOS far& windowPos);

Handles WM_WINDOWPOSCHANGED to make sure that the dockable client gets a chance to do final layout.

EvWindowPosChanging
void EvWindowPosChanging(WINDOWPOS far& windowPos);

Handles WM_WINDOWPOSCHANGING to make sure that the frame is properly constrained by the dimensions of the dockable client.

EvWinIniChange

void EvWinIniChange(char far*);

Event handler for the .INI file changed message. The window may have resized because the user has changed the caption size.

TFont class

TFont derived from *TGdiObject* provides constructors for creating font objects from explicit information or indirectly.

Public constructors

Form 1 TFont(THandle handle, TAutoDelete autoDelete = NoAutoDelete);

Creates a *TFont* object and sets the *Handle* data member to the given borrowed *handle*. The *ShouldDelete* data member defaults to false, ensuring that the borrowed handle will not be deleted when the C++ object is destroyed.

Form 2 TFont(const char far* facename=0, int height=0, int width=0, int escapement=0, int orientation=0,
        int weight=FW_NORMAL, uint8 pitchAndFamily=DEFAULT_PITCHIFF_DONTCARE,
        uint8 italic=false, uint8 nderline=false, uint8 strikeout=false, uint8 charSet=1,
        uint8 outputPrecision=OUT_DEFAULT_PRECIS, uint8 clipPrecision=CLIP_DEFAULT_PRECIS,
        uint8 quality=DEFAULT_QUALITY);

Creates a *TFont* object with the given values.

Form 3 TFont(int height, int width, int escapement=0, int orientation=0, int weight=FW_NORMAL,
        uint8 underline=false, uint8 strikeout=false, uint8 charSet=1,
        uint8 italic=false, uint8 outputPrecision=OUT_DEFAULT_PRECIS,
        uint8 clipPrecision=CLIP_DEFAULT_PRECIS, uint8 quality=DEFAULT_QUALITY,
        uint8 pitchAndFamily=DEFAULT_PITCHIFF_DONTCARE, const char far* facename=0);

Creates a *TFont* object with the given values. The constructor parameter list and default values match the Windows API *CreateFont* call.

Form 4 TFont(const LOGFONT far* logFont);

Creates a *TFont* object from the given *logFont*.

Form 5 TFont(const TFont& src);

The *TFont* copy constructor.

See also ::CreateFont (Windows API), ::CreateFontIndirect (Windows API), TGdiObject::Handle, TGdiObject::ShouldDelete

Public member functions

GetAveWidth

Form 1 int GetAveWidth(TDC& dc) const;

Returns the average width of the characters in the font if selected into the DC.

Form 2 int GetAveWidth() const;

Returns the average width of the characters in the font.

GetHandle

THandle GetHandle() const;

Returns the handle of the font with type HFONT.

GetHeight

Form 1   int GetHeight(TDC& dc) const;

Return the height of the font if selected into the DC.

Form 2   int GetHeight() const;

Returns the height of the font.

GetMaxWidth

Form 1   int GetMaxWidth(TDC& dc) const;

Returns the maximum width of the characters in the font if selected into the DC.

Form 2   int GetMaxWidth() const;

Returns the maximum width of the characters in the font.

GetObject

bool GetObject(LOGFONT far& logFont) const;

Retrieves information about this pen object and places it in the given *LOGFONT* structure. Returns true if successful and false if unsuccessful.

See also   TGdiObject::GetObject, LOGFONT struct

GetTextMetrics

Form 1   void GetTextMetrics(TEXTMETRIC& tm) const;

Retrieves information about this font when selected in a screen DC.

Form 2   TEXTMETRIC GetTextMetrics() const;

Retrieves information about this font when selected in a screen DC.

Form 3   void GetTextMetrics(TEXTMETRIC& tm, TDC& dc) const;

Retrieves information about this font when selected in the specified *dc*.

Form 4   TEXTMETRIC GetTextMetrics(TDC& dc) const;

Retrieves information about this font when selected in the specified *dc*.

operator HFONT()

operator HFONT() const;

Typecasting operator that converts this font's *Handle* to type *HFONT* (the data type representing the handle to a physical font).

THandle

operator THandle() const;

Returns the handle of the font with type HFONT.

TFormatRange class   richedit.h

TFormatRange encapsulates the FORMATRANGE structure, which contains information that a rich edit control uses to format its output for a particular device.

Public constructor

TFormatRange
TFormatRange(HDC renderDC, HDC targetDC, const TRect& renderArea, const TRect& entireArea,
    const TCharRange& txtRange);
Constructs a *TFormatRange* object initializing data members with the specified
parameters.

Public member functions

SetPageRect
void SetPageRect(const TRect&);
Sets the entire area of the rendering device.

Note   The specified units are in twips.

SetRange
Form 1   void SetRange(long, long);
Sets the range of text to format, specifying the starting and ending character offsets.

Form 2   void SetRange(const TCharRange&);
Sets the range of text to format.

SetRenderDC
void SetRenderDC(HDC);
Sets the device context of the device to render to.

SetRenderRect
void SetRenderRect(const TRect&);
Sets the area to render to.

Note   The specified units are in twips.

SetTargetDC
void SetTargetDC(HDC);
Sets the device context of the target device to format for.

TFrameWindow class   framewin.h

Derived from *TWindow*, *TFrameWindow* controls such window-specific behavior as
keyboard navigation and command processing for client windows. For example, when
a window is reactivated, *TFrameWindow* is responsible for restoring a window's input
focus and for adding menu bar and icon support. *TFrameWindow* is a streamable class.

In terms of window areas, the frame area consists of the border, system menus, toolbars
and status bars whereas the client area excludes these areas. Although frame windows
can support a client window, the frame window remains separate from the client
window so that you can change the client window without affecting the frame window.

ObjectWindows uses this frame and client structure for both *TFrameWindow* and *TMDIChild* classes. Both these classes can hold a client class. Having a separate class for the client area of the window adds more flexibility to your program. For example, this separate client area, which might be a dialog box, can be moved into another frame window, either a main window or an MDI child window.

See *TFloatingFrame* for a description of a floating frame with the same default functionality as a frame window.

Public data member

KeyboardHandling
bool KeyboardHandling;

Indicates if keyboard navigation is required.

Public constructors and destructor

Form 1   TFrameWindow(TWindow* parent, const char far *title = 0, TWindow* clientWnd = 0, bool shrinkToClient = false,
     TModule* module = 0);

Constructs a window object with the parent window supplied in *parent*, which is zero if this is the main window. *title*, which by default is zero, contains the title displayed in the window's caption bar. *clientWnd* is the client window for this frame window or zero if none exists. *shrinkToClient* controls whether the client window will size to fit the frame or the frame window will fit the client. Note that this parameter only affects the size of the main window. When a client window is used in a frame window that doesn't have *shrinktoClient* set, the client window resizes to fit the frame window. When a client window is used in a frame window that has the *shrinktoClient* set, the frame window shrinks to fit the size of the client window.

Form 2   TFrameWindow(HWND hWnd, TModule* module = 0);

Constructor for a *TFrameWindow* that is being used as an alias for a non-ObjectWindows window. *hWnd* is the handle to the existing window object that *TFrameWindow* controls; *module* contains the module passed to the base class's contructor.

Destructor
~TFrameWindow();

Deletes any associated menu descriptor.

See also   TWindow::TWindow, TFloatingFrame::TFloatingFrame

Public member functions

AssignMenu
virtual bool AssignMenu(TResId menuResId);

Sets *Attr.Menu* to the supplied *menuResId* and frees any previous strings pointed to by *Attr.Menu*. If *HWindow* is nonzero, loads and sets the menu of the window, destroying any previously existing menu.

See also   TMDIFrameWindow::SetMenu, TFrameWindow::SetMenuDescr

EnableKBHandler
void EnableKBHandler();

Sets a flag indicating that the receiver has requested keyboard navigation (translation of keyboard input into control selections). By default, the keyboard interface, which lets users use the tab and arrow keys to move between the controls, is disabled for windows and dialog boxes.

GetClientWindow
virtual TWindow* GetClientWindow();

Returns a pointer to the client window. If you are trying to access a window-based object in a *TMDIChild* (which is a frame window), you can use this function.

See also   TMDIChild

GetCommandTarget
virtual HWND GetCommandTarget();

Locates and returns the child window that is the target of the command and command enable messages. If the current application does not have focus or if the focus is within a toolbar in the application, *GetCommandTarget* returns the most recently active child window.

If an alternative form of command processing is desired, a user's main window class can override this function. TFrameWindow's *EvCommand* and *EvCommandEnable* functions use *GetCommandTarget* to find the command target window. This member is not available under Presentation Manager.

GetKeyboardHandling
bool GetKeyboardHandling() const;

Returns flag indicating that the receiver has requested "keyboard handling" (translation of keyboard input into control selections).

GetMenuDescr
const TMenuDescr* GetMenuDescr();

Returns a pointer to the menu descriptor.

See also   TFrameWindow::SetMenuDescr, TMenuDescr

HoldFocusHwnd
bool HoldFocusHWnd(HWND hWndLose, HWND hWndGain);

Overrides *TWindow*'s virtual function. Responds to a request by a child window to hold its HWND when it is losing focus. Stores the child's HWND in *HwndRestoreFocus*.

See also   TWindow::HoldFocusHwnd

IdleAction
void IdleAction(long idleCount);

Overrides *TWindow*'s virtual function. *TApplication* calls the main window's *IdleAction* when no messages are waiting to be processed. *TFrameWindow* uses this idle time to perform command enabling for the menu bar. It also forwards *IdleAction* to each of its children. *IdleAction* can be overridden to do background processing.

See also   TApplication::IdleAction

MergeMenu
bool MergeMenu(const TMenuDescr& childMenuDescr);

Merges the given menu descriptor with this frame's own menu descriptor and displays the resulting menu in this frame. See *TMenuDescr* for a description of menu bar types that can be merged.

See also   TMenuDescr

PreProcessMsg
bool PreProcessMsg(MSG& msg);

Overrides *TWindow's* virtual function. Performs preprocessing of window messages. If the child window has requested keyboard navigation, *PreProcessMsg* handles any accelerator key messages and then processes any other keyboard messages.

See also   TWindow::PreProcessMsg

RemoveChild
void RemoveChild(TWindow* child);

Removes the client, updates the client, and restores the focus pointers.

RestoreMenu
bool RestoreMenu();

Restores the default menu of the frame window.

SetClientWindow
virtual TWindow* SetClientWindow(TWindow* clientWnd);

Sets the client window to the specified window. Users are responsible for destroying the old client window if they want to eliminate it.

SetDocTitle
bool SetDocTitle(const char far* docname, int index);

Overrides *TWindow's* virtual function. Pastes the number of the view into the caption and then shows the number on the screen. This function can be overridden if you don't want to use the default implementation, which displays a number on the screen. That is, you might want to write "Two" instead of ":2" on the screen. For an example of the behavior of this function, see step 12 of the ObjectWindows tutorial, which renumbers the views if one of them is closed.

SetIcon
bool SetIcon(TModule* iconModule, TResId iconResId);

Sets the icon in the module specified in *iconModule* to the resource ID specified in *iconResId*. See the sample file BMPVIEW.CPP for an example of painting an icon from a bitmap. You can set the *iconResId* to one of these predefined values as well as user-defined values:

IDI_APPLICATION	Default icon used for applications
IDI_ASTERISK	Asterisk used for an informative message
IDI_EXCLAMATION	Exclamation mark used for a warning message

IDI_HAND   Hand used for warning messages

IDI_QUESTION   Question mark used for prompting a response

See also TFrameWindow::EvQueryDragIcon

SetIconSm
bool SetIconSm(TModule* iconModule, TResId iconResIdSm);
Set the Small Icon (16 x 16).

SetKeyboardHandling
void SetKeyboardHandling(bool kh=true);
Sets flag indicating that the receiver has requested "keyboard handling" (translation of keyboard input into control selections).

SetMenu
virtualBOOL SetMenu(HMENU newMenu);
Overrides *TWindow's* non-virtual *SetMenu* function, thus allowing derived classes the opportunity to implement this function differently from *TWindow*. *SetMenu* sets the window's menu to the menu indicated by *newMenu*. If *newMenu* is 0, the window's current menu is removed. *SetMenu* returns 0 if the menu remains unchanged; otherwise, it returns a nonzero value.

SetMenuDescr
void SetMenuDescr(const TMenuDescr& menuDescr);
Sets the menu descriptor to the new menu descriptor.

See also TFrameWindow::GetMenuDescr, TMenuDescr

Protected data members

ClientWnd
TWindow* ClientWnd;
ClientWnd points to the frame's client window.

DocTitleIndex
int DocTitleIndex;
Holds the index number for the document title.

HWndRestoreFocus
HWND HWndRestoreFocus;
Stores the handle of the child window whose focus gets restored.

See also TFrameWindow::HoldFocusHwnd

MergeModule
TModule* MergeModule;
Tells the frame window which module the menu comes from. *TDecoratedFrame* uses this member to get the menu hints it displays at the bottom of the screen. It assumes that the menu hints come from the same place the menu came from.

Protected constructor

TFrameWindow
TFrameWindow();
Protected constructor used in conjunction with *Init* function for initializing virtually derived classes.

Protected member functions

CleanupWindow
void CleanupWindow();
Cleans up any associated icons.

EvCommand
LRESULT EvCommand(uint id, HWND hWndCtl, uint notifyCode);
Provides extra processing for commands and lets the focus window and its parent windows handle the command first.

EvCommandEnable
void EvCommandEnable(TCommandEnabler& ce);
Handles checking and unchecking of the frame window's menu items. *EvCommandEnable* uses *TWindow*'s *RouteCommandEnable* member function to perform the majority of this command enabling work.

See also   TWindow::RouteCommandEnable

EvEnterIdle
void EvEnterIdle(uint source, HWND hWndDlg);
Watches for WM_ENTERIDLE messages from idling modal dialog boxes so that background processing can continue when they are up.

EvEraseBkgnd
bool EvEraseBkgnd(HDC);
EvEraseBkgnd erases the background of the window specified in *HDC*. It returns true if the background is erased; otherwise, it returns false.

EvInitMenuPopup
HANDLE EvInitMenuPopup(HMENU hPopupMenu, uint index, bool sysMenu);
Sent before a pop-up menu is displayed, *EvInitMenuPopup* lets an application change the items on the menu before the menu is displayed. *EvInitMenuPopup* controls whether the items on the pop-up menu are enabled or disabled, checked or unchecked, or strings. *HMENU* indicates the menu handle. *index* is the index of the pop-up menu. *sysMenu* indicates if the pop-up menu is the system menu.

EvPaint
void EvPaint();
Responds to a WM_PAINT message in the client window in order to paint the iconic window's icon or to allow client windows a change to paint the icon.

See also   TWindow::Paint, TScroller::BeginView, TScroller::EndView

EvPaletteChanged
void EvPaletteChanged(THandle hWndPalChg);
Forwards the WM_PALETTECHANGED message to the client window.

EvParentNotify
void EvParentNotify(uint event, uint childHandleOrX, uint childIDOrY);
Responds to a message to notify the parent window that a given event has occurred. If the client window is destroyed, closes the parent window. If *shrinkToClient* is set and the child window has changed size, the frame is adjusted.

When a *TFrameWindow*'s client window is destroyed, the *TFrameWindow* object sees the WM_PARENTNOTIFY message and posts a close message to itself. Without this message, an empty frame would remain and the client window would then have to determine how to destroy the frame. If you don't want this to happen, you can derive from the frame window and have your application handle the *EvParentNotify* or *EvClose* messages.

EvQueryDragIcon
HANDLE EvQueryDragIcon();
Responds to a WM_QUERYDRAGICON message sent to a minimized (iconic) window that is going to be dragged. Instead of the default icon, *EvQueryDragIcon* uses the icon that was set using *SetIcon*.

This member is not available under Presentation Manager.

See also   TFrameWindow::SetIcon

EvQueryNewPalette
bool EvQueryNewPalette();
Forwards the WM_QUERYNEWPALETTE message to the client window.

EvSetFocus
void EvSetFocus(HWND hWndLostFocus);
Restores the focus to the active window. *hWndLostFocus* contains the handle for the window that lost focus.

EvSize
void EvSize(uint sizeType, TSize& size);
Resizes the client window so that it is equivalent to the client rectangle's size. Calls *TWindow::EvSize)* in response to an incoming WM_SIZE message.

See also   TSize

GetDocTitleIndex
int GetDocTitleIndex() const;
Returns the document title index.

GetHWndRestoreFocus
HWND GetHWndRestoreFocus();
Returns the handle of the window to restore the focus to.

GetMergeModule
TModule* GetMergeModule();

Returns the module of the merge menu.

Init
void Init (TWindow* clientWnd, bool shrinkToClient);

This initialize function is for use with virtually derived classes, which must call *Init* before construction is completed. This procedure provides necessary data to virtually derived classes and takes care of providing the data in the appropriate sequence.

SetDocTitleIndex
void SetDocTitleIndex(int index);

Sets the current document's title index.

SetHWndRestoreFocus
void SetHWndRestoreFocus(HWND hwndRestoreFocus);

Sets the remembered focused window.

SetMergeModule
void SetMergeModule(TModule* module);

Remembers where the merged menu came from.

SetupWindow
void SetupWindow();

Calls *TWindow::SetUpWindow* to create windows in a child list. *SetupWindow* performs the initial adjustment of the client window if one exists, assigns the frame's menu based on the menu descriptor, and initializes *HwndRestoreFocus*.

See also   TWindow::SetUpWindow

Response table entries

Response table entry	Member function
EV_WM_ERASEBKGND	EvEraseBkgnd
EV_WM_INITMENUPOPUP	EvInitMenuPopup
EV_WM_PAINT	EvPaint
EV_WM_PARENTNOTIFY	EvParentNotify
EV_WM_QUERYDRAGICON	EvQueryDragIcon (Windows only)
EV_WM_SETFOCUS	EvSetFocus
EV_WM_SIZE	EvSize

TGadget class

TGadget is the base class for the following derived gadget classes:

Class	Description
TBitmapGadget	Displays a bitmap
TButtonGadget	Uses a bitmap to simulate a button gadget
TControlGadget	Encapsulates inserting a control such as an edit control or a combo box, into a gadget window
TTextGadget	Displays text
TSeparatorGadget	Separates logical groups of gadgets

TGadget interface objects belong to a gadget window, have borders and margins, and have their own coordinate system. The margins are the same as those for *TGadgetWindow* and borders are always measured in border units.

To set the attributes for the gadget, you can either choose a border style (which automatically sets the individual border edges) or set the borders and then override the member function *PaintBorder* to create a custom look for your gadget. If you change the borders, margins, or border style, the gadget window's *GadgetChangedSize* member function is invoked.

Although, by default, gadgets shrink-wrap to fit around their contents, you can control this attribute by setting your own values for *ShrinkWrapWidth* and *ShrinkWrapHeight*.

A gadget window, being an actual window, receives messages from the mouse. After the gadget window receives the message, it decides which gadget should receive the message by calling the member function directly instead of sending or posting a message.

Public data members

Clip
bool Clip;

If *Clip* is false, clipping borders have not been established. If *Clip* is true, the drawing for each gadget is restrained by the gadget's border.

WideAsPossible
bool WideAsPossible;

Initially set to **false**, *WideAsPossible* indicates whether the gadget width will be adjusted by the gadget window to be as wide as possible in the remaining space.

See also   TGadgetWindow::WideAsPossible

Public enums and structures

TBorders struct

struct TBorders
  unsigned Left;
  unsigned Right;
  unsigned Top;
  unsigned Bottom;

Holds the values for the left, right, top, and bottom measurements of the gadget.

TBorderStyle enum

enum TBorderStyle {None, Plain, Raised, Recessed, Embossed, Grooved, ButtonUp, ButtonDn, WndRaised, WndRecessed, WellSet};

Enumerates an exclusive list of border styles. For an example of border styles, see the sample ObjectWindows program, MDIFILE.CPP, on your distribution disk.

Table 2.9   Border Style Constants

Constant	Meaning if set
None	No border painted at all.
Plain	Plain border.
Raised	Raised above the gadget window.
Recessed	Recessed into the window.
Embossed	Painted with an embossed border.
Grooved	Grouping groove.
ButtonUp	Button is in up position.
ButtonDn	Button in down position (pressed).
WndRaised	Inner and outer edge of the window is raised.
WndRecessed	Input field and other window is recessed.
WellSet	Well option set (auto grows + 1).

TMargins struct

struct TMargins {
  enum TUnits {Pixels, LayoutUnits, BorderUnits};
  TUnits Units;
  int Left;
  int Right;
  int Top;
  int Bottom;
};

Used by the *TGadgetWindow* and *TGadget* classes, *TMargins* contains the measurements of the margins for the gadget. The constructor initializes *Units* to *LayoutUnits* and sets *Left*, *Right*, *Top*, and *Bottom* equal to 0.

See also   TGadgetWindow::SetMargins

Public constructor and destructor

Constructor
TGadget(int id = 0, TBorderStyle = None);
Constructs a *TGadget* object with the specified ID and border style.

Destructor
virtual ~TGadget();
Destroys a *TGadget* interface object and removes it from its associated window.

Public member functions

CommandEnable
virtual void CommandEnable();
Provided so that the gadget can perform command enabling (so it can handle an incoming message if it's appropriate to do so).

GetBorders
TBorders& GetBorders();
Gets the gadget's borders measured in border units that are based on SM_CXBORDER and SM_CYBORDER.

See also   TGadget::SetBorders

GetBorderStyle
TBorderStyle GetBorderStyle();
Gets the style for the gadget's borders.

See also   TGadget::SetBorderStyle

GetBounds
TRect& GetBounds();
Returns the boundary rectangle for the gadget.

See also   TButtonGadget::SetNotchCorners

GetDesiredSize
virtual void GetDesiredSize(TSize& size);
Determines how big the gadget can be. The gadget window sends this message to query the gadget's size. If shrink-wrapping is requested, *GetDesiredSize* returns the size needed to accommodate the borders and margins. If shrink-wrapping is not requested, it returns the gadget's current width and height. *TGadgetWindow* needs this information to determine how big the gadget needs to be, but it can adjust these dimensions if necessary. If *WideAsPossible* is true, then the width parameter (*size.cx*) is ignored.

GetEnabled
bool GetEnabled() const;

Determines whether keyboard and mouse input have been enabled for the specified gadget. If the gadget is enabled, *GetEnabled* returns true; otherwise, it returns false. By default, keyboard and mouse input are enabled.

See also   TGadget::SetEnabled

GetId
int GetId() const;
Gets the ID for the gadget.

GetInnerRect
void GetInnerRect(TRect& rect);
Computes the area of the gadget's rectangle excluding the borders and margins.

GetMargins
TMargins& GetMargins();
Gets the margin dimensions.

GetOuterSizes
void GetOuterSizes(int& left, int& right, int& top, int& bottom);
Returns the amount of space (in pixels) taken up by the borders and margins.

IdleAction
virtual bool IdleAction(long idleCount);
Called during idle time to allow the gadget to perform any idle actions. *TGadget* performs command enabling on first call in each idle period.

IsEndOfRow
bool IsEndOfRow() const;
Returns true if this gadget is at the end of a row.

IsVisible
bool IsVisible() const;
Returns true if the gadget is visible.

NextGadget
TGadget* NextGadget();
Returns the next gadget in the list of gadgets.

SetBorders
void SetBorders(const TBorders& borders);
Sets the borders for the gadget. If the borders are changed, *SetBorders* calls *TGadgetWindow::GadgetChangedSize* to notify the gadget window of the change.

See also   TGadget::GetBorders

SetBorderStyle
void SetBorderStyle(TBorderStyle bs);
Sets the border style for the gadget.

See also   TGadget::GetBorderStyle, TGadget::TBorderStyle

SetBounds

virtual void SetBounds(const TRect& rect);

Informs the gadget of a change in its bounding rectangle. Although the default behavior updates only the instance variable *Bounds,* you can override this method to also update the internal state of the gadget.

SetEnabled

virtual void SetEnabled(bool enabled);

Enables or disables keyboard and mouse input for the gadget. By default, the gadget is disabled when it is created and must be enabled before it can be activated.

See also   TGadget::GetEnabled

SetEndOfRow

void SetEndOfRow(bool eor);

Sets the end of row property for the gadget. The end of row property is used to tile gadgets.

SetMargins

void SetMargins(const TMargins& margins);

Sets the margins of the gadget. If the margins are changed, *SetMargins* calls *TGadgetWindow::GadgetChangedSize* to notify the gadget window.

See also   TGadget::GetMargins

SetShrinkWrap

void SetShrinkWrap(bool shrinkWrapWidth, bool shrinkWrapHeight);

Sets the *ShrinkWrapWidth* and *ShrinkWrapHeight* data members. Your derived class can call *TGadgetWindow::GadgetChangedSize* if you want to change the size of the gadget.

SetSize

void SetSize(TSize& size);

Alters the size of the gadget and then calls *TGadgetWindow::GadgetChangedSize* for the size change to take effect.

This function is needed only if you have turned off shrink-wrapping in one or both dimensions; otherwise, use the *GetDesiredSize* member function to return the shrink-wrapped size.

SetVisible

void SetVisible(bool visible);

Changes the visibility of the gadget.

SysColorChange

virtual void SysColorChange();

Called when the system colors have been changed so that gadgets can rebuild and repaint, if necessary.

Protected data members

Borders
TBorders Borders;
Contains the border measurements of *TGadget::GetInnerRect*.

BorderStyle
TBorderStyle BorderStyle;
Contains the border style for the gadget.

Bounds
TRect Bounds;
Contains the bounding rectangle for the gadget in gadget window coordinates.

See also   TGadget::GetInnerRect

Id
int Id;
Contains the gadget's ID.

Margins
TMargins Margins;
Contains the margin measurements of the rectangle or the gadget.

See also   TGadget::GetInnerRect

ShrinkWrapHeight
bool ShrinkWrapHeight;
Indicates if the gadget is to be shrink-wrapped to fit around its contents.

ShrinkWrapWidth
bool ShrinkWrapWidth;
Indicates if the gadget is to be shrink-wrapped to fit around its contents.

TrackMouse
bool TrackMouse;
Initialized to **false**. When *TrackMouse* is true, the gadget captures the mouse on *LButtonDown* by calling *TGadgetWindow*'s *GadgetSetCapture* and releases the mouse on *LButtonUp* by calling *GadgetReleaseCapture*.

Window
TGadgetWindow* Window;
References the owning or parent window for the gadget.

Protected member functions

Created
virtual void Created();
This is the virtual called after the window holding a gadget has been created.

Inserted
virtual void Inserted();
Called after a gadget is inserted into a window.

Invalidate
void Invalidate(bool erase = true);
Used to invalidate the active (usually nonborder) portion of the gadget, *Invalidate* calls *InvalidateRect* and passes the boundary width and height of the area to erase.

InvalidateRect
void InvalidateRect(const TRect& rect, bool erase = true);
Invalidates the gadget-relative rectangle in the parent window.

LButtonDown
virtual void LButtonDown(uint modKeys, TPoint& point);
Captures the mouse if *TrackMouse* is set. *point* is located in the gadget's coordinate system.

LButtonUp
virtual void LButtonUp(uint modKeys, TPoint& point);
Releases the mouse capture if *TrackMouse* is set. *point* is located in the gadget's coordinate system.

MouseEnter
virtual void MouseEnter(uint modKeys, TPoint& point);
Called when the mouse enters the gadget.

See also TGadget::MouseLeave

MouseLeave
virtual void MouseLeave(uint modKeys, TPoint& point);
Called when the mouse leaves the gadget.

See also TGadget::MouseEnter

MouseMove
virtual void MouseMove(uint modKeys, TPoint& point);
If mouse events are captured, *MouseMove* responds to a mouse dragging message. *point* is located in the receiver's coordinate system.

See also TGadget::MouseEnter, TGadget::MouseLeave

Moved
virtual void Moved();
This is the virtual called when a gadget is relocated.

Paint
virtual void Paint(TDC&);
Calls *PaintBorder* to paint the indicated device context.

See also TTextGadget::Paint

PaintBorder
virtual void PaintBorder(TDC& dc);

Used to paint the border, *PaintBorder* determines the width and height of the gadget and uses the color returned by *GetSyscolor* to paint or highlight the area with the specified brush. Depending on whether the border style is raised, embossed, or recessed, *PaintBorder* paints the specified boundary. You can override this function if you want to implement a border style that is not supported by ObjectWindows' gadgets.

PtIn
virtual bool PtIn(TPoint& point);

Determines if the point is within the receiver's bounding rectangle and returns **true** if this is the case; otherwise, returns **false**.

Removed
virtual void Removed();

Called after a gadget is removed from a window.

Update
void Update();

Repaints the gadget if possible.

TGadgetControl class   gadgetwi.h

TGadgetControl is a specialized, easily constructed gadget window that holds one gadget for use as a control in a window.

Public constructor

TGadgetControl
TGadgetControl(TWindow* parent = 0, TGadget* soleGadget = 0, TFont* font = new TGadgetWindowFont, TModule* module = 0);

Constructs a control out of a gadget.

TGadgetList class   gadgetwi.h

TGadgetList is a list of gadgets with management functions.

Public member functions

FirstGadget
TGadget* FirstGadget() const;

Returns the first gadget of the list.

GadgetCount
uint GadgetCount() const;

Returns the number of gadgets in the list.

GadgetFromPoint
TGadget* GadgetFromPoint(TPoint& point) const;

Returns the gadget that a given window-relative point is in, or 0 if none is found.

GadgetWithId
TGadget* GadgetWithId(int id) const;

Returns the gadget with a given ID, or 0 if none is found.

Insert
virtual void Insert(TGadget& gadget, TPlacement = After, TGadget* sibling = 0);

Inserts a Gadget. Caller also needs to call *LayoutSession()* after inserting gadgets if this window has already been created.

Inserted
virtual void Inserted(TGadget& gadget);

Callback invoked when a gadget is inserted. (A gadget has been inserted into this gadget window.)

InsertFrom
virtual void InsertFrom(TGadgetList& list, TPlacement = After, TGadget* sibling = 0);

Inserts a list of gadgets. Caller also needs to call *LayoutSession()* after inserting gadgets if this window has already been created.

NextGadget
TGadget* NextGadget(TGadget& gadget) const;

Returns the next gadget.

operator []
TGadget* operator [](uint index);

Returns gadget at a given index.

Remove
virtual TGadget* Remove(TGadget& gadget);

Remove (unlinks) a gadget from this gadget window. The gadget is returned but not destroyed. Returns 0 if gadget is not in this window. Caller also needs to call *LayoutSession()* after inserting/removing gadgets if this gadget window has already been created.

Removed
virtual void Removed(TGadget& gadget);

A gadget has been removed from this gadget window.

Protected data members

Gadgets
TGadget* Gadgets;

Called by a gadget that wants to capture the mouse. *Gadgets* always get notified when a left button down occurs within their bounding rectangle. If you want mouse drags and a mouse up, then you need to capture the mouse. Fails if it's already captured.

NumGadgets
uint NumGadgets;

Total number of gadgets.

TGadgetWindow class   gadgetwi.h

Derived from *TWindow*, *TGadgetWindow* maintains a list of tiled gadgets for a window and lets you dynamically arrange tool bars. You can specify the following attributes of these gadgets:

- Horizontal or vertical tiling. Positions the gadgets horizontally or vertically within the inner rectangle (the area excluding borders and margins).

- Gadget font. Default font to use for gadgets and for calculating layout units. For font information, see the description of *TGadgetWindowFont*.

- Left, right, top, and bottom margins. Specified in pixels, layout units (based on the window font), or border units (the width or height of a thin window border).

- Measurement units. Specified in pixels, layout units, or border units.

- Gadget window size. A gadget window can shrink-wrap its width, height, or both to fit around its gadgets. By default, horizontally tiled gadgets shrink-wrap to fit the height of the window and vertically tiled gadgets shrink-wrap to fit the width of the window.

TGadgetWindow is the base class for the following derived classes: *TControlBar*, *TMessageBar*, *TToolBox*, and *TStatusBar*.

Type definitions

THintMode enum
enum THintMode {NoHints, PressHints, EnterHints};

Enumerates the hint mode settings of the gadget.

Table 2.10   Hint mode constants

Constant	Meaning if set
NoHints	No hints.
PressHints	Hints when a button is pressed.
EnterHints	Hints when the mouse passes over a gadget.

See also   TGadgetWindow::GetHintMode

TTileDirection enum
enum TTileDirection {Horizontal, Vertical, Rectangular};

Enumerates the two directions the gadget can be tiled. *TGadgetWindow::TileGadgets* actually tiles the gadgets in the direction requested.

Table 2.11   Constants

Constant	Meaning if set
Horizontal	Tiles the gadgets horizontally.
Vertical	Tiles the gadgets vertically.
Rectangular	Arranges the gadgets in rows and columns (grid).

See also   TGadgetWindow::TileGadgets

Public constructor and destructor

Constructor
TGadgetWindow(TWindow* parent = 0, TTileDirection direction = Horizontal, TFont* font = new
   TGadgetWindowFont, TModule* module = 0);

Creates a *TGadgetWindow* interface object with the default tile direction and font and passes *module* with a default value of 0.

Destructor
~TGadgetWindow();

Destructs the *TGadgetWindow* object by deleting all of its gadgets and fonts.

Public member functions

Create
bool Create();

Overrides *TWindow* member function and chooses the initial size of the gadget if shrink-wrapping was requested.

See also   TGadgetWindow::SetShrinkWrap

FirstGadget
TGadget* FirstGadget() const;

Returns the *FirstGadget* in the list.

See also   TGadgetWindow::FirstGadget

GadgetChangedSize

void GadgetChangedSize(TGadget& gadget);

Used to notify the gadget window that a gadget has changed its size, *GadgetChangedSize* calls *LayoutSession* to re-layout all gadgets.

See also   TGadget::SetShrinkWrap, TGadgetWindow::GadgetChangedSize

GadgetFromPoint

TGadget* GadgetFromPoint(TPoint& point);

Returns the gadget at the given window coordinates.

GadgetReleaseCapture

void GadgetReleaseCapture(TGadget& gadget);

Releases the capture so that other windows can receive mouse messages.

See also   TGadgetWindow::GadgetSetCapture

GadgetSetCapture

bool GadgetSetCapture(TGadget& gadget);

GadgetSetCapture reserves all mouse messages for the gadget window until the capture is released. Although gadgets are always notified if a left button-down event occurs within the rectangle, the derived gadget class must call *GadgetSetCapture* if you want the gadget to be notified when a mouse drag and a mouse button-up event occurs.

See also   TGadgetWindow::GadgetReleaseCapture

GadgetWithId

TGadget* GadgetWithId(int id) const;

Returns a pointer to the gadget associated with the given ID (*id*).

GetCelArray

TCelArray& GetCelArray(int minX = 0, int minY = 0);

Gets the Shared CelArray for this gadget window. Makes an empty one "on the fly" if needed.

GetDesiredSize

virtual void GetDesiredSize(TSize& size);

If shrink-wrapping was requested, *GetDesiredSize* returns the size needed to accommodate the borders and the margins of the widest and highest gadget; otherwise, it returns the width and height in the window's *Attr* structure.

If you want to leave extra room for a specific look (for example, a separator line between gadgets, a raised line, and so on), you can override this function. However, if you override *GetDesiredSize*, you will probably also need to override *GetInnerRect* to calculate your custom inner rectangle.

See also   TGadgetWindow::GetInnerRect

GetDirection

TTileDirection GetDirection() const;

Gets the horizontal or vertical orientation of the gadgets.

See also   TGadgetWindow::SetDirection

GetFont

TFont& GetFont();

Returns the font (which is *Sans Serif* by default).

See also   TGadgetWindowFont::TGadgetWindowFont

GetFontHeight

uint GetFontHeight() const;

Gets the height of the window's font.

GetHintMode

THintMode GetHintMode();

Returns the hint mode.

GetTooltip

TTooltip* GetTooltip() const;

Retrieves the tooltip of gadget window.

IdleAction

bool IdleAction(long idleCount);

While no messages are waiting to be processed, *IdleAction* is called and iterates through the gadgets, invoking their *CommandEnable* member function.

See also   TGadget::CommandEnable

Insert

void Insert(TGadget& gadget, TPlacement = After, TGadget* sibling = 0);

Inserts a gadget before or after a sibling gadget (*TPlacement*). If *sibling* is 0, then the new gadget is inserted at either the beginning or the end of the gadget list. If this window has already been created, *LayoutSession* needs to be called after inserting gadgets.

See also   TGadgetWindow::LayoutSession, TGadgetWindow::Remove

Inserted

void Inserted(TGadget& gadget);

This indicates that a gadget has been inserted into this gadget window.

InsertFrom

void InsertFrom(TGadgetList& list, TPlacement = After, TGadget* sibling = 0);

Inserts a list of Gadgets. The caller needs also to call *LayoutSession()* after inserting gadgets if this window has already been created.

LayoutSession

virtual void LayoutSession();

LayoutSession is typically called when a change occurs in the size of the margins or gadgets, or when gadgets are added or deleted. *LayoutSession* calls *TileGadgets* to tile the gadgets in the specified direction and *Invalidate* to mark the area as invalid (needs repainting).

See also   TGadgetWindow::Insert, TGadgetWindow::Remove, TWindow::Invalidate

NextGadget

TGadget* NextGadget(TGadget& gadget) const;

Returns the next gadget after *gadget* or 0 if none exists.

Remove

TGadget* Remove(TGadget& gadget);

Removes a gadget from the gadget window. The gadget is returned but not destroyed. *Remove* returns 0 if the gadget is not in the window.

If this window has already been created, the calling application must call *LayoutSession* after any gadgets have been removed.

See also   TGadgetWindow::Insert, TGadgetWindow::LayoutSession

Removed

void Removed(TGadget& gadget);

This indicates that a gadget has been removed from this gadget window.

SetCelArray

void SetCelArray(TCelArray* sharedCels);

Sets a new Shared CelArray for this gadget window. Allows a predefined array of images to be shared by the gadgets. This GadgetWindow assumes ownership of the passed CelArray pointer.

SetDirection

virtual void SetDirection(TTileDirection direction);

Sets the horizontal or vertical orientation of the gadgets. If the gadget window is already created, *SetDirection* readjusts the dimensions of the gadget window to fit around the gadgets.

The setting of the direction parameter is also related to the setting of the second parameter (*Tlocation*) in *TDecoratedFrame's Insert* function, which specifies where the decoration is added in relation to the frame window's client window. If the second parameter in *TDecoratedFrame::Insert* is set to top or bottom, the direction parameter in *SetDirection* must be horizontal. If the second parameter in *TDecoratedFrame::Insert* is set to left or right, the direction parameter in *SetDirection* must be vertical.

See also   TGadgetWindow::GetDirection

SetHintCommand

void SetHintCommand(int id);

Simulates menu selection messages so that ObjectWindows command processing can display command hints for the given command *id* (CM_xxxx).

See also   CM_xxxx edit constants, CM_xxxx edit file constants -

SetHintMode

void SetHintMode(THintMode hintMode);

Sets the mode of the hint text. Defaults to *PressHints* (displays hint text when a button is pressed).

See also   THintMode enum

SetMargins
void SetMargins(TMargins& margins);
Sets or changes the margins for the gadget window and calls *LayoutSession*.

See also   TGadgetWindow::Margins

SetRectangularDimensions
void SetRectangularDimensions(int width, int height, int rowMargin= -1);
Sets the maximum width for each row used for rectangular layout.

SetShrinkWrap
void SetShrinkWrap(bool shrinkWrapWidth, bool shrinkWrapHeight);
Sets the width and height of the data members. By default, if the tile direction is horizontal, *ShrinkWrapWidth* is false and *ShrinkWrapHeight* is true. Also by default, if the direction is vertical, *ShrinkWrapWidth* is true and *ShrinkWrapHeight* is false.

Protected data members

AtMouse
TGadget* AtMouse;
The last gadget at the mouse position.

BkgndBrush
TBrush* BkgndBrush;
The color of the background brush.

Capture
TGadget* Capture;
Points to the gadget that currently has the mouse capture; otherwise, if no gadget has the mouse capture, *Capture* is 0.

See also   TGadgetWindow::GadgetSetCapture

Direction
TTileDirection Direction;
The direction of the tiling—either horizontal or vertical.

DirtyLayout
bool DirtyLayout;
Indicates the layout has changed and gadgets need to be re-tiled. Using *DirtyLayout* avoids redundant tiling when gadget windows are created.

See also   TGadgetWindow::LayoutSession

Font
TFont* Font;
Points to the font used to calculate layout units.

See also   TGadgetWindow::GetFont

FontHeight
uint FontHeight;
Holds the height of the gadget window's font.

See also TGadgetWindow::GetFont

Gadgets
TGadget* Gadgets;
Points to the first gadget in the gadget list.

HintMode
THintMode HintMode;
Holds the hint text mode.

See also THintMode enum

Margins
TMargins Margins;
Holds the margin values for the gadget window.

See also TGadgetWindow::SetMargins

NumGadgets
uint NumGadgets;
The number of gadgets in the window.

SharedCels
TCelArray* SharedCels;
A CelArray that can be shared by gadgets.

ShrinkWrapHeight
bool ShrinkWrapHeight;
If *ShrinkWrapHeight* is true, the window will shrink its width to fit the tallest gadget for horizontally tiled gadgets.

See also TGadgetWindow::SetShrinkWrap

ShrinkWrapWidth
bool ShrinkWrapWidth;
If *ShrinkWrapWidth* is true, the window will shrink its width to fit the widest gadget for vertically tiled gadgets.

See also TGadgetWindow::SetShrinkWrap

Tooltip
TTooltip* Tooltip;
Gadget window's tooltip.

WideAsPossible
uint WideAsPossible;
The number of gadgets that are as wide as possible.

Protected member functions

EvCommand

TResult EvCommand(uint id, HWND hWndCtl, uint notifyCode);

When the gadget window receives a WM_COMMAND message, it is likely from a gadget or control within a *TControlGadget*. This reroutes it to the command target.

EvCommandEnable

void EvCommandEnable(TCommandEnabler& ce);

When the gadget window receives a WM_COMMAND_ENABLE message, it is likely from a gadget or control within a *TControlGadget*. This reroutes it to the command target.

EvLButtonDblClk

void EvLButtonDblClk(uint modKeys, TPoint& point);

Passes double clicks through as if they were just a second click; finishes the first click, and begins the second: Dn + Dbl + Up -> Dn + Up+Dn + Up.

EvLButtonDown

void EvLButtonDown(uint modKeys, TPoint& point);

Responds to a left button-down mouse message by forwarding the event to the gadget positioned under the mouse.

EvLButtonUp

void EvLButtonUp(uint modKeys, TPoint& point);

Responds to a left button-up mouse message by forwarding the event to the gadget that has the capture.

EvMouseMove

void EvMouseMove(uint modKeys, TPoint& point);

Forward mouse moves to the gadget that has captured the mouse, if any. Otherwise checks for mouse entering and leaving gadgets. This could be enhanced by delaying mouse enter messages until the mouse has been in the same area for a while, or by looking ahead in the queue for mouse messages.

EvNotify

TResult EvNotify(uint id, TNotify far& notifyInfo);

Catches tooltip requests for text and forwards them to the parent instead.

EvSysColorChange

void EvSysColorChange();

Responds to WM_SYSCOLORCHANGE to let the gadgets update their UI colors, and to let this gadget window update its background color.

Note This is an obsolete function retained for compatibility. New *TWindow*, *TColor*, and other UI support makes this unecessary.

EvWindowPosChanging

void EvWindowPosChanging(WINDOWPOS far& windowPos);

Intercepts window size changes to make sure that this gadget window follows its own sizing rules. Also gives it a chance to layout wide-as-possible gadgets.

GetInnerRect

virtual void GetInnerRect(TRect& rect);

GetInnerRect computes the rectangle inside of the borders and margins of the gadget.

If you want to leave extra room for a specific look (for example, a separator line between gadgets, a raised line, and so on), you can override this function. If you override *GetInnerRect*, you will probably also need to override *GetDesiredSize* to calculate your custom total size.

See also   TGadgetWindow::GetDesiredSize

GetMargins

void GetMargins(const TMargins& margins, int& left, int& right, int& top, int& bottom);

Returns the left, right, top, and bottom margins in pixels.

LayoutUnitsToPixels

int LayoutUnitsToPixels(int units);

Converts layout units to pixels. A layout unit is determined by dividing the window font height by eight.

See also   TGadgetWindow::LayoutSession

Paint

void Paint(TDC& dc, bool erase, TRect& rect);

Puts the font into the device context and calls *PaintGadgets*.

See also   TGadgetWindow::PaintGadgets

PaintGadgets

virtual void PaintGadgets(TDC& dc, bool erase, TRect& rect);

Called by *Paint* to repaint all of the gadgets, *PaintGadgets* iterates through the list of gadgets, determines the gadget's area, and repaints each gadget.

You can override this function to implement a specific look (for example, separator line, raised, and so on).

PositionGadget

virtual void PositionGadget(TGadget* previous, TGadget* next, TPoint& point);

PositionGadget is called to allow spacing adjustments to be made before each gadget is positioned.

See also   TGadgetWindow::TileGadgets

PreProcessMsg

bool PreProcessMsg(MSG& msg);

Relays 'interesting' messages to the tooltip window.

SetupWindow

void SetupWindow();

Overrides *TWindow::SetupWindow* to create tooltips for the gadget window.

TileGadgets

virtual TRect TileGadgets();

Tiles the gadgets in the direction requested (horizontal or vertical). Calls *PositionGadget* to give derived classes an opportunity to adjust the spacing between gadgets in their windows.

See also   TGadgetWindow::PositionGadget

UseDesiredSize

void UseDesiredSize();

Updates the Size in Attr.W and Attr.H to match that obtained using *GetDesiredSize* for each dimension that is shrink-wrapped.

Response table entries

Response table entry	Member function
EV_WM_LBUTTONDOWN	EvLButtonDown
EV_WM_LBUTTONUP	EvLButtonUp
EV_WM_MOUSEMOVE	EvMouseMove
EV_WM_SIZE	EvSize
EV_WM_SYSCOLORCHANGE	EvSysColorChange

TGadgetWindowFont class   gadgetwi.h

Derived from *TFont*, *TGadgetWindowFont* is a specific font used in gadget windows for sizing and default text. You can specify the point size of the font (not the size in pixels) and whether it is bold or italic. You can use one of the following *FF_xxxx* constants to indicate the font family type:

Value	Meaning
FF_DECORATIVE	Specialty fonts such as Old English.
FF_DONTCARE	The font type does not matter.
FF_MODERN	Fonts such as Pica, Elite, or Courier with a constant stroke, width, and with or without serifs.
FF_ROMAN	Fonts such as Times New Roman and New Century Schoolbook with varied stroke and with serifs.
FF_SCRIPT	Fonts such as Script that are designed to resemble handwriting.
FF_SWISS	Fonts such as MS Sans Serif with variable stroke width and without serifs.

Depending on the typeface, the font weight can be one of the following *FW_xxxx* constants:

Value	Meaning
FW_DONTCARE	Does not matter
FW_THIN	Thin
FW_EXTRALIGHT	Extra light
FW_ULTRALIGHT	Extra light
FW_LIGHT	Light
FW_NORMAL	Normal
FW_REGULAR	Normal font weight
FW_MEDIUM	Medium
FW_SEMIBOLD	Somewhat bold
FW_DEMIBOLD	Somewhat bold
FW_BOLD	Bold
FW_EXTRABOLD	Extra bold
FW_ULTRABOLD	Extra bold
FW_BLACK	Heavy weight
FW_HEAVY	Heavy weight

Because the font's appearance depends on the typeface, some fonts have only FW_NORMAL, FW_REGULAR, and FW_BOLD available. If FW_DONTCARE is indicated, the default font weight is used.

Public constructor

TGadgetWindowFont
TGadgetWindowFont(int pointSize = 10, bool bold = false, bool italic = false);

Constructs a *TGadgetWindowFont* interface object with a default point size of 10 picas without bold or italic typeface. By default, the constructor creates the system font: a variable-width, sans-serif Helvetica.

See also   TFont

TGauge class   gauge.h

A streamable class derived from *TControl*, *TGauge* defines the basic behavior of gauge controls. Gauges are display-only horizontal or vertical controls that provide duration or analog information about a particular process. A typical use of a gauge occurs in installation programs where a control provides a graphical display indicating the percentage of files copied. In general, horizontal gauges with a broken (dashed-line) bar are used to display short-duration, process information, and horizontal gauges with a solid bar are used to illustrate long-duration, process information. Usually, vertical gauges are preferred for displaying analog information.

Public constructors

Form 1   TGauge(TWindow* parent, const char far* title, int id, int x, int y, int w, int h = 0, bool isHorizontal = true,
         int margin = 1, TModule* module = 0);

Constructs a *TGauge* object with borders that are determined by using the value of SM_CXBORDER. Sets IsHorizontal to *isHorizontal*. Sets border thickness and spacing between dashed borders (LEDs) to 0. Sets the range of possible values from 0 to 100.

Form 2   TGauge(TWindow* parent, int id, int x, int y, int w, int h = 0, TModule* module = 0);

Simplified constructor for a *TGauge* object. Creates a horizontal LED style gauge, using a system control when available.

Public member functions

DeltaValue
void DeltaValue(int delta);

Changes the value of the gauge by the given delta.

GetRange
void GetRange(int& min, int& max) const;

This inline implementation gets the minimum and maximum values for the gauge.

GetStep
int GetStep() const;

Returns the step factor.

GetValue
int GetValue() const;

Returns the current value of the gauge.

operator ++
void operator ++(int);

Another way of stepping (calls *StepIt*).

SetColor
void SetColor(const TColor& color);

Sets the *BarColor* data member to the value specified in *color*.

SetLed
void SetLed(int spacing, int thickPercent = 90);

Sets the *LedSpacing* and *LedThick* data members to the values *spacing* and *thick*.

SetNativeUse
static void SetNativeUse(TNativeUse nu);

Specifies whether the class uses the native (operating system) implementation or emulates it.

SetRange

void SetRange(int min, int max);

Sets the *Min* and *Max* data members to *min* and *max* values returned by the constructor. If *Max* is less than or equal to *Min*, *SetRange* resets *Max* to *Min* + 1.

SetStep

void SetStep(int step);

Sets the *Step* amount of the gauge for *StepIt* operations.

SetValue

void SetValue(int value);

Sets the value of the gauge.

Restricts *value* to be within the minimum and maximum values established for the gauge. If the current value has changed, *SetValue* marks the old position for repainting. Then, it sets the data member *Value* to the new value.

StepIt

void StepIt();

Adjusts the active gauge value by the *Step* increment. If the new value exceeds the *Max* value of the gauge, *StepIt* wraps the setting of the gauge to its *Min* value.

Protected data members

BarColor

TColor BarColor;

Holds the bar or LED color, which defaults to blue.

ClassNativeUse

static TNativeUse ClassNativeUse;

The gauge doesn't "know" if the native implementation will work. That is, if more features are requested than the native control can provide, the class will emulate the gauge rather than relying on the operating systems.

IsHorizontal

int IsHorizontal;

Set to the *isHorizontal* argument of the constructor. *IsHorizontal* is **true** if the gauge is horizontal and **false** if it is vertical.

LedSpacing

int LedSpacing;

Holds the integer value (in gauge units) of the spacing between the broken bars of the gauge. Note that *TGauge* does not paint the title while using LED spacing.

LedThick

int LedThick;

Holds the thickness of the broken bar.

Margin

int Margin;

Contains the border width and height of the gauge.

Max

int Max;

Holds the maximum value (in gauge units) displayed on the gauge.

Min

int Min;

Holds the minimum value (in gauge units) displayed on the gauge.

Step

int Step;

Holds the step factor to be used by *StepIt* operations.

Value

int Value;

Holds the current value of the gauge.

Protected member functions

EvEraseBkgnd

bool EvEraseBkgnd(HDC);

Overrides the *TWindow::EvEraseBkgnd* function and erases the background of the gauge. Whenever the background is repainted, *EvEraseBkgnd* is called to avoid flickering.

GetClassName

char far* GetClassName();

Returns the class name of the native control or emulation, depending on NativeUse.

Paint

void Paint(TDC& dc, bool erase, TRect& rect);

Overrides *TWindow::Paint* and paints the area and the border of the gauge. Uses the values supplied in *rect* and *dc* to paint the given rectangle on the given device context. Uses the values in *LedSpacing* and *IsHorizontal* to draw a horizontal or vertical gauge with solid or broken bars.

See also   TDC, TRect

PaintBorder

virtual void PaintBorder(TDC& dc);

Paints the border (bevel and margin).

Paints the gauge border using the specified device context. Depending on whether the border style is raised, embossed, or recessed, *PaintBorder* paints the specified boundary. You can override this function if you want to implement a border style that is not supported by ObjectWindows' gauges.

SetupWindow
void SetupWindow();
If a system control is being used, updates it to match our member settings.

Response table entries

Response table entry	Member function
EV_WM_ERASEBKGND	EvEraseBkgnd

TGdiObject class   gdiobjec.h

GdiObject is the root, pseudo-abstract base class for ObjectWindows' GDI (Graphics Device Interface) wrappers. The *TGdiOject*-based classes let you work with a GDI handle and construct a C++ object with an aliased handle. Some GDI objects are also based on *TGdiObject* for handle management. Generally, the *TGdiObject*-based class hierarchy handles all GDI objects apart from the DC (Device Context) objects handled by the *TDC*-based tree.

The five DC selectable classes *(TPen, TBrush, TFont, TPalette,* and *TBitmap),* and the *TIcon, TCursor, TDib,* and *TRegion* classes, are all derived directly from *TGdiObject*.

TGdiObject maintains the GDI handle and a *ShouldDelete* flag that determines if and when the handle and object should be destroyed. Protected constructors are provided for use by the derived classes: one for borrowed handles, and one for normal use.

An optional orphan control mechanism is provided. By default, orphan control is active, but you can turn it off by defining the NO_GDI_ORPHAN_CONTROL identifier:

    #define NO_GDI_ORPHAN_CONTROL

With orphan control active, the following static member functions are available:

RefAdd, RefCount, RefDec, RefFind, RefInc, and *RefRemove.*

These maintain object reference counts and allow safe orphan recovery and deletion. Macros, such as OBJ_REF_ADD, let you deactivate or activate your orphan control code by simply defining or undefining NO_GDI_ORPHAN_CONTROL. When NO_GDI_ORPHAN_CONTROL is undefined, for example, *OBJ_REF_ADD(handle, type)* expands to *TGdiObject::RefAdd((handle),(type)),* but when NO_GDI_ORPHAN_CONTROL is defined, the macro expands to *handle.*

Public destructor

~TGdiObject();
If *ShouldDelete* is false no action is taken. Otherwise with *ShouldDelete* true, the action of the destructor depends on whether orphan control is active or not. If orphan control is inactive (that is, if NO_ORPHAN_CONTROL is defined) ~*TGdiObject* deletes the GDI

object. If orphan control is active (the default) the object is deleted only if its reference count is 0.

Type definitions

TAutoDelete enum
enum TAutoDelete{NoAutoDelete, AutoDelete};

This **enum**, which is defined in the private base class, gdibase.h, enumerates the flag values for GDI handle constructors. This flag is used to control GDI object deletion in the destructors.

TType enum
enum TType{None, Pen, Brush, Font, Palette, Bitmap, TextBrush};

This enumeration is used to store the object type in the **struct** *TObjInfo*. This internal structure is used to track object reference counts during debugging sessions.

See also   TGdiObject::RefCount

Public member functions

GetGdiHandle
THandle GetGdiHandle() const;

Returns the handle of the GDI object.

GetObject
int GetObject(int count, void far* object) const;

Obtains information about this GDI object and places it in the *object* buffer. If the call succeeds and *object* is not 0, *GetObject* returns the number of bytes copied to the object buffer. If the call succeeds and *object* is 0, *GetObject* returns the number of bytes needed in the object buffer for the type of object being queried. Depending on what type of GDI object is derived, this function retrieves a *LOGPEN*, *LOGBRUSH*, *LOGFONT*, or *BITMAP* structure through *object*.

See also   TPen::GetObject, BITMAP struct, LOGBRUSH struct, LOGFONT struct, LOGPEN struct

GetObjectType
uint32 GetObjectType() const;

Returns the type of the GDI object.

IsGDIObject
bool IsGDIObject() const;

Returns true if this represents a real GDI object.

operator ==
bool operator ==(const TGdiObject& other) const;

Returns true if the handles are equal. This is a binary compare.

RefAdd

static void RefAdd(HANDLE handle, TType type);

Available only if orphan control is active (that is, if NO_GDI_ORPHAN_CONTROL is undefined). *RefAdd* adds a reference entry for the object with the given *handle* and *type* to the *ObjInfoBag* table and sets the reference count to 1. If the table already has a matching entry, no action is taken.

See also TGdiObject::RefCount, macro OBJ_REF_ADD

RefCount

static int RefCount(HANDLE handle);

Available only if orphan control is active, that is, if NO_GDI_ORPHAN_CONTROL is undefined. *RefCount* returns this object's current reference count or -1 if the object is not in the *ObjInfoBag* table.

See also macro OBJ_REF_COUNT

RefDec

static void RefDec(HANDLE handle);
static void RefDec(HANDLE handle, bool wantDelete);

Available only if orphan control is active, that is, if NO_GDI_ORPHAN_CONTROL is undefined. *RefDec* decrements this object's reference count by 1 and deletes the object when the reference count reaches zero. A warning is issued if the deletion was supposed to happen but didn't. Likewise, a warning is issued if the deletion wasn't supposed to happen but did. The deleted object is also detached from the *ObjInfoBag* table.

The second version of *RefDec* is available only if the _ _TRACE identifier is defined. You can vary the normal deletion strategy by setting *wantDelete* to true or false.

See also TGdiObject::RefCount, macro OBJ_REF_DEC

RefFind

static TObjInfo* RefFind(HANDLE object);

Available only if orphan control is active (that is, if NO_GDI_ORPHAN the given object is undefined). If found, the object's type and reference count are returned in the specified *TObjInfo* object. *RefFind* returns 0 if no match is found.

See also TGdiObject::RefCount

RefInc

static void RefInc(HANDLE handle);

Available only if orphan control is active (that is, if NO_GDI_ORPHAN_CONTROL is undefined). *RefInc* increments by 1 the reference count of the object associated with *handle*.

See also TGdiObject::RefCount, macro OBJ_REF_INC

RefRemove

static void RefRemove(HANDLE handle);

Available only if orphan control is active (that is, if NO_GDI_ORPHAN_CONTROL is undefined). *RefRemove* removes the reference entry to the object with the given *handle* from the *ObjInfoBag* table. If the given handle is not found, no action is taken.

See also TGdiObject::RefCount, macro OBJ_REF_REMOVE

THandle

operator THandle() const;

Returns the handle of the GDI object. *TGdiObject* encapsulates an HGDIOBJ.

operator HGDIOBJ

operator HGDIOBJ() const

Typecasting operator that converts this GDI object handle to type HGDIOBJ.

Protected data members

Handle

HANDLE Handle;

The GDI handle of this object.

See also   TGdiObject Protected Constructors

ShouldDelete

bool ShouldDelete;

Set true if the destructor needs to delete this object's GDI handle.

See also   TGdiObject Protected Constructors

Protected member functions

CheckValid

Form 1   void CheckValid(uint resId=IDS_GDIFAILURE)

Form 2   static void CheckValid(HANDLE handle, uint resId=IDS_GDIFAILURE)

Both versions of *CheckValid* check for a valid GDI object handle. If one is not found a GDI exception is thrown for the given resource id.

Protected constructors

Form 1   TGdiObject();

This default constructor sets *Handle* to 0 and *ShouldDelete* to true. This constructor is intended for use by derived classes that must set the *Handle* member.

Form 2   TGdiObject(HANDLE handle, TAutoDelete autoDelete = NoAutoDelete);

This constructor is intended for use by derived classes only. The *Handle* data member is "borrowed" from an existing handle given by the argument *handle*. The *ShouldDelete* data member defaults to false ensuring that the borrowed handle will not be deleted when the object is destroyed.

See also   TGdiObject::enumTAutoDelete, TGdiObject::Handle, TGdiQbject::RefCount, TGdiObject::ShouldDelete

Macros

OBJ_REF_ADD

OBJ_REF_ADD(handle, type)

If orphan control is active (the default), *OBJ_REF_ADD(handle, type)* is defined as *TGdiObject::RefAdd((handle), (type))*. The latter adds to the *ObjInfoBag* table a reference entry for the object with the given *handle* and *type*, and sets its count to 1. If orphan control is inactive, *OBJ_REF_ADD(handle)* is defined as *handle*. This macro lets you write orphan control code that can be easily deactivated with the single statement *#define NO_GDI_ORPHAN_CONTROL*.

See also   TGdiObject::RefAdd

OBJ_REF_COUNT

OBJ_REF_COUNT(handle)

If orphan control is active (the default), *OBJ_REF_COUNT(handle)* is defined as *TGdiObject::RefCount((handle))*. The latter returns the reference count of the object with the given handle, or -1 if no such object exists. If orphan control is inactive, *OBJ_REF_COUNT(handle)* is defined as -1. This macro lets you write orphan control code that can be easily deactivated with the single statement *#define NO_GDI_ORPHAN_CONTROL*.

See also   TGdiObject::RefCount

OBJ_REF_DEC

OBJ_REF_DEC(handle, wantDelete)

If orphan control is active (the default), *OBJ_REF_DEC(handle, wantDelete)* is defined as either *TGdiObject::RefDec((handle))* or *TGdiObject::RefDec((handle), (wantDelete))*. The latter format occurs only if _ _TRACE is defined. *RefDec(handle)* decrements the reference count of the object associated with *handle* and optionally deletes orphans or warns you of their existence. If orphan control is inactive, *OBJ_REF_DEC(handle)* is defined as *handle*. This macro lets you write orphan control code that can be easily deactivated with the single statement *#define NO_GDI_ORPHAN_CONTROL*.

See also   TGdiObject::RefDec

OBJ_REF_INC

OBJ_REF_INC(handle)

If orphan control is active (the default), *OBJ_REF_INC(handle)* is defined as *TGdiObject::RefInc((handle))*. The latter increments the reference count of the object associated with *handle*. If orphan control is inactive, *OBJ_REF_DEC(handle)* is defined as *handle*. This macro lets you write orphan control code that can be easily deactivated with the single statement *#define NO_GDI_ORPHAN_CONTROL*.

See also   TGdiObject::RefInc

OBJ_REF_REMOVE

OBJ_REF_REMOVE(handle)

If orphan control is active (the default), *OBJ_REF_REMOVE(handle)* is defined as *TGdiObject::RefRemove((handle))*. The latter removes from the *ObjInfoBag* table the reference entry for the object associated with *handle*. If orphan control is inactive,

OBJ_REF_REMOVE(handle) is defined as *handle*. This macro lets you write orphan control code that can be easily deactivated with the single statement #*define NO_GDI_ORPHAN_CONTROL*.

See also   TGdiObject::RefRemove

TGlyphButton class   glyphbtn.h

TGlyphButton encapsulates a control which is capable of displaying a bitmap (or glyph) and/or text.

Type definitions

TButtonInfo enum
enum TButtonInfo {biPushed = 0x0001, biFocus = 0x0002, biDefault = 0x0004, biDisabled = 0x0008, biShowT=0x0010, biShowGlyph= 0x0020};
TButtonInfo is used to describe the current state of the button.

Table 2.12   Button info constants

Constant	Meaning if set
biPushed	Button is currently depressed
biFocus	Button has focus
biDefault	Button is a DefaultPushButton
biDisabled	Button is disabled
biShowText	Button should display its caption
biShowGlyph	Button should draw its glyph

TGlyphType enum
enum TGlyphType {gtUp = TUIFace::Normal, gtDisabled = TUIFace::Disabled, gtDown, gtFocus};
TGlyphType is used to describe the state when a particular bitmap should be displayed. If only a single bitmap (*gtUp*) is specified, *TGlyphButton* automatically generates the bitmaps for the other states.

Table 2.13   Glyph type constants

Constant	Meaning if set
gtUp	Bitmap for when the button is up
gtDisabled	Bitmap for when the button is disabled
gtDown	Bitmap for when the button is depressed
gtFocus	Bitmap for when the button has focus

See also   TGlyphButton::SetGlyph

TLayoutStyle enum

enum TLayoutStyle {lsNone, lsH_SGST, lsH_GST, lsH_STSG, lsH_TSGS, lsV_SGST, lsV_GST,
lsV_STSG, lsV_TSGS};

TLayoutStyle enumerates the constants that control the layout of the items on a glyph
button as follows:

Table 2.14   Layout constants

Constant	Meaning if set
lsNone	Use specified coordinates
lsH_SGST	Space, Glyph, Space, Text (Horizontal).
lsH_GST	Glyph, Space, Text (Horizontal).
lsH_STSG	Space, Text, Space, Glyph (Horizontal).
lsH_TSGS	Text, Space, Glyph, Space (Horizontal).
lsV_SGST	Space, Glyph, Space, Text (Vertical).
lsV_GST	Glyph, Space, Text (Vertical).
lsV_STSG	Space, Text, Space, Glyph (Vertical).
lsV_TSGS	Text, Space, Glyph, Space (Vertical).

Public constructor and destructor

Constructor
Form 1   TGlyphButton(TWindow* parent, int id, const char far* text, int X, int Y, int W, int H, bool isDefault = false,
TModule* module = 0);

Constructor of *TGlyphButton*. Use this constructor to create a GlyphBtn from scratch.

Form 2   TGlyphButton(TWindow* parent, int resourceId, TModule* module = 0);

Constructor of *TGlyphButton*. Use this constructor to alias a glyph button control
specified in a dialog template.

Destructor
~TGlyphButton();

Destructor. Cleans up resources used by glyph button object.

Public member functions

SetGlyph
Form 1   void SetGlyph(TResId resId, TModule* module = 0, TGlyphType = gtUp);

Specifies the resource identifier of a bitmap to be used as glyph.

Form 2   void SetGlyph(TBitmap* bitmap, TGlyphType = gtUp);

Specifies a bitmap object to be used as glyph.

Note   The *bitmap* parameter can be 0 to reset the glyph stored by the glyph button object.

Form 3   void SetGlyph(HBITMAP hBitmap, TGlyphType = gtUp, TAutoDelete autoDelete = NoAutoDelete);

Specifies a bitmap to be used as glyph.

SetGlyphOrigin

void SetGlyphOrigin(int x, int y);

Sets the upper left corner of glyphs and invalidates window if necessary.

SetLayoutStyle

void SetLayoutStyle(TLayoutStyle style);

Specifies a *style* describing how text and glyph should be laid out. Invalidates the window if necessary.

SetTextOrigin

void SetTextOrigin(int x, int y);

Sets text coordinates and invalidates window if necessary.

Protected member functions

BmGetState

TResult BmGetState(TParam1 param1, TParam2 param2);

BM_GETSTATE handler. Returns the current state of the window.

BmSetState

TResult BmSetState(TParam1 param1, TParam2 param2);

BM_SETSTATE handler. Updates internal state flags based on parameters and redraws control if necessary.

BmSetStyle

TResult BmSetStyle(TParam1 param1, TParam2 param2);

BM_SETSTYLE handler. Updates internal flags to match specified parameters and invalidates the window if necessary.

ClearCapture

void ClearCapture();

Releases caption if we are in "capture" mode. Resets internal flags appropriately.

EvCancelMode

void EvCancelMode();

WM_CANCELMODE handler. Releases capture if currently in capture mode and terminates any internal operation on the button.

EvEnable

void EvEnable(bool enabled);

WM_ENABLE handler. Updates internal flags and invalidates control if necessary.

EvEraseBkgnd

bool EvEraseBkgnd(HDC);

WM_ERASEBKGND handler. Returns true to prevent background from being erased. (WM_PAINT handler paints whole client area).

EvGetDlgCode

uint EvGetDlgCode(MSG far* msg);

WM_GETDLGCODE handler. Informs dialog manager of a "normal" push button or the default push button according to the style.

EvGetFont

HFONT EvGetFont();

WM_GETFONT handler. Returns font used by control if one was specified earlier. Otherwise, returns 0.

EvKeyDown

void EvKeyDown(uint key, uint repeatCount, uint flags);

WM_KEYDOWN handler. Updates the state of the button upon detecting that the user pressed the space bar.

EvKeyUp

void EvKeyUp(uint key, uint repeatCount, uint flags);

WM_KEYUP handler. Restores state of button and notify parent.

EvKillFocus

void EvKillFocus(THandle hWndGetFocus);

WM_KILLFOCUS handler. Updates internal flag and forces button to redraw.

EvLButtonDblClk

void EvLButtonDblClk(uint modKeys, TPoint& point);

WM_LBUTTONDBLCLK handler. Simply forwards to LBUTTONDOWN handler.

EvLButtonDown

void EvLButtonDown(uint modKeys, TPoint& point);

WM_LBUTTONDOWN handler. Grabs focus and updates button's state to be in "pushed" mode.

EvLButtonUp

void EvLButtonUp(uint modKeys, TPoint& point);

WM_LBUTTONUP handler. Restores state of button and notifies parent with a CLICKED message if necessary.

EvMouseMove

void EvMouseMove(uint modKeys, TPoint& point);

WM_MOUSEMOVE handler. Updates state of button if it is in "capture" mode.

EvPaint

void EvPaint();

WM_PAINT handler. Invokes *Paint* method to display glyph and/or text.

EvSetFocus

void EvSetFocus(THandle hWndLostFocus);

WM_SETFOCUS handler. Updates internal flag and forces button to redraw.

EvSetFont
void EvSetFont(HFONT hFont, bool redraw);
WM_SETFONT handler. Deletes any cached font and stores a copy of the new one.

GetClassName
char far* GetClassName();
Returns name of window class associated with a glyph button control.

GetWindowClass
void GetWindowClass(WNDCLASS& wndClass);
Overrides virtual of *TWindow*. Fills out information about the Window class associated with a glyph button.

Note   The class information is based on the system's *BUTTON* class.

InitVars
void InitVars();
Method used to initialized variables used by GlyphButton's implementation.

LayoutTextGlyph
void LayoutTextGlyph(const TRect& faceRect, TRect& textRect, TRect& glyphRect);
Virtual routine invoked to retrieve the placement of text and glyph when drawing the button.

Paint
void Paint(TDC& dc, bool erase, TRect& rect);
Invokes *PaintButton* to display glyph and/or text.

PaintButton
void PaintButton(TDC& dc);
Paints the button into a memory DC and bitblt the final rendering to the specified *dc*.

PaintDefaultRect
void PaintDefaultRect(TDC& dc, TRect& rect);
Draws a frame around the button if it's a default push button.

PaintFace
void PaintFace(TDC& dc, TRect& rect);
Draws the face of the button [i.e. text and glyph portions].

PaintFocusRect
void PaintFocusRect(TDC& dc, const TRect& faceRect);
Displays a focus rectangle.

PaintFrame
void PaintFrame(TDC& dc, TRect& rect);
Draws the border of the button.

PaintNow

void PaintNow();

Repaints window right away by retrieving a client DC and invoking the *Paint* method.

SetupWindow

void SetupWindow();

Overrides virtual of *TWindow*. Updates internal flags based on style of underlying window.

TGroupBox class   groupbox.h

An instance of a *TGroupBox* is an interface object that represents a corresponding group box element. Generally, *TGroupBox* objects are not used in dialog boxes or dialog windows (*TDialog*), but are used when you want to create a group box in a window.

Although group boxes do not serve an active purpose onscreen, they visually unify a group of selection boxes such as check boxes and radio buttons or other controls. Behind the scenes, however, they can take an important role in handling state changes for their group of controls (normally check boxes or radio buttons).

For example, you might want to respond to a selection change in any one of a group of radio buttons in a similar manner. You can do this by deriving a class from *TGroupBox* that redefines the member function *SelectionChanged*.

Alternatively, you could respond to selection changes in the group of radio buttons by defining a response for the group box's parent. To do so, define a child-ID-based response member function using the ID of the group box. The group box will automatically send a child-ID-based message to its parent whenever the radio button selection state changes. This class is streamable.

Public constructors

Form 1   TGroupBox(TWindow* parent, int Id, const char far *text, int x, int y, int w, int h, TModule* module = 0);

Constructs a group box object with the supplied parent window (*Parent*), control ID (*Id*), associated text (*text*), position (*x, y*) relative to the origin of the parent window's client area, width (*w*), and height (*h*). Invokes the *TControl* constructor with similar parameters, then modifies *Attr.Style*, adding BS_GROUPBOX and removing WS_TABSTOP. *NotifyParent* is set to **true**; by default, the group box's parent is notified when a selection change occurs in any of the group box's controls.

Form 2   TGroupBox(TWindow* parent int resourceId, TModule* module = 0);

Constructs a *TGroupBox* object to be associated with a group box control of a *TDialog* object. Invokes the *TControl* constructor with identical parameters. *resourceID* must correspond to a group box resource that you define.

See also   TControl::TControl, TWindow::DisableTransfer

Public member functions

NotifyParent
bool NotifyParent;

Flag that indicates whether parent is to be notified when the state of the group box's selection boxes has changed. *NotifyParent* is **true** by default.

GetNotifyParent
bool GetNotifyParent() const;

Returns the flag that indicates whether or not the parent is notified.

SelectionChanged
virtual void SelectionChanged(int controlId);

If *NotifyParent* is **true**, *SelectionChanged* notifies the parent window of the group box that one of its selections has changed by sending it a child-ID-based message. This member function can be redefined to allow the group box to handle selection changes in its group of controls.

SetNotifyParent
void SetNotifyParent(bool notifyparent);

Sets the flag that indicates whether or not the parent is notified.

Protected member functions

GetClassName
char far* GetClassName();

GetClassName returns the name of *TGroupBox*'s Windows registration class, *BUTTON*. If Borland Windows Custom Controls (BWCC) is enabled, *GetClassName* returns BUTTON_CLASS.

THarbor class
docking.h

THarbor is the object that holds all the docking slips. It performs the actual docking insertion and coordination. It is never visible; it is a window in order to capture the mouse.

Public constructor and destructor

Constructor
THarbor(TDecoratedFrame& df);

Creates the harbor. The harbor is where the slips can go dock.

Destructor
~THarbor();

Destructor. Currently does nothing.

Public member functions

DockDraggingBegin
bool DockDraggingBegin(TDockable& dockable, TPoint& pt, TAbsLocation location,
     TDockingSlip* dockingNotify = 0);
Begins a dockable window tracking session. Returns true if started satisfactorily.

Insert
void Insert(TDockable& dockable, TAbsLocation location, const TPoint* where = 0,
     TRelPosition position = rpNone, TDockable* relativeTo = 0);
Inserts a dockable into the appropriate docking area indicated by the given location and
either a point or a relative dockable and position.

Move
void Move(TDockable& dockable, TAbsLocation location, const TPoint* where = 0,
     TRelPosition position = rpNone, TDockable* relativeTo = 0);
Moves a dockable from one slip to another.

Remove
void Remove(TDockable& dockable);
Removes a dockable from the harbor.

Protected member functions

ConstructEdgeSlip
virtual TEdgeSlip* ConstructEdgeSlip(TDecoratedFrame& df, TAbsLocation location);
Creates an edge slip at a location.

ConstructFloatingSlip
virtual TFloatingSlip* ConstructFloatingSlip(TDecoratedFrame& df, int x, int y, TWindow* dockableWindow);
Constructs a floating slip with a particular window at a location.

EvLButtonDblClk
void EvLButtonDblClk(uint modKeys, TPoint& point);
Handles the left button double click and forwards the message to the dockable window.

EvLButtonUp
void EvLButtonUp(uint modKeys, TPoint& point);
Handles mouse up to drop a dockable window being dragged.

EvMouseMove
void EvMouseMove(uint modKeys, TPoint& point);
Handles *MouseMove* to perform dockable dragging if a drag is in progress.

GetEdgeSlip
TEdgeSlip* GetEdgeSlip(TAbsLocation location);
Returns the slip at the location.

GetSlipPosition
TRelPosition GetSlipPosition(TAbsLocation location);

Returns the default docking relative position for a given slip location.

SetEdgeSlip
void SetEdgeSlip(TAbsLocation location, TEdgeSlip* slip);

Sets a new edge slip for a given location. Also lets the edge slip know who we are.

SetupWindow
void SetupWindow();

Ensures that all decorations in the docking window are abutted against each other (both horizontally and vertically). There should be no gaping holes.

THatch8x8Brush class
gdiobjec.h

Derived from *TBrush*, *THatch8x8Brush* defines a small, 8x8, monochrome, configurable hatch brush. Because the hatch brush is a logical brush created from device-independent bitmaps (DIBs), it can be passed to any device context (DC), which then renders the brush into the appropriate form for the device.

Although the default brush color is a white foreground and a black background, you can vary the colors of the hatched brush. The colors can be any one of the *TColor* object encapsulated colors, namely the standard RGB values.

THatch8x8Brush contains static arrays that define common hatched brush patterns. The hatched brush patterns you can select are:

Standard

Forward diagonal

Backward diagonal

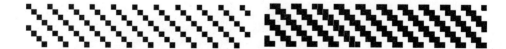

You can use *THatch8x8Brush* to design a variety of hatched brush border patterns around a simple rectangle or an OLE container. You can also use *THatch8x8Brush* in conjunction with *TUIHandle*.

Public data members

Hatch11F1[8]

const static uint8 Hatch11F1[8];

The static array *Hatch11F1[8]* holds the logical hatched brush pattern of one pixel on and one pixel off in monochrome, offset one per row as the following pattern illustrates:

Hatch13B1[8]

const static uint8 Hatch13B1[8];

The static array *Hatch13B1[8]* holds a hatched brush pattern of one pixel on and three pixels off in backward diagonal hatch marks, offset one per row as the following pattern illustrates:

Hatch13F1[8]

const static uint8 Hatch13F1[8];

The static array *Hatch13F1[8]* holds a hatched brush pattern of one pixel on and three pixels off in forward diagonal hatch marks, offset one per row as the following pattern illustrates:

Hatch22B1[8]

const static uint8 Hatch22B1[8];

The static array *Hatch22B1[8]* holds a hatched brush pattern of two pixels on and two off in backward diagonal hatch marks, offset one per row as the following pattern illustrates:

Hatch22F1[8]

const static uint8 Hatch22F1[8];

The static array *Hatch22F1[8]* holds a monochrome hatched brush pattern of two pixels on and two off in forward diagonal hatch marks, offset one per row as the following pattern illustrates:

Public constructors

THatch8x8Brush(const uint8 hatch[], const TColor& fgColor=TColor::White,
        const TColor&bgColor=TColor::Black);

Constructs a *THatchBrush* object with the specified hatched pattern and colors. Although the hatched brush is, by default, white on a black background, you can control the displayed colors by passing different colors in the constructor, where *fgColor* represents the foreground color and *bgColor* represents the background color of a TColor object type.

Note that colors can be specified in either palette mode (a reference to a corresponding color palette entry in the currently realized palette) or RGB mode (an actual red, green, or blue color value).

Public member functions

Reconstruct

void Reconstruct(const uint8 hatch[], const TColor& fgColor, const TColor& bgColor);

Reconstructs the hatched brush with a new pattern or new set of colors.

See also TBrush, TColor, TUIHandle

THdrItem class   colmnhdr.h

THdrItem contains information about an item in a header control.

Public constructors

Form 1   THdrItem(const char far* str);

Constructs a *THdrItem* object for an item which has a string. Defaults to left alignment and the default string item size.

Form 2　　THdrItem(const char far* str, HBITMAP hbm);

Constructs a *THdrItem* object for an item consisting of both a string and a bitmapped image.

Form 3　　THdrItem(HBITMAP hbm);

Constructs a *THdrItem* object for an item which has a bitmapped image. Defaults to left alignment and the default bitmap item size.

Form 4　　THdrItem(char far* buffer, int len, uint msk = HDI_TEXT);

Constructs an "empty" *THdrItem* with the specified *msk* enabled. This form of the constructor is mainly used to construct an object which is used to retrieve information about an existing item. *buffer* specifies a location which will receive the text of the item and *len* specifies the size of the buffer.

Form 5　　THdrItem(uint msk = 0);

Constructs an "empty" *THdrItem* with the specified *msk* enabled. This form of the constructor is mainly used to construct an object which is used to retrieve information about an existing item.

Public member functions

SetBitmap
void SetBitmap(HBITMAP hbm);
Sets the bitmap handle of the *HeaderItem* object.

Note　The format flags is not updated to contain any alignment flags.

SetDefBitmapSize
static void SetDefBitmapSize(int size);
API to allow the user to update ObjectWindows' default bitmap item size.

Note　Because the variable maintaining that information is shared by every instance of this class, use this function with caution.

SetDefStringSize
static void SetDefStringSize(int size);
API to allow user to update ObjectWindows' default string size.

Note　Because the variable maintaining that information is shared by every instance of this class, use this function with caution.

SetHeight
void SetHeight(int cy);
Sets the height of the item.

SetMask
void SetMask(int msk);
Updates the mask member of the structure. The latter indicates which other members of the structure contain valid data.

SetText
void SetText(const char far* str);
Sets the text of the *HeaderItem* object.

Note The format flags are not updated to contain any alignment flags.

SetWidth
void SetWidth(int cx);
Sets the width of the item.

Protected member functions

DefBitmapItemSize
static int DefBitmapItemSize;
Returns default size of bitmap item.

DefStringItemSize
static int DefStringItemSize;
Default size of string item.

THdrNotify class   commctrl.h

THdrNotify encapsulates the *HD_NOTIFY* structure which is sent with the WM_NOTIFY messages sent by the HeaderControl to its parent.

Public member functions

operator NMHDR&
operator NMHDR&();
Allows the notification structure to be transparently treated as an NMHDR structure, thereby eliminating the need to explicitly refer to the NMHDR data member (which is always the first member of notification structures).

THelpContext class   hlpmanag.h

THelpContext is a class that maintains information about a menu item ID and a child control ID with a help context ID. As particular windows get and lose focus, their context tables are removed from a global context table.

Public constructors and destructor

Constructors

Form 1   THelpContext();

Default constructor that initializes every data member to zero.

Form 2   THelpContext(TWindow* window, int helpId, int menuId, int controlId);

Convenient constructor to initialize the context entry with the proper IDs.

Form 3   THelpContext(const THelpContext&);

Makes a copy of the context entry.

Destructor

~THelpContext();

Does nothing.

Public member functions

GetControlContextId

int GetControlContextId() const;

Returns the child control ID for this context entry.

GetHelpFileContextId

int GetHelpFileContextId() const;

Returns the help file context ID for the context entry.

GetMenuContextId

int GetMenuContextId() const;

Returns the menu ID for this context entry.

GetWindow

TWindow* GetWindow() const;

Returns the window this entry is associated with.

operator =

THelpContext& operator = (const THelpContext&);

Makes a copy of the context entry.

operator ==

int operator == (const THelpContext&) const;

Returns true if the context entries match.

SetWindow

void SetWindow(TWindow* window);

Sets the window for this context entry.

THelpFileManager class

hlpmanag.h

THelpFileManager, which is designed to be a mix-in for *TApplication*, uses the global context table. *THelpFileManager* looks for the WM_HELP message and calls the help file with the associated context ID.

Type definitions

TType enum
enum TType {Control, Menu};

Public constructors

Form 1   THelpFileManager(const string helpFileName);
Constructor. Saves the name of the help file and creates the global context table.

Form 2   virtual ~THelpFileManager();
Deletes the allocated context table.

Public member functions

ActivateHelp
virtual void ActivateHelp(TWindow*, int helpFileContextId);
Called by *EvHelp()* to activate the help file with the help context ID.

AddContextInfo
void AddContextInfo(TWindow*, int helpId, int menuId, int controlId);
Adds an entry into the global context table.

DeactivateHelp
virtual void DeactivateHelp();
Deactivates the help.

GetHelpContextFromControl
bool GetHelpContextFromControl(THelpContext&, int controlId, HWND ctrl) const;
Returns true if a match for the control ID was found.

GetHelpContextFromMenu
bool GetHelpContextFromMenu(THelpContext&, int menuId) const;
Returns true if a match for the menu item ID was found.

GetHelpFile
string GetHelpFile() const;
Returns the name of the help file.

RemoveContextInfo
void RemoveContextInfo(TWindow*);
Removes all the entries in the context table for the window.

SetHelpFile
void SetHelpFile(const string helpFileName);
Changes the name of the help file.

THotKey class   hotkey.h

THotKey encapsulates the hot-key control, a window that allows the user to enter a combination of keystrokes to be used as a hot key. (A hot key is a key combination that the user can press to perform an action quickly.)

Public constructors

Form 1   THotKey(TWindow* parent, int id, int x, int y, int w, int h, TModule* module = 0);
Constructors for *THotKey* initialize data fields using parameters passed and default values. By default, a Hotkey control associated with the *TColumnHeader* will be visible upon creation and will have a border.

Form 2   THotKey(TWindow* parent, int resourceId, TModule* module = 0);
Constructs a hot key control from resource.

Public member functions

GetHotKey
uint16 GetHotKey();
Returns the 16-bit virtual key code for the control.

SetHotKey
Form 1   void SetHotKey(uint8 vk, uint8 mods);
Sets the virtual key code and modifier flags for the hot key.

Form 2   void SetHotKey(uint16 hotKey);
Sets the virtual key code and modifier flags for the hot key. See the Windows API for more details on VK_xxxx and modifier flags.

SetRules
void SetRules(uint16 invalid, uint16 defFlag);
Sets the invalid key combinations for the hot key control.

Protected member functions

GetClassName
char far* GetClassName();
Returns the class name for a hot key control.

Transfer
uint Transfer(void* buffer, TTransferDirection direction);
Transfers a uint16 (the virtual key code) for the control.

THostEntry class   wskhostm.h

THostEntry encapsulates the attributes of a host (hostent).

Public constructor

THostEntry();
Constructor of *THostEntry* object. Initializes members describing host to 0.

Public member functions

GetAddressCount
int GetAddressCount();
Returns the number of pointers to addresses in the hostent (parent class of *THostEntry*).

GetINetAddress
ulong GetINetAddress();
Returns the Internet address of the host.

GetNthINetAddress
ulong GetNthINetAddress(int nIndex = 0);
This function is flawed in that it is Internet addressing-specific (AF_INET/PF_INET). The proper way to implement this function would be to look at h_addrtype and h_length to determine the nature of the address type and return something useful or make a derived class that knows about each address family.

THostInfoManager class   wskhostm.h

THostInfoManager encapsulates the host (hostent) database functions.

Public constructor and destructor

Constructor
THostInfoManager();
This function initializes the hidden window.

Destructor
~THostInfoManager();
With this destructor, you need to clear any pending requests before the deletion.

Public member functions

CancelHostRequest
int CancelHostRequest(HANDLE hTheHostRequest=0);
The caller can use this call to cancel the last pending request.

GetHostAddress
Form 1   int GetHostAddress(TSocketAddress& sAddress, const char far* szHostName);
This function effectively converts *szHostName* to a socket address. If you have a name such as "joe_schmoe@borland.com," and you want the *TSocketAddress* for it, you can call this function. This function, like most of Windows Sockets, currently works only with IP addresses. Thus, the *szHostAddress* is always going to be dotted-decimal format in Windows Sockets.

This function returns an error value of WINSOCK_ERROR or WINSOCK_NOERROR.

Form 2   int GetHostAddress(char far* szHostAddress, const char far* szHostName);
This function effectively converts *szHostName* to *szHostAddress*. If you have a name such as "joe_schmoe@borland.com" and you want the dotted-decimal IP address for it, you can call this function. This function assumes that there is enough space in *szHostAddress* for the address. This function, like most of Windows Sockets, currently works only with IP addresses. Thus, the *szHostAddress* is always going to be dotted-decimal format in Windows Sockets.

Note that when using the *inet_ntoa()* function, the char* string returned resides in Windows Sockets memory space, the *szHostAddress* returned is allocated and owned by the caller of this function and can be manipulated any way the caller wants.

This function returns an error value of WINSOCK_ERROR or WINSOCK_NOERROR.

GetHostInfo
Form 1   int GetHostInfo(THostEntry*& hEntry, const char far* szName);
Windows Sockets can block a call until the other end finishes the transaction. Entry is a pointer passed by reference. The system will change that pointer to point to an internal Windows Sockets data structure. The contents must not be modified. Name is a preallocated string that holds a string. The address of the host can be in string format or in binary format.

The caller of this function passes a pointer to a *THostEntry* struct, for example:

```
THostEntry* tempTHostEntry;
GetHostInfo(tempTHostEntry, "JoeShmoe@anywhere.com");
printf("%s", tempTHostEntry->h_name); //h_name should be "joeSchmoe@anywhere.com"
```

Form 2 int GetHostInfo(THostEntry*& hEntry, const TSocketAddress& sAddress);

The caller of this function supplies a pointer to be assigned by this function. The caller need not allocate space for any *THostEntry* structure. Because of this, the data needs to be read immediately or copied for later use. Address is a preallocated SocketAddress reference.

Due to the design of the socket API, the call to *gethostbyaddr* currently requires a pointer to the Internet address, rather than a sockaddr or even a sockaddr_in. Because passing a ulong pointer would most likely not work (for example, if the socket API was to support something other than IP), this issue is fixed by making a sockaddr interface to this API. The address is in network byte ordering.

GetHostInfoAsync

Form 1 int GetHostInfoAsync(TWindow& wndNotify, HANDLE& hTheHostRequest, char far* szName,
        uint nMessage=MSG_HOST_INFO_NOTIFY, char far* chBuffer=0);

This function notifies the given window that a request has completed, *hwndNotify* is the window that will get the message that the request has completed. *nMessage* is the message that the *hwndNotify* will receive. It defaults to MSG_HOST_INFO_NOTIFY, which is defined in the *THostInfoManager's* header file. *hTheHostRequest* is the asynchrous request handle that will be a reference to the request. *szName* is the name of the host, as in "coyote@acme.com." The *chBuffer* is a pointer to buffer that will be filled in with a hostent. It needs to be at least MAXGETHOSTSTRUCT bytes. If *chBuffer* is 0 (or not specified), the *THostInfoManager's* internal buffer will be used. The returned address is in network byte ordering.

Form 2 int GetHostInfoAsync(TWindow& wndNotify, HANDLE& hTheHostRequest, TSocketAddress& sAddress,
        uint nMessage=MSG_HOST_INFO_NOTIFY, char far* chBuffer=0);

This function notifies the given window that a request has completed. *nMessage* is the message that the *hwndNotify* will receive. It defaults to MSG_HOST_INFO_NOTIFY, which is defined in the *THostInfoManager's* header file. The *chBuffer* is a pointer to the buffer that will be filled in with a hostent. It needs to be at least MAXGETHOSTSTRUCT bytes. If *chBuffer* is 0 (or not specified), the *THostInfoManager's* internal buffer is used. The *hTheHostRequest* will hold a handle that the caller can use to reference the request on call-back. *wParam* will be equal to the *hService* returned.

WSAGETSYNCERROR (*lParam*) holds an error, if any (0 is OK). WSAGETSYNCBUFLEN (*lParam*) holds actual length of the buffer. When this function returns, *myTHostEntry* holds the appropriate information. Since this information belongs to this object, you can delay reading it as long as you want. Note that while the *sAddress* should be passed in network byte ordering, the output on callback is also in network ordering.

Form 3 int GetHostInfoAsync(HANDLE& hTheHostRequest, char far* szName);

Returns the same information as the other versions of *GetHostInfoAsync*. The difference is that the host name can be a string, rather than a *TSocketAddress*.

Form 4   int GetHostInfoAsync(HANDLE& hTheHostRequest, TSocketAddress& sAddress);

The *TheHostRequest* parameter is returned to the caller with the asynchrous request handle. Address needs to be in network byte ordering. Note that due to the design of this class, you cannot have two outstanding service requests that get notified directly to this class. You can use the hwnd-specific notification version of this function to manage multiple requests. You can also create more than one instance of this class. The service is complete when *HostRequestCompleted* is true. Look at *LastError* in this case to see if there was an error.

Do not issue any asynchrous calls that post to this class hwnd until the previous request is completed. The alternative is to create multiple *THostInfoManagers* or manage the call-backs yourself. See the comments about the non-asynchronous version of this call (*THostInfoManager::GetHostInfo*) for more information.

GetHostName
int GetHostName(char far* name, int nameLength = N_MAX_HOST_NAME);

This function returns the name of the computer on which this program is running. The *szName* parameter is set to the name. The return value is either WINSOCK_ERROR or WINSOCK_NOERROR. You can call *THostInfoManager::GetLastError()* to get the actual error value. *name* is a pointer to a preallocated buffer of minimum size of *nNameLength*. *nameLength* should be at least N_MAX_HOST_NAME.

GetHostRequestCompleted
short GetHostRequestCompleted();

This function returns true if the host completed the last requested transaction.

GetLastError
int GetLastError();

This function returns the last error code.

HostEntryToAddress
Form 1   static intHostEntryToAddress(THostEntry* hEntry, TSocketAddress& sAddress);

Given a *THostEntry**, this function converts it to a socket address. Because Windows Sockets supports only IP addressing, this function uses IP addressing and the address is an INetSocketAddress. The return value is WINSOCK_ERROR or WINSOCK_NOERROR.

Form 2   static int HostEntryToAddress(THostEntry* hEntry, char far* szAddress);

Given a THostEntry*, this function converts it to a dotted-decimal *szAddress*. Because Windows Sockets supports only IP addressing, this function uses IP addressing and the address is always dotted-decimal. The return value is WINSOCK_ERROR or WINSOCK_NOERROR.

Protected data members

HostWindow
THostInfoWindow HostWindow;

This function is a hidden window to catch notifications.

LastError
int LastError;
This function supplies the last error code.

HostInfoBuffer
char HostInfoBuffer[MAXGETHOSTSTRUCT];
This function is used for calls to *WSAAsync...()*.

SetHostRequestCompleted
void SetHostRequestCompleted(int error);
This function is called whenever an asynchronous request is completed. You may want to override this function in your *THostInfoManager*-derived class. If you do, you must call the base version.

THostInfoWindow class   wskhostm.h

THostInfoWindow is a private class created by *THostInfoManager* to catch Windows Sockets messages.

Public constructor

THostInfoWindow
THostInfoWindow(THostInfoManager* hostInfoManagerParent);
The *HostInfoWindow* requires a *HostInfoManager*, so it can relay messages to it.

Public member functions

DoNotification
TResult DoNotification(TParam1 param1, TParam2 param2);
This is a relay function.

HostInfoManagerParent
THostInfoManager* HostInfoManagerParent;
This is an object to notify of Windows Sockets events.

TIC class   dc.h

Derived from *TDC*, *TIC* is a device context (DC) class that provides a constructor for creating a DC object from explicit driver, device, and port names.

Public constructor

TIC

TIC(const char far* driver, const char far* device, const char far* output, const DEVMODE far* initData=0);

Creates a DC object with the given driver, device, and port names and initialization values.

See also   TDC::GetDeviceCaps, DEVMODE struct

TIcon class   gdiobjec.h

TIcon, derived from *TGdiObject*, represents the GDI object icon class. *TIcon* constructors can create icons from a resource or from explicit information. Because icons are not real GDI objects, the *TIcon* destructor overloads the base destructor, *~TGdiObject*.

Public constructors and destructor

Constructors

Form 1   TIcon(HICON handle, TAutoDelete autoDelete = NoAutoDelete);

Creates a *TIcon* object and sets the *Handle* data member to the given borrowed handle. The *ShouldDelete* data member defaults to false, ensuring that the borrowed handle will not be deleted when the C++ object is destroyed.

Form 2   TIcon(HINSTANCE instance, const TIcon& icon);

Creates a copy of the given *icon* object.

Form 3   TIcon(HINSTANCE instance, TResID resID);

Creates an icon object from the given resource.

Form 4   TIcon(HINSTANCE instance, const char far* filename, int index);

Creates an icon object from the given resource file.

Form 5   TIcon(HINSTANCE instance, const TSize& size, int planes, int bitsPixel, const void far* andBits, const void far* xorBits);

Creates an icon object with the given values.

Form 6   TIcon(const void* resBits, uint32 resSize);

Creates an icon object of the given size from the bits found in the *resBits* buffer.

Form 7   TIcon(const ICONINFO* iconInfo);

Creates an icon object with the given ICONINFO information.

Destructor

~TIcon();

Destroys the icon and frees any memory that the icon occupied.

See also   ~TGdiObject, TGdiObject::Handle, TGdiObject::ShouldDelete, TResID, TSize, ICONINFO structure

Public member functions

GetHandle
THandle GetHandle() const;

Returns the handle of the icon with type HICON.

GetIconInfo
bool GetIconInfo(ICONINFO* iconInfo) const;

Retrieves information about this icon and copies it into the given ICONINFO structure. Returns true if the call is successful; otherwise returns false.

See also   ICONINFO structure

operator HICON()
operator HICON() const;

Typecasting operator that converts this icon's *Handle* to type *HICON* (the data type representing the handle to an icon resource).

operator ==
bool operator ==(const TIcon& other) const;

Returns true if the handles of two icons are identical.

THandle
operator THandle() const;

Returns the handle of the icon with type HICON.

TIdentityPalette class   dibitmap.h

TIdentityPalette is a palette in which the colors and order of those colors match the physical palette. If the identity palette is used whenever possible, the system does not have to map colors, and so can speed up bitmap drawing.

Public constructor

TIdentityPalette
TIdentityPalette(const TPalette& palette);

Implementation of (WinG) Identity Palette object, *TIdentityPalette*. Use of an identity palette allows objects to be blitted without having the color mapper come into play. The overall effect is faster graphics. *TIdentityPalette* returns an identity palette to be used by bitmaps, ensuring speed and color accuracy.

TImageInfo class   imagelst.h

TImageInfo is a wrapper class for a structure that describes an image within an image list.

Public constructors

Form 1   TImageInfo();
          Constructs an empty image info.

Form 2   TImageInfo(const TImageList& list, int index=0);
          Construct based on an image within the image list.

Public member functions

GetImageBM
HBITMAP GetImageBM() const;
Gets the image bitmap.

GetImageRect
TRect GetImageRect() const;
Gets the area of the image.

GetMaskBM
HBITMAP GetMaskBM() const;
Gets the image's mask.

_IMAGEINFO&
operator _IMAGEINFO&();
Converts to an _IMAGEINFO structure.

TImageList class   imagelst.h

TImageList is a wrapper class for the ImageList common "control".

Public constructors and destructor

Form 1   TImageList(const TSize& size, uint flags, int initCount, int growBy);
          Constructs an empty *ImageList* of a given size.

Form 2   TImageList(const TBitmap& bmp, uint flags, int initCount, int growBy);
          Constructs a *TImageList* from a bitmap, slicing a portion of the bitmap up into a
          horizontal array of specified, sized images.

Form 3   TImageList(const TDib& dib, uint flags, int initCount, int growBy);
          Constructs a *TImageList* from a dib, slicing the dib up into a horizontal array of evenly
          sized images.

Form 4   TImageList(HINSTANCE hI, TResId resName, int w, int growBy, const TColor& mask, uint type, uint flags);

Constructs an *ImageList* right from a bmp, icon, or cursor resource in a file. *type* should be one of the consts from winuser.h:

- IMAGE_BITMAP
- IMAGE_ICON
- IMAGE_CURSOR
- IMAGE_ENHMETAFILE

Form 5   TImageList(HIMAGELIST imageList)

Constructs a C++ alias for an existing imagelist.

Form 6   TImageList(const TImageList& src);

Constructs a *TImageList* as a copy of an existing one.

Form 7   TImageList(TPoint& pt, TPoint& hotspot);

Constructs a wrapper for the current drag imagelist and specifies the location and hotspot of the imagelist.

Destructor

~TImageList();

Destructs the *ImageList* and cleans up the image list handle.

Public member functions

Add

Form 1   int Add(const TIcon&);

Adds an icon to the *ImageList*. Returns index of new addition.

Form 2   int Add(const TBitmap& image, const TColor& mask);

Adds new image(s) to *ImageList*, specifying a mask color to generate a mask. Returns index of the new addition.

Form 3   int Add(const TBitmap& image, const TBitmap& mask);

Adds new image/mask pair(s) to the *ImageList*. Returns index of new addition.

Form 4   int Add(const TBitmap& image);

Adds new image(s) to the *ImageList*. Returns index of new addition. No mask bitmap is added.

BeginDrag

bool BeginDrag(int index, int dxHotspot, int dyHotspot);

BeginDrag sets this imagelist to be the drag imagelist. There can only be one drag imagelist at any time.

DragEnter

static bool DragEnter(HWND hwndLock, int x, int y);

Typically, this function is called in response to a WM_LBUTTONDOWN message. The *x* and *y* parameters are relative to the upper-left corner of the window's rectangle and NOT the client area. The window *hWndLock* is locked from further updates.

DragLeave
static bool DragLeave(HWND hwndLock);

DragLeave is typically called when receiving a WM_LBUTTONUP message. The *hWndLock* window is unlocked from updates.

DragMove
static bool DragMove(int x, int y);

DragMove is typically called when receiving a WM_MOUSEMOVE message. The *x* and *y* parameters are generally passed from the message to this function.

DragShowNolock
static bool DragShowNolock(bool show);

Locks or unlocks the window from updates.

Draw

Form 1   bool Draw(int index, TDC&, int x, int y, int dx, int dy, const TColor& bgClr, const TColor& fgClr,
         uint style=ILD_NORMAL, int overlay=0);

Extended version of *draw* that takes a foreground color and background color.

Form 2   bool Draw(int index, TDC&, int x, int y, uint style=ILD_NORMAL, int overlay=0);

Draws an image onto a target DC at a given coordinate and with a given style.

EndDrag
static void EndDrag();

EndDrag removes the current drag imagelist from the system.

GetBkColor
TColor GetBkColor() const;

Gets the current background color for this *ImageList*.

GetIcon
HICON GetIcon(int index, uint flags) const;

Creates and retrieves an icon from an image and mask in the *ImageList*.

GetIconSize
bool GetIconSize(int& cx, int& cy);

Returns the icon size.

GetImageCount
int GetImageCount() const;

Returns number of images currently in this *ImageList*.

GetImageInfo
bool GetImageInfo(int index, TImageInfo& cellInfo) const;

Gets general information about a given image.

GetImageOffset
TPoint GetImageOffset(int cel) const;

Returns the offset of a given image in the *ImageList*'s bitmap.

GetImageRect
TRect GetImageRect(int cel) const;
Returns the bounding rect of a given image in the *ImageList*'s bitmap.

GetImageSize
TSize GetImageSize() const;
Returns the size each image. Each image of the list must be the same size.

HIMAGELIST
operator HIMAGELIST() const;
Converts to the HIMAGELIST structure.

operator [ ]
TRect operator [](int cel) const;
Returns the rectangle of the image at index *index*.

operator =
TImageList& operator =(const TImageList&);
Assigns an *ImageList* over this *ImageList*, replacing all contents.

Remove
bool Remove(int index);
Removes an image (or all images if index is -1) from this *ImageList*.

RemoveAll
bool RemoveAll();
Removes all images from the list.

Replace
Form 1   bool Replace(int index, const TBitmap& image, const TBitmap& mask);
Replaces an image and mask in the *ImageList*.

Form 2   bool Replace(int index, const TBitmap& image);
Replaces an image in this *ImageList*.

ReplaceIcon
int ReplaceIcon(int index, HICON hicon);
Replaces the image at index *index* with the icon or cursor.

SetBkColor
TColor SetBkColor(const TColor& newColor);
Sets the current background color for this *ImageList*, returning the previous color.

SetDragCursorImage
bool SetDragCursorImage(int drag, int dxHotspot, int dyHotspot);
Combines the current drag image with another image in the list. Typically, a mouse cursor would be added to the image list and merged with the drag image list.

SetOverlayImage
bool SetOverlayImage(int index, int overlay);
Selects an image for use as an overlay. Up to four can be selected.

TBitmap&
operator TBitmap&();
Returns the image bitmap used by this *ImageList*.

Protected data members

Handle
HIMAGELIST Handle;
Handle of *ImageList*.

Protected member functions

CheckValid
void CheckValid();
Throws an exception if this image list handle is invalid.

TINetSocketAddress class   wskaddr.h

TINetSocketAddress encapsulates the Internet socket address structure (sockaddr_in).

Type definitions

TINetClass enum
enum TINetClass {ClassA, ClassB, ClassC, ClassUnknown};

Public constructors

Form 1   TINetSocketAddress();
Empty constructor. Useful for creating a *TInetSocketAddress*, but delaying the actual assignment of addressing data until later.

Form 2   TINetSocketAddress(sockaddr& newSockaddr);
The argument should be in network byte ordering.

Form 3   TINetSocketAddress(ushort nNewPort, ulong lNewAddress=INADDR_ANY, ushort nNewFamily = AF_INET);
newPort should be passed in network byte ordering. *newAddress* is in the format of numerical IP addressing (e.g. *132.212.43.1*). It cannot be in the form of *user@place*. *nFamily* is in the form of AF_INET, etc.

Form 4   TINetSocketAddress(ushort nNewPort, char* szNewAddress, ushort nNewFamily = AF_INET);

All arguments should be in network byte ordering. *newFamily* is an enumeration, so there is no specific byte ordering.

Note   Address can also be INADDR_ANY, INADDR_LOOPBACK, INADDR_BROADCAST, INADDR_NONE.

Also note that in winsock.h (1.1), Microsoft defines these addresses in network byte ordering format, so you don't need to convert to network byte ordering upon passing to this function, or any other that expects network byte ordering.

Public member functions

ConvertAddress
Form 1   static char far* ConvertAddress(ulong lAddress);

This function accepts a ulong in the form of an IP binary address and converts it to a character string IP address (e.g. *123.213.132.122*), if possible. The *lAddress* parameter must be given in network byte ordering to work properly. Note that this function returns a character pointer to a string allocated by the system. It is imperative that the caller immediately copy this data, and neither modify it nor de-allocate it. This restriction is imposed by WinSock.

Form 2   static ulong ConvertAddress(char far* szAddress);

This function accepts a string in the form of *162.132.211.204* and converts it to an IP address (ulong) if possible. The returned value will be in network byte ordering. It should be INADDR_NONE if there was an error.

GetClass
TINetClass GetClass();

This function uses WinSock macros to get standard class information. It knows nothing about subnetting, nor about any classes beyond class C.

GetNetwork
Form 1   ulong GetNetwork(ulong lSubnet);

Returns the network ID masked with the subnet.

Form 2   ulong GetNetwork();

This function returns 0 if the network cannot be determined.

GetNetworkAddress
ulong GetNetworkAddress();

Returns IP binary address in network byte ordering.

GetNode
Form 1   ulong GetNode(ulong lSubnet);

Returns the node of this address.

Form 2   ulong GetNode();

This function returns the node component of the address with the subnet masked out.

GetPort
ushort GetPort();

Returns port in network byte ordering.

IsAddressDottedDecimal
static short IsAddressDottedDecimal(char far* szAddress);

This function can be used to tell if a character string points to an address in dotted-decimal IP format (e.g. *162.132.211.204*) or in name format (e.g. *jimmy_carter@wh.com*). You could call this function if the user typed in a destination address in one of either of the above formats, and you need to know which one it is, so you can know how to convert it to a ulong IP address. If the address is dotted-decimal, then you can simpoy use the *TINetSocketAddress::ConvertAddress()* function. Otherwise, you need to use one of the *HostInfoManager* functions. The *szAddress* is a pointer to a string that can be in any format, but most likely, one of either the dotted-decimal or the name formats mentioned above. This function's job is only to tell you if it is in dotted-decimal format or not. The return value is 1 if in dotted-decimal format, and 0 if not.

operator =
TINetSocketAddress& operator =(const sockaddr& newSockaddr);

The argument should be in the same byte ordering (network) as this object.

SetAddress
void SetAddress(ushort nNewFamily, ushort nNewPort, ulong lNewAddress);

This function makes an address out of the necessary IP address components. *newFamily* is an enumeration, e.g. AF_INET. *newPort* is in network byte ordering, as is *lNewAddress*.

SetFiller
void SetFiller();

This is an internal function. It is merely used to zero out the unused data of the address.

SetNetworkAddress
Form 1   void SetNetworkAddress(char* szAddressDottedDecimal);

Sets the network address.

Form 2   void SetNetworkAddress(ulong lAddress);

This function expects the argument to be in network byte ordering.

SetPort
void SetPort(ushort nPort);

This function expects the argument to be in network byte ordering.

sockaddr_in
operator sockaddr_in() const;

Converts this address to the sockaddr_in structure.

TInputDialog class

Provides a generic dialog box to retrieve text input by a user. When the input dialog box is constructed, its title, prompt, and default input text are specified. *TInputDialog* is a streamable class.

Public data members

buffer
char far* buffer;

Pointer to the buffer that returns the text retrieved from the user. When passed to the constructor of the input dialog box, contains the default text to be initially displayed in the edit control.

BufferSize
int BufferSize;

Contains the size of the buffer that returns user input.

prompt
char far* prompt;

Points to the prompt for the input dialog box.

Public constructor and destructor

Constructor
TInputDialog(TWindow* parent, const char far *title, const char far *prompt, char far* buffer, int buffersize,
TModule* module = 0, TValidator* valid = 0)

Invokes *TDialog*'s constructor, passing it *parent*, the resource identifier, and *module*. Sets the caption of the dialog box to *title* and the prompt static control to *prompt*. Sets the *Buffer* and *BufferSize* data members to *buffer* and *bufferSize*.

Destructor
~TInputDialog();

Destructor for this class.

Public member functions

GetBuffer
const char far* GetBuffer() const;

Returns the buffer.

GetBufferSize
int GetBufferSize() const;

Returns the size of the buffer.

GetPrompt
const char far* GetPrompt() const;
Returns the prompt for the dialog.

TransferData
void TransferData(TTransferDirection);
Transfers the data of the input dialog box. If *direction* is *tdSetData*, sets the text of the static and edit controls of the dialog box to the text in *prompt* and *buffer*.

Protected member function

SetupWindow
void SetupWindow();
Calls *TDialog::SetupWindow* to set up the window, then limits the number of characters the user can enter to *bufferSize - 1*.

TInStream class   docview.h

Derived from *TStream* and *istream*, *TInStream* is a base class used to define input streams for documents.

Public constructor

TInStream
TInStream(TDocument& doc, const char far* name, int mode);
Constructs a *TInStream* object. *doc* refers to the document object, *name* is the user-defined name of the stream, and *mode* is the mode of opening the stream.

See also   TOutStream, ofXXXX document open enum, shdocument sharing enum

TLayoutConstraint struct   layoutco.h

TLayoutConstraint is a structure that defines a relationship (a layout constraint) between an edge or size of one window and an edge or size of one of the window's siblings or its parent. If a parent-child relationship is established between windows, the dimensions of the child windows are dependent on the parent window. A window can have one of its sizes depend on the size of the opposite dimension. For example, the width can be twice the height. *TLayoutMetrics* lists the relationships you can have among size and edge constraints

The following window is displayed by the sample program LAYOUT.CPP, which demonstrates layout constraints:

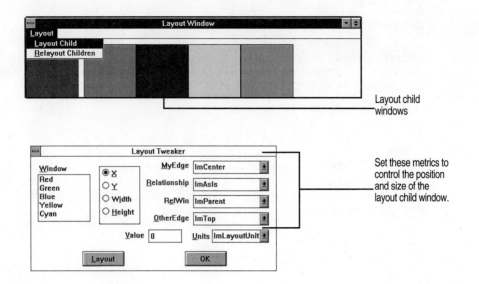

Layout child windows

Set these metrics to control the position and size of the layout child window.

Public data members

Margin
int Margin;

MyEdge
uint MyEdge;

MyEdge contains the name of the edge or size constraint (*lmTop, lmBottom, lmLeft, lmRight, lmCenter, lmWidth,* or *lmHeight*) for your window.

See also TWidthHeight enum

OtherEdge
uint OtherEdge;

OtherEdge contains the name of the edge or size constraint (*lmTop, lmBottom, lmLeft, lmRight, lmCenter, lmWidth,* or *lmHeight*) for the other window.

See also TWidthHeight enum

Percent
int Percent;

Relationship
TRelationship Relationship;

Relationship specifies the type of relationship that exists between the two windows (that is, *lmRightOf, lmLeftOf, lmAbove, lmBelow, lmSameAs,* or *lmPercentOf*). A value of *lmAbsolute* actually indicates that no relationship exists.

See also TRelationship enum

RelWin

TWindow* RelWin;

RelWin is a pointer to the sibling windows or *lmParent* if the child is a proportion of the parent's dimensions. *RelWin* points to the window itself (**this**) if a child window's dimension is a proportion of one of its other dimensions (for example, its height is a proportion of its width).

See also   TRelationship enum

Units

TMeasurementUnits Units;

Units enumerates the units of measurement (either pixels or layout units) used to measure the height and width of the windows. Unlike pixels, layout units are based on system font size and will be consistent in their perceived size even if the screen resolution changes.

See also   TMeasurementUnits enum

union

```
union {
    int  Margin;
    int  Value;
    int  Percent;
};
```

This **union** is included for the convenience of naming the layout constraints. *Margin* is used for the *lmAbove*, *lmLeftOf*, *lmLeftOf*, or *lmRightOf* enumerated values in *TRelationship*. *Value* is used for the *lmSameAs* or *lmAbsolute* enumerated values in *TRelationship*. *Percent* is used for the *lmPercentOf* enumerated value in *TRelationship*.

Value

int Value;

See also   TMeasurementUnits enum

TLayoutMetrics class   layoutwi.h

Contains the four layout constraints used to define the layout metrics for a window. The following table lists the constraints you can use for the *X*, *Y*, *Height*, and *Width* fields.

Field	Constraints
X	lmLeft, lmCenter, lmRight
Y	lmTop, lmCenter, lmBottom
Height	lmCenter, lmRight, lmWidth
Width	lmCenter, lmBottom, lmHeight

If the metrics for the child window are relative to the parent window, the relation window pointer needs to be *lmParent* (not the actual parent window pointer). For example,

```
TWindow* child = new TWindow(this, "");
TLayoutMetrics metrics;
metrics.X.Set(lmCenter, lmSameAs, lm()t, lmCenter);
metrics.Y.Set(lmCenter, lmSameAs, lm()t, lmCenter);
SetChildLayoutMetrics(*child, metrics);
```

The parent window pointer (**this**) should not be used as the relation window pointer of the child window.

Public data members

Height
TEdgeOrWidthConstraint Height;
Contains the height size constraint, center edge constraint, or bottom edge constraint of the window.

Width
TEdgeOrWidthConstraint Width;
Contains the width size constraint, center edge constraint, or right edge (*lmRight*) constraint of the window.

X, Y
TEdgeConstraint X, Y;
X contains the *X* (left, center, right) edge constraint of the window. *Y* contains the *Y* (top, center, bottom) edge constraint of the window.

Public constructors

TLayoutMetrics();
Creates a *TLayoutMetrics* object and initializes the object. It sets the units for the child and parent window to the specified layout units, and the relationship between the two windows to what is defined in *lmAsIs* (of *TRelationship*). *TLayoutMetrics* sets the following default values:

```
X.RelWin = 0;
X.MyEdge = lmLeft;
X.Relationship = lmAsIs;
X.Units = lmLayoutUnits;
X.Value = 0;
Y.RelWin = 0;
Y.MyEdge = lmTop;
Y.Relationship = lmAsIs;
Y.Units = lmLayoutUnits;
Y.Value = 0;
Width.RelWin = 0;
Width.MyEdge = lmWidth;
```

```
      Width.Relationship = lmAsIs;
      Width.Units = lmLayoutUnits;
      Width.Value = 0;
      Height.RelWin = 0;
      Height.MyEdge = lmHeight;
      Height.Relationship = lmAsIs;
      Height.Units = lmLayoutUnits;
      Height.Value = 0;
```

The following program creates two child windows and a frame into which you can add
layout constraints.

```
#include <owl\owl.h>
#include <owl\framewin.h>
#include <owl\applicat.h>
#include <owl\layoutwi.h>
#include <owl\decorate.h>
#include <owl\decmdifr.h>
#include <owl\layoutco.h>
#pragma hdrstop

// Create a derived class. //

class TMyDecoratedFrame : public TDecoratedFrame {
public:
   TMyDecoratedFrame(TWindow* parent, const char far* title,
                     TWindow& clientWnd, TWindow* MyChildWindow);
   void SetupWindow();
   {
     TDecoratedFrame::SetupWindow();
     MyChildWindow->ShowWindow(SW_NORMAL);
     MyChildWindow->BringWindowToTop();
   }
};

// Setup a frame window. //

TMyDecoratedFrame::TMyDecoratedFrame(TWindow * parent,
                                     const char far * title,
                                     TWindow& clientWnd)
   : TDecoratedFrame(parent, title, clientWnd),
     TFrameWindow(parent, title, &clientWnd),
     TWindow(parent, title)
{
// Create a new TMyChildWindow. //

   MyChildWindow = new TWindow(this, "");
   MyChildWindow->Attr.Style |=  WS_BORDER |WS_VISIBLE |WS_CHILD;
   MyChildwindow->SetBkgndColor(RGB(0,100,0));

// Establish metrics for the child window. //

   TLayoutMetrics  layoutMetrics;
```

```
    layoutMetrics.X.Absolute(lmLeft, 10);
    layoutMetrics.Y.Absolute(lmTop, 10);
    layoutMetrics.Width.Absolute( 80 );
    layoutMetrics.Height.Absolute( 80 );
}
    SetChildLayoutMetrics(*MyChildWindow, layoutMetrics);
class TMyApp : public TApplication {
public:

    virtual void InitMainWindow()
    {
      TWindow* client = new TWindow(0, "title");
      MainWindow = new TMyDecoratedFrame(0,
                               "Layout Window Ex",
                               *client);

    }
};
int OwlMain(int, char**) {
    return TMyApp.Run();
}
```

TLayoutWindow class   layoutwi.h

Derived from TWindow, *TLayoutWindow* provides functionality for defining the layout
metrics for a window. By using layout constraints, you can create windows whose
position and size are proportional to another window's dimensions, so that one window
constrains the size of the other window. Toolbars and status bars are examples of
constrained windows.

TLayoutWindow examples

The following examples show how to set up various metrics using edge constraints. For
purposes of illustration, these examples use a parent-child relationship, but you can also
use a child-to-child (sibling) relationship. Keep in mind that moving the parent's origin
(the left and top edges) also moves the child window.

Example 1

To create windows that can grow, set the top and left edges of the child window's
boundaries in a fixed relationship to the top and left edges of the parent's window. In
this example, if you expand the bottom and right edges of the parent, the child's bottom
and right edges grow the same amount. Both the X and Y constraints are 10 units from
the parent window's edges. Both the *Width* and *Height* constraints are 40 layout units
from the parent window's edges. Specifically, *Width (lmWidth)* is 40 units to the left of
the parent's right edge (*lmLeftOf* = *lmSameAs* + *offset* or *sameas - 40*).

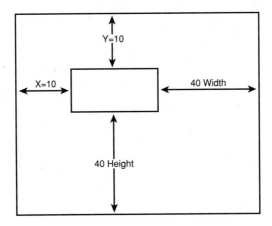

Use the following layout constraints:

```
layoutmetrics.X.Set(lmLeft, lmRightOf, lmParent, lmLeft, 10);
layoutmetrics.Y.Set(lmTop, lmBelow, lmParent, lmTop, 10);
layoutmetrics.Width.Set(lmRight, lmLeftOf, lmParent, lmRight, 40);
layoutmetrics.Height.Set(lmBottom, lmAbove, lmParent, lmBottom, 40);
SetChildLayoutMetrics(*MyChildWindow, layoutMetrics);
```

Example 2

To create fixed-size and fixed-position windows, set the child's right edge a fixed distance from the parent's left edge, and the child's bottom edge a fixed distance from the parent's top edge. In this example, both the *X* and *Y* edge constraints are set to 10 and both the *Width* and *Height* edge constraints are set to 100.

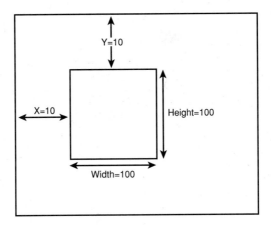

Use the following layout constraints:

```
layoutmetrics.X.Set(lmLeft, lmRightOf, lmParent, lmLeft, 10);
layoutmetrics.Y.Set(lmTop, lmBelow, lmParent, lmTop, 10);
layoutmetrics.Width.Absolute(100);
```

```
layoutmetrics.Height.Absolute(100);
SetChildLayoutMetrics(*MyChildWindow, layoutMetrics);
```

Example 3

To create a fixed-size window that remains a constant distance from the parent's right corner, set the child's top and bottom edges a fixed distance (*lmLayout* unit or pixels) from the parent window's bottom. Also, set the child's left and right edges a fixed distance from the parent's right edge. In this example, both the *Width* and the *Height* edge constraints are set to 100 and the *X* and *Y* edge constraints are set to 10. In this case, the child window, which stays the same size, moves with the lower right corner of the parent.

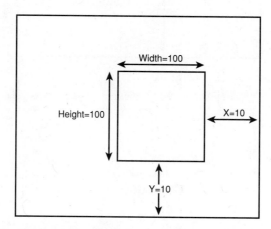

Use the following layout constraints:

```
layoutmetrics.X.Set(lmRight, lmLeftOf, lmParent, lmRight, 10);
layoutmetrics.Y.Set(lmBottom, lmAbove, lmParent, lmBottom, 10);
layoutmetrics.Width.Absolute(100);
layoutmetrics.Height.Absolute(100);
SetChildLayoutMetrics(*MyChildWindow, layoutMetrics);
```

Example 4

To create a window in which the child's edges are a percentage of the parent's window, set the child's edges a percentage of the distance from the parent's edges. Specifically, the child's top and bottom edges are a percentage of the parent's bottom edge. The child's left and right edges are a percentage of the parent's right edge.

If you resize the parent window, the child window will change size and origin (that is, the top and left edges will also change).

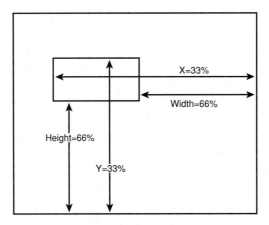

Use the following layout constraints:

```
layoutmetrics.X.Set(lmLeft, lmPercentOf, lmParent, lmRight, 33);
layoutmetrics.Y.Set(lmTop, lmPercentOf, lmParent, lmBottom, 33);
layoutmetrics.Width.Set(lmRight, lmPercentOf, lmParent, lmRight, 66);
layoutmetrics.Height.Set(lmBottom, lmPercentOf, lmParent, lmBottom, 66);
SetChildLayoutMetrics(*MyChildWindow, layoutMetrics);
```

Public constructor and destructor

Constructor
TLayoutWindow(TWindow* parent, const char far* title = 0, TModule* module = 0);
Creates a *TLayoutWindow* object with specified parent, window caption, and library ID.

Destructor
~TLayoutWindow();
Deletes variables and frees the child metrics and constraints.

Public member functions

GetChildLayoutMetrics
bool GetChildLayoutMetrics(TWindow &child, TLayoutMetrics &metrics);
Gets the layout metrics of the child window.

Layout
void Layout();
Causes the window to resize and position its children according to the specified metrics.
You can call *Layout* to implement changes that occur in the layout metrics.

RemoveChildLayoutMetrics
bool RemoveChildLayoutMetrics(TWindow &child);
Removes the layout metrics for a child window.

SetChildLayoutMetrics
void SetChildLayoutMetrics(TWindow &child, TLayoutMetrics &metrics);

Sets the metrics for the window and removes any existing ones. Set the metrics as shown:

```
layoutMetrics->X.Absolute(lmLeft, 10);
layoutMetrics->Y.Absolute(lmTop, 10);
layoutMetrics->Width.Set(lmWidth, lmRightOf, GetClientWindow(), lmWidth, -40);
layoutMetrics->Height.Set(lmHeight, lmRightOf, GetClientWindow(), lmHeight, -40);
```

Then call *SetChildLayoutMetrics* to associate them with the position of the child window:

```
SetChildLayoutMetrics(* MyChildWindow, * layoutMetrics);
```

Protected data members

ClientSize
TSize ClientSize;

Contains the size of the client area.

Protected member functions

EvSize
void EvSize(uint sizeType, TSize& size);

Responds to a change in window size by calling *Layout* to resize the window.

RemoveChild
void RemoveChild(TWindow* child);

Overrides *TWindow* virtual to allow cleanup of child metrics.

Response table entries

Response table entry	Member function
EV_WM_SIZE	EvSize

See also   *TLayoutConstraint* defines layout constraints. *TLayoutMetrics* describes the metrics you can use to set up layout constraints.

TListBox class   listbox.h

An interface object that represents a corresponding list box element. A *TListBox* must be used to create a list box control in a parent *TWindow*. A *TListBox* can be used to facilitate communication between your application and the list box controls of a *TDialog* object. *TListBox*'s member functions also serve instances of its derived class *TComboBox*. From within MDI child windows, you can access a *TListBox* object by using *TFrameWindow::GetClientWindow*. *TListBox* is a streamable class.

Public constructors

Form 1   TListBox(TWindow* parent, int Id, int x, int y, int w, int h, TModule* module = 0);

Constructs a list box object with the supplied parent window (*parent*) library ID (*module*), position (*x, y*) relative to the origin of the parent window's client area, width (*w*), and height (*h*). Invokes a *TControl* constructor. Adds LBS_STANDARD to the default styles for the list box to provide it with

- A border (WS_BORDER)
- A vertical scroll bar (WS_VSCROLL)
- Automatic alphabetic sorting of list items (LBS_SORT)
- Parent window notification upon selection (LBS_NOTIFY)

The *TListBox* member functions that are described as being for single-selection list boxes are inherited by *TComboBox* and can also be used by combo boxes. Also, these member functions return -1 for multiple-selection list boxes.

Form 2   TListBox(TWindow* parent, int resourceId, TModule* module = 0)

Constructs a *TListBox* object to be associated with a list box control of a *TDialog* object. Invokes the *TControl* constructor with similar parameters. The *module* parameter must correspond to a list box resource that you define.

See also   GetSelIndex, GetSelString

Public member functions

AddString
virtual int AddString(const char far* str);

Adds *string* to the list box, returning its position in the list (0 is the first position). Returns a negative value if an error occurs. The list items are automatically sorted unless the style LBS_SORT is not used for list box creation.

See also   TListBox::DeleteString, TListBox::InsertString

ClearList
virtual void ClearList();

Clears all items in the list.

DeleteString
virtual int DeleteString(int index);

Deletes the item in the list at the position (starting at 0) supplied in *index*. *DeleteString* returns the number of remaining list items, or a negative value if an error occurs.

See also   TListBox::AddString, TListBox::InsertString

DirectoryList
virtual int DirectoryList(uint attrs, const char far* fileSpec)

Adds a list of file names to a list box.

FindExactString
int FindExactString(const char far* str, int searchIndex) const;

Starting at the line number passed in *searchIndex*, searches the list box for an exact match with the string *str*. If a match is not found after the last string has been compared, the search continues from the beginning of the list until a match has been found or until the list has been completely traversed. Searches from the beginning of the list when -1 is supplied as *searchIndex*. Returns the index of the first string found if successful, or a negative value if an error occurs.

See also   TListBox::AddString, TListBox::DeleteString

FindString
virtual int FindString(const char far* str, int Index) const;

Searches the list box as described under *FindExactString*, but looks for the first entry that begins with *str*.

See also   TListBox::AddString, TListBox::DeleteString, TListBox::InsertString

GetCaretIndex
int GetCaretIndex() const;

Returns the index of the currently focused list-box item. For single-selection list boxes, the return value is the index of the selected item, if one is selected.

See also   TListBox::SetCaretIndex

GetCount
virtual int GetCount() const;

Returns the number of items in the list box, or a negative value if an error occurs.

GetHorizontalExtent
int GetHorizontalExtent() const;

Returns the number of pixels by which the list box can be scrolled horizontally.

See also   TListBox::SetHorizontalExtent

GetItemData
virtual uint32 GetItemData(int index) const;

Returns the 32-bit value of the list box item set by *SetItemData*.

See also   TListBox::SetItemData

GetItemHeight
virtual int GetItemHeight(int index) const;

Returns the height in pixels of the specified list box items.

See also   TListBox::SetItemHeight

GetItemRect

int GetItemRect(int index, TRect& rect) const;

Returns the dimensions of the rectangle that surrounds a list-box item currently displayed in the list-box window.

GetSel

bool GetSel(int index) const;

Returns the selection state of the list-box item at location *index*. Returns **true** if the list-box item is selected, **false** if not selected.

See also   TListBox::SetSel

GetSelCount

int GetSelCount() const;

Returns the number of selected items in the single- or multiple-selection list box or combo box.

GetSelIndex

virtual int GetSelIndex() const;

For single-selection list boxes. Returns the nonnegative index (starting at 0) of the currently selected item, or a negative value if no item is selected.

See also   TListBox::SetSelIndex

GetSelIndexes

int GetSelIndexes(int* indexes, int maxCount) const;

For multiple-selection list boxes. Fills the *indexes* array with the indexes of up to *maxCount* selected strings. Returns the number of items put in *indexes* (-1 for single-selection list boxes and combo boxes).

See also   TListBox::SetSelIndexes

GetSelString

int GetSelString(char far* str, int maxChars) const;

Retrieves the currently selected items, putting up to *maxChars* of them in *str*. Each entry in the *str* array should have space for *maxChars* characters and a terminating null. For single-selection list boxes, *GetSelString* returns one of the following: the string length, a negative value if an error occurs, or 1 if no string is selected. For multiple-selection list boxes, it returns -1.

See also   TListBox::SetSelString

GetSelStrings

int GetSelStrings(char far** strs, int maxCount, int maxChars) const;

Retrieves the total number of selected items for a multiselection list and copies them into the buffer. The *strs* parameter is an array of pointers to chars. Each of the pointers to the buffers is of *maxChars*. *maxCount* is the size of the array.

See also   TListBox::SetSelStrings

GetString

virtual int GetString(char far* str, int index) const;

Retrieves the item at the position (starting at 0) supplied in *index* and returns it in *str*. *GetString* returns the string length, or a negative value if an error occurs.

GetStringLen

virtual int GetStringLen(int Index) const;

Returns the string length (excluding the terminating NULL) of the item at the position index supplied in *Index*. Returns a negative value in the case of an error.

GetTopIndex

int GetTopIndex() const;

Returns the index of the first item displayed at the top of the list box.

See also   TListBox::SetTopIndex

InsertString

virtual int InsertString(const char far* str, int index);

Inserts *str* in the list box at the position supplied in *index*, and returns the item's actual position (starting at 0) in the list. A negative value is returned if an error occurs. The list is not resorted. If *index* is -1, the string is appended to the end of the list.

See also   TListBox::AddString, TListBox::DeleteString, TListBox::FindString

SetCaretIndex

int SetCaretIndex(int index, bool partScrollOk);

Sets the focus to the item specified at *index*. An item that is not visible is scrolled into view.

See also   TListBox::GetCaretIndex

SetColumnWidth

void SetColumnWidth(int width);

Sets the width in pixels of the items in the list box.

SetHorizontalExtent

void SetHorizontalExtent(int horzExtent);

Sets the number of pixels by which the list box can be scrolled horizontally.

See also   TListBox::GetHorizontalExtent

SetItemData

virtual int SetItemData(int index, uint32 itemData);

Sets the 32-bit value of the list box item at the specified *index* position.

See also   TListBox::GetItemData

SetItemHeight

virtual int SetItemHeight(int index, int height);

Sets the height in pixels of the items in the list box.

See also   TListBox::GetItemHeight

SetItemRect

int SetItemRect(int index, TRect& rect) const;

Sets the dimensions of the rectangle that surrounds a list-box item currently displayed in the list-box window.

SetSel

int SetSel(int index, bool select);

For multiple-selection list boxes. Selects an item at the position specified in *index*.

See also   TListBox::GetSel

SetSelIndex

virtual int SetSelIndex(int index);

For single-selection list boxes. Forces the selection of the item at the position (starting at 0) supplied in *index*. If *index* is -1, the list box is cleared of any selection. *SetSelIndex* returns a negative number if an error occurs.

SetSelIndexes

int SetSelIndexes(int* indexes, int numSelections, bool shouldSet);

For multiple-selection list boxes. Selects or deselects the strings in the associated list box at the indexes specified in the *Indexes* array. If *ShouldSet* is **true**, the indexed strings are selected and highlighted; if *ShouldSet* is **false** the highlight is removed and they are no longer selected. Returns the number of strings successfully selected or deselected (-1 for single-selection list boxes and combo boxes). If *NumSelections* is less than 0, all strings are selected or deselected, and a negative value is returned on failure.

SetSelItemRange

int SetSelItemRange(bool select, int first, int last);

Selects the range of items specified from *first* to *last*.

SetSelString

int SetSelString(const char far* str, int searchIndex);

For single-selection list boxes. Forces the selection of the first item beginning with the text supplied in *str* that appears beyond the position (starting at 0) supplied in *SearchIndex*. If *SearchIndex* is -1, the entire list is searched, beginning with the first item. *SetSelString* returns the position of the newly selected item, or a negative value in the case of an error.

SetSelStrings

int SetSelStrings(const char far** prefixes, int numSelections, bool shouldSet);

For multiple-selection list boxes, selects the strings in the associated list box that begin with the prefixes specified in the *prefixes* array. For each string the search begins at the beginning of the list and continues until a match is found or until the list has been completely traversed. If *shouldSet* is **true**, the matched strings are selected and highlighted; if *shouldSet* is **false**, the highlight is removed from the matched strings and they are no longer selected. Returns the number of strings successfully selected or deselected (-1 for single-selection list boxes and combo boxes). If *numSelections* is less than 0, all strings are selected or deselected, and a negative value is returned on failure.

SetTabStops

bool SetTabStops(int numTabs, int far* tabs);

Sets tab stops. *numTabs* is the number of tab stops. *tabs* is the array of integers representing the tab positions.

SetTopIndex

int SetTopIndex(int index);

Sets *index* to the first item displayed at the top of the list box.

See also   TListBox::GetTopIndex

Transfer

uint Transfer(void *buffer, TTransferDirection direction);

Transfers the items and selection(s) of the list box to or from a transfer buffer if *tdSetData* or *tdGetData*, respectively, is passed as the *direction*. *buffer* is expected to point to a pointer to a *TListBoxData* structure.

Transfer, which overrides the *TWindow* virtual member function, returns the size of *TListBoxData* (the pointer, not the structure). To retrieve the size without transferring data, pass *tdSizeData* as the *direction*.

You must use a pointer in your transfer buffer to these structures. You cannot embed copies of the structures in your transfer buffer, and you cannot use these structures as transfer buffers.

See also   TWindow::Transfer

Protected member functions

GetClassName

char far* GetClassName();

Returns the name of *TListBox's* registration class, *LISTBOX*.

TListBoxData class   listbox.h

Used to transfer the contents of a list box.

Public constructor and destructor

Constructor

TListBoxData();

Constructs *Strings* and *SelStrings*. Initializes *SelCount* to 0.

Destructor

~TListBoxData();

Deletes the space allocated for *Strings* and *SelStrings*.

Public member functions

AddString
void AddString(const char *str, bool isSelected = false);

Adds the specified string to *Strings*. If *IsSelected* is true, adds the string to *SelStrings* and increments *SelCount*.

AddStringItem
void AddStringItem(const char* str, uint32 itemData, bool isSelected = false));

Adds a string to the *Strings* array, optionally selects it, and adds item data to the *ItemDatas* array.

Clear
void Clear();

Resets the list box by flushing the *ItemDatas* and *Strings* arrays and calling *ResetSelections*.

See also   TListBoxData::Strings, TListBoxData::ItemDatas, TListBoxData::ResetSelections

GetItemDatas
TDwordArray& GetItemDatas();

Returns a pointer to the ItemDatas array.

See also   TListBoxData::ItemDatas

GetSelCount
int GetSelCount() const;

GetSelIndices
TIntArray& GetSelIndices();

Returns a pointer to the SelIndices array.

See also   TListBoxData::SelIndices

GetSelString
Form 1   void GetSelString(string& str, int index=0) const;

Returns the length of the string at the passed selection index, excluding the terminating 0.

Form 2   void GetSelString(char far* buffer, int bufferSize, int index = 0) const;

Locates the string at the specified *index* in *SelStrings* and copies it into *buffer*. *bufferSize* includes the terminating NULL.

GetSelStringLength
int GetSelStringLength(int index = 0) const;

Returns the length (excluding the terminating NULL) of the string at the specified *index* in *SelStrings*.

GetStrings
TStringArray& GetStrings();

Returns a pointer to the Strings array.

See also   TListBoxData::Strings

ResetSelections
void ResetSelections();

Removes all strings from *SelStrings* and sets *SelCount* to 0.

Select
void Select(int index);

Selects the string at the given *index*.

SelectString
void SelectString(const char far* str);

Adds *str* to *SelStrings* and increments *SelCount*.

Protected data members

ItemDatas
TDwordArray* ItemDatas;

Contains all **uint32** item data for each item in the list box.

SelCount
int SelCount;

Holds the number of selected items.

SelIndices
TIntArray* SelIndices;

Contains the indexes of all the selected strings in a multiple-selection list box.

SelStrings
TStringArray* SelStrings;

Pointer to an array of the strings to select when data is transferred into the list box. When data is transferred out of the list box, *SelStrings* returns the current selection(s).

Strings
TStringArray* Strings;

Pointer to an array of strings to be transferred into a *TListBox*.

TListView class   listview.h

Provides views for list boxes.

Public constructor and destructor

Constructor
TListView(TDocument& doc, TWindow* parent = 0);

Creates a *TListView* object associated with the specified document and parent window. Sets *Attr.AccelTable* to IDA_LISTVIEW to identify the edit view. Sets the view style to WS_HSCROLL | LBS_NOINTEGRALHEIGHT.

Sets *TView::ViewMenu* to the new *TMenuDescr* for this view.

Destructor
~TListView();

After checking to see if there is an open view, this destructor destroys the *TListView* object.

Public data members

DirtyFlag
bool DirtyFlag;

Has a nonzero value if the data in the list view has been changed; otherwise, is 0.

Public member functions

AddString
int AddString(const char far* str);

Add a string into the view. Returns the index at which the string is added.

CanClose
bool CanClose();

Checks to see if all child views can be closed before closing the current view. If any child returns 0, *CanClose* returns 0 and aborts the process. If all children return nonzero, it calls *TDocManager::FlushDoc*.

Create
bool Create();

Overrides *TWindow::Create* and creates the view's window. Determines if the file is new or already has data. If there is data, calls *LoadData* to add the data to the view. If the view's window can't be created, *Create* throws a *TXWindow* exception.

GetViewName
const char far* GetViewName();

Overrides *TView's* virtual *GetViewName* function and returns the descriptive name of the class (*StaticName*).

GetWindow
TWindow* GetWindow();

Overrides *TView's* virtual *GetWindow* function and returns the list view object as a *TWindow*.

SetDocTitle
bool SetDocTitle(const char far* docname, int index);

Overrides *TView's* virtual *SetDocTitle* function and stores the document title. This name is forwarded up the parent chain until a *TFrameWindow* object accepts the data and displays it in its caption.

StaticName
static const char far* StaticName();

Returns a constant string for the view name, *ListView*. This information is displayed in the user interface selection box.

See also   TView::GetViewName

Protected data members

MaxWidth
int MaxWidth;

Holds the maximum horizontal extent (the number of pixels by which the view can be scrolled horizontally).

Origin
long Origin;

Holds the file position at the beginning of the display.

Protected member functions

CmEditAdd
void CmEditAdd();

Automatically responds to CM_LISTADD message by getting the length of the input string and inserting the text string into the list view. Sets the data member *DirtyFlag* to **true**.

CmEditClear
void CmEditClear();

Automatically responds to a menu selection with a menu ID of CM_EDITCLEAR by clearing the items in the list box using functions in *TListBox*.

CmEditCopy
void CmEditCopy();

Automatically responds to a menu selection with a menu ID of CM_EDITCOPY and copies the selected text to the Clipboard.

CmEditCut
void CmEditCut();

Automatically responds to a menu selection with a menu ID of CM_EDITCUT by calling *CmEditCopy* and *CmEditDelete* to delete a text string from the list view. Sets the data member DirtyFlag to **true**.

CmEditDelete
void CmEditDelete();

Automatically responds to a menu selection with a menu ID of CM_EDITDELETE by deleting the currently selected text.

CmEditItem
void CmEditItem();

Automatically responds to a CM_LISTEDIT message by getting the input text and inserting the text into the list view. Sets *DirtyFlag* to a nonzero value to indicate that the view has been changed and not saved.

CmEditPaste
void CmEditPaste();

Automatically responds to a menu selection with a menu ID of CM_EDITPASTE by inserting text into the list box using functions in *TListBox*.

CmEditUndo
void CmEditUndo();

Handler to undo the last operation performed on the underlying list box.

Note   This feature is not implemented in the current version of ObjectWindows.

CmSelChange
void CmSelChange();

Automatically responds to a LBN_SELCHANGE message (which indicates that the contents of the list view have changed) by calling *TWindow::DefaultProcessing*.

EvGetDlgCode
uint EvGetDlgCode(MSG far*);

Overrides *TWindow*'s response to a WM_GETDLGCODE message (an input procedure associated with a control that isn't a check box) by calling *TWindow::DefaultProcessing*.

EvGetDlgCode returns a code that indicates how the list box control message is to be treated.

See also   TButton::EvGetDlgCode

GetMaxWidth
int GetMaxWidth() const;

Returns the maximum width of the strings.

GetOrigin
long GetOrigin() const;

Returns the origin position on the persistent stream.

LoadData
bool LoadData(int top, int sel);

Reads the view from the stream and closes the file. Returns **true** if the view was successfully loaded.

Throws an *xmsg* exception and displays the error message *TListView initial read error* if the file can't be read. Returns **false** if the view can't be loaded.

SetExtent
void SetExtent(const char far* str);

Sets the maximum horizontal extent for the list view window.

SetMaxWidth
void SetMaxWidth(int maxwidth);

Sets the maximum width of the strings.

SetOrigin
void SetOrigin(long origin);

Sets the position of the object.

VnCommit
bool VnCommit(bool force);

Commits changes made in the view to the document. If *force* is nonzero, all data, even if it's unchanged, is saved to the document.

See also   TListView::vnRevert, vnxxxx view notification constants

VnDocClosed
bool VnDocClosed(int omode);

Indicates that the document has been closed.

See also   vnxxxx view notification constants

VnIsDirty
bool VnIsDirty();

Returns a nonzero value if changes made to the data in the view have not been saved to the document; otherwise, returns 0.

See also   vnxxxx view notification constants

VnIsWindow
bool VnIsWindow(HWND hWnd);

Returns a nonzero value if the window's handle passed in *hWnd* is the same as that of the view's display window.

See also   vnxxxx view notification constants

VnRevert
bool VnRevert(bool clear);

Indicates if changes made to the view should be erased, and if the data from the document should be restored to the view. If *clear* is a nonzero value, the data is cleared instead of restored to the view.

See also   TListView::vnCommit

Response table entries

Entry	Member function
EV_COMMAND(CM_LISTUNDO, CmEditUndo)	CmEditUndo
EV_COMMAND(CM_LISTCUT, CmEditCut)	CmEditcut
EV_COMMAND(CM_LISTCOPY, CmEditCopy)	CmEditCopy
EV_COMMAND(CM_LISTPASTE, CmEditPaste)	CmEditPaste
EV_COMMAND(CM_LISTCLEAR, CmEditClear)	CmEditClear
EV_COMMAND(CM_LISTDELETE, CmEditDelete)	CmEditDelete
EV_COMMAND(CM_LISTADD, CmEditAdd)	CmEditAdd
EV_COMMAND(CM_LISTEDIT, CmEditItem)	CmEditItem
EV_WM_GETDLGCODE	EvGetDlgCode
EV_NOTIFY_AT_CHILD(LBN_DBLCLK, CmEditItem)	CmEditItem
EV_NOTIFY_AT_CHILD(LBN_SELCHANGE, CmSelChange)	CmSelchange
EV_VN_DOCCLOSED	VnDocClosed
EV_VN_ISWINDOW	VnIsWindow
EV_VN_ISDIRTY	VnIsDirty
EV_VN_COMMIT	VnCommit
EV_VN_REVERT	VnRevert

See also   TView describes the view functions, TListBox describes the list box functions

TListWindColumn class   listwind.h

TListWindColumn is a column in the *TListWindow*.

Type definitions

TFormat enum
enum TFormat {Left, Center, Right};

TFormat is used to describe the alignment of a column in a list window.

Table 2.15   Constants

Table 2.15   Constants

Constant	Meaning if set
Left	Left aligned
Center	Centered
Right	Right aligned

Public constructors

Form 1   TListWindColumn();

This is the default constructor for the class.

Form 2   TListWindColumn(LV_COLUMN);

Constructor based on existing structure.

Form 3   TListWindColumn(char far*, int width, TFormat how = Left, int subItem = 0);

Constructor based on the text, width of the column, alignment, and column number.

Public member functions

SetFormat
void SetFormat(TFormat how);

Sets the alignment for the column.

SetSubItem
void SetSubItem(int);

Sets the column number.

SetText
void SetText(char far*, int = 0);

Sets the text and buffer size of the column.

SetWidth
void SetWidth(int pixels);

Sets the width of the column.

Protected member functions

Init
void Init();

Private *Init* to zero out data members.

TListWindItem class
listwind.h

TListWindItem is an item in the *TListWindow*.

Type definitions

TListState enum
enum TListState {Focus, Selected, Cut, DropHilited, OverlayMask, StateImageMask};

TListState is used to describe the state of an item.

Table 2.16   Constants

Constant	Meaning if set
Focus	Only one item has focus
Selected	Marked as selected
Cut	Marked for cut and paste
DropHilited	Marked as a drop target
OverlayMask	Retrieve one-based overlay image index
StateImageMask	Retrieve one-based state image index

Public constructors

Form 1   TListWindItem();

Default constructor.

Form 2   TListWindItem(LV_ITEM);

Constructor based on an existing structure.

Form 3   TListWindItem(char far*, int subitem = 0, int len = 0);

Constructor based on text, column number, and length of text.

Public member functions

GetImageIndex
int GetImageIndex() const;

Returns the image list index.

GetIndex
int GetIndex() const;

Returns the item's index.

GetItemData
uint32 GetItemData() const;

Returns the additional data value.

GetState
int GetState() const;

Returns the state of the item.

GetSubItem
int GetSubItem() const;

Returns the column number for the item.

GetText
void GetText(char far*, int len = 0);
Returns the text of the item.

SetImageIndex
void SetImageIndex(int index);
Sets the image list index for the item.

SetIndex
void SetIndex(int);
Sets the item's index number.

SetItemData
void SetItemData(uint32);
Sets the additional data value.

SetState
void SetState(TListState state);
Sets the state of the item.

SetSubItem
void SetSubItem(int);
Sets the column number.

SetText
void SetText(char far*, int len = 0);
Sets the text buffer.

Protected member functions

Init
void Init();
Private Init to zero out data members.

TListWindow class

listwind.h

TListWindow encapsulates the *ListView*. The *ListWindow* has four views: Icon, Small Icon, Report, and List. The view is determined by the style of the *ListWindow*, set either with *Attr.Style* or *SetWindowLong*.

Type definitions

TArrangeCode enum
enum TArrangeCode {Default, Left, Top, SnapToGrid};
TArrangeCode is used to describe how to arrange the items in a list window control.

Table 2.17   Arrangement constants

Constant	Meaning if set
Default	Use default for control style
Left	Align items to the left edge
Top	Align items to the right edge
SnapToGrid	Snap icons to nearest grid position

TImageListType enum
enum TImageListType {Normal, Small, State};

TImageListType is used to describe the type of iamge list for use with the list window control.

Table 2.18   List type constants

Constant	Meaning if set
Normal	Normal image list
Small	Small icons for LVS_SMALLICON
State	State image

TItemRectType enum
enum TItemRectType {Bounds, Icon, Label};

TItemRectType is used to describe the type of rectangle boundaries to retrieve.

Table 2.19   Boundary constants

Constant	Meaning if set
Bounds	Entire boundary (icon and label)
Icon	Only the icon
Label	Only the label

TNextItemCode enum
enum TNextItemCode {Above, All, Below, ToLeft, ToRight, Cut, DropHilited, Focused, Selected};

TNextItemCode is used to describe the next item to retrieve from current item.

Table 2.20   Next item constants

Constant	Meaning if set
Above	Directly above
All	By index
Below	Directly below
ToLeft	Left of
ToRight	Right of
Cut	Marked for cut and paste
DropHilited	Marked for drop target
Focused	Marked as having focus
Selected	Marked as selected

Public constructors and destructor

Form 1   TListWindow(TWindow* parent, int id, int x, int y, int w, int h, TModule* module = 0);

Constructor that creates a window.

Form 2   TListWindow(TWindow* parent, int resourceId, TModule* module = 0);

Constructor from resource.

Destructor
~TListWindow();

Destructor.

Public member functions

TListWindow helper classes
TLwFindInfo

TLwHitTestInfo

TLwComparer

TListWindItem

TListWindColumn

Arrange
bool Arrange(ArrangeCode code);

Rearranges the *ListWindow*.

CreateDragImage
HIMAGELIST CreateDragImage(int itemIndex, TPoint* upLeft);

Creates a drag image. The returned HIMAGELIST should be deleted.

DeleteAllItems
bool DeleteAllItems();

Removes all items from the *ListWindow*.

DeleteAnItem
bool DeleteAnItem(int itemIndex);

Removes one item from the *ListWindow*.

DeleteColumn
bool DeleteColumn(int colNum);

Deletes the column number *colNum*.

EditLabel
HWND EditLabel(int itemIndex);

Edits the text associated with the item number *itemIndex*. This is similar to clicking on the label of an icon on the new shell.

EnsureVisible
bool EnsureVisible(int index, bool partialOk);

Makes sure the item number *index* is visible; will scroll the item into view if necessary.

FindItem
int FindItem(int startIndex, const TLvFindInfo far* findInfo);

Locates the item indicated by *findInfo*. Returns the index of the item if found. Returns -1 if not found.

GetBkColor
COLORREF GetBkColor();

Returns the background color of the *List Window*.

GetCallBackMask
uint GetCallBackMask();

Returns the callback mask.

GetColumn
bool GetColumn(int index, LV_COLUMN far*);

Returns the column information of column number *index*.

GetColumnWidth
int GetColumnWidth(int index);

Returns the width of the column *index*.

GetCountPerPage
int GetCountPerPage();

Returns the number of fully visible items that can fit vertically in list or report view.

GetEditControl
HWND GetEditControl();

Returns the HWND of the edit control used for editing labels.

GetImageList
HIMAGELIST GetImageList(ImageListType);

Returns the IMAGELIST for the type.

GetItem
bool GetItem(TLvItem&);

Returns the information specified by item.

GetItemCount
int GetItemCount();

Returns the number of items total in the *List Window*.

GetItemPosition
bool GetItemPosition(int index, POINT far*);

Returns the item's position.

GetItemRect
bool GetItemRect(int index, RECT far*, ItemRectType);

Returns the item's size. *TItemRectType* indicates what type of rectangle to return.

GetItemState
uint GetItemState(int index, uint mask);

Returns the current state of the item (selected, focused, etc.).

GetItemText
int GetItemText(int index, int subItem, char far* text, int size);

Returns the text of the item.

GetNextItem
int GetNextItem(int index, NextItemCode code);

Returns the index of the *next* item after item *index*. See *TNextItemCode* for more details.

GetOrigin
bool GetOrigin(POINT far*);

Retrieves the current view origin of the *ListWindow*. Returns false if current *ListWindow* is in list or report view.

GetStringWidth
int GetStringWidth(char far* text);

Returns the width of the text using the current *ListWindow*'s font.

GetTextBkColor
COLORREF GetTextBkColor();

Returns the text background color of the *ListWindow*.

GetTextColor
COLORREF GetTextColor();

Returns the text color of the *ListWindow*.

GetTopIndex
int GetTopIndex();

Returns the index of the topmost visible item.

GetViewRect
bool GetViewRect(RECT far*);

Returns the bouding rectangle of all items in the *ListWindow*. *ListWindow* must be in icon or small icon view.

HitTest
int HitTest(TLvHitTestInfo&);

Returns the index of the item indicated by *info*.

InsertColumn
int InsertColumn(int colNum, TLvColumn&);

Inserts the column *colItem* into column number *colNum*.

InsertItem
int InsertItem(TLvItem&);

Inserts the item into the position indicated by *item.iItem*.

RedrawItems
bool RedrawItems(int startIndex, int endIndex);

Invalidates rectangle between the items between *startIndex* and *endIndex*.

Scroll
bool Scroll(int dx, int dy);

Scroll the contents of the *ListWindow*. The parameters *dx* and *dy* are in pixels.

SetBkColor
bool SetBkColor(COLORREF c);

Sets the background color of the *ListWindow*.

SetCallBackMask
bool SetCallBackMask(uint mask);

Sets the callback mask.

SetColumn
bool SetColumn(int index, TLvColumn&);

Sets the attributes of the column *index*.

SetColumnWidth
bool SetColumnWidth(int index, int width);

Sets the column width of *index*.

SetImageList
bool SetImageList(HIMAGELIST list, ImageListType type);

Sets the imagelist for the type.

SetItem
bool SetItem(TLvItem&);

Sets the attributes of the item *item*.

SetItemCount
void SetItemCount(int numItems);

Optimizes inserting a large number of items.

SetItemPosition
bool SetItemPosition(int index, POINT p);

Sets the item to a particular point. Only valid for icon or small icon view.

SetItemState
bool SetItemState(int index, uint state, uint mask);

Sets the state of the item.

SetItemText
void SetItemText(int index, TLvItem&);

Sets the text for the item.

SetTextBkColor
bool SetTextBkColor(COLORREF c);

Sets the background color of the *ListWindow*.

SetTextColor
bool SetTextColor(COLORREF c);

Sets the text color of the items.

SortItems
bool SortItems(const TLvComparer& comparer, uint32 lParam = 0);

Sorts the items within the *ListWindow*. *TLwComparer* is the base class for the comparison function

Update
bool Update(int index);

Updates the *ListWindow*. If the list window has LVS_AUTOARRANGE, the items are automatically arranged to their proper locations.

Protected member functions

GetClassName
char far* GetClassName();

Returns the proper class name.

TLookupValidator class   validate.h

A streamable class, *TLookupValidator* compares the string typed by a user with a list of acceptable values. *TLookupValidator* is an abstract validator type from which you can derive useful lookup validators. You will never create an instance of *TLookupValidator*. When you create a lookup validator type, you need to specify a list of valid items and override the *Lookup* method to return true only if the user input matches an item in that list. One example of a working descendant of *TLookupValidator* is *TStringLookupValidator*.

Public constructor

TLookupValidator
TLookupValidator();

Constructs a *TLookupValidator* object.

Public member functions

IsValid
bool IsValid(const char far* str);

IsValid overrides *TValidator*'s virtual function and calls *Lookup* to find the string *str* in the list of valid input items. *IsValid* returns true if *Lookup* returns true, meaning *Lookup* found *str* in its list; otherwise, it returns false.

Lookup
virtual bool Lookup(const char far* str);

Searches for the string *str* in the list of valid entries and returns true if it finds *str*; otherwise, returns false. *TLookupValidator*'s *Lookup* is an abstract method that always returns false. Descendant lookup validator types must override *Lookup* to perform a search based on the actual list of acceptable items.

TLwComparer class   listwind.h

TLwComparer is a base class for comparisons to sort items.

Public member functions

Compare
virtual int Compare(uint32 item1, uint32 item2, uint32 IParam) const;

Override this to compare two items for sorting items. If item1 < item2, it returns -1. If item1 == item2, it return 0. Otherwise, it returns 1.

TLwDispInfoNotify class   listwind.h

TLwDispInfoNotify is a *TListWindow* notification to repaint an item.

Public data members

item
LV_ITEM item;

The item to repaint.

TLwFindInfo class   listwind.h

TLwFindInfo is used to find an item in a *TListWindow*.

Public constructors

Form 1 TLwFindInfo(LV_FINDINFO);
Constructor based on existing structure.

Form 2 TLwFindInfo();
Constructor to initialize every data member to 0.

Public member functions

SetData
void SetData(TParam2 param);
Sets extra information.

SetPartial
void SetPartial(char far* text = 0);
Finds a partial string.

SetString
void SetString(char far* text = 0);
Finds based on string information.

SetSubstring
void SetSubstring(char far* text = 0);
Finds exact substring.

SetWrap
void SetWrap(bool = true);
Continues to search at beginning if end has been reached.

Protected member functions

Init
void Init();
Private Init to zero out all data members.

TLwHitTestInfo class   listwind.h

TLwHitTestInfo determines if a point is somewhere on an item or not.

Public constructors

Form 1 TLwHitTestInfo();
Default constructor. Zeros out everything.

Form 2   TLwHitTestInfo(TPoint& p);
         Initializes the point.

Form 3   TLwHitTestInfo(LV_HITTESTINFO);
         Construct based on an existing structure.

Public member functions

GetFlags
uint GetFlags();
Returns the flag for the item.

GetIndex
int GetIndex();
Returns the item's index.

SetPoint
void SetPoint(TPoint& p);
Sets the point information.

Protected member functions

Init
void Init();
Private *Init()* to zero out data members.

TLwKeyDownNotify class   listwind.h

TLwKeyDownNotify is a *TListWindow* notification that a key has been pressed.

Public member functions

flags
uint flags;
Flags of the key.

wVKey
uint16 wVKey;
Which key was pressed.

TLwNotify class

listwind.h

TLwNotify is a basic *TListWindow* notification.

Public data members

iItem
int iItem;
The index of the item.

iSubItem
int iSubItem;
The index of the subitem (column).

lParam
TParam2 lParam;
Additional data member. Only valid for LVN_DELETEITEM.

ptAction
POINT ptAction;
Point action occurred. Valid for LVN_BEGINDRAG and LVN_BEGINRDRAG.

uChanged
uint uChanged;
A member indicating what changed.

uNewState
uint uNewState;
Combination of LVIS_* (if uChanged & LVIF_STATE). New state of the item.

uOldState
uint uOldState;
Combination of LVIS_*. Old state of the item.

TMailer class

mailer.h

The *TMailer* class encapsulates the MAPI DLL (MAPI [32].DLL). It provides an easy method to dynamically test for the availability of the DLL and bind to its exported functions at runtime. By using the *TMailer* class instead of direct calls to the MAPI DLL, ObjectWindows applications can provide the appropriate behavior when running in an environment where the DLL is not available.

Each data member of the *TMailer* class corresponds to the API with a similar name exposed by the MAPI DLL. For example, *TMailerDll::MAPISendDocuments* corresponds to the *MAPISendDocuments* API exported by the MAPI DLL.

The following is a list of the members of the *TMailer* class corresponding to functions exposed by the DLL. For more information about these members, consult the documentation about the corresponding API exposed by the MAPI DLL.

- *TMailer::TMailer*
- *MAPISendDocuments*
- *SendDocuments*

TMci class   mci.h

TMci is a Windows MCI (Media Control Interface) encapsulation class.

Public constructors

Form 1   TMci();
Creates a hidden window for catching messages.

Form 2   ~TMci();
If the MCI device is still open, this closes it now. Deletes the hidden window.

Public member functions

Close
uint32 Close();
Stops the MCI device and closes it.

GetCallback
uint32 GetCallback() const;
Returns the callback. If the window exists, the handle of the window is returned.

GetDeviceId
uint GetDeviceId() const;
Returns the ID of the open MCI device.

IsBusy
bool IsBusy() const;
Returns true if the MCI is currently busy doing something.

Load
uint32 Load(const char far* fileName, uint32 flags = 0);
Loads the file into the MCI device.

MciNotify
virtual TResult MciNotify(TParam1, TParam2);
The default *MciNotify* is to return 0.

Open

uint32 Open(MCI_OPEN_PARMS, uint32 command = 0);

Opens the MCI device.

Pause

uint32 Pause(uint32 flags = 0);

Pauses the MCI device.

Play

uint32 Play(MCI_PLAY_PARMS, uint32 flags = 0);

Plays the MCI device.

Resume

uint32 Resume(uint32 flags = 0);

Resumes playing of the MCI device.

Seek

Form 1   uint32 Seek(uint32 to, uint32 flags = 0);

Seeks a particular position on the MCI device. This function is provided for convenience.

Form 2   uint32 Seek(MCI_SEEK_PARMS, uint32 flags = 0);

Seeks a particular position on the MCI device. This function requires the parameters to be specified in a structure.

SendCommand

Form 1   static uint32 SendCommand(uint deviceId, uint msg, uint32 command, uint32 param);

Sends the MCI command to the opened device.

Form 2   uint32 SendCommand(uint msg, uint32 command, uint32 param);

Sends the MCI command to the device if it's not busy.

SetBusy

void SetBusy(bool);

Sets the busy flag for the MCI device.

Stop

uint32 Stop(uint32 flags = 0);

Stops the MCI device.

TMciHiddenWindow class

mci.h

TMciHiddenWindow is a private *TWindow* derivative used by *TMci* to capture events.

Public constructors

TMciHiddenWindow(TMci&, TModule* = 0);

A hidden window created for the sole purpose of catching MCI messages.

Public member functions

MciNotify
TResult MciNotify(TParam1, TParam2);

Notifies the MCI class that the MCI event has finished.

Response table entries

Response table entry	Member function
EV_MESSAGE (MM_MCINOTIFY, MciNotify)	MciNotify

TMciWaveAudio class   mci.h

TMciWaveAudio is a wrapper to play .WAV files.

Public constructors

TMciWaveAudio(const char far* elementName = 0, const char far* deviceName = 0, uint16 id = 0);

Constructs an MCI waveaudio (.WAV) device.

Public member functions

Play
uint32 Play(uint32 flags = 0, uint32 from = 0, uint32 to = 0);

Plays the file on the waveaudio device.

TMDIChild class   mdichild.h

TMDIChild defines the basic behavior of all MDI child windows. Child windows can be created inside the client area of a parent window. Because child windows exist within, and are restricted to the parent window's borders, the parent window defined before the child is defined. For example, a dialog box is a window that contains child windows, often referred to as dialog box controls.

To be used as MDI children, classes must be derived from *TMDIChild*. MDI children can inherit keyboard navigation, focus handling, and icon support from *TFrameWindow*. *TMDIChild* is a streamable class.

Public constructors and destructor

Constructors

Form 1   TMDIChild(TMDIClient& parent, const char far* title = 0, TWindow* clientWnd = 0, bool shrinkToClient = false,
          TModule* module = 0);

Creates an MDI child window of the MDI client window specified by *parent*, using the specified *title*, client window (*clientWnd*) and instance (*inst*). Invokes the *TFrameWindow* base class constructor, supplying *parent*, *title*, *clientWnd*, *inst*, and indicating that the child window is not to be resized to fit. Invokes the *TWindow* base class constructor, specifying *parent*, *title*, and *inst*. The window attributes are then adjusted to include WS_VISIBLE, WS_CHILD, WS_CLIPSIBLINGS, WS_CLIPCHILDREN, WS_SYSMENU, WS_CAPTION, WS_THICKFRAME, WS_MINIMIZEBOX, and WS_MAXIMIZEBOX. The dimensions of the window are set to the system default values.

Form 2   TMDIChild(HWND hWnd, TModule* module = 0);

Creates an MDI child window object from a preexisting window, specified by *hWnd*. The base class *TFrameWindow* constructor is invoked, specifying this *hWnd*, as well as the specified *inst*. The base class *TWindow* constructor is invoked, supplying the *hWnd* and *inst* parameters.

Destructor
~TMDIChild();

Destructs the MDI child window object.

Public member functions

Destroy
void Destroy(retVal = 0);

Destroys the interface element associated with the *TMDIChild*. Calls *EnableAutoCreate* for each window in the child list so that the children are also re-created when the parent window is re-created.

See also   TWindow::EnableAutoCreate

EnableWindow
bool EnableWindow(bool enable);

Overrides *TWindow*'s virtual function. *Enables* a child window.

PreProcessMsg
bool PreProcessMsg (MSG& msg);

Performs preprocessing of window messages for the MDI child window. If keyboard handling is enabled the parent client window's *TMDIClient_PreProcessMsg* member function is called to preprocess messages. In this case, the return value is true. Otherwise, *TFrameWindow::PreProcessMsg* is called and its return value becomes the return value of this member function.

See also   TMDIClient::PreProcessMsg, TFrameWindow::PreprocessMsg

ShowWindow
bool ShowWindow(int cmdShow);

Overrides *TWindow*'s virtual function. Displays a child window according to the value of *cmdShow*.

Protected member functions

DefWindowProc
LRESULT DefWindowProc (uint msg, WPARAM wParam, LPARAM lParam);

Overrides *TWindow::DefWindowProc* to provide default processing for any incoming message the MDI child window does not process. In addition, DefWindowProc handles the following messages: WM_CHILDACTIVATE, WM_GETMINMAXINFO, WM_MENUCHAR, WM_MOVE, WM_SETFOCUS, WM_SIZE, and WM_SYSCOMMAND.

See also TWindow::DefWindowProc

EvMDIActivate
void EvMDIActivate(HWND hWndActivated, HWND hWndDeactivated);

Instructs a client window to activate or deactivate an MDI child window and then sends a message to the child window being activated and the child window being deactivated.

EvNCActivate
void EvNCActivate(bool activate);

Responds to a request to change a title bar or icon.

PerformCreate
void PerformCreate(int menuOrId);

Creates the interface element associated with the MDI child window. Otherwise, it notifies the parent MDI client window to create the child window's interface element. The supplied *menuOrId* parameter is ignored because MDI child windows cannot have menus.

Response table entries

Response table entry	Member function
EV_WM_MDIACTIVATE	EvMDIActivate
EV_WM_NCACTIVATE	EvNCActivate

TMDIClient class   mdi.h

Multiple Document Interface (MDI) client windows (represented by a *TMDIClient* object) manage the MDI child windows of a *TMDIFrame* parent. *TMDIClient* is a streamable class.

Public data members

ClientAttr
LPCLIENTCREATESTRUCT ClientAttr;
ClientAttr holds a pointer to a structure of the MDI client window's attributes.

Public constructor and destructor

Constructor
TMDIClient(TModule* module = 0);
Creates an MDI client window object by invoking the base class *TWindow* constructor, passing it a null parent window, a null title, and the specified library ID. Sets the default client window identifier (IDW_MDICLIENT) and sets the style to include MDIS_ALLCHILDSTYLES, WS_GROUP, WS_TABSTOP, WS_CLIPCHILDREN, WS_VSCROLL, and WS_HSCROLL. Initializes the *ClientAttr* data member, setting its *idFirstChild* member to IDW_FIRSTMDICHILD.

Destructor
~TMDIClient();
Frees the *ClientAttr* structure.

See also TWindow::TWindow

Public member functions

ArrangeIcons
virtual void ArrangeIcons();
Arranges the MDI child window icons at the bottom of the MDI client window.

CascadeChildren
virtual void CascadeChildren();
Sizes and arranges all of the non-iconized MDI child windows within the MDI client window. The children are overlapped, although each title bar is visible.

CloseChildren
virtual bool CloseChildren();
First calls *CanClose* on each of the MDI child windows owned by this MDI client. Returns true if all MDI children are closed; otherwise returns false.

See also TWindow::CanClose

Create
bool Create();
Creates the interface element associated with the MDI client window. Calls *TWindow::Create* after first setting the child window menu in *ClientAttr* to the parent frame window's child menu.

See also TWindow_Create, TFrameWindow_GetMenuDescr

CreateChild
virtual TWindow* CreateChild();

Overrides member function defined by *TWindow*. Constructs and creates a new MDI child window by calling *InitChild* and *Create*. Returns a pointer to the new MDI child window.

See also   TMDIClient::InitChild, TModule::MakeWindow, TWindow::Create

GetActiveMDIChild
TMDIChild *GetActiveMDIChild();

GetActiveMDIChild points to the *TMDIClient*'s active MDI child window. *GetActiveMDIChild* is set by the child in its *EvMDIActivate* message response member function. *TMDIClient*'s constructors initialize *GetActiveChild*.

GetClientAttr
LPCLIENTCREATESTRUCT GetClientAttr();

Returns the client create struct for the MDI client.

InitChild
virtual TMDIChild *InitChild();

Constructs an instance of *TWindow* as an MDI child window and returns a pointer to it. Children must be created with MDI client as the parent window. Redefine this member function in your derived MDI window class to construct an instance of a derived MDI child class. For example,

```
PTWindowsObject TMyMDIClient::InitChild()
{
  return new TMyMDIChild(this, "");
}
```

See also   TMDIClient::CreateChild

PreProcessMsg
bool PreProcessMsg(MSG &msg);

If the specified *msg* is one of WM_KEYDOWN or WM_SYSKEYDOWN, then the keyboard accelerators are translated for the MDI client.

See also   TWindow::PreProcessMsg

SetClientAttr
void SetClientAttr(LPCLIENTCREATESTRUCT clientattr);

Sets the client create struct for the MDI client.

TileChildren
virtual void TileChildren(int tile = MDITILE_VERTICAL);

Sizes and arranges all of the non-iconized MDI child windows within the MDI client window. The children fill up the entire client area without overlapping.

Protected member functions

CmArrangeIcons
void CmArrangeIcons();

Calls *ArrangeIcons* in response to a menu selection with an ID of
CM_ARRANGEICONS.

See also   TMDIClient::ArrangeIcons

CmCascadeChildren
void CmCascadeChildren();

Calls *CascadeChildren* in response to a menu selection with an ID of
CM_CASCADECHILDREN.

See also   TMDIClient::CascadeChildren

CmChildActionEnable
void CmChildActionEnable(TCommandEnabler& commandEnabler);

If there are MDI child windows, *CmChildActionEnable* enables any one of the child
window action menu items.

CmCloseChildren
void CmCloseChildren();

Calls *CloseChildren* in response to a menu selection with an ID of
CM_CLOSECHILDREN.

See also   TMDIClient::CloseChildren

CmCreateChild
void CmCreateChild();

Calls *CreateChild* to produce a new child window in response to a menu selection
with a menu ID of CM_CREATECHILD.

See also   TMDIClient::CreateChild

CmTileChildren
void CmTileChildren();

Calls *TileChildren* in response to a menu selection with an ID of
CM_TILECHILDREN.

See also   TMDIClient::TileChildren

CmTileChildrenHoriz
void CmTileChildrenHoriz();

Calls *TileChildren* in response to a menu selection with an ID of
CM_TILECHILDREN and passes MDI child tile flag as MDITILE_HORIZONTAL.

EvDropFiles
void EvDropFiles(TDropInfo);

Forwards dropped file messages by default to the parent (MDI Frame) where they
can be handled, or be allowed to forward to the application where they can be handled more easily.

EvMDICreate

LRESULT EvMDICreate(MDICREATESTRUCT far& createStruct);

Intercepts the WM_MDICREATE message sent when MDI child windows are created, and, if the client's style includes MDIS_ALLCHILDSTYLES, and the child window's specified style is 0, then changes the child window style attributes to WS_VISIBLE, WS_CHILD, WS_CLIPSIBLINGS, WS_CLIPCHILDREN, WS_SYSMENU, WS_CAPTION, WS_THICKFRAME, WS_MINIMIZEBOX, and WS_MAXIMIZEBOX.

See also   TWindow::DefaultProcessing, MDICREATE struct

EvMDIDestroy

void EvMDIDestroy(HWND hWnd);

Intercepts the WM_MDIDESTROY message.

GetClassName

char far *GetClassName();

Returns *TMDIClient's* registration class name, "MDICLIENT."

Response table entries

Response table entry	Member function
EV_COMMAND (CM_ARRANGEICONS, CmArrangeIcons)	CmArrangeIcons
EV_COMMAND (CM_CASCADECHILDREN, CmCascadeChildren)	CmCascadeChildren
EV_COMMAND (CM_CLOSECHILDREN, CmCloseChildren)	CmCloseChildren
EV_COMMAND (CM_CREATECHILD, CmCreateChild)	CmCreateChild
EV_COMMAND (CM_TILECHILDREN, CmTileChildren)	CmTileChildren
EV_COMMAND(CM_TILECHILDRENHORIZ,CmTileChildrenHoriz)	CmTileChildrenHoriz
EV_COMMAND_ENABLE(CM_TILECHILDREN, CmChildActionEnable)	CmChildActionEnable
EV_COMMAND_ENABLE(CM_CASCADECHILDREN, CmChildActionEnable)	CmChildActionEnable
EV_COMMAND_ENABLE(CM_ARRANGEICONS, CmChildActionEnable)	CmChildActionEnable
EV_COMMAND_ENABLE(CM_CLOSECHILDREN, CmChildActionEnable)	CmChildActionEnable
EV_WM_MDICREATE	EvMDICreate
EV_WM_MDIDESTROY	EvMDIDestroy

TMDIFrame class   mdi.h

Multiple Document Interface (MDI) frame windows, represented by *TMDIFrame*, are overlapped windows that serve as main windows of MDI-compliant applications. *TMDIFrame* objects automatically handle creating and initializing an MDI client window (represented by a *TMDIClient* object) required by Windows. *TMDIFrame* sets window style WS_CLIPCHILDREN by default so that minimal flicker occurs when the MDI frame erases its background and the backgrounds of its children. *TMDIFrame* is a streamable class.

Because *TMDIFrame* is derived from *TFrameWindow*, it inherits keyboard navigation. As a result, all children of the MDI frame acquire keyboard navigation. However, it's best to enable keyboard navigation only for those children who require it.

To create an OLE-enabled MDI frame window, use *TOleMDIFrame*, which inherits functionality from both *TMDIFrame* and *TOleFrame*.

Public constructors

TMDIFrame
Form 1   TMDIFrame(const char far *title, TResId menuResId, TMDIClient &clientWnd = *new TMDIClient,
         TModule* module = 0);

Constructs an MDI frame window object using the caption (*title*) and resource ID (*menuResId*). If no client window is specified (*clientWnd*), then an instance of TMDIClient is created automatically and used as the client window of the frame. The supplied library ID (*module*) is passed to the *TFrameWindow* constructor along with a null parent window pointer, caption, client window, and a flag indicating that the client window is not to be resized to fit. The TWindow constructor is also invoked; it passes the supplied caption and library ID, as well as a null parent window pointer. Then the child menu position is initialized to be the leftmost menu item, and the supplied menu resource ID is used in a call to *TFrameWindow::AssignMenu*.

Form 2   TMDIFrame(HWND hWindow, HWND clientHWnd, TModule* module = 0);

Constructs an MDI frame window using an already created non-ObjectWindows window. Invokes the *TFrameWindow* and *TWindow* constructors, passing in the window handle (*hWindow*) and library ID (*module*). Initializes the child menu position to the leftmost menu item and constructs a TMDIClient object that corresponds to the supplied *clientHWnd*.

Public member functions

FindChildMenu
static HMENU FindChildMenu(HMENU newMenu);

FindChildMenu searches, from right to left, the pop-up child menus contained in the *newMenu* menu resource for a child menu containing command items with one of the following identifiers: CM_CASCADECHILDREN, CM_TITLECHILDREN, or CM_ARRANGEICONS. The return value of *FindChildMenu* is the HMENU of the first child menu containing one of these identifiers. If one of these identifiers is not found, *FindChildMenu* returns 0.

FindChildMenu is used to locate the menu to which the MDI child window list will be appended. This call to *FindChildMenu* is made from within the *TMDIClient* class.

GetClientWindow
Form 1   TMDIClient *GetClientWindow();

Returns a pointer to the MDI client window.

Form 2   TWindow* GetClientWindow();

Returns the client window of this MDI frame.

See Also   TFrameWindow::GetClientWindow

GetCommandTarget
virtual HWND GetCommandTarget();

Locates and returns the child window that is the target of the command and the command enabling messages. If the current application does not have focus or if the focus is within a toolbar in the application, *GetCommandTarget* returns the most recently active child window. If an alternative form of command processing is desired, a user's main window class can override this function.

PerformCreate
void PerformCreate(int menuOrId);

Overrides *TWindow*'s virtual *PerformCreate* function. Creates the interface element associated with the MDI frame window.

SetMenu
bool SetMenu (HMENU);

Searches for the MDI child menu in the new menu bar and updates the child menu position with the specified menu *index*. Then sends the client window an WM_MDISETMENU message to set the new menu and invokes *TWindow::DrawMenuBar* to redraw the menu. Returns false if the MDI client indicates that there was no previous menu; otherwise returns true.

Protected member function

DefWindowProc
LRESULT DefWindowProc (uint message, WPARAM wParam, LPARAM lParam);

Overrides *TWindow::DefWindowProc* and provides default processing for any incoming message the MDI frame window does not process.

TMemoryDC class   dc.h

A device context (DC) class derived from TDC, *TMemoryDC* provides access to a memory DC.

Public constructors and destructor

Constructors
Form 1   TMemoryDC();

Default constructor for a memory device context (DC) object.

Form 2   TMemoryDC(const TDC& DC);

Creates a memory DC object compatible with the given *DC* argument.

Form 3   TMemoryDC(HDC handle, TAutoDelete AutoDelete);

Creates a memory DC object from an existing *DC* handle.

Form 4   TMemoryDC(TBitmap& bitmap);

Selects a bitmap right away.

Destructor
~TMemoryDC();

Destructor for this class.

See also   TDC::TDC

Public member functions

RestoreBitmap
void RestoreBitmap();

Restores the originally selected bitmap object for this device context.

See also   TDC::RestoreObjects

RestoreObjects
void RestoreObjects();

Restores the originally selected brush, pen, font, palette, and bitmap objects for this device context.

See also   TDC::RestoreObjects, TMemoryDC::RestoreBitmap

SelectObject
void SelectObject(const TBrush& brush);
void SelectObject(const TPen& pen);
void SelectObject(const TFont& font);
void SelectObject(const TPalette& palette, bool forceBackground=false);
void SelectObject(const TBitmap& bitmap);

Selects the given GDI object into this DEVICE CONTEXT.

See also   TDC::SelectObject, TMemoryDC::RestoreBitmap, TMemoryDC::Restore-Objects

Protected data members

OrgBitmap
HBITMAP OrgBitmap;

The original bitmap selected into this device context.

See also   TMemoryDC::SelectObject, TMemoryDC::RestoreBitmap

TMemoryDC
TMemoryDC(const char far* driver, const char far* device, const char far* output,
   const DEVMODE far* initData=0);

A protected pass-thru constructor for use by derived classes.

TMenu class   menu.h

The *TMenu* class encapsulates window menus. You can use *TMenu* member functions to construct, modify, query, and create menu objects. You can also use *TMenu* to add bitmaps to your menu or to specify if a menu item is checked or unchecked. *TMenu* includes two versions of a helper function, *DeepCopy*, designed to make copies of menus and insert them at a specified position on the menu bar. See the *ObjectWindows Programmer's Guide* for information about how to create menu objects.

Public constructors

Form 1   TMenu(TAutoDelete autoDelete = AutoDelete);

Creates an empty menu and sets *autoDelete*, by default, so that the menu is automatically deleted when the object is destroyed.

Form 2   TMenu(const TMenu& original, TAutoDelete autoDelete = NoAutoDelete);

Creates a complete copy of an existing menu and sets *autoDelete*, by default, so that the menu is not automatically deleted when the object is destroyed.

Form 3   TMenu(HWND wnd, TAutoDelete autoDelete = NoAutoDelete);

Creates a menu object representing the window's current menu and sets *autoDelete*, by default, so that the menu is not automatically deleted when the object is destroyed.

Form 4   TMenu(HMENU handle, TAutoDelete autoDelete = NoAutoDelete);

Creates a menu object from an already loaded menu and sets *autoDelete*, by default, so the menu is not automatically deleted when the object is destroyed.

Form 5   TMenu(const void far* menuTemplate);

Creates a menu object from a menu template in memory. This constructor is not available under Presentation Manager.

Form 6   TMenu(HINSTANCE instance, TResId resId);

Creates a menu object from a specified resource ID.

Form 7   virtual ~TMenu();

Destroys the menu.

See also   TResId

Public member functions

AppendMenu

Form 1   bool AppendMenu(uint flags, uint newItem, const TBitmap& newBmp);

Adds a bitmap menu item at the end of the menu. See *TMenu::GetMenuState* for a description of the flag values that specify the attributes of the menu; for example, menu item is checked, menu item is disabled, and so on.

Form 2   bool AppendMenu(uint flags, uint newItem = -1, const char far* newItem = 0);

Adds a text menu item to the end of the menu. See *TMenu::GetMenuState* for a description of the flag values that specify the attributes of the menu, for example, menu item is checked, menu item is a a bitmap, and so on.

See also   TBitmap, TMenu::GetMenuState

CheckMenuItem

bool CheckMenuItem(uint item, uint check);

Checks or unchecks the menu item. By combining flags with the bitwise OR operator (|) *check* specifies both the position of *item* (MF_BYCOMMAND, MF_BYPOSITION) and whether *item* is to be checked (MF_CHECKED) or unchecked (MF_UNCHECKED).

CheckValid

void CheckValid(uint resId = IDS_MENUFAILURE);

Throws a *TXMenu* exception if the menu object is invalid.

See also   TMenu::TXMenu

DeleteMenu

bool DeleteMenu(uint item, uint flags);

Removes the menu item (*item*) from the menu or deletes the menu item if it's a pop-up menu. *flags* is used to identify the position of the menu item by its relative position in the menu (MF_BYPOSITION) or by referencing the handle to the top-level menu (MF_BYCOMMAND).

See also   TMenu::RemoveMenu

DrawItem

virtual void DrawItem(DRAWITEMSTRUCT far& drawItem);

DrawItem responds to a message forwarded to a drawable control by *TWindow* when the control needs to be drawn.

See also   DRAWITEMSTRUCT struct

EnableMenuItem

bool EnableMenuItem(uint item, uint enable);

Enables, disables, or grays the menu item specified in the *item* parameter. If a menu item is enabled (the default state), it can be selected and used as usual. If a menu item is grayed, it appears in grayed text and cannot be selected by the user. If a menu item is disabled, it is not displayed. Returns true if successful.

GetHandle
virtual HMENU GetHandle();

Returns the handle to the menu.

See also   TMenu::IsOK

GetMenuCheckMarkDimensions

Form 1   static bool GetMenuCheckMarkDimensions(TSize& size);

Gets the size of the bitmap used to display the default check mark on checked menu items.

Always returns true. The size reference stores the dimensions of the checkmark bitmaps.

Form 2   static TSize GetMenuCheckMarkDimensions();

Return the dimensions of the check mark bitmaps.

See also   TMenu::SetMenuItemBitmaps, TSize

GetMenuItemCount
uint GetMenuItemCount() const;

Returns the number of items in a top-level or pop-up menu.

GetMenuItemID
uint GetMenuItemID(int posItem) const;

Returns the ID of the menu item at the position specified by *posItem*. If the menu is a pop-up menu, *GetMenuItemID* returns the ID of the menu's first item minus one.

GetMenuState
uint GetMenuState(uint item, uint flags) const;

Returns the menu flags for the menu item specified by *item*. *flags* specifies how the *item* is interpreted, and is one of the following values:

Flag	Description
MF_BYCOMMAND	Interpret *item* as a menu command ID. Default it neither MF_BYCOMMAND nor MF_BYPOSITION is specified.
MF_BYPOSITION	Interpret *item* as the zero-base relative postion of the menu item within the menu.

If *item* is found, and is a pop-up menu, the low-order byte of the return value contains the flags associated with *item*, and the high-order byte contains the number of items in the pop-up menu. If *item* is not a pop-up menu, the return value specifies a combination of these flags:

Flag	Description
MF_BITMAP	Menu item is a bitmap.
MF_CHECKED	Menu item is checked (pop-up menus only).
MF_DISABLED	Menu item is disabled.
MF_ENABLED	Menu item is enabled. Note: this constant's value is 0.
MF_GRAYED	Menu item is disabled and grayed.

Flag	Description
MF_MENUBARBREAK	Same as MF_MENUBREAK except pop-up menu columns are separated by a vertical dividing line.
MF_MENUBREAK	Static menu items are placed on a new line, pop-up menu items are placed in a new column, without separating columns.
MF_SEPARATOR	A horizontal dividing line is drawn, which cannot be enabled, checked, grayed, or highlighted. Both *item* and *flags* are ingonred.
MF_UNCHECKED	Menu item check mark is removed (default). Note: this constant value is 0.

Returns -1 if *item* doesn't exist.

GetMenuString
uint GetMenuString(uint item, char* str, int count, uint flags) const;

Returns the label (*str*) of the menu item (*item*).

GetSubMenu
HMENU GetSubMenu(int posItem) const;

Returns the handle of the menu specified by *posItem*.

InsertMenu
Form 1   bool InsertMenu(uint item, uint flags, uint newItem, const TBitmap& newBmp);

Adds a bitmap menu item after the menu item specified in *item*. The *flags* parameter contains either the MF_BYCOMMAND or MF_BYPOSITION values that indicate how to interpret the item parameter. If MF_BYCOMMAND, item is a command ID; if MF_BYPOSITION, item holds a relative position within the menu.

Form 2   bool InsertMenu(uint item, uint flags, uint newItem = -1, const char far* newItem = 0);

Inserts a new text menu item or pop-up menu into the menu after the menu item specified in *item*. The *flags* parameter contains either the MF_BYCOMMAND or MF_BYPOSITION values that indicate how to interpret the item parameter. If MF_BYCOMMAND, *item* is a command ID; if MF_BYPOSITION, *item* holds a relative position within the menu.

See also   TMenu::GetMenuState

IsOK
bool IsOK() const;

Returns true if the menu has a valid handle.

See also   TMenu::GetHandle

MeasureItem
virtual void MeasureItem(MEASUREITEMSTRUCT far& measureItem);

measureItem is used by owner-drawn controls to store the dimensions of the specified item.

See also   MEASUREITEMSTRUCT struct

ModifyMenu

Form 1 bool ModifyMenu(uint item, uint flags, uint newItem, const TBitmap& newBmp);

Changes an existing menu item into a bitmap. The *flags* parameter contains either the MF_BYCOMMAND or MF_BYPOSITION values that indicate how to interpret the item parameter. If MF_BYCOMMAND, item is a command ID; if MF_BYPOSITION, item holds a relative position within the menu.

Form 2 bool ModifyMenu(uint item, uint flags, uint newItem = -1, const char far* newItem = 0);

Changes an existing menu item from the item specified in *item* to *newItem*. The *flags* parameter contains either the MF_BYCOMMAND or MF_BYPOSITION values that indicate how to interpret the item parameter. If MF_BYCOMMAND, item is a command ID; if MF_BYPOSITION, item holds a relative position within the menu.

See also TMenu::GetMenuState

operator HMENU
operator HMENU()const;

Returns the menu's handle.

See also TMenu::operator uint

operator =
TMenu& operator =(const TMenu&);

Copies an existing menu onto this menu, using *DeepCopy*.

See also TMenu::operator uint

operator uint
operator uint()const;

Returns the menu's handle. This function provides compatibility with functions that require a uint menu parameter.

See also TMenu::operator HMenu

RemoveMenu
bool RemoveMenu(uint item, uint flags);

Removes the menu item from the menu but does not delete it if it is a submenu.

See also TMenu::DeleteMenu

SetMenuItemBitmaps
bool SetMenuItemBitmaps(uint item, uint flags, const TBitmap* bmpUnchecked=0,
    const TBitmap* bmpChecked=0);

Specifies the bitmap to be displayed when the menu item is checked and unchecked. *item* indicates the menu item to be associated with the bitmap. *flags* indicates how the *size* parameter is interpreted (whether by MF_BYPOSITION or by MF_BYCOMMAND). *GetMenuCheckMarkDimensions* gets the size of the bitmap.

See also TMenu::GetMenuCheckmarkDimensions, TBitmap

Protected data members

Handle
HMENU Handle;

Holds the handle to the menu.

ShouldDelete
bool ShouldDelete;

ShouldDelete is set to true if the destructor needs to delete the handle to the menu.

See also   TMenu::DeleteMenu, TMenu::RemoveMenu

Protected member functions

DeepCopy
Form 1 static void DeepCopy(TMenu& dest, const TMenu& source, int offset = 0, int count = -1);

Makes a deep copy (that is, an actual copy of the menu, not just a copy of pointers or handles to a menu) of the menu. This form of *DeepCopy* copies *count* number of pop-up menus or menu items from *src* beginning at *offset* and appends the items or menus to the destination menu. If *count* is passed as -1, all source menu items are copied.

Form 2 static void DeepCopy(TMenu& dst, int dstOff, const TMenu& src, int srcOff = 0, int count = -1);

Makes a deep copy (that is, an actual copy of the menu, not just a copy of pointers or handles to a menu) of the menu. This form of *DeepCopy* copies *count* number of pop-up menus or menu items from *source* beginning at *offset* and inserts the items or menus at the *dstOffset* position specified in the destination menu (*dest*). If *count* is passed as -1, all source menu items are copied.

TMenuDescr class   menu.h

Derived from *TMenu*, *TMenuDescr* describes your menu bar and its functional groups. *TMenuDescr* provides an easy way for you to group menus on your menu bar and to add new groups to an existing menu bar. It uses a resource ID to identify the menu resource and an array of count values to indicate the number of pop-up menus in each group on the menu bar.

The *TGroup* enum enumerates the six basic functional groups on a menu bar: File, Edit, Container, Object, Window, and Help. *TMenuDescr*'s constructors simply initialize the members based on the arguments passed. *TFrameWindow::MergeMenu* actually performs the real work of merging the menu groups.

For a single document application (SDI), the menus are merged as soon as you load the application. However, for a multiple-document application (MDI), you do not see the final menu until you invoke a child menu. See the sample program, mdifile.cpp, for an example of MDI menu merging.

One technique you can use to create a menu involves invoking the *TMenuDescr* constructor and passing the number of group counts for each menu selection.

For example, if your original menu groups included these items:

File	Edit Search	View	Page Paragraph Word	Window	Help

you might use the following group counts:

Group	Count	Menu
FileGroup	1	File
EditGroup	2	Edit Search
ContainerGroup	1	View
ObjectGroup	3	Page Paragraph Word
WindowGroup	1	Window
HelpGroup	1	Help

You would then invoke the constructor this way:

```
TMenuDescr(IDM_MYMENU, 1, 2, , 3, 1, 1)
```

You can build the previous menu by merging two menus. When a zero is passed in the parent menu's constructor, the group indicated by the zero is filled in by the child menu's group, if an item is specified, when the menu merging occurs. Set your application's parent frame menu bar by specifying these menu groups:

File	View	Window	Help

and passing these group counts in the constructor:

```
TMenuDescr(IDM_FRAME, 1, 0, 1, 0, 1, 1)
```

Set the word-processor child menu bar this way:

Edit Search	Page Paragraph Word	Help

and pass these values in the constructor:

```
TMenuDescr(IDM_WPROC, 0, 2, 0, 3, 0, 1)
```

If no child is active, only the frame menu will be active. When the word processor's child window becomes active, the child menu bar is merged with the frame menu. Every group that is 0 in the child menu bar leaves the parent's group intact. The previous example interleaves every group except for the last group, the Help group, in which the child replaces the frame menu.

By convention, the even groups (File, Container, Window) usually belong to the outside frame or container, and the odd groups (Edit, Object, Help) belong to the child or contained group.

If a -1 is used in a group count, the merger eliminates the parent's group without replacing it. For example, another child menu bar, such as a calculator, could be added to your application in this way:

```
TMenuDescr(IDM_WCALC, 0, 1, -1, 1, 0, 1)
```

In this example, the child's menu group contributes nothing from the container group, and the parent's container group is removed. This produces a merged menu (with the View menu selection eliminated as a result of the -1) that looks like this:

If you want to merge the following parent menu groups

with these paint window menu groups,

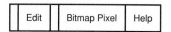

pass the following group counts in the constructor:

```
TMenuDescr(IDM_WPAINT, 0, 1, 0, 2, 0, 1)
```

This produces the following merged menu:

The simplest way to add groups to a menu bar involves defining the menu groups and adding separators in a resource file. Insert the term MENUITEM SEPARATOR between each menu group and an additional separator if one of the menu groups is not present. For example, the resource file for Step 14 of the ObjectWindows tutorial defines the following menu groups and separators:

```
IDM_MDICMNDS MENU
{
// Display a grayed File menu
  MENUITEM "File",   0,GRAYED  ;placeholder for File menu from DocManager
```

```
  MENUITEM SEPARATOR
  MENUITEM "Edit",  CM_NOEDIT ;placeholder for Edit menu from View
  MENUITEM SEPARATOR
  MENUITEM SEPARATOR
  MENUITEM SEPARATOR
  POPUP "&Window"
{
// Options within the Window menu group
   MENUITEM  "&Cascade",        CM_CASCADECHILDREN
   MENUITEM  "&Tile",              CM_TILECHILDREN
   MENUITEM  "Arrange &Icons", CM_ARRANGEICONS
   MENUITEM  "C&lose All",        CM_CLOSECHILDREN
   MENUITEM  "Add &View",       CM_VIEWCREATE
   }
  MENUITEM SEPARATOR
  POPUP "&Help"
  {
   MENUITEM "&About",  CM_ABOUT
   }
}
```

You can see the separators by loading Step14.rc into Resource Workshop and disabling the View as Popup Option in the View menu. This resource file defines an Edit group, a File group, a Window group, and a Help group, but no entries for Container or Object groups.

Step14.cpp uses these commands from the resource file to set the main window and its menu, passing IDM_MDICMNDS as the parameter to *SetMenuDescr* function, as follows:

```
SetMainWindow(frame);
GetMainWindow()->SetMenuDescr(TMenuDescr(IDM_MDICMNDS));
```

It produces the following menu groups:

TMenuDescr's functions let you perform menu merging similar to that of OLE 2. That is, you can merge menus from a container's document (the MDI frame window) with those of an embedded object (the MDI child window). When the embedded object is activated in place by double-clicking the mouse, the menu of the child window merges with that of the frame window.

Public constructors and destructor

Constructors
Form 1   TMenuDescr();

Default constructor for a *TMenuDescr* object. No menu resources or groups are specified. Constructs an empty menu bar.

Form 2   TMenuDescr(TResId id, int fg, int eg, int cg, int og, int wg, int hg, TModule* module = ::Module);

Constructs a menu descriptor from the resource indicated by *id*. Places the pop-up menus in groups according the values of the *fg, eg, cg, of, wg,* and *hg* parameters. The *fg, eg, cg, of, wg,* and *hg* parameters represent the functional groups identified by the TGroup enum. Calls the function *ExtractGroups* to extract the group counts based on the separator items in the menu bar.

Form 3   TMenuDescr(const TMenuDescr& original);

Copies the menu descriptor object specified in the *original* parameter.

Form 4   TMenuDescr(TResId id, TModule* module = ::Module);

Creates a menu descriptor from the menu resource specified in the *id* parameter. Calls the function *ExtractGroups* to extract the group counts based on the separator items in the menu bar.

Form 5   TMenuDescr(HMENU hMenu, int fg, int eg, int cg, int og, int wg, int hg, TModule* module = ::Module);

Constructs a menu descriptor from the menu handle indicated in the *hMenu* parameter. The menu descriptor can have zero or more pop-up menus in more than one functional group. The *fg, eg, cg, of, wg,* and *hg* parameters represent the functional groups identified by the *TGroup* enum. Calls the function *ExtractGroups* to extract the group counts based either on the separator items in the menu bar or on the group count parameters specified if there are no separators in the menu bar.

Destructor
~TMenuDescr();

Destroys the *TMenuDescr* object.

Type definitions

TGroup enum
enum TGroup{FileGroup, EditGroup, ContainerGroup, ObjectGroup, WindowGroup, HelpGroup, NumGroups};

Used by *TMenuDescr,* the *TGroup* enum describes the following constants that define the index of the entry in the *GroupCount* array.

Constant	Meaning
FileGroup	Index of the File menu group count
EditGroup	Index of the Edit menu group count
ContainerGroup	Index of the Container menu group count
ObjectGroup	Index of the Object group count
WindowGroup	Index of the Window menu group count
HelpGroup	Index of the Help menu group count
NumGroups	Total number of groups

See also   TMenuDescr::GroupCount

Public member functions

GetHandle
HMENU GetHandle() const;

Gets the handle to the menu, possibly causing any deferred menu acquisition to occur.

GetModule
TModule* GetModule() const;

Returns a pointer to the module object.

SetModule
void SetModule(TModule* module);

Sets the default module object for this menu descriptor.

GetId
TResId GetId() const;

Gets the menu resource ID used to construct the menu descriptor.

GetGroupCount
int GetGroupCount(int group) const;

Gets the number of menus in a specified group within the menu bar. There are a maximum of six functional groups as defined by the *TGroup* enum. These groups include *FileGroup, EditGroup, ContainerGroup, ObjectGroup, WindowGroup,* and *Help-Group.*

ClearServerGroupCount
void ClearServerGroupCount();

Clears the odd groups (that is, 1, 3, 5 or Edit Group, Object Group, and Help Group) in the menu bar for a server application.

See also   TGroup enum, TOcMenuDescr

ClearContainerGroupCount
void ClearContainerGroupCount();

Clears the even groups (that is, 0, 2, 4 or File Group, Container Group, Window Group) in the menu bar for a container application.

See also   TGroup enum, TOcMenuDescr

Merge
Form 1   bool Merge(const TMenuDescr& sourceMenuDescr);

Merges the functional groups of another menu descriptor into this menu descriptor.

Form 2   bool Merge(const TMenuDescr& sourceMenuDescr, TMenu& destMenu);

Merges the functional groups of this menu descriptor and another menu descriptor into an empty menu.

See also   TMenuDesc::TGroup enum

Protected data members

Id
TResId Id;

The resource ID for the menu. The resource ID is passed in the constructors to identify the menu resource.

operator =
TMenuDescr& operator =(const TMenuDescr& original);

operator <<
Form 1   friend opstream& operator <<(opstream& os, const TMenuDescr& m);

Form 2   friend ipstream& operator >>(ipstream& is, TMenuDescr& m);

operator >>
friend ipstream& operator >>(ipstream& is, TMenuDescr& m);

GroupCount
int GroupCount[NumGroups];

An array of values indicating the number of pop-up menus in each group on the menu bar.

See also   TGroup enum

Module
TModule* Module

Points to the *TModule* object that owns this *TMenuDescr*.

Protected member functions

ExtractGroups
bool ExtractGroups();

Extracts the group counts from the loaded menu bar by counting the number of menus between separator items. After the group counts are extracted, the separators are removed.

See also   TMenu, TOcMenuDescr

TMenuGadget class   menugadg.h

TMenuGadget is a text gadget that, when pressed, acts as a pop-up menu.

Public constructors

TMenuGadget
Form 1   TMenuGadget(TMenu& menu, TWindow* window, int id = 0, TBorderStyle borderStyle = TGadget::ButtonUp,
            char far* text = 0, TFont* font = new TGadgetWindowFont);

Creates the pop-up menu and initializes the text gadget.

Form 2   ~TMenuGadget();

Deletes the allocated pop-up menu.

Public member functions

LButtonDown
void LButtonDown(uint modKeys, TPoint& p);

This is a pop-up menu on LButtonDown.

TMenuItemEnabler class   framewin.h

Derived from *TCommandEnabler*, *TMenuItemEnabler* is a command enabler for menu items. The functions in this class modify the text, check state, and appearance of a menu item.

Public constructors

TMenuItemEnabler
TMenuItemEnabler(HMENU hMenu, uint id, HWND hWndReceiver, int position);

Constructs a *TMenuItemEnabler* with the specified command ID, for the menu item, message responder (*hWndReceiver*), and position on the menu.

Protected data members

HMenu
HMENU HMenu;

The menu that holds the item being enabled or disabled.

Position
int Position;

The position of the menu item.

Public member functions

Enable
void Enable(bool enable);

Overrides *TCommandEnable::Enable*. Enables or disables the menu options that control the appearance of the corresponding menu item.

GetMenu
HMENU GetMenu();

Returns the menu that holds the item being enabled or disabled.

GetPosition
int GetPosition();

Returns the position of the menu item.

SetText
void SetText(LPCSTR);

Overrides *TCommandEnable::SetText*. Changes the text of the corresponding menu item.

SetCheck
void SetCheck(int state);

Overrides *TCommandEnable::SetCheck*. Checks or unchecks the corresponding menu item. The *state* parameter reflects the menu item's state, which can be checked, unchecked, or indeterminate.

TMessageBar class   messageb.h

Derived from *TGadgetWindow*, *TMessageBar* implements a message bar with one text gadget as wide as the window and no border. Normally positioned at the bottom of the window, the message bar uses the default gadget window font and draws a highlighted line at the top.

Public constructor and destructor

Constructor
TMessageBar(TWindow* parent = 0, TFont* font = new TGadgetWindowFont, TModule* module = 0);

Constructs a *TMessageBar* object with the gadget window font. Sets IDW_STATUSBAR, *HighlightLine* to true, and *TTextGadget's* member *WideAsPossible* to true, making the text gadget as wide as the window.

Destructor
~TMessageBar();

The destructor for this class.

See also   TGadgetWindowFont::TGadgetWindowFont

Public member functions

SetHintText
virtual void SetHintText(const char* text);

Sets or clears the menu hint text for the message bar. Hint text is displayed over all other gadgets and is used for menu and control bar button help.

SetMessageText
void SetMessageText(int id, const char* text);

Sets the text for the default text message gadget by specifying the id.

SetText
void SetText(const char* text);

Forwards the message in the message bar to the text gadget for formatting.

See also   TTextGadget::SetText

Protected data members

HighlightLine
bool HighlightLine;

Is true if a highlighted line is drawn.

HintText
char* HintText;

Stores the command hint text, if any, that's currently being displayed.

Protected member functions

GetDesiredSize
void GetDesiredSize(TSize& rect);

Calls *TGadgetWindow's GetDesiredSize* to get the size of the message bar. Then, if a highlighting line is drawn, adjusts the size of the message bar.

See also   TGadgetWindow::GetDesiredSize

GetHighlightLine
bool GetHighlightLine() const;

Returns true if the message bar has an upper highlight line.

GetHintText
const char* GetHintText() const;

Returns the cached hint text for the current message.

GetInnerRect
void GetInnerRect(TRect& rect);

GetInnerRect computes the rectangle inside the borders and margins of the message bar.

See also   TGadgetWindow::GetInnerRect

PaintGadgets
void PaintGadgets(TDC& dc, bool erase, TRect& rect);

Adjusts the message bar and paints a highlight line. Then, *PaintGadgets* either paints the hint text if any is set or calls *TGadgetWindow::PaintGadgets* to repaint each gadget.

See also   TGadgetWindow::PaintGadgets

SetHighlightLine
void SetHighlightLine(bool highlightline);

Sets the flag for the message bar to have an upper highlight line.

TMetaFileDC class

Derived from *TDC*, *TMetaFileDC* provides access to a device context with a metafile selected for drawing.

Public constructors and destructor

Constructor

Form 1   TMetaFileDC(const char far* filename = 0);

Creates a *TMetaFileDC* object with the data written to the named file if one is provided.

Form 2   TMetaFileDC(const TDC& dc, const char far* filename = 0, TRect* rect = 0, const char far* description = 0);

For Win32. Provides access to a DC with a metafile selected into it for drawing into.

Destructor
~TMetaFileDC();

Destroys this object.

See also   TDC::TDC

Public member functions

Close
HMETAFILE Close();

Closes this metafile DC object. Sets the *Handle* data member to 0 and returns a pointer to a new *TMetaFilePict* object.

See also   TMetaFilePict

CloseEnh
HENHMETAFILE CloseEnh();

Closes the enhanced metafile DC.

Comment
bool Comment(uint bytes, const void* data);

Inserts a comment record into the enhanced metafile.

IsEnhanced
bool IsEnhanced() const;

Returns true if the device context contains an enhanced metafile.

TMetaFilePict class

metafile.h

TMetaFilePict is a support class used with *TMetaFileDC* to simplify metafile operations, such as playing into a device context (DC) or storing data on the Clipboard. *TMetaFilePict* automatically handles the conversion between a metafile and a metafilepict.

Public constructors and destructor

Constructors

Form 1   TMetaFilePict(HMETAFILE handle, TAutoDelete autoDelete);

Creates a *TMetaFilePict* object using the given *handle* argument.

Form 2   TMetaFilePict(const TClipboard& clipboard);

Creates a *TMetaFilePict* object from the contents of the specified Clipboard.

Form 3   TMetaFilePict(const char* filename);

Creates a *TMetaFilePict* object for the metafile stored in the named file.

Form 4   TMetaFilePict(uint size, void far* data);

Creates a *TMetaFilePict* object for the memory-based metafile specified by *data*. The *data* buffer must hold a metafile of length *size* bytes.

Form 5   TMetaFilePict(HGLOBAL data);

Creates a *TMetaFilePict* object for the memory-based metafile specified by *data*. The *data* global memory block must hold a metafile.

Form 6   TMetaFilePict(const TMetaFilePict& orig, const char far* fileName = 0);

Copies the metafile *orig* to the named file. If *filename* is 0 (the default), the metafile is copied to a memory-based metafile.

Destructor

~TMetaFilePict()

Destroys this object.

See also   TClipboard

Public member functions

CalcPlaySize

TSize CalcPlaySize(TDC& dc, const TSize& defSize) const;

Calculates the size of this metafile when played on a given DC.

See also   TDC, TSize

GetMetaFileBits
HANDLE GetMetaFileBits();

Returns a handle to a global memory block containing this metafile as a collection of bits. The memory block can be used to determine the size of the metafile or to save the metafile as a file.

GetMetaFileBitsEx
uint32 GetMetaFileBitsEx(uint size, void* data);

(32-bit only) Retrieves the contents of the metafile associated with this object and copies them (up to *size* bytes) to the *data* buffer. If *data* is nonzero and the call succeeds, the actual number of bytes copied is returned. If *data* is 0, a successful call returns the number of bytes required by the buffer. A return value of 0 always indicates a failure.

Height
int Height() const;

Retrieves the height of this metafile.

MappingMode
unsigned MappingMode()const;

Retrieves the mapping mode of this metafile.

operator HMETAFILE()
operator HMETAFILE() const;

Type-conversion operator.

operator <<
TClipboard& operator <<(TClipboard& clipboard, TMetaFilePict& mfp);

Places the *TMetaFilePict* object onto the Clipboard. Returns a reference to the resulting Clipboard, allowing the usual chaining of << operations.

See also   TClipboard

PlayOnto
bool PlayOnto(TDC& dc, const TSize& defSize) const;

Plays the metafile into a device context.

See also   TDC

SetMappingMode
void SetMappingMode(unsigned mm);

Sets the mapping mode of this metafile.

SetSize
void SetSize(const TSize& size);

Sets the size of this metafile.

Size
TSize Size() const;

Retrieves the size of this metafile.

ToClipboard
void ToClipboard(TClipboard& clipboard, unsigned mapMode = MM_ANISOTROPIC,
    const TSize& extent=TSize(0,0));

Puts this metafile onto the Clipboard.

See also   TClipboard, TSize

Width
int Width() const;

Retrieves the width of this metafile.

Protected data members

Extent
TSize Extent;

Holds the extent or size of the metafile.

Mm
int Mm;

Stores the mapping mode for the metafile.

TModeGadget class   modegad.h

TModeGadget is a mode-tracking text gadget class.

Public constructors

TModeGadget
TModeGadget(int vkKey, char far* text, int id = 0, TBorderStyle = Recessed, TAlign = Center,
    TFont* font = new TGadgetWindowFont);

Initializes the text gadget with the text key's text.

Public member functions

IdleAction
bool IdleAction(long count);

Override from *TGadget* to update the state of the key.

TModule class

ObjectWindows dynamic-link libraries (DLLs) construct an instance of *TModule*, which acts as an object-oriented stand-in for the library (DLL) module. *TModule* defines behavior shared by both library and application modules. ObjectWindows applications construct an instance of *TApplication*, derived from *TModule*. *TModule*'s constructors manage loading and freeing external DLLs, and the member functions provide support for default error handling.

Public data members

lpCmdLine
char far* lpCmdLine;
A null-terminated string, *lpCmdLine* points to a copy of the command-line arguments passed when the module is loaded. Notice that *lpCmdLine* is different from the WIN32 *lpCmdLine* in which the full path name of the module is appended to the command-line arguments. Whether running under WIN16 or WIN32, ObjectWindows *TModule::lpCmdLine* data member includes only the command-line arguments. Note that the run-time library global variables **_argv***[] and **_argc** contain identical information for both WIN16 and WIN32 APIs, and that **_argv[0]** points to the full path name of the module.

See also   TApplication

Module
extern TModule *Module;
Holds a global pointer to the current module.

Status
TStatus Status;
Status contains the module status and is included for backward compatibility with ObjectWindows 1.0 applications. ObjectWindows 2.0, and later, uses exceptions to handle errors. Setting *Status* to any nonzero value will throw a *TXCompatibility* exception.

See also   TXCompatibility::MapStatusCodeToString

Public constructors and destructor

Constructors
Form 1   TModule(const char far* name, HINSTANCE hInstance, const char far* cmdLine);
Constructs a *TModule* object for an ObjectWindows DLL or program from within *LibMain* or *WinMain*. Calls *InitModule* to initialize *hInstance* and *cmdLine*.

Form 2   TModule(const char far* name, HINSTANCE hInstance);
Constructs a *TModule* object that is an alias for an already loaded DLL or program with an available *HInstance*. When the *TModule* is destructed, the instance isn't automatically freed. *name*, which is optional, can be 0.

Form 3   TModule(const char far* name, bool shouldLoad = true);

Constructs a *TModule* object that is used as an alias for a DLL. If *shouldLoad* is true, *TModule* will automatically load and free the DLL. If *shouldLoad* is false, then the *HInstance* needs to be set later using *InitModule*.

Destructor

virtual ~TModule();

Destroys a *TModule* object and deletes *lpCmdLine*.

Public member functions

AccessResource

int AccessResource(HRSRC hRsrc) const;

Used for 16-bit applications, *AccessResource* finds the specified resource. The preferred method is to use *FindResource*.

See also   TModule::FindResource

AllocResource

HGLOBAL AllocResource(HRSRC hRsrc, uint32 size) const;

Used for 16-bit applications, *AllocResource* loads a resource into memory. The preferred method is to use *LoadResource*.

See also   TModule::LoadResource

CopyCursor

HCURSOR CopyCursor(HCURSOR hCursor) const;

Used for 16-bit applications, *CopyCursor* copies the cursor specified in *hCursor*. The return value is a handle to the duplicate cursor.

See also   TIcon

CopyIcon

HICON CopyIcon(HICON hIcon) const;

Copies the icon specified in *hIcon*. The return value is a handle to the icon or 0 if unsuccessful. When no longer required, the duplicate icon should be destroyed.

Error

Form 1   virtual void Error(int errorCode);

Processes errors identified by the error value supplied in *errorCode*. *Error* displays the error code in a message box and asks the user if it is OK to continue. If the user does continue, the program might or might not be able to recover. If the user does not continue, the program terminates. *Error* can be overridden with another kind of exception handler. This function is included only for backward compatibility with ObjectWindows 1.0. If you are writing ObjectWindows 2.0 (and later) applications, use the following *Error* function instead.

Form 2   virtual int Error(xmsg& x, unsigned captionResId, unsigned promptResId=0);

Called when fatal exceptions occur, *Error* takes an *xmsg* exception object, a resource ID for a message box caption, and an optional resource ID for a user prompt. By default, *Error* calls *HandleGlobalException* with the *xmsg* object and the strings obtained from the resources. An application (derived from *TApplication* which is derived from *TModule*) can reimplement this function to provide alternative behavior.

A nonzero status code is returned to indicate that an error condition is to be propagated; a zero status indicates that the condition has been handled and that it is OK to proceed. ObjectWindows uses this status code inside its message loop to allow the program to resume. The global error handler (defined in except.h), which displays the message text, is

```
int _OWLFUNC HandleGlobalException(xmsg& x, char* caption, char* canResume);
```

ExecDialog
int ExecDialog(TDialog* dialog);
Executes a dialog box. This function is included only for backward compatibility. Use *TDialog::Execute* instead.

FindResource
HRSRC FindResource(TResId id, const char far* type) const;
Finds the resource indicated by *id* and *type* and, if successful, returns a handle to the specified resource. If the resource cannot be found, the return value is zero. The *id* and *type* parameters either point to zero-terminated strings or specify an integer value. *type* can be one of the standard resource types defined below.

Value of type	Resource
RT_ACCELERATOR	Accelerator table
RT_BITMAP	Bitmap
RT_CURSOR	Cursor
RT_DIALOG	Dialog box
RT_FONT	Font
RT_FONTDIR	Font directory
RT_ICON	Icon
RT_MENU	Menu
RT_RCDATA	User-defined resource
RT_STRING	String

See also   TResID

GetClientHandle
HWND GetClientHandle(HWND hWnd);
Gets the handle to the client window. This function is included only for backward compatibility with ObjectWindows 1.0.

GetClassInfo
bool GetClassInfo(const char far* name, WNDCLASS far* wndclass) const;
Used particularly for subclassing, *GetClassInfo* gets information about the window class specified in *wndclass*. *name* points to a 0-terminated string that contains the name of the class. *wndclass* points to the WNDCLASS structure that receives information about the class. If successful, *GetClassInfo* returns nonzero. If a matching class cannot be found, *GetClassInfo* returns zero.

See also   WNDCLASS struct

GetHandle
THandle GetHandle() const;
Gets the module instance handle.

GetInstance
HINSTANCE GetInstance() const;
Returns the instance handle for this module.

GetInstanceData
int GetInstanceData(void* data, int len) const;
Used only for 16-bit applications, *GetInstanceData* gets data from an already running instance of an application. *len* is the size of the buffer.

GetModuleFileName
int GetModuleFileName(char far* buff, int maxChars);
Returns the expanded file name (path and file name) of the file from which this module was loaded. *buff* points to a buffer that holds the path and file name. *maxChars* specifies the length of the buffer. The expanded filename is truncated if it exceeds this limit. *GetModeFileName* returns 0 if an error occurs.

GetModuleUsage
int GetModuleUsage() const;
Used only for 16-bit applications, *GetModuleUsage* returns the reference count of the module, if successful. The reference count is incremented by one each time a module is loaded, and decremented by one each time a module is freed.

GetName
const char far* GetName() const;
Gets the name of the module.

See also   ::GetName (Windows API)

GetParentObject
TWindow* GetParentObject(HWND hWndParent);
Gets a handle to the parent window. This function is included only for backward compatibility with ObjectWindows 1.0.

See also   ::GetParentObject (Windows API)

GetProcAddress
FARPROC GetProcAddress(const char far* fcnName) const;
Returns the entry-point address of the exported function *fcnName* if the function is found. Returns NULL otherwise.

InitModule
void InitModule(HINSTANCE hInstance, const char far* cmdLine);
Performs any instance initialization necessary for the module. If the module cannot be created, a *TXInvalidModule* exception is thrown.

IsLoaded
bool IsLoaded() const;
Returns a nonzero value if the instance handle is loaded. Use this function primarily to ensure that a given instance is loaded.

LoadAccelerators
HACCEL LoadAccelerators(TResId id) const;
Loads the accelerator table resource specified by *id*. *LoadAccelerators* loads the table only if it has not been previously loaded. If the table has already been loaded, *LoadAccelerators* returns a handle to the loaded table.

LoadBitmap
HBITMAP LoadBitmap(TResId id) const;
Loads the bitmap resource specified by *id*. If the bitmap cannot be found, *LoadBitmap* returns 0.

See also   TBitMap, TResID, ::LoadBitmap (Windows API), OBM_XXXX values (Windows API)

LoadCursor
HCURSOR LoadCursor(TResId id) const
Loads the cursor resource specified by *id* into memory and returns a handle to the cursor resource. If the cursor resource cannot be found or identifies a resource that is not a cursor, *LoadCursor* returns 0.

See also   TCursor, TResID, ::LoadCursor (Windows API)

LoadIcon
HICON LoadIcon(const char far* name) const;
Loads the icon resource indicated by the parameter, *name*, into memory. *LoadIcon* loads the icon only if it has not been previously loaded. If the icon resource cannot be found, *LoadIcon* returns 0.

LoadIcon can be used to load a predefined Windows icon if *name* points to one of the Windows IDI_XXXX values.

See also   TIcon, ::LoadIcon (Windows API), IDI_XXXX values (Windows API)

LoadMenu
HMENU LoadMenu(TResId id) const;
Loads the menu resource indicated by *id* into memory. If the menu resource cannot be found, *LoadMenu* returns 0.

See also   TMenu, ::LoadMenu (Windows API)

LoadResource
HGLOBAL LoadResource(HRSRC hRsrc) const;
Loads a resource indicated by *hRsrc* into memory and returns a handle to the memory block that contains the resource. If the resource cannot be found, the return value is 0. The *hRsrc* parameter must be a handle created by *FindResource*.

LoadResource loads the resource into memory only if it has not been previously loaded. If the resource has already been loaded, *LoadResource* increments the reference count by one and returns a handle to the existing resource. The resource remains loaded until it is discarded.

LoadString

Form 1   int LoadString(uint id, char far* buff, int maxChars) const;

Loads a string resource identified by *id* into the buffer pointed to by *buff*. *maxChars* indicates the size of the buffer to which the zero-terminated string is copied. A string longer than the length specified in *maxChars* is truncated. The return value is the number of characters copied into the buffer, or 0 if the string resource does not exist.

Form 2   string LoadString(uint id) const;

Loads a string resource identified by *id*

LowMemory

bool LowMemory();

This function, which is obsolete, always returns 0.

MakeWindow

TWindow* MakeWindow(TWindow* win);

This function is obsolete. Use the *TWindow::Create* function instead.

operator ==

bool operator ==(const TModule& other) const;

Returns true if this instance is equal to the other instance; otherwise, returns false.

operator HINSTANCE

operator HINSTANCE() const;

Returns the handle of the application or DLL module represented by this *TModule*. The handle must be supplied as a parameter to Windows when loading resources.

RestoreMemory

void RestoreMemory();

This function, which is obsolete, restores memory.

SetInstance

void SetInstance(HINSTANCE hInstance);

Sets the instance handle for this *TModule*. *SetInstance* is used for special cases in which the *hInstance* is not known when the module is constructed.

SetName

void SetName(const char far* name);

Accessor function that sets the name of the module.

SetResourceHandler

const RSRCHDLRPROC SetResourceHandler(const char far* type, RSRCHDLRPROC loadProc) const;

Used for 16-bit applications, *SetResourceHandler* installs a callback function that loads resources. *type* points to a resource type. *loadProc* is the address of the callback procedure. If successful, *SetResourceHandler* returns a pointer to a previously installed resource handler. If no resource handler has been installed, *SetResourceHandler* returns a pointer to the default handler. This function is useful for handling user-defined resource types.

SizeOfResource
uint32 SizeofResource(HRSRC hRsrc) const;
Returns the size, in bytes, of the resource indicated by *hRscr*. The resource must be a resource handle created by *FindResource*. If the resource cannot be found, the return value is 0.

Because of alignment in the executable file, the returned size might be larger than the actual size of the resource. An application cannot rely on *SizeofResource* for the exact size of a resource.

THandle
operator THandle() const;
Returns the instance handle of the library module represented by the *TModule* object.

ValidWindow
TWindow* ValidWindow(TWindow* win);
This function, which is obsolete, returns a handle to the valid window.

Protected data members

HInstance
HINSTANCE HInstance;
Contains the executing instance of either the application or DLL module. The instance must be supplied as a parameter to Windows when loading resources.

Name
char far* Name;
Holds the name of the application or DLL module.

TModuleProc class   module.h

TModuleProc is a base module procedure class that does initial binding. It throws an exception if it cannot bind.

Public constructor

TModuleProc
TModuleProc(const TModule& module, const char far* id);
Constructs a module entry object from a function name string or ordinal.

Protected member functions

Proc
FARPROC Proc;
Derived template classes perform type-safe parameter passing on call. Different class for each number of parameters, 'V' version for void return.

TModuleVersionInfo class   module.h

TModuleVersionInfo provides access to a *TModule*'s VERSIONINFO resource.

Public constructors

Form 1 TModuleVersionInfo(TModule::THandle module);
Access to a *TModule*'s VERSIONINFO resource.

Form 2 TModuleVersionInfo(const char far* modFName);
Access to a *TModule*'s VERSIONINFO resource.

~TModuleVersionInfo();
Access to a *TModule*'s VERSIONINFO resource.

Public member functions

GetFileDescription
bool GetFileDescription(const char far*& fileDesc, uint lang=0);
Commonly used, predefined info string queries. Passes requested language through, may be 0 to signify default.

GetFileVersion
bool GetFileVersion(const char far*& fileVersion, uint lang=0);
Retrieves the file version information in the requested language id.

GetFileVersionLS
uint32 GetFileVersionLS() const;
Gets the minor file version (last 32-bits).

GetFileVersionMS
uint32 GetFileVersionMS() const;
Gets the major product version number (first 32-bits).

GetFixedInfo
VS_FIXEDFILEINFO far& GetFixedInfo();
Returns the version information about this module.

GetInfoString
bool GetInfoString(const char far* str, const char far*& value, uint lang=0);
Queries any given "\StringFileInfo\lang-charset\<str>" version. Info string lang indicates the language translation, may be 0 to signify file default.

GetInternalName
bool GetInternalName(const char far*& internalName, uint lang=0);
Retrieves the internal name of the module.

GetLanguage
uint GetLanguage() const;
Returns the language id of this module.

GetLanguageName

Form 1   static string GetLanguageName(uint language);

Gets the language name string associated with a language/charset code.

Form 2   string GetLanguageName() const;

Returns the language name of this module.

GetLegalCopyright

bool GetLegalCopyright(const char far*& copyright, uint lang=0);

Retrieves the copyright message.

GetOriginalFilename

bool GetOriginalFilename(const char far*& originalFilename, uint lang=0);

Retrieves the original file name.

GetProductName

bool GetProductName(const char far*& prodName, uint lang=0);

Retrieves the product name this module is associated with.

GetProductVersion

bool GetProductVersion(const char far*& prodVersion, uint lang=0);

Retrieves the version of the product.

GetProductVersionLS

uint32 GetProductVersionLS() const;

Gets the minor product version number (last 32-bits).

GetProductVersionMS

uint32 GetProductVersionMS() const;

Gets the major product version number (first 32-bits).

GetSpecialBuild

bool GetSpecialBuild(const char far*& debug, uint lang=0);

Retrieves the special build number.

IsFileFlagSet

bool IsFileFlagSet(uint32 flag) const;

Returns true if the flag has been set in the version info.

Protected member functions

Buff

void far* Buff;

Renews file version info buffer.

FixedInfo

VS_FIXEDFILEINFO far* FixedInfo;

Fixed file info structure.

Lang
uint32 Lang;
Default language translation.

TMsgFilter class   commctrl.h

TMsgFilter is a structure sent with EN_MSGFILTER notification.

Public member functions

operator NMHDR&
operator NMHDR&();
Allows the notification structure to be transparently treated as an NMHDR structure, thereby eliminating the need to explicitly refer to the NMHDR data member (which is always the first member of notification structures).

TNoteTab class   notetab.h

TNoteTab encapsulates a tab control with each tab item along the bottom of the window.

Public constructors and destructor

Constructors
Form 1 TNoteTab(TWindow* parent, int id, int x, int y, int w, int h, TWindow* buddy = 0, bool dialogBuddy = true,
            TModule* module = 0);
Constructor of *NoteTab* object. Use this constructor when creating a notetab control from scratch.

Form 2 TNoteTab(TWindow* parent, int resourceId, TWindow* buddy = 0, bool dialogBuddy = true,
            TModule* module = 0);
Constructor of *NoteTab* object. Use this constructor when aliasing a control defined within a dialog template.

Destructor
~TNoteTab();
Destructor of *NoteTab* object—cleans up allocated resources.

Public member functions

Add
int Add(const char* txt, uint32 clientData = 0);
Removes tab items.

AdjustRect
void AdjustRect(bool clientInWindowOut, TRect& rect);
Sets/queries attributes of control window.

Delete
bool Delete(int index);
Removes tab items.

DeleteAll
bool DeleteAll();
Removes all tab items.

GetBuddy
HWND GetBuddy() const;
Sets/queries buddy window.

GetCount
int GetCount() const;
Set/query attributes of *TabControl*.

GetItem
bool GetItem(int index, TNoteTabItem& item) const;
Sets/queries attributes of tab items.

GetSel
int GetSel() const;
Returns the index of the selected tabitem.

Note Returns a zero-based index or -1 if there are no tab items in the notetab control.

GetStyle3d
bool GetStyle3d() const;
Returns the flag specifying whether the note tab control should draw a 3D border.

GetWindowFace
bool GetWindowFace() const;
Returns the flag specifying whether the active tab should use the system's window color.

Insert
int Insert(const char* txt, int index, uint32 clientData = 0);
Inserts a new tabitem at the specified index.

IsVisible
bool IsVisible(int index);
Returns true if the tab item at the specified index is visible. Returns false otherwise.

SetBuddy
void SetBuddy(HWND buddy);
Sets handle of the buddy window associated with this notetab control.

SetItem
bool SetItem(int index, const TNoteTabItem& item);
Updates information about the tab item at the specified index.

SetSel
int SetSel(int index);
Selects the tabitem at the specified index.

Note *SetSel* does not send any notifications to the parent and/or buddy.

SetStyle3d
void SetStyle3d(bool);
Specifies whether the note tab should draw a 3D edge. If "st" is true, the control displays a 3D edge.

SetWindowFace
void SetWindowFace(bool);
Specifies whether active tab should use the system's window color. If the "wf" parameter is true, the system's window color is used.

Transfer
uint Transfer(void* buffer, TTransferDirection direction);
Overrides *TWindow* virtual member function to handle transfers.

Protected data members

Style3d
bool Style3d;
Draws with 3D style.

TopMargin
int TopMargin;
Amount of a extra space to be left between the tab items and the top of the control when computing the location of the tabs.

WindowFace
bool WindowFace;
Active tab should use window color.

Protected member functions

EvGetDlgCode
uint EvGetDlgCode(MSG far* msg);
WM_GETDLGCODE handler. Informs dialog manager that arrow keys are to be used.

EvKeyDown
void EvKeyDown(uint key, uint repeatCount, uint flags);
WM_KEYDOWN handler. Handles arrow keys to allow user to navigate through tab items.

EvLButtonDown

void EvLButtonDown(uint modKeys, TPoint& point);

WM_LBUTTONDOWN handler. Checks whether the mouse was clicked on a tab item and selects it.

Note   A notification is sent to the parent before and after selecting the tab. The parent may choose to veto the selection after receiving the first notification.

EvSize

void EvSize(uint sizeType, TSize& size);

GetClassName

char far* GetClassName();

GetScrollerArea

void GetScrollerArea(TRect& rect);

Retrieves the desired location of the scrollers within the tab.

GetTabsArea

void GetTabsArea(TRect& rect);

If there are no tabs in the control, then only the left, top, and right sides are valid as the bottom requires tabs to be computed.

InitCtrl

void InitCtrl();

Routines handling underlying implementation.

InvalidateTabRect

void InvalidateTabRect(int index);

Invalidates the rectangle occupied by the tab at the specified index.

Paint

void Paint(TDC& dc, bool erase, TRect& rect);

Overriden Paint routine.

SetTabRects

void SetTabRects(int firstTab);

Lays out tab items with the specified index at the leftmost.

SetTabSize

void SetTabSize(int index);

Updates the internal information stored about the label of a particular tab item.

SetupFont

void SetupFont(HFONT font = 0);

Sets the specified font handle as the one to be used when drawing the labels of tab items.

SetupWindow

void SetupWindow();

Overriden virtual of *TWindow*. Initializes font used by control and resize accordingly.

TabFromPoint
int TabFromPoint(const TPoint& pt);
Returns the index of the tab item at the specified window coordinate.

TNoteTabItem struct   notetab.h

TNoteTabItem holds information about each tab in a notetab control. For example, the structure contains information about the title and size of each tab item.

Public constructors

Form 1   TNoteTabItem(const char* label, uint32 clientData = 0);
Constructor of Notetab Item object. Initializes object with specified string label and optional user-defined data.

Form 2   TNoteTabItem();
Default constructor of Notetab Item object.

Public data members

ClientData
uint32 ClientData;
User-defined data associated with item.

Label
string Label;
Label of tab.

LabelSize
TSize LabelSize;
Width and height of label.

Rect
TRect Rect;
Location of tab [client-area base coordinates].

TNotify class   commctrl.h

TNotify is a thin wrapper around the NMHDR structure. It's a placeholder for future enhancements for handling notifications.

Public constructors

Form 1   TNotify();
Constructor to create a *TNotify* object whose members are initialized to zero.

Form 2   TNotify(HWND ctl, uint id, uint code);
Constructor to create a *TNotify* object (NMHDR wrapper) from the specified window handle, control ID, and notification code.

TOleClientDC class   olewindo.h

Derived from *TClientDC*, *TOleClientDC* is a helper class that translates between two different coordinate systems. For example, the window's logical points may be measured in HIMETRIC or *twips*, whereas the coordinates of the actual output device (the viewport) may be measured in pixels. Without the help of this class, you would need to create a client DC and then setup the window's logical coordinates (its *origin*) and its width and height (its *extent*) as well as the viewport's origin (measured in device coordinates) and extent. Instead, *TOleClientDC* performs these calculations for you by mapping logical points to device points and vice versa.

TOleClientDC works with a *TOleWindow* object. By default, *TOleClientDC* takes care of both scaling (adjusting the extents of the window and the viewport) and scrolling (adjusting the origins of the window and the viewport).

Public constructor

TOleClientDC(TOleWindow& win, bool scale = true);
Constructs a *TOleClientDC* object . The parameter *win* references the window that *TOleClientDC* uses to create a device context (DC). If the *scale* parameter is **true**, *TOleClientDC* takes care of scaling. However, if your application handles scaling, you can pass *scale* as **false**.

Scrolling is controlled by the presence of a scroller (*TScroller*). *TOleClientDC* by default takes care of both scaling and scrolling.

Public member functions

DOWNCAST
return TYPESAFE_DOWNCAST(OcView, TOcRemView);

GetOcDoc
inline TOcDocument* TOleWindow::GetOcDoc() {

GetOcRemView
inline TOcRemView* TOleWindow::GetOcRemView() {

GetOcView
inline TOcView* TOleWindow::GetOcView() {

TOleDocument class   oledoc.h

Derived from *TStorageDocument*, *TOleDocument* implements the document half of the Doc/View pair. It manages the document's data while the corresponding *TOleView* object determines how the data is displayed on the screen. Basically, *TOleDocument* is a *TStorageDocument* with a knowledge of *TOcDocument* through its pointer to *TOcDocument*.

TOleDocument is responsible for creating compound documents, closing documents, reading documents from storage, and writing documents to storage. In the case of a server, the document consists of a single object. In the case of a container, the document can consist of one or more embedded objects (also referred to as *parts*).

To accomplish these tasks, *TOleDocument* talks to the underlying *ObjectComponents* classes through the use of functions such as *GetOcApp*, *GetOcDoc*, and *SetOcDoc*.

See also   TOcRemView

Public constructor and destructor

Constructor
TOleDocument(TDocument* parent = 0);
Constructs a *TOleDocument* object associated with the given parent *TDocument* object.

Destructor
~TOleDocument();
Destroys the *TOleDocument* object. In the case of an OLE container, the compound file remains open until all the views shut down.

Public member functions

CanClose
virtual bool CanClose();
Prepares the document for closing. Before closing the current document, checks to see if all child documents can be closed. If any child returns **false**, *CanClose* returns **false** and aborts the process. If all children return **true**, *CanClose* checks to see if the document has been changed. If so, it asks the user to save the document, discard any changes, or cancel the operation. If the document has not been changed and all child documents return **true**, this *CanClose* function returns **true**, thus indicating that the document can be closed.

CanClose also calls ReleaseDoc on its associated ObjectComponents document to make sure that all the embedded objects are closed properly.

Close
bool Close();
Ensures that the *IStorage* is released properly and disconnects any active server in the document. A compound file must be closed before it is reopened.

Commit
bool Commit(bool force);
Commits the current document's data to storage. If *force* is **true** and the data is not dirty, all data is written to storage and *Commit* returns **true**. If *force* is **false**, the data is written only if it is dirty.

CommitSelection
virtual bool CommitSelection(TOleWindow& oleWin, void* userData);
Virtual function to be overriden in *TOleDocument*-derived class that serves or supports linking to portions of a document's data.

GetNewStorage
virtual IStorage* GetNewStorage();
Typically used in a SaveAs menu selection, *GetNewStorage* gets a new storage for the document. For example, if the document's path changes, use this function to create a new storage.

GetOcApp
TOcApp* GetOcApp();
Returns the ObjectComponents application associated with this *TOleDocument* object.

See also   TOcApp

GetOcDoc
TOcDocument* GetOcDoc();
Returns the ObjectComponents document associated with this *TOleDocument* object.

See also   TOleDocument::SetOcDoc

InitDoc
virtual bool InitDoc();
Overrides the *TDocument::InitDoc* function and creates or opens a compound file so that there is an *IStorage* associated with this document's embedded objects. Uses a *TOcDocument* object to perform the actual interaction with the OLE *IStorage* and *IStream* interfaces, which are ultimately responsible for establishing the relationship between a compound file and its storage.

OleViewClose
void OleViewClose();
Shuts down the *TOleView*'s.

Open
bool Open(int mode, const char far* path);
Loads the embedded objects, if any, using the path specified in *path*. *mode* is a combination of bits that specify how the embedded objects are opened (for example, read only, read/write, and so on). By default, objects are opened in *ofReadWrite* and *ofTransacted* modes.

See also   ofxxxx document open enum

PathChanged
bool PathChanged();
Checks to see if the current document's path is the same as the *TOcDocument*'s path. If the paths are not the same, *PathChanged* returns **true**.

PreOpen
virtual void PreOpen();
Before the document is actually opened, *PreOpen* gives the derived class a chance to perform a particular operation; for example, setting a different open mode for the compound document.

See also   dtxxxx document constants, ofxxxx document open enum

Read
virtual bool Read();
Loads the embedded objects from the compound file. A container should call this function to load any embedded objects.

See also   TOleDocument::Write

ReleaseDoc
virtual bool ReleaseDoc();
Releases the ObjectComponents document when the server is finished using the document.

See also   TOleDocument::CanClose

RestoreStorage
bool RestoreStorage();
Restores the original root *IStorage* before the save operation.

Revert
bool Revert(bool clear);
Performs the reverse of *Commit*. *Revert* cancels any changes made to the document since the last time the document was saved to storage.

SetOcDoc
void SetOcDoc(TOcDocument* doc);
Sets the ObjectComponents document associated with this *TOleDocument* object.

See also   TOleDocument::GetOcDoc

SetStorage
virtual bool SetStorage(IStorage* stg);
Attaches the *IStorage* pointer (*stg*) to this document. If successful, *SetStorage* returns **true**.

Write
virtual bool Write();
Saves the embedded objects to the compound file. A container should call this function to save its embedded objects to storage.

See also   TOleDocument::Read

TOleFactoryBase<> class

olefacto.h

A template class, *TOleFactoryBase<>* creates callback code for ObjectWindows classes. The main purpose of the factory code is to provide a callback function, *Create*, that ObjectComponents calls to create objects.

Just as a recipe consists of a list of instructions about how to make a particular kind of food, a template, such as *TOleFactoryBase<>*, contains instructions about how to make an object, in this case, a factory object. *TOleFactoryBase<>* includes two public member functions. The three additional functions are passed as template arguments. Although these template arguments actually belong to the class that is instantiated when you fill in the arguments to *TOleFactoryBase<>*, they are described here for convenience.

Use *TOleFactoryBase<>* to manufacture objects in general, whether or not they are embedded, OLE-enabled, or use the Doc/View model. These objects might or might not be connected to OLE.

The callouts are supplied through the arguments passed to the template class. The factory base class takes three template parameters: the application type, a set of functions to create the object, and a set of functions to create an automation object. Depending on the arguments passed, you can make the following OLE-enabled components:

- Doc/View components that are automated

- Doc/View components that are not automated

- Non-Doc/View components that are automated

- Non-Doc/View components that are not automated

ObjectWindows provides a standard implementation for object creation and automation. Factory Template Classes gives an overview of these classes.

By using *TOleFactoryBase<>* to obtain an OLE interface for your application, you can make objects that are accessible to OLE. That is, *TOleFactoryBase<>* handles any relationships with *IUnknown*, a standard OLE interface.

See also   TComponentFactory typedef, TOcRegistrar class, TAutoFactory class

Public member functions

TComponentFactory
operator TComponentFactory();
Converts the object into a pointer to the factory. ObjectComponents uses this pointer to create the object.

Create
static IUnknown* Create(IUnknown* outer, uint32 options, uint32 id);
A *TComponentFactory* callback function that creates or destroys the application or creates objects. If an application object does not already exist, *Create* creates a new one. The *outer* argument points to the OLE 2 *IUnknown* interface with which this object aggregates itself. If *outer* is 0, the object will become an independent object.

The *options* argument indicates the application's mode while it is running. The values for *options* are either set from the command line or set by ObjectComponents. They are passed in by the *Registrar* to this callback. The application looks at these flags in order to know how to operate, and the factory callback looks at them in order to know what to do. For example, a value of *amExeMode* indicates that the server is running as an .EXE either because it was built as an .EXE or because it is a DLL that was launched by an .EXE stub and is now running as an executable program. The *TOcAppMode enum* description shows the possible values for the *options* argument.

If the application already exists and the object ID (*id*) equals 0, *Create* returns the application's OLE interface. Otherwise, it calls *OCInit* to create a new *TOcApp* and register the options from *TOcAppMode* enum, which contains OLE-related flags used in the application's command line. (These flags tell the application whether it has been run as a server, whether it needs to register itself, and so on.) If a component ID was passed, that becomes the component; otherwise, *Create* runs the application itself based on the values of the *TOcAppMode* enum and returns the OLE interface.

See also   TOleFactoryBase::DestroyApp, TOcAppMode enum

Template arguments

CreateApp
static T* CreateApp(options);
Creates a new application. By default, it creates a new application of template type *T* with no arguments. This is a static function that you can override in your application.

The *options* are those passed to the factory. They can be one of the *TOcAppMode* enum values (for example, *amRun*, *amEmbedding*, and so on) that indicate the application's mode when running and indicate the options to the factory.

See also   TOleFactoryBase::DestroyApp

CreateObject
static IUnknown* CreateObject(TApplication* app, TDocTemplate* tpl, IUnknown* outer);
Creates an object using the document template referred to in *tpl* and the application specified in *app*. The *outer* parameter refers to the controlling *IUnknown* interface of the object with which this object is going to be aggregated. If *outer* is 0, the object is an independent object.

You can override this static function to create your own object at run-time.

See also   TOleFactoryBase::DestroyApp, TOcView class

DestroyApp
static void DestroyApp(T* app);
Destroys the application (*app*) by unregistering the object and deleting it.

See also   TOleFactoryBase::CreateApp

TOleFrame class

Derived from *TDecoratedFrame*, *TOleFrame* provides user-interface support for the main window of a Single Document Interface (SDI) OLE application. Because it inherits *TDecoratedFrame*'s functionality, *TOleFrame* is able to position decorations, such as toolbars, around the client window. Because of its OLE frame functionality, you will always want to create a *TOleFrame* as a main frame. For example, *TOleFrame* supports basic container operations, such as

- Creating space in a container's frame window that the server has requested

- Merging the container's menu and the server's menu

- Processing accelerators and other messages from the server's message queue

In addition to supporting the customary frame window operations and event-handling, *TOleFrame* provides functionality that supports OLE 2 menu merging for pop-up menus.

Through the use of the EvOcXxxx event-handling member functions, *TOleFrame* responds to ObjectComponents messages sent to both the server and the container applications. Although most of the messages and functions provide container support, one message, *EvOcAppShutDown*, is server related, and one function, *GetRemViewBucket*, supplies server support. Whether *TOleFrame* functions as a container or a server, it always has a pointer to a corresponding *TOcApp*.

Public constructor and destructor

Constructor
TOleFrame(const char far* title, TWindow* clientWnd, bool trackMenuSelection = false, TModule* module = 0);
Constructs a *TOleFrame* object with the specified caption for the frame window (*title*), the client window (*clientWnd*), and module instance. The *trackMenuSelection* parameter indicates whether or not the frame window should track menu selections (that is, display hint text in the status bar of the window when a menu item is highlighted).

Destructor
~TOleFrame();
Destroys a *TOleFrame* object.

Public member functions

AddUserFormatName
void AddUserFormatName(char far* name, char far* resultName, char far* id);
Adds user-defined formats and the corresponding names to the list of Clipboard formats. Use this function if you want to associate a Clipboard data format (*name*) with the description of the data format as it appears to users in the Help text of the Paste Special dialog box (*resultName*). To use a standard Clipboard format, set the *id* parameter to an appropriate constant (for example, CF_TEXT). Otherwise, if the format is identified by a string, pass the string as the name and omit the ID.

See also TOcApp::AddUserFormatName

GetOcApp
TOcApp* GetOcApp();
Gets the ObjectComponents application associated with this frame window.

See also TOcApp, TOleFrame::SetOcApp

GetRemViewBucket
TWindow* GetRemViewBucket();
Returns a pointer to the OLE frame's hidden helper window that holds all inactive server windows. It can also hold in-place tool bars and *TOleView* windows.

SetOcApp
void SetOcApp(TOcApp* app);
Sets the ObjectComponents application associated with this frame window to the applications specified in the *app* parameter.

See also TOcApp, TOleFrame::GetOcApp

Protected member functions

CanClose
bool CanClose();
Returns true if the frame window can be closed. Tests to see if both the *TOcApp* and all child windows can close. If the application and all child windows return true, *CanClose* closes the frame window.

See also TOcApp

CleanupWindow
void CleanupWindow();
Performs normal window cleanup of any HWND-related resources. For DLL servers, *CleanupWindow* destroys the idle timer.

See also TWindow::CleanupWindow, TOleFrame::EvTimer

Destroy
void Destroy(int retVal);
Checks with all the connected servers to ensure that they can close before destroying the frame window. If the user closes the application with objects still embedded, *Destroy* hides the frame window instead of destroying it.

DestroyStashedPopups
void DestroyStashedPopups();
Destroys the previously stored shared pop-up menus. Checks to see if *StashCount* is 0 before destroying the menus.

See also TOleFrame::StashContainerPopups, TOleFrame::StashCount

EvActivateApp
void EvActivateApp(bool active, HTASK hTask);

Responds to a EV_WM_ACTIVATEAPP message sent when a window is activated or deactivated. If active is **true**, the window is being activated.

This message is sent to the top-level window being deactivated before it is sent to the top-level window being activated. *hTask* is a handle to the current process.

This event is forwarded to the *TOcApp* object, which activates an in-place server if one exists.

See also   TOcApp

EvOcAppBorderSpaceReq
bool EvOcAppBorderSpaceReq(TRect far* rect);
Responds to an OC_APPBORDERSPACEREQ message sent to a container. The response is to ask the container if it can give border space in its frame window to the server.

See also   TOcApp::BorderSpaceSet

EvOcAppBorderSpaceSet
bool EvOcAppBorderSpaceSet(TRect far* rect);
Responds to an OC_APPBORDERSPACESET message by making room in the container's frame window for the border space that the server has requested.

See also   TOcApp::BorderSpaceReq

EvOcAppDialogHelp
void EvOcAppDialogHelp(TOcDialogHelp far& dh);
Responds to an OC_APPDIALOGHELP message. The *dh* parameter refers to one of the *TOcDialogHelp* enum constants that indicate the kind of dialog box the user has open. For example, *dhBrowseLinks* indicates that the Links dialog box is open. The *TOcDialogHelp* enum lists the help constants and their dialog box equivalents.

See also   TOcDialogHelp enum

EvOcAppFrameRect
bool EvOcAppFrameRect(TRect far* rect);
Responds to an OC_APPFRAMERECT message sent to a container. The response is to get the coordinates of the client area rectangle of the application's main window.

EvOcAppInsMenus
bool EvOcAppInsMenus(TOcMenuDescr far& sharedMenu);
Responds to an EV_OC_APPINSMENUS message by merging the container's menu into the shared menu. The *sharedMenu* parameter refers to this merged menu.

EvOcAppMenus
bool EvOcAppMenus(TOcMenuDescr far& md);
Responds to an OC_OCAPPMENUS sent to the container. The response is to install a merged menu bar.

EvOcAppProcessMsg
bool EvOcAppProcessMsg(MSG far* msg);
Responds to an EV_OC_APPROCESSMSG message sent to the container asking the server to process accelerators and other messages from the container's message queue.

EvOcAppRestoreUI
void EvOcAppRestoreUI();
Responds to an OC_APPRESTOREUI message by restoring the container's normal menu and borders because in-place editing has finished.

EvOcAppShutdown
bool EvOcAppShutdown();
Responds to an OC_APPSHUTDOWN message indicating that the last embedded object has been closed. The response is to shut down the server.

EvOcAppStatusText
void EvOcAppStatusText(const char far*);
Responds to an OC_APPSTATUSTEXT message by displaying text from the server on this container's status bar.

EvOcEvent
LRESULT EvOcEvent(WPARAM wParam, LPARAM lParam);
Responds to a WM_OCEVENT message and subdispatches it to one of the EvOcXxxx event-handling functions based on the value of *wParam*. WM_OCEVENT messages are sent by ObjectComponents when it needs to communicate with an OLE-generated event; for example, if a server wants to display toolbars.

EvSize
void EvSize(uint sizeType, TSize& size);
Responds to an EV_WM_SIZE message indicating a change in the frame window's size and forwards this information to the *TOcApp*, which then notifies any in-place server. The server uses this information to change the size of its toolbar, if necessary.

See also   TOcApp::EvActivate

EvTimer
void EvTimer(uint timerId);
If this is a DLL server, *EvTimer* responds to a timer message by running an idle loop if the message queue is empty.

See also   TOleFrame::CleanupWindow

SetupWindow
void SetupWindow();
Associates the ObjectComponents application with the window's HWND so that the *TOcApp* and the window can communicate. Prepares a place to insert the server's toolbars when in-place editing of the embedded object occurs.

See also   TOcApp

StashContainerPopups
void StashContainerPopups(const TMenuDescr& shMenuDescr);
Stores a local copy of the pop-up menus so they can be used for menu merging and then destroyed later by *DestroyStashedPopups*. *shMenuDescr* is the shared menu descriptor to be stored. Increments *StashCount* each time the pop-up menus are saved.

See also   TOleFrame::DestroyStashedPopups, TMenuDescr

Protected data members

HoldMenu
HMENU HoldMenu;
Holds the handle to the container's previously saved copy of the menu.

OcApp
TOcApp* OcApp;
Points to the ObjectComponents application associated with this frame window.

See also   TOcApp

StashCount
int StashCount;
Holds the number of menu bars that have been stored. This number indicates how many active in-place editing sessions you have open.

See also   StashContainerPopups, TOleFrame::DestroyStashedPopups

StashedContainerPopups
TMenu StashedContainerPopups;
Holds the stored, shared pop-up menus.

See also   StashContainerPopups, TOleFrame::StashCount

Response table entries

Response table entry	Member function
EV_WM_SIZE	EvSize
EV_WM_ACTIVATEAPP	EvActivateApp
EV_MESSAGE(WM_OCEVENT, EvOcEvent)	EvOcEvent
EV_OC_APPINSMENUS	EvOcAppInsMenus
EV_OC_APPMENUS	EvOcAppMenus
EV_OC_APPROCESSMSG	EvOcAppProcessMsg
EV_OC_APPFRAMERECT	EvOcAppFrameRect
EV_OC_APPBORDERSPACEREQ	EvOcAppBorderspaceReq
EV_OC_APPBORDERSPACESET	EvOcAppBorderSpaceSet
EV_OC_APPSTATUSTEXT	EvOcAppStatusText
EV_OC_APPRESTOREUI	EvOcAppRestoreUI
EV_OC_APPSHUTDOWN	EvOcAppShutDown

TOleLinkView class   oleview.h

Derived from TView, *TOleLinkView* provides embedding and linking support for a portion of a document instead of an entire document. With the added functionality of *TOleLinkView*, a container gains the ability to embed or link to a selection within the server document.

The main purpose of a class derived from *TOleLinkView* is to attach a view to a portion of a document whenever a link is created to a selection within a server document. After this link is established, any changes made to the linked selection in the server document are sent to the container via the following sequence of steps:

1 When a user changes the server document, *TOleLinkView* receives a notification message.

2 *TOleLinkView* checks to see if the selection it represents has changed. If the selection has changed, *TOleLinkView* notifies *TOcLinkView* about the change.

3 When *TOcLinkView* receives the change message, it notifies the container that the selection has changed.

4 Non-Doc/View servers need to maintain a list of the *TOleLinkView*s attached to the document so that change notifications can be sent to each one of the views.

See also   TOleView, TOleWindow, TOcView, TOcRemView

Public constructor and destructor

Constructor
TOleLinkView(TDocument& doc, TOcLinkView& view);
Constructs a *TOleLinkView* object associated with the given document object (*doc*) and view (*view*).

Destructor
~TOleLinkView();
Destroys the *TOleLinkView* object and detaches the view from the associated document.

Public member functions

GetMoniker
TString GetMoniker();
Returns the moniker for the selection in a server document associated with this *TOleLinkView* container's view. By looking at the moniker, the application can find the corresponding objects in its document.

See also   TOcLinkView:GetMoniker

GetViewName
const char far* GetViewName();
Overrides *TView*'s virtual GetViewName function and returns the static name, "Link View."

StaticName
static const char far* StaticName();
Returns the constant string *"Link View"* that is displayed in the user interface selection box.

See also   TListView::StaticName

UpdateLinks

virtual bool UpdateLinks();

When any changes occur to the server document, *UpdateLinks* updates all containers linked to the view of the server document. If successful, it returns **true**.

See also TOcLinkView::Invalidate

VnLinkMoniker

virtual bool VnLinkMoniker(TString moniker);

Returns **true** if a *TOleLinkView* object is associated with the given server's *TOcRemView*. In contrast to *VnLinkView*, this function searches for the view using the specified server's moniker.

When the document receives a request for the *TOleLinkView* associated with a particular moniker, the document sends a *vnLinkView* notification message to all its attached views. The handler for *vnLinkMoniker* in *TOleLinkView* simply returns **true** if the handler finds a view associated with the moniker.

See also TOcLinkView::GetMoniker

VnLinkView

virtual bool VnLinkView(TOcLinkView& view);

Returns **true** if a *TOleLinkView* object is associated with the server's *TOcRemView*, the server's remote link view object. A *TOcRemView* is the object created by a linking and embedding server so that the server can draw its OLE object in a metafile used by the container. In contrast to *VnLinkMoniker*, this function searches for the *TOleLinkView* object using a reference to the view.

See also TOcLinkView

Protected member functions

OcLinkView

TOcLinkView& OcLinkView;

The *TOcLinkView* connector object associated with this view.

Response table entries

Response table entry	Member function
EV_VN_LINKVIEW	VnLinkView
EV_VN_LINKMONIKER	VnLinkMoniker

TOleMDIFrame class   olemdifr.h

Derived from *TMDIFrame* and *TOleFrame*, *TOleMDIFrame* provides OLE user-interface support for the main window of a Multiple Document Interface (MDI) application. *TOleMDIFrame* also talks directly to the ObjectComponents classes through the use of a pointer to the *OcApp* object.

TOleMDIFrame inherits functionality from *TMDIFrame* that supports the use of MDI frame windows designed to serve as the main windows of an MDI-compliant application. It also inherits decorated frame window functionality that supports the addition of decorations (such as toolbars and status lines) to the frame window. In addition, *TOleMDIFrame* inherits the ability to

- Create space that the server has requested in a container's frame window

- Merge the container's menu into the server's menu

- Process accelerators and other messages from the server's message queue

- Support OLE 2 menu merging for pop-up menus

TOleMDIFrame also inherits from *TOleFrame* the ability to talk directly to the ObjectComponents classes through the use of a pointer to the *OcApp* object.

See Step 14 of the ObjectWindows tutorial for an example of a program that uses *TOleMDIFrame* to create an OLE-enabled decorated MDI frame window.

Public constructor and destructor

Constructor
TOleMDIFrame(const char far* title, TResIdmenuResId, TMDIClient& clientWnd = *new TMDIClient,
    bool trackMenuSelection = false, TModule* module = 0);
Constructs a *TOleMDIFrame* object with the indicated title, menu resource ID, client window, and module instance. By default, because *trackMenuSelection* is **false**, menu hint text is not displayed. (These parameters coincide with those of TMDIFrame's constructor.)

Destructor
~TOleMDIFrame();
Destroys the OLE MDI frame window object.

See also   TDecoratedMDIFrame

Protected member functions

DefWindowProc
LRESULT DefWindowProc(uint message, WPARAM wParam, LPARAM lParam);
Allows default processing for all messages except for a resizing message concerning the frame window, in which case *DefWindowProc* returns nothing.

EvActivateApp
void EvActivateApp(bool active, HTASK hTask);
Responds to a message indicating that the frame window of this application (*hTask*) is going to be either activated (*active* is **true**) or deactivated (*active* is **false**), and forwards this information to the TOcApp object.

EvOcAppInsMenus
bool EvOcAppInsMenus(TOcMenuDescr far*);

Inserts menus into a provided menu bar, or merges them with a child window and servers. To do this, *EvOcAppInsMenus* creates a temporary composite menu for the frame and MDI child windows, then copies the shared menu widths to the ObjectComponents structure. It saves the container popups so they can be destroyed later.

Response table entries

Response table entry	Member function
EV_WM_ACTIVATEAPP	EvActivateApp
EV_OC_APPINSMENUS	EvOcAppInsMenus

See also   TMDIFrame, TDecoratedMDIFrame, TOleFrame, TOleFrame::SetOcApp

TOleView class   oleview.h

Derived from *TWindowView* and *TView*, *TOleView* supports the View half of the Doc/View pair and creates a window with a view that can display an associated document. Documents use views to display themselves to a user. Regardless of whether a view belongs to a server or a container, *TOleView* sets up a corresponding TOcDocument object (an entire compound document).

In the case of an OLE-enabled container application, *view* refers to the window where the container application draws the compound document, which may consist of one or more linked and embedded objects. To display these objects in different formats, a container can be associated with more than one view. Similarly, to display the data properly, each embedded object can also have its own view. Each container view creates a corresponding ObjectComponents *TOcView* object.

If the view belongs to an OLE-enabled server application, *TOleView* creates a remote view on the server's document (a *TOcRemView* object). *TOleView* takes care of transmitting messages from the server to the container, specifically in the case of merging menus and redrawing embedded objects, and supports merging the server's and the container's pop-up menu items to form a composite menu. Because it knows the dimensions of the server's view, *TOleView* is responsible for telling the container how to redraw the embedded object.

Similarly to *TView*, *TOleView* supports the creation of views and provides several event handling functions that allow the view to query, commit, and close views. *TOleView* also manages the writing to *storage* of documents that belong to a container or a server.

Note   *Storage* is a compartment or area within a compound file structure.

Public constructor and destructor

Constructor
TOleView(TDocument& doc, TWindow* parent = 0);

Constructs a *TOleView* object associated with the given document object (*doc*) and parent window (*parent*).

Destructor
~TOleView();
Destroys the *TOleView* object and detaches the view from the associated document.

Public member functions

GetViewName
const char far* GetViewName();
Overrides *TView*'s virtual *GetViewName* function and returns the name of the class (*TOleView*).

GetWindow
TWindow* GetWindow();
Overrides *TView*'s virtual *GetWindow* function and returns the *TWindow* instance associated with this view.

OleShutDown
bool OleShutDown();
Shuts down the associated OCF partners if possible.

SetDocTitle
bool SetDocTitle(const char far* docname, int index);
Overrides *TView*'s and *TWindow*'s virtual *SetDocTitle* function and stores the title of the document associated with this view.

See also   TView::SetdocTitle, TWindow::SetdocTitle

StaticName
static const char far* StaticName();
Returns the constant string "Ole View" that is displayed in the user interface selection box.

See also   TListView::StaticName

Protected member functions

CanClose
bool CanClose();
A view uses this function to verify whether or not it can shut down. If this is a server's view window, *CanClose* checks to see if any *open-editing* is occurring on any of the embedded objects in the frame window. If so, *CanClose* closes this open-editing session by disconnecting the embedded object from its server. Then, it hides the server's frame window and returns **true** when appropriate. If this is a container, *CanClose* queries all documents and views and returns **true** when all documents and views can be closed.

Note   Unlike in-place editing, which takes place in the container's window, open-editing occurs in the server's frame window.

CleanupWindow

void CleanupWindow();

Performs a normal *CleanupWindow*. Also lets the *OcView* object know that we have closed.

CreateOcView

TOcView* CreateOcView(TDocTemplate* tpl, bool isEmbedded, IUnknown* outer);

Creates an ObjectComponents view associated with the embedded object. Associates the view with the document template specified in *tpl*. The *isEmbedded* parameter is true if the view is an embedded object. The *outer* parameter refers to the *IUnknown* interface with which the view will aggregate itself.

EvOcViewAttachWindow

bool EvOcViewAttachWindow(bool attach);

Attaches this view to its ObjectWindows parent window so the embedded object can be either opened and edited or deactivated. To attach a view to an embedded object, set the *attach* parameter to **true**. To detach the embedded object, set the *attach* parameter to **false**.

EvOcViewBreakLink

bool EvOcViewBreakLink(TOcLinkView& view);

Responds to an OC_VIEWBREAKLINK message that *TOcLinkView* sends when the server document that provides the link shuts down. *EvOcViewBreakLink* breaks the link with a server document or a selection by deleting the *TOleLinkView* associated with the *TOcLinkView* (*view*). After the link is broken, the container application is left holding a static representation (that is, a metafile) of the linked document. Returns **false** if unsuccessful.

Non-Doc/View applications use *TOleWindow*'s implementation of this function.

See also TOleWindow::EvOcViewBreakLink, TOleView::EvOcViewSetLink

EvOcViewGetItemName

bool EvOcViewGetItemName(TOcItemName& item);

Finds the item name for whole document or for the selection.

EvOcViewInsMenus

bool EvOcViewInsMenus(TOcMenuDescr far& sharedMenu);

Inserts the server's menu into the composite menu. Determines the number of groups and the number of pop-up menu items to insert within each group. The shared menu (*sharedMenu*) is the container's menu merged with the server's menu groups.

See also TMenuDescr has more information about menu merging, TOcMenuDescr struct

EvOcViewClose

bool EvOcViewClose();

Asks the server to close the view associated with this document. Tests to see if the document has been changed since it was last saved. Returns **true** if the document and its associated view are closed.

See also TOleView::EvOcViewSavePart

EvOcViewLoadPart

bool EvOcViewLoadPart(TOcSaveLoad far& ocLoad);
Asks the server to load itself from storage. Loads the document and its associated view.

EvOcViewOpenDoc

bool EvOcViewOpenDoc(const char far* path);
Asks the container application to open an existing document so the document can receive embedded and linked objects. (Actually, *TOleView* calls on the TOleDocument object to read the document from storage, using the standard OLE *IStorage* and *IStream* interfaces). Assigns a unique string identifier to the document and returns **true** if successful.

See also TOleView::EvOcViewClose

EvOcViewPartInvalid

bool EvOcViewPartInvalid(TOcPart far& changeInfo);
Notifies the active view of any changes made to the embedded object's data (*changeInfo*). Also, notifies any other views associated with this document that the bounding rectangle for the document is invalid and needs to be repainted. *EvOcViewPartInvalid* always returns **true**.

EvOcViewSavePart

bool EvOcViewSavePart(TOcSaveLoad far& ocSave);
Asks the server to save the embedded object's data to storage. To save the object, *EvOcViewSavePart* calls upon the *TOleDocument* object, which creates storage as necessary for each embedded object. Saves the dimensions of the server's view, which the server uses to tell the container how to redraw the embedded object in the container's window.

See also TOleView::EvOcViewClose, TOleView::EvOcViewOpenDoc, TOleDocument

EvOcViewSetLink

bool EvOcViewSetLink(TOcLinkView& view);
Responds to an OC_VIEWSETLINK message *TOcLinkView* sends when the server document provides a link to a container document. *EvOcViewSetLink* establishes the link between a *TOleLinkView* and a *TOcLinkView*. The *view* parameter references the view with which the document or selection is associated. Returns **false** if unsuccessful.

Non-Doc/View applications use *TOleWIndow*'s implementation of the function.

See also TOleView::EvOcViewBreakLink, TOleWindow::EvOcViewSetLink

GetViewMenu

TMenuDescr* GetViewMenu();
Overrides TView's *GetViewMenu* to make an on-the-fly decision about which menu to use: normal, or embedded.

OtherViewExists

bool OtherViewExists();
Checks whether another *TOleView* already exists.

VnDocOpened

bool VnDocOpened(int omode);

Ensures that *TOleView*'s data members, such as *DragPart*, *Pos*, and *Scale*, are initialized properly after a revert operation, which cancels any changes made to the document since the last time the document was saved to storage.

VnInvalidateRect

bool VnInvalidateRect(LPARAM p);

Invalidates the view region specified by *p*. Use this function to invalidate the bounding rectangle surrounding an embedded object if the object has been changed, usually as a result of in-place editing. If successful, returns **true**.

Response table entries

Response table entry	Member function
EV_OC_VIEWOPENDOC	EvOcViewOpenDoc
EV_OC_VIEWINSMENUS	EVOcViewInsMenus
EV_OC_VIEWCLOSE	EvOcViewClose
EV_OC_VIEWSAVEPART	EvOcViewSavePart
EV_OC_VIEWLOADPART	EvOcViewLoadPart
EV_OC_VIEWATTACHWINDOW	EvOcViewAttachWindow
EV_OC_VIEWBREAKLINK	EvOcViewBreakLink
EV_OC_VIEWSETLINK	EvOcViewSetLink

TOleWindow class   olewindo.h

Derived from *TWindow*, *TOleWindow* provides support for embedding objects in a compound document and serves as the client of a frame window. A compound document, such as the one *TOleWindow* supports, can contain many different types of embedded objects, from spreadsheets to bitmaps. In addition to providing support for a variety of basic window operations, *TOleWindow* also implements several OLE-related operations, among them

- Responding to drag-and-drop events

- In-place editing (the process whereby an embedded object can be edited without having to switch to its associated server application)

- Activating an embedded object's server application

- Creating views for the container application

- Transmitting a document's scaling information between a container's and a server's view windows

TOleWindow has the ability to determine whether it's acting as a server or a container. If it is a container, *TOleWindow* has a pointer to a *TOcView* or if it is a server, *TOleWindow* establishes a pointer to a *TOcRemView*. From the server's point of view, every remote view has a corresponding *TOleWindow*.

Through its many event-handling member functions, *TOleWindow* communicates with ObjectComponents to implement container and server support for embedded objects, update views, and respond to a variety of menu commands associated with the typical command identifiers (for example, CM_FILEMENU). It also supports OLE-specific verbs such as those activated from the Edit menu (for example, Edit and Open). These commands and verbs can originate from various sources such as a menu selection, a radio button, or even an internal program message.

Conversely, ObjectComponents talks to ObjectWindows by means of the various EV_OC_Xxxx messages. Some of these messages, such as EV_OC_VIEWPARTINVALID, implement container support while others, such as EV_OC_VIEWCLOSE, implement server support.

For any user-defined classes derived from *TOleWindow*, you need to choose which functions are appropriate. If you want to provide additional server support, you need to define only those functions that implement server messages; if you want to provide container support, you need to define only those functions that provide additional container support.

For example, the data embedded in the container application (a compound document having one or more embedded objects) and the data embedded in the server application (a single OLE object with or without other embedded objects) can be written to storage and loaded from storage. If you're using *TOleWindow* without *TOleView*, you have to manipulate the storage by talking directly to the ObjectComponents class, *TOcDocument*.

In addition to communicating with ObjectComponents classes, *TOleWindow* supports many transactions as a result of its interaction with other ObjectWindows classes. By virtue of its derivation from *TWindow*, naturally it inherits much of *TWindow*'s functionality.

See also   TWindowView

Public constructor and destructor

Constructor
TOleWindow(TWindow* parent = 0, TModule* module = 0);
Constructs a *TOleWindow* object associated with the specified parent window and module instance.

Destructor
~TOleWindow();
Checks to see if there are any open views, and, if no open views exist, destroys the *TOleWindow* object.

Public member functions

CreateOcView
virtual TOcView* CreateOcView(TDocTemplate* tpl, bool isEmbedded, IUnknown* outer);

Creates an ObjectComponents view associated with the embedded object. Associates the view with the document template specified in *tpl*. If *isEmbedded* is **true**, a remote view is created (that is, a *TOcRemView* instead of a *TOcView*). The *outer* parameter refers to the *IUnknown* interface with which the view will aggregate itself.

See also   TOcView, TOcRemView

GetOcApp
TOcApp* GetOcApp();
Returns the ObjectComponents application associated with this window. Every ObjectComponents application that supports linking and embedding has an associated *TOcApp* object.

See also   TOcApp

GetOcDoc
TOcDocument* GetOcDoc();
Returns the ObjectComponents document associated with this window. This document can be either a container's or a server's document. If this is a *TOcDocument* created by the container, the document is an entire compound document, which may consist of one or more embedded objects. If this is a *TOcDocument* created by the server, the document is a single OLE object's data.

See also   TOcDocument

GetOcRemView
TOcRemView* GetOcRemView();
Returns the server's view associated with this window. In order to draw the OLE object in the container's window, the server creates a remote view.

See also   TOcRemView

GetOcView
TOcView* GetOcView();
Points to the ObjectComponents container view associated with this window. The container view holds the compound document (that is a document containing one or more embedded objects).

See also   TOcView

HasActivePart
bool HasActivePart();
Returns **true** if the container's view holds an in-place active embedded object.

See also   TOcView::GetActivePart, InvalidatePart

IsOpenEditing
bool IsOpenEditing() const;
Checks whether the window is in Open-Edit mode.

IsRemote
bool IsRemote() const;
Returns **true** if the window represents an embedded server. Returns **false** otherwise.

OleShutDown
virtual bool OleShutDown();
Shuts down the associated ObjectComponents partners, if possible.

PaintMetafile
virtual void PaintMetafile(TDC& dc, bool erase, TRect& rect);
Repaints the area of the server where the embedded object resides. The *dc* parameter points to the device context. *erase* is **true** if the background of the embedded object is to be repainted. *rect* refers to the area to be repainted.

See also   InvalidatePart

SelectEmbedded
bool SelectEmbedded();
Selects the embedded object and returns **true** to indicate that the object has been selected.

SetupDC
virtual void SetupDC(TDC& dc, bool scale = true);
Determines the viewport's origin and extent (the logical coordinates and the size of the device context). Sets up the device context (DC) before painting the embedded object. *dc* refers to the DC and *scale* indicates that the scaling factor to use when painting the embedded object is a ratio between the site and the embedded object.

See also   TOcScaleFactor, SetScale

Protected data members

ContainerName
string ContainerName;
Holds the name of the container. The server displays the container's name when an embedded object is being edited in the server's window (referred to as *out-of-place editing*).

DragDC
TDC* DragDC;
Points to the device context used while an object is being dragged.

See also   DragPt

DragHit
TUIHandle::TWhere DragHit;
Indicates the position in the embedded object where the user points and clicks the mouse. This can be any one of the *TUIHandle::TWhere* enumerated values, for example, *TopLeft, TopCenter, TopRight, MidLeft, MidCenter, MidRight, BottomLeft, BottomCenter, BottomRight*, or *Outside* when no dragging is taking place.

See also   TUIHandle::TWhere enum

DragPart
TOcPart* DragPart;
Points to the embedded object (the part) being dragged.

DragPt

TPoint DragPt;

Indicates the point (in logical units) where the mouse is over the dragged object.

See also   DragDC

DragRect

TRect DragRect;

Holds the rectangle being dragged.

See also   DragDC

DragStart

TPoint DragStart;

Holds the point where the dragging of the embedded object began.

See also   DragPt

Embedded

bool Embedded;

Is **true** if this *TOleWindow* is an embedded window. As a result, a *TocRemView* is created because the data is being displayed in a server's window.

MinHeight

int MinHeight;

The minimum height of the part.

MinWidth

int MinWidth;

The minimum width of the part.

OcApp

TOcApp* OcApp;

Holds the ObjectComponents application associated with this *TOleWindow*.

See also   TOcView::OcApp, TOcApp

OcDoc

TOcDocument* OcDoc;

Holds the ObjectComponents document associated with this *TOleWindow*.

See also   TOcDocument, TOcView::OcDocument

OcView

TOcView* OcView;

Holds the ObjectComponents view or remote view (the server's) associated with the *TOleWindow* view.

See also   TOcView

Pos

TRect Pos;

Holds the current area in the window where the object is embedded. *Pos* reflects the area where the object is moved if you move the object.

Remote
bool Remote;
Returns **true** if the window represents an embedded server. Returns **false** otherwise.

Scale
TOcScaleFactor Scale;
Holds the current scaling factor. The server uses this information to determine how to scale the document.

See also   TOcScaleFactor, EvOcViewGetScale, SetScale

ShowObjects
bool ShowObjects;
Is **true** if the embedded object's frame (the gray or shaded brushes around the object) is displayed. The frame can be turned on or off depending on how you want the object to appear.

Protected member functions

CanClose
bool CanClose();
Returns **true** if the window can be closed. Checks all the server's child windows' *CanClose* functions, which must return **true** before the window can be closed. Terminates any open editing transactions before closing the window; otherwise, passes control to *TWindow::CanClose*.

CeEditConvert
void CeEditConvert(TCommandEnabler&);
Enables a command with an ID of CM_EDITCONVERT, which lets the user convert the selected object from one format to another. This is an OLE-specific pop-up menu option.

CeEditCopy
void CeEditCopy(TCommandEnabler&);
Enables a command with an ID of CM_EDITCOPY, which lets the user copy selected object to the clipboard.

CeEditCut
void CeEditCut(TCommandEnabler&);
Enables a command with an ID of CM_EDITCUT, which lets a user copy and delete the selected object from the view.

CeEditDelete
void CeEditDelete(TCommandEnabler&);
Enables a command with an ID of CM_EDITDELETE, which lets the user delete the selected object from the view.

CeEditInsertControl
void CeEditInsertControl(TCommandEnabler& ce);
Enables a command with an ID of CM_EDITINSERTCONTROL if the *OcApp* and *OcView* objects exist. Disables the command otherwise.

See also TOleWindow::CmEditInsertControl, TOleWindow::OcApp, TOleWindow::OcView

CeEditInsertObject
void CeEditInsertObject(TCommandEnabler&);
Enables a command with an ID of CM_EDITINSERTOBJECT if the *OcApp* and *OcView* objects exist. Disables the command otherwise.

CeEditLinks
void CeEditLinks(TCommandEnabler&);
Enables a command with an ID of CM_EDITLINKS, which lets the user manually update the list of linked items in the current view.

CeEditObject
void CeEditObject(TCommandEnabler&);
Enables a command with an ID of CM_EDITOBJECT, which lets the user edit the embedded object.

CeEditPaste
void CeEditPaste(TCommandEnabler&);
Enables a command with an ID of CM_EDITPASTE, which lets the user paste the embedded object from the clipboard.

CeEditPasteLink
void CeEditPasteLink(TCommandEnabler&);
Enables a PasteLink command with an ID of CM_EDITPASTELINK, which lets the user link to the embedded object on the clipboard. See the ocrxxxx Clipboard Constants for a description of the available clipboard formats.

See also TOleWindow::CeEditPasteSpecial, ocrxxxx Clipboard Constants

CeEditPasteSpecial
void CeEditPasteSpecial(TCommandEnabler&);
Enables the PasteSpecial command, which lets the user select a clipboard format to be pasted or paste linked. See the ocrxxxx Clipboard Constants for a description of the available clipboard formats.

See also TOleWindow::CeEditPasteLink, ocrxxxx Clipboard Constants

CeEditShowObjects
void CeEditShowObjects(TCommandEnabler& ce);
Checks or unchecks the Edit I Show Objects menu command according to the value of the ShowObjects data member.

See also TOleWindow::CmEditShowObjects, TOleWindow::OcApp, TOleWindow::OcView

CeEditVerbs
void CeEditVerbs(TCommandEnabler& ce);
Enables the Edit I Verbs command, which lets the user select one of the OLE-specific verbs from the Edit menu: for example, Edit, Open, or Play.

CeFileClose

void CeFileClose(TCommandEnabler& ce);
Enables the FileClose command, which lets the user exit from the window view.

CleanupWindow

void CleanupWindow();
Performs normal window cleanup and informs the *TOcView* object that the window is closed.

See also   TWindow::CleanupWindow, TOcView

CmEditConvert

void CmEditConvert();
Responds to a command with an ID of CM_EDITCONVERT by converting an object from one type to another.

CmEditCopy

void CmEditCopy();
Responds to a command with an ID of CM_EDITCOPY by copying the selected text to the clipboard.

CmEditCut

void CmEditCut();
Responds to a command with an ID of CM_EDITCUT by copying the selected text to the clipboard before cutting the text.

CmEditDelete

void CmEditDelete();
Responds to a command with an ID of CM_EDITDELETE by deleting the selected text.

CmEditInsertControl

void CmEditInsertControl();
Responds to a command with an ID of CM_EDITINSERTCONTROL by creating, initializing, painting, and selecting an OCX control (*TOcControl* object).

CmEditInsertObject

void CmEditInsertObject();
Responds to a command with an ID of CM_EDITINSERTOBJECT by creating, initializing, painting, and selecting an OLE object (*TOcPart* object).

CmEditLinks

void CmEditLinks();
Responds to a command with an ID of CM_EDITLINKS by updating the user-selected list of linked items in the current view.

CmEditPaste

void CmEditPaste();
Responds to a command with an ID of CM_EDITPASTE by pasting an object from the clipboard into the document.

CmEditPasteLink

void CmEditPasteLink();

Responds to a command with an ID of CM_EDITPASTELINK by creating a link between the current document and the object on the clipboard.

See also TOleWindow::CmEditPasteSpecial, ocrxxxx Clipboard Constants

CmEditPasteSpecial

void CmEditPasteSpecial();

Responds to a command with an ID of CM_EDITPASTESPECIAL by letting the user select an object from a list of available formats for pasting from the clipboard onto the document.

See also TOleWindow::CmEditPasteLink, ocrxxxx Clipboard Constants

CmEditShowObjects

void CmEditShowObjects();

Responds to a command with an ID of CM_EDITSHOWOBJECTS by toggling the value of the *ShowObjects* data member.

CmFileClose

void CmFileClose();

Responds to a command with an ID of CM_FILECLOSE by posting a WM_CLOSE message to the parent window to close the application.

CreateVerbPopup

TPopupMenu* CreateVerbPopup(const TOcVerb& ocVerb);

Creates and enables a pop-up menu option (*ocVerb*) on the Edit menu. The verb describes an action (for example, Edit, Open, Play) that is appropriate for the embedded object.

See also EvDoVerb

Deactivate

virtual bool Deactivate();

If an embedded object is no longer the active embedded object, either because the user has ended an in-place editing session or because the user has clicked outside the embedded object, call *Deactivate* to unselect the object. Returns **true** if successful.

EvCommand

LRESULT EvCommand(uint id, HWND hWndCtl, uint notifyCode);

Overrides the usual EvCommand message to handle the OLE verbs from CM_EDITFIRSTVERB to CM_EDITLASTVERB. These commands, which are defined in oleview.rh, correspond to the OLE-specific Edit menu selections such as Edit, Open, and Play. All of the other commands are passed to *TWindow::EvCommand* for normal processing.

See also CM_xxxx Edit View Constants, TOleWindow::EvCommandEnable, TWindow::EvCommand

EvCommandEnable

void EvCommandEnable(TCommandEnabler& commandEnabler);

Overrides the usual *EvCommandEnable* message in order to enable the OLE verbs from CM_EDITFIRSTVERB to CM_EDITLASTVERB. These commands enable the OLE-specific Edit menu selections, such as Edit, Open, and Play. Many of the other commands are passed to *TWindow::EvCommand* for normal processing.

If a window is embedded, however, *TOleWindow* calls upon *TWindow*'s *RouteCommandEnable* to perform command enabling.

See also   TOleWindow::EvCommand, TWindow::EvCommand, TWindow::RouteCommandEnable

EvDoVerb

void EvDoVerb(uint whichVerb);

Executes an OLE-related menu option from the Edit menu (for example, Edit, Copy, or Play) that is associated with the selected object.

See also   CreateVerbPopupTOleWindow_CreateVerbPopup

EvDropFiles

void EvDropFiles(TDropInfo dropInfo);

This is a response method for an incoming EV_WM_DROPFILES message.

EvHScroll

void EvHScroll(uint scrollCode, uint thumbPos, HWND hWndCtl);

In response to a WM_HSCROLL message, *EvHScroll* calls *TWindow::EvHScroll* and invalidates the window.

EvLButtonDblClk

void EvLButtonDblClk(uint modKeys, TPoint& point);

Responds to a mouse button double click message. *EvLButtonDblClk* performs hit testing to see which embedded object, if any, is being clicked on, then in-place activates the embedded object.

EvLButtonDown

void EvLButtonDown(uint modKeys, TPoint& point);

Responds to a left button down message by beginning a mouse drag transaction at the given point. Performs additional hit testing to see which embedded object, if any, is being clicked on. The *modKeys* parameter holds the values for a key combination such as a shift and double click of the mouse button.

See also   EvRButtonDown

EvLButtonUp

void EvLButtonUp(uint modKeys, TPoint& point);

Responds to a left button up message by ending a mouse drag action. *point* refers to the place where the mouse is located. *modKeys* holds the values for a combined key and mouse transaction.

EvMDIActivate

void EvMDIActivate(HWND hWndActivated, HWND hWndDeactivated);

Responds to a message forwarded from the MDI child window (if one exists) and lets the *TOcView* class know that the view window child window frame has been activated or deactivated.

The *hWndActivated* parameter contains a handle to the MDI child window being activated. Both the child window being activated being activated and the child window (*hWndDeactivated*) being deactivated receive this message.

See also   TOcView

EvMenuSelect
void EvMenuSelect(uint menuItemId, uint flags, HMENU hMenu);
Handles WM_MENUSELECT to provide hint text in the container's status bar, based on the menu item id. It treats popup items separately and asks them for their ids. This implementation is similar to the code in TDecoratedFrame.

EvMouseActivate
uint EvMouseActivate(HWND topParent, uint hitCode, uint msg);
Forwards the WM_MOUSEACTIVATE message to the top parent of the *TOleWindow* object.

EvMouseMove
void EvMouseMove(uint modKeys, TPoint& point);
Responds to a mouse move message with the appropriate transaction. If the mouse is being dragged, the embedded object is moved. If a resizing operation occurs, then the embedded object is resized. This message is handled only when a mouse dragging or resizing action involving the embedded object occurs.

EvOcAmbientGetBackColor
virtual bool EvOcAmbientGetBackColor(long* rgb);
Handles the EV_OC_AMBIENT_GETBACKCOLOR message, which is sent by an OCX control. Returns **false** by default. You should override the default implementation so the function stores the window background color in *rgb* and returns **true**.

EvOcAmbientGetDisplayAsDefault
virtual bool EvOcAmbientGetDisplayAsDefault(bool* disp);
Handles the EV_OC_AMBIENT_GETDISPLAYASDEFAULT message, which is sent by an OCX control. Returns **false** by default. You should override the default implementation so the function stores whether or not the control is a default control (buttons only) in *disp* and returns **true**.

EvOcAmbientGetDisplayName
virtual bool EvOcAmbientGetDisplayName(TString** name);
Handles the EV_OC_AMBIENT_GETDISPLAYNAME message, which is sent by an OCX control. Returns **false** by default. You should override the default implementation so the function stores a control name (used in error messages) in *name* and returns **true**.

EvOcAmbientGetFont
virtual bool EvOcAmbientGetFont(IDispatch** font);
Handles the EV_OC_AMBIENT_GETFONT message, which is sent by an OCX control. Returns **false** by default. You should override the default implementation so the function stores the window font information in *font* and returns **true**.

EvOcAmbientGetForeColor
virtual bool EvOcAmbientGetForeColor(long* rgb);
Handles the EV_OC_AMBIENT_GETFORECOLOR message, which is sent by an OCX control. Returns **false** by default. You should override the default implementation so the function stores the window forecolor in *rgb* and returns **true**.

EvOcAmbientGetLocaleID
virtual bool EvOcAmbientGetLocaleID(long* locale);
Handles the EV_OC_AMBIENT_GETLOCALEID message, which is sent by an OCX control. Returns **false** by default. You should override the default implementation so the function stores the window locale ID in *locale* and returns **true**.

EvOcAmbientGetMessageReflect
virtual bool EvOcAmbientGetMessageReflect(bool* msgReflect);
Handles the EV_OC_AMBIENT_GETMESSAGEREFLECT message, which is sent by an OCX control. Returns **false** by default. You should override the default implementation so the function stores whether or not the window reflects messages back to the control in *msgReflect* and returns **true**.

EvOcAmbientGetScaleUnits
virtual bool EvOcAmbientGetScaleUnits(TString** units);
Handles the EV_OC_AMBIENT_GETSCALEUNITS message, which is sent by an OCX control. Returns **false** by default. You should override the default implementation so the function stores the window scale units in *units* and returns **true**.

EvOcAmbientGetShowGrabHandles
virtual bool EvOcAmbientGetShowGrabHandles(bool* show);
Handles the EV_OC_AMBIENT_GETSHOWGRABHANDLES message, which is sent by an OCX control. Returns **false** by default. You should override the default implementation so the function stores whether or not the window shows grab handles in *show* and returns **true**.

EvOcAmbientGetShowHatching
virtual bool EvOcAmbientGetShowHatching(bool* show);
Handles the EV_OC_AMBIENT_GETSHOWHATCHING message, which is sent by an OCX control. Returns **false** by default. You should override the default implementation so the function stores whether or not the window shows hatching in *show* and returns **true**.

EvOcAmbientGetSupportsMnemonics
virtual bool EvOcAmbientGetSupportsMnemonics(bool* support);
Handles the EV_OC_AMBIENT_GETSUPPORTSMNEMONICS message, which is sent by an OCX control. Returns **false** by default. You should override the default implementation so the function stores whether or not the window supports mnemonics in *support* and returns **true**.

EvOcAmbientGetTextAlign
virtual bool EvOcAmbientGetTextAlign(short* align);
Handles the EV_OC_AMBIENT_GETTEXTALIGN message, which is sent by an OCX control. Returns **false** by default. You should override the default implementation so the function stores the window text alignment in *show* and returns **true**.

EvOcAmbientGetUIDead

virtual bool EvOcAmbientGetUIDead(bool* dead);

Handles the EV_OC_AMBIENT_GETUIDEAD message, which is sent by an OCX control. Returns **false** by default. You should override the default implementation so the function stores whether or not the window's user interface is disabled in *dead* and returns **true**.

EvOcAmbientGetUserMode

virtual bool EvOcAmbientGetUserMode(bool* mode);

Handles the EV_OC_AMBIENT_GETUSERMODE message, which is sent by an OCX control. Returns **false** by default. You should override the default implementation so the function stores whether or not the window is in user mode in *mode* and returns **true**.

EvOcAmbientSetBackColor

virtual bool EvOcAmbientSetBackColor(long rgb);

Handles the EV_OC_AMBIENT_SETBACKCOLOR message, which is sent by an OCX control. Returns **false** by default. You can override the default implementation so the window changes its background color to *rgb* and returns **true**.

EvOcAmbientSetDisplayAsDefault

virtual bool EvOcAmbientSetDisplayAsDefault(bool disp);

Handles the EV_OC_AMBIENT_SETDISPLAYASDEFAULT message, which is sent by an OCX control. Returns **false** by default. You can override the default implementation so the window displays itself as a default control (if the window represents a button control) if disp is **true**.

EvOcAmbientSetDisplayName

virtual bool EvOcAmbientSetDisplayName(TString* name);

Handles the EV_OC_AMBIENT_SETDISPLAYNAME message, which is sent by an OCX control. Returns **false** by default. You can override the default implementation so the window changes its display name (for error messages) to *name* and returns **true**.

EvOcAmbientSetFont

virtual bool EvOcAmbientSetFont(IDispatch* font);

Handles the EV_OC_AMBIENT_SETFONT message, which is sent by an OCX control. Returns **false** by default. You can override the default implementation so the window changes its font to *font* and returns **true**.

EvOcAmbientSetForeColor

virtual bool EvOcAmbientSetForeColor(long rgb);

Handles the EV_OC_AMBIENT_SETFORECOLOR message, which is sent by an OCX control. Returns **false** by default. You can override the default implementation so the window changes its background color to *rgb* and returns **true**.

EvOcAmbientSetLocaleID

virtual bool EvOcAmbientSetLocaleID(long locale);

Handles the EV_OC_AMBIENT_SETLOCALEID message, which is sent by an OCX control. Returns **false** by default. You can override the default implementation so the window changes its locale ID to *locale* and returns **true**.

EvOcAmbientSetMessageReflect

virtual bool EvOcAmbientSetMessageReflect(bool msgReflect);

Handles the EV_OC_AMBIENT_SETMESSAGEREFLECT message, which is sent by an OCX control. Returns **false** by default. You can override the default implementation so the window does or doesn't reflect messages according to the value in *msgReflect*.

EvOcAmbientSetScaleUnits

virtual bool EvOcAmbientSetScaleUnits(TString* units);

Handles the EV_OC_AMBIENT_SETSCALEUNITS message, which is sent by an OCX control. Returns **false** by default. You can override the default implementation so the window sets its scale units equal to *units* and returns **true**.

EvOcAmbientSetShowGrabHandles

virtual bool EvOcAmbientSetShowGrabHandles(bool show);

Handles the EV_OC_AMBIENT_SETSHOWGRABHANDLES message, which is sent by an OCX control. Returns **false** by default. You can override the default implementation so the window shows or hides grab handles according to the value in *show*.

EvOcAmbientSetShowHatching

virtual bool EvOcAmbientSetShowHatching(bool show);

Handles the EV_OC_AMBIENT_SETSHOWHATCHING message, which is sent by an OCX control. Returns **false** by default. You can override the default implementation so the window shows or hides hatching according to the value in *hatching*.

EvOcAmbientSetSupportsMnemonics

virtual bool EvOcAmbientSetSupportsMnemonics(bool support);

Handles the EV_OC_AMBIENT_SETSUPPORTSMNEMONICS message, which is sent by an OCX control. Returns **false** by default. You can override the default implementation so the window turns its support for mnemonics on or off according to the value in *support*.

EvOcAmbientSetTextAlign

virtual bool EvOcAmbientSetTextAlign(short align);

Handles the EV_OC_AMBIENT_SETTEXTALIGN message, which is sent by an OCX control. Returns **false** by default. You can override the default implementation so the window aligns text according to the value in *align* and returns **true**.

EvOcAmbientSetUIDead

virtual bool EvOcAmbientSetUIDead(bool dead);

Handles the EV_OC_AMBIENT_SETUIDEAD message, which is sent by an OCX control. Returns **false** by default. You can override the default implementation so the window enables or disables itself according to the value in *dead*.

EvOcAmbientSetUserMode

virtual bool EvOcAmbientSetUserMode(bool mode);

Handles the EV_OC_AMBIENT_SETUSERMODE message, which is sent by an OCX control. Returns **false** by default. You can override the default implementation so the window sets user mode equal to the value in *mode*.

EvOcCtrlClick

virtual bool EvOcCtrlClick(TCtrlEvent* pev);

Handles the EV_OC_CTRLCLICK message, which is sent by an OCX control. Returns **false** by default. You can override the default implementation so the window responds to the message and returns **true**.

EvOcCtrlCustomEvent

virtual bool EvOcCtrlCustomEvent(TCtrlCustomEvent* pev);

Handles the EV_OC_CTRLCUSTOMEVENT message, which is sent by an OCX control. Returns **false** by default. You can override the default implementation so the window responds to the message and returns **true**.

EvOcCtrlDblClick

virtual bool EvOcCtrlDblClick(TCtrlEvent* pev);

Handles the EV_OC_CTRLDBLCLICK message, which is sent by an OCX control. Returns **false** by default. You can override the default implementation so the window responds to the message and returns **true**.

EvOcCtrlErrorEvent

virtual bool EvOcCtrlErrorEvent(TCtrlErrorEvent* pev);

Handles the EV_OC_CTRLERROREVENT message, which is sent by an OCX control. Returns **false** by default. You can override the default implementation so the window responds to the message and returns **true**.

EvOcCtrlFocus

virtual bool EvOcCtrlFocus(TCtrlFocusEvent* pev);

Handles the EV_OC_CTRLFOCUS message, which is sent by an OCX control. Returns **false** by default. You can override the default implementation so the window responds to the message and returns **true**.

EvOcCtrlKeyDown

virtual bool EvOcCtrlKeyDown(TCtrlKeyEvent* pev);

Handles the EV_OC_CTRLKEYDOWN message, which is sent by an OCX control. Returns **false** by default. You can override the default implementation so the window responds to the message and returns **true**.

EvOcCtrlKeyUp

virtual bool EvOcCtrlKeyUp(TCtrlKeyEvent* pev);

Handles the EV_OC_CTRLKEYUP message, which is sent by an OCX control. Returns **false** by default. You can override the default implementation so the window responds to the message and returns **true**.

EvOcCtrlMouseDown

virtual bool EvOcCtrlMouseDown(TCtrlMouseEvent* pev);

Handles the EV_OC_CTRLMOUSEDOWN message, which is sent by an OCX control. Returns **false** by default. You can override the default implementation so the window responds to the message and returns **true**.

EvOcCtrlMouseMove

virtual bool EvOcCtrlMouseMove(TCtrlMouseEvent* pev);

Handles the EV_OC_CTRLMOUSEMOVE message, which is sent by an OCX control. Returns **false** by default. You can override the default implementation so the window responds to the message and returns **true**.

EvOcCtrlMouseUp

virtual bool EvOcCtrlMouseUp(TCtrlMouseEvent* pev);

Handles the EV_OC_CTRLMOUSEUP message, which is sent by an OCX control. Returns **false** by default. You can override the default implementation so the window responds to the message and returns **true**.

EvOcCtrlPropertyChange

virtual bool EvOcCtrlPropertyChange(TCtrlPropertyEvent* pev);

Handles the EV_OC_CTRLPROPERTYCHANGE message, which is sent by an OCX control. Returns **false** by default. You can override the default implementation so the window responds to the message and returns **true**.

EvOcCtrlPropertyRequestEdit

virtual bool EvOcCtrlPropertyRequestEdit(TCtrlPropertyEvent* pev);

Handles the EV_OC_PROPERTYREQUESTEDIT message, which is sent by an OCX control. Returns **false** by default. You can override the default implementation so the window responds to the message and returns **true**.

EvOcEvent

LRESULT EvOcEvent(WPARAM wParam, LPARAM lParam);

Responds to a WM_OCEVENT message and subdispatches the message based on *wParam*. ObjectComponents sends WM_OCEVENT messages when it needs to communicate with an OLE-generated event; for example, if a server wants to display toolbars.

EvOcPartInvalid

bool EvOcPartInvalid(TOcPart far&);

Handles a WM_OCEVENT message concerning the embedded or linked object in the document and invalidates the part.

If the *TOleWindow* object is unable to handle the message, *EvOcPartInvalid* returns **false**.

EvOcViewAttachWindow

bool EvOcViewAttachWindow(bool attach);

Attaches the view to its ObjectWindows parent window so that the user can perform open editing on the embedded object, or if the embedded object has been de-activated while in-place editing was occurring.

If the *TOleWindow* object is unable to handle the message, *EvOcViewAttachWindow* returns **false**.

EvOcViewBorderSpaceReq

bool EvOcViewBorderSpaceReq(TRect far*);

Requests that the server create space for a tool bar in the view of an embedded object.

If the *TOleWindow* object is unable to handle the message, *EvOcViewBorderSpaceReq* returns **false**, the default value.

See also   EvOcViewBorderSpaceSet

EvOcViewBorderSpaceSet
bool EvOcViewBorderSpaceSet(TRect far*);
Requests that the server's tool bar be placed in the container's view of an embedded object.

If the *TOleWindow* object is unable to handle the message, *EvOcViewBorderSpaceSet* returns **false**, the default value.

See also   EvOcViewBorderSpaceReq

EvOcViewBreakLink
bool EvOcViewBreakLink(TOcLinkView& view);
EvOcViewBreakLink responds to an OC_VIEWBREAKLINK message that *TOcLinkView* sends when the server document that provides the link shuts down. *EvOcViewBreakLink* breaks the link with a server document or a selection by deleting the *TOleLinkView* associated with the *TOcLinkView* (*view*). Returns **false** if unsuccessful. Doc/View applications use *TOleView*'s *EvOcViewBreakLink*, which overrides *TOleWindow*'s version.

See also   TOleWindow::EvOcViewSetLink, TOleView::EvOcViewBreakLink

EvOcViewClipData
HANDLE EvOcViewClipData(TOcFormat far& format);
Requests clipboard data in the specified format.

If the *TOleWindow* object is unable to handle the message, *EvOcViewClipData* returns **false**.

See also   ocrxxxx Clipboard Constants, TOcFormat

EvOcViewClose
bool EvOcViewClose();
Asks the server to close a currently open document and its associated view.

If the *TOleWindow* object is unable to handle the message, *EvOcViewClose* returns **false**.

EvOcViewDoVerb
bool EvOcViewDoVerb(uint verb);
Handles the EV_OC_VIEWDOVERB message. Returns **false**. Implement your own event handler to control how the window responds to verbs selected by the user.

EvOcViewDrag
bool EvOcViewDrag(TOcDragDrop far&);
Handles an OC_VIEWDRAG message asking the container to provide visual feedback while the user is dragging the embedded object.

If the *TOleWindow* object is unable to handle the message, *EvOcViewDrag* returns **false**.

EvOcViewDrop
bool EvOcViewDrop(TOcDragDrop far&);
Requests a given object be dropped at a specified place on the container's window.

If the *TOleWindow* object is unable to handle the message, *EvOcViewDrop* returns **false**.

EvOcViewGetItemName
bool EvOcViewGetItemName(TOcItemName& item);
Handles the EV_OC_VIEWGETITEMNAME. Returns **false**.

EvOcViewGetPalette
bool EvOcViewGetPalette(LOGPALETTE far* far* palette);
Requests the color palette to draw the object.

If the *TOleWindow* object is unable to handle the message, *EvOcViewGetPalette* returns **false**.

EvOcViewGetScale
bool EvOcViewGetScale(TOcScaleFactor& scaleFactor);
Responds to an OC_VIEWGETSCALE message and gets the scaling for the server object, causing the embedded object to be displayed using the correct scaling value (for example, 120%). *scaleFactor* indicates the scaling factor, the ratio between the size of the embedded object and the size of the site where the object is to be displayed.

If the *TOleWindow* object is unable to handle the message, *EvOcViewGetScale* returns **false**.

See also   Scale, TOcScaleFactor

EvOcViewGetSiteRect
bool EvOcViewGetSiteRect(TRect far* rect);
Gets the size of the rectangle (the site) where the embedded object is to be placed. *rect* refers to the size of the bounding rectangle that encloses the embedded object.

See also   EvOcViewSetSiteRect

EvOcViewInsMenus
bool EvOcViewInsMenus(TOcMenuDescr far&);
Requests that the menus in a composite menu (a menu composed of both the server's and the container's menus).

If the *TOleWindow* object is unable to handle the message, *EvOcViewInsMenus* returns **false**.

EvOcViewLoadPart
bool EvOcViewLoadPart(TOcSaveLoad far* ocLoad);
Requests that an embedded object load itself.

If the *TOleWindow* object is unable to handle the message, *EvOcViewLoadPart* returns **false**.

EvOcViewOpenDoc
bool EvOcViewOpenDoc(const char far*);

Asks the container to open an existing document, which will be used for linking from the embedding site.

If the *TOleWindow* object is unable to handle the message, *EvOcViewOpenDoc* returns **false**.

EvOcViewPaint
bool EvOcViewPaint(TOcViewPaint far&);
Asks the server to paint an object at a given position on a specified device context.

If the *TOleWindow* object is unable to handle the message, *EvOcViewPaint* returns **false**.

EvOcViewPartActivate
bool EvOcViewPartActivate(TOcPart& ocPart);
Notifies ObjectWindows container applications that an embedded object is active. *ocPart* is the embedded object that has been activated. *EvOcViewPartActivate* returns **true** after the embedded object has been activated.

EvOcViewPartInvalid
bool EvOcViewPartInvalid(TOcPart far& changeInfo);
Informs an active container that one of its embedded objects needs to be redrawn. Changes in the container's part should be reflected in any other, non-active views. Returns **true** after all views have been notified of the necessary changes.

If the *TOleWindow* object is unable to handle the message, *EvOcViewPartInvalid* returns **false**.

EvOcViewPartSize
bool EvOcViewPartSize(TRect far*);
The server asks itself the size of its current rectangle and lets the container know about the size of the server's view in pixels.

If the *TOleWindow* object is unable to handle the message, *EvOcViewPartSize* returns **false**.

EvOcViewPasteObject
bool EvOcViewPasteObject(TOcInitInfo& init);
Pastes an OLE object into the document pointed to by the *TOleWindow::OcDoc* data member.

EvOcViewSavePart
bool EvOcViewSavePart(TOcSaveLoad far& ocSave);
Asks the server to write an embedded object's data (the part as represented by the *ocSave* parameter) into storage.

If the *TOleWindow* object is unable to handle the message, *EvOcViewSavePart* returns **false**.

EvOcViewScroll

bool EvOcViewScroll(TOcScrollDir);

Asks the container to scroll the view window and updates any internal state as needed. *EvOcViewScroll* is called when the server is resizing or a drop interaction occurs near the edge of the window.

If the *TOleWindow* object is unable to handle the message, *EvOcViewScroll* returns **false**.

EvOcViewSetLink

bool EvOcViewSetLink(TOcLinkView& view);

Responds to an OC_VIEWSETLINK message *TOcLinkView* sends when the server document provides a link to a container document. *EvOcViewSetLink* establishes the link between a *TOleLinkView* and a *TOcLinkView*. *view* references the view with which the document or selection is associated. Returns **false** if unsuccessful.

Doc/View applications use *TOleView*'s implementation of this function.

See also   TOleWindow::EvOcViewBreakLink, TOleView::EvOcViewSetLink

EvOcViewSetScale

bool EvOcViewSetScale(TOcScaleFactor& scaleFactor);

Responds to an OC_VIEWSETSCALE message and handles the scaling for server application, ensuring that the embedded object is displayed using the correct scaling values (for example, 120%). The server uses this value in its paint procedure when the embedded object needs to be redrawn. *scaleFactor* indicates the scaling factor, the ratio between the size of the embedded object and the size of the site where the object is to be displayed.

If the *TOleWindow* object is unable to handle the message, *EvOcViewSetScale* returns **false**.

See also   EvOcViewGetScale, TOcScaleFactor

EvOcViewSetSiteRect

bool EvOcViewSetSiteRect(TRect far* rect);

Converts the *rect* to logical units. This area, referred to as the *site*, is measured in logical units that take into account any scaling factor. *rect* refers to the size of the bounding rectangle that encloses the embedded object.

See also   EvOcViewGetSiteRect

EvOcViewSetTitle

bool EvOcViewSetTitle(const char far* title);

Sets the window's caption to *title*. The new caption is the name of the in-place active server merged with the caption of the container's window. In the case of an MDI child window, the new caption is the in-place server's name merged with the caption of the MDI child window. When the child window is maximized, the merged caption is appended to the end of the main frame window's caption.

EvOcViewShowTools

bool EvOcViewShowTools(TOcToolBarInfo far& tbi);

Asks the server to provide its tool bars for display in the container's window. Returns **true** if tool bars are supplied.

If the *TOleWindow* object is unable to handle the message, *EvOcViewShowTools* returns **false**.

EvOcViewTitle
const char far* EvOcViewTitle();
Asks the container for the caption in its frame window. Returns the frame window's caption.

EvPaint
void EvPaint();
Sets up the dc for proper scaling and scrolling and then calls the derived class's *Paint* method to paint the contents of the dc.

See also   TGadget::Paint, TPreviewPage::Paint, TUIHandle::Paint, TWindow::Paint

EvRButtonDown
void EvRButtonDown(uint modKeys, TPoint& point);
Responds to a right button down message. Performs additional hit testing to see which embedded object, if any, is being clicked on and displays a local menu with appropriate options for the embedded object.

point refers to the place where the mouse is located. *modKeys* holds the values for a combined key and transaction, such as a *Shift+Double-click* of the mouse button.

See also   EvLButtonDown

EvSetCursor
bool EvSetCursor(HWND hWndCursor, uint hitTest, uint mouseMsg);
Performs hit testing to tell where the cursor is located within the window and what object the cursor is moving over. If the cursor is within an embedded object, *EvSetCursor* changes the shape of the cursor.

When the cursor is over an inactive part and not on a handle, *EvSetCursor* uses an arrow cursor. If the cursor is on one of the handles of the embedded part, *EvSetCursor* changes the cursor to a resizing cursor.

EvSetFocus
void EvSetFocus(HWND hWndLostFocus);
Responds to a change in focus of the window. *hWndLostFocus* contains a handle to the window losing the focus. *EvSetFocus* checks to see if an in-place server exists and, if so, passes the focus to the in-place server.

EvSize
void EvSize(uint sizeType, TSize& size);
Passes the event to *TWindow::EvSize* for normal processing and forwards the event to *TOcView::EvResize* to let a possible in-place server adjust its size.

See also   TOcView::EvSize

EvVScroll
void EvVScroll(uint scrollCode, uint thumbPos, HWND hWndCtl);
In response to a WM_VSCROLL message, *EvVScroll* calls *TWindow::EvVScroll* and invalidates the window.

GetInsertPosition

virtual void GetInsertPosition(TRect& rect);

Gets the position (*rect*) where the embedded object is inserted. You need to override this function if you want to override any default position.

GetLogPerUnit

virtual void GetLogPerUnit(TSize& logPerUnit);

Gets the logical units (typically pixels) per inch for a document so that the document's embedded objects can be painted correctly on the screen device context.

IdleAction

bool IdleAction(long idleCount);

Returns TWindow::IdleAction(idleCount).

InClient

bool InClient(TDC& dc, TPoint& point);

Returns **true** if *point* is inside the client area of the window. Returns **false** otherwise.

Init

void Init();

Initializes the *TOleWindow* object with the appropriate window style and initializes the necessary data members (for example, sets the accelerator ID to IDA_OLEVIEW).

InvalidatePart

virtual void InvalidatePart(TOcInvalidate invalid);

Invalidates the area where the embedded object exists. The server uses this function to tell OLE that the part (the embedded object) has changed. OLE then asks the server to redraw the part into a new metafile so that OLE can redraw the object for the container application even when the server application is not active.

See also   PaintMetafile, TOcView_GetActivePart

PaintLink

virtual bool PaintLink(TDC& dc, bool erase, TRect& rect, TString& moniker);

Repaints part of an object on the given device context. The *erase* parameter is **true** if the background of the part is to be repainted. *rect* indicates the area that needs repainting. *metafile* indicates whether or not the part is a metafile.

By default, *PaintLink* returns **false**. If your application supports working with parts of an object, you should override the *PaintLink* function, providing your own implementation for painting an object part.

For more information, see Step 17 of the OWL tutorial.

PaintParts

virtual bool PaintParts(TDC& dc, bool erase, TRect& rect, bool metafile);

Repaints the embedded objects on the given device context. The *erase* parameter is **true** if the background of the embedded object is to be repainted. *rect* indicates the area that needs repainting. *metafile* indicates whether or not the object is a metafile.

PaintSelection
virtual bool PaintSelection(TDC& dc, bool erase, TRect& rect, void* userData = 0);
Repaints the selected portion of a document on the given device context. The parameter *userData*, which *TocDataProvider* passes to the application, contains information the application uses to repaint the selection. Similar to a moniker, this information tells the application where to find the selection and how to repaint it.

See also   PaintParts, TOleLinkView

PreProcessMsg
bool PreProcessMsg(MSG& msg);
Calls the *TWindow::PreProcessMsg* function. Returns *true* if accelerators are processed. Returns **false** otherwise.

See also   TWindow::PreProcessMsg

Select
virtual bool Select(uint modKeys, TPoint& point);
Selects the embedded object at the specified point (measured in logical units). Returns **true** if the object is captured by the mouse drag; otherwise, returns **false**.

SetScale
virtual void SetScale(uint16 percent);
Sets the ratio of the embedded object's size to the size of the site.

See also   SetupDC

SetSelection
void SetSelection(TOcPart* part);
Selects the embedded object indicated in the *part* parameter. When the embedded object is selected, a selection box is drawn around the area. After an embedded object is selected, the user can perform operations on the embedded object: for example, moving, sizing, or copying the embedded object to the clipboard.

SetupWindow
void SetupWindow();
Establishes a connection between the *TOcView* object and the view's HWND so the view can send notification messages to the window.

See also   TWindow::SetupWindow, TOcView::SetupWindow

ShowCursor
virtual bool ShowCursor(HWND wnd, uint hitTest, uint mouseMsg);
Handles the WM_NCHITTEST message, setting the cursor according to its position on the screen. By default, the cursor is always an arrow. But by overriding the *ShowCursor* function, you can specify the conditions under which the cursor should change and to which bitmap it should change.

HWND is the window containing the cursor, *hitTest* is a constant that represents the current position of the mouse (for a list of possible values, see the WM_NCHITTEST topic), and *mouseMsg* is a constant that represents the current mouse action, such as WM_MOUSEACTIVATE.

For an example of an implementation of the *ShowCursor* function, see Step 17 of the OWL tutorial.

See also   WM_NCHITTEST, WM_MOUSEACTIVATE

VnInvalidateRect
bool VnInvalidateRect(LPARAM p);

When the embedded object is modified, *VnInvalidateRect* sends a message to the View portion of the Doc/View pair. When *TOleWindow* receives this message, the view region is marked for erasing. *VnInvalidateRect* always returns **true**.

TOpenSaveDialog class   opensave.h

TOpenSaveDialog is the base class for modal dialogs that let you open and save a file under a specified name. *TOpenSaveDialog* constructs a *TData* structure and passes it the *TOpenSaveDialog* constructor. Then the dialog is executed (modal) or created (modeless). Upon return, the necessary fields are updated, including an error field that contains 0, or a common dialog extended error.

Public constructors

TOpenSaveDialog
TOpenSaveDialog(TWindow* parent, TData& data, TResId templateId = 0, const char far* title = 0,
    TModule* module = 0);

Constructs an open save dialog box object with the supplied parent window, data, resource ID, title, and current module object.

See also   TData struct

Public member functions

GetFileTitle
static int GetFileTitle(const char far* fileName, char far* fileTitle, int fileTitleLen)

Stores the name of the file to be saved or opened.

GetFileTitleLen
static int GetFileTitleLen(const char far* fileName);

Stores the length of the file name to be saved or opened.

Protected data members

Data
TData& Data;

Stores the file name, its length, extension, filter, initial directory, default file name, extension, and any error messages.

ofn
OPENFILENAME ofn;
Contains the attributes of the file name such as length, extension, and directory. *ofn* is initialized using the fields in the *TOpenSaveDialog::TData class*. This member is not available under Presentation Manager.

See also   TData struct

ShareViMsgId
static uint ShareViMsgId;
Contains the message ID of the registered *ShareViolation* message. This member is not available under Presentation Manager.

See also   TData struct, ShareViolation

Protected constructor

TOpenSaveDialog
TOpenSaveDialog(TWindow* parent, TData& data, TModule* module);
Constructs a *TOpenSaveDialog* box object with the supplied parent, data, and current module object.

See also   TData struct

Protected member functions

CmLbSelChanged
void CmLbSelChanged();
Indicates that the selection state of the file name list box in the *GetOpenFileName* or *GetSaveFileName* dialog boxes has changed. *CmLbSelChanged* is a default handler for command messages sent by *lst1* or *lst2* (the file and directory list boxes, respectively).

CmOk
void CmOk();
Responds to a click on the dialog box's OK button (with the identifier IDOK). Calls *CloseWindow* (passing IDOK).

See also   TDialog::CloseWindow

DialogFunction
bool DialogFunction(uint message, WPARAM, LPARAM);
Returns true if a message is handled, returns *ShareViMsgId* if a sharing violation occurs, otherwise returns false.

DoExecute
int DoExecute();
Creates and executes a modal dialog box.

GetData
TData& GetData();
Retrieves the transfer buffer for the dialog.

GetOFN
OPENFILENAME& GetOFN();
Returns the OPENFILENAME structure.

GetShareViMsgId
static uint GetShareViMsgId();
Returns the sharing violation message ID.

Init
void Init(TResId templateId);
Initializes a *TOpenSaveDialog* object with the current resource ID.

SetData
void SetData(TData& data);
Sets the transfer buffer for the dialog.

SetOFN
void SetOFN(const OPENFILENAME& _ofn);
Sets the OPENFILENAME structure for the dialog.

ShareViolation
virtual int ShareViolation();
If a sharing violation occurs when a file is opened or saved, *ShareViolation* is called to obtain a response. The default return value is OFN_SHAREWARN. Other sharing violation responses are listed in the following table. This member is not available under Presentation Manager.

Constant	Meaning
OFN_SHAREFALLTHROUGH	Specifies that the file name can be used and that the dialog box should return it to the application.
OFN_OFN_SHARENOWARN	Instructs the dialog box to perform no further action with the file name and not to warn the user of the situation.
OFN_SHAREWARN	This is the default response that is defined as 0. Instructs the dialog box to display a standard warning message.

See also   TData struct, ShareViMsgId

Response table entries

The *TOpenSaveDialog* response table has no entries.

TOpenSaveDialog::TData struct   opensave.h

TOpenSaveDialog structure contains information about the user's file open or save selection. Specifically, this structure stores a user-specified file name filter, file extension, file name, the initial directory to use when displaying file names, any error codes, and various file attributes that determine, for example, if the file is a read-only file. The classes *TFileOpenDialog* and *TFileSaveDialog* use the information stored in this structure when a file is opened or saved.

Data members

TData::CustomFilter
char* CustomFilter;
CustomFilter stores the user-specified file filter; for example, *.CPP.

TData::DefExt
char* DefExt;
DefExt stores the default extension.

TData::Error
uint32 Error;
Error contains one or more of the following error codes:

Constant	Meaning
CDERR_DIALOGFAILURE	Failed to create a dialog box.
CDERR_LOCKRESOURCEFAILURE	Failed to lock a specified resource.
CDERR_LOADRESFAILURE	Failed to load a specified resource.
CDERR_LOADSTRFAILURE	Failed to load a specified string.

TData::Flags
uint32 Flags;
Flag contains one or more of the following constants:

Constant	Meaning
OFN_HIDEREADONLY	Hides the read-only check box.
OFN_FILEMUSTEXIST	Lets the user enter only names of existing files in the File Name entry field. If an invalid file name is entered, a warning message is displayed.
OFN_PATHMUSTEXIST	Lets the user enter only valid path names. If an invalid path name is entered, a warning message is displayed.
OFN_NOVALIDATE	Performs no check of the file name and requires the owner of a derived class to perform validation.
OFN_NOCHANGEDIR	Sets the current directory back to what it was when the dialog was initiated.
OFN_ALLOWMULTISELECT	Allows multiple selections in the File Name list box.
OFN_CREATEPROMPT	Asks if the user wants to create a file that does not currently exist.
OFN_EXTENSIONDIFFERENT	Idicates the user entered a file name different from the specified in DefExt. This message is returned to the caller.
OFN_NOREADONLYRETURN	The returned file does not have the Read Only attribute set and is not in a write-protected directory. This message is returned to the caller.
OFN_NOTESTFILECREATE	The file is created after the dialog box is closed. If the application sets this flag, there is no check against write protection, a full disk, an open drive door, or network protection. For certain network environments, this flag should be set.

Constant	Meaning
OFN_OVERWRITEPROMPT	The Save As dialog box displays a message asking the user if it's OK to overwrite an existing file.
OFN_SHAREAWARE	If this flag is set and a call to open a file fails because of a sharing violation, the error is ignored and the dialog box returns the given file name. If this flag is not set, the virtual function ShareViolation is called, which returns OFN_SHAREWARN (by default) or one of the following values:
	OFN_SHAREFALLTHROUGH: File name is returned from the dialog box.
	OFN_SHARENOWARN No further action is taken.
	OFN_SHAREWARN: User receives the standard warning message for this type of error.
OFN_SHOWHELP	Shows the Help button in the dialog box.

TData::FileName
char* FileName;
Holds the name of the file to be saved or opened.

TData::Filter
char* Filter;
Filter holds the filter to use initially when displaying file names.

TData::FilterIndex
int FilterIndex;
FilterIndex indicates which filter to use initially when displaying file names.

TData::InitialDir
char* InitialDir;
InitialDir holds the directory to use initially when displaying file names.

Public member functions

TData::SetFilter
void SetFilter(const char*filter = 0);
Makes a copy of the filter list used to display the file names.

TData::TData
TData(uint32 flags=0, const char* filter=0, char* customFilter=0, char* initialDir=0, char* defExt=0);

Constructor
~TData();
Constructs a *TOpenSaveDialog::TData* structure.

Destructor
Destructs a *TOpenSaveDialog::TData* structure.

See also   TEditFile::FileData

TOutStream class

docview.h

Derived from *TStream* and *ostream*, *TOutStream* is a base class used to create output storage streams for a document.

Public constructor

TOutStream
TOutStream(TDocument& doc, const char far* name, int mode);
Constructs a *TOutStream* object. *doc* refers to the document object, *name* is the user-defined name of the stream, and *mode* is the mode of opening the stream.

See also   TInStream, ofXXXX document open enum, shxxx document sharing enum

TPaintDC class

dc.h

A DC class derived from *TWindowDC* that wraps begin and end paint calls for use in a WM_PAINT response function.

Public data members

Ps
PAINTSTRUCT Ps;
The paint structure associated with this *TPaintDC* object.

See also   PAINTSTRUCT struct

Public constructor and destructor

Constructor
TPaintDC(HWND wnd);
Creates a *TPaintDC* object with the given owned window. The data member *Wnd* is set to *wnd*.

Destructor
~TPaintDC();
Destructor for this class.

See also   TWindowDC::Wnd, TDC::TDC

Protected data members

Wnd
HWND Wnd
The associated window handle.

TPalette class
gdiobjec.h

TPalette is the GDI Palette class derived from *TGdiObject*. The *TPalette* constructors can create palettes from explicit information or indirectly from various color table types that are used by DIBs.

Public constructors

Form 1 | TPalette(HPALETTE handle, TAutoDelete autoDelete = NoAutoDelete);
Creates a *TPalette* object and sets the *Handle* data member to the given borrowed *handle*. The *ShouldDelete* data member defaults to **false**, ensuring that the borrowed handle will not be deleted when the C++ object is destroyed.

Form 2 | TPalette(const TClipboard&);
Creates a *TPalette* object with values taken from the given clipboard.

Form 3 | TPalette(const TPalette& palette);
This public copy constructor creates a complete copy of the given *palette* object as in

```
TPalette myPalette = yourPalette;
```

Form 4 | TPalette(const LOGPALETTE far* logPalette);
Creates a *TPalette* object from the given *logPalette* array.

Form 5 | TPalette(const PALETTEENTRY far* entries, int count);
Creates a *TPalette* object with *count* entries from the given *entries* array.

Form 6 | TPalette(const BITMAPINFO far* info, uint flags = 0);
Creates a *TPalette* object from the color table following the given BITMAPINFO structure. This constructor works only for 2-color, 16-color, and 256-color bitmaps. A handle with value 0 (zero) is returned for other bitmaps, including 24-bit DIBs.

Form 7 | TPalette(const BITMAPCOREINFO far* core, uint flags = 0);
For Presentation Manager (PM) 1.x DIBs only, creates a *TPalette* object from the color table following the given BITMAPCOREINFO structure. This constructor works only for 2-color, 16-color, and 256-color bitmaps. A handle with value 0 (zero) is returned for other bitmaps, including 24-bit DIBs. Note that every color in a PM 1.x table must be present because there is no *ClrUsed* field in the DIB header.

Form 8 | TPalette(const TDib& dib, uint flags = 0);
Creates a *TPalette* object from the given DIB object. The *flags* argument represents the values of the LOGPALETTE data structure used to create the palette.

Form 9 | TPalette();
For Presentation Manager only, creates a *TPalette* object that uses the default system palette.

See also   TClipboard::GetClipboardData, TGdiObject::Handle, TGdiObject::ShouldDelete, TPalette::GetPaletteEntries, PALETTEENTRY struct

Public member functions

AnimatePalette
void AnimatePalette(uint start, uint count, const PALETTEENTRY far* entries);
Replaces entries in this logical palette from the *entries* array of PALETTEENTRY structures. The parameter *start* specifies the first entry to be animated, and *count* gives the number of entries to be animated. The new entries are mapped into the system palette immediately.

GetHandle
THandle GetHandle() const;
Returns the handle of the palette.

GetNearestPaletteIndex
uint GetNearestPaletteIndex(TColor color) const;
Returns the index of the color entry that represents the closest color in this palette to the given *color*.

See also   TColor

GetNumEntries
uint GetNumEntries() const;
Returns the number of entries in this palette, or 0 if the call fails.

See also   TGdiObject::GetObject

GetObject
bool GetObject(uint16 far& numEntries) const;
Finds the number of entries in this logical palette and sets the value in the *numEntries* argument. To find the entire LOGPALETTE structure, use GetPaletteEntries. Returns **true** if the call is successful; otherwise returns **false**.

See also   TGdiObject::GetObject

GetPaletteEntries
uint GetPaletteEntries(uint16 start, uint16 count, PALETTEENTRY far* entries) const;
Retrieves a range of entries in this logical palette and places them in the *entries* array. The *start* parameter specifies the first entry to be retrieved, and *count* gives the number of entries to be retrieved. Returns the number of entries actually retrieved, or 0 if the call fails.

See also   PALETTEENTRY struct

GetPaletteEntry
uint GetPaletteEntry(uint16 index, PALETTEENTRY far& entry) const;
Retrieves the entry in this logical palette at *index* and places it in the *entries* array. Returns the number of entries actually retrieved: 1 if successful or 0 if the call fails.

See also   TPalette::SetPaletteEntry, PALETTEENTRY struct

operator <<
TClipboard& operator << (TClipboard& clipboard, TPalette& palette);

Copies the given *palette* to the given *clipboard* argument. Returns a reference to the resulting Clipboard, which allows normal chaining of <<.

See also   TClipboard

operator HPALETTE()
operator HPALETTE() const;
Typecasting operator. Converts this palette's *Handle* to type HPALETTE, which is the data type representing the handle to a logical palette.

ResizePalette
bool ResizePalette(uint numEntries);
Changes the size of this logical palette to the number given by *numEntries*. Returns **true** if the call is successful; otherwise returns **false**.

See also   TPalette::AnimatePalette

SetPaletteEntries
uint SetPaletteEntries(uint16 start, uint16 count, const PALETTEENTRY far* entries);
Sets the RGB color values in this palette from the *entries* array of PALETTEENTRY structures. The *start* parameter specifies the first entry to be animated, and *count* gives the number of entries to be animated. Returns the number of entries actually set, or 0 if the call fails.

SetPaletteEntry
uint SetPaletteEntry(uint16 index, const PALETTEENTRY far& entry);
Sets the RGB color value at *index* in this palette from the *entry* argument. The *start* parameter specifies the first entry to be animated, and *count* gives the number of entries to be animated. Returns 1, the number of entries actually set if successful, or 0 if the call fails.

See also   PALETTEENTRY struct

THandle
operator THandle() const;
Returns the handle of the palette. TPalette encapsulates an HPALETTE.

ToClipboard
void ToClipboard(TClipboard& clipboard);
Moves this palette to the *target* Clipboard argument. If a copy is to be put on the Clipboard, use *TPalette(myPalette).ToClipboard* ; to make a copy first. The handle in the temporary copy of the object is moved to the clipboard. *ToClipboard* sets *ShouldDelete* to **false** so that the object on the clipboard is not deleted. The handle will still be available for examination.

See also   TClipBoard::SetClipBoardData

UnrealizeObject
bool UnrealizeObject();
Directs the GDI to completely remap the logical palette to the system palette on the next *RealizePalette(HDC)* or *TDC::RealizePalette* call. Returns **true** if the call is successful; otherwise **false**.

See also   TDC::RealizePalette

Protected member functions

Create
Form 1   void Create(const BITMAPINFO far* info, uint flags);

Form 2   void Create(const BITMAPCOREINFO far* core, uint flags);
Sets values in this palette from the given bitmap structure. These functions are usually called by the constructor rather than directly.

See also   BITMAPCOREINFO struct, BITMAPINFO struct

TPaneSplitter class   panespli.h

TPaneSplitter is a class that acts as a container for child windows (called panes) and splitters (pane mover, separator). It supports operations for manipulating panes (add, remove, move, resize, etc) and splitters (drawing, width, etc). Splitters can be moved (thereby resizing the panes) by function call or mouse input. Using the mouse, multiple splitters can be moved simultaneously.

Public constructors

TPaneSplitter
TPaneSplitter(TWindow* parent, const char far* title = 0, int splitterWidth = 0, TModule* module = 0);
Initializes data members.

Public member functions

DelObj
bool DelObj(TDelete dt);
Returns true if the object should be deleted.

ForEachPane
void ForEachPane(TForEachPaneCallback callback, void* p);
Iterates over each pane. If *callback* returns 0, then iteration stops.

GetSplitterWidth
int GetSplitterWidth();
Returns the width of the splitter widget.

MoveSplitter
bool MoveSplitter(TWindow* pane, int dist);
Moves *pane* a given distance. If *pane* does not exist, or there are no splitters, or removal of a pane has failed, then false is returned. Otherwise, true is returned.

PaneCount
int PaneCount();
Returns the number of panes in *TPaneSplitter*.

RemoveAllPanes
void RemoveAllPanes(TDelete dt = TShouldDelete::DefDelete);
Removes all the panes (and their splitters). If any pane can't close, the operation is aborted.

RemovePane
bool RemovePane(TWindow* pane, TDelete dt = TShouldDelete::DefDelete);
Removes a pane from this splitter.

ReplacePane
bool ReplacePane(TWindow* target, TWindow* newPane, TDelete dt = TShouldDelete::DefDelete);
Replaces *target* pane (must exist) with *newPane* (does not exist). *target* may be deleted; it depends on 'dt'.

SetSplitterWidth
int SetSplitterWidth(int newWidth);
Sets the splitter width and adjusts all splitters. Takes effect immediately.

SplitPane
bool SplitPane(TWindow* target, TWindow* newPane, TSplitDirection splitDir);
Splits given *pane, target,* with *newPane,* in either the vertical or horizontal direction. Creates a new splitter.

SwapPanes
bool SwapPanes(TWindow* pane1, TWindow* pane2);
Swaps given panes (must exist). Panes take on each others' layout metrics.

Protected member functions

CleanupWindow
void CleanupWindow();
Removes all panes (and related splitters). Destroys cursors.

DrawSplitter
virtual void DrawSplitter(TDC& dc, const TRect& splitter);
Called by *TSplitter* when it needs to draw itself. The default behavior provided in this base class is to draw a 3dface splitter.

EvSize
void EvSize(uint sizeType, TSize& size);
Sets data member *PaneSplitterResizing* to indicate that contained splitters should adjust themselves according to their percentage.

SetupWindow
void SetupWindow();
Loads cursors and sets *TSplitter*'s pane splitter object.

Response table entries

Response table entry	Member function
EV_WM_SIZE	EvSize

TParaFormat class   richedit.h

TParaFormat encapsulates the PARAFORMAT structure, which contains information about paragraph formatting attributes of a rich edit control.

Public constructors

Form 1 TParaFormat(ulong mask = 0);
Constructs a default *TParaFormat* structure.

Form 2 TParaFormat(const TRichEdit&, ulong mask = CFM_ALL);
Constructs a *TParaFormat* structure whose members are initialized with the paragraph formatting attributes of the current selection of a rich edit control.

Public member functions

SetAlignment
void SetAlignment(uint16);
Sets the alignment option. The 'opt' parameter can be one of the following values:

PFA_LEFT   Paragraphs are aligned with the left margin.
PFA_RIGHT   Paragraphs are aligned with the right margin.
PFA_CENTER   Paragraphs are centered.

SetNumbering
void SetNumbering(uint16);
Sets the numbering options. The only valid parameter is '0' or PFN_BULLET.

SetOffset
void SetOffset(long);
Sets the indentation of the second line and subsequent lines, relative to the starting indentation. The first line is indented if the 'offset' parameter is negative, or outdented if it is positive.

SetRightIndent
void SetRightIndent(long);
Sets the size of the right identation, relative to the right margin.

SetStartIndent
void SetStartIndent(long, bool relative = false);

Sets the indentation of the first line in the paragraph. If the paragraph formatting is being set and the 'relative' parameter is true, the 'start' value is treated as a relative value that is added to the starting indentation of each affected paragraph.

SetTabCount
void SetTabCount(short, long*);
Sets the number and absolute positions of the tab stops.

ToggleMaskBit
void ToggleMaskBit(ulong flag);
Toggles the specified flag in the member which describes which information of the PARAFORMAT structures is valid.

TPen class   gdiobjec.h

TPen is derived from *TGdiObject*. It encapsulates the GDI pen tool. Pens can be constructed from explicit information or indirectly. *TPen* relies on the base class's destructor, *~TGdiObject*.

Public constructors

Form 1   TPen(HPEN handle, TAutoDelete autoDelete = NoAutoDelete);
Creates a *TPen* object and sets the *Handle* data member to the given borrowed *handle*. The *ShouldDelete* data member defaults to false, ensuring that the borrowed handle will not be deleted when the C++ object is destroyed.

Form 2   TPen(TColor color, int width=1, int style=PS_SOLID);
Creates a *TPen* object with the given values. The *width* argument is in device units, but if set to 0, a 1-pixel width is assumed. Sets *Handle* with the given default values. If *color* is black or white, *width* is one, *style* is solid, a stock pen handle is returned. The values for *style* are listed in the following table.

Value	Meaning
PS_SOLID	Creates a solid pen.
PS_DASH	Creates a dashed pen. Valid only when the pen width is one or less in device units.
PS_DOT	Creates a dotted pen. Valid only when the pen width is one or less in device units.
PS_DASHDOT	Creates a pen with alternating dashes dots. Valid only when the pen width is one or less in device units.
PS_DASHDOTDOT	Creates a pen with alternating dashes double-dots. Valid only when the pen width is one or less in device units.
PS_NULL	Creates a null pen.
PS_INSIDEFRAME	Creates a solid pen. When this pen is used in any GDI drawing function that takes a bounding rectangle, the dimensions of the figure will be shrunk so that it fits entirely in the bounding rectangle, taking into account the width of the pen.

Form 3   TPen(const LOGPEN far* logPen);
         Creates a *TPen* object from the given *logPen* values.

Form 4   TPen(const Tpen& pen);
         The *TPen* copy constructor.

Form 5   TPen(uint32 penStyle, uint32 width, const TBrush& brush, uint32 styleCount, uint32 style);
         (32-bit) Creates a *TPen* object with the given values.

Form 6   TPen(uint32 penStyle, uint32 width, const LOGBRUSH& logBrush, uint32 styleCount, uint32 style);
         (32-bit) Creates a *TPen* object with the given values.

See also   TColor, TGdiObject::Handle, TGdiObject::ShouldDelete, LOGBRUSH struct, LOGPEN struct

Public member functions

GetHandle
THandle GetHandle() const;
Returns the handle of the pen with type *HPEN*.

GetObject
bool GetObject(LOGPEN far& logPen) const;
Retrieves information about this pen object and places it in the given *LOGPEN* structure. Returns true if the call is successful, otherwise false.

See also   TGdiObject::GetObject, LOGPEN struct

operator HPEN()
operator HPEN() const;
Typecasting operator. Converts this pen's *Handle* to type *HPEN* (the data type representing the handle to a logical pen).

THandle
operator THandle() const;
Returns the handle of the pen with type *HPEN*.

TPickListDialog class   picklist.h

TPickListDialog allows selection of an item from a list in a dialog with OK and Cancel buttons. An initial string list and selection can be provided. Also, the dialog template and title can be overriden. Strings can be added after construction using *AddString()*. The 0-based selection is returned from *Execute()*, or can be retrieved later using *GetResult()*.

Public constructor and destructor

Constructor
TPickListDialog(TWindow* parent, TStringArray& stringArray, int* result, TModule* module = 0);
Constructor for this class.

Destructor

~TPickListDialog();
Destructor for this class.

Public member functions

AddString
int AddString(const char far* str);
Adds a string to the Strings list, and to the List box if it has already been created.

ClearStrings
void ClearStrings();
Clears all strings from the list.

GetResult
int GetResult() const;
Returns the result of the selection.

Protected member functions

CmCancel
void CmCancel();
User-selected Cancel. Returns < 0. (-1 can't be used since it signals a dialog failure.)

CmOk
void CmOk();
User-selected OK. Gets selection from the listbox and returns it.

SetupWindow
void SetupWindow();
Override from *TDialog*. Adds each string into the listbox.

Response table entries

Response table entry	Member function
EV_COMMAND (IDOK, CmOK)	CmOK
EV_COMMAND (IDCANCEL, CmCancel)	CmCancel
EV_LBN_DBLCLK (IDC_LIST,CmOK)	CmOK

TPickListPopup class
picklist.h

TPickListPopup allows selection of an item from a pop-up list. The list can have an optional title, provided by string or string resource id. Strings can be added after construction using *AddString()*. The 0-based selection is returned from *Execute()*, or can be retrieved later using *GetResult()*.

Public constructors

Form 1 TPickListPopup(TWindow* parent, const char far* title = 0);
Constructs a pop-up menu, adding the title at the top of the menu.

Form 2 TPickListPopup(TWindow* parent, uint titleId);
Constructs a pop-up menu, adding the title from the resource at the top of the menu.

Public member functions

AddString
int AddString(const char far* str);
Adds a string to the pop-up.

ClearStrings
void ClearStrings();
Clears all strings from the pop-up.

Execute
int Execute();
Displays the pop-up menu and returns the command ID of the menu item the user selected.

GetResult
int GetResult() const;
Returns the result of the selection.

Protected member functions

EvCommand
TResult EvCommand(uint id, THandle hWndCtl, uint notifyCode);
Generic handler for WM_COMMAND messages. Result is set to the ID of the menu item clicked.

TPictureWindow class   pictwind.h

TPictureWindow displays a DIB in a window in different ways. The DIB is owned by the window and will be deleted when the window is deleted.

Type definitions

TDisplayHow enum
enum TDisplayHow {UpperLeft = 0, Center, Stretch};

Enumerates the following constants that define the DIB window's properties:

Constant	Meaning
UpperLeft	Displays the DIB in the upper left corner of the window.
Center	Always centered.
Stretch	Stretch or shrink to fit.

Public constructor and destructor

Constructor
TPictureWindow(TWindow* parent, TDib* dib, TDisplayHow = UpperLeft, const char far* title = 0,
    TModule* module = 0);
Constructor for this class. Assumes ownership of the DIB passed in.

Destructor
~TPictureWindow();
Destructor for this class. Deletes the owned DIB.

Public member functions

GetClassName
char far* GetClassName();
Overridden from *TWindow*. Returns a unique name to force *GetWindowClass* to be called.

GetWindowClass
void GetWindowClass(WNDCLASS& wndClass);
Overridden from *TWindow*.

SetDib
TDib* SetDib(TDib* newDib);
Allows changing of the DIB. Returns the old DIB.

SetHowToDisplay
void SetHowToDisplay(TDisplayHow how);
Changes the formatting of the DIB.

Protected member functions

Paint
void Paint(TDC& dc, bool erase, TRect& rect);
Paints the DIB onto the window.

TPidl class

shellitm.h

TPidl is an item identifier list class (ITEMIDLIST). Its constructor takes an ITEMIDLIST* (a.k.a., pidl). The copy constructor and assignement operators supplied function to manipulate the ITEMIDLIST, get the size, get the number of items in the list, etc, supplied. Normally, the programmer will not have to be concerned with ITEMIDLISTs nor with the *TPidl* class. The *TShellItem* class hides all this.

Public constructors and destructor

Constructors

Form 1   TPidl(ITEMIDLIST* pidl = 0);
Constructs a *TPidl* from an ITEMIDLIST* (pidl).

Form 2   TPidl(const TPidl& source);
TPidl copy constructor.

Destructor

virtual ~TPidl();
TPidl destructor.

Public member functions

CopyPidl
ITEMIDLIST* CopyPidl() const;
Copies a pidl (allocates memory with the shell's allocator).

GetItemCount
long GetItemCount() const;
Returns the number of identifiers in the identifier list (pidl).

GetLastItem
TPidl GetLastItem() const;
GetLastItem returns the last item in an identifier list for file system items. This is the rightmost part of a path (e.g., *GetLastItem()* on a pidl representing "c:\\dir1\\dir2\\dir3\\file1") returns "file1").

GetSize
ulong GetSize() const;
GetSize returns the size (in bytes) of the PIDL.

ITEMIDLIST*
operator const ITEMIDLIST* () const;
Uses *TPidl* in place of ITEMIDLIST* (pidl).

ITEMIDLIST**
Form 1   operator ITEMIDLIST** ();
Use to set the ITEMIDLIST*.

Form 2   operator const ITEMIDLIST** () const;

Use *TPidl* in place of ITEMIDLIST** (pinter to pidl) (const).

Next
static ITEMIDLIST* Next(ITEMIDLIST *pidl);
Returns next item id (in the list).

operator !
operator !() const;
Checks to see if *TPidl* represents an ITEMIDLIST. (Returns true if it does not.)

operator =
Form 1   TPidl& operator = (ITEMIDLIST* pidl);
TPidl assignment operator (from an ITEMIDLIST* (pidl)).

Form 2   TPidl& operator = (const TPidl& source);
TPidl assignment operator (from another *TPidl*).

StripLastItem
TPidl StripLastItem() const;
StripLastItem returns a pidl stipped of its last (rightmost) item.

TPopupMenu class   menu.h

TPopupMenu creates an empty pop-up menu to add to an existing window or pop-up menu.

Public constructors

Form 1   TPopupMenu(TAutoDelete autoDelete = AutoDelete);
Constructs an empty pop-up menu.

Form 2   TPopupMenu(HMENU handle, TAutoDelete autoDelete = NoAutoDelete);
Alias constructor for a pop-up menu.

Form 3   TPopupMenu(TMenu& menu, TAutoDelete autoDelete = AutoDelete);
Creates a pop-up menu from an existing menu.

Public member functions

TrackPopupMenu
Form 1   bool TrackPopupMenu(uint flags, int x, int y, int rsvd, HWND wnd, TRect* rect = 0);
Allows the application to create a pop-up menu at the specified location in the specified window. *flags* specifies a screen position and can be one of the TPM_*xxxx* values(TPM_CENTERALIGN, TPM_LEFTALIGN, TPM_RIGHTALIGN, TPM_LEFTBUTTON, or TPM_RIGHTBUTTON). *wnd* is the handle to the window that receives messages about the menu.*x*specifies the horizontal position in screen coordinates of the left side of the menu. *y* species the vertical position in screen coordinates of the top of the menu (for example, 0,0 specifies that a menu's left corner is

in the top left corner of the screen). *rect* defines the area that the user can click without dismissing the menu.

Form 2   bool TrackPopupMenu(uint flags, TPoint& point, int rsvd, HWND wnd, TRect* rect = 0);
This function is the same as the previous *TrackPopupMenu* except that the *x* and *y* positions are specified in *point*.

See also   TPM_ (Windows API)

TPreviewDCBase class   preview.h

TPreviewDCBase is the base class encapsulating a "dual" device context, i.e., a DC which is tied to the screen but responds as if it were tied to a printer or some other device. A dual DC is schizophrenic and maintains two personalities: Dr. Screen and Mr. Printer. When queried about its attributes, a dual DC acts as a printer DC. When requested to modify some attributes, a dual DC acts as both a printer DC and a screen DC. When sent output, a dual DC acts as a screen DC.

Note   The *TPreviewDCBase* provides the basics of a "dual" device context object. However, this base object does not attempt to map the screen DC to correspond to the attributes of the printer's device context.

Public constructors

TPreviewDCBase
TPreviewDCBase(TDC& screen, TPrintDC& printdc);
Constructs a basic Preview DC.

Public member functions

GetAttributeHDC
HDC GetAttributeHDC() const;
Overriden to return printer's HDC.

Protected member functions

PrnDC
TPrintDC& PrnDC;
DC of "real" device (that is, the *TargetDevice*) whose output is being previewed.

TPreviewPage class   preview.h

TPreviewPage displays a page of a document in a print preview window. To obtain the information needed to display the page, *TPreviewPage* interacts with *TPrintPreviewDC* and *TPrintout*. Specifically, it creates a *TPrintPreviewDC* from the window DC provided in *Paint* and passes that *TPrintPreviewDC* object to *TPrintout*'s *SetPrintParams* member function. The sample program PRINT.CPP displays the following print preview window:

Figure 2.1   Sample Print Preview window

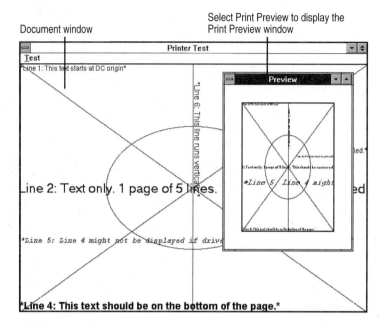

Public constructor

Constructor
TPreviewPage(TWindow* parent, TPrintout& printout, TPrintDC& prndc, TSize& printExtent, int pagenum = 1);
Constructs a *TPreviewPage* object where *parent* is the parent window, printout is a reference to the corresponding *TPrintout* object, *prndc* is a reference to the *TPrintPreviewDC* object, *printExtent* is the extent (width and height) in logical units of the printed page, and *pagenum* is the number of the preview page. *TPreviewPage* has the attributes of a visible child window with a thin border. Sets the background color of the preview page window to white.

Public member functions

GetPageNumber
int GetPageNumber() const;
Retrieves the index of the page currently being previewed (painted) on the preview page window.

Paint
void Paint(TDC& dc, bool, TRect& clip);
Displays the page in the preview window. To determine the preview page's attributes (line width, and so on), *Paint* calls several of *TPrintout's* member functions. Then, to

adjust the printer object for previewing, *Paint* determines if the page fits in the preview window or if clipping is necessary. Finally, *Paint* passes clipping and banding information to *TPrintout's PrintPage* function, which is called to display the page in the preview window.

See also   TPrintout::BeginPrinting, TPrintout::EndPrinting, TPrintout::PrintPage

SetPageNumber
void SetPageNumber(int newNum);
Sets *newNum* to the number of the page currently displayed in the preview window.

Protected data members

PageNum
int PageNum;
Number of the page displayed in the preview window.

PrintDC
TPrintDC& PrintDC;
PrintDC& is a handle to the device context to use for printing.

PrintExtent
TSize PrintExtent;
Contains the extent (width and height) in logical units of the page.

Printout
TPrintout& Printout;
Holds a reference to the *TPrintout* object.

Protected member functions

EvSize
void EvSize(uint sizeType, TSize& size);
Invalidates the entire window when the size of the page displayed in the preview window changes.

Response table entries

Response table entry	Member function
EV_WM_SIZE	EvSize

TPreviewWin class   prevwin.h

TPreviewWin encapsulates a simple preview window frame. It contains one or two preview pages as well as a simple toolbar.

Public constructor and destructor

Constructor
TPreviewWin(TWindow* parentWindow, TPrinter& printer, TPrintout& printout, TWindow& dataWindow, const char far* title, TLayoutWindow* client);
Constructor of a Preview frame window.

Destructor
~TPreviewWin();
Destructor of Preview frame window. Performs general cleanup.

Protected member functions

DataWindow
TWindow& DataWindow;
Window with data being previewed.

FirstPage
int FirstPage;
First Page displayed.

GetNewPreviewPage
virtual TPreviewPage* GetNewPreviewPage(TWindow* parent, TPrintout& printout, TPrintDC& prndc,
     TSize& printExtent, int pagenum = 1);
Returns a pointer to a *TPreviewPage* object.

Note   This default version simply returns a 'true' *TPreviewPage*. However, derived *TPreviewWin* classes can return a more sophisticated preview page (e.g., one that can handle zooming).

LastPage
int LastPage;
Last Page displayed.

LayoutPages
virtual void LayoutPages();
Repositions the preview page(s) using the aspect ratio of the printer when determining the dimensions of the pages.

Page1
TPreviewPage* Page1;
Pointer to the first preview page.

Page2
TPreviewPage* Page2;
Pointer to the second preview page.

PreviewSpeedBar
TControlBar* PreviewSpeedBar;
Pointer to toolbar object.

Printer
TPrinter& Printer;
Printer device object.

PrinterPageSize
TSize PrinterPageSize;
The printer's page size.

Printout
TPrintout& Printout;
Printer document object.

PrnDC
TPrintDC* PrnDC;
Retrieves the device context of the default printer.

SetupWindow
void SetupWindow();
Overriden virtual of *TWindow* to allow preview frame to create the preview page(s).

TPrintDC class   dc.h

Derived from *TDC*, *TPrintDC* provides access to a printer.

Public constructors

Form 1   TPrintDC(HDC handle, TAutoDelete autoDelete = NoAutoDelete);
Creates a *TPrint* object for the DC given by *handle*.

Form 2   TPrintDC(const char far* driver, const char far* device, const char far* output, const DEVMODE far* initData);
Creates a *TPrint* object given print driver, device, output, and data from the DEVMODE structure.

See also   TDC, DEVMODE struct

Public member functions

AbortDoc
int AbortDoc();
Aborts the current print job on this printer and erases everything drawn since the last call to *StartDoc*. *AbortDoc* calls the user-defined function set with *TPrintDC::SetAbortProc* to abort a print job because of error or user intervention. *TPrintDC::EndDoc* should be used to terminate a successfully completed print job.

If successful, *AbortDoc* returns a positive or zero value; otherwise a negative value is returned.

See also   TPrintDC::EndDoc, TPrintDC::SetAbortProc, TPrintDC::Escape

BandInfo

int BandInfo(TBandInfo& bandInfo);

Retrieves information about the banding capabilities of this device, and copies it to the given *bandInfo* structure. Returns 1 if the call is successful; returns 0 if the call fails or if this device does not support banding.

See also   TBandInfo, TPrintDC::Escape

DeviceCapabilities

static uint32 DeviceCapabilities(const char far* driver, const char far* device, const char far* port, int capability, char far* output=0, LPDEVMODE devmode=0);

Retrieves data about the specified *capability* of the named printer *driver*, *device*, and *port*, and places the results in the *output* **char** array. The driver, device, and port names must be zero-terminated strings. The *devmode* argument points to a DEVMODE **struct**. If *devmode* is 0 (the default), *DeviceCapabilities* retrieves the current default initialization values for the specified printer driver; otherwise, it retrieves the values contained in the DEVMODE structure. The format of the *output* array depends on the capability being queried. If *output* is 0 (the default), *DeviceCapabilities* returns the number of bytes required in the *output* array. Possible values for *capability* are as follows:

Value	Meaning
DC_BINNAMES	The function enumerates the paper bins on the given device. If a device driver supports this constant, the *output* array is a data structure that contains two members. The first member is an array identifying valid paper bins:
	short BinList[cBinMax]
	The second member is an array of character strings specifying the bin names:
	char PaperNames[cBinMax][cchBinName]
	If a device driver does not support this value, the *output* array is empty and the return value is NULL.
	If *output* is NULL, the return value specifies the number of bins supported.
DC_BINS	The function retrieves a list of constants that identify the available bins and copies the list to the *output* array. If this array is NULL, the function returns the number of supported bins. The following bin identifiers can be returned:
	DMBIN_AUTO
	DMBIN_CASSETTE
	DMBIN_ENVELOPE
	DMBIN_ENVMANUAL
	DMBIN_FIRST
	DMBIN_LARGECAPACITY
	DMBIN_LARGEFMT
	DMBIN_LAST
	DMBIN_LOWER
	DMBIN_MANUAL
	DMBIN_MIDDLE
	DMBIN_ONLYONE

Value	Meaning
	DMBIN_SMALLFMT
	DMBIN_TRACTOR
	DMBIN_UPPER
DC_DRIVER	The function returns the driver version number.
DC_DUPLEX	The function returns the level of duplex support. The return value is 1 if the function supports duplex output; otherwise it is 0.
DC_ENUMRESOLUTIONS	The function copies a list of available printer resolutions to the *output* array. The resolutions are copied as pairs of int32 integers; the first value of the pair specifies the horizontal resolution and the second value specifies the vertical resolution. If *output* is 0, the function returns the number of supported resolutions.
DC_EXTRA	The function returns the number of bytes required for the device-specific data that is appended to the DEVMODE structure.
DC_FIELDS	The function returns a value indicating which members of the DEVMODE structure are set by the device driver. This value can be one or more of the following constants: DM_ORIENTATION DM_PAPERSIZE DM_PAPERLENGTH DM_PAPERWIDTH DM_SCALE DM_COPIES DM_DEFAULTSOURCE DM_PRINTQUALITY DM_COLOR DM_DUPLEX DM_YRESOLUTION DM_TTOPTION
DC_FILEDEPENDENCIES	The function returns a list of files that must be loaded when the device driver is installed. If *output* is 0 and this value is specified, the function returns the number of file names that must be loaded. If *output* is nonzero, the function returns the specified number of 64-character file names.
DC_MAXEXTENT	The function returns the maximum supported paper-size. These dimensions are returned in a POINT structure; the *x* member gives the maximum paper width and the *y* member gives the maximum paper length.
DC_MINEXTENT	The function returns the minimum supported paper-size. These dimensions are returned in a POINT structure; the *x* member gives the minimum paper width and the *y* member gives the minimum paper length.
DC_ORIENTATION	This function returns the number of degrees that a portrait-oriented paper is rotated counterclockwise to produce landscape orientation. if the return value is 0, there is no landscape orientation. If the return value is 90, the portrait-oriented paper is rotated 90 degrees (as is the case when HP laser printers are used). if the return value is 270, the portrait-oriented paper is rotated 270 degrees (as is the case when dot-matrix printers are used).

Value	Meaning
DC_PAPERNAMES	This function returns a list of supported paper names such as Letter size or Legal size. The *output* array points to an array containing the paper names. If the *output* array is 0, the function returns the number of available paper sizes.
DC_PAPERS	The function retrieves a list of supported paper sizes and copies it to the *output* array. The function returns the number of sizes identified in the array. If *output* is 0, the function returns the number of supported paper sizes.
DC_PAPERSIZE	The function retrieves the supported paper sizes (specified in .1 millimeter units) and copies them to the *output* array.
DC_SIZE	The function returns the size of the DEVMODE structure required by the given device driver.
DC_TRUETYPE	This function returns the printer driver's TrueType font capabilities. The values returned can be one or more of the following constants:
	DCTT_BITMAP: Device supports printing TrueType fonts as graphics. (Dot-matrix and PCL printers)
	DCTT_DOWNLOAD: Device supports downloading TrueType fonts. (PostScript and PCL printers)
	DCTT_SUBDEV: Device supports substituting device fonts for TrueType fonts. (PostScript printers)
DC_VERSION	The function returns the device driver version number.

If *DeviceCapabilities* succeeds, the return value depends on the value of *capability*, as noted above. Otherwise, the return value is GDI_ERROR.

See also   TDC::GetDeviceCaps, DEVMODE struct

EndDoc
int EndDoc();
Ends the current print job on this printer. *EndDoc* should be called immediately after a successfully completed print job. *TPrintDC::AbortDoc* should be used to terminate a print job because of error or user intervention.

If successful, *EndDoc* returns a positive or zero value; otherwise a negative value is returned.

See also   TPrintDC::StartDoc, TPrintDC::AbortDoc, TPrintDC::Escape

EndPage
int EndPage();
Tells this printer's device driver that the application has finished writing to a page. If successful, *EndPage* returns a positive or zero value; otherwise a negative value is returned. Possible failure values are listed below:

Value	Meaning
SP_ERROR	General error.
SP_APPABORT	Job terminated because the application's print-canceling function returned 0.
SP_USERABORT	User terminated the job.
SP_OUTOFDISK	Insufficient disk space for spooling.
SP_OUTOFMEMORY	Insufficient memory for spooling.

See also   TPrintDC::StartPage, TPrintDC::Escape

Escape

int Escape(int escape, int count=0, const void* inData=0, void* outData=0);

Allows applications to access the capabilities of a particular device that are not directly available through the GDI of this DC. The *Escape* call is specified by setting a mnemonic value in the *escape* argument. In Win32 the use of *Escape* with certain *escape* values has been replaced by specific functions. The names of these new functions are based on the corresponding *escape* mnemonic, as shown in the following table:

Value	Action
ABORTDOC	Superseded by *TPrintDC_AbortDoc* in Win32.
BANDINFO	Obsolete in Win32. Because all printer drivers for Windows version 3.1 and later set the text flag in every band, this escape is useful only for older printer drivers.
BEGIN_PATH	No changes for Win32. This escape is specific to PostScript printers.
CLIP_TO_PATH	No changes for Win32. This escape is specific to PostScript printers.
DEVICEDATA	Superseded in Win32. Applications should use the PASSTHROUGH escape to achieve the same functionality.
DRAFTMODE	Superseded in Win32. Applications can achieve the same functionality by setting the dmPrintQuality member of the DEVMODE structure to DMRES_DRAFT and passing this structure to the *CreateDC* function.
DRAWPATTERNRECT	No changes for Win32.
ENABLEDUPLEX	Superseded in Win32. Applications can achieve the same functionality by setting the *dmDuplex* member of the DEVMODE structure and passing this structure to the *CreateDC* function.
ENABLEPAIRKERNING	No changes for Win32.
ENABLERELATIVEWIDTHS	No changes for Win32.
ENDDOC	Superseded by *TPrintDC_EndDoc* in Win32.
END_PATH	No changes for Win32. This escape is specific to PostScript printers.
ENUMPAPERBINS	Superseded in Win32. Applications can use *TPrintDC::DeviceCapabilities* to achieve the same functionality.
ENUMPAPERMETRICS	Superseded in Win32. Applications can use *TPrintDC::DeviceCapabilities* to achieve the same functionality.
EPSPRINTING	No changes for Win32. This escape is specific to PostScript printers.
EXT_DEVICE_CAPS	Superseded in Win32. Applications can use *TDC::GetDeviceCaps* to achieve the same functionality. This escape is specific to PostScript printers.
EXTTEXTOUT	Superseded in Win32. Applications can use *TDC::ExtTextOut* to achieve the same functionality. This escape is not supported by the version 3.1 PCL driver.
FLUSHOUTPUT	Removed for Win32.
GETCOLORTABLE	Removed for Win32.
GETEXTENDEDTEXTMETRICS	No changes for Win32. Support for this escape might change in future versions of Windows.
GETEXTENTTABLE	Superseded in Win32. Applications can use *::GetCharWidth* to achieve the same functionality. This escape is not supported by the version 3.1 PCL or PostScript drivers.
GETFACENAME	No changes for Win32. This escape is specific to PostScript printers.

Value	Action
GETPAIRKERNTABLE	No changes for Win32.
GETPHYSPAGESIZE	No changes for Win32. Support for this escape might change in future versions of Windows.
GETPRINTINGOFFSET	No changes for Win32. Support for this escape might change in future versions of Windows.
GETSCALINGFACTOR	No changes for Win32. Support for this escape might change in future versions of Windows.
GETSETPAPERBINS	Superseded in Win32. Applications can achieve the same functionality by calling *TPrintDC::DeviceCapabilities* to find the number of paper bins, calling *::ExtDeviceMode* to find the current bin, and then setting the *dmDefaultSource* member of the DEVMODE structure and passing this structure to the *CreateDC* function. GETSETPAPERBINS changes the paper bin only for the current device context. A new device context will use the system-default paper bin until the bin is explicitly changed for that device context.
GETSETPAPERMETRICS	Obsolete in Win32. Applications can use *TPrintDC::DeviceCapabilities* and *::ExtDeviceMode* to achieve the same functionality.
GETSETPAPERORIENT	Obsolete in Win32. Applications can achieve the same functionality by setting the *dmOrientation* member of the DEVMODE structure and passing this structure to the *CreateDC* function. This escape is not supported by the Windows 3.1 PCL driver.
GETSETSCREENPARAMS	No changes for Win32.
GETTECHNOLOGY	No changes for Win32. Support for this escape might change in future versions of Windows. This escape is not supported by the Windows 3.1 PCL driver.
GETTRACKKERNTABLE	No changes for Win32.
GETVECTORBRUSHSIZE	No changes for Win32. Support for this escape might change in future versions of Windows.
GETVECTORPENSIZE	No changes for Win32. Support for this escape might change in future versions of Windows.
MFCOMMENT	No changes for Win32.
NEWFRAME	No changes for Win32. Applications should use *::StartPage* and *::EndPage* instead of this escape. Support for this escape might change in future versions of Windows.
NEXTBAND	No changes for Win32. Support for this escape might change in future versions of Windows.
PASSTHROUGH	No changes for Win32.
QUERYESCAPESUPPORT	No changes for Win32.
RESTORE_CTM	No changes for Win32. This escape is specific to PostScript printers.
SAVE_CTM	No changes for Win32. This escape is specific to PostScript printers.
SELECTPAPERSOURCE	Obsolete in Win32. Applications can achieve the same functionality by using *TPrintDC::DeviceCapabilities*.
SETABORTPROC	Superseded in Win32 by *::SetAbortProc*. See *TPrintDC::SetAbortProc*.
SETALLJUSTVALUES	No changes for Win32. Support for this escape might change in future versions of Windows. This escape is not supported by the Windows 3.1 PCL driver.
SET_ARC_DIRECTION	No changes for Win32. This escape is specific to PostScript printers.
SET_BACKGROUND_COLOR	No changes for Win32. Applications should use *::SetBkColor* instead of this escape. Support for this escape might change in future versions of Windows.
SET_BOUNDS	No changes for Win32. This escape is specific to PostScript printers.

Value	Action
SETCOLORTABLE	No changes for Win32. Support for this escape might change in future versions of Windows.
SETCOPYCOUNT	Superseded in Win32. An application should call *TPrintDC::DeviceCapabilities*, specifying DC_COPIES for the *capability* parameter, to find the maximum number of copies the device can make. Then the application can set the number of copies by passing to the *CreateDC* function a pointer to the DEVMODE structure.
SETKERNTRACK	No changes for Win32.
SETLINECAP	No changes for Win32. This escape is specific to PostScript printers.
SETLINEJOIN	No changes for Win32. This escape is specific to PostScript printers.
SETMITERLIMIT	No changes for Win32. This escape is specific to PostScript printers.
SET_POLY_MODE	No changes for Win32. This escape is specific to PostScript printers.
SET_SCREEN_ANGLE	No changes for Win32.
SET_SPREAD	No changes for Win32.
STARTDOC	Superseded in Win32. Applications should call ::*StartDoc* instead of this escape.
TRANSFORM_CTM	No changes for Win32. This escape is specific to PostScript printers.

Escape calls are translated and sent to the printer device driver. The *inData* buffer lets you supply any data needed for the escape. You must set *count* to the size (in bytes) of the *inData* buffer. If no input data is required, *inData* and *count* should be set to the default value of 0. Similarly, you must supply an *outData* buffer for those *Escape* calls that retrieve data. If the escape does not supply output, set *outData* to the default value of 0.

NextBand
int NextBand(TRect& rect);

Tells this printer's device driver that the application has finished writing to a band. The device driver sends the completed band to the Print Manager and copies the coordinates of the next band in the rectangle specified by *rect*.

If successful, *NextBand* returns a positive or zero value; otherwise a negative value is returned. Possible failure values are listed below:

Value	Meaning
SP_ERROR	General error.
SP_APPABORT	Job terminated because the application's print-canceling function returned 0.
SP_USERABORT	User terminated the job.
SP_OUTOFDISK	Insufficient disk space for spooling.
SP_OUTOFMEMORY	Insufficient memory for spooling.

See also   TPrintDC::Escape, TPrintDC::BandInfo

QueryAbort
bool QueryAbort(int rsvd=0);

16-bit applications only. Tries to call the *AbortProc* callback function for this printer to determine if a print job should be aborted or not. *QueryAbort* returns the value returned by *AbortProc* or true if no such callback function exists. true indicates that printing should continue; false indicates that the print job should be terminated. The *rsvd* argument is a reserved value that should be set to 0.

See also   TPrintDC::SetAbortProc, TPrintDC::AbortDoc

QueryEscSupport
uint QueryEscSupport(int escapeNum);
Returns true if the escape specified by *escapeNum* is implemented on this device; otherwise false.

See also   TPrintDC::Escape

SetAbortProc
int SetAbortProc(ABORTPROC proc);
Establishes the user-defined *proc* as the printer-abort function for this printer. This function is called by *TPrintDC::AbortDoc* to cancel a print job during spooling.

SetAbortProc returns a positive (nonzero) value if successful; otherwise it returns a negative (nonzero) value.

See also   TPrintDC::Escape

SetCopyCount
int SetCopyCount(int reqestCount, int& actualCount);
Sets *requestCount* to the number of uncollated copies of each page that this printer should print. The actual number of copies to be printed is copied to *actualCount*. The actual count will be less than the requested count if the latter exceeds the maximum allowed for this device. *SetCopyCount* returns 1 if successful; otherwise, it returns 0.

See also   TPrintDC::DeviceCapabilities, TPrintDC::Escape

StartDoc
int StartDoc(const char far* docName, const char far* output);
Starts a print job for the named document on this printer DC. If successful, *StartDoc* returns a positive value, the job ID for the document. If the call fails, the value SP_ERROR is returned. Detailed error information can be obtained by calling *GetLastError*.

This function replaces the earlier *::Escape* call with value STARTDOC.

See also   TPrintDC::EndDoc, TPrintDC::Escape

StartPage
int StartPage();
Prepares this device to accept data. The system disables *::ResetDC* between calls to *StartPage* and *EndPage*, so that applications cannot change the device mode except at page boundaries. If successful, *StartPage* returns a positive value; otherwise, a negative or zero value is returned.

See also   TPrintDC::EndPage

Protected data members

DocInfo
DOCINFO DocInfo;
Holds the input and output file names used by *TPrintDC::StartDoc*. The DOCINFO structure is defined as follows:

```
typedef struct {
    int cbSize;              // size of the structure, bytes
    DocInfo lpszDocName;     // document name <= 32 chars inc. final 0
    DocInfo lpszOutput;      // output file name
} DOCINFO;
```

The *lpszOutput* field allows a print job to be redirected to a file. If this field is NULL, the output will go to the device for the specified DC.

See also   TPrintDC::StartDoc

Protected member functions

GetDocInfo
DOCINFO& GetDocInfo();
Returns the DOCINFO structure.

SetDocInfo
void SetDocInfo(const DOCINFO& docinfo);
Sets the DOCINFO structure.

TPrintDialog class   printdia.h

TPrintDialog displays a modal print or a print setup dialog box for 16-bit applications. For 32-bit applications, it displays a modal print or a page setup dialog. The print dialog box lets you print a document. The print setup dialog box lets you configure the printer and specify additional print job characteristics. The page setup dialog lets you specify page settings, such as margins, and paper orientation. You can also use *TPrinter* and *TPrintout* to provide support for printer dialog boxes. *TPrintDialog* uses the *TPrintDialog::TData* structure to initialize the dialog box with the user's printer options, such as the number of pages to print, the output device, and so on.

Public constructor

TPrintDialog
TPrintDialog(TWindow* parent, TData& data, const char far* printTemplateName=0,
        const char far* setupTemplateName=0, const char far* title=0, TModule* module=0);
Constructs a print or print setup dialog box with specified data from the *TPrintDialog::TData* struct structure, parent window, window caption, print and setup templates, and module.

Public member functions

DoExecute
int DoExecute();
If no error occurs, *DoExecute* copies flags and print specifications into the *data* argument in the constructor. If an error occurs, *DoExecute* sets the error number of *data* to an error code from *TPrintDialog::TData::Error*.

GetDefaultPrinter
bool GetDefaultPrinter();
Without displaying a dialog box, *GetDefaultPrinter* gets the device mode and name that are initialized for the system default printer.

Protected data members

Data
TData& Data;
Data is a reference to the *TData* object passed in the constructor. The *TData* object contains print specifications such as the number of copies to be printed, the number of pages, the output device name, and so on.

See also   TPrintDialog::TData struct

pd
PRINTDLG pd;
Specifies the dialog box print job characteristics such as page range, number of copies, device context, and so on necessary to initialize the print or print setup dialog box.

See also   TPrintDialog::TData struct

Protected member functions

CmSetup
void CmSetup();
Responds to the click of the setup button with an EV_COMMAND message.

DialogFunction
bool DialogFunction(uint message, WPARAM, LPARAM);
Returns **true** if a message is handled.

See also   TDialog::DialogFunction

GetData
TData& GetData();
Returns the transfer data of the dialog.

GetPD
PRINTDLG& GetPD();
Returns the PRINTDLG structure used by the dialog.

SetData
void SetData(const TData& data);
Sets the transfer data of the dialog.

SetPD
void SetPD(const PRINTDLG& _pd);
Sets the PRINTDLG structure used by the dialog.

Response table entries

The *TPrintDialog* response table has no entries.

TPrintDialog::TData class   printdia.h

TPrintDialog::TData contains information required to initialize the printer dialog box
with the user's print selections. This information consists of the number of copies to be
printed, the first and last pages to print, the maximum and minimum number of pages
that can be printed and various flag values that indicate whether the Pages radio button
is displayed, the Print to File check box is enabled, and so on. *TPrintDialog* uses this
struct to initialize the print dialog box. Whenever the user changes the print
requirements, this struct is updated.

If an error occurs, *TPrintDialog::TData* returns one of the common dialog extended error
codes. *TPrintDialog::TData* also takes care of locking and unlocking memory associated
with the DEVMODE and DEVNAMES structures, which contain information about the
printer driver, the printer, and the output printer port.

TPrinter has access to this information through its data member, *Data*.

See also   TPrintDialog, TPrinter

Public data members

TData::Copies
int Copies;
Copies indicates the actual number of pages to be printed.

TData::DoPageSetup
bool DoPageSetup;
Flag to do page setup.

TData::Error
uint32 Error;

If the dialog box is successfully executed, *Error* returns 0. Otherwise, it contains one of the following error codes.

Constant	Meaning
CDERR_DIALOGFAILURE	Failed to create a dialog box.
CDERR_FINDRESFAILURE	Failed to find a specified resource.
CDERR_INITIALIZATION	Failed to initialize the common dialog box function. A lack of sufficient memory can generate this error.
CDERR_LOCKRESOURCEFAILURE	Failed to lock a specified resource.
CDERR_LOADRESFAILURE	Failed to load a specified resource.
CDERR_LOADSTRFAILURE	Failed to load a specified string.
CDERR_MEMALLOCFAILURE	Unable to allocate memory for internal data structures.
CDERR_MEMLOCKFAILURE	Unable to lock the memory associated with a handle.
CDERR_REGISTERMSGFAIL	A message, designed for the purpose of communicating between two applications, could not be registered.
PDERR_CREATEICFAILURE	*TPrintDialog* failed to create an information context.
PDERR_DEFAULTDIFFERENT	The printer described by structure members doesn't match the default printer. This error message can occur if the user changes the printer specified in the control panel.
PDERR_DNDMMISMATCH	The printer specified in *DevMode* and in *DevNames* is different.
PDERR_GETDEVMODEFAIL	The printer device-driver failed to initialize the *DevMode* structure.
PDERR_INITFAILURE	The *TPrintDialog* structure could not be initialized.
PDERR_LOADDRVFAILURE	The specified printer's device driver could not be loaded.
PDERR_NODEFAULTPRN	A default printer could not be identified.
PDERR_NODEVICES	No printer drivers exist.
PDERR_PARSEFAILURE	The string in the [devices] section of the WIN.INI file could not be parsed.
PDERR_PRINTERNOTFOUND	The [devices] section of the WIN.INI file doesn't contain the specified printer.
PDERR_RETDEFFAILURE	Either *DevMode* or *DevNames* contain zero.
PDERR_SETUPFAILURE	*TPrintDialog* failed to load the required resources.

TData::Flags
uint32 Flags;

Flags, which are used to initialize the printer dialog box, can be one or more of the following values that control the appearance and functionality of the dialog box:

Constant	Meaning
PD_ALLPAGES	Indicates that the All radio button was selected when the user closed the dialog box.
PD_COLLATE	Causes the Collate checkbox to be checked when the dialog box is created.
PD_DISABLEPRINTTOFILE	Disables the Print to File check box.
PD_HIDEPRINTTOFILE	Hides and disables the Print to File check box.
PD_NOPAGENUMS	Disables the Pages radio button and the associated edit control.
PD_NOSELECTION	Disables the Selection radio button.

Constant	Meaning
PD_NOWARNING	Prevents the warning message from being displayed when there is no default printer.
PD_PAGENUMS	Selects the Pages radio button when the dialog box is created.
PD_PRINTSETUP	Displays the Print Setup dialog box rather than the Print dialogbox.
PD_PRINTTOFILE	Checks the Print to File check box when the dialog box is created.
PD_RETURNDC	Returns a device context matching the selections that the user made in the dialog box.
PD_RETURNDEFAULT	Returns DevNames structures that are initialized for the default printer without displaying a dialog box.
PD_RETURNIC	Returns an information context matching the selections that the user made in the dialog box.
PD_SELECTION	Selects the Selection radio button when the dialog box is created.
PD_SHOWHELP	Shows the Help button in the dialog box.
PD_USEDEVMODECOPIES	If a printer driver supports multiple copies, setting this flag causes the requested number of copies to be stored in the dmCopies member of the DevMode structure and 1 in Copies. If a printer driver does not support multiple copies, setting this flag disables the Copies edit control. If this flag is not set, the number 1 is stored in DevMode and the requested number of copies in Copies.

TData::FromPage
int FromPage;
FromPage indicates the beginning page to print.

See also TPrintDialog::TData::ToPage

TData::Margin
TRect Margin;
The initial margins for the paper.

TData::MaxPage
int MaxPage;
MaxPage indicates the maximum number of pages that can be printed.

TData::MinMargin
TRect MinMargin;
The minimum allowable margins of the paper.

TData::MinPage
int MinPage;
MinPage indicates the minimum number of pages that can be printed.

TData::PageSetupFlags
uint32 PageSetupFlags;
Additional page setup dialog flags.

TData::PaperSize
TPoint PaperSize;
The size of the paper that the user has chosen.

TData::ToPage
int ToPage;
ToPage indicates the ending page to print.

See also   TPrintDialog::TData::FromPage

Public member functions

TData::ClearDevMode
void ClearDevMode();
Clears device mode information (information necessary to initialize the dialog controls).

TData::ClearDevNames
void ClearDevNames();
Clears the device name information (information that contains three strings used to specify the driver name, the printer name, and the output port name).

TData::GetDeviceName
const char far* GetDeviceName() const;
Gets the name of the output device.

TData::GetDevMode
const DEVMODE far* GetDevMode() const;
Gets a pointer to a DEVMODE structure (a structure containing information necessary to initialize the dialog controls).

TData::GetDevNames
const DEVNAMES far* GetDevNames() const;
Gets a pointer to a DEVNAMES structure (a structure containing three strings used to specify the driver name, the printer name, and the output port name).

TData::GetDriverName
const char far* GetDriverName() const;
Gets the name of the printer device driver.

TData::GetOutputName
const char far* GetOutputName() const;
Gets the name of the physical output medium.

TData::Lock
void Lock();
Locks memory associated with the DEVMODE and DEVNAMES structures.

TData::Read
void* Read(ipstream& is, uint32 version);
Reads the persistent object from the stream.

TData::SetDevMode
void SetDevMode(const DEVMODE far* devMode);
Sets the values for the DEVMODE structure.

TData::SetDevNames
void SetDevNames(const char far* driver, const char far* device, const char far* output);
Sets the values for the DEVNAMES structure.

TData::TransferDC
TPrintDC* TransferDC();
Creates and returns a *TPrintDC* with the current settings.

TData::Unlock
void Unlock();
Unlocks memory associated with the DEVMODE and DEVNAMES structures.

TData::Write
void Write(opstream& os);
Writes the object to a peristent stream.

TPrinter class   printer.h

TPrinter represents the physical printer device. To print or configure a printer, initialize an instance of *TPrinter*.

Public constructor and destructor

Constructor
TPrinter();
Constructs an instance of *TPrinter* associated with the default printer. To change the printer, call *SetDevice* after the object has been initialized or call *Setup* to let the user select the new device through a dialog box.

Destructor
virtual ~TPrinter();
Frees the resources allocated to *TPrinter*.

Public member functions

ClearDevice
virtual void ClearDevice();
Called by *SetPrinter* and the Destructor, *ClearDevice* disassociates the device with the current printer. *ClearDevice* changes the current status of the printer to PF_UNASSOCIATED, which causes the object to ignore all calls to *Print* until the object is reassociated with a printer.

GetSetup
TPrintDialog::TData& GetSetup();
Returns a reference to the *TPrintDialog* data structure.

GetUserAbort
static bool GetUserAbort();

Returns **true** if the user has chosen to stop printing through the printing dialog. Returns **false** otherwise.

Print
virtual bool Print(TWindow* parent, TPrintout& printout, bool prompt);
Print renders the given printout object on the associated printer device and displays an Abort dialog box while printing. It displays any errors encountered during printing. Prompt allows you to show the user a window.

See also   TPrinter::Error

ReportError
virtual void ReportError(TWindow* parent, TPrintout& printout);
Print calls *ReportError* if it encounters an error. By default, it brings up the system message box with an error string created from the default string table. This function can be overridden to show a custom error dialog box.

Setup
virtual void Setup(TWindow* parent);
Setup lets the user select and/or configure the currently associated printer. *Setup* opens a dialog box as a child of the given window. The user then selects one of the buttons in the dialog box to select or configure the printer. The form of the dialog box is based on *TPrintDialog*, the common dialog printer class.

SetUserAbort
static void SetUserAbort(bool abort=true);
Sets the printing abort flag.

Protected data members

BandRect
TRect BandRect;
BandRect specifies the size of the banding rectangle.

Data
TPrintDialog::TData* Data;
Data is a pointer to the *TPrintDialog* data structure that contains information about the user's print selection.

See also   TPrintDialog::TData struct

Error
int Error;
Error is the error code returned by GDI during printing. This value is initialized during a call to *Print*.

FirstBand
bool FirstBand;
FirstBand is set to **true** if the first band of the print job is being printed, otherwise **false**.

Flags
unsigned Flags;
The *Flags* data member specifies whether the printout bands contain graphics bands, text bands, or both. The valid flag values are enumerated by *TPrintoutFlags*:

```
enum TPrintoutFlags {
    pfGraphics // Current band accepts graphics
    pfText     // Current band accepts text
    pfBoth     // Current band accepts either graphics or text
};
```

PageSize
TSize PageSize;
PageSize specifies the size of the printed page, as specifed in the device context.

UseBandInfo
bool UseBandInfo;
UseBandInfo is set to true if the printer supports banding, otherwise it's set to false.

Protected member functions

CalcBandingFlags
void CalcBandingFlags(TPrintDC& prnDC);
CalcBandingFlags determines if there are either text and graphics bands, and sets data member *Flags* accordingly.

CreateAbortWindow
virtual TWindow* CreateAbortWindow(TWindow* parent, TPrintout& printout);
Creates a printer abort dialog message box.

ExecPrintDialog
virtual bool ExecPrintDialog(TWindow* parent);
Executes a *TPrintDialog*.

GetDefaultPrinter
virtual void GetDefaultPrinter();
Updates the *printer* structure with information about the user's default printer.

SetPrinter
virtual void SetPrinter(const char* driver, const char* device, const char* output);
SetPrinter changes the printer device association. *Setup* calls *SetPrinter* to change the association interactively. The valid parameters to this method can be found in the [devices] section of the WIN.INI file.

Entries in the [devices] section have the following format:

```
<device name>=<driver>, <port> {, <port>}
```

TPrinterAbortDlg class   printer.h

TPrinterAbortDlg is the object type of the default printer-abort dialog box. This dialog box is initialized to display the title of the current printout, as well as the device and port currently used for printing.

TPrinterAbortDlg expects to have three static text controls, with control IDs of 101 for the title, 102 for the device, and 103 for the port. These controls must have "%s" somewhere in the text strings so that they can be replaced by the title, device, and port. The dialog-box controls can be in any position and tab order.

Public constructor

TPrinterAbortDlg(TWindow* parent, TResId resId, const char far* title, const char far* device, const char far* port);
Constructs an Abort dialog box that contains a Cancel button and displays the given title, device, and port.

Protected member functions

CmCancel
void CmCancel();
Handles the print-cancel button by setting the user print abort flag in the application.

SetupWindow
void SetupWindow();
Overrides *SetupWindow*. This function disables the Close system menu option.

Protected data members

PrnDC
HDC PrnDC;
Device context to print on.

TPrintout class   printer.h

TPrintout represents the physical printed document that is to sent to a printer to be printed. *TPrintout* does the rendering of the document onto the printer. Because this object type is abstract, it cannot be used to print anything by itself. For every document, or document type, a class derived from *TPrintout* must be created and its *PrintPage* function must be overridden.

Public constructor and destructor

Constructor
TPrintout(const char far* title);
Constructs an instance of *TPrintOut* with the given title.

Destructor
virtual ~TPrintout();
Destroys the resources allocated by the constructor.

Public member functions

BeginDocument
virtual void BeginDocument(int startPage, int endPage, unsigned flags);
The printer object's *Print* function calls *BeginDocument* once before printing each copy of
a document. The *flags* field indicates if the current print band accepts graphics, text, or
both.

The default *BeginDocument* does nothing. Derived objects can override *BeginDocument* to
perform any initialization needed at the beginning of each copy of the document.

See also   TPrintoutFlags enum

BeginPrinting
virtual void BeginPrinting();
The printer object's *Print* function calls *BeginPrinting* once at the beginning of a print job,
regardless of how many copies of the document are to be printed. Derived objects can
override *BeginPrinting* to perform any initialization needed before printing.

EndDocument
virtual void EndDocument();
The printer object's *Print* function calls *EndDocument* after each copy of the document
finishes printing. Derived objects can override *EndDocument* to perform any needed
actions at the end of each document.

EndPrinting
virtual void EndPrinting();
The printer object's *Print* function calls *EndPrinting* after all copies of the document
finish printing. Derived objects can override *EndPrinting* to perform any needed actions
at the end of each document.

GetDialogInfo
virtual void GetDialogInfo(int& minPage, int& maxPage, int& selFromPage, int& selToPage);
Retrieves information needed to allow the printing of selected pages of the document
and returns **true** if page selection is possible. Use of page ranges is optional, but if the
page count is easy to determine, *GetDialogInfo* sets the number of pages in the
document. Otherwise, it sets the number of pages to 0 and printing will continue until
HasPage returns **false**.

GetTitle
const char far* GetTitle() const;
Returns the title of the current printout.

HasPage
virtual bool HasPage(int pageNumber);
HasPage is called after every page is printed. By default, it returns **false**, indicating that only one page is to be printed. If the document contains more than one page, this function must be overridden to return **true** while there are more pages to print.

PrintPage
virtual void PrintPage(int page, TRect& rect, unsigned flags);
PrintPage is called for every page (or band, if *Banding* is **true**) and must be overridden to print the contents of the given page. The *rect* and *flags* parameters are used during banding to indicate the extent and type of band currently requested from the driver (and should be ignored if *Banding* is false). *page* is the number of the current page.

SetPrintParams
virtual void SetPrintParams(TPrintDC* dc, TSize pageSize);
SetPrintParams sets DC to *dc* and *PageSize* to *pageSize*. The printer object's *Print* function calls *SetPrintParams* to obtain the information it needs to determine pagination and page count. Derived objects that override *SetPrintParams* must call the inherited function.

See also TPreviewPage::Paint

WantBanding
bool WantBanding() const;
Returns the value of data member *Banding*.

WantForceAllBands
bool WantForceAllBands() const;
Returns the value of data member *ForceAllBands*.

Type definitions   printer.h

TPrintoutFlags enum
enum{pfGraphics, pfText, pfBoth};
ObjectWindows defines the following banding constants used to set flags for printout objects.

Constant	Meaning
pfGraphics	Current band accepts only graphics.
pfText	Current band accepts only text.
pfBoth	Current band accepts both text and graphics.

See also TPrinter, TPrintOut

Protected data members

Banding
bool Banding;

If *Banding* is **true**, the printout is banded and the *PrintPage* function is called once for every band. Otherwise, *PrintPage* is called only once for every page. Banding a printout is more memory- and time-efficient than not banding. By default, *Banding* is set to **false**.

DC
TPrintDC* DC;

DC is the handle to the device context to use for printing.

ForceAllBands
bool ForceAllBands;

Many device drivers do not provide all printer bands if both text and graphics are not performed on the first band (which is typically a text-only band). Leaving *ForceAllBands* **true** forces the printer driver to provide all bands regardless of what calls are made in the *PrintPage* function. If *PrintPage* does nothing but display text, it is more efficient for *ForceAllBands* to be **false**. By default, it is true. *ForceAllBands* takes effect only if *Banding* is **true**.

PageSize
TSize PageSize;

PageSize is the size of the print area on the printout page.

Title
const char far* GetTitle( ) const;

Returns the title of the current printout.

TPrintPreviewDC class
preview.h

Derived from *TPrintDC*, *TPrintPreviewDC* maps printer device coordinates to logical screen coordinates. It sets the extent of the view window and determines the screen and printer font attributes. Many of *TPrintPreviewDC's* functions override *TDC's* virtual functions.

Public constructor and destructor

Constructor
TPrintPreviewDC(TDC& screen, TPrintDC& printdc, const TRect& client, const TRect& clip);

TPrintPreviewDC's constructor takes a screen DC as well as a printer DC. The screen DC is passed to the inherited constructor while the printer DC is copied to the member, *PrnDC*.

Destructor
~TPrintPreviewDC();

Destroys a *TPrintPreviewDC* object.

Public member functions

GetDeviceCaps
int GetDeviceCaps(int index) const;
GetDeviceCaps returns capability information, such as font and pitch attributes, about the printer DC. The *index* argument specifies the type of information required.

See also TDC::GetDeviceCaps

LPtoSDP
Form 1 bool LPtoSDP(TPoint* points, int count = 1) const;
Converts each of the *count* points in the *points* array from logical points of the printer DC to screen points. Returns a nonzero value if the call is successful; otherwise, returns 0.

Form 2 bool LPtoSDP(TRect& rect) const;
Converts each of the points in the *rect* from logical points of the printer DC to screen device points. Returns a nonzero value if the call is successful; otherwise, returns 0.

See also TPrintPreviewDC::SDPtoLP, TDC::LPtoDP

OffsetViewportOrg
bool OffsetViewportOrg(const TPoint& delta, TPoint far* oldOrg = 0);
Modifies this DC's viewport origin relative to the current values. The *delta* x- and y-components are added to the previous origin and the resulting point becomes the new viewport origin. The previous origin is saved in *oldOrg*. Returns nonzero if the call is successful; otherwise, returns 0.

See also TPrintPreviewDC::SetViewportOrg, TDC::OffsetViewportOrg

ReOrg
virtual void ReOrg();
Gets the x- and y- extents of the viewport, equalizes the logical and screen points, and resets the x- and y- extents of the viewport.

ReScale
virtual void ReScale();
Maps the points of the printer DC to the screen DC. Sets the screen window extent equal to the maximum logical pointer of the printer DC.

RestoreFont
void RestoreFont();
Restores the original GDI font object to this DC.

See also TPrintPreviewDC::SelectObject, TDC::OrgFont

ScaleViewportExt
bool ScaleViewportExt(int xNum, int xDenom, int yNum, int yDenom, TSize far* oldExtent = 0);
Modifies this DC's viewport extents relative to the current values. The new extents are derived as follows:

$$xNewVE = (xOldVE * xNum) / xDenom$$

$$yNewVE = (yOldVE * yNum) / yDenom$$

The previous extents are saved in *oldExtent*. Returns nonzero if the call is successful; otherwise returns 0.

See also TDC::ScaleViewportExt, TPrintPreviewDC::SetViewportExt

ScaleWindowExt
bool ScaleWindowExt(int xNum, int xDenom, int yNum, int yDenom, TSize far* oldExtent = 0);
Modifies this DC's window extents relative to the current values. The new extents are derived as follows:

$$xNewWE = (xOldWE * xNum) / xDenom$$

$$yNewWE = (yOldWE * yNum) / yDenom$$

The previous extents are saved in *oldExtent*. Returns nonzero if the call is successful; otherwise returns 0.

See also TDC::SetWindowExt, TPrintPreviewDC::ScaleWindowExt

SDPtoLP
Form 1   bool SDPtoLP(TPoint* points, int count = 1) const;
Converts each of the *count* points in the *points* array from screen device points to logical points of the printer DC. Returns a nonzero value if the call is successful; otherwise, returns 0.

Form 2   bool SDPtoLP(TRect& rect) const;
Converts each of the points in the *rect* from screen device points to logical points of the printer DC. Returns a nonzero value if the call is successful; otherwise, returns 0.

See also TPrintPreviewDC::LPtoSDP, TDC::DPtoLP

SelectObject
void SelectObject(const TFont& newFont);
Selects the given font object into this DC.

See also TPrintPreviewDC::SelectStockObject, TDC::SelectObject

SelectStockObject
void SelectStockObject(int index);
Retrieves a handle to a predefined stock font.

See also TDC::SelectStockObject

SetBkColor
TColor SetBkColor(TColor color);
Sets the current background color of this DC to the given *color* value or the nearest available. Returns 0x80000000 if the call fails.

See also TDC::SetBkColor

SetMapMode
int SetMapMode(int mode);
Sets the current window mapping mode of this DC to *mode*. Returns the previous mapping mode value. The mapping mode defines how logical coordinates are mapped to device coordinates. It also controls the orientation of the device's x- and y-axes.

See also TDC::GetMapMode, TDC::SetMapMode

SetTextColor

TColor SetTextColor(TColor color);
Sets the current text color of this DC to the given *color* value. The text color determines the color displayed by *TDC::TextOut* and *TDC::ExtTextOut*.

See also   TDC::GetTextColor, TDC::SetTextColor

SetViewportExt

bool SetViewportExt(const TSize& extent, TSize far* oldExtent = 0);
Sets the screen's viewport x- and y-extents to the given *extent* values. The previous extents are saved in *oldExtent*. Returns nonzero if the call is successful; otherwise, returns 0. The *extent* value determines the amount of stretching or compression needed in the logical coordinate system to fit the device coordinate system. *extent* also determines the relative orientation of the two coordinate systems.

See also   TDC::GetViewportExt, TDC::SetViewportExt

SetViewportOrg

bool SetViewportOrg(const TPoint& origin, TPoint far* oldOrg=0);
Sets the printer DC's viewport origin to the given *origin* value, and saves the previous origin in *oldOrg*. Returns nonzero if the call is successful; otherwise returns 0.

See also   TPrintPreviewDC::OffsetViewportOrg, TDC::GetViewportOrg, TDC::SetViewportOrg

SetWindowExt

bool SetWindowExt(const TSize& extent, TSize far* oldExtent=0);
Sets the DC's window x- and y-extents to the given *extent* values. The previous extents are saved in *oldExtent*. Returns nonzero if the call is successful; otherwise, returns 0. The *extent* value determines the amount of stretching or compression needed in the logical coordinate system to fit the device coordinate system. *extent* also determines the relative orientation of the two coordinate systems.

See also   TDC::GetWindowExt, TDC::SetWindowExt, TPrintPreviewDC::ScaleWindowExt

SyncFont

virtual void SyncFont();
Sets the screen font equal to the current printer font.

Protected data members

CurrentPreviewFont

TFont* CurrentPreviewFont;
The current view font.

PrnDC

TPrintDC& PrnDC;
Holds a reference to the printer DC.

PrnFont
HFONT PrnFont;
The current printer font.

Protected member functions

GetAttributeHDC
HDC GetAttributeHDC() const;
Returns the attributes of the printer DC (*PrnDC*).

See also   TDC::GetAttributeHDC

TPropertyPage class   propsht.h

The *TPropertyPage* object represents a dialog box found within a property sheet. Each 'page' contains controls for setting a group of related properties. Each page has a tab that the user can select to bring the page to the foreground of the property sheet.

Public constructors and destructor

Constructors
Form 1   TPropertyPage(TPropertySheet* parent, TResId resid, const char far*title, TResId iconRes, TModule* module)
Constructor for *TPropertyPage*.

Form 2   TPropertyPage(TPropertySheet* parent, const PROPSHEETPAGE& pgInfo, TModule* module);
Constructor to create a property page object using the information stored in the *pgInfo* parameter.

Destructor
~TPropertyPage();
Destructor of *TPropertyPage*. Cleans up allocated buffers used when ObjectWindows provides implementation of property pages.

Public member functions

Create
bool Create();
Creates the page.

CreatePropertyPage
HPROPSHEETPAGE CreatePropertyPage();
CreatePropertyPage is called by the *Sheet* object requesting the page to return a handle used to represent this dialog when it's inserted into the *Sheet*.

DestroyPropertyPage
bool DestroyPropertyPage();
Destroys the page represented by this object.

DialogFunction

virtual bool DialogFunction(uint msg, TParam1 p1, TParam2 p2);

As with *TDialog*, most of the page's events are dispatched directly from *StdWndProc*. Although the *Sheet* has each page's *DialogProc*, the notifications are not (or don't seem to be) funneled directly to the *dialogProc*.

EvNotify

virtual TResult EvNotify(uint id, TNotify far& notifyInfo);

WM_NOTIFY handler: Scans for property sheet notifications to 'patch' the 'idFrom' member to the predefined *PropPageID*.

Note   This is necessary because WM_NOTIFY subdispatching relies on the ID of the sender.

GetPageInfo

void GetPageInfo(PROPSHEETPAGE& pgInfo) const;

'GetPageInfo' is called by the 'Sheet' object requesting the page to fill out a 'PROPSHEETPAGE' structure that describes the attributes of the page.

HPROPSHEETPAGE

operator HPROPSHEETPAGE() const;

Returns the HPROPSHEETPAGE handle representing an underlying PropertyPage.

Note   This method is only functional when the Common Control library provides the underlying implementation of PropertyPages.

Note   The 'CreatePropertyPage' method also returns the HPROPSHEETPAGE. However, it will attempt to create the page if the latter had not been created beforehand. The HPROPSHEETPAGE operator simply returns the page handle without attempting to create the page.

SetIcon

Form 1   void SetIcon(TResId iconResId);

Specifies the icon to be used for this page.

Note   This routine must be invoked before the page is created.

Form 2   void SetIcon(const TIcon&);

Specifies the icon to be used for this page.

Note   This routine must be invoked before the page is created.

SetTitle

Form 1   void SetTitle(int txtResId);

Sets the caption of this page.

Note   This routine must be invoked before the page is created.

Form 2   void SetTitle(const char far*);

Sets the caption of this page.

Note   This routine must be invoked before the page is created.

Protected member functions

HPropPage
HPROPSHEETPAGE HPropPage;
Handle of this property page.

PageInfo
PROPSHEETPAGE PageInfo;
A structure that holds information about this dialog when it is inserted into a *PropertySheet*.

UseNative
bool UseNative;
Flags if native implementation is used.

Response table entries

Response table entry	Member function
EV_COMMAND(CM_EDITCONVERT, CmEditConvert)	CmEditConvert
EV_COMMAND(CM_EDITCOPY, CmEditCopy)	CmEditCopy
EV_COMMAND(CM_EDITCUT, CmEditCut)	CmEditCut
EV_COMMAND(CM_EDITDELETE, CmEditDelete)	CmEditDelete
EV_COMMAND(CM_EDITINSERTCONTROL, CmEditInsertControl)	CmEditInsertControl
EV_COMMAND(CM_EDITINSERTOBJECT, CmEditInsertObject)	CmEditInsertObject
EV_COMMAND(CM_EDITLINKS, CmEditLinks)	CmEditLinks
EV_COMMAND(CM_EDITPASTE, CmEditPaste)	CmEditPaste
EV_COMMAND(CM_EDITPASTELINK, CmEditPasteLink)	CmEditPasteLink
EV_COMMAND(CM_EDITPASTESPECIAL, CmEditPasteSpecial)	CmEditPasteSpecial
EV_COMMAND(CM_EDITSHOWOBJECTS, CmEditShowObjects)	CmEditShowObjects
EV_COMMAND(CM_EXIT, CmFileClose)	CmFileClose
EV_COMMAND_ENABLE(CM_EDITCONVERT, CeEditConvert)	CeEditConvert
EV_COMMAND_ENABLE(CM_EDITCOPY, CeEditCopy)	CeEditCopy
EV_COMMAND_ENABLE(CM_EDITCUT, CeEditCut)	CeEditCut
EV_COMMAND_ENABLE(CM_EDITDELETE, CeEditDelete)	CeEditDelete
EV_COMMAND_ENABLE(CM_EDITINSERTCONTROL, CeEditInsertControl)	CeEditInsertControl
EV_COMMAND_ENABLE(CM_EDITINSERTOBJECT, CeEditInsertObject)	CeEditInsertObject
EV_COMMAND_ENABLE(CM_EDITLINKS, CeEditLinks)	CeEditLinks
EV_COMMAND_ENABLE(CM_EDITOBJECT, CeEditObject)	CeEditObject
EV_COMMAND_ENABLE(CM_EDITPASTE, CeEditPaste)	CeEditPaste
EV_COMMAND_ENABLE(CM_EDITPASTELINK, CeEditPasteLink)	CeEditPasteLink
EV_COMMAND_ENABLE(CM_EDITPASTESPECIAL, CeEditPasteSpecial)	CeEditPasteSpecial

Response table entry	Member function
EV_COMMAND_ENABLE(CM_EDITSHOWOBJECTS, CeEditShowObjects)	CeEditShowObjects
EV_COMMAND_ENABLE(CM_EXIT, CeFileClose)	CeFileClose
EV_DROPFILES	EvDropFiles
EV_HSCROLL	EvHScroll
EV_MESSAGE(WM_OCEVENT, EvOcEvent)	EvOcEvent
EV_OC_VIEWATTACHWINDOW	EvOcViewAttachWindow
EV_OC_VIEWBORDERSPACEREQ	EvOcViewBorderSpaceReq
EV_OC_VIEWBORDERSPACESET	EvOcViewBorderSpaceSet
EV_OC_VIEWBREAKLINK	EvOcViewBreakLink
EV_OC_VIEWCLIPDATA,	EvOcViewclipData
EV_OC_VIEWCLOSE	EvOcViewClose
EV_OC_VIEWDRAG	EvOcViewDrag
EV_OC_VIEWDROP	EvOcViewDrop
EV_OC_VIEWGETPALETTE	EvOcViewGetPalette
EV_OC_VIEWGETSCALE	EvOcViewGetScale
EV_OC_VIEWGETSITERECT	EvOcViewGetSiteRect
EV_OC_VIEWINSMENUS	EvOcViewInsMenus
EV_OC_VIEWLOADPART	EvOcViewLoadPart
EV_OC_VIEWOPENDOC	EvOcViewOpenDoc
EV_OC_VIEWPAINT	EvOcViewPaint
EV_OC_VIEWPARTINVALID	EvOcViewPartInvalid
EV_OC_VIEWPARTSIZE	EvOcViewPartSize
EV_OC_VIEWPASTEOBJECT	EvOcViewPasteObject
EV_OC_VIEWSAVEPART	EvOcViewSavePart
EV_OC_VIEWSCROLL	EvOcViewScroll
EV_OC_VIEWSETLINK	EvOcViewSetLink
EV_OC_VIEWSETSCALE	EvOcViewSetScale
EV_OC_VIEWSETSITERECT	EvOcViewSetSiteRect
EV_OC_VIEWSETTITLE	EvOcViewSetTitle
EV_OC_VIEWSHOWTOOLS,	EvOcViewshowTools
EV_OC_VIEWTITLE	EvOcViewTitle
EV_OWLNOTIFY(vnInvalidate)	VnInvalidateRect
EV_WM_LBUTTONDBLCLK	EvLButtonDblClk
EV_WM_LBUTTONDOWN	EvLButtonDown
EV_WM_LBUTTONUP	EvLButtonUp
EV_WM_MDIACTIVATE	EvMDIActivate
EV_WM_MOUSEMOVE	EvMouseMove
EV_WM_PAINT	EvPaint
EV_WM_RBUTTONDOWN	EvRButtonDown
EV_WM_SETCURSOR	EvSetCursor

FALSE, the property sheet sends the PSN_APPLY notification message to all pages. Returns true if all pages successfully applied the changes, or false otherwise.

CancelToClose
void CancelToClose();
Disables the 'Cancel' button and changes the text of the 'OK' button to 'Close'. You must invoke this method after applying a change that cannot be canceled.

DoExecute
int DoExecute();
Executes the sheet.

Execute
int Execute();
Updates the member that contains the window handle of the sheet's parent and then executes the sheet via a call to *DoExecute*.

FirstPageThat
TPropertyPage* FirstPageThat(TCondPageFunc cond, void* paramList = 0);
Applies the specified 'test' function to each *TPropertyPage* of the sheet and returns the first page which causes the 'test' function to return true. Returns '0' if no page meets the condition.

ForEachPage
void ForEachPage(TActionPageFunc action, void* paramList = 0);
Applies the specified 'action' function to each *TPropertyPage* child of the sheet.

GetPageCount
int GetPageCount() const;
Retrieves the number of pages within a particular sheet.

GetTabControl
HWND GetTabControl() const;
Retrieves the handle to a tab control of a property sheet.

IndexOfPage
int IndexOfPage(TPropertyPage* page) const;
Returns the index of the specified page, or '-1' if the specified page could not be found in the child list of the sheet object.

IsDialogMessage
bool IsDialogMessage(MSG far& msg);
Passes a message to a property sheet dialog box and indicates whether the dialog processed the message. Returns true if the message was processed or false otherwise.

PageAtIndex
TPropertyPage* PageAtIndex(int index) const;
Returns the *TPropertyPage** object representing the page at the specified index.

PageChanged
void PageChanged(const TPropertyPage&);

Informs the sheet that information in a sheet has changed. The sheet enables the 'Apply' button.

PageUnchanged
void PageUnchanged(const TPropertyPage&);
Informs the sheet that the information in the specified page has reverted to the previously saved state. The sheet disables the 'Apply' button if no other pages have registered changes with the property sheet.

PressButton
void PressButton(int button);
Simulates the choice of a property sheet button. The button parameter can be one of the following:

- PSBTN_APPLYNOW Apply Now button
- PSBTN_BACK Back button
- PSBTN_CANCEL Cancel button
- PSBTN_FINISH Finish button
- PSBTN_HELP Help button
- PSBTN_NEXT Next button
- PSBTN_OK OK button

QuerySiblings
int QuerySiblings(TParam1, TParam2);
Forwards the 'PSM_QUERYSIBLINGS' message to each page in the property sheet. If a page returns a nonzero value, the property sheet does not send the message to subsequent pages. Returns the nonzero value from a page in the property sheet, or zero if no page returns a nonzero value.

RebootSystem
void RebootSystem();
Indicates that the system needs to be restarted for the changes to take effect. You should invoke this method only in response to the PSN_APPLY or PSN_KILLACTIVE notifications.

Note It's your responsibility to reboot the system (via *ExitWindowEx*, for example).

Note Invoking this method causes the *TPropertySheet::Execute* method to return ID_PSREBOOTSYSTEM.

RemovePage
Form 1 void RemovePage(int pgIndex);
Removes the page from the property sheet at the specified index.

Form 2 void RemovePage(const TPropertyPage&);
Removes the specified page from the property sheet.

RestartWindows
void RestartWindows();

Indicates that the system needs to be restarted for the changes to take effect. You should invoke this method only in response to the PSN_APPLY or PSN_KILLACTIVE notifications.

Note It's your responsibility to reboot the system (via *ExitWindowEx* for example).

Note Invoking this method causes the *TPropertySheet::Execute* method to return ID_PSRESTARTWINDOWS.

SelectPage
Form 1   bool SelectPage(TResId pgRes);

Activates the page with the specified resource identifier. Returns true if successful or false otherwise.

Note The page that's losing activation receives a PSN_KILLACTIVE notification while the window that's gaining activation receives a PSN_SETACTIVE notification.

Form 2   bool SelectPage(int pgIndex);

Activates the page at the specified index in the property sheet. Returns true if successful or false otherwise.

Note The page that's losing activation receives a PSN_KILLACTIVE notification while the window that's gaining activation receives a PSN_SETACTIVE notification.

Form 3   bool SelectPage(const TPropertyPage&);

Activates the specified page in the property sheet. Returns true if successful or false otherwise.

Note The page that's losing activation receives a PSN_KILLACTIVE notification while the window that's gaining activation receives a PSN_SETACTIVE notification.

SetCaption
void SetCaption(const char far* title);

Updates the caption of the property sheet.

SetFinishText
void SetFinishText(const char far* txt);

Sets the text for the 'Finish' button in a Wizard property sheet.

Note The button is enabled while the 'Next' and 'Back' buttons are hidden.

SetTitle
void SetTitle(const char far* txt, uint32 style = PSH_PROPTITLE);

Sets the title of a property sheet. If 'style' parameter is the PSH_PROPTITLE value, the prefix "Properties of" is included with the specified title ('txt') parameter.

SetupWindow
void SetupWindow();

Updates the style/size of the dialog [PropertyPage].

Protected member functions

HeaderInfo
PROPSHEETHEADER HeaderInfo;

Holds information necessary to create the property sheet.

UseNative
bool UseNative;
Flags if native implementation is used.

TPXPictureValidator class   validate.h

TPXPictureValidator objects compare user input with a picture of a data format to determine the validity of entered data. The pictures are compatible with the pictures Borland's Paradox relational database uses to control data entry. For a complete description of picture specifiers, see the *Picture* member function.

Public constructors

TPXPictureValidator
TPXPictureValidator(const char far* pic, bool autoFill=false);
Constructs a picture validator object by first calling the constructor inherited from *TValidator* and setting *pic* to point to it. Then sets the *voFill* bit in *Options* if *AutoFill* is true and sets *Options* to *voOnAppend*. Throws a *TXValidator* exception if the picture is invalid.

Public member functions

Adjust
int Adjust(string& text, uint& begPos, uint& endPos, int amount);
Adjusts the 'value' of the text, given a cursor position and an amount. Returns the actual amount adjusted.

Error
void Error();
Overrides *TValidator's* virtual function and displays a message box that indicates an error in the picture format and displays the string pointed to by *Pic*.

See also   TValidator::Error

IsValid
bool IsValid(const char far* str);
IsValid overrides *TValidator's* virtual function and compares the string passed in *str* with the format picture specified in *Pic*. *IsValid* returns true if *Pic* is NULL or if *Picture* returns *Complete* for *str*, indicating that *str* needs no further input to meet the specified format; otherwise, it returns false.

See also   TPXPictureValidator::Picture

IsValidInput
bool IsValidInput(char far* str, bool suppressFill);
IsValidInput overrides *TValidator's* virtual function and checks the string passed in *str* against the format picture specified in *Pic*. *IsValid* returns true if *Pic* is NULL or *Picture*

does not return *Error* for *str*; otherwise, it returns false. The *suppressFill* parameter overrides the value in *voFill* for the duration of the call to *IsValidInput*.

If *suppressFill* is false and *voFill* is set, the call to *Picture* returns a filled string based on *str*, so the image in the edit control automatically reflects the format specified in *Pic*.

See also   TPXPictureValidator::Picture

Picture
virtual TPicResult Picture(char far* input, bool autoFill=false);

Formats the string passed in *input* according to the format specified by the picture string pointed to by *Pic*. *Picture* returns *prError* if there is an error in the picture string or if *input* contains data that cannot fit the specified picture. Returns *prComplete* if *input* can fully satisfy the specified picture. Returns *prIncomplete* if *input* contains data that incompletely fits the specified picture.

The following characters are used in creating format pictures:

Type of character	Character	Description
Special	#	Accept only a digit
	?	Accept only a letter (case_insensitive)
	&	Accept only a letter, force to uppercase
	@	Accept any character
	!	Accept any character, force to uppercase
Match	;	Take next character literally
	*	Repetition count
	[]	Option
	{}	Grouping operators
	,	Set of alternatives
	All others	Taken literally

See also   TPicResultenum

Protected data members

Pic
string Pic;

Points to a string containing the picture that specifies the format for data in the associated edit control. The constructor sets *Pic* to a string that is passed as one of the parameters.

Protected member functions

GetPic
const string& GetPic() const;

Returns the picture mask used by the validator.

SetPic
void SetPic(const string& pic);
Sets the picture mask for the validator.

TRadioButton class   radiobut.h

Defines an interface object that represents a corresponding radio button element in Windows. Use *TRadioButton* to create a radio button control in a parent *TWindow* object. A *TRadioButton* object can also be used to facilitate communication between your application and the radio button controls of a *TDialog* object.

Radio buttons have two states: checked and unchecked. *TRadioButton* inherits its state management member functions from its base class, *TCheckBox*. Optionally, a radio button can be part of a group (*TGroupBox*) that visually and logically groups its controls. *TRadioButton* is a streamable class.

Public constructors

Form 1   TRadioButton(TWindow* parent, int id, const char far* title, int x, int y, int w, int h, TGroupBox *group = 0, TModule* module = 0);
Constructs a radio button object with the supplied parent window (*parent*), control ID (*id*), associated text (*title*), position (*x, y*) relative to the origin of the parent window's client area, width (*w*), height (*h*), and associated group box (*group*). Invokes the TCheckBox constructor with similar parameters. The style is set to WS_CHILD | WS_VISIBLE | BS_AUTORADIOBUTTON.

Form 2   TRadioButton(TWindow* parent,int resourceId,TGroupBox *group, TModule* module = 0);
Constructs a *TRadioButton* object to be associated with a radio button control of a TDialog object. Invokes the *TCheckBox* constructor with identical parameters. The *resourceId* parameter must correspond to a radio button resource that you define.

See also   TControl::TControl

Protected member functions

BNClicked
void BNClicked();
Responds to an incoming BN_CLICKED message.

See also   BN_xxxx Button Message Constants

GetClassName
char far* GetClassName();
Returns "BUTTON", the name of the predefined radio button class.

Response table entries

Response table entry	Member function
EV_MESSAGE (BM_SETSTYLE, BMSetStyle)	BMSetStyle
EV_WM_GETDLGCODE	EvGetDlgCode

TRangeValidator class   validate.h

Determines whether the data typed by a user falls within a designated range of integers. *TRangeValidator* is a streamable class.

Public constructor

TRangeValidator
TRangeValidator(long min, long max);
Constructs a range validator object by first calling the constructor inherited from *TFilterValidator*, passing a set of characters containing the digits '0'..'9' and the characters '+' and '-'. Sets Min to *min* and Max to *max*, establishing the range of acceptable long integer values.

See also   TFilterValidator::TFilterValidator

Public member functions

Adjust
int Adjust(string& text, uint& begPos, uint& endPos, int amount);
Adjusts the 'value' of the text, given a cursor position and an amount. Returns the actual amount adjusted.

Error
void Error();
Overrides *TValidator*'s virtual function and displays a message box indicating that the entered value does not fall within the specified range.

IsValid
bool IsValid(const char far* str);
Converts the string *str* into an integer number and returns **true** if the result meets all three of these conditions:

- It is a valid integer number.

- Its value is greater than or equal to *min*.

- Its value is less than or equal to *max*.

- If any of those tests fails, *IsValid* returns **false**.

Transfer
uint Transfer(char far* str, void* buffer, TTransferDirection direction);
Incorporates the three types, *tdSizeData*, *tdGetData*, and *tdSetData*, that a range validator can handle for its associated edit control. The parameter *str* is the edit control's string value, and *buffer* is the data passed to the edit control. Depending on the value of *direction*, *Transfer* either sets *str* from the number in *buffer* or sets the number at *buffer* to the value of the string *str*. If *direction* is *tdSetData*, *Transfer* sets *str* from *buffer*. If *direction* is *tdGetData*, *Transfer* sets *buffer* from *str*. If *direction* is *tdSizeData*, *Transfer* neither sets nor reads data.

Transfer always returns the size of the data transferred.

See also   TTransferDirection enum, TWindow::Transfer

Protected data members

Max
long Max;
Max is the highest valid **long** integer value for the edit control.

Min
long Min;
Min is the lowest valid **long** integer value for the edit control.

Protected member functions

GetMax
long GetMax();
Returns the maximum number the validator can accept.

GetMin
long GetMin();
Returns the minimum number the validator can accept.

SetMax
void SetMax(long max);
Sets the maximum number the validator can accept.

SetMin
void SetMin(long min);
Sets the minimum number the validator can accept.

TRecentFiles class   rcntfile.h

TRecentFiles implements a most-recent files list, designed to be mixed in with TApplication. The list is appended to the menu with CM_FILEOPEN and CM_FILECLOSE options.

Public constructors

Constructor
TRecentFiles(const char far* iniName, int numSavedFiles = MaxMenuItems);
Constructor to initialize the external storage and the maximum number of items to save in the most-recently-used (MRU) list.

Destructor
~TRecentFiles();
Deletes the allocated profile.

Public member functions

GetMenuText
bool GetMenuText(int id, char far* text, int maxTextLen);
Retrieves the text of the choice based on the ID.

SaveMenuChoice
void SaveMenuChoice(const char far* text);
Saves the menu choice into the profile.

SetMaxMruItems
void SetMaxMruItems(int max);
Sets the maximum number of items that can be saved with this MRU.

Protected member functions

AddMruItem
void AddMruItem(const char far* text);
Adds an item to the top of the MRU list. If there is a duplicate, the item is moved from its current position to the top of the list.

CeExit
void CeExit(TCommandEnabler& ce);
Reads information in the *TProfile* to display the menu choices.

CmFile
void CmFile(uint id);
Responds to a menu item selection.

ExistMruItem
bool ExistMruItem(const char far* text);
Returns true if there are any items in the MRU list that match the text.

GetExitMenuPos
int GetExitMenuPos(HMENU hMenu);
Retrieves the menu position of the CM_EXIT menu item. Returns -1 if not found.

GetMenuPos
int GetMenuPos(HMENU hMenu, uint id);
Searches the menu to find the position of a menu item.

GetMruCount
int GetMruCount();
Returns the number of files that are currently in the MRU list.

GetMruItemIndex
int GetMruItemIndex(const char far* text);
Returns the index of the MRU item containing text. Returns -1 if not found.

InsertMruItemsToMenu
void InsertMruItemsToMenu(HMENU hMenu);
Reads external information and adds the MRU items into the menu. Adds a separator between the MRU items and the exit menu item.

MruItemsInsertedIntoMenu
bool MruItemsInsertedIntoMenu(HMENU hMenu);
Returns true if the menu has any MRU items in it.

RemoveMruIndex
void RemoveMruIndex(int index);
Removes the MRU item at index. Shuffles the items below index up.

RemoveMruItemsFromMenu
void RemoveMruItemsFromMenu(HMENU hMenu);
Removes the MRU items from the menu.

TRegion class   gdiobjec.h

TRegion, derived from *TGdiObject*, represents GDI abstract shapes or regions. *TRegion* can construct region objects with various shapes. Several operators are provided for combining and comparing regions.

Type definition

enum TEllipse
enum TEllipse{Ellipse};
Defines the class-specific constant *Ellipse*, used to distinguish the ellipse constructor from the rectangle copy constructor.

See also   TRegion::TRegion

Public constructors

Form 1   TRegion();

The default constructor creates an empty *TRegion* object. *Handle* is set to 0 and *ShouldDelete* is set to **true**.

Form 2   TRegion(HRGN handle,TAutoDelete autoDelete = NoAutoDelete);
Creates a *TRegion* object and sets the *Handle* data member to the given borrowed *handle*. The *ShouldDelete* data member defaults to **false**, ensuring that the borrowed handle is not deleted when the C++ object is destroyed. *HRGN* is the data type representing the handle to an abstract shape.

Form 3   TRegion(const TRegion& region);
This public copy constructor creates a copy of the given *TRegion* object as in:
TRegion myRegion = yourRegion;

Form 4   TRegion(const TRect& rect);
Creates a region object from the given *TRect* object as in:

```
TRegion myRegion(rect1);
TRegion* pRegion;
pRegion = new TRegion(rect2);
```

Form 5   TRegion(const TRect& E, TEllipse);
Creates the elliptical *TRegion* object that inscribes the given rectangle *E*. The *TEllipse* argument distinguishes this constructor from the *TRegion(const TRect& rect)* constructor.

Form 6   TRegion(const TRect& rect, const TSize& corner);
Creates a *TRegion* object from the given *rect* corner.

Form 7   TRegion(const TPoint* points,int count,int fillMode);
Creates a filled *TRegion* object from the polygons given by *points* and *fillMode*.

Form 8   TRegion(const TPoint* points, const int* polyCounts, int count,int fillMode);
Creates a filled *TRegion* object from the polygons given by *points* and *fillMode*.

See also   TGdiObject::Handle, TGdiObject::ShouldDelete, TPoint, TRect, TSize

Public member functions

Contains
bool Contains(const TPoint& point) const;
Returns **true** if this region contains the given point.

See also   TPoint

GetHandle
THandle GetHandle() const;
Returns the handle of the region with type HREGION.

GetRgnBox
Form 1   int GetRgnBox(TRect& box) const;

Finds the bounding rectangle (the minimum rectangle containing this region). The resulting rectangle is placed in *box* and the returned values are as follows:

Value	Meaning
COMPLEXREGION	Region has overlapping borders.
NULLREGION	Region is empty.
SIMPLEREGION	Region has no overlapping borders.

Form 2   TRect GetRgnBox() const;
Returns the resulting rectangle.

See also   TRect

operator ==
bool operator ==(const TRegion& other) const;
Returns **true** if this region is equal to the *other* region.

See also   TRegion::operator !=

operator !=
bool operator !=(const TRegion& other) const;
Returns **true** if this region is not equal to the *other* region.

See also   TRegion::operator ==

operator =
TRegion& operator =(const TRegion& source);
Assigns the *source* region to this region. A reference to the result is returned, allowing chained assignments.

operator +=
TRegion& operator +=(const TSize& delta);
Adds the given *delta* to each point of this region to displace (translate) it by *delta.x* and *delta.y*. Returns a reference to the resulting region.

See also   TSize, TRegion::operator -=

operator -=
Form 1   TRegion& operator -=(const TSize& delta);

Form 2   TRegion& operator -=(const TRegion& source);
The first form subtracts the given *delta* from each point of this region to displace (translate) it by *-delta.x* and *-delta.y*. The second form creates a "difference" region consisting of all parts of this region that are not parts of the *source* region. Both forms return a reference to the resulting region.

See also   TSize, TRegion::operator +=

operator &=
Form 1   TRegion& operator &=(const TRegion& source);

Form 2   TRegion& operator &=(const TRect& source);

Creates the intersection of this region with the given *source* region or rectangle, and returns a reference to the result.

See also   TRect

operator |=

Form 1   TRegion& operator |=(const TRegion& source);

Form 2   TRegion& operator |=(const TRect& source);
Creates the union of this region and the given *source* region or rectangle, and returns a reference to the result.

See also   TRect

operator ^=

Form 1   TRegion& operator ^=(const TRegion& source);

Form 2   TRegion& operator ^=(const TRect& source);
Creates the union of this region and the given *source* region or rectangle, but excludes any overlapping areas. Returns a reference to the resulting region object.

See also   TRect

operator HRGN()
operator HRGN() const;
Typecast operator. *HRGN* is the data type representing the handle to a physical region.

SetRectRgn
void SetRectRgn(const TRect& rect);
Creates a rectangle of the size given by *rect*.

See also   TRect

THandle
operator THandle() const;
Returns the handle of the region with type HREGION.

Touches
bool Touches(const TRect& rect) const;
Returns **true** if this region touches the given rectangle.

See also   TRect

TRegisterOcxWnd class   oledialg.h

Registers an OCX window for a subsequent call to the *TOLEDialog::SetupWindow* function.

Public constructor and destructor

Constructor
TRegisterOcxWnd(HINSTANCE);

Class for registering and unregistering OCX window classes.

Destructor
~TRegisterOcxWnd();
Unregisters OCX window.

Protected member functions

HAppInst
HINSTANCE HAppInst;

TReplaceDialog class   findrepl.h

TReplaceDialog creates a modeless dialog box that lets the user enter a selection of text to replace. Because these are model dialog boxes, you can search for text, edit the text in the window, and return to the dialog box to enter another selection. *TReplaceDialog* uses the *TFindReplaceDialog::TData* class to set the user-defined values for the dialog box, such as the text strings to search for and replace.

Public constructors

TReplaceDialog
TReplaceDialog(TWindow* parent, TData& data, TResID templateName=0, const char far* title=0,
    TModule* module=0);
Constructs a *TReplaceDialog* object with a parent window, resource ID, template name, caption, and module instance. The *data* parameter is a reference to the *TFindReplaceDialog::TData* class that contains information about the appearance and functionality of the dialog box, such as the user-entered text strings to search for and replace.

See also   TFindReplaceDialog::TData

Protected member functions

DoCreate
HWND DoCreate();
Creates a modeless find and replace dialog box.

See also   TDialog::DoCreate

TReqResize class   commctrl.h

TReqResize is a structure sent with EN_REQUESTRESIZE notification.

Public member functions

operator NMHDR&
operator NMHDR&();

Allows the notification structure to be transparently treated as an NMHDR structure, thereby eliminating the need to explicitly refer to the NMHDR data member (which is always the first member of notification structures).

TResponseTableEntry class   eventhan.h

A template class, *TResponseTableEntry* lets you define a pattern for entries into a response table. Entries consist of a message, a notification code, a resource ID, a dispatcher type, and a pointer to a member function.

See DECLARE_RESPONSE_TABLE and DEFINE_RESPONSE_TABLE for additional information about the macros in the response tables.

Public data members

Dispatcher
TAnyDispatcher Dispatcher;

An abstract dispatcher type that points to one of the dispatcher functions.

Id
uint Id;

Contains the menu or accelerator resource ID (CM_xxxx) for the message response member function.

Msg
uint Msg;

Contains the ID of the message sent. These can be command messages, child id messages, notify-based messages such as LBN_SELCHANGE, or messages such as LBUTTONDOWN.

NotifyCode
uint NotifyCode;

Stores the control notification code (for example, ID_LISTBOX) for the response table entry. These can be button, combo box, edit control, or list box notification codes.

Pmf
PMF Pmf;

Points to the actual handler or member function.

Type definitions

T
typedef void(T_*PMF)();

Type for a generic member function that responds to notification messages. *T* is the template for the response table.

TRichEdit class   richedit.h

TRichEdit encapsulates a rich edit control, a window in which a user can enter, edit, and format text.

Type definitions

TFmtStatus enum
enum TFmtStatus {No, Yes, Partly};

TFmtStatus enumerates the flags that can be returned when querrying a RichEdit control. This is useful to determine the status of a particular character attribute for a chunk of selected text.

Table 2.21   Format status constants

Constant	Meaning if set
No	The whole selection has the attribute.
Yes	The attribute is absent from the selection.
Partly	Part of the selection has the attribute.

Public constructors

TRichEdit
TRichEdit(TWindow* parent, int id, const char far* text, int x, int y, int w, int h, const char far* fileName = 0,
        TModule* module = 0);

Constructor for a *TRichEdit* object. By default, edit control has a border and its text is left-justified. Multiline edit control has horizontal vertical scroll bars.

Public member functions

ChangeCharPointSize
bool ChangeCharPointSize(int pointSizeDelta);

Increases or decreases (using a positive or negative value, respectively) the point size of the current selection.

FindText
Form 1   int FindText(uint flags, const TCharRange far&, const char far* text);

Finds text within the rich edit control. The 'flags' parameter can be a combination of the following values:

FT_MATCHCASE   Performs a case sensitive search.

FT_MATCHWORD   Matches whole words.

Form 2   int FindText(uint flags, const TFindText far&);
Finds text within the rich edit control. The 'flags' parameter can be a combination of the following values:

FT_MATCHCASE   Performs a case sensitive search.

FT_MATCHWORD   Matches whole words.

GetCharFormat
ulong GetCharFormat(TCharFormat far&, bool selection = false) const;
Retrieves the current character formatting in an edit control. If 'selection' parameter is 'true', the attribute of the current selection is retrieved. Otherwise, the default formatting attribute is retrieved.

GetParaFormat
ulong GetParaFormat(TParaFormat far&) const;
Retrieves the paragraph formatting of the current selection of the rich edit control.

Note   If more than one paragraph is selected, the structure receives the attributes of the first paragraph, and the dwMask member specifies which attributes are consistent throughout the entire selection.

GetSelectedText
int GetSelectedText(char far* buffer) const;
Retrieves the currently-selected text of the rich edit control.

GetSelection
void GetSelection(uint& startPos, uint& endPos) const;
Retrieves the starting and ending character position of the selection in the rich edit control.

GetSelectionType
ulong GetSelectionType() const;
Returns the selection type of the rich edit control. Returns SEL_EMPTY if the selection is empty, or one or more of the following values:

Value	Contents of the selection
SEL_TEXT	Text
SEL_OBJECT	At least one OLE object
SEL_MULTICHAR	More than one character of text
SEL_MULTIOBJECT	More than one OLE object

GetSelRange
void GetSelRange(TCharRange far&) const;
Retrieves the starting and ending character positions of the selection of the rich edit control.

GetSubText
virtual void GetSubText(char far* str, uint startPos, uint endPos) const;
Retrieves a specified range of text from the rich edit control.

GetTextRange

Form 1   int GetTextRange(const TCharRange far&, char far* buffer) const;
Retrieves a specified range of text from the rich edit control.

Form 2   int GetTextRange(TTextRange far&) const;
Retrieves a specified range of text from the rich edit control.

HasCharAttribute

uint HasCharAttribute(ulong mask, ulong effects);
Function returns whether or not the current selection has a particular attribute. The 'mask' identifies the attribute of interest. The 'effects' contains the state of the attributes. The function returns

- *TFmtStatus::Yes*: if the attribute is enabled.

- *TFmtStatus::No*: if the attribute is absent.

- *TFmtStatus::Partly*: if the attribute is partly present.

HasSelection

bool HasSelection() const;
Returns true if the rich edit control has an active selection. Returns false otherwise.

HideSelection

void HideSelection(bool hide, bool changeStyle);
Shows or hides the selection in the rich edit control. The 'hide' parameter specifies whether to hide or show the selection. If it is 'false' the selection is shown. Otherwise, the selection is hidden. The 'changeStyle' parameter specifies whether to change the control's ES_NOHIDESEL window style. If this parameter is 'false', the selection is temporarily shown or hidden. Otherwise, the style is changed. If this parameter is 'true' and the control has the focus, the selection is hidden or shown as appropriate.

LimitText

void LimitText(long max);
Sets an upper limit to the amount of text in the rich edit control.

SetBkgndColor

TColor SetBkgndColor(const TColor& = TColor::None);
Sets the background color of the rich edit control.

Note   If *TColor::None* is specified, the color is set to the window background system color.

SetCharFormat

bool SetCharFormat(const TCharFormat far&, uint flags= SCF_SELECTION);

Sets the character formatting of a rich edit control. The 'flags' parameter can be one of the following:

SCF_SELECTION — Applies the formatting to the current selection, or sets the default formatting if the selection is empty.

SCF_WORD — Applies the formatting to the selected word or words. If the selection is empty but the insertion point is inside a word, the formatting is applied to the word. . This value must be used in conjunction with the SCF_SELECTION value.

SetParaFormat
bool SetParaFormat(const TParaFormat far&);
Sets the paragraph formatting of the current selection of the rich edit control.

SetSelection
bool SetSelection(uint startPos, uint endPos);
Selects a range of characters in the rich edit control.

SetSelRange
int SetSelRange(const TCharRange far&);
Selects a range of characters in the rich edit control.

ToggleCharAttribute
bool ToggleCharAttribute(ulong mask, ulong effects);
Toggles a set of character attributes. The 'mask' identifies the attributes of interest while 'effects' identifies the state of the attributes.

Protected member functions

CmCharsEnable
void CmCharsEnable(TCommandEnabler& commandHandler);
This function is called for the Clear menu item to determine whether or not the item is enabled.

CmEditClear
void CmEditClear();
Handles the CM_EDITCLEAR command; invokes the 'Clear' method.

CmEditCopy
void CmEditCopy();
Handles the CM_EDITCOPY command; invokes the 'Copy' method.

CmEditCut
void CmEditCut();
Handles the CM_EDITCUT command; invokes the 'Cut' method.

CmEditDelete
void CmEditDelete();
Handles the CM_EDITDELETE command; invokes the 'DeleteSelection'.

CmEditPaste
void CmEditPaste();
Handles the CM_EDITPASTE command; invokes the 'Paste' method.

CmEditUndo
void CmEditUndo();
Handles the CM_EDITUNDO command; invokes the 'Undo' method.

CmModEnable
void CmModEnable(TCommandEnabler& commandHandler);
This function is called for the Undo menu item to determine whether or not the item is enabled.

CmPasteEnable
void CmPasteEnable(TCommandEnabler& commandHandler);
This function is called for the Paste menu item to determine whether or not the item is enabled.

CmSelectEnable
void CmSelectEnable(TCommandEnabler& commandHandler);
This function is called for Cut/Copy/Delete menu items to determine whether or not the item is enabled.

ENErrSpace
void ENErrSpace();
Child ID notification handled at the child.

EvChar
void EvChar(uint key, uint repeatCount, uint flags);
WM_CHAR handler to bypass *TEdit*'s handler (which caters to validators).

EvGetDlgCode
uint EvGetDlgCode(MSG far*);
WM_GETDLGCODE handler to bypass *TEdit*'s handler (which caters to validators).

EvKeyDown
void EvKeyDown(uint key, uint repeatCount, uint flags);
WM_KEYDOWN handler to bypass *TEdit*'s handler (which caters to validators).

EvKillFocus
void EvKillFocus(HWND hWndGetFocus);
WM_KILLFOCUS handler to bypass *TEdit*'s handler (which caters to validators).

EvSetFocus
void EvSetFocus(HWND hWndLostFocus);
WM_SETFOCUS handler to bypass *TEdit*'s handler (which caters to validators).

GetClassName
char far* GetClassName();
Returns name of predefined Windows edit class.

SetupWindow
void SetupWindow();
Limits the amount of text that an edit control can have to the value of *TextLimit*.

TRichEdit helper classes

TCharFormat

TCharRange

TParaFormat

TFormatRange

TEditStream

TTextRange

TFindText

TEnDropFiles

TRichEditPreviewFrame

TRichEditPagePreview

TRichEditPrintout

TSelChange

TRichEditPagePreview class   richedpr.h

TRichEditPagePreview is a window which displays rich edit data formatted for a
particular printer DC.

Public constructor

TRichEditPagePreview
TRichEditPagePreview(TWindow* parent, TPrintout& printout, TPrintDC& prndc, TSize& printExtent,
    int pagenum = 1);
Constructor of *RichEdit PagePreview* object.

Protected member functions

Paint
void Paint(TDC& dc, bool, TRect& clip);
WM_PAINT handler of *RichEdit PagePreview* window. Displays a preview of the page if
the printout can handle it. Otherwise, simply fills the window with a white background.

TRichEditPreviewFrame class   richedpr.h

TRichEditPreviewFrame is a window object which contains preview pages displaying data from a rich edit control. It contains a simple preview toolbar and one or two preview pages.

Public constructor

TRichEditPreviewFrame
TRichEditPreviewFrame(TWindow* parentWindow, TPrinter& printer, TPrintout& printout, TRichEdit& richEdit, const char far* title, TLayoutWindow* client = new TLayoutWindow(0));
Constructor of a *RichEdit* Preview Frame.

Protected member functions

GetNewPreviewPage
TPreviewPage* GetNewPreviewPage(TWindow* parent, TPrintout& printout, TPrintDC& prndc, TSize& printExtent, int pagenum = 1);
Returns pointer to a preview page object.

TRichEditPrintout class   richedpr.h

TRichEditPrintout encapsulates the information to print/preview data from a rich edit control. For example, it holds the offset of pages, the range of data to be printer/previewed, etc.

Public constructors

Constructor
TRichEditPrintout(TPrinter& printer, TRichEdit& richEdit, const char far *title);
Constructs a Printout object which represent a RICHEDIT's document.

Destructor
~TRichEditPrintout();
Destructor of *RichEdit PrintOut*. Flushes any cached formatting information.

Public member functions

BeginPrinting
void BeginPrinting();
This routine is invoked to inform the printout that a printing operation has started.

CleanupPrintParams
void CleanupPrintParams();
This is an overriden virtual method of *TPrintout*.

EndPrinting
void EndPrinting();
This routine is invoked to inform the printout that the printint operation has ended.

GetDialogInfo
void GetDialogInfo (int& minPage, int& maxPage, int& selFromPage, int& selToPage);
This method is invoked by the printer or print-preview classes to allow the printout to update the page range information.

HasPage
bool HasPage(int pageNumber);
This routine is invoked to asked the printout object whether it has necessary information to print the specified page.

PageOfOffset
int PageOfOffset(int offset);
Returns the index of the page at the particular offset within the buffer of an edit control.

PrintPage
void PrintPage(int page, TRect& rect, unsigned flags);
This routine is invoked to request the printout object to print a page.

SetPrintParams
void SetPrintParams(TPrintDC* dc, TSize pageSize);
This method is invoked by the printer or print-preview objects to hand the printout object the target device context and the size of its pages.

Protected member functions

FlushCache
bool FlushCache;
Flags that the control needs to be reset.

FmtRange
TFormatRange FmtRange;
Range of text to format.

PageCount
int PageCount;
Number of pages formatted.

PageIndices
TDynArray<int> PageIndices;
Index of page offsets.

Printer
TPrinter& Printer;
Constructs a Printout object which represents a RICHEDIT's document.

RichEdit
TRichEdit& RichEdit;

Reference to associated control.

SizePhysInch
TSize SizePhysInch;
Size of printer in inches.

SizePhysPage
TSize SizePhysPage;
Physical size of printer (pels).

TextLen
int TextLen;
Length of text formatted.

TRollDialog class   rolldial.h

TRollDialog allows a dialog to "roll" up and down, similar to the Corel interface. This class is best used for modeless dialog boxes. When the dialog is created, a menu item is appended to the system menu. This menu choice will be either Shrink or Expand depending upon which state the dialog is currently in. If the dialog contains minimize or maximize buttons, the behavior of those buttons map to shrink and expand respectively.

Public constructors

TRollDialog
TRollDialog(TWindow* parent, TResId resId, bool animated = true, bool fullSize = true, TModule* module = 0);
Sets up data members for the various properties of the dialog.

Public member functions

SetupWindow
void SetupWindow();
Adds the shrink system menu option, if desired. This also shrinks the dialog if that option was chosen.

Protected member functions

EvSysCommand
void EvSysCommand(uint, TPoint&);
Event handler for the system menu choice. Calls either *TRollDialog::Shrink* or *TRollDialog::Expand*.

Expand
void Expand();
Event handler for the system menu option "expand". Toggles the system menu choice to "shrink".

IsFullSize
bool IsFullSize;
Tracks if the dialog is currently full-size.

Shrink
void Shrink();
Event handler for the system menu option "shrink". Toggles the system menu choice to "expand".

Response table entries

Response table entry	Member function
EV_WM_SYSCOMMAND	EvSysCommand

TScreenDC class   dc.h

Derived from *TWindowDC*, *TScreenDC* is a DC class that provides direct access to the screen bitmap. *TScreenDC* gets a DC for handle 0, which is for the whole screen with no clipping. Handle 0 paints on top of other windows.

Public constructors

TScreenDC
TScreenDC();
Default constructor for *TScreenDC* objects.

TScrollBar class   scrollba.h

TScrollBar objects represent standalone vertical and horizontal scroll bar controls. Most of *TScrollBar's* member functions manage the scroll bar's sliding box (thumb) position and range.

One special feature of *TScrollBar* is the notify-based set of member functions that automatically adjust the scroll bar's thumb position in response to scroll bar messages.

Never place *TScrollBar* objects in windows that have either the WS_HSCROLL or WS_VSCROLL styles in their attributes.

TScrollBar is a streamable class.

Public data members

LineMagnitude
int LineMagnitude;

The number of range units to scroll the scroll bar when the user requests a small movement by clicking on the scroll bar's arrows. *TScrollBar*'s constructor sets *LineMagnitude* to 1 by default. (The scroll range is 0-100 by default.)

See also   TScrollBar::SetupWindow

PageMagnitude
int PageMagnitude;
The number of range units to scroll the scroll bar when the user requests a large movement by clicking in the scroll bar's scrolling area. *TScrollBar*'s constructor sets *PageMagnitude* to 10 by default. (The scroll range is 0-100 by default.)

Public constructors

TScrollBar
Form 1   TScrollBar(TWindow* parent, int id, int x, int y, int w, int h, bool isHScrollBar, TModule* module = 0);
Constructs and initializes a *TScrollBar* object with the given parent window (*parent*), a control ID (*id*), a position (*x, y*), and a width and height (*w, h*). Invokes the *TControl* constructor with similar parameters. If *isHScrollBar* is **true**, the constructor adds SBS_HORZ to the window style. If it is **false**, the constructor adds SBS_VERT. If the supplied height for a horizontal scroll bar or the supplied width for a vertical scroll bar is 0, a standard value is used. *LineMagnitude* is initialized to 1 and *PageMagnitude* is set to 10.

Form 2   TScrollBar(TWindow* parent,int resourceId,TModule* module = 0);
Constructs a *TScrollBar* object to be associated with a scroll bar control of a *TDialog* object. Invokes the *TControl* constructor with identical parameters.

The *resourceId* parameter must correspond to a scroll bar resource that you define.

Public member functions

DeltaPos
virtual int DeltaPos(int delta);
Calls *SetPosition* to change the scroll bar's thumb position by the value supplied in *delta*. A positive *delta* moves the thumb down or right. A negative *delta* value moves the thumb up or *left*. *DeltaPos* returns the new thumb position.

See also   TScrollBar::SetPosition

EvHScroll
void EvHScroll(uint scrollCode, uint thumbPos, HWND hWndCtl);
Response table handler that calls the virtual function (*SBBottom, SBLineDown*, and so on) in response to messages sent by *TWindow::DispatchScroll*.

EvVScroll
void EvVScroll(uint scrollCode, uint thumbPos, HWND hWndCtl);
Response table handler that calls the virtual function (*SBBottom, SBLineDown*, and so on) in response to messages sent by *TWindow::DispatchScroll*.

GetLineMagnitude
int GetLineMagnitude() const;
Returns the current delta to move the thumb when line up/line down is received.

GetPageMagnitude
int GetPageMagnitude() const;
Returns the current delta to move the thumb when page up/page down is received.

GetPosition
virtual int GetPosition() const;
Returns the scroll bar's current thumb position.

See also   TScrollBar::SetPosition, TScrollBarData struct

GetRange
virtual void GetRange(int& min, int& max) const;
Returns the end values of the present range of scroll bar thumb positions in *min* and *max*.

See also   TScrollBar::SetPosition, TScrollBar::SetRange, TScrollBarData struct

SBBottom
virtual void SBBottom();
Calls *SetPosition* to move the thumb to the bottom or right of the scroll bar. *SBBottom* is called to respond to the thumb's being dragged to the bottom or rightmost position of the scroll bar.

SBEndScroll
virtual void SBEndScroll();
User released the mouse after scrolling.

SBLineDown
virtual void SBLineDown();
Calls *SetPosition* to move the thumb down or right (by *LineMagnitude* units). *SBLineDown* is called to respond to a click on the bottom or right arrow of the scroll bar.

SBLineUp
virtual void SBLineUp();
Calls *SetPosition* to move the thumb up or left (by *LineMagnitude* units). *SBLineUp* is called to respond to a click on the top or left arrow of the scroll bar.

SBPageDown
virtual void SBPageDown();
Calls *SetPosition* to move the thumb down or right (by *PageMagnitude* units). *SBPageDown* is called to respond to a click in the bottom or right scrolling area of the scroll bar.

SBPageUp
virtual void SBPageUp();
Calls *SetPosition* to move the thumb up or left (by *PageMagnitude* units). *SBPageUp* is called to respond to a click in the top or left scrolling area of the scroll bar.

SBThumbPosition
virtual void SBThumbPosition(int thumbPos);
Calls *SetPosition* to move the thumb. *SBThumbPosition* is called to respond when the thumb is set to a new position.

SBThumbTrack
virtual void SBThumbTrack(int thumbPos);
Calls *SetPosition* to move the thumb as it is being dragged to a new position.

SBTop
virtual void SBTop();
Calls *SetPosition* to move the thumb to the top or right of the scroll bar. *SBTop* is called to respond to the thumb's being dragged to the top or rightmost position on the scroll bar.

SetLineMagnitude
void SetLineMagnitude(int linemagnitude);
Sets the delta to move the thumb when line up/line down is received.

SetPageMagnitude
void SetPageMagnitude(int pagemagnitude);
Sets the delta to move the thumb when page up/page down is received.

SetPosition
virtual void SetPosition(int thumbPos);
Moves the thumb to the position specified in *thumbPos*. If *thumbPos* is outside the present range of the scroll bar, the thumb is moved to the closest position within range.

See also   TScrollBar::GetPosition

SetRange
virtual void SetRange(int min, int max);
Sets the scroll bar to the range between *min* and *max*.

See also   TScrollBar::GetRange

Transfer
uint Transfer(void* buffer, TTransferDirection direction);
Transfers scroll-bar data to or from the transfer buffer pointed to by *buffer,* which is expected to point to a *TScrollBarData* structure.

Data is transferred to or from the transfer buffer if *tdGetData* or *tdSetData* is supplied as the direction.

Transfer always returns the size of the transfer data (the size of the *TScrollBarData* structure). To retrieve the size of this data without transferring data, pass *tdSizeData* as the *direction*.

Protected member functions

GetClassName
char far* GetClassName();
Returns the name of *TScrollBar's* registration class, "SCROLLBAR".

SetupWindow
void SetupWindow();
Sets the scroll bar's range to 0, 100. To redefine this range, call *SetRange*.

Response table entries

Response table entry	Member function
EV_WM_HSCROLL	EvHScroll
EV_WM_VSCROLL	EvVScroll

TScrollBarData struct   scrollba.h

The *TScrollBarData* structure contains integer values that represent a range of thumb positions on the scroll bar. *TScrollBar*'s function *GetRange* calls *TScrollBarData* to obtain the highest and lowest thumb positions on the scroll bar. *GetPosition* calls *TScrollBarData* to obtain the current thumb position on the scroll bar.

See also   TScrollBar::Transfer

Public data members

HighValue
int HighValue;
Contains the highest value of the thumb position in the scroll bar's range.

See also   TScrollBar::GetRange

LowValue
int LowValue;
Contains the lowest value of thumb position in the scroll bar's range.

See also   TScrollBar::GetRange

Position
int Position;
Contains the scroll bar's thumb position.

See also   TScrollBar::GetPosition

TScroller class   scroller.h

TScroller supports an automatic window-scrolling mechanism (referred to as autoscrolling) that works in conjunction with horizontal or vertical window scroll bars. (It also works if there are no scroll bars.) When autoscrolling is activated, the window automatically scrolls when the mouse is dragged from inside the client area of the window to outside that area. If the *AutoMode* data member is true, *TScroller* performs autoscrolling.

To use *TScroller*, set the *Scroller* member of your *TWindow* descendant to a *TScroller* object instantiated in the constructor of your *TWindow* descendant. *TScroller* is a streamable class.

Public data members

AutoMode
bool AutoMode;
Is true if automatic scrolling is activated.

AutoOrg
bool AutoOrg;
Is true if scroller offsets original.

HasHScrollBar, HasVScrollBar
bool HasHScrollBar, HasVScrollBar;
Is true if scroller has horizontal or vertical scroll.

TrackMode
bool TrackMode;
Is true if track scrolling is activated.

Window
TWindow* Window;
Points to the window whose client area scroller is to be managed.

XLine, YLine
int XLine, YLine;
Specifies the number of logical device units per line to scroll the rectangle in the horizontal (X) and vertical (Y) directions.

XPage, YPage
int XPage, YPage;
Specifies the number of logical device units per page to scroll the rectangle in the horizontal (X) and vertical (Y) directions.

XPos,YPos
long XPos, YPos;
Specifies the current position of the rectangle in horizontal (*XPos*) and vertical (*YPos*) scroll units.

XRange, YRange
long XRange, YRange;
Specifies the number of horizontal and vertical scroll units.

XUnit, YUnit
int XUnit, YUnit;
Specifies the amount (in logical device units) to scroll the rectangle in the horizontal (X) and vertical (Y) directions. The rectangle is scrolled right if *XUnit* is positive and left if

XUnit is negative. The rectangle is scrolled down if *YUnit* is positive and up if *YUnit* is negative.

Public constructor and destructor

Constructor
TScroller(TWindow* window, int xUnit, int yUnit, long xRange, long yRange);
Constructs a *TScroller* object with *window* as the owner window, and *xUnit*, *yUnit*, *xRange*, and *yRange* as *xUnit*, *yUnit*, *xRange* and *yRange*, respectively. Initializes data members to default values. *HasHScrollBar* and *HasVScrollBar* are set according to the scroll bar attributes of the owner window.

Destructor
virtual ~TScroller();
Destructs a *TScroller* object. Sets owning window's *Scroller* number variable to 0.

Public member functions

AutoScroll
virtual void AutoScroll();
Scrolls the owner window's display in response to the mouse being dragged from inside to outside the window. The direction and the amount by which the display is scrolled depend on the current position of the mouse.

BeginView
virtual void BeginView(TDC& dc, TRect& rect);
If *TScroller_AutoOrg* is true (default condition), *BeginView* automatically offsets the origin of the logical coordinates of the client area by *XPos*, *YPos* during a paint operation. If *AutoOrg* is false (for example, when the scroller is larger than 32,767 units), you must set the offset manually.

EndView
virtual void EndView();
Updates the position of the owner window's scroll bars to be coordinated with the position of the *TScroller*.

HScroll
virtual void HScroll(uint scrollEvent, int thumbPos);
Responds to the specified horizontal *scrollEvent* by calling *ScrollBy* or *ScrollTo*. The type of scroll event is identified by the corresponding SB_ constants. *thumbPos* contains the current thumb position when the scroller is notified of SB_THUMBTRACK and SB_THUMBPOSITION scroll events.

IsAutoMode
virtual bool IsAutoMode();
IsAutoMode is true if automatic scrolling is activated.

See also   TScroller::AutoMode

IsVisibleRect

bool IsVisibleRect(long x, long y, int xExt, int yExt);

Is true if the rectangle (*x*, *y*, *xExt*, and *yExt*) is visible.

SetPageSize

virtual void SetPageSize();

Sets the *XPage* and *YPage* data members to the width and height (in *XUnits* and *YUnits*) of the owner window's client area.

See also   TScroller::XPage, YPage, TScroller::XUnit, YUnit

SetRange

virtual void SetRange(long xRange, long yRange);

Sets the *xRange* and *yRange* of the *TScroller* to the parameters specified. Then calls *SetSBarRange* to synchronize the range of the owner window's scroll bars.

See also   TScroller::SetSBarRange

SetSBarRange

virtual void SetSBarRange();

Sets the range of the owner window's scroll bars to match the range of the *TScroller*.

SetUnits

virtual void SetUnits(int xUnit, int yUnit);

Sets the *XUnit* and *YUnit* data members to *TheXUnit* and *TheYUnit*, respectively. Updates *XPage* and *YPage* by calling *SetPageSize*.

See also   TScroller::XPage, YPage, TScroller::XUnit, YUnit

ScrollBy

void ScrollBy(long dx, long dy);

Scrolls to a position calculated using the passed delta values (*dx* and *dy*). A positive delta position moves the thumb position down or right. A negative delta position moves the thumb up or left.

ScrollTo

virtual void ScrollTo(long x, long y);

Scrolls the rectangle to the position specified in *x* and *y*.

SetWindow

void SetWindow(TWindow* win);

Sets the owning window to *win*.

VScroll

virtual void VScroll(uint scrollEvent, int thumbPos);

Responds to the specified vertical *scrollEvent* by calling *ScrollBy* or *ScrollTo*. The type of scroll event is identified by the corresponding SB_ constants. *thumbPos* contains the current thumb position when the scroller is notified of SB_THUMBTRACK and SB_THUMBPOSITION scroll events.

See also   TScroller::ScrollTo

XScrollValue
int XScrollValue(long rangeUnit);
XScrollValue converts a horizontal range value from the scroll bar to a horizontal scroll value.

See also   TScroller::YScrollValue

XRangeValue
int XRangeValue(int scrollUnit);
XRangeValue converts a horizontal scroll value from the scroll bar to a horizontal range value.

See also   TScroller::YRangeValue

YScrollValue
int YScrollValue(long rangeUnit);
YScrollValue converts a vertical range value from the scroll bar to a vertical scroll value.

See also   TScroller::XScrollValue

YRangeValue
int YRangeValue(int scrollUnit);
YRangeValue converts a vertical scroll value from the scroll bar to a vertical range value.

See also   TScroller::XRangeValue

TSelChange class   commctrl.h

TSelChange is a structure sent with EN_SELCHANGE notification.

Public member functions

operator NMHDR&
operator NMHDR&();
Allows the notification structure to be transparently treated as an NMHDR structure, thereby eliminating the need to explicitly refer to the NMHDR data member (which is always the first member of notification structures).

TSeparatorGadget class   gadget.h

TSeparatorGadget is a simple class you can use to create a separator between gadgets. To do so, you must specify the size of the separator in units of SM_CXBORDER (width of the window frame) and SM_CYBORDER (height of the window frame). Determines the width and height of the gadget and sets the right and bottom boundaries of the separator. By default, the separator disables itself and turns off shrink-wrapping. Note that the default border style is *none*.

Public constructors

TSeparatorGadget
TSeparatorGadget(int size = 6);
Used for both the width and the height of the separator, *size* is initialized at 6 border units (the width or height of a thin window border).

Public member functions

Inserted
void Inserted();
This is an overridden virtual, called after a gadget is inserted into a window.

See also TGadget::TBorderStyle enum

TSerializer class   serialze.h

TSerializer sends a block of data to another window.

Type definitions

TBlock enum
enum TBlock {End = 0, Data1, Data2, Data3, Data4, Begin};
TBlock is used to define the different types of blocks sent from one window to another. This enum is sent as the *wParam*.

Table 2.22   Constants

Constant	Meaning if set
End	End of data (lParam == 0)
Data1	Data is stored in bits 0x000000FF of lParam
Data2	Data is stored in bits 0x0000FFFF of lParam
Data3	Data is stored in bits 0x00FFFFFF of lParam
Data4	Data is stored in bits 0xFFFFFFFF of lParam
Begin	Beginning of data (lParam length of data)

Public constructors

TSerializer
TSerializer(HWND hwndTarget, uint32 length, void far* data);
Breaks down the data into blocks and sends each block to the window via *SendMessage*. *wParam* of the *SendMessage* is of type *TBlock*, which signifies what *lParam* contains.

TSerializeReceiver class   serialze.h

TSerializeReceiver is a mix-in class that automatically puts together the block of data sent by *TSerializer*.

Public constructors

TSerializeReceiver
TSerializeReceiver();
Constructor for this class.

Public member functions

DataReceived
virtual void DataReceived(uint32 length, void far* data);
This virtual function will be called whenever the data has been reconstructed. Derived classes should override this function to copy the data because it will be deleted when this function returns.

Protected member functions

BlockReceived
int32 BlockReceived(TParam1, TParam2);
Automatically puts the data blocks back together.

Response table entries

Response table entry	Member function
EV_REGISTERED (SerializeMessage, BlockReceived)	BlockReceived

TServiceEntry class   wskservm.h

TServiceEntry encapsulates information about a service.

Public constructors

TServiceEntry
TServiceEntry();
Initializes all data members of service to 0.

TServiceManager class

wskservm.h

TServiceManager encapsulates service database functions.

Public constructors

Form 1   TServiceManager();
Creates the hidden window and initialize data members.

Form 2   virtual ~TServiceManager();
If there are any outstanding requests, cancel them.

Public member functions

CancelServiceRequest
int CancelServiceRequest(HANDLE hService=0);
Cancels a pending service that equals the *hService*. Note that if the service is 0 or unspecified, then this function uses its own current service.

GetLastError
int GetLastError();
Returns the last error code.

GetLastServiceCompletion
int GetLastServiceCompletion();
Returns the last service completion.

GetService
Form 1   int GetService(TServiceEntry*& sEntry, const char* szName, const char* szProtocol=0);
Implements the blocking *getservbyname()*. 'entry' is a pointer to a *ServiceEntry**. The caller does not allocate a *ServiceEntry*; it will be set by the system. Do not change any data in the returned structure. The 'name' argument points to the string representing the service name, such as "ftp." It is generally case-sensitive. 'protocol' is the protocol name, but may be passed as 0 to mean default or first found. The returned entry has the port in network byte order.

Form 2   int GetService(TServiceEntry*& sEntry, int nPort, const char* szProtocol=0);
Implements the blocking *getservbyport()*. 'entry' is a pointer to a *ServiceEntry**. The caller does not allocate a *ServiceEntry*; it will be set by the system. Do not change any data in the returned structure. 'port' is passed to this function in network byte ordering. 'protocol' is the protocol name, but may be passed as 0 to mean default or first found. The returned entry has the port in network byte order.

GetServiceAsync
Form 1   int GetServiceAsync(TWindow& wndNotify, HANDLE& hService, char* szName, const char* szProtocol=0,
           uint nMessage=MSG_SERVICE_NOTIFY, char* chBuffer=0);
This function notifies the given *wndNotify* about the completion of the request. *nMessage* is the message that the *hwndNotify* will receive. It defaults to MSG_SERVICE_NOTIFY, which is defined in the *TServiceManager*'s header file. The *hService* will hold a handle

that the caller can use to reference the request on callback. The *chBuffer* is a pointer to a buffer that will be filled in with a SERVENT. It needs to be at least MAXGETHOSTSTRUCT bytes. If *chBuffer* is 0 (or not specified), then the *TServiceManager*'s internal buffer will be used. 'name' is a pointer to a c string service name, such as "ftp." 'protocol' is the protocol name, but may be passed as 0 to mean default or first found. This class will NOT save the *hService* for itself. *wParam* will be equal to the *hService* returned. WSAGETSYNCERROR(*lParam*) holds an error, if any (0 is OK). WSAGETSYNCBUFLEN(*lParam*) holds actual length of the buffer.

Form 2   int GetServiceAsync(TWindow& wndNotify, HANDLE& hService, int nPort, const char* szProtocol=0,
            uint nMessage=MSG_SERVICE_NOTIFY, char* chBuffer=0);

This function notifies the given *wndNotify* about the completion of the request. *nMessage* is the message that the *hwndNotify* will receive. It defaults to MSG_SERVICE_NOTIFY, which is defined in the *TServiceManager*'s header file. The hService will hold a handle that the caller can use to reference the request on callback. port should be passed in network byte ordering. The *chBuffer* is a pointer to buffer that will be filled in with a SERVENT. It needs to be at least MAXGETHOSTSTRUCT bytes. If *chBuffer* is 0 (or not specified), then the *TServiceManager*'s internal buffer will be used. protocol is the protocol name, but may be passed as 0 to mean default or first found. This class will NOT save the *hService* for itself. *wParam* will be equal to the *hService* returned. WSAGETSYNCERROR(*lParam*) holds an error, if any (0 is OK). WSAGETSYNCBUFLEN(*lParam*) holds actual length of the buffer.

Form 3   int GetServiceAsync(HANDLE& hService, char* szName, const char* szProtocol=0);

This call is non-blocking. It sets up a callback to its own member window. *hService* is a HANDLE reference. If the call is successful, it will hold the handle for the asynchrous call. Note that the caller can save the handle, but also that this class stores the handle for itself as well. port is passed into this function in network byte ordering. Note that due to the design of this class, you cannot have two outstanding service requests that get notified directly to this class. You may use the hwnd-specific notification version of this function to manage multiple requests at a time. You may also simply create more than one instance of this class. The service is complete when *bServiceRequestCompleted* is TRUE. You must look at *nLastError* in this case to see if there was an error.

Form 4   int GetServiceAsync(HANDLE& hService, int nPort, const char* szProtocol=0);

This call is non-blocking. It sets up a callback to its own member window. *hService* is a HANDLE reference. If the call is successful, it will hold the handle for the asynchrous call. Note that the caller can save the handle, but also that this class stores the handle for itself as well. port is passed into this function in network byte ordering. Note that due to the design of this class, you cannot have two outstanding service requests that get notified directly to this class. You may use the hwnd-specific notification version of this function to manage multiple requests at a time. You may also simply create more than one instance of this class. The service is complete when *bServiceRequestCompleted* is TRUE. You must look at *nLastError* in this case to see if there was an error.

GetServiceName

int GetServiceName(int nPort, char* szName, const char* szProtocol=0);

This function is blocking. 'name' needs to be big enough to hold the service's name (N_MAX_SERVICE_NAME). 'port' must be passed in network byte ordering. 'protocol' is the protocol name, but may be passed as 0 to mean default or first found.

GetServicePort
int GetServicePort(char* szName, int& nPort, const char* szProtocol=0);

This function is blocking. Given an input service in 'name', this function fills in *nPort* with the port (in network order). 'port' is a reference to an int. If the call retuns OK, then this will be the port in network ordering. protocol is the protocol name, but may be passed as 0 to mean default or first found.

GetServiceRequestCompleted
bool GetServiceRequestCompleted();

Returns true if the last service requested has been completed.

ServiceEntry
TServiceEntry* ServiceEntry;

Set to point to *chServiceBuffer*.

Protected member functions

LastError
int LastError;

Last error code.

LastServiceRequest
HANDLE LastServiceRequest;

Handle of last service request.

LastServiceRequestCompleted
bool LastServiceRequestCompleted;

Is the last request done?

ServiceBuffer
char ServiceBuffer[MAXGETHOSTSTRUCT];

Used for calls to *WSAAsync...()*

OutstandingServiceRequests
int OutstandingServiceRequests;

Keeps track of count of total requests that haven't completed yet.

ServiceCompleted
void ServiceCompleted(int nError);

This function is called whenever an internal window callback is used for an async call. When this function is called, the *ServiceRequestCompleted* member will be true (it got set to true right before this function was called). You may want to override this function. If you do, you will probably want to call this function as part of the subclassed function.

TServiceWindow
friend class TServiceWindow;

Window
TServiceWindow Window;

This function is a private window for catching notifications.

TServiceWindow class

TServiceWindow is a private class created by the *TServiceManager* to catch notifications.

Public constructors

TServiceWindow
TServiceWindow(TServiceManager* newServiceManagerParent);
A *TServiceWindow* requires a *TServiceManager* parent.

Protected member functions

DoNotification
TResult DoNotification(TParam1 param1, TParam2 param2);
This function merely calls the parent notification function. Since Windows is designed to receive only system messages, there is a dummy window that does nothing but simulate the concept of Objects receiving messages (in this case, the *ServiceManager* object). The *TServiceWindow* hides this from the user (programmer).

ServiceManagerParent
TServiceManager* ServiceManagerParent;
Object to pass notifications.

TShellItem class

TShellItem is an item in the shell's name space. All items in the shell's name space can be identified by a fully qualified pidl. Another way to uniquely identify an item is via it's parent and an item id (i.e., a single item rather than a list). A *TShellItem* contains a parent (*TComRef<IShellFolder> ParentFolder*) and the item id (*TPidl* pidl).

Type definitions

TAttribute enum
enum TAttribute {atCapabilityMask, atCanBeCopied, atCanBeDeleted, atCanCreateShortcut, atCanBeMoved, atCanBeRenamed, atIsADropTarget, atHasAPropertySheet, atDisplayAttributeMask, atDisplayGhosted, atIsShortcut, atIsReadOnly, atIsShared, atContentsMask, atContainsSubFolder, atContainsFileSystemFolder, atIsPartOfFileSystem, atIsFolder, atCanBeRemoved};
TAttribute is used by *TShellItem::GetAttributes* to retrieve the attributes of one or more shell items.

Table 2.23   Attribute constants

Constant	Meaning if set
atCapabilityMask	Mask for the capability flags
atCanBeCopied	The shell item can be copied

Constant	Meaning if set
atCanBeDeleted	The shell item can be deleted
atCanCreateShortcut	Shortcuts can be created for the shell item
atCanBeMoved	The shell item can be moved
atCanBeRenamed	The shell item can be renamed
atIsADropTarget	The shell item is a drop target
atHasAPropertySheet	The shell item has a property sheet
atDisplayAttributeMask	Mask for the display attributes
atDisplayGhosted	The shell item should be displayed using a ghosted icon
atIsShortcut	The shell item is a shortcut
atIsReadOnly	The shell item is readonly
atIsShared	The shell item is shared
atContentsMask	Mask for the contents attributes
atContainsSubFolder	The shell item has subfolders
atContainsFileSystemFolder	The shell item contains one or more system folders
atIsPartOfFileSystem	The shell item is part of the file system
atIsFolder	The shell item is a folder
atCanBeRemoved	The shell item is on removable media

See also   TShellItem::GetAttributes

TBrowseFlags enum

enum TBrowseFlags {OnlyComputers, OnlyPrinters, NoNetorkFoldersBelowDomain, OnlyFSAncestors, OnlyFSDirs};

TBrowseFlags is used by *TShellItem::BrowseForFolder* to receive information about the selected shell item.

Table 2.24   Browse flag constants

Constant	Meaning if set
OnlyComputers	Returns only computers
OnlyPrinters	Returns only printers
NoNetworkFoldersBelowDomain	Does not return network folders below the domain.
OnlyFSAncestors	Returns only file system ancestors
OnlyFSDirs	Returns only file system directories

See also   TShellItem::BrowseForFolder

TDisplayNameKind enum

enum TDisplayNameKind {Normal, InFolder, ForParsing};

TDisplayNameKind defines flags that are used by *TShellItem::GetDisplayName* and *TShellItem::Rename*.

Table 2.25 Display kind constants

Constant	Meaning if set
Normal	File object displayed by itself.
InFolder	File object displayed within a folder.
ForParsing	File object suitable for parsing.

See also TShellItem::GetDisplayName, TShellItem::Rename

TExeKind enum
enum TExeKind {NonExecutable, WindowsNE, WindowsPE, MSDOS, Win32Console};
TExeKind is returned by *TShellItem::GetExeType* to specify the executable file type.

Table 2.26 Executable Type Constants

Constant	Meaning if set
NonExecutable	Nonexecutable file or an error condition
WindowsNE	Windows-based application
WindowsPE	Windows level (3.0, 3.5, or 4.0)
MSDOS	MS-DOS .EXE, .COM, or .BAT file
Win32Console	Win32-based console application

See also TShellItem::GetExeType

TFileOpFlags enum
enum TFileOpFlags {AllowUndo, NoConfirmation, NoConfirmMkDir, RenameOnCollision, Silent, SimpleProgress};
TFileOpFlags contains information that *TShellItem::Rename, Copy, Move, Delete* use to perform file operations.

Table 2.27 File operation constants

Constant	Meaning if set
AllowUndo	Preserves undo information (if possible)
NoConfirmation	Responds with "yes to all" for any dialog
NoConfirmMkDir	No confirmation on the creation of a new directory
RenameOnCollision	Renames the file being operated on if a file of the same name already exists (i.e., Copy #1 of ...)
Silent	No progess dialog box is displayed
SimpleProgress	A simple progress dialog box is diaplayed (no file names)

See also TShellItem::Rename, TShellItem::Copy, TShellItem::Move, TShellItem::Delete

TIconKind enum
enum TIconKind {Link, Open, Selected};
TIconKind is used by *TShellItem::GetIcon* to determine how to display the shell item's icon.

Table 2.28   Icon Kind Constants

Constant	Meaning if set
Link	Adds the link overlay to the shell item's icon
Open	Retrieves the shell item's open icon
Selected	Blends the shell item's icon with the system highlight color

See also   TShellItem::GetIcon

TIconSize enum
enum TIconSize {Large , Small , Shell};
TIconSize is used by *TShellItem::GetIcon* to determine the display size of the shell item's icon.

Table 2.29   Icon Size Constants

Constant	Meaning if set
Large	Retrieves the shell item's large icon
Small	Retrieves the shell item's small icon
Shell	Retrieves the shell-sized icon (if unavailable, the normal icon is sized according to the system metric values)

See also   TShellItem::GetIcon

TSpecialFolderKind enum
enum TSpecialFolderKind {RecycleBin, ControlPanel, Desktop, DesktopFileDir, MyComputer, Fonts, NetworkNeighborhoodFileDir, NetworkNeighborhood, CommonDocuments, Printers, Programs, RecentDocuments, SendTo, StartMenu, Startup, CommonTemplates, Favorites};
TSpecialFolderKind is used by the constructor for *TShellItem* to specify the type of shell item to construct.

Table 2.30   Folder Kind Constants

Constant	Meaning if set
RecycleBin	Directory containing file objects in the user's recycle bin
ControlPanel	Virtual folder containing icons for the Control Panel
Desktop	Virtual folder at the root of the namespace
DesktopFileDir	Directory used to physically store file objects on the desktop
MyComputer	Virtual folder containing everything on the local computer
Fonts	Virtual folder containing fonts
NetworkNeighborhoodFileDir	Directory containing objects that appeat in the Network Neighborhood
NetworkNeighborhood	Virtual folder representing the top level of the network hierarchy
CommonDocuments	Directory that serves as a repository for common documents
Printers	Virtual folder containing installed printers

Constant	Meaning if set
Programs	Directory containing the user's program groups
RecentDocuments	Directory containing the user's most recently used documents
SendTo	Directory containing Send To menu items
StartMenu	Directory containing Start menu items
Startup	Directory that corresponds to the user's Startup program group
CommonTemplates	Directory that serves as a repository for document templates
Favorites	

See also   TShellItem::TShellItem

Public constructors

TShellItem

Form 1   TShellItem (const char* path, bool throwOnInvalidPath = true, HWND windowOwner = 0);
TShellItem constructor makes a *TShellItem* for a file or directory in the file system. If the *throwOnInvalidPath* argument is true, an exception is raised if the path is not valid or if the file or directory does not exist. If this argument is false, no exception is raised and the *Valid()* function should be called to make sure it returns true. If *Valid()* returns false, the *TShellItem* does not represent an object in the shell namespace.

Form 2   TShellItem(const TSpecialFolderKind kind, HWND windowOwner = 0);
TShellIterm constructor makes a *TShellItem* for a special folder. Special folders can be any specified in the *TSpecialFolderKind* enum.

Form 3   TShellItem(const TCreateStruct& cs);
TShellItem constructor to make a *TShellItem* from a *TCreateStruct*. *TCreateStruct* contains a *TPidl* and a *TComRef<IShellFolder>ParentFolder*, which represents the parent folder.

TCreateStructs are returned by *TShellItem::GetParentFolder()* and by the following *TShellItemIterator* functions: operator ++(pre- &post-fix), operator -- (pre- & post-fix), operator [](), and *Current()*.

TCreateStructs are also returned as out parameters of the following *TShellItem* functions: *BrowseForFolder()*, *ParseDisplayName()*.

Form 4   TShellItem(const TPidlPtr& Pidl, const TComRef<IShellFolder>& parentFolder);
TShellItem constructor to make a *TShellItem* from a *TPidl* and a *ComRef<IShellFolder>* (parent folder).

Form 5   TShellItem(ITEMIDLIST* pidl = 0, const TComRef<IShellFolder>& parentFolder = 0);
TShellIterm constructor to make a *TShellItem* from a ITEMIDLIST(pidl) and a *ComRef<IShellFolder>* (parent folder).

Form 6   TShellItem(const TShellItem& source);
TShellItem copy constructor.

Public member functions

AddToRecentDocs
void AddToRecentDocs() const;
Adds the *TShellItem* to the taskbar's recent document list.

BrowseForFolder
bool BrowseForFolder(TCreateStruct& cs, HWND windowOwner = 0, const char* title = 0,
    const uint flags = 0,,int* image = 0, const bool includeStatus = false, BFFCALLBACK func = 0,
    const LPARAM param = 0) const;
BrowseForFolder presents a dialog box to the user in which he can select a subfolder. The root of the dialog box is this *TShellItem* folder.

Note It is only meaningful to call this function if the *TShellItem* is a folder; consequently, if this function is called on a *TShellItem* that is not a folder, an exception is thrown.

CanBeRemoved
bool CanBeRemoved() const;
Returns true if the *TShellItem* represents an item that can be removed.

ContainsSubFolder
bool ContainsSubFolder() const;
Returns true if the *TShellItem* represents an item that contains a subfolder.

Copy
Form 1   bool Copy(const TShellItem& dest, const bool destIsFolder = true, const ushort flags = 0,
    const char* title = 0, HWND windowOwner = 0) const;
Copy copies this *TShellItem* to destination *TShellItem*. Flags are any combination of *TFileOpFlags*.

Title is the title displayed in the progress dialog box. *windowOwner* should be set to the owner of the progress dialog box.

Form 2   bool Copy(const char* dest, const bool destIsFolder = true, const ushort flags = 0, const char* title = 0,
    HWND windowOwner = 0) const;
Copy copies this *TShellItem* to destination path. *destIsFolder* must tell whether or not dest is a folder. Flags are any combination of *TFileOpFlags*.

Title is the title displayed in the progress dialog box. *windowOwner* should be set to the owner of the progress dialog box.

Delete
bool Delete(const ushort flags = 0, const char* title = 0, HWND windowOwner = 0);
Delete deletes this *TShellItem*. Flags are any combination of *TFileOpFlags*.

Title is the title displayed in the progress dialog box. *windowOwner* should be set to the owner of the progress dialog box.

EnumObjects
void EnumObjects(IEnumIDList** iface, HWND windowOwner = 0, const uint kind = Folders | NonFolders) const;
EnumObjects is a protected function that returns an *IEnumIDList* enumerator on a folder.

Note This function is only meaningful for folders; consequently, if this function is called on a *TShellItem* that is not a folder, an exception is thrown.

GetAttributes

ulong GetAttributes(const ulong reqAttrib) const;

GetAttributes gets Capabilities, Display, Contents, and Misc. Attributes with a single call. *validateCachedInfo* defaults to false. If true, the shell will not rely on cached information.

GetContextMenu

TContextMenu GetContextMenu(HWND windowOwner = 0);

GetContextMenu returns an interface pointer to this *TShellItem*'s *IContextMenu* OLE interface.

GetDataObject

TDataObject GetDataObject(HWND windowOwner = 0);

GetDataObject returns an interface pointer to this *TShellItem*'s *IDataObject* OLE interface.

GetDisplayName

TString GetDisplayName(const TDisplayNameKind kind = Normal) const;

GetDisplayName returns a name for this *TShellItem* that is suitable to display to the user.

The three options are:

- Normal - Suitable for displaying by itself.

- InFolder - Suitable for displaying within its parent folder.

- ForParsing - Suitable to pass to the ParseDisplayName member function.

GetDropTarget

TDropTarget GetDropTarget(HWND windowOwner = 0);

GetDropTarget returns an interface pointer to this *TShellItem*'s *IDropTarget* OLE interface.

GetExtractIcon

TExtractIcon GetExtractIcon(HWND windowOwner = 0);

GetExtractIcon returns an interface pointer to this *TShellItem*'s *IExtractIcon* OLE interface.

GetFullyQualifiedPidl

TPidlPtr GetFullyQualifiedPidl() const;

GetFullyQualifiedPidl returns a *TPidl* that is fully qualified (from the desktop).

GetIcon

bool GetIcon(HICON* largeIcon, HICON* smallIcon, HWND windowOwner = 0, const TIconKind kind = ForShell, const uint reqLargeIconSize = 0, bool* dontCache = 0, bool* perInstance = 0);

GetIcon returns a handle to an icon representing this *TShellItem*. The size can be Large, Small, or Shell. The kind can be Link, Open, or Selected.

GetParentFolder

TCreateStruct GetParentFolder() const;

GetParentFolder returns a *TCreateStruct* representing the folder that contains the *TShellItem*.

GetPath

TString GetPath() const;

GetPath returns the fully qualified path representing this *TShellItem*.

GetPidl
TPidlPtr GetPidl() const;
Get fully qualified *TPidl*.

IsDesktop
bool IsDesktop() const;
IsDesktop returns true if the *TShellItem* respresents the shell's desktop.

IsFolder
bool IsFolder() const;
Return true if the *TShellItem* represents an item that is a folder.

ITEMIDLIST
operator ITEMIDLIST*();
Get *TExtractIcon, TContextMenu, TDataObject, TDropTarget* for a *TShellItem*.

Move
Form 1   bool Move(const TShellItem& destFolder, const ushort flags = 0, const char* title = 0, HWND windowOwner = 0);
Move moves this *TShellItem* to destination *TShellItem* (which must be a folder). Flags are any combination of *TFileOpFlags*.

Title is the title displayed in the progress dialog box. *windowOwner* should be set to the owner of the progress dialog box.

Form 2   bool Move(const char* destFolder, const ushort flags = 0, const char* title = 0, HWND windowOwner = 0);
Move moves this *TShellItem* to destination path (which must be a folder). Flags are any combination of *TFileOpFlags*.

Title is the title displayed in the progress dialog box. *windowOwner* should be set to the owner of the progress dialog box.

operator !=
bool operator!=(const TShellItem& rhs) const;
Compare sort order of this *TShellItem* is not equal to another *TShellItem*.

operator <
bool operator<(const TShellItem& rhs) const;
Compare sort order of this *TShellItem* is less than another *TShellItem*.

operator <=
bool operator<=(const TShellItem& rhs) const;
Compare sort order of this *TShellItem* <= another *TShellItem*.

operator =
Form 1   TShellItem& operator= (const TCreateStruct& cs);
Assignment operator.

Form 2   TShellItem& operator= (const TShellItem &source);
Assignment operator.

operator ==
bool operator==(const TShellItem& rhs) const;
Compare sort order of this *TShellItem* equals another *TShellItem*.

operator >
bool operator>(const TShellItem& rhs) const;
Compare sort order of this *TShellItem* is greater than another *TShellItem*.

operator >=
bool operator>=(const TShellItem& rhs) const;
Compare sort order of this *TShellItem* >= another *TShellItem*.

ParseDisplayName
HRESULT ParseDisplayName(TCreateStruct& cs, const char* displayName, ulong* eaten = 0,
        HWND windowOwner = 0, ulong* attrib = 0) const;
ParseDisplayName parses a "for parsing" display name into a *TCreateStruct* (which can
be used to create a *TShellItem*). In general, it is not necessary to call this function when
using OWL's shell classes.

Note   It is only meaningful to call this function if the *TShellItem* is a folder; consequently, if this
function is called on a *TShellItem* that is not a folder, an exception is thrown.

Rename
void Rename(const char* newName, HWND windowOwner = 0, const TDisplayNameKind kind = Normal);
Rename renames this *TShellItem* to *newName*. *kind* indicates the kind of name being
passed (Normal, InFolder, or ForParsing).

TShellItemIterator   shellitm.h

TShellItemIterator is an iterator for walking through the contents of a folder. A folder is a
TShellItem whose *IsFolder* or *ContainsSubFolder* attributes are true.

Type definitions

TIncludeKind enum
enum TIncludeKind {Folders, NonFolders, HiddenAndSystem};
TIncludeKind is used by the constructor for *TShellItemIterator* to determine what type of
shell items to include.

See also   TShellItemIterator::TShellItemIterator

Public constructors

Form 1   TShellItemIterator(const TShellItem& folder, HWND windowOwner = 0,
        const uint kind = TShellItem::Folders | TShellItem::NonFolders);
TShellItemIterator constructor.

Note   It is only meaningful to construct iterators on folders; therefore, if this constructor is
passed a *TShellItem* that is not a folder, an exception will be thrown.

Form 2   TShellItemIterator(const TShellItemIterator& source);
TShellItemIterator copy constructor.

Note This function does not work with the intial release of Win95 because Win95's *IEnumIDList::Clone* is broken (it returns E_FAIL (unspecified error)).

Public member functions

Current
TShellItem::TCreateStruct Current();
Operator *Current* returns the item pointed to by the "cursor." The item is returned as a *TShellItem::TCreateStruct* structure.

GetCount
long GetCount() const;
GetCount returns the number of items in the iterator's list.

Note This function does not work with the initial release of Win95 because Clone and Reset are broken in the initial Win95 release.

operator ++
TShellItem::TCreateStruct operator ++(int);
Operator ++ increments the "cursor" in the iterator, then returns the item pointed to by the cursor. The item is returned as a *TShellItem::TCreateStruct* structure.

operator --
Form 1 TShellItem::TCreateStruct operator --(int);
Operator --(int) returns the item pointed to by the "cursor," then decrements the cursor. The item is returned as a *TShellItem::TCreateStruct* structure.

Note This function does not work with the initial release of Win95 because it requires *IEnumIDList::Reset* to be called and *IEnumIDList::Reset* returns E_NOTIMPL (not implemented) in the initial Win95 release.

Form 2 TShellItem::TCreateStruct operator --();
Operator -- decrements the "cursor" in the iterator, then returns the item pointed to by the cursor. The item is returned as a *TShellItem::TCreateStruct* structure.

Note This function does not work with the initial release of Win95 because it requires *IEnumIDList::Reset* to be called and *IEnumIDList::Reset* returns E_NOTIMPL (not implemented) in the initial Win95 release.

operator []
TShellItem::TCreateStruct operator [] (const long index);
Operator [] returns the item at the *<index>* location. Index is zero based. The item is returned as a *TShellItem::TCreateStruct* structure.

Note operator [] doesn't work with the initial release of Win95 because it calls Skip and Reset, which are broken in the initial Win95 release. Both of these functions return E_NOTIMPL (not implemented). The only way operator [] will work is to call it sequentially, beginning at index 0, i.e., to use it like operator ++().

operator=
TShellItemIterator& operator= (const TShellItemIterator &source);
TShellItem assignment operator (from another *TShellItem*).

Reset
void Reset();
Resets the cursor to the beginning.

Note This function does not work with the initial release of Win95 because *IEnumIDList::Reset* returns E_NOTIMPL (not implemented) in the initial Win95 release.

Skip
void Skip(const ulong count);
Skip advances the cursor *<count>* times. Equivalent to calling Next *<count>* times.

Note This function does not work with the initial release of Win95 because *IEnumIDList::Skip* returns E_NOTIMPL (not implemented) in the initial Win95 release.

Valid
bool Valid() const;
Returns true if *TShellItemIterator* is valid and not at the end of the list of items.

TShellMalloc class   shellitm.h

TShellMalloc wraps the shell's *IMalloc* interface. The default constructor obtains shell's *IMalloc interface. TComRef<IMalloc> and copy constructors are supplied. TComRef<IMalloc>* and *TShellMalloc* assignment operators are also supplied.

Public constructors

TShellMalloc
Form 1   TShellMalloc();
Default constructor for *TShellMalloc*.

Form 2   TShellMalloc(const TComRef<IMalloc>& source);
TShellMalloc constructor to construct from *TComRef<IMalloc>*.

Form 3   TShellMalloc(const TShellMalloc& source);
TShellMalloc copy constructor.

Public member functions

operator=
Form 1   TShellMalloc& operator= (const TShellMalloc& source);
TShellMalloc assignment operator (from another *TShellMalloc*).

Form 2   TShellMalloc& operator= (const TComRef<IMalloc>& source);
TShellMalloc assignment operator (from *TComRef<IMalloc>*).

TSizeGripGadget class   gadget.h

TSizeGripGadget is a gadget that is used on the far right of a status bar to provide re-sizing grip for the host window.

Public constructors

TSizeGripGadget
TSizeGripGadget(int id = IDG_SIZEGRIP);
Constructs a gadget that can be grabbed to resize the frame.

Public member functions

Paint
void Paint(TDC& dc);
Draws the resize gadget.

TSlider class   slider.h

An abstract base class derived from *TScrollBar*, *TSlider* defines the basic behavior of sliders (controls that are used for providing nonscrolling, position information). Like scroll bars, sliders have minimum and maximum positions as well as line and page magnitude. Sliders can be moved using either the mouse or the keyboard. If you use a mouse to move the slider, you can drag the thumb position, click on the slot on either side of the thumb position to move the thumb by a specified amount (*PageMagnitude*), or click on the ruler to position the thumb at a specific spot on the slider. The keyboard's *Home* and *End* keys move the thumb position to the minimum (*Min*) and maximum (*Max*) positions on the slider.

You can use *TSlider*'s member functions to cause the thumb positions to automatically align with the nearest tick positions. (This is referred to as snapping.) You can also specify the tick gaps (the space between the lines that separate the major divisions of the X- or Y-axis).

The sample program SLIDER.CPP on your distribution disk displays the following thermostat that uses sliders:

See also   TVSlider, THSlider

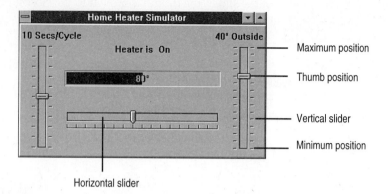

Public constructor and destructor

Constructor
TSlider(TWindow* parent, int id, int X, int Y, int W, int H, TResId thumbResId, TModule* module = 0);
Constructs a slider object setting *Pos* and *ThumbRgn* to 0, *TicGap* to *Range* divided by 10, *SlotThick* to 17, *Snap* to true, and *Sliding* to **false**. Sets *Attr.W* and *Attr.H* to the values in *X* and *Y*. *ThumbResId* is set to *thumbResId*.

Destructor
~TSlider();
Destructs a *TSlider* object and deletes *ThumbRgn*.

Public member functions

GetPosition
int GetPosition() const;
Returns the slider's current thumb position. Overloads *TScrollBar*'s virtual function.

See also   TSlider::SetPosition

GetRange
void GetRange(int &min, int &max) const;
Returns the end values of the present range of slider thumb positions in *min* and *max*. Overloads *TScrollBar*'s virtual function.

See also   TSlider::SetRange

SetNativeUse
static void SetNativeUse(TNativeUse nu);
Specifies whether the class uses the native (operating system) implementation or emulates it.

SetPosition
void SetPosition(int thumbPos);
Sets the position of the thumb and always redraws.

Moves the thumb to the position specified in *thumbPos*. If *thumbPos* is outside the present range of the slider, the thumb is moved to the closest position within the specified range. Overloads *TScrollBar*'s virtual function.

See also   TSlider::GetPosition

SetRange
void SetRange(int min, int max);
Checks and sets the slider range.

Sets the slider to the range between *min* and *max*. Overloads *TScrollBar*'s virtual function.

See also   TSlider::GetRange

SetRuler
Form 1   void SetRuler(int ticGap, bool snap = false);
Sets the slider's ruler. Each slider has a built-in ruler that is drawn with the slider. The ruler, which can be blank or have tick marks on it, can be created so that it forces the thumb to snap to the tick positions automatically.

Form 2   void SetRuler(int tics[], bool snap = false);
Sets the ruler's custom tics and snap. Snapping is not currently supported in native.

SetSel
void SetSel(int start, int end, bool redraw);
Set a selection range for the slider. Requires that TBS_ENABLESELRANGE style attribute be set.

See also   TSlider::EvPaint

Protected member functions

EvEraseBkgnd
bool EvEraseBkgnd(HDC hDC);

EvGetDlgCode
uint EvGetDlgCode(MSG far* msg);
Responds to a WM_GETDLGCODE message and let the dialog manager control the response to a DIRECTION key or TAB key input. Captures cursor-movement keys to move the thumb by returning a DLGC_WANTARROWS message, which indicates that direction keys are desired.The *msg* parameter indicates the kind of message (for example, a control or a command message) sent to the dialog box manager.

EvGetDlgCode returns a code that indicates how the control message is to be treated.

See also   TButton::EvGetDlgCode, TWindow::DefaultProcessing, DLGC_xxxxdialogcontrolmessageconstants

EvKeyDown
void EvKeyDown(uint key, uint repeatCount, uint flags);
Translates the virtual key code into a movement and then moves the thumb. *key* indicates the virtual key code of the pressed key, *repeatCount* holds the number of times

the same key is pressed, and *flags* contains one of the following messages, which translate to virtual key (VK) codes:

Value	Virtual key code
SB_PAGEUP	VK_PRIOR
SB_PAGEDOWN	VK_NEXT
SB_BOTTOM	VK_END
SB_TOP	VK_HOME
SB_LINEUP	VK_LEFT(same as SB_LINELEFT)
SB_LINEUP	VK_UP
SB_LINEDOWN	VK_RIGHT(same as SB_LINERIGHT)
SB_LINEDOWN	VK_DOWN

EvKillFocus
void EvKillFocus(HWND hWndGetFocus);
In response to a WM_KILLFOCUS message sent to a window that is losing the keyboard, *EvKillFocus* hides and then destroys the caret.

EvLButtonDblClk
void EvLButtonDblClk(uint modKeys, TPoint& point);
Responds to a WM_LBUTTONDBLCLK message (which indicates the user double-clicked the left mouse button), then throws away the messages so the base class does not receive them.

EvLButtonDown
void EvLButtonDown(uint modKeys, TPoint& point);
Responds to a mouse press by positioning the thumb or beginning a mouse drag. If the mouse is pressed down while it is over the thumb, *EvLButtonDown* enters sliding state. If the mouse is in the slot, *EvLButtonDown* pages up or down. If the mouse is on the ruler, *EvLButtonDown* jumps to that position. *EvLButtonDown* generates a scroll code of SB_THUMBPOSITION, SB_LINEUP, SB_LINEDOWN, SB_PAGEUP, SB_PAGEDOWN, or SB_THUMBTRACK.

See also   TSlider::EvLButtonUp

EvLButtonUp
void EvLButtonUp(uint modKeys, TPoint& point);
If the mouse button is released, *EvLButtonUp* ends sliding, paging, or jumping to a position on the ruler.

See also   TSlider::EvLButtonDown

EvMouseMove
void EvMouseMove(uint modKeys, TPoint& point);
Moves the mouse to the indicated position. If the mouse is being dragged, *EvMouseMove* positions the thumb and sends the appropriate message to the parent window. It also detects a lost button up and simulates it.

EvPaint
void EvPaint();

Paints the entire slider—ruler, slot, and thumb. Calls the virtual functions *PaintRuler*, *PaintSlot*, and *PaintThumb* to paint the components of the slider.

EvSetFocus
void EvSetFocus(HWND hWndLostFocus);
Paints a focus rect when we have focus. Removes it when we lose focus.

GetBkColor
void GetBkColor(TDC& dc);
Sends a WM_CTLCOLOR message to the parent and calls *dc::GetBkColor* to extract the background color for the slider. Gets and releases a brush obtained from our parent window for use in painting background areas in this control.

GetClassName
char far* GetClassName();
Returns the windows system class name that this slider is basing itself on. It depends on whether or not *NativeUse&nuUsing* is set.

HitTest
virtual int HitTest(TPoint& point) = 0;
Gets information about where a given X,Y location falls on the slider. The return value is in *scrollCodes*. Each of the derived classes performs comparisons to return a scroll code.

See also   TSlider::NotifyParent

NotifyParent
virtual void NotifyParent(int scrollCode, int pos=0) = 0;
Sends a WS_HSCROLL or WS_VSCROLL message to the parent window.

See also   TVSlider::HitTest

PaintRuler
virtual void PaintRuler(TDC& dc) = 0;
Paints the ruler. It is assumed that the slot or thumb do not overlap the ruler.

PaintSlot
virtual void PaintSlot(TDC& dc) = 0;
Paints the slot in which the thumb slides.

PaintThumb
virtual void PaintThumb(TDC& dc);
Paints the thumb itself using a resource DIB that overlaps the slot and is translated to the current system button colors.

PointToPos
virtual int PointToPos(const TPoint& point) = 0;
Translates an X,Y point to a position in slider units.

See also   TSlider::PosToPoint

PosToPoint
virtual TPoint PosToPoint(int pos) = 0;
Translates a position in slider units to an X,Y point.

See also   TSlider::PointToPos

SetupThumbRgn
virtual void SetupThumbRgn();
Creates the region that defines the thumb shape for this slider class. Although the default region is a simple bounding rectangle, it can be any shape. While the slider thumb is being moved, this region is used for testing the mouse position and updating the thumb position.

See also   TSlider::ThumbRgn

SetupWindow
void SetupWindow();
Calls *TScrollBar::SetupWindow* and *SetupThumbRgn* to set up the slider window.

SlideThumb
virtual void SlideThumb(TDC& dc, int thumbPos);
Slides the thumb to a given position and performs the necessary blitting and painting. Assumes that *Pos*, *Min*, and *Max* are up to date.

SnapPos
int SnapPos(int pos);
Constrains *pos* so it is in the range from *Min* to *Max* and (if snapping is enabled) performs snapping by rounding *pos* to the nearest *TicGap*.

See also   TSlider::TicGap

Protected data members

Bkcolor
TColor BkColor;
Gets and releases a brush obtained from our parent window for use in painting background areas in this control.

CaretRect
TRect CaretRect;
Refers to the position of the caret's rectangle. It's the bounding rect of Thumb's blink caret.

ClassNativeUse
static TNativeUse ClassNativeUse;
Always uses the common control when available for sliders.

Max
int Max;
Contains the maximum value of the slider position.

Min
int Min;
Contains the minimum value of the slider position.

MouseOffset
static TSize MouseOffset;
Shows the offset from the rectangle's original top left position to the position where the mouse is clicked. When the rectangle is moved, it can maintain a set relationship to the position of the mouse click.

Pos
int Pos;
Indicates where the thumb is positioned on the slider.

See also TSlider::GetPosition

Range
uint Range;
Contains the difference between the maximum and minimum range of the slider.

SlideDC
static TDC* SlideDC;
Used while the mouse is down and the thumb is sliding, *SlideDC* reflects the movement of the mouse on the DC.

Sliding
bool Sliding;
true if the thumb is sliding. Otherwise, **false**.

SlotThick
int SlotThick;
Indicates the thickness of the slot. Set to 17 by default.

Snap
bool Snap;
true if snapping is activated; otherwise **false**.

ThumbRect
TRect ThumbRect;
Holds the thumb's bounding rectangle.

ThumbResId
TResId ThumbResId;
The bitmap resource ID for the thumb knob.

ThumbRgn
TRegion* ThumbRgn;
Refers to the region, if any, that defines the thumb shape for this slider class.

See also TSlider::SetupThumbRgn

TicGap
int TicGap;
Specifies the amount of space in pixels between ticks.

Response table entries

Response table entry	Member function
EV_WM_GETDLGCODE	EvGetDlgCode
EV_WM_KEYDOWN	EvKeyDown
EV_WM_KILLFOCUS	EvKillFocus
EV_WM_LBUTTONDBLCLK	EvLButtonDblClk
EV_WM_LBUTTONDOWN	EvLButtonDown
EV_WM_LBUTTONUP	EvLButtonUp
EV_WM_MOUSEMOVE	EvMouseMove
EV_WM_PAINT	EvPaint
EV_WM_SETFOCUS	EvSetFocus
EV_WM_SIZE	EvSize

THSlider class   slider.h

Derived from *TSlider*, *THSlider* provides implementation details for horizontal sliders. See *TSlider* for an illustration of a horizontal slider.

Public constructor

Constructor
THSlider(TWindow* parent, int id, int X, int Y, int W, int H, TResId thumbResId = IDB_HSLIDERTHUMB,
    TModule* module = 0);
Constructs a slider object with a default bitmap resource ID of IDB_HSLIDERTHUMB for the thumb knob.

Protected member functions

HitTest
int HitTest(TPoint& point);
Overrides *TSlider*'s virtual *HitTest* function and gets information about where a given X,Y location falls on the slider. The return value is in *scrollCodes*.

NotifyParent
void NotifyParent(int scrollCode, int pos=0);
Overrides *TSlider*'s virtual *NotifyParent* function and sends a WS_HSCROLL message to the parent window.

PaintRuler
void PaintRuler(TDC&);
Overrides *TSlider*'s virtual *PaintRuler* function and paints the horizontal ruler.

PaintSlot
void PaintSlot(TDC&);

Overrides *TSlider*'s virtual *PaintSlot* function and paints the slot in which the thumb slides.

PointToPos
int PointToPos(TPoint& point);
Overrides *TSlider*'s virtual *PointToPos* function and translates an X,Y point to a position in slider units.

PosToPoint
TPoint PosToPoint(int pos);
Overrides *TSlider*'s virtual *PosToPoint* function and translates a position in slider units to an X,Y point.

TSocket class   wsksock.h

TSocket encapsulates the basic attributes of a socket. A socket is an endpoint of communication to which a name may be bound. Each socket in use has a type and an associated process.

Type definitions

TShutMode enum
enum TShutMode {ShutModeNoRecv = 0, ShutModeNoSend = 1, ShutModeNoRecvSend = 2};
TShutMode can be one of the following constants:

• ShutModeNoRecv

• ShutModeNoSend

• ShutModeNoRecvSend

Public constructors and destructor

Constructors
Form 1   TSocket();
Default constructor for a socket. The individual members of the *TSocket* can be set later.

Form 2   TSocket(SOCKET& newS);
TSocket(SOCKET&) is a constructor based on a Winsock SOCKET descriptor.

Form 3   TSocket(TSocketAddress& newSocketAddress, int nNewFamily=PF_INET, int nNewType=SOCK_STREAM,
int nNewProtocol=0);
This is the standard constructor for a *TSocket*. It doesn't call *socket()* or *bind()*. These must be done independently.

Destructor
virtual ~TSocket();
This *TSocket* destructor will close the socket it if has not be closed already. It will also delete the friend notification window.

Public member functions

BindSocket

Form 1   virtual int BindSocket();

This *BindSocket* simply binds with the previously defined member data socket address.

Form 2   virtual int BindSocket(TSocketAddress& addressToBindTo);

BindSocket is much like the Winsock bind() function. Regardless of what mySocketAddress may have been previously, a call to *bind()* immediately makes the socket's address the one put into the bind() call. Thus, *mySocketAddress* is always assigned to be *boundSocketAddress*. The address argument must be in network byte ordering. On the other hand, the *SocketAddress* class always keeps its addresses in network byte ordering.

CancelNotification

virtual int CancelNotification();

CancelNotification() turns off the notification to this window. This also changes the socket to be blocking.

The return value is WINSOCK_ERROR or WINSOCK_NOERROR. You can then examine *GetLastError()*.

CloseSocket

virtual int CloseSocket();

The *CloseSocket()* function is much like the Winsock *closesocket()* function.

ConvertProtocol

virtual int ConvertProtocol(char* protocol);

Converts a string protocol to integer value. Makes assumptions about the protocol string. Only "tcp" and udp return valid values.

CreateSocket

virtual int CreateSocket();

The *CreateSocket* function is much like the Winsock *socket()* function. This function assumes that *nFamily*, *nType*, and *nProtocol* are already set properly. Note also that since the return of *socket()* is assigned to *s*, that *s* must not already be used. This is another way of saying that there can only be one SOCKET for each *TSocket* object.

GetBroadcastOption

int GetBroadcastOption(bool& bBroadcast);

Retrieves the current broadcast option.

GetDebugOption

int GetDebugOption(bool& bDebug);

Retrieves the current debugging option.

GetDriverWaitingSize

virtual ulong GetDriverWaitingSize();

GetDriverWaitingSize() is much like calling *ioctlsocket(s, FIONREAD,...)* in Winsock. It returns the number of bytes waiting to be read on the socket. For datagrams, it is the size of the next datagram. For streams, it should be the total waiting bytes.

GetKeepAliveOption

int GetKeepAliveOption(bool& bKeepAlive);

Retrieves the *keepAlive* option.

GetLastError

int GetLastError();

Returns the last error of the socket.

GetLingerOption

int GetLingerOption(bool& bLinger, ushort& nLingerTime);

Retreives the current linger option.

GetMyAddress

Form 1   virtual int GetMyAddress(TSocketAddress& socketAddress, int& nAddressLength);

This function stores the address into the reference argument *socketAddress*. *addressLength* will hold the length of the address. Uses the SOCKET in my member data as the socket to get the address of.

Form 2   virtual int GetMyAddress(TSocketAddress& socketAddress, int& nAddressLength, SOCKET& socket);

This function stores the address into the reference argument *socketAddress*. *addressLength* will hold the length of the address. *socket* refers to the socket whose address will be examined.

GetOOBOption

int GetOOBOption(bool& bSendOOBDataInline);

Retrieves the out-of-band (OOB) option.

GetPeerAddress

Form 1   virtual int GetPeerAddress(TSocketAddress& socketAddress, int& nAddressLength);

This version of *GetPeerAddress()* works on our own socket descriptor.

Form 2   virtual int GetPeerAddress(TSocketAddress& socketAddress, int& nAddressLength, SOCKET& socket);

The *GetPeerAddress()* function is much like the Winsock *getpeername()* function. The Winsock *getpeername()* function is misnamed; it should be *getpeeraddress()*. *socketAddress* will be changed to have the right addressing info, and *nAddressLength* will be set to be the address length.

Note that this function can be used to get the address for any socket descriptor, not just our own socket descriptor.

GetReceiveBufferOption

int GetReceiveBufferOption(int& nReceiveBufferSize);

Retrieves the current receiving buffer size.

GetReuseAddressOption

int GetReuseAddressOption(bool& bAllowReuseAddress);

Retrieves the reusable address option.

GetRouteOption

int GetRouteOption(bool& bRoute);

Retrieves the routing option.

GetSendBufferOption
int GetSendBufferOption(int& nSendBufferSize);
Retrieves the current sending buffer size.

GetTotalWaitingSize
virtual ulong GetTotalWaitingSize();
Returns the total number of bytes waiting to be read.

operator =
TSocket& operator =(TSocket& newSocket);
Does a deep copy of the TSocket—as much as possible.

operator ==
friend bool operator ==(const TSocket& socket1, const TSocket& socket2);
While it's possible that two sockets could refer to the same SOCKET (though this would likely create a mess if not governed with care), it's defined as not possible that two sockets could have the same window member. This is because the window is created uniquely on construction for each *TSocket*.

operator SOCKET
operator SOCKET() const;
Returns the handle of the socket.

SetBroadcastOption
int SetBroadcastOption(bool bBroadcast);
Allows transmission of broadcast messages.

SetDebugOption
int SetDebugOption(bool bDebug);
Records debugging info.

SetKeepAliveOption
int SetKeepAliveOption(bool bKeepAlive);
Sends *keepAlive* messages.

SetLingerOption
int SetLingerOption(bool bLinger, ushort nLingerTime=0);
If you set *linger* to true, then that means to linger for *lingerTime* seconds. Examples:

- *linger*=true, *lingerTime*=0. Hard immediate close. All queued data for sending gets canned immediately.

- *linger*=true, *lingerTime*=2. Graceful close. Waits 2 seconds to try to send any pending data.

- *linger*=false, *lingerTime*=<any>. "Graceful" immediate close. Causes data to be still in queue to send when ready.

SetMaxReadBufferSize
virtual void SetMaxReadBufferSize(int nNewMaxReadBufferSize);
This should be called by someone who knows what the correct value is.

SetMyAddress
virtual void SetMyAddress(TSocketAddress& newSocketAddress);
This may be useful for changing the address or setting the address before binding. It's no good to change this after binding, as a binding is a permanent association between a socket descriptor and a full address (for IP, this is a ushort port and ulong address).

SetNotificationSet
virtual void SetNotificationSet(int notificationSet);
Returns the set of notifications the socket will catch.

SetNotificationWindow
virtual void SetNotificationWindow(TWindow* windowNotification);
Sets the new notification window.

SetOOBOption
int SetOOBOption(bool bSendOOBDataInline);
Receives out-of-band (OOB) data in the normal data stream.

SetPeerSocketAddress
virtual void SetPeerSocketAddress(TSocketAddress& newPeerSocketAddress);
The *myPeerSocketAddress* member variable is useful for Datagram sockets because it allows them to specify a default destination to send datagrams to. With a default destination, a datagram socket that always or often sends to one address can simply call the *Write()* or *Send()* functions with no address arguments and the data will send to the default address. This function can also be used by a stream socket to set the address for a peer that it wants to connect to.

SetReceiveBufferOption
int SetReceiveBufferOption(int nReceiveBufferSize);
Sets the buffer size for receiving messages.

SetReuseAddressOption
int SetReuseAddressOption(bool bAllowReuseAddress);
Allows the socket to bind to an already-bound address.

SetRouteOption
int SetRouteOption(bool bRoute);
A false argument means don't route.

SetSaveSocketOnDelete
bool SetSaveSocketOnDelete(bool saveSocket=true);
Saves the socket on deletion.

SetSendBufferOption
int SetSendBufferOption(int nSendBufferSize);
Sets the buffer size for sending messages.

SetSocketStyle
virtual void SetSocketStyle(int nNewFamily=PF_INET, int nNewType=SOCK_STREAM, int nNewProtocol=0);

The *SetSocketStyle* function can be used to set or change some *TSocket* member data. Note that the *newFamily* is also represented in the *TSocketAddress* member, and so they should match.

ShutDownSocket
virtual int ShutDownSocket(TShutMode shutMode = ShutModeNoRecvSend);
The *ShutDownSocket()* function is much like the Winsock *shutdown()* function. Note that shutting down a socket essentially means that you can't un-shut it down. It's a graceful way of preparing to end a session, somewhat like a yellow stoplight. Use this function to close your socket, while still allowing data be received from the network. This is as opposed to *CloseSocket()*, which kills all transfers in both directions. shutMode is one of the enumerations: *ShutModeNoRecv*, *ShutModeNoSend*, or *ShutModeNoRecvSend*.

StartAcceptNotification
virtual int StartAcceptNotification();
This function says to listen only to FD_ACCEPT messages. Note that a socket set up to be a listening socket will never be a connected socket, and a connected socket will never receive FD_ACCEPT messages. Thus all stream sockets are implicitly either connected sockets or listening sockets. Since the accepted socket needs a different notification window from the listening socket, and the sockets specification says that an accepted socket inherits the notification properties of the listening socket, the listening socket must not be set to receive FD_READ, etc, notifications. This is because it's possible that between the *accept()* call for the new socket and the *WSAAsyncSelect()* call for the new socket, data may be received for the new socket. Thus the listening socket may get sent the message and it would never get routed to the new socket. Calling this function is saying that this SocketWindow is for listening for connections.

The return value is WINSOCK_ERROR or WINSOCK_NOERROR. You can then examine *GetLastError()*.

StartCustomNotification
virtual int StartCustomNotification(int nSelectionOptions);
The return value is WINSOCK_ERROR or WINSOCK_NOERROR. You can then examine *GetLastError()*.

StartRegularNotification
virtual int StartRegularNotification();
This function turns on all Winsock notifications except FD_ACCEPT. Calling this function is saying that this *SocketWindow* is for connections rather than for listening. Since a Winsock socket cannot be a listening socket and a connected socket at the same time, the notification functions are separated from each other: *StartAcceptNotification()* and *StartRegularNotification()*.

The return value is WINSOCK_ERROR or WINSOCK_NOERROR. You can then examine *GetLastError()*.

Protected data members

Family
int Family;

PF_INET, etc. (This is the protocol family.)

LastError
int LastError;
The last error.

MaxReadBufferSize
int MaxReadBufferSize;
Maximum buffer size.

Protocol
int Protocol;
IPPROTO_TCP, etc.

SaveSocket
short SaveSocket;
Saves the socket on deletion.

Type
int Type;
SOCK_STREAM, etc.

Protected member functions

DoAcceptNotification
virtual DoAcceptNotification(const SOCKET& s, int nError);
This isn't responded to in the generic *TSocket* class.

DoCloseNotification
virtual DoCloseNotification(const SOCKET& s, int nError);
This isn't responded to in the generic *TSocket* class.

DoConnectNotification
virtual DoConnectNotification(const SOCKET& s, int nError);
This isn't responded to in the generic *TSocket* class.

DoOOBNotification
virtual DoOOBNotification(const SOCKET& s, int nError);
This isn't responded to in the generic *TSocket* class.

DoReadNotification
virtual DoReadNotification(const SOCKET& s, int nError);
This function gets called whenever the socket gets a read notification. This means that data on the port is ready to be read. Thus this function must be subclassed by a *DatagramSocket* and *StreamSocket*.

DoWriteNotification
virtual DoWriteNotification(const SOCKET& s, int nError);
The generic socket doesn't know how many bytes it can send, since this limit is dependent on whether the socket is a stream or datagram socket. Thus this function must be subclassed by a *DatagramSocket* and *StreamSocket*.

Init

void Init();

This function is an intitialization function called by the *TSocket* constructors. It simply creates the friend window that the *TSocket* needs for Winsock notifications.

SocketsCallCheck

int SocketsCallCheck(int error);

Checks the return error value from a sockets call, caching the last error if one occured (i.e., error is non-zero). Returns a Winsock error/noerror code.

TSocketAddress class   wskaddr.h

TSocketAddress normally stores its data in network byte ordering, as opposed to host byte ordering.

Public constructors

Form 1   TSocketAddress();
Only the family is specified. The rest of the data is currently undefined.

Form 2   TSocketAddress::TSocketAddress(const sockaddr& src)
The argument is a socket address in network byte ordering.

Form 3   TSocketAddress::TSocketAddress(const TSocketAddress& src)
The argument address should be in network byte ordering.

Form 4   TSocketAddress(ushort family, char* data, short dataLength);
The argument address should be in network byte ordering.

Public member functions

GetFamily

ushort GetFamily();

Returns the family of addressing this address belongs to.

operator =

TSocketAddress& operator =(const sockaddr& src);

The argument address should be in network byte ordering.

SetAddress

void SetAddress(ushort family, const char* data, short dataLength);

newFamily is AF_INET, etc. *data* is a pointer to data in the same format as sockaddr.sa_data[]. *dataLength* is the length of data. It is limited to 14 bytes in WinSock 1.1. The passed data should be in network byte ordering.

SetFamily

void SetFamily(ushort family);

Sets the family of addressing this address belongs to.

TSocketError class

TSocketError converts Windows Sockets errors to string messages.

Public constructors

Form 1   TSocketError(int nNewError=0, int nNewSizeToAllocate=128);
This function constructs with the error code and the size of the buffer to allocate.

Form 2   virtual ~TSocketError();
This function destroys the allocated string.

Public member functions

AppendError
Form 1   char* AppendError(int nStringResourceToAppendErrorTo, char* szDestination=0);
This function is similar to *AppendError(char*)*, but the pre-string comes from a string resource and *szStringToAppendErrorTo* will be overwritten with what is in the string resource and appended to the Windows Sockets Error description. *stringToAppendErrorTo* must be able to hold at least 128 characters.

Form 2   char* AppendError(char* szStringToAppendErrorTo, char* szDestination=0);
This function appends an error string to whatever is in the string *stringToAppendErrorTo* and puts the result in destination. You may want to put something specific about the error in the string and then use *AppendError()* to add the Windows Sockets error code and description to it.

For example:

MessageBox(TSocketError(WSAENOTCONN). AppendError(Unable to send your mail), Error, MB_OK); and *AppendError()* will put "\n\nWinsock Error 10057: Socket is not presently connected" after the Unable to send you mail string.

szStringToAppendErrorTo must be able to hold at least 128 characters.

GetReasonString
char* GetReasonString();
This function hands the pointer to the string to the caller. The caller shouldn't alter this string (because it doesn't belong to the caller).

GetReasonValue
int GetReasonValue();
This function returns the error code.

Init
void Init(int newError);
This function initializes the error code.

operator =
TSocketError& operator =(TSocketError& newSocketError);
This function copies the error code and string.

operator ==
friend bool operator ==(TSocketError& socketError1, TSocketError& socketError2);
The important criteria for determining equality is the error value. The string is unimportant.

Protected member functions

GetErrorString
void GetErrorString();
This function gets a string, suitable for display, based on the *nError* value. The previous string is deleted if necessary. Note that the string allocated must be at least 128 characters long. Note that even though the error strings you see don't have error numbers associated with them, the function pre-pends the error number to the *szString* before returning. If you are writing string resources for the error strings, don't put error numbers in the string, because that will be done for you later.

SizeToAllocate
int SizeToAllocate;
This function specifies the size to allocate for a string.

TSocketInfo class   wsksockm.h

TSocketInfo encapsulates the structure that contains details of the Windows Socket implementation. For example, it contains the version of the Windows Socket specification implemented and the maximum number of sockets that a single process can open.

Public constructor

TSocketInfo
TSocketInfo();
Default constructor. Initializes all data members to 0.

TSocketManager class   wsksockm.h

TSocketManager is a class that starts up WinSock and provides information about the system's WinSock.

Public constructors and destructor

Constructor
TSocketManager(short nVersionMajor=1, short nVersionMinor=1, short bAutoStartup=1);

The *SocketManager* constructor takes a major and minor version as parameters. These version parameters are the WinSock versions that can be requested, as with *WSAStartup()* calls.

Destructor
virtual ~TSocketManager();
The *TSocketManager* destructor cleans up after itself. Every time *Startup()* (same as *WSAStartup()*) is called, this destructor will call *ShutDown* (same as *WSACleanup()*).

Public member functions

GetDescription
char* GetDescription();
Returns the system's description of WinSock.

GetLastError
int GetLastError();
Returns the last error code.

GetMajorVersion
int GetMajorVersion();
Returns the major version of WinSock support.

GetMaxSocketsAvailable
ushort GetMaxSocketsAvailable();
Returns maximum number of WinSock connections avaialble.

GetMaxUdpDgAvailable
ushort GetMaxUdpDgAvailable();
Returns maximum number of bytes each UDP packet can be.

GetMinorVersion
int GetMinorVersion();
Returns the minor version of WinSock support.

GetSystemStatus
char* GetSystemStatus();
Returns the status of WinSock.

GetVendorInfo
char far* GetVendorInfo();
Returns this WinSocket's vendor's information.

Information
void Information(TSocketInfo& socketInfo);
Sets the information about this WinSocket.

Init
void Init(short versionMajor=1, short versionMinor=1);
The *ITSocketManager* function does some initialization for the *TSocketManager*. This function is separate from the constructor so it can be called at any time to re-specify the

desired major and minor versions before a call to *Startup()*. *nNewVersionMajor* and *nNewVersionMinor* will be the values specified in the WinSock *WSAStartup()* call that *TSocketManager::Startup()* makes. The return value is true or false.

IsAvailable
int IsAvailable();
Returns true if WinSock is available.

ShutDown
int ShutDown();
The *ShutDown()* function is the equivalent to the WinSock *WSACleanup()* function. You can call this function if you want, but in its destructor, the *TSocketManager* will automatically call it once for every time *Startup()* was called. Of course, the *TSocketManager* cannot know about any independent *WSAStartup()* direct calls that are made.

Startup
int Startup();
The *Startup()* function is equivalent to the WinSock *WSAStartup()* function. This function fills out the *TSocketManager's SocketInfo* structure (same as a *WSAData* structure) with the return information. *GetMaxSocketsAvailable()*, *GetVendorInfo()*, *Available()*, *GetMajorVersion()*, *GetMinorVersion()*, or *Information()* functions can then be called to get the results of the call.

Protected data members

Available
short Available;
Flag for WinSock availability.

LastError
int LastError;
Last error code.

SocketInfo
TSocketInfo SocketInfo;
Information about this WinSocket implementation.

StartupCount
short StartupCount;
Make sure to not overflow number of connects.

VersionMajor
short VersionMajor;
Major version number.

VersionMinor
short VersionMinor;
Minor version number.

TSortedStringArray class

validate.h

Implements a list of ASCII characters stored as a sorted array of elements that are string objects. *TSortedStringArray* can perform many of the string manipulation functions, such as adding and removing elements from the array, and provides many of the common C++ functions implemented by container classes.

See also   TValidator, TLookupValidator

Public constructors

TSortedStringArray
TSortedStringArray(int upper, int lower, int delta);
Constructs a *TSortedStringArray* object with an upper boundary of *upper*, a lower boundary of *lower*, and a growth delta of *delta*.

Type definitions

void
typedef void (*IterFunc)(string&, void*);
Function type used as a parameter to the *ForEach* member function.

int
typedef int (*CondFunc)(const string&, void*);
Function type used as a parameter to the *FirstThat* and *LastThat* member functions.

Public member functions

Add
int Add(const string& t);
Adds an element to the array at the next available index position. Adding an element beyond the upper boundary leads to an overflow condition. If this condition occurs and the growth delta, *delta*, (from the constructor) is nonzero, the array is expanded (by sufficient multiples of *delta* bytes) to accommodate the addition. If *delta* is zero, *Add* fails. *Add* returns 0 if the object could not be added.

ArraySize
unsigned ArraySize() const;
Returns the size of the array.

Destroy
Form 1   int Destroy(const string& t);
Removes the element specified by *t* and deletes it.

Form 2   int Destroy(int loc);
Removes an element from the array at the specified index location, *loc*, and deletes it.

Detach

Form 1   int Detach(const string& t);

Removes the specified element from the array. Returns 1 if successful; otherwise, returns 0.

Form 2   int Detach(int loc);

Removes an element from the array at the specified index location, *loc*. Returns 1 if successful; otherwise, returns 0.

Find

int Find(const string& t) const;

Finds the first element represented by *t* and returns the index where the element is located.

FirstThat

string* FirstThat(CondFunc cond, void* args) const;

Returns a pointer to the first element in the array that satisfies a specified condition. *cond* is the test function pointer that returns true for a specified condition. *args* contains the various arguments passed. Returns 0 if no element in the array satisfies the given condition. Because *FirstThat* creates its own internal iterator, you can use it as a search function also.

Flush

void Flush();

Removes all elements from the array without destroying the array itself.

ForEach

void ForEach(IterFunc iter, void* args);

Creates an internal iterator to execute the specified function, *iter*, for each element in the array. Use the *args* argument to pass various kinds of data to this function.

GetItemsInContainer

unsigned GetItemsInContainer() const;

Returns the number of elements in the array.

HasMember

int HasMember(const string& t) const;

Returns 1 if the element specified by *t* exists in the array; otherwise returns 0.

IsEmpty

int IsEmpty() const;

Returns 1 if the array is empty; otherwise, returns 0.

IsFull

int IsFull() const

Returns 1 if the array is full; otherwise, returns 0.

LastThat

string* LastThat(CondFunc cond, void* args) const;

Returns a pointer to the last element in the array that satisfies a specified condition. *cond* is the test function pointer that returns true for a specified condition. *args* contains the various arguments passed. Returns 0 if no element in the array satisfies the given condition. Because *LastThat* creates its own internal iterator, you can use it as a search function also.

LowerBound
int LowerBound() const;
Returns the array's lower boundary.

UpperBound
int UpperBound() const;
Returns the array's upper boundary.

operator [ ]
Form 1   string& operator [](int loc);
Returns a reference to the element at the location specified by *loc*. This version resizes the array if it is necessary to make *loc* a valid index.

Form 2   string& operator [](int loc) const;
Returns a reference to the element at the location specified by *loc*. This version throws an exception in the debugging version on an attempt to index out of bounds.

TSplashWindow class   splashwi.h

TSplashWindow creates a layout window that contains a *TPictureWindow* and optionally, a *TStatic* and a *TGauge*.

Type definitions

TStyle enum
enum TStyle {None, ShrinkToFit, MakeGauge, MakeStatic, CaptureMouse};
TStyle is used to describe the styles for a splash window.

Table 2.31   Style constants

Constant	Meaning if set
None	No styles are applied.
ShrinkToFit	Resizes the window to fit bitmap
MakeGauge	Displays a gauge to indicate progress
MakeStatic	Display a static window
CaptureMouse	Captures mouse clicks

Public constructors

Form 1   TSplashWindow(TDib& dib, int width, int height, int style = None, uint timeOut = 0, const char far* title = 0, TModule* module = 0);
Constructor to create a splash screen. The parameters width and height are the dimensions of the window unless the style *ShrinkToFit* is used (in which case, the size of

the DIB is used). The *timeOut* parameter is the number of milliseconds to wait until the splash screen closes itself. Use 0 to not automatically close the splash screen. The splash screen does not assume ownership of the DIB. The lifetime of the DIB must be as long as the lifetime of the splash screen.

Form 2   ~TSplashWindow();
Deletes the child controls.

Public member functions

SetPercentDone
void SetPercentDone(int percent);
Sets the percentage done for the gauge control. If the splash screen does not have a gauge control, this doesn't do anything.

SetText
void SetText(const char far* text);
Changes the text within the static control. If the splash screen does not have a static control, this doesn't do anything.

Protected member functions

CleanupWindow
void CleanupWindow();
Before the window closes, and if the mouse has been captured, this releases it now.

EvLButtonDown
void EvLButtonDown(uint modKeys, TPoint& point);
If the user clicks on the splash screen and the *CaptureMouse* style is on, this closes the splash screen.

EvTimer
void EvTimer(uint timerId);
Handler for the timer event. Closes the window.

GetGauge
TGauge* GetGauge();
Returns the gauge used by the splash window. The gauge control is only created if the style includes *MakeGauge*.

GetStatic
TStatic* GetStatic();
Returns the static control used by the splash window. The static control is only created if the style includes *MakeStatic*.

GetStyle
uint GetStyle() const;
Returns the current style of the splash window.

GetTimeOut
uint GetTimeOut() const;
Returns the number of milliseconds for the splash window to automatically close.

HasStyle
bool HasStyle(TStyle) const;
Determines if the splash window has a particular style.

SetupWindow
void SetupWindow();
After the window has been created, this centers the window and makes it topmost.

Response table entries

Response table entry	Member function
EV_WM_LBUTTONDOWN	EvLButtonDown
EV_WM_TIMER	EvTimer

TStatic class   static.h

An interface object that represents a static text interface element. Static elements consist of text or graphics that the user does not change. An application, however, can modify the static control. You must use a *TStatic* object, for example, to create a static control that's used to display a text label such as a copyright notice in a parent *TWindow* object. *TStatic* can also be used to make it easier to modify the text of static controls in *TDialog* objects. See the sample program in the EXAMPLES\OWL\OWLAPI\STATIC directory for an example of a static control.

Public data members

TextLimit
uint TextLimit;
Holds the size of the text buffer for static controls. Because of the null terminator on the string, the number of characters that can be stored in the static control is one less than *TextLimit*. *TextLimit* is also the number of bytes transferred by the *Transfer* member function.

Public constructors

Form 1   TStatic(TWindow* parent, int id, const char far* title, int x, int y, int w, int h, uint textLimit = 0,
            TModule* module = 0);
Constructs a static control object with the supplied parent window (*parent*), control ID (*Id*), text (*title*), position (*x, y*) relative to the origin of the parent window's client area, width (*w*), height (*h*), and default text length (*textLimit*) of zero. By default, the static control is visible upon creation and has left-justified text. (Set to WS_CHILD |

WS_VISIBLE | WS_GROUP | SS_LEFT.) Invokes a *TControl* constructor. You can change the default style of the static control via the control object's constructor.

Form 2   TStatic(TWindow* parent, int resourceId, uint textLimit = 0, TModule* module = 0);
Constructs a *TStatic* object to be associated with a static control interface control of a *TDialog* object. Invokes the *TControl* constructor with similar parameters, then sets *TextLimit* to *textLimit*. Disables the data transfer mechanism by calling *DisableTransfer*. The *resourceId* parameter must correspond to a static control resource that you define.

Public member functions

Clear
virtual void Clear();
Clears the text of the associated static control.

GetIcon
HICON GetIcon() const;
Returns the handle of the icon used for this static control.

GetText
int GetText(char far* str, int maxChars);
Retrieves the static control's text, stores it in the *str* argument of *maxChars* size, and returns the number of characters copied.

GetTextLimit
int GetTextLimit() const;
Returns the length of the static control's text.

SetIcon
HICON SetIcon(HICON);
Sets the handle of the icon.

SetText
void SetText(const char far* str);
Sets the static control's text to the string supplied in *str*.

SetTextLimit
void SetTextLimit(uint textlimit);
Sets the maximum number of characters to display in the control.

Transfer
uint Transfer(void* buffer, TTransferDirection direction);
Transfers *TextLimit* characters of text to or from a transfer buffer pointed to by *buffer*. If *direction* is *tdGetData*, the text is transferred to the buffer from the static control. If *direction* is *tdSetData*, the static control's text is set to the text contained in the transfer buffer. *Transfer* returns *TextLimit*, the number of bytes stored in or retrieved from the buffer. If *direction* is *tdSizeData*, *Transfer* returns *TextLimit* without transferring data.

Protected member functions

EvSize
void EvSize (uint sizeType, TSize& size);
Overrides *TWindow*'s virtual *EvSize* function. When the static control is resized, *EvSize* ensures that it is repainted.

GetClassName
virtual char far* GetClassName();
Returns the name of *TStatic's* registration class (STATIC), or returns STATIC_CLASS if Borland Windows Custom Controls (BWCC) is enabled.

Response table entries

Response table entry	Member function
EV_WM_SIZE	EvSize

TStatus class   except.h

Used primarily for backward compatibility with previous versions of ObjectWindows, *TStatus* is used by *TModule* and *TWindow* to indicate an error in the initialization of an interface object. If *Status* is set to a nonzero value, a *TXCompatibility* exception is thrown.

Public constructors

TStatus
TStatus();
Constructs a *TStatus* object and initializes the status code to 0.

See also   TModule::Status, TWindow::Status

Public data members

operator =
TStatus& operator =(int statusCode);
Sets the status code and throws a *TXCompatibility* exception.

operator int
operator int() const;
Returns the status code.

TStatusBar class

statusba.h

Type definitions

TModeIndicator enum
enum TModeIndicator {ExtendSelection = 1, CapsLock = 1 << 1, NumLock = 1 << 2, ScrollLock = 1 << 3,
Overtype = 1 << 4, RecordingMacro = 1 << 5, SizeGrip = 1 << 6};
Enumerates the keyboard modes. By default, these are arranged horizontally on the
status bar from left to right. Sets the extended selection, CapsLock, NumLock,
ScrollLock, Overtype, recording macro, and size grip indicators.

Public constructors

TStatusBar
TStatusBar(TWindow* parent = 0, TGadget_TBorderStyle borderStyle = TGadget_Recessed,
uint modeIndicators = 0, TFont* font = new TGadgetWindowFont, TModule* module = 0);
Constructs a *TStatusBar* object in the *parent* window and creates any new gadgets and
mode indicator gadgets. Sets *BorderStyle* to *borderStyle*, *ModeIndicators* to *modeIndicators*,
and *NumModeIndicators* to 0. *borderStyle* can be any one of the values of the *BorderStyle*
enum (for example, *Plain, Raised, Recessed,* or *Embossed*). The parameter mode indicators
can be one of the values of the *TModeIndicator* enum, such as CapsLock, NumLock,
ScrollLock, or Overtype. The parameter *font* points to a font object that contains the type
of fonts used for the gadget window. The parameter, *module*, which defaults to 0, is
passed to the base *TWindow*'s constructor in the *module* parameter. Sets the values of the
margins and borders depending on whether the gadget is raised, recessed, or plain.

Public member functions

GetModeIndicator
bool GetModeIndicator(TModeIndicator i) const;
Returns the current status bar mode indicator.

Insert
void Insert(TGadget& gadget, TPlacement = After, TGadget* sibling = 0);
Inserts the gadget (objects derived from class *TGadget*) in the status bar. By default, the
new gadget is placed just after any existing gadgets and to the left of the status mode
indicators. For example, you can insert a painting tool or a happy face that activates a
recorded macro.

operator [ ]
TGadget* operator[](uint index);
Returns a gadget at a given index, but cannot access mode indicator gadgets.

SetModeIndicator
void SetModeIndicator(TModeIndicator, bool state);

Sets *TModeIndicator* to a given text gadget and set the status (on, by default) of the mode indicator. For the mode indicator to appear on the status bar, you must specify the mode when the window is constructed.

See also   TStatusBar::TModeIndicator

SetSpacing
void SetSpacing(TSpacing& spacing);

Uses the *TSpacing* values to set the spacing to be used between mode indicator gadgets. *TSpacing* sets the status-bar margins in layout units. Typically, the message indicator (the leftmost text gadget) is left-justified on the status bar and the other indicators are right-justified. See *TLayoutMetrics* for a detailed explanation of layout units and constraints.

```
struct TSpacing {
    TMargins::TUnits  Units;
    int Value;
    TSpacing() {Units = TMargins::LayoutUnits; Value = 0;}
};
```

See also   TStatusBar::TModeIndicator

ToggleModeIndicator
void ToggleModeIndicator(TModeIndicator);

Toggles the *ModeIndicator*.

Protected data members

BorderStyle
TGadget::TBorderStyle BorderStyle;

One of the enumerated border styles—*None, Plain, Raised, Recessed,* or *Embossed*—used by the mode indicators on the status bar.

ModeIndicators
uint ModeIndicators;

The *ModeIndicators* bit field indicates which mode indicators have been created for the status bar.

ModeIndicatorState
uint ModeIndicatorState;

Specifies the mode of the status bar. This can be any one of the values of *TModeIndicator* enum, such as *CapsLock, NumLock, ScrollLock, Overtype, RecordingMacro,* or *ExtendSelection*.

NumModeIndicators
uint NumModeIndicators;

Specifies the number of mode indicators, which can range from 1 to 5.

Spacing
TSpacing Spacing;

Specifies the spacing between mode indicators on the status bar.

Protected member functions

EvNCHitTest
uint EvNCHitTest(TPoint& point);
If the status bar has a size grip gadget and the mouse is over the gadget, simulates resizing of the frame.

IdleAction
bool IdleAction(long);
If more than one application is running, *TStatusBar* calls *IdleAction* instead of *PreProcessMsg* to check the state of the *NumLock*, *CapsLock*, or *ScrollLock* keys and to update the mode indicators if they do not reflect the current status of these keys.

See also   TStatusBar::PreProcessMsg

GetModeIndicators
uint GetModeIndicators() const;
Returns the bit flags for which indicator is on.

GetNumModeIndicators
uint GetNumModeIndicators();
Returns the number of mode indicators that are on.

GetSpacing
TSpacing& GetSpacing();
Returns the spacing between the mode indicator gadgets.

PositionGadget
void PositionGadget(TGadget* previous, TGadget* next, TPoint& point);
Determines the position of the new gadget in relation to any previously existing gadgets and uses the *Pixels*, *LayoutUnits*, and *BorderUnits* fields of *TMargins* to determine the amount of spacing to leave between the mode indicators.

PreProcessMsg
bool PreProcessMsg(MSG& msg);
Overrides *TWindow::PreProcessMsg* to process keyboard messages and update the mode indicators when the *NumLock*, *CapsLock*, or *ScrollLock* keys are pressed.

See also   TStatusBar::IdleAction

SetModeIndicators
void SetModeIndicators(uint modeindicators);
Sets the bit flags for which indicator is on.

TStorageDocument class   stgdoc.h

Derived from *TDocument*, *TStorageDocument* supplies functionality that supports OLE's compound file structure. A compound file structure is a file-management system that stores files in a hierarchical structure within a root file. This storage structure is analagous to the directory or folder and file scheme used on a disk, except that a directory is called a storage and a file is called a stream.

In addition, *TStorageDocument* provides support for OLE's compound document mechanism. A compound document can store many different kinds of embedded objects, for example, spreadsheets as well as bitmaps.

Basically, *TStorageDocument* supports having a document read and write its own storage. In order to provide this functionality, *TStorageDocument* overrides several virtual methods from *TDocument* and, following *TDocument*'s strategy, also applies property lists both to documents and to their views. In this way, documents can use these attributes to read files in from storage and write files out to storage

Messages are sent to the application, which queries the properties in order to determine how to process the document or view. Each derived class must implement its own property attribute types—either string or binary data.

See also   TDocument, TOleDocument

Type definitions

TStgDocProp enum
enum TStgDocProp {PrevProperty, CreateTime, ModifyTime, AccessTime, StorageSize, IStorageInstance, NextProperty};
Enumerates the following constants that define the document's properties:

Constant	Meaning
PrevProperty	Should always have a value of TDocument::NextProperty - 1. This is the initial value in any document's property list.
CreateTime	The time the file is created.
ModifyTime	The time the file is modified.
AccessTime	The last time the file was accessed.
StorageSize	The size of the storage buffer.
IStorageInstance	The storage instance for the document.
NextProperty	The final value for any document's list of properties.

Public constructor and destructor

Constructor
TStorageDocument(TDocument* parent = 0): TDocument(parent), StorageI(0), OpenCount(0), CanRelease(false);
Constructs a *TStorageDocument* object with the specified *TDocument* parent window. Sets the data members *StorageI* and *OpenCount* to 0. Sets *CanRelease* to false. Later, the member function *ReleaseDoc* sets this flag to true so that the document can be closed.

Destructor
~TStorageDocument();
Destroys a *TStorageDocument* object.

Public member functions

Close
bool Close();
Releases the *IStorage* if *CanRelease* is **true**. (*CanRelease* is set to **true** when *ReleaseDoc* is called.) Before closing the document, *Close* checks any child documents and tries to close them.

See also   TStorageDocument::Open, TStorageDocument::ReleaseDoc, TOutStream, ofxxxx Document Open Enum

Commit
bool Commit(bool force = false);
Saves the current data to storage. When a file is closed, the document manager calls either *Commit* or *Revert*. If *force* is **true**, all data is written to storage. *TDocument*'s *Commit* checks any child documents and commits their changes to storage also. Before the current data is saved, all child documents must return **true**. If all child documents return **true**, *Commit* flushes the views for any operations that occurred since the last time the view was checked. Once all data for the document object is updated and saved, *Commit* returns **true**.

CommitTransactedStorage
bool CommitTransactedStorage();
If a file is opened or created in transacted mode, call *CommitTransactedStorage* to commit a document to permanent storage. By default, a document uses transacted instead of direct storage. With transacted storage, a document written to IStorage is only temporary until it is committed permanently. If a compound file is opened or created in direct mode, then *CommitTransactedStorage* does not need to be called.

FindProperty
int FindProperty(const char far* name);
Gets the property index, given the property name. Returns the integer index number that corresponds to the name. If the name isn't found in the list of properties, returns 0.

See also   pfxxxx property attribute constants

GetHandle
virtual bool GetHandle(HGLOBAL* handle);
Gets the global handle from *ILockBytes*.

GetNewStorage
virtual IStorage* GetNewStorage();
Gets a new *IStorage*, typically in a *SaveAs* situation. Releases *StorageI* and sets it to the new storage if all OK.

GetProperty
int GetProperty(int index, void far* dest, int textlen=0);
Returns the total number of properties for this storage document, where *index* is the property index, *dest* contains the property data, and *textlen* is the size of the property array. If *textlen* is 0, the property data is returned as binary data; otherwise, the property data is returned as text data.

See also   pfxxxx property attribute constants, TStorageDocument::SetProperty

GetStorage
IStorage* GetStorage();
Returns the document's root *IStorage*.

See also   TStorageDocument::SetStorage

InStream
TInStream* InStream(int omode, const char far* strmId=0);
Provides an input stream for the *TStorageDocument* object. Returns a pointer to a
TInStream object. The parameter *omode* contains a combination of the document open
and sharing modes (for example, *ofReadWrite*) defined in docview.h. The *strmId*
parameter is used for documents that support named streams.

See also   TStorageDocument::OutStream, TInStream, ofxxxx Document Open Enum

IsOpen
bool IsOpen();
Checks to see if the storage document has any *IStorage* created. If there is no storage,
IsOpen returns **false**; otherwise, it returns **true**.

Open
bool Open(int omode, const char far* name);
Opens or creates a document based on *IStorage*. The *name* parameter specifies the name
of the document, if any, to open. The *omode* parameter contains a combination of the
document open and sharing modes (for example, *ofReadWrite*) defined in docview.h.

See also   TStorageDocument::Close, TOutStream, ofxxxx Document Open Enum,
TOleDocument::Open

OpenHandle
virtual bool OpenHandle(int omode, HANDLE hGlobal);
OpenHandle writes data to a memory block. *OpenHandle* first creates an *ILockBytes*
interface on the global handle and then creates an *IStorage* based on the *ILockBytes*
interface. The parameter *omode* contains a combination of the document open and
sharing modes (for example, *ofReadWrite*) defined in docview.h.

See also   ofxxxx Document Open Enum

Note   *ILockBytes* is an OLE 2 interface that implements reading, writing, and locking a series of
bytes in a file.

OutStream
TOutStream* OutStream(int omode, const char far* strmId=0);
Provides an output stream for a particular storage medium. Returns a pointer to a
TOutStream. The parameter *omode* contains a combination of the document open and
sharing modes (for example, *ofReadWrite*) defined in docview.h. The *strmId* parameter is
used for documents that support named streams.

See also   TStorageDocument::InStream, TOutStream, ofxxxx Document Open Enum

PropertyCount
int PropertyCount();

Gets the total number of properties for the *TStorageDocument* object. Returns *NextProperty* - 1.

See also   pfxxxx property attribute constants

PropertyFlags
int PropertyFlags(int index);
Returns the attributes of a specified property given the index of the property whose attributes you want to retrieve.

See also   pfxxxx property attribute constants

PropertyName
const char* PropertyName(int index);
Returns the name of the property given the index value.

See also   pfxxxx property attribute constants

ReleaseDoc
virtual bool ReleaseDoc();
Releases the storage for the document and closes the document.

Revert
bool Revert(bool clear = false);
Performs the reverse of *Commit* and cancels any changes made to the storage document since the last commit. If *clear* is **true**, data is not reloaded for views. Revert also checks all child documents and cancels any changes if all children return **true**. When a file is closed, the document manager calls either *Commit* or *Revert*. *Revert* returns **true** if the revert operation is successful.

SetDocPath
bool SetDocPath(const char far* path);
Sets the document path for the Open and Save file operations.

SetHandle
virtual bool SetHandle(int omode, HANDLE hGlobal, bool create = false, bool remember = false);
Replaces the *IStorage* with an istorage based on a memory handle.

SetProperty
bool SetProperty(int index, const void far* src);
Sets the value of the property, given the index of the property, and *src*, the data type (either binary or text) to which the property must be set.

See also   pfxxxx property attribute constants, TStorageDocument::GetProperty

SetStorage
IStorage* SetStorage(IStorage* stg);
Attaches an *IStorage* pointer (*stg*) to this document.

See also   TStorageDocument::GetStorage, TStorageDocument::StorageI

Protected data members

LockBytes
ILockBytes* LockBytes;
Pointer to *ILockBytes* used, if any.

OrgStorageI
IStorage* OrgStorageI;
Pointer to the original *IStorage* interface.

StorageI
IStorage* StorageI;
Holds the current *IStorage* instance. (If no storage is open, *StorageI* is 0.)

See also   TStorageDocument::GetStorage, TStorageDocument::SetStorage

ThisOpen
int ThisOpen;
Holds the actual mode bits used for opening the storage. The mode bits determine how the file is opened: for example, read only, read and write, and so on.

See also   ofxxxx Document Open Enum

Protected member functions

GetLockBytes
ILockBytes* GetLockBytes();
Returns a pointer to the *ILockBytes* interface currently being used by this storage document object. Returns 0 if no *ILockBytes* interface is in use.

GetOrgStorageI
IStorage* GetOrgStorageI();
Returns a pointer to the original IStorage interface associated with this storage document object.

GetThisOpen
int GetThisOpen();
Returns the mode bits used to open the storage currently associated with this storage object.

TStream class   docview.h

An abstract base class, *TStream* provides links between streams and documents, views, and document files.

Public destructor

~TStream();

Closes the stream. Derived classes generally close the document if it was opened especially for this stream.

Public member functions

GetDocument
TDocument& GetDocument();
Returns the current document that is open for streaming.

GetOpenMode
int GetOpenMode();
Gets mode flags used when opening document streams. For example, the stream can be opened in *ofRead* mode to allow reading, but not changing (writing to) the file.

See also ofxxxx document open enum

GetStreamName
const char far* GetStreamName();
Gets the name of the stream used for opening the document.

Protected data members

Doc
TDocument& Doc;
Stores the document that owns this stream.

NextStream
TStream* NextStream;
Points to the next stream in the list of active streams.

Protected constructors

TStream
TStream(TDocument& doc, const char far* name,int mode);
Constructs a *TStream* object. The *doc* parameter refers to the document object, *name* is the user-defined name of the stream, and *mode* is the mode used for opening the stream.

See also TInStream, TOutStream, ofXXXX document open enum, shXXXX document sharing enum

TStreamSocket class   wsksockd.h

TStreamSocket encapsulates a Windows Sockets stream socket.

Type definitions

TConnectStatus enum
enum TConnectStatus {NotConnected, ConnectPending, Connected, Listening};
TConnectStatus can be one of the following constants:

- NotConnected

- ConnectPending

- Connected

- Listening

Public constructors

Form 1   TStreamSocket();
This function calls *TSocket* constructor and initializes the state of the connection to not connected.

Form 2   TStreamSocket(SOCKET& src);
This function is an alias constructor.

Form 3   TStreamSocket(TSocketAddress& socketAddress, int addressFormat=PF_INET, int Type=SOCK_STREAM,
                int protocol=0);
This function is a constructor for a protocol defined by an integer.

Public member functions

Accept
Form 1   int Accept(SOCKET& socket, sockaddr& sAddress);
This function tries to accept a connection with the first connecting peer that is waiting in the queue. If successful, the socket reference argument is set to a new connected socket. The *sAddress* reference argument is set to the address of the connecting peer. The caller of this function may immediately use the new socket with data sends, etc.

Note that the caller may want to flag the socket as connected. If the socket belongs to a *StreamSocket*, its *nConnectionStatus* can be set as *nConnected*. The return value is either WINSOCK_ERROR or WINSOCK_NOERROR. If there is an error, then nLastError will be set with the appropriate error.

Note that this call could be made when no pending socket connections are in the queue. If this is the case, the call will block if the socket is marked as blocking, and will return WINSOCK_ERROR with WSAEWOULDBLOCK if the socket is marked as non-blocking. This function is usually called in response to an accept notification. A socket is set up as a stream socket and *listen()* is called. When a connection is ready, the driver notifies the listening socket with a *DoAcceptNotification()* call. (See the *DoAcceptNotification()* call documentation.) This *Accept()* function should be called as a result.

Form 2   int Accept(TStreamSocket& socket);

This function will try to accept a connection with the first connecting peer that is waiting in the queue. If successful, the *TStreamSocket&* socket will have a valid and connected socket, a proper status of nConnected, and the correct peer socket address. The caller usually calls this function in response to an Accept notification. The caller merely needs to create a new *TStreamSocket* and pass it to this function. The default constructor for *TStreamSocket* can be used, because this function fixes up the missing parts.

Connect

Form 1   int Connect(TSocketAddress& addressToConnectTo);

This function sets *myPeerSocketAddress* to *sAddressToConnectTo* then calls *Connect()*. (See *Connect()* for more details.)

Form 2   int Connect();

This function uses *myPeerSocketAddress*, which needs to be set before calling this function. The connection attempt (and this function) should return right away, without blocking. When actually connected, a notification comes from the driver at the *DoConnectNotification()* function. Upon receiving that notification, the *nConnectStatus* is set to *nConnected*. Technically, a datagram socket can call connect; doing this sets the default address for future send()/recv() calls that the datagram socket might use. It's in the *TStreamSocket* class for simplicity, and because the *TDatagramSocket* class already supports its own default address system.

Listen

int Listen(int nMaxQueuedConnections=N_DEF_MAX_QUEUED_CONNECTIONS);

This function puts this socket into a passive "listening" mode.

operator =

TStreamSocket& operator =(TStreamSocket& src);

This function copies the socket connection information.

Read

int Read(char* data, int& charsToRead);

This reads from the already received and queued data. This data has already been received from the socket driver.

ReadOOB

int ReadOOB(char* data, int& charsToRead);

This function works just like the *Read()* function, but it works on the OOB queue.

Write

int Write(char* data, int& charsToWrite, int flags=0, bool becomeOwnerOfData=true, bool copyData=true);

This function writes the buffer into the stream.

WriteOOB

int WriteOOB(char* data, int& charsToWrite, int nFlags=MSG_OOB, bool becomeOwnerOfData=true,
        bool copyData=true);

Works just like *TStreamSocket::Write()*, except it adds in the MSG_OOB into the flags.

Protected member functions

DoAcceptNotification
DoAcceptNotification(const SOCKET& s, int nError);
This notification occurs when a client socket on the network is attempting to connect to you. Code needs to be written to intercept this notification.

DoCloseNotification
DoCloseNotification(const SOCKET& s, int nError);
This notification gets called when the socket has been closed. The socket is marked as not connected, so the user can find out about it. It is important to read any data that may be waiting in the queue before changing the status of the connection and doing any notification.

DoConnectNotification
DoConnectNotification(const SOCKET& s, int nError);
This means that the connection attempted with a server on the network has completed. This function gets called sometime after this object makes a *connect()* attempt. If the connect attempt was non-blocking, a notification is posted. When this function gets called, the *nConnectStatus* should be *nConnecting*.

DoOOBNotification
DoOOBNotification(const SOCKET& s, int nError);
This notification appears when OOB data is ready to be received on the socket port.

DoReadNotification
DoReadNotification(const SOCKET& s, int nError);
This function is called when the socket receives a read notification unless there is an error. This means that data on the port is ready to be read.

This function doesn't do much with the nError parameter. It doesn't do the read if there is an error value.

DoWriteNotification
DoWriteNotification(const SOCKET& s, int nError);
This function is called when the socket receives a write notification. This means that data on the port is ready to be written.

TStringLookupValidator class   validate.h

Derived from *TLookupValidator*, *TStringLookupValidator* is a streamable class. A *TStringLookupValidator* object verifies the data in its associated edit control by searching through a collection of valid strings. You can use string-lookup validators when your edit control needs to accept only members of a certain set of strings.

Public constructor and destructor

Constructor
TStringLookupValidator(TSortedStringArray* strings);
Constructs a string-lookup object by first calling the constructor inherited from *TLookupValidator* and then setting *Strings* to *strings*.

Destructor
~TStringLookupValidator();
This destructor disposes of a list of valid strings by calling *NewStringList* and then disposes of the string-lookup validator object by calling the Destructor inherited from *TLookupValidator*.

Public member functions

Adjust
int Adjust(string& text, uint& begPos, uint& endPos, int amount);
Adjusts the 'value' of the text, given a cursor position and an amount. Returns the actual amount adjusted.

Error
void Error();
Overrides *TValidator's* virtual function and displays a message box indicating that the typed string does not match an entry in the string list.

See also   TValidator::Error

Lookup
bool Lookup(const char far* str);
Overrides *TLookupValidator's* virtual function. Returns true if the string passed in *str* matches any of the *strings*. Uses the search method of the string collection to determine if str is present.

See also   TLookupValidator::Lookup

NewStringList
void NewStringList(TSortedStringArray* strings);
Sets the list of valid input string for the string-lookup validator. Disposes of any existing string list and then sets *Strings* to *strings*.

Protected data members

Strings
TSortedStringArray* Strings;
Points to a string collection containing all the valid strings the user can type. If *Strings* is NULL, all input is validated.

Protected member functions

GetStrings
const TSortedStringArray* GetStrings() const;
Returns the set of valid strings used by the validator.

SetStrings
void SetStrings(TSortedStringArray* strings);
Sets the valid strings used by the validator.

TSystemFont class   gdiobjec.h

TSystemFont is the default system font class. Use it to get a standard system font.

Public constructors

TSystemFont
TSystemFont(int height=0, int width=0, int escapement=0, int orientation=0, int weight=FW_NORMAL,
    uint8 italic=false, uint8 underline=false, uint8 strikeout=false,
    uint8 outputPrecision=OUT_DEFAULT_PRECIS, uint8 clipPrecision=CLIP_DEFAULT_PRECIS,
    uint8 quality=DEFAULT_QUALITY);
Convenient font ctor. Make a standard system font.

TSystemMenu class   menu.h

TSystemMenu creates a system menu object that then becomes the existing system menu.

Public constructors

TSystemMenu
TSystemMenu(HWND wnd, bool revert = false);
Constructs a system menu object. If *revert* is true, then the menu created is a default
system menu. Otherwise, it is the menu currently in the window.

See also   TPopupMenu::TPopupMenu

TTabControl class   tabctrl.h

TTabControl encapsulates the Tab Control, a window that provides a UI analogous to
dividers in a notebook.

Public constructors

Form 1   TTabControl(TWindow* parent, int id, int x, int y, int w, int h, TModule* module = 0);

Constructor for *TTabControl*. Initializes its data fields using parameters passed and default values by default. A Tab Control associated with the *TTabControl* will:

- be visible upon creation

- display only one row of tabs

Form 2   TTabControl(TWindow* parent, int resourceId, TModule* module = 0);
Constructor for a *TTabControl* object associated with a Tab Control specified in a dialog resource.

Form 3   ~TTabControl();
Cleans up if underlying Tab support was provided by ObjectWindows.

Public member functions

Add
Form 1   int Add(const char far* tabText);
Adds a new tab with the 'tabText' caption to the tab control returns the index of the new tab, if successful or -1 otherwise.

Form 2   int Add(const TTabItem&);
Inserts a new tab described by the *item* parameter to the tab control at the position specified by the *index* parameter. The return value is the index of the new tab or -1 in case of error.

AdjustRect
void AdjustRect(bool clientInWindowOut, TRect& rect);
If the *clientInWindowOut* parameter is false, this method calculates the display area of a tab control's display from a window rectangle specified by the *rect* parameter. Otherwise, the method calculates the window rectangle that would correspond to the display area specified by the *rect* parameter. The *rect* parameter receives the newly computed rectangle.

Delete
bool Delete(int index);
Removes the item at the position specified by the *index* parameter. Returns *true* if successful or *false* otherwise.

DeleteAll
bool DeleteAll();
Removes all items from the tab control. Returns *true* if successful or *false* if otherwise.

GetCount
int GetCount() const;
Returns the number of tab items in the tab control.

GetImageList
HIMAGELIST GetImageList() const;
Retrieves the ImageList associated with a tab control. Returns 0 if unsuccessful.

GetItem
bool GetItem(int index, TTabItem& item) const;
Retrieves information about the tab at the position specified by the *index* parameter. Returns true if successful or false if otherwise.

Note The *mask* member of the *item* structure specifies which attributes of the tab to return. When specifying TCIF_TEXT, item's *pszText* member must point to a valid buffer and *cchTextMax* must specify the size of the buffer.

GetItemRect
bool GetItemRect(int index, TRect& rect) const;
Retrieves the bounding rectangle of a tab within a tab control. Returns true if successful or false if otherwise.

Note *rect* receives the position in viewport coordinates.

GetRowCount
int GetRowCount() const;
Retrieves the current number of rows in the tab control.

Note Only tabs with the TCS_MULTILINE style can have multiple rows.

GetSel
int GetSel() const;
Returns the index of the currently selected tab item in the tab control.

Returns -1 if no tab is selected.

GetToolTips
HWND GetToolTips() const;
Retrieves the handle of the tooltip control associated with the tab control. Returns 0 if unsuccessful.

HitTest
int HitTest(TTabHitTestInfo&);
Determines the index of the tab which is at the location specified in the *pt* member of the *htInfo* parameter. Returns -1 if no tab is at the specified position.

Insert
Form 1 int Insert(const char far* tabText, int index);
Inserts a new tab with the caption *tabText* at the specified *index*. Returns the index of the new tab, if successful.

Form 2 int Insert(const TTabItem&, int index);
Inserts a new tab described by the *item* parameter to the tab control at the position specified by the *index* parameter. The return value is the index of the new tab or -1 in case of error.

RemoveImage
void RemoveImage(int index);
Removes the image at the position specified by *index* from the imagelist associated with the tab control.

Note The tab automatically updates each tab's image index so each tab remains associated with the same image it had been.

SetImageList
HIMAGELIST SetImageList(HIMAGELIST);
Assigns an imagelist to the tab control. Returns the handle of the previous imagelist or 0 if there is no previous image list.

SetItem
bool SetItem(int index, const TTabItem& item);
Sets some or all of a tab's attributes. The *mask* member of the *item* parameter specifies which attributes to set. Returns true if successful or false if otherwise.

SetItemExtra
bool SetItemExtra(int extra);
Sets the number of bytes per tab reserved for application-defined data in a tab control. Returns true if successful or false if otherwise.

Note This method should be invoked only when the tab control does not contain any tabs.

SetItemSize
TSize SetItemSize(const TSize& size);
Sets the size (width/height) of tabs in a fixed-width or owner-drawn tab control. Returns a *TSize* object containing the old width and height.

SetPadding
TSize SetPadding(const TSize& size);
Sets the amount of space around each tab's icon and label in a tab control.

SetSel
int SetSel(int index);
Selects the tab item at the position specified by the *index* parameter. The return value is the index of the previously selected tab item if successful, or -1 if otherwise.

Note A tab control does not send TCN_SELCHANGING or TCN_SELCHANGE notifications when a tab item is selected via this method.

SetToolTips
void SetToolTips(HWND toolTip);
Assigns a tooltip control to the tab control.

Transfer
uint Transfer(void* buffer, TTransferDirection direction);
Transfer is not implemented in *TTabControl*, given that each item interacts with settings outside of the TC_ITEM members. (For example, the image index points to the ImageList.)

Protected member functions

EvHScroll
void EvHScroll(uint scrollCode, uint thumbPos, THandle hWndCtl);

Keeps *TWindow* from rerouting this message. It must be left as is for the tab control, as it may originate from the control's spin.

EvVScroll
void EvVScroll(uint scrollCode, uint thumbPos, THandle hWndCtl);
Handler for WM_VSCROLL messages.

GetClassName
char far* GetClassName();
Returns the class name of the underlying control associated with the *TTabControl* object.

Note   The logic used depends on the availability of native Common Control support. In the case where OWL provides the underlying support, we'll specify a *TTabControl*-specific classname. (Although it's not necessary, it eases debugging.)

TTabHitTestInfo class   tabctrl.h

TTabHitTestInfo is a very thin wrapper around the TC_HITTESTINFO structure. It's a place-holder for future ObjectWindows enhancements for tabcontrol hit testing.

TTabItem class   tabctrl.h

TTabItem encapsulates the attributes of a single tab within a tab control. For example, it holds the string containing the tab's text.

Public constructors

Form 1   TTabItem(uint mask);
Constructor for a *TabItem*. This constructor is useful when creating a *TabItem* (TC_ITEM) structure which will be filled with information about an existing tab in a tab control. For example,

- *TTabItem item(TCIF_IMAGE | TCIF_PARAM);*

- *tabCtrl.GetItem(index, item);*

Form 2   TTabItem(const TC_ITEM& tblItem);
Constructs a *TTabItem* object from a *TC_ITEM* structure using the assignment operator.

Note   Default assignment operator is fine, even if we get a shallow copy for *pszText*, since the effective lifetime of a *TTabItem* is rather short and the underlying control copies/caches the item's label.

Form 3   TTabItem(const TTabControl& ctl, int index, uint mask, int buffLen = 0, char far* buffer = 0);
The item is initialized with the state of an actual tab in a created tab control.

Form 4   TTabItem(const char far* str, int buffLen = 0, TParam2 param = 0);
The tab item's label field is initialized to the specified buffer and extra parameter set to the *param* parameter.

Form 5   TTabltem(int imageIndex, TParam2 param);
          The tab item is initialized with the IMAGELIST index and the extra parameter specified.

Form 6   TTabltem(int imageIndex, const char far*str);
          The tab item is initialized with the IMAGELIST index and label specified.

Public member functions

SetIcon
void SetIcon(int imageIndex);
Sets the index of the image associated with the tab represented by this item structure.

SetLabel
void SetLabel(const char far* str, int len = 0);
Initializes the structure member representing the tab's text.

SetParam
void SetParam(TParam2 lp);
Sets the user-defined data associated with the tab represented by this item structure.

TTabKeyDown class   commctrl.h

TTabKeyDown is a wrapper of the TC_KEYDOWN structure sent to the parent of a tab control to notify that a key has been pressed.

Public constructors

Form 1   TTabKeyDown();
          TTabKeyDown contains information about a key press in a tab control. This constructor initializes the structure NUL value for the virtual *wVKey* and flags members.

Form 2   TTabKeyDown(HWND ctl, uint id, uint code, uint16 vk, uint flg);
          TTabKeyDown contains information about a key press in a tab control. This constructor initializes the members to the specified parameters.

Public member functions

operator NMHDR&
operator NMHDR&();
Allows the notification structure to be transparently treated as an NMHDR structure, thereby eliminating the need to explicitly refer to the NMHDR data member (which is always the first member of notification structures).

TTextGadget class
textgadg.h

Derived from *TGadget*, *TTextGadget* is a text gadget object. When you construct a text gadget, you must specify how many characters you want to reserve space for and how the text should be aligned horizontally. The inner boundaries of the text gadget are computed by multiplying the number of characters by the maximum character width.

Type definitions

TTileDirection enum

Header File
gadgetwi.h

enum TTileDirection{Horizontal, Vertical};
Enumerates the two directions the gadget can be tiled. *TGadgetWindow::TileGadgets* actually tiles the gadgets in the direction requested.

See also   TGadgetWindow::Direction, TGadgetWindow::TileGadgets

TAlign enum
enum TAlign {Left, Center, Right};
Enumerates the text-alignment attributes.

Table 2.32   Constants

Constant	Meaning if set
Left	Aligns the text at the left edge of the bounding rectangle.
Center	Aligns the text horizontally at the center of the bounding rectangle.
Right	Aligns the text at the right edge of the bounding rectangle.

Public constructor and destructor

Constructor
TTextGadget(int id = 0, TBorderStyle = Recessed, TAlign = Left, uint numChars = 10, const char* text = 0);
Constructs a *TTextGadget* object with the specified ID, border style, and alignment. Sets *Margins.Left* and *Margins.Right* to 2. Sets *Text* and *TextLen* to 0.

Destructor
~TTextGadget();
Destroys a *TTextGadget* object.

Public member functions

GetText
char* GetText();
Returns the text for the gadget.

SetText

void SetText(const char* text);

If the text stored in *Text* is not the same as the new text, *SetText* deletes the text stored in *Text*. Then, it sets *TextLen* to the length of the new string. If no text exists, it sets both *Text* and *TextLen* to 0 and then calls *Invalidate* to invalidate the rectangle.

Protected data members

Align

TAlign Align;

Text alignment attribute—left, center, or right-aligned.

Font

TFont* Font;

The display font.

NumChars

uint NumChars;

Holds the number of text characters.

Text

char* Text;

Points to the text for the gadget.

TextLen

uint TextLen;

Stores the length of the text.

Protected member functions

GetDesiredSize

void GetDesiredSize(TSize &size);

If shrink-wrapping is requested, *GetDesiredSize* returns the size needed to accommodate the borders, margins, and text; otherwise, if shrink-wrapping is not requested, it returns the gadget's current width and height.

See also   TGadget::GetDesiredSize

Invalidate

void Invalidate();

Calls *TGadget::GetInnerRect* to compute the area of the text for the gadget and then *TGadget::InvalidateRect* to invalidate the rectangle in the parent window.

See also   TGadget::GetInnerRect, TGadget::Invalidate

Paint

void Paint(TDC& dc);

Calls *TGadget::PaintBorder* to paint the border. Calls *TGadget::GetInnerRect* to calculate the area of the text gadget's rectangle. If the text is left-aligned, *Paint* calls *dc.GetTextExtent* to compute the width and height of a line of the text. To set the background color, *Paint* calls *dc.GetSysColor* and sets the default background color to face shading (COLOR_BTNFACE). To set the button text color, *Paint* calls *dc.SetTextColor* and sets the default button text color to COLOR_BTNTEXT. To draw the text, *Paint* calls *dc.ExtTextOut* and passes the parameters ETO_CLIPPED (so the text is clipped to fit the rectangle) and ETO_OPAQUE (so the rectangle is filled with the current background color).

See also   TGadget::Paint

TTextRange class   richedit.h

TTextRange encapsulates the TEXTRANGE structure, which contains information about a range of text in a rich edit control.

Public constructors

Form 1   TTextRange();
Constructs a default *TTextRange* structure with the data members describing the range and text initialized to zero.

Form 2   TTextRange(const TCharRange&, char far* buffer);
Constructs a *TTextRange* structure by initializing the range and text members with the *rng* and *buffer* parameters respectively.

Form 3   TTextRange(long beg, long end, char far* buffer);
Constructs a *TTextRange* structure by initializing the text with the *buffer* parameter, and the range using *beg* and *end*.

TTimeGadget class   timegadg.h

TTimeGadget is a gadget for displaying a time and/or date message.

Type definitions

TGetTimeFunc
typedef void _CALLCNVN (*TGetTimeFunc)(string&);
Function prototype of callback invoked to retrieve the correct time.

Public constructors

TTimeGadget
TTimeGadget(TGetTimeFunc timeFunc = &TTimeGadget::GetTTime, int id = 0, TBorderStyle = Recessed,
        TAlign = Center, uint numChars = 12, const char* text = 0, TFont* font = new TGadgetWindowFont);
Constructor for *TTimeGadget*.

Public member functions

GetSystemTime
static void GetSystemTime(string&);
Retrieves the system time using the Win32 API.

GetTTime
static void GetTTime(string&);
Retrieves the current time.

IdleAction
bool IdleAction(long count);
Override from *TGadget*.

TTinyCaption class   tinycapt.h

Derived from *TWindow*, *TTinyCaption* is a mix-in class that handles a set of non-client events to produce a smaller caption bar for a window. Whenever it displays the caption bar, *TTinyCaption* checks the window style and handles the WS_SYSMENU, WS_MINIMIZEBOX, WS_MAXIMIZEBOX display attributes. Thus, you can use *TTinyCaption* to set the attributes of the tiny caption bar before enabling the caption. For example,

```
Attr.Style = WS_POPUP | WS_BORDER | WS_SYSMENU | WS_MINIMIZEBOX | WS_MAXIMIZEBOX;
```

TTinyCaption provides functions that let you manipulate frame types, border styles, and menus. You can adjust the height of the caption bar or accept the default height, which is about one-half the height of a standard caption bar. If you set *CloseBox* to **true**, then the window will close when you click the close box instead of displaying the system menu.

The sample program OWLCMD.CPP on your distribution disk displays the following tiny caption bar:

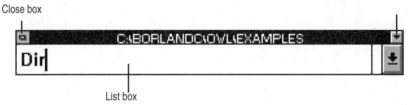

Close box

C:\BORLAND\OWL\EXAMPLES

Dir

List box

If you are using *TTinyCaption* as a mix-in class that does partial event handling, call the *DoXxxx* function in the mix-in class (instead of the *EvXxxx* function) to avoid duplicating default processing. The following example from OWLCMD.CPP (a sample program on your distribution disk) illustrates this process:

```
void TMyFrame::EvSysCommand(uint cmdType,TPoint& p)
{
  if (TTinyCaption::DoSysCommand(cmdType, p) == esPartial)
    FrameWindow::EvSysCommand(cmdType, p);
```

The TFloatingFrame class can be used with *TTinyCaption* to produce a close box. See the sample programs OWLCMD.CPP and MDIFILE.CPP on your distribution disk for examples of how to use *TTinyCaption*.

Protected data members

Border
TSize Border;
Thin frame border size for dividers.

CaptionFont
TFont* CaptionFont;
Font used for the text in the tiny caption bar.

CaptionHeight
int CaptionHeight;
Height of the caption bar.

CloseBox
bool CloseBox;
If **true**, the window will close when the close box is clicked.

DownHit
uint DownHit;
Location of mouse-button press or cursor move.

Frame
TSize Frame;
Actual left and right, top and bottom dimensions of the caption bar.

IsPressed
bool IsPressed;
Is **true** if a mouse button is pressed.

TCEnabled
bool TCEnabled;
Is **true** if the tiny caption bar is displayed.

WaitingForSysCmd
bool WaitingForSysCmd;
Is **true** if *TTinyCaption* is ready to receive system messages.

Protected constructor and destructor

Constructor
TTinyCaption();
Constructs a *TTinyCaption* object attached to the given parent window. Initializes the caption font to 0 and *TCEnabled* to **false** so that the tiny caption bar is not displayed automatically.

Destructor
~TTinyCaption();
Destroys a *TTinyCaption* object and deletes the caption font.

Protected member functions

DoCommand
TEventStatus DoCommand(uint id, HWND hWndCtl, uint notifyCode, LRESULT& evRes);
Displays the system menu using *::TrackPopup* so that *TTinyCaption* sends
WM_COMMAND instead of WM_SYSCOMMAND messages. If a system menu
command is received, it's then transformed into a WM_SYSCOMMAND message. If the
tiny caption bar is **false**, *DoCommand* returns *esPartial*.

See also   TTinyCaption::EvCommand, TEventStatus enum

DoLButtonUp
TEventStatus DoLButtonUp(uint hitTest, TPoint& screenPt);
Releases the mouse capture if the caption bar is enabled and a mouse button is pressed.
Sets *hitTest*, indicating the mouse button has been pressed. Captures the mouse message
and repaints the smaller buttons before returning *esComplete*.

See also   TTinyCaption::EvLButtonUp

DoMouseMove
TEventStatus DoMouseMove(uint hitTest, TPoint& screenPt);
Returns *TEventStatus*.

DoNCActivate
TEventStatus DoNCActivate(bool active, bool& evRes);
If the tiny caption is not enabled or is iconic, returns *esPartial*. Otherwise, repaints the
caption as an active caption and returns *esComplete*.

See also   TTinyCaption::EvNCActivate

DoNCCalcSize
TEventStatus DoNCCalcSize(bool calcValidRects, NCCALCSIZE_PARAMS far& calcSize, uint& evRes);
If the caption bar is not enabled or is iconic, returns *esPartial*. Otherwise, calculates the
dimensions of the caption and returns *esComplete*.

See also   TTinyCaption::EvNCCalcSize

DoNCHitTest
TEventStatus DoNCHitTest(TPoint& screenPt, uint& evRes);
If the caption bar is not enabled, returns *esPartial*. Otherwise, sends a message to the
caption bar that the mouse or the cursor has moved, and returns *esComplete*.

See also   TTinyCaption::EvNCHitTest

DoNCLButtonDown
TEventStatus DoNCLButtonDown(uint hitTest, TPoint& screenPt);
If the caption bar is not enabled, returns *esPartial*. Otherwise, determines if the user
released the button outside or inside a menu, and returns *esComplete*.

See also   TTinyCaption::EvNCLButtonDown

DoNCPaint
TEventStatus DoNCPaint();
If the caption bar is not enabled or is iconized, returns *esPartial*. Otherwise, gets the focus, paints the caption, and returns *esPartial*, thus indicating that a separate paint function must be called to paint the borders of the caption.

See also   TTinyCaption::EvNCPaint

DoSysCommand
TEventStatus DoSysCommand(uint cmdType, TPoint& p);
If the caption bar is not enabled, returns *esPartial*. If the caption bar is iconized and the user clicks the icon, calls *DoSysMenu* to display the menu in its normal mode and returns *esComplete*.

See also   TTinyCaption::EvSysCommand

DoSysMenu
void DoSysMenu;
Gets the system menu and sets up menu items. *DoSysMenu* is also responsible for displaying and tracking the status of the menu.

EnableTinyCaption
void EnableTinyCaption(int ch=58, bool closeBox=false);
Activates the tiny caption bar. By default, *EnableTinyCaption* replaces the system window with a tiny caption window that does not close when the system window is clicked. If the *closeBox* argument is **true**, clicking on the system menu will close the window instead of bringing up the menu. You can use *EnableTinyCaption* to hide the window if you are using a tiny caption in a derived class. To diminish the tiny caption bar, try the following values:

```
EnableTinyCaption(30, true);
```

To maximize the tiny caption bar, use these values:

```
EnableTinyCaption(48, true);
```

EvCommand
LRESULT EvCommand(uint id, HWND hWndCtl, uint notifyCode);
EvCommand provides extra processing for commands, but lets the focus window and its parent windows handle the command first.

See also   TTinyCaption::DoCommand

EvLButtonUp
void EvLButtonUp(uint hitTest, TPoint& screenPt);
Responds to a mouse button-up message by calling *DoLButtonUp*. If *DoLButtonUp* does not return *IsComplete*, *EvLButtonUp* calls *TWindow::EvLButtonUp*.

EvMouseMove
void EvMouseMove(uint hitTest, TPoint& screenPt);
Responds to a mouse-move message by calling *DoMouseMove*. If *DoMouseMove* does not return *IsComplete*, *EvMouseMove* calls *TWindow::EvMouseMove*.

EvNCActivate

bool EvNCActivate(bool active);

Responds to a request to change a title bar or icon by calling *DoNCActivate*. If *DoNCActivate* does not return *esComplete*, *EvNCActivate* calls *TWindow::EvNCActivate*.

EvNCCalcSize

uint EvNCCalcSize(bool calcValidRects, NCCALCSIZE_PARAMS far& calcSize);

Responds to a request to change a title bar or icon by calling *DoNCActivate*. If *DoNCActivate* does not return *esComplete*, *EvNCActivate* calls *TWindow::EvNCActivate*.

Calculates the size of the command window including the caption and border so that it can fit within the window.

EvNCHitTest

uint EvNCHitTest(TPoint& screenPt);

Responds to a cursor move or press of a mouse button by calling *DoNCHitTest*. If *DoNCHitTest* does not return *esComplete*, *EvNCHitTest* calls *TWindow::EvNCHitTest*.

EvNCLButtonDown

void EvNCLButtonDown(uint hitTest, TPoint& screenPt);

Responds to a press of the left mouse button while the cursor is within the nonclient area of the caption bar by calling *DoNCLButtonDown*. If *DoNCLButtonDown* does not return *esComplete*, *EvNCLButtonDown* calls *TWindow::EvNCLButtonDown*.

EvNCPaint

void EvNCPaint();

Responds to a request to change a title bar or icon. Paints the indicated device context or display screen and does any special painting required for the caption.

See also TTinyCaption::DoNCActivate

EvSysCommand

void EvSysCommand(uint cmdType, TPoint& p);

Responds to a WM_SYSCOMMAND message by calling *DoSysCommand*. If *DoSysCommand* returns *esPartial*, *EvSysCommand* calls *TWindow::EvSysCommand*.

GetCaptionRect

TRect GetCaptionRect();

Gets the area of the caption for changing or repainting.

See also TTinyCaption::PaintCaption

GetMaxBoxRect

TRect GetMaxBoxRect();

Returns the size of the maximize box rectangle.

See also TTinyCaption::PaintMaxBoxRect

GetMinBoxRect

TRect GetMinBoxRect();

Returns the size of the minimize box rectangle.

See also TTinyCaption::PaintMinBoxRect

GetSysBoxRect
TRect GetSysBoxRect();
Returns the size of the system box rectangle.

See also   TTinyCaption::PaintSysBoxRect

PaintButton
void PaintButton(TDC& dc, TRect& boxRect, bool pressed);
Paints a blank button.

PaintCaption
void PaintCaption(bool active);
Calls *dc.SelectObject* to select the given rectangle and *dc.PatBlt* to paint the tiny caption bar using the currently selected brush for this device context.

See also   TDC::SelectObject, TDC::PatBlt

PaintCloseBox
void PaintCloseBox(TDC& dc, TRect& boxRect, bool pressed);
Paints a close box on the tiny caption bar. You can override the default box if you want to design your own close box.

See also   TTinyCaption::GetSysBoxRect

PaintMaxBox
void PaintMaxBox(TDC& dc, TRect& boxRect, bool pressed);
Paints a maximize box on the tiny caption bar.

See also   TTinyCaption::GetMaxBoxRect

PaintMinBox
void PaintMinBox(TDC& dc, TRect& boxRect, bool pressed);
Paints a minimize box on the tiny caption bar.

See also   TTinyCaption::GetMinBoxRect

PaintSysBox
void PaintSysBox(TDC& dc, TRect& boxRect, bool pressed);
Paints the system box.

See also   TTinyCaption::GetSysBoxRect

Response table entries

Response table entry	Member function
EV_WM_NCACTIVATE	EvNCActivate
EV_WM_NCCALCSIZE	EvNcCalcSize
EV_WM_NCHITTEST	EvNcHitTest
EV_WM_NCPAINT	EvNcPaint
EV_WM_NCLBUTTONDOWN	EvNclButtonDown
EV_WM_LBUTTONUP	EvLButtonUp
EV_WM_MOUSEMOVE	EvMouseMove
EV_WM_SYSCOMMAND	EvSysCommand

TToolBox class   toolbox.h

Derived from *TGadgetWindow*, *TToolBox* arranges gadgets in a matrix in which all columns are the same width (as wide as the widest gadget) and all rows are the same height (as high as the highest gadget).

You can specify exactly how many rows and columns you want for your toolbox, or you can let *TToolbox* calculate the number of columns and rows you need. If you specify AS_MANY_AS_NEEDED, the *TToolBox* calculates how many rows or columns are needed based on the opposite dimension. For example, if there are twenty gadgets, and you requested four columns, your matrix would have five rows.

Public constructor

```
TToolBox(TWindow* parent, int numColumns = 2, int numRows = AS_MANY_AS_NEEDED,
    TTileDirection direction = Horizontal, TModule* module = 0);
```
Constructs a *TToolBox* object with the specified number of columns and rows and tiling direction. Overlaps the borders of the toolbox with those of the gadget and sets *ShrinkWrapWidth* to true.

Public member functions

GetDesiredSize
```
void GetDesiredSize(TSize& size);
```
Overrides *TGadget*'s *GetDesiredSize* function and computes the size of the cell by calling *GetMargins* to get the margins.

See also   TGadgetWindow::GetDesiredSize

Insert
```
void Insert(TGadget& gadget, TPlacement = After, TGadget* sibling = 0);
```
Overrides *TGadget*'s *Insert* function and tells the button not to notch its corners.

See also   TGadgetWindow::Insert

LayoutSession

void LayoutSession();

Called when a change occurs in the size of the margins of the tool box or size of the gadgets, *LayoutSession* gets the desired size and moves the window to adjust to the desired change in size.

SetDirection

virtual void SetDirection(TTileDirection direction);

Sets the direction of the tiling—either horizontal or vertical.

Protected data members

NumColumns

int NumColumns;

Contains the number of columns for the toolbox.

NumRows

int NumRows;

Contains the number of rows for the toolbox.

Protected member functions

GetNumColumns

int GetNumColumns() const;

Returns the number of columns the tool box is using.

GetNumRows

int GetNumRows() const;

Returns the number of rows the tool box is using.

TileGadgets

TRect TileGadgets;

Tiles the gadgets in the direction requested (horizontal or vertical). Derived classes can adjust the spacing between gadgets.

See also   TGadgetWindow::TileGadget

TToolInfo class

tooltip.h

TToolInfo contains information about a particular tool. (A tool is either a window or an application-defined rectangular area within a window's client area.) For example, it contains the text to be displayed in the tooltip window.

Public constructors

Form 1   TToolInfo();

This is the default constructor of *TToolInfo*. It's used mainly when retrieving information about the current tool of the tooltip control or for initializing a brand new tool to be registered with the control. For example,

- *TToolInfo ti;*

- *tooltip.GetCurrentTool(ti);*

Form 2   TToolInfo(HWND window, const TRect&, uint toolId, char far* txt = LPSTR_TEXTCALLBACK);

Constructor for a tool implemented as a rectangular area within a window's client area. *window* receives the 'TTN_NEEDTEXT' notification in case of *txt* default to LPSTR_TEXTCALLBACK.

Form 3   TToolInfo(HWND window, const TRect&, uint toolId, int resId, HINSTANCE txtResModule);

Constructor for a tool implemented as a rectangular area within a window's client area. *strRes* and *hInst* specify a string resource of the message to be used by the tooltip window.

Form 4   TToolInfo(HWND parent, HWND toolHwnd, char far* txt = LPSTR_TEXTCALLBACK);

Constructor for a tool implemented as windows (eg. child/controls). *parent* receives the *TTN_NEEDTEXT* notification in case of *txt* defaults to the LPSTR_TEXTCALLBACK.

Form 5   TToolInfo(HWND parent, HWND toolHwnd, int resId, HINSTANCE strResModule);

Constructor for a tool implemented as a window (child/control). *strRes* and *hInst* specify a string resource to be used by the tooltip window.

Public member functions

GetToolRect
void GetToolRect(TRect& rect) const;

This method retrieves the actual RECT linked to a tool. For tools implemented as a rectangle within a client area, that rectangle is retrieved. For tools associated with a control, the latter's client area is retrieved.

GetToolWindow
HWND GetToolWindow() const;

This method returns the actual HWND linked to a tool. For tools implemented as a rectangle within a client area, the window's handle is returned. For tools associated with a control, the handle of the control is returned.

IsPointInTool
bool IsPointInTool(HWND win, const TPoint& pt) const;

This method determines whether a particular location of a window is relevant to this tool. For tools implemented as a rectangle within a window's client area, simply check that *pt* is within that rectangle. For tools representing a child window, check that *pt* is within the client area of the child window.

Note   *pt* must be relative to the window's client area.

Returns true if successful, or false otherwise.

SetRect

void SetRect(const TRect& rect);

Sets the bounding rectangle of the tool. The coordinates are relative to the upper-left corner of the client area of the window.

Note   This flag is only valid if the tool is a rectangle within the window and not a control parented to the window.

SetText

Form 1   void SetText(char far* text);

Sets the text of this tool by providing a buffer that contains the string.

Note   The string passed is not copied. Only a pointer to the buffer is set. You must therefore ensure that the buffer remains valid until the *TToolInfo* structure is no longer used.

Form 2   void SetText(int resId, HINSTANCE hinstance);

Sets the text of this tool by providing a string resource identifier and the handle of the instance containing that resource.

SetToolId

void SetToolId(uint id);

Sets the identifier of the tool.

Note   The *uFlags* member is cleared because otherwise the *uId* member is expected to contain a window handle (i.e., *uFlags* includes the TTF_IDISHWND value).

SetToolInfo

Form 1   void SetToolInfo(HWND toolWin, HWND parent);

Form 2   void SetToolInfo(HWND toolWin, uint id);

Form 3   void SetToolInfo(HWND toolWin, uint id, const TRect& rc);

TTooltip class   tooltip.h

TTooltip encapsulates a tooltip window. A tooltip window is a small popup window that displays a single line of descriptive test giving the purpose of the item underneath the current cursor location.

Public constructors and destructor

Constructors

Form 1   TTooltip(TWindow* parent, bool alwaysTip = true, TModule* module = 0);

Constructor for *Ttooltip*. Initializes its data fields using parameters passed and default values. By default, a tooltip associated with the *TTooltip* will be active regardless of whether its owner is active or inactive.

Form 2   TTooltip(HWND hWnd, TModule* module = 0);

Constructor to alias a non-OWL tooltip control. Especially useful when used with controls that automatically create a tooltip (eg *TabControls* with TCS_TOOLTIPS style).

Destructor
~TTooltip();
Destructor of *TTooltip* class.

Public member functions

Activate
void Activate(bool activate = true);
Activates or deactivates the tooltip control. If *activate* is true, the tooltip control is activated, If it is false, the tooltip control is deactivated.

AddTool
bool AddTool(const TToolInfo&);
Registers a tool with the tooltip control. The *TToolInfo* parameter contains information that the tooltip control needs to display text for the tool.

Note   This method does not check for duplicate tool ids!

Cleanup
void Cleanup();
Cleans up internal variables.

CleanupWindow
void CleanupWindow();
Overridden to clean up internal variables when providing underlying implementation of tooltips.

DeleteTool
void DeleteTool(const TToolInfo&);
Removes a tool from the tooltip control. You must invoke the *SetToolHandle* or *SetToolId* method of *TToolInfo* to identify the tool to remove (i.e., the *hwnd* or *uId* members of the *TToolInfo* must identify the tool).

DisableTimer
void DisableTimer();
Kills the timer if it was enabled.

EnableTimer
void EnableTimer();
Sets on a timer and updates the state variable.

EnumTools
bool EnumTools(uint index, TToolInfo&) const;
Retrieves the information that the tooltip control maintains about the specified tool. Returns true if successul or false otherwise.

Note   The index is zero-based and the *TToolInfo* structure receives the information about the tool.

EvGetFont
HFONT EvGetFont();

WM_GETFONT handler: Returns font used by tooltip.

EvSetFont
void EvSetFont(HFONT hFont, bool redraw);

WM_SETFONT handler: Sets a new font to be used by the handler.

EvTimer
void EvTimer(uint timerId);

WM_TIMER handler: Displays a tip if the appropriate timeout has occured for a tool.

GetClassName
char far* GetClassName();

Returns the native class of the tooltip control or the class implementing OWL's version of tooltips.

GetToolCount
uint GetToolCount() const;

Returns the number of tools currently registered with the tooltip control.

GetToolInfo
bool GetToolInfo(TToolInfo&) const;

Retrieves the information that the tooltip control maintains about a tool. You must invoke the *SetToolHandle* or *SetToolId* method of *TToolInfo* to identify the tool (i.e., the *hwnd* or *uId* members of the *TToolInfo* must identify the tool).

GetToolText
void GetToolText(TToolInfo&) const;

Retrieves the text associated with the specified tool. You must invoke the *SetToolHandle* or *SetToolId* method of *TToolInfo* to identify the tool (i.e., the *hwnd* or *uId* members of the *TToolInfo* must identify the tool).

GetWindowClass
void GetWindowClass(WNDCLASS& wc);

Updates the CLASSINFO to be registered to include SAVEBITS and a NUL brush.

HideActiveTip
void HideActiveTip();

Hides the tooltip window.

HitTest
bool HitTest(TTooltipHitTestInfo&) const;

Determines whether a tool is within a specified point. The method also retrieves information about the tool if one is identified at that location. Returns true if a tool is found at the location, or false otherwise.

Init
void Init();

Initializes internal variables.

NewToolRect
void NewToolRect(const TToolInfo&);

Updates the bounding rectangle of a tool. You must invoke the *SetToolId* method of *TToolInfo* to identify the tool (i.e., the *uId* member of the *TToolInfo* must identify the tool).

Paint

void Paint(TDC& dc, bool erase, TRect& rect);

WM_PAINT handler: Displays tip if there's an active tool.

RelayEvent

Form 1   void RelayEvent(MSG&);

Passes a mouse message to the tooltip control for processing.

Form 2   void RelayEvent(HWND receiver, uint msg, const TPoint& pt);

Checks relayed events and filters the ones that matter to the tooltip.

SetupWindow

void SetupWindow();

Overridden to initialize internal variables when providing underlying implementation of tooltips.

SetDelayTime

void SetDelayTime(int delay);

Sets the initial, reshow, and autopopup durations for a tooltip control. The *flag* parameter can be one of the following:

- TTDT_AUTOMATIC: Automatically calculates the initial, reshow, and autopopup duration based on *delay*.

- TTDT_AUTOPOP: Sets the length of time before the tooltip window is hidden if the cursor remains:

  - stationary in the tool's bounding rectangle

  - after the tooltip window has disappeared

- TTDT_INITIAL: Sets the length of time that the cursor must remain stationary within the bounding rectangle before the tooltip window is displayed.

- TTDT_RESHOW: Sets the length of time before subsequent tooltip windows are displayed when the cursor is moved from one tool to another.

Note   The *delay* duration is in milliseconds.

SetToolInfo

void SetToolInfo(const TToolInfo&);

Sets the information that the tooltip control maintains for a particular tool. You must invoke the *SetToolHandle* or *SetToolId* method of *TToolInfo* to identify the tool (i.e., the *hwnd* or *uId* members of the *TToolInfo* must identify the tool).

ShowActiveTip

void ShowActiveTip(TPoint& pt);

Displays the tip of the current tool at the specified location.

UpdateTipText

void UpdateTipText(const TToolInfo&);

Sets the text of a tool. You must invoke the *SetToolHandle* or *SetToolId* method of *TToolInfo* to identify the tool (i.e., the *hwnd* or *uId* members of the *TToolInfo* must identify the tool).

TTooltipEnabler class tooltip.h

TTooltipEnabler is the object forwarded along the command-chain to retrieve the tip text of a tool. The object is not a 'true' command enabler (i.e., invoking *SetCheck* or *Enable* does not modify the state of the command associated with the tool); however, by using the 'CommandEnabler' setup to retrieve the text of tools, the commands are potentially given first crack at customizing the text.

Public constructor

TTooltipEnabler
TTooltipEnabler(TTooltipText& tt, TWindow::THandle hReceiver);
Constructs enabler object to be sent to a window so that the latter can provide the text of the specified tool.

Public member functions

SetCheck
void SetCheck(int);
SetCheck does nothing but serve as a place-holder function.

SetText
void SetText(const char far* text);
Sets the text of a tooltip to a specified buffer.

Note The buffer pointed to by the specified parameter must be valid for as long as the *TTooltipText* points to it.

For temporary buffers, use the *CopyText* method instead.

Protected data member

TipText
TTooltipText& TipText;
A reference to the notification structure accompanying a runtime request for the text of a particular tool.

TTooltipHitTestInfo class

TTooltipHitTestInfo is a very thin wrapper around the TTHITTESTINFO structure, used to determined whether a point is within the bounding rectangle of a particular tool. It's a place-holder for future ObjectWindows enhancements to tooltip hit-testing.

TTooltipText class

TTooltipText identifies a tool for which text is to be displayed. It is sent to the parent of the tooltip via a WM_NOTIFY/TTN_NEEDTEXT notification. It receives the text to be displayed.

Public member functions

CopyText
void CopyText(char* buff);
Sets the text of the tooltip. The text is copied into the buffer owned by the *TTooltipText*.

SetText
Form 1   void SetText(int resId, HINSTANCE hInstance);
Sets the text of the tooltip. The *resId* identifies a string resource found in the module pointed to by the *hInstance* parameter.

Form 2   void SetText(char far* buff);
Sets the text of the tool specified by the *TTooltipEnabler* object.

Note   The text is copied to the *TTooltipText* structure.

TTreeItem class

TTreeItem is used to represent the data to be stored in the *TTreeWindow*.

Public constructors

Form 1   TTreeItem();
Default constructor.

Form 2   TTreeItem(TV_ITEM item);
Initializes based on an existing item.

Form 3   TTreeItem(const char far*, int len = 0);
Constructor using only text.

Form 4   TTreeItem(const char far*, int index, int selIndex);
Constructor based on text, an image index, and a selected index.

Public member functions

GetHTreeitem
HTREEITEM GetHTreeitem();
Returns the magic cookie of the item.

GetItemData
uint32 GetItemData();
Returns the extra data.

GetText
void GetText(char far*, int len);
Returns the text of the item.

SetHTreeItem
void SetHTreeItem(HTREEITEM hItem);
Sets the magic cookie for the item.

SetImageIndex
void SetImageIndex(int index);
Sets the image index of the item.

SetItemData
void SetItemData(uint32);
Sets the extra data of the item.

SetSelectedImageIndex
void SetSelectedImageIndex(int index);
Sets the selected image index of the item.

SetText
void SetText(const char far*, int len = -1);
Sets the text of the item.

Protected member function

Init
void Init();
Private *Init* function to zero out the data members.

TTreeNode class   treewind.h

TTreeNode is used to navigate the *TTreeWindow*. Each node conceptually contains a pointer to a *TTreeItem*.

Type definitions

TExpandCode enum

enum TExpandCode {Collapse, Expand, Toggle, CollapseReset};

TExpandCode can be one of the following constants:

- Collapse
- Expand
- Toggle
- CollapseReset (only available for 32-bit applications)

THowToInsert enum

enum THowToInsert {First, Last, Sort};

THowToInsert can be one of the following constants:

- First
- Last
- Sort

TNextCode enum

enum TNextCode {Root, Next, Previous, Parent, Child, FirstVisible, NextVisible, PreviousVisible, DropHilite, Caret};

TNextCode can be one of the following constants:

- Root
- Next
- Previous
- Parent
- Child
- FirstVisible (only available for 32-bit applications)
- NextVisible (only available for 32-bit applications)
- PreviousVisible (only available for 32-bit applications)
- DropHilite (only available for 32-bit applications)
- Caret

Public constructors

Form 1   TTreeNode(TTreeWindow&, HTREEITEM = TVI_ROOT);
Constructs based on an item.

Form 2   TTreeNode(const TTreeNode&, TNextCode);
Constructs on a next node.

Form 3   TTreeNode(const TTreeNode&);
Copies a node.

Public member functions

AddChild
TTreeNode AddChild(TTreeItem&);
Adds an item to the end of the child list.

AddSibling
TTreeNode AddSibling(TTreeItem&);
Adds the item above this item.

CreateDragImage
HIMAGELIST CreateDragImage();
Returns the image list used for dragging purposes.

Delete
bool Delete();
Deletes the item from the control.

EditLabel
HWND EditLabel();
Returns the HWND of the edit control to change the text.

EnsureVisible
bool EnsureVisible();
Makes sure the item is visible. Scrolls the item(s) if necessary.

ExpandItem
bool ExpandItem(TExpandCode flag);
Expands or contracts a parent node; similar to the user clicking on the - or + area of the control.

GetChild
TTreeNode GetChild();
Gets the first child of the current node.

GetItem
bool GetItem(TTreeItem* item);
Returns the item associated with the node.

GetNextItem
TTreeNode GetNextItem(TNextCode flag);
Returns the next item.

GetNextSibling
TTreeNode GetNextSibling();
Returns the next sibling.

GetNextVisible
TTreeNode GetNextVisible();
Returns the next visible item.

GetParent
TTreeNode GetParent();
Returns the parent of the current node.

GetPrevSibling
TTreeNode GetPrevSibling();
Returns the previous sibling.

GetPrevVisible
TTreeNode GetPrevVisible();
Returns the next previous item.

InsertChild
TTreeNode InsertChild(TTreeItem&, THowToInsert);
Inserts a child before the passed item.

InsertItem
TTreeNode InsertItem(TTreeItem&);
Inserts an item before this item.

SelectItem
bool SelectItem(TNextCode flag);
Makes the next item selected.

SetItem
bool SetItem(TTreeItem* item);
Sets the item associated with this node.

SortChildren
Form 1   bool SortChildren(const TTwComparer& comparer, bool recurse = false, uint32 extraParam = 0);
Recursively sorts the children of the nodes.

Form 2   bool SortChildren(bool recurse = false);
Sorts the children of *item*. Recursively sorts each child if *recurse* is true.

Protected data member

HtItem
HTREEITEM HtItem;
Wrapper for the tree item.

TTreeWindow class   treewind.h

TTreeWindow is a window that displays information in a hierarchical manner with the concept of parent/child relationships. It's usually used to display a directory structure.

Type definitions

TImageListType enum
enum TImageListType {Normal, State};
TImageListType can be one of the following constants:

- Normal

- State

TStyle enum
enum TStyle {twsNone, twsHasButtons, twsHasLines, twsLinesAtRoot, twsEditLabels, twsDisableDragDrop, twsShowSelAlways};
TStyle can be one of the following constants:

- twsNone

- twsHasButtons

- twsHasLines

- twsLinesAtRoot (only available for 32-bit applications)

- twsEditLabels (only available for 32-bit applications)

- twsDisableDragDrop (only available for 32-bit applications)

- twsShowSelAlways (only available for 32-bit applications)

Public constructors and destructor

Constructors
Form 1   TTreeWindow(TWindow* parent, int id, int x, int y, int w, int h, TModule* module = 0);
Dynamically creates the window.

Form 2   TTreeWindow(TWindow* parent, int resourceId, TModule* module = 0);
Creates the *TTreeWindow* object from a resource.

Destructor

~TTreeWindow();
Destructor.

Public member functions

CreateDragImage
HIMAGELIST CreateDragImage(HTREEITEM item);
Creates a drag image.

Delete
bool Delete(HTREEITEM);
Deletes the item.

DeleteAllItems
bool DeleteAllItems();
Removes all items from the control.

EditLabel
HWND EditLabel(HTREEITEM item);
Enables the user to edit the text of an item.

EnsureVisible
bool EnsureVisible(HTREEITEM);
Makes sure the item is visible.

ExpandItem
bool ExpandItem(TTreeItem::ExpandCode flag, HTREEITEM);
Expands and contracts the parent node.

GetDropHilite
TTreeItem GetDropHilite();
Returns the drop target node.

GetEditControl
HWND GetEditControl();
Returns the edit control used for editing the text.

GetFirstVisible
TTreeItem GetFirstVisible();
Returns the first visible node.

GetImageList
HIMAGELIST GetImageList(ImageListType type);
Returns the image list used by the control.

GetIndent
uint GetIndent();
Returns the number of pixels per indent level.

GetItemCount
uint GetItemCount();
Returns the number of items in the control.

GetNextItem
HTREEITEM GetNextItem(TTreeItem::NextCode nc, HTREEITEM);
Returns the next item.

GetRoot
TTreeItem GetRoot();
Returns the root node.

GetSelection
TTreeItem GetSelection();
Returns the selected node.

GetVisibleCount
uint GetVisibleCount();

Returns the number of the fully visible items in the control.

HasStyle
bool HasStyle(TStyle style);

Returns true if a particular style is set.

HitTest
HTREEITEM HitTest(TTwHitTestInfo* info);

Returns the item that contains the point.

InsertItem
HTREEITEM InsertItem(TV_INSERTSTRUCT far*);

Inserts an item.

SelectItem
bool SelectItem(TTreeItem::NextCode flag, HTREEITEM hItem);

Selects the next item.

SetImageList
HIMAGELIST SetImageList(ImageListType type, HIMAGELIST newList);

Sets the image list used by the control.

SetIndent
void SetIndent(uInt);

Sets the number of pixels per indent level.

SetStyle
void SetStyle(TStyle style);

Sets the style of the control.

SortChildren
Form 1   bool SortChildren(HTREEITEM item, bool recurse = false);

Sorts the children of *item*.

Form 2   bool SortChildren(PFNTVCOMPARE, HTREEITEM parent, bool recurse = false, uint32 lParam = 0);

Recursively sorts each set of children if *recurse* is true.

Update
void Update();

Compatability for Win32.

Protected member function

GetClassName
char far* GetClassName();

Returns the common control class name WC_TREEVIEW.

TTreeWindow helper classes

- *TTwHitTestInfo*
- *TTreeItem*
- *TTwComparer*
- *TTreeNode*

TTwComparer class   treewind.h

TTwComparer is a base class for comparisons of sort items.

Public member function

Compare
virtual int Compare(uint32 item1, uint32 item2, uint32 lParam) const;
Default comparison function that makes every item equal to every other item. Derived classes should override this to return proper sorting codes.

TTwDispInfoNotify class   treewind.h

TTwDispInfoNotify is a *TTreeWindow* notification to repaint an item.

Public data member

item
TV_ITEM item;
Item to repaint.

TTwHitTestInfo class   treewind.h

TTwHitTestInfo is a *TTreeWindow* notification for hit-testing (a C++ type used for notification dispatching).

TTwKeyDownNotify class   treewind.h

TTwKeyDownNotify is a *TTreeWindow* notification that a key has been pressed.

Public data members

flags
uint flags;
Keyboard flags for the notification.

wVKey
uint16 wVKey;
Virtual key.

TTwNotify class   treewind.h

TTwNotify is a basic *TTreeWindow* notification.

Public member functions

action
uint action;
Notification-specific flag.

itemNew
TV_ITEM itemNew;
New item state.

itemOld
TV_ITEM itemOld;
Old item state.

ptDrag
TPoint ptDrag;
Point at the time of drag.

TUDAccel class   updown.h

TUDAccel is a very thin wrapper for the UDACCEL structure which contains information about updown accelarators. The main purpose of this class is to have a placeholder for future abstraction/encapsulation.

TUIBorder class   uihandle.h

TUIBorder assists in drawing borders of many styles. It uses win4.0 calls when available.

Public constructors

Form 1   TUIBorder(const TRect& frame, TStyle style, uint flags = 0);

Constructs a *UIBorder* object given a frame and a high-level style type. Calculates edge and modifier flags internally, as needed.

Form 2   TUIBorder(const TRect& frame, TEdge edge, uint flags = 0);

Constructs a *UIBorder* object given a frame, edge, and modifier flags.

Public member functions

DrawEdge
static bool DrawEdge(TDC& dc, const TRect& frame, uint edge, uint flags);

This is a static function that performs the actual drawing of edges for a *UIBorder* or an external client. It uses the system *::DrawEdge* if available.

GetBoundingRect
TRect GetBoundingRect() const;

Calculates the outside frame rectangle.

GetClientRect
TRect GetClientRect() const;

Calculates the rectangle within the border.

Move
void Move(int dx, int dy);

Moves the frame rect by (*dx,dy*).

MoveTo
void MoveTo(int x, int y);

Moves the frame rect to (*x,y*).

Paint
void Paint(TDC& dc) const;

Paints this *UIBorder* object onto a given device context.

PaintFrame
static void PaintFrame(TDC& dc, const TRect& frame, uint flags, const TColor& tlColor, const TColor& brColor);

Paints a 2-color single pixel-thick frame. Bevel corners get brush color.

PaintFrameC
static void PaintFrameC(TDC& dc, const TRect& frame, uint flags, const TColor& tlColor, const TColor& brColor, const TColor& bcColor);

Paints a 2-color single pixel-thick frame. Bevel corners get their own color.

Size
void Size(int w, int h);

Resizes the frame rect to (*w,h*).

TUIFace class

uihandle.h

TUIFace assists in painting UI elements in various states.

Type definitions

TState enum
enum TState {Normal, Down, Indeterm, Disabled, Default};
TState is used to describe the state of the bitmap to be drawn.

Table 2.33   State Constants

Constant	Meaning if set
Normal	Normal state
Down	Down or Option set state
Indeterm	Indeterminant, or mixed-value state
Disabled	Disabled or Unavailable state
Default	Default button state (bold)

Public constructors

Form 1   TUIFace(const TRect& faceRect, const TBitmap& bm);
Initializes the button face with a bitmap.

Form 2   TUIFace(const TRect& faceRect, const char far* text);
Initializes the button face with a text string.

Form 3   TUIFace(const TRect& faceRect, const TIcon& icon);
Initializes the button face with an icon.

Public member functions

Paint
void Paint(TDC& dc, const TPoint& pt, TState state, bool pressed);
This is the internal bitmap painting function.

PaintMask
void PaintMask(TDC& dc, const TPoint& pt);
Paints the mask onto a DC.

TUIHandle class

uihelper.h

TUIHandle manages and draws various kinds of UI handles, including hatched border handles, and resizing grapples (small squares that appear along the edges) on a rectangle. You can use this class to create a hatched border that encloses various kinds of drawing objects you want to manipulate.

With the help of this class, you can create an application that lets you

- Resize the shape of the rectangle by pointing to and grabbing one of the grapples on the border

- Move the entire rectangle by clicking in the middle of the rectangle

Although by default a hatched border with eight grapples is created, you can control whether grapples appear. In addition, you can vary the pattern of the border by drawing a dashed frame enclosing a rectangle or a rectangle filled with hatch marks. *TuiHandle* uses *THatch8x8Brush* to draw the hatched border.

TUIHandle uses the **enum** *TWhere* to return the area where the user points and clicks the mouse (referred to as a *hit area*).

The following diagram displays a UI handle and identifies several small square grapples where hit testing occurs:

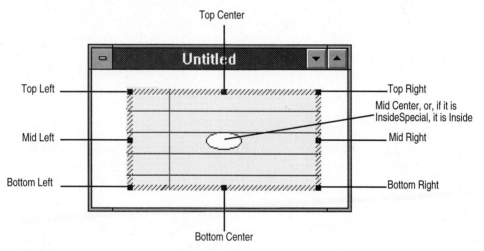

The following code fragment sets up a hatched border and UI grapples for an OLE 2 container application:

```
// Do the default rectangle painting.

TRect r //...; Insert your rectangle drawing code here.

// Draw 8 grapples with a border on top of the object.
TUIHandle handle(r, TUIHandle::HandlesIn|
                TUIHandle::Grapples|
                TUIHandle::HatchBorder, 5);
handle.Paint(dc);
// Insert your code here....

// Draw a hatched border.
TUIHandle handle(r, TUIHandle::HatchBorder, 5);
handle.Paint(dc);
```

See also   THatch8x8Brush

Type definitions

TStyle enum

enum TStyle{HandlesIn, HandlesOut, Framed, DashFramed, Grapples, HatchBorder, HatchRect, InsideSpecial};

Enumerates the style of the border around the rectangle with combinations of the following styles:

Value	Description
Select one of the following styles:	
HandlesIn	Draw handles inside the rectangle
HandlesOut	Draw handles outside the rectangle
Select zero or one of the following styles:	
Framed	Draw a solid frame around the rectangle
DashFramed	Draw a dashed frame around the rectangle
Grapples	Draw eight grapples for resizing
Select zero or one of the following styles:	
HatchBorder	Draw a hatched handle for moving the border
HatchRect	Draw the entire rectangle filled in with hatch marks
InsideSpecial	Treat the inside hit area in a special way

If a hatched border with grapples is drawn inside a rectangle, it sits within the borders of the outer frame of the rectangle. If a hatched border with grapples is drawn outside the rectangle, it is drawn outside the boundary of the rectangle's frame. In the latter case, the function *GetBoundingRect* returns a larger rectangle.

TWhere enum

enum TWhere {TopLeft, TopCenter, TopRight, MidLeft, MidCenter, MidRight, BottomLeft, BottomCenter, BottomRight, Outside, Inside};

TWhere indicates which one of the grapples or handle was hit. *TWhere* can contain one of the following values:

Value	Description
TopLeft	The grapple in the top left corner of the border was hit.
TopCenter	The grapple in the top center of the border was hit.
TopRight	The grapple in the top left right corner of the border was hit.
MidLeft	The grapple in the middle of the left border was hit.
MidCenter	The area in the middle of the rectangle was hit. This indicates that either the hatched frame was hit or inside, non-special area was hit.
MidRight	The grapple in the middle of the right border was hit.
BottomLeft	The grapple in the left corner of the bottom border was hit.
BottomCenter	The grapple in the center of the bottom border was hit.
BottomRight	The grapple in the right corner of the bottom border was hit.

Value	Description
Outside	The hit area is completely outside the object.
Inside	The hit area for the grapple is inside the object and *InsideSpecial* is set.

The *InsideSpecial* designation refers to the area inside the rectangle when the hit area needs to be treated specially (for example, because it might contain text or graphics). Normally, if the area inside the rectangle is hit, it means that user wants to move the rectangle. However, if there is text inside the rectangle, the user might click on this area in order to enter text. This latter situation is referred to as an *inside special* case.

The hit area (*Where*) can be converted to a row and a column by using the following equations:

- Row = Where / 3
- Column = Where mod 3

The value of *Where* ranges from 0 (*TopLeft*) to 8 (*BottomRight*) and corresponds to the following areas of a rectangle:

Column

	0	1	2
Row 0	TopL	TopC	TopR
1	MidL	MidC	MidR
2	BottomL	BottomC	BottomR

You can then use these values to calculate the movement of the object and to resize the object.

Public constructor

TUIHandle

TUIHandle(const TRect& frame, uint style = HandlesIn|Grapples|HatchBorder, int thickness = 5);

Constructs a *TUIHandle* object for the specified frame, with eight grapples drawn in a hatched border and a default thickness of 5 pixels drawn to the inside.

Public member functions

GetBoundingRect

GetBoundingRect()const;

GetBoundingRect returns a rectangle with the size adjusted according to the thickness. For example, if the handles are outside the rectangle, *GetboundingRect* returns a larger rectangle. The enum *TStyle* defines the positions of the handles (whether the handles are defined as *HandlesIn* or *HandlesOut*).

GetCursorId

static uint16 GetCursorId(TWhere where);

Returns the ID of a standard cursor that is appropriate for use over the location specified in the *where* parameter.

HitTest

TWhere HitTest(const TPoint& point)const;

Compares a given point (*point*) to various parts of the rectangle. If the hit was outside the rectangle, *HitTest* returns *Outside*. If the hatched border handle of the rectangle was hit, returns *MidCenter* (inside). For any other hits, *HitTest* returns the location of the grapple that was hit. The **enum** *TWhere* defines the possible hit areas.

Move

void Move(int dx, int dy);

Moves the rectangle relative to the values specified in *dx* and *dy*.

See also   TUIHandle::MoveTo

MoveTo

void MoveTo(int x, int y);

Moves the rectangle to the given *x* and *y* coordinates.

See also   TUIHandle::Move

Paint

void Paint(TDC& dc) const;

Paints the *TUIHandle* object onto the specified device context, *dc*.

Size

void Size(int w, int h);

Sets the size of the rectangle according to the measurements specified in *w*, the width, and *h*, the height.

TUIPart class   uihelper.h

TUIPart encapsulates the DrawFrameControl 32-bit API.

Public constructor

TUIPart

TUIPart();

This is an empty constructor.

Public enums

TState enum

enum TState {Button3State, ButtonCheck, ButtonPush, ButtonRadio, ButtonRadioImage, ButtonRadioMask, Checked, Flat, Inactive, Mono, Pushed, CaptionClose, CaptionHelp, CaptionMax, CaptionMin, CaptionRestore, MenuArrow, MenuBullet, MenuCheck, ScrollCombo, ScrollDown, ScrollLeft, ScrollRight, ScrollSizeGrip, ScrollUp};

TState is used to describe the various glyphs available for buttons, captions, menus, and scrollbar parts.

Table 2.34   State constants

Constant	Meaning if set
Button3State	Three-state button
ButtonCheck	Check box
ButtonPush	Push button
ButtonRadio	Radio button
ButtonRadioImage	Image for radio button (nonsquare needs image)
ButtonRadioMask	Mask for radio button (nonsquare needs mask)
Checked	Draw button as checked
Flat	Draw button with flat border
Inactive	Draw button grayed
Mono	Draw button with monochrome border
Pushed	Draw button pushed
CaptionClose	Close button
CaptionHelp	Help button
CaptionMax	Maximize button
CaptionMin	Minimize button
CaptionRestore	Restore button
MenuArrow	Submenu arrow
MenuBullet	Bullet
MenuCheck	Check mark
ScrollCombo	Combo box scroll bar
ScrollDown	Down arrow of scroll bar
ScrollLeft	Left arrow of scroll bar
ScrollRight	Right arrow of scroll bar
ScrollSizeGrip	Size grip in bottom-right corner of window
ScrollUp	Up arrow of scroll bar

TType enum

enum TType {uiButton = DFC_BUTTON, uiCaption = DFC_CAPTION, uiMenu = DFC_MENU};

TType is used to describe the part to be drawn. *TState* then refines the exact glyph of the selected part.

Table 2.35   Type constants

Constant	Meaning if set
uiButton	Draw a button glyph
uiCaption	Draw a caption glyph
uiMenu	Draw a menu glyph
uiScroll	Draw a scroll bar glyph

See also   TUIPart::TState enum

Public member functions

DrawFrameControl
bool DrawFrameControl(TDC& dc, TRect& rect, TType type, TState state);

This is the wrapper for the DrawFrameControl API.

Paint
bool Paint(TDC& dc, TRect& rect, TType type, TState state);

Draws the part onto a DC. The type and state control how the part should be painted.

TUpDown class   updown.h

TUpDown encapsulates an up-down control, which is a window with a pair of arrow buttons that the user can click to increment or decrement a value.

Type definitions

TCtlState enum
enum TCtlState {csGrayed = 0x0001, csHidden = 0x0002, csMouseOut = 0x0004, csIncrement = 0x0008, csDecrement = 0x0010, csTimer1On = 0x0020, csTimer2On = 0x0040};

TCtlState is used to describe the state and attributes of the updown control.

Table 2.36   Control state constants

Constant	Meaning if set
csGrayed	Control is grayed
csHidden	Control is hidden
csMouseOut	Mouse is outside client area
csIncrement	Control is currently incrementing
csDecrement	Control is currently decrementing
csTimer1On	Initial/delayed timer is enabled
csTimer2On	Repeat/hold timer is enabled

Public constructors

Form 1   TUpDown(TWindow* parent, int id, int x, int y, int w, int h, TWindow* buddy = 0, TModule* module = 0);
Constructor of *UpDown* control.

Form 2   TUpDown(TWindow* parent, int resourceId, TWindow* buddy = 0, TModule* module = 0);
Constructor to an alias of an up-down control that is part of a dialog resource.

Public member functions

GetAccel
int GetAccel(int count, TUDAccel far* accels) const;
Retrieves acceleration information for the underlying up-down control.

GetBase
int GetBase() const;
Retrieves the current radix base of the underlying up-down control. Return value is either 10 or 16.

GetBuddy
HWND GetBuddy() const;
Retrieves handle of buddy window of underlying up-down control.

GetPos
int32 GetPos() const;
Returns current position of underlying up-down control. The high-order word is non-zero in case of an error. The current position is in the low-order word.

GetRange
Form 1   void GetRange(int& lower, int& upper) const;
Retrieves the minimum and maximum range of the underlying up-down control into the specified 'lower' and 'upper' variables, respectively.

Form 2   uint32 GetRange() const;
Retrieves the minimum and maximum range of the underlying up-down control. The low-order word contains the maximum position while the high-order word contains the minimum position.

SetAccel
bool SetAccel(int count, const TUDAccel far* accels);
Sets the acceleration of the underlying up-down control. *count* specifies the number of structures specified in *accels* while the latter is the address of an array of *TUDAccel* structures.

SetBase
int SetBase(int base);
Sets the radix of the underlying up-down control. The *base* parameter should be either *10* or *16* for decimal and hexadecimal, respectively.

SetBuddy
HWND SetBuddy(HWND hBuddy);
Sets the buddy window of the underlying up-down control.

SetPos
int32 SetPos(int pos);
Sets the current position of the underlying up-down control. The return value is the previous position.

SetRange
void SetRange(int lower, int upper);
Sets the minimum and maximum positions of the up-down control.

Note Neither *lower* nor *upper* can be greater than UD_MAXVAL or less than UD_MINVAL. Futhermore, the difference between the two positions must not exceed UD_MAXVAL.

Protected member functions

Action
void Action();
Sends UP or DOWN notifications.

EvCancelMode
void EvCancelMode();
Handles WM_CANCELMODE messages to reset current processing.

EvEnable
void EvEnable(bool enabled);
Handles WM_ENABLE messages to allow control to paint according to its current state.

EvHScroll
void EvHScroll(uint, uint, HWND);
Keeps *TWindow* from rerouting these; must be left as is for updown control.

EvLButtonDblClk
void EvLButtonDblClk(uint modKeys, TPoint& point);
Handles WM_LBUTTONDBLCLK, which is handled just like a regular LBUTTONDOWN.

EvLButtonDown
void EvLButtonDown(uint modKeys, TPoint& point);
Handles WM_LBUTTONDOWN to process up/down scroll mouse requests.

EvLButtonUp
void EvLButtonUp(uint modKeys, TPoint& point);
Handles WM_LBUTTONUP to reset mouse down/dblclk processing.

EvMouseMove
void EvMouseMove(uint modKeys, TPoint& point);

Handles WM_MOUSEMOVE to monitor mouse location when processing mouse down/dblclk requests.

EvShowWindow

void EvShowWindow(bool show, uint status);

Enables WM_SHOWWINDOW to keep track of the window's visibility.

EvTimer

void EvTimer(uint timerId);

Handles WM_TIMER messages to send periodic notifications.

EvVScroll

void EvVScroll(uint, uint, HWND);

Keeps *TWindow* from rerouting these. Must be left as is for updown control.

GetBuddyInt

void GetBuddyInt();

Retrieves current position from buddy's caption.

GetClassName

char far* GetClassName();

Returns the *ClassName* of the underlying control.

Note   The name returned depends upon whether you're using an operating system which provides the underlying implementation of updown controls. Also, when emulating, we choose to return a distinct class name. Although this is not strictly necessary with ObjectWindows, it facilitates the debugging process.

GetSpinRect

void GetSpinRect(TRect& rect, bool incRect);

Retrieves the rectangle of either 'up' or 'down' button.

GetSpinRectFromPoint

uint GetSpinRectFromPoint(TRect& rect, const TPoint& pt);

Retrieves the rectangle of the 'active' button based on the location specified via *pt*. Returns either *csIncrement* or *csDecrement* to indicate which area the point was in.

GetSpinRectFromState

void GetSpinRectFromState(TRect& rect);

Retrieves the rectangle of the 'active' button, based on the current state of the control.

Paint

void Paint(TDC& dc, bool erase, TRect& rect);

Handles WM_PAINT messages. Paints control, based on the state of the latter.

Note   We do not have to check for *NativeUse* here since the virtual method *Paint* is not called for predefined classes (i.e., it's not invoked when we use the Native implementation).

PerformCreate

void PerformCreate(int);

Overridden to invoke the OS' *CreateUpDownControl* method on systems that use the native implementation of Updown controls.

SetBuddyInt
void SetBuddyInt() const;

Update buddy's caption based on current position.

SetupWindow
void SetupWindow();

Overridden to initialize members when ObjectWindows provides the underlying implementation of the updown control.

TUpDownNotify class   commctrl.h

TUpDownNotify is a wrapper of the NM_UPDOWN structure sent with notifications from an *UpDown* control.

Public member function

operator NMHDR&
operator NMHDR&();

Allows the notification structure to be transparently treated as an NMHDR structure, thereby eliminating the need to explicitly refer to the NMHDR data member (which is always the first member of notification structures).

TValidator class   validate.h

A streamable class, *TValidator* defines an abstract data validation object. Although you will never actually create an instance of *TValidator*, it provides the abstract functions for the other data validation objects.

The VALIDATE.CPP sample program on your distribution disk derives *TValidateApp* from *TApplication* in the following manner:

```
class TValidateApp : public TApplication {
  public:
    TValidateApp() : TApplication("ValidateApp") {}
    void InitMainWindow() {
      MainWindow = new TTestWindow(0, "Validate Dialog Input");
    }
}
```

The program displays the following message box if the user enters an invalid employee ID:

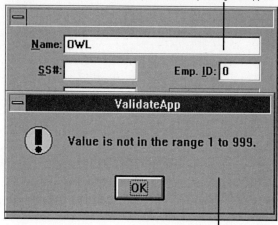

After you choose Input|Employee from the menu, the Employee Data Entry dialog box appears.

If an invalid employee ID is entered, the ValidateApp message box appears.

See also   TValidatorOptions

Public constructor and destructor

Constructor
TValidator();
Constructs an abstract validator object and sets *Options* fields to 0.

Destructor
virtual ~TValidator();
Destroys an abstract validator object.

Public member functions

Adjust
virtual int Adjust(string& text, uint& begPos, uint& endPos, int amount);
Adjusts the 'value' of the text, given a cursor position and an amount. Returns the actual amount adjusted.

Error
virtual void Error();
Error is an abstract function called by *Valid* when it detects that the user has entered invalid information. By default, *TValidator::Error* does nothing, but derived classes can override *Error* to provide feedback to the user.

HasOption
bool HasOption(int option);

Gets the *Options* bits. Returns **true** if a specified option is set.

See also   TValidatorOptions enum

IsValid

virtual bool IsValid(const char far* str);

By default, returns **true**. Derived validator types can override *IsValid* to validate data for a completed edit control. If an edit control has an associated validator object, its *Valid* method calls the validator object's *Valid* method, which in turn calls *IsValid* to determine whether the contents of the edit control are valid.

IsValidInput

virtual bool IsValidInput(char far* str, bool suppressFill);

If an edit control has an associated validator object, it calls *IsValidInput* after processing each keyboard event, thus giving validators such as filter validators an opportunity to catch errors before the user fills the entire item or screen.

By default, *IsValidInput* returns **true**. Derived data validators can override *IsValidInput* to validate data as the user types it, returning **true** if *str* holds valid data and **false** otherwise.

str is the current input string. *suppressFill* determines whether the validator should automatically format the string before validating it. If *suppressFill* is **true**, validation takes place on the unmodified string *str*. If *suppressFill* is **false**, the validator should apply any filling or padding before validating data. Of the standard validator objects, only *TPXPictureValidator* checks *suppressFill*.

IsValidInput can modify the contents of the input string; for example, it can force characters to uppercase or insert literal characters from a format picture. *IsValidInput* should not, however, delete invalid characters from the string. By returning **false**, *IsValidInput* indicates that the edit control should erase the incorrect characters.

SetOption

void SetOption(int option);

Sets the bits for the *Options* data member.

See also   TValidator::Options, TValidatorOptions enum

Transfer

virtual uint Transfer(char far* str, void* buffer, TTransferDirection direction);

Allows a validator to set and read the values of its associated edit control. This is primarily useful for validators that check non-string data, such as numeric values. For example, *TRangeValidator* uses *Transfer* to read and write values instead of transferring an entire string.

By default, edit controls with validators give the validator the first chance to respond to *DataSize*, *GetData*, and *SetData* by calling the validator's *Transfer* method. If *Transfer* returns anything other than 0, it indicates to the edit control that it has handled the appropriate transfer. The default action of *TValidator::Transfer* is always to return 0. If you want the validator to transfer data, you must override its *Transfer* method.

Transfer's first two parameters are the associated edit control's text string and the *tdGetData* or *tdSetData* data record. Depending on the value of *direction*, *Transfer* can set *str* from buffer or read the data from *str* into *buffer*. The return value is always the number of bytes transferred.

If direction is *tdSizeData*, *Transfer* doesn't change either *str* or *buffer*; it just returns the data size. If *direction* is *tdSetData*, *Transfer* reads the appropriate number of bytes from *buffer*, converts them into the proper string form, and sets them into *str*, returning the number of bytes read. If *direction* is *tdGetData*, *Transfer* converts *str* into the appropriate data type and writes the value into *buffer*, returning the number of bytes written.

See also   TTransferDirection enum

UnsetOption
void UnsetOption(int option);

Unsets the bits specified in the *Options* data member.

See also   TValidator::Options, TValidatorOptions enum

Valid
bool Valid(const char far* str);

Returns **true** if *IsValid* returns **true**. Otherwise, calls *Error* and returns **false**. A validator's *Valid* method is called by the *Valid* method of its associated edit control.

Edit controls with associated validator objects call the validator's *Valid* method under two conditions. The first condition is when the edit control's *ofValidate* option is set and the edit control calls *Valid* when it loses focus. The second condition is when the dialog box that contains the edit control calls *Valid* for all its controls, usually because the user requested to close the dialog box or to accept an entry screen.

Protected data member

Options
uint16 Options;

A bitmap member used to control options for various descendants of *TValidator*. By default, the *TValidator* constructor clears all the bits in *Options*.

See also   TValidatorOptions enum, TValidator::SetOption, TValidator::UnsetOption

TVbxControl class   vbxctl.h

Derived from TControl, *TVbxControl* provides the interface for Visual Basic (VBX) controls. You can use this class to get or set the properties of VBX controls. Under certain conditions, you can also use additional methods for processing controls. Both 16- and 32-bit programs can use these VBX controls.

You can manipulate the control's properties using either an index value or a name. Several overloaded *GetProp* functions are provided so that you can access different types of properties. Similarly, several overloaded *SetProp* functions let you set the properties of controls using either the name of the VBX control or the index value. Consult the documentation for your VBX controls to find the name that corresponds to the property you want to manipulate.

The VBXCTLX.CPP sample program on your distribution disks displays the following VBX controls:

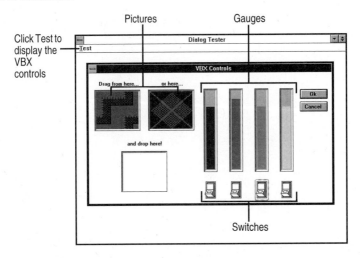

TVbxControl provides event-handling functions that process requests to compare, delete, draw, or measure VBX controls. If you want the *TVbxControl* object to process additional VBX events, you can derive a class from *TVbxControl* and add a response table that has entries for the events you want processed. For information about creating response tables and handling VBX messages, see *TVbxEventHandler*.

See also   Visual Basic Control Objects Overview

Public constructors and destructor

Constructors

Form 1   TVbxControl(TWindow* parent, int id, const char far* vbxName, const char far* vbxClass, const char far* title, int x, int y, int w, int h, long initLen = 0, void far* initData = 0, TModule* module = 0);

Constructs a VBX control where *parent* points to the parent window, *id* is the control's ID, *vbxName* is the name of the file containing the VBX control, *vbxClass* is the VBX class name, *title* is the control's caption, *x* and *y* are the coordinates in the parent window where the controls are to be placed, *w* and *h* are the width and height of the control, and *module* is the library resource ID for the control.

Form 2   TVbxControl(TWindow* parent, int resourceId, TModule* module = 0);

If a VBX control is part of a dialog resource, its ID can be used to construct a corresponding (or alias) ObjectWindows object. You can use this constructor if a VBX control has already been defined in the application's resource file. *resourceId* is the resource ID of the VBX control in the resource file.

Destructor

~TVbxControl();

Destroys the *TVbxControl* object.

Public member functions

AddItem
bool AddItem(int index, const char far* item);

Adds an item (*item*) to the list of VBX control items at the specified index (*index*). Returns nonzero if successful.

Drag
bool Drag(int action);

Controls the drag and drop state of the VBX control according to the value of *action*, which can be 0 (cancel a drag operation), 1 (begin dragging a control), or 2 (end dragging a control).

GetEventIndex
int GetEventIndex(const char far* name);

Returns the index of the event associated with the name of the event passed in *name*. Returns -1 if an error occurs.

GetEventName
Form 1   const char far* GetEventName(int eventindex);

Returns a string containing the name of an event associated with the integer event index number (*eventindex*). Returns 0 if an error occurs.

Form 2   void GetEventName(int eventIndex, string& str);

Retrieves the name of the event at a particular index.

GetHCTL
HCTL GetHCTL();

Returns a handle to a VBX control associated with this *TVbxControl* object.

GetNumEvents
int GetNumEvents();

Returns the total number of events associated with the VBX control.

GetNumProps
int GetNumProps();

Returns the total number of properties associated with the VBX control.

GetProp
Form 1   bool GetProp(int propIndex, int& value, int arrayIndex = -1);

Gets an integer property value. An overloaded function, *GetProp* gets a VBX control property using an index value. *propIndex* is the index value of the property whose value you want to get. *value* is a reference to the variable that will receive the property values. *arrayIndex*, an optional argument, specifies the position of the value in an array property if the property is an array type. If the property isn't an array type, *arrayIndex* defaults to -1. See the third-party reference guide for your VBX controls to determine a property's data type. *GetProp* returns nonzero if successful. To get the property by specifying the property index, use one of the following six *GetProp* functions.

Form 2   bool GetProp(int propIndex, long& value, int arrayIndex = -1);

Gets a *long* property value.

Form 3   bool GetProp(int propIndex, ENUM& value, int arrayIndex=-1);

Gets an enumerated property value. For example, a list of options associated with a font style might be defined as an enumerated type.

Form 4   bool GetProp(int propIndex, HPIC& value, int arrayIndex=-1);

Gets a picture (*value*). HPIC is a handle to the picture.

Form 5   bool GetProp(int propIndex, float& value, int arrayIndex = -1);

Gets a floating-point property value.

Form 6   bool GetProp(int propIndex, string& value, int arrayIndex = -1);

Gets a string property value.

Form 7   bool GetProp(int propIndex, COLORREF& value, int arrayIndex = -1);

Gets a color property value.

Form 8   bool GetProp(const char far* name, int& value, int arrayIndex = -1);

Returns an integer data value. An overloaded function, *GetProp* gets a VBX control property. *propIndex* is the index value of the property whose value you want to get. *value* is a reference to the variable that will receive the property value. *arrayIndex*, an optional argument, specifies the position of the value in an array property if the property is an array type. If the property isn't an array type, *arrayIndex* defaults to -1. *GetProp* returns nonzero if successful. To get the property by specifying the name of the property, use one of the following five *GetProp* functions.

Form 9   bool GetProp(const char far* name, long& value, int arrayIndex = -1);

Gets a **long** property value.

Form 10   bool GetProp(const char far* name, float& value, int arrayIndex = -1);

Gets a floating-point property value.

Form 11   bool GetProp(const char far* name, ENUM& value, int arrayIndex=-1);

Gets an enumerated property value.

Form 12   bool Getprop(const char far* name, HPIC& value, int arrayIndex=-1);

Gets a picture (*value*) property value. HPIC is a handle to the picture.

Form 13   bool GetProp(const char far* name, string& value, int arrayIndex = -1);

Gets a string property value.

Form 14   bool GetProp(const char far* name, COLORREF& value, int arrayIndex = -1);

Gets a string color property value.

Form 15   bool GetProp(const char far* name, bool& value, int arrayIndex=-1);

Gets properties by name.

Form 16   bool GetProp(int propIndex, bool& value, int arrayIndex=-1);

Retrieves the boolean property at a particular index.

See also   TVbxControl::SetProp

GetPropIndex
int GetPropIndex(const char far* name);

Gets the integer index value for the property name passed in *name*. Returns -1 if an error occurs. This usually indicates that the property name passed in *name* couldn't be located.

GetPropName

Form 1   const char far* GetPropName(int propIndex);

Gets the name for the property index passed in *index*. Returns 0 if an error occurs.

Form 2   void GetPropName(int propIndex, string& str);

Retrieves the name of the property at a particular index.

GetPropType

Form 1   int GetPropType(int propIndex);

Gets the type for the property specified by *index*.

Form 2   int GetPropType(char far* name);

Gets the property string type specified by *name*. Returns 0 if an error occurs. The following table lists the names of the property types and their corresponding C++ data types.

Property type	C++ type
PTYPE_CSTRING	HSZ
PTYPE_SHORT	short
PTYPE_LONG	int32
PTYPE_BOOL	bool
PTYPE_COLOR	uint32 or COLORREF
PTYPE_ENUM	uint8 or ENUM
PTYPE_REAL	float
PTYPE_XPOS	int32 (Twips)
PTYPE_XSIZE	int32(Twips)
PTYPE_YPOS	int32 (Twips)
PTYPE_YSIZE	int32 (Twips)
PTYPE_PICTURE	HPIC
PTYPE_BSTRING	HLSTR

IsArrayProp

Form 1   bool IsArrayProp(int propIndex);

Returns true if the property specified by *index* is an array property.

Form 2   bool IsArrayProp(char far* name);

Returns true if the property specified by *name* is an array property.

Move

bool Move(long x, long y, long w, long h);

Moves a VBX control to the coordinates specified in *x* and *y*, which designate the upper left corner screen coordinates. Resizes the VBX control to *w twips* wide by *h twips* high. Returns nonzero if successful.

Refresh

bool Refresh();

Repaints the control's display area.

RemoveItem

bool RemoveItem(int index);

Removes an item (specified by *index*). The item could be removed from a list box, a combo box, or a database, for example.

SetProp

Form 1   bool SetProp(int propIndex, int value, int arrayIndex = -1);

Sets the property to an integer value. An overloaded function, *SetProp* sets a VBX control property. *propIndex* is the index number of the property whose value you want to set. *value* specifies the new value for the property. *arrayIndex* specifies the position of the value in an array property if the property is an array type. If the property isn't an array type, *arrayIndex* defaults to -1. To set the property by passing the property's index value, use one of the following six *SetProp* functions.

Form 2   bool SetProp(int propIndex, long value, int arrayIndex = -1);

Sets the property to a **long** value.

Form 3   bool SetProp(int propIndex, ENUM value, int arrayIndex=-1);

Sets the property to an enumerated value.

Form 4   bool SetProp(int propIndex, HPIC value, int arrayIndex=-1);

Sets a picture to an HPIC, or picture, value.

Form 5   bool SetProp(int propIndex, float value, int arrayIndex = -1);

Sets the property to a floating-point value.

Form 6   bool SetProp(int propIndex, const string& value, int arrayIndex = -1);

Sets the property to a string value.

Form 7   bool SetProp(int propIndex, const char far* value, int arrayIndex = -1);

Sets the property to a character string value.

Form 8   bool SetProp(int propIndex, COLORREF value, int arrayIndex = -1);

Sets the property to a color value.

Form 9   bool SetProp(const char far* name, int value, int arrayIndex = -1);

Sets the property to an integer value. An overloaded function, *SetProp* sets a VBX control property. *arrayIndex* specifies the position of the value in an array property if the property is an array type. If the property isn't an array type, *arrayIndex* defaults to -1. To set the property by using the property's name, use one of the following six *SetProp* functions.

Form 10   bool SetProp(const char far* name, long value, int arrayIndex = -1);

Sets the property to a *long* value.

Form 11   bool SetProp(const char far* name, ENUM value, int arrayIndex=-1);

Sets the property to an enumerated value.

Form 12   bool SetProp(const char far* name, HPIC value, int arrayIndex = -1);

Sets the picture property to an HPIC, or picture, value.

Form 13   bool SetProp(const char far* name, float value, int arrayIndex = -1);

Sets the property to a floating-point value.

Form 14   bool SetProp(const char far* name, const string& value, int arrayIndex = -1);
Sets the property to a string value.

Form 15   bool SetProp(const char far* name, const char far* value, int arrayIndex = -1);
Sets the property to a character string value.

Form 16   bool SetProp(const char far* name, COLORREF value, int arrayIndex = -1);
Sets the property to a color string value.

See also   TVbxControl::GetProp

SetupWindow
void SetupWindow();
A VBX control has an HWND plus a VBX handle. Usually, the VBX control handle is created first. However, if the window has already been created, you can use this function to extract the VBX control handle.

Protected member functions

GetClassName
char far* GetClassName();
Gets the name of the VBX window class.

GetVBXProperty
bool GetVBXProperty(int propIndex, void far* value, int arrayIndex = -1);
Returns nonzero if the specified property exists. *propIndex* specifies the index value of the integer property whose value you want to get. *value* points to the variable where the value will be stored.

PerformCreate
void PerformCreate(int menuOrId);
Creates a new control window and associates the VBX control with the window. Establishes the control ID, the VBX control name and class, and the window caption. Sets *Attr.style* to the window style of the control, *Attr.X* and *Attr.Y* to the upper-left screen coordinates of the control, and *Attr.W* and *Attr.H* to the width and height of the control.

SetVBXProperty
bool SetVBXProperty(int propIndex, int32 value, int arrayIndex=-1);
Returns nonzero if the specified property value is set, or 0 if unsuccessful. *propindex* is the index number of the property whose value you want to set. *value* is the value to be stored. An optional argument, *arrayIndex*, which is -1 by default, specifies the index value in an array of values of the property to be set.

Response table entries

The *TVbxControl* class has no response table entries.

TVbxEventHandler class

vbxctl.h

Derived from *TEventHandler*, *TVbxEventHandler* handles events from VBX controls. Although you never need to modify this class, *TVbxEventHandler* needs to be mixed in with your window class so that your window class can receive events from VBX controls. For example,

```
class TMyWindow:public TWindow, public TVbxEventHandler
{
// Include class definition here.
}
```

The following diagram illustrates the flow of information between VBX controls, parent windows, and response tables:

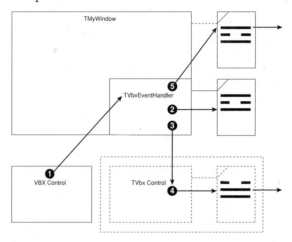

When a VBX control fires an event (sends an event message), the following sequence of events occurs:

1   The VBX Control sends a WM_VBXFIREEVENT message to *TMyWindow*.

2   *TMyWindow*'s *TVbxEventHandler* finds a WM_VBXFIREEVENT message in its response table and calls *EvVbxDispatch*.

3   If a child window is present, *EvVbxDispatch* dispatches the event to the child.

4   If there is an event-handling function in the child window's response table, the child window handles the event.

5   If there is no child window, or the child window doesn't handle the event, *EvVbxDispatch* dispatches the event to *TMyWindow*'s response table.

In other words, when a VBX control sends a WM_VBXFIREEVENT message, the parent window's *TVbxEventHandler* catches this message first, converts it into a form understood by a window's response table, and attempts to send the converted message to the child window. If there is no child window or if the child window doesn't handle the message, *TVbxEventHandler* sends the converted message to the parent window.

When the parent window receives the message, it calls the handler function that corresponds to the message.

Two response table macros, EV_VBXEVENTNAME and EV_VBXEVENTINDEX, map VBX events to handler functions. Of the two macros, EV_VBXEVENTNAME is more commonly used. EV_VBXEVENTINDEX is intended for use with code generators, which can determine the event index values for a VBX control. Both macros call an event handler function and point to the VBXEVENT structure. A typical EV_VBXEVENTNAME response table entry might be

```
EV_VBXEVENTNAME(IDC_BUTTON1, "MouseMove", EvMouseMove);
```

In this response table, IDC_BUTTON1 is the event ID, "MouseMove" is the event name, and *EvMouseMove* is the handler function.

The *lparam* of a WM_VBXFIREEVENT message points to a VBXEVENT structure, which holds information about the event and the control that generated the event. The VBXEVENT structure contains the following members:

```
typedef struct VBXEVENT {
    HCTL    Control;
    HWND    Window;
    int     ID;
    int     EventIndex;
    LPCSTR  EventName;
    int     NumParams;
    LPVOID  ParamList;
} VBXEVENT;
```

The structure members are described in the following table:

Member	Description
Control	A handle to the VBX control sending the message.
Window	The handle of the VBX control window.
ID	The ID of the VBX control.
EventIndex	The event index.
EventName	The name of the event.
NumParams	The number of event arguments.
ParamList	A pointer to a list of pointers to the event's arguments. The *ParamList* data member provides access to the actual arguments of the event.

To handle VBX events, your program uses an event-handling function. In the following example, *EvMouseMove* is the name of the handler function, which passes a pointer to the VBXEVENT event structure. VBX_EVENTARGNUM is the macro that takes *event*, *type*, and an index number as its parameters. *event* references the VBXEVENT structure, **short** is the event argument type, and 0 and 1 are the index numbers of the argument. The argument types and indexes can be found in the documentation for the VBX control.

```
void EvMouseMove(VBXEVENT FAR* event)
{
    short X = VBX_EVENTARGNUM(event, short, 0);
    short Y = VBX_EVENTARGNUM(event, short, 1);
}
```

Because VBX controls were originally designed to be used with Visual Basic, their event arguments are documented in terms of Basic data types. The following table lists the Basic types, their C++ equivalents, and macros:

Basic	C++	Macro
Boolean	short	VBX_EVENTARGNUM(*event, short, index*)
Control	HCTL	VBX_EVENTARGNUM(*event, HCTL, index*)
Double	double	VBX_EVENTARGNUM(*event, double, index*)
Enum	short	VBX_EVENTARGNUM(*event, short, index*)
Integer	short	VBX_EVENTARGNUM(*event, short, index*)
Long	long	VBX_EVENTARGNUM(*event, long, index*)
Single	float	VBX_EVENTARGNUM(*event, float, index*)
String	HLSTR	VBX_EVENTARGSTR(*event, index*)

The following table lists the standard VBX events and corresponding arguments that the Borland C++ VBX emulation library supports:

Event	Arguments
Click	None
DblClick	None
DragDrop	Source as Control, X as Integer, Y as Integer
DragOver	Source as Control, X as Integer, Y as Integer, State as Integer
GotFocus	None
KeyDown	Key as Integer, Shift as Integer
KeyPress	Key as Integer, Shift as Integer
KeyUp	Key as Integer, Shift as Integer
LostFocus	None
MouseDown	X as Integer, Y as Integer
MouseMove	X as Integer, Y as Integer, Shift as Integer, Button as Integer
MouseUp	X as Integer, Y as Integer, Shift as Integer, Button as Integer

For the *DragOver* event, the state argument can be one of the following values:

- 0, where the source control is being dragged within a target's range.

- 1, where the source control is being dragged out of a target's range.

- 2, where the source control is being moved from one position in the target to another.

For both the *DragOver* and *DragDrop* events, the *Control* argument type should be translated to HCTL (a handle to the VBX control) for C++. The X and Y values are in pixels, not twips.

If a standard VBX event has a Shift key argument, the argument has these bit values:

Key	Bit value
Shift	0x1
Ctrl	0x2
Alt	0x4 (Used in connection with a Menu selection)

If a standard VBX event has a Button key argument, the argument has these bit values:

Button	Bit value
Left	0x1
Right	0x2
Middle	0x4

The following example shows how you might use the Shift key arguments. For example, if you want the VBX control to perform some action when the mouse is moved and the Shift key is pressed, you could write a function such as

```
void EvMouseMove(VBXEVENT FAR* event)
{
    short X = VBX_EVENTARGNUM(event, short, 0);
    short Y = VBX_EVENTARGNUM(event, short, 1);
    short Shift = VBX_EVENTARGNUM(event, short, 2);
    short Button = VBX_EVENTARGNUM(event, short, 3);
    if (shift & 0x2)
        MessageBox ("The control key is pressed.");
}
```

Borland C++ uses pixels to express the X and Y coordinate arguments of standard VBX events. This differs from Visual Basic, which expresses coordinates in twips (1/20th of a point or 1/1440 of an inch). Custom events are usually expressed in terms of twips. You can use these functions to convert between pixels and twips:

Function	Meaning
VBXPix2TwpX	Converts an X argument from pixels to twips
VBXPix2TwpY	Converts a Y argument from pixels to twips
VBXTwp2PixX	Converts an X argument from twips to pixels
VBXTwp2PixY	Converts a Y argument from twips to pixels

Protected member functions

EvVbxDispatch
LRESULT EvVbxDispatch(WPARAM wp, LPARAM lp);

After *TVbxEventHandler* receives a WM_VBXFIREEVENT message from the parent window, it calls *EvVbxDispatch*, which sends the message to the correct event-handling function and passes a pointer to the VBXEVENT structure.

EvVbxInitForm
LRESULT EvVbxInitForm(WPARAM wp, LPARAM lp);
Initializes a dialog box that contains VBX controls.

Response table entries

Response table entry	Member function
EV_MESSAGE(WM_VBXFIREEVENT, EvVbxDispatch)	EvVbxDispatch
EV_MESSAGE(WM_VBXINITFORM, EvVbxinitForm)	EvVbxInitForm

See also   Visual Basic Control Objects Overview

TView class   docview.h

Derived virtually from both *TEventHandler* and *TStreamableBase*, *TView* is the interface presented to a document so it can access its client views. Views then call the document functions to request input and output streams. Views own the streams and are responsible for attaching and deleting them.

Instead of creating an instance of *TView*, you create a derived class that can implement *TView*'s virtual functions. The derived class must have a way of knowing the associated window (provided by *GetWindow*) and of describing the view (provided by *GetViewName*). The view must also be able to display the document title in its window (*SetDocTitle*).

Classes derived from *TView* may need to handle several notification messages. For example, if a view is associated with a window that can gain focus, then the view should handle the *vnIsWindow* notification message.

View classes can take various forms. For example, a view class can be a window (through inheritance), can contain a window (an embedded object), can reference a window, or can be contained within a window object. A view class might not even have a window, as in the case of a voice mail or a format converter. Some remote views (for example, those displayed by DDE servers) might not have local windows.

Other viewer classes derived from *TView* include *TEditView*, *TListView*, and *TWindowView*. These classes display different types of data: *TEditView* displays unformatted text files, *TListView* displays text information in a list box, and *TWindowView* is a basic viewer from which you can derive other types of viewers such as hexadecimal file viewers.

For OLE-enabled applications, use *TOleView*, which supports views for embedded objects and compound documents.

Type definitions

TNewEnum enum
enum TNewEnum {PrevProperty, ViewClass, ViewName, NextProperty};

TNewEnum can be one of the following constants:

- PrevProperty
- View Class
- ViewName
- NextProperty

Public data member

Tag
void far* Tag;

Holds a pointer to the application-defined data. Typically, you can use *Tag* to install a pointer to your own application's associated data structure. *TView* zeros *Tag* during construction and does not access it again.

Public constructor and destructor

Constructor
TView(TDocument& doc);

Constructs a *TView* object of the document associated with the view. Sets the private data member *ViewId* to *NextViewId*. Calls *TDocument*'s private member function *AttachView* to attach the view to the associated document.

Destructor
virtual ~TView();

Frees a *TView* object and calls *TDocument*'s private member function *DetachView* to detach the view from the associated document.

Public member functions

BumpNextViewId
static void BumpNextViewId();

Increments an internal count used by the Doc/View subsystem to identify each view.

FindProperty
virtual int FindProperty(const char far* name);

Gets the property index, given the property name (*name*). Returns 0 if the name is not found.

See also   pfxxxx property access constants

GetDocument
TDocument& GetDocument();

Returns a reference to the view's document.

GetNextView
TView* GetNextView();
Returns the next global view ID to be assigned.

GetNextViewId
static unsigned GetNextViewId{};
Returns the next view ID to be assigned.

GetProperty
virtual int GetProperty(int index, void far* dest, int textlen=0);
Returns the total number of properties, where *index* is the property index, *dest* contains the property data, and *textlen* is the size of the property array. If *textlen* is 0, property data is returned as binary data; otherwise, property data is returned as text data.

See also   pfxxxx property access constants, TView::SetProperty

GetTag
void far* GetTag() const;
Retrieves the user-defined pointer attached to this view.

GetViewId
unsigned GetViewId();
Returns the unique ID for this view.

GetViewMenu
TMenuDescr* GetViewMenu();
Returns the menu descriptor for this view. This can be any existing *TMenuDescr* object. If no descriptor exists, *ViewMenu* is 0.

GetViewName
virtual const char far* GetViewName()=0;
Pure virtual function that returns 0. Override this function in your derived class to return the name of the class.

See also   TEditView::StaticName, TEditView::GetViewName

GetWindow
virtual TWindow* GetWindow()
Returns the *TWindow* instance associated with the view, or 0 if no view exists.

See also   TeditView::GetWindow

IsOK
bool IsOK();
Returns a nonzero value if the view is successfully constructed.

See also   TView::NotOK

PropertyCount
virtual int PropertyCount();
Gets the total number of properties for the *TDocument* object. Returns *NextProperty* -1.

See also   pfxxxx property access constants

PropertyFlags
virtual int PropertyFlags(int index);

Returns the attributes of a specified property given the index of the property whose attributes you want to retrieve.

See also   pfxxxx property access constants, TView::FindProperty, TView::PropertyName

PropertyName
virtual const char* PropertyName(int index);

Returns the text name of the property given the index value.

See also   pfxxxx property access constants, TView::FindProperty

SetDocTitle
virtual bool SetDocTitle(const char far* docname, int index)

Stores the document title.

See also   TWindow::SetDocTitle

SetProperty
virtual bool SetProperty(int index, const void far* src);

Sets the value of the property, given the index of the property, and *src*, the data type (either binary or text) to which the property must be set.

See also   pfxxxx property access constants, TView::GetProperty

SetTag
void SetTag(void* far* tag);

Associates an arbitrary (user-defined) pointer with this view.

Note   The *Tag* is not used by the Doc/View subsystem.

SetViewMenu
void SetViewMenu(TMenuDescr* menu);

Sets the menu descriptor for this view. This can be any existing *TMenuDescr* object. If no descriptor exists, *ViewMenu* is 0.

See also   TView::GetViewMenu

Protected data member

Doc
TDocument* Doc;

Holds the current document.

Protected member function

NotOK
void NotOK();

Sets the view to an invalid state, causing *IsOK* to return 0.

TVSlider class

slider.h

Derived from *TSlider*, *TVSlider* provides implementation details for vertical sliders. See *TSlider* for an illustration of a vertical slider.

Public constructor

TVSlider(TWindow* parent, int id, int X, int Y, int W, int H, TResId thumbResId = IDB_VSLIDERTHUMB,
    TModule* module = 0);
Constructs a vertical slider object with a default bitmap resource ID of IDB_VSLIDERTHUMB for the thumb knob.

Protected member functions

HitTest
int HitTest(TPoint& point);
Overrides *TSlider*'s virtual function and gets information about where a given X, Y location falls on the slider. The return value is in *scrollCodes*.

See also   TSlider::HitTest

NotifyParent
void NotifyParent(int scrollCode, int pos=0);
Overrides *TSlider*'s virtual function and sends a WS_VSCROLL message to the parent window.

See also   TSlider::NotifyParent

PaintRuler
void PaintRuler(TDC& dc);
Overrides *TSlider*'s virtual function and paints the vertical ruler.

See also   TSlider::PaintRuler

PaintSlot
void PaintSlot(TDC& dc);
Overrides *TSlider*'s virtual function and paints the slot in which the thumb slides.

See also   TSlider::PaintSlot

PointToPos
int PointToPos(TPoint& point);
Overrides *TSlider*'s virtual function and translates an X,Y point to a position in slider units.

See also   TSlider::PointToPos

PosToPoint
TPoint PosToPoint(int pos);
Overrides *TSlider*'s virtual function and translates a position in slider units to an X,Y point.

See also   TSlider::PosToPoint

TWindow class

window.h

TWindow, derived from *TEventHandler* and *TStreamableBase*, provides window-specific behavior and encapsulates many functions that control window behavior and specify window creation and registration attributes.

TWindow is a generic window that can be resized and moved. You can construct an instance of *TWindow*, though normally you use *TWindow* as a base for your specialized window classes. In general, to associate and disassociate a *TWindow* object with a window element, you need to follow these steps:

1 Construct an instance of a *TWindow*.

2 Call *Create* or *Execute*, which creates the interface element (HWND) and then calls *SetupWindow*, which calls the base *SetupWindow* for normal processing, which in turn involves

- Creating the *HWindow* and any child *HWindow*s.

- Calling *TransferData* to setup the transfer of data between the parent and child windows.

3 To destroy the interface element, choose one of the following actions, depending on your application:

- Call *Destroy* to destroy the interface element unconditionally.

- Call *CloseWindow*, which calls *CanClose* to test if it is OK to destroy the interface element.

4 There are two ways to destroy the interface object:

- If the object has been **new**'d, use **delete**.

- If the object has not been **new**'d, the compiler automatically destructs the object.

The ObjectWindows destroy process consists of two parts: (1) call *Destroy* to destroy the interface element and (2) then delete the C++ object. However, it is perfectly valid to call *Destroy* on the interface element without deleting the C++ object and then to call *Create* at a later time to re-create the window. Because it is also valid to construct a C++ window object on the stack or as an aggregated member, the *Destroy* function cannot assume it should delete the C++ object.

The user-generated WM_CLOSE event handler, *EvClose*, also causes a C++ object to be deleted by passing the **this** pointer to the application. The C++ object is deleted automatically because the *EvClose* event frequently occurs in response to a user action, and this is the most convenient place for the deletion to take place. Later, when it's safe to do so, the application then deletes the window pointer. Because the stack often contains selectors that refer to the addresses of objects that may become invalid during the delete process, it is not safe to delete the **this** pointer while events are still being processed. If the addresses become invalid, they could cause trouble when they are reloaded from the stack.

TWindow is the base class for all window classes, including *TFrameWindow*, *TControl*, *TDialog*, and *TMDIChild*. The ObjectWindows hierarchy diagram shows the many classes that are derived from *TWindow*.

Public data members

Attr
TWindowAttr Attr;

Holds a *TWindowAttr* structure, which contains the window's creation attributes. These attributes, which include the window's style, extended style, position, size, menu ID, child window ID, and menu accelerator table ID, are passed to the function that creates the window.

See also   TWindow::TWindow, Window::Create

DefaultProc
WNDPROC DefaultProc;

Holds the address of the default window procedure. *DefWindowProc* calls *Default-Proc* to process Windows messages that are not handled by the window.

HWindow
HWND HWindow;

Holds the handle to the associated MS-Windows window, which you'll need to access if you make calls directly to Windows API functions.

Parent
TWindow* Parent;

Points to the interface object that serves as the parent window for this interface object.

Scroller
TScroller* Scroller;

Points to the scroller object that supports either the horizontal or vertical scrolling for this window.

Status
TStatus Status;

Used to signal an error in the initialization of an interface object. Setting *Status* to a nonzero value causes a *TXCompatibility* exception to be thrown. Classes derived from *TWindow* do not attempt to associate an interface element with an object whose previous initialization has failed. *Status* is included only to provide backward compatibility with previous versions of ObjectWindows.

Title
char far* Title;

Points to the window's caption. When there is a valid *HWindow*, *Title* will yield the same information as *::GetWindowText* if you use *TWindow::SetCaption* to set it.

See also   ::GetWindowText, TDialog::SetCaption, TDialog::SetupWindow, TWindow::GetWindowTextTitle

Public constructors and destructor

The following paragraphs describe procedures common to both constructor syntaxes. *module* specifies the application or DLL that owns the *TWindow* instance. ObjectWindows needs the correct value of *module* to find needed resources. If *module* is 0, *TWindow* sets its module according to the following rules:

- If the window has a parent, the parent's module is used.

- If the *TWindow* constructor is invoked from an application, the module is set to the application.

- If the *TWindow* constructor is invoked from a DLL that is dynamically linked with the ObjectWindows DLL and the currently running application is linked the same way, the module is set to the currently running application.

- If the *TWindow* constructor is invoked from a DLL that is statically linked with the ObjectWindows library or the invoking DLL is dynamically linked with ObjectWindows DLL but the currently running application is not, no default is used for setting the module. Instead, a *TXInvalidModule* exception is thrown and the object is not created.

Form 1   TWindow(THandle handle, TModule* module = 0);

Constructs a *TWindow* that is used as an alias for a non-ObjectWindows window, and sets wfAlias. Because the HWND is already available, this constructor, unlike the other *TWindow* constructor, performs the "thunking" and extraction of HWND information instead of waiting until the function *Create* creates the interface element.

Form 2   TWindow(TWindow* parent, const char far* title = 0, TModule* module = 0);

Adds **this** to the child list of *parent* if nonzero, and calls *EnableAutoCreate* so that **this** will be created and displayed along with *parent*. Also sets the title of the window and initializes the window's creation attributes.

Destructor
virtual ~TWindow();

Destroys a still-associated interface element by calling *Destroy*. Deletes the window objects in the child list, then removes **this** from the parent window's child list. Deletes the *Scroller* if it is nonzero. Frees the cursor, if any exists, and the object instance (thunk).

See also   TWindowFlag enum, TWindow::EnableAutoCreate

Public member functions

AdjustWindowRect
static void AdjustWindowRect(TRect& rect, uint32 style, bool menu);

Calculates the size of the window rectangle according to the indicated client-rectangle size. *rect* refers to the structure that contains the client rectangle's coordinates. *style* specifies the style of the window. *menu* is **true** if the window has a menu.

AdjustWindowRectEx
static void AdjustWindowRectEx(TRect& rect, uint32 style, bool menu, uint32 exStyle);

Calculates the size of a window rectangle that has an extended style. *TRect* refers to the class that contains the client rectangle's coordinates. *style* specifies the window styles of the window to be adjusted. *menu* returns **true** if the window has a menu. *exStyle* indicates the extended styles to be used for the window. Extended styles include the following styles:

Value	Meaning
WS_EX_ACCEPTFILES	The window can make use of drag and drop files.
WS_EX_DLGMODALFRAME	The window has a double border that can be created with a title bar if the WS_CAPTION style flag is specified.
WS_EX_NOPARENTNOTIFY	The child window created from this style does not send parent notify messages to the parent window when the child is created or destroyed.
WS_EX_TOPMOST	A window having this style is placed above windows that are not topmost and remains above the non-topmost windows even when it's deactivated.
WS_EX_TRANSPARENT	A window having this style is transparent, that is, any windows beneath this window are not concealed by this window.

See also TWindowAttr struct

AssignContextMenu
void AssignContextMenu(TPopupMenu* menu);

Associates a popup menu with the window so that it can automatically handle a WM_CONTEXTMENU message.

BringWindowToTop
void BringWindowToTop();

Brings a pop-up or child window to the top of the stack of overlapping windows and activates it.

CanClose
virtual bool CanClose();

Use this function to determine if it is okay to close a window. Returns **true** if the associated interface element can be closed. Calls the *CanClose* member function of each of its child windows. Returns **false** if any of the *CanClose* calls returns **false**.

In your application's main window, you can override *TWindow*'s *CanClose* and call *TWindow::MessageBox* to display a YESNOCANCEL message prompting the user as follows:

YES	Save the data
NO	Do not save the data, but close the window
CANCEL	Cancel the close operation and return to the edit window

The following example shows how to write a *CanClose* function that displays a message box asking if the user wants to save a drawing that has changed. To save time, *CanClose* uses the *IsDirty* flag to see if the drawing has changed. If so, *CanClose* queries the user before closing the window.

```
bool TMyWindow::CanClose()
{
  if (IsDirty)
    switch(MessageBox("Do you want to save?", "Drawing has changed.",
                      MB_YESNOCANCEL | MB_ICONQUESTION)) {
      case IDCANCEL:
        // Choosing Cancel means to abort the close -- return false.
        return false;

      case IDYES:
        // Choosing Yes means to save the drawing.
        CmFileSave();
    }
  return true;
}
```

CheckDlgButton
void CheckDlgButton(int buttonId, uint check);

Places a check mark in (or removes a check mark from) the button specified in *buttonId*. If *check* is nonzero, the check mark is placed next to the button; if 0, the check mark is removed. For buttons having three states, *check* can be 0 (clear), 1 (checked), or 2 (gray).

CheckRadioButton
void CheckRadioButton(int firstButtonId, int lastButtonId, int checkButtonId);

Checks the radio button specified by *checkButtonId* and removes the check mark from the other radio buttons in the group. *firstButtonId* and *lastButtonId* specify the first and last buttons, respectively, in the group.

ChildBroadcastMessage
void ChildBroadcastMessage(uint msg, TParam1 wParam=0, TParam2 lParam=0);

Sends the specified message to all immediate children using *SendMessage*.

See also   TWindow::SendMessage

ChildWindowFromPoint
THandle ChildWindowFromPoint(const TPoint& point) const;

Determines which of the child windows contains the point specified in *TPoint*. Returns a handle to the window that contains the point, or 0 if the point lies outside the parent window.

See also   TWindow::WindowFromPoint

ChildWithId
TWindow* ChildWithId(int id) const;

Returns a pointer to the window in the child window list that has the supplied *id*. Returns 0 if no child window has the indicated *id*.

ClearFlag
void ClearFlag(TWindowFlag mask);

Clears the specified *TWindow wfXxxx* constant flags (for example *wfAlias*, *wfTransfer*, and so on) in the *Flags* member.

See also TWindowFlag enum

ClientToScreen
void ClientToScreen(TPoint& point) const;

Converts the client coordinates specified in *point* to screen coordinates for the new window.

CloseWindow
virtual void CloseWindow(int retVal = 0);

Determines if it is okay to close a window before actually closing the window. If **this** is the main window of the application, calls *GetApplication->CanClose*. Otherwise, calls **this**->*CanClose* to determine whether the window can be closed. After determining that it is okay to close the window, *CloseWindow* calls *Destroy* to destroy the HWND.

See also TApplication::CanClose, TWindow::CanClose

Create
virtual bool Create();

Creates the window interface element to be associated with this ObjectWindows interface element. Specifically, *Create* performs the following window creation tasks:

1 If the HWND already exists, *Create* returns **true**. (It is perfectly valid to call *Create* even if the window currently exists.)

2 If the *wfFromResource* flag is set, then *Create* grabs the HWND based on the window ID. Otherwise, *Create* registers the window, sets up the window thunk, loads accelerators and menus, and calls *PerformCreate* in the derived class to create the HWND.

3 If class registration fails for the window, *Create* calls *TXWindow* with IDS_CLASSREGISTERFAIL. If the window creation fails, *Create* calls *TXWindow* with IDS_WINDOWCREATEFAIL.

4 If the window is created for a predefined Window class (for example, a button or dialog class) registered outside of ObjectWindows, then ObjectWindows thunks the window so that it can intercept messages and obtains the state of the window (the window's attributes) from the HWND.

See also TWindowFlag enum

CreateCaret
Form 1 void CreateCaret(HBITMAP hBitmap);

Creates a new caret for the system. *HBITMAP* specifies the bit mapped caret shape.

Form 2   void CreateCaret(bool isGray, int width, int height);

Create a new caret for the system with the specified shape, bitmap shade, *width*, and *height*. If *width* or *height* is 0, the corresponding system-defined border size is used.

CreateChildren
bool CreateChildren();

Creates the child windows in the child list whose auto-create flags (with *wfAutoCreate* mask) are set. If all of the child windows are created successfully, *CreateChildren* returns **true**.

See also   TWindow::EnableAutoCreate, TWindow::DisableAutoCreate, TWindow-Flag enum

DefaultProcessing
TResult DefaultProcessing();

Serves as a general-purpose default processing function that handles a variety of messages. After being created and before calling *DefaultProcessing*, however, a window completes the following sequence of events (illustrated in the Default Message-Processing Flowchart).

- If the window is already created, *SubclassWindow* is used to install *StdWndProc* in place of the window's current procedure. The previous window procedure is saved in *DefaultProc*.

- If the window has not been created, *InitWndProc* is set up as the window proc in the class. Then, when the window first receives a message, *InitWndProc* calls *GetThunk* to get the window's instance thunk (created by the constructor by calling *CreateInstanceThunk*). *InitWndProc* then switches the message-receiving capability from the window's procedure to *StdWndProc*.

After this point, *StdWndProc* responds to incoming messages by calling the window's virtual *WindowProc* to process the messages. ObjectWindows uses the special registered message *::GetWindowPtrMsgId* to get the **this** pointer of an HWND. *StdWndProc* responds to this message by returning the **this** pointer obtained from the thunk.

If the incoming message is not a command or command enable message, *WindowProc* immediately searches the window's response table for a matching entry. If the incoming message is a command or command enable message, *WindowProc* calls *EvCommand* or *EvCommandEnable*. *EvCommand* and *EvCommandEnable* begin searching for a matching entry in the focus window's response table. If an entry is found, the corresponding function is dispatched; otherwise ObjectWindows calls *DefaultProcessing* to finish the recursive walk back up the parent chain, searching for a match until the receiving window (the window that initially received the message) is reached. At this point, one of the following actions occurs:

- If there is still no match and this is the *MainWindow* of the application, the window searches the application's response table.

- If there are no matches and this is a command, *DefWindowProc* is called.

- If this is a *CommandEnable* message, no further action is taken.

- If this is not a command, and if a response table entry exists for the window, *WindowProc* dispatches the corresponding *EvXxxx* function to handle the message.

- If this is the application's *MainWindow*, and the message is designed for the application, the message is forwarded to the application.

- For any other cases, the window calls *DefWindowProc*.

The following diagram illustrates this sequence of message-processing events:

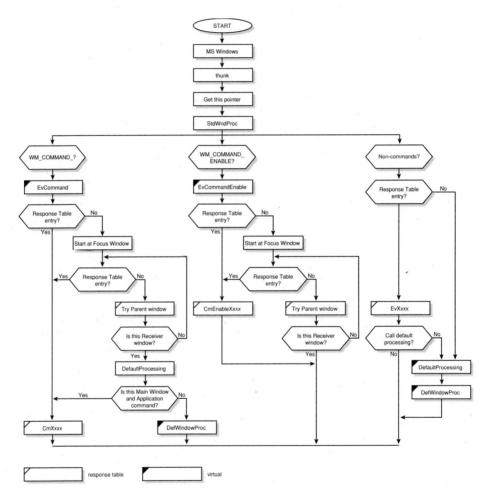

See also TWindow::DefWindowProc, TWindow::EnableAutoCreate, TWindow::DisableAutoCreate, TWindow::WindowProc

DefWindowProc

virtual TResult DefWindowProc(uint msg, TParam1 p1, TParam2 p2);

Performs default Windows processing and passes the incoming Windows message. You usually do not need to call this function directly. Classes such as *TMDIFrame* and *TMDIChild* override this function to perform specialized default processing.

See also   TWindow::DefaultProc, TWindow::WindowProc

Destroy
virtual void Destroy(int retVal = 0);

First, *Destroy* calls *EnableAutoCreate* for each window in the child list to ensure that windows in the child list will be re-created if **this** is re-created. Then, it destroys the associated interface element.

If a derived window class expects to be destructed directly, it should call *Destroy* as the first step in its destruction so that any virtual functions and event handlers can be called during the destroy sequence.

DestroyCaret
static void DestroyCaret();

DestroyCaret first checks the ownership of the caret. If a window in the current task owns the caret, *DestroyCaret* destroys the caret and removes it from the screen.

See also   TWindow::CreateCaret

DisableAutoCreate
void DisableAutoCreate();

Disables the feature that allows an associated child window interface element to be created and displayed along with its parent window. Call *DisableAutoCreate* for pop-up windows and controls if you want to create and display them at a time later than their parent windows.

See also   TWindow::EnableAutoCreate

DisableTransfer
void DisableTransfer();

Disables (for the interface object) the transfer mechanism, which allows state data to be transferred to and from a transfer buffer.

See also   TWindowFlag enum

Dispatch
virtual TResult Dispatch(TEventInfo& info, TParam1 wp, TParam2 lp = 0);

Cracks and dispatches a *TWindow* message. The *info* parameter is the event-handling function. The *wp* and *lp* parameters are the message parameters the dispatcher cracks.

DoExecute
virtual int DoExecute();

Do actual modal execution using the Begin/End Modal support of *TApplication*.

Defaults to TASKMODAL.

DragAcceptFiles
void DragAcceptFiles(bool accept);

If a window can process dropped files, *DragAcceptFiles* sets *accept* to **true**.

DrawMenuBar
void DrawMenuBar();

DrawMenuBar redraws the menu bar. This function should be called to redraw the menu if the menu is changed after the window is created.

EnableAutoCreate
void EnableAutoCreate();

Ensures that an associated child window interface element is created and displayed along with its parent window. By default, this feature is enabled for windows and controls, but disabled for dialog boxes.

See also   TWindow::DisableAutoCreate

EnableScrollBar
bool EnableScrollBar(uint sbFlags=SB_BOTH, uint arrowFlags=ESB_ENABLE_BOTH);

Disables or enables one or both of the scroll bar arrows on the scroll bars associated with this window. *sbFlags*, which specifies the type of scroll bar, can be one of the Scroll Bar constants (SB_CTL, SB_HORZ, SB_VERT, or SB_BOTH). By default, the arrows on both the horizontal and vertical scroll bars are either enabled or disabled. *arrowFlags*, which indicates whether the scroll bar arrows are enabled or disabled, can be one of the Enable Scroll Bar constants (ESB_ENABLE_BOTH, ESB_DISABLE_LTUP, ESB_DISABLE_RTDN, ESB_DISABLE_BOTH). By default, the arrows on both the horizontal and vertical scroll bars are enabled.

See also   SB_Xxxx scroll bar constants

EnableTransfer
void EnableTransfer();

Enables the transfer mechanism, which allows state data to be transferred between the window and a transfer buffer.

EnableWindow
virtual bool EnableWindow(bool enable);

Allows the given window to receive input from the keyboard or mouse. If enable is **true**, the window can receive input. Use the function *IsWindowEnabled* to determine if the window has been enabled.

EnumProps
int EnumProps(PROPENUMPROC proc);

Enumerates all the items in the property list of the current window and passes them one by one to the callback function indicated in *proc*. The process continues until every item has been enumerated or until *proc* returns zero. *proc* holds the address of the callback function.

EvCommand
virtual TResult EvCommand(uint id, THandle hWndCtl, uint notifyCode);

WindowProc calls *EvCommand* to handle WM_COMMAND messages. *id* is the identifier of the menu item or control. *hWndCtl* holds a value that represents the control sending the message. If the message is not from a control, it is 0. *notifyCode* holds a value that represents the control's notification message. If the message is from an accelerator, *notifyCode* is 1; if the message is from a menu, *notifyCode* is 0.

See also   TWindow::DefaultProcessing

EvCommandEnable
virtual void EvCommandEnable(TCommandEnabler& ce);

Called by *WindowProc* to handle WM_COMMAND_ENABLE messages, *EvCommandEnable* calls the *CmXxxx* command-handling function or calls *DefaultProcessing* to handle the incoming message.

See also   TCommandEnabler

EvNotify
virtual TResult EvNotify(uint id, TNotify far& notifyInfo);

Handles WM_NOTIFY and subdispatch messages from child controls. This is the default message handler for WM_NOTIFY.

Execute
virtual int Execute();

Creates the underlying HWND and makes it modal with the help of *TApplication*'s *BeginModal* support.

FirstThat
Form 1   TWindow* FirstThat(TCondFunc test, void* paramList = 0);

Form 2   TWindow* FirstThat(TCondMemFunc test, void* paramList = 0);

There are two *FirstThat* functions, both of which pass a pointer to an iterator function. The first *FirstThat* points to a nonmember function as its first parameter; the second *FirstThat* points to a member function instead.

Both *FirstThat* functions iterate over the child list, calling a Boolean *test* function and passing each child window in turn as an argument (along with *paramList*). If a *test* call returns **true**, the iteration is stopped and *FirstThat* returns the child window object that was supplied to test. Otherwise, *FirstThat* returns 0.

In the following example, *GetFirstChecked* calls *FirstThat* to obtain a pointer (*p*) to the first check box in the child list that is checked:

```
bool IsThisBoxChecked(TWindow* p, void*) {
    return ((TCheckBox*)p)->GetCheck() == BF_CHECKED;
}
TCheckBox* TMyWindow::GetFirstChecked() {
    return FirstThat(IsThisBoxChecked);
}
```

See also   TCondFunc type

FlashWindow
bool FlashWindow(bool invert);

Changes the window from active to inactive or vice versa. If *invert* is nonzero, the window is flashed. If *invert* is 0, the window is returned to its original state—either active or inactive.

ForEach

Form 1   void ForEach(TActionFunc action, void* paramList = 0);

There are two *ForEach* functions. This *ForEach* takes a nonmember function as its first parameter; the other *ForEach* (see the following entry) takes a member function instead. This version of *ForEach* iterates over the child list, calling a nonmember function supplied as the action to be performed and passing each child window in turn as the argument (along with *paramList*).

In the following example, *CheckAllBoxes* calls *ForEach*, checking all the check boxes in the child list:

```
void CheckTheBox(TWindow* p, void*) {
  ((TCheckBox*)p)->Check();
}
void CheckAllBoxes() {
  ForEach(CheckTheBox);
}
```

Form 2   void ForEach(TActionMemFunc action, void* paramList = 0);

Refer to the *ForEach* description for Syntax 1. The difference between the two *ForEach* members is that the first *ForEach* takes a nonmember function as a parameter and this *ForEach* takes a member function as a parameter.

See also   TActionFunc typedef, TActionMemFunc typedef

ForwardMessage

Form 1   TResult ForwardMessage(bool send = true);

Forwards the window's current message. Calls *SendMessage* if send is **true**; otherwise calls *PostMessage*.

Form 2   TResult ForwardMessage(THandle handle, bool send = true);

Forwards the window's current message to another HWND. Calls *SendMessage* if send is **true**; otherwise calls *PostMessage*.

GetActiveWindow

static THandle GetActiveWindow();

Retrieves the handle of the active window. Returns 0 if no window is associated with the calling thread.

GetApplication

TApplication* GetApplication() const;

Gets a pointer to the *TApplication* object associated with **this**. Use *GetApplication* to obtain access to data and functions in the *TApplication* object.

GetCapture

static THandle GetCapture();

Returns the handle of the window that has captured the mouse.

GetCaretBlinkTime
static uint GetCaretBlinkTime();

Retrieves the caret blink rate in milliseconds.

See also   TWindow::SetCaretBlinkTime

GetCaretPos
static void GetCaretPos(TPoint& point);

Gets the position of the caret in the coordinates of the client window. *point* refers to the structure that receives the client coordinates of the caret.

See also   TWindow::SetCaretPos

GetClassLong
long GetClassLong(int index) const;

Retrieves the 32-bit value containing information about the window class. If unsuccessful, returns 0. Depending on the value of *index*, *GetClassLong* can retrieve the following information:

Value	Meaning
GCL_CBCLSEXTRA	Size in bytes of memory associated with this class
GCL_CBWINDEXTRA	Size of extra window memory associated with each window
GCL_HBRBACKGROUND	Handle of the background brush associated with the class
GCL_HCURSOR	Handle of the cursor
GCL_HICON	Handle of the icon
GCL_HMODULE	Handle of the module that registered the class
GCL_MENUNAME	Address of the menu name string
GCL_STYLE	The style bits associated with a window class
GCL_WNDPROC	Address of the window procedure associated with this class

See also   Twindow::SetClassLong

GetClassName
long GetClassName(char far* className, int maxCount) const;

Returns the class name for a generic OWL window.

GetClassWord
uint16 GetClassWord(int index) const;

Gets a 16-bit value containing information about the class or style of the window. If unsuccessful; returns 0. Depending on the value of *index*, *GetClassWord* can retrieve the following information:

Value	Meaning
GCW_CBCLSEXTRA	Number of additional class information
GCW_CBWINDEXTRA	Number of bytes of additional window information
GCW_HBRBACKGROUND	Handle of the background brush

Value	Meaning
GCW_HCURSOR	Handle of the cursor
GCW_HICON	Handle of the icon
GCW_HMODULE	Handle of the module
GCW_STYLE	The style bits associated with a window class

See also   TWindow::SetClassWord

GetClientRect

Form 1   TRect GetClientRect() const;

Gets the coordinates of the window's client area (the area in a window you can use for drawing).

Form 2   void GetClientRect(TRect& rect) const;

Gets the coordinates of the window's client area and then copies them into the object referred to by *TRect*.

GetContextMenu

TPopupMenu* GetContextMenu() const;

Returns the associated popup menu used by the window.

GetCurrentEvent

TCurrentEvent& GetCurrentEvent();

Returns the current event to be processed in the message queue.

GetCursorPos

static void GetCursorPos(TPoint& pos);

Retrieves the cursor's current position (in window screen coordinates) and copies the values into the structure pointed to by *pos*.

GetDesktopWindow

static THandle GetDesktopWindow();

Returns a handle to the desktop window.

GetDlgCtrlID

int GetDlgCtrlID() const;

Returns the ID of the control.

GetDlgItem

THandle GetDlgItem(int childId) const;

Retrieves the handle of a control specified by *childId*.

See also   TWindow::GetDlgItemInt

GetDlgItemInt

uint GetDlgItemInt(int childId, bool* translated = 0, bool isSigned = true) const;

Retrieves the text of a control specified by *childId*. *translated* points to the variable that receives the translated value. *isSigned* indicates that the retrieved value is signed (the default).

See also   TWindow::GetDlgItem

GetDlgItemText
int GetDlgItemText(int childId, char far* text, int max) const;

Retrieves the text of a control specified by *childId*. *text* points to the text buffer to receive the text. *max* specifies the maximum length of the caption, which is truncated if it exceeds this length.

See also   TWindow::SetDlgItemText

GetExStyle
uint32 GetExStyle() const;

Gets the extra style bits of the window.

GetFirstChild
TWindow* GetFirstChild()

Returns a pointer to the first child window, which is the first window created in the interface object's child list.

See also   TWindowAttr struc

GetFocus
static THandle GetFocus();

Gets a handle to the window that has the focus. Use the function *SetFocus* to set the keyboard focus to this window.

GetHandle
THandle GetHandle() const;

Returns the handle of the window.

GetHWndState
void GetHWndState();

Copies the style, coordinate, and the resource *id* (but not the title) from the existing *HWnd* into the *TWindow* members.

GetId
int GetId() const;

Returns *Attr.Id*, the ID used to find the window in a specified parent's child list.

See also   TWindowAttr struct

GetLastActivePopup
THandle GetLastActivePopup() const;

Returns the last active pop-up window in the list.

GetLastChild
TWindow* GetLastChild();

Returns a pointer to the last child window in the interface object's child list.

GetMenu
HMENU GetMenu() const;

Returns the handle to the menu of the indicated window. If the window has no menu, the return value is 0.

See also   TWindow::SetMenu

GetModule
TModule* GetModule() const;

Returns a pointer to the module object.

GetNextDlgGroupItem
THandle GetNextDlgGroupItem(THandle hWndCtrl, bool previous = false) const;

Returns either the next or the previous control in the dialog box. *hWndCtrl* identifies the control in the dialog box where the search begins. If *previous* is 0, *GetNextDlg-GroupItem* searches for the next control. If *previous* is nonzero, it searches for the previous control.

GetNextDlgTabItem
THandle GetNextDlgTabItem(THandle hWndCtrl, bool previous = false) const;

Returns the handle of the first control that lets the user press the Tab key to move to the next control (that is, the first control with the WS_TABSTOP style associated with it). *hWndCtrl* identifies the control in the dialog box where the search begins. If *previous* is 0, *GetNextDlgTabItem* searches for the next control. If *previous* is nonzero, it searches for the previous control.

GetNextWindow
THandle GetNextWindow(uint dirFlag) const;

Finds the handle associated with either the next or previous window in the window manager's list. *dirFlag* specifies the direction of the search. Under the Win 32 API, *GetNextWindow* returns either the next or the previous window's handle. If the application is not running under Win32, *GetNextWindow* returns the next window's handle.

GetParent
Form 1   TWindow* GetParent();

Retrieves the OWL object of the parent window. If none exists, returns 0.

Form 2   THandle GetParent() const;

Retrieves the handle of the parent window. If none exists, returns 0.

See also   TWindow::SetParent

GetParentH
THandle GetParentH() const;

Returns the handle of this window's parent. This can return either the handle of native window, or a pointer to the OWL object. It may return different objects in some cases.

Use either *GetParentH* or *GetParentO* to avoid change across versions.

GetParentO
TWindow* GetParentO() const;

Returns the OWL's parent for this window. This can return either the handle of native window, or a pointer to the OWL object. It may return different objects in some cases.

Use either *GetParentH* or *GetParentO* to avoid change across versions.

GetProp
Form 1   HANDLE GetProp(uint16 atom) const;

Returns a handle to the property list of the specified window. *atom* contains a value that identifies the character string whose handle is to be retrieved. If the specified string is not found in the property list for this window, returns NULL.

Form 2   HANDLE GetProp(const char far* str) const;

Returns a handle to the property list of the specified window. Unlike the Syntax 1 *GetProp* function, *string* points to the string whose handle is to be retrieved. If the specified string is not found in the property list for this window, returns NULL.

See also   TWindow::SetProp

GetScroller
TScroller* GetScroller();

Returns the associated scroller object for this window.

GetScrollPos
int GetScrollPos(int bar) const;

Returns the thumb position in the scroll bar. The position returned is relative to the scrolling range. If *bar* is SB_CTL, it returns the position of a control in the scroll bar. If *bar* is SB_HORZ, it returns the position of a horizontal scroll bar. If *bar* is SB_VERT, it returns the position of a vertical scroll bar.

See also   TWindow::SetScrollPos, SB_Xxxx scroll bar constants

GetScrollRange
void GetScrollRange(int bar, int& minPos, int& maxPos) const;

Returns the minimum and maximum positions in the scroll bar. If *bar* is SB_CTL, it returns the position of a control in the scroll bar. If *bar* is SB_HORZ, it returns the position of a horizontal scroll bar. If *bar* is SB_VERT, it returns the position of a vertical scroll bar. *minPos* and *maxPos* hold the lower and upper range, respectively, of the scroll bar positions. If there are no scroll bar controls or if the scrolls are non-standard, *minPos* and *maxPos* are zero.

See also   TWindow::SetScrollRange, SB_Xxxx scroll bar constants

GetStyle
uint32 GetStyle() const;

Gets the style bits of the underlying window or the *Style* member of the attribute structure associated with this *TWindow* object.

GetSysModalWindow
static THandle GetSysModalWindow();

Retrieves the handle of the system-modal window.

See also   TWindow::SetSysModalWindow

GetSystemMenu
HMENU GetSystemMenu(bool revert = false) const;

Returns a handle to the system menu so that an application can access the system menu.

GetThunk
WNDPROC GetThunk()const;

Gets the instance thunk, a small piece of code created for use with exported callback functions.

GetTopWindow
THandle GetTopWindow() const;

Returns a handle to the top window currently owned by this parent window. If no children exist, *GetTopWindow* returns 0.

GetUpdateRect
bool GetUpdateRect(TRect& rect, bool erase = true) const;

Retrieves the screen coordinates of the rectangle that encloses the updated region of the specified window. *erase* specifies whether *GetUpdateRect* should erase the background of the updated region.

See also   TWindow::RedrawWindow

GetUpdateRgn
bool GetUpdateRgn(TRegion& rgn, bool erase = true) const;

Copies a window's update region into a region specified by *region*. If *erase* is **true**, *GetUpdateRgn* erases the background of the updated region and redraws nonclient regions of any child windows. If *erase* is **false**, no redrawing occurs.

If the call is successful, *GetUpdateRgn* returns a value indicating the kind of region that was updated. If the region has no overlapping borders, it returns SIMPLEREGION; if the region has overlapping borders, it returns COMPLEXREGION; if the region is empty, it returns NULLREGION; if an error occurs, it returns ERROR.

See also   TWindow::RedrawWindow

GetWindow
THandle GetWindow(uint cmd) const;

Returns the handle of the window that has the indicated relationship to this window. *cmd*, which indicates the type of relationship to be obtained, can be one of the following values:

Value	Meaning
GW_CHILD	If the given window is a parent window, the return value indicates the child window at the top of the Z order (the position of a window in a series of overlapping windows arranged in a stack). Otherwise, the return value is 0. Only child windows are examined.
GW_HWNDFIRST	The return value indicates the window at the top of the Z order. If this window is a topmost window, the return value identifies the topmost window at the top of the Z order. If this window is a top-level window, the return value identifies the top-level window at the bottom of the Z order. If this window is a child window, the return value indicates the sibling window at the bottom of the Z order.
GW_HWNDNEXT	The return value identifies the window below the given window in the Z order. If this window is a topmost window, the return value identifies the topmost window below this window. If this window is a top-level window, the return value indicates the top-level window below this window. If this window is a child window, the return value indicates the sibling window below this window.
GW_HWNDPREV	The return value identifies the window above the given window in the Z order. If this window is a topmost window, the return value identifies the topmost window above this window. If this window is a top-level window, the return value indicates the top-level window above this window. If this window is a child window, the return value indicates the sibling window above this window.
GW_OWNER	The return value identifies this window's owner window, if one exists.

GetWindowFont
HFONT GetWindowFont();

Gets the font the control uses to draw text. The return value is a handle of the font the control uses. If a system default font is being used, *GetWindowFont* returns NULL.

GetWindowLong
long GetWindowLong(int index) const;

Retrieves information about the window depending on the value stored in *index*. The values returned, which provide information about the window, include the following GWL_Xxxx window style constants:

Value	Description
GWL_EXSTYLE	The extended window style
GWL_STYLE	The window style (position, device context creation, size, and so on)
GWL_WNDPROC	The address of the window procedure being processed

In the case of a dialog box, additional information can be retrieved, such as:

Value	Description
DWL_DLGPROC	The address of the procedure processed by the dialog box
DWL_MSGRESULT	The value that a message processed by the dialog box returns
DWL_USER	Additional information that pertains to the application, such as pointers or handles the application uses

See also   TWindow::GetClassLong

GetWindowPlacement
bool GetWindowPlacement(WINDOWPLACEMENT* place) const;

Retrieves display and placement information (normal, minimized, and maximized positions) about the window and stores that information in the argument, *place*.

See also   TWindow::SetWindowPlacement, TWindow::Show

GetWindowRect
Form 1   void GetWindowRect(Trect& rect) const;

Gets the screen coordinates of the window's rectangle and copies them into *rect*.

Form 2   TRect GetWindowRect() const;

Gets the screen coordinates of the window's rectangle.

See also   TWindow::GetClientRect

GetWindowTask
HTASK GetWindowTask() const;

Returns a handle to the task that created the specified window.

GetWindowText
int GetWindowText(char far* str, int maxCount) const;

Copies the window's title into a buffer pointed to by *string*. *maxCount* indicates the maximum number of characters to copy into the buffer. A string of characters longer than *maxCount* is truncated. *GetWindowText* returns the length of the string or 0 if no title exists.

See also   TWindow::SetWindowText, TWindow::GetWindowTextTitle, TWindow::SetCaption

GetWindowTextLength
int GetWindowTextLength() const;

Returns the length, in characters, of the specified window's title. If the window is a control, returns the length of the text within the control. If the window does not contain any text, *GetWindowTextLength* returns 0.

See also   TWindow::SetWindowText

GetWindowTextTitle
void GetWindowTextTitle();

Updates the *TWindow* title data member (*Title*) from the current window's caption. *GetWindowTextTitle* is used to keep *Title* synchronized with the actual window state when there is a possibility that the state might have changed.

See also   TWindow::SetCaption, TWindow::Title

GetWindowWord
uint16 GetWindowWord(int index) const;

Retrieves information about this window depending on the value of *index*. *GetWindowWord* returns one of the following values that indicate information about the window:

Value	Meaning
GWW_HINSTANCE	The instance handle of the module owning the window
GWW_HWNDPARENT	The handle of the parent window
GWW_ID	The ID number of the child window

See also   TWindow::GetWindowLong, TWindow::SetWindowWord, TWindow::SetParent

HandleMessage
TResult HandleMessage(uint msg, TParam1 p1 = 0, TParam2 p2 = 0);

Handles message sent to a window. *HandleMessage* can be called directly to handle Windows messages without going through *SendMessage*.

HideCaret
void HideCaret();

Removes the caret from the specified display screen. The caret is hidden only if the current task's window owns the caret. Although the caret is not visible, it can be displayed again using *ShowCaret*

See also   TWindow::CreateCaret, TWindow::ShowCaret

HiliteMenuItem
bool HiliteMenuItem(HMENU hMenu, uint idItem, uint hilite);

Either highlights or removes highlighting from a top-level item in the menu. *idItem* indicates the menu item to be processed. *hilite* (which contains a value that indicates if the *idItem* is to be highlighted or is to have the highlight removed) can be one or more of the following constants:

Value	Meaning
MF_BYCOMMAND	The *idItem* parameter contains the menu item's identifier.
MF_BYPOSITION	The *idItem* parameter contains the zero-based relative position of the menu item.
MF_HILITE	Highlights the menu item. If this value is not specified, highlighting is removed from the item.
MF_UNHILITE	Removes the menu item's highlighting.

If the menu is set to the specified condition, *HiliteMenuItem* returns **true**; otherwise, it returns **false**.

See also   TWindow::GetMenu

HoldFocusHwnd

virtual bool HoldFocusHWnd(THandle hLose, THandle hGain);

Responds to a request by a child window to hold its HWND when it is losing focus. Stores the child's HWND in *HoldFocusHwnd*.

IdleAction

virtual bool IdleAction(long idleCount);

Called when no messages are waiting to be processed, *IdleAction* performs idle processing as long as **true** is returned. *idleCount* specifies the number of times *idleAction* has been called between messages.

Invalidate

void Invalidate(bool erase = true);

Invalidates (marks for painting) the entire client area of a window. The window then receives a message to redraw the window. By default, the background of the client area is marked for erasing.

See also   TWindow::Validate, TWindow::InvalidateRect

InvalidateRect

void InvalidateRect(const TRect& rect, bool erase = true);

Invalidates a specified client area. By default, the background of the client area to be invalidated is marked for erasing.

See also   TWindow::ValidateRect, TWindow::Invalidate

InvalidateRgn

void InvalidateRgn(HRGN hRgn, bool erase = true);

Invalidates a client area within a region specified by the *hRgn* parameter when the application receives a WM_PAINT message. The region to be invalidated is assumed to have client coordinates. If *hRgn* is 0, the entire client area is included in the region to be updated. The parameter *erase* specifies whether the background with the update region needs to be erased when the region to be updated is determined. If *erase* is **true**, the background is erased; if *erase* is **false**, the background is not erased when the *Paint* function is called. By default, the background within the region is marked for erasing.

See also   TWindow::ValidateRgn

IsChild

bool IsChild(THandle hWnd) const;

Returns **true** if the window is a child window or a descendant window of this window. A window is considered a child window if it is the direct descendant of a given parent window and the parent window is in a chain of windows leading from the original overlapped or pop-up window down to the child window. *hWnd* identifies the window to be tested.

IsDlgButtonChecked

uint IsDlgButtonChecked(int buttonId) const;

Indicates if the child button specified in the integer parameter, *buttonId*, is checked, or if a button is grayed, checked, or neither. If the return value is 0, the button is unchecked. If the return value is 1, the button is checked. If the return value is 3, the button state is undetermined. This function sends a BM_GETCHECK message to the specified button control.

IsFlagSet
bool IsFlagSet(uint mask);

Returns the state of the bit flag in *Attr.Flags* whose *mask* is supplied. Returns **true** if the bit flag is set, and **false** if not set.

See also   TWindowAttr struc

IsIconic
bool IsIconic() const;

Returns **true** if window is iconic or minimized.

IsWindow
bool IsWindow() const;

Returns **true** if an HWND is being used.

IsWindowEnabled
bool IsWindowEnabled() const;

Returns **true** if the window is enabled. Use the function *EnableWindow* to enable or disable a window.

IsWindowVisible
bool IsWindowVisible() const;

Returns **true** if the window is visible. By default, *TWindow*'s constructor sets the window style attribute (WS_VISIBLE) so that the window is visible.

IsZoomed
bool IsZoomed() const;

Returns **true** if window is zoomed or maximized.

KillTimer
bool KillTimer(uint timerId);

Gets rid of the timer and removes any WM_TIMER messages from the message queue. *timerId* contains the ID number of the timer event to be killed.

See also   TWindow::SetTimer

LockWindowUpdate
bool LockWindowUpdate();

Prevents or enables window drawing for one window at a time. If the window is locked, returns **true**; otherwise, returns **false**, which indicates either that an error occurred or that some other window is already locked.

If any drawing is attempted within a locked window or locked child windows, the extent of the attempted operation is saved within a bounding rectangle. When the window is then unlocked, the area within the rectangle is invalidated, causing a paint message to be sent to this window. If any drawing occurred while the window was locked for updates, the area is invalidated.

MapWindowPoints

void MapWindowPoints(THandle hWndTo, TPoint* pts, int count) const;

Maps a set of points in one window to a relative set of points in another window. *hWndTo* specifies the window to which the points are converted. *points* points to the array containing the points. If *hWndTo* is 0, the points are converted to screen coordinates. *count* specifies the number of *points* structures in the array.

MessageBox

int MessageBox(const char far* text, const char far* caption = 0, uint type = MB_OK);

Creates and displays a message box that contains a message (*text*), a title (*caption*), and icons or push buttons (*type*). If *caption* is 0, the default title is displayed. Although *type* is set to one push button by default, it can contain a combination of the MB_Xxxx message constants. This function returns one of the following constants:

Value	Description
IDABORT	User selected the abort button.
IDCANCEL	User selected the cancel button.
IDIGNORE	User selected the ignore button.
IDNO	User selected the no button.
IDOK	User selected the OK button
IDRETRY	User selected the retry button.
IDYES	User selected the yes button.

If BWCC is already enabled, the message box will be BWCC-enabled. If CTRL 3D is already enabled, the message box will be CTRL-3D-enabled. If neither BWCC nor CTRL 3D is enabled, the message box will be displayed as a standard windows message box.

See also   TWindow::PostMessage, MB_Xxxx message constants

ModifyExStyle

bool ModifyExStyle(uint32 offBits, uint32 onBits, uint swpFlags = 0);

Modifies the style bits of the window.

ModifyStyle

bool ModifyStyle(uint32 offBits, uint32 onBits, uint swpFlags = 0);

Modifies the style bits of the window.

MoveWindow

Form 1   bool MoveWindow(int x, int y, int w, int h, bool repaint = false);

Repositions the specified window. *x* and *y* specify the new upper left coordinates of the window; *w* and *h* specify the new width and height, respectively. If *repaint* is **false**, the window is not repainted after it is moved.

Form 2   bool MoveWindow(const TRect& rect, bool repaint = false);

Repositions the window. *rect* references the left and top coordinates and the width and height of the new screen rectangle. If *repaint* is **false**, the window is not repainted after it is moved.

See also   TWindow::RedrawWindow

Next
TWindow* Next();

Returns a pointer to the next sibling window in the window's sibling list.

See also   TWindow::Previous

NumChildren
uint NumChildren();

Returns the number of child windows of the window.

OpenClipboard
TClipboard& OpenClipboard();

Opens the Clipboard and prevents another application from changing the contents of the Clipboard. This function fails if another window has already opened the Clipboard.

Operator HWND
operator HWND()const;

Allows a *TWindow&* to be used as an HWND in Windows API calls by providing an implicit conversion from *TWindow* to HWND.

Paint
virtual void Paint(TDC& dc, bool erase, TRect& rect);

Repaints the client area (the area you can use for drawing) of a window. Called by base classes when responding to a WM_PAINT message, *Paint* serves as a placeholder for derived types that define *Paint* member functions. *Paint* is called by *EvPaint* and requested automatically by Windows to redisplay the window's contents. *dc* is the paint display context supplied to text and graphics output functions. The supplied reference to the *rect* structure is the bounding rectangle of the area that requires painting. *erase* indicates whether the background needs erasing.

PerformCreate
virtual void PerformCreate(int menuOrId);

Called from *Create* to perform the final step in creating an MS-Windows interface element to be associated with an ObjectWindows window. *PerformCreate* can be overridden to provide alternate HWND implementation.

PostMessage
bool PostMessage(uint msg, TParam1 p1 = 0, TParam2 p2 = 0);

Posts a message (*msg*) to the window in the application's message queue. *PostMessage* returns without waiting for the corresponding window to process the message.

See also   TWindow::ForwardMessage, TWindow::MessageBox

PreProcessMsg
virtual bool PreProcessMsg(MSG& msg);

Allows preprocessing of queued messages prior to dispatching. If you override this method in a derived class, be sure to call the base class's *PreProcessMsg* because it handles the translation of accelerator keys. When a nonzero value is returned, message processing stops.

See also   TApplication::ProcessAppMsg

Previous
TWindow* Previous();

Returns a pointer to the previous window in the window's sibling list.

See also   TWindow::Next

ReceiveMessage
TResult ReceiveMessage(uint msg, TParam1 p1 = 0, TParam2 p2 = 0);

Called from *StdWndProc*, *ReceiveMessage* is the first member function called when a message is received. It calls *HandleMessage* from within the **try** block of the exception-handling code. In this way, exceptions can be caught and suspended before control is returned to exception-unsafe Windows code.

RedrawWindow
bool RedrawWindow(TRect* update, HRGN hUpdateRgn, uint redrawFlags = RDW_INVALIDATE |
RDW_UPDATENOW | RDW_ERASE);

Redraws the rectangle specified by *update* and the region specified by *hUpdateRgn*. *redrawFlags* can be a combination of one or more of the following RDW_Xxxx redraw window constants used to invalidate or validate a window:

Table 2.37   Flags that invalidate a window

Value	Description
RDW_ERASE	When the window is repainted, it receives a WM_ERASEBKGND message. If RDW_INVALIDATE is not also specified, this flag has no effect.
RDW_FRAME	Any part of the non-client area of the window receives a WM_NCPAINT message if it intersects the region to be updated.
RDW_INTERNALPAINT	A WM_PAINT message is posted to the window whether or not it contains an invalid region.
RDW_INVALIDATE	Invalidates either *hUpdateRgn* or *update*. In cases where both are 0, the entire window becomes invalid.

Table 2.38 Flags that validate a window

Value	Description
RDW_NOERASE	The window is prevented from receiving any WM_ERASEBKGND messages.
RDW_NOFRAME	The window is prevented from receiving any WM_NCPAINT messages. The flag RDW_VALIDATE must also be used with this flag.
RDW_NOINTERNALPAINT	The window is prevented from receiving internal WM_PAINT messages, but does not prevent the window from receiving WM_PAINT messages from invalid regions.
RDW_VALIDATE	Validates *update* and *hUpdateRgn*. However, if both are 0, the entire window area is validated. The flag does not have any effect on internal WM_PAINT messages.

Table 2.39 Flags that control when the window is repainted

Value	Description
RDW_ERASENOW	Before the function returns, the specified windows will receive WM_NCPAINT and WM_ERASEBKGND messages.
RDW_UPDATENOW	Before the function returns, the specified windows will receive WM_NCPAINT, WM_ERASEBKGND, as well as WM_PAINT messages.

See also   TWindow::GetUpdateRect

Register
virtual bool Register();

Registers the Windows registration class of this window, if this window is not already registered. Calls *GetClassName* and *GetWindowClass* to retrieve the Windows registration class name and attributes of this window. Register returns **true** if this window is registered.

See also   TWindow::GetClassName, TWindow::GetWindowClass, WNDCLASS struct

RegisterHotKey
bool RegisterHotKey(int idHotKey, uint modifiers, uint virtKey);

Registers a hotkey ID with the current application. *modifiers* can be a combination of keys that must be pressed to activate the specified *hotkey*, such as HOTKEYF_SHIFT, HOTKEYF_CONTROL, and HOTKEYF_ALT.

See also   TWindow::UnRegisterHotKey

ReleaseCapture
static void ReleaseCapture();

Releases the mouse capture from this window.

RemoveProp
Form 1   HANDLE RemoveProp(uint16 atom) const;

Removes the property specified by *atom* from the application's property list. *atom* indicates the string to be removed. Returns the handle of the given string or NULL if no string exists in the window's property list.

Form 2   HANDLE RemoveProp(const char far* str) const;

Removes the property specified by *str*, a null-terminated string, from the application's property list. Returns the handle of the given string or NULL if no string exists in the window's property list.

See also   TWindow::GetProp

RouteCommandEnable
void RouteCommandEnable(THandle hInitCmdTarget, TCommandEnabler& ce);

Walks the chain of windows from the initial target window to **this** window. If it finds a window to receive the message, *RouteCommandEnable* dispatches the command enabler to that window. *hInitCmdTarget* is the handle to the initial command target window, which can be focus window but does not need to be. *ce* is a reference to the command enabler.

Other classes use this function to perform particular command enabling tasks: For example, *TFrameWindow* calls *RouteCommandEnable* to perform the majority of its menu command enabling tasks. When it is an embedded window, *TOleWindow* also uses *RouteCommandEnable* to perform command enabling.

See also   TFrameWindow::EvCommandEnable, TOleWindow::EvCommandEnable, TCommandEnabler class

ScreenToClient
void ScreenToClient(TPoint& point) const;

Uses the screen coordinates specified in *point* to calculate the client window's coordinates and then places the new coordinates into *point*.

ScrollWindow
void ScrollWindow(int dx, int dy, const TRect far* scroll = 0, const TRect far* clip = 0);

Scrolls a window in the vertical (*dx*) and horizontal (*dy*) directions. *scroll* indicates the area to be scrolled. If 0, the entire client area is scrolled. *clip* specifies the clipping rectangle to be scrolled. Only the area within *clip* is scrolled. If *clip* is 0, the entire window is scrolled.

See also   TWindow::ScrollWindowEx

ScrollWindowEx
void ScrollWindowEx(int dx, int dy, const TRect far* scroll = 0, const TRect far* clip = 0, HRGN hUpdateRgn = 0, TRect far* update = 0, uint flags = 0);

Scrolls a window in the vertical (*dx*) and horizontal (*dy*) directions. *scroll* indicates the area to be scrolled. If 0, the entire client area is scrolled. *clip* specifies the clipping rectangle to be scrolled. Only the area within *clip* is scrolled. If *clip* is 0, the entire window is scrolled. *update* indicates the region that will receive the boundaries of the area that becomes invalidated as a result of scrolling. *flags*, which determines how the window's children are scrolled, can be one of the following SW_Xxxx scroll window constants:

Value	Description
SW_ERASE	Erases the invalidated region after sending an erase background message to the window indicated by the SW_INVALIDATE flag value.
SW_INVALIDATE	Invalidates the region indicated by the *hUpdate* parameter.
SW_SCROLLCHILDREN	Scrolls all the child window intersecting the rectangle pointed to by the *scroll* parameter.

See also   TWindow::ScrollWindow, TWindow::Show

SendDlgItemMessage
TResult SendDlgItemMessage(int childId, uint msg, TParam1 p1 = 0, TParam2 p2 = 0);

Sends a message (*msg*) to the control specified in *childId*.

See also   TWindow::SendMessage

SendMessage
TResult SendMessage(uint msg, TParam1 p1 = 0, TParam2 p2 = 0);

Sends a message (*msg*) to a specified window or windows. After it calls the window procedure, it waits until the window procedure has processed the message before returning.

See also   TWindow::ChildBroadcastMessage, TWindow::HandleMessage, TWindow::SendDlgItemMessage

SendNotification
Form 1   uint32 SendNotification(THandle receiver, uint id, NMHDR& nmhdr, uint msg = WM_NOTIFY);

Repacks a command message (*msg*) so that a child window (*hCtl*) can send a message to its parent regardless of whether this is a Win16 or Win32 application.

Form 2   uint32 SendNotification(int id, NMHDR& nmhdr, uint msg = WM_NOTIFY);

Form 3   void SendNotification(THandle receiver, int id, int notifyCode, THandle hCtl, uint msg = WM_COMMAND);

Form 4   void SendNotification(int id, int notifyCode, THandle hCtl, uint msg = WM_COMMAND);

SetActiveWindow
THandle SetActiveWindow();

Activates a top-level window. Returns a handle to the previously active window.

See also   TWindow::GetActiveWindow

SetBkgndColor
void SetBkgndColor(const TColor& color);

Sets the background color for the window. You can also get the current color of an element displayed on the screen. For example,

```
layout -> SetBkgndColor(GetSysColor(COLOR_APPWORKSPACE));
```

Uses one of the Windows COLOR values (in this case, the color of multiple document interface (*MDI*) applications).

See also   TWindow::BkgndColor

SetCaption
void SetCaption(const char far* title);

Copies *title* to an allocated string pointed to by *title*. Sets the caption of the interface element to *title*. Deletes any previous title.

See also   TWindow::GetWindowTextTitle, TWindow::Title

SetCapture
THandle SetCapture();

Sets the mouse capture to the current window. All mouse input is directed to this window.

SetCapture
THandle SetCapture();

Wrapper for Windows API.

SetCaretBlinkTime
static void SetCaretBlinkTime(uint16 milliSecs);

Sets the caret blink rate in milliseconds.

See also   TWindow::GetCaretBlinkTime

SetCaretPos
Form 1   static void SetCaretPos(int x, int y);

Sets the position of the caret in the coordinates of the client window. *x* and *y* indicate the client coordinates of the caret.

Form 2   static void SetCaretPos(const TPoint& pos);

Sets the position of the caret in the coordinates of the client window. *pos* indicates the client coordinates of the caret.

See also   TWindow::GetCaretPos, TWindow::ShowCaret

SetClassLong
long SetClassLong(int index, long newLong);

Sets the **long** value at the specified offset (*index*). Depending on the value of *index*, *SetClassLong* sets a handle to a background brush, cursor, icon, module, menu, window function, or extra class bytes.

See also   TWindow::GetClassLong

SetClassWord
uint16 SetClassWord(int index, uint16 newWord);

Sets the word value at the specified offset (*index*). Depending on the value of *index*, *SetClassLong* sets the number of bytes of class information, of additional window information, or the style bits. Unlike *SetClassLong*, *SetClassWord* uses one of the following GCW_xxxx class word constants:

Value	Meaning
GCW_HBRBACKGROUND	Sets a handle for a background brush.
GCW_HCURSOR	Sets a handle of a cursor.
GCW_HICON	Sets a handle of an icon.
GCW_STYLE	Sets a style bit for a window class.

See also   TWindow::GetClassWord

SetCursor
bool SetCursor(TModule* module, TResId resId);

Sets the cursor position for the window using the given *module* and *ResId*. If the *module* parameter is 0, *CursorResId* can be one of the IDC_xxxx constants that represent different kinds of cursors. See the data member for a list of these cursor values. If the mouse is over the client area, *SetCursor* changes the cursor that is displayed.

See also   TWindow::GetCursorPos, TWindow::CursorResId

SetDlgItemInt
void SetDlgItemInt(int childId, uint value, bool isSigned = true) const;

Sets the child window with the ID (*childId*) in the window to the integer value specified in *value*. If *isSigned* is **true**, the value is signed.

See also   TWindow::GetDlgItem

SetDlgItemText
void SetDlgItemText(int childId, const char far* text) const;

Sets the title or text of a control in a dialog box. *childId* identifes the control. *text* points to the text buffer containing the text that is to be copied into the control.

See also   TWindow::GetDlgItemText

SetDocTitle
virtual bool SetDocTitle(const char far* docname, int index);

Stores the title of the document (*docname*). *index* is the number of the view displayed in the document's caption bar. In order to determine what the view number should be, *SetDocTitle* makes two passes: the first pass checks to see if there's more than one view, and the second pass, if there is more than one view, assigns the next number to the view. If there is only one view, *index* is 0; therefore, the document does not display a view number. When *TDocument* is checking to see if more than one view exists, *index* is -1. In such cases, only the document's title is displayed in the caption bar.

SetDocTitle returns **true** if there is more than one view and *TDocument* displays the number of the view passed in *index*.

SetExStyle
uint32 SetExStyle(uint32 style);

Sets the extra style bits of the window.

SetFlag
void SetFlag(uint mask);

If **true** is supplied, the bits in *Attr.Flags* in *Mask* are set. Otherwise, the bit is cleared. *Mask* can be any one, or a combination, of the *wfXxxx* constants.

See also   TWindow::IsFlagSet, TWindow::Flag enum

SetFocus
THandle SetFocus();

Sets the keyboard focus to current window and activates the window that receives the focus by sending a WM_SETFOCUS message to the window. All future keyboard input is directed to this window, and any previous window that had the input focus loses it. If successful, *SetFocus* returns a handle to the window that has the focus; otherwise, it returns NULL.

See also   TWindow::GetFocus

SetMenu
bool SetMenu(HMENU hMenu);

Sets the specified window's menu to the menu indicated by *hMenu*. If *hMenu* is 0, the window's current menu is removed. *SetMenu* returns 0 if the menu remains unchanged; otherwise, it returns a nonzero value.

See also   TWindow::GetMenu, TMDIFrame::SetMenu

SetModule
void SetModule(TModule* module);

Sets the default module for this window.

See also   TWindow::GetModule

SetNext
void SetNext(TWindow* next);

Sets the next window in the sibling list.

SetParent
virtual void SetParent(TWindow* newParent);

Sets the parent for the specified window by setting *Parent* to the specified new *Parent* window object. Removes this window from the child list of the previous parent window, if any, and adds this window to the new parent's child list.

See also   TWindow::GetParent

SetProp
Form 1   bool SetProp(uint16 atom, HANDLE data) const;

Adds an item to the property list of the specified window. *atom* contains a value that identifies the data entry to be added to the property list.

Form 2   bool SetProp(const char far* str, HANDLE data) const;

Adds an item to the property list of the specified window. *str* points to the string used to identify the entry data to be added to the property list.

See also   TWindow::GetProp

SetRedraw
void SetRedraw(bool redraw);

Sends a WM_SETREDRAW message to a window so that changes can be redrawn (redraw = **true**) or to prevent changes from being redrawn (redraw = **false**).

SetScroller
void SetScroller(TScroller* scroller);

Sets the scroller object for this window. This window assumes ownership of the scroller object, and will delete it when done and on subsequent sets.

SetScrollPos
int SetScrollPos(int bar, int pos, bool redraw = true);

Sets the thumb position in the scroll bar. *bar* identifies the position (horizontal, vertical, or scroll bar control) to return and can be one of the SB_Xxxx scroll bar constants.

See also   TWindow::GetScrollPos

SetScrollRange
void SetScrollRange(int bar, int minPos, int maxPos, bool redraw = true);

Sets the thumb position in the scroll bar. *bar* identifies the position (horizontal, vertical, or scroll bar control) to set and can be one of the SB_Xxxx scroll bar constants. *minPos* and *maxPos* specify the lower and upper range, respectively, of the scroll bar positions.

See also   TWindow::GetScrollRange, TWindow::SetScrollRange

SetStyle
uint32 SetStyle(uint32 style);

Sets the style bits of the underlying window or the *Style* member of the attribute structure associated with this *TWindow* object.

SetSysModalWindow
THandle SetSysModalWindow();

Makes the indicated window a system-modal window.

See also   TWindow::GetSysModalWindow

SetTimer
uint SetTimer(uint timerId, uint timeout, TIMERPROC proc = 0);

Creates a timer object associated with this window. *timerID* contains the ID number of the timer to be created, *timeout* specifies the length of time in milliseconds, and *proc* identifies the address of the function that's to be notified when the timed event occurs. If *proc* is 0, WM_TIMER messages are placed in the queue of the application that called *SetTimer* for this window.

See also TWindow::KillTimer

SetTransferBuffer
void SetTransferBuffer(void* transferBuffer);

Sets *TransferBuffer* to *transferBuffer*.

See also TWindow::Transfer, TWindow::TransferData

SetWindowFont
void SetWindowFont(HFONT font, bool redraw);

Sets the font that a control uses to draw text. *font*, which specifies the font being used, is NULL if the default system font is used. If *redraw* is **true**, the control redraws itself after the font is set; if **false**, the control does not redraw itself. See the sample program, FILEBROW.CPP, for an example of how to set the font for a file browser list box.

SetWindowLong
long SetWindowLong(int index, long newLong);

Changes information about the window. Depending on the value of *index*, *SetWindowLong* sets a handle to a background brush, cursor, icon, module, menu, or window function. The window style can be one of the GWL_xxxx values that represent styles.

See also TWindow::SetWindowWord

SetWindowPlacement
bool SetWindowPlacement(const WINDOWPLACEMENT* place);

Sets the window to a display mode and screen position. *place* points to a window placement structure that specifies whether the window is to be hidden, minimized or displayed as an icon, maximized, restored to a previous position, activated in its current form, or activated and displayed in its normal position.

See also TWindow::GetWindowPlacement, TWindow::Show

SetWindowPos

Form 1 bool SetWindowPos(THandle hWndInsertAfter, const TRect& rect, uint flags);

Changes the size of the window pointed to by *rect*. *flags* contains one of the SWP_Xxxx set window position constants (described below) that specify the size and position of the window. If *flags* is set to SWP_NOZORDER, *SetWindowPos* ignores the *hWndInsertAfter* parameter and retains the current ordering of the child, pop-up, or top-level windows.

Form 2 bool SetWindowPos(THandle hWndInsertAfter, int x, int y, int w, int h, uint flags);

Changes the size of the window pointed to by *x*, *y*, *w*, and *h*. *flags* contains one of the SWP_Xxxx set window position constants that specify the size and position of the window. If *flags* is set to SWP_NOZORDER, *SetWindowPos* ignores the *hWndInsertAfter* parameter and retains the current ordering of the child, pop-up, or top-level windows.

Table 2.40 SWP_Xxxx set window position constants

Value	Description
SWP_DRAWFRAME	Draws a frame around the window.
SWP_FRAMECHANGED	Sends a message to the window to recalculate the window's size. If this flag is not set, a recalculate size message is sent only at the time the window's size is being changed.
SWP_HIDEWINDOW	Hides the window.
SWP_NOACTIVATE	Does not activate the window. If this flag is not set, the window is activated and moved to the top of the stack of windows.
SWP_NOCOPYBITS	Discards the entire content area of the client area of the window. If this flag is not set, the valid contents are saved and copied into the window after the window is resized or positioned.
SWP_NOMOVE	Remembers the window's current position.
SWP_NOSIZE	Remembers the window's current size.
SWP_NOREDRAW	Does not redraw any changes to the window. If this flag is set, no repainting of any window area (including client, nonclient, and any window part uncovered as a result of a move) occurs. When this flag is set, the application must explicitly indicate if any area of the window is invalid and needs to be redrawn.
SWP_NOZORDER	Remembers the current Z-order (window stacking order).
SWP_SHOWWINDOW	Displays the window.

See also   TWindow::GetWindowPlacement

SetWindowText
void SetWindowText(const char far* str);

Sets the window title to a buffer pointed to by *str*. *maxCount* indicates the number of characters to copy into the buffer. Note that this does not update this window's *Title* member. Use *SetCaption* if the window's *Title* member needs to be synchronized with the window's title.

See also   TWindow::GetWindowText

SetWindowWord
uint16 SetWindowWord(int index, uint16 newWord);

Changes information about the window. *index* specifies a byte offset of the word to be changed to the new value (*newWord*).

See also   TWindow::GetWindowWord, TWindow::SetWindowLong

Show
void Show(int cmdShow);

After ensuring that the *TWindow* interface element has a valid handle, *Show* displays the *TWindow* on the screen in a manner specified by *cmdShow*, which can be one of the following SW_Xxxx show window constants:

Value	Description
SW_SHOWDEFAULT	Show the window in its default configuration. Should be used at startup.
SW_HIDE	Hide the window and activate another window.

Value	Description
SW_MINIMIZE	Minimize the window and activate the top-level window in the list.
SW_RESTORE	Same as SW_SHOWNORMAL.
SW_SHOW	Show the window in the window's current size and position.
SW_SHOWMAXIMIZED	Activate and maximize the window.
SW_SHOWMINIMIZED	Activate window as an icon.
SW_SHOWNA	Display the window as it is currently.
SW_SHOWMINNOACTIVE	Display the window as an icon.
SW_SHOWNORMAL	Activate and display the window in its original size and position.
SW_SHOWSMOOTH	Show the window after updating it in a bitmap.

ShowCaret
void ShowCaret();

Displays the caret in the specified shape in the active window at the current position.

See also   TWindow::CreateCaret, TWindow::HideCaret

ShowOwnedPopups
void ShowOwnedPopups(bool show);

Shows or hides all owned popup windows according to the value of *show*.

See also   TWindow::Show

ShowScrollBar
void ShowScrollBar(int bar, bool show = true);

Displays or hides the scroll bar. *bar* specifies whether the bar is a control itself or part of the window's nonclient area. If *bar* is part of the nonclient area, it can be one of the SB_Xxxx scroll bar constants (specifically, SB_BOTH, SB_HORZ, or SB_VERT). If it is a control, it should be SB_CTRL. If *show* is **true**, the scroll bar is displayed; if **false**, it is hidden.

See also   TWindow::GetScrollRange

ShowWindow
virtual bool ShowWindow(int cmdShow);

Displays the window according to the value of *cmdShow*. *Show* describes the SW_xxxx constants passed in *cmdShow* and is the preferred method of showing the window.

ShutDownWindow
Form 1   void ShutDownWindow(int retVal = 0);

This inline version of *ShutDownWindow* calls the static version of *ShutDownWindow*.

Form 2   static void ShutDownWindow(TWindow* win, int retVal = 0);

This version of *ShutDownWindow* unconditionally shuts down a given window, calls *Destroy* on the interface element, and then deletes the interface object. Instead of using *ShutDownWindow*, you can call *Destroy* directly and then delete the interface object.

SubclassWindowFunction
void SubclassWindowFunction();

Installs the instance thunk as the *WindowProc* and saves the old window function in *DefaultProc*.

See also   TWindow::DefaultProcessing

THandle
operator THandle() const;

Transfer
virtual uint Transfer(void* buffer, TTransferDirection direction);

Transfers data to or from any window with or without children and returns the total size of the data transferred. *Transfer* is a general mechanism for data transfer that can be used with or without using *TransferData*. The *direction* supplied specifies whether data is to be read from or written to the supplied buffer, or whether the size of the transfer data is simply to be returned. Data is not transferred to or from any child windows whose *wfTransfer flag* is not set. The return value is the size (in bytes) of the transfer data.

See also   TWindow::TransferData

TransferData
virtual void TransferData(TTransferDirection direction);

A window usually calls *TransferData* during setup and closing of windows and relies on the constructor to set *TransferBuffer* to something meaningful. *TransferData* calls the *Transfer* member function of each participating child window, passing a pointer to *TransferBuffer* as well as the direction specified in *direction* (*tdSetData*, *tdGetData*, or *tdSizeData*).

See also   TWindow::EnableTransfer, TWindow::DisableTransfer, TWindow::Setup-Window

UnregisterHotKey
bool UnregisterHotKey(int idHotKey);

Unregisters a hotkey ID with the current application.

See also   TWindow::RegisterHotKey

UpdateWindow
void UpdateWindow();

Updates the client area of the specified window by immediately sending a WM_PAINT message.

Validate
void Validate();

Calls the function *ValidateRect* to validate (that is, remove from the area to be updated) the entire client area (the area you can use for drawing).

See also   TWindow::InValidate

ValidateRect

void ValidateRect(const TRect& rect);

Validates a portion of the client area indicated by *rect*.

See also   TWindow::InvalidateRect

ValidateRgn

void ValidateRgn(HRGN hRgn);

Validates the client area within a region of the current window. *hRgn* is a handle to the client area that is to be removed from the region to be updated. If *hRgn* is NULL, the entire client area is removed from the region to be updated.

See also   TWindow::InvalidateRgn

WindowFromPoint

static THandle WindowFromPoint(const TPoint& point);

Returns the handle of the window in which the specified point (*point*) lies.

See also   TWindow::ChildWindowFromPoint

WindowProc

virtual TResult WindowProc(uint msg, TParam1 p1, TParam2 p2);

Processes incoming messages by calling *EvCommand* to handle WM_COMMAND messages, *EvCommandEnable* to handle WM_COMMAND_ENABLE messages, and dispatching for all other messages.

See also   TWindow::DefWindowProc

WinHelp

bool WinHelp(const char far* helpFile, uint command, uint32 data);

Invokes a specified help system. *helpFile* points to a string containing the directory path and name of the help file. *command*, which indicates the type of help requested, can be one of the Windows Help_xxxx constants such as HELP_CONTEXT, HELP_HELPONHELP, HELP_INDEX, HELP_MULTIKEY, HELP_QUIT, or HELP_SETINDEX. *data* contains keywords that indicate the help topic items.

For example, in the sample ObjectWindows file, HELP.CPP, WinHelp is called with the arguments HELP_CONTEXT and HELP_MENUITEMA if the *F1* key is pressed.

```
void TOwlHelpWnd::CmMenuItemA()
{
   if (F1Pressed) {
     WinHelp(HelpFile, HELP_CONTEXT, HELP_MENUITEMA);
     F1Pressed = false;
   } else {
      MessageBox("In Menu Item A command", Title, MB_ICONINFORMATION);
   }
}
```

You can also include bitmaps in your Help file by referencing their file names or by copying them from the Clipboard. For more information about how to create Help files, see the online Help documentation.

Protected data members

BkgndColor
TColor BkgndColor;

Stores the current background color set by *TWindow::SetBkgndColor*.

ContextPopupMenu
TPopupMenu* ContextPopupMenu;

Returns the associated popup menu used by the window.

CursorModule
TModule* CursorModule;

Holds the module ID for the specified cursor. A value of 0 indicates a standard system cursor.

See also   TWindow::CursorResId

CursorResId
TResId CursorResId;

Holds the cursor resource ID for the window's cursor. If the data member *Cursor-Module* is 0, *CursorResId* can be one of the following IDC_Xxxx constants that represent different kinds of cursors:

Value	Meaning
IDC_ARROW	Customary arrow cursor
IDC_CROSS	Crosshair cursor
IDC_IBEAM	I-beam cursor
IDC_ICON	Unfilled icon cursor
IDC_SIZE	A smaller square in the right inside corner of a larger square
IDC_SIZENESW	Dual-pointing cursor with arrows pointing southwest and northeast
IDC_SIZENS	Dual-pointing cursor with arrows pointing south and north
IDC_SIZENWSE	Dual-pointing cursor with arrows pointing southeast and northwest
IDC_SIZEWE	Dual-pointing cursor with arrows pointing east and west
IDC_UPARROW	Vertical arrow cursor
IDC_WAIT	Hourglass cursor

See also   TWindow::SetCursor

hAccel
HACCEL hAccel;

Holds the handle to the current Windows accelerator table associated with this window.

HCursor
HCURSOR HCursor;

Holds a handle to the window's cursor. The cursor is retrieved using *CursorModule* and *CursorResId* and set using *SetCursor*.

TransferBuffer

void* TransferBuffer;

Points to a buffer to be used in transferring data in and out of the *TWindow* object. A *TWindow* object assumes that the buffer contains data used by the windows in its child list. If *TransferBuffer* is 0, no data is to be transferred.

See also   tdxxxx constants

Protected constructor

TWindow();

Constructor used with virtually derived classes. Immediate derived classes must call *Init* before the construction of the object is finished.

Protected member functions

CleanupWindow

virtual void CleanupWindow();

Always called immediately before the HWindow becomes invalid, *CleanupWindow* gives derived classes an opportunity to clean up HWND related resources. This function is the complement to *SetupWindow*.

Override this function in your derived class to handle window cleanup. Derived classes should call the base class's version of *CleanupWindow* as the last step before returning. The following example from the sample program, APPWIN.CPP, illustrates this process:

```
//
Tell windows that we are not accepting drag and drop transactions any more and per
form other window cleanup.
void
TAppWindow::CleanupWindow()
{
  AppLauncherCleanup();
  DragAcceptFiles(false);
  TWindow::CleanupWindow();
}
```

See also   TWindow::SetupWindow

DispatchScroll

void DispatchScroll(uint scrollCode, uint thumbPos, THandle hWndCtrl);

Called by *EvHScroll* and *EvVScroll* to dispatch messages from scroll bars.

EvActivate

void EvActivate(uint active, bool minimized, THandle hWndOther /* may be 0 */);

Default message handler for WM_ACTIVATE.

EvActivateApp

void EvActivateApp(bool active, HTASK hTask);

The default message handler for WM_ACTIVATEAPP.

EvAskCBFormatName
void EvAskCBFormatName(uint bufLen, char far* buffer);

The default message handler for WM_ASKCBFORMATNAME.

EvCancelMode
void EvCancelMode();

The default message handler for WM_CANCELMODE.

EvChangeCBChain
void EvChangeCBChain(THandle hWndRemoved, THandle hWndNext);

The default message handler for WM_CHANGECBCHAIN.

EvChar
void EvChar(uint key, uint repeatCount, uint flags);

The default message handler for WM_CHAR.

EvCharToItem
int EvCharToItem(uint key, THandle hWndListBox, uint caretPos);

The default message handler for WM_CHARTOITEM.

EvChildInvalid
void EvChildInvalid(THandle hWnd);

Responds to a WM_CHILDINVALID message posted by a child edit control. Indicates that the contents of the child window are invalid.

EvClose
void EvClose();

The default message handler for WM_CLOSE.

EvCommNotify
void EvCommNotify(uint commId, uint status);

The default message handler for WM_COMMNOTIFY.

EvCompacting
void EvCompacting(uint compactRatio);

The default message handler for WM_COMPACTING.

EvCompareItem
TResult EvCompareItem(uint ctrlId, COMPAREITEMSTRUCT far& compareInfo);

The default message handler for WM_COMPAREITEM.

EvContextMenu
void EvContextMenu(HWND childHwnd, int x, int y);

The default message handler for WM_CONTEXTMENU.

EvCreate
int EvCreate(CREATESTRUCT far& createStruct);

The default message handler for WM_CREATE.

EvCtlColor
HBRUSH EvCtlColor(HDC hDC, THandle hWndChild, uint ctlType);

The default message handler for WM_CTLCOLOR.

EvDeadChar
void EvDeadChar(uint deadKey, uint repeatCount, uint flags);

The default message handler for WM_DEADCHAR.

EvDeleteItem
void EvDeleteItem(uint ctrlId, DELETEITEMSTRUCT far& deleteInfo);

The default message handler for WM_DELETEITEM.

EvDestroy
void EvDestroy();

The default message handler for WM_DESTROY.

EvDestroyClipboard
void EvDestroyClipboard();

The default message handler for WM_DESTROYCLIPBOARD.

EvDevModeChange
void EvDevModeChange(char far* devName);

The default message handler for WM_DEVMODECHANGE.

EvDrawClipboard
void EvDrawClipboard();

The default message handler for WM_DRAWCLIPBOARD.

EvDrawItem
void EvDrawItem(uint ctrlId, DRAWITEMSTRUCT far& drawInfo);

The default message handler for WM_DRAWITEM.

EvDropFiles
void EvDropFiles(TDropInfo dropInfo);

The default message handler for WM_DROPFILES.

EvEnable
void EvEnable(bool enabled);

The default message handler for WM_ENABLE.

EvEndSession
void EvEndSession(bool endSession);

The default message handler for WM_ENDSESSION.

EvEnterIdle
void EvEnterIdle(uint source, THandle hWndDlg);

The default message handler for WM_ENTERIDLE.

EvEraseBkgnd
bool EvEraseBkgnd(HDC);

The default message handler for WM_ERASEBKGND.

EvFontChange
void EvFontChange();

The default message handler for WM_FONTCHANGE.

EvGetDlgCode
uint EvGetDlgCode(MSG far* msg);

The default message handler for WM_GETDLGCODE.

EvGetFont
HFONT EvGetFont();

The default message handler for WM_GETFONT.

EvGetIcon
HICON EvGetIcon(bool largeIcon);

The default message handler for WM_GETICON.

EvGetMinMaxInfo
void EvGetMinMaxInfo(MINMAXINFO far& minmaxinfo);

The default message handler for WM_GETMINMAXINFO.

EvGetText
void EvGetText(uint buffSize, char far* buff);

The default message handler for WM_GETTEXT.

EvGetTextLength
uint EvGetTextLength();

The default message handler for WM_GETTEXTLENGTH.

EvHotKey
void EvHotKey(int idHotKey);

The default message handler for WM_HOTKEY.

EvHScroll
void EvHScroll(uint scrollCode, uint thumbPos, THandle hWndCtl);

The default message handler for WM_HSCROLL.

EvHScrollClipboard
void EvHScrollClipboard(THandle hCBViewer, uint scrollCode, uint pos);

The default message handler for WM_HSCROLLCLIPBOARD.

EvIconEraseBkgnd
void EvIconEraseBkgnd(HDC hDC);

The default message handler for WM_ICONERASEBKGND.

EvInitMenu
void EvInitMenu(HMENU hMenu);

The default message handler for WM_INITMENU.

EvInitMenuPopup
void EvInitMenuPopup(HMENU hPopupMenu, uint index, bool sysMenu);

The default message handler for WM_INITMENUPOPUP.

EvInputFocus
void EvInputFocus(bool gainingFocus);

The default message handler for WM_INPUTFOCUS.

EvKeyDown
void EvKeyDown(uint key, uint repeatCount, uint flags);

The default message handler for WM_KEYDOWN.

EvKeyUp
void EvKeyUp(uint key, uint repeatCount, uint flags);

The default message handler for WM_KEYUP.

EvKillFocus
void EvKillFocus(THandle hWndGetFocus /* may be 0 */);

The default message handler for WM_KILLFOCUS.

EvLButtonDblClk
void EvLButtonDblClk(uint modKeys, TPoint& point);

The default message handler for WM_LBUTTONDBLCLK.

EvLButtonDown
void EvLButtonDown(uint modKeys, TPoint& point);

The default message handler for WM_LBUTTONDOWN.

EvLButtonUp
void EvLButtonUp(uint modKeys, TPoint& point);

The default message handler for WM_LBUTTONUP.

EvMButtonDblClk
void EvMButtonDblClk(uint modKeys, TPoint& point);

The default message handler for WM_MBUTTONDBLCLK.

EvMButtonDown
void EvMButtonDown(uint modKeys, TPoint& point);

The default message handler for WM_MBUTTONDOWN.

EvMButtonUp
void EvMButtonUp(uint modKeys, TPoint& point);

The default message handler for WM_MBUTTONUP.

EvMeasureItem

void EvMeasureItem(uint ctrlId, MEASUREITEMSTRUCT far& measureInfo);

The default message handler for WM_MEASUREITEM.

EvMenuChar

int32 EvMenuChar(uint nChar, uint menuType, HMENU hMenu);

The default message handler for WM_MENUCHAR.

EvMenuSelect

void EvMenuSelect(uint menuItemId, uint flags, HMENU hMenu);

The default message handler for WM_MENUSELECT.

EvMouseActivate

uint EvMouseActivate(THandle hTopLevel, uint hitCode, uint msg);

The default message handler for WM_MOUSEACTIVATE.

EvMouseMove

void EvMouseMove(uint modKeys, TPoint& point);

The default message handler for WM_MOUSEMOVE.

EvMove

void EvMove(TPoint& clientOrigin);

The default message handler for WM_MOVE.

EvNCActivate

bool EvNCActivate(bool active);

The default message handler for WM_NCACTIVATE.

EvNCCalcSize

uint EvNCCalcSize(bool calcValidRects, NCCALCSIZE_PARAMS far& params);

The default message handler for WM_NCCALCSIZE.

EvNCCreate

bool EvNCCreate(CREATESTRUCT far& createStruct);

The default message handler for WM_NCCREATE.

EvNCDestroy

void EvNCDestroy();

The default message handler for WM_NCDESTROY.

EvNCHitTest

uint EvNCHitTest(TPoint& point);

The default message handler for WM_NCHITTEST.

EvNCLButtonDblClk

void EvNCLButtonDblClk(uint hitTest, TPoint& point);

The default message handler for WM_NCLBUTTONDBLCLK.

EvNCLButtonDown
void EvNCLButtonDown(uint hitTest, TPoint& point);

The default message handler for WM_NCLBUTTONDOWN.

EvNCLButtonUp
void EvNCLButtonUp(uint hitTest, TPoint& point);

The default message handler for WM_NCLBUTTONUP.

EvNCMButtonDblClk
void EvNCMButtonDblClk(uint hitTest, TPoint& point);

The default message handler for WM_NCMBUTTONDBLCLK.

EvNCMButtonDown
void EvNCMButtonDown(uint hitTest, TPoint& point);

The default message handler for WM_NCMBUTTONDOWN.

EvNCMButtonUp
void EvNCMButtonUp(uint hitTest, TPoint& point);

The default message handler for WM_NCMBUTTONUP.

EvNCMouseMove
void EvNCMouseMove(uint hitTest, TPoint& point);

The default message handler for WM_NCMOUSEMOVE.

EvNCPaint
void EvNCPaint();

The default message handler for WM_NCPAINT.

EvNCRButtonDblClk
void EvNCRButtonDblClk(uint hitTest, TPoint& point);

The default message handler for WM_NCRBUTTONDBLCLK.

EvNCRButtonDown
void EvNCRButtonDown(uint hitTest, TPoint& point);

The default message handler for WM_NCRBUTTONDOWN.

EvNCRButtonUp
void EvNCRButtonUp(uint hitTest, TPoint& point);

The default message handler for WM_NCRBUTTONUP.

EvNextDlgCtl
void EvNextDlgCtl(uint hctlOrDir, uint isHCtl);

The default message handler for WM_NEXTDLGCTL.

EvOtherWindowCreated
void EvOtherWindowCreated(THandle hWndOther);

The default message handler for WM_OTHERWINDOWCREATED.

EvOtherWindowDestroyed

void EvOtherWindowDestroyed(THandle hWndOther);

The default message handler for WM_OTHERWINDOWDESTROYED.

EvPaint

void EvPaint();

The default message handler for WM_PAINT.

EvPaintClipboard

void EvPaintClipboard(THandle hWnd, HANDLE hPaintStruct);

The default message handler for WM_PAINTCLIPBOARD.

EvPaintIcon

void EvPaintIcon();

The default message handler for WM_PAINTICON.

EvPaletteChanged

void EvPaletteChanged(THandle hWndPalChg);

The default message handler for WM_PALETTECHANGED.

EvPaletteIsChanging

void EvPaletteIsChanging(THandle hWndPalChg);

The default message handler for WM_PALETTEISCHANGING.

EvParentNotify

void EvParentNotify(uint event, uint childHandleOrX, uint childIDOrY);

The default message handler for WM_PARENTNOTIFY.

EvPower

int EvPower(uint powerEvent);

The default message handler for WM_POWER.

EvQueryDragIcon

HANDLE EvQueryDragIcon();

The default message handler for WM_QUERYDRAGICON.

EvQueryEndSession

bool EvQueryEndSession();

The default message handler for WM_QUERYENDSESSION.

EvQueryNewPalette

bool EvQueryNewPalette();

The default message handler for WM_QUERYNEWPALETTE.

EvQueryOpen

bool EvQueryOpen();

The default message handler for WM_QUERYOPEN.

EvQueueSync
void EvQueueSync();

The default message handler for WM_QUEUESYNC.

EvRButtonDblClk
void EvRButtonDblClk(uint modKeys, TPoint& point);

The default message handler for WM_RBUTTONDBLCLK.

EvRButtonDown
void EvRButtonDown(uint modKeys, TPoint& point);

The default message handler for WM_RBUTTONDOWN.

EvRButtonUp
void EvRButtonUp(uint modKeys, TPoint& point);

The default message handler for WM_RBUTTONUP.

EvRenderAllFormats
void EvRenderAllFormats();

The default message handler for WM_RENDERALLFORMATS.

EvRenderFormat
void EvRenderFormat(uint dataFormat);

The default message handler for WM_RENDERFORMAT.

EvSetCursor
bool EvSetCursor(THandle hWndCursor, uint hitTest, uint mouseMsg);

The default message handler for WM_SETCURSOR.

EvSetFocus
void EvSetFocus(THandle hWndLostFocus /* may be 0 */);

The default message handler for WM_SETFOCUS.

EvSetFont
void EvSetFont(HFONT hFont, bool redraw);

The default message handler for WM_SETFONT.

EvSetIcon
HICON EvSetIcon(bool largeIcon, HICON icon);

The default message handler for WM_SETICON.

EvSetRedraw
void EvSetRedraw(bool redraw);

The default message handler for WM_SETREDRAW.

EvSetText
void EvSetText(const char far* text);

The default message handler for WM_SETTEXT.

EvShowWindow
void EvShowWindow(bool show, uint status);

The default message handler for WM_SHOWWINDOW.

EvSize
void EvSize(uint sizeType, TSize& size);

The default message handler for WM_SIZE.

EvSizeClipboard
void EvSizeClipboard(THandle hWndViewer, HANDLE hRect);

The default message handler for WM_SIZECLIPBOARD.

EvSpoolerStatus
void EvSpoolerStatus(uint jobStatus, uint jobsLeft);

The default message handler for WM_SPOOLERSTATUS.

EvSysChar
void EvSysChar(uint key, uint repeatCount, uint flags);

The default message handler for WM_SYSCHAR.

EvSysColorChange
void EvSysColorChange();

The default message handler for WM_SYSCOLORCHANGE.

EvSysCommand
void EvSysCommand(uint cmdType, TPoint& point);

Responds to a user-selected command from the System menu or when the user selects the maximize or minimize box. Applications that modify the system menu must process *EvSysCommand* messages. Any *EvSysCommand* messages not handled by the application must be passed to *DefaultProcessing*. The parameter *cmdType* can be one of the following system commands:

Constant	Meaning
SC_CLOSE	Close the window.
SC_HOTKEY	Activate the specified window.
SC_HSCROLL	Scroll horizontally.
SC_KEYMENU	Retrieve a menu through a keystroke.
SC_MAXIMIZE (or SC_ZOOM)	Maximize the window.
SC_MINIMIZE (or SC_ICON)	Minimize the window.
SC_MOUSEMENU	Retrieve a menu through a mouse click.
SC_NEXTWINDOW	Move to the next window.
SC_PREVWINDOW	Move to the previous window.
SC_SCREENSAVE	Execute the specified screen saver.
SC_SIZE	Size the window.
SC_TASKLIST	Activate the Windows Task Manager.
SC_VSCROLL	Scroll vertically.

In the following example, *EvSysCommand* either processes system messages or calls *DefaultProcessing*:

```
void MyWindow::EvSysCommand(uint cmdType, TPoint&)
{
    switch (cmdType& 0xFFF0) {
        case SC_MOUSEMENU:
        case SC_KEYMENU:
            break;
        default:
            DefaultProcessing();
    }
}
```

EvSysDeadChar
void EvSysDeadChar(uint key, uint repeatCount, uint flags);

The default message handler for WM_SYSDEADCHAR.

EvSysKeyDown
void EvSysKeyDown(uint key, uint repeatCount, uint flags);

The default message handler for WM_SYSKEYDOWN.

EvSysKeyUp
void EvSysKeyUp(uint key, uint repeatCount, uint flags);

The default message handler for WM_SYSKEYUP.

EvSystemError
void EvSystemError(uint error);

The default message handler for WM_SYSTEMERROR.

EvTimeChange
void EvTimeChange();

The default message handler for WM_TIMECHANGE.

EvTimer
void EvTimer(uint timerId);

The default message handler for WM_TIMER.

EvVKeyToItem
int EvVKeyToItem(uint key, THandle hWndListBox, uint caretPos);

The default message handler for WM_VKEYTOITEM.

EvVScroll
void EvVScroll(uint scrollCode, uint thumbPos, THandle hWndCtl);

The default message handler for WM_VSCROLL.

EvVScrollClipboard
void EvVScrollClipboard(THandle hCBViewer, uint scrollCode, uint pos);

The default message handler for WM_VSCROLLCLIPBOARD.

EvWin32CtlColor
TResult EvWin32CtlColor(TParam1, TParam2);

The default message handler for WM_WIN32CTLCOLOR.

EvWindowPosChanged
void EvWindowPosChanged(WINDOWPOS far& windowPos);

The default message handler for WM_WINDOWPOSCHANGED.

EvWindowPosChanging
void EvWindowPosChanging(WINDOWPOS far& windowPos);

The default message handler for WM_WINDOWPOSCHANGING.

EvWinIniChange
void EvWinIniChange(char far* section);

The default message handler for WM_WININICHANGE.

GetClassName
virtual char far* GetClassName();

Returns the Windows registration class name. The default class name is generated using the module name plus *Window*. If you are registering a new class or changing the name of an existing window class, override this function in your derived class.

See also   TWindow::GetWindowClass, WNDCLASS struct

GetWindowClass
virtual void GetWindowClass(WNDCLASS& wndClass);

Redefined by derived classes, *Get WindowClass* fills the supplied MS-Windows registration class structure with registration attributes, thus allowing instances of *TWindow* to be registered. This function, along with *GetClassName*, allows Windows classes to be used for the specified ObjectWindows class and its derivatives. It sets the fields of the passed *WNDCLASS* parameter to the default attributes appropriate for a *TWindow*. The fields and their default attributes for the class are the following:

Value	Meaning
cbClsExtra	0 (the number of extra bytes to reserve after the window class structure). This value is not used by ObjectWindows.
cbWndExtra	0 (the number of extra bytes to reserve after the window instance). This value is not used by ObjectWindows.
hInstance	The instance of the class in which the window procedure exists.
hIcon	0 (Provides a handle to the class resource.) By default, the application must create an icon if the application's window is minimized.
hCursor	IDC_ARROW (provides a handle to a cursor resource).
hbrBackground	COLOR_WINDOW + 1 (the system background color).
lpszMenuName	0 (Points to a string that contains the name of the class's menu.) By default, the windows in this class have no assigned menus.
lpszClassName	Points to a string that contains the name of the window class.
lpfnWndProc	The address of the window procedure. This value is not used by ObjectWindows.
style	CS_DBLCLKS
	The style field can contain one or more of the following values:

Value	Meaning
	CS_BYTEALIGNCLIENT
	Aligns the window's client on a byte boundary in the x direction. This alignment, designed to improve performance, determines the width and horizontal position of the window.
	CS_BYTEALIGNWINDOW
	Aligns a window on a byte boundary in the x direction. This alignment, designed to improve performance, determines the width and horizontal position of the window
	CS_CLASSDC
	Allocates a single device context (DC) that's going to be shared by all of the window in the class. This style controls how multi-threaded applications that have windows belonging to the same class share the same DC.
	CS_DBLCLKS
	Sends a double-click mouse message to the window procedure when the mouse is double-clicked on a window belonging to this class.
	CS_GLOBALCLASS
	Allows an application to create a window class regardless of the instance parameter. You can also create a global class by writing a DLL that contains the window class.
	CS_HREDRAW
	If the size of the window changes as a result of some movement or resizing, redraws the entire window.
	CS_NOCLOSE
	Disables the Close option on this window's system menu.
	CS_OWNDC
	Enables each window in the class to have a different DC.
	CS_PARENTDC
	Passes the parent window's DC to the child windows.
	CS_SAVEBITS
	Saves the section of the screen as a bitmap if the screen is covered by another window. This bitmap is later used to recreate the window when it is no longer obscured by another window.
	CS_VREDRAW
	If the height of the client area is changed, redraws the entire window.

After the Windows class structure has been filled with default values by the base class, you can override this function to change the values of the Windows class structure. For example, you might want to change the window's colors or the cursor displayed.

See also TWindow::GetClassName, WNDCLASS struct

GetWindowPtr
TWindow* GetWindowPtr(THandle hWnd) const;

Calls *TApplication::GetWindowPtr* on the application associated with this window. Then, given the handle to this window (*hWnd*), *GetWindowPtr* returns the *TWindow* pointer associated with this window.

Init
Form 1   void Init(THandle hWnd, TModule* module);

Form 2   void Init(TWindow* parent, const char far* title, TModule* module);

Allows for further initialization after default construction of a window in virtually derived classes.

InitWndProc
static TResult CALLBACK InitWndProc(THandle, uint, TParam1, TParam2);
Callback process for hooking *TWindow* to native window.

LoadAcceleratorTable
void LoadAcceleratorTable();
Loads a handle to the window's accelerator table specified in the *TWindowAttr* structure (*Attr.AccelTable*). If the accelerator does not exist, *LoadAcceleratorTable* produces an "Unable to load accelerator table" diagnostic message.

RemoveChild
virtual void RemoveChild(TWindow* child);
Removes a child window. Uses the ObjectWindows list of objects rather the window's HWND list.

See also TWindow::GetFirstChild, TWindow::GetLastChild, TWindow::Next, TWindow::Previous

SetHandle
void SetHandle(THandle handle);
Sets the window handle in a derived class. Used by derived classes that create their window handle in a class-specific way.

SetupWindow
virtual void SetupWindow();
The first virtual function called when the *HWindow* becomes valid. *TWindow*'s implementation performs window setup by iterating through the child list, attempting to create an associated interface element for each child window object for which autocreation is enabled. (By default, autocreation is enabled for windows and controls, and disabled for dialog boxes.) *SetupWindow* then calls *TransferData*. If a child window cannot be created, *SetupWindow* calls *TXWindow* with an IDS_CHILDCREATEFAIL message.

SetupWindow can be redefined in derived classes to perform additional special initialization. Note that the *HWindow* is valid when the overridden *SetupWindow* is called, and that the children's *HWindow*s are valid after calling the base classes' *SetupWindow* function.

The following example from the sample program, APPWIN.CPP, illustrates the use of an overridden *SetupWindow* to setup a window, initialize .INI entries, and tell Windows that we want to accept drag and drop transactions:

```
void TAppWindow::SetupWindow()
{
  TFloatingFrame::SetupWindow();
  InitEntries();    // Initialize .INI entries.
  RestoreFromINIFile(); // from APPLAUNC.INI in the startup directory
  UpdateAppButtons();
  DragAcceptFiles(true);
}
```

See also   TFrameWindow::SetupWindow, TComboBox::SetupWindow, TWindow::CleanupWindow

StdWndProc
static TResult CALLBACK StdWndProc(THandle, uint, TParam1, TParam2);
Callback process for hooking *TWindow* to native window.

Response table entries

There are two tables. The first one shows the standard response table entries. The second shows the Win32 response table entries.

Table 2.41   Standard response table entries.

Response table entry	Member function
EV_WM_CREATE	EvCreate
EV_WM_CLOSE	EvClose
EV_WM_DESTROY	EvDestroy
EV_WM_SIZE	EvSize
EV_WM_MOVE	EvMove
EV_WM_NCDESTROY	EvNcDestroy
EV_WM_QUERYENDSESSION	EvQueryEndSession
EV_WM_COMPAREITEM	EvCompareItem
EV_WM_DELETEITEM	EvDeleteItem
EV_WM_DRAWITEM	EvDrawItem
EV_WM_MEASUREITEM	EvMeasureItem
EV_WM_CHILDINVALID	EvChildInvalid
EV_WM_VSCROLL	EvVScroll
EV_WM_HSCROLL	EvHScroll
EV_WM_PAINT	EvPaint
EV_WM_SETCURSOR	EvSetCursor
EV_WM_LBUTTONDOWN	EvLButtonDown
EV_COMMAND(CM_EXIT, CmExit)	CmExit
EV_WM_SYSCOLORCHANGE	EvSysColorChange
EV_WM_KILLFOCUS	EvKillFocus
EV_WM_ERASEBKGND	EvEraseBkgnd

Table 2.42   Win32 response table entries

Response table entry	Member function
EV_MESSAGE(WM_CTLCOLORMSGBOX, EvWin32CtlColor)	EvWin32CtlColor
EV_MESSAGE(WM_CTLCOLOREDIT, EvWin32CtlColor)	EvWin32CtlColor
EV_MESSAGE(WM_CTLCOLORLISTBOX, EvWin32CtlColor)	EvWin32CtlColor
EV_MESSAGE(WM_CTLCOLORBTN, EvWin32CtlColor)	EvWin32CtlColor
EV_MESSAGE(WM_CTLCOLORDLG, EvWin32CtlColor)	EvWin32CtlColor

Response table entry	Member function
EV_MESSAGE(WM_CTLCOLORSCROLLBAR, EvWin32CtlColor)	EvWin32CtlColor
EV_MESSAGE(WM_CTLCOLORSTATIC, EvWin32CtlColor)	EvWin32CtlColor

TWindowAttr struct   window.h

Holds *TWindow* attributes set during construction of a window. Your program controls a window's creation by passing these values to one of *TWindow*'s creation routines. If the window is streamed, these attributes are also used for re-creation.

Public data members

AccelTable
TResID AccelTable;
Holds the resource ID for the window's accelerator table.

See also TApplication::HAccTable, TWindow::LoadAcceleratorTable

ExStyle
uint32 ExStyle;
Contains the extended style values of your window. These can be any one of the extended style constants (WS_EX_DLGMODALFRAME, WS_EX_NOPARENTNOTIFY, WS_EX_TOPMOST, WS_EX_SHADOW). See *TWindow::AdjustWindowRectEx* for a description of these constants.

See also TWindow::AdjustWindowRectEx

Id
int Id;
Contains the identifier of the child window. For a dialog box control, *Id* is its resource identifier. If Win32 is defined, *Id* is set to *GetWindowLong*; otherwise *Id* is set to *GetWindowWord*.

Menu
TResId Menu;
Contains the resource ID for the menu associated with this window. If no menu exists, Menu is 0.

Param
char far* Param;
Contains a value that is passed to Windows when the window is created. This value identifies a data block that is then available in the message response functions associated with WM_CREATE. *Param* is used by *TMDIClient* and can be useful when converting non-ObjectWindows code.

Style
uint32 Style;

Contains the values that define the style, shape, and size of your window. Although *TWindow* sets *Attr.Style* to WS_CHILD and WS_VISIBLE, you can also use other combinations of the following style constants:

Value	Meaning
WS_BORDER	Creates a window with a thin lined border.
WS_CAPTION	Creates a window with a title bar.
WS_CHILD	Creates a child windows. Cannot be used with popup styles.
WS_CHILDWINDOW	Creates a child window.
WS_CLIPCHILDREN	Used when creating a parent window. Excludes the area occupied by child windows when drawing takes place within the parent window.
WS_CLIPSIBLINGS	Clips child windows relative to the child window that receives a paint message.
WS_DISABLED	Creates a window that cannot receive user input.
WS_DLGFRAME	Creates a window having a typical dialog box style (without a title bar).
WS_GROUP	Indicates the first control in a group of controls, which the user can change by pressing the direction keys.
WS_HSCROLL	Window has a horizontal scroll bar.
WS_MAXIMIZE	Window is initially maximized.
WS_MAXIMIZEBOX	Window has a maximize button.
WS_MINIMIZE	Window is initially minimized.
WS_MINIMIZEBOX	Window has a minimize button.
WS_OVERLAPPED	Creates an overlapped window with a title bar and a border.
WS_OVERLAPPEDWINDOW	Overlapped window has the WS_OVERLAPPED, WS_CAPTION, WS_SYSMENU, WS_THICKFRAME, WS_MINIMIZEBOX, and WS_MAXIMIZEBOX styles.
WS_POPUP	Creates a popup window. Cannot be used with child window styles.
WS_POPUPWINDOW	Creates a popup window with WS_BORDER, WS_POPUP, and WS_SYSMENU styles. The WS_CAPTION and WS_POPUPWINDOW styles combine to create a system menu.
WS_SYSMENU	Window has a system menu box in its title bar. Must also indicate the WS_CAPTION style.
WS_TABSTOP	Control can receive the keyboard focus when TAB key is pressed.
WS_THICKFRAME	Window has a border that lets you change the window size.
WS_VISIBLE	Window is initially visible.
WS_VSCROLL	Window has a vertical scroll bar.

See also   TWindow::IsWindowVisible

X, Y, W, H
int X, Y, W, H;

X and Y contain the screen coordinates of the top left corner of the window. W and H contain the width and height values of the window.

TWindowDC class   dc.h

Derived from TDC, *TWindowDC* is a device context (DC) class that provides access to the entire area owned by a window. *TWindowDC* is the base class for any DC class that releases its handle when it is finished.

Public constructor and destructor

Constructor
TWindowDC(HWND wnd);
Creates a TWindow object with the given owned window. The data member Wnd is set to *wnd*.

Destructor
~TWindowDC();
Destroys this object.

Protected constructor

TWindowDC();
Used for derived classes only.

Protected data members

Wnd
HWND Wnd;
Holds a handle to the window owned by this device context.

See also   TWindowDC::TWindowDC

TWindowView class   docview.h

Derived from both TWindow and TView, *TWindowView* is a streamable base class that can be used for deriving window-based views. *TWindowView*'s functions override *TView*'s virtual function to provide their own implementation. By deriving a window-view class from *TWindow* and *TView*, you add window functionality to the view of your document.

Public constructor and destructor

Constructor
TWindowView (TDocument& doc, TWindow* parent = 0);
Constructs a *TWindowView* interface object associated with the window view. Sets ViewId to NextViewId. Calls the associated document's *AttachView* function (a private *TDocument* function) to attach the view to the document.

Destructor
~TWindowView();
Destroys a *TWindowView* object and calls the associated document's *DetachView* function (a private *TDocument* function) to detach the view from the associated document.

Public member functions

CanClose
bool CanClose();
Overrides *TWindow::CanClose* and returns a nonzero value if the window can be closed. *CanClose* checks all the associated document's *CanClose* functions. These must return nonzero values before the window view can be closed.

See also   TWindow::CanClose

GetViewName
const char far* GetViewName();
Overrides *TView::GetViewName* and returns *StaticName*, the name of the view.

GetWindow
TWindow* GetWindow()
Overrides *TView::GetWindow* and returns the *TWindowView* object as a TWindow.

See also   TEditView::GetWindow

SetDocTitle
bool SetDocTitle(const char far* docname, int index)
Overrides *TView::SetDocTitle* and stores the document title. This name is forwarded up the parent chain until a *TFrameWindow* object accepts the data and displays it in its caption.

See also   TView::SetDocTitle, TWindow::SetDocTitle

StaticName
static const char far* StaticName();
Returns "Window View," the descriptive name of the view. This title is displayed in the user-interface box.

Response table entries

Response table entry	Member function
EV_VN_ISWINDOW	VnIsWindow

TWinG class   wing.h

bool IsAvailable();
Returns true if the DLL implementing WinG is available and loaded, or false otherwise.

Class description

TWinG is an alias for an instance of the TDllLoader template which ensures the underlying DLL is loaded and available. The *IsAvailable* method (defined by the TDllLoader template) can be used to load the DLL. For example,

```
if (TWinG::IsAvailable()) {
    // DLL is loaded - Proceed with WinG calls
} else {
    // Error - Underlying DLL is not available.
}
```

TWinGDll class   wing.h

The *TWinGDll* class encapsulates the WinG DLL (WING [32].DLL). It provides an easy method to dynamically test for the availability of the DLL and bind to its exported functions at runtime. By using the *TWinGDll* class instead of direct calls to the WinG DLL, ObjectWindows applications can provide the appropriate behavior when running in an environment where the DLL is not available.

Each data member of the TWinGDll class corresponds to the API with a similar name exposed by the WinG DLL. For example, *TWinGDll::CreateDC* corresponds to the WinGCreateDC API exported by the WinG DLL.

TWinSock class   winsock.h

bool IsAvailable();
Returns true if the DLL implementing WinSock is available and loaded, or false otherwise.

Class description

TWinSock is an alias for an instance of the TDllLoader template which ensures the underlying DLL is loaded and available. The *IsAvailable* method (defined by the TDllLoader template) can be used to load the DLL. For example,

```
if (TWinSock::IsAvailable()) {
    // DLL is loaded - Proceed with WinSock calls
} else {
```

```
        // Error - Underlying DLL is not available.
    }
```

TWinSockDll class   winsock.h

The *TWinSockDll* class encapsulates the WinSock DLL (WINSOCK.DLL). It provides an easy method to dynamically test for the availability of the DLL and bind to its exported functions at runtime. By using the *TWinSockDll* class instead of direct calls to the WinSock DLL, ObjectWindows applications can provide the appropriate behavior when running in an environment where the DLL is not available.

Each data member of the *TWinSockDll* class corresponds to the API with a similar name exposed by the WinSock DLL. For example, *TWinSockDll::WSAStartup* corresponds to the WSAStartup API exported by the WinSock DLL.

TXClipboard class   clipboar.h

TXClipboard creates the TXClipboard exception with a string resource.

Public constructors

TXClipboard
TXClipboard(uint resourceId = IDS_CLIPBOARDBUSY);
Creates the TXClipboard exception with a string resource.

Public member functions

Clone
Form 1   TXClipboard* Clone();
Clones the exception for safe throwing in Windows.

Form 2   TXBase* Clone();
Clones the exception for safe throwing in Windows.

Raise
static void Raise(uint resourceId = IDS_CLIPBOARDBUSY);
Raises the exception.

Throw
void Throw();
Throws the exception.

TXCommCtrl class

commctrl.h

TXCommCtrl is an exception object thrown by the Common Control wrappers of ObjectWindows.

Public constructors

TXCommCtrl
TXCommCtrl();
Constructor of the Object thrown by the Common Control wrappers of ObjectWindows.

Public member functions

Clone
Form 1 TXCommCtrl* Clone();
Routine to copy an exception object. The *Clone* method is invoked when an exception must be suspended. The cloned copy can latter be used to resume the exception.

Form 2 TXBase* Clone();
Routine to copy an exception object. The Clone method is invoked when an exception must be suspended. The cloned copy can latter be used to resume the exception.

Raise
static void Raise();
Constructs a TXCommCtrl exception from scratch, and throws it.

Throw
void Throw();
Method to localize the actual call to 'throw' a *TXCommCtrl* object.

Note Localizing the call to *throw* is a size optimization: the overhead of a *throw* statement is generated only once.

TXCompatibility class

except.h

Describes an exception that results from setting *TModule::Status* to nonzero. This exception is included for backward compatibility with ObjectWindows 1.0.

Public constructors

Form 1 TXCompatibility(int statusCode);
Constructs a *TXCompatibility* object.

Form 2 TXCompatibility(const TXCompatibility& src);
Constructs a *TXCompatibility* object with the window that failed.

Public member functions

Clone
TXOwl* Clone();
Makes a copy of the exception object. *Clone* must be implemented in any class derived from *TXOwl*.

MapStatusCodeToString
static string MapStatusCodeToString(int statusCode);
Retrieves *Tmodule*'s status code and coverts it to a string.

Status
int Status;
Contains an OWL-1 compatible status code representing an error condition.

Throw
void Throw();
Throws the exception object. *Throw* must be implemented in any class derived from *TXOwl*.

Unhandled
int Unhandled(TModule* app, unsigned promptResId);
If an exception caught in the message loop has not been handled, *Unhandled* is called. *Unhandled* deletes the window. This type of exception could occur if a window can't be created.

TGdiBase::TXGdi class   gdibase.h

Describes an exception resulting from GDI failures such as creating too many TWindow device contexts (DCs). This exception occurs, for example, if a DC driver cannot be located or if a device-independent bitmap (DIB) file cannot be read.

The following code from the PAINT.CPP sample program on your distribution disk throws a *TXGdi* exception if a new DIB cannot be created.

```
void TCanvas::NewDib(int width, int height, int nColors)
{
  TDib* dib;
  try {
    dib = new TDib(width, height, nColors);
  }
  catch (TGdiBase::TXGdi& x) {
    MessageBox("Could Not Create DIB", GetApplication()->Name,   MB_OK);
    return;
  }
}
```

Public constructors

TXGdi
TXGdi(uint resId = IDS_GDIFAILURE, HANDLE handle = 0);
Constructs a *TXGdi* object with a default IDS_GDIFAILURE message.

Public member functions

Clone
Form 1   TXOwl* Clone();
Makes a copy of the exception object. *Clone* must be implemented in any class derived from TXOwl.

Form 2   TXGdi* Clone();
Clones the exception object for safe-throwing across Windows.

Form 3   TXBase* Clone();
Clones the exception object for safe-throwing across Windows.

Msg
static string Msg(uint resId, HANDLE);
Converts the resource ID to a string and returns the string message.

Raise
static void Raise(uint resId = IDS_GDIFAILURE, HANDLE handle = 0);
Throws the exception.

Throw
void Throw();
Throws the exception object. *Throw* must be implemented in any class derived from TXOwl.

TApplication::TXInvalidMainWindow class   applicat.h

A nested class, *TXInvalidMainWindow* describes an exception that results from an invalid Window. This exception is thrown if there is not enough memory to create a window or a dialog object. TApplication::InitInstance throws this exception if it can't initialize an instance of an application object.

Public constructor

TXInvalidMainWindow();
Constructs a *TXInvalidMainWindow* object with a default IDS_INVALIDMAINWINDOW message.

Public member functions

Clone
virtual TXOwl* Clone();
Makes a copy of the exception object. *Clone* must be implemented in any class derived from TXOwl.

Raise
static void Raise();
Throws a TXInvalidMainWindow exception.

Throw
virtual void Throw();
Throws the exception object. *Throw* must be implemented in any class derived from TXOwl.

TModule::TXInvalidModule class   module.h

A nested class, *TXInvalidModule* describes an exception that results from an invalid module. A window throws this exception if it can't create a valid *TModule* object.

Public constructors

Form 1   TXInvalidModule();
Constructs a *TXInvalidModule* object.

Form 2   TXInvalidModule(const char far* name = 0);
Creates the Invalid Module exception.

Public member functions

TXInvalidModule::Clone
Form 1   TXOwl* Clone();
Makes a copy of the *TXInvalidModule* exception object.

Form 2   TXInvalidModule* Clone();
Creates a copy of exception for 16-bit Windows.

TXInvalidModule::Raise
static void Raise(const char far* name = 0);
Throws the exception.

TXInvalidModule::Throw
void Throw();
Throws the *TXInvalidModule* exception object.

TMenu::TXMenu class
menu.h

A nested class, *TXMenu* describes an exception that occurs when a menu item cannot be constructed.

Public constructor

TXMenu(unsigned resId = IDS_GDIFAILURE);
Constructs a *TXMenu* exception object with a default IDS_GDIFAILURE message.

Public member functions

Clone
Form 1   TXMenu* Clone();
Creates a copy of the *TXMenu* exception.

Form 2   TXBase* Clone();
Creates a copy of the *TXMenu* exception.

Raise
static void Raise(uint resId = IDS_MENUFAILURE);
Creates a *TXMenu* exception and throws it.

Throw
void Throw();
Throws a *TXMenu* exception.

TXOutOfMemory class
except.h

Describes an exception that results from running out of memory.

Public constructors

TXOutOfMemory();
Constructs a *TXOutOfMemory* object.

Public member functions

Clone
TXOwl* Clone();
Makes a copy of the exception object. *Clone* must be implemented in any class derived from *TXOwl*.

Raise
static void Raise();
Constructs a *TXOutOfMemory* exception from scratch.

Throw
void Throw();
Throws the exception object. *Throw* must be implemented in any class derived from
TXOwl.

TXOwl class   except.h

TXOwl is a parent class for several classes designed to describe exceptions. In most
cases, you derive a new class from *TXOwl* instead of using this one directly. The
ObjectWindows classes derived from *TXOwl* include

Class	Description
TXCompatibility	Describes an exception that occurs if TModule::Status is not zero
TValidator::TXValidator	Describes an exception that occurs if there is an invalid validator expression
TWindow::TXWindow	Describes an exception that results from trying to create an invalid window
TGdiObject::TXGdi	Describes an exception that results from creating an invalid GDI object
TApplication::TXInvalidMainWindow	Describes an exception that results from creating an invalid main window
TMenu::TXMenu	Describes an exception that occurs when a menu object is invalid
TModule::TXInvalidModule	Describes an exception that occurs if a TModule object is invalid
TPrinter::TXPrinter	Describes an exception that occurs if a printer device context is invalid
TXOutOfMemory	Describes an exception that occurs if an out of memory error occurs

Each of the exception classes describes a particular type of exception. When your
program encounters a given situation that's likely to produce this exception, it passes
control to the specified exception-handling object. If you use exceptions in your code,
you can avoid having to scatter error-handling procedures throughout your program.

To create an exception handler, place the keyword **try** before the block of code that
might produce the abnormal condition (the code that might generate an exception
object) and the keyword **catch** before the block of code that follows the **try** block. If an
exception is thrown within the **try** block, the classes within each of the subsequent **catch**
clauses are checked in sequence. The first one that matches the class of the exception
object is executed.

The following example from MDIFILE.CPP, a sample program on your distribution
disk, shows how to set up a **try/catch** block around the code that might throw an
exception.

```
void TMDIFileApp::CmRestoreState()
{
    char* errorMsg = 0;
```

```
        ifpstream is(DskFile);
        if (is.bad())
            errorMsg = "Unable to open desktop file.";
    // try block of code //
        else {
        if (Client->CloseChildrenParen) {
            try {
                is >>* this;
                if (is.bad())
                    errorMsg = "Error reading desktop file.";
                else
                    Client->CreateChildren();
            }
    // catch block of code //
        catch (xalloc) {
            Client->CloseChildren();
            errorMsg = "Not enough memory to open file.";
          }
        }
      }
    if (errorMsg)
        MainWindow->MessageBox(errorMsg, "Error",
            MB_OK | MB_ICONEXCLAMATION);
    }
```

See also   TXBase

Public data members

ResId
unsigned ResId;
Resource ID for a *TXOwl* object.

Public constructors and destructor

Form 1   TXOwl(const string& msg, unsigned resId = 0);
Constructs a *TXOwl* object with a string message (*msg*).

Form 2   TXOwl(unsigned resId, TModule* module = ::module);
Loads the string resource identified by the *resId* parameter and uses this *resId* to initialize the *TXBase* object.

Destructor
~TXOwl();
Destroys a *TXOwl* object.

Public member functions

Clone
TXOwl* Clone();

Makes a copy of the exception object. *Clone* must be overridden in any class derived from *TXOwl*.

GetErrorCode
unsigned GetErrorCode() const;
Returns the resource ID.

MakeMessage
static string MakeMessage(uint resId, uint infoNum, TModule* module = ::Module);
This extension to the string loader adds the feature of *sprintf*'ing an additional information string into the resource message string.

Raise
Form 1   static void Raise(uint resId, TModule* module = ::Module);

Form 2   static void Raise(const string& msg, uint resId = 0);
Construct a *TXOwl* exception from scratch, and throw it. There are two versions, corresponding to the two constructor signatures.

ResourceIdToString
static string ResourceIdToString(bool* found, unsigned resId, TModule* module = ::module);
Converts the resource ID to a string and returns a string that identifies the exception. If the string message cannot be loaded, returns a "not found" message. Sets the *found* parameter to true if the resource is located; otherwise, sets *found* to false.

Throw
void Throw();
Throws the exception object. *Throw* must be implemented in any class derived from *TXOwl*.

Unhandled
virtual int Unhandled(TModule* app, unsigned promptResId);
Called when an unhandled exception is caught at the main message loop level.

TPrinter::TXPrinter class   printer.h

A nested class, *TXPrinter* describes an exception that results from an invalid printer object. This type of error can occur when printing to the physical printer.

Public constructor

TXPrinter(uint resId = IDS_PRINTERERROR);
Constructs a *TXPrinter* object with a default IDS_PRINTERERROR message.

Public member functions

TXPrinter::Clone
Form 1   TXPrinter* Clone();

Clones the exception object for safe throwing across Win16 stack frames.

Form 2   TXBase* Clone();
Clones the exception object for safe throwing across Win16 stack frames.

TXPrinter::Raise
static void Raise(uint resId = IDS_PRINTERERROR);
Creates the exception object and throws it.

TXPrinter::Throw
void Throw();
Throws the exception.

TXShell class   shellitm.h

TXShell is the base Shell exception class. It handles all *TShellItem* and related class exceptions.

Public constructors

TXShell
TXShell(uint resId = IDS_SHELLFAILURE, HANDLE handle = 0);
Constructs a *TXShell* object with a default IDS_SHELLFAILURE message.

Public member functions

Check
static void Check(HRESULT hr, uint resId = IDS_SHELLFAILURE, HANDLE handle = 0);
Checks an HResult and throws a *TXShell* if not SUCCEEDED(hr).

Clone
TXShell* Clone();
Makes a copy of the exception object.

Raise
static void Raise(uint resId = IDS_SHELLFAILURE, HANDLE handle = 0);
Constructs a *TXShell* exception from scratch, and throws it.

Throw
void Throw();
Throws the exception object.

TValidator::TXValidator class   validate.h

A nested class, *TXValidator* describes an exception that results from an invalid validator object. That is, if a validator expression is not valid, this exception is thrown.

Public constructor

TXValidator(uint resId = IDS_VALIDATORSYNTAX);
Constructs a *TXValidator* object, setting the resource ID to IDS_VALIDATORSYNTAX
string resource.

Public member functions

Clone
Form 1   TXValidator* Clone();
Copies the exception so it can be rethrown at a safer time.

Form 2   TXBase* Clone();
Copies the exception so it can be rethrown at a safer time.

Raise
static void Raise();
Creates an instance of TXValidator and throws it.

Throw
void Throw();
Creates an instance of TXValidator and throws it.

TWindow::TXWindow class   window.h

A nested class, *TXWindow* describes an exception that results from trying to create an
invalid window.

Public constructors

Form 1   TXWindow(TWindow* win = 0, uint resourceId = IDS_INVALIDWINDOW);
Constructs a *TXWindow* object with a default resource ID of IDS_INVALIDWINDOW.

Form 2   TXWindow(const TXWindow& src);
Constructs a *TXWindow* object with the window that failed.

Public data members

TXWindow::Window
TWindow* Window;
Points to the window object that is associated with the exception.

Public member functions

TXWindow::Clone
TXOwl* Clone();

Makes a copy of the exception object. *Clone()* must be implemented in any class derived from TXOwl.

TXWindow::Msg
static string Msg(TWindow*, uint resourceid);
Converts the resource ID to a string and returns the string message.

TXWindow::Raise
static void Raise(TWindow* win = 0, uint resourceId = IDS_INVALIDWINDOW);
Creates the *TXWindow* exception and throws it.

TXWindow::Throw
void Throw();
Throws the exception object. *Throw()* must be implemented in any class derived from *TXOwl*.

TXWindow::Unhandled
int Unhandled(TModule* app, unsigned promptResId);
Called if an exception caught in the window's message loop has not been handled. *Unhandled()* deletes the window. This type of exception can occur if a window cannot be created.

ObjectWindows constants

This chapter is an alphabetical summary of the ObjectWindows constants.

BF_xxxx button flag constants   checkbox.h

Check box and radio button objects use the button flag constants to indicate the state of a selection box.

Table 3.1   Button flag constants

Constant	Meaning
BF_CHECKED	Item is checked.
BF_GRAYED	Item is grayed.
BF_UNCHECKED	Item is unchecked.

See also   TCheckbox::GetCheck, TCheckbox::SetCheck

CM_xxxx edit constants   window.rh

These command-based member functions are invoked in response to a particular edit menu selection or command.

Table 3.2   Command-based constants

Constant	Member function	Menu equivalent
CM_EXIT	TWindow::CmExit	File I Exit
CM_EDITCLEAR	TEdit::CMEditClear	Edit I Clear
CM_EDITCOPY	TEdit::CMEditCopy	Edit I Copy
CM_EDITCUT	TEdit::CMEditCut	Edit I Cut

Constant	Member function	Menu equivalent
CM_EDITDELETE	TEdit::CMEditDelete	Edit	Delete
CM_EDITPASTE	TEdit::CMEditPaste	Edit	Paste
CM_EDITUNDO	TEdit::CMEditUndo	Edit	Undo
CM_EDITADD	*	Edit	Add
CM_EDITEDIT	*	Edit	Edit

Note * CM_EDITADD and CM_EDITEDIT do not have predefined handlers in ObjectWindows. If you derive a class that provides these functions, it is suggested that you associate functions with these constants in an EV_COMMAND response table entry.

CM_xxxx edit file constants   docview.rh

These command-based member functions are invoked in response to open, close, print, and save commands.

Table 3.3   Command-based constants

Constant	Member function	Menu equivalent
CM_FILECLOSE	TDocManager::CmFileClose	File	Close
CM_FILENEW	TEditFile::CmFileNew	File	New
CM_FILEOPEN	TEditFile::CmFileOpen	File	Open
CM_FILEPRINT	*	File	Print
CM_FILEPRINTERSETUP	*	File	PrinterSetup
CM_FILEPPAGESETUP	*	File	PrinterSetup
CM_FILEREVERT	TDocManager::CmFileRevert	File	Revert
CM_FILESAVE	TEditFile::CmFileSave	File	Save
CM_FILESAVEAS	TEditFile::CmFileSaveAs	File	Save As
CM_VIEWCREATE	TDocManager::CmViewCreate	File	View Create

Note * CM_FILEPRINT, CM_FILEPRINTERSETUP, and CM_FILEPAGESETUP do not have predefined handlers in ObjectWindows. If you derive a class that provides a function that prints files or sets up printers, it is suggested that you associate the function with one of these constants in an EV_COMMAND response table entry.

CM_xxxx edit replace constants   editsear.rh

These command-based member functions are invoked when the corresponding find and replace command is received.

Table 3.4   Command-based constants

Constant	Member function	Menu equivalent
CM_EDITFIND	TEditSearch::CMEditFind	Edit I Find
CM_EDITFINDNEXT	TEditSearch::CMEditFindNext	Edit I Find I Next
CM_EDITREPLACE	TEditSearch::CMEditReplace	Edit I Replace

CM_xxxx edit view constants   oleview.rh

These command-based view functions are invoked in response to menu and accelerator key commands. The Edit I Verbs selection refers to one of the OLE-specific menu commands, such as Edit or Open.

Constant	Member function	Menu equivalent
CM_EDITPASTESPECIAL	TOleWindow::CmEditPasteSpecial	Paste I Special
CM_EDITPASTELINK	TOleWindow::CmEditPasteLink	Paste I Link
CM_EDITINSERTOBJECT	TOleWindow::CmEditInsertObject	Insert I Object
CM_EDITINSERTCONTROL	TOleWindow::CmEditInsertControl	Insert I Control
CM_EDITLINKS	TOleWindow::CmEditLinks	Edit I Links
CM_EDITOBJECT	TOleWindow::CeEditObject	Edit I Object
CM_EDITFIRSTVERB	TOleWindow::EvCommandEnable	Edit I Verbs
CM_EDITLASTVERB	TOleWindow::EvCommandEnable	Edit I Verbs
CM_EDITCONVERT	TOleWindow::CmEditConvert	Edit I Convert
CM_EDITSHOWOBJECTS	TOleWindow::CmEditShowObjects	Show I Objects

CM_xxxx MDI constants   mdi.rh

These MDI functions are invoked when the corresponding MDI command message is received.

Table 3.5   Command message constants

Constant	Member function	Menu equivalent
CM_ARRANGEICONS	TMDIClient::CmArrangeIcons	Window I Arrange Icons
CM_CASCADECHILDREN	TMDIClient::CmCascadeChildren	Window I Cascade
CM_CLOSECHILDREN	TMDIClient::CmCloseChildren	Window I Close All
CM_CREATECHILD	TMDIClient::CmCreateChild	
CM_TILECHILDREN	TMDIClient::CmTileChildren	Window I Tile
CM_TILECHILDRENHORIZ	TMDIClient::CmTileChildren	Window I Tile

ID_xxxx file constants   inputdia.rh

Resource and control IDs for the input dialog box.

Constant	Meaning
IDD_INPUTDIALOG	Resource ID number for the input dialog box
ID_INPUT	Control ID for the user input
ID_PROMPT	Control ID for the static text

See also   TInputDialog::SetUpWindow

ID_xxxx printer constants   printer.rh

Resource and control IDs for the printer abort dialog box.

Constant	Meaning
IDD_ABORTDIALOG	Resource ID number for the abort dialog box.
ID_TITLE	Control ID for the selected printer driver.
ID_DEVICE	Control ID for the selected printer.
ID_PAGE	ID number for the page number text control.
ID_PORT	Control ID for the selected printer port.
ID_TOPAGE	ID number for the ending page.

IDA_EDITFILE accelerator ID constant   editfile.rh

Resource ID for accelerator keys.

Constant	Meaning
IDA_EDITFILE	Resource ID for accelerator keys.

IDA_OLEVIEW OLE accelerator ID constant   oleview.rh

Resource ID for accelerator keys.

Constant	Meaning
IDA_OLEVIEW	Resource ID for accelerator keys for OLE enabled applications.

IDG_xxxx gadget ID constants

gadget.h

Identifiers of predefined gadgets created by ObjectWindows.

Constant	Meaning
IDG_FIRST	First predefined gadget ID
IDG_LAST	Last predefined gadget ID
IDG_MESSAGE	For backward compatability
IDG_STATUS_EXT	The ID for an extended selection gadget
IDG_STATUS_CAPS	The ID for a capslock gadget
IDG_STATUS_NUM	The ID for a numlock gadget
IDG_STATUS_SCRL	The ID for a scroll lock gadget
IDG_STATUS_OVR	The ID for an overwrite gadget
IDG_STATUS_REC	The ID for a record gadget
IDG_SIZEGRIP	The ID for a size grip gadget

IDM_EDITFILE menu ID constant

editfile.rh

Resource ID for menu selections.

Constant	Meaning
IDM_EDITFILE	Resource ID for menu selections.

IDM_xxxx OLE menu ID constants

oleview.rh

Menu IDs for OLE-enabled applications.

Constant	Meaning
IDM_OLEPOPUP	The ID for the context menu of an OLE object
IDM_OLEVIEW	The ID for the edit popup menu of an OLE container
IDM_OLEVIEWEMBED	The ID for the default menu of an OLE server

IDS_xxxx edit view ID constants

oleview.rh

String constants used to respond to edit view commands.

Constant	Meaning
IDS_EDITOBJECT	Edit the object
IDS_EDITCONVERT	Convert the object
IDS_CLOSESERVER	Close the server application
IDS_EXITSERVER	Exit the server application

IDS_Mode constants

Resource and command IDs to use with *TStatusBar*.

Constant	Meaning
IDS_MODES	String resource to define mode On indicators
IDS_MODESOFF	String resource to define mode Off indicators

IDS_xxxx document string ID constants

String IDs that define resource IDs used to determine the status of the document.

Constant	Displays these messages
IDS_DOCCHANGED	If the document has been changed, displays the message, "Do you want to save the changes?"
IDS_DOCLIST	Document is a document type.
IDS_DOCMANAGERFILE	This is a document manager file.
IDS_DUPLICATEDOC	This is a duplicate document.
IDS_NODOCMANAGER	There is no document manager.
IDS_NOMEMORYFORVIEW	Not enough memory to view the document.
IDS_NOTCHANGED	The document has not been changed.
IDS_READERROR	Error while reading the file.
IDS_WRITEERROR	Error while writing the file.
IDS_UNABLECLOSE	Document manager is unable to close the document.
IDS_UNABLEOPEN	Document manager is unable to open the document.
IDS_UNTITLED	Document is untitled.
IDS_VIEWLIST	Document is a view type.
IDS_WRITEERROR	Error while writing the file.

IDS_xxxx edit file ID constants

String constants used by edit and file classes to display information about files.

Constant	Meaning
IDS_FILECHANGED	The text in the file has changed. Do you want to save the changes?
IDS_FILEFILTER	Use this filter to display text files.
IDS_UNABLEREAD	Unable to read the file from the disk.
IDS_UNABLEWRITE	Unable to write the file to the disk.
IDS_UNTITLEDFILE	The default window title unless the file is being edited.
IDS_RICHEDITFILTER	Filter containing a list of file types supported by a rich edit control.

IDS_xxxx exception message constants   except.rh

General and application exception message constants. When an exception occurs in the creation of a child window, for example, *TWindow::Create* calls *TXWindow* with an IDS_WINDOWCREATEFAIL message. The following list groups the constants according to message type:

Constant	Meaning
IDS_INVALIDMAINWINDOW	Invalid MainWindow
IDS_INVALIDMODULE	Invalid module specified for window
IDS_NOAPP	No application object
IDS_OKTORESUME	Resume in spite of error
IDS_OWLEXCEPTION	Unknown exception
IDS_OUTOFMEMORY	Out of memory
IDS_UNHANDLEDXMSG	Unhandled xmsg error
IDS_UNKNOWNERROR	Unknown error
IDS_UNKNOWNEXCEPTION	Unknown exception error
IDS_VBXLIBRARYFAIL	VBX library initialization error
IDS_INVALIDMODULEFCN	Function not found in module
IDS_INVALIDMODULEORD	Ordinal not found in module
IDS_COMMCTRL	Failure in the Common Control DLL
Owl 1 compatibility messages:	
IDS_INVALIDCHILDWINDOW	Invalid child window
IDS_INVALIDCLIENTWINDOW	Invalid client window
IDS_INVALIDWINDOW	Invalid window
TXWindow messages:	
IDS_CHILDCREATEFAIL	Child create fail for window
IDS_CHILDREGISTERFAIL	Child class registration fails for window
IDS_CLASSREGISTERFAIL	Class registration fails for window
IDS_LAYOUTCOMPLETE	Layout window failure
IDS_LAYOUTBADRELWIN	Layout window failure
IDS_MENUFAILURE	Menu creation failure
IDS_PRINTERERROR	Printer error
IDS_VALIDATORSYNTAX	Validator syntax error
IDS_WINDOWCREATEFAIL	Create fail for window
IDS_WINDOWEXECUTEFAIL	Execute fail for window
GDI messages:	
IDS_GDIALLOCFAIL	GDI allocate failure
IDS_GDICREATEFAIL	GDI creation failure
IDS_GDIDELETEFAIL	GDI object delete failure
IDS_GDIDESTROYFAIL	GDI object destroy failure
IDS_GDIFAILURE	GDI failure
IDS_GDIFILEREADFAIL	GDI file read failure
IDS_INVALIDDIBHANDLE	Invalid DIB handle

Constant	Meaning
IDS_GDIRESLOADFAIL	GDI resource load failure
IDS_WINGNOTAVAILABLE	WING system DLL is not installed or is corrupted
IDS_WINGFAILURE	An error occured in the WING DLL
TXShell messages:	
IDS_SHELLFAILURE	Shell failure
IDS_SHELLALLOCFAIL	TShellMalloc::Alloc failed
IDS_INVALIDPATH	Invalid path
IDS_BINDTOOBJECTFAIL	IShellFolder::BindToObject failed
IDS_SHGETDESKTOPFAIL	SHGetDesktopFolder failed
IDS_SHGETSPECIALFAIL	SHGetSpecialFolderLocation failed
IDS_GETATTRIBUTESOFFAIL	IShellFolder::GetAttributesOf failed
IDS_GETFILEINFOFAIL	SHGetFileInfo failed
IDS_GETDISPLAYNAMEFAIL	IShellFolder::GetDisplayNameOf failed
IDS_GETPATHFROMPIDLFAIL	SHGetPathFromIDList failed
IDS_SETNAMEOFFAIL	IShellFolder::SetNameOf failed
IDS_GETUIOBJECTOFFAIL	IShellFolder::GetUIObjectOf failed
IDS_COMPAREIDSFAIL	IShellFolder::CompareIDs failed
IDS_TSHELLITEMINVALID	TShellItem is invalid
IDS_ENUMOBJECTSFAIL	IShellFolder::EnumObjects failed
IDS_CLONEFAIL	IEnumIDList::Clone failed
IDS_SHELLITERATORATEND	Attempt to read past end of TShellItemIterator list
IDS_IDLISTNEXTFAIL	IEnumIDList::Next failed
IDS_IDLISTSKIPFAIL	IEnumIDList::Skip failed
IDS_IDLISTRESETFAIL	IEnumIDList::Reset failed
IDS_IDLISTZEROPOINTER	IEnumIDList pointer is zero
IDS_SHGETMALLOCFAIL	SHGetMalloc failed
IDS_GETICONLOCFAIL	IExtractIcon::GetIconLocation failed
IDS_EXTRICONEXTRACTFAIL	IExtractIcon::Extract failed
IDS_SHELLRENAMEFAIL	TShellItem::Rename attempted on item that cannot be renamed
IDS_SHELLCOPYFAIL	TShellItem::Copy attempted on item that cannot be copied
IDS_SHELLMOVEFAIL	TShellItem::Move attempted on item that cannot be moved
IDS_SHELLDELETEFAIL	TShellItem::Delte attempted on item that cannot be deleted
IDS_CREATESHELLLINKFAIL	CoCreateInstance(IShellLink) failed
IDS_LINKQUERYINTRFCFAIL	IShellLink::QueryInterface(IPersistFile) failed
IDS_PERSISTFILELOADFAIL	IPersistFile::Load failed
IDS_LINKGETIDLISTFAIL	IPersistFile::Load failed
IDS_CLIPBOARDBUSY	IShellLink::GetIDList failed

IDS_xxxx listview ID constants

listview.rh

Defines the ID of the string resource used to display selected line entries in a list view.

Constant	Meaning
IDS_LISTNUM	Resource ID of string resource.

IDS_xxxx printer string ID constants

printer.rh

Constants used by printer classes to determine the printer status.

Constant	String displayed
IDS_PRNNODEFAULT	No default printer is configured on this machine.
IDS_PRNCANCEL	Printing is canceled.
IDS_PRNERRORCAPTION	Printer error occurred.
IDS_PRNERRORTEMPLATE	Document was not printed.
IDS_PRNGENERROR	Error encountered during printing.
IDS_PRNMGRABORT	Printing aborted in Print Manager.
IDS_PRNON	Printer is on.
IDS_PRNOUTOFDISK	Out of disk space.
IDS_PRNOUTOFMEMORY	Out of memory.

IDS_xxxx validator ID constants

validate.rh

Defines several constants used by validator classes to determine the validator status.

Constant	Meaning
IDS_VALPXPCONFORM	Item doesn't conform to correct picture format.
IDS_VALINVALIDCHAR	Character isn't one of the valid entries.
IDS_VALNOTINRANGE	Entry isn't within the specified range.
IDS_VALNOTINLIST	String isn't found in the list of valid entries.

IDW_MDICLIENT constant

framewin.h

IDW_MDICLIENT
Child ID constant used to identify MDI client windows.

IDW_FIRSTMDICHILD constant

framewin.h

IDW_FIRSTMDICHILD
Child ID constant used to identify the first MDI client window.

ImParent constant layoutco.h

#define ImParent 0
LmParent is used to construct layout metrics (for example, edge and size constraints).

See also   TLayoutConstraint struct

MSG_SOCKET_NOTIFY constant wsksock.h

#define MSG_SOCKET_NOTIFY ((UINT)(WM_USER+301))
User-defined message used for socked notifications.

MruFileMessage constant rcntfile.h

#define MruFileMessage "MRUFILEMESSAGE"
String that OWL uses to register the message used by the MRU classes.

pfxxxx property attribute constants docview.h

Define document and view property attributes. Documents, views, and applications use these attributes to determine how to process a document or view.

Constant	Meaning
pfGetText	Property is accessible in a text format.
pfGetBinary	Property is accessible as a native nontext format.
pfConstant	Property cannot be changed after the object is created.
pfSettable	Property can be set. Must supply a native format.
pfUnknown	Property is defined but unavailable for the object.
pfHidden	Property should be hidden from the user during normal browsing. (Do not let the user see its name or value.)
pfUserDef	Property has been user-defined at run time.

See also   TDocument, TView

vnxxxx view notification constants docview.h

The view notification constants are used to notify the view of a given event.

Constant	Meaning
vnCommit	Changes are committed to the document.
vnCustomBase	Base event for document notifications.
vnDocOpened	Document has been opened.

Constant	Meaning
vnDocClosed	Document has been closed.
vnIsDirty	Is true if uncommitted changes are present.
vnIsWindow	Is true if the HWND passed belongs to this view.
vnRevert	Document's previous data is reloaded and overwrites the view's current data.
vnViewOpened	A new view has been constructed.
vnViewClosed	A view is about to be destroyed.

See also   TListView, TEditView

4

ObjectWindows enumerated types

This chapter lists in alphabetical order the ObjectWindows enumerated types.

dnxxxx document message enumerator   docmanag.h

Used by *TDocManager* to indicate that a document or view has been created or closed. You can set up response table entries for these messages using the EV_OWLVIEW or EV_OWLDOCUMENT macros.

Constant	Meaning
dnCreate	A new document or view has been created.
dnClose	A document or view has been closed.

See also   TDocManager::TDocManager

ofxxxx document open enumerator   docview.h

Defines the document and open sharing modes used for constructing streams and storing data. Any constants that have the same functionality as those used by OLE 2.0 doc files are indicated in the following table; for example, STGM_TRANSACTED, STGM_CONVERT, STGM_PRIORITY, and STGM_DELETEONRELEASE.

Although files are typically used for data storage, databases or spreadsheets can also be used. I/O streams rather than DOS use these bit values. Documents open the object used for storage in one of the following modes:

Constant	Meaning
ofParent	A storage object is opened using the parent's mode.
ofRead	A storage object is opened for reading.

Constant	Meaning
ofWrite	A storage object is opened for writing.
ofReadWrite	A storage object is opened for reading and writing.
ofAtEnd	Seek to end-of-file when opened originally.
ofAppend	Data is appended to the end of the storage object.
ofTruncate	An already existing file is truncated.
ofNoCreate	Open fails if file doesn't exist.
ofNoReplace	Open fails if file already exists.
ofBinary	Data is stored in a binary, not text, format. Carriage returns are not stripped.
ofIosMask	All of the above bits are used by the *ios* class.
ofTransacted	Changes to the storage object are preserved until the data is either committed to permanent storage or discarded. (STGM_TRANSACTED)
ofPreserve	Backs up previous storage data using before creating a new storage object with the same name. (STGM_CONVERT)
ofPriority	Supports temporary, efficient reading before opening the storage. (STGM_PRIORITY)
ofTemporary	The storage or stream is automatically destroyed when it is destructed. (STGM_DELETEONRELEASE)

See also   TStream, TInStream, TOutStream

shxxxx document sharing enumerator   docview.h

The following file-sharing modes are available when opening document streams.

Constant	Meaning
shCompat	Used for noncompliant applications, but should be avoided if possible.
shNone	DENY_ALL functionality.
shRead	DENY_WRITE functionality.
shWrite	DENY_READ functionality.
shReadWrite	DENY_NONE functionality.
shDefault	Use stream implementation default value.
shMask	Mask for file-sharing bits.

TAbsLocation enumerator   decframe.h

enum TAbsLocation {alNone , alTop , alBottom , alLeft, alRight};

TAbsLocation contains general-use absolute two-dimensional rectangular locations. It is used primarily to describe the locations of a gadget window, such as a tool bar or a status bar, within a decorated frame.

Table 4.1   Constants

Constant	Meaning if set
alNone	No location specified
alTop	Refers to the top edge of the frame
alBottom	Refers to the bottom edge of the frame
alLeft	Refers to the left edge of the frame
alRight	Refers to the right edge of the frame

See also   TDockingSlip, TEdgeSlip, TFloatingSlip, THarbor

TEdge enumerator

latoutc.h

enum TEdge{lmLeft, lmTop, lmRight, lmBottom, lmCenter};
The *TEdge* **enum** describes the following constants that define the boundaries of a window:

Table 4.2   Edge constants

Constant	Meaning
lmLeft	The left edge of the window
lmTop	The top edge of the window
lmRight	The right edge of the window
lmBottom	The bottom edge of the window
lmCenter	The center of the window. The object that owns the constraint, such as TLayoutMetrics, determines whether the center of window is the vertical center or the horizontal center.

See also   TEdgeConstraint

TEventStatus enumerator

window.h

enum TEventStatus{esPartial, esComplete};
Event status constants indicate the status of a mix-in window event implementation, for example, a keyboard event. The *TEventStatus* constants indicate whether or not additional handlers are needed.

Table 4.3   Event status constants

Constant	Meaning
esPartial	Additional handlers can be invoked
esComplete	No additional handlers are needed

See also   TEventHandler::TEventInfo

TMeasurementUnits enumerator

layoutco.h

enum TMeasurementUnits{lmPixels, lmLayoutUnits};

Used by the *TLayoutConstraint* struct, *TMeasurementUnits* enumerates the measurement units (*lmPixels* or *lmLayoutUnits*) that control the dimension of the window. These can be either pixels or layout units that are obtained by dividing the font height into eight vertical and eight horizontal segments.

See also   TLayoutConstraint struct

TNativeUse enumerator

control.h

enum TNativeUse {nuNever, nuAvoid, nuDontCare, nuAttempt, nuAlways, nuSuggestion, nuUsing};
Enumerates the native usage for common controls.

Table 4.4   Constants

Constant	Meaning if set
nuNever	Instance should never use the native control.
nuAvoid	Avoid if possible, unless options require the native control.
nuDontCare	Don't care—control uses whatever is best.
nuAttempt	Attempt to use the native control, unless options are not supported.
nuAlways	Always use the native control, when available.
nuUsing	This bit contains the native control usage for an instance, once it has been determined. It also provides a simple test for usage (NativeUse & nuUsing).
nuSuggestion	The bit mask for getting the suggestion values (NativeUse & nuSuggestion).

TNotificationSet enumerator

wsksock.h

enum TNotificationSet {NotifyNone, NotifyRead, NotifyWrite, NotifyOOB, NotifyAccept, NotifyConnect, NotifyClose, NotifyAll};
TNotificationSet contains enumerations that describe the type of event notifications you want to receive for a given socket. You can OR or add these together to make a notification set.

Table 4.5   Notification constants

Constant	Meaning if set
NotifyNone	No notifications
NotifyRead	Notification of readiness for reading
NotifyWrite	Notification of readiness for writing
NotifyOOB	Notification of the arrival of out-of-band data
NotifyAccept	Notification of incoming connections
NotifyConnect	Notification of completed connections

Constant	Meaning if set
NotifyClose	Notification of socket closure
NotifyAll	All notifications

See also   TSocket

TPicResult enumerator   validate.h

enum TPicResult{prComplete, prIncomplete, prEmpty, prError, prSyntax, prAmbiguous, prIncompNoFill};
TPicResult is the result type returned by the *Picture* member function of
TPXPictureValidator. The result type indicates whether the data entered into the edit
control matches a specified format. For example, *prIncomplete* indicates that the data
entered is missing some information that was specified in the format picture of the data.

See also   TPXPictureValidator::Picture

TPlacement enumerator   gadgetwi.h

enum TPlacement {Before, After};
Enumerates the placement of a gadget. The new gadget is inserted either before or after
another gadget.

You can control the placement of the new gadget by specifying a *sibling* gadget that the
new gadget is inserted before or after. If the sibling argument in *TGadgetWindow::Insert*
is 0 then the new gadget is inserted at the beginning or the end of the existing gadgets.
By default, the new gadget is inserted at the end of the existing gadgets.

See also   TPicResult enum, TGadgetWindow::Insert, TGadgetList

TPrintoutFlags enumerator   printer.h

enum{pfGraphics, pfText, pfBoth};
ObjectWindows defines the following banding constants used to set flags for printout
objects.

Constant	Meaning
pfGraphics	Current band accepts only graphics.
pfText	Current band accepts only text.
pfBoth	Current band accepts both text and graphics.

See also   TPrinter, TPrintOut

TRelationship enumerator
layoutco.h

enum TRelationship {lmAsIs, lmPercentOf, lmAbove, lmLeftOf = lmAbove, lmBelow, lmRightOf = lmBelow, lmSameAs, lmAbsolute};

Used by the *TLayoutConstraint* struct, *TRelationship* specifies the relationship between the edges and sizes of one window and the edges and sizes of another window (which can be a parent or sibling). These relationships can be specified as either the same value as the sibling or parent window (*lmAsIs*), an absolute value (*lmAbsolute*), a percent of one of the windows (*lmPercentOf*), a value that is either added above (*lmAbove*) or left (*lmLeftOf*) of one of the windows, or a value that is subtracted from below (*lmBelow*) or right (*lmRightOf*) of one of the windows.

See also   TLayoutConstraint struct

TRelPosition enumerator
docking.h

enum TRelPosition {rpNone, rpAbove, rpBelow, rpRightOf, rpLeftOf};
TRelPosition contains general use two-dimensional rectangular relative positions. The values are used to describe the location of a docking window; more specifically the location of the EdgeSlip containing docking windows.

Table 4.6   Relative position constants

Constant	Meaning if set
rpNone	No location specified
rpAbove	Refers to the top edge of the frame
rpBelow	Refers to the bottom edge of the frame
rpRightOf	Refers to the right edge of the frame
rpLeftOf	Refers to the Left edge of the frame

See also   TDecoratedFrame::TLocation enum, TDockingSlip, TEdgeSlip, TFloatingSlip, THarbor

TSplitDirection enumerator
splitter.h

enum TSplitDirection {psHorizontal, psVertical, psNone};
TSplitDirection is used to describe whether to split a window in the X or Y plane.

Table 4.7   Split direction constants

Constant	Meaning if set
psHorizontal	Horizontal split
psVertical	Vertical split
psNone	Unspecified split

See also   TSplitter

TTransferDirection enumerator

window.h

enum TTransferDirection {tdGetData, tdSetData, tdSizeData};

The *TTransferDirection* enum describes the following constants that the transfer function uses to determine how to transfer data to and from the transfer buffer:

Constant	Meaning
tdGetData	Retrieve data from the class.
tdSetData	Send data to the class.
tdSizeData	Return the size of data transferred by the class.

See also   TWindow::Transfer, TWindow::TransferData

TValidatorOptions enumerator

validate.h

enum TValidatorOptions {voFill, voTransfer, voOnAppend, voReserved };

Constants that represent bits in the bitmapped Options word in validator objects.

Constant	Meaning
voFill	Used by picture validators to indicate whether to fill in literal characters as the user types.
voTransfer	The validator handles data transfer for the input line. Currently only used by range validators.
voOnAppend	Used by picture validators to determine how to interact with edit controls.
voReserved	The bits in this mask are reserved.

See also   TValidator

TWidthHeight enumerator

layoutco.h

enum TWidthHeight{lmWidth = lmCenter = 1, lmHeight};

Used by the *TLayoutConstraint* struct, *TWidthHeight* enumerates the values that control the width (*lmWidth*) and height (*lmHeight*) of the window.

See also   TLayoutConstraint struct

TWindowFlag enumerator

window.h

enum TWindowFlag{wfAlias, wfAutoCreate, wfDeleteOnClose, wfFromResource, wfShrinkToClient, wfMainWindow, wfFullyCreated, wfStreamTop, wfPredefinedClass, wfTransfer, wfUnHidden, wfUnDisabled};

Define bit masks for the internally used flag attributes of *TWindow*. A *wfXxxx* mask is defined for each of these attributes:

Table 4.8   TWindow attribute masks

Constant	Meaning if set
wfAlias	The window object is an alias for an existing HWND.
wfAutoCreate	Create the HWindow when the parent window is created.
wfDeleteOnClose	Indicates that a modeless dialog's pointer is to be deleted when it receives a WM_CLOSE message, causing its class's destructor to be called immediately. Default behavior is to leave the dialog pointer alone. Setting this flag has no effect on modal dialogs. To set this flag for a modeless dialog object, add the following statement to the constructor of your TDialog -derived class: `SetFlag(wfDeleteOnClose);`
wfFullyCreated	Window is fully created and not being destroyed.
wfFromResource	HWindow comes from an HWND created from a resource definition.
wfMainWindow	Window is a main window.
wfPredefinedClass	The window belongs to a predefined Windows class, not an ObjectWindows class.
wfShrinkToClient	Tells a frame window to shrink itself to fit around the client window.
wfStreamTop	Indicates the topmost window of the collection of windows to be streamed.
wfTransfer	Participates in the *Transfer* mechanism.
wfUnDisabled	Temporarily used when an MDI child window is destroyed.
wfUnHidden	Temporarily used when an MDI child window is destroyed.

See also   TWindow::CreateChildren, TWindow::EnableAutoCreate

xs exception status enumerator   applicat.h

enum {xsUnknown, xsBadCast, xsBadTypeid, xsMsg, xsAlloc, xsBase, xsOwl};
These bit flags define the types of exceptions that are caught and suspended. *SuspendThrow* and *QueryThrow* return the values of these bit flags.

The following table shows the xs exception enum constants:

Constant	Meaning
xsUnknown	Unknown exception
xsBadCast	*Bad_cast* exception
xsBadTypeid	*Bad_typeid* exception
xsMsg	Any exception derived from *xmsg*
xsAlloc	*xalloc* exception
xsBase	TXBase exception
xsOwl	TXOwl exception (for compatibility)

5

ObjectWindows event handlers

These topics include several tables that list predefined ObjectWindows response-table macros and event-handling functions. Each table lists the name of the ObjectWindows macro, any required macro arguments, and the associated event-handling function. The tables are organized in alphabetical order.

Some event-handling functions or messages have no predefined names. In these cases, the generic term *UserName* is used to indicate that you can use any function name you want to as long as the function's signature matches the signature required by the response table macro. Similarly, the term *UserMessage* indicates that you can define your own message ID.

The descriptions of these macros and functions use the following conventions when listing the arguments of the message macros:

- ID refers to the child window's ID (for example, ID_GROUPBOX)

- CMD ID refers to the command ID (for example, CM_FILENEW)

- Code refers to the notification code (for example, BN_CLICKED) that is being sent.

See also   Event Handling Overview

Button notification messages

These button macros handle BN_xxxx notification codes. To determine the name of the notification code that corresponds to the EV_XXXX macro, remove the EV_ prefix.

Macro	Macro arguments	Response function declaration
EV_BN_CLICKED	ID, *UserName*	void *UserName*()
EV_BN_DISABLE	ID, *UserName*	void *UserName*()
EV_BN_DOUBLECLICKED	ID, *UserName*	void *UserName*()

Macro	Macro arguments	Response function declaration
EV_BN_HILITE	ID, *UserName*	void *UserName()*
EV_BN_PAINT	ID, *UserName*	void *UserName()*
EV_BN_UNHILITE	ID, *UserName*	void *UserName()*

Child ID notification messages

The following macros handle messages that a child window sends to its parent:

Macro	Macro arguments	Response function declaration
EV_CHILD_NOTIFY_AND_CODE	ID, Code, *UserName*	void *UserName(WPARAM)*
EV_CHILD_NOTIFY_ALL_CODES	ID, *UserName*	void *UserName(UINT)*
EV_NOTIFY_AT_CHILD	Code, *UserName*	void *UserName*
EV_CHILD_NOTIFY	ID, Code, *UserName*	void *UserName*

Combo box notification messages

These combo box macros handle CBN_xxxx notification codes. To determine the name of the notification code that corresponds to the EV_XXXX macro, remove the EV_ prefix.

Macro	Macro arguments	Response function declaration
EV_CBN_CLOSEUP	ID, *UserName*	void *UserName()*
EV_CBN_DBLCLK	ID, *UserName*	void *UserName()*
EV_CBN_DROPDOWN	ID, *UserName*	void *UserName()*
EV_CBN_EDITCHANGE	ID, *UserName*	void *UserName()*
EV_CBN_EDITUPDATE	ID, *UserName*	void *UserName()*
EV_CBN_ERRSPACE	ID, *UserName*	void *UserName()*
EV_CBN_KILLFOCUS	ID, *UserName*	void *UserName()*
EV_CBN_SELCHANGE	ID, *UserName*	void *UserName()*
EV_CBN_SELENDCANCEL	ID, *UserName*	void *UserName()*
EV_CBN_SELENDOK	ID, *UserName*	void *UserName()*
EV_CBN_SETFOCUS	ID, *UserName*	void *UserName()*

Command messages

These macros handle WM_COMMAND messages:

Macro	Macro arguments	Response function declaration
EV_COMMAND	CMD ID, *UserName*	void *UserName()*
EV_COMMAND_AND_ID	CMD ID, *UserName*	void *UserName*(WPARAM)
EV_COMMAND_ENABLE	CMD ID, *UserName*	void *UserName*(TCommandEnabler&)

Common control notification messages

These common control macros handle NM_xxxx notification codes. To determine the name of the notification code that corresponds to the EV_XXXX macro, remove the EV_ prefix.

Macro	Macro arguments	Response function declaration
EV_NM_CLICK	ID, *UserName*	void *UserName*()
EV_NM_DBLCLK	ID, *UserName*	void *UserName*()
EV_NM_KILLFOCUS	ID, *UserName*	void *UserName*()
EV_NM_OUTOFMEMORY	ID, *UserName*	void *UserName*()
EV_NM_RCLICK	ID, *UserName*	void *UserName*()
EV_NM_RDBLCLK	ID, *UserName*	void *UserName*()
EV_NM_RETURN	ID, *UserName*	void *UserName*()
EV_NM_SETFOCUS	ID, *UserName*	void *UserName*()

Custom OWL window messages

These macros handle OWL-defined window messages used internally by the framework:

Macro	Macro arguments	Response function declaration
EV_WM_CANCLOSE	ID, *UserName*	bool EvCanClose()
EV_WM_PREPROCMENU	ID, *UserName*	void EvPreProcMenu(HMENU)
EV_WM_WAKEUP	ID, *UserName*	void EvWakeUp()

Document manager messages

These macros handle messages generated by the document manager:

Macro	Macro arguments	Response function declaration
EV_OWLDOCUMENT	ID, *UserName*	`void UserName(TDocument& document)`
EV_OWLNOTIFY	ID, *UserName*	`bool UserName(LPARAM&)`
EV_OWLVIEW	ID, *UserName*	`void UserName(TView& view)`
EV_VIEWNOTIFY	ID, *UserName*	`bool UserName(int32)`

Document view messages

These macros handle view-related messages generated by the document manager. *VnHandler* is a generic term for the view notification handler function.

Macro	Response function declaration
EV_VN_COMMIT	`bool VnCommit(bool force)`
EV_VN_DOCCLOSED	`bool VnDocClosed(int openMode)`
EV_VN_DOCOPENED	`bool VnDocOpened(int openMode)`
EV_VN_ISDIRTY	`bool VnIsDirty()`
EV_VN_ISWINDOW	`bool VnIsWindow(HWND hWnd)`
EV_VN_VIEWCLOSED	`bool VnViewClosed(TView* view)`
EV_VN_VIEWOPENED	`bool VnViewOpened(TView* view)`
EV_VN_REVERT	`bool VnRevert(bool clear)`

Edit control notification messages

These edit control macros handle EN_xxxx notification codes. To determine the name of the notification code that corresponds to the EV_XXXX macro, remove the EV_ prefix.

Macro	Macro arguments	Response function declaration
EV_EN_CHANGE	ID, *UserName*	`void UserName()`
EV_EN_ERRSPACE	ID, *UserName*	`void UserName()`
EV_EN_HSCROLL	ID, *UserName*	`void UserName()`
EV_EN_KILLFOCUS	ID, *UserName*	`void UserName()`
EV_EN_MAXTEXT	ID, *UserName*	`void UserName()`
EV_EN_SETFOCUS	ID, *UserName*	`void UserName()`
EV_EN_UPDATE	ID, *UserName*	`void UserName()`
EV_EN_VSCROLL	ID, *UserName*	`void UserName()`

Header control notification messages

These header control macros handle EN_xxxx notification codes. To determine the name of the notification code that corresponds to the EV_XXXX macro, remove the EV_ prefix.

Macro	Macro arguments	Response function declaration
EV_HDN_BEGINTRACK	ID, *UserName*	void *UserName*(THdrNotify& nmHdr)
EV_HDN_DIVIDERDBLCLICK	ID, *UserName*	void *UserName*(THdrNotify& nmHdr)
EV_HDN_ENDTRACK	ID, *UserName*	void *UserName*(THdrNotify& nmHdr)
EV_HDN_ITEMCHANGED	ID, *UserName*	void *UserName*(THdrNotify& nmHdr)
EV_HDN_ITEMCHANGING	ID, *UserName*	bool *UserName*(THdrNotify& nmHdr)
EV_HDN_ITEMCLICK	ID, *UserName*	void *UserName*(THdrNotify& nmHdr)
EV_HDN_TRACK	ID, *UserName*	bool *UserName*(THdrNotify& nmHdr)

List box notification messages

These list box macros handle LBN_xxxx notification codes. To determine the name of the notification code that corresponds to the EV_XXXX macro, remove the EV_ prefix.

Macro	Macro arguments	Response function declaration
EV_LBN_DBLCLK	ID, *UserName*	void *UserName*()
EV_LBN_ERRSPACE	ID, *UserName*	void *UserName*()
EV_LBN_KILLFOCUS	ID, *UserName*	void *UserName*()
EV_LBN_SELCANCEL	ID, *UserName*	void *UserName*()
EV_LBN_SELCHANGE	ID, *UserName*	void *UserName*()
EV_LBN_SETFOCUS	ID, *UserName*	void *UserName*()

List view notification messages

These list view macros handle LVN_xxxx notification codes. To determine the name of the notification code that corresponds to the EV_XXXX macro, remove the EV_ prefix.

Macro	Macro arguments	Response function declaration
EV_LVN_KEYDOWN	ID, *UserName*	void *UserName*(TTwKeyDownNotify& nbHdr)
EV_LVN_BEGINDRAG	ID, *UserName*	void *UserName*(TLwNotify& nmHdr)
EV_LVN_BEGINLABELEDIT	ID, *UserName*	bool *UserName*(TLwDispInfoNotify& nmHdr)
EV_LVN_BEGINRDRAG	ID, *UserName*	void *UserName*(TLwNotify& nmHdr)
EV_LVN_COLUMNCLICK	ID, *UserName*	void *UserName*(TLwNotify& nmHdr)
EV_LVN_DELETEALLITEMS	ID, *UserName*	void *UserName*(TLwNotify& nmHdr)

Macro	Macro arguments	Response function declaration
EV_LVN_DELETEITEM	ID, *UserName*	void *UserName*(TLwNotify& nmHdr)
EV_LVN_ENDDRAG	ID, *UserName*	void *UserName*(TLwNotify& nmHdr)
EV_LVN_ENDLABELEDIT	ID, *UserName*	void *UserName*(TLwDispInfoNotify& nmHdr)
EV_LVN_GETDISPINFO	ID, *UserName*	void *UserName*(TLwDispInfoNotify& nmHdr)
EV_LVN_INSERTITEM	ID, *UserName*	void *UserName*(TLwNotify& nmHdr)
EV_LVN_ITEMCHANGED	ID, *UserName*	void *UserName*(TLwNotify& nmHdr)
EV_LVN_ITEMCHANGING	ID, *UserName*	bool *UserName*(TLwDispInfoNotify& nmHdr)
EV_LVN_SETDISPINFO	ID, *UserName*	void *UserName*(TLwDispInfoNotify& nmHdr)

ObjectComponents messages

The following macros handle ObjectComponents messages:

Macro	Response function declaration
EV_OC_APPBORDERSPACEREQ	bool EvOcAppBorderSpaceReq(TRect far* rect)
EV_OC_APPBORDERSPACESET	bool EvOcAppBorderSpaceSet(TRect far* rect)
EV_OC_APPDIALOGHELP	void EvOcAppDialogHelp(TOcDialogHelp far& dh)
EV_OC_APPFRAMERECT	bool EvOcAppFrameRect(TRect far* rect)
EV_OC_APPINSMENUS	bool EvOcAppInsMenus(TOcMenuDescr far&)
EV_OC_APPMENUS	bool EvOcAppMenus(TOcMenuDescr far& md)
EV_OC_APPPROCESSMSG	bool EvOcAppProcessMsg(MSG far* msg)
EV_OC_APPRESTOREUI	void EvOcAppRestoreUI()
EV_OC_APPSHUTDOWN	void EvOcAppShutDown()
EV_OC_APPSTATUSTEXT	void EvOcAppStatusText(const char far* rect)
EV_OC_VIEWATTACHWINDOW	bool EvOcViewAttachWindow()
EV_OC_VIEWBORDERSPACEREQ	bool EvOcViewBorderSpaceReq(TRect far* rect)
EV_OC_VIEWBORDERSPACESET	bool EvOcViewBorderSpaceSet(TRect far& rect)
EV_OC_VIEWBREAKLINK	bool EvOcViewBreakLink(TOcLinkView& view)
EV_OC_VIEWCLIPDATA	HANDLE EvOcViewClipData(TOcFormat far& format)
EV_OC_VIEWCLOSE	bool EvOcViewClose()
EV_OC_VIEWDOVERB	bool EvOcViewDoVerb(UINT)
EV_OC_VIEWDRAG	bool EvOcViewDrag(TOcDragDrop far& ddInfo)
EV_OC_VIEWDROP	bool EvOcViewDrop(TOcDragDrop far& ddInfo)
EV_OC_VIEWGETITEMNAME	bool EvOcViewGetItemName(TOcItemName&)
EV_OC_VIEWGETPALETTE	bool EvOcViewGetPalette(LOGPALETTE far* far*)
EV_OC_VIEWGETSCALE	bool EvOcViewGetScale(TOcScaleFactor&)
EV_OC_VIEWGETSITERECT	bool EvOcViewGetSiteRect(TRect far* rect)
EV_OC_VIEWINSMENUS	bool EvOcViewInsMenus(TOcMenuDescr far&)
EV_OC_VIEWLOADPART	bool EvOcViewLoadPart(TOcSaveLoad far& ocLoad)
EV_OC_VIEWOPENDOC	bool EvOcViewOpenDoc(const char far* path)

Macro	Response function declaration
EV_OC_VIEWPAINT	bool EvOcViewPaint(TOcViewPaint far& vp)
EV_OC_VIEWPARTACTIVATE	bool EvOcViewPartActivate(TOcPart& ocPart)
EV_OC_VIEWPARTINVALID	bool EvOcViewPartInvalid(TOcPart far& part)
EV_OC_VIEWPARTSIZE	bool EvOcViewPartSize(TRect far* size)
EV_OC_VIEWPASTEOBJECT	bool EvOcViewPasteObject(TOcInitInfo&)
EV_OC_VIEWSAVEPART	bool EvOcViewSavePart(TOcSaveLoad far& ocSave)
EV_OC_VIEWSCROLL	bool EvOcViewScroll (TOcScrollDir scrollDir)
EV_OC_VIEWSETDATA	bool EvOcViewSetData(TOcFormatData&)
EV_OC_VIEWSETLINK	bool EvOcViewSetLink(TOcLinkView& view)
EV_OC_VIEWSETSCALE	bool EvOcViewSetScale(TOcScaleFactor&)
EV_OC_VIEWSETSITERECT	bool EvOcViewSetSiteRect(TRect far* rect)
EV_OC_VIEWSETTITLE	void EvOcViewSetTitle(CONST char far*)
EV_OC_VIEWSHOWTOOLS	bool EvOcViewShowTools(TOcToolBarInfo far& tbi)
EV_OC_VIEWTITLE	const char far* EvOcViewTitle()

Property sheet notification messages

The following property sheet macros handle PSN_xxxx notification codes. To determine the name of the notification code that corresponds to the EV_XXXX macro, remove the EV_ prefix.

Macro	Macro arguments	Response function declaration
EV_PSN_APPLY	UserName	int UserName(TNotify& nmHdr)
EV_PSN_HASHELP	UserName	bool UserName(TNotify& nmHdr)
EV_PSN_HELP	UserName	void UserName(TNotify& nmHdr)
EV_PSN_KILLACTIVE	UserName	bool UserName(TNotify& nmHdr)
EV_PSN_QUERYCANCEL	UserName	bool UserName(TNotify& nmHdr)
EV_PSN_RESET	UserName	void UserName(TNotify& nmHdr)
EV_PSN_SETACTIVE	UserName	int UserName(TNotify& nmHdr)
EV_PSN_WIZBACK	UserName	int UserName(TNotify& nmHdr)
EV_PSN_WIZFINISH	UserName	bool UserName(TNotify& nmHdr)
EV_PSN_WIZNEXT	UserName	int UserName(TNotify& nmHdr)

Rich edit notification messages

The following rich edit macros handle EN_xxxx notification codes. To determine the name of the notification code that corresponds to the EV_XXXX macro, remove the EV_ prefix.

Macro	Macro arguments	Response function declaration
EV_EN_DROPFILES	ID, *UserName*	`bool` *UserName*`(TEnDropFiles& nmHdr)`
EV_EN_MSGFILTER	ID, *UserName*	`bool` *UserName*`(TMsgFilter& nmHdr)`
EV_EN_PROTECTED	ID, *UserName*	`bool` *UserName*`(TEnProtected& nmHdr)`
EV_EN_REQRESIZE	ID, *UserName*	`void` *UserName*`(TReqSize& nmHdr)`
EV_RICHED_EN_SELCHANGE	ID, *UserName*	`bool` *UserName*`(TSelChange& nmHdr)`

Caution   EV_EN_SELCHANGE is not a valid message for *rich edit* controls. It is reserved for edit controls. Make sure that you use EV_RICHED_EN_SELCHANGE when using a rich edit control.

Scroll bar notification messages

The following scrollbar control macros handle SB_xxxx notification codes. To determine the name of the notification code that corresponds to the EV_XXXX macro, remove the EV_ prefix.

Macro	Macro arguments	Response function declaration
EV_SB_BEGINTRACK	ID, *UserName*	`void` *UserName*`()`
EV_SB_BOTTOM	ID, *UserName*	`void` *UserName*`()`
EV_SB_ENDSCROLL	ID, *UserName*	`void` *UserName*`()`
EV_SB_LINEDOWN	ID, *UserName*	`void` *UserName*`()`
EV_SB_LINEUP	ID, *UserName*	`void` *UserName*`()`
EV_SB_PAGEDOWN	ID *UserName*	`void` *UserName*`()`
EV_SB_PAGEUP	ID, *UserName*	`void` *UserName*`()`
EV_SB_THUMBPOSITION	ID, *UserName*	`void` *UserName*`()`
EV_SB_TOP	ID, *UserName*	`void` *UserName*`()`

Standard Windows messages

These macros handle Windows messages. These macros are defined in windowev.h. To determine the name of the Windows message that corresponds to the EV_XXXX macro, remove the EV_ prefix. For example, WM_ACTIVATE is the name of the Windows message that the EV_WM_ACTIVATE macro handles. These macros, which crack the standard Windows messages (break the LPARAM and WPARAM parameters into separate parts), take no arguments. They pass the cracked parameters directly to the predefined *EVxxxx* message function. The standard Windows messages are described in your Windows documentation.

Macro	Response function declaration
EV_WM_ACTIVATE	void EvActivate(uint active, bool minimized, HWND hWndOther)
EV_WM_ACTIVATEAPP	void EvActivateApp(bool active, HANDLE threadId) (WIN32 only)
EV_WM_ACTIVATEAPP	void EvActivateApp(bool active, HTASK hTask) (WIN16 only)
EV_WM_ASKCBFORMATNAME	void EvAskCBFormatName(uint bufLen, char far* buffer)
EV_WM_CANCELMODE	void EvCancelMode()
EV_WM_CHANGECBCHAIN	void EvChangeCBChain(uint bufLen, char far* buffer)
EV_WM_CHAR	void EvChar(uint key, uint repeatCount, uint flags)
EV_WM_CHARTOITEM	int EvCharToItem(uint key, HWND hWndListBox, uint caretPos)
EV_WM_CHILDACTIVATE	void EvChildActivate()
EV_WM_CHILDINVALID	void EvChildInvalid(HWND)
EV_WM_CLOSE	void EvClose()
EV_WM_COMMNOTIFY	void EvCommNotify(UINT, UINT)
EV_WM_COMPACTING	void EvCompacting(uint compactRatio)
EV_WM_COMPAREITEM	LRESULT EvCompareItem(uint ctrlId, COMPAREITEMSTRUCT far& compareInfo)
EV_WM_CREATE	int EvCreate(CREATESTRUCT far &)
EV_WM_CTLCOLOR	HBRUSH EvCtlColor(HDC, HWND hWndChild, uint ctlType)
EV_WM_DEADCHAR	void EvDeadChar(uint deadKey, uint repeatCount, uint flags)
EV_WM_DELETEITEM	void EvDeleteItem(uint ctrlId, DELETEITEMSTRUCT far& deleteInfo)
EV_WM_DESTROY	void EvDestroy()
EV_WM_DESTROYCLIPBOARD	void EvDestroyClipboard()
EV_WM_DEVMODECHANGE	void EvDevModeChange(char far* devMode)
EV_WM_DRAWCLIPBOARD	void EvDrawClipboard()
EV_WM_DRAWITEM	void EvDrawItem(uint ctrlId, DRAWITEMSTRUCT far& drawInfo)
EV_WM_DROPFILES	void EvDropFiles(TDropInfo dropInfo)
EV_WM_ENABLE	void EvEnable(bool enabled)
EV_WM_ENDSESSION	void EvEndSession(bool endSession)
EV_WM_ENTERIDLE	void EvEnterIdle(uint source, HWND hWndDlg)
EV_WM_ERASEBKGND	bool EvEraseBkgnd(HDC)
EV_WM_FONTCHANGE	void EvFontChange()
EV_WM_GETDLGCODE	uint EvGetDlgCode(MSG far*)
EV_WM_GETFONT	HFONT EvGetFont();
EV_WM_GETMINMAXINFO	void EvGetMinMaxInfo(MINMAXINFO far &)
EV_WM_GETTEXT	void EvGetText(uint bufLen, char far* buffer)

Macro	Response function declaration
EV_WM_GETTEXTLENGTH	uint EvGetTextLength() (WIN32 only)
EV_WM_HOTKEY	void EvHotKey(int idHotKey)
EV_WM_HSCROLL	void EvHScroll(uint scrollCode, uint thumbPos, HWND hWndCtl)
EV_WM_HSCROLLCLIPBOARD	void EvHScrollClipboard(HWND hWndCBViewer, uint scrollCode, uint pos)
EV_WM_ICONERASEBKGND	void EvIconEraseBkgnd(HDC)
EV_WM_INITMENU	void EvInitMenu(HMENU)
EV_WM_INITMENUPOPUP	void EvInitMenuPopup(HMENU hPopupMenu, uint index, bool sysMenu)
EV_WM_INPUTFOCUS	void EvInputFocus(bool gainingFocus) (WIN32 only)
EV_WM_KEYDOWN	void EvKeyDown(uint key, uint repeatCount, uint flags)
EV_WM_KEYUP	void EvKeyUp(uint key, uint repeatCount, uint flags)
EV_WM_KILLFOCUS	void EvKillFocus(HWND hWndGetFocus)
EV_WM_LBUTTONDBLCLK	void EvLButtonDblClk(uint modKeys, TPoint& point)
EV_WM_LBUTTONDOWN	void EvLButtonDown(uint modKeys, TPoint& point)
EV_WM_LBUTTONUP	void EvLButtonUp(uint modKeys, TPoint& point)
EV_WM_MBUTTONDBLCLK	void EvMButtonDblClk(uint modKeys, TPoint& point)
EV_WM_MBUTTONDOWN	void EvMButtonDown(uint modKeys, TPoint& point)
EV_WM_MBUTTONUP	void EvMButtonUp(uint modKeys, TPoint& point)
EV_WM_MDIACTIVATE	void EvMDIActivate(HWND hWndActivated, HWND hWndDeactivated)
EV_WM_MDICREATE	LRESULT EvMDICreate(MDICREATESTRUCT far& createStruct)
EV_WM_MDIDESTROY	void EvMDIDestroy(HWND hWnd)
EV_WM_MENUCHAR	uint EvMenuChar(uint nChar, uint menuType, HMENU hMenu)
EV_WM_MENUSELECT	void EvMenuSelect(uint menuItemId, uint flags, HMENU hMenu)
EV_WM_MEASUREITEM	void EvMeasureItem(uint ctrlId, MEASUREITEMSTRUCT far& measureInfo)
EV_WM_MOUSEACTIVATE	uint EvMouseActivate(HWND hWndTopLevel, uint hitTestCode, uint msg)
EV_WM_MOUSEMOVE	void EvMouseMove(uint modKeys, TPoint& point)
EV_WM_MOVE	void EvMove(TPoint &clientOrigin)
EV_WM_NCACTIVATE	bool EvNCActivate(bool active)
EV_WM_NCCALCSIZE	uint EvNCCalcSize(bool calcValidRects, NCCALCSIZE_PARAMS far &)
EV_WM_NCCREATE	bool EvNCCreate(CREATESTRUCT far &)
EV_WM_NCDESTROY	void EvNCDestroy()
EV_WM_NCHITTEST	uint EvNCHitTest(TPoint& point)

Macro	Response function declaration
EV_WM_NCLBUTTONDBLCLK	void EvNCLButtonDblClk(uint hitTest, TPoint& point)
EV_WM_NCLBUTTONDOWN	void EvNCLButtonDown(uint hitTest, TPoint& point)
EV_WM_NCLBUTTONUP	void EvNCLButtonUp(uint hitTest, TPoint& point)
EV_WM_NCMBUTTONDBLCLK	void EvNCMButtonDblClk(uint hitTest, TPoint& point)
EV_WM_NCMBUTTONDOWN	void EvNCMButtonDown(uint hitTest, TPoint& point)
EV_WM_NCMBUTTONUP	void EvNCMButtonUp(uint hitTest, TPoint& point)
EV_WM_NCMOUSEMOVE	void EvNCMouseMove(uint hitTest, TPoint& point)
EV_WM_NCPAINT	void EvNCPaint()
EV_WM_NCRBUTTONDBLCLK	void EvNCRButtonDblClk(uint hitTest, TPoint& point)
EV_WM_NCRBUTTONDOWN	void void EvNCRButtonDown(uint hitTest, TPoint& point)
EV_WM_NCRBUTTONUP	void EvNCRButtonUp(uint hitTest, TPoint& point)
EV_WM_NEXTDLGCTL	void EvNextDlgCtl(UINT, UINT)
EV_WM_OTHERWINDOWCREATED	void EvOtherWindowCreated(HWND hWndOther) (WIN32 only)
EV_WM_OTHERWINDOWDESTROYED	void EvOtherWindowDestroyed(HWND hWndOther) (WIN32 only)
EV_WM_PAINT	void EvPaint()
EV_WM_PAINTCLIPBOARD	void EvPaintClipboard(HWND, HANDLE hPaintStruct) (WIN32 only)
EV_WM_PAINTICON	void EvPaintIcon()
EV_WM_PALETTECHANGED	void EvPaletteChanged(HWND hWndPalChg)
EV_WM_PALETTEISCHANGING	void EvPaletteIsChanging(HWND hWndPalChg)
EV_WM_PARENTNOTIFY	void EvParentNotify(uint event, uint childHandleOrX, uint childIDOrY)
EV_WM_POWER	int EvPower(uint powerEvent)
EV_WM_QUERYDRAGICON	HANDLE EvQueryDragIcon()
EV_WM_QUERYENDSESSION	bool EvQueryEndSession()
EV_WM_QUERYNEWPALETTE	bool EvQueryNewPalette()
EV_WM_QUERYOPEN	bool EvQueryOpen()
EV_WM_QUEUESYNC	void EvQueueSync()
EV_WM_RBUTTONDBLCLK	void EvRButtonDblClk(uint modKeys, TPoint& point)
EV_WM_RBUTTONDOWN	void EvRButtonDown(uint modKeys, TPoint& point)
EV_WM_RBUTTONUP	void EvRButtonUp(uint modKeys, TPoint& point)
EV_WM_RENDERALLFORMATS	void EvRenderAllFormats()
EV_WM_RENDERFORMAT	void EvRenderFormat(uint dataFormat)
EV_WM_SETCURSOR	bool EvSetCursor(HWND hWndCursor, uint hitTest, uint mouseMsg)

Macro	Response function declaration
EV_WM_SETFOCUS	void EvSetFocus(HWND hWndLostFocus)
EV_WM_SETFONT	void EvSetFont(HFONT hFont, bool redraw)
EV_WM_SETREDRAW	void EvSetRedraw(bool)
EV_WM_SETTEXT	void EvSetText(CONST char far* text)
EV_WM_SHOWWINDOW	void EvShowWindow(bool show, uint status)
EV_WM_SIZE	void EvSize(uint sizeType, TSize& size)
EV_WM_SIZECLIPBOARD	void EvSizeClipboard(HWND hWndViewer, HANDLE hRect)
EV_WM_SPOOLERSTATUS	void EvSpoolerStatus(uint jobStatus, uint jobsLeft)
EV_WM_SYSCHAR	void EvSysChar(uint key, uint repeatCount, uint flags)
EV_WM_SYSCOLORCHANGE	void EvSysColorChange()
EV_WM_SYSCOMMAND	void EvSysCommand(uint cmdType, TPoint& point)
EV_WM_SYSDEADCHAR	void EvSysDeadChar(uint key, uint repeatCount, uint flags)
EV_WM_SYSKEYDOWN	void EvSysKeyDown(uint key, uint repeatCount, uint flags)
EV_WM_SYSKEYUP	void EvSysKeyUp(uint key, uint repeatCount, uint flags)
EV_WM_SYSTEMERROR	void EvSystemError(uint error)
EV_WM_TIMECHANGE	void EvTimeChange()
EV_WM_TIMER	void EvTimer(uint timerId)
EV_WM_VKEYTOITEM	int EvVKeyToItem(uint key, HWND hWndListBox, uint caretPos)
EV_WM_VSCROLL	void EvVScroll(uint scrollCode, uint thumbPos, HWND hWndCtl)
EV_WM_VSCROLLCLIPBOARD	void EvVScrollClipboard(HWND hWndCBViewer, uint scrollCode, uint pos)
EV_WM_WINDOWPOSCHANGED	void EvWindowPosChanged(WINDOWPOS far &windowPos)
EV_WM_WINDOWPOSCHANGING	void EvWindowPosChanging(WINDOWPOS far &windowPos)
EV_WM_WININICHANGE	void EvWinIniChange(char far* section)

Standard Windows messages 4.0

These macros handle Windows messages (4.0). These macros are defined in windowev.h. To determine the name of the Windows message that corresponds to the EV_XXXX macro, remove the EV_ prefix. For example, WM_CAPTURECHANGED is the name of the Windows message that the EV_WM_CAPTURECHANGED macro handles. These macros, which crack the standard Windows messages (break the LPARAM and WPARAM parameters into separate parts), take no arguments. They pass the cracked parameters directly to the predefined *EVxxxx* message function. The standard Windows messages are described in your Windows documentation.

Macro
EV_WM_CAPTURECHANGED
EV_WM_CONTEXTMENU
EV_WM_DEVICECHANGE
EV_WM_DISPLAYCHANGE
EV_WM_ENTERMENULOOP
EV_WM_EXITMENULOOP
EV_WM_EXITSIZEMOVE
EV_WM_GETICON
EV_WM_HELP
EV_WM_INPUTLANGCHANGE
EV_WM_INPUTLANGCHANGEREQUEST
EV_WM_MOVING
EV_WM_NEXTMENU
EV_WM_POWERBROADCAST
EV_WM_PRINT
EV_WM_PRINTCLIENT
EV_WM_SETICON
EV_WM_SETTINGCHANGE
EV_WM_SIZING
EV_WM_STYLECHANGED
EV_WM_STYLECHANGING
EV_WM_TCARD
EV_WM_USERCHANGED

Tab control notification messages

The following tab control macros handle TCN_xxxx notification codes. To determine the name of the notification code that corresponds to the EV_XXXX macro, remove the EV_ prefix.

Macro	Macro arguments	Response function declaration
EV_TCN_KEYDOWN	ID, *UserName*	void *UserName*(THdrNotify& nmHdr)
EV_TCN_SELCHANGE	ID, *UserName*	void *UserName*(TNotify& nmHdr)
EV_TCN_SELCHANGING	ID, *UserName*	bool *UserName*(TNotify& nmHdr)

Tree view notification messages

The following tree view macros handle TVN_xxxx notification codes. To determine the name of the notification code that corresponds to the EV_XXXX macro, remove the EV_ prefix.

Macro	Macro arguments	Response function declaration
EV_TTN_NEEDTEXT	ID, *UserName*	`void UserName(TTooltipText& nmHdr)`
EV_TVN_BEGINDRAG	ID, *UserName*	`void UserName(TTwNotify& nmHdr)`
EV_TVN_BEGINLABELEDIT	ID, *UserName*	`bool UserName(TTwDispInfoNotify& nmHdr)`
EV_TVN_DELETEITEM	ID, *UserName*	`void UserName(TTwNotify& nmHdr)`
EV_TVN_ENDLABELEDIT	ID, *UserName*	`void UserName(TTwNotify& nmHdr)`
EV_TVN_GETDISPINFO	ID, *UserName*	`void UserName(TTwNotify& nmHdr)`
EV_TVN_ITEMEXPANDED	ID, *UserName*	`void UserName(TTwNotify& nmHdr)`
EV_TVN_ITEMEXPANDING	ID, *UserName*	`bool UserName(TTwNotify& nmHdr)`
EV_TVN_SELCHANGED	ID, *UserName*	`void UserName(TTwNotify& nmHdr)`
EV_TVN_SELCHANGING	ID, *UserName*	`bool UserName(TTwNotify& nmHdr)`
EV_TVN_SETDISPINFO	ID, *UserName*	`void UserName(TTwNotify& nmHdr)`
EV_TVN_KEYDOWN	ID, *UserName*	`void UserName(TTwKeyDownNotify&nmHdr)`

UpDown notification messages

The following Up/Down control macro handles UDN_xxxx notification codes. To determine the name of the notification code that corresponds to the EV_XXXX macro, remove the EV_ prefix.

Macro	Macro arguments	Response function declaration
EV_UDN_DELTAPOS	ID, *UserName*	`void UserName()`

User-defined messages

The following macros handle user-defined messages:

Macro	Macro arguments	Response function declaration
EV_MESSAGE	UserMessage, *UserName*	`LRESULT UserName(WPARAM, LPARAM)`
EV_REGISTERED	Registered name, *UserName*	`LRESULT UserName(WPARAM, LPARAM)`

VBX messages

The following macros handle WM_VBXFIREEVENT messages generated by VBX controls. *EvHandler* is a generic term for a specific VBX control message (such as *EvClick*).

Macro	Macro arguments	Response function declaration
EV_VBXEVENTINDEX	ID, event, *EvHandler*	void *EvHandler*(VBXEVENT FAR *event)
EV_VBXEVENTNAME	ID, event, *EvHandler*	void *EvHandler*(VBXEVENT FAR *event)

6

ObjectWindows global functions

This chapter is an alphabetical summary of the ObjectWindows global functions.

GetApplicationObject function   appdict.h

TApplication* GetApplicationObject(unsigned pid = 0);
This global function is included mainly for backward compatibility with previous
ObjectWindows applications. To find the application object associated with a process
ID, *GetApplicationObject* calls *TAppDictionary::GetApplication* on an application
dictionary.

See also   GetWindowPtr function, TAppDictionary::GetApplication

GetWindowPtr function   window.h

TWindow* GetWindowPtr(HWND hWnd);
This global function is included mainly for backward compatibility with previous
ObjectWindows applications. First, *GetWindowPtr* calls the global function
GetApplicationObject to find the application. It then calls *TApplication::GetWindowPtr* to
get the TWindow pointer associated with the window.

See also   GetApplicationObject function, TApplication::GetWindowPtr

LongMulDiv function   scroller.h

inline long LongMulDiv(long mul1, long mul2, long div1);
TScroller uses this function to convert horizontal range values (*XRange*) from the scroll
bar to horizontal scroll values (*XScrollValue*) and vice versa, or to convert vertical range

values (*YRange*) from the scroll bar to vertical scroll values (*YScrollValue*) and vice versa. It multiplies *mul1* by *mul2* and divides the result by *div1*.

See also TScroller

OWLGetVersion function defs.h

uint16 far _OWLFUNC OWLGetVersion();
Returns the version number of the ObjectWindows library. The version number is represented as an unsigned short.

ObjectWindows macros

This section describes the ObjectWindows macros. The chapter is divided into sections, each of which describes a macro type. The macros are listed alphabetically within each section.

Build macros

The following macros are used when building ObjectWindows libraries and DLLs.

_BUILDOWLDLL macro   defs.h

_BUILDOWLDLL
Used internally to control values for the _OWLCLASS, _OWLDATA, and _OWLFUNC macros. This macro is defined when building the ObjectWindows DLL. It must be defined and included in ObjectWindows makefiles to build the ObjectWindows DLL.

NATIVE_CTRL macro   defs.h

NATIVE_CTRL
Causes ObjectWindows to be built to only use the system's implementation of common controls.

See also   _OWLDLL macro

Common control macros

The following macros are used to specify how ObjectWindows implements common control classes.

_OWL_NATIVECTRL_ALWAYS macro   commctrl.h

_OWL_NATIVECTRL_ALWAYS
Used during compile-time to tell ObjectWindows to *always* use native controls and not encapsulation.

_OWL_NATIVECTRL_MAYBE macro   commctrl.h

_OWL_NATIVECTRL_MAYBE
Used during compile-time to tell ObjectWindows to determine native control usage vs. emulation during runtime.

_OWL_NATIVECTRL_NEVER macro   commctrl.h

_OWL_NATIVECTRL_NEVER
Used during compile-time to tell ObjectWindows to *never* use native controls, but to use encapsulation.

Configuration macros

The following macros are used as function, class, or data modifiers for symbols defined by ObjectWindows.

_OWLCLASS macro   defs.h

_OWLCLASS
Used internally by ObjectWindows to modify an entire class for use in a DLL. It is the ObjectWindows version of _RTLCLASS adjusted to export and import WIN32 DLLs.

For static WIN16 and WIN32 , the default models are used. When ObjectWindows is being built, this macro evaluates to **_export** for WIN16 and WIN32 DLLs. For WIN32 DLLs, this macro evaluates to **_import** and performs necessary operations for WIN32 DLLs. For WIN16 DLL use, this macro evaluates to **_import**, which is essentially the same as **_huge**.

_OWLCLASS_RTL macro   defs.h

_OWLCLASS_RTL
Same as _OWLCLASS macro.

See also   _OWLCLASS macro

_OWLDATA macro
defs.h

_OWLDATA
The ObjectWindows version of _RTLDATA adjusted to export and import WIN32 DLLs for ObjectWindows. _OWLDATA modifies a specific data declaration.

For static WIN16 and WIN32, the default models are used. When ObjectWindows is being built, this macro evaluates to **_export** for WIN16 and WIN32 DLLs. For WIN32 DLLs, this macro evaluates to **_import** and performs necessary operations for WIN32 DLLs. For WIN16 DLLs, this macro evaluates to nothing.

_OWLDLL macro
defs.h

_OWLDLL
_OWLDLL, which is automatically defined if _RTLDLL is turned on, controls values for the _OWLCLASS, _OWLDATA, and _OWLFUNC macros. It is also automatically defined if the user _OWLDLL module is used as a DLL from another user module. It must be defined if you are writing ObjectWindows applications or DLLs that use DLLs. This macro can also be turned on by a makefile.

_OWL_EXPORT macro
defs.h

_OWL_EXPORT
This macro expands to the appropriate modifier in structuring the compiler to export a function or class.

_OWL_EXPORT16 macro
defs.h

_OWL_EXPORT16
Same as _OWL_EXPORT macro.

See also _OWL_EXPORT macro

_OWLFAR macro
defs.h

_OWLFAR
The macro _OWLFAR is the ObjectWindows version of _RTLFAR adapted to promote far data pointers in DLLs for ObjectWindows.

_OWLFARVTABLE macro
defs.h

_OWLFARVTABLE
Moves the ObjectWindows virtual function tables (vtables) out of the DGROUP of the data segment and stores them in the code segment. Use this macro in conjunction with the _OWLCLASS macro to add the **_huge** option when static models are compiled.

_OWLFUNC macro defs.h

_OWLFUNC

The ObjectWindows function version of _RTLFUNC adapted to export and import functions for building WIN32 DLLs for ObjectWindows. _OWLFUNC modifies a specific member or global function for use in a DLL.

For static WIN16 and WIN32 DLLs, the default models are used. When ObjectWindows is being built, this macro evaluates to **_export** for WIN16 and WIN32 DLLs. For WIN32 DLLs, this macro evaluates to **_import** and performs necessary operations for WIN32 DLLs. For WIN16 DLL use, this macro evaluates to nothing.

_OWL_INI macro defs.h

_OWL_INI

Name of the file where ObjectWindows runtime options are stored. It is used mainly for diagnostic libraries.

_USERCLASS macro defs.h

_USERCLASS

Modifier to be used for classes that are derived from ObjectWindows classes. For example:

```
class _USERCLASS TMyWindow : public TWindow {
   .
   .
   .
};
```

Doc/View macros

The following macros are used by ObjectWindow's Doc/View subsystem.

DEFINE_DOC_TEMPLATE_CLASS macro doctpl.h

Creates a document template. Takes three arguments: the name of the document class that holds the data, the name of the view class that displays the data, and the name of the template class, and then associates the document with one or more views. The following example illustrates how you can associate document and view classes with new template classes.

```
DEFINE_DOC_TEMPLATE_CLASS(TFileDocument, TListView, ListTemplate);
DEFINE_DOC_TEMPLATE_CLASS(TFileDocument, TEditView, EditTemplate);
```

DOCVIEWCLASS macro docmanag.h

Modifier to be used for user-defined doc/view classes.

DOCVIEWENTRY macro   doctpl.h

Modifier to be used for doc/view templates residing in a DLL.

EV_xxxx macros   windowev.h

The following macros are used to create response table entries that match events to member functions.

Macro	Meaning
EV_CHILD_NOTIFY(id,notifyCode,method)	Handles child ID notifications (for example, button, edit control, list box, combo box, and scroll bar notification messages) at the child's parent window. Passes no arguments.
EV_CHILD_NOTIFY_ALL_CODES (method)	Passes all notifications to the response function and passes the notification code in as an argument.
EV_CHILD_NOTIFY_AND_CODE (id, notifyCode, method)	Handles child ID notifications at the child's parent window and passes the notification code as an argument.
EV_COMMAND(id, method)	Handler for menu selections, accelerator keys, and push buttons.
EV_COMMAND_AND_ID(id, method)	Handler for multiple commands using a single response function. Passes the menu ID in as an argument.
EV_COMMAND_ENABLE(id, method)	Enables and disables commands such as buttons and menu items.
EV_MESSAGE(message, method)	General purpose macro for Windows WM_xxxx messages.
EV_NOTIFY_AT_CHILD (notifyCode, method)	Handles all child ID notifications at the child window.
EV_OWLDOCUMENT(id, method)	Handles new document notifications.
EV_OWLNOTIFY(id, method)	Generic document handler.
EV_OWLVIEW(id, method)	Handles view notifications.
EV_REGISTERED(str, method)	Handles registered MSG messages.
EV_VIEWNOTIFY	Sends a notification message from the document to the views.

OLE macros

The following macros are used when building OLE-enabled apllications.

DEFINE_APP_DICTIONARY macro   appdict.h

This macro defines an *AppDictionary* reference and object as needed for use in component DLLs and EXEs. Unless a user dictionary is specified, the macro defines the dictionary as *OwlAppDictionary*, which is a globally exported *TAppDictionary*. The macro is defined as follows:

```
#define DEFINE_APP_DICTIONARY(AppDictionary)
```

See also   TAppDictionary

_OCMCLASS macro

appdict.h

_OWLCLASS
Same as _OWLCLASS macro.

See also   _OWLCLASS macro

Registration macros

locale.h

The following macros take care of performing various OLE-related registration procedures. These macros simplify the process of building a registration table (a specific kind of lookup table) either for an automation server or for a non-automated application or document associated with a container or server. A collection of vital statistics about an object, the registration table provides an external description associated with an object. Some of the information goes into the system registry and is used by OLE. Some of the information is displayed in the File | Open dialog box when the user selects the Insert Object selection.

The registration macros build a *TRegList* structure containing entries of type *TRegItem*, a structure defined as follows:

```
struct TRegItem {
    char*  Key;              //Item name
    TLocaleString Value;     //String value for the item
};
```

Using these macros saves you the trouble of having to build the *TRegItem* and *TRegList* structures directly.

Although servers and containers use the same macros, they pass different kinds of information to the registration structures. The number of registration macros you use depends on the amount of information you want associated with your application and whether you want to set up a structure with document or application information.

Table 7.1   Registration macros

Macro	Meaning
BEGIN_REGISTRATION	Begins a registration macro table.
END_REGISTRATION	Ends a registration macro table.
REGDATA	Registers information about the application such as class ID, description, document filter, and debugger options.
REGDOCFLAGS	Registers a series of document flags. Required for a document registration table.
REGFORMAT	Registers a data format.
REGICON	Registers an icon.
REGITEM	Registers a customized format.
REGSTATUS	Registers an aspect status.
REGVERBOPT	Registers an option for a verb.
REGISTRATION_FORMAT_BUFFER	Sets the size of the buffer space needed for expansion.

REGDATA, the main macro used in the registration table, passes string data in its arguments. The REGFORMAT, REGDOCFLAG, REGICON, REGSTATUS, and REGVERBOPT macros format numeric values as string values.

For a list of which item names (referred to as keys) are required in the application and document registration tables, see "Registration Keys." For information about how to use these macros in your OLE-enabled applications, see "Registering a Linking and Embedding Server" and "Registering a Container." The sample applications REGTEST.CPP and STEP15DV.CPP on your distribution disk provide examples of registration tables designed for different kinds of applications and documents.

See also "Registering a Linking and Embedding Server," "Registration Keys," "Registering a Container," TLocaleString struct

BEGIN_REGISTRATION macro   locale.h

BEGIN_REGISTRATION(regname)
Indicates the beginning of a registration macro table. The macro takes one argument (*regname*), which is the name of the structure to be built. Within the registration table macro, there are several macros that build the registration structure. Depending on the type of application or document, different macros are used. The following example from STEP15.CPP registers the drawing pad as a server application and builds an *AppReg* structure:

```
BEGIN_REGISTRATION(AppReg)
  REGDATA(clsid,       "{5E4BD320-8ABC-101B-A23B-CE4E85D07ED2}")
  REGDATA(description,"OWL Drawing Pad Server")
END_REGISTRATION
```

See also END_REGISTRATION macro, REGDATA macro

END_REGISTRATION macro   locale.h

END_REGISTRATION
Indicates the end of a registration macro table. You can insert the registration macros within the BEGIN_REGISTRATION and END_REGISTRATION macros to build a registration structure.

See also BEGIN_REGISTRATION macro

REGDATA macro   locale.h

REGDATA(var,val)
The main registration macro, REGDATA registers information about an application or a document. The macro always takes an item name (for example, *clsid)* and a corresponding string value (for example, 5E4BD320-8ABC-101B-A23B-CE4E85D07ED2). The following example from STEP15.CPP on your distribution disk passes the class ID and description to build an *AppReg* application registration structure:

```
BEGIN_REGISTRATION(AppReg)
  REGDATA(clsid, "{5E4BD320-8ABC-101B-A23B-CE4E85D07ED2}")
  REGDATA(description, "OWL Drawing Pad Server")
END_REGISTRATION
```

For an automation server application, the registration structure includes the following REGDATA macros:

```
BEGIN_REGISTRATION(myappreg)
  REGDATA(clsid,       "{01234567-1234-5678-1122-334455667788}")
  REGDATA(progid,      "MySample")
  REGDATA(description, "My Sample 1.0 Application")
  REGDATA(cmdline,     "/automation")
  REGDATA(version,     "1.2")
END_REGISTRATION
```

Each object that can be automated requires a unique program ID, a description, and a command-line argument that is placed on the server's command line. As usual, only one class ID is defined for the entire application. See the *ObjectWindows Programmer's Guide* for detailed information about how to register an automation server.

For each application registration structure, you may have one or more document registration structures. The following example uses the data from several REGDATA macros to build a *DocReg* registration structure:

```
BEGIN_REGISTRATION(mydocreg)
  REGDATA(description, "My Sample 1.0 Document")
  REGDATA(extension,  "myd") //Do not use a period before extension.
  REGDATA(directory,  "C:\temp")
  REGDATA(docfilter,  "*.drw;*.drx")
  ...//Insert additional macros here.
  REGDATA(debugger,   "tdw -t") // Sets debugger option
  REGDATA(progid,     "MyDocument") //For servers only
  REGDATA(menuname,   "My Document") //For servers only
  REGDATA(insertable,0) // For servers only
  REGDATA(usage,      ocrMultipleUse) // For servers only
  REGDATA(verb0,      "&Edit") //For servers only
  REGDATA(verb1,      "&Open") //For servers only
  REGDATA(verb2,      "&Play") //For servers only
  ...//Insert additional macros here.
END_REGISTRATION
```

See also   BEGIN_REGISTRATION macro, END_REGISTRATION macro

REGDOCFLAGS macro   locale.h

REGDOCFLAGS(i)

Indicates options for the document and defines the characteristics of document templates. The REGDOCFLAGS arguments tell the document manager how to display and manage the documents and views. Although for backward compatibility you can still pass this information to the document template by using the separate parameters in the constructor, newer programs should use the REGFORMAT, REGDOCFLAGS, and REGDATA macros to create a document template object.

The sample program REGTEST.CPP on your distribution disk includes the following REGDOCFLAGS macro declaration within the document registration structure:

```
BEGIN_REGISTRATION(mytplreg)
  REGDATA(description,"My Sample Draw View")
  REGDATA(filter,      "*.drw;*.drx")
  REGDATA(defaultext, "dvw")
  REGDATA(directory,  0)
  REGDOCFLAGS(dtAutoDelete | dtUpdateDir | dtCreatePrompt)
END_REGISTRATION
```

The arguments to REGDOCFLAGS define the document's characteristics. In the case of dtAutoDelete, for example, the document is deleted when the last view is deleted:

Certain documents must be registered with different options. For example, to register a Doc/View application used with a TOleDocument object, you must specify the dtRegisterExt and dtAutoOpen flags. If this is a Doc/View application, and if the document template is not hidden, you must register the description, filter, and extension.

See also   BEGIN_REGISTRATION macro, REGFORMAT macro, REGDATA macro

REGFORMAT macro   locale.h

REGFORMAT(i,f,a,t,d)
The data formats that the server or container can support. REGFORMAT has the following parameters:

Parameter	Description
i	Order of priority for the designated data format, with 0 being the highest fidelity rendered.
f	The data format, for example, *ocrText*, *ocrTiff*, *ocrDib*, and so on. (ocrxxxx Clipboard Constants describes the data formats.)
a	The format used to present the data
t	Medium to use to transfer the data, such as *ocrMfPict* (METAFILEPICT structure), *ocrGDI* (GDI object such as a bitmap), *ocrIStream* (Stream object in a compound file), and so on. (ocrxxxx Medium Constants describes the medium formats.)
d	Whether or not data is provided as well as received in the designated format.The accepted values are *ocrGet* (imports data in the specified format), *ocrSet* (exports data in the specified format), or *ocrGetSet* (both exports and imports data in the specified format).

For example, STEP15DV.CPP registers several clipboard formats:

```
REGFORMAT(0, ocrEmbedSource,  ocrContent,  ocrIStorage,  ocrGet)
REGFORMAT(1, ocrMetafilePict, ocrcontent,  ocrMfPict,  ocfSet)
```

The later code generates the string "format1, 3, 1, 1056,1". Although you could enter the string yourself, it is much easier to use the enumerated values.

To build a registration structure, use REGFORMAT within the BEGIN_REGISTRATION and END_REGISTRATION macros in a registration macro table. Any formats registered using REGFORMAT are also registered automatically on the Windows Clipboard. You can register your own formats by inserting a string indicating your own format. For example,

```
REGFORMAT(2, "ANewFormat", ocrContent, ocrIStorage, ocrGetSet)
```

To provide names for your own formats, call TOleFrame::AddUserFormatName. This function associates a clipboard data format with the description of the data format as it appears to users in the Help text of the Paste Special dialog box.

See also   BEGIN_REGISTRATION macro, TOleFrame::AddUserFormatName

REGICON macro   locale.h

REGICON(i)
Registers an icon so the object is displayed as an icon. The sample program REGTEST.CPP on your distribution disk includes the following REGICON macro:

REGICON(1)
The macro takes one argument, the index of the default icon to use. This argument indicates which icon is to be retrieved from the resource file when the document is displayed as an icon.

See also   BEGIN_REGISTRATION macro

REGITEM macro   locale.h

REGITEM(key,val)
Lets you write customized entries for the system registry. The following example from REGTEST.CPP registers conversion formats:

REGITEM("CLSID\\<clsid>\\Conversion\\Readable\\Main","FormatX,FormatY")
The first string is the registry key, which has one parameter (*<clsid>*). When the registry information is generated, an actual value is substituted for the template parameters.

See also   BEGIN_REGISTRATION macro, END_REGISTRATION macro

REGSTATUS macro   locale.h

REGSTATUS(a,f)
Indicates the way in which the view (the *aspect*) of an object behaves. REGSTATUS has the following arguments:

Parameter	Description
a	The content of the object.
f	One of the ocrxxxx Object Status enum values indicating the status of the object, such as *ocrOnlyIconic*, *ocrActivateWhenVisible*, and so on.

The object can be defined to have many different behaviors. For example, an object registered as *ocrActivateWhenVisible* is active whenever it is visible.

Servers that support linked and embedded objects use this macro to register the behavior an object exhibits when it is viewed. This behavior is referred to as the *aspect status*, or simply aspect, of the object.

The sample program REGTEST.CPP on your distribution disk includes the following REGSTATUS macros:

```
REGSTATUS(all, ocrNoSpecialRendering)
REGSTATUS(icon, ocrOnlyIconic)
```

The first macro registers flags for all aspects of the object. The second macro registers flags for the iconic aspect of the object. (The icon used in the REGSTATUS macro must have been defined and registered.)

See also   BEGIN_REGISTRATION macro, REGICON macro

REGVERBOPT macro   locale.h

REGVERBOPT(v,mf,sf)

Registers the actions a server can perform on its objects. The arguments control how the verbs appear on the container's menu. The macro has the following arguments:

Parameter	Description
v	The verb key, for example, *verb1* or *verb2*.
mf	A value that describes how a server's verbs appear on the container's menu. This value must be one of the ocrxxxx Verb Menu constants, such as *ocrGrayed*, which makes the verb appear gray on the menu and disables the verb.
sf	A value that tells the container how to use the verb. This value must be one of the ocrxxxx Verb Attribute constants, such as *ocrNeverDirties*, which indicates that the verb never modifies the object. These options can be **OR**ed together.

The sample program REGTEST.CPP on your distribution disk includes the following REGVERBOPT macro:

```
REGVERBOPT(verb1, ocrGrayed, ocrOnContainerMenu | ocrNeverDirties)
```

These verb options are optional and are only valid if the verb is registered in the document registration table for the server application. To register the verb, use

```
REGDATA(verb1, "&Open")
```

See also   BEGIN_REGISTRATION macro

REGISTRATION_FORMAT_BUFFER macro   locale.h

REGISTRATION_FORMAT_BUFFER(n);

Allocates space in memory (*n*) for the expansion of the values passed in the registration macros that control the formatting of a document or application. Generally, allow 10 bytes for each value passed in the REGFORMAT macro in addition to the space required for strings passed in the REGSTATUS, REGVERBOPT, REGICON, or REGFORMAT macros. For example, the sample program, STEP15.CPP uses this macro to declare 100 bytes of space:

```
REGISTRATION_FORMAT_BUFFER(100);
```

Response table macros

The following macros are used to create message handlers.

DECLARE_RESPONSE_TABLE macro   eventhan.h

Declares a response table in the class definition. To handle events for a class, you need to both declare a response table with this macro and define the response table using one of the DEFINE_RESPONSE_TABLE macros. For example, to declare a response table, use the following declaration, where the single parameter, *Class*, represents the name of the current class:

```
DECLARE_RESPONSE_TABLE(Class);
```

ObjectWindows' response tables define the relationship between a window message and a corresponding event-handling function. The description of *TEventHandler* has more information about how ObjectWindows associates a response table entry with the appropriate function.

See also   DEFINE_RESPONSE_TABLE macros, END_RESPONSE_TABLE macro, TEventHandler class

DEFINE_RESPONSE_TABLE macros   eventhan.h

Defines a response table. Takes one plus x number of arguments: one is the name of the class that is defining the response table and x is the immediate base class as well as any virtual base classes. Use the END_RESPONSE_TABLE macro to end the definition for the response table. Between the DEFINE_RESPONSE_TABLE macro and the END_RESPONSE_TABLE macro, insert the message response entries for the messages you want the class to handle. For example,

```
DEFINE_RESPONSE_TABLE1(TMyClass, TWindow)
  EV_WM_PAINT,
  EV_WM_LBUTTONDOWN,
END_RESPONSE_TABLE;
```

In this example, EV_WM_PAINT and EV_WM_LBUTTONDOWN illustrate the message response entries for the class *TMyClass* derived from *TWindow*. These macros call the corresponding event-handling functions, *EvPaint* and *EvLButtonDown*, respectively. Note that response tables are sometimes defined, but have no entries. In such cases, the base class's response table entries are searched for the appropriate event-handling function. You can also associate more than one message with an event-handling function.

The following table shows the form the DEFINE_RESPONSE_TABLE macro takes depending on the number of base classes.

Number of Base Classes	Macro
0	DEFINE_RESPONSE_TABLE(Class)
1	DEFINE_RESPONSE_TABLE1(Class, Base)
2	DEFINE_RESPONSE_TABLE2(Class, Base1, Base2)
3	DEFINE_RESPONSE_TABLE3(Class, Base1, Base2, Base3)

See also   DECLARE_RESPONSE_TABLE macro, END_RESPONSE_TABLE macro, TEventHandler class

END_RESPONSE_TABLE macro   eventhan.h

END_RESPONSE_TABLE;
Indicates the end of a response table. For each class that contains a response table, add this macro to the class definition.

See also   DEFINE_RESPONSE_TABLE macro

WinSock macros

The following macro is used by ObjectWindow's WinSock encapsulation.

WINSOCK_NOERROR macro   wsksock.h

WINSOCK_NOERROR (int)0
Macro that defines a successful code from a WinSock API.

ObjectWindows type definitions

This chapter lists the ObjectWindows type definitions in alphabetical order.

TActionFunc typedef   window.h

typedef void(*TActionFunc)(TWindow* win, void* param);
Defines the signature of the callback function passed to the *ForEach* method of *TWindow*.

See also   TWindow::ForEach

TActionMemFunc typedef   window.h

typedef void(TWindow::*TActionMemFunc)(TWindow* win, void* param);
Defines the signature of the callback function passed to the *ForEach* method of *TWindow*.

See also   TWindow::ForEach

TActionPageFunc typedef   propsht.h

typedef void (*TActionPageFunc)(TPropertyPage* pPage, void* param);
Defines the prototype of the callback function invoked when an action must be
performed on every page of a property sheet.

See also   TPropertySheet::ForEachPage

TAnyDispatcher typedef   dispatch.h

typedef int32 _OWLFUNC (*TAnyDispatcher)(GENERIC&, TAnyPMF, uint, int32);

A message dispatcher type. All message dispatcher functions conform to this type and take four parameters:

- A reference to an object
- A pointer to the member function in which the signature varies according to the cracking that the function performs
  - WPARAM
  - LPARAM

TAnyPMF typedef   dispatch.h

typedef void(GENERIC::*TAnyPMF)();
A generic pointer to a member function.

TCondFunc typedef   window.h

typedef bool (*TCondFunc) (Twindow* win, void* param);
Defines the signature of the callback function used by the *FirstThat* function of *TWindow*.

See also   TWindow::FirstThat

TCondMemFunc typedef   window.h

typedef bool (TWindow::*TCondMemFunc)(TWindow* win, void* param);
Defines the signature of the member function used by the *FirstThat* function of *TWindow*.

See also   TWindow::FirstThat

TCondPageFunc typedef   propsht.h

typedef bool (*TCondPageFunc)(TPropertyPage* pPage, void* param);
Defines the prototype of the callback function invoked for the *FirstPageThat* method of *TPropertySheet*.

See also   TPropertySheet::FirstPageThat

TEqualOperator typedef   eventhan.h

typedef bool(*TEqualOperator)(TGenericTableEntry __RTFAR&, TEventInfo&);
TEqualOperator is used to perform special kinds of searches and to facilitate finding response table entries. *TEqualOperator* compares a particular message event

(*TEventInfo&*) with a response table entry (*TGenericTableEntry*) to determine if they match.

See also   TResponseTableEntry

ObjectWindows dispatch functions

Dispatch functions separate the *lParam* and *wParam* parameters of Windows messages into their respective data types and pass control to an ObjectWindows member function.

For example, when Windows sends an application a WM_CTLCOLOR message, the *wParam* is really an HDC, and the *lParam* has a HWND and a **uint** hidden inside. After the dispatch function cracks the *wParam* and *lParam* parameters into their constituent parts, it dispatches the Windows WM_CTLCOLOR message to the following ObjectWindows member function:

```
HBRUSH EvCtlColor(HDC, HWND, uint);
```

Although dispatch functions are written for specific Windows API messages, they have no knowledge of the actual Windows messages they are cracking. Instead, at run time, *TEventHandler::Dispatch* calls the appropriate dispatch function which then cracks the message and calls the appropriate member function, using the response table's *pmf* (pointer to a member function). These dispatch functions are never called directly.

The following four parameters are common to all dispatch functions:

- *GENERIC& generic* is the pointer to the object (for example, *TEdit*).
- *GENERIC::*pmf* is the pointer to the member function (for example, *EvActivate*).
- *WPARAM* is one of the message parameters the dispatch function cracks.
- *LPARAM* is one of the message parameters the dispatch function cracks.

The name of the dispatch function used in the response table entry or macro depends on the type of message cracking the function performs. The first letter of the name indicates the return type (for example, U indicates an unsigned integer). The second group of letters signifies the arguments of the function (for example, *POINT* of type TPOINT, or

U of type **uint**). The following table lists the abbreviations of the member functions' signatures and their corresponding data types.

Abbreviation	Data type
i	**int**
v	**void**
H	HANDLE (same as **uint** in size)
I32	**int32**
POINT	*TPoint*& (*TPoint* object constructed)
POINTER	**void*** (model's ambient size)
U	**uint**

Message crackers that serve customized messages have names based on the specific message they crack. For example, the message cracker for WM_MDIACTIVATE messages has the following prototype:

```
int32_v_MdiActivate_Dispatch(GENERIC& generic, HBRUSH (GENERIC::*pmf)(uint, uint),
                             uint wParam, int32 lParam);
```

ObjectWindows uses the same dispatch functions for messages that require the same type of cracking. For example, both the WM_HSCROLL and WM_VSCROLL event handlers have `void (*)( uint, uint, HWND)` as their signature. The Windows message also has the *wParam* and *lParam* parameters in the same place. Therefore, ObjectWindows uses the same dispatch functions for both of these messages.

The following aliases have been defined for purposes of backward compatibility:

```
#define HBRUSH_HDC_W_U_Dispatch          U_U_U_U_Dispatch
#define LRESULT_U_U_W_Dispatch           I32_MenuChar_Dispatch
#define LRESULT_WPARAM_LPARAM_Dispatch   I32_WPARAM_LPARAM_Dispatch
#define v_U_B_W_Dispatch                 v_Activate_Dispatch
#define v_W_W_Dispatch                   v_MdiActivate_Dispatch
```

See also   TEventHandler

i_LPARAM_Dispatch   Dispatch.h

int32 i_LPARAM_Dispatch(GENERIC& generic, int (GENERIC::*pmf)(int32), uint wParam, int32 lParam);
Passes *lParam* as an **int32** and returns an **int**.

i_U_W_U_Dispatch   Dispatch.h

int32 i_U_W_U_Dispatch(GENERIC& generic, int (GENERIC::*pmf)(uint, uint, uint), uint wParam, int32 lParam);
For Win32, passes *wParam.lo* (the LOWORD of *wParam*) as a **uint**, *lParam* as a **uint** and *wParam.hi* (the HIWORD of *wParam*) as a **uint** and returns an **int**. For Win16, passes *wParam* as a **uint**, *lParam.lo* as a **uint** and *lParam.hi* as a **uint,** and returns an **int**. This is a semi-customized dispatch function used for WM_CHARTOITEM and WM_KEYTOITEM messages.

i_WPARAM_Dispatch
Dispatch.h

> int32 i_WPARAM_Dispatch(GENERIC& generic, int (GENERIC::*pmf)(uint), uint wParam, int32 lParam);
> Passes *wParam* as a **uint** and returns an **int**.

I32_Dispatch
Dispatch.h

> int32 I32_Dispatch(GENERIC& generic, int32 (GENERIC::*pmf)(), uint, int32);
> This dispatcher passes nothing and returns an **int32**.

I32_LPARAM_Dispatch
Dispatch.h

> int32 I32_LPARAM_Dispatch(GENERIC& generic, int32 (GENERIC::*pmf)(int32), uint, int32 lParam);
> This dispatcher passes *lParam* as an **int32** and returns an **int32**.

I32_WPARAM_LPARAM_Dispatch
Dispatch.h

> int32 I32_WPARAM_LPARAM_Dispatch(GENERIC& generic, int32 (GENERIC::*pmf)(uint, int32),
>   uint wParam, int32 lParam);
> This dispatcher passes *wParam* as a **uint** and *lParam* as an **int32**, and returns an **int32**.

I32_MenuChar_Dispatch
Dispatch.h

> int32 I32_MenuChar_Dispatch(GENERIC& generic, uint (GENERIC::*pmf) (uint, uint, uint), uint wParam,
>   int32 lParam);
> Cracker for WM_PARENTNOTIFY messages. Passes three **uints** and returns an **int32**.
> Under Win32, the first **uint** is *wParam.lo*, the second **uint** is *wParam.hi*, and the third **uint**
> is *lParam*. Under Win 16, the first **uint** is *wParam*, the second **uint** is *lParam.lo*, and the
> third **uint** is *lParam.hi*.

I32_U_Dispatch
Dispatch.h

> int32 I32_U_Dispatch(GENERIC& generic, int32 (GENERIC::*pmf)(uint), int32 lParam);
> This dispatcher passes *lParam* and **uint** and returns an **int32**.

U_Dispatch
Dispatch.h

> int32 U_Dispatch(GENERIC& generic, uint (GENERIC::*pmf) (), uint wParam, int32 lParam);
> Passes no arguments and returns a **uint**.

U_LPARAM_Dispatch   Dispatch.h

int32 U_LPARAM_Dispatch(GENERIC& generic, uint (GENERIC::*pmf) (int32), uint wParam, int32 lParam);
Passes *lParam* as an **int32** and returns a **uint**.

U_POINT_Dispatch   Dispatch.h

int32 U_POINT_Dispatch(GENERIC& generic, uint (GENERIC::*pmf) (TPoint&), uint wParam, int32 lParam);
Passes *lParam* as a *TPoint&* and returns a **uint**.

U_POINTER_Dispatch   Dispatch.h

int32 U_POINTER_Dispatch(GENERIC& generic, uint (GENERIC::*pmf) (void*), uint, int32 lParam);
Passes *lParam* as a **void*** and returns a **uint**.

U_U_Dispatch   Dispatch.h

int32 U_U_Dispatch(GENERIC& generic, uint (GENERIC::*pmf) (uint), uint, int32 lParam);
Passes *lParam* as a **uint** and returns a **uint**.

U_U_U_U_Dispatch   Dispatch.h

int32 U_U_U_U_Dispatch(GENERIC& generic, uint (GENERIC::*pmf) (uint, uint, uint), uint wParam, int32 lParam);
Passes three **uints** and returns a **uint**. The first **uint** is *wParam*, the second **uint** is the LOWORD of *lParam*, and the third **uint** is the HIWORD of *lParam*.

U_WPARAM_LPARAM_Dispatch   Dispatch.h

int32 U_WPARAM_LPARAM_Dispatch(GENERIC& generic, uint (GENERIC::*pmf) (uint, int32), uint wParam,
    int32 lParam);
Passes *wParam* as a **uint** and *lParam* as an **int32** and returns a **uint**.

v_Activate_Dispatch   Dispatch.h

int32 v_Activate_Dispatch(GENERIC& generic, void (GENERIC::*pmf) (uint, uint, uint), uint wParam,
    int32 lParam);
Cracker for WM_ACTIVATE messages. Passes three **uints** and always returns 0. Under Win32, the first **uint** is *wParam.lo*, the second **uint** is *wParam.hi*, and the third **uint** is *lParam*. Under Win16, the first **uint** is *wParam*, the second **uint** is *lParam.hi*, and the third **uint** is *lParam.lo*.

v_Dispatch
Dispatch.h

int32 v_Dispatch (GENERIC& generic, void (GENERIC::*pmf) (), uint uint, int32);
Passes nothing and always returns 0.

v_LPARAM_Dispatch
Dispatch.h

int32 v_LPARAM_Dispatch (GENERIC& generic, void (GENERIC::*pmf) (int32), uint wParam, int32 lParam);
Passes *lParam* as an **int32** and always returns 0.

v_MdiActivate_Dispatch
Dispatch.h

int32 v_MdiActivate_Dispatch(GENERIC& generic, void (GENERIC::*pmf)(uint, uint), uint wParam, int32 lParam);
Specifically designed to handle *EvMDIActivate* messages, *v_MdiActivate_Dispatch* passes two **uint**s and always returns 0. Under Win32, the first **uint** is *lParam* and the second **uint** is *wParam*. Under Win16, the first **uint** is *lParam.lo*. If *lParam* is nonzero, the second **uint** is *lParam.hi*; otherwise, the second **uint** is *wParam*.

v_ParentNotify_Dispatch
Dispatch.h

int32 v_ParentNotify_Dispatch(GENERIC& generic, int(GENERIC::*pmf) (uint, uint, uint), uint wParam,
    int32 lParam);
Performs message cracking for WM_PARENTNOTIFY messages, which notify a parent window that a given event has occurred in the child window. Passes three **uint**s and always returns 0. For Win16, the first **uint** is *wParam*, the second **uint** is *lParam.lo*, and the third **uint** is *lParam.hi*. For Win32, if *wparam.lo* is a mouse message, then the first **uint** is *wparam*, the second **uint** is *lparam.lo*, and the third **uint** is *lParam.hi*. Otherwise, the first **uint** is *wparam.lo*, the second **uint** is *lParam*, and the third **uint** is *wParam.hi*.

v_POINT_Dispatch
Dispatch.h

int32 v_POINT_Dispatch (GENERIC& generic, void (GENERIC::*pmf) (TPoint&), uint wParam, int32 lParam);
Passes a reference to a *POINT* (*TPoint&*) and always returns 0. Under Win32, passes *lParam*; under Win16, passes a reference to *lParam*.

v_POINTER_Dispatch
Dispatch.h

int32 v_POINTER_Dispatch(GENERIC& generic, void (GENERIC::*pmf)(void*), uint wParam, int32 lParam);
Passes an *lParam* as a **void*** pointer and always returns 0.

v_U_Dispatch

Dispatch.h

int32 v_U_Dispatch(GENERIC& generic, void (GENERIC::*pmf) (uint, int32 lParam);
Passes *lParam* as a **uint** and always returns 0.

v_U_POINT_Dispatch

Dispatch.h

int32 v_U_POINT_Dispatch(GENERIC& generic, void (GENERIC::*pmf) (uint, TPoint&), uint wParam,
int32 lParam);
Passes *wparam* as a **uint** and *lParam* as a reference to a *POINT* and always returns 0.

v_U_U_Dispatch

Dispatch.h

int32 v_U_U_Dispatch(GENERIC& generic, void (GENERIC::*pmf) (uint, uint), uint wParam, int32 lParam);
Passes two **uints** and always returns 0. The first **uint** is *wParam* and the second **uint** is
lParam.

v_U_U_U_Dispatch

Dispatch.h

int32 v_U_U_U_Dispatch(GENERIC& generic, void (GENERIC::*pmf) (uint, uint, uint), uint wParam, int32 lParam);
Passes three **uints** and always returns 0. The first **uint** is *wParam*, the second **uint** is
lParam.lo, and the third **uint** is *lParam.hi.*

v_U_U_W_Dispatch

Dispatch.h

int32 v_U_U_W_Dispatch(GENERIC& generic, void (GENERIC::*pmf) (uint, uint, uint), uint wParam, nt32 lParam);
Passes three **uints** and always returns 0. Under Win32, the first **uint** is *wParam.lo.*, the
second **uint** is *wParam.hi*, and the third **uint** is *lParam*. Under Win16, the first **uint** is
wParam, the second **uint** is *lParam.lo*, and the third **uint** is *lParam.hi*. This is a semi-
customized message cracker for WM_HSCROLL, WM_VSCROLL, and
WM_MENUSELECT messages.

v_WPARAM_Dispatch

Dispatch.h

int32 v_WPARAM_Dispatch(GENERIC& generic, void (GENERIC::*pmf) (uint), uint wParam, int32 lParam);
Passes *wParam* as a **uint** and always returns 0.

v_WPARAM_LPARAM_Dispatch

Dispatch.h

int32 v_WPARAM_LPARAM_Dispatch(GENERIC& generic, void (GENERIC::*pmf) (uint, int32),
uint wParam, int32 lParam);
Passes *wParam* as a **uint** and *lParam* as an **int32** and always returns 0.

ObjectComponents programmer's reference

Part II describes all the ObjectComponents classes, structures, constants, types, and macros. It is organized into the following chapters:

- **Chapter 10, "Overview of ObjectComponents,"** provides an overview of the ObjectComponents classes, libraries, and header files. It describes the classes according to their functional groups and explains their purpose within that group.

- **Chapter 11, "ObjectComponents library reference,"** is an alphabetical listing of all the standard ObjectComponents classes, including explanations of their purpose, usage, and members. It also describes the non-object elements such as structures, constants, variables, and macros that classes use.

Chapter

10

Overview of ObjectComponents

This chapter lists alphabetically the ObjectComponents classes, macros, constants, data types, and registration keys. The header file that defines each entry is listed opposite the entry name. Class members are grouped according to their access specifiers—**public** or **protected**. Within these categories, data members, then constructors and destructors, and member functions are grouped separately and listed alphabetically.

The members listed for each class include only those that are new or redefined in the class itself. Members inherited from a base class are not listed again in the derived class. No private members are listed. In some cases members that are public or protected are omitted as well because they are meant only for the use of other ObjectComponents classes.

Some entries related to ObjectComponents programs appear in other sections of this book. OLE-enabled ObjectWindows classes, such as *TOleWindow* and *TOleFactory*, are listed with the other ObjectWindows classes.

ObjectComponents libraries

These are the libraries an ObjectComponents application uses for linking.

Medium model	Large model	DLL libraries	Description
OCFWM.LIB	OCFWL.LIB	OCFWI.LIB	ObjectComponents
OWLWM.LIB	OWLWL.LIB	OWLWI.LIB	ObjectWindows
BIDSM.LIB	BIDSL.LIB	BIDSI.LIB	Class libraries
OLE2W16.LIB	OLE2W16.LIB	OLE2W16.LIB	OLE system DLLs
IMPORT.LIB	IMPORT.LIB	IMPORT.LIB	Windows system DLLs
MATHWM.LIB	MATHWL.LIB		Math support
CWM.LIB	CWL.LIB	CRTLDLL.LIB	C run-time libraries

ObjectComponents header files

Header files, located in your INCLUDE/OCF subdirectory, contain declarations for class functions and definitions for data types and constants.

File	Contents
appdesc.h	*TAppDescriptor, TComponentFactory*
autodefs.h	Classes and **struct**s used for automation
automacr.h	Macros for automation declarations and definitions
ocapp.h	OC_APPxxxx messages, *TOcApp, TOcFormatName, TOcHelp, TOcMenuDescr, TOcModule, TOcNameList, TOcRegistrar*, WM_OCEVENT message
ocapp.rh	IDS_CFxxxx resource IDs for strings describing standard Windows clipboard formats
occtrl.h	*TOcControl, TOcControlEvent, TOcxView*
ocdefs.h	*TXObjComp*, HR_xxxx result codes, declaration specifiers
ocdoc.h	*TOcDocument*
ocfevx.h	Message cracker macros for WM_OCEVENT messages
ocfpch.h	**#include** statements for all ObjectComponents headers, used with pre-compiled headers
oclink.h	*TOcLinkView, TOcLinkCollection, TOcLinkCollectionIter*
ocobject.h	*TOcAspect, TOcDialogHelp, TOcDropAction, TOcInitHow, TOcInitInfo, TOcInitWhere, TOcInvalidate, TOcPartName, TOcScrollDir*
ocpart.h	*TOcPart, TOcPartCollection, TOcPartCollectionIter, TOcVerb*
ocreg.h	OCxxxx global functions, ocrxxxx registration constants, *TAppMode* **enum**, *TRegistrar, TXRegistry*
ocremvie.h	*TOcRemView*
ocstorag.h	*TOcStream, TOcStorage*
ocview.h	OC_VIEWxxxx messages, *TOcDragDrop, TOcFormat, TOcFormatList, TOcFormatListIter, TOcSaveLoad, TOcScaleFactor, TOcToolBarInfo, TOcView, TOcViewPaint*
oleutil.h	DECLARE_COMBASES# macros, *TOleAllocator, TUnknown, TXOle*

General OLE classes, macros, and type definitions

ObjectComponents provides the following utility items for use in building OLE applications, whether they support linking and embedding or automation.

Item	Meaning
HR_xxxx macros	Return values from OLE functions
_ICLASS macro	Specifier for declaring a class that implements an OLE interface
_IFUNC macro	Specifier for declaring OLE functions
_OCFxxxx macros	Specifiers for declaring ObjectComponents classes
TComponentFactory typedef	Callback function where an application creates objects that OLE requests
TLocaleId typedef	Data type for language setting identifiers
TOleAllocator class	Establishes a memory allocator for OLE to use
TUnknown class	Implements the fundamental *IUnknown* interface required of all OLE objects

Global utility functions

The items in this table are utility functions that ObjectComponents declares globally.

Item	Purpose
DynamicCast	Converts a pointer from one type to another if both types are related through inheritance
MostDerived	Returns a pointer to the most derived class type that fits a given object

ObjectComponents exception classes

ObjectComponents throws the types of exceptions shown in this list. All the exception classes derive from TXBase.

Class	Purpose
TXAuto	Exceptions that occur during automation
TXObjComp	Exceptions that occur during ObjectComponents linking and embedding operations
TXOle	Exceptions that occur while processing OLE API commands
TXRegistry	Exceptions that occur while using the system registration database

Automation classes

ObjectComponents provides the following classes that support automation.

Class	Purpose
TAutoBase	Base class for deriving automated objects
TAutoCommand	Holds all the data for one command received by an automation server
TAutoEnumerator<>	Lets an automation controller enumerate items in a server's collection
TAutoIterator	Lets an automation server iterate items in an automated collection
TAutoObject<>	Creates a smart pointer to an automated object
TAutoObjectByVal<>	Lets an automation server automate a method that returns an object by value (not by reference)
TAutoObjectDelete	Lets an automation server automate a method that returns an object
TAutoProxy	Base class for deriving the C++ objects an automation controller creates to represent the OLE objects it wants to control
TAutoStack	Holds a set of *TAutoCommand* objects each representing a command received by an automation server
TAutoVal	Holds the data from a VARIANT union, the data format OLE uses for sending automation commands
TRegistrar	Manages system registration tasks for an automation application

Automation enumerated types and type definitions

ObjectComponents provides the following items that support automation.

Item	Purpose
AutoDataType enum	Identifiers for automation data types
ObjectPtr typedef	**void** pointer to a C++ object

Automation data types

ObjectComponents provides the following data types that support automation. To use these data types, see "Declarations and definitions of automation data types."

Data type
TAutoBool struct
TAutoCurrency struct
TAutoDate struct
TAutoDouble struct
TAutoFloat struct
TAutoInt
TAutoLong struct
TAutoShort struct
TAutoString struct
TAutoStruct struct
TAutoVoid struct

Declarations and definitions of automation data types ocf/autodefs.h

An automation data type is a structure that exists solely to describe a single type of data. Automation definitions use these structures to assist in converting parameters and return values between the VARIANT unions that OLE uses and the C++ data types that your programs use.

For the most part, although they are structures, you cannot create instances of them because they lack constructors and contain only a single static member. They all derive from TAutoType and inherit its *GetType* method. The only thing most of these structures do is respond to *GetType* calls by returning the static ID for a data type.

The following table lists C++ data types that might appear in your programs and the corresponding data types that you should use in automation declarations (DECLARE_AUTOCLASS) and definitions. (DEFINE_AUTOCLASS.)

C++ type	Declaration type	Definition type
short	short	TAutoShort
unsigned short	short or unsigned	TAutoShort or TAutoLong

C++ type	Declaration type	Definition type
long	long	TAutoShort
unsigned long	unsigned long	TAutoLong (treated as signed long)
int	int	TAutoInt
unsigned int	int or long	TAutoInt or TAutoLong
float	float	TAutoFloat
double	double	TAutoDouble
bool (or int)	TBool	TAutoBool
TAutoDate	TAutoDate	TAutoDate
TAutoDate far *	TAutoDate far*	TAutoDateRef
TAutoCurrency far*	TAutoCurrency far*	TAutoCurrencyRef
char*	TAutoString	TAutoString
const char*	TAutoString	TAutoString
char far*	TAutoString	TAutoString
const char far*	TAutoString	TAutoString
string	string	TAutoString
enum	short or int	TAutoShort or user-defined AUTOENUM
T*	TAutoObject<T>	T (class T must be automated)
T&	TAutoObject<T>	T (class T must be automated)
const T*	TAutoObject<const T>	T (class T must be automated)
const T&	TAutoObject<const T>	T (class T must be automated)
T* (returned)	TAutoObjectDelete<T>	(C++ object deleted if no refs)
T& (returned)	TAutoObjectDelete<T>	(C++ object deleted if no refs)
T (returned)	TAutoObjectByVal<T>	T (T copied, deleted when refs==0)
void (no return)	(use AUTOFUNCxV macros)	TAutoVoid
short far*	short far*	TAutoShortRef
long far*	long far*	TAutoLongRef
float far*	float far*	TAutoFloatRef
double far*	double far*	TAutoDouble Ref

Automation declaration macros   ocf/automacr.h

To make parts of an automated class accessible to OLE, an automation server adds declaration macros to the declaration of the C++ class and definition macros to the implementation of the C++ class. The declaration macros create command objects for executing commands sent by the controller.

The block of automation declaration macros always begins with DECLARE_AUTOCLASS. There is no need for a matching END macro to close the declaration.

Macro	Meaning
DECLARE_AUTOCLASS(cls)	The macros that follow declare automatable members of the user-defined class *cls*.

Declaration macros
After DECLARE_AUTOCLASS comes a series of macros, one for each class member that you choose to expose. Which particular macros you choose depends on what the members are.

Declaration macro	Member
AUTODATA	Data
AUTOFLAG	A bit flag
AUTOFUNC	Function
AUTOITERATOR	Iterator object
AUTOPROP	Property
AUTOSTAT	Static member or global function
AUTOTHIS	***this**

AUTODETACH macro
In addition, an automation declaration can also include the AUTODETACH macro. This macro does not expose a class member. It invalidates external references when the object is destroyed.

Automation definition macros
ocf/automacr.h

To make parts of an automated class accessible to OLE, an automation server adds declaration macros to the declaration of the C++ class and definition macros to the implementation of the C++ class.

The block of automation definition macros begins with DEFINE_AUTOCLASS and ends with END_AUTOCLASS, unless the object is, inherits from, or delegates to a Component Object Model (COM) object. In that case, the block of automation definition macros begins with DEFINE_AUTOAGGREGATE and ends with END_AUTOAGGREGATE.

Macro	Meaning
DEFINE_AUTOCLASS(cls)	The macros that follow define automatable members of the user-defined class *cls*.
END_AUTOCLASS(cls, name, doc, help)	The C++ class *cls* is exposed to OLE controllers under the name *name*. If the user asks OLE about the object name, the system returns the string in *doc*. If a .HLP file is registered for the object, then the context ID in *help* points to a screen that describes the object.

Macro	Meaning
DEFINE_AUTOAGGREGATE(cls, aggregator)	The macros that follow define automatable members of the user-defined class *cls*, which is, inherits from, or delegates to a COM object.
END_AUTOAGGREGATE(cls, name, doc, help)	Same as END_AUTOCLASS.

Between the DEFINE and END macros comes a series of other macros describing each exposed data member or function. The macros implement methods for a class nested within your automated class. When ObjectComponents receives commands from a controller, it passes them to the nested class. The macros build wrapper functions in the nested class that enable it to call your own class directly.

Which particular macros you choose depends on what the members are.

Member	Declaration macro
Automated application	EXPOSE_APPLICATION Macro
Auxiliary class	EXPOSE_DELEGATE Macro
Base class	EXPOSE_INHERIT Macro
Collection iterator	EXPOSE_ITERATOR Macro
Method	EXPOSE_METHOD Macro
Read-only property	EXPOSE_PROPRO
Read-write property	EXPOSE_PROPRW
Write-only property	EXPOSE_PROPWO
Shutdown method	EXPOSE_QUIT

Automation hook macros   ocf/automacr.h

These macros establish hooks to be invoked every time a particular automation command is executed. They are never used by themselves but always as the last parameter of some other automation declaration macro. If you add one of these hooks to the declaration of some exposed class member, then every time an automation controller attempts to execute that command, ObjectComponents first executes the code in the hook. The code can be a simple expression or it can contain calls to other functions.

Most of the macros expect to receive some expression or code as a parameter. Often the code or expression in the macro needs to refer to the arguments passed in or to the value of an automated data member. Within the macro expression, write *Arg1*, *Arg2*, *Arg3*... to refer to the received arguments. Write *Val* to refer to an automated data member.

Macro	Meaning
AUTONOHOOK	Use this macro, without arguments, to prevent anyone from hooking the command. Not even ObjectComponents can monitor the call. (For advanced uses only.)
AUTOINVOKE(code)	The code here is executed each time the automation command is executed. Create an AUTOINVOKE hook if you want to override the normal execution sequence.

Macro	Meaning
AUTORECORD(code)	The code inserted here creates a record of the commands executed so that the sequence can be stored and replayed.
AUTOREPORT(code)	The code inserted here returns an error code from the automated member. If *code* evaluates to 0, OLE assumes the command succeeded. If *code* evaluates to a nonzero value, then OLE throws an exception that returns an error code to the controller.
	Within the code expression, use *Val* to refer to the actual value returned.
AUTOUNDO(code)	The code inserted here creates a *TAutoCommand* object that will undo the action of the current command.
AUTOVALIDATE(condition)	The code here should evaluate to **true** if the arguments received are valid for the command and **false** otherwise. If the expression returns **false**, OLE throws an exception that returns an error code to the controller application.

Example

This declaration ensures that an automated data member is never assigned a value outside a given range.

```
AUTODATA(Number, Number, short,
 AUTOVALIDATE(Val>=NUM_MIN && NotTooBig(Val)));
```

Automation proxy macros   ocf/automacr.h

An automation controller creates a proxy object (derived from *TAutoProxy*) to represent an automated OLE object. For every command the controller wants to send the object, it adds a method to the proxy object. The proxy methods mimic the commands the object supports. When the controller calls proxy methods, ObjectComponents sends automation commands through OLE.

The implementation of a proxy method always contains three macros: an AUTONAMES macro, an AUTOARGS macro, and an AUTOCALL macro. AUTONAMES associates names with arguments. AUTOARGS describes any arguments that do not have names. The use of names makes it possible to send partial sets of arguments and let the server assign default values to the remaining arguments.

The third macro, AUTOCALL, tells whether the command represents a method or a property of the automated object and whether the command returns a value.

To generate proxy object declarations and definitions directly, use the TYPEREAD.EXE tool (located in the OCTOOLS subdirectory). TYPEREAD scans the type library of an automation server and generates complete proxy code for controlling the server.

You are free to substitute your own code for the standard macros in order to handle special situations.

Macro	Description
AUTONAMES	Associates names with arguments so the caller can choose to pass only selected arguments

Macro	Description
AUTOARGS	Describes arguments that do not have names
AUTOCALL	Tells whether the command is a method or a property and whether it returns a value

Registration keys

Most ObjectComponents programs build registration tables describing their OLE capabilities. (Only automation controllers can omit this step.) The registration tables contain keys paired with values. The keys are standard. You decide which ones to register and you supply values for them.

Which keys you choose depends on whether your application is a server, a container, or an automation program. Some keys must be registered and some are optional. Furthermore, some apply only to the application's primary registration table, and others apply to the tables for each of the application's document types.

A registration table starts with the BEGIN_REGISTRATION macro and ends with END_REGISTRATION. In between is one macro for each key you want to register. The macro depends on the key. Most keys use the REGDATA macro, but there are others such as REGFORMAT and REGSTATUS.

If your application is a server, most of the information in its registration tables is recorded in the system's registration database. Putting the information there makes it possible for OLE to learn much about the server without actually loading the application into memory. For example, if an automation controller asks for information about the commands an automation server supports, OLE can locate the server's type library from an entry in the database.

Key	Meaning
aspectall	Option flags that apply to all presentation aspects.
aspectcontent	Option flags for the content view of an object.
aspectdocprint	Option flags for the printed document view of an object.
aspecticon	Option flags for the iconic view of an object.
aspectthumbnail	Option flags for the thumbnail view of an object.
clsid	A GUID identifying the application.
cmdline	Arguments OLE should place on the command line when it launches the server.
debugclsid	A GUID identifying the debugging version of a server. This is always generated internally. You should never specify it directly.
debugdesc	A **long** string describing the debugging version of a program.
debugger	The file name and command line switches for loading your debugger.
debugprogid	A string naming the debugging version of a program. Defining this forces ObjectComponents to register debugging and non-debugging versions.
description	A string describing the application.
directory	The default directory for browsing document files.
docfilter	File specification for listing files created by the application.
docflags	Option flags for the application's documents.
extension	A three-letter file-name extension for files created by the server.

Key	Meaning
filefmt	Name of default file format.
format*n*	A Clipboard format the application supports. (Use REGFORMAT to register Clipboard formats.)
handler	A full path pointing to a library that can draw objects created by the server. Defaults to OLE2.DLL.
helpdir	Full directory where online Help for the type library resides.
iconindex	An index telling which of the icons in the server's resources represents the type of objects the server produces. (Use REGICON to register an icon.)
insertable	Indicates that the application serves its document for linking and embedding in container documents.
language	Locale ID currently in effect. (Set internally during automation.)
menuname	A short name for the server, used in a container's menu.
path	The path where OLE looks to find the server. This key is set internally during registration.
permid	A string that names the application without indicating any version.
permname	A string that describes the application without indicating any version.
progid	A string uniquely naming the application.
typehelp	Name of the file where online Help for the type library resides.
usage	Indicates the whether the server can support concurrent clients with a single application instance.
verb*n*	A string naming an action the server can perform with its objects.
verb*n*opt	Option flags describing the server's verbs. (Use REGVERBOPT to register verb options.)
version	Version string for the application and type library.

Linking and embedding classes

ObjectComponents provides the following classes for use by applications that support linking and embedding.

Class	Purpose
TOcApp	Connector object that implements BOCOLE interfaces for the application
TOcContainerHost	Contains virtual functions that handle container events
TOcContainerHostMsg	Forwards container events to the view window
TOcControl	Connector object that a container uses to represent an embedded OCX control
TOcControlEvent	Forwards OCX control messages to the container
TOcDocument	Manages the parts in a container's compound document
TOcFormatList	List of Clipboard data formats a document supports
TOcFormatListIter	Iterator for the list of Clipboard data formats a document supports
TOcFormatName	Holds strings describing a single data format that an application might encounter on the Clipboard (see *TOcNameList*)
TOcModule	Base class for deriving OLE-enabled application objects
TOcNameList	Contains a collection of strings describing all the data formats that an application might find on the Clipboard

Class	Purpose
TOcPart	Connector object that a container uses to represent an object linked or embedded in one of its documents
TOcPartCollection	Manages a collection of linked or embedded parts
TOcPartCollectionIter	Iterator for the collection of parts linked or embedded in a single document
TOcRegistrar	Manages OLE registration tasks for a linking and embedding application
TOcRemView	Connector object that a server uses to draw an object linked or embedded in a container's document
TOcScaleFactor	Carries information from a container to a server requesting that linked or embedded objects be drawn to a certain scale
TOcServerHost	Contains virtual functions that handle server events
TOcServerHostMsg	Forwards server events to the view window
TOcVerb	Holds information about an action that a server is able to perform with its own objects when they are linked or embedded in a container
TOcView	A connector object that an application uses to draw its own documents in its own frame window
TOcxView	A TOcView-derived class that handles OCX control messages

A few of the ObjectComponents classes used for linking and embedding implement COM interfaces. (COM stands for Component Object Model. COM is the standard that defines what an OLE object is.) Most of the supported interfaces are not standard OLE interfaces; they are custom interfaces that communicate with OLE through the BOCOLE support library. But like any COM object they do implement *IUnknown* (by deriving from *TUnknown*).

The classes that define COM objects for linking and embedding are *TOcApp*, *TOcView*, *TOcRemView*, and *TOcPart*. These classes connect your application to OLE. They are called *connector objects*. An ObjectComponents application must create connector objects in order to interact with other OLE applications.

Figure 10.1 shows how the connector objects are related.

Figure 10.1   Hierarchy of ObjectComponents connector classes

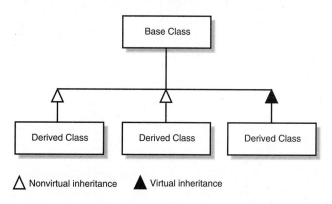

Linking and embedding enums

ObjectComponents provides the following enumerated types for use by applications that support linking and embedding.

Item	Description
TOcAppMode enum	Flags identifying the application's running conditions
TOcAspect enum	Flags identifying object presentation aspects
TOcDialogHelp enum	Constants identifying standard OLE dialog boxes where a user can ask for help
TOcDropAction enum	Constants identifying actions that can result from dropping an object on a window
TOcInitHow enum	Constants identifying the action a container is to take on receiving a new object— either link or embed
TOcInitWhere enum	Constants identifying places the data for an object can reside
TOcInvalidate enum	Flags indicating whether an object is invalid because of a change in its data or just in its appearance
TOcPartName enum	Constants identifying different strings a container might request when asking for the name of an object linked or embedded in it
TOcScrollDir enum	Constants identifying directions a container might be asked to scroll its window
TOcViewOptions	Constants identifying view options

Linking and embedding messages

ObjectComponents provides the following messages for use by applications that support linking and embedding.

Message	Purpose
OC_APPxxxx	Messages sent to an application object
OC_CTRLxxxx	Messages sent to an OCX control
OC_VIEWxxxx	Messages sent to a view object
WM_OCEVENT	Carries event signals from ObjectComponents to an application

Linking and embedding structs

ObjectComponents provides the following structs for use by applications that support linking and embedding.

Item	Purpose
TOcDragDrop struct	Holds information a container needs in order to receive an object dropped on its window
TOcInitInfo struct	Holds information a container needs in order to place a new object in its document
TOcMenuDescr struct	Holds information about a shared menu where the container and server merge their commands for in-place editing

Item	Purpose
TOcSaveLoad struct	Carries information an application needs to save or load a linked or embedded object
TOcToolbarInfo struct	Carries handles to a server's tool bars to be displayed in the container's window during in-place editing
TOcViewPaint struct	Carries information that tells a server how to repaint a linked or embedded object when the container invalidates part of the object's surface

ocrxxxx constants   ocf/ocreg.h

The ocreg.h header defines a number of constants used in constructing an application's registration tables. These constants all begin with *ocr*. They fall into several groups. Most of them are used with the REGFORMAT macro to describe the kinds of data transfers a document supports.

Group	Meaning
Aspect constants	Data presentation modes (such as icon, content, or thumbnail)
Clipboard constants	Clipboard data formats (such as text, bitmap, or link source)
Direction constants	Data transfer directions (getting or setting)
Limit constants	Maximum number of items that can be registered
Medium constants	Data transfer mediums (such as disk file or Clipboard)
Object status constants	Aspect options (such as showing icon only or redrawing on resize)
Usage constants	Support for multiple clients (single use or multiple use)
Verb attributes constants	Verb option flags (never dirties and show on menu)
Verb menu flags	Verb display options (such as grayed, disabled, or menu bar break)

ObjectComponents library reference

This chapter describes all the standard ObjectComponents classes, including their purpose, usage, and members. It also describes the non-object elements, such as structures, constants, variables, and macros that classes use.

_ICLASS macro   ocf/oleutil.h

Modifies the declaration of an interface class, one that defines or implements an interface for OLE or for the BOCOLE support library.

_IFUNC macro   ocf/oleutil.h

Modifies the declaration of an OLE function.

The _IFUNC macro controls function calling conventions and export declarations. Placing these macros in a keyword allows the compiler to choose the right combination of modifiers for a particular platform.

ObjectComponents uses the macro to declare OLE and BOCOLE functions as well as member functions that wrap direct OLE and BOCOLE calls.

_IFUNC serves the same purpose in Borland headers that the STDMETHODCALLTYPE serves in OLE system headers.

_OCFxxxx macros   ocf/ocfdefs.h

These macros are used internally to declare classes, functions, and data members in ObjectComponents classes. Their definitions vary depending on whether you build a 16- or 32-bit EXE or DLL. Some of them also force the declaration to __huge.

These macros closely match the corresponding _OWLxxxx macros.

Constant	Meaning
_OCFCLASS	Exports or imports classes for DLLs.
_OCFDATA	Exports or imports data members for DLLs.
_OCFFUNC	Exports or imports member functions for DLLs.

aspectall registration key

Registers option flags that affect all views of an object. The flags control how all views of the object are presented.

Linking and embedding servers can optionally register aspect status in their document registration tables. Aspect status does not apply to application registration tables, containers, or automation servers.

To register flags for all aspects, use the REGSTATUS macro, passing "all" as the first parameter and an *ocrxxxx* object status **enum** value as the second parameter.

```
REGSTATUS(all, ocrNoSpecialRendering)
```

See also   aspectcontent registration key, aspectdocprint registration key, aspecticon registration key, aspectthumbnail registration key, ocrxxxx Object Status enum, REGSTATUS macro

aspectcontent registration key

Registers option flags for the content view of an object. The content view usually shows all the data in an object (or as much of the data as fits in the available space.) The option flags control how the content view is used.

Linking and embedding servers can optionally register aspect status in their document registration tables. Aspect status does not apply to application registration tables, containers, or automation servers.

To register flags for the content aspect, use the REGSTATUS macro, passing *content* as the first parameter and an *ocrxxxx* object status **enum** value as the second parameter.

```
REGSTATUS(content, ocrRecomposeOnResize)
```

See also   aspectall registration key, aspectdocprint registration key, aspecticon registration key, aspectthumbnail registration key, ocrxxxx object status enum, REGSTATUS macro

aspectdocprint registration key

Registers option flags that affect the printed document view of an object. The printed document view usually approximates how the object will appear if sent to the current printer. The option flags control how the docprint view is presented.

Linking and embedding servers can optionally register aspect status in their document registration tables. Aspect status does not apply to application registration tables, containers, or automation servers.

To register flags for the printed document aspect, use the REGSTATUS macro, passing *docprint* as the first parameter and an *ocrxxxx* object status **enum** value as the second parameter.

See also   aspectall registration key, aspectcontent registration key, aspecticon registration key, aspectthumbnail registration key, ocrxxxx object status enum, REGSTATUS macro

aspecticon registration key

Registers option flags that affect the iconic view of an object. The icon view, rather than showing the object's contents, displays an icon that represents a particular kind of object. The option flags control how the icon view is presented.

Linking and embedding servers can optionally register aspect status in their document registration tables. Aspect status does not apply to application registration tables, containers, or automation servers.

To register flags for the icon aspect, use the REGSTATUS macro, passing *icon* as the first parameter and an *ocrxxxx* object status **enum** value as the second parameter.

```
REGSTATUS(icon, ocrOnlyIconic)
```

See also   aspectall registration key, aspectcontent registration key, aspectdocprint registration key, aspectthumbnail registration key, ocrxxxx object status enum, REGSTATUS macro

aspectthumbnail registration key

Registers option flags that affect the thumbnail view of an object. The thumbnail view usually shows a miniature representation of the object's contents. The flags control how the thumbnail view is presented.

Linking and embedding servers can optionally register aspect status in their document registration tables. Aspect status does not apply to application registration tables, containers, or automation servers.

To register flags for the thumbnail aspect, use the REGSTATUS macro, passing *thumbnail* as the first parameter and an *ocrxxxx* object status **enum** value as the second parameter.

See also   aspectall registration key, aspectcontent registration key, aspectdocprint registration key, aspecticon registration key, ocrxxxx object status enum, REGSTATUS macro

AUTOARGS macros   ocf/automacr.h

An automation controller uses AUTOARGS to implement methods in its proxy objects. AUTOARGS macros list all the arguments that the controller passes to an automation command, identifying them by the dummy parameter names used in the function definition.

AUTOARGS macros are the second in three sets of macros used to implement methods in proxy objects. The first, AUTONAMES, assigns names to any arguments that the controller wants to reference by name. The third set, AUTOCALL, tells whether the command is a method or a property and whether it returns a value.

The automacr.h header defines AUTOARG macros that accept up to six arguments. To generate versions that accept more arguments, use the MACROGEN.EXE utility.

Macro	Meaning
AUTOARGS0()	The automation command has no required arguments.
AUTOARGS1(a1)	The automation command requires argument *a1*.
AUTOARGS2(a1, a2)	The automation command requires arguments *a1* and *a2*.
AUTOARGS3(a1, a2, a3)	The automation command requires arguments *a1*, *a2*, and *a3*.
AUTOARGS4(a1, a2, a3, a4)	The automation command requires arguments *a1*, *a2*, *a3*, and *a4*.

AUTOCALxos   ocf/automacr.h

AUTOCALL is the third of three sets of macros that an automation controller uses to implement automation commands in proxy objects. The first two sets, AUTONAMES and AUTOARGS, describe the command's arguments. AUTOCALL macros tell whether the command represents a method or a property of the automated object and whether the command returns a value. Commands whose return values are themselves automated objects must also be specially marked.

Macro	Meaning
AUTOCALL_METHOD_REF(prx)	The command is a method that returns a reference to an object. *prx* is an object derived from *TAutoProxy* and receives the return value.
AUTOCALL_METHOD_RET	The command is a method that returns a value.
AUTOCALL_METHOD_VOID	The command is a method that returns no value.
AUTOCALL_PROP_GET	The command returns the value of a property of the automated object.

Macro	Meaning
AUTOCALL_PROP_REF(prx)	The command returns the value of a property and the value is itself an object. *prx* is an object derived from *TAutoProxy* and receives the return value.
AUTOCALL_PROP_SET(val)	The command assigns *val* to a property of the automated object.

_AUTOCLASS macro   ocf/autodefs.h

_AUTOCLASS is the class modifier that ObjectComponents uses to declare the base classes and member objects it creates inside your classes for automation. As long as your own classes use the application's ambient memory model, you do not have to worry about _AUTOCLASS, which by default is defined as nothing. If, however, you declare your automation classes with a modifier that differs from the ambient class model, then the classes (such as *TAutoBase*) that ObjectComponents defines must be modified to match. To accomplish the modification, define _AUTOCLASS yourself. For example:

```
#define _AUTOCLASS __far
```

AUTODATA macros   ocf/automacr.h

An automation server uses AUTODATA macros in an automation declaration (after DECLARE_AUTOCLASS) to make data members of an automated class accessible through OLE.

Both forms take the same four parameters. *name* is the internal name that you assign to the data member. ObjectComponents uses the internal names to keep track of all the automated members. The only other place you use this name is in the subsequent automation definition (after DEFINE_AUTOCLASS).

member is the C++ name of the data member, the name you normally use in your source code.

In most cases, *type* should be a normal C++ data type, but if the data member is a string or an object then specify *TAutoString* or one of the *TAutoObject* classes instead. See "Automation data types" for more details.

options is a place to insert a hook, code to be called each time the automation command is executed. Hooks can record, undo, or validate commands. See "Automation hook macros" for more details. *options* can be omitted, but a comma must follow the preceding argument anyway.

Macro	Meaning
AUTODATA(name, member, type, options)	The command permits read and write access to a data member.
AUTODATARO(name, member, type, options)	The command permits read-only access to a data member.

AutoDataType enum

ocf/autodefs.h

enum AutoDataType

These flags identify automation data types. The types correspond to standard OLE 2 data types. The *TAutoVal* class uses the flags to guide its conversions to and from the VARIANT unions that OLE passes between programs.

Constant	Meaning
atVoid	**void**
atNull	SQL-style null
atShort	2-byte **signed int**
atLong	4-byte **signed int**
atFloat	4-byte real
atDouble	8-byte real
atCurrency	currency
atDatetime	datetime as **double**
atString	BSTR, string preceded by length
atObject	*IDispatch**
atError	SCODE
atBool	**True** = –1, **false** = 0
atVariant	VARIANT FAR*
atUnknown	*IUnknown**
atTypeMask	Base type code without bit flags
atOLE2Mask	Type code with bit flags

The preceding flags are mutually exclusive. A value can belong to only one type. Any of the type flags can, however, be combined with the following bit flags.

Bit Flag	Meaning
atByRef	The value is a reference to an object.
atEnum	The value is an enumeration of some type.

See also   TAutoVal class, TAutoEnumTpublic constructor

AUTODETACH macro

ocf/automacr.h

AUTODETACH

An automation server uses this macro in its automation declaration (after DECLARE_AUTOCLASS) to ensure that whenever the automated object is destroyed OLE receives notification. Sending the object's obituary to OLE prevents crashes should a controller attempt to manipulate the nonexistent object. The obituary is necessary only if the logic of your program makes it possible for the automated object to be destroyed by non-automated means while still connected to the controller.

Deriving a class from *TAutoBase* serves exactly the same purpose. The advantage of AUTODETACH is that you can use it to automate classes you did not create and whose derivation you cannot control.

AUTOENUM macros   ocf/automacr.h

An automation server uses the AUTOENUM macros to expose enumerated values to automation controllers. For example, if the server wants the controller to pass actions into a DoThis command, the server might create an enumerated type containing values such as Play, Stop, and Rewind. To make these values available to the controller, the server must create an AUTOENUM table. In this example, the table consists of three AUTOENUM macros, one for each enumerated value.

```
DEFINE_AUTOENUM(TAction, TAutoShort);
  AUTOENUM("Play", Play)
  AUTOENUM("Stop", Stop)
  AUTOENUM("Rewind", Rewind);
  END_AUTOENUM(TAction, TAutoShort)
```

Macro	Meaning
DEFINE_AUTOENUM(cls, type)	Begins an AUTOENUM table. *cls* is the name of the automated enumeration type (not the name of the C++ enumerated type). You invent this name. The only other place it appears is in the application's automation definition.
	type is the automation data type that describes what kind of values are being enumerated. For more information, see "Automation data types."
AUTOENUM(name, val)	*name* is the public string that a controller uses to refer to one in a series of enumerated values. *val* is the internal value the server associates with *name*.
END_AUTOENUM(cls, type)	Ends an AUTOENUM table. *cls* and *type* are the same as for DEFINE_AUTOENUM.

AUTOFLAG macro   ocf/automacr.h

AUTOFLAG(name, data, mask, options)
An automation server uses AUTOFLAG in an automation declaration (after DECLARE_AUTOCLASS) to expose for automation a single bit from a set of bit flags.

name is an internal name that you assign to the bit. ObjectComponents uses the internal names to keep track of all the automated members. The only other place you use this name is in the subsequent automation definition (after DEFINE_AUTOCLASS).

data is the C++ name of a data member that holds a set of bit flags.

mask is a value with one bit set marking the position of the exposed flag in *data*.

options is a place to insert a hook, code to be called each time the automation command is executed. Hooks can record, undo, or validate commands. See "Automation hook macros" for more details. *options* can be omitted, but a comma must follow the preceding argument anyway.

AUTOFUNC macros   ocf/automacr.h

An automation server uses AUTOFUNC macros in an automation declaration (after DECLARE_AUTOCLASS) to make member functions of an automated class accessible through OLE.

In every version of the macro the first parameter, *name*, is an internal name that you assign to the function. ObjectComponents uses the internal names to keep track of all the automated members. The only other place you use this name is in the subsequent automation definition (after DEFINE_AUTOCLASS).

func is the C++ name of the member function, the name you normally use in your source code.

ret is the type of data the function returns. *type1*, *t1*, *t2*, *t3*, and *t4* represent the data types of the parameters. In most cases, all these data types should be normal C++ data types, but if the data member is a string or an object then specify *TAutoString* or one of the *TAutoObject* classes instead. See "Automation data types" for more details. Also, automated functions cannot return **const** values. Do not use const in a *ret* type.

options is a place to insert a hook, code to be called each time the automation command is executed. Hooks can record, undo, or validate commands. See "Automation hook macros" for more details. *options* can be omitted, but a comma must follow the preceding argument anyway.

The automacr.h header defines versions of this macro that accept up to three arguments. To generate versions that accept more arguments, use the MACROGEN.EXE utility.

Macro	Meaning
AUTOFUNC0(name, func, ret, options)	The function takes no parameters and returns a value of type *ret*.
AUTOFUNC0V(name, func, options)	The function takes no parameters and returns **void**.
AUTOFUNC1(name, func, ret, type1, options)	The function takes one parameter of type *type1* and returns a value of type *ret*.
AUTOFUNC1V(name, func, type1, options)	The function takes one parameter of type *type1* and returns **void**.
AUTOFUNC2(name, func, ret, t1, t2, options)	The function takes two parameters of types *t1* and *t2*. It returns a value of type *ret*.
AUTOFUNC2V(name, func, t1, t2, options)	The function takes two parameters and returns **void**.
AUTOFUNC3(name, func, ret, t1, t2, t3, options)	The function takes three parameters and returns a value.
AUTOFUNC3V(name, func, t1 ,t2, t3, options)	The function takes three parameters and returns **void**.
AUTOFUNC4(name, func, ret, t1, t2, t3, t4, options)	The function takes four parameters and returns a value.
AUTOFUNC4V(name, func, t1, t2, t3, t4, options)	The function takes four parameters and returns **void**.

AUTOINVOKE macro

ocf/automacr.h

AUTOINVOKE(code)

An automation server uses AUTOINVOKE in an automation declaration macro to hook in user-defined code for ObjectComponents to execute every time the application receives a particular automation command. *code* is the expression or function call to execute on each command.

Create an AUTOINVOKE hook if you want to override the normal execution sequence.

AUTOITERATOR macros

ocf/automacr.h

An iterator is an object used to enumerate a collection of objects. An iterator's methods let the caller step through a list of objects and examine each one in turn.

An automation server needs to create an iterator in any automated object that represents a collection of other objects. To create an iterator, the server adds one of the AUTOITERATOR macros to the class's automation definition (after DEFINE_AUTOCLASS). The iterator must also be exposed in the automation definition with the EXPOSE_ITERATOR macro.

Macro	Meaning
AUTOITERATOR(state, init, test, step, extract)	Implements a collection iterator within the automated class.
AUTOITERATOR_DECLARE(state)	Declares but does not implement a collection iterator within the automated class. Use this if your iterator's implementation is too complex for AUTOITERATOR.

The five arguments of AUTOITERATOR define the iteration algorithm for the collection class. Only one auto-iterator can exist within a class, so there is no need for a special internal name. The five arguments each represent a code fragment, and they follow the sequence of code in a **for** loop. As the examples show, because the iterator object is nested within the automated collection class, it can refer to members of the class.

Parameter	Example	Meaning
state	int Index	Declaration of state variables. This must be the same declaration previously given in AUTOITERATOR_DECLARE.
init	Index = 0	Statements (usually assignments) executed to initialize the loop.
test	Index < This->Total	Boolean expression tested each time through the loop.
step	Index++	Statements executed each time through the loop.
extract	(This->Array)[Index]	Expression that returns the successive objects in the collection.

Within the parameters, *This* (note the capital T) points to the enclosing collection object, not to the nested iterator object.

Commas cannot be used except inside parentheses. Semicolons can be used to separate multiple statements, but not to end a macro argument.

If you use AUTOITERATOR_DECLARE instead of AUTOITERATOR, then you must implement the state variables and these methods, corresponding to the steps described for AUTOITERATOR.

```
void Init();
bool Test();
void Step();
void Return(TAutoVal& v);
```

AUTONAMES macros   ocf/automacr.h

The AUTONAMES macros are the first in three sets of macros that an automation controller uses to implement methods in its proxy objects. AUTONAMES macros assign names to any arguments that the controller wants to reference by name. Named parameters have default values and are not required in a command. If a command has fifteen parameters and ten of them have names and default values, then the controller must always pass the five unnamed parameters and can choose to pass any subset of the remaining ten, identifying them by their names.

The second set of macros, AUTOARGS, describe the data types of unnamed arguments that must always be passed in the command. The third set, AUTOCALL, tells whether the command is a method or a property and what it returns.

In the macros that follow, *id* is a numeric ID for a method, *fname* is a string naming a method, and *n1*, *n2*, *n3*, and *n4* are strings assigned as argument names. Most of the macros need the function name to identify the function, but if a function has no named arguments, then you can pass its identifying number instead.

The automacr.h header defines AUTONAMES macros that accept up to ten arguments. To generate versions that accept more arguments, use the MACROGEN.EXE utility.

Macro	Meaning
AUTONAMES0(id)	Function *id* has no named arguments.
AUTONAMES0(fname)	Function *fname* has no named arguments.
AUTONAMES1(fname, n1)	Function *fname* has one named argument, *n1*.
AUTONAMES2(fname, n1, n2)	Function *fname* has two named arguments, *n1* and *n2*.
AUTONAMES3(fname, n1, n2, n3)	Function *fname* has three named arguments, *n1*, *n2*, and *n3*.
AUTONAMES4(fname, n1, n2, n3, n4)	Function *fname* has four named arguments, *n1*, *n2*, *n3*, and *n4*.

AUTONOHOOK macro   ocf/automacr.h

AUTONOHOOK

An automation server uses AUTONOHOOK in an automation declaration macro to prevent anyone from hooking the command. Not even ObjectComponents can monitor the call.

AUTONOHOOK is for advanced uses only.

AUTOPROP macros
ocf/automacr.h

An automation server uses AUTOPROP macros in its automation declaration (after DECLARE_AUTOCLASS) to make properties of an automated class accessible to OLE. A property is data that cannot be read or written directly, only through a set of access functions (for example, *GetPosition* and *SetPosition*).

A server can implement the access functions any way it likes. Because only the access functions are exposed, the property does not have to be a data member. In other words, *GetPosition* and *SetPosition* would not have to refer to a data member of type *TPoint*. They might query the system for the cursor position and return the answer.

The three AUTOPROP macros have similar parameters. *name* is an internal name you assign to the property. ObjectComponents uses the name to keep track of all the automated members. The only other place you use this internal name is in the corresponding automation definition.

get and *set* are the access functions. A read-only property has just a get function. A write-only property has just a set function.

type is the property's data type. This is usually a C++ data type, but string and object properties require special treatment.

options is a place to insert a hook, code to be called each time the automation command is executed. Hooks can record, undo, or validate commands. See "Automation hook macros" for more details. *options* can be omitted, but a comma must follow the preceding argument anyway.

Macro	Meaning
AUTOPROP(name, get, set, type, options)	The property can be read and written.
AUTOPROPRO(name, get, type, options)	The property can only be read, not changed.
AUTOPROPWO(name, set, type, options)	The property can be changed but not read (rare).

AUTORECORD macro
ocf/automacr.h

AUTORECORD(code)

An automation server uses AUTORECORD in an automation declaration macro to hook in user-defined code that creates a record of each call made to a particular automation command. *code* is the expression or function call to execute on each command. It should store whatever information the application would need to play back the same command later.

Recording is not supported in the current version of ObjectComponents.

AUTOREPORT macro
ocf/automacr.h

AUTOREPORT(code)

An automation server uses AUTOREPORT in an automation declaration macro to hook in user-defined code that checks the error code from an automated member function. If *code* evaluates to 0, OLE assumes the command succeeded. If *code* evaluates to a nonzero value, then OLE throws an exception in the controller. Within the code expression, use *Val* to refer to the actual value returned.

AutoSymFlag enum   ocf/autodefs.h

enum AutoSymFlag

These flags are used in the *TAutoCommand* class to describe attributes of an automation command. The flags tell whether the command is a method or a property, whether arguments are passed by value or by reference, and whether it should be visible in type information browsers.

Constant	Meaning
asAnyCommand	Any command: method, property access, object builder.
asOleType	Method or property exposed for OLE.
asMethod	Method.
asGet	Returns the value of a property.
asIterator	Iterator property; used to enumerate items in a collection.
asSet	Set property value.
asGetSet	Get or set a property value.
asBuild	Constructor command (not supported by OLE 2.01).
asArgument	Property that returns an object.
asArgByVal	The value of the argument is passed.
asArgByRef	The argument is a pointer to a value.
asFactory	For creating objects or determining class.
asClass	Extension to another class symbol table.
asBindable	Sends *OnChanged* notification.
asRequestEdit	Sends *OnRequest* edit before change.
asDisplayBind	User-display of bindable.
asDefaultBind	This property only is the default (redundant).
asHidden	Not visible to normal browsing.
asPersistent	Property is persistent.

See also   TAutoCommand public constructor

AUTOSTAT macros   ocf/automacr.h

Use the AUTOSTAT in an automation declaration (after DECLARE_AUTOCLASS) to make static member functions and global functions accessible to OLE.

All versions of the AUTOSTAT macro have similar parameters. *name* is an internal name you assign to the function. ObjectComponents uses the name to keep track of all the automated members. The only other place you use this internal name is in the corresponding automation definition.

func is the name of the static or global function.

ret is the type of value the function returns.

type1, t1, t2, t3, and *t4* are the types of the function's arguments.

options is a place to insert a hook, code to be called each time the automation command is executed. Hooks can record, undo, or validate commands. See "Automation hook macro" for more details. *options* can be omitted, but a comma must follow the preceding argument anyway.

The return types and argument types are usually normal C++ data types, but string and object values require special treatment. See "Automation data types" for more information.

Macro	Meaning
AUTOSTAT0(name, func, ret, options)	The static function *func* is assigned the symbol *name*. It takes no arguments and returns a value of type *ret*.
AUTOSTAT0V(name, func, options)	The static function *func* takes no arguments and returns no value.
AUTOSTAT1(name, func, ret, type1, options)	*func* takes one argument of type *type1* and returns a value of type *ret*.
AUTOSTAT1V(name, func, type1, options)	*func* takes one argument of type *type1* and returns no value.
AUTOSTAT2(name, func, ret, t1, t2, options)	*func* takes two arguments of types *t1* and *t2* and returns a value of type *ret*.
AUTOSTAT2V(name, func, t1,t2, options)	*func* takes two arguments and returns no value.
AUTOSTAT3(name, func, ret, t1,t2, t3, options)	*func* takes three arguments and returns a value.
AUTOSTAT3V(name, func, t1, t2, t3, options)	*func* takes three arguments and returns no value.
AUTOSTAT4(name, func, ret, t1, t2, t3, t4, options)	*func* takes four arguments and returns a value.
AUTOSTAT4V(name, func, t1, t2, t3, t4, options)	*func* takes four arguments and returns no value.

AUTOTHIS macro ocf/automacr.h

AUTOTHIS(name, type, options)
An automation server uses the AUTOTHIS macro in its automation declaration (after DECLARE_AUTOCLASS) if it wants to expose the C++ object itself as a member of the automated OLE object.

name is an internal name you assign to the property. ObjectComponents uses the name to keep track of all the automated members. The only other place you use this internal name is in the corresponding automation definition.

type must be *TAutoObject<T>*, where *T* is the type of the automated class.

options is a place to insert a hook, code to be called each time a controller asks for this property. Hooks can record, undo, or validate commands. See "Automation hook macros" for more details. *options* can be omitted, but a comma must follow the preceding argument anyway.

AUTOUNDO macro

ocf/automacr.h

AUTOUNDO(code)

An automation server uses AUTOUNDO in an automation declaration macro to hook in user-defined code that records whatever information the application needs to reverse the command later. Usually it adds information to a user-maintained undo stack. The information might include the parameters that execute the inverse of the original command, for example. To undo a series of actions, the program can pop commands off the undo stack and execute them. *code* is the expression or function that records information.

Undoing commands is not supported in the current version of ObjectComponents.

AUTOVALIDATE macro

ocf/automacr.h

AUTOVALIDATE(condition)

An automation server uses AUTOVALIDATE in an automation declaration macro to hook in user-defined code that confirms the validity of received arguments before passing them on to be processed in a command. *condition* is an expression or function that evaluates to true if the arguments received are valid for the command and false if not. If the expression returns false, OLE throws an exception in the controller application.

clsid registration key

Registers a globally unique identifier (GUID) for the application's class ID. A GUID is a 16-byte value and can be represented as a string.

A *clsid* GUID is required in every application registration table. You never need to specify any others. If others are needed for your documents, type library, automated classes, or debugging invocation, ObjectComponents automatically increments the low-order field of the first GUID to produce them. Be sure to allow for the full range of numbers your application actually uses when determining the next available GUID for another program.

There are several ways to acquire a *clsid*. One is to run the GUIDGEN tool in the OCTOOLS directory. Also, AppExpert automatically generates a GUID for any applications it creates that support OLE. Another way to get a GUID is to call the OLE API *CoCreateGuid*, as documented in the Help file OLE2HELP.HLP. Finally, you can contact Microsoft to have a block of GUIDs assigned to you permanently.

Every application must have its own absolutely unique *clsid* string, so never use values pasted in from example programs.

To register a *clsid*, use the REGDATA macro with *clsid* as the first parameter and a GUID string as the second parameter.

```
REGDATA(clsid, "{CDE7F941-544B-101B-A9C1-04021C007002}")
```

cmdline registration key

Registers arguments OLE should place on the command line when it launches the server's executable file.

The *cmdline* key is valid in application registration tables but is ignored for DLL servers. Any application can register it, but normally only automation servers have a use for it.

Automation servers can use the *cmdline* key to set up the **–Automation** switch. When the registrar object sees this switch, it overrides the application's registered *usage* setting and forces the program to run in single-use mode. This is useful in a server that supports linking and embedding as well as automation. As a linking and embedding server, it might support concurrent client applications with a single instance. When running as an automation server, however, most applications don't want concurrent client programs to control exactly the same instance of an object.

To register command-line options, use the REGDATA macro with *cmdline* as the first parameter and a string containing command-line arguments as the second parameter.

```
REGDATA(cmdline, "/automation")
```

debugclsid registration key

A GUID identifying the debugging version of a server. You should never register this key directly. It is always generated for you automatically if you register *debugprogid*.

This key is ignored in DLL servers.

See also debugprogid registration key

debugdesc registration key

A string describing the debugging version of your program. When used in registering a document, this string appears in the Insert Object menu. When used in registering an application, it appears in object browsers. The string can contain up to 40 characters and can be localized.

The *debugdesc* key is required in application and document registration tables for any program that registers the *debugprogid* key. Otherwise it is irrelevant.

To register the *debugdesc* key, use the REGDATA macro, passing *debugdesc* as the first parameter and the descriptive string as the second parameter.

```
REGDATA(debugdesc, "My Application (debugging)")
```

This key is ignored in DLL servers.

See also debugclsid registration key, debugger registration key, debugprogid registration key, REGDATA macro

debugger registration key

Registers the path and filename for loading your debugger.

The *debugger* key is valid in any registration table. It is required if you also register *debugprogid*. Otherwise it is irrelevant.

To register the *debugger* key, use the REGDATA macro, passing *debugger* as the first parameter and the command-line string for the debugger application as the second parameter. When OLE invokes the debugger, it places the second parameter string on the command line ahead of the server's .EXE path. The debugger string can optionally contain a full path and debugger command-line switches.

```
REGDATA(debugger, "TDW") // assumes TDW is somewhere on the path
```

This key is ignored in DLL servers.

See also   debugclsid registration key, debugdesc registration key, debugprogid registration key, REGDATA macro

debugprogid registration key

A string identifying the debugging version of a program. Just as a *progid* string does, this string has two parts divided by a period. The first part is your program's name, and the second part is *.debug*.

Assigning a value to the *debugprogid* key causes ObjectComponents to create two sets of entries for the server in the registration database. When you choose Insert Object from the Edit menu, both entries appear in the list. Choosing the debugging entry causes ObjectComponents to invoke your debugger together with the server. Without the ability to register a duplicate debugging entry, it is difficult to debug the server when OLE invokes it.

ObjectComponents generates a *clsid* for the debugger entry automatically.

The *debugprogid* key is optional for application registration tables and irrelevant for document registration tables. If you register *debugprogid*, you also need to register *debugdesc* and *debugger*.

To register a *debugprogid*, use the REGDATA macro, passing *debugprogid* as the first parameter and the ID string as the second parameter.

```
REGDATA(debugprogid, "MyApp.Debug")
```

This key is ignored in DLL servers.

See also   debugclsid registration key, debugdesc registration key, debugger registration key, progid registration key, REGDATA macro

DECLARE_AUTOCLASS macro

ocf/automacr.h

DECLARE_AUTOCLASS(cls)

DECLARE_AUTOCLASS(cls) introduces a block of macros that declare automatable members of the user-defined class *cls*.

An automation server uses DECLARE_AUTOCLASS to begin a block of macros that make automatable members of a user-defined C++ class accessible to OLE. *cls* is the name of the user's C++ class.

The block of declaration macros usually appears in the definition of the automatable C++ class. A corresponding block of automation definition macros must appear in the implementation of the automatable C++ class.

DECLARE_COMBASES*n*macros

ocf/oleutil.h

Use the COMBASES macros to create C++ objects that conform to the OLE Component Object Model (COM). COM objects support OLE interfaces and let you derive classes that interact with OLE directly, not through ObjectComponents. These macros are meant for advanced users.

COM objects are used as base classes for other objects. The derived class must inherit from both your COM class and from the ObjectComponents *TUnknown* class. *TUnknown* implements the controlling *IUnknown* interface for your object.

To create a COM class:

1 Precede the declaration of the class with one of the DECLARE_COMBASES macros. Which you choose depends on how many interfaces (besides *IUnknown)* the COM class supports.

2 Precede the implementation of your COM class with the corresponding DEFINE_COMBASES macro.

3 Derive your final class multiply from *TUnknown* and your new COM class (in that order).

The first macro argument is *name.* It is the name of the COM class you are creating. *i1, i2, i3,* and *i4* are the names of the interfaces your COM class supports.

Macro	Meaning
DECLARE_COMBASES1(name, i1)	Declare a COM class *name* that inherits from the *i1* interface class.
DECLARE_COMBASES2(name, i1, i2)	Declare a COM class *name* that inherits from the *i1* and *i2* interface classes.
DECLARE_COMBASES3(name, i1, i2, i3)	Declare a COM class *name* that inherits from the *i1, i2,* and *i3* interface classes.
DECLARE_COMBASES4(name, i1, i2, i3, i4)	Declare a COM class *name* that inherits from the *i1, i2, i3,* and *i4* interface classes.

DEFINE_AUTOAGGREGATE macro ocf/automacr.h

DEFINE_AUTOAGGREGATE(cls, AggregatorFunction)

An automation server uses DEFINE_AUTOAGGREGATE to begin a block of macros that define automatable members of *cls*, a user-defined C++ class. The block ends with the END_AUTOAGGREGATE macro.

DEFINE_AUTOCLASS does the same thing but without the extra *AggregatorFunction* parameter. Use DEFINE_AUTOAGGREGATE when the C++ class you are automating is, inherits from, or delegates to a Component Object Model (COM) object. The *AggregatorFunction* parameter points to the aggregating function for reaching the COM object. For example, if *Aggregate* is the name of the COM object, the aggregator function might be any of these expressions:

```
Aggregate          // automated C++ object is the COM object
OcApp->Aggregate   // automated C++ object delegates to COM object
MyBase::Aggregate  // automated C++ object inherits from COM object
```

See also DEFINE_AUTOCLASS, END_AUTOAGGREGATE

DEFINE_AUTOCLASS macro ocf/automacr.h

DEFINE_AUTOCLASS(cls)

Introduces a block of macros in an automation server. Each macro in the block defines an automatable member of *cls*, a user-defined C++ class. The block ends with the END_AUTOCLASS macro.

The block of definition macros appears in the implementation of the automatable C++ class. A corresponding block of automation declaration macros must appear in the definition of the same class.

See also END_AUTOCLASS macro

DEFINE_COMBASES*n*macros ocf/oleutil.h

Implements the *IUnknown* interface for each of the OLE interfaces that your COM object supports.

Use the COMBASE macros to create C++ objects that conform to the OLE Component Object Model (COM). COM objects support OLE interfaces and let you derive classes that interact with OLE directly, not through ObjectComponents. These macros are meant for advanced users.

Automated objects can delegate to COM objects using the DEFINE_AUTOAGGREGATE and DECLARE_AUTOAGGREGATE macros.

To create a COM class,

1 Precede the declaration of the class with one of the DECLARE_COMBASES macros. Which you choose depends on how many interfaces (besides *IUnknown*) the COM class supports.

2 Precede the implementation of your COM class with the corresponding DEFINE_COMBASES macro.

3 Derive your final class multiply from your new COM class and from *TUnknown*.

COM objects can delegate to other COM objects using another set of related macros also defined in oleutil.h. For more information, look in the header file for the DEFINE_QI_xxxx macros.

Macro	Meaning
DEFINE_COMBASES1(name, i1)	Define *IUnknown* for the *i1* interface in the COM class *name*.
DEFINE_COMBASES2(name, i1, i2)	Define *IUnknown* for the *i1* and *i2* interfaces in the COM class *name*.
DEFINE_COMBASES3(name, i1, i2, i3)	Define *IUnknown* for the *i1*, *i2*, and *i3* interfaces in the COM class *name*.
DEFINE_COMBASES4(name, i1, i2, i3, i4)	Define *IUnknown* for the *i1*, *i2*, *i3*, and *i4* interfaces in the COM class *name*.

See also   DECLARE_COMBASES*n* macros

description registration key

Registers a long descriptive name, up to 40 characters, meant for the user to see. The string describes the application or its document types and appears in the Insert Object dialog box. This value should be localized.

A description string is required in every registration table. To register a description string, use the REGDATA macro, passing *description* as the first parameter and the descriptive string as the second parameter.

```
REGDATA(description, "OWL Drawing Pad 2.0")
```

See also   REGDATA macro

directory registration key

Registers the default directory for document files. The document template class refers to this path when it invokes a File Open common dialog box. The directory path is not used by OLE.

The directory key is valid in any document registration table. It is always optional.

To register a directory, use the REGDATA macro, passing *directory* as the first parameter and a path name as the second parameter.

```
REGDATA(directory, "C:\\temp")
```

docfilter registration key

Registers a file specification for listing files created by the application. This information is used by the document template class when it creates a File Open common dialog box. It is not used by OLE.

docfilter is valid in any document registration table. It is required unless the corresponding *docflags* key includes the *dtHidden* flag. If you register a document filter, you might also want to register the *extension* key.

To register a document filter, use the REGDATA macro, passing *docflags* as the first parameter and a filter string as the second parameter.

```
REGDATA(docfilter, "*.txt")
```

See also   docflags registration key, dt document view constants, extension registration key, REGDATA macro

docflags registration key

Registers document view option flags for the application's documents. This information is used by the document template class, not by OLE. The document template uses the flags to control its display of the File Open common dialog box. For a list of all the flags, see the description of *dtxxxx* Document View Constants.

The *docflags* key is valid in any document registration table. It is always optional.

To register document flags, use the REGDOCFLAGS macro.

```
REGDOCFLAGS(dtAutoOpen | dtAutoDelete | dtUpdateDir | dtCreatePrompt)
```

See also   docfilter registration key, dt document view constants, REGDOCFLAGS macro

DynamicCast function   ocf/autodefs.h

```
const void far* DynamicCast(const void far* obj, const typeinfo& src, const typeinfo& dst);
```
Attempts to convert a pointer from one type to another. The attempt succeeds only if the old type and the new type are related through inheritance.

obj is the pointer you want to cast to a new type. *src* is type information about the source object. *dst* is information about the destination type.

If the conversion succeeds, *DynamicCast* returns a pointer to the new type. If it fails, the return is zero.

You can generate the *src* and *dst* parameters with the *typeid* parameter. (ObjectComponents requires the use of RTTI.)

See also   MostDerived function, typeid, typeinfo class

END_AUTOAGGREGATE macro   ocf/automacr.h

END_AUTOAGGREGATE(cls, name, doc, help)

Terminates a block of macros that an automation server uses to define automatable methods in *cls*, a user-defined C++ class. The definition block begins with DEFINE_AUTOAGGREGATE.

The related DEFINE_AUTOCLASS and END_AUTOCLASS macros also mark an automation definition block. Use the aggregation macros when *cls* is, inherits from, or delegates to a Component Object Model (COM) object.

name is the string that automation controllers use to identify objects of type *cls*. If the user asks OLE about the object name, the system returns the string in *doc*. If an .HLP file is registered for the object, then the context ID in *help* points to a screen that describes the object.

See also   DEFINE_AUTOAGGREGATE macro, END_AUTOCLASS macro

END_AUTOCLASS macro   ocf/automacr.h

END_AUTOCLASS(cls, name, doc, help)

Terminates the block of macros an automation server uses to define automatable methods in *cls*, a user-defined C++ class. The definition block begins with DEFINE_AUTOCLASS.

name is the string that automation controllers use to identify objects of type *cls*. If the user asks OLE about the object name, the system returns the string in *doc*. If an .HLP file is registered for the object, then the context ID in *help* points to a screen that describes the object.

See also   DEFINE_AUTOCLASS macro

EXPOSE_APPLICATION macro   ocf/automacr.h

EXPOSE_APPLICATION(cls, extName, doc, help)

An automation server uses EXPOSE_APPLICATION in its automation definition (after DEFINE_AUTOCLASS) if it chooses to expose the application itself as a member of its automated object. OLE conventions suggest that each automation object should have this member.

cls is the class name of the application.

extName is the external, public name you assign to this member. Automation controllers use this string to refer to the application member. The string can be localized.

doc is a string that describes this member to the user. An automation controller can ask OLE for this string if the user requests help.

help is a context ID for an .HLP file. This parameter, which can be omitted, is useful only if you register an .HLP file to document your server. If you do, then when the user asks the controller for help, the controller passes this context ID to the Help system to display a screen describing the object member.

EXPOSE_DELEGATE macro ocf/automacr.h

EXPOSE_DELEGATE(cls, extName, locator)
An automation server uses EXPOSE_DELEGATE in its automation definition (after DEFINE_AUTOCLASS) in order to combine two unrelated C++ classes into a single OLE automation object. In effect, the application's primary automated class delegates some tasks to another automated class. This macro tells ObjectComponents to search both classes to determine what commands the automated OLE object can perform.

cls is the name of the auxiliary class, which must also be automated. In other words, it must contain its own automation declaration and definition.

extName is an external, public name that an OLE controller uses to refer to this member of the object.

locator is a function that returns a pointer to an auxiliary object. In order to call members of that class, ObjectComponents needs a pointer to an object of that type. The conversion function should follow this prototype:

```
auxclass *locator( autoclass *this );
```

auxclass is the name of the auxiliary class and *autoclass* is the name of the primary automated class. *locator* in effect converts a *this* pointer to a *that* pointer.

See also EXPOSE_INHERIT macro

EXPOSE_INHERIT macro ocf/automacr.h

EXPOSE_INHERIT(cls, extName);
An automation server uses EXPOSE_INHERIT in its automation definition (after DEFINE_AUTOCLASS) in order to combine two related C++ classes into a single OLE automation object. In effect, the application's primary automated class delegates some tasks to its base class. This macro tells ObjectComponents to search both classes to determine what commands the automated OLE object can perform.

cls is the name of the base class, which must also be automated. In other words, it must contain its own automation declaration and definition.

extName is an external, public name that an OLE controller uses to refer to this member of the object. It can be localized.

See also EXPOSE_DELEGATE macro

EXPOSE_ITERATOR macro   ocf/automacr.h

EXPOSE_ITERATOR(retType, doc, help);

An automation server uses EXPOSE_ITERATOR in its automation definition (after DEFINE_AUTOCLASS) in order to expose an iterator object to enumerate objects in a collection. An iterator is useful only when the automated object itself represents a collection of other objects. The controller uses methods of the nested iterator object to retrieve and examine successive objects in a list.

retType is an automated data type that describes the type of the objects in the collection. For example, if the collection is an array of short integers, then *retType* should be *TAutoShort*. For more information, see "Automation data types."

doc is a string that describes the iterator to the user. An automation controller can ask OLE for this string if the user requests help.

help is a context ID for an .HLP file. This parameter, which can be omitted, is useful only if you register an .HLP file to document your server. If you do, then when the user asks the controller for help, the controller passes this context ID to the Help system to display a screen describing the iterator.

See also
AUTOITERATOR macros

EXPOSE_METHOD macros   ocf/automacr.h

EXPOSE_METHOD(intName, retType, extName, doc, help);
EXPOSE_METHOD_ID(id, intName, retType, extName, doc, help);

An automation server uses EXPOSE_METHOD macros in its automation definition (after DEFINE_AUTOCLASS) to expose a member function of an object to OLE for automation.

intName is an internal name that you assign to identify the method. ObjectComponents uses the internal name to keep track of all the automated members. This name must match the name assigned to the method with the AUTOFUNC macro in the automation declaration.

retType is a data type that describes the type of value the method returns. For example, if the method returns a long integer, then *retType* should be *TAutoLong*. For more information, see "Automation data types."

extName is the external, public name that a controller uses to specify this method. The string can be localized.

doc is a string that describes this method to the user. An automation controller can ask OLE for this string if the user requests help. This string can also be localized.

help is a context ID for an .HLP file. This parameter, which can be omitted, is useful only if you register an .HLP file to document your server. If you do, then when the user asks the controller for help, the controller passes this context ID to the Help system to display a screen describing the method.

id is a dispatch identifier that you can choose to assign explicitly by using one of the EXPOSE_METHOD_ID macros. The dispatch ID is what OLE passes to identify commands requested by a controller. The OLE system header files define several standard dispatch ID values. For example, –5 is the default evaluation method. Standard dispatch IDs are always negative numbers. By default, dispatch IDs are assigned low positive numbers incremented from 1. If you want to specify explicit dispatch IDs for your applications, choose high positive values in order not to collide with the low positive numbers ObjectComponents assigns to exposed members without explicit IDs.

0 is the ID of the default method or property. ObjectComponents never automatically assigns 0 as a dispatch ID. To have a default method, you need to assign 0 yourself.

An EXPOSE_METHOD or EXPOSE_METHOD_ID macro must always be followed immediately by one macro for each of the method's arguments.

Type of Argument	Declaration Macro
Required	REQUIRED_ARG
Optional	OPTIONAL_ARG
Object passed by reference	REQBYREF_ARG

See also   AUTOFUNC macros, OPTIONAL_ARG macro, REQBYREF_ARG macro, REQUIRED_ARG macro

EXPOSE_PROPxxxx macros
ocf/automacr.h

An automation server uses EXPOSE_PROPxxxx macros in its automation definition (after DEFINE_AUTOCLASS) to expose properties of an object to OLE for automation. A property is data that can be read or written only through a set of access functions (for example, *GetPosition* and *SetPosition*).

intName is an internal name that you assign to identify the property. ObjectComponents uses the internal name to keep track of all the automated members. This name must match the name assigned to the method with the AUTOPROP macro in the automation declaration.

type is a data type that describes the type of value the property holds. For example, if the property is a string, then *type* should be *TAutoString*. For more information, see "Automation data types."

extName is the public name that a controller uses to refer to this property. The string can be localized.

doc is a string that describes this property to the user. An automation controller can ask OLE for this string if the user requests help. This string can also be localized.

help is a context ID for an .HLP file. This parameter, which can be omitted, is useful only if you register an .HLP file to document your server. If you do, then when the user asks the controller for help, the controller passes this context ID to the Help system to display a screen describing the property.

id is a dispatch identifier that you can choose to assign explicitly by using one of the EXPOSE_xxxx_ID macros. The dispatch ID is what OLE passes to identify commands requested by a controller. The OLE system header files define several standard dispatch ID values. For example, –5 is the default evaluation method. Standard dispatch IDs are always negative numbers. By default, dispatch IDs are assigned low positive numbers incremented from 1. If you want to specify explicit dispatch IDs for your applications, choose high positive values in order not to collide with the low positive numbers ObjectComponents assigns to exposed members without explicit IDs.

0 is the ID of the default method or property. ObjectComponents never automatically assigns 0 as a dispatch ID. To have a default property, you need to assign 0 yourself.

Macro	Meaning
EXPOSE_PROPRW(intName, type, extName, doc, help)	The property can be read and written.
EXPOSE_PROPRW_ID(id, intName, type, extName, doc, help)	The property can be read and written. Its dispatch ID is *id*.
EXPOSE_PROPRO(intName, type, extName, doc, help)	The property is read-only.
EXPOSE_PROPRO_ID(id, intName, type, extName, doc, help)	The property is read-only. Its dispatch ID is *id*.
EXPOSE_PROPWO(intName, type, extName, doc, help)	The property is write-only and cannot be read (rarely used).

EXPOSE_QUIT macro   ocf/automacr.h

EXPOSE_QUIT(extName, docString, helpContext)

An automation server that exposes the application itself as an automated object uses the EXPOSE_QUIT macro to make a safe shutdown method available to the controller. The shutdown method implemented by this macro checks whether the application was originally invoked by OLE for automation. If so, it unregisters the active object and shuts down the server. If the user invoked the server before the controller connected to it, however, then the shutdown method does nothing because the application should continue to run.

Every automated application should include EXPOSE_QUIT in the application object's automation definition (after DEFINE_AUTOCLASS). EXPOSE_QUIT is not needed in the automation definition of other automated objects the server might create.

extName is the external, public name that a controller uses to call this method. The string can be localized.

doc is a string that describes the shutdown method to the user. An automation controller can ask OLE for this string if the user requests help. This string can also be localized.

help is a context ID for an .HLP file. This parameter, which can be omitted, is useful only if you register an .HLP file to document your server. If you do, then when the user asks the controller for help, the controller passes this context ID to the Help system to display a screen describing the shutdown method.

extension registration key

A file name extension. This extension becomes the default extension assigned to file names in the File Open common dialog box. It is also recorded in the system registration database so that OLE can find the right server for a file based on the file's extension.

extension is valid in document registration tables of servers that support linking and embedding. It is always optional. If you register an extension, you might also want to register a *docfilter*.

To register a file extension, use the REGDATA macro, passing *extension* as the first parameter and the extension string as the second parameter. In 16-bit Windows, the extension is limited to three characters.

```
REGDATA(extension, "TXT")
```

See also   docfilter registration key, REGDATA macro

filefmt registration key

Registers a name for a server's default file format. This string appears in dialog boxes where the user selects file types.

filefmt is valid in document registration tables for servers that support linking and embedding. It is always optional.

To register a file format, use the REGDATA macro, passing *filefmt* as the first parameter and the name string as the second parameter.

See also   REGDATA macro

format*n*registration key

Registers a Clipboard format the application supports. An application registers the formats that it can put on or take from the Clipboard. A server can register different sets of formats for different document types.

Clipboard format keys are valid in any document registration table. Any application that supports linking and embedding should register at least some Clipboard formats. ObjectComponents supports up to eight formats using the keys *format0* through *format7*. The *ocrFormatLimit* constant, defined in ocf/ocreg.h, represents the maximum number of formats allowed (8).

To register a Clipboard format, use the REGFORMAT macro. The first parameter assigns a priority to the format. Give your preferred format highest priority. Programs that support OLE usually prefer to export their data as OLE objects, and so they make *ocrEmbedSource* priority 0. The second parameter identifies a particular data format. For explanations of the other parameters, see the description of the REGFORMAT macro.

```
REGFORMAT(0, ocrEmbedSource,  ocrContent, ocrIStorage, ocrGet)
REGFORMAT(1, ocrMetafilePict, ocrContent, ocrMfPict, ocrGet)
```

See also   ocrxxxx aspect constants, ocrxxxx Clipboard constants, ocrxxxx direction constants, ocrxxxx medium constants, REGFORMAT macro

handler registration key

A full path pointing to a library that can draw objects created by the server.

A path for the library that OLE can call to draw objects without having to launch the server as a separate process. By default this value is "OLE2.DLL." OLE itself can render cached formats such as metafiles and bitmaps.

The *handler* key is valid in document registration tables for servers that support linking and embedding. It is always optional, but if you omit it OLE cannot use your handler library.

To register a handler, use the REGDATA macro, passing *handler* as the first parameter and the path of the handler DLL in the second parameter. If the path does not begin with a drive or root directory, ObjectComponents determines the full path by starting at the place where the server itself is installed. For example, if the server is at C:\MYDIR and the handler path is HELPERS\MYHANDLR, then the full path is assumed to be C:\MYDIR\HELPERS\MYHANDLR.DLL.

See also   REGDATA macro

helpdir registration key

Directory where online Help for the type library resides. (The name of the Help file is registered separately with the *typehelp* key.)

This key matters only in the application registration table of an automation controller. It is always optional. If you register a type library Help file without registering a Help directory, ObjectComponents automatically assumes the same directory registered for *path*.

To register a Help directory, use the REGDATA macro, passing *helpdir* as the first parameter and the path string as the second parameter.

If the path does not begin with a drive or root directory, ObjectComponents determines the full path by starting at the place where the server itself is installed. For example, if the server is at C:\MYDIR and the Help path is HELP, then the Help file is assumed to be at C:\MYDIR\HELP.

See also   path registration key, typehelp registration key

HR_xxxx return constants   ocf/ocfdefs.h

OLE system calls return HRESULT values that sometimes encode detailed information about the result of the call. ObjectComponents sometimes passes HRESULT values back to you. These macros simplify the task of testing for some common results. Each represents a possible return value. For a complete listing of HRESULT return values, see the scode.h header file.

Constant	Meaning
HR_ABORT	The operation was aborted.
HR_FAIL	An unspecified error occurred.
HR_FALSE	An action did not complete in the usual way but no error occurred. For example, an enumeration reached the end of its list.
HR_HANDLE	A handle is invalid.
HR_INVALIDARG	One or more arguments are invalid.
HR_NOERROR	No error occurred.
HR_NOINTERFACE	The requested interface is not supported.
HR_NOTIMPL	The requested service is not implemented.
HR_OK	Same as HR_NOERROR.
HR_OUTOFMEMORY	Not enough memory is available to complete the operation.
HR_POINTER	A pointer is invalid.

iconindex registration key

A zero-based index telling which of the icons in the server's resources represents the type of objects the server produces.

Use *iconindex* in the document registration tables of a linking and embedding server. It is always optional.

To register an icon index, use the REGICON macro, passing the index value as the parameter.

```
REGICON(1)
```

See also   REGICON macro

insertable registration key

Indicates the application is a server and allows its document to be linked or embedded in other applications. Registering this key makes the document type show up in dialog boxes listing objects that can be inserted. The value assigned to this key is ignored.

insertable is valid in the document registration tables of a linking and embedding server. An application must register *insertable* for at least one document type in order to be a linking and embedding server. A server need not make all its document types insertable, however.

To register the *insertable* key, use the REGDATA macro, passing *insertable* as the first parameter and 0 as the second parameter.

```
REGDATA(insertable, 0)
```

See also   REGDATA macro

language registration key

Overrides the locale ID currently in effect. By default, the *language* key takes its value from the system's default language setting for the current user. Registering a language setting directs ObjectComponents to choose a particular language for registration strings you have localized.

During automation this value is reset internally at the request of the automation controller.

menuname registration key

A short name for the server. The name appears as a menu item in container programs. For consistency in the user interface, the suggested maximum length is 15 characters.

menuname is required in the document registration tables of a linking and embedding server. In other places it is irrelevant. The *menuname* string can be localized.

To register the *menuname* key, use the REGDATA macro, passing *menuname* as the first parameter and a name string as the second parameter.

```
REGDATA(menuname, "OWL Drawing Pad")
```

See also   REGDATA macro

MostDerived function

ocf/autodefs.h

const void far* MostDerived(const void far* obj, const typeinfo& src);

Returns a pointer to the most derived class type that fits the given object. This is useful when dealing with polymorphic objects. Use it to obtain a consistent pointer to an object, regardless of the type of pointer used to reach the object.

obj is the pointer whose most derived type you want to determine. *src* holds type information about the *obj* object. The return value points to the most derived class that can be made out of *obj*. If *obj* is already the object's most derived type, then the return value is *obj*.

Use *typeid* to generate the *src* parameter.

See also   DynamicCast function, typeid, typeinfo class

ObjectPtr typedef

ocf/autodefs.h

typedef void* ObjectPtr;

ObjectPtr is a void* that points to a C++ object.

OC_APPxxxx messages

ocf/ocapp.h

These messages are sent from ObjectComponents to the application's main window. They notify the application of signals and events that come from the OLE system. The actual message sent is WM_OCEVENT. The constants in the table below are carried in the message's *wParam* and identify particular events. To find out what each message carries in its *lParam*, look up the corresponding event handlers (such as *EvOcAppBorderSpaceSet* and *EvOcAppMenus*.)

Applications that use the ObjectWindows Library can set up event handlers in their response tables using the EV_OC_xxxx macros defined in ocfevent.h. For more information about the data each message carries, see the descriptions of the corresponding event handlers.

The constants beginning OC_APP indicate events typically handled in the main frame window. Another set of constants beginning OC_VIEW indicate events typically handled in the view object.

Messages	Meaning
OC_APPDIALOGHELP	The user pressed the Help button in one of the standard OLE dialog boxes.
OC_APPBORDERSPACEREQ	Asks the container whether it can give the server border space in its frame window.
OC_APPBORDERSPACESET	Asks the container to give the server border space in its frame window.
OC_APPFRAMERECT	Requests coordinates for the inner rectangle of the container's main window.
OC_APPINSMENUS	Asks the container to merge its menu into the shared menu bar.
OC_APPMENUS	Asks the container to install the merged menu bar.

Messages	Meaning
OC_APPPROCESSMSG	Asks the container to process accelerators and other messages from the server's message queue.
OC_APPRESTOREUI	Tells the container to restore its normal menu and borders because in-place editing has ended.
OC_APPSHUTDOWN	Tells the server when its last linked or embedded object closes down. If the user did not launch the server directly, the server can terminate.
OC_APPSTATUSTEXT	Passes text for the status bar from the server to the container during in-place editing.

See also   OC_VIEWxxxx messages, WM_OCEVENT message

OC_VIEWxxxx messages   ocf/ocview.h

These messages are sent from ObjectComponents to the application's window procedure. They notify the application of signals and events that come from the OLE system. The actual message sent is WM_OCEVENT. The constants in the table below are carried in the message's *wParam* and identify particular events. To find out what each message carries in its *lParam*, look up the corresponding event handlers (such as *EvOcViewBorderSpaceSet* and *EvOcViewDrag*.)

Applications that use the ObjectWindows Library can set up event handlers in their response tables using the EV_OC_xxxx macros defined in ocfevent.h. For more information about the data each message carries, see the descriptions of the corresponding event handlers.

The constants beginning OC_VIEW indicate events typically handled in the view object. Another set of constants beginning OC_APP indicate events that typically concern the application object.

Constant	Meaning
OC_VIEWATTACHWINDOW	Asks the server window to attach to its own frame window or the container's window.
OC_VIEWBORDERSPACEREQ	Requests border space for in-place editing tools in the container's view.
OC_VIEWBORDERSPACESET	Sets border space for in-place editing tools in the container's view.
OC_VIEWCLIPDATA	Asks the server for Clipboard data in a particular format.
OC_VIEWCLOSE	Tells server to close this remote view.
OC_VIEWDRAG	Requests visual feedback during a drag operation.
OC_VIEWDROP	Accepts a dropped object.
OC_VIEWGETPALETTE	Asks the server for the palette it uses to paint its object.
OC_VIEWGETSCALE	Asks the container to give scaling information.
OC_VIEWGETSITERECT	Asks container for the site rectangle.
OC_VIEWINSMENUS	Asks the server to insert its menus in the menu bar for in-place editing.
OC_VIEWLOADPART	Asks the server to load its document. (The server's document contains one part.)
OC_VIEWOPENDOC	Asks the server for the extents of its open document.
OC_VIEWPAINT	Asks the server to paint a remote view of its document.
OC_VIEWPARTINVALID	Indicates that a part needs repainting.

Constant	Meaning
OC_VIEWPARTSIZE	Asks the server for the extents of its object.
OC_VIEWSAVEPART	Asks the server to save its document. (The server's document contains one part.)
OC_VIEWSCROLL	Asks the client to scroll its view because the user is trying to drag something off the edge.
OC_VIEWSETSCALE	Asks the server to handle scaling.
OC_VIEWSETSITERECT	Asks the container to set the site rectangle.
OC_VIEWSHOWTOOLS	Asks the server to display its tool bars in the container's window for in-place editing.
OC_VIEWTITLE	Gets the title displayed in the view's window.

See also   OC_APPxxxx constants

ocrxxxx aspect constants   ocf/ocreg.h

These constants identify modes of presenting data. A server might be able to draw the same object several different ways, such as displaying its full content, creating a miniature representation of the content, or representing the type of object with an icon.

When a server registers a data format, it also registers the aspects it supports for each format. The values of these constants are flags and can be combined with the bitwise OR operator (|).

Constant	OLE equivalent	Meaning
ocrContent	DVASPECT_CONTENT	Show the full content of the object at its normal size.
ocrThumbnail	DVASPECT_THUMBNAIL	Show the content of the object shrunk to fit in a smaller space.
ocrIcon	DVASPECT_ICON	Show an icon representing the type of object.
ocrDocPrint	DVASPECT_DOCPRINT	Show the object as it would look if sent to the printer.

See also   ocrxxxx constants, REGFORMAT macro, TOcAspect enum

ocrxxxx Clipboard constants   ocf/ocreg.h

These constants identify standard data formats for data that applications might share with each other. Use them in the REGFORMAT macro to describe the formats that your documents can import and export.

Constant	Windows format name	Meaning
ocrText	CF_TEXT	Array of text characters
ocrBitmap	CF_BITMAP	Device-dependent bitmap
ocrMetafilePict	CF_METAFILEPICT	A Windows metafile wrapped in a METAFILEPICT structure

Constant	Windows format name	Meaning
ocrSylk	CF_SYLK	Symbolic Link Format
ocrDif	CF_DIF	Data Interchange Format
ocrTiff	CF_TIFF	Tag Image File Format
ocrOemText	CF_OEMTEXT	Text containing characters in the original equipment manufacturer's character set (usually ASCII)
ocrDib	CF_DIB	Device-independent bitmap
ocrPalette	CF_PALETTE	GDI palette object
ocrPenData	CF_PENDATA	Data for pen extensions to the operating system
ocrRiff	CF_RIFF	Resource Interchange File Format (often used for multimedia)
ocrWave	CF_WAVE	A sound wave file (uses a subset of the RIFF format)
ocrUnicodeText	CF_UNICODETEXT	Wide-character Unicode text (32-bit only)
ocrEnhMetafile	CF_ENHMETAFILE	Enhanced metafile (32-bit only)
ocrRichText	"Rich Text Format"	RTF tagged text format
ocrEmbedSource	"Embed Source"	OLE object that can be embedded
ocrEmbeddedObject	"Embedded Object"	OLE object that is already embedded
ocrLinkSource	"Link Source"	OLE object that can be linked
ocrObjectDescriptor	"Object Descriptor"	Descriptive information about an OLE object that can be embedded
ocrLinkSrcDescriptor	"Link Source Descriptor"	Descriptive information about an OLE object that can be linked

See also   ocrxxxx constants, REGFORMAT macro

ocrxxxx direction constants   ocf/ocreg.h

These constants identify directions for passing data. For example, a server might be able to export and import bitmaps but only import metafiles. In that case, it uses *ocrGetSet* for the bitmap format and *ocrGet* for metafiles.

When a server registers a data format, it also specifies whether it can get or set each format.

Constant	Meaning
ocrGet	Imports data in the given format
ocrSet	Exports data in the given format
ocrGetSet	Both exports and imports data in the given format

See also   ocrxxxx constants, REGFORMAT macro

ocrxxxx limit constants
ocf/ocreg.h

These constants set the maximum number of verbs and data formats that an application is allowed to register for any one document type. Currently these limits are both set to 8.

Constant	Meaning
ocrVerbLimit	Maximum number of verbs a server can register for a document
ocrFormatLimit	Maximum number of data formats an application can register for a document

See also   ocrxxxx constants

ocrxxxx medium constants
ocf/ocreg.h

These constants identify channels for passing data. A server might be able to pass a particular kind of object as a global memory handle, as a disk file handle, or through a data stream, for example.

When a server registers a data format, it also registers the transfer channels it supports for each format. The values of these constants are flags and can be combined with the bitwise OR operator (|).

Constant	OLE equivalent	Meaning
ocrHGlobal	TYMED_HGLOBAL	Handle to global memory object
ocrFile	TYMED_FILE	Handle to disk file
ocrIStream	TYMED_ISTREAM	Stream object in a compound file
ocrIStorage	TYMED_ISTORAGE	Storage object in a compound file
ocrGDI	TYMED_GDI	GDI object (such as a bitmap)
ocrMfPict	TYMED_MFPICT	METAFILEPICT structure

See also   ocrxxxx constants, REGFORMAT macro

ocrxxxx object status constants
ocf/ocreg.h

These constants describe how an object behaves when presented in particular aspects. Register these options for documents using the REGSTATUS macro.

The values of these constants are flags and can be combined with the bitwise OR operator (|).

Constant	Meaning
ocrActivateWhenVisible	Applies only if *ocrInsideOut* is set. Indicates that the object prefers to be active whenever it is visible. The container is not obliged to comply.
ocrCanLinkByOle1	Used only in OBJECTDESCRIPTOR. Indicates that an OLE 1 container can link to the object.
ocrCantLinkInside	This object, when embedded, should not be made the source of a link.
ocrInsertNotReplace	This object, when placed in a document, should not replace the current selection but be inserted next to it.
ocrInsideOut	The object can be activated and edited without having to install menus or toolbars. Objects of this type can be active concurrently.
ocrIsLinkObject	Set by an OLE 2 link for OLE 1 compatibility. The system sets this bit automatically.
ocrNoSpecialRendering	Same as *ocrRenderingIsDeviceIndependent*.
ocrOnlyIconic	The only useful way the server can draw this object is as an icon. The content view looks like the icon.
ocrRecomposeOnResize	When container site changes size, the server would like to redraw its object. (Presumably the server wants to do something other than scale.)
ocrRenderingIsDeviceIndependent	The object makes no presentation decisions based on the target device. Its presentation data is always the same.
ocrStatic	The object is an OLE static object and cannot be edited.

See also   ocrxxxx constants, REGSTATUS macro

ocrxxxx usage constants   ocf/ocreg.h

These constants tell how a server supports concurrent clients. Use them to register the usage key for a server.

Constant	Meaning
ocrSingleUse	One client per application instance
ocrMultipleUse	Multiple clients per application instance
ocrMultipleLocal	Multiple clients supported by separate in-proc server

See also   ocrxxxx constants, usage registration key

ocrxxxx verb attributes constants   ocf/ocreg.h

enum ocrVerbAttributes
These constants give the container hints about how a verb is used. Register these options for documents using the REGVERBOPT macro.

The values of these constants are flags and can be combined with the bitwise OR operator (|).

Constant	Meaning
ocrNeverDirties	The verb never modifies the object in such a way that it needs to be saved again.
ocrOnContainerMenu	The verb should be displayed on the container's menu of object verbs when the object is active. The standard verbs Hide, Show, and Open should not have this flag set.

See also   ocrxxxx constants, REGVERBOPT macro

ocrxxxx verb menu flags   ocf/ocreg.h

These constants describe how a server's verbs should appear on the container's menu. Register these options for documents using the REGVERBOPT macro.

The values of these constants are flags and can be combined with the bitwise OR operator (|).

Constant	Windows equivalent	Meaning
ocrGrayed	MF_GRAYED	Makes the verb appear gray on the menu. This also disables the verb.
ocrDisabled	MF_DISABLED	Disables the verb so the user cannot choose it.
ocrChecked	MF_CHECKED	Places a check by the verb.
ocrMenuBarBreak	MF_MENUBARBREAK	Places the verb in a new column and adds a vertical line to separate the columns.
ocrMenuBreak	MF_MENUBREAK	Places the verb in a new column without separating the columns.

See also   ocrxxxx constants, REGVERBOPT macro

OPTIONAL_ARG macro   ocf/automacr.h

OPTIONAL_ARG(cls, extName, default)

An automation server uses this macro in its automation definition (after DEFINE_AUTOCLASS) in order to describe one argument in an exposed method.

After an EXPOSE_METHOD or EXPOSE_METHOD_ID macro, you need to add a list of argument macros, one for each parameter in the method. If the argument has a default value, then use the OPTIONAL_ARG macro.

type is an automation class that describes the argument's data type. For example, if the argument is Boolean value, then *type* should be *TAutoBool*. For more information, see Automation Data Types.

extName is the public name that a controller uses to refer to this argument. The string can be localized.

default is the default value assigned if the caller chooses to omit the argument.

path registration key

The path where OLE looks to find and load the server.

The path is optional for any server's application registration table. Usually you can omit the path because by default ObjectComponents records the actual path and file name of the server when it registers itself.

To register a path, use the REGDATA macro, passing *path* as the first parameter and the full path string, including .EXE name, as the second parameter.

See also   REGDATA macro

permid registration key

A string that names the application without indicating any version. The *permid* is just like the *progid* but without a version number. It always represents the latest installed version of a class.

The *permid* key is valid in any registration table. It is always optional. If you register *permid*, you should also register *permname*. Like the *progid*, the *permid* cannot be localized.

To register *permid*, use the REGDATA macro, passing *permid* as the first parameter and the ID string as the second parameter.

See also   permname registration key, progid registration key, REGDATA macro, version registration key

permname registration key

A string that describes the application without indicating any version. The *permname* is just like the *description* but without a version number. It always represents the latest installed version of a class. A *permname* value can contain up to 40 characters.

The *permname* key is valid in any registration table. It is always optional. If you register *permname*, you should also register *permid*. The *permname* string should be localized.

To register *permname*, use the REGDATA macro, passing *permname* as the first parameter and the descriptive string as the second parameter.

See also   description registration key, permid registration key, REGDATA macro, version registration key

progid registration key

Registers a string which uniquely identifies the class.

The string can contain up to 39 characters. The first character must be a letter. Subsequent characters can be letters, digits, or periods (no spaces or other delimiters). Conventionally, the *progid* value has three parts separated by periods. They are the program name, an object name, and a version number. The value of the *progid* cannot be localized.

A *progid* string is required in every application registration table. To register a *progid*, use the REGDATA macro, passing *progid* as the first parameter and the identifier string as the second parameter.

```
REGDATA(progid, "DrawingPad.Application.2")
```

See also   REGDATA macro

REQUIRED_ARG macro   ocf/automacr.h

REQUIRED_ARG(type, extName);
An automation server uses this macro in its automation definition (after DEFINE_AUTOCLASS) in order to describe one argument in an exposed method.

After an EXPOSE_METHOD or EXPOSE_METHOD_ID macro, you need to add a list of argument macros, one for each parameter in the method. If the argument does not have a default value and is not an object, then use the REQUIRED_ARG macro.

type is an automation class that describes the argument's data type. For example, if the argument is Boolean value, then *type* should be *TAutoBool*. For more information, see "Automation data types."

extName is the external, public name that a controller uses to refer to this argument. The string can be localized.

TAutoBase class   ocf/autodefs.h

TAutoBase is a base class for deriving automatable objects. The class does only one thing: whenever an object of *TAutoBase* is destroyed, the destructor notifies OLE that the object is no longer available.

Automated objects are not required to derive from *TAutoBase*. Doing so is simply a safeguard and matters only if the logic of the program makes it possible for the automated object to be destroyed by non-automated means while still connected to an OLE controller.

If you are using *TAutoBase* to derive classes with explicit class specifiers that do not match the default specifiers for the application's model, then be sure to define the _AUTOCLASS macro.

See also   _AUTOCLASS macro

Public destructor

Destructor
virtual ~TAutoBase();

The virtual destructor—the only member of class *TAutoBase*—sends OLE an obituary when the object is destroyed. The notification matters in cases where the object might be destroyed by non-automated means, without the knowledge of OLE, while still connected to an automation controller. Sending the obituary prevents a crash if OLE subsequently sends a command to the nonexistent object.

TAutoBool struct   ocf/autodefs.h

Use *TAutoBool* in an automation definition to describe the parameters and return values of automated methods.

Public data member

ClassInfo
static TAutoType ClassInfo;

The *ClassInfo* member of *TAutoBool* holds information that identifies the Boolean data type.

TAutoCommand class   ocf/autodefs.h

TAutoCommand is an abstract base class for automation command objects. An automation server constructs a command object whenever it receives a command from an automation controller. The command object receives all parameters as VARIANT unions from OLE. The compiler generates calls to command object conversion functions in order to extract the proper C++ data type from the union.

All this happens internally. Normally you should not have to construct or manipulate *TAutoCommand* objects directly.

Public constructor and destructor

Constructor
TAutoCommand(int attr);

Creates a command having the attributes set in the *attr* flag mask. The flags are defined in the *AutoSymFlag* enum.

Destructor
virtual ~TAutoCommand();
Destroys the *TAutoCommand* object.

See also   AutoSymFlag enum

Type definitions

TCommandHook
typedef bool (*TCommandHook)(TAutoCommand& cmdObj);
Describes the prototype for a user-defined callback function called during *Invoke*, before executing the automation command object. *cmdObj* is the object about to be executed. If the callback returns **false**, *Invoke* does not execute the command.

See also   TAutoCommand::Invoke, TAutoCommand::SetCommandHook

TErrorMsgHook
typedef const char* (*TErrorMsgHook)(long errCode);
Describes the prototype for a user-defined callback function called after *Invoke* to process any error code the command might return. *errCode* is the status result. The callback is expected to return a string describing the error for the user.

See also   TAutoCommand::LookupError, TAutoCommand::SetErrorMsgHook

Public member functions

ClearFlag
void ClearFlag(int mask);
Clears all the flags in *mask*. The flags are defined in the *AutoSymFlag* enum.

See also   AutoSymFlag enum

Execute
virtual void Execute();
Executes the automation command by invoking the internal C++ member of the automated class to which the command belongs.

Fail
void Fail(TXAuto::TError);
Throws whatever exception is indicated by the parameter.

See also   TXAuto::TError enum

GetSymbol
TAutoSymbol* GetSymbol();
Retrieves the symbol that generates this command.

Invoke
virtual TAutoCommand& Invoke();

Initiates the process of executing a command. The user can override the usual process by supplying a hook with the AUTOINVOKE macro.

See also   AUTOINVOKE macro, TAutoCommand::SetCommandHook

IsPropSet
bool IsPropSet();

Returns **true** if the *asSet* property flag is set. This flag indicates that the command assigns a value to some property of the automated class and does not return a value.

LookupError
static const char* LookupError(long errCode);

Translates an error code from a function into a message string for the user. *errCode* is a function status value sent by *Report*. *LookupError* works by calling a function you have installed with *SetErrorMsgHook*. You do not have to call *LookupError* directly. If you have installed an error message hook, *LookupError* is called for you at the right time.

See also   TAutoCommand::Report

Record
virtual int Record(TAutoStack& q);

Records the command and its arguments by calling any hook the programmer might have supplied in the automation declaration with the AUTORECORD macro.

Recording is not supported in the current version of ObjectComponents.

See also   AUTORECORD macro

Report
virtual long Report();

The AUTOREPORT macro invokes this function to translate the status code a command returns into an error code.

See also   AUTOREPORT MacroTAutoCommand::SetErrorMsgHook

Return
virtual void Return(TAutoVal& v);

Converts whatever value the internal C++ command returned into a VARIANT union. The converted value is passed to OLE. This is what the automation controller receives as its return value.

SetCommandHook
static TCommandHook SetCommandHook(TCommandHook callback);

Installs a user-defined callback function of type *TCommandHook* to be called whenever the command is executed. The command hook is useful for monitoring automation calls.

See also   TAutoCommand::Invoke, TAutoCommand::SetErrorMsgHook, TAutoCommand::TCommandHook typedef

SetErrorMsgHook
static TErrorMsgHook SetErrorMsgHook(TErrorMsgHook callback);

Installs a user-defined callback function of type *TErrorMsgHook* to be called if the command returns an error code.

See also TAutoCommand::LookupError, TAutoCommand::Report, TAutoCommand::SetCommandHook, TAutoCommand::TErrorMsgHook typedef

SetFlag
void SetFlag(int mask);

Sets all the flags in *mask*. The flags are defined in the *TAutoSymFlag* enum.

See also AutoSymFlag enum

SetSymbol
void SetSymbol(TAutoSymbol* sym);

Assigns a symbol to the command object. The symbol is set internally. It is taken from the tables built by the automation definition and declaration of the automated class.

TestFlag
bool TestFlag(int mask);

Returns **true** if any of the flags in *mask* are set for this command. The flags are defined in the *AutoSymFlag* enum.

See also AutoSymFlag enum

Undo
virtual TAutoCommand* Undo();

Generates a command for the undo stack by calling any hook the programmer might have supplied in the automation declaration with the AUTOUNDO macro. Undoing commands is not supported in the current version of ObjectComponents.

See also AUTOUNDO macro

Validate
virtual bool Validate();

Tests the validity of the command's parameters by executing whatever validation function or expression the programmer supplied in the automation declaration with the AUTOVALIDATE macro.

See also AUTOVALIDATE macro

Protected data members

Attr
int Attr;

Attribute and state flags. The flags are defined in the *AutoSymFlag* enum.

See also AutoSymFlag enum

Symbol
TAutoSymbol* Symbol;

The symbol entry that generates this command. OLE passes this symbol to make this command execute.

TAutoCurrency struct   ocf/autodefs.h

TAutoCurrency is an automation data type that helps ObjectComponents provide type checking for members of an automated class exposed to OLE. Use *TAutoCurrency* in an automation definition to identify currency values.

Public data member

ClassInfo
static TAutoType ClassInfo;

The *ClassInfo* member of *TAutoCurrency* holds information that identifies data as a currency value.

TAutoDate struct   ocf/autodefs.h

TAutoDate is an automation data type that helps ObjectComponents provide type checking for members of an automated class exposed to OLE. Use *TAutoDate* in an automation definition to identify date values stored as type double.

Public data members

ClassInfo
static TAutoType ClassInfo;

The *ClassInfo* member of *TAutoDate* holds information that identifies the date data type.

Date
double Date;

Stores a date as a 32-bit value.

Public constructors

Constructors
Form 1   TAutoDate();

Creates an empty *TAutoDate*.

Form 2   TAutoDate(double d);

Creates a *TAutoDate* that initially holds the value in *d*, assumed to be a date.

Public member function

operator double
operator double();

Returns the value stored in the Date field of *TAutoDate*.

TAutoDouble struct

ocf/autodefs.h

TAutoDouble is an automation data type that helps ObjectComponents provide type checking for members of an automated class exposed to OLE. Use *TAutoDouble* in an automation definition to identify **double** values.

Public data member

ClassInfo
static TAutoType ClassInfo;

The *ClassInfo* member of *TAutoDouble* holds information that identifies the **double** data type.

TAutoEnumerator<> class

ocf/autodefs.h

An automation controller creates a *TAutoEnumerator* object to enumerate items in a collection held by an automation server. A collection can contain any set of similar values or objects that the server chooses to expose as a group. The items in the collection might be numbers in an array, for example, or each one might be an automated object.

The type you pass to the template is the type of value the collection holds. If the collection is a set of integer values, pass **int**. If the collection holds automated objects, pass the controller's proxy class (derived from *TAutoProxy*).

At first, a newly created enumerator is empty. After you call *Step*, the enumerator holds the first value in the collection. To see the value, call *Value* if the collection contains values of intrinsic data types, such as int or **float**, or call *Object* if the collection contains automated objects. *Step*, *Value*, and *Object* are the most important methods of *TAutoEnumerator*. The others are generally called for you at the right time.

Public constructors and destructor

Constructors
Form 1 TAutoEnumerator();

Constructs an enumerator object but does not attach it to any automated collection.

Form 2 TAutoEnumerator(const TAutoEnumerator& copy);

Constructs a new enumerator object by copying an existing one. Both enumerators are attached to the same collection of objects.

However it is constructed, a newly created *TAutoEnumerator* object does not yet hold any value. Always call *Step* to get the first item before calling *Value* or *Object* to see the item.

Destructor

~TAutoEnumerator();

Detaches the enumerator from its collection before allowing the enumerator to be destroyed.

See also   TAutoEnumerator::StepTAutoEnumerator_Step

Public member functions

Bind

void Bind(TAutoVal& val);

Connects the enumerator to the collection object, *val*. *Bind* is called internally when the controller passes the enumerator object to a method that returns a collection.

See also   TAutoEnumerator::Unbind

Clear

void Clear();

Empties the enumerator so that it no longer points to any item in the collection. This method is called internally during *Step*.

See also   TAutoEnumerator::Step

Object

void Object(TAutoProxy& prx);

Returns in *prx* the current object from the collection. Use *Object* if the items in the collection are automated objects. If the collection contains data values, then call *Value* instead.

To advance the enumerator so that *Object* returns the next object, call *Step*.

See also   TAutoEnumerator::Step, TAutoEnumerator::Value

Step

bool Step();

Advances the enumerator object one step so that *Value* returns the next item in the collection. *Step* returns **false** when called after the enumerator has reached the last item in the collection.

See also   TAutoEnumerator::Object, TAutoEnumerator::Value

Unbind

void Unbind();

Disconnects the enumerator object from the collection it currently enumerates.

See also   TAutoEnumerator::Bind

Value

void Value(T& v);

Returns in *v* the current item from the collection. Use *Value* if the items in the collection are data values. If the collection contains objects, then call *Object* instead.

To advance the enumerator so that *Value* returns the next item, call *Step*.

See also   TAutoEnumerator::Object, TAutoEnumerator::Step

TAutoFloat struct   ocf/autodefs.h

TAutoFloat is an automation data type that helps ObjectComponents provide type checking for members of an automated class exposed to OLE. Use *TAutoFloat* in an automation definition to identify **float** values.

Public data member

ClassInfo
static TAutoType ClassInfo;
The *ClassInfo* member of *TAutoFloat* holds information that identifies the **float** data type.

TAutoIterator class   ocf/autodefs.h

TAutoIterator is a pure virtual base class for iterator objects. An iterator is used to enumerate a collection of other objects. The iterator's methods let the caller step through a list of objects and examine each one in turn.

An automation server needs to create an iterator in any automated object that represents a collection of other objects. To create an iterator, the server usually inserts an AUTOITERATOR macro in the automation definition of the collection class (after DEFINE_AUTOCLASS).

In most cases, you do not need to work with the iterator class directly because the AUTOITERATOR macro implements the object for you. In cases where the iterator requires a more complex implementation, however, you might need to define the class directly yourself.

You can still declare the class using AUTOITERATOR_DECLARE instead of AUTOITERATOR. This is just a shortcut for writing out all the standard members of an iterator object by hand.

TAutoIterator has five pure virtual members that any derived class must implement. These five functions compose a standard interface for iterators in automated collection objects. They are *Init*, *Test*, *Step*, *Return*, and *Copy*. The first four correspond to steps in a *for* loop that steps through the collection. (See AUTOITERATOR for a description of the correspondence.) *Copy* creates a duplicate iterator.

The constructors are protected because *TAutoIterator* should be constructed only by a derived class.

Besides implementing the inherited virtual functions, a class derived from *TAutoIterator* also typically declares one or more data members that record the iterator's current state. Usually the state variable remembers a position in the sequence of enumerated objects.

TAutoIterator is a COM object and implements the *IUnknown* interface.

Public member functions

Copy
virtual TAutoIterator* Copy()=0;

Returns a copy of the iterator object. Your implementation should copy the iterator's state variables.

See also   TAutoIterator::Init, TAutoIterator::Return, TAutoIterator::Step, TAutoIterator::Test

GetSymbol
TAutoSymbol* GetSymbol();

Retrieves the automation symbol associated with the iterator. Usually you do not need to call this function.

See also   TAutoIterator::SetSymbol

Init
virtual void Init()=0;

Initializes any state variables in the iterator. The primary task of an iterator is to loop through a list of objects enumerating them one by one. *Init* tells the iterator to prepare for beginning a new pass through the loop. For example, if the iterator's state variable is called *index*, *Init* might say

```
index = 0;
```

See also   TAutoIterator::Copy, TAutoIterator::Return, TAutoIterator::Step, TAutoIterator::Test

IUnknown()
operator IUnknown*();

Returns a pointer to the iterator's *IUnknown* OLE interface and calls *AddRef* on the interface pointer. This operator is called internally to return the iterator to OLE. Usually you do not need to call it directly yourself.

Return
virtual void Return(TAutoVal& value)=0;

Extracts one item from a collection and returns a reference to it in the value parameter. The primary task of an iterator is to loop through a list of objects enumerating them one by one. *Return* is the command that retrieves a different item from the collection on each pass through the loop. For example, *Return* might look like this:

```
value = (Collection->Array)[Index]
```

value is the function's parameter, *Collection* points to the enclosing collection object, *Array* is a member of *Collection*, and *Index* is the iterator's state variable.

value is type *TAutoVal* and represents a VARIANT union, which is the format in which OLE passes values. *TAutoVal* defines conversion operators to handle standard C++ data types as well as C++ strings, *TAutoCurrency*, *TAutoData*, and automated C++ objects. The items in a collection can be any of these types.

See also   TAutoIterator::Copy, TAutoIterator::Init, TAutoIterator::Step, TAutoIterator::Test

SetSymbol
void SetSymbol(TAutoSymbol* sym);

Associates an automation symbol with the iterator. *SetSymbol* is called internally during the construction of the iterator. Usually you do not need to call it directly yourself.

See also   TAutoIterator::GetSymbol

Step
virtual void Step()=0;

Advances the iterator to point to the next item in a collection. The primary task of an iterator is to loop through a list of objects enumerating them one by one. *Step* is like the *i++* statement in a **for** loop. It changes the state of the iterator to focus on the next item. For example, if the iterator's state variable is called *index*, *Step* might simply say

```
index++;
```

See also   TAutoIterator::Copy, TAutoIterator::Init, TAutoIterator::Return, TAutoIterator::Test

Test
virtual bool Test()=0;

Tests whether all items have been enumerated. The primary task of an iterator is to loop through a list of objects, enumerating them one by one. *Test* returns **true** if more objects remain to be enumerated and **false** when it reaches the end of the list. For example, if the iterator's state variable is called *index*, *Test* might say

```
return (index >= NUM_ITEMS);
```

See also   TAutoIterator::Copy, TAutoIterator::Init, TAutoIterator::Return, TAutoIterator::Step

Protected constructors

Constructors
Form 1   TAutoIterator (TServedObject& owner);

Constructs an iterator to enumerate items held in the *owner* class. *owner* can be any automated class.

Form 2   TAutoIterator (TAutoIterator& copy);

Constructs an iterator by creating a copy of another iterator. Both iterators enumerate the same collection of objects.

The constructors are protected because only a derived class should construct a *TAutoIterator*.

Protected data member

Owner
TServedObject& Owner;

Holds a reference to the collection object that encloses the iterator. *Owner* is initialized by the constructor. The undocumented *TServedObject* class implements the interfaces that a client expects to find on an OLE object. ObjectComponents uses this class internally. *Owner* can be any automated object.

TAutoLong struct   ocf/autodefs.h

TAutoLong is an automation data type that helps ObjectComponents provide type information for members of an automated class exposed to OLE. Use *TAutoLong* in an automation definition to identify **long** values.

Public data member

ClassInfo
static TAutoType ClassInfo;

The *ClassInfo* member of *TAutoLong* holds information that identifies the **long** data type.

TAutoObject <> class   ocf/autodefs.h

TAutoObject holds a pointer to a C++ object. *TAutoObject* casts the pointer to different data types appropriately when an automation operation requires conversion. It also retrieves type information about the object when needed during automation. Think of *TAutoObject* as a smart pointer.

ObjectComponents often creates smart pointers for you. Usually you do not need to manipulate *TAutoObject* objects directly.

Public constructors

Constructors
Form 1   TAutoObject();

Constructs an empty *TAutoObject* that contains no pointer.

Form 2   TAutoObject(T* point);

Constructs a *TAutoObject* that holds the pointer *point*.

Form 3   TAutoObject(T& ref);

Constructs a *TAutoObject* that holds a pointer to the object *ref*.

Form 4   TAutoObject(IDispatch* dispatch);

Attempts to read type information from the object that owns the *IDispatch* interface. If it succeeds, the constructor builds a *TAutoObject* around a pointer to the C++ object. If it fails, the constructor throws a *TXAuto::xTypeMismatch* exception.

Public member functions

operator *()
T& operator *();

The dereference operator returns a reference to the object whose pointer *TAutoObject* holds.

operator =
Form 1   void operator =(T* point);

Places the *point* pointer in the *TAutoObject*.

Form 2   void operator =(T& ref);

Places a pointer to the object *ref* in the *TAutoObject*.

Form 3   void operator =(IDispatch* dispatch);

Attempts to read type information from the object that owns the *IDispatch* interface. If it succeeds, the operator places in the *TAutoObject* a pointer to the C++ object. If it fails, the constructor throws a *TXAuto::xTypeMismatch* exception.

The assignment operators place a pointer to a C++ object in the *TAutoObject*. They are usually used to initialize the *TAutoObject* after creating it with the default constructor.

operator T& ()
T& operator*();

The dereference operator returns a reference to the object whose pointer *TAutoObject* holds.

operator T* ()
operator T*();

Returns a pointer to the object *TAutoObject* holds.

TObjectDescriptor()
operator TObjectDescriptor();

Constructs and returns a new object descriptor object based on the pointer that *TAutoObject* holds. This operator is called internally to obtain type information for constructing an automation object.

Protected data member

operator P
T* P;
Returns the pointer that *TAutoObject* holds.

TAutoObjectByVal<> class   ocf/autodefs.h

Base class
TAutoObjectDelete

An automation server uses this class when an automated method needs to return a copy of an object. Usually you do not have to use the class directly because the automation macros make the proper declarations for you.

To return an object, *TAutoObjectByVal* clones the object by calling its copy constructor. The clone is passed to the automation controller as the return value from some automation command. *TAutoObjectByVal* holds on to the cloned object until the controller releases it. Then it destroys the object by calling its destructor.

In other respects, *TAutoObjectByVal* closely resembles its parent class, *TAutoObjectDelete*.

See also   TAutoObjectDelete

Public data member

operator =
void operator =(T obj);
This operator creates a new object of type *T* by copying the original object, *obj*. The copy is passed to an automation controller as the return value from an automated method. *T* is the data type passed into the template.

Public constructors

Constructors
Form 1   TAutoObjectByVal();
Creates an empty *TAutoObjectByVal*.

Form 2   TAutoObjectByVal(T obj);
Creates a *TAutoObjectByVal* that holds a copy of the object *obj*. *T* is the data type passed into the template.

TAutoObjectDelete <> class   ocf/autodefs.h

Base class
TAutoObject

An automation server uses this class when an automated method needs to return an object to an automation controller. Usually you do not have to use the class directly because the automation macros make the proper declarations for you.

Like its parent class *TAutoObject*, *TAutoObjectDelete* exists in order to hold a pointer to an object and convert it as necessary when the object is passed from server to client through automation calls. The difference between the two classes is that when the automation controller is through with the automated object, *TAutoObjectDelete* informs the connector object that it can let the automated C++ object call its destructor.

See also   TAutoObject class

Public constructors

Constructors
Form 1   TAutoObjectDelete();
Creates an empty *TAutoObjectDelete* object.

Form 2   TAutoObjectDelete(T* p);
Creates a *TAutoObjectDelete* object from a pointer to another object.

Form 3   TAutoObjectDelete(T& r);
Creates a *TAutoObjectDelete* object from a reference to another object.

The *TAutoObjectDelete* constructors do nothing but pass their parameters back to the parent class, *TAutoObject*.

Public member functions

operator =
Form 1   void operator =(T& r);
Tells *TAutoObjectDelete* to hold a pointer to the object referred to by *r*.

Form 2   void operator =(T* p);
Tells TAutoObjectDelete to hold the pointer *p*.

TObjectDescriptor()
operator TObjectDescriptor();
Returns type information describing the object.

TAutoProxy class   ocf/autodefs.h

An automation controller derives classes from *TAutoProxy* to represent automated OLE objects that it wants to command. To send commands to an automated object, the controller invokes methods on the proxy that represents the object. ObjectComponents connects the proxy to the original so that invoking members of the proxy also invokes members of the automated object.

A proxy object must inherit from *TAutoProxy*. In the derived class, the controller declares one method for each command it wants to send. The declared methods must match the prototypes of the desired commands. To implement these proxy methods, the controller uses three macros: AUTONAMES, AUTOARGS, and AUTOCALL. The macros insert code that calls down to the base class. *TAutoProxy* passes the commands to OLE.

Usually you do not have to call anything in *TAutoProxy* directly. All you have to do is derive your proxy class from *TAutoProxy* and implement the methods with the proxy macros.

To generate proxy classes quickly and easily, use the AUTOGEN.EXE tool in the OCTOOLS directory. AUTOGEN reads the automation server's type library and writes all the necessary headers and source files for your proxy objects.

Public destructor

Destructor
~TAutoProxy();
Destroys the *TAutoProxy* object.

The constructors are protected because only derived proxy classes should call them.

Public member functions

Bind

Form 1   void Bind(IUnknown* obj);

Binds the proxy object to a server identified by a pointer to its *IUnknown* interface. Throws a *TXOle* exception for failure.

Form 2   void Bind(IUnknown& obj);

Binds the proxy object to a server identified by a reference to its *IUnknown* interface. Throws a *TXOle* exception for failure.

Form 3   void Bind(const GUID& guid);

Binds the proxy object to a server identified by its globally unique ID (GUID). This is the *clsid* that the server registered for objects of the type you want to control. Throws a *TXOle* exception for failure.

Form 4   void Bind(char far* progid);

Binds the proxy object to a server identified by its *progid*. (This is the GUID that the server registered to identify the application itself.) Throws a *TXOle* exception for failure.

Form 5   void Bind(TAutoVal& val);

Attempts to intrepret the value in the *TAutoVal* union as a reference to an *IDispatch* object and bind to the *IDispatch* directly. Throws a *TXAuto* exception if the object does not support *IDispatch*.

Form 6   void Bind(IDispatch* obj);

Accepts *obj* as the proxy object's server.

Form 7   void Bind(IDispatch& obj);

Accepts *obj* as the proxy object's server.

The *Bind* function attempts to open a channel of communication to the automation server in order to send commands. More specifically, *Bind* requests a pointer to the server's *IDispatch* interface.

Bind is called internally when the object is passed as the return object for another proxy method. Which form of *Bind* is used depends on what information is available to identify the server.

See also   TAutoProxy::Bind

IDispatch&()
operator IDispatch&();

Returns a reference to the *IDispatch* interface of the proxy object's server.

IDispatch*()
operator IDispatch*();

Returns a pointer to the *IDispatch* interface of the proxy object's server and calls *AddRef* on the interface pointer.

IsBound
bool IsBound();

Returns **true** if the server already has a pointer to the *IDispatch* interface of its server and **false** if it does not.

Lookup
Form 1   long Lookup(char far* name);

Calls the server to get the ID that matches the name.

Form 2   long Lookup(const long id);

Returns the value passed in as *id*.

Form 3   void Lookup(const char* names, long* ids, unsigned count);

Looks up a series of names and returns all their IDs at once. *names* and *ids* point to two parallel arrays. *count* gives the number of elements in both arrays. With a single call to OLE, *Lookup* fills the *ids* array with numbers to identify all the names.

Given the name of a command or an argument, *Lookup* calls the server to ask for the corresponding ID values. Although commands and arguments have names for the convenience of programmers, OLE actually identifies them by numbers. A server must find out the ID number in order to execute the command.

MustBeBound
void MustBeBound();

Throws a *TXAuto* exception if the *TAutoProxy* object does not have an *IDispatch* interface for its server. *TAutoProxy* calls this method internally before performing actions that assume the object is already bound to the server.

SetLang
void SetLang(TLangId lang);

Sets the locale ID that the controller will pass to the server with each command. The locale ID tells the server what language the controller is using.

See also   Locale IDs, TAutoStack

Unbind
void Unbind();

Decrements the reference count of the proxy object's server and erases internal references to the server.

See also   TAutoProxy::Bind

Protected constructor

Constructor
TAutoProxy(TLangId lang);

Constructs a *TAutoProxy* object and sets the object to use the language identified by the *lang* locale ID.

See also   Locale IDs

Protected member function

Invoke
TAutoVal& Invoke(int attr, TAutoProxyArgs& args, long* ids, unsigned named=0);

Sends a command to the automation server. *Invoke* is called by the AUTOCALL macros.

attr describes the type of command being issued and can be a combination of the *AutoCallFlag* **enum** values.

The *args* object contains all the values passed as arguments to the command.

ids points to an array of ID values identifying the command and the arguments. There should be one ID value for each element in the *args* array.

names tells how many arguments in *args* are identified by name.

See also   AutoCallFlag enum, AUTOCALL_xxxx macros

TAutoShort struct

ocf/autodefs.h

TAutoShort is an automation data type that helps ObjectComponents provide type
checking for members of an automated class exposed to OLE. Use *TAutoShort* in an
automation definition to identify **short** values.

Public data member

ClassInfo
static TAutoType ClassInfo;
The *ClassInfo* member of *TAutoShort* holds information that identifies the **short** data
type.

TAutoStack class

ocf/autodefs.h

TAutoStack processes the command stack that an automation controller sends to an
automation server through OLE. The command stack contains a dispatch ID identifying
a particular command and a set of VARIANT unions containing all the arguments
needed to execute the command.

ObjectComponents interprets the dispatch ID and extracts the proper C++ value from
each union. It builds a command object (*TAutoCommand*) and calls the command's
Execute method. *TAutoCommand* in turn invokes the methods you have exposed by
declaring them and defining them in your automated classes.

The stack also carries a locale ID identifying the language used in the command.
ObjectComponents takes the locale into account when interpreting strings it extracts
from the stack. If you have provided localization resources, then ObjectComponents
translates to the requested language for you.

Usually you do not have to work with *TAutoStack* directly. ObjectComponents
automatically passes a stack in to the proper command object for you. The command
objects are created by the automation declaration macros.

See also   TAutoCommand class

Public constructor and destructor

Constructor
TAutoStack(TServedObject& owner, VARIANT far* stack, TLocaleId locale,int argcount, int namedcount,
    long far* map);
The constructor is called only internally. You should not need to construct your own
stack.

owner is the automated object to which the command is directed.

stack points to a series of contiguous unions of type VARIANT. The unions contain values or object references passed in automation commands.

locale is a locale ID describing the language the controller is using.

argcount tells how many arguments follow the dispatch ID in the stack.

namedcount tells how many of the arguments were passed with their names. A controller can pass arguments in any order, and even omit optional arguments, if it identifies the arguments it does pass explicitly by the name the server gives them.

If *namedcount* is greater than zero, then *map* points to an array of ID values corresponding to the argument names passed by the constructor.

map is a table for translating named argument IDs to argument positions.

Destructor
~TAutoStack();
Destroys the *TAutoStack* object.

Public member function

operator []
TAutoVal& operator[](int index);

Extracts individual arguments from the command stack for use as C++ function arguments. *index* is a zero-based index into the command's argument list, which follows the order established in the corresponding EXPOSE macro of the automation definition. This operator is called by the command objects generated in the automation declaration.

If *index* is out of range, the operator throws a *TXAuto::xNoArgSymbol* exception.

Public data members

ArgCount
const int ArgCount;
Holds the number of arguments passed on the command stack (named or unnamed).

ArgSymbolCount
int ArgSymbolCount;
Holds the number of command arguments exposed to automation.

CurrentArg
int CurrentArg;
As ObjectComponents processes the arguments on the stack one by one, this member indexes the current argument. When *CurrentArg* reaches *ArgCount*, all the arguments have been processed.

LangId
TLangId LangId;
Holds a number that identifies the language the controller is using to send commands.

Owner
TServedObject& Owner;
Refers to the automated object that is processing the command on the stack.

Symbol
int ArgSymbolCount;
Holds the number of command arguments exposed to automation.

Constant

SetValue
TAutoStack::SetValue
SetValue is a predefined standard dispatch ID. The dispatch ID is a number that identifies a particular command that an automated object can execute. The only two standard dispatch IDs used in ObjectComponents are 0 for an object's default action and –3 for a command that sets the value of a property. *SetValue* is –3.

See also   TAutoVal class, TLocaleId

TAutoString struct   ocf/autodefs.h

An automation server uses *TAutoString* to describe C string types in an automation definition. The member functions of the *TAutoString* structure facilitate copying and assigning string values with minimal memory reallocations when strings are passed back and forth between servers and controllers.

You do not need to use *TAutoString* with C++ *string* objects. For more information, see Automation Data Types.

TAutoString works best with **const** string values. When passed a non-constant string, *TAutoString* must make an internal copy. When the string is **const**, *TAutoString* knows the value will not change and can skip the copying step. The performance improvement is significant.

Public constructors and destructor

Constructors
Form 1   TAutoString(const string& s);
Creates a *TAutoString* and assigns it the string held in a C++ *string* object.

Form 2   TAutoString(const TAutoString& copy);
Creates a new *TAutoString* that holds the same string value as the *copy* object.

Form 3   TAutoString(TAutoVal& val);
Initializes the new object with the value in a *TAutoVal* union. *TAutoVal* represents the VARIANT data type OLE uses to pass values between two applications. It is a union of many types. This constructor extracts the value from the union as a string.

Form 4   TAutoString(const char far* str);

Initializes the new object with the value in a **const** C string.

Form 5   TAutoString(BSTR s, bool loan)

Initializes the new object with the value in a BASIC-style string, one preceded by its length and not terminated by null. That is the format OLE uses for passing strings. Set *loan* to **true** if the *TAutoString* object owns the BSTR and **false** if it only references the BSTR.

Destructor
~TAutoString();

TAutoString maintains a reference count on the string object it contains. The destructor decrements the reference count.

Public member functions

int()
operator int()

Returns the length of the string value (as *strlen* would calculate the length).

operator =
Form 1   TAutoString& operator =(const char far* str);

Accepts a C-style **const** string as the new value of the *TAutoString*.

Form 2   TAutoString& operator =(char* s);

Accepts a C-style non-**const** string as the new value of *TAutoString*. Because the string is not constant, *TAutoString* must create a new copy of the string for itself. This makes Form 3 significantly slower than Form 1. Try to pass **const** strings where possible.

Form 3   TAutoString& operator =(const TAutoString& copy)

Sets the value of the *TAutoString* object to be a string copied from another *TAutoString* object.

char*()
operator char*();

Returns the object's string value in the form of a non-**const** C-style string. To do this, *TAutoString* must create a new copy of the string. It is faster to assign to a **const char*** where possible.

const char far*()
operator const char far*();

Returns the object's string value in the form of a **const** C-style string.

Public data member

ClassInfo
static TAutoType ClassInfo;

This static structure holds a number that identifies the data type as a string. All the automation data types hold a similar static identifier so that ObjectComponents can query any of them to determine what they are.

TAutoType struct   ocf/autodefs.h

The *TAutoType* structure is a static data member of all the automation data type classes, such as *TAutoBool* and *TAutoString*. *TAutoType* makes all these data types self-describing. This is an essential quality for dealing with the VARIANT unions that OLE uses to pass values during automation. Because all the automation types derive from *TAutoType*, ObjectComponents can process values of any type with the same code. Because *TAutoType* is self-describing, ObjectComponents can always determine the actual type of any particular item.

Usually you do not have to work with *TAutoType* directly, just with the automation types that derive from it.

Public member function

GetType
short GetType();

Returns an integer that identifies a particular data type. The identifiers are defined in the *AutoDataType* **enum**.

See also   AutoDataType enum

TAutoVal class   ocf/autodefs.h

TAutoVal duplicates the VARIANT type that OLE uses to pass values between an automation server and controller. It also adds access methods to retrieve the value in the VARIANT. A VARIANT can be cast to type *TAutoVal*, and *TAutoVal* can be cast to a VARIANT.

A VARIANT is a large union with fields of many different data types. A large set of overloaded assignment operators allow many different kinds of values to be stored in a *TAutoVal* object. Each assignment operator also records internally a number that identifies the type of value just received. A similar set of conversion operators allows the value in the object to be cast to different types of values. Whether a particular conversion succeeds depends on the type of value in the object. A *string* cannot be cast to some other object, for example. If the conversion fails, *TAutoVal* throws an exception of type *TXAuto::xConversionFailure*.

ObjectComponents treats the data passed between an automation server and controller as a stack of unions. The stack is *TAutoStack,* and the items on the stack are *TAutoVal.* Because the server and controller are built separately and can use different programming languages, data passed between them cannot retain an intrinsic type. Command identifiers and argument values are passed as VARIANTs. The recipient of a VARIANT value must rely on the item's context in order to determine what type the value is supposed to be. For example, when it sees a dispatch ID for a command that expects two integer arguments, the application extracts integers from the next two VARIANTs.

Public member functions

operator =
void operator=(int i);
void operator=(int far* p);
void operator=(long i);
void operator=(long far* p);
void operator=(unsigned long i);
void operator=(unsigned long far* p);
void operator=(short i);
void operator=(short far* p);
void operator=(float i);
void operator=(float far* p);
void operator=(double i);
void operator=(double far* p);
void operator=(TBool i);
void operator=(TBool far* p);
void operator=(const char far* s);
void operator=(string s);
void operator=(TAutoString s);
void operator=(TAutoCurrency i);
void far* operator=(TAutoCurrency far* p);
void operator=(TAutoDate i);
void far* operator=(TAutoDate far* i);
void operator=(TAutoVoid);
void operator=(IDispatch* ifc);
void operator=(IUnknown* ifc);
void operator=(TObjectDescriptor od);

Assignment operators initialize *TAutoVal* by placing in the object both the assigned value and an ID to show the type of the assigned value.

This table describes those data types that are not standard C types.

Type	Description
IDispatch	A class ObjectComponents uses internally to implement the standard OLE interface called *IDispatch*, supported by automatable objects.
IUnknown	A class that ObjectComponents uses internally to implement the standard *IUnknown* OLE interface, supported by all OLE objects.
string	C++ *string* object.
TAutoCurrency	An automation data type that holds a currency value.
TAutoString	An automation data type that holds a C-style string value.
TAutoVoid	An automation data type that represents a **void** return.
TObjectDescriptor	A class that ObjectComponents uses internally to hold information about an OLE object.

See also Automation data types, String class

Clear

void Clear();

Clears the value stored in the object, leaving it empty. This method cannot be called on the objects managed by *TAutoStack*.

See also TAutoStack class

Copy

void Copy(const TAutoVal& copy);

Copies the *TAutoVal* object into *copy*. Intelligently allocates space for a string, if needed, and calls *AddRef* if the value in the union is an OLE object.

double far*()

operator double far*();

Returns a pointer to a **double** value.

double()

operator double();

Returns the value in the object as a **double** value.

int far*()

operator int far*();

Returns a pointer to an **int**.

float far*()

operator float far*();

Returns a pointer to a floating-point value.

float()

operator float();

Returns the value in the object as a floating-point value.

GetDataType

int GetDataType();

Returns an integer identifying the type of value that was assigned to the union.

IDispatch&()

operator IDispatch&();

Extracts an *IDispatch* interface from the value in the *TAutoVal* object. *IDispatch* is the standard OLE interface supported by automatable objects. This method does not call *AddRef* on the *IDispatch* interface.

See also TAutoVal::IDispatch*()

IDispatch*()

operator IDispatch*();

Extracts an *IDispatch* interface from the value in the *TAutoVal* object. *IDispatch* is the standard OLE interface supported by automatable objects. This function also calls the interface's *AddRef* method.

See also TAutoVal::IDispatch&()

int()
operator int();
Returns the value in the object as an integer.

int far*()
operator int far*();
Returns a pointer to an **int**.

IsRef
bool IsRef();
Returns **true** if the value assigned to the union is a reference to a value.

IUnknown&()
operator IUnknown&();
Extracts an *IUnknown* interface from the value in the *TAutoVal* object. *IUnknown* is the standard OLE interface supported by all objects. This method does not call *AddRef* on the *IUnknown* interface.

See also   TAutoVal::IUnknown*()

IUnknown*()
operator IUnknown*();
Extracts an *IUnknown* interface from the value in the *TAutoVal* object. *IUnknown* is the standard OLE interface supported by all objects. This method calls *AddRef* on the *IUnknown* interface.

See also   TAutoVal::IUnknown&()

long()
operator long();
Returns the value in the object as a **long** integer.

long far*()
operator long far*();
Returns a pointer to a **long** integer.

short()
operator short();
Returns the value in the object as a **short** integer.

short far*()
operator short far*();
Returns a pointer to a **short** integer.

string()
operator string();
Returns the value in the object as a C++ *string* object.

TAutoCurrency()
operator TAutoCurrency();
Returns the value in the object as a currency value.

See also   TAutoCurrency class

TAutoCurrency far*()
operator TAutoCurrency far*();
Returns a pointer to a currency value.

See also   TAutoCurrency

TAutoDate()
operator TAutoDate();
Returns the value in the object as a date value.

See also   TAutoDate class

TAutoDate far*()
operator TAutoDate far*();
Returns a pointer to a date value.

See also   TAutoDate class

TBool()
operator TBool();
Returns the value in the object as a Boolean value.

TBool far*()
operator TBool far*();
Returns a pointer to a Boolean value.

TUString*()
operator TUString*();
Returns the value in the object as a *TUString* object. *TUString* is a reference-counted union of various string representations. It is used internally by ObjectComponents for implementing *TAutoString*.

unsigned long()
operator unsigned long();
Returns the value in the object as an **unsigned long** integer.

unsigned long far*()
operator unsigned long far*();
Returns a pointer to a **long** integer. (*TAutoVal* does not distinguish **long** from **unsigned long**.)

See also   TAutoStack class

TAutoVoid struct   ocf/autodefs.h

TAutoVoid is an automation data type like *TAutoShort* and *TAutoBool*. Use it in an automation definition to describe functions that return no value.

The purpose of the structure is to implement the assignment of **void** to a *TAutoVal*.

See also TAutoVal struct

Public data member

ClassInfo
static TAutoType ClassInfo;
As with any automation data type, the *ClassInfo* member holds a value that identifies a data type, in this case **void**.

See also TAutoType struct

TComponentFactory type definition   ocf/ocreg.h

typedef IUnknown* (*TComponentFactory)(IUnknown* outer, uint32 options, uint32 id = 0);
TComponentFactory is a type definition for a callback function.

outer points to the *IUnknown* interface of an external OLE object under which the application is asked to aggregate. If *outer* is 0, then either the new object is independent or it will become the outer object in an aggregation.

options contains bit flags indicating the application's running state. To test the flags, use the *TOcAppMode* **enum** constants.

id is a number ObjectComponents assigns to identify a particular type of object the application can create. If *id* is 0, the application is asked to create itself. To request particular document types, ObjectComponents passes the document template ID.

The return value is a pointer to the *IUnknown* interface of whatever object the callback function creates, either the application itself or one of its objects. During aggregation, the return value becomes the inner *IUnknown* pointer in some other object. (*IUnknown* is a standard OLE type declared in compobj.h.)

A callback of type *TComponentFactory* is passed to the constructor of an application's registrar object (either *TOcRegistrar* for a linking and embedding application or *TRegistrar* for an application that supports automation only).

See also TOcAppMode enum, TOcRegistrar class, TRegistrar class

TLocaleId type definition   ocf/autodefs.h

typedef unsigned long TLocaleId;
A locale ID is a 32-bit value that identifies a language. The low half of the value is a 16-bit language ID. In the current OLE definition, the upper word is reserved, so in effect a locale ID is a 32-bit language ID.

Windows uses locale IDs to set the system's default language. ObjectComponents uses locale IDs in automation. An automation controller passes a locale ID to the server with every command. The server is expected to interpret the commands it receives as strings in the given language.

There are two predefined system locale settings in the olenls.h header.

Constant	Meaning
LOCALE_SYSTEM_DEFAULT	The default locale set for the system.
LOCALE_USER_DEFAULT	The default locale set for a particular user (which can differ from the system setting on multiuser systems).

See also   Langxxxx language ID constants, TLangId typedef

TOcApp class   ocf/ocapp.h

Base class
TUnknown

TOcApp is an ObjectComponents connector object for a linking and embedding application. It implements the interfaces an application needs for communicating with OLE. Any ObjectComponents application that supports linking and embedding needs to have a *TOcApp* object. Usually it is created for you by your *TOcRegistrar* object.

Applications that support automation but do not support linking and embedding do not need a *TOcApp* object. They create a *TRegistrar* instead of a *TOcRegistrar*.

TOcApp is a COM object and implements the *IUnknown* interface.

See also
TOcModule::OnInit, TOcRegistrar class, TOleFactory<> class, TRegistrar class, TUnknown class

Type definitions

TOcMenuEnable
enum TOcMenuEnable

These enumeration values are flags that can be combined with the bitwise OR operator (|). A container passes them to the *EnableEditMenu* function in order to determine which OLE commands on the Edit menu should be enabled. The answer depends on whether the container supports any of the data formats currently present on the Clipboard.

Constant	Menu command enabled
EnablePaste	The Paste command places an object from the Clipboard in the open document. The format of the new data object depends on what the server prefers and the container supports.
EnablePasteLink	The Paste Link command adds to the open document a link to the object on the Clipboard.
EnableBrowseClipboard	The Paste Special command invokes a standard dialog box that shows all the data formats available for the object currently on the Clipboard and lets the user choose among them.
EnableBrowseLinks	The Links command displays a list of all the linked objects in the open document, allowing the user to update or delete them.

See also   REGFORMAT macro, TOcApp::EnableEditMenu

Public member functions

AddUserFormatName
void AddUserFormatName(char far* name, char far* resultName, char far* id = 0);

Call this function to associate a result name with a Clipboard format. The *resultName* parameter describes the data format to users and appears in Help text of the Paste Special dialog box. Use one of the other two parameters to identify the associated Clipboard format. This method is used only if you have a non-standard, private Clipboard format that you want to associate with names used in the Paste Special dialog box.

A custom format must first be entered in the application's registration tables using the REGFORMAT macro. For example,

```
REGFORMAT(0, "DrawingClip", ocrContent, ocrIStorage, ocrGet);
```

"DrawingClip" becomes the ID string that Windows uses internally to identify the custom format. To associate more descriptive strings with the custom format, call *AddUserFormatName*:

```
AddUserFormatName("DrawingPad", "a freehand drawing", "DrawingClip");
```

The name of the "DrawingClip" format is now "DrawingPad". If the user chooses Paste Special when data of this type is on the Clipboard, the name in the dialog box is "DrawingPad". It is perfectly legal for the ID and the name to be the same string.

The result string, "a freehand drawing", typically appears in the Help text during a Paste Special operation.

See also   REGFORMAT macro

Browse
bool Browse(TOcInitInfo& initInfo);

Displays the Insert Object dialog box allowing the user to choose from available servers to create a new object in the open document. Returns **true** if the user inserts an object and **false** if the user cancels.

Create *initInfo* first by passing to its constructor the view object where the new object will be inserted. *Browse* fills *initInfo* with information about the object. Then use *initInfo* to create a new *TOcPart*.

See also   TOcInitInfo, TOcPart, TOcView

BrowseClipboard
bool BrowseClipboard(TOcInitInfo& initInfo);

Displays the Paste Special dialog box showing the available formats for the data currently on the Clipboard, allowing the user to choose what format to paste. Returns **true** if the user pastes data and **false** if the user cancels.

Create *initInfo* first by passing to its constructor the view object where the new object will be inserted. *Browse* fills *initInfo* with information about the object. Then use *initInfo* to create a new *TOcPart*.

This function is called by *TOcView::BrowseClipboard*.

See also TOcInitInfo, TOcPart, TOcView

CanClose
bool CanClose();

A container calls this function to determine whether it can shut down. *CanClose* polls all the connected servers and attempts to close them. It returns **true** if it is safe to close the application.

Clip
bool Clip(IBPart far* part, bool link, bool embed, bool delay = false);

Copies the currently selected object to the Clipboard. Usually you do not have to call *Clip* directly because *TOcView::Copy* does it for you.

part points to the linked or embedded object. You can pass an object of type *TOcPart* for this parameter. (*TOcPart* supports the *IBPart* interface, which is defined in the BOCOLE library.) If *link* and *embed* are both **true**, then other applications can either link or embed the object when they paste it from the Clipboard. Make delay **true** to have ObjectComponents provide delayed rendering of alternate data formats. (Delayed rendering saves memory. For more information, refer to the Clipboard Overview in the API Help file. Look for the topic "Clipboard Operations.")

See also TOcPart, TOcView::Copy

Convert
bool Convert(TOcPart* ocPart, bool activate);

Displays the Convert dialog box where the user can alter the aspect or format of a linked or embedded object. *ocPart* points to the object the user wants to modify.

Make *activate* **true** if you want ObjectComponents to activate the object after converting it. Generally *activate* should be **false** if the user has chosen Links from the Edit menu. If the user tries to activate an object whose server is not present, you can offer the option of converting the object to another server, and in that case *activate* should be **true**.

See also TOcPart

Drag
bool Drag(IBPart far* part, TOcDropAction inAction, TOcDropAction& outAction);

A container calls this function when the user wants to drag one of the container's objects. The first parameter, *part*, is the object the user is trying to drag. Usually this is an object of type *TOcPart*. (*TOcPart* supports the *IBPart* interface, which is defined in the BOCOLE library.)

inAction combines bit flags indicating possible drag actions the application supports. The flags indicate whether the user can move, copy, or link the object. The value returned in *outAction* contains just one of the action flags indicating what actually did happen.

See also TOcDropAction enum, TOcPart

EnableEditMenu
uint EnableEditMenu(TOcMenuEnable enable, IBDataConsumer far* ocview);

An application calls *EnableEditMenu* to find out which of the OLE-related commands on its Edit menu should currently be enabled. The flags combined in *enable* indicate the commands to be tested, and the return value uses the same bit flags to indicate which commands to enable. *ocview* is usually an object of type *TOcView*. (*TOcView* supports the *IBDataConsumer* interface, which is defined in the BOCOLE library.)

TOleContainer and *TOleView* call *TOcApp::EnableEditMenu* in the command enabler functions for the Edit menu.

See also   TOcApp::TOcMenuEnable enum, TOcView

EvActivate
void EvActivate(bool active);

A container calls this function to tell OLE when its frame window becomes active or inactive. Make *active* **true** if the window was activated or **false** if it was deactivated.

See also   TOcApp::EvResize, TOcApp::EvSetFocus

EvResize
void EvResize();

A container calls this function to tell OLE when the size of its frame window (the main window) has changed. OLE might need this information to let a server modify its tool bar during in-place editing.

See also   TOcApp::EvActivate, TOcApp::EvSetFocus

EvSetFocus
bool EvSetFocus(bool set);

A container calls this function to tell OLE that its frame window has either received or yielded the input focus. Make *set* **true** if the window gained the focus or **false** if it lost the focus.

See also   TOcApp::EvActivate, TOcApp::EvResize

GetName
string GetName() const;

Returns a string object containing the application's name.

GetNameList
TOcNameList& GetNameList();

Returns an array of *TOcNameList* objects containing the names of all the Clipboard formats the application supports. The *TOcView* class uses this list when executing the Paste Special command. The list provides the names and Help strings associated with the formats.

See also   TOcNameList

GetRegistrar()
TOcRegistrar& GetRegistrar();

Returns the application's registrar object. This is the same object passed into the *TOcApp* constructor.

See also   TOcApp public constructor and destructor, TOcRegistrar class

IsOptionSet

bool IsOptionSet(uint32 option) const;

Tests the application mode flags and returns **true** if those set in *option* are set for the application. The application mode flags are defined in the *TOcAppMode* enum.

See also   TOcApp::SetOption, TOcAppMode enum

Paste

bool Paste(TOcInitInfo& initInfo);

Fills *initInfo* with information about the object on the Clipboard. Returns **true** if it succeeds in gathering information and **false** if it fails.

Create *initInfo* first. The *TOcInitInfo* constructor receives the view object where the new part will be inserted. Then call *Paste* to put information in *initInfo*. Finally, call *TOcView::Drop* to put the object in the view.

This function is called by *TOcView::Paste*.

See also   TOcInitInfo, TOcView, TOcView::Drop, TOcView::Paste

RegisterClass

bool RegisterClass(const string& progid, BCID classId, bool multiUse);

Tells OLE that the application is capable of producing objects of a certain type. What objects a server can produce depend on the types of documents it registers.

progid is the registered string that identifies a type of object.

RegisterClasses loops through the application's document templates and calls *RegisterClass* once for each type. The call is made internally and usually you do not need to invoke either function directly.

See also   TOcApp::RegisterClasses, TOcApp::UnregisterClass, TOcApp::UnregisterClasses

RegisterClasses

void RegisterClasses(const TDocTemplate* tplHead = ::DocTemplateStaticHead);

Announces to OLE that the application is running and tells OLE about each type of document the application has registered. The document types are exposed to OLE as kinds of objects the application can produce. *RegisterClasses* tells OLE who you are and what you can make.

tplHead points to the beginning of the application's list of document templates. ObjectWindows stores this list in the global variable *DocTemplateStaticHead*. *UnregisterClasses* loops through the list of document types and calls *UnregisterClass* for each one that has a registered *progid*.

RegisterClasses loops through the document structures in *tplHead* and calls *RegisterClass* once for each type that has a *progid*. The call is made internally, and usually you do not need to invoke either function directly.

See also   progid registration key, TOcApp::RegisterClass, TOcApp::UnregisterClass, TOcApp::UnregisterClasses

ReleaseObject

virtual void ReleaseObject();

ReleaseObject notifies the object that the application's main window is gone. If the application is not serving a client, *ReleaseObject* also decrements the TOcApp object's internal reference count. The object will destroy itself when the count reaches zero. The destructor of *TOcModule* calls this function.

See also   TOcModule

SetOption
void SetOption(uint32 bit, bool state);

Modifies the application's running mode flags. *bit* contains bit flags from the *TOcAppMode* enum. If *state* is **true**, *SetOption* turns the flags on. If *state* is **false**, it turns the flags off. You should never have to call this function because ObjectComponents always maintains the mode flags.

See also   TOcApp::IsOptionSet, TOcAppMode enum

SetupWindow
void SetupWindow(HWND frameWnd);

Tells the *TOcApp* object what window to associate with the application. Usually *frameWnd* is the application's main window. Usually this function is called from the *SetupWindow* function associated with the application's main window.

TranslateAccel
bool TranslateAccel(MSG far* msg);

A container application adds *TranslateAccel* to its Windows message loop if it wants to make a DLL server's accelerator keystrokes available to the user during in-place editing. DLL servers require this cooperation because they do not have message loops of their own, as an .EXE server does.

If you call *TranslateAccel* after the usual call to the Windows API *TranslateAccelerator*, then your own accelerators will have priority if they happen to conflict with the server's.

msg holds a Windows message structure. The return value is **true** if the server translates the accelerator and **false** if it does not.

UnregisterClass
bool UnregisterClass(const string& progid);

Notifies OLE when the application is no longer available to produce objects of a certain type. *progid* is the registered string that identifies a type of object.

UnregisterClasses loops through all the documents the application registered and calls *UnregisterClass* for each one. The destructor of *TOcApp* calls *UnregisterClasses*.

See also   TOcApp::RegisterClass, TOcApp::RegisterClasses, TOcApp::UnregisterClasses

UnregisterClasses
void UnregisterClasses(const TDocTemplate* tplHead = ::DocTemplateStaticHead);

Announces to the system that the application is no longer available for OLE interactions. *tplHead* points to the beginning of the application's list of document templates. ObjectWindows stores this list in the global variable *DocTemplateStaticHead*.

UnregisterClasses loops through the list of document types and calls *UnregisterClass* for each one that has a registered *progid*. *UnregisterClasses* is called from the *TOcApp* destructor.

See also   progid registration key, TOcApp::RegisterClass, TOcApp::RegisterClasses, TOcApp::UnregisterClass

Protected constructor and destructor

Constructor
TOcApp(TOcRegistrar& registrar, uint32 options = ULONG_MAX, IUnknown* outer = 0,
    const TDocTemplate* tplHead = ::DocTemplateStaticHead);

The constructor for a *TOcApp* object expands the application's message queue if necessary to accommodate OLE message traffic and builds the application's list of supported Clipboard formats.

registrar is a registration object that processes the command line. Create the registrar first.

options is a set of application mode bit flags. The *TOcApp* object is usually created in the *TComponentFactory* callback function. The constructor's *options* parameter is the same as the callback's *options* parameter.

outer points to the *IUnknown* interface of the outer object inside which the new application is asked to aggregate itself.

tplHead points to the head of an application's list of document templates. The ObjectWindows Library stores an application's document template list in the global variable *DocTemplateStaticHead*.

Destructor
~TOcApp();

The *TOcApp* destructor notifies OLE that the application is no longer available.

Usually the creation and destruction of an application's *TOcApp* object are managed by the *TOcRegistrar* object.

See also   TComponentFactory typedef, TOcRegistrar class, TOcApp::ReleaseObject

Protected member functions

ForwardEvent

Form 1   uint32 ForwardEvent(int eventId, const void far* param);

Form 2   uint32 ForwardEvent(int eventId, uint32 param = 0);

Both forms send a WM_OCEVENT message to the application's main window. The *eventId* parameter becomes the message's *wParam* and should be one of the

OC_APPxxxx or OC_VIEWxxxx constants. The second parameter becomes the message's *lParam* and can be either a pointer (Form 1) or an integer (Form 2). Which form you use depends on the information a particular event needs to send in its *lParam*.

See also WM_OCEVENT message, OC_APPxxxx messages, OC_VIEWxxxx messages, TOcRegistrar class

TOcAppMode enum   ocf/ocreg.h

enum TOcAppMode

The enumerated values of *TOcAppMode* represent flags that ObjectComponents sets to indicate an application's running modes. Some flags are set in response to command-line switches that OLE places on a server's command line. Others are set as the application registers itself.

To determine whether a particular mode flag is set, call *TOcApp::IsOptionSet* or *TOcModule::IsOptionSet*. The *TOcApp* object holds the mode flags for each instance of the application. *TOcModule* simply queries the *TOcApp*.

The enumerated values are bit flags and can be combined with the bitwise OR operator (|). Flags marked with an asterisk can differ for each instance of an application.

Constant	What the Server Should Do
amAnyRegOption	Combine the *RegServer*, *UnregServer*, and *TypeLib* bits.
amAutomation	Register itself as single-use (one client only). Always accompanied by –**Embedding**.
amDebug	Enter a debugging session.
amExeMode	*Nothing. This flag is set to indicate that the server is running as an .EXE. Either the server was built as an .EXE, or it is a DLL that was launched by an .EXE stub and is running as an executable program.
amExeModule	Nothing. This flag is set to indicate that the server was built as a .EXE program.
amEmbedding	*Consider remaining hidden because it is running for a client, not for itself.
amLangId	Use the locale ID that follows this switch when creating registration and type libraries. (Useless without the –**RegServer** or –**TypeLib** switches.)
amNoRegValidate	Omit the usual validation check comparing the server's *progid*, *clsid*, and *path* to those registered with the system. The registrar object responds to this flag.
amRegServer	Register itself in the system registration database and quit.
amRun	Run its message loop. This is used by the factory callback function.
amServedApp	*Avoid deleting itself (a client is using the application and holds a reference to it).
amShutdown	*When the *TComponentFactory* callback sees this flag, it should terminate the application.
amSingleUse	*Register itself as a single-use (one client only) application.
amTypeLib	Create and register a type library.
amUnregServer	Remove all its entries from the system registration database and quit.

See also TOcModule::IsOptionSet, TOcApp::IsOptionSet

TOcAspect enum   ocf/ocobject.h

enum TOcAspect

A container uses these values to request that objects in its documents be presented in particular ways. An object might be asked to show all its content, to show a miniature representation of its content, or an icon that represents the type of object it is. A server is not obliged to support all the possible aspects.

The values are flags and can be combined with the bitwise OR operator (|).

Constant	Meaning
asContent	Show the full content of the object at its normal size.
asThumbnail	Show the content of the object shrunk to fit in a smaller space.
asIcon	Show an icon representing the type of object.
asDocPrint	Show the object as it would look if sent to the printer.
asDefault	Continue to use the last aspect specified.
asMaintain	Preserve the object's original aspect ratio. Do not alter the aspect ratio to fit the rectangle where the client chooses to show the object.

See also   TOcPart::Draw, ocrxxxx aspect constants

TOcDialogHelp enum   ocf/ocobject.h

enum TOcDialogHelp

The OC_APPDIALOGHELP event tells the container when the user clicks the Help button in a standard OLE dialog box. The *lParam* of the WM_OCEVENT message carries one of these values to indicate which dialog box the user has open.

Constant	Dialog box	Purpose
dhBrowse	Insert Object dialog box	Choose an object to insert.
dhBrowseClipboard	Paste Special dialog box	Choose the data format for pasting an object.
dhConvert	Convert dialog box	Convert an object to work with a different server.
dhBrowseLinks	Links dialog box	Update links to objects.
dhChangeIcon	Change Icon dialog box	Used internally by Insert Object and Paste Special dialog boxes.
dhFileOpen	File Open dialog box	Choose a file to open.
dhSourceSet	Change Source dialog box	Assign a new link source to a linked object.
dhIconFileOpen	File Open dialog box	Confirm that the chosen file contains an icon resource.

See also   EvOcAppDialogHelp event handler, OC_APPxxxx messages, TOleFrame::EvOcAppDialogHelp, WM_OCEVENT message

TOcDocument class

ocf/ocdoc.h

The primary responsibility of a *TOcDocument* is to save and load data in a compound file using hierarchically ordered storages. (A storage is a compartment within a file, just as a directory is a compartment on a disk.) By default the application's native data always goes in the document's root storage, but the application is free to create its own storages in the same file. *TOcDocument* creates new storages below the root as necessary for OLE objects that the user inserts into the compound document. The new storages take their names from the names of the objects they store. *TOcView* automatically assigns a unique string identifier to each new object.

Both servers and containers can create objects of type *TOcDocument*. In the container, this object represents an entire compound document. In the server, it represents the data for a single OLE object. (The server's single OLE object can have other OLE objects linked or embedded in it.)

A *TOcDocument* object manages the collection of *TOcPart* objects that are deposited in one of the container's documents. It does not draw the data on the screen. To do that, every *TOcDocument* needs a corresponding *TOcView* or *TOcRemView* object. An application can possess multiple pairs of associated document and view objects, one for each open document.

A container creates a *TOcView* object to draw its compound document in the container's own window. Because the window where the server draws belongs to the container (it is a child of the container's window), the server must create a remote view object (*TOcRemView*) for each document.

In spite of the similar names, *TOcDocument* and *TOcView* are not part of the ObjectWindows Doc/View model. The nature of OLE makes it useful to separate data from its graphical representation, and the terms *document* and *view* express that separation even outside of ObjectWindows.

To execute its tasks, a *TOcDocument* must use the standard OLE interfaces *IStorage* and *IStream*. Usually it is not necessary to use these interfaces directly because ObjectComponents implements them for you in its undocumented *TOcStorage* and *TOcStream* classes. These classes are thin wrappers around standard OLE interfaces. The implementation of *TOcDocument* makes use of both objects.

See also
TOcRemView class, TOcView class

Public constructors and destructor

Constructors

Form 1   TOcDocument(TOcApp& app, const char far* fileName = 0);

Creates a new document object for the application and optionally assigns a file name for storing the document. A container uses this constructor for each document the user opens.

Form 2   TOcDocument(TOcApp& app, const char far* fileName, IStorage far* storageI);

Creates a new document object for the application and assigns a particular file and storage object to hold the document. The container calls this constructor when opening an existing file. The server and the container each create their own *TOcDocument* object for the object they share, but both their objects point to the same file for storing the object.

IStorage is the standard OLE storage interface. ObjectComponents implements this interface in its internal, undocumented *TOcStorage* class. It is usually not necessary to manipulate the *IStorage* interface or the *TOcStorage* class directly in an ObjectComponents application.

Destructor
~TOcDocument();
Destroys the *TDocument* object.

Public member functions

Close
void Close();
A container calls *TOcPart::Close* for each object in the compound document to release its servers. *TOleDocument* calls this function automatically when asked to close down.

See also   TOcPart::Close, TOleDocument class

GetActiveView
TOcView* GetActiveView();
Returns a pointer to the active view. *TOcPart* calls this method to coordinate changing focus among active parts.

See also   TOcDocument::SetActiveView

GetName
string GetName() const;
Returns the name of the file where the document will be stored. ObjectComponents keeps track of the name in order to create links correctly.

See also   TOcDocument::SetName

GetParts
TOcPartCollection& GetParts();
Returns an object with information about all the parts in the document. Each part corresponds to a linked or embedded object. Create an iterator of type *TOcPartCollectionIter* to loop through the collection and extract information about individual parts.

See also   TOcPart class, TOcPartCollection class, TOcPartCollectionIter class

GetStorage
TOcStorage* GetStorage();
Returns the document file's root storage.

See also   TOcDocument::SetStorage

LoadParts

bool LoadParts();

Reads all the linked and embedded parts saved in a compound file. *LoadParts* does not necessarily load all the data from all the parts into memory immediately. The data is needed only if the object is visible.

LoadParts returns **true** if all the parts are read successfully. If no file has yet been assigned to the document, then there is nothing to load and the function still returns **true**. (A document can acquire a file from its constructor, from *SaveToFile*, or from *SetStorage*.)

See also   TOcDocument public constructors and destructors, TOcDocument::SaveParts, TOcDocument::SaveToFile, TOcDocument::SetStorage

RenameParts

void RenameParts(IBRootLinkable far* BLDocumentl);

Call this whenever the name of the document file changes. *RenameParts* updates the internal name stored with each part so that other applications can still link to them correctly.

IBRootLinkable is a custom OLE interface defined in the BOCOLE support library. Objects of type *TOcView* implement this interface, so it is usually not necessary to implement it yourself. Simply pass the document's view object to *RenameParts*.

TOcView calls this function automatically if the view is renamed.

See also   TOcDocument::SetName, TOcView::Rename

SaveParts

bool SaveParts(IStorage* storage = 0, bool sameAsLoaded = true);

Writes all the document's linked and embedded objects to the document's file. *storage* is the root storage in the file. A container's *TOcDocument* creates the storage object when the document is created or the first time it is saved. Find the object by calling *GetStorage*. A server gets the storage object from the container. It is usually not necessary to manipulate the *storage* object directly.

sameAsLoaded should be **true** unless the name of the document file has changed since the last time the document was loaded or saved.

SaveParts returns **true** if all the objects are successfully written to the file.

LoadParts and *SaveParts* are called by the *Open* and *Commit* methods in *TOleDocument*.

See also   TOcDocument::GetStorage, TOcDocument::LoadParts, TOcDocument::SaveToFile

SaveToFile

bool SaveToFile(const char far* newName);

Saves the document in the file named by *newName*. Usually a container calls this function when the user chooses File | Save for an unnamed document or File | Save As for any document. *SaveToFile* creates a new storage object and then calls *SaveParts*. It returns **true** if all the linked and embedded parts are successfully saved.

See also   TOcDocument::SaveParts

SetActiveView

void SetActiveView(TOcView* view);

A *TOcView* object calls this method when it is activated so that the document can locate the active view. *TOcDocument* communicates only with the active view. The active view sends messages to the corresponding window, perhaps a *TOleView* window. This window is responsible for telling other windows about changes.

See also   TOcDocument::GetActiveView

SetName

void SetName(const string& newName);

Tells the document the name of the file where it will be stored. ObjectComponents needs to know the name in order to create links correctly. More specifically, *SetName* causes ObjectComponents to update the OLE moniker that a link server must provide.

See also   TOcDocument::GetName

SetStorage

Form 1   void SetStorage(const char far* path);

Creates a compound file using the name in *path* and assigns the root storage of the new file to be the root storage of the document. Usually a container calls this function when the user chooses File | Save for an unnamed document or File | Save As for any document.

Form 2   void SetStorage(IStorage* storage);

Assigns *storage* to be the document's root storage. Usually a server calls this function when the container passes it an *IStorage* object. (An *IStorage* object implements the standard OLE interface *IStorage*. Usually it is not necessary to manipulate this object directly.)

Assigns the document a storage for writing its data. *storage* becomes the document's root storage. Each linked or embedded object gets its own substorage under the root storage.

See also   TOcDocument::GetStorage

TOcDragDrop struct   ocf/ocview.h

Holds information that a view or a window needs in order to accept a drag and drop object. The OC_VIEWDRAG and OC_VIEWDROP messages carry a reference to this structure in their *lParams*. *TOleView* and *TOleWindow* process these messages for you, so you should not need to use *TOcDragDrop* directly unless you are programming without ObjectWindows. For examples of how to process OC_VIEWDRAG and OC_VIEWDROP messages, look at the source code for the *EvOcViewDrag* and *EvOcViewDrop* methods in *TOleView* and *TOleWindow*.

See also   OC_VIEWxxxx messages, TOleView::EvOcViewDrag, TOleView::EvOcViewDrop, TOleWindow::EvOcViewDrag, TOleWindow::EvOcViewDrop

Public data members

InitInfo
TOcInitInfo far* InitInfo;

When carried in an OC_VIEWDROP message, this field describes an object about to be dropped on the view. When carried in an OC_VIEWDRAG message, this field is zero.

See also   OC_VIEWxxxx messages, TOcInitInfo class

Pos
TRect Pos;

The coordinates in *Pos* indicate the area of the view where the user has dropped an object. The position is given in device coordinates relative to the client area.

See also   TRect class

Where
TPoint Where;

The coordinates in *Where* indicate the point on the view where the mouse released the object. The position is given in client area coordinates.

See also   TPoint class

TOcDropAction enum   ocf/ocobject.h

enum TOcDropAction

TOcApp::Drag uses these values to describe what actions are allowed and what actions actually occur during a drag and drop operation. The values are flags and can be combined with the bitwise OR operator (|).

Constant	Meaning
daDropCopy	Copy the object to the drop site.
daDropMove	Move the object to the drop site.
daDropLink	Create a link to the object at the drop site.
daDropNone	No action occurred.

See also   TOcApp::Drag

TOcFormatList class   ocf/ocview.h

Manages a list of Clipboard formats that a particular view supports.

TOcFormat, *TOcFormatList*, and *TOcFormatListIter* all work together to maintain the list of formats. *TOcFormatList* adds and deletes *TOcFormat* objects from the list. *TOcFormatListIter* enumerates the items in the list whenever the view needs to examine them one by one. Because *TOcView* creates and maintains this list internally, it is usually not necessary for you to use any of these classes directly.

When ObjectComponents receives your document registration table, it sees entries for each Clipboard format that the document receives or produces. From these entries, *TOcView* creates a list of objects of type *TOcFormat*, each object representing one format. The view needs this list to know when a Clipboard command or drag-and-drop operation can succeed. For example, if the user drags a bitmap over a view that accepts only text, *TOcView* knows the object cannot be dropped and adjusts the cursor accordingly.

See also   TOcFormat class, TOcFormatListIter class, TOcView class

Public constructor and destructor

Constructor
TOcFormatList( );
Creates an empty list object. To insert items in the list, call the *Add* method.

Destructor
~TOcFormatList( );
Deletes all the items in the list.

See also   TOcFormatList::Add

Public member functions

Add
int Add(TOcFormat* format);
Inserts a new Clipboard format item in the list. Returns 0 for failure and 1 for success.

See also   TOcFormatList::Clear

Clear
void Clear(int del = 1);
Removes all the items from the list. If *del* is 1, *Clear* also deletes all the *TOcFormat* objects.

See also   TOcFormatList::Add, TOcFormatList::Detach

Count
virtual uint Count( ) const;
Returns the number of items in the list.

See also   TOcFormatList::IsEmpty

Detach
int Detach(const TOcFormat* format, int del = 0);
Removes one format item from the list. If *del* is 1, then *Detach* also deletes the *TOcFormat* object.

See also   TOcFormatList::Add, TOcFormatList::Clear

Find

unsigned Find(const TOcFormat* format) const;

Searches the list for the object passed as format. If the object is found, then *Find* returns the object's position in the list. (The first position is 0.) If format is not in the list, *Find* returns UINT_MAX.

IsEmpty

int IsEmpty() const;

Returns 1 if the list object currently contains no *TOcFormat* items and 0 if the list is not empty.

See also   TOcFormatList::Count

operator [ ]

TOcFormat*& operator [(unsigned index)];

Retrieves a Clipboard format by its position in the list. If *index* is 1, for example, the [] returns the second item in the list. The order of items depends on the priority assigned to them when they are registered.

TOcFormatListIter class   ocf/ocview.h

Enumerates all the Clipboard formats that a particular view supports.

TOcFormat, *TOcFormatList*, and *TOcFormatListIter* all work together to manage the list of formats. *TOcFormatList* adds and deletes *TOcFormat* objects from the list. *TOcFormatListIter* enumerates the items in the list whenever the view needs to examine them one by one. Because *TOcView* creates and maintains this list internally, it is usually not necessary for you to use any of these classes directly.

When ObjectComponents receives your document registration table, it sees entries for each Clipboard format that the document receives or produces. From these entries, *TOcView* creates a list of objects of type *TOcFormat*, each object representing one format. The view needs this list to know when a Clipboard command or drag-and-drop operation can succeed. For example, if the user drags a bitmap object over a view that accepts only text, *TOcView* knows the object cannot be dropped and adjusts the cursor accordingly.

See also   TOcFormat class, TOcFormatList class, TOcView class

Public constructor

Constructor

TOcFormatListIter(const TOcFormatList& collection)

Constructs an iterator to enumerate the Clipboard formats contained in collection.

Public member functions

Current
TOcFormat* Current() const;

Returns the format that the iterator currently points to.

operator ++
Form 1   TOcFormat* operator++();

Returns the current format and then advances the iterator to point to the next format (postincrement).

Form 2   TOcFormat* operator++(int);

Advances the iterator to point to the next format in the list and then returns that format (preincrement).

operator int()
operator int() const;

Converts the iterator to an integer value in order to test whether the iterator has finished enumerating the collection. If parts remain unenumerated, the operator returns the iterator's current position in the list of parts. If the iterator has reached the end of the list, the operator returns zero.

Restart
Form 1   void Restart();

Resets the iterator to begin again with the first format in the list.

Form 2   void Restart(unsigned start, unsigned stop);

Resets the iterator to enumerate a subset of the format list, beginning with the object at position *start* and ending with the object at position *stop*.

TOcFormatName class   ocf/ocapp.h

TOcApp uses this class internally to hold the strings that describe a Clipboard data format such as text or bitmap. *TOcApp* displays these strings in standard OLE dialog boxes such as Paste Link.

Every Clipboard format has three associated pieces of information: an ID value, a name string, and a result name. For standard formats, the ID is a constant such as CF_SYLK. The name string is a short name such as "Sylk." The result name is a longer string that tells the user what pasting this data produces—for example, "a spreadsheet." A *TOcFormatName* object holds all three values for one format.

TOcApp makes a *TOcNameList* object to hold all the format names it needs. It loads descriptive strings into *TOcFormatName* objects and adds the objects one by one to its name list. Both objects are created and managed inside *TOcApp*. Usually you do not have to manipulate either of them directly.

See also   TOcApp class, TOcNameList class

Public constructors and destructor

Constructors

Form 1   TOcFormatName();

Constructs an empty format name object.

Form 2   TOcFormatName(char far* fmtName, char far* fmtResultName, char far* id = 0);

Constructs a format name object and initializes it with three values that describe a Clipboard format. *fmtName* is the name of the format ("metafile"). *fmtResultName* describes what the user gets by pasting this format ("a Windows metafile picture"). *id* is the value that Windows assigns to identify the format (CF_METAFILEPICT) but expressed as a string of decimal digits ("3").

Destructor

~TOcFormatName();

Releases the object.

Public member functions

GetId

const char far* GetId();

Returns a pointer to the string that the system uses to designate the format.

GetName

const char far* GetName();

Returns a pointer to the name of the format.

GetResultName

const char far* GetResultName();

Returns the descriptive string that tells the user what pasting data of this format produces.

operator ==

bool operator ==(const TOcFormatName& other);

Returns **true** if *other* is the same object as **this**.

TOcInitHow enum   ocf/ocobject.h

enum TOcInitHow

These values tell whether a container is to link or embed a new object it is receiving. The container passes this information to a *TOcInitInfo* object when it receives a new OLE object.

Constant	Meaning
ihLink	Link to the object. Create a reference in the container's document that points to the place in the server's document where the data actually resides.
ihEmbed	Embed the object. Copy the object's data directly into the container's document.

Constant	Meaning
ihMetafile	Embed a static object that draws itself as a metafile.
ihBitmap	Embed a static object that draws itself as a bitmap.

See also
TOcInitInfo public constructors, TOcInitWhere enum

TOcInitInfo class   ocf/ocobject.h

TOcInitInfo holds information that tells ObjectComponents how to create a new part. When the user pastes, inserts, or drops an object into a container, ObjectComponents creates a *TOcInitInfo* object, initializes it with information about the incoming OLE object, and passes the info object to the *TOcPart* constructor. The info object tells the part where to find its data and how to create itself.

If you are using ObjectWindows, *TOleView* manages these details for you. If you are programming without ObjectWindows, you can find sample code for using *TOcInitInfo* objects in the *TOleView* methods that insert objects: look at the code for *CmEditInsertObject* and *CmEditPasteSpecial*. Look also at the code for *TOcView::Drop*.

See also
TOcPart Class, TOcView::Drop, TOleView::CmEditInsertObject,
TOleView::CmEditPasteSpecial

Public data members

Container
IBContainer far* Container;

Container is the view object that is about to receive the object. *IBContainer* is an undocumented custom OLE interface defined in the BOCOLE support library and implemented in *TOcView*. The *Container* data member can hold an object of type *TOcView*.

See also   TOcView class

HIcon
HICON HIcon;

HIcon holds the icon to draw if the user chooses the Display As Icon option from the Insert Object dialog box. The *HIcon* handle is actually a global memory handle to a metafile containing the icon. The *Browse* and *BrowseClipboard* functions in *TOcApp* handle the Insert Object dialog box for you, so usually you do not need to display the icon directly yourself.

How
TOcInitHow How;

Tells whether the object should be linked or embedded when it is added to the document.

See also   TOcInitHow enum

Storage

IStorage far* Storage;

Storage is the storage object in a compound file. The container provides the storage to hold data transferred from the server. *IStorage* is a standard OLE interface. ObjectComponents implements the *IStorage* interface in *TOcStorage*, so *Storage* usually holds a *TOcStorage* object.

Where

TOcInitWhere Where;

Tells where the server will place the object's data. For example, the server can choose to transfer data by placing it in a file, in a storage, or in a memory handle.

See also   TOcInitWhere enum

Data

IDataObject* Data;

One of four data fields in an anonymous union, this field is used when *Where* is *iwDataObject*, indicating that the server has created an OLE data object to transfer the data for the incoming object. *Data* points to the *IDataObject* interface on the server's data transfer object. (*IDataObject* is a standard OLE interface.) This is the normal transfer method for objects received from the Clipboard or through a drag-and-drop operation.

Path

LPCOLESTR Path;

One of four data fields in an anonymous union, this field is used when *Where* is *iwFile*, indicating that the server has placed the data for the incoming object in a file. *Path* points to the name of the file where the data is stored.

CId

BCID CId;

One of four data fields in an anonymous union, this field is used when *Where* is *iwNew*, indicating that the incoming object is brand new, being freshly created. *CId* is the class ID that the server registered for one of its document factories. It tells the server what kind of object to create.

See also   TOcApp::RegisterClasses, TOcInitInfo::Where

Handle

```
struct{
  HANDLE Data;
  uint DataFormat;
} Handle;
```

One of four data fields in an anonymous union, this structure is used when *Where* is *iwHandle*, indicating that the server has placed the data for the incoming object in a memory handle. *Data* is the handle itself and *DataFormat* identifies a Clipboard format for the data in the handle.

Public constructors

TOcInitInfo
IBContainer far* Container;

Container is the view object that is about to receive the object. *IBContainer* is an undocumented custom OLE interface defined in the BOCOLE support library and implemented in *TOcView*. The *Container* data member can hold an object of type *TOcView*.

See also   TOcView class

TOcInitInfo
Form 1   TOcInitInfo(IBContainer far* container);

Use Form 1 when invoking the server to create a new object from scratch—for example, when processing the Insert Object command. The new part will be embedded, not linked.

Form 2   TOcInitInfo(TOcInitHow how, TOcInitWhere where, IBContainer far* container);

Use Form 2 when creating a part to hold an object that already exists—for example, when loading a part from a storage in a compound document. *how* tells whether the object will be linked or embedded. *where* tells what medium the server will use to transfer data from the existing object.

Both forms of the constructor create a *TOcInitInfo* object for placing a new part in *container*. *container* is the view that will hold the new part. *IBContainer* is a custom OLE interface defined in the BOCOLE support library and implemented in *TOcView*. *container* can be an object of type *TOcView*.

Public member function

ReleaseDataObject
uint32 ReleaseDataObject();

If the *TOcInitInfo* object holds a pointer to the data object from which the new part is about to be created, then *ReleaseDataObject* decrements the data object's reference count. Call this when you are through with the data object.

See also   TOcInitInfo::Data

TOcInitWhere enum   ocf/ocobject.h

enum TOcInitWhere

These values tell where the data for an object resides. A container passes this information to a *TOcInitInfo* object when it receives a new OLE object for linking or embedding. The server can choose any of several available channels for transferring the data in the object.

Constant	Meaning
iwFile	The server passes the data in a disk file.
iwStorage	The server passes the data in a storage object (part of a compound file).
iwDataObject	The server passes the data in a data transfer object, one that supports the standard *IDataObject* OLE interface. (Objects transferred through the Clipboard or by dragging support this interface. *TOcInitInfo* holds a pointer to the interface.)
iwNew	The server will be asked to create a new object.
iwHandle	The server passes a memory handle for the data.

See also
TOcInitInfo public constructors, TOcInitHow enum

TOcInvalidate enum   ocf/ocobject.h

enum TOcInvalidate

Functions that invalidate an object use these enumeration values to indicate whether the data in the object has changed or the appearance of the object has changed. It is possible for the data in an object to change without invalidating the view of the object. For example, if the object is drawn as an icon, then editing the data probably does not call for an update to the view. If both the data and the view change, then combine both flags with the bitwise OR operator (|).

If the view is invalid, the object needs to be redrawn. If the data is invalid, then the object needs saving. (It is not necessary to save the object right away. *invData* simply indicates that the object is dirty and needs to be saved before the document is closed.)

Constant	Meaning
invData	The data in an object has changed and should be updated in the container.
invView	The appearance of an object needs to change and should be updated in the container.

See also
TOcRemView::InvalidateTOc, TOleView::InvalidatePart, TOleWindow::InvalidatePart

TOcMenuDescr struct   ocf/ocapp.h

The menu descriptor structure is used when merging the menus of a container and server for in-place editing. The structure holds a handle to a shared Windows menu object and a count of the number of drop-down menus in each group.

If you are using ObjectWindows, use the information in the structure to construct a *TMenuDescr* object for the other application. To merge two menus, call *TMenuDescr::Merge*. If you are not using ObjectWindows, call the Windows API routines such as *InsertMenu* to place your own commands in the shared menu.

The following messages carry a *TOcMenuDescr* **struct** in their *lParams*: OC_APPINSMENUS, OC_APPMENUS, and OC_VIEWINSMENUS. The ObjectWindows OLE-enabled window and view classes process these messages for you. Unless you are programming without ObjectWindows, you usually will not have to use *TOcMenuDescr* directly. For examples of how to process the messages, see the source code for the relevant event handlers in *TOleView*, *TOleWindow*, *TOleFrame*, and *TOleMDIFrame*.

See also   OC_APPxxxx messages, OC_VIEWxxxx messages, TMenuDescr class

Public data members

HMenu
HMENU HMenu;

Holds a handle to the shared menu. The handle is valid only while the menu is constructed. Do not store it for later use.

Width
int Width[6];

The *Width* array contains the number of pop-up menus in each menu group. The groups, in order, are File, Edit, Container, Object, Windows, and Help.

The array is meant to help you construct a *TMenuDescr* object. The numbers it holds control how the menu is merged.

See also   TMenuDescr public constructors and destructors

TOcModule class   ocf/ocapp.h

TOcModule is a mix-in class for deriving OLE-enabled application classes. Any ObjectComponents application that supports linking and embedding should derive its application class from both *TApplication* and *TOcModule*. The ObjectComponents module class coordinates some basic housekeeping chores related to registration and memory management. It also holds a pointer to the *TOcApp* object that connects your application object to OLE through ObjectComponents. Allowing *TOcModule* to do this work also makes it easy to use the same code for both .EXE and .DLL versions of the same server.

See also   TApplication class, TOcApp class

Public constructor and destructor

Constructor
TOcModule();

Builds a *TOcModule*. After creating a *TOcModule* object, you need to call *OcInit*.

Destructor

~TOcModule();

Releases the *TOcApp* object. An application that derives from *TOcModule* does not need to call the *TOcApp::ReleaseObject* method when it closes down. (Never call **delete** to destroy a *TOcApp* object, either.)

See also   TOcModule::OcInitTOcModuleOcInit

Public member functions

GetRegistrar

TRegistrar& GetRegistrar();

Returns the application's registrar object. Be sure to call *OcInit* first.

See also   TOcModule::OcInit, TRegistrar class

IsOptionSet

bool IsOptionSet(uint32 option) const;

Returns **true** if the command-line flag indicated by *option* is set and **false** if it is not. The registrar sets the flags for you when it interprets OLE-related switches on the application's command line. The possible values for *option* are enumerated in *TOcAppMode*.

See also   TOcAppMode class, TOcRegistrar class

OcInit

void OcInit(TOcRegistrar& registrar, uint32 options);

Initializes ObjectComponents support for the code module. This call causes ObjectComponents to create the *TOcApp* connector object that attaches the application to the OLE system. Always call *OcInit* right after constructing the module object.

registrar is the application registrar object. It must be created before you call *OcInit*.

options is a set of bit flags describing command-line options set for this instance of the program. To test for particular options, call *IsOptionSet*. The possible option flags are defined in *TOcAppMode*.

See also   TOcApp class, TOcAppMode enum, TOcModule::IsOptionSet, TOcModule::IsOptionSet,, TOcRegistrar class

Public data members

OcApp

TOcApp* OcApp;

Holds the *TOcApp* object that is the ObjectComponents partner object for your *TApplication*-derived class. This member is initialized when you call *OcInit*.

See also   TOcApp class, TOcModule::OcInit

OleMalloc

TOleAllocator OleMalloc;

Sets up an allocator object that initializes the OLE system and sets up the memory allocator. OLE allows each program to set up a memory manager for OLE to use when allocating and de-allocating memory on behalf of that application.

TOcModule simply chooses the default allocator. If you have unusual memory management needs and want to supply your own custom memory allocator, set its *IMalloc* interface in *OleMalloc::Mem*.

See also   TOleAllocator class, TOleAllocator::Mem

TOcNameList class   ocf/ocapp.h

TOcApp uses this class internally to manage a collection of *TOcFormatName* objects. Each format name object holds three strings that describe a Clipboard data format such as text or bitmap. *TOcApp* displays these strings in standard OLE dialog boxes such as Paste Link.

The list of format names is created and managed inside *TOcApp*. Usually you do not have to manipulate the list directly. To put your own custom formats in the list, however, you do have to register them. See *TOcApp::AddUserFormatName* for more information about setting up custom formats.

Standard Windows Clipboard formats are always added to the list for you. The name and result strings for standard formats are defined in OLEVIEW.RC. To localize the strings, edit this file. (Standard formats do not have an identifier string. Instead they have a registration number, such as CF_TEXT.)

See also   TOcApp class, TOcApp::AddUserFormatName, TOcFormatName class

Public constructor and destructor

Constructor
TOcNameList();

Constructs a name list containing no items. To insert names in the list, call *Add*.

Destructor
~TOcNameList();

Destroys the list and the objects in the list.

See also   TOcNameList::Add

Public member functions

operator []
Form 1   TOcFormatName*& operator[](unsigned index);

Returns the item at position *index* in the list of format name objects. The first object is at index 0. If *index* points past the end of the list, the function throws a precondition exception.

Form 2   TOcFormatName* operator[](char far* id);

Returns the format name object whose format ID string matches *id*. The return value is 0 if no match is found.

See also   TOcFormatName

Add
int Add(TOcFormatName* name);

Inserts the object *name* into the list. Returns 1 for success and 0 for failure.

See also   TOcNameList::Clear, TOcNameList::Detach

Clear
void Clear(int del = 1);

Empties the list. If *del* is 1, *Clear* also deletes each object in the list.

See also   TOcNameList::Add, TOcNameList::Detach

Count
virtual uint Count( ) const;

Returns the number of items in the list.

See also   TOcNameList::IsEmpty

Detach
int Detach(const TOcFormatName* name, int del = 0);

Removes the single object *name* from the list. If *del* is 1, *Detach* also deletes the object *name*.

See also   TOcNameList::Clear, TOcNameList::Add

Find
unsigned Find(const TOcFormatName* name) const;

Searches the list and returns the position of *name*. If the *name* object is not in the list, *Find* returns UINT_MAX.

IsEmpty
int IsEmpty( ) const;

Returns 1 if the list currently contains no items and 0 if it contains at least one item.

See also   TOcNameList::Count

TOcPart class   ocf/ocpart.h

Base class
TUnknown

A *TOcPart* object represents a linked or embedded object in a document. It represents the linked or embedded object as the container sees it. From the server's side, the same linked or embedded OLE object has two parts: data (*TOcDocument*) and a graphical representation of the data (*TOcRemView*). *TOcPart* manages a site in the container's document where a server places an OLE object.

TOcPart is a COM object and implements the *IUnknown* interface.

See also   TOcDocument class, TOcPartCollection class, TOcRemView class, TUnknown class

Public constructors

Constructors

Form 1   TOcPart(TOcDocument& document, TOcInitInfo far& initInfo, TRect pos, int id = 0);

document is the container's *TOcDocument* object representing the compound document that will hold the newly created part. *initInfo* contains information about the object being inserted. It is usually obtained during a paste, drop, or insertion operation. The coordinates in *pos* designate the area where the new object will be drawn. *id* is any arbitrary unique integer used to distinguish this object from others in the same document. If *id* is 0, *TOcPart* generates a new ID automatically.

Form 2   TOcPart(TOcDocument& document, const char far* name);

document is the same as for Form 1. The *name* string is the name of a linked or embedded part. The second form is used when loading a part from a compound document. The name of the part is also the name of the storage where the part was written.

Both constructors expect to receive the container's own *TOcDocument* object. This represents the compound document where the new object will be placed.

See also   TOcDocument class, TOcInitInfo class, TOcPart::Delete, TRect class

Public member functions

operator ==
bool operator==(const TOcPart& other);

Returns **true** if *other* is the same *TOcPart* as **this**. This operator is defined for the use of the *TOcPartCollection* class.

Activate
bool Activate(bool activate);

If *activate* is **true**, this function activates the part by asking the server to execute its primary (or default) verb for the object. If the default verb is *Edit*, for example, *Activate* initiates an in-place editing session. If *activate* is **false**, then this function deactivates an in-place editing session.

Activate returns **true** if the server is able to execute the command.

See also   TOcPart::IsActive, TOcPart::Open

Close
bool Close();

Disconnects the embedded object from its server. Returns **true** if the server closes successfully.

Delete
void Delete();

Delete is used when the user selects an embedded object and presses the Delete key (or does a cut operation). It first calls *Close* to disconnect the container from the embedded object. Then it releases the reference to the embedded part.

See also   TOcPart::Close

Detach
int Detach();

Separates a part from its document. Call *Detach* before cutting a part to the Clipboard, for example.

DoVerb
bool DoVerb(uint whichVerb);

Tells the server to execute one of its commands on the part. A verb is usually an action such as Edit or Play. One server can support several verbs, and *whichVerb* identifies a particular verb by its ordinal value. (The first verb, the primary or default verb, is zero.) *DoVerb* returns **true** if the server is able to complete the requested action. Executing a verb can cause the part to become activated.

See also   TOcPart::EnumVerbs

Draw
bool Draw(HDC dc, const TRect& pos, const TRect& clip, TOcAspect aspect = asDefault);

Draws the part on the screen. If the part has not yet been loaded, *Draw* loads it first.

dc is a Windows device context where the part is to be drawn. The coordinates in *pos* tell where in the window to place the part. The *clip* rectangle designates an area outside of which the server cannot draw. *clip* and *pos* can be the same. If *clip* describes an empty rectangle, then the server can draw anywhere. *aspect* controls how the data were presented—as an icon, for example.

See also   TOcAspect enum, TRect class

EnumVerbs
bool EnumVerbs(const TOcVerb& verb);

Call *EnumVerbs* to find out what verbs the server supports for a particular part. Each call to *EnumVerbs* places another verb in the *verb* parameter. When all the server's verbs have been enumerated, *EnumVerbs* returns **false**.

TOleWindow calls *EnumVerbs* in order to place verbs for the active object on the container's Edit menu.

GetName
LPCOLESTR GetName();

Returns the string that identifies the part. Every part in a document has a different name. ObjectComponents creates the names for you automatically by incrementing an internal ID number for each new part.

See also   TOcPart::GetNameLen, TOcPart::Rename

GetNameLen

int GetNameLen();

Returns the number of characters in the name string that identifies the part. The count does not include the terminating null character.

See also   TOcPart::GetName, TOcPart::Rename

GetPos

TPoint GetPos() const;

Returns the part's position within its container document. The position specifies the part's upper-left corner in client area coordinates. The coordinates take into account any scaling set for the *TOcView* object that holds the part.

See also   TOcPart::GetRect, TOcPart::GetSize, TOcPart::SetPos, TPoint class

GetRect

TRect GetRect() const;

Returns the rectangle that bounds the image of the part in the container's client area. The position of the rectangle is given in client area coordinates.

See also   TOcPart::GetPos, TOcPart::GetSize, TOcPart::UpdateRect, TRect class

GetServerName

LPCOLESTR GetServerName(TOcPartName partName);

Asks OLE for the name of the object or of the object's server, depending on the value of *partName*. A container might want to display this information in its title bar.

In the current implementation of ObjectComponents, this function is not used. The *TOcView* object automatically updates the container window title.

See also   TOcPartName enum

GetSize

TSize GetSize() const;

Returns the size of the part's image in the container document. The fields of the return value give the width and height of the part in client area coordinates. If there is scaling, the coordinates take that into account.

See also   TOcPart::GetPos, TOcPart::GetRect, TOcPart::SetSize, TSize class

IsActive

bool IsActive() const;

Returns **true** if the part is currently active and **false** if it is not.

See also   TOcPart::SetActive

IsLink

bool IsLink() const;

Returns **true** if the part represents a linked OLE object and **false** if it represents an embedded OLE object. A container might use this method to distinguish visually between linked and embedded objects. For an example, look at the source code for *TOleWindow::PaintParts*.

IsSelected

bool IsSelected() const;

Returns **true** if the part is currently selected and **false** if it is not. This function is frequently called in loops that process all the selected objects in a document. For example, when *TOleView* paints the parts in a document, it calls *IsSelected* for each one to determine where to paint selection boxes.

Selection state information is maintained entirely in *TOcPart* and does not affect the OLE object itself.

See also   TOcPart::Select

IsVisible

Form 1   bool IsVisible() const;

Returns **true** if the part is currently visible and **false** if it is hidden.

Form 2   bool IsVisible(const TRect& logicalRect) const;

Returns **true** if the part is currently visible within the given *logicalRect* area of the container's window. Returns **false** if the part is not visible, perhaps because the user has scrolled to another part of the document.

See also   TOcPart::SetVisible

Load

bool Load();

Initializes a *TOcPart* object with information read from a storage.

See also   TOcPart::Save

Open

bool Open(bool open);

If *Open* is **true**, the *Open* command invokes the server to initiate an out-of-place editing session. More specifically, it asks the server to execute its Open verb. If *Open* is **false**, the command tells the server to hide its open editing window but does not end the session. *Open* returns **true** for success. If the server does not support editing, *Open* returns **false**.

Note   *TOcPart::Close* is not the opposite of *TOcPart::Open*. To terminate editing, pass **false** to *Open*.

See also   TOcPart::Activate

Rename

void Rename();

Causes the part to update the internal name that ObjectComponents generates to distinguish the parts in a document. Call *Rename* whenever you rename the document's file. OLE uses the object's name when creating links, so the object name must accurately reflect the file name in order for links to work.

See also   TOcPart::GetName, TOcPart::GetNameLen

Save

Form 1   bool Save(bool sameAsLoaded = true);

Causes the part to write itself into the document's file stream. If *sameAsLoaded* is **true**, then the part saves itself in the same storage where it was last written. Setting *sameAsLoaded* to **false** causes the part to create a new storage for itself under the document's new root storage. Usually *sameAsLoaded* should be **true** in response to a File | Save command and **false** in response to File | Save As.

(A storage is a compartment within a compound file. ObjectComponents manages the storages for you. Usually you do not have to give explicit instructions about where to store parts.)

Form 2   bool Save(IStorage* storage, bool sameAsLoaded, bool remember);

The second form accepts a pointer to an *IStorage* interface, allowing you to control where the object is written. *sameAsLoaded* is the same as in Form 1. *remember* tells the part whether or not to remember the object in *storage*. When saving a part to its usual file, you typically want it to remember its own storage. When copying a part, on the other hand, you typically want the part to keep its original storage object, not the one where you are saving the copy. When saving a copy to a file for the Clipboard, for example, *remember* should be **false**.

See also   TOcPart::Load

Select

void Select(bool select);

Tells the part whether or not it is currently selected. Make *select* **true** to select the part and **false** to deselect it. The user selects objects in order to perform operations on them. For example, the user selects an object before copying it to the Clipboard. When *TOleView* paints its parts, it queries each one and draws a selection box around any that the user has selected.

See also   TOcPart::IsSelected

SetActive

void SetActive();

Synchronizes an internal flag with the object's actual state, active or inactive. Usually you should not have to call this function. To make a part active, call *TOcPart::Activate* instead.

See also   TOcPart::Activate, TOcPart::IsActive

SetHost

bool SetHost(IBContainer far* container);

Moves the part from one container to another. *container* can be an object of type *TOcView* (or one derived from *TOcView*). It designates the view that receives the part. *SetHost* is not usually called from within the application.

IBContainer is a custom interface defined within the BOCOLE support library. *TOcView* implements this interface.

SetPos

void SetPos(const TPoint& pos);

Sets the part's position within its container document. The position specifies the part's upper left corner in pixels measured from the upper-left corner of the container's client window. If there is scaling, the coordinates take that into account.

See also   TOcPart::GetPos, TOcPart::SetSize, TOcPart::UpdateRect, TPoint class

SetSize
void SetSize(const TSize& size);

Sets the size of the part's image in the container document. *size* sets the width and height of the part in client area coordinates. The coordinates take into account any scaling set for the *TOcView* object that holds the part.

See also   TOcPart::GetPos, TOcPart::SetSize, TOcPart::UpdateRect, TSize class

SetVisible
void SetVisible(bool visible);

Shows or hides the part, according to the value of *visible*.

See also   TOcPart::IsVisible

Show
bool Show(bool show);

Makes the part visible. *Show* is used to ask the Link Source to show itself in the container window. If *show* is **false**, the part hides itself. The return value is **true** for success.

See also   TOcPart::IsVisible

UpdateRect
void UpdateRect();

Sets the part to a new rectangle when its size or position changes. Called by *SetPos* and *SetRect*.

See also   TOcPart::GetRect, TOcPart::SetPos, TOcPart::SetSize

Protected destructor

Destructor
~TOcPart();

Destroys the *TOcPart* object.

TOcPartCollection class   ocf/ocpart.h

Manages a set of *TOcPart* objects. Every *TOcDocument* creates a part collection object to maintain the set of OLE objects linked or embedded in the document. The part collection object adds parts, deletes parts, finds them, counts them, and generally helps the document keep track of what it has.

Because *TOcDocument* contains a part collection object, usually you do not have to create or manipulate the collection directly yourself.

See also   TOcPart class, TOcPartCollectionIter class

Public constructor and destructor

Constructor
TOcPartCollection();
Creates an empty collection. Call *Add* to insert parts in the collection.

Destructor
~TOcPartCollection();
Releases all the servers that supply the linked or embedded objects.

Public member functions

Add
int Add(TOcPart* const& part);
Adds a new part to the collection. Returns 1 for success and 0 for failure.

See also   TOcPart class

Clear
void Clear();
Disconnects all the parts in the collection from their servers, removes them from the collection, and releases them. Tells OLE that this collection has no further need for the servers.

Count
virtual unsigned Count() const;
Returns the number of parts currently in the collection.

Detach
int Detach(TOcPart* const& part, int del = 0);
Removes *part* from the collection. If *del* is nonzero, then *Detach* also releases *TOcPart* object. If the part's internal reference count reaches zero as a result, the part deletes itself. Returns 1 for success and 0 for failure.

See also   TOcPart class

Find
unsigned Find(TOcPart* const& part) const;
Searches for *part* and returns its position in the collection. If *part* is not in the collection, *Find* returns UINT_MAX.

See also   TOcPart class

IsEmpty
int IsEmpty() const;
Returns **true** if the collection currently contains no objects and **false** if it does contain at least one object.

Locate

TOcPart* Locate(TPoint& point);

Returns the part object visible at a particular point on the screen. The numbers in point are interpreted as logical coordinates. If no part in the collection occupies the given point, *Locate* returns 0.

See also   TPoint class

SelectAll

bool SelectAll(bool select = false);

Sets the selection state of all the parts in the collection. If *select* is **true**, *SelectAll* selects them all. If *select* is **false**, it deselects all the parts. The user can perform actions (such as dragging, deleting, and copying) that affect all the selected objects.

The container conventionally marks selected objects by drawing a rectangle with grapples (handles for moving the rectangle) around each of them. The *TOleWindow* class does this automatically in ObjectWindows programs.

TOcPartCollectionIter class   ocf/ocpart.h

A part collection iterator enumerates the objects embedded in a compound document.

A compound document can contain many linked and embedded objects. Within the container, each object is represented by an object of type *TOcPart*. To manage all the parts it contains, *TOcDocument* creates a collection object of type *TOcPartCollection*. The collection object takes care of adding and deleting members of the collection. In order to walk through the current list of its parts, *TOcDocument* also creates a part collection iterator. An iterator basically points to an element in the collection. You can increment the iterator to walk through the list of objects. The iterator signals when it reaches the end (the ++ operator returns 0).

Together the collection and its iterator give the document much flexibility in managing its objects.

See also   TOcPart class, TOcPartCollection class

Public constructor

Constructor

TOcPartCollectionIter(const TOcPartCollection& coll);

Constructs an iterator to enumerate the objects contained in the collection *coll*.

See also   TOcPartCollection class

Public member functions

operator ++

Form 1   TOcPart* operator++(int);

Returns the current part and then advances the iterator to point to the next part (postincrement).

Form 2   TOcPart* operator++();

Advances the iterator to point to the next part in the list and then returns that part (preincrement).

Current
TOcPart* Current() const;

Returns the part that the iterator currently points to.

operator int()
operator int() const;

Converts the iterator to an integer value in order to test whether the iterator has finished enumerating the collection. Returns zero if the iterator has reached the end of the list and a nonzero value if it has not.

Restart
Form 1   void Restart();

Resets the iterator to begin again with the first part in the document.

Form 2   void Restart(unsigned start, unsigned stop);

Resets the iterator to enumerate a partial range of objects in the document, beginning with the object at position *start* in the list and ending with the object at position *stop*.

TOcPartName enum   ocf/ocobject.h

enum TOcPartName
When a container asks the server for the name of a part, it might want any of several possible answers. These values indicate which name the container wants to see.

Constant	Meaning
pnLong	The string the server registered as the *description* for this type of object.
pnShort	The string the server registered as the *progid* for this type of object.
pnApp	The string the server registered as the *description* for the server application as a whole.

See also   description registration key, progid registration key, TOcPart::GetServerName

TOcRegistrar class   ocf/ocapp.h

Base class
TRegistrar

TOcRegistrar manages all the registration tasks for an application. It processes OLE-related switches on the command line and records any necessary information about the application in the system registration database. If the application is already registered in the database, the registrar confirms that the registered *path*, *progid*, and *clsid* are still accurate. If not, it reregisters the application.

Every ObjectComponents application needs to create a registrar object. If your application supports linking and embedding, then create a *TOcRegistrar* object. If your application supports automation but not linking and embedding, then you should create a *TRegistrar* object instead. *TOcRegistrar* extends *TRegistrar* by connecting the application to the BOCOLE support library interfaces that support linking and embedding.

An application's main procedure usually performs these actions with its registrar:

- Constructs the registrar, passing it a pointer to the application's factory callback.

- Calls *IsOptionSet* to check for options that might affect how the application chooses to start (for example, remaining invisible if invoked for embedding).

- Calls *Run* to enter the program's message loop.

TOcRegistrar inherits both *IsOptionSet* and *Run* from its base class, *TRegistrar*.

See also clsid registration key, path registration key, progid registration key, TRegistrar class

Public constructor and destructor

Constructor
TOcRegistrar(TRegList& regInfo, TComponentFactory callback, string& cmdLine,
    HINSTANCE hInst = _hInstance);

regInfo is the application registration structure (conventionally named *appReg*).

callback is the factory callback function that ObjectComponents invokes when it is time for the application to create an object. An ObjectWindows program can use the *TOleFactory* class to implement this callback.

cmdLine holds the command-line string that invoked the application.

hInst is the application's instance.

Destructor
~TOcRegistrar();
Destroys objects the registrar uses internally.

See also TComponentFactory typedef, TOleFactory<> class

Public member functions

BOleComponentCreate
HRESULT BOleComponentCreate(IUnknown far* far* retIface, IUnknown far* outer, BCID idClass);

Calls the BOCOLE support library to create one of the helper objects that ObjectComponents uses internally. Usually you do not need to call *BOleComponentCreate* yourself.

retIface receives an interface to the requested component.

outer is the *IUnknown* interface of the outer object that you want the new component to become a part of.

idClass identifies the particular component you want to create. The possible values are defined as *cidBolexxxx* constants in ocf/boledefs.h.

The return value is an OLE result, either HR_OK for success or HR_FAIL for failure.

See also HR_xxxx result macros

CreateOcApp
void CreateOcApp(uint32 options, TOcApp*& ret);

Creates the connector object that attaches an application to OLE. *options* is a set of bit flags indicating the application's running mode. The possible option flags are defined in *TOcAppMode*. *ret* is where *CreateOcApp* places a pointer to the newly created *TOcApp* connector object.

CreateOcApp is called during *TOcModule::OcInit*. You shouldn't have to call it directly yourself.

The purpose of *CreateOcApp* is to shield you from the details of the *TOcApp* connector object. *TOcApp* is closely tied to the implementation of ObjectComponents, and the details of initializing an OLE session are subject to change.

See also TOcApp class, TOcAppMode enum, TOcModule::OcInit

GetAppDescriptor
TAppDescriptor& GetAppDescriptor();

Returns the application descriptor. ObjectComponents uses an application descriptor internally to hold information about a module. (A DLL gets an application descriptor of its own.) *TAppDescriptor* is undocumented because it is used only internally and is subject to change. The registrar classes, *TOcRegistrar* and *TRegistrar,* are the supported interfaces to the application descriptor. The registrar constructs the descriptor and most of its member functions call descriptor functions to perform the work.

Usually you will not need to call this method yourself.

Protected member functions

CanUnload
bool CanUnload();

Returns **true** if the application is not currently serving any OLE clients and **false** otherwise.

GetFactory
void far* GetFactory(const GUID& clsid, const GUID far& iid);

Returns a pointer to the factory interface for creating the type of object indicated by *clsid*. *iid* names the particular interface you want to receive. If the registrar is unable to find an *iid* interface for *clsid* objects, it returns zero.

ObjectComponents calls a DLL's *GetFactory* member every time a new client loads the DLL. Usually you do not need to call *GetFactory* yourself.

LoadBOle
void LoadBOle();

Loads and initializes the ObjectComponents support library (BOCOLE.DLL). *LoadBOle* throws a *TXObjComp* exception if it cannot find BOCOLE.DLL, or if the installed version is not compatible with the application's version of the library.

TOcRemView class   ocf/ocremvie.h

Base class
TOcView

A linking and embedding server creates a remote view object in order to draw its OLE object in the container's window. *TOcRemView* only draws the object. To load and save the data in the object, the server also needs to create a *TOcDocument* object. The document and the remote view together represent an OLE object as the server sees it.

The container creates a *TOcPart* object for every OLE object it receives. The container's part object communicates with the server's document and view objects through OLE. The part tells the server's view when and where to draw the object. It tells the server's document when and where to load or save the object.

Do not confuse the two kinds of views, *TOcView* with *TOcRemView*. A container creates a single view (*TOcView*) for its compound document. This view can contain parts received from other applications. Each part draws itself by invoking a remote view from its server. Containers create *TOcView* objects and servers create *TOcRemView* objects. (A *TOcRemView* object can become a container also, however, if the user embeds objects within objects.)

In spite of the similar names, *TOcDocument*, *TOcView*, and *TOcRemView* are not part of the ObjectWindows Doc/View model. The nature of OLE makes it beneficial to separate data from its graphical representation, and the terms *document* and *view* express that separation even outside of ObjectWindows.

TOcRemView is a COM object and implements the *IUnknown* interface.

See also   TOcDocument class, TOcView class

Public constructor

Constructor
TOcRemView(TOcDocument& doc, TRegList* regList = 0, IUnknown* outer = 0);

A remote view is always associated with a *TOcDocument* object. The document loads and saves data in an OLE object and the remote view draws the data in the container's window. In both forms of the constructor, *doc* is the document to associate with the view. That means the document must always be created first.

Also, in both forms *regList* is a document registration table. A server that creates different kinds of objects needs several document registration tables, one for each type. The *regList* parameter determines the type of object that the view represents. *outer* points to the *IUnknown* interface of a master object under which the new object is asked to aggregate itself.

Registration tables are built with the BEGIN_REGISTRATION and END_REGISTRATION macros.

The destructor for *TOcRemView* is private. ObjectComponents releases the object when it is no longer needed.

See also   BEGIN_REGISTRATION macro, TAutoObject class, TOcDocument class

Public member functions

Copy
virtual bool Copy();
Copies the object to the Clipboard. Returns **true** for success.

EvClose
virtual void EvClose();
The application's remote view window calls this function when it closes. *EvClose* disconnects the view from any parts displayed in it.

GetContainerTitle
virtual LPCOLESTR GetContainerTitle();
Asks the container for its name. The server usually includes this string in its own title bar during out-of-place editing (when the user edits a linked or embedded object in the server's own window, not in the container's).

GetInitialRect
void GetInitialRect();
Requests the initial size and position of the area where the server can draw its object. The function initializes *Extent*, a protected data member that *TOcRemView* inherits from *TOcView*.

See also   TOcView::Extent

Invalidate
void Invalidate(TOcInvalidate invalid);
Notifies the container's active view that the server has changed either the contents or the appearance of the object. The *invalid* parameter indicates what needs changing. It can be *invData*, *invView*, or both combined with the OR operator (|). If the container is an ObjectComponents application, its active view generates an OC_VIEWPARTINVALID message.

See also   OC_VIEWxxxx messages, TOcInvalidate enum

IsOpenEditing
bool IsOpenEditing() const;

Returns **true** if the view is currently engaged in an open editing session. Open editing occurs when the user chooses an object's Open verb. Open editing takes place in the server's own frame window, unlike in-place editing, which takes place in the container's window. Remote view objects are used in both kinds of editing.

Load

bool Load(IStorage* storageI);

Reads from *storageI* information specific to the remote view. This information is part of the data the server stores in the container's file when asked to save an object. *Load* returns **true** for success.

IStorage is a pointer to an OLE interface. *storageI* can be a pointer to a *TOcStorage* object, the ObjectComponents implementation of that interface.

See also   TOcRemView::Save

Rename

virtual void Rename( );

Updates the name string ObjectComponents generates to distinguish the parts in a compound document. *TOcRemView* calls *Rename* during construction to find out what the container wants to call the object. It is usually not necessary for you to call *Rename* directly.

Save

bool Save(IStorage* storageI);

Writes to *storageI* information specific to the remote view. This information becomes part of the object data stored in the container's compound document file. Returns **true** for success.

IStorage is a pointer to an OLE interface. *storageI* can be a pointer to a *TOcStorage* object, the ObjectComponents implementation of that interface.

See also   TOcRemView::Load

TOcSaveLoad struct   ocf/ocview.h

Holds information that a view uses when loading and saving its OLE object parts. The OC_VIEWLOADPART and OC_VIEWSAVEPART messages carry a pointer to this structure in their *lParam*s.

The *TOleView* processes the load and save messages for you. If you are programming with the ObjectWindows Doc/View model, then you do not need to use the *TOcSaveLoad* structure directly. For examples that show how to process the load and save messages, look at the source code for the *EvViewSavePart* and *EvViewLoadPart* methods in *TOleView*.

See also   OC_VIEWxxxx messages, TOleView::EvViewSavePart, TOleView::EvViewLoadPart

Public data members

Release
bool Release;

Is **true** if the view should keep the storage object for future file operations and **false** if it should forget the storage object after using it once.

StorageI
IStorage far* StorageI;

Points to the storage object assigned to hold the part. ObjectComponents implements the standard OLE *IStorage* interface in *TOcStorage*, so *TOcStorage* can be used to construct an *IStorage*.

TOcScaleFactor class   ocf/ocview.h

The *TOcScaleFactor* class carries information from a container to a server about how the container wants to scale its document. For example, if the container has a Zoom command and the user chooses to magnify the document to 120%, the server should match the scaling factor when it draws objects embedded in the container.

ObjectComponents passes a reference to an *TOcScaleFactor* object in the *lParam* of OC_VIEWGETSCALE and OC_VIEWSETSCALE messages. When a container receives OC_VIEWGETSCALE, it fills in the object with scaling information. When a server receives the OC_VIEWSETSCALE information, it reads the scaling values and can use them in its paint procedure.

TOcScaleFactor stores scaling information in its two *TSize* members, *SiteSize* and *PartSize*. The names refer to the area where the container wants to draw an object (the site) and the object itself (the part). The values in the members need not be the actual size of the site or the part, however. What matters is the ratio of the two sizes. If the *SiteSize* values are twice as large as the *PartSize* values, then the server is being asked to draw the object at twice its default size.

If you are programming with ObjectWindows, then the *TOleWindow* class takes care of scaling for you. For examples showing how to handle scaling without the benefit of ObjectWindows, look at the source code for the following *TOleWindow* methods: *EvViewGetScale*, *EvViewSetScale*, and *SetupDC*.

See also   OC_VIEWxxxx messages, TOleWindow::EvViewGetScale, TOleWindow::EvViewSetScale, TOleWindow::SetupDC, TSize class

Public constructors

Constructors
Form 1   TOcScaleFactor();

Initializes the site and part extents to 1 so the scaling factor is 100%.

Form 2   TOcScaleFactor(const RECT& siteRect, const TSize& partSize);

Bases the initial scaling factor on the values in the given rectangle structure and size object. Calculates the extents of the rectangle *siteRect* and sets them in *SiteSize*. Copies *partSize* to *PartSize*.

Form 3   TOcScaleFactor(const BOleScaleFactor far& scaleFactor);

Bases the initial scaling factor on the values in *scaleFactor*. *BOleScaleFactor* is a structure that the BOCOLE support library uses internally to carry scaling information. You should not have to use the structure directly.

Usually you do not have to construct a *TOcScaleFactor* object directly. ObjectComponents creates it for you and passes it in the OC_VIEWGETSCALE or OC_VIEWSETSCALE message.

Destructor
~TOcScaleFactor();

See also   TOcScaleFactor::PartSize, TOcScaleFactor::SiteSize, TSize class

Public data members

PartSize
TSize PartSize;

Holds two values describing the default horizontal and vertical extent of a server's object. The values in *PartSize* do not need to be actual measurements. What matters is the ratio of the values here to the values in *SiteSize*. That ratio determines how an image should be scaled.

See also   TOcScaleFactor::SiteSize, TSize class

SiteSize
TSize SiteSize;

Holds two values describing the horizontal and vertical extent of the area a container has allotted for displaying a linked or embedded object. The values in *SiteSize* do not need to be actual measurements. What matters is the ratio of the values here to the values in *PartSize*. That ratio determines how an image should be scaled.

See also   TOcScaleFactor::PartSize, TSize class

Public member functions

operator =
Form 1   TOcScaleFactor& operator =(const BOleScaleFactor far& scaleFactor);

Copies the values in a *BOleScaleFactor* structure. The BOCOLE support library uses this structure internally to carry scaling information.

Form 2   TOcScaleFactor& operator =(const TOcScaleFactor& scaleFactor);

Copies one *TOcScaleFactor* into another.

Both forms of the assignment operator copy the values from one scaling object into another.

See also   OC_VIEWxxxx messages

GetScale
uint16 GetScale();

Retrieves a percentage value expressing the ratio of the part's size to the site's size. For example, if the part size is 20 x 20 and the site size is 40 x 40, then *GetScale* returns 200.

See also   TOcScaleFactor::SetScale

GetScaleFactor
void GetScaleFactor(BOleScaleFactor far& scaleFactor) const;

Fills in *scaleFactor* with values from the *TOcScaleFactor* object. *BOleScaleFactor* is a structure that the BOCOLE library uses to hold the same scaling information. Usually you do not have to call this function directly.

IsZoomed
bool IsZoomed();

Returns **true** if the sizes stored for the part and the site do not match.

SetScale
void SetScale(uint16 percent);

Sets the ratio of the part's size to the site's size. More specifically, *SetScale* sets the size of the part to 100 and the size of the site to *percent*.

See also   TOcScaleFactor::GetScale

TOcScrollDir enum   ocf/ocobject.h

enum TOcScrollDir

The OC_VIEWSCROLL event tells the container when the user performs a drag movement that should scroll the window. The *lParam* of the WM_OCEVENT message carries one of these values to indicate which direction the window has been asked to scroll.

Constant	Meaning
sdScrollUp	Scroll toward the top of the document.
sdScrollDown	Scroll toward the bottom of the document.
sdScrollLeft	Scroll toward the left edge of the document.
sdScrollRight	Scroll toward the right edge of the document.

See also   EvOcViewScroll event handler, OC_VIEWxxxx messages, TOleView::EvOcViewScroll, TOleWindow::EvOcViewScroll, WM_OCEVENT message

TOcToolbarInfo struct

ocf/ocview.h

The OC_VIEWSHOWTOOLS message carries a pointer to this structure in its *lParam*. The message asks a server for handles to its tool bars so the container can display them in its own window. This happens during in-place editing when the user opens an object in the container in order to modify it.

The structure has four fields, allowing the server to return handles for up to four tool bars. Each tool bar occupies a different edge of the container's client area.

For examples, look at the source code for *TOleWindow::EvOcViewShowTools* and *TOleView::EvOcViewShowTools*. The default implementations of these methods allow a single tool bar at the top of the client area. To give the container more tool bars, handle the OC_VIEWSHOWTOOLS message directly yourself.

See also   TOleView::EvOcViewShowTools, TOleWindow::EvOcViewShowTools

Public data members

HBottomTB
HWND HBottomTB;

Holds a handle to the tool bar that the server wants to place at the bottom of the container's client area.

HFrame
HWND HFrame;

If *Show* is **true** and the server is being asked to display its tool bar, then *HFrame* holds a handle to the frame window where the tool bar is to appear. If *Show* is **false**, then *HFrame* holds a handle to the server's own frame window.

See also   TOcToolbarInfo::Show

HLeftTB
HWND HLeftTB;

Holds a handle to the tool bar that the server wants to place at the left edge of the container's client area.

HRightTB
HWND HRightTB;

Holds a handle to the tool bar that the server wants to place at the right edge of the container's client area.

HTopTB
HWND HTopTB;

Holds a handle to the tool bar that the server wants to place at the top of the container's client area.

Show
bool Show;

Is **true** to ask that the server display its tool bar or **false** to request that the server hide the tool bar.

TOcVerb class

Holds information about a single verb that a server supports for its objects.

A verb is an action the server can perform with one of its objects. A server that creates text objects, for example, might support an Edit verb. A server for sound objects might support Edit, Play, and Rewind.

When the user selects an object in a compound document, the container asks the *TOcPart* object for a list of the verbs it can execute. The container displays the verbs on its Edit menu. The command for enumerating verbs is *TOcPart::EnumVerbs*.

Whenever the user selects a part, the container modifies its Edit menu by adding an item for manipulating the object. If the object is part of a Quattro Pro spreadsheet, for example, the container adds the command Notebook Object to its Edit menu. If the user selects this command, then the container shows a pop-up menu with the notebook's verbs, Edit and Open.

For an example of how to implement these items on the Edit menu, look at the source code for *TOleWindow::CeEditObject* in OLEWINDO.CPP.

See also   TOcPart::EnumVerbs

Public constructor

Constructor
TOcVerb();
Creates an empty verb object.

Public data members

CanDirty
bool CanDirty;
Is **true** if executing the verb can modify the object so that it might need to be saved or redrawn afterwards. For example, the *CanDirty* field of an Edit verb is always **true**, and the *CanDirty* field of a Play verb is usually **false**.

TypeName
LPCOLESTR TypeName;
Points to the name of the type of object to which this verb belongs. The container usually shows this name in the Object item of its Edit menu. For example, if the user has selected an object inserted from the server in Chapter 15 of the *ObjectWindows Programmer's Guide, TypeName* is "Drawing Pad," and the container's Edit menu should have an item saying "Drawing Pad." Choosing this item leads to a pop-up menu with all the picture's verbs on it.

The *TypeName* string comes from the value the server registered for the *menuname* key in its document registration table.

See also   TOcPart::EnumVerbs, menuname registration key

VerbIndex
uint VerbIndex;

Holds the index number that identifies this verb in the server's list of possible verbs. The first verb is always 0 and is considered the default verb. If the user double-clicks the object, the container should ask the server to execute its default verb.

VerbName
LPCOLESTR VerbName;

Points to the name of the verb. This is the string that the container adds to its Edit menu.

TOcView class   ocf/ocview.h

Base class
TUnknown

TOcView manages the presentation of a container's compound document containing linked and embedded objects. Each object in the document is represented by an object of type *TOcPart*. The document view knows which parts are selected or activated. It scrolls the window and remembers which parts are visible. It transfers parts to and from the document through the Clipboard or through drag-and-drop operations.

Every *TOcView* has a corresponding *TOcDocument*. The ObjectComponents document object implements the OLE interfaces that manipulate the data in a compound document. *TOcView* implements the interfaces that manipulate the appearance of a compound document.

TOcView is a COM object and implements the *IUnknown* interface.

See also   TOcApp class, TOcDocument class, TOcPart class, TUnknown class

Public constructor

Constructor
TOcView(TOcDocument& doc, TRegList* regList = 0, IUnknown* outer=0);

doc refers to the *TOcDocument* object that corresponds to the view. *TOcDocument* manages the data in a compound document, and *TOcView* manages the appearance of the document on the screen.

regList is the registration structure for a particular document. Use the BEGIN_REGISTRATION and END_REGISTRATION macros to create an object of type *TRegList*.

outer is the root interface of an outer object inside which the new view is asked to aggregate itself.

See also   BEGIN_REGISTRATION macro, TAutoObject class, TOcDocument class

Public member functions

ActivatePart

bool ActivatePart(TOcPart* part);

Attempts to activate the given part (by calling *TOcPart::Activate*). Returns **true** if the designated part becomes active and **false** otherwise. If any other part was already active, it is deactivated first.

See also   TOcPart::Activate, TOcView::ActivePart, TOcView::GetActivePart

BrowseClipboard

bool BrowseClipboard(TOcInitInfo& initInfo);

Displays the Paste Special dialog box showing the available formats for the data currently on the Clipboard, allowing the user to choose what format to paste. Returns **true** if the user pastes data and **false** if the user cancels or the dialog box fails.

Create *initInfo* first by passing the view to the *TOcInitInfo* constructor. *BrowseClipboard* fills *initInfo* with information about the object. Then use *initInfo* to create a new *TOcPart*.

This function calls *TOcApp::BrowseClipboard*.

See also   TOcApp::BrowseClipboard, TOcApp::BrowseLinks, TOcInitInfo class, TOcPart class

BrowseLinks

bool BrowseLinks();

Displays the Links dialog box showing all the linked objects in the compound document and what they are linked to. The user can modify the displayed links, perhaps to reconnect with a file that was moved. Returns **false** if an error prevents the dialog box from being displayed or if the user cancels the dialog box.

See also   TOcApp::BrowseClipboard

Copy

bool Copy(TOcPart* part);

Creates a copy of a linked or embedded object and places it on the Clipboard. Returns **true** if the operation succeeds. Call *Copy* in response to Cut or Copy commands from the Edit menu.

EvActivate

void EvActivate(bool activate);

A container calls this function if any of its windows gains focus while any of its linked or embedded objects is being edited in place. *EvActivate* restores focus to the in-place activated view. If the user clicks in the client window of an MDI frame, for example, the client window needs to shift the focus back to the view, which in turn restores focus to the activated part. A part engaged in in-place editing should always retain the focus.

activate should be **true** if the window is gaining focus and **false** if it is losing it.

See also   TOcView::EvClose, TOcView::EvResize, TOcView::EvSetFocus

EvClose

virtual void EvClose( );

A container calls this function to tell ObjectComponents that the window associated with the view has closed.

See also   TOcView::EvActivate, TOcView::EvResize, TOcView::EvSetFocus

EvResize

void EvResize( );

A container calls this function to tell OLE when the window associated with the view changes size. OLE might need this information to let a server modify its tool bar during in-place editing.

See also   TOcView::EvActivate, TOcView::EvClose, TOcView::EvSetFocus

EvSetFocus

bool EvSetFocus(bool set);

A container calls this function to tell OLE that the window associated with the view has either received or lost the input focus. Make *set* **true** if the window gained the focus or **false** if it lost the focus.

The function returns **false** if the view is unable to receive the focus. That happens if an object in the view is engaged in in-place editing. Such objects retain the focus until the editing session ends.

See also   TOcView::EvActivate, TOcView::EvResize, TOcView::EvSetFocus

GetActivePart

TOcPart* GetActivePart( );

Returns the currently active part. If the view does not contain an active part, the return value is 0.

See also   TOcView::ActivePart, TOcView::ActivatePart

GetOcDocument

TOcDocument& GetOcDocument( );

Returns the ObjectComponents document associated with the view. Views and documents work in pairs. *TOcView* manages the appearance of a compound document and *TOcDocument* manages the data in it.

See also   TOcDocument class, TOcView::OcDocument

GetOrigin

TPoint GetOrigin( ) const;

Returns the physical coordinates currently mapped to the upper-left corner of the container window's client area. ObjectWindows programmers can ignore this method because *TOleWindow* performs scrolling for you.

See also   TOcView::Origin, TOcView::ScrollWindow, TPoint class

GetWindowRect

TRect GetWindowRect( ) const;

Returns the client rectangle for the view window.

See also   TOcView::GetOrigin, TRect class

InvalidatePart

void InvalidatePart(const TOcPart* part);

Sends an OC_VIEWPARTINVALID message to the container window. If the container window responds with **false** to indicate it has not processed the message, *InvalidatePart* tells the system that the area inside the part's bounding rectangle is invalid and needs repainting.

Paste

bool Paste(bool linking = false);

Inserts an object from the Clipboard into the compound document. If *linking* is **true**, *Paste* will try to create a link rather than embedding the new object. Make *linking* **true** when processing the Paste Link command.

RegisterClipFormats

bool RegisterClipFormats(TRegList& regList);

Tells OLE what Clipboard formats the document understands. The list of formats comes from *regList*, the document's registration structure. Use the BEGIN_REGISTRATION and END_REGISTRATION macros to create *regList*. Also, the REGFORMAT macro places Clipboard format entries in the structure. To register custom Clipboard formats, be sure to call *TOcApp::AddUserFormatName* as well.

RegisterClipFormats is called automatically when the view is constructed.

See also   BEGIN_REGISTRATION macro, REGFORMAT macro, TOcApp::AddUserFormatName, TOcView::FormatList

ReleaseObject

virtual void ReleaseObject();

Call this instead of delete to destroy a *TOcView* object when you are through with it. *ReleaseObject* decrements the view's internal reference count and dissociates the view from its window.

See also   TOcView::SetupWindow

Rename

virtual void Rename();

Tells OLE when the name assigned to a compound document has changed. OLE updates its internal records. Also, the associated *TOcDocument* object passes the new name to any linked or embedded objects it contains.

ScrollWindow

void ScrollWindow(int dx, int dy);

Brings new areas of a document into view by adjusting the origin of the container window. *dx* and *dy* are horizontal and vertical offsets added to the origin. This function is usually called in response to messages from the window scroll bars or from the arrow keys.

See also   TOcView::GetOrigin, TOcView::Origin

SetLink

void SetLink(bool pasteLink);

Sets an internal flag that determines whether Paste operations create linked or embedded objects. More specifically, *SetLink* alters the priority of the document's registered Clipboard formats. You set the original priorities with the first parameter of the REGFORMAT macro. If *pasteLink* is **true**, then *SetLink* moves the Link Source format to the top of the list. If *pasteLink* is **false**, it restores the Link Source format to its original position behind Embed Source.

It is usually not necessary to call *SetLink* directly because the *Paste* method calls it for you.

See also   REGFORMAT macro, TOcView::Paste

SetupWindow

void SetupWindow(HWND hWin);

Tells the view what window is associated with it. The view sometimes sends notification messages to its window. Usually this function should be called from the *SetupWindow* member of the container's window class. *TOleWindow* performs this task automatically.

See also   OC_VIEWxxxx messages, TOleWindow::SetupWindow, TOcView::Win

Protected destructor

Protected Destructor

~TOcView();

Destroys the view object.

Protected member functions

ForwardEvent

Form 1   uint32 ForwardEvent(int eventId, const void far* param);

Form 2   uint32 ForwardEvent(int eventId, uint32 param = 0);

Both forms send a WM_OCEVENT message to the container's window. The *eventId* parameter becomes the message's *wParam* and should be one of the OC_APPxxxx or OC_VIEWxxxx constants. The second parameter becomes the message's *lParam* and may be either a pointer (Form 1) or an integer (Form 2). Which form you use depends on the information a particular event needs to send in its *lParam*.

See also   OC_APPxxxx messages, OC_VIEWxxxx messages, TOcView::Win, WM_OCEVENT message

Init

void Init(TRegList* regList);

Initializes a newly created view object. *Init* is called by both of the *TOcView* constructors. Usually you don't need to call it directly yourself. *TRegList* is the data type that holds all the registry keys and associated values for a single registration table. *regList* must be a document registration table (the structure created by the registration macros and conventionally named *DocReg*).

Init makes this view the document's active view, connects with the BOCOLE support library, and registers supported Clipboard formats.

Shutdown

void Shutdown();

Called by the destructor of derived classes to release helper objects that the view holds internally.

See also   TOcView public constructors and destructor

Protected data members

ActivePart

TOcPart* GetActivePart();

Returns the currently active part. If the view does not contain an active part, the **return** value is 0.

See also   TOcView::ActivePart, TOcView::ActivatePart

Extent

TSize Extent;

Holds the current width and height of the container window's client area. Both are measured in device units.

See also   TOcView::GetWindowRect

FormatList

TOcFormatList FormatList;

Holds information about all the Clipboard formats the compound document supports. The list is generated from information the application registers for the types of documents it supports.

See also   TOcFormatList class, TOcView::RegisterClipFormats

Link

int Link;

Used internally by the *Paste* method to adjust the priority of link source format.

OcApp

TOcApp& OcApp;

A view stores the application that owns it in this protected data member.

OcDocument

TOcDocument& OcDocument;

A view stores the document object that owns the view in this protected data member. The view object manages the appearance of a compound document, and the document object manages the data.

See also   TOcView::GetOcDocument

Origin

TPoint Origin;

Holds the coordinates of the point currently mapped to the upper-left corner of the container window's client area.

See also   TOcView::GetOrigin

Win
HWND Win;

Holds a handle to the window where the view draws itself. The *ForwardEvent* method sends messages to this window.

See also   TOcView::ForwardEvent, TOcView::SetupWindow

WinTitle
string WinTitle;

Holds the original caption string of the container's window. The caption is usually modified as the user moves from part to part within the document. When no part is active, the view restores the window's title to this original string.

TOcViewPaint struct   ocf/ocview.h

The OC_VIEWPAINT message carries a pointer to this structure in its *lParam*. The message notifies a server that it should update its painting of an object. The structure carries information about the area that needs repainting. Generally a program should respond by calling paint methods on the window or view that receives the message. For examples, look at the source code for *TOleWindow::EvOcViewPaint* and *TOleView::EvOcViewPaint*.

See also   OC_VIEWxxxx messages, TOleView::EvOcViewPaint, TOleWindow::EvOcViewPaint

Public data members

Aspect
TOcAspect Aspect;

Holds an enumerated value that tells how the part is to be drawn. A single object can often be drawn in more than one way. For example, the server might show the object's full contents, a miniature representation of the contents, or an icon that represents the type of object without indicating its specific contents.

See also   TOcAspect enum

Clip
TRect* Clip;

Designates the area where the part should be allowed to draw. The server can clip the output to this area to avoid drawing outside its allotted space.

See also   TRect class

DC
HDC DC;

Contains a handle to the device context where the repainting should occur.

Part

TOcPart* Part;

Points to the part that needs to be redrawn. This member can be used to ask the part to repaint itself. In the current implementation of ObjectComponents, this member is not used.

See also   TOcPart class

Pos

TRect* Pos;

Specifies the upper-left corner of the server object that has become invalid and needs repainting.

See also   TRect class

TOleAllocator class   ocf/oleutil.h

A linking and embedding .EXE application creates a memory allocator object in order to tell OLE what memory manager the system should use when allocating and deallocating memory on behalf of the server. Unless you have particular memory management needs, it's easiest to let OLE use its default allocator.

When writing a linking and embedding application, you usually do not need to create a memory allocator object directly because your registrar object takes care of it for you. The only applications that create memory allocators directly are automation servers that do not support linking and embedding. Because automation servers don't create *TOcApp* objects, they do need to create *TOleAllocator*s.

DLL servers do not need a memory allocator because the system uses whatever allocator the .EXE client designates.

See also   TOcRegistrar class, TRegistrar class

Public constructors and destructor

Constructor

Form 1   TOleAllocator(IMalloc* mem = 0);

Initializes the OLE system library and, if *mem* is nonzero, registers a custom memory allocator. Unless you have particular memory management needs, it is easiest to let OLE use its default allocator. To implement your own allocator, refer to the OLE documentation on the *IMalloc* interface.

Form 2   TOleAllocator();

Tells OLE to use the custom memory allocator. Does not initialize the OLE system library. In .EXE applications, the registrar object initializes the OLE library. In DLL servers, the .EXE client provides the allocator.

Destructor

~TOleAllocator();

Releases the memory allocator (either the default allocator or a custom allocator) and uninitializes the OLE system.

See also   TOcRegistrar Class, TRegistrar Class

Public member functions

Alloc

void far* Alloc(unsigned long size);

Calls the *Alloc* method on the active memory allocator to request a block of memory. *size* gives the size of the block. Unless you have registered a custom memory allocator, *Alloc* calls OLE's default allocator. If the request fails, *Alloc* returns 0.

See also   TOleAllocator::Free_

Free

void Free(void far* block);

Calls the *Free* method on the active memory allocator to release a block of memory previously allocated with *Alloc*. *block* points to the base of the area to be released. Unless you have registered a custom memory allocator, *Free* calls OLE's default allocator.

See also   TOleAllocator::Alloc_

Public data member

Mem

IMalloc* Mem;

Points to the active memory allocator object. Unless you have registered a custom memory allocator, *Mem* points to OLE's default allocator.

TRegistrar class   ocf/ocreg.h

TRegistrar manages all the registration tasks for an application. It processes OLE-related switches on the command line and records any necessary information about the application in the system registration database. If the application is already registered in the database, the registrar confirms that the registered *path*, *progid*, and *clsid* are still accurate. If not, it reregisters the application.

Every ObjectComponents application needs to create a registrar object. If your application supports automation but not linking and embedding, then create a *TRegistrar* object. To support linking and embedding—alone or along with automation—then create a *TOcRegistrar* instead. *TOcRegistrar* extends *TRegistrar* by connecting the application to the BOCOLE support library interfaces that support linking and embedding.

An application's main procedure usually performs these actions with its registrar:

- Construct the registrar, passing it a pointer to the application's factory callback.

- Call *IsOptionSet* to check for options that might affect how the application chooses to start (for example, remaining invisible if invoked for embedding).

- Call *Run* to enter the program's message loop.

See also   TOcRegistrar class

Public constructor and destructor

Constructor
TRegistrar(TRegList& regInfo, TComponentFactory callback, string& cmdLine, HINSTANCE hInst);

regInfo is the application registration structure (conventionally named *appReg*). *callback* is the factory callback function that ObjectComponents invokes when it is time for the application to create a document. An ObjectWindows program can use the *TOleFactory* class to create this callback. *cmdLine* points to the command line received when the application was invoked. *hInst* is the application instance.

Destructor
virtual ~TRegistrar();
Deletes objects the registrar maintains internally.

The constructor processes OLE-related switches and removes them from the command line. (Call *IsOptionSet* to determine what switches were found.) It also initializes some settings from the application registration table. If the application is a DLL, the constructor initializes the global *DllRegistrar* variable.

See also   string class, TComponentFactory typedef, TOleFactory class, TRegistrar::IsOptionSet

Public member functions

CanUnload
virtual bool CanUnload();
Returns **true** if the application is not currently serving any OLE clients and **false** otherwise.

CreateAutoApp
TUnknown* CreateAutoApp(TObjectDescriptor app, uint32 options, IUnknown* outer = 0);
Creates an instance of an automated application. This method is usually called from the application's *TComponentFactory* callback function.

app is the automation server's primary automated class created from the *TAutoObjectDelete<>* template.

options contains the application's mode flags. This is usually the same value passed in to the factory callback function. The possible values are enumerated in *TOcAppMode*.

outer points to the *IUnknown* interface of an outer component under which the application is asked to aggregate.

The return value points to the new OLE application object.

See also   TAutoObjectDelete<> class, TComponentFactory typedef, TRegistrar::CreateAutoObject

CreateAutoObject

Form 1   TUnknown* CreateAutoObject(TObjectDescriptor obj, TServedObject& app);

app is the automated OLE application object.

obj is the automated C++ object.

Form 2   TUnknown* CreateAutoObject(const void* obj, const typeinfo& objInfo, const void* app, const typeinfo& appInfo);

app and *obj* are the same as in Form 1.

objInfo identifies the type of object in *obj*. *appInfo* identifies the type of object in *app*. Both values can be obtained using *typeid*.

CreateAutoObject asks an automated application to instantiate one of its automated objects. It is usually called from the application's *TComponentFactory* callback function. Which form you call depends on what information you have to identify the kind of object you want to create.

See also   TComponentFactory typedef, TRegistrar::CreateAutoApp, typeid, typeinfo class

GetFactory

virtual void far* GetFactory(const GUID& clsid, const GUID far& iid);

Returns a pointer to the factory interface for creating type object indicated by *clsid*. *iid* names the particular interface you want to receive. If the registrar is unable to find an *iid* interface for *clsid* objects, it returns zero.

ObjectComponents calls a DLL's *GetFactory* member every time a new client loads the DLL. Usually you do not need to call *GetFactory* yourself.

GetOptions

uint32 GetOptions() const;

Returns a 32-bit integer containing bit flags that reflect the application's running mode. Some of the flags are set in response to command-line switches. Others are set directly by ObjectComponents. For a list of the mode flags, see the *TOcAppMode* enum.

See also   TOcAppMode enum, TRegistrar::IsOptionSet, TRegistrar::ProcessCmdLine, TRegistrar::SetOption

IsOptionSet

bool IsOptionSet(uint32 option) const;

Returns **true** if a particular option was set as a flag on the application's command line, and **false** if the option was not set. The flags are set by the *ProcessCmdLine* method.

For a list of possible values *option* can assume, see the *TOcAppMode* enum.

See also   TOcApp::IsOptionSet, TOcAppMode enum, TRegistrar::GetOptions, TRegistrar::ProcessCmdLine, TRegistrar::SetOption

ProcessCmdLine
void ProcessCmdLine(string& cmdLine);

Locates any OLE-related switches on the application's command line (or passed in to a DLL server from ObjectComponents). The switches tell the program whether it has been launched independently or as a server, whether it should register or unregister itself, whether to create a type library, and signal other running conditions as well. *ProcessCmdLine* records the presence of each flag it finds. You can call *IsOptionSet* to determine the results.

The command line is always processed for you when the registrar object is constructed. Usually you do not need to call this function directly.

cmdLine contains the string of arguments passed to the program on its command line. *ProcessCmdLine* removes OLE-related switches from the command line. That lets you process *cmdLine* afterwards for any of your own arguments without worrying about OLE arguments.

See also   string class, TRegistrar::IsOptionSet

ReleaseAutoApp
void ReleaseAutoApp(TObjectDescriptor app);

This method is used by an application's factory callback function if the application must detach itself from OLE before it can shut down. Detaching the application is necessary when an automated application has registered its application object for its class, allowing the controller to manipulate it.

RegisterAppClass
void RegisterAppClass();

Tells OLE that an automated application is up and ready to create an application instance. Has no effect if called from an application that does not support automation.

For convenience, it is recommended that every ObjectComponents application, even those that do not support automation, call *RegisterAppClass* on starting up and *UnregisterAppClass* when closing down. This habit is harmless even if sometimes unnecessary and ensures that you will not forget to include registration functions if you later add automation.

See also   TRegistrar::UnregisterAppClass

Run
virtual int Run();

Call this function to execute your program. If the application was built as an .EXE file, then *Run* lets the application enter its message loop. If the application was built as a DLL, then *Run* returns without entering the message loop. DLL servers must wait for OLE to call their factory before they run. The purpose of the *Run* function is to let you build your applications as either an .EXE or a DLL without having to modify your code.

In .EXE programs, *Run* performs the following steps:

- If the application is automated, call *RegisterAppClass*.

- Call the factory function to run the application. The application enters its message loop.

- Call the factory function to shut down the application.

- Ensure that the application's *TOcApp* connector object is properly released.

See also   TOcApp, TRegistrar::RegisterApp, TRegistrar::Shutdown

SetOption
void SetOption(uint32 bit, bool state);

Modifies the application's running mode flags. *bit* contains bit flags from the *TOcAppMode* enum. If *state* is **true**, *SetOption* turns the flags on. If *state* is **false**, it turns the flags off. You should never have to call this function because ObjectComponents always maintains the mode flags.

See also   TOcAppMode enum, TRegistrar::GetOptions, TRegistrar::IsOptionSet, TRegistrar::ProcessCmdLine

Shutdown
virtual void Shutdown(IUnknown* releasedObj, uint32 options);

Calls the application's factory function and asks it to make the application stop. Ensures that the application's *TOcApp* connector object is properly released. In the normal path of execution, the Run command performs the same tasks. Call *Shutdown* to terminate the application directly.

See also   TOcApp, TRegistrar::Run

UnregisterAppClass
void UnregisterAppClass();

Announces that the application is no longer available for OLE interactions.

See also   TRegistrar::RegisterAppClass

Protected data member

AppDesc
TAppDescriptor& AppDesc;

Holds the application descriptor. ObjectComponents uses an application descriptor internally to manage information about a component. (Like .EXEs, each DLL gets an application descriptor of its own.) *TAppDescriptor* is undocumented because it is used only internally and is subject to change. The registrar classes, *TOcRegistrar* and *TRegistrar*, are the supported interfaces to the application descriptor. The registrar constructs the descriptor, and most of its member functions call descriptor functions to perform the work.

Usually you will not need to manipulate this data member directly.

Protected constructor

Constructor
TRegistrar(TAppDescriptor& appDesc);

The protected constructor is used only by the derived class *TOcRegistrar*. *TAppDescriptor* is a class that both registrar objects (*TRegistrar* and *TOcRegistrar*) use internally to hold information about an application.

TUnknown class   ocf/oleutil.h

Implements the standard OLE *IUnknown* interface. ObjectComponents derives some of its own classes from *TUnknown*, so usually you do not need to use it directly yourself. Advanced users, however, might find *TUnknown* helpful in creating their own custom Component Object Model (COM) objects.

The *TUnknown* class is the basis for the ObjectComponents implementation of object aggregation. With aggregation, you can make distinct components work together as a single OLE object. A single primary object becomes the outer object, and secondary objects behave as though they are parts of the primary object. For this to work, whenever any inner object is asked for its *IUnknown* interface, it must return the *IUnknown* that belongs to the outer object. If the outer object is asked for an interface it does not support, it forwards the request to the chain of attached inner objects. All the interfaces supported by any object in the aggregation are available through the *QueryInterface* method of the outer object.

Aggregation is established in the *TComponentFactory* callback function. Each component receives the *IUnknown* pointer to its outer object and returns its own *IUnknown* pointer to be placed in the chain of secondary objects.

See also   TComponentFactory typedef

Public member functions

Aggregate
IUnknown& Aggregate(TUnknown& inner);

Aggregates a new object under the current object. *inner* points to the *IUnknown* interface of the new object. The current object stores *inner* for use in responding to future *QueryInterface* calls. It also calls *AddRef* on the inner pointer.

If **this** is already part of an aggregation, *inner* is passed down to the last inner object in the chain.

Aggregate returns a reference to the object's own outer *IUnknown* interface. The newly added object should use the return value as its *Outer* pointer, too. To aggregate **this** under an object that is not a *TUnknown*, call *SetOuter* instead.

See also   TUnknown::SetOuter, TUnknown::Outer

GetOuter

IUnknown* GetOuter();

Returns a pointer to the object's outer *IUnknown* interface, the one that belongs to the primary object in a group of aggregated objects.

See also   TUnknown::SetOuter, TUnknown::Outer

GetRefCount

unsigned long GetRefCount();

Returns the reference count of the outer object. If **this** is not aggregated, then *GetRefCount* returns the object's own reference count.

The reference count tells how many clients hold pointers to the object. The destructor prevents the object from being destroyed if the reference count is not 0.

operator IUnknown&()

operator IUnknown&();

Returns a reference to the object's outer *IUnknown* interface. Does not increment the object's reference count.

operator IUnknown*()

operator IUnknown*();

Returns a pointer to the object's outer *IUnknown* interface. Increments the object's reference count first.

See also   TUnknown::operator IUnknown&()

SetOuter

IUnknown* SetOuter(IUnknown* outer);

Tells the object to aggregate itself under the object *outer*. When asked for its *IUnknown* interface, **this** always returns *outer*. *SetOuter* returns the object's own *IUnknown* interface to the outer object. It does not call *AddRef* before returning the pointer.

If *outer* is 0, *SetOuter* ignores *outer* but still returns its own *IUnknown* interface.

SetOuter is called to make the object aggregate under an unknown outer object. If the outer object is also a TUnknown, call Aggregate instead. Aggregate sets the object's inner pointer as well as its outer pointer.

See also   TUnknown::Aggregate, TUnknown::GetOuter, TUnknown::Outer, TUnknown::operator IUnknown*()

Protected constructor and destructor

Constructor

TUnknown();

Creates a *TUnknown* object with an initial reference count of 0. Initially the object is not aggregated with any other object.

These members are protected because only a derived class should be able to construct a *TUnknown* object. *TUnknown* is meant to be a base for other objects, not an independent object.

Destructor
virtual ~TUnknown();
Deletes the object.

See also   TUnknown::Aggregate

Protected member functions

QueryObject
virtual HRESULT QueryObject(const GUID far& iid, void far* far* pif);
Asks whether the object supports the interface identified by *iid*. If the object supports the interface, the function returns HR_NOERROR and places a pointer to the interface in *pif*.

The implementation of *QueryObject* in *TUnknown* always fails. It always returns HR_NOINTERFACE. Classes derived from *TUnknown* should override this function.

For examples of override functions, look at the source code for classes such as *TOcApp* and *TOcView*.

ThisUnknown
IUnknown& ThisUnknown();
Returns a reference to the *IUnknown* interface for **this**, not to the outer or inner aggregated objects.

Protected data member

Outer
IUnknown* Outer;
Holds a pointer to the *IUnknown* interface of the outer object in a group of aggregated objects.

See also   TUnknown::GetOuter, TUnknown::SetOuter

TXAuto class   ocf/autodefs.h

Base class
TXBase

TXAuto is the exception object that ObjectComponents throws when it encounters an unexpected error while processing automation calls. The possible errors are indicated by the *TError* nested **enum** values.

See also   TXBase class (OWL.HLP), TXObjComp class, TXOle class, TXRegistry class

Public constructor

Constructor
TXAuto(TXAuto::TError err);
Constructs an exception object to describe the problem indicated by *err*.

See also   TXAuto::TError enum

Public data member

ErrorCode
TError ErrorCode;
Holds the code that identifies the problem this object was constructed to describe.

See also   TXAuto::TError enum

Type definition

TError
enum TError
The values of the enumeration identify possible errors that can occur during automation.

Constant	Meaning
xNoError	No error occurred.
xConversionFailure	Problem converting a value from a VARIANT union to the expected data type.
xNotIDispatch	Attempted to send an automation command to an object that does not execute commands.
xForeignIDispatch	Attempted to send an automation command to an automated object that does not derive from *TAutoProxy*.
xTypeMismatch	A supplied argument cannot be converted to the required type.
xNoArgSymbol	A command attempted to use more arguments than the server recognizes.
xParameterMissing	An automation call failed to provide a required argument when setting a property value.
xNoDefaultValue	A parameter is missing and no default value was supplied.
xValidateFailure	The code in a user-defined validation hook indicated that the argument values it received are unacceptable.

TXObjComp class   ocf/ocdefs.h

Base class
TXBase
TXObjComp is the exception object that ObjectComponents throws when it encounters an unexpected error while processing its own internal code. The possible errors are indicated by the *TError* nested **enum** values.

See also TXAuto class, TXBase class, TXOle class, TXRegistry class

Public constructor

Constructor
TXObjComp(TXObjComp::TError err, const char* msg = 0);

Constructs an exception object to describe the problem indicated by *err*. Associates the optional *msg* string with the error.

See also TXObjComp::TError

Public member function

ErrorCode
TError ErrorCode;

Holds the error code that identifies the problem this object was constructed to describe.

See also TXObjComp::TError enum

Type definition

TError
enum TError

The values of the enumeration identify possible errors that can occur inside ObjectComponents.

Constant	Meaning
Application Errors	
xNoError	No error occurred.
xBOleLoadFail	The BOCOLE support library could not be loaded.
xBOleBindFail	ObjectComponents could not get a necessary interface from the BOCOLE support library.
xDocFactoryFail	TOcApp was unable to register or unregister the application with OLE.
xRegWriteFail	The registrar could not write to the system registration database.
Document and Part Errors	
xMissingRootIStorage	The document where a part was asked to construct itself does not possess a root storage object. (Without a storage, the document has nowhere to store its parts.)
xInternalPartError	ObjectComponents was unable to create a part object.
xPartInitError	ObjectComponents was unable to initialize a newly created part.
xDocSaveError	A *TOcDocument* could not write itself to a file.
Storage Errors	
xStorageOpenError	A document was unable to open its storage object.
xStreamOpenError	A document was unable to open the stream object it needs for file I/O.
xStreamWriteError	A document was unable to write to the stream object it needs for file I/O.

TXOle class

ocf/oleutil.h

Base class

TXBase

TXOle is the exception object that ObjectComponents throws when it encounters an unexpected error while executing an OLE API call.

The object's *Check* method is static so that you can call it without actually creating a *TXOle* object. If the parameters you pass indicate an error has occurred, *Check* creates a *TXOle* object and throws the exception for you.

See also TXAuto class, TXObjComp class, TXRegistry class

Public constructors and destructor

Constructors

Form 1 TXOle(const char far* msg, HRESULT stat);

Creates an OLE exception object. *msg* points to an error message and *stat* holds the return value from an OLE API call.

Form 2 TXOle(const TXOle& copy);

Constructs a new OLE exception object by copying the one passed as *copy*.

Usually you do not need to construct an OLE exception object directly. Call *Check* instead.

Destructor

~TXOle();

Destroys the *TXOle* object.

See also TXOle::Check

Public member functions

Check

Form 1 static void Check(HRESULT stat, const char far* msg);

If *stat* indicates an error, Form 1 throws a *TXOle* exception containing the *msg* error string.

Form 2 static void Check(HRESULT stat);

If *stat* indicates an error, Form 2 throws a *TXOle* exception containing the error string "OLE call FAILED, ErrorCode = *stat*" where *stat* is shown as an eight-digit hexadecimal value.

If you see this error message when running programs, you can look it up in the OLE_ERRS.TXT file, which for convenience matches the error codes to corresponding comments from the OLE system header files.

Checks whether an error has occurred and if so throws an exception. *stat* is the value returned by an OLE API call. *Check* is static so that you can call it without actually creating a *TXOle* object first. If *stat* indicates an error, then *Check* creates a *TXOle* object and throws an exception.

Public data member

Stat
long Stat;

Stat ("status") holds the result code returned from an OLE API.

TXRegistry class   ocf/ocdefs.h

Base class
TXBase

TXRegistry is the exception object that ObjectComponents throws when it encounters an unexpected error while reading from or writing to the system registration database.

The object's *Check* method is static so that you can call it without actually creating a *TXRegistry* object. If the parameters you pass indicate an error has occurred, *Check* creates a *TXRegistry* object and throws the exception for you.

See also   TXAuto class, TXObjComp class, TXOle class

Public constructors

Constructors
Form 1   TXRegistry(const char* msg, const char* key);

Creates a registry exception object. *msg* points to an error message and *key* points to the name of the registry key that ObjectComponents was processing when the exception occurred.

Form 2   TXRegistry(const TXRegistry& copy);

The copy constructor constructs a new registry exception object by copying the one passed as *copy*.

Usually you do not need to construct a registry exception directly. Call *Check* instead.

See also   TXRegistry::Check

Public member functions

Check
static void Check(long stat, const char* key);

Tests the value of *stat* to determine if an error has occurred and if so throws an exception. *stat* is the return value from a registration command. *key* is the name of the key that the registration command was processing.

Check is static so that you can call it without actually creating a *TXRegistry* object first. If *stat* is nonzero, then *Check* creates a *TXRegistry* object and throws an exception. The exception carries the message string "Registry failure on key: *key*, ErrorCode = *stat*."

Key
const char* Key;

Points to the name of the registration key that ObjectComponents was processing when the exception occurred.

typehelp registration key

Registers the name of a Help file (.HLP) containing information about the methods and properties your program exposes for automation. If the file is not in the same directory as the executable, be sure to register *helpdir* as well.

typehelp is valid in the application registration table of an automation server. It is optional. Also, the file name can be localized, making it easy to have different Help files for different languages.

To register *typehelp*, use the REGDATA macro, passing *typehelp* as the first parameter and file name as the second parameter.

See also helpdir registration key, REGDATA macro, typelib registration key

usage registration key

Determines whether a single instance of your application is allowed to support multiple users or whether a new instance should be launched for each new OLE client. The *–Automation* command-line switch overrides this setting and forces single use when an automation server is invoked.

The *usage* key is valid in any server registration table. It is always optional. If you omit it, ObjectComponents by default registers the application to support only one client per instance.

To register the *usage* key, use the REGDATA macro, passing *usage* as the first parameter and one of the *ocrxxxx* Usage constants as the second parameter.

```
REGDATA(usage, ocrSingleUse)   // one client per instance (default)
```

See also ocrxxxx usage constants, REGDATA macro

verb*n*registration keys

A string naming an action the server can perform with its objects. Containers add the active object's verbs to their Edit menus.

verb0 is the name of the primary (default) verb for the class. The primary verb is executed if the user double-clicks the object. Use *verb1* through *verb7* to register additional verbs. The *ocrVerbLimit* constant, defined in ocf/ocreg.h, represents the maximum number of verbs allowed (8).

The *verbn* keys are valid in the document registration tables of a server that supports linking and embedding. Every server should register a default verb. Other verbs are optional.

To register a verb, use the REGDATA macro, passing *verbn* as the first parameter and a menu item string as the second parameter.

```
REGDATA(verb0, "&Edit")   // default action
REGDATA(verb1, "&Open")   // another possible action (optional)
```

See also   REGDATA macro, verb*n*opt registration keys

verb*n* opt registration keys

Registers option flags describing the server's verbs. The flags determine how the verbs appear on the container's menu. They can be grayed or disabled, for example.

Verb options are valid in the document registration table of any server that supports linking and embedding. They are always optional. Verb options are meaningless unless you also register verbs.

To register verb options, use the REGVERBOPT macro, passing a verb key (such as *verb0* or *verb1)* as the first parameter. For the second parameter, use *ocrxxxx* verb menu constants. For the third parameter, use *ocrxxxx* verb attribute constants.

```
REGVERBOPT(verb2, ocrGrayed, ocrOnContainerMenu | ocrNeverDirties)
```

See also   ocrxxxx verb menu constants, ocrxxxx verb attribute constants, REGVERBOPT macro, verb*n* registration keys

version registration key

Registers a version string for the application and type library. The string can include minor version numbers delimited by periods. OLE ignores version numbers after the first two (the major and minor version numbers).

The version key is valid in any registration table. It is always optional.

To register *version*, use the REGDATA macro, passing *version* as the first parameter and a version number string as the second parameter.

```
REGDATA(version, "1.0.5")
```

See also   description registration key, permid registration key, permname registration key

WM_OCEVENT message   ocf/ocapp.h

ObjectComponents defines the WM_OCEVENT message in order to notify an application's window when significant OLE-related events occur.

Message	Meaning
WM_OCEVENT	Notification of an OLE event from ObjectComponents. The *wParam* value identifies the particular event.

See also   OC_APPxxxx messages, OC_VIEWxxxx messages

Windows System classes reference

Use the Window System classes to perform low-level Windows system functions. The Windows System class library contains many separate independent classes with no rigid hierarchy.

Part III presents the Windows System classes, structures, and typedefs alphabetically. Class members are grouped according to their access specifiers—public or protected. Within these categories, data members, then constructors and destructors, and member functions are grouped separately and listed alphabetically.

12

Windows system classes

The Windows system classes encapsulate various aspects of the API for both 16-bit and 32-bit versions of Windows. This includes classes used to define rectangles, register applications, manipulate initialization files, utilize color palettes, and enable drag-and-drop.

This section lists the Windows System classes, structures, and typedefs alphabetically. The header file that defines each entry is opposite the entry name.

Class members are grouped according to their access specifiers—public or protected. Within these categories, data members, then constructors and destructors, and member functions are grouped separately and listed alphabetically.

The members listed for each class include only those that are new or redefined in the listed class. Members inherited from a base class are not listed again in the derived class. No private members are listed. In some cases, public or protected members are omitted as well because they are meant only for the use of other ObjectWindow classes.

TColor class   color.h

TColor is a support class used in conjunction with the classes *TPalette*, *TPaletteEntry*, *TRgbQuad*, and *TRgbTriple* to simplify all color operations. *TColor* has ten static data members representing the standard RGB COLORREF values, from *Black* to *White*. Constructors are provided to create *TColor* objects from COLORREF and RGB values, palette indexes, palette entries, and RGBQUAD and RGBTRIPLE values.

See the entries for *NBits* and *NColors* for a description of *TColor*-related functions.

Public data members

Black
static const TColor Black;
The static *TColor* object with fixed *Value* set by RGB(0, 0, 0).

Gray
static const TColor Gray;
Contains the static *TColor* object with fixed *Value* set by RGB(128, 128, 128).

LtBlue
static const TColor LtBlue;
Contains the static *TColor* object with the fixed *Value* set by RGB(0, 0, 255).

LtCyan
static const TColor LtCyan;
Contains the static *TColor* object with the fixed *Value* set by RGB(0, 255, 255).

LtGray
static const TColor LtGray;
Contains the static *TColor* object with the fixed *Value* set by RGB(192, 192, 192).

LtGreen
static const TColor LtGreen;
Contains the static *TColor* object with the fixed *Value* set by RGB(0, 255, 0).

LtMagenta
static const TColor LtMagenta;
Contains the static *TColor* object with the fixed *Value* set by RGB(255, 0, 255).

LtRed
static const TColor LtRed;
Contains the static *TColor* object with the fixed *Value* set by RGB(255, 0, 0).

LtYellow
static const TColor LtYellow;
Contains the static *TColor* object with the fixed *Value* set by RGB(255, 255, 0).

None
static const TColor None;
These are special marker colors, using flag bit pattern. *Value* is never really used. *Value* must not change for streaming compatibility with OWL's TWindow.

Sys3dDkShadow
static const TColor Sys3dDkShadow;
For Windows 95 only. The symbolic system color value for dark shadow regions of 3-dimensional display elements. Performs GetSysColor() on conversion to COLORREF.

Sys3dFace
static const TColor Sys3dFace;

For Windows 95 only. The symbolic system color value for the face color of 3-dimensional display elements. Performs GetSysColor() on conversion to COLORREF.

Sys3dHilight
static const TColor Sys3dHilight;
For Windows 95 only. The symbolic system color value for highlighted 3-dimensional display elements (for edges facing the light source). Performs GetSysColor() on conversion to COLORREF.

Sys3dLight
static const TColor Sys3dLight;
For Windows 95 only. The symbolic system color value for the light color for 3-dimensional display elements (for edges facing the light source). Performs GetSysColor() on conversion to COLORREF.

Sys3dShadow
static const TColor Sys3dShadow;
For Windows 95 only. The symbolic system color value for the shadow regions of 3-dimensional display elements (for edges facing away from the light source). Performs GetSysColor() on conversion to COLORREF.

SysActiveBorder
static const TColor SysActiveBorder;
The symbolic system color value for the borders of the active window. Performs GetSysColor() on conversion to COLORREF.

SysActiveCaption
static const TColor SysActiveCaption;
The symbolic system color value for the caption of the active window. Performs GetSysColor() on conversion to COLORREF.

SysAppWorkspace
static const TColor SysAppWorkspace;
The symbolic system color value for the background of multiple document interface (MDI) applications. Performs GetSysColor() on conversion to COLORREF.

SysBtnText
static const TColor SysBtnText;
The symbolic system color value for the text on buttons. Performs GetSysColor() on conversion to COLORREF.

SysCaptionText
static const TColor SysCaptionText;
The symbolic system color value for text in captions and size boxes, and for the arrow boxes on scroll bars. Performs GetSysColor() on conversion to COLORREF.

SysDesktop
static const TColor SysDesktop;
The symbolic system color value for the desktop. Performs GetSysColor() on conversion to COLORREF.

SysGrayText
static const TColor SysGrayText;
The symbolic system color value for grayed (disabled) text. Performs GetSysColor() on conversion to COLORREF.

This color is set to 0 if the current display driver does not support a solid gray color.

SysHighlight
static const TColor SysHighlight;
The symbolic system color value for items selected in a control. Performs GetSysColor() on conversion to COLORREF.

SysHighlightText
static const TColor SysHighlightText;
The symbolic system color value for text selected in a control. Performs GetSysColor() on conversion to COLORREF.

SysInactiveBorder
static const TColor SysInactiveBorder;
The symbolic system color value for the borders of every inactive window. Performs GetSysColor() on conversion to COLORREF.

SysInactiveCaption
static const TColor SysInactiveCaption;
The symbolic system color value for the caption background of every inactive window. Performs GetSysColor() on conversion to COLORREF.

SysInactiveCaptionText
static const TColor SysInactiveCaptionText;
The symbolic system color value for the caption text of every inactive window. Performs GetSysColor() on conversion to COLORREF.

SysInfoBk
static const TColor SysInfoBk;
For Windows 95 only. The symbolic system color value for the background of tooltip controls. Performs GetSysColor() on conversion to COLORREF.

SysInfoText
static const TColor SysInfoText;
For Windows 95 only. The symbolic system color value for text shown on tooltip controls. Performs GetSysColor() on conversion to COLORREF.

SysMenu
static const TColor SysMenu;
The symbolic system color value for the background of menus. Performs GetSysColor() on conversion to COLORREF.

SysMenuText
static const TColor SysMenuText;
The symbolic system color value for the text shown on menus. Performs GetSysColor() on conversion to COLORREF.

SysScrollbar

static const TColor SysScrollbar;

The symbolic system color value for what is usually the gray area of scrollbars. This is the region that the scrollbar slider slides upon. Performs GetSysColor() on conversion to COLORREF.

SysWindow

static const TColor SysWindow;

The symbolic system color value for the background of each window. Performs GetSysColor() on conversion to COLORREF.

SysWindowFrame

static const TColor SysWindowFrame;

The symbolic system color value for the frame around each window. The frame is not the same as the border. Performs GetSysColor() on conversion to COLORREF.

SysWindowText

static const TColor SysWindowText;

The symbolic system color value for text in every window. Performs GetSysColor() on conversion to COLORREF.

Transparent

static const TColor Transparent;

Non-painting marker color using the flag bit pattern. This value is never really used. This value must not change, for streaming compatibility with OWL's *TWindow*.

White

static const TColor White;

Contains the static *TColor* object with the fixed *Value* set by RGB(255, 255, 255).

Public constructors

Form 1   TColor();
The default constructor sets *Value* to 0.

Form 2   TColor(COLORREF value);
Creates a *TColor* object with *Value* set to the given value.

Form 3   TColor(long value);
TColor(long value) : Value((COLORREF)value) {}
Creates a *TColor* object with *Value* set to (COLORREF)*value*.

Form 4   TColor(int r, int g, int b);
Creates a *TColor* object with *Value* set to RGB(r,g,b).

Form 5   TColor(int r, int g, int b, int f);
Creates a *TColor* object with *Value* set to RGB(r,g,b) with the flag byte formed from *f*.

Form 6   TColor(int index);
Creates a *TColor* object with *Value* set to *PALETTEINDEX(index)*.

Form 7   TColor(const PALETTEENTRY far& pe);

Creates a *TColor* object with *Value* set to:

```
RGB(pe.peRed, pe.peGreen, pe.peBlue)
```

Form 8 TColor(const RGBQUAD far& q);
Creates a *TColor* object with *Value* set to:

```
RGB(q.rgbRed, q.rgbGreen, q.rgbBlue)
```

Form 9 TColor(const RGBTRIPLE far& t);
Creates a *TColor* object with *Value* set to:

```
RGB(t.rgbtRed, t.rgbtGreen, t.rgbtBlue)
```

See also COLORREF typedef, PALETTEENTRY struct, RGBQUAD struct, RGBTRIPLE struct, TColor::Value

Public member functions

Blue
uint8 Blue() const;
Returns the blue component of this color's *Value*.

See also TColor::Red, TColor::Green, COLORREF typedef

Flags
uint8 Flags() const;
Returns the *peFlags* value of this object's *Value*.

See also TPaletteEntry

GetSysColor
static TColor GetSysColor(int uiElement);
(Presentation Manager only) Returns the color of the given *uiElement*.

GetValue
COLORREF GetValue() const;
Gets a 32bit COLORREF type from this color object. Performs a GetSysColor() lookup if the object represents a symbolic sys-color index.

Green
uint8 Green() const;
Returns the green component of this color's *Value*.

See also TColor::Red, TColor::Blue, COLORREF typedef

IsSysColor
bool IsSysColor() const;
Returns true if the color is a system color, false otherwise.

See also TColor::Value

operator ==
This function compares between two binary representation of colors; it does not compare colors logically.

For example, if palette entry 4 is solid red (rgb components (255, 0, 0)), the following will return false:

```
if (TColor(4) == TColor(255, 0, 0))
```

Form 1   bool operator ==(const TColor& other) const;
Returns true if two colors are equal.

Form 2   bool operator ==(COLORREF cr) const;
Returns true if this color matches a COLORREF.

operator =
TColor& operator =(const TColor& src);
Sets the value of color after it has been initialized.

operator !=
This function compares between two binary representation of colors; it does not compare colors logically.

Form 1   bool operator !=(const TColor& other) const;
Returns true if two colors are not equal.

Form 2   bool operator !=(COLORREF cr) const;
Returns true if this color does not match a COLORREF.

operator COLORREF()
operator COLORREF() const;
Type-conversion operator that returns *Value*.

See also   TColor::Value

Index
int Index() const;
Returns the index value corresponding to this color's *Value* by masking out the two upper bytes. Used when color is a palette index value.

See also   TColor::Value, COLORREF typedef

PalIndex
TColor PalIndex() const;
Returns the palette index corresponding to this color's *Value*. The returned color has the high-order byte set to 1.

See also   TColor::Value, TColor::Index, COLORREF typedef

PalRelative
TColor PalRelative() const;
Returns the palette-relative RGB corresponding to this color's *Value*. The returned color has the high-order byte set to 2.

See also   TColor::Value, TColor::Rgb, COLORREF typedef

Red
uint8 Red() const;
Returns the red component of this color's *Value*.

See also   TColor::Blue, TColor::Green

Rgb
TColor Rgb() const;
Returns the explicit RGB color corresponding to this color's *Value* by masking out the high-order byte.

See also TColor::Value, COLORREF typedef

SetSysColors
static bool SetSysColors(unsigned nelems, const int uiElementIndices[], const TColor colors[]);
(Presentation Manager only) Sets groups of UI element colors. *nelems* indicates the number of element colors to change and the size of the array parameters, *uiElementIndices* indicates which elements to change, and *colors* indicates what color to change the corresponding element to. Returns true if successful.

SetValue
void SetValue(const COLORREF& value);
Changes the color after it has been initialized.

Private data members

Value
COLORREF Value;
The color value of this *TColor* object. *Value* can have three different forms, depending on the application:

- Explicit values for RGB (red, green, blue)

- An index into a logical color palette

- A palette-relative RGB value.

See also COLORREF typedef

TDropInfo class   wsyscls.h

TDropInfo is a simple class that supports file-name drag and drop operations using the WM_DROPFILES message. Each *TDropInfo* object has a private handle to the HDROP structure returned by the WM_DOPFILES message.

Public constructors

TDropInfo
TDropInfo(HDROP handle);
Creates a *TDropInfo* object with *Handle* set to the given *handle*.

Public member functions

DragFinish
void DragFinish();
Releases any memory allocated for the transferring of this *TDropInfo* object's files during drag operations.

DragQueryFile
uint DragQueryFile(uint index, char far* name, uint nameLen);
Retrieves the name of the file and related information for this *i* object. If *index* is set to -1 (0xFFFF), *DragQueryFile* returns the number of dropped files. This is equivalent to calling *DragQueryFileCount*.

If *index* lies between 0 and the total number of dropped files for this object, *DragQueryFile* copies to the *name* buffer (of length *nameLen* bytes) the name of the dropped file that corresponds to *index*, and returns the number of bytes actually copied.

If *name* is 0, *DragQueryFile* returns the required buffer size (in bytes) for the given *index*. This is equivalent to calling *DragQueryFileNameLen*.

See also   TDropInfo::DragQueryPoint, TDropInfo::DragQueryFileCount

DragQueryFileCount
uint DragQueryFileCount();
Returns the number of dropped files in this *TDropInfo* object. This call is equivalent to calling *DragQueryFile(-1, 0, 0)*.

See also   TDropInfo::DragQueryFile

DragQueryFileNameLen
uint DragQueryFileNameLen(uint index);
Returns the length of the name of the file in this *TDropInfo* object corresponding to the given index. This call is equivalent to calling *DragQueryFile(index, 0, 0)*.

See also   TDropInfo::DragQueryFile

DragQueryPoint
bool DragQueryPoint(TPoint& point);
Retrieves the mouse pointer position when this object's files are dropped and copies the coordinates to the given *point* object. *point* refers to the window that received the WM_DROPFILES message. *DragQueryPoint* returns true if the drop occurs inside the window's client area, otherwise false.

See also   Tpoint

operator HDROP()
operator HDROP();
Typecasting operator that returns *Handle*.

TFileDroplet class
wsyscls.h

TFileDroplet encapsulates information about a single dropped file, its name, where it was dropped, and whether or not it was in the client area.

Public constructors and destructor

Constructors
Form 1   TFileDroplet(const char* fileName, TPoint& p, bool inClient);
Supports drag and drop.

Form 2   TFileDroplet(TDropInfo& drop, int i);
Constructs a *TFileDroplet* given a *DropInfo* and a file index.

The location is relative to the client coordinates, and will have negative values if dropped in the non-client parts of the window.

DragQueryPoint copies that point where the file was dropped and returns whether or not the point is in the client area. Regardless of whether the file is dropped in the client or non-client area of the window, you will still receive the file name.

Destructor
~TFileDroplet();
The destructor for this class.

Public member functions

GetInClientArea
bool GetInClientArea() const;
Returns **true** if the drop occurred in the client area.

GetName
const char* GetName() const;
Returns the name of the file dropped.

GetPoint
TPoint GetPoint() const;
Returns the cursor position at which the file was dropped.

operator ==
operator ==(const TFileDroplet& other) const;
Returns **true** if the address of this object is equal to the address of the compared object.

TLangId typedef

typedef unsigned short TLangId;

Holds a language ID, a predefined number that represents a base language and dialect. For example, the number 409 represents American English. *TLocaleString* uses the language ID to find the correct translation for strings.

See also TLocaleString

TLocaleString struct

Designed to provide support for localized registration parameters, the *TLocaleString* Struct defines a localizable substitute for **char*** strings. These strings, which describe both OLE and non-OLE enabled objects to the user, are available in whatever language the user needs. This Struct supports ObjectWindows' Doc/View as well as ObjectComponents' OLE-enabled applications. The public member functions, which supply information about the user's language, the native language, and a description of the string marked for localization, simplify the process of translating and comparing strings in a given language.

To localize the string resource, *TLocaleString* uses several user-entered prefixes to determine what kind of string to translate. Each prefix must be followed by a valid resource identifier (a standard C identifier).The following table lists the prefixes *TLocaleString* uses to localize strings. Each prefix is followed by a sample entry.

Prefix	Description
@TXY	The string is a series of characters interpreted as a resource ID and is accessed only from a resource file. It is never used directly.
1045	The string is a series of digits interpreted as a resource ID and is accessed from a resource file. It is never used directly.
!MyWindow	The string is translated if it is not in the native language; otherwise, this string is used directly.

See the section on localizing symbol names in the *ObjectWindows Programmer's Guide* for more information about localizing strings.

See also TLangId typedef, LangXxxx_ID constants

Public Member Functions

Compare
int Compare(const char far* str, TLangId lang);

Using the specified language (*lang*), *Compare* compares *TLocaleString* with another string. It uses the standard string compare and the language-specific collation scheme. It returns one of the following values.

Return value	Meaning
0	There is no match between the two strings.
1	This string is greater than the other string.
-1	This string is less than the other string.

CompareLang
static int CompareLang(const char far* s1, const char far* s2, TLangId);
This function may be re-implemented with enhanced NLS support in another module.

Note That module must be linked in before the library, to override this default implementation.

GetSystemLangId
static TLangId GetSystemLangId();
Returns the system language ID, which can be the same as the *UserLangId*.

See also TLocaleString::GetUserLangId

GetUserLangId
static TLangId GetUserLangId();
Returns the user language ID. For single user systems, this is the same as *LangSysDefault*. The language ID is a predefined number that represents a base language and dialect.

See also TLocaleString::GetSystemLangId

IsNativeLangId
static int IsNativelangId(TLangId lang);
Returns **true** if *lang* equals the native system language.

operator =
void operator = (const char* str);
Assigns the string (*str*) to this locale string.

operator const char*
operator const char* ();
Returns the current character string in the translation.

Translate
const char* Translate(TLangId lang);
Translates the string to the given language. *Translate* follows this order of preference in order to choose a language for translation:

1 Base language and dialect.

2 Base language and no dialect.

3 Base language and another dialect.

4 The native language of the resource itself.

5 Returns 0 if unable to translate the string. (This can happen only if an @ or # prefix is used; otherwise, the ! prefix indicates that the string following is the native language itself.)

Public data members

Module
static HINSTANCE Module;
The handle of the file containing the resource.

NativeLangId
static TLangId NativeLangId;
The base language ID of non-localized strings.

Null
static TLocaleString Null;
A null string.

Private
const char* Private;
A string pointer used internally.

SystemDefaultLangId
static TLangId SystemDefaultLangId;
The default language identifier.

UserDefaultLangId
static TLangId UserDefaultLangId;
The user-defined default language identifier.

TMsgThread class   msgthred.h

TMsgThread implements basic behavior for threads that own message queues, including mutex locking for the queue. This class provides message queue oriented thread class support. *TMsgThread* degenerates to a simple message queue owner under non-threaded environments.

Type definitions

TCurrent enum
enum TCurrent {Current};

Public constructor

TMsgThread(TCurrent);

Attaches to the current running thread. This is often the initial process thread, or even the only thread for non-threaded systems.

Public data members

BreakMessageLoop
bool BreakMessageLoop;
The message loop is broken via WM_QUIT.

LoopRunning
bool LoopRunning;
Tracks whether the loop is running.

MessageLoopResult
int MessageLoopResult;
Returns the value from the message loop.

Public member functions

EnableMultiThreading
void EnableMultiThreading(bool enable);
Enables or disables the use of the mutex to synchronize access to the message queue. *TMsgThread* will only lock its message queue mutex when enabled. Real multi-threading requires compiler and RTL support.

FlushQueue
void FlushQueue();
Flushes all real messages from the message queue.

GetMutex
TMutex* GetMutex();
Gets this message thread's mutex. Returns 0 if mutexes are not supported, or are not enabled for this thread.

IdleAction
virtual bool IdleAction(long idleCount);
Called each time there are no messages in the queue. Idle count is incremented each time, and zeroed when messages are pumped. Returns whether or not more processing needs to be done.

IsRunning
bool IsRunning() const;
Returns true if this queue thread is running its message loop.

MessageLoop
virtual int MessageLoop();
Retrieves and processes messages from the thread's message queue using *PumpWaitingMessages()* until *BreakMessageLoop* becomes true. Catches exceptions to post a quit message and cleanup before resuming.

ProcessMsg
virtual bool ProcessMsg(MSG& msg);
Called for each message that is pulled from the queue, to perform all translation and dispatching.

Returns *true* to drop out of the pump.

PumpWaitingMessages
bool PumpWaitingMessages();
The inner message loop. Retrieves and processes messages from the OWL application's message queue until it is empty. Set BreakMessageLoop if a WM_QUIT passes through.

Call *ProcessAppMsg()* for each message to allow special pre-handling of the message.

Protected constructors

TMsgThread
TMsgThread();

Protected member functions

InitInstance
virtual void InitInstance();
Handles initialization for each executing instance of the message thread. Derived classes can override this to perform initialization for each instance.

Mutex
TAppMutex Mutex;
Prevents multiple threads from processing messages at the same time.

Run
virtual int Run();
Runs this message thread, returns when the message queue quits Initialize instances. Runs the thread's message loop. Each of the virtual functions called are expected to throw an exception if there is an error.

Exceptions that are not handled, that is, where the status remains non-zero, are propagated out of this function. The message queue is still flushed and *TermInstance* called.

TermInstance
virtual int TermInstance(int status);
Handles termination for each executing instance of the message thread. Called at the end of a *Run()* with the final return status.

TPaletteEntry class   color.h

TPaletteEntry is a support class derived from the structure *tagPALETTEENTRY*. The latter is defined as follows:

```
typedef struct tagPALETTEENTRY {
    uint8  peRed;
    uint8  peGreen;
    uint8  peBlue;
    uint8  peFlags;
} PALETTEENTRY;
```

The members *peRed*, *peGreen*, and *peBlue* specify the red, green, and blue intensity-values for a palette entry.

The *peFlags* member can be set to NULL or one of the following values:

Value	Meaning
PC_EXPLICIT	Specifies that the low-order word of the logical palette entry designates a hardware palette index. This flag allows the application to show the contents of the display device palette.
PC_NOCOLLAPSE	Specifies that the color be placed in an unused entry in the system palette instead of being matched to an existing color in the system palette. If there are no unused entries in the system palette, the color is matched normally. Once this color is in the system palette, colors in other logical palettes can be matched to this color.
PC_RESERVED	Specifies that the logical palette entry be used for palette animation; this prevents other windows from matching colors to this palette entry since the color frequently changes. If an unused system-palette entry is available, this color is placed in that entry. Otherwise, the color is available for animation.

TPaletteEntry is used in conjunction with the classes *Tpalette* and *Tcolor* to simplify logical color-palette operations. Constructors are provided to create *TPaletteEntry* objects from explicit COLORREF and RGB values, or from *TColor* objects.

Public constructors

Form 1   TPaletteEntry(int r, int g, int b, int f = 0);
Creates a palette entry object with *peRed*, *peGreen*, *peBlue*, and *peFlags* set to *r*, *g*, *b*, and *f*, respectively.

Form 2   TPaletteEntry(TColor c);
Creates a palette entry object with *peRed*, *peGreen*, *peBlue*, and *peFlags* set to *r*, *g*, *b*, and *f*, respectively.

Public member functions

operator ==
bool operator ==(COLORREF cr) const;
Returns true if the palette entries have the same color components.

See also   TColor::Red, TColor::Green, TColor::Blue

TPoint class geometry.h

TPoint is a support class, derived from *tagPOINT*. The *tagPOINT* struct is defined as

```
struct tagPOINT {
    int x;
    int y;
};
```

TPoint encapsulates the notion of a two-dimensional point that usually represents a screen position. *TPoint* inherits two data members, the coordinates *x* and *y*, from *tagPOINT*. Member functions and operators are provided for comparing, assigning, and manipulating points. Overloaded << and >> operators allow chained insertion and extraction of *TPoint* objects with streams.

Public constructors

Form 1   TPoint();
The default *TPoint* constructor.

Form 2   TPoint(int _x, int _y);
Creates a *TPoint* object with the given coordinates.

Form 3   TPoint(const POINT& point);
Creates a *TPoint* object with $x = point.x$, $y = point.y$.

Form 4   TPoint(const SIZE& size);
Creates a *TPoint* object with $x = size.cx$ and $y = size.cy$.

Form 5   TPoint(uint32 dw);
Creates a *TPoint* object with $x = $ LOWORD(*dw*), $y = $ HIWORD(*dw*)).

See also   TSize

Public member functions

Magnitude
int Magnitude() const;
Returns the distance between the origin and the point.

Offset
TPoint& Offset(int dx, int dy);
Offsets this point by the given delta arguments. This point is changed to $(x + dx, y + dy)$. Returns a reference to this point.

See also   TPoint::OffsetBy, TPoint::operator +=

OffsetBy
TPoint OffsetBy(int dx, int dy) const;
Calculates an offset to this point using the given displacement arguments. Returns the point $(x + dx, y + dy)$. This point is not changed.

See also TPoint::operator +, TPoint::Offset

operator +
TPoint operator +(const TSize& size) const;
Calculates an offset to this point using the given size argument as the displacement. Returns the point (x + $size.cx$, y + $size.cy$). This point is not changed.

See also TPoint::OffsetBy, TSize

operator -
Form 1   TPoint operator -(const TSize& size) const;
Calculates a negative offset to this point using the given *size* argument as the displacement. Returns the point (x - $size.cx$, y - $size.cy$). This point is not changed.

Form 2   TSize operator -(const TPoint& point) const;
Calculates a distance from this point to the *point* argument. Returns the *TSize* object (x - $point.x$, y - $point.y$). This point is not changed.

Form 3   TPoint operator -() const;
Returns the point ($-x$, $-y$). This point is not changed.

See also TPoint::operator +, TSize

operator ==
bool operator ==(const TPoint& other) const;
Returns true if this point is equal to the *other* point; otherwise returns false.

See also TPoint::operator !=

operator +=
TPoint& operator +=(const TSize& size);
Offsets this point by the given *size* argument. This point is changed to(x + $size.cx$, y + $size.cy$). Returns a reference to this point.

See also TPoint::Offset, TPoint::operator -=, TSize

operator -=
TPoint& operator -=(const TSize& size);
Negatively offsets this point by the given *size* argument. This point is changed to (x - $size.cx$, y - $size.cy$). Returns a reference to this point.

See also TPoint::Offset, TPoint::operator +=, TSize

operator !=
bool operator !=(const TPoint& other) const;
Returns false if this point is equal to the *other* point; otherwise returns true.

See also TPoint::operator ==

operator >>
Form 1   ipstream& operator >>(ipstream& is, TPoint& p);
Extracts a *TPoint* object from persistent stream *is*, and copies it to *p*. Returns a reference to the resulting stream, allowing the usual chaining of << operations.

Form 2   istream& operator >>(istream& is, TPoint& p);
Extracts a *TPoint* object from stream *is,* and copies it to *p.* Returns a reference to the resulting stream, allowing the usual chaining of >> operations.

See also   TPoint operator <<

operator <<
Form 1   opstream& operator <<(opstream& os, const TPoint& p);
Inserts the given *TPoint* object *p* into persistent stream *os.* Returns a reference to the resulting stream, allowing the usual chaining of >> operations.

Form 2   ostream& operator <<(ostream& os, const TPoint& p);
Formats and inserts the given *TPoint* object *p* into the *ostream os.* The format is "(x,y)." Returns a reference to the resulting stream, allowing the usual chaining of << operations.

See also   TPoint operator >>

X
int X() const;
Returns the x coordinate of the point.

Y
int Y() const;
Returns the y coordinate of the point.

TPointF class   **geometry.h**

TPointF is similar to *TPoint,* but uses floating variables rather than integers.

Public constructors

Form 1   TPointF();
Default constructor that does nothing.

Form 2   TPointF(float _x, float _y);
Constructor that initializes the location.

Form 3   TPointF(const TPointF far& point);
Constructor that copies the location.

Public member functions

Offset
TPointF& Offset(float dx, float dy);
Moves the point by an offset.

OffsetBy
TPointF OffsetBy(float dx, float dy) const;
Creates a new point that is offset from the current point.

operator !=
bool operator !=(const TPointF& other) const;
Returns true if the points are not at the same location.

operator +
TPointF operator +(const TPointF& size) const;
Returns a new point (x+cx, y+cy).

operator +=
TPointF& operator +=(const TPointF& size);
Returns the new point moved by the offset.

operator -
TPointF operator -() const;
Returns the new point subtracted from the current.

operator -
TPointF operator -(const TPointF& point) const;
Returns the negative of the point.

operator -=
TPointF& operator -=(const TPointF& size);
Returns the new point subtracted from the current.

operator ==
bool operator ==(const TPointF& other) const;
Returns true if the points are at the same location.

X
float X() const;
Returns the X component of the point.

Y
float Y() const;
Returns the Y component of the point.

TPointL class

geometry.h

TPointL is similar to *TPoint*, but uses long rather than int variables.

Public constructors

Form 1   TPointL();
Default constructor that does nothing.

Form 2   TPointL(long _x, long _y);
Constructs the point to a specific location.

Form 3   TPointL(const POINTL far& point);
Alias constructor that initializes from an existing point.

Form 4   TPointL(const TPointL far& point);
Makes a copy of the location.

Public member functions

Offset
TPointL& Offset(long dx, long dy);
Returns the point (x+dx, y+dy), shifting the point by the offset.

OffsetBy
TPointL OffsetBy(long dx, long dy) const;
Returns the new point (x+dx, y+dy). Creates a new point shifted by the offset, preserving the original point.

operator !=
bool operator !=(const TPointL& other) const;
Returns true if the positions are not the same.

operator +
TPointL operator +(const TSize& size) const;
Returns the new point (x+cx, y+cy).

operator +=
TPointL& operator +=(const TSize& size);
Returns the point (x+cx, y+cy).

operator -
Form 1   TPointL operator -() const;
Returns the negative of the point.

Form 2   TPointL operator -(const TSize& size) const;
Returns the new point (x-cx, y-cy).

Form 3   TPointL operator -(const TPointL& point) const;
Returns the difference between the two points.

operator -=
TPointL& operator -=(const TSize& size);
Returns the point (x-cx, y-cy).

operator ==
bool operator ==(const TPointL& other) const;
Returns true if positions are the same.

X
long X() const;
Returns the X component of the point.

Y
long Y() const;
Returns the Y component of the point.

TProcInstance class

A *ProcInstance* object. This encapsulates the *MakeProcInstance* call, which is really only needed in old Win3.X real mode. This exists now for OWL 2.x compatibility only.

Designed for Win16 applications, *TProcInstance* handles creating and freeing an instance thunk, a piece of code created for use with exported callback functions. (A callback function is a function that exists within a program but is called from outside the program by a Windows library routine, for example, a dialog box function.)

For Win32 applications, *TProcInstance* is non-functional. The address returned from *TProcInstance* can be passed as a parameter to callback functions, window subclassing functions, or Windows dialog box functions.

See the Windows API online Help for more information about *MakeProcInstance*, which creates an instance thunk for the function and *FreeProcInstance*, which frees an instance thunk. For more information about exporting callback functions, see the *Borland C++ Programmer's Guide*.

Public constructor and destructor

Constructor
TProcInstance(FARPROC p);
Makes a *TProcInstance*, passing *p* as the address of the procedure. Under Win16, calls *::MakeProcInstance* to make an instance thunk for *p*. Under Win32, the constructor just saves *p*.

Destructor
~TProcInstance()
Under WIN16, frees the instance thunk.

See also   ::MakeProcInstance (Windows API), ::FreeProcInstance (Windows API)

Public member functions

operator FARPROC
operator FARPROC();
Under Win16, returns the instance thunk. Under Win32, returns *p* from the constructor.

TProfile class

An instance of *TProfile* encapsulates a setting within a system file, often referred to as a *profile* or *initialization* file. Examples of this type of file include the Windows initialization files SYSTEM.INI and WIN.INI. Within the system file itself, the individual settings are grouped within sections. For example,

```
[Diagnostics]; section name
Enabled=0     ; setting
```

For a setting, the value to the left of the equal sign is called the *key*. The value to the right of the equal sign, the *value*, can be either an integer or a string data type.

Public constructor and destructor

Constructor
TProfile(const char* section, const char* filename=0);
Constructs a *TProfile* object for the indicated *section* within the profile file specified by *filename*. If the file name is not provided, the file defaults to the system profile file; for example, WIN.INI under Windows .

Destructor
~TProfile();
Destroys the *TProfile* object.

Public member functions

Flush
void Flush();
Makes sure that all written profile values are flushed to the actual file.

GetInt
int GetInt(const char* key, int defaultInt = 0);
Looks up and returns the integer value associated with the given string, *key*. If *key* is not found, the default value, *defaultInt*, is returned.

GetString
bool GetString(const char* key, char buff[], unsigned buffSize, const char* defaultString = "");
Looks up and returns the string value associated with the given *key* string. The string value is copied into *buff*, up to *buffSize* bytes. If the key is not found, *defaultString* provides the default value. If a 0 key is passed, all section values are returned in *buff*.

WriteInt
bool WriteInt(const char* key, const char* int value);
Looks up the key and replaces its value with the integer value passed (*int*). If the key is not found, *WriteInt* makes a new entry. Returns **true** if successful.

WriteString
bool WriteString(const char* key, const char* str);
Looks up the key and replaces its value with the string value passed (*str*). If the key is not found, *WriteString* makes a new entry. Returns **true** if successful.

TRect class   geometry.h

TRect is a mathematical class derived from *tagRect*. The *tagRect* struct is defined as

```
struct tagRECT {
    int left;
```

```
    int top;
    int right;
    int bottom;
};
```

TRect encapsulates the properties of rectangles with sides parallel to the x- and y-axes. In ObjectWindows, these rectangles define the boundaries of windows, boxes, and clipping regions. *TRect* inherits four data members from *tagRect left, top, right*, and *bottom*. These represent the top left and bottom right *(x, y)* coordinates of the rectangle. Note that *x* increases from left to right, and *y* increases from top to bottom.

TRect places no restrictions on the relative positions of top left and bottom right, so it is legal to have *left > right* and *top > bottom*. However, many manipulations--such as determining width and height, and forming unions and intersections--are simplified by normalizing the *TRect* objects involved. Normalizing a rectangle means interchanging the corner point coordinate values so that *left < right* and *top < bottom*. Normalization does not alter the physical properties of a rectangle. *myRect.Normalized* creates normalized copy of *myRect* without changing *myRect*, while *myRect.Normalize* changes *myRect* to a normalized format. Both members return the normalized rectangle.

TRect constructors are provided to create rectangles from either four **int**s, two *TPoint* objects, or one *TPoint* and one TSize object. In the latter case, the *TPoint* object specifies the top left point (also known as the rectangle's origin) and the *TSize* object supplies the width and height of the rectangle. Member functions perform a variety of rectangle tests and manipulations. Overloaded << and >> operators allow chained insertion and extraction of *TRect* objects with streams.

Public constructors

Form 1   TRect();
The default constructor.

Form 2   TRect(const tagRECT far& rect);
Copies from an existing rectangle.

Form 3   TRect(const TRect far& rect);
Copies the given *rect* to this object.

Form 4   TRect(int _left, int _top, int _right, int _bottom);
Creates a rectangle with the given values.

Form 5   TRect(const TPoint& upLeft, const TPoint& loRight);
Creates a rectangle with the given top left and bottom right points.

Form 6   TRect(const TPoint& origin, const TSize& extent);
Creates a rectangle with its origin (top left) at *origin*, width at *extent.cx*, height at *extent.cy*.

See also   TPoint, TSize

Public member functions

Area
long Area() const;
Returns the area of this rectangle.

See also   TRect::Size

Bottom
int Bottom() const;
Returns the bottom value.

BottomLeft
TPoint BottomLeft() const;
Returns the *TPoint* object representing the bottom left corner of this rectangle.

See also   TRect::TopLeft, TRect::TopRight, TRect::BottomRight, TPoint

BottomRight
Form 1   const TPoint& BottomRight() const;

Form 2   TPoint& BottomRight();
Returns the *TPoint* object representing the bottom right corner of this rectangle.

See also   TRect::TopRight, TRect::BottomLeft, TRect::TopLeft, TPoint

Contains
Form 1   bool Contains(const TPoint& point) const;
Returns **true** if the given *point* lies within this rectangle; otherwise, it returns **false**. If *point* is on the left vertical or on the top horizontal borders of the rectangle, *Contains* also returns **true**, but if *point* is on the right vertical or bottom horizontal borders, *Contains* returns **false**.

Form 2   bool Contains(const TRect& other) const;
Returns **true** if the other rectangle lies on or within this rectangle; otherwise, it returns **false**.

See also   TRect::Touches, TPoint, TRect

Height
int Height() const;
Returns the height of this rectangle (*bottom - top*).

See also   TRect::Width

Inflate
Form 1   TRect& Inflate(int dx, int dy);

Form 2   TRect& Inflate(const TSize& delta);
Inflates a rectangle inflated by the given delta arguments. In the first version, the top left corner of the returned rectangle is (*left - dx, top - dy*), while its bottom right corner is (*right + dx, bottom + dy*). In the second version the new corners are (*left - size.cx, top - size.cy*) and (*right + size.cx, bottom + size.cy*).

See also   TRect, TSize

InflatedBy

Form 1   TRect InflatedBy(int dx, int dy) const;

Form 2   TRect InflatedBy(const TSize& size) const;

Returns a rectangle inflated by the given delta arguments. In the first version, the top left corner of the returned rectangle is (*left - dx, top - dy*), while its bottom right corner is (*right + dx, bottom + dy*). In the second version the new corners are (*left - size.cx, top - size.cy*) and (*right + size.cx, bottom + size.cy*). The calling rectangle object is unchanged.

See also   TRect::OffsetBy, TRect, TSize

IsEmpty

bool IsEmpty() const;

Returns **true** if *left* >= *right* or *top* >= *bottom*; otherwise, returns **false**.

See also   TRect::SetEmpty, TRect::IsNull

IsNull

bool IsNull() const;

Returns **true** if left, *right, top,* and *bottom* are all 0; otherwise, returns **false**.

See also   TRect::IsEmpty, TRect::SetEmpty

Left

int Left() const;

Returns the left value.

MovedTo

TRect MovedTo(int x, int y);

Moves the upper left point of the rectangle while maintaining the current dimensions.

MoveTo

TRect& MoveTo(int x, int y);

Move the upper left corner of the rectangle to a new location and maintain the current dimensions.

Normalize

TRect& Normalize();

Normalizes this rectangle by switching the *left* and *right* data member values if *left* > *right*, and switching the *top* and *bottom* data member values if *top* > *bottom*. *Normalize* returns the normalized rectangle. A valid but nonnormal rectangle might have *left* > *right* or *top* > *bottom* or both. In such cases, many manipulations (such as determining width and height) become unnecessarily complicated. Normalizing a rectangle means interchanging the corner point values so that *left* < *right* and *top* < *bottom*. The physical properties of a rectangle are unchanged by this process.

See also   TRect::Normalized, TRect

Normalized

TRect Normalized() const;

Returns a normalized rectangle with the top left corner at (*Min(left, right), Min(top, bottom)*) and the bottom right corner at (*Max(left, right), Max(top, bottom)*). The calling rectangle object is unchanged. A valid but nonnormal rectangle might have *left* > *right* or *top* > *bottom* or both. In such cases, many manipulations (such as determining width and height) become unnecessarily complicated. Normalizing a rectangle means interchanging the corner point values so that *left* < *right* and *top* < *bottom*. The physical properties of a rectangle are unchanged by this process.

Note that many calculations assume a normalized rectangle. Some Windows API functions behave erratically if an inside-out *Rect* is passed.

See also   TRect::Normalize, TRect

Offset
TRect& Offset(int dx, int dy);
Changes this rectangle so its corners are offset by the given delta values. The revised rectangle has a top left corner at (*left* + *dx*, *top* + *dy*) and a right bottom corner at (*right* + *dx*, *bottom* + *dy*). The revised rectangle is returned.

See also   TRect::operator +, TRect::operator +=, TRect::OffsetBy

OffsetBy
TRect OffsetBy(int dx, int dy) const;
Returns a rectangle with the corners offset by the given delta values. The returned rectangle has a top left corner at (*left* + *dx*, *top* + *dy*) and a right bottom corner at (*right* + *dx*, *bottom* + *dy*).

See also   TRect::operator +

operator +
TRect operator +(const TSize& size) const;
Returns a rectangle offset positively by the delta values' given sizes. The returned rectangle has a top left corner at (*left* + *size.x*, *top* + *size.y*) and a right bottom corner at (*right* + *size.x*, *bottom* + *size.y*). The calling rectangle object is unchanged.

See also   TRect::OffsetBy, TSize

operator -
TRect operator -(const TSize& size) const;
Returns a rectangle offset negatively by the delta values' given sizes. The returned rectangle has a top left corner at (*left* - *size.cx*, *top* - *size.cy*) and a right bottom corner at (*right* - *size.cx*, *bottom* - *size.cy*). The calling rectangle object is unchanged.

See also   TRect::OffsetBy, TSize

operator &
TRect operator &(const TRect& other) const;
Returns the intersection of this rectangle and the *other* rectangle. The calling rectangle object is unchanged. Returns a NULL rectangle if the two don't intersect.

See also   TRect::operator |, TRect::operator &=

operator |
TRect operator |(const TRect& other) const;
Returns the union of this rectangle and the *other* rectangle. The calling rectangle object is unchanged.

See also   TRect::operator &, TRect::operator |=

operator ==
bool operator ==(const TRect& other) const;
Returns **true** if this rectangle has identical corner coordinates to the *other* rectangle; otherwise, returns **false**.

See also   TRect::operator !=

operator !=
bool operator !=(const TRect& other) const;
Returns **false** if this rectangle has identical corner coordinates to the *other* rectangle; otherwise, returns **true**.

See also   TRect::operator ==

operator +=
TRect& operator +=(const TSize& delta);
Changes this rectangle so its corners are offset by the given delta values, *delta.x* and *delta.y*. The revised rectangle has a top left corner at (*left + delta.x, top + delta.y*) and a right bottom corner at (*right + delta.x, bottom + delta.y*). The revised rectangle is returned.

See also   TRect::operator +, TRect::OffsetBy, TRect::Offset

operator -=
TRect& operator -=(const TSize& delta);
Changes this rectangle so its corners are offset negatively by the given delta values, *delta.x* and *delta.y*. The revised rectangle has a top left corner at (*left - delta.x, top - delta.y*) and a right bottom corner at (*right - delta.x, bottom - delta.y*). The revised rectangle is returned.

See also   TRect::operator -, TRect::operator +=, TRect::OffsetBy, TRect::Offset

operator &=
TRect& operator &=(const TRect& other);
Changes this rectangle to its intersection with the *other* rectangle. This rectangle object is returned. Returns a NULL rectangle if there is no intersection.

See also   TRect::operator &, TRect::operator |=

operator |=
TRect& operator |=(const TRect& other);
Changes this rectangle to its union with the *other* rectangle. This rectangle object is returned.

See also   TRect::operator |, TRect::operator &=

operator >>
ipstream& _BIDSFUNC operator >>(ipstream& is, TRect& r);
Extracts a *TRect* object from *is*, the given input stream, and copies it to *r*. Returns a reference to the resulting stream, allowing the usual chaining of >> operations.

See also   TRect operator <<

operator <<

Form 1   opstream& _BIDSFUNC operator <<(opstream& os, const TRect& r);

Inserts the given *TRect* object, *r*, into the *opstream*, *os*. Returns a reference to the resulting stream, allowing the usual chaining of << operations.

Form 2   ostream& _BIDSFUNC operator <<(ostream& os, const TRect& r);

Formats and inserts the given *TRect* object, *r*, into the *ostream*, *os*. The format is (*r.left*, *r.top*)(*r.right*, *r.bottom*). Returns a reference to the resulting stream and allows the usual chaining of << operations.

See also   TRect operator >>

operator TPoint*()

Form 1   operator const TPoint*() const;

Form 2   operator TPoint*()

Type conversion operators converting the pointer to this rectangle to type pointer to *TPoint*.

See also   TPoint

Right

int Right() const;

Returns the right value.

Set

void Set(int _left, int _top, int _right, int _bottom);

Repositions and resizes this rectangle to the given values.

SetEmpty

void SetEmpty();

Empties this rectangle by setting *left*, *top*, *right*, and *bottom* to 0.

SetNull

void SetNull();

Sets the *left*, *top*, *right*, and *bottom* of the rectangle to 0.

SetWH

void SetWH(int _left, int _top, int w, int h);

Determines the rectangle, given its upper-left point, width, and height.

Size

TSize Size() const;

Returns a *TSize* object representing the width and height of this rectangle.

See also   TSize

Subtract

int Subtract(const TRect& other, TRect result[]) const;

Determines the parts of this rect that do not lie within "other" region. The resulting rectangles are placed in the "result" array.

Returns the resulting number of rectangles. This number will be 1, 2, 3, or 4.

Top
int Top() const;
Returns the top value.

TopLeft
Form 1   const TPoint& TopLeft() const;

Form 2   TPoint& TopLeft();
Returns the *TPoint* object representing the top left corner of this rectangle.

See also   TRect::TopRight, TRect::BottomLeft, TRect::BottomRight, TPoint

TopRight
TPoint TopRight() const;
Returns the *TPoint* object representing the top right corner of this rectangle.

See also   TRect::TopLeft, TRect::BottomLeft, TRect::BottomRight

Touches
bool Touches(const TRect& other) const;
Returns **true** if the *other* rectangle shares any interior points with this rectangle; otherwise, returns **false**.

See also   TRect::Contains

Width
int Width() const;
Returns the width of this rectangle (*right - left*).

See also   TRect::Height

X
int X() const;
Returns the left value.

Y
int Y() const;
Returns the top value.

TRegistry class   registry.h

TRegistry provides high level stream and list access to the registry.

Public member functions

Unregister
static int Unregister(TRegList& regInfo, TUnregParams* params, TRegItem* overrides = 0);
Unregisters entries given a reglist. An optional overrides regItem. Returns the number of errors from deleting keys.

Update
static void Update(TRegKey& baseKey, istream& in);

Walks through an input stream and uses *basekey\key\key=data* lines to set registry entries.

Has named value support in the form: *basekey\key\key | valuename=data*.

Validate
static int Validate(TRegKey& baseKey, istream& in);

Walks through an input stream and uses *basekey\key\key=data* lines to check registry entries.

Returns the number of differences. Zero means a complete match.

Has named value support in the following form:

```
basekey\key\key|valuename=data
```

TRegItem struct

TRegItem defines localizable values for parameters or subkeys. These values can be passed to *TLocaleString*, which defines a localizable substitute for **char***. *TRegItem* contains several undocumented functions that are used privately by the registration macros REGFORMAT and REGSTATUS.

Public data members

Key
char* Key;

Contains a non-localizable item name, such as *clsid* or *progid*.

See also   Registration macros, TLocaleString struct

Value
TLocaleString Value;

Contains a localizable value (for example, "My Sample App") associated with an item name.

See also   Registration macros, TLocaleString struct

Public member functions

OverflowCheck
static void OverflowCheck();

RegFlags
static char* RegFlags(long flags, TRegFormatHeap& heap);

RegFormat
Form 1   static char* RegFormat(const char* f, int a, int t, int d, TRegFormatHeap& heap);
Registers data formats for the object.

Form 2　static char* RegFormat(int f, int a, int t, int d, TRegFormatHeap& heap);
Registers data formats for the object.

RegVerbOpt
static char* RegVerbOpt(int mf, int sf, TRegFormatHeap& heap);
Registers the verb option.

See also　Registration macros, TRegLink struct, TRegList class

TRegKey class   registry.h

TRegKey is the encapsulation of a registration key.

Public constructors and destructor

Constructors
Form 1　TRegKey(THandle baseKey, const char far* keyName, REGSAM samDesired = KEY_ALL_ACCESS,
　　　　TCreateOK createOK = CreateOK);
Creates or opens a key given a base key and a subkeyname. Security information is
ignored in 16-bit (and under Win95). This can also provide an ok-to-create or open-only
indicator.

Form 2　TRegKey(const TRegKeyIterator& iter, REGSAM samDesired = KEY_ALL_ACCESS);
Constructs a key given the current position of a regkey iterator.

Form 3　TRegKey(THandle aliasKey, bool shouldClose=false, const char far* keyName = 0);
Contructs a key that is an alias to an existing HKEY.

Destructor
~TRegKey();
The destructor for this class.

Public member functions

ClassesRoot
static TRegKey ClassesRoot;
Special predefined root key used by shell and OLE applications.

ClassesRootClsid
static TRegKey ClassesRootClsid;
A subkey commonly used by shell and OLE applications.

CurrentConfig
static TRegKey CurrentConfig;
Special predefined root key.

CurrentUser
static TRegKey CurrentUser;
Special predefined root key defining the preferences of the current user.

DeleteKey

long DeleteKey(const char far* subKeyName);

Deletes the specified subkey of this registry key.

DeleteValue

long DeleteValue(const char far* valName) const;

Removes a named value from this registry key.

DynData

static TRegKey DynData;

Special predefined root key.

EnumKey

long EnumKey(int index, char far* subKeyName, int subKeyNameSize) const;

Enumerates the subkeys of this registry key.

EnumValue

long EnumValue(int index, char far* valueName, uint32& valueNameSize, uint32* type=0, uint8* data=0, uint32* dataSize=0) const;

Flush

long Flush() const;

Writes the attribute of this key into the registry.

GetName

const char far* GetName() const;

Returns a string identifying this key.

GetSecurity

long GetSecurity(SECURITY_INFORMATION secInf, PSECURITY_DESCRIPTOR secDesc, uint32* secDescSize);

Retrieves a copy of the security descriptor protecting this registry key.

GetSubkeyCount

uint32 GetSubkeyCount() const;

Returns the number of subkeys attached to this key.

GetValueCount

uint32 GetValueCount() const;

Returns the number of values attached to this key.

LoadKey

long LoadKey(const char far* subKeyName, const char far* fileName);

Creates a subkey under HKEY_USER or HKEY_LOCAL_MACHINE and stores registration information from a specified file into that subkey. This registration information is in the form of a hive. A hive is a discrete body of keys, subkeys, and values that is rooted at the top of the registry hierarchy. A hive is backed by a single file and a .LOG file.

LocalMachine
static TRegKey LocalMachine;
Special predefined root key defining the physical state of the computer.

NukeKey
long NukeKey(const char far* subKeyName);
Completely eliminates a child key, including any of its subkeys. *RegDeleteKey* fails if a key has subkeys, so must tail-recurse to clean them up first.

PerformanceData
static TRegKey PerformanceData;
Special predefined root key used to obtain performance data.

QueryDefValue
long QueryDefValue(const char far* subkeyName, char far* data, uint32* dataSize) const;
Retrieves the default [unnamed] value associated with this key.

QueryInfo
long QueryInfo(char far* class_, uint32* classSize, uint32* subkeyCount, uint32* maxSubkeySize, uint32* maxClassSize, uint32* valueCount, uint32* maxValueName, uint32* maxValueData, uint32* secDescSize, FILETIME far* lastWriteTime);
Retrieves information about this registry key.

QueryValue
long QueryValue(const char far* valName, uint32* type, uint8* data, uint32* dataSize) const;
Retrieves the value associated with the unnamed value for this key in the registry.

ReplaceKey
long ReplaceKey(const char far* subKeyName, const char far* newFileName, const char far* oldFileName);
Replaces the file backing this key and all of its subkeys with another file, so that when the system is next started, the key and subkeys will have the values stored in the new file.

Restore
long Restore(const char far* fileName, uint32 options=0);
Reads the registry information in a specified file and copies it over this key. This registry information may be in the form of a key and multiple levels of subkeys.

Save
long Save(const char far* fileName);
Saves this key and all of its subkeys and values to the specified file.

SetDefValue
long SetDefValue(const char far* subkeyName, uint32 type, const char far* data, uint32 dataSize);
Sets the default [unnamed] value associated with this key.

SetSecurity
long SetSecurity(SECURITY_INFORMATION secInf, PSECURITY_DESCRIPTOR secDesc);
Sets the security descriptor of this key.

SetValue

Form 1 long SetValue(const char far* valName, uint32 data) const;
Associates a 4-byte value with this key.

Form 2 long SetValue(const char far* valName, uint32 type, const uint8* data, uint32 dataSize) const;
Associates a value with this key.

THandle

operator THandle() const;
Returns the HANDLE identifying this registry key.

UnLoadKey

long UnLoadKey(const char far* subKeyName);
Unloads this key and its subkeys from the registry.

Users

static TRegKey Users;
Special predefined root key defining the default user configuration.

Protected member functions

Key

THandle Key;
This key's handle.

Name

char far* Name;
This key's name.

ShouldClose

bool ShouldClose;
Whether this key should be closed on destruction.

SubkeyCount

uint32 SubkeyCount;
The number of subkeys.

ValueCount

uint32 ValueCount;
The number of value entries.

TRegLink struct

registry.h

TRegLink is a linked structure in which each node points to a list of TRegList objects (or *TRegList*-derived objects) or TDocTemplate objects. Each object has an item name and a string value associated with the item name. The structure forms a typical linked list as the following diagram illustrates:

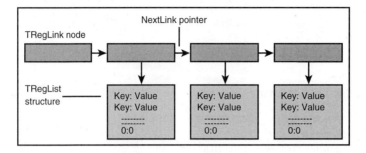

A *TDocTemplate* object uses the following variation of the *TRegLink* structure:

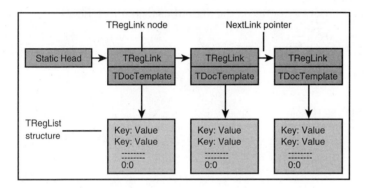

See also   Registration macros, TLocaleString struct, TRegItem struct

Public constructor and destructor

Constructor
TRegLink(TRegList& regList, TRegLink*& head);
Constructs a reglink pointing to a reglist, and adds it to the end of the list.

Destructor
~TRegLink();
The destructor for this class.

Public data members

NextLink
TRegLink* NextLink;
Points to the next link that references a list of items.

Public member functions

AddLink
static void AddLink(TRegLink*& head, TRegLink& newLink);
Adds a new link to the end of the link list.

GetNext
TRegLink* GetNext() const;
Returns a pointer to the next link.

GetRegList
TRegList& GetRegList() const;
Returns a pointer to the registration parameter table (reglist).

RemoveLink
static bool RemoveLink(TRegLink*& head, TRegLink& remLink);
Removes a link from the link list. Returns true if the link is found and removed.

Protected member functions

RegList
TRegList* RegList;
Points to the list of item value pairs.

See also   Registration macros

Next
TRegLink* Next;
The next *RegLink*.

Protected constructor

TRegLink

TRegList class   locale.h

Holds an array of items of type *TRegItem*. Provides functionality that lets you access each item in the array and return the name of the item. Instead of creating a *TRegList* directly, you can use ObjectWindows' registration macros to build a *TRegList* for you.

See also   Registration macros, TLocaleString struct, TRegLink class

Public data members

Items
TRegItem* Items;
References the item value pair respectively; for example, *Prgid* and "My Sample Application."

See also   Registration macros

Public constructor

TRegList(TRegItem* list):Items(List);
Constructs a *TRegList* object from an array of *TRegItems* terminated by a NULL item name.

See also   Registration macros, TRegList::TRegList

Public member functions

Lookup
const char* Lookup(const char* key, TLangId lang = TLocaleString::UserDefaultLangId);
Performs the lookup of the *TRegItems* using a *key* (an item name such as *progid*) and returns the value associated with the *key* (for example, "My Sample Application"). The value is returned in the language specified in *lang* (for example, French Canadian).

See also   TLangId, TLocaleString struct

LookupRef
TLocaleString& LookupRef(const char* key);
Looks up and returns a reference to a local string value associated with a particular item name (*key*). You can then translate this string into the local language as necessary.

See also   Registration macros, TLocaleString struct

operator [ ]
const char* operator[](const char* key);
The array operator uses an item name (*key*) to locate an item in the array.

TRegValue class   registry.h

TRegValue encapsulates a value-data entry within one registration key.

Public constructor and destructor

Constructor
Form 1   TRegValue(const TRegKey& key, const char far* name);
Creates a registry value object from the specified registry key and name.

Form 2   TRegValue(const TRegValueIterator& iter);
Creates a registry object from the current location of the specified iterator.

Destructor
~TRegValue();
The destructor for this class.

Public member functions

Delete
long Delete();
Removes this value from its associated key.

Note   The state of this value object becomes undefined.

GetData
const uint8* GetData() const;
Returns the type code for the data associated with this value.

GetDataSize
const uint32 GetDataSize() const;
Returns the size in bytes of the data associated with this value.

GetDataType
const uint32 GetDataType() const;
Returns the type code for the data associated with this value.

GetName
const char far* GetName() const;
Returns a string identifying this value.

operator *
operator const char far*() const;
Returns the data associated with this value as a const char*.

operator =
Form 1   void operator =(const char far* v);
Sets the data for this value to v.

Form 2   void operator =(uint32 v);
Sets the data for this value to v.

RetrieveOnDemand
void RetrieveOnDemand() const;
Flag specifying whether data should be read upon construction of object or only when data is requested.

Set
Form 1   long Set(const char far* data);
Sets the data associated with this value.

Form 2   long Set(uint32 data);
Sets the data associated with this value.

Note   For 32-bit only.

Form 3   long Set(uint32 type, uint8* data, uint32 dataSize);
Sets the data associated with this value. 'type' describes the type of the value. 'data' is the address of the data. 'size' specifies the length in characters.

uint32
operator uint32() const;
Returns the data associated with this value as a 32-bit unsigned integer.

TRegValueIterator class   registry.h

TRegValueIterator is an iterator for walking through the values of a key.

Public constructor

TRegValueIterator(const TRegKey& regKey);
Creates a subkey iterator for a registration key.

Public member functions

BaseKey
const TRegKey& BaseKey() const;
Returns the registration key that this iterator is bound to.

Current
int Current() const;
Returns the index to the current subkey.

operator ++
Form 1   uint32 operator ++();
Pre-increments to the next value.

Form 2   uint32 operator ++(int);
Post-increments to the next value

operator --
Form 1   uint32 operator --();
Pre-decrements to the previous value.

Form 2   uint32 operator --(int);
Post-decrements to the previous value.

operator [ ]
uint32 operator [](int index);
Sets the index of the iterator to the passed value. Return the new index.

operator bool()
operator bool();
Tests the validity of this iterator. Returns **true** if the iterator's index is greater than or equal to 0 and less than the number of subkeys.

Reset
void Reset();
Resets the value index to zero.

TResId class

geometry.h

A simple support class, *TResId* creates a resource ID object from either an integer or an actual string identifier. For example, *TResId* encapsulates the use of *LPSTR (char_far*)* as a resource identifier. This resource identifier can be passed to various ObjectWindows classes. To handle these two different types of resource identifiers, *TResId* defines a conversion operator and provides two constructors that convert and use these native data types. One constructor accepts a 16-bit integer and the other accepts a character string.

Public constructors

Form 1   TResId();
The default *TResId* constructor.

Form 2   TResId(int resNum);
Creates a *TResId* object with the given *resNum*.

Form 3   TResId(const char far* resString);
Creates a *TResId* object with the given *resString*.

Public member functions

operator char far*()
operator char far*();
Typecasting operator that converts *Id* (a *TResId* private data member) to type **char far*** so that instances of *TResId* can be used in places where **char far*** data types are expected.

IsString
bool IsString() const;
Returns **true** if this resource ID was created from a string; otherwise, returns **false**.

Friend functions

operator >>
friend ipstream& operator >>(ipstream& is, TResId& id);
Extracts a *TResId* object from *is* (the given input stream), and copies it to *id*. Returns a reference to the resulting stream, allowing the usual chaining of >> operations.

See also   TResId friend operator <<

operator <<
Form 1   friend opstream& operator <<(opstream& os, const TResId& id);
Inserts the given *TResId* object (*id*) into the *opstream* (*os*). Returns a reference to the resulting stream, allowing the usual chaining of << operations.

Form 2   friend ostream& operator <<(ostream& os, const TResId& id);
Formats and inserts the given *TResId* object (*id*) into the *ostream* (*os*). Returns a reference to the resulting stream, allowing the usual chaining of << operations.

See also   TResId friend operator >>

TResource class

wsyscls.h

TResource simplifies access to a resource by encapsulating the find, load, lock, and free steps for accessing a resource.

T represents a structure which defines the binary layout of the resource.

resType is a constant string that defines the resource type.

For example,

```
typedef TResource<DLGTEMPLATE, RT_DIALOG> TDlgResource;
TDlgResource dlgInfo(hInstance, IDD_ABOUTDLG);
DLGTEMPLATE* pDlgTmpl = dlgInfo;
```

Public constructors and destructor

Constructors

Form 1   TResource(HINSTANCE hModule, TResId resId);
Creates an object based on the module information and the resource identifier.

Form 2   TResource(HINSTANCE hModule, TResId resid, LANGID langid);
Creates an object based on the module information and the resource identifier.

Destructor
~TResource();
The destructor for this class.

Public member functions

T*
operator T*();
Conversion operator to point to the structure representing the binary layout of the resource.

IsOK
bool IsOK() const;
Confirms whether the resource was found.

Protected member functions

MemHandle
HGLOBAL MemHandle;
The handle of the resource.

MemPtr
T* MemPtr;
Pointer to the locked resource.

TRgbQuad class

TRgbQuad is a support class derived from the structure *tagRGBQUAD*, which is defined as follows:

```
typedef struct tagRGBQUAD {
    uint8   rgbBlue;
    uint8   rgbGreen;
    uint8   rgbRed;
    uint8   rgbReserved;
} RGBQUAD;
```

The elements *rgbBlue*, *rgbGreen*, and *rgbRed* specify the relative blue, green, and red intensities of a color. *rgbReserved* is not used and must be set to 0.

TRgbQuad is used in conjunction with the classes TPalette and *TColor* to simplify RGBQUAD-based color operations. Constructors are provided to create *TRgbQuad* objects from explicit RGB values, from *TColor* objects, or from other *TRgbQuad* objects.

Public constructors

TRgbQuad
Form 1   TRgbQuad(int r, int g, int b);
Creates a *TRgbQuad* object with *rgbRed*, *rgbGreen*, and *rgbBlue* set to *r*, *g*, and *b* respectively. Sets *rgbReserved* to 0.

Form 2   TRgbQuad(TColor c);
Creates a *TRgbQuad* object with *rgbRed*, *rgbGreen*, *rgbBlue* set to *c.Red*, *c.Green*, *c.Blue* respectively. Sets *rgbReserved* to 0.

Form 3   TRgbQuad(const RGBQUAD far& q);
Creates a *TRgbQuad* object with the same values as the referenced RGBQUAD object.

Public member functions

operator ==
bool operator ==(COLORREF cr) const;
Returns true if the RGBQUAD has the same color components.

See also   TColor::Red, TColor::Green, TColor::Blue

TRgbTriple class

TRgbTriple is a support class derived from the structure *tagRgbTriple*, which is defined as follows:

```
typedef struct tagRGBTRIPLE {
    uint8   rgbBlue;
    uint8   rgbGreen;
    uint8   rgbRed;
} RGBTRIPLE;
```

The members *rgbBlue*, *rgbGreen*, and *rgbRed* specify the relative blue, green, and red intensities for a color.

TRgbTriple is used in conjunction with the classes *TPalette* and *TColor* to simplify bmci-color-based operations. Constructors are provided to create *TRgbTriple* objects from explicit RGB values, from *TColor* objects, or from other *TRgbTriple* objects.

Public constructors

Form 1   TRgbTriple(int r, int g, int b);
Creates a *TRgbTriple* object with *rgbRed*, *rgbGreen*, and *rgbBlue* set to *r*, *g*, and *b* respectively.

Form 2   TRgbTriple(TColor c);
Creates a *TRgbTriple* object with *rgbRed*, *rgbGreen*, *rgbBlue* set to *c.Red*, *c.Green*, and *c.Blue* respectively.

Form 3   TRgbTriple(const RGBTRIPLE far& t);
Creates a *TRgbTriple* object with the same values as the referenced RGBTRIPLE object.

See also   tag RGBTRIPLE struct, TColor::Red, TColor::Green, TColor::Blue

Public member functions

operator ==
bool operator ==(COLORREF cr) const;
Returns true if the triple match color components.

TSize class   geometry.h

TSize is a mathematical class derived from the structure *tagSIZE*.

The *tagSIZE* struct is defined as

```
struct tagSIZE {
    int cx;
    int cy;
};
```

TSize encapsulates the notion of a two-dimensional quantity that usually represents a displacement or the height and width of a rectangle. *TSize* inherits the two data members *cx* and *cy* from *tagSIZE*. Member functions and operators are provided for comparing, assigning, and manipulating sizes. Overloaded << and >> operators allow chained insertion and extraction of *TSize* objects with streams.

Public constructors

Form 1   TSize();
The default *TSize* constructor.

Form 2   TSize(int dx, int dy);
Creates a *TSize* object with $cx = dx$ and $cy = dy$.

Form 3   TSize(const POINT& point);
Creates a *TSize* object with $cx = point.x$ and cy = *point.y*.

Form 4   TSize(const SIZE& size);
Creates a *TSize* object with $cx = size.cx$ and $cy = size.cy$.

Form 5   TSize(uint32 dw);
Creates a *TSize* object with $cx = \text{LOWORD}(dw)$ and $cy = \text{HIWORD}(dw)$).

See also   TPoint

Public member functions

Magnitude
int Magnitude() const;
Returns the length of the diagonal of the rectangle represented by this object. The value returned is an **int** approximation to the square root of ($cx2 + cy2$).

operator +
TSize operator +(const TSize& size) const;
Calculates an offset to this *TSize* object using the given *size* argument as the displacement. Returns the object ($cx + size.cx$, $cy + size.cy$). This *TSize* object is not changed.

See also   TSize::operator -

operator -
Form 1   TSize operator -(const TSize& size) const;
Calculates a negative offset to this *TSize* object using the given *size* argument as the displacement. Returns the point ($cx - size.cx$, $cy - size.cy$). This object is not changed.

Form 2   TSize operator -() const;
Returns the *TSize* object ($-cx$, $-cy$). This object is not changed.

See also   TSize::operator +

operator ==
bool operator ==(const TSize& other) const;
Returns **true** if this *TSize* object is equal to the *other* TSize object; otherwise returns **false**.

See also   TSize::operator !=

operator !=
bool operator !=(const TSize& other) const;
Returns **false** if this *TSize* object is equal to the *other* TSize object; otherwise returns **true**.

See also   TSize::operator ==

operator +=
TSize& operator +=(const TSize& size);
Offsets this *TSize* object by the given *size* argument. This *TSize* object is changed to ($cx + size.cx$, $cy + size.cy$). Returns a reference to this object.

See also   TSize::operator -=

operator -=
TSize& operator -=(const TSize& size);
Negatively offsets this *TSize* object by the given *size* argument. This object is changed to (*cx - size.cx, cy - size.cy*). Returns a reference to this object.

See also   TSize::operator +=

operator >>
ipstream& operator >>(ipstream& is, TSize& s);
Extracts a *TSize* object from *is*, the given input stream, and copies it to *s*. Returns a reference to the resulting stream, allowing the usual chaining of >> operations.

See also   TSize operator <<

operator <<

Form 1   opstream& operator <<(opstream& os, const TSize& s);
Inserts the given *TSize* object *s* into the *opstream os*. Returns a reference to the resulting stream, allowing the usual chaining of << operations.

Form 2   ostream& operator <<(ostream& os, const TSize& s);
Formats and inserts the given *TSize* object *s* into the *ostream os*. The format is "(*cx x cy*)." Returns a reference to the resulting stream, allowing the usual chaining of << operations.

X
int X() const;
Returns the width.

Y
int Y();
Returns the height.

See also   TSize operator >>

TString class   string.h

TString is a flexible universal string envelope class. It facilitates efficient construction and assignment of many string types.

Public constructors and destructor

Constructors
Form 1   TString(const char far* s = 0);
Constructs a *TString* from a character array.

Form 2   TString(const wchar_t* s);
Constructs a *TString* from a wide character array.

Form 3 TString(BSTR s, bool loan);
Constructs a *TString* from a BSTR (OLE string).

Form 4 TString(TSysStr& s, bool loan);
Constructs a *TString* from a system string (BSTR).

Form 5 TString(const string& s);
Constructs a *TString* from a string.

Form 6 TString(TUString* s);
Constructs a *TString* from a *TUString*.

Form 7 TString(const TString& src);
Constructs a *TString* from a *TString*; this is the copy constructor.

Destructor
~TString();
The destructor for this class.

Public member functions

GetLangId
TLangId GetLangId();
Gets the Language ID of this string.

IsNull
bool IsNull() const;
Returns true if the string is empty.

IsWide
bool IsWide() const;
Returns true if the string uses a wide character set.

Length
int Length() const;
Returns the length of the string.

operator *
Form 1 operator wchar_t*();
Returns the string as a wchar_t*.

Form 2 operator const wchar_t*() const;
Returns the string as a const wchar_t*.

Form 3 operator char*();
Returns the string as a char*.

Form 4 operator const char far*() const;
Returns the string as a const char far*.

operator =
Form 1 TString& operator =(wchar_t* s);
Copies the contents of wchar_t* s into this string.

Form 2   TString& operator =(const wchar_t* s);
          Copies the contents of const wchar_t* s into this string.

Form 3   TString& operator =(char* s);
          Copies the contents of char* s into this string.

Form 4   TString& operator =(const char far* s);
          Copies the contents of const char* s into this string.

Form 5   TString& operator =(const string& s);
          Copies the contents of string s into this string.

Form 6   TString& operator =(const TString& s);
          Copies the contents of TString s into this string.

Relinquish
Form 1   wchar_t* Relinquish() const;
          Returns a pointer of type wchar_t to a copy of the string.

Form 2   char* Relinquish() const;
          Returns a pointer of type char to a copy of the string.

RelinquishNarrow
char* RelinquishNarrow() const;
Returns a pointer (char*) to a copy of the string.

RelinquishSysStr
BSTR RelinquishSysStr() const;
Returns a pointer (BSTR) to a copy of the string.

RelinquishWide
wchar_t* RelinquishWide() const;
Returns a pointer (wchar_t*) to a copy of the string.

SetLangId
void SetLangId(TLangId id);
Sets the language ID of this string.

Protected data member

S
TUString* S;
Instance of a helper object that implements functionality of a string object.

TXBase class   except.h

Derived from xmsg, *TXBase* is the base class for ObjectWindows and ObjectComponents exception-handling classes. The ObjectWindows classes that handle specific kinds of exceptions, such as out-of-memory or invalid window exceptions, are derived from TXOwl, which is in turn derived from *TXBase*. The ObjectComponents classes *TXOle* and *TXAuto* are derived directly from *TXBase*.

TXBase contains the functions *Clone* and *Throw*, which are overridden in all derived classes, as well as two constructors. The constructors increment *InstanceCount*, and the destructor decrements *InstanceCount*.

See also   Working with TXBase

Public constructors and destructor

Constructors
Form 1   TXBase(const string& msg);
Calls the *xmsg* class's constructor that takes a string parameter and initializes *xmsg* with the value of the string parameter.

Form 2   TXBase(const TXBase& src);
Creates a copy of the *TXBase* object passed in the *TXBase* parameter.

Destructor
virtual ~TXBase;
Destroys the *TXBase* object and decrements the *InstanceCount* data member.

See also   TXOwl::TXOwl

Public data member

InstanceCount
static int InstanceCount;
Counts the number of *TXBase* and *TXBase*-derived objects existing in a single application.

Public member functions

Clone
virtual TXBase* Clone();
Makes a copy of the exception object.

Raise
static void Raise(const string& msg);
Constructs a *TXBase* exception from scratch, and throws it.

Throw
virtual void Throw();
Throws the exception object.

TXRegistry class   registry.h

TXRegistry is the object thrown when exceptions are encountered within the WinSys Registry classes.

Public constructors

TXRegistry
Form 1   TXRegistry(const TXRegistry& copy);
The copy constructor. Constructs a new registry exception object by copying the one passed as *copy*.

Form 2   TXRegistry(const char* msg, const char* key);
Creates a registry exception object. *msg* points to an error message, and *key* points to the name of the registry key that ObjectComponents was processing when the exception occurred.

Public member functions

Check
static void Check(long stat, const char* key);
Registry exception checking. Throws a *TXRegistry* if the argument is non-zero.

Key
const char* Key;
Identifies the registry which caused the exception.

Index